Introduction to Law
and the Legal System

Introduction to Law and the Legal System

ELEVENTH EDITION

FRANK AUGUST SCHUBERT
Professor Emeritus
Northeastern University

CENGAGE
Learning·

Australia • Brazil • Canada • Mexico • Singapore • Spain • United Kingdom • United States

**Introduction to Law and the Legal System
Eleventh Edition**
Frank August Schubert

Product Manager: Carolyn Merrill

Content Developer: Jennifer Jacobson, Ohlinger
Publishing Services

Content Coordinator: Jessica Wang

Product Assistant: Abigail Hess

Market Development Manager: Courtney Wolstoncroft

Art Director: Linda May

Print Buyer: Fola Orekoya

Senior Rights Acquisition Specialist, Image:
Jennifer Meyer Dare

Production Service/Compositor: S4Carlisle

Cover Image: Mesut Dogan/Shutterstock
Sebastian Duda/Shutterstock

© 2015, 2012, 2008, 2004 Cengage Learning

ALL RIGHTS RESERVED. No part of this work covered by the copyright herein may be
reproduced, transmitted, stored, or used in any form or by any means graphic,
electronic, or mechanical, including but not limited to photocopying, recording,
scanning, digitizing, taping, web distribution, information networks, or information
storage and retrieval systems, except as permitted under Section 107 or 108 of the
1976 United States Copyright Act, without the prior written permission of the
publisher.

For product information and technology assistance, contact us at
Cengage Learning Customer & Sales Support, 1-800-354-9706

For permission to use material from this text or product, submit
all requests online at **www.cengage.com/permissions**.
Further permissions questions can be emailed to
permissionrequest@cengage.com.

Library of Congress Control Number: 2013946033

ISBN-13: 978-1-285-43825-2
ISBN-10: 1-285-43825-6

Cengage Learning
200 First Stamford Place, 4th Floor
Stamford, CT 06902
USA

Cengage Learning is a leading provider of customized learning solutions with office
locations around the globe, including Singapore, the United Kingdom, Australia,
Mexico, Brazil and Japan. Locate your local office at **international.cengage.com/
region**.

Cengage Learning products are represented in Canada by Nelson Education, Ltd.

For your course and learning solutions, visit **www.cengage.com**.

Purchase any of our products at your local college store or at our preferred online store
www.cengagebrain.com.

Instructors: Please visit **login.cengage.com** and log in to access instructor-specific
resources.

Printed in the United States of America
1 2 3 4 5 6 7 17 16 15 14 13

*To the memories of the late Elizabeth Josephine Neal
and Ethel L. Neal.*
F. A. S.

Brief Contents

Contents

(Please note that cases are shown in italics, and those indicated with an asterisk reflect cases that are new to this edition.)

VIII Criminal Law and Procedure   **254**

Preface

Welcome to the eleventh edition of *Introduction to Law and the Legal System*! The first edition was published 38 years ago.

Suited for undergraduate or graduate programs, this text is a survey of the American legal system and can be used in a variety of courses such as Survey of Law, Introduction to Law and the Legal System, Law and Society, Legal Environment and Business, and Legal Process. This text could be an integral part of business, criminal justice, political science, interdisciplinary, paralegal, or other similar courses in an institution of higher learning.

From its first edition to the present, the goal has been to provide readers with a general understanding of American substantive and procedural law. The premise is that this kind of knowledge is basic to a well-rounded education. Because this book is used in a wide variety of academic settings and disciplines, it is expected that instructors will select topics and cases that are appropriate to the course and students. The length and complexity of cases varies from case to case because it is difficult to reduce a fifty-page opinion to three or four pages and still include all the fodder for class discussion. While it is true that many topics included in the text are fundamental to the typical law school's curriculum, this is not a textbook for law students. This book explains in a few pages fundamental principles that law students study for an entire semester. Law students study law so that they can become practitioners. Undergraduate students—and graduate students in fields other than law—study law in order to obtain a basic understanding of law. This presentation's strength is that it provides readers with a brief peek at what are inherently complex concepts without getting students in over their heads.

Because this is an undergraduate- and graduate-level text, it also tries to show readers connections between law and topics typically covered in more detail in undergraduate or graduate courses taught in history, philosophy, political science, sociology–anthropology, and business departments. Thus, the text includes some legal and cultural history, jurisprudence, ethics, and similar topics in the hope that students will get a taste of the bigger picture and perhaps enroll in a corresponding course. Showing these connections helps to promote a better understanding of the role law plays in a complex modern society. From this understanding, students can decide for themselves whether lawmaking institutions—the legislative, judicial, and administrative agencies—are adequately addressing our society's problems.

By reading cases and studying statutes in this text, students will learn to exercise their own powers of reasoning. Because the cases are continuously updated in every edition, students read about real-world problems and study appellate court discussions about how the problems should be resolved. This promotes class discussions about the relative strengths and weaknesses of the competing arguments made by the parties.

New to the Eleventh Edition

The eleventh edition has been updated with 34 new cases including many recent, controversial cases such as the 2012 U.S. Supreme Court case, *National Federation of Independent Business v. Sebelius,* related to whether Congress had the constitutional authority to establish an individual mandate within the Patient Protection and Affordable Care Act (ACA, popularly known as "Obamacare"); the 2013 U.S. Supreme Court case *United States v. Windsor,* concerning the Defense of Marriage Act's constitutionality; and the 2013 U.S. Supreme Court case *Hollingsworth v. Perry,* in which the court ruled on whether California was violating the Fourteenth Amendment rights of same-sex couples by restricting marriage to heterosexual couples.

Comments from reviewers and users have been carefully considered as decisions were made with respect to the replacement or retention of particular cases. As always, the goal has been to select cases that are interesting, teachable, and controversial, and that illustrate the theory being discussed in the corresponding chapter section. Some of the retained cases are classics and have proven to be useful for many years. *Katko v. Briney, Strunk v. Strunk,* and *Campbell Soup Company v. Wentz,* for example, have appeared in all eleven editions. Other older cases have been included because they better illustrate the legal principle being addressed in the text than did the removed case.

Some instructors will be pleased to find the return of a long-standing favorite case, *E. I. DuPont de Nemours & Co., Inc. v. Christopher,* which now appears in an appendix after having been removed from the tenth edition. Other favorites that have been "retired" from the textbook can be found on the textbook's website, along with additional cases, statutes, and materials that could not be included in the textbook because of space limitations. This website will be updated periodically with new and relevant cases, and often will include concurring and dissenting opinions that would be too lengthy to be included in the textbook. Additionally, students will find open access to learning objectives, tutorial quizzes, chapter glossaries, flash cards, and crossword puzzles, all correlated by chapter, as well as additional cases on the website. Instructors also have access to the Instructor's Manual which includes chapter objectives, court cases, and answers to chapter questions. The test bank available to instructors has been updated with a large array of well-crafted true-false, multiple choice, and essay questions, along with their answers and page references.

Teaching and Learning Aids

The text includes a glossary that was substantially expanded in the ninth edition. Please note that it focuses on terms as they are used in the text and is not intended to be as comprehensive as a legal dictionary. The Constitution of the United States is also reprinted for easy reference.

All cases have been edited to frame issues for classroom discussion and for length and readability. Most case footnotes have been deleted. Most citations similarly have been omitted, as well as less important portions of majority opinions. Ellipses have been inserted to indicate such omissions. Academic works that were relied upon as sources within each chapter have been acknowledged with endnotes. Case citations are provided occasionally so that interested students can consult the official reports for unedited cases.

Acknowledgments

This revision would not have been possible without the valuable contributions of many people. The following reviewers were instrumental in shaping the eleventh edition:

Russell J. Ippolito, Westchester Community College

Paul Chen, Western Washington University

Brett Curry, Georgia Southern University

Brian J. McCully, Fresno City College

Stephanie Delaney, Seattle Central Community College

I am most pleased and proud that my daughter, Tracy, has again prepared the index for this text. Her excellent assistance has made the eleventh edition both better and more memorable. Finally, I'd like to thank my wife, Barbara. Once again she has adjusted to life with a husband who is deeply involved in the long process of researching and writing another edition of this textbook. Barbara has always encouraged me and shown patience and steadfastness as I have labored away. I could not have completed this work without her constant love and support. This edition is dedicated to the memories of my late mother, Elizabeth Josephine Neal and my maternal grandmother, Ethel L. Neal.

F.A.S.

I

Introduction

CHAPTER OBJECTIVES

1. *Understand each of five jurisprudential approaches to answering the question, What is law?*

2. *Explain the legal objectives that are common to American public and private law.*

3. *Understand how our nation's legal history and culture have contributed to law and legal institutions as we know them today.*

4. *Develop the ability to read and brief an appellate court opinion.*

5. *Explain in general terms the concepts underlying the Due Process and Equal Protection Clauses.*

6. *Understand the basic differences between civil and criminal law.*

7. *Understand the basic differences between tort and contract law.*

WHAT IS LAW?

The study of legal philosophy is called **jurisprudence.** Many of the world's greatest philosophers have theorized about the nature and meaning of law. Jurisprudential philosophers ask questions like these: What is law? Is bad law still law? Is custom law? Is law what it says in the statute books, or what really happens in practice? Philosophers have debated the essential nature of law for centuries, yet there is no single commonly accepted definition. This chapter begins by summarizing some of the schools of legal philosophy in order to introduce students to different ways of answering this fundamental question: What is law?[1]

Law as Power

According to this view, the validity of a law does not depend on whether it is socially good or bad. It is apparent, for example, that tyrannies, monarchies, and democracies have produced socially beneficial laws. They have also produced laws that are unjust and "wrongful." What these different forms of government have in common is that each is based on power and that possessing the power to enforce its laws is central to each government's existence. This philosophy can be criticized for ignoring arbitrariness, abuses of power, and tyranny, and for producing bad law.

Natural Law

Natural law philosophers argued that law is that which reflects, or is based on, the built-in sense of right and wrong that exists within every person at birth. This moral barometer, which operates through the functioning of conscience, gives each person the capacity to discover moral truth independently. Some believed this sense was God-given; others believed it was an intrinsic part of human nature.[2] Natural law philosophers argued that moral goodness is conceptually independent of institutional views of goodness or evil. Thus, no government can make a morally evil law good or a morally good law evil. Moral goodness exists prior to institutional lawmaking and sets a moral standard against which positive law should be measured. Thus, even though during apartheid the all-white South African government may have had the power to enact racially discriminatory statutes, such statutes were not truly "law" because they were morally abhorrent. This natural law philosophy was very influential in seventeenth- and eighteenth-century Europe. Revolutionaries who sought to overthrow established monarchies were attracted to natural law because it established a philosophical foundation for political reform.

Natural law thinking has greatly influenced American law as well. American civil rights advocates currently use the same time-tested natural law arguments that were used thirty and forty years ago to oppose racial discrimination. They argue that discriminatory statutes should not be respected as law because they are so blatantly unfair. Constitutional provisions that require government to treat all persons fairly and impartially (the Due Process and Equal Protection Clauses) are other examples.

Our tort system is also a reflection of natural law thinking. It is "right" that people who intend no harm but who carelessly cause injury to other people should have to pay compensation for the damages. Similarly, if two people voluntarily enter into a contract, it is "right" that the parties comply with its terms or pay damages for the breach. (However, our law confers power in our judges to refuse to enforce contractual provisions that are too one-sided.) Finally, it is "right" to punish persons who commit crimes for those acts.

When there is no consensus in society about what is morally right and wrong, natural law loses its effectiveness as a basis for law. Current examples of this problem include issues such as abortion, physician-assisted suicide, and capital punishment.

Historical Jurisprudence

Historical jurisprudence evolved in response to the natural law philosophy. Aristocrats were attracted to this school because it provided a justification for preserving the status quo and the preferential treatment of powerful elites that was deeply rooted in cultural tradition. The historical philosophy of law integrated the notion that law is the will of the sovereign with the idea of the "spirit of the people."[3] That is, law is only valid to the extent that the will of the sovereign is compatible with long-standing social practices, customs, and values. Law, according to this view, could not be arbitrarily imposed by legislators whose legal source was "right" reasoning. Instead, the historical school insisted that only practices that have withstood the test of time could be thought of as law.[4] Further, these philosophers believed that law changes slowly and invisibly as human conduct changes.

A major advantage of historical jurisprudence is that it promotes stability in law. In fact, much law is largely grounded in judicially approved custom.

Our contemporary American real estate law,[5] property law,[6] and contract law[7] are some of the areas in which long-standing practices continue to be recognized as law. Custom has also played an important role in determining the meaning of the Constitution. Appellate courts such as the U.S. Supreme Court trace provisions of the Bill of Rights to their historical statutory and case law antecedents. They do this because they recognize that some beliefs, practices, procedures, and relationships between people and the state have become fundamental to our culture.

Occasionally a sovereign will enact legislation that significantly contravenes long-standing custom. A few years ago, the Massachusetts legislature enacted a mandatory seat belt law. Many citizens believed that the state was infringing on a matter of personal choice. They insisted that the matter be placed on the ballot, and the law was repealed in a statewide referendum.[8]

A major problem with historical jurisprudence is determining at what point a practice has become a custom. How long must a practice have been followed, and how widely must it be accepted, before it is recognized as customary?

Utilitarian Law

The **utilitarian** conception of law focused on the social usefulness of legislation rather than on metaphysical notions of goodness and justice.[9] Utilitarians thought that government was responsible for enacting laws that promote the general public's happiness. They believed that the desire to maximize pleasure and minimize pain is what motivates people, and that legislatures were responsible for inducing people to act in socially desirable ways through a legislated system of incentives and disincentives.[10] For example, if the pain imposed by a criminal sentence exceeds the gain realized by an offender in committing the offense, future criminal actions will be deterred. Additionally, they thought that law should focus on providing people with security and equality of opportunity. They maintained that property rights should be protected because security of property is crucial to attaining

happiness. People, they thought, should perform their contracts because increased commercial activity and economic growth produce socially beneficial increases in employment.

Utilitarians also favored the simplification of legal procedures. They opposed checks and balances, legal technicalities, and complex procedures. They believed that these "formalities" increased the costs and length of the judicial process and made the justice system ineffective and unresponsive to the needs of large numbers of average people. Modern utilitarians would favor small claims courts, with their simplified pleading requirements, informality, low cost, and optional use of lawyers.

Utilitarian influence can be found in legislative enactments that require the nation's broadcasters to operate "in the public interest," in "lemon laws," and in other consumer protection legislation. A major problem with utilitarianism is that not everyone agrees about what is pleasurable and what is painful. And many, if not most, political scientists would dispute that legislators actually make decisions according to the pleasure–pain principle.

Analytical Positivism

Analytical positivism asserted that law was a self-sufficient system of legal rules that the sovereign issued in the form of commands to the governed. These commands did not depend for legitimacy on extraneous considerations such as reason, ethics, morals, or even social consequences.[11] However, the sovereign's will was law only if it was developed according to duly established procedures, such as the enactments of a national legislature.

Thus, the apartheid laws passed by the previously all-white South African legislature were "the law" of that country at that time to the same extent that civil rights legislation enacted by the U.S. Congress was the law of this country. Each of these lawmaking bodies was exercising sovereign power in accordance with provisions of a national constitution. Positivists would maintain that individuals and governmental officials have no right to disobey laws with which they personally disagree due to moral, ethical, or policy objections. Positivists also would maintain that trial jurors have a legal obligation to apply the law according to the judge's instructions, even if that means disregarding strongly held personal beliefs about the wisdom of the law or its application in a particular factual dispute.

Members of this philosophical school would view disputes about the goodness or badness of legal rules as extra-legal.[12] They would maintain that such issues do not relate to the law as it is. This approach promotes stability and security. It also legitimizes governmental line drawing (such as laws that specify the age at which people can lawfully drink or vote, or those that determine automobile speed limits).

In the United States, people often disagree with governmental decisions about foreign policy, as well as about such issues as housing, the financing of public education, health care, abortion, environmental protection, and the licensing of nuclear power plants. Many contend that governmental officials are pursuing wrongful, and sometimes immoral, objectives. Such concerns, however, are generally unpersuasive in our courts. If governmental officials are authorized to make decisions, act within constitutional limitations, and follow established procedures, even decisions that are unpopular with some segments of society are nevertheless law.

But is law really just a closed system of rules and the product of a sovereign? Doesn't international law exist despite the absence of a sovereign? Don't contracting parties routinely create their own rules without any sovereign's involvement unless a dispute arises that results in litigation? And is law really morally neutral? Shouldn't the positivist approach be criticized if it protects governmental officials who act unfairly?

SOCIOLOGICAL JURISPRUDENCE, LEGAL REALISM, AND LEGAL SOCIOLOGY

After the Civil War, the nation's economy rapidly expanded, and America moved toward a market economy. Along with this expansion came new technologies, new products, and changing legal attitudes about government's rights to interfere with private property. Laissez-faire was in vogue, and although it contributed to expanding the economy, it also produced monopolies, political corruption, environmental pollution, hazardous working conditions, and labor–management conflict. The U.S. Supreme Court often opposed social reforms initiated by state governments. In *Lochner v. New York,* for example, the Court struck down a reform statute that limited bakers to ten-hour workdays and sixty-hour work weeks.[13] The majority ruled that this statute unreasonably infringed on the rights of employees and employers to negotiate their own contracts. The Court also declared the Erdman Act unconstitutional in *Adair v. United States.*[14] Congress enacted the Erdman Act to stop the railroad monopolies from discharging employees who joined labor unions. Congress, said the Supreme Court, had no right under the Interstate Commerce Clause to regulate labor relations in the railroad industry.

The excesses of laissez-faire produced social and economic unrest among farmers and laborers in particular, and produced political pressure for reforms. These factors culminated in the rise of the Progressive Movement. The Progressives sought an expanded governmental role in the economy. They wanted government to pay attention to reforming and to enact laws that would regulate special interests. The Progressives rejected the notion that law is based on immutable principles and deductive reasoning, and therefore is unrelated to political, social, and economic factors in society. Too often, they contended, the courts had ignored what Benjamin Cardozo would call the "pursuit of social justice."[15]

Sociological Jurisprudence

Roscoe Pound, of Harvard Law School, published an article in the 1911 *Harvard Law Review* that picked up on Progressive themes and announced a philosophy of law called sociological jurisprudence.[16] Pound argued against what he called "mechanical jurisprudence," with its backwardness and unjust outcomes in individual cases. He advocated that governments become proactive in working to promote social and economic reforms and that judges become more socially aware of the impact of their decisions on society.[17]

Early sociologists were interested in examining jurisprudence from a social-scientific perspective. They focused on what they called the living law—not just the law declared by legislatures and courts, but also the informal rules that actually influence social behavior. The sociological school maintains that law can only be understood when the formal system of rules is considered in conjunction with social realities (or facts). In this sense, it is similar to the historical school. However, the historical school approached time in terms of centuries, whereas the sociological school focused on ten- or twenty-year segments.

Sociological jurisprudence theorists, for example, would note that during the last sixty years the courts and legislatures have made many attempts to eliminate racial discrimination in voting, housing, employment, and education, and that the law on the books has changed significantly. It is equally clear from scholarly studies, however, that discrimination continues. The written law provides for equal opportunity, and on the surface racial discrimination is not as obvious as it once was. But the social facts continue to reveal subtle forms of racism that law has not been able to legislate or adjudicate away. Similarly, employment discrimination against women, older workers, and persons with disabilities continues despite the enactment of federal and state legislation that legally puts an end to such practices. Informally enforced social norms that condone bigotry and inflict personal indignities and economic inequities on targeted segments of society are not easily legislated away.

Although this approach effectively points out the discrepancies between the promise and the reality of enacted law, it often fails to produce practical solutions to the problems. Should judges be encouraged to consider social consequences in addition to legal rules in reaching decisions? If so, might this not result in arbitrary, discretionary decisions that reflect only the personal preferences of one particular jurist or group of jurists?

Legal Realists

During the early decades of the twentieth century, the social sciences were emerging. Academics and judges were attempting to borrow the scientific methods that had been used to study the natural and physical sciences and use them to examine social institutions. From the late 1920s through the middle 1930s, juries, and judges in particular, were subjected to empirical scrutiny by reformists such as Jerome Frank and Karl Llewellyn, who called themselves **legal realists.** The realists focused on the extent to which actual practices varied from the formal legal rules.[18] They believed that judges were influenced more by their personal convictions than by established and immutable rules. Llewellyn made a very important distinction between the legal rules and precedent-setting cases that were often cited as the basis for deciding why cases were won and lost (which he called "paper" rules) and the "real" rules of decisions that were undisclosed unless revealed by behavioral research.[19] Llewellyn believed that judges made law instead of discovering it, and he went so far as to proclaim that law was merely "what officials do about disputes."[20] Rules, the realists pointed out, do not adequately account for witness perjury and bias, and neither do rules compensate for the differing levels of ability, knowledge, and prejudice of individual lawyers, judges, and jurors. Because the realists produced little theory and research, they primarily blazed a trail for the legal sociologists to follow.

Legal Sociologists

Legal sociologists such as Donald Black have gone beyond the legal realists. Using quantitative methodological tools, they examine such factors as the financial standing, race, social class, respectability, and cultural differences of those involved in disputes.[21] In addition, they evaluate the social facts of the lawyers and judges working on the case, as well as those of the parties. In theory, legal outcomes should not be affected by differences in the socioeconomic status of the litigants, because all are "equal" before the law. Individual plaintiffs, for example, should be able to win when suing multinational corporations. But legal sociologists claim that the facts do not support this theory.[22] The rule of law is a myth, they say, because legal rules fail to take into account the impact of social diversity on litigation. Discrimination is a fact of modern life, and different combinations of social factors will produce disparate legal outcomes.[23] Donald Black points out that disputes between friends, neighbors, and family members are rarely litigated because "law varies directly with relational distance."[24] It can be argued persuasively that well-trained lawyers should decide only after carefully considering the relevant social factors and relationships whether to settle a case or go to trial, whether to try a case to a judge or a jury, and whether to appeal.[25]

Legal sociologists raise issues that challenge fundamental postulates of our society. If people become convinced that legal outcomes are largely a function of sociological considerations, rather than the application of impartial rules, the integrity of the judicial process itself will be undermined, as will the legitimacy of government. If research, however, can reveal more precisely how various combinations of sociological factors influence legal outcomes, this information could be used either to eliminate the bias or to develop alternative mechanisms for resolving particular types of disputes.

OBJECTIVES OF LAW

One of the foundations of our society is the belief that ours is a nation committed to the rule of law. No person is above the law. Our shared legal heritage binds us together as Americans. We use law to regulate people in their relationships with each other and in their relationships with government. Law reflects our societal aspirations, our culture, and our political and economic beliefs. It provides mechanisms for resolving disputes and for controlling government officials. Private law includes property, family, tort, probate, and corporate law. Public law includes constitutional, criminal, and administrative law. Common to both, however, are certain legal objectives.

Continuity and Stability

It is important that established laws change gradually. Litigants have greater confidence that justice has been done when preexisting rules are used to determine legal outcomes. Laws work best when people become aware of them and learn how they work and why they are necessary. Stable laws are also more likely to be applied uniformly and consistently throughout a jurisdiction and will be better understood by those charged with enforcement.

Stable laws are also very important to creating and maintaining a healthy economy because they are predictable and serve as a guide for conduct. Businesspeople, for example, are not likely to incur risk in a volatile legal and political environment. They are likely to feel more comfortable in making investments and taking economic risks where it appears likely that the future will resemble the present and the recent past. This stability is threatened by society's appetite for producing rules. Various state and federal legislative and administrative rule-making bodies are currently promulgating so many regulations that it is difficult, if not impossible, for affected citizens to stay current.

Adaptability

In one sense, it would be desirable if society could create a great big "legal cookbook" that contained a prescribed law or rule for every conceivable situation. We would then only have to look in the cookbook for definitive answers to all legal problems. In reality, there is no such cookbook. Legislators produce statutes that have a broad scope and that are designed to promote the public's health, safety, welfare, and morals. Judges make law in conjunction with resolving disputes that have been properly brought before the court. Experience has shown that legislative enactments and judicial opinions produce imperfect law. Lawmakers cannot anticipate every factual possibility. Courts, in particular, often feel compelled to recognize exceptions to general rules in order to provide justice in individual cases. Judges often find that there are gaps in the law that they have to fill in order to decide a case, or that a long-standing rule no longer makes any sense, given current circumstances and societal values. In this way, law adapts to social, environmental, and political changes within our evolving society.

Justice, Speed, and Economy

Although most people would agree with the preamble to the U.S. Constitution that it is the role of the government "to establish justice," there is no consensus about what that means. Some see justice as a natural law–type settlement, which means each party to a dispute receives what he or she is due. To other people justice means that a specified process was followed by governmental institutions. In some situations, justice requires the elimination of discretion so that law is applied more equally. In other situations, justice requires the inclusion of discretion (equity) so that the law is not applied too mechanically. In this respect, it is helpful to look at recent history. Our current notions of justice with respect to race, gender, sexual orientation, and class differ from the views of many of our forebears. Posterity will probably have a concept of justice that differs from our own.

Rule 1 of the Federal Rules of Civil Procedure provides that procedural rules should be construed "to secure the just, speedy and inexpensive determination of every action." Although it would be desirable if our judicial systems could satisfy all three of these objectives, they are often in conflict. As a society we continually have to make choices about how much justice we desire and can afford.

Consider a society dedicated to achieving the highest possible levels of justice in its judicial system. Elaborate measures would be required to ensure that all relevant evidence has been located and all possible witnesses identified and permitted to testify. In such a society, all litigants would be entitled to the services of investigators, thorough pretrial discovery procedures, and qualified and experienced trial attorneys. Great care would have to be taken to ensure that jurors were truly unbiased and competent to render a fair verdict. Only highly probative evidence would be permitted as proof, and various levels of appellate review would be required to consider carefully whether significant substantive or procedural errors were made at trial. Obviously, such a process would be very slow and very expensive. Denying deserving plaintiffs a recovery until the process had run its course could itself be unfair, because a recovery would be denied for several years.

Instead, some judicial systems build in cost-cutting measures such as six-person instead of twelve-person juries. They also make it easier for juries to reach decisions by permitting less-than-unanimous verdicts. Although each cost-cutting step risks more error in the system, there are limits to how much justice society is willing to provide. People have a multitude of needs, including medical care, housing, education, and defense, as well as a limited interest in paying taxes. These competing needs have to be prioritized. In recent years, governmental funding of poverty lawyers has been greatly reduced. This has occurred at a time when the cost of litigating average cases has risen substantially. As the costs of using the legal system increase, fewer persons will be able to afford to use litigation to resolve their disputes. Private attorneys often decline to represent a potential client if the likely recovery in the case will not produce an acceptable profit.

An example of how law balances the desire for justice with a concern for cost appears in the case of *Goss v. Lopez* (which can be read on the textbook website). In that case the U.S. Supreme Court determined that public school administrators only have to provide rudimentary procedural due process to students who face short suspensions. The Supreme Court explained that requiring schools to provide students with extensive trial-type procedures would make the disciplinary process too expensive. In Chapter XIV we examine alternative methods for resolving disputes.

Determining Desirable Public Policy

Historically, law has been used to determine desirable public policy. It has been used to establish and then abolish discrimination on the basis of race, gender, age, and sexual preference. Law has been used to promote environmental protection and to permit resource exploitation. Through law, society determines whether doctors can assist in suicides, whether people of the same sex can marry, and which kinds of video games minors can purchase.

ORIGIN OF LAW IN THE UNITED STATES

The British victory over the French in the French and Indian War and the signing of the Treaty of Paris (1763) concluded the competition between the two nations for domination of North America. A French victory might well have resulted in the establishment of the French legal system in the colonies along the Atlantic seaboard. The British victory, however, preserved the English common law system for what would become the United States. The following discussion highlights some of the important milestones in the development of the common law.

The Origins of English Common Law

Anglo-Saxon kings ruled England prior to 1066. During the reign of Edward the Confessor (1042–1066), wealthy landowners and noblemen, called earls, gained power over local affairs. There was no central legislature or national judicial court. Instead, the country was organized into communal units, based on population. Each unit was called a hundred and was headed by an official called the reeve. The primary function of the hundred was judicial; it held court once each month and dealt with routine civil and criminal matters. Local freemen resolved these cases in accordance with local custom.[26]

The hundreds were grouped into units called shires (counties), which in earlier times often had been Anglo-Saxon kingdoms. The shire was of much greater importance than the hundred. The king used it for military, administrative, and judicial purposes. The king administered the shires through the person of the shire reeve (sheriff). Royal sheriffs existed in each of the shires throughout the country. The sheriff was the king's principal judicial and administrative officer at the local level. Sheriffs collected taxes, urged support of the king's administrative and military policies, and performed limited judicial functions.[27] The shire court, composed of all the freemen in the county, was held twice a year and was presided over by the bishop and the sheriff.[28] It handled criminal, civil, and religious matters that were too serious or difficult for the hundred court, as well as disputes about land ownership.[29] The freemen in attendance used local custom as the basis for making decisions, even in religious matters, resulting in a variety of regional practices throughout the country. Anglo-Saxon law did not permit a person to approach the king to appeal the decisions of these communal courts.[30]

The Anglo-Saxon king had a number of functions. He raised armies and a navy for the defense of the kingdom. He issued writs, which were administrative letters containing the royal seal.[31] The **writs** were used to order courts to convene and sheriffs to do justice, and to award grants of land and privileges.[32] The king administered the country with the assistance of the royal household, an early form of king's council.[33] He also declared laws (called dooms),[34] sometimes after consulting with the Witan, a national assembly of important nobles.[35]

When Edward the Confessor died childless in 1066, the candidates to succeed him were his brother-in-law, Harold, Earl of Wessex, and his cousin, William, Duke of Normandy (a French duchy). Harold was English and the most powerful baron in the country. William was French. Each claimed that Edward had selected him as the next king. William also claimed that Harold had agreed to support William's claim to the throne.[36] Harold, however, was elected king by the Witan and was crowned. William's response was to assemble an army, cross the English Channel, and invade England.

The Norman Invasion

In 1066, Duke William of Normandy, with 5,000 soldiers and 2,500 horses, defeated the Anglo-Saxons and killed King Harold at the Battle of Hastings.[37] William became king of England, and the Normans assumed control of the country. Although the Anglo-Saxons had implemented a type of feudalism before the invasion, the Normans developed and refined it. Feudalism was a military, political, and social structure that ordered relationships among people. Under feudalism, a series of duties and obligations existed between a lord and his vassals. In England, the Normans merged feudalism with the Anglo-Saxon institution of the national king. William insisted, for example, that all land in England belonged ultimately to the king, and in 1086 he required all landholders to swear allegiance to him.[38] In this way, all his barons and lords and their vassals were personally obligated to him by feudal law. At his coronation, King William decreed that Englishmen could keep the customary laws that had been in force during the reign of the Anglo-Saxon King Edward the Confessor. This meant that the hundred and shire courts could continue to resolve disputes between the English as they had in the past.[39] William did, however, make one significant change in the jurisdiction of the communal courts: he rejected the Anglo-Saxon practice of allowing church officials to use the communal courts to decide religious matters. Instead, he mandated that the church should establish its own courts and that religious matters should be decided according to canon (church) law, rather than customary law.[40] William also declared that the Normans would settle their disputes in the courts of the lords and barons, in agreement with feudal law.

England at that time consisted of two societies, one French and the other English.[41] French was the language spoken by the victorious Normans, as well as by the king, the upper classes, the clergy, and scholars.[42] Following the invasion, English was only spoken by the lower classes, and it did not achieve prominence and become the language of the courts and the "common law" until 1362.[43] The French legacy can be seen in many words used by lawyers today. *Acquit, en banc, voir dire, demurrer, embezzle,* and *detainer* are some examples of English words that were borrowed from the French. Although the Normans spoke French, formal documents were written in Latin. This may help to explain why students reading judicial opinions in the twenty-first century encounter Latin words such as *certiorari, subpoena, mens rea, actus reus, in camera, mandamus, capias,* and *pro se.*

The Development of the Common Law

Over time, marriages between Norman and English families blurred the old class system. William's son Henry (who became Henry I), for example, married a descendant of the Anglo-Saxon royal house.[44] It was not until after 1453, when the French drove the English out of France (except for Calais), however, that the Normans and English were unified as one nation.

William died in 1100. The most important of his successors—in terms of the development of the common law—were Henry I and Henry's grandson, Henry II. After the death of the very unpopular William II, the nobles elected Henry I as king. Henry I had promised the nobles that if elected he would issue a charter in which he pledged to respect the rights of the nobles.[45] He also promised to be a fair ruler in the manner of William I. This charter is significant because it was a model for the most famous of all charters, the Magna Carta.[46]

Henry I ruled during a prosperous period and strengthened the king's powers while making peace with the church and feudal barons. He also strengthened the judiciary by requiring members of his council, the Curia Regis, to ride circuit occasionally throughout the country to listen to pleas and supervise the local courts. During this period, the communal courts, the religious courts, and the feudal courts of the barons were still meeting, and there was much confusion over jurisdiction.[47] Henry I encouraged people who distrusted the local courts to turn to the king for justice.

Henry II was the king most involved in the development of the central judiciary and the common law.[48] He created a professional royal court to hear civil litigation between ordinary parties (common pleas) and staffed this court with barons who had learned how to judge from working as members of the Curia Regis.[49] The king had some of his judges sit with him at Westminster (in London), and others traveled throughout the country listening to pleas and supervising local courts.[50] These royal judges applied the same law in each of the jurisdictions in which they held court.[51]

They did not treat each case as if it were a case of first impression or apply the customary law of the particular region. Decisions were not based on abstract principles and theories. The royal judges decided disputes in a consistent manner throughout the country, based on slowly evolving legal rules adopted by the members of the court.[52]

There were important procedural incentives for bringing suit in the royal courts rather than in the local courts. One was that the losing party in a communal or feudal court could have the decision reviewed by common pleas. Another was that the king enforced royal court judgments. Last, royal courts used juries instead of trials by battle and ordeal.[53]

One type of problem that was often brought to the king involved land disputes between neighboring nobles. One noble would claim part of his neighbor's land and seize it without bringing the matter to the attention of any court. Henry II's response was to allow victims to petition him for issuance of a writ of right. This writ, which was purchased from the king, directed the communal courts to do full justice without delay or to appear in a royal court and give an explanation.[54] The development of the writ of right resulted in a law making it illegal to dispossess someone of land without a trial conducted according to a royal writ.

The Normans became very creative in the way they used writs. Under the Norman kings, prospective plaintiffs had to obtain writs in order to litigate any claim. As the demand for writs increased, the responsibility for issuing them was transferred from the king to the chancellor,[55] and in later years to the courts themselves. Each writ conferred jurisdiction on a designated court to resolve a particular dispute. It also specified many of the procedures to be followed since there was no general code of civil procedure to regulate the conduct of litigation.[56] A writ, for example, would often be addressed to the sheriff and would require him to summons in the defendant and convene a jury. In Henry I's era, there were very few writs. By Henry III's reign, many writs existed, including entry, debt, detinue, account, replevin, covenant, and novel disseisin (wrongful ejection).[57] A few master registers of writs were developed to form a primitive "law library."

By roughly 1200, the principal components of the common law system were in place. National law had replaced local and regional customs of the shire and hundred. A body of royal judges applied a common law throughout the nation, a tradition of respecting precedent was established, and the writ system was functioning.[58]

The development of legal literature was important to the development and improvement of the common law.[59] Henry Bracton, a thirteenth-century English lawyer, wrote commentaries on the writs of the day during the reign of Henry III (Henry II's grandson) and collected cases from the preceding twenty years.[60] During the fourteenth and fifteenth centuries, lawyers and law students began a series of "Year Books," a collection of the cases that had been heard in the most important courts for each year. The Year Books were discontinued in 1535 and were replaced by case reports, which were informal collections by various authors. Some of these authors, such as Chief Justice Edward Coke (pronounced "cook"), were well known and highly respected.[61] Coke published thirteen volumes of cases between 1572 and 1616. The reports established a process that in 1865 resulted in the publication of official law reports. In 1765, Sir William Blackstone, an Oxford professor, published a collection of his lectures in a book titled *Commentaries on the Laws of England,* which was immensely popular in the American colonies. The first American judicial reports were published in

1789, and James Kent's influential *Commentaries on American Law* was published between 1826 and 1830.[62]

The common law came to what is now the United States as a result of Britain's colonization policies. In the early 1600s, British monarchs began awarding charters to merchants and proprietors to establish colonies along the Atlantic coast of North America. Over the next 150 years, a steady flow of immigrants, most of whom were British, crossed the Atlantic, bringing the English language, culture, law books, and legal tradition. The common law was one major component of that tradition; another was the court of equity.

The Origin of the English Equitable Court

Until the fourteenth century, the common law courts were willing to consider arguments based on conscience as well as law. The judges were concerned with equity (fairness and mercy) as well as legality. By the fifteenth century, however, the common law courts were sometimes less concerned with justice than with technicalities. Common law pleading was complex and jury tampering was common.[63] The courts often refused to allow parties to testify, and there were no procedures for discovering an opponent's evidence. Although the common law courts were able to act against land and would award money judgments, they refused to grant injunctive relief (court orders directing individuals to perform or refrain from engaging in certain acts).[64] Unusual situations arose for which there was no common law relief, or for which the relief available was inadequate as a remedy. In addition, the law courts were often slow, and litigation was very costly. Increasingly, dissatisfied parties began to petition the king and his council to intervene in the name of justice. As the number of petitions rose, the king and council forwarded the petitions to the chancellor.[65]

The **chancellor,** originally a high-ranking member of the clergy, was part of the royal household. He was the king's leading advisor in political matters and was a professional administrator. The chancellor's staff included people with judicial

experience who issued the writs that enabled suitors to litigate in the common law courts.[66] Because they were ecclesiastics, the early chancellors were not trained as common law lawyers. They were well educated,[67] however, and were familiar with the canon law of the Roman Catholic Church.[68] As a result, the chancellors were often more receptive to arguments based on morality than to arguments based exclusively on legality.

As chancellors began to hear petitions, the **court of chancery,** or **equity court,** came into being. It granted relief based on broad principles of right and justice in cases in which the restrictions of the common law prevented it. Chancellors began to use the **writ of subpoena** to speed up their hearings and the **writ of summons** to require people to appear in the chancery.[69] Chancery trials were conducted before a single judge who sat without a jury. The chancellor, who exercised discretion and did not rely on precedent in granting relief, would only act where extraordinary relief was required because no writ applied to the wrong from which the petitioner sought relief. One such area was specific performance of contracts. Although a suit for what we would call breach of contract could be maintained in a common law court, that court could not require a contracting party to perform his bargain. The chancellor, however, could issue such an order directed to the nonperforming person and could enforce it with the contempt power.

The equity court became very popular and was very busy by the middle 1500s. For centuries, common law and equity were administered in England by these two separate courts. Each court applied its own system of jurisprudence and followed its own judicial rules and remedies. Much of traditional equity is based on concepts such as adequacy, practicality, clean hands, and hardship (matters we discuss in Chapter VII). The equity court's workload continued to grow, as did the chancellor's staff. By the seventeenth century, the most important of the chancellor's staff clerks were called masters in chancery. The chief master was called the Master of the Rolls. Masters in chancery helped the chancellor conduct the equity court, particularly while the chancellor was performing nonjudicial duties for the king.

Initially, despite their differing aims, the common law courts and the equity court cooperated with each other. Starting with Henry VIII's reign, common law lawyers rather than ecclesiastics were named chancellor, which improved relations between courts of law and equity.[70] Sir Thomas More, as chancellor, invited the common law judges to incorporate the notion of conscience into the common law, but the judges declined, preferring to stand behind the decisions of the juries. Gradually, however, this dual-court system created a competition for business, and the common law courts became more flexible by borrowing from equity. The equitable courts were also changing, and chancellors began to identify jurisdictional boundaries between the equitable and common law courts. Equity, for example, agreed to furnish a remedy only when the common law procedure was deficient or the remedy at common law was inadequate.[71]

Beginning in 1649, the decisions of the chancellors were sporadically collected and published, a process that led to the establishment of equitable precedent.[72] Eventually, equitable precedent made the equity courts as formalistic and rigid as the common law courts had been in equity's early days.[73] This dual-court system continued in England until the passage by Parliament of the Judicature Acts of 1873 and 1875, which merged the equitable and common law courts into a unified court.

Some North American colonies along the Atlantic coast diverged from British precedent when it came to the establishment of equity courts. Massachusetts never established an equity court, and its trial courts were not permitted to exercise the equitable powers of the chancellor until 1870. Maryland, New York, New Jersey, Delaware, North Carolina, and South Carolina initially established separate courts for common law and equity. However, by 1900 common law and equity had merged into a single judicial system in most states.

As you read the cases included in this textbook, you will notice that plaintiffs often request legal and equitable relief in the same complaint. A plaintiff may demand money damages (common law relief), a declaratory judgment (equitable relief), and an injunction (equitable relief) in the complaint. This creates no problem for the courts. The legal issues will be tried by a jury (unless the parties prefer a bench trial), and the equitable issues will be decided by the judge sitting as a chancellor according to the rules of equity. In Chapter VII we look more closely at the differences between the common law and equitable remedies.

A PROCEDURAL PRIMER

The following highly simplified overview of litigation is intended to give you a sense of the big picture before we examine each stage of the process in more detail. Like a trial attorney's opening statement in a jury trial, it is intended to help you see how the various procedural stages fit together. This abbreviated treatment omits many of the details and is intentionally very limited in scope.

Every lawsuit is based on some event that causes a person to feel that he or she has been legally injured in some manner by another. The injured party will often contact an attorney to discuss the matter. The attorney will listen to the facts, make a determination about whether the client has a case, and present the client with a range of options for pursuing a claim. These options will often include informal attempts to settle the claim, alternative dispute resolution methods such as those discussed in Chapter XIV, and filing suit in court. After weighing the costs and benefits of each option and listening to the advice of the attorney, the client will make a decision as to how to proceed. If the decision is made to file suit, the lawyer will draft a document called a **complaint** and a writ of summons and serve them on the defendant in accordance with the law. The complaint will explain the plaintiff's claims and requested relief. The summons will tell the defendant to serve a document called an answer, in which the defendant responds to the claims made in the complaint, on the plaintiff's attorney by a statutorily determined date. If the defendant's attorney finds any legal defects in jurisdiction, venue, form, or substance in either the summons or the complaint, he or she can make motions seeking modification or dismissal of the action. Assuming that the motions are denied and any defects are corrected, the defendant will then draft and serve the **answer.** If the defendant fails to file a timely answer, the court can declare the plaintiff the winner by default due to the defendant's inaction.

Once the complaint has been properly served and filed with the court, the **discovery** phase begins. This is where each party learns as much as possible about the case. Virtually all relevant information can be obtained from friendly, neutral, or adverse sources, such as the opposing party. Obviously some information is not discoverable, such as an attorney's trial strategy, research notes (work product), and other material that is classified as privileged. In Chapter V, we learn specific techniques lawyers use during the discovery phase.

After the facts have been sufficiently investigated, one or both parties will frequently request the court to dispose of the case and award a **judgment** (the court's final decision in a case), rather than proceeding to trial. This request, called a **motion for summary judgment,** is properly granted when the plaintiff and defendant substantially agree about the important facts in the case. If there is no dispute about the significant facts, there is no reason to conduct a trial. In that situation, the judge can resolve any dispute about what legal rule applies to this particular set of facts and award a judgment to the deserving party.

It is important to note that informal discussions between the attorneys often take place at all stages of the process, up to and even during the course of the trial, in an effort to settle the case. These discussions usually intensify once motions for summary judgment have been denied and it appears that the case will be tried. Assuming that summary judgment is denied and there is no negotiated settlement, what usually follows is the pretrial conference.

At a **pretrial conference,** the court and the attorneys will meet to define the issues, prepare for the trial, and discuss the possibility of settlement. At this meeting, the parties can indicate how many days they believe it will take to try the case, try to resolve evidentiary and discovery problems, and schedule any necessary pretrial hearings. After the meeting, the judge will sign a pretrial order that records the decisions that were made at the conference.

Before proceeding to trial, many jurisdictions will require or encourage the litigating parties to participate in **alternative dispute resolution (ADR).** Some form of ADR is practiced in every state, but it is more commonly used in some jurisdictions than in others. The situation in the federal district courts is somewhat similar. Although all districts are required by federal statute to offer at least one ADR procedure, its use varies greatly by district.[74] ADR is an umbrella concept for a variety of procedures designed to help parties resolve their disputes without trials. Jurisdictions participate in ADR to differing degrees. Some mandate cooperation, and others make participation optional. In Chapter XIV we explain such ADR techniques as mediation, arbitration, summary jury trials, and minitrials, but we emphasize that any party dissatisfied with the ADR process can insist on proceeding to trial. There is a continuing dispute as to whether ADR is living up to its proponents' claims and producing faster, less expensive, and higher-quality justice than litigation.[75]

Less than 2 percent of all federal lawsuits filed actually are decided at trial.[76] Nonjury trials (also known as bench trials), in which a judge decides the factual issues, are conducted differently from trials in which juries render a verdict. In bench trials, for example, there are no jurors to select, the attorneys generally do not make opening statements, the rules of evidence are often relaxed, and there are no jury instructions to prepare and deliver. The judge will consider the evidence presented by each party and determine whether the plaintiff has satisfied the burden of proof. At the end of a bench trial, the judge will announce findings of fact, state conclusions of law, and award a judgment.

Additional procedures are necessary for jury trials. The jurors have to be carefully selected, and in major trials, the lawyers may seek help from trial consultants. Because jurors generally know little about rules of evidence and the applicable law, the lawyers do not present their cases as they would in a bench trial. Judges must keep the lawyers in check and ensure that the jury is exposed only to evidence that is relevant, material, and competent (legally adequate). After each side has had the opportunity to present evidence and cross-examine opposing witnesses, the attorneys will conclude by arguing their cases to the jury. After the closing arguments, the judge instructs the jury on the law and sends it out to deliberate. The jury deliberates until it reaches a verdict, which it reports to the court. After deciding any postverdict motions, the court will enter a **judgment** in favor of one of the parties and award relief accordingly. Normally any party dissatisfied with the judgment will have a specified number of days after the entry of judgment in which to make an appeal, provided timely objections were made during the trial.

READING CASES - PART I

The application of law to factual situations is necessary when there is a controversy between two or more people or when parties seek guidance concerning the consequences of their conduct or proposed conduct. The court cases in this text involve disputes that the parties were unable to resolve by themselves and that were brought to the trial and appellate courts for a decision. Most disputes, however, are settled by the parties outside court based on professional predictions of what a court would do.

Students learn to understand the legal process and the relationship between judicial theories and practical legal problems by analyzing actual court cases. The cases in this text illustrate particular points of law. They also convey current legal theory. These cases should serve as points of departure for discussions about the legal response to current social problems. It is important to understand the strengths and weaknesses of law as an instrument of social change.

Case reports are official explanations of a court's decision-making process. They explain which legal principles are applicable and why they are controlling under the particular circumstances of each case. Thus, in analyzing each case decision, students should focus on the underlying factual situation, the law that the court applied, whether the decision was just, and the impact the decision will have when it is used as precedent.

Because U.S. Supreme Court opinions tend to be quite long, the author omits portions of an opinion that do not contribute to the resolution of the most important issue in the case and omits portions of opinions that only marginally advance the discussion or are likely to confuse readers.

Author's Introduction to *Evan Miller v. Alabama* and *Kuntrell Jackson v. Ray Hobbs, Director, Arkansas Department of Correction*

Our first case explores whether the Cruel and Unusual Punishments Clause of the Eighth Amendment permits the mandatory sentencing of juveniles who have been convicted of murder to life imprisonment without possibility of parole. As of 2012, twenty-eight states and the federal government had statutorily mandated such sentences. Two juveniles, one from Alabama (Evan Miller) and the other from Arkansas (Kuntrell Jackson), were prosecuted, convicted, and sentenced in adult courts for capital murder. Miller's offense involved extreme brutality and cruelty on his part and occurred in conjunction with an arson. Miller was originally charged in juvenile court and then transferred into adult court. Jackson, although found by the jury not to have been the shooter, was convicted of aiding and abetting the person who shot and killed the victim in conjunction with the armed robbery of a video store. Jackson, although fourteen, was initially prosecuted in adult court. Miller and Jackson were sentenced in adult courts to mandatory terms of life in prison without possibility of parole. The appellate courts of the States of Alabama and Arkansas confirmed the convictions and sentences.

Miller and Jackson, acting independently, successfully petitioned the U.S. Supreme Court, which agreed to review both of their cases. The two cases were consolidated by the Supreme Court for decision. The Supreme Court ruled on the following issue:

> Does the Eighth Amendment's Cruel and Unusual Punishments Clause prohibit the sentencing of juveniles convicted of capital murder to mandatory sentences of life in prison without possibility of parole?

The mandatory nature of the sentences was the most contentious issue before the Court. The jurors in both states had convicted Miller and Jackson of murders that included "aggravating circumstances," a finding required in all death penalty cases (the Arkansas statute lists ten circumstances that permit an offender's execution, and the Alabama aggravating circumstances list contains eighteen such offenses). Despite their capital murder convictions and the findings of aggravated circumstances, Miller and Jackson (unlike adults under the same circumstances) could not be sentenced to death, because of a U.S. Supreme Court ruling. In *Roper v. Simmons* the Court held that a juvenile under the age of eighteen when the crime was committed could not be sentenced to death.

But as juveniles convicted of capital offenses, they were still subject to a mandatory sentence of life in prison without possibility of parole under Alabama and Arkansas law. Neither state had established any special provisions for juveniles. Nor had either state permitted the sentencing entity (a judge and advisory jury in Alabama and a jury in Arkansas) to consider any mitigating factors that might warrant a sentence less than the mandated sentence. The Alabama and Arkansas legislatures, in enacting mandatory sentences, had chosen the inflexible per se ("one size fits all") approach over the alternative individualized sentencing ("case-by-case") approach. Where individualized sentencing is permitted at sentencing hearings, judges can consider as part of the decision-making process the facts and circumstances of the offenses, the nature and extent of the juvenile offender's participation in the commission of the crime, the juvenile's background,

intent, or lack of intent, and any other relevant mitigating or aggravating factors that might have influenced the sentencing determination. The Alabama and Arkansas judges who sentenced these convicted juveniles had no discretion. They were compelled by state statutes to impose the mandated sentences.

The U.S. Supreme Court decided these cases in favor of Miller and Jackson, by a slim 5-4 margin. The five justices constituting the majority were Justices Kagan, Kennedy, Ginsburg, Breyer, and Sotomayor. Justice Kagan wrote the Opinion of the Court (the majority opinion), in which she explained the Court's rationale (the reasoning that supports the decision).

Nomenclature Tips

The following brief explanation will help readers who are unfamiliar with courtroom terminology to better understand the various labels that are attached to the litigants as the legal process moves from the initiation of the prosecution through the trial and appellate levels all the way to the U.S. Supreme Court.

The States of Alabama and Arkansas became the **plaintiffs** in their respective jurisdictions when state prosecutors filed criminal complaints in court naming Miller and Jackson as **defendants.** Miller and Jackson became **appellants** when they filed appeals in the aftermath of their trials, and their opponents on appeal, the States of Arkansas and Alabama, became the **appellees.** Miller and Jackson became the **petitioners** when they filed a petition for **writ of certiorari** in the U.S. Supreme Court (a necessary step in obtaining review in that court), and the States of Alabama and Arkansas became the **respondents** in the U.S. Supreme Court.

What follows is an edited version of Justice Kagan's Opinion of the Court. Part III of the majority opinion, in which Justice Kagan rebuts the arguments of the dissenting justices, has been omitted in the interest of conserving space. An edited version of the omitted content can be found on this textbook's website.

Miller v. Alabama
_____ U.S. _____
Supreme Court of the United States
June 25, 2012

Justice Kagan delivered the opinion of the Court.
The two 14-year-old offenders in these cases were convicted of murder and sentenced to life imprisonment without the possibility of parole. In neither case did the sentencing authority have any discretion to impose a different punishment. State law mandated that each juvenile die in prison even if a judge or jury would have thought that his youth and its attendant characteristics, along with the nature of his crime, made a lesser sentence ... more appropriate....

I

A
In November 1999, petitioner Kuntrell Jackson, then 14 years old, and two other boys decided to rob a video store. En route to the store, Jackson learned that one of the boys, Derrick Shields, was carrying a sawed-off shotgun in his coat sleeve. Jackson decided to stay outside when the two other boys entered the store. Inside, Shields pointed the gun at the store clerk, Laurie Troup, and demanded that she "give up the money."... Troup refused. A few moments later, Jackson went into the store to find Shields continuing to demand money. At trial, the parties disputed whether Jackson warned Troup that "[w]e ain't playin'," or instead told his friends, "I thought you all was playin'." ... When Troup threatened to call the police, Shields shot and killed her. The three boys fled empty-handed....

Arkansas law gives prosecutors discretion to charge 14-year-olds as adults when they are alleged to have committed certain serious offenses.... The prosecutor here exercised that authority by charging Jackson with capital felony murder and aggravated robbery. Jackson moved to transfer the case to juvenile court ... , but ... the trial court denied the motion, and an appellate court affirmed.... A jury later convicted Jackson of both crimes.... [T]he judge sentenced Jackson to life without parole ... see Ark. Code Ann. §5-4-104(b) (1997) ("A defendant convicted of capital murder or treason shall be sentenced to death or life imprisonment without parole").... [T]he Arkansas Supreme Court affirmed the convictions....

Following *Roper v. Simmons*, 543 U. S. 551 (2005), in which this Court invalidated the death penalty for all juvenile offenders under the age of 18, Jackson filed a state petition for habeas corpus. He argued, based on Roper's reasoning, that a mandatory sentence of life without parole for a 14-year-old also violates the Eighth Amendment. The circuit court rejected that argument and granted the State's motion to dismiss.... While that ruling was on appeal, this Court held in *Graham v. Florida* that life without parole violates the Eighth Amendment when imposed on juvenile non-homicide offenders. After the parties filed briefs addressing that decision, the Arkansas Supreme Court affirmed the dismissal of Jackson's petition.... Two justices dissented. They noted that Jackson was not the shooter and that "any evidence of intent to kill was severely lacking." ... And they argued that Jackson's mandatory sentence ran afoul of *Graham's* admonition that " '[a]n offender's age is relevant to the Eighth Amendment, and criminal procedure laws that fail to take defendants' youthfulness into account at all would be flawed.' "...

B
Like Jackson, petitioner Evan Miller was 14 years old at the time of his crime. Miller had by then been in and out of foster care because his mother suffered from alcoholism and drug addiction and his stepfather abused him. Miller, too, regularly used drugs and alcohol; and he had attempted suicide four times, the first when he was six years old....

One night in 2003, Miller was at home with a friend, Colby Smith, when a neighbor, Cole Cannon, came to make a drug deal with Miller's mother.... The two boys followed Cannon back to his trailer, where all three smoked marijuana and played drinking games. When Cannon passed out, Miller stole his wallet, splitting about $300 with Smith. Miller then tried to put the wallet back in Cannon's pocket, but Cannon awoke and grabbed Miller by the throat. Smith hit Cannon with a nearby baseball bat, and once released, Miller grabbed the bat and repeatedly struck Cannon with it. Miller placed a sheet over Cannon's head, told him " 'I am God, I've come to take your life,' " and delivered one more blow.... The boys then retreated to Miller's trailer, but soon decided to return to Cannon's to cover up evidence of their crime. Once there, they lit two fires. Cannon eventually died from his injuries and smoke inhalation....

Alabama law required that Miller initially be charged as a juvenile, but allowed the District Attorney to seek removal of the case to adult court.... The D. A. did so, and the juvenile court agreed ... , the Alabama Court of Criminal Appeals affirmed.... The State accordingly charged Miller as an adult with murder in the course of arson. That crime … carries a mandatory minimum punishment of life without parole.… See Ala. Code §§13A-5-40(9), 13A-6-2(c) (1982).

… [A] jury found Miller guilty. He was therefore sentenced to life without the possibility of parole. The Alabama Court of Criminal Appeals affirmed.… The Alabama Supreme Court denied review.

We granted certiorari in both cases [the Court grants "certiorari" when it agrees to decide a case].…

II
The Eighth Amendment's prohibition of cruel and unusual punishment "guarantees individuals the right not to be subjected to excessive sanctions."… That right, we have explained, "flows from the basic 'precept of justice that punishment for crime should be graduated and proportioned' " to both the offender and the offense.… And we view that concept less through a historical prism than according to " 'the evolving standards of decency that mark the progress of a maturing society.' "…

The cases before us implicate two strands of precedent.… The first has adopted categorical bans on sentencing practices based on mismatches between the culpability of a class of offenders and the severity of a penalty.… So, for example, we have held that imposing the death penalty for non-homicide crimes against individuals, or imposing it on mentally retarded defendants, violates the Eighth Amendment.… Several of the cases in this group have specially focused on juvenile offenders, because of their lesser culpability. Thus, *Roper* held that the Eighth Amendment bars capital punishment for children, and *Graham* concluded that the Amendment also prohibits a sentence of life without the possibility of parole for a child who committed a non-homicide offense. *Graham* further likened life without parole for juveniles to the death penalty itself, thereby evoking a second line of our precedents. In those cases, we have prohibited mandatory imposition of capital punishment, requiring that sentencing authorities consider the characteristics of a defendant and the details of his offense before sentencing him to death.… Here, the confluence of these two lines of precedent leads to the conclusion that mandatory life-without-parole sentences for juveniles violate the Eighth Amendment.

To start with the first set of cases: *Roper* and *Graham* establish that children are constitutionally different from adults for purposes of sentencing. Because juveniles have diminished culpability and greater prospects for reform, we explained, "they are less deserving of the most severe punishments."… Those cases relied on three significant gaps between juveniles and adults. First, children have a " 'lack of maturity and an underdeveloped sense of responsibility,' " leading to recklessness, impulsivity, and heedless risk-taking.… Second, children "are more vulnerable … to negative influences and outside pressures," including from their family and peers; they have limited "contro[l] over their own environment" and lack the ability to extricate themselves from horrific, crime-producing settings.… And third, a child's character is not as "well formed" as an adult's; his traits are "less fixed" and his actions less likely to be "evidence of irretrievabl[e] deprav[ity]."…

Nor can deterrence do the work in this context, because " 'the same characteristics that render juveniles less culpable than adults' "—their immaturity, recklessness, and impetuosity—make them less likely to consider potential punishment.… Similarly, incapacitation could not support the life-without-parole sentence … [because] [d]eciding that a "juvenile offender forever will be a danger to society" would require "mak[ing] a judgment that [he] is incorrigible"—but " 'incorrigibility is inconsistent with youth.' "… And for the same reason, rehabilitation could not justify that sentence. Life without parole … reflects "an irrevocable judgment about [an offender's] value and place in society," at odds with a child's capacity for change.…

Most fundamentally, *Graham* insists that youth matters in determining the appropriateness of a lifetime of incarceration without the possibility of parole.… "An offender's age," we made clear in *Graham*, "is relevant to the Eighth Amendment," and so "criminal procedure laws that fail to take defendants' youthfulness into account at all would be flawed."… But the mandatory penalty schemes at issue here prevent the sentencer from taking account of these central considerations. By removing youth from the balance—by subjecting a juvenile to the same life-without-parole sentence applicable to an adult—these laws prohibit a sentencing authority from assessing whether the law's harshest term of imprisonment proportionately punishes a juvenile offender. That contravenes *Graham*'s (and also *Roper*'s) foundational principle: that imposition of a State's most severe penalties on juvenile offenders cannot proceed as though they were not children.

And *Graham* makes plain these mandatory schemes' defects in another way: by likening life-without-parole sentences imposed on juveniles to the death penalty itself. Life-without-parole terms, the Court wrote, "share some characteristics with death sentences that are shared by no other sentences."… And this lengthiest possible incarceration is an "especially harsh punishment for a juvenile," because he will almost inevitably serve "more years and a greater percentage of his life in prison than an adult offender."... The penalty when imposed on a teenager, as compared with an older person, is therefore "the same ... in name only."... All of that suggested a distinctive set of legal rules: In part because we viewed this ultimate penalty for juveniles as akin to the death penalty, we treated it similarly to that most severe punishment. We imposed a categorical ban on the sentence's use, in a way unprecedented for a term of imprisonment....

... *Graham*'s "[t]reat[ment] [of] juvenile life sentences as analogous to capital punishment..."... makes relevant here a second line of our precedents, demanding individualized sentencing when imposing the death penalty. In *Woodson*, 428 U. S. 280, we held that a statute mandating a death sentence for first-degree murder violated the Eighth Amendment. We thought the mandatory scheme flawed because it gave no significance to "the character and record of the individual offender or the circumstances" of the offense, and "exclud[ed] from consideration ... the possibility of compassionate or mitigating factors."... Subsequent decisions have elaborated on the requirement that capital defendants have an opportunity to advance, and the judge or jury a chance to assess, any mitigating factors, so that the death penalty is reserved only for the most culpable defendants committing the most serious offenses....

In light of *Graham*'s reasoning, these decisions too show the flaws of imposing mandatory life-without-parole sentences on juvenile homicide offenders. Such mandatory penalties, by their nature, preclude a sentencer from taking account of an offender's age and the wealth of characteristics and circumstances attendant to it. Under these schemes, every juvenile will receive the same sentence as every other—the 17-year-old and the 14-year-old, the shooter and the accomplice, the child from a stable household and the child from a chaotic and abusive one. And still worse, each juvenile (including these two 14-year-olds) will receive the same sentence as the vast majority of adults committing similar homicide offenses—but really, as *Graham* noted, a greater sentence than those adults will serve....

So *Graham* and *Roper* and our individualized sentencing cases alike teach that in imposing a State's harshest penalties, a sentencer misses too much if he treats every child as an adult.... And finally, this mandatory punishment disregards the possibility of rehabilitation even when the circumstances most suggest it.

Both cases before us illustrate the problem. Take Jackson's first. As noted earlier, Jackson did not fire the bullet that killed Laurie Troup; nor did the State argue that he intended her death. Jackson's conviction was instead based on an aiding-and-abetting theory; and the appellate court affirmed the verdict only because the jury could have believed that when Jackson entered the store, he warned Troup that "[w]e ain't playin'," rather than told his friends that "I thought you all was playin'."... To be sure, Jackson learned on the way to the video store that his friend Shields was carrying a gun, but his age could well have affected his calculation of the risk that posed, as well as his willingness to walk away at that point. All these circumstances go to Jackson's culpability for the offense.... ("[W]hen compared to an adult murderer, a juvenile offender who did not kill or intend to kill has a twice diminished moral culpability"). And so too does Jackson's family background and immersion in violence: Both his mother and his grandmother had previously shot other individuals.... At the least, a sentencer should look at such facts before depriving a 14-year-old of any prospect of release from prison.

That is true also in Miller's case. No one can doubt that he and Smith committed a vicious murder. But they did it when high on drugs and alcohol consumed with the adult victim. And if ever a pathological background might have contributed to a 14-year-old's commission of a crime, it is here. Miller's stepfather physically abused him; his alcoholic and drug-addicted mother neglected him; he had been in and out of foster care as a result; and he had tried to kill himself four times, the first when he should have been in kindergarten.... Nonetheless, Miller's past criminal history was limited—two instances of truancy and one of "second-degree criminal mischief."... That Miller deserved severe punishment for killing Cole Cannon is beyond question. But once again, a sentencer needed to examine all these circumstances before concluding that life without any possibility of parole was the appropriate penalty.

We therefore hold that the Eighth Amendment forbids a sentencing scheme that mandates life in prison without possibility of parole for juvenile offenders.... By making youth (and all that accompanies it) irrelevant to imposition of that harshest prison sentence, such a scheme poses too great a risk of disproportionate punishment. Because that holding is sufficient to decide these cases, we do not consider Jackson's and Miller's alternative argument that the Eighth Amendment requires a categorical bar on life without parole for juveniles, or at least for those 14 and younger. But given all we have said in *Roper*, *Graham*, and this decision about children's diminished culpability and heightened capacity for change, we think appropriate occasions for sentencing juveniles to this harshest possible penalty will be uncommon.... Although we do not foreclose a sentencer's ability to make that judgment in homicide cases, we require it to take into account how children are different, and how those differences counsel against irrevocably sentencing them to a lifetime in prison....

IV

Graham, *Roper*, and our individualized sentencing decisions make clear that a judge or jury must have the opportunity to consider mitigating circumstances before imposing the harshest possible penalty for juveniles. By requiring that all children convicted of homicide receive lifetime incarceration without possibility of parole, regardless of their age and age-related characteristics and the nature of their crimes, the mandatory sentencing schemes before us violate this principle of proportionality, and so the Eighth Amendment's ban on cruel and unusual punishment. We accordingly reverse the judgments of the Arkansas Supreme Court and Alabama Court of Criminal Appeals and remand the cases for further proceedings not inconsistent with this opinion.

It is so ordered.

In *Miller v. Alabama* four opinions were written in addition to Justice Kagan's Opinion of the Court. Justice Breyer wrote what is called a concurring opinion, in which he expressed additional views going beyond what Justice Kagan said in the majority opinion. Justice Breyer's concurrence was joined by Justice Sotomayor.

A Short Excerpt from Justice Breyer's Concurring Opinion, Which Also Was Joined by Justice Sotomayor

Justice Breyer wrote:

> [T]o be found guilty, Jackson did not need to kill the clerk (it is conceded he did not), nor did he need to have intent to kill or even "extreme indifference." As long as one of the teenage accomplices in the robbery acted with extreme indifference to the value of human life, Jackson could be convicted of capital murder.

Justice Breyer argued that "those that do not intend to kill are 'categorically less deserving of the most serious forms of punishment than are murderers.'"

> [I]f the State continues to seek a sentence of life without the possibility of parole for Kuntrell Jackson, there will have to be a determination whether Jackson "kill[ed] or intend[ed] to kill" the robbery victim.... In my view, without such a finding, the Eighth Amendment as interpreted in *Graham* forbids sentencing Jackson to such a sentence, regardless of whether its application is mandatory or discretionary under state law....

"I Respectfully Dissent"

The three dissenting opinions are excerpted below. Interested readers can find edited versions of these additional opinions included on the textbook's website. Three of the justices who voted in favor of Alabama and Arkansas in *Miller* wrote opinions explaining why they disagreed with the Court's majority. Because of the length of the dissents it is not possible to include even edited versions in this textbook even though all readers would benefit from having read and understood why four justices completely disagreed with the majority justices. The following excerpts are intended to provide a glimpse into what is in the dissents in the hopes that this will encourage readers to go to the website and read the edited versions of the dissents.

A Short Excerpt from Chief Justice Roberts's Dissent

Chief Justice Roberts asserts that the majority did not establish a traditional basis for its conclusions that the sentences in question were "cruel and unusual." He observed that the accepted process courts are expected to follow when determining whether a given punishment is constitutionally "cruel and unusual" is to find the relevant "objective indicia." Roberts noted that twenty-nine jurisdictions had adopted statutes like those of Alabama and Arkansas and that evidence alone was sufficient to show that such a penalty was neither "unusual" nor unrepresentative of " 'the evolving standards of decency that mark the progress of a maturing society.' "

The Chief Justice also rejected the majority's argument that many juvenile murderers may have received "automatic" mandatory sentences of life without parole because of the coupling of mandatory "waiver into adult court" statutes with mandatory "life without parole at sentencing" statutes. The minority noted the majority was not showing the appropriate level of deference and respect that the Supreme Court historically has afforded legislative bodies. He also rejected any suggestion that the lawmakers in the twenty-nine jurisdictions were unaware of the consequences of their statutes on sentencing decisions—and isn't the constitutionality of legislation supposed to be presumed?

Chief Justice Roberts concluded as follows:

> In recent years, our society has moved toward requiring that the murderer, his age notwithstanding, be imprisoned for the remainder of his life. Members of this Court may disagree with that choice. Perhaps science and policy suggest society should show greater mercy to young killers, giving them a greater chance to reform themselves at the risk that they will kill again.... But that is not our decision to make. Neither the text of the Constitution nor our precedent prohibits legislatures from requiring that juvenile murderers be sentenced to life without parole. I respectfully dissent.

A Short Excerpt from Justice Thomas's Dissent

According to Justice Thomas the Court's majority had in *Miller* "[upset] the legislatively enacted sentencing regimes of 29 jurisdictions without constitutional warrant." In particular he disagreed with recent Supreme Court decisions that interpreted the Cruel and Unusual Punishments Clause

differentially. He pointed to previous decisions in which the Court interpreted the Eighth Amendment as prohibiting the imposition of certain sentences with specified categories of offenders. He pointed to the *Roper* case, which held that offenders who were not yet eighteen when their offenses were committed could not be executed, and the *Graham* case, in which the Court prohibited sentencing offenders under eighteen convicted of nonhomicide offenses to life without parole.

Justice Thomas wrote:

> As I have previously explained, "the Cruel and Unusual Punishments Clause was originally understood as prohibiting torturous methods of punishment—specifically methods akin to those that had been considered cruel and unusual at the time the Bill of Rights was adopted."... The Clause does not contain a "proportionality principle." ... [I]n short, it does not authorize courts to invalidate any punishment they deem disproportionate to the severity of the crime or to a particular class of offenders. Instead, the Clause "leaves the unavoidably moral question of who 'deserves' a particular nonprohibited method of punishment to the judgment of the legislatures that authorize the penalty."

He concluded his dissent with the following:

> Today's decision invalidates a constitutionally permissible sentencing system based on nothing more than the Court's belief that "its own sense of morality ... preempts that of the people and their representatives."... Because nothing in the Constitution grants the Court the authority it exercises today, I respectfully dissent.

A Short Excerpt from Justice Alito's Dissent

In his dissenting opinion Justice Alito criticized the Court's methodology for determining the direction and extent to which our society's moral standards have changed over the last fifty years. He also argued that the Court has "abandoned the original meaning" of what constitutes "cruel and unusual punishment" and the traditional precedents for how "objective indicia of our society's moral standards and the trajectory of our moral 'evolution' are determined."

The justice wrote:

> What today's decision shows is that our Eighth Amendment cases are no longer tied to any objective indicia of society's standards. Our Eighth Amendment case law is now entirely inward looking. After entirely disregarding objective indicia of our society's standards in *Graham*, the Court now extrapolates from *Graham*. Future cases may extrapolate from today's holding, and this process may continue until the majority brings sentencing practices into line with whatever the majority views as truly evolved standards of decency…. Unless our cases change course, we will continue to march toward some vision of evolutionary culmination that the Court has not yet disclosed. The Constitution does not authorize us to take the country on this journey.

CASE QUESTIONS

1. According to the majority, exactly what legal principle was violated by the mandatory nature of these sentences?

2. What reasons did the majority give for ruling as they did?

3. What does the Court require in future cases?

4. Do you agree or disagree with the majority of justices? What is your reasoning?

5. What impact do you believe the decision will have on sentencing in the future?

READING CASES - PART II

Because *Miller v. Alabama* is the first reported judicial decision in this book, a brief introduction to

case analysis is appropriate. The case heading consists of four items. The first line contains the names of the parties. In this instance there are two sets of parties whose claims are before the U.S. Supreme Court, Miller v. Alabama and Jackson v. Arkansas. For the U.S. Supreme Court's convenience these two cases were consolidated for decision, and although both cases were decided at the same time by the Court, for purposes of citation "they" are referred to as *Miller v. Alabama*.

The next item in the heading describes the volume and page where the judicial opinion in the case can be found. In this instance, the case is reported in volume 567 of the United States Reports (U.S.), on page XXX. The name of the reviewing court that decided the case or ruled on a motion is next in the heading, followed by the date the decision was published.

The first item in the body of the court opinion is the name of the justice or judge who wrote the reviewing court's majority opinion (also called the opinion for the court). Generally only one of the judges voting with the majority of the court is selected to write the majority opinion. The other members of the court who constitute the majority are said to have "joined in the opinion." The majority opinion explains the court's decision in the case and the majority's reasoning for reaching that outcome. A concurring opinion is written by a judge who, while voting with the majority, has additional comments that go beyond what is included in the majority opinion. Sometimes the majority will agree on the decision but disagree on the reasons for that result. In such a case, the court will announce the decision, but there will be no majority opinion. The judges constituting the majority will write concurring opinions explaining their differing reasons for what they agree is the correct result. A judge who disagrees with the majority opinion can explain why in a dissenting opinion.

Only courts with appellate jurisdiction are entitled to decide cases on appeal. Appeals courts review the decisions of lower courts to see if substantial error was committed in those lower courts. An appellate court can affirm, reverse, and/or remand a lower court's decision. It can also, when appropriate, dismiss an appeal. If a reviewing court affirms the lower court, it rules that the lower court's decision is valid and reasserts the judgment. If it reverses, it vacates and sets aside the lower court's judgment. Note that a decision can be reversed in part. When a case is remanded, it is returned to the lower court, generally with instructions as to further proceedings to be undertaken by the lower court.

In order to maximize the benefits of the case study method, one must read each case carefully and pay close attention to detail. After reading a case, one should have not merely a general sense or the gist of what the case says, but also a precise understanding of what the court did.

Careful attention should be given to the **holding** of the case—the rule of law that the court says applies to the facts of the case. Majority opinions are often discursive, and their authors often stray into writing about issues not actually before the court for decision. Such unnecessary comments are classified as **dicta.** Although these statements may appear to be important, if they are dicta they lack the authority of the case's holding.

BRIEFING A CASE

Most students new to reading judicial opinions often find it helpful to **brief** a case. With practice it becomes possible to write a brief without having to refer back constantly to the judicial opinion itself. Briefing with the case set aside provides a check on understanding and encourages careful reading. A brief should contain the parts of the case selected as important, organized for the purpose at hand rather than in the haphazard order in which they may be reported.

The following brief of *Miller v. Alabama* illustrates one way of briefing. The elements in the example are usually found in most briefs, though writing style is often a matter of individual preference. It is usually desirable to keep copying from the text of the case to a minimum; briefs are not exercises in stenography. This brief was written to help students who have not previously read a judicial opinion. It is intended to help these students understand what is important in the case reports they are reading.

Sample Brief

Miller v. Alabama

Facts: Two juveniles, one from Alabama (Evan Miller) and the other from Arkansas (Kuntrell Jackson), were prosecuted, convicted, and sentenced in adult courts for capital murder. Miller's offense involved extreme brutality and cruelty on his part and occurred in conjunction with an arson. Miller was originally charged in juvenile court and then transferred into adult court. Jackson, although found by the jury to not have been the shooter, was convicted of aiding and abetting the person who shot and killed the victim in conjunction with the armed robbery of a video store. Jackson, although fourteen, was initially prosecuted in adult court. Miller and Jackson were sentenced in adult courts to mandatory terms of life in prison without possibility of parole. The appellate courts of the States of Alabama and Arkansas confirmed the convictions and sentences.

Miller and Jackson, acting independently, successfully petitioned the U.S. Supreme Court, which agreed to review both of their cases. The two cases were consolidated by the Supreme Court and were decided concurrently.

Issue(s) Presented:

Does the Eighth Amendment's Cruel and Unusual Punishments Clause prohibit the sentencing of juveniles convicted of capital murder to mandatory sentences of life in prison without possibility of parole?

Holding: The Eighth Amendment's Cruel and Unusual Punishments Clause prohibits the sentencing of juveniles convicted of capital murder to mandatory sentences of life in prison without possibility of parole.

Rationale: The Supreme Court explained the reasoning behind its holding as follows:

1. The Eighth Amendment differentiates juveniles from adults when determining whether a punishment is so excessive as to be constitutionally disproportionate because juvenile offenders differ significantly from their adult counterparts. Juveniles are immature, lack a developed sense of responsibility, are often impulsive and engage in risky behavior, and are impressionable and vulnerable to what Justice Kagan referred to as "negative influences and outside pressures." The constitutional significance of the differences between juveniles and adults in sentencing has been well established by the Supreme Court in such cases as *Roper v. Simmons* and *Graham v. Florida.*

2. The Court noted that mandatory sentences of life in prison without the possibility of parole have much in common with capital punishment. Such a sentence is the most severe sanction that a juvenile can receive. Because juveniles are always younger than adults, a juvenile who receives a mandatory life without parole sentence will end up serving more time in prison than an adult who has committed an equivalent offense. The Court noted that it had previously ruled that individualized sentencing is constitutionally required for convicted individuals who have been targeted for the death penalty (*Woodson v. North Carolina*) and for juveniles committing nonhomicide offenses (*Graham v. Florida*). Justice Kagan wrote about *Woodson*:

   [W]e held that a statute mandating a death sentence for first-degree murder violated the Eighth Amendment. We thought the mandatory scheme flawed because it gave no significance to "the character and record of the individual offender or the circumstances" of the offense, and "exclud[ed] from consideration … the possibility of compassionate or mitigating factors."… Subsequent decisions have elaborated on the requirement that capital defendants have an opportunity to advance, and the judge or jury a chance to assess, any mitigating factors, so that the death penalty is reserved only for the most culpable defendants committing the most serious offenses.

Justice Kagan's conclusion was that since individualized sentencing is required when an adult is facing the possibility of the ultimate punishment, individualized sentencing should also be required for juveniles convicted of capital murder facing the possibility of the ultimate sentence available to persons under eighteen.

DUE PROCESS

The **Due Process Clauses** of the Fifth and Fourteenth Amendments to the U.S. Constitution provide that no person shall be "deprived of life, liberty, or property, without due process of law." These clauses are deeply embedded in Anglo-American legal history, going back to 1215. In June of that year, English barons decided that King John had been acting arbitrarily and in violation of their rights. They sought protection from the king in the Magna Carta, a charter containing sixty-three chapters that limited the king's powers.[77]

Chapter XXXIX of the Magna Carta is the predecessor of our Due Process Clauses. It provided that "no man shall be captured or imprisoned or disseised or outlawed or exiled or in any way destroyed, nor will we go against him or send against him, except by the lawful judgment of his peers or by the law of the land."[78]

The barons amassed an army, confronted the king, and forced him to agree to the Magna Carta. Subsequent monarchs reissued the Magna Carta many times over the next two centuries.[79] In 1354 the words "by the law of the land" (which were initially written in Latin) were translated into English to mean "by due process of the law."[80] In the seventeenth century, these words were interpreted to include the customary rights and liberties of Englishmen.[81] English legal commentators further expanded the scope of due process by arguing that it included what philosopher John Locke called each individual's natural right to "life, liberty, and property."[82]

The Magna Carta's influence in this country is apparent in the 1776 constitutions of Maryland and North Carolina, which contain due process language taken verbatim from the Magna Carta. In 1791 the Due Process Clause was included in the Fifth Amendment to the U.S. Constitution. Every person in our society has an inherent right to due process of law, which protects him or her from arbitrary, oppressive, and unjust governmental actions. If a proceeding results in the denial of fundamental fairness and shocks the conscience of a court, a violation of due process has occurred. In addition, under both the Fifth and Fourteenth Amendments, a corporation, as well as a partnership or unincorporated association, is a person to whom that protection applies.

Due process of law focuses on deprivations of "life, liberty, and property." "Life" refers to deprivation of biological life and to a person's right to have a particular lifestyle. "Liberty," as is further explained below, covers a vast scope of personal rights. It also implies the absence of arbitrary and unreasonable governmental restraints on an individual's person, as well as the freedom to practice a trade or business, the right to contract, and the right to establish a relationship with one's children. "Property" is everything that may be subject to ownership, including real and personal property, obligations, rights, legal entitlements such as a public education, and other intangibles.

Determining what due process means in a given factual situation has been a matter for the judiciary. In this, the courts are influenced by procedures that were established under English common law prior to the enactment of our constitution. They are also influenced by contemporary events, values, and political and economic conditions.

The due process guarantee protects people from unfairness in the operation of both substantive and procedural law. Substantive law refers to the law that creates, defines, and regulates rights. It defines the legal relationship between the individual and the state and among individuals themselves and is the primary responsibility of the legislative branch of the government. Procedural law prescribes the method used to enforce legal rights. It provides the machinery by which individuals can enforce their rights or obtain redress for the invasion of such rights.

The Fifth and Fourteenth Amendments

The Fifth Amendment guarantee of due process of law was included in the Bill of Rights in order to place limits on the federal government. It was intended to control the Congress, and prior to the Civil War, it was primarily used to protect property rights from governmental regulation. The Due Process Clause was also interpreted by the Supreme Court to overrule those parts of the Missouri Compromise that prohibited slavery. In the *Dred Scott* case (60 U.S. 393 [1861]), the Supreme Court ruled that slaves were property, and thus the Due Process Clause prohibited Congress from making slavery illegal. This is a historical irony given the role due process has played in promoting civil rights in recent decades. Even during the Civil War era, many abolitionists interpreted due process differently and identified this Fifth Amendment clause as the basis for their convictions, maintaining that states had no right to deny slaves, or any other person, the right to life, liberty, or property without due process of law.

The addition of the Fourteenth Amendment to the Constitution in 1868 reflected the abolitionists' position. From that point forward, state governments were constitutionally required to provide due process of law and equal protection of the law to all people.

The Meaning of Substantive Due Process

The Bill of Rights contains many specifics regarding procedural fairness, particularly in criminal cases, but the meaning of substantive due process is less obvious. In our system of government, the

U.S. Supreme Court has historically borne the responsibility for determining the degree to which the concept of due process includes a substantive dimension.

In **substantive due process** cases, the claimant challenges a statute on the grounds that the law excessively intrudes on individual decision making. The claimant argues that the infringement is against that person's due process liberty interest. When the court examines the facts, it often discovers that the government has no legitimate interest in the matter and is acting arbitrarily, and the claimant has an important, historically validated interest (a "fundamental right," in legalese) to make the decision. The court decides these claims on a case-by-case basis, and the claimant wins when a majority of justices conclude that the claimed right should be classified as fundamental given these particular circumstances.

An example of such a case is found in Chapter IX of this textbook in a case decided by the U.S. Supreme Court in 1967, titled *Loving v. Virginia.* Richard Loving, who was white, and his wife, Mildred, who was black, brought suit challenging Virginia's antimiscegenation laws (statutes making it illegal for white people to marry black people). The U.S. Supreme Court ruled in favor of the Lovings. It concluded that the decision as to whether to enter into an interracial marriage was a matter for Richard and Mildred, not the Commonwealth of Virginia. The Court said that Virginia had no legitimate interest in the races of married people and could not categorically prohibit black and white people from marrying one another.

But most persons seeking federal due process protection are unsuccessful. You will soon read the case of *Washington v. Glucksberg,* in which doctors unsuccessfully argued before the U.S. Supreme Court that they had a constitutionally protected due process right to assist their terminally ill patients to commit suicide. The Supreme Court ultimately decided that the doctors' claim was not within the scope of due process protection.

U.S. Supreme Court Justice David H. Souter commented in *Washington v. Glucksberg,* 521 U.S. 702 (1997), on substantive due process in his concurring opinion. Souter, although voting with the majority to sustain Washington's statute, recognized the conceptual legitimacy of substantive due process. He referred to substantive due process as the long-standing "American constitutional practice ... [of] recognizing unenumerated substantive limits on governmental action" (e.g., rights not explicitly included in the text of the Constitution).

This "American constitutional practice" was also acknowledged by the late Chief Justice Rehnquist in *Cruzan v. Missouri Department of Health,* 497 U.S. 261 (1990), where he asserted in his opinion for the Court that "the principle that a competent person has a constitutionally protected liberty interest in refusing unwanted medical treatment may be inferred from our prior decisions." In *Cruzan,* as in *Glucksberg* and *Loving,* the fact that the Due Process Clauses were textually silent about a substantive due process claim did not preclude the Court from recognizing that such an unenumerated right is protected within the scope of substantive due process.

Substantive Due Process and Economic and Social Regulation

In the years following the enactment of the Fourteenth Amendment, the U.S. Supreme Court began a slow process of expanding the substantive meaning of due process. As we learned in the earlier discussion of sociological jurisprudence, the Supreme Court in the 1890s was unsympathetic to the Progressives and state reform legislation. In the early cases, the states usually won if they were legislating to protect the public's health, welfare, safety, or morals. Gradually, however, the Court began using the Fourteenth Amendment to strike down state social and economic legislation. The justices often concluded that these laws exceeded the state's legislative power because they infringed upon the individual's due process right to contract. They maintained that the individual had the right to determine how many hours he or she wanted to work, at least in nonhazardous occupations. And legislative attempts to set minimum wages for women hospital workers were viewed by the Court as "price fixing." The Court was, in effect, sitting in judgment on the legislative policies themselves. The Court used the Due Process Clause as an instrument for striking down social and economic legislation with which it disagreed.

The depression of the 1930s resulted in New Deal legislative initiatives that were intended to stimulate the economy. Congress created numerous agencies and programs in order to benefit industry, labor, savers and investors, farmers, and the needy. However, the Supreme Court struck down many of these New Deal laws between 1934 and 1936. This made the Court very unpopular in the "court" of public opinion, and the president responded by proposing that Congress increase the size of the Court, presumably so that he could nominate people for the new seats who were sympathetic to New Deal legislation. In 1936, the Supreme Court began to reverse itself and uphold New Deal legislation. In 1937, the Court's majority began using the Commerce Clause to sustain federal legislation, and they were no longer using the Due Process Clause to overturn state reforms. The Court replaced the dual federalism doctrine, which attempted to enforce strict boundaries around the federal and state "zones of interest," with a general policy of deference to legislative preferences with respect to social and economic policies that are in its view neither arbitrary nor irrational.

However, the traditional deference shown to Congress was called into question in 1995 in the case of *United States v. Lopez* (a Commerce Clause case that can be read on this textbook's website), in which the Supreme Court explicitly held that Congress did not have the right under the Commerce Clause to criminalize the possession of a gun within a local school zone because there was no connection between the legislation and commerce. The Court also used this same rationale in 2000 to strike down a portion of the Violence Against Women Act in the case of *United States v. Morrison.* But in *Gonzales v. Raich,* the Supreme Court in 1995 upheld Congress's right to make it a crime for someone to grow their own marijuana for personal medicinal purposes. More recently in 2012, Chief Justice Roberts and

Justices Breyer, Ginsburg, Kagan, and Sotomayor relied on Congress's powers under the Taxing Clause to sustain the constitutionality of "Obamacare," in *National Federation of Independent Business v. Sebelius.* However, the Chief Justice also opined that he agreed with Justices Alito, Kennedy, Scalia, and Thomas that there was no authority under the Commerce Clause for Congress to mandate that anyone purchase health care insurance. It is unlikely that the existing ambiguity about the scope of the Commerce Clause will be resolved in a clear-cut, doctrinaire manner. Rather, its meaning probably will continue to evolve slowly on a case-by-case basis in the traditional manner of the common law.

The Scope of Substantive Due Process

In the 1920s, the Supreme Court began to recognize that an individual's liberty rights included more than just property rights. Individual "liberty" also required the constitutional protection of certain kinds of conduct. The justices of the U.S. Supreme Court differed, however, about whether such rights could be "found" within the meaning of due process. Although various justices on the Court proposed limits on the scope of substantive due process, the majority on the Court adopted what is called the selective incorporation approach. This approach recognizes that all rights that the Court deems to be fundamental are included in the concept of due process.

Fundamental rights include those that historically have been part of our legal tradition, such as the First Amendment freedoms. Other fundamental rights include intimate decisions relating to marriage, procreation, contraception, family relations, child rearing, and education. The determination of whether a right is fundamental is made by the U.S. Supreme Court on a case-by-case basis.

The following case of *Washington v. Glucksberg* illustrates conflicting approaches to the meaning of substantive due process. In this case, Dr. Harold Glucksberg and four other doctors brought suit for declaratory and injunctive relief against the State of Washington. They sought to enjoin the enforcement of a Washington statute that made it a crime for the doctors to help three of their mentally competent but terminally ill patients to commit suicide. The late Chief Justice Rehnquist first explains his views on the proper scope of substantive due process under the Fourteenth Amendment. Recently retired Associate Justice David Souter then explains that although he agrees with Rehnquist as to the correct decision in the case, he profoundly disagrees with the Chief Justice about the proper scope of substantive due process.

Washington et al. v. Harold Glucksberg et al.
521 U.S. 702
Supreme Court of the United States
June 26, 1997

Chief Justice Rehnquist delivered the opinion of the Court.

The question presented in this case is whether Washington's prohibition against "causing" or "aiding" a suicide offends the Fourteenth Amendment to the United States Constitution. We hold that it does not.

It has always been a crime to assist a suicide in the State of Washington. In 1854, Washington's first Territorial Legislature outlawed "assisting another in the commission of self murder." Today, Washington law provides: "A person is guilty of promoting a suicide attempt when he knowingly causes or aids another person to attempt suicide."... "Promoting a suicide attempt" is a felony, punishable by up to five years' imprisonment and up to a $10,000 fine.... At the same time, Washington's Natural Death Act, enacted in 1979, states that the "withholding or withdrawal of life sustaining treatment" at a patient's direction "shall not, for any purpose, constitute a suicide"....

Petitioners in this case are the State of Washington and its Attorney General. Respondents Harold Glucksberg, M.D., Abigail Halperin, M.D., Thomas A. Preston, M.D., and Peter Shalit, M.D., are physicians who practice in Washington. These doctors occasionally treat terminally ill, suffering patients, and declare that they would assist these patients in ending their lives if not for Washington's assisted suicide ban. In January 1994, respondents, along with three gravely ill, pseudonymous plaintiffs who have since died and Compassion in Dying, a nonprofit organization that counsels people considering physician assisted suicide, sued in the United States District Court, seeking a declaration that Wash Rev. Code 9A.36.060(1) (1994) is, on its face, unconstitutional.

The plaintiffs asserted "the existence of a liberty interest protected by the Fourteenth Amendment which extends to a personal choice by a mentally competent, terminally ill adult to commit physician assisted suicide."... Relying primarily on *Planned Parenthood v. Casey*, 505 U.S. 833 (1992), and *Cruzan v. Director, Missouri Dept. of Health*, 497 U.S. 261 (1990), the District Court agreed ... and concluded that Washington's assisted suicide ban is unconstitutional because it "places an undue burden on the exercise of [that] constitutionally protected liberty interest."... The District Court also decided that the Washington statute violated the Equal Protection Clause's requirement that "all persons similarly situated ... be treated alike"....

A panel of the Court of Appeals for the Ninth Circuit reversed, emphasizing that "in the two hundred and five years of our existence no constitutional right to aid in killing oneself has ever been asserted and upheld by a court of final jurisdiction."... The Ninth Circuit reheard the case en banc, reversed the panel's decision, and affirmed the District Court.... Like the District Court, the en banc Court of Appeals emphasized our *Casey* and *Cruzan* decisions.... The court also discussed what it described as "historical" and "current societal attitudes" toward suicide and assisted suicide ... and concluded that "the Constitution encompasses a due process liberty interest in controlling the time and manner of one's death—that there is, in short, a constitutionally recognized 'right to die.'"... After "weighing and then balancing" this interest against Washington's various interests, the court held that the State's assisted suicide ban was unconstitutional "as applied to terminally ill competent adults who wish to hasten their deaths with medication prescribed by their physicians."... The court did not reach the District Court's equal protection holding.... We granted certiorari ... and now reverse.

I

We begin, as we do in all due process cases, by examining our Nation's history, legal traditions, and practices.... In almost every State—indeed, in almost every western democracy—it is a crime to assist a suicide. The States' assisted suicide bans are not innovations. Rather, they are long-standing expressions of the States' commitment to the protection and preservation of all human life.... Indeed, opposition to and condemnation of suicide—and, therefore, of assisting suicide—are consistent and enduring themes of our philosophical, legal, and cultural heritages....

More specifically, for over 700 years, the Anglo American common law tradition has punished or otherwise disapproved of both suicide and assisting suicide.... In the thirteenth century, Henry de Bracton, one of the first legal treatise writers, observed that "just as a man may commit felony by slaying another so may he do so by slaying himself."... The real and personal property of one who killed himself to avoid conviction and punishment for a crime were forfeit to the king; however, thought Bracton, "if a man slays himself in weariness of life or because he is unwilling to endure further bodily pain ... [only] his movable goods [were] confiscated."... Thus, "the principle that suicide of a sane person, for whatever reason, was a punishable felony was ... introduced into English common law." Centuries later, Sir William Blackstone, whose *Commentaries on the Laws of England* not only provided a definitive summary of the common law but was also a primary legal authority for 18th and 19th century American lawyers, referred to suicide as "self murder" and "the pretended heroism, but real cowardice, of the Stoic philosophers, who destroyed themselves to avoid those ills which they had not the fortitude to endure...." Blackstone emphasized that "the law has ... ranked [suicide] among the highest crimes," although, anticipating later developments, he conceded that the harsh and shameful punishments imposed for suicide "borde[r] a little upon severity."...

For the most part, the early American colonies adopted the common law approach....

Over time, however, the American colonies abolished these harsh common law penalties. William Penn abandoned the criminal forfeiture sanction in Pennsylvania in 1701, and the other colonies (and later, the other States) eventually followed this example....

Nonetheless, although States moved away from Blackstone's treatment of suicide, courts continued to condemn it as a grave public wrong....

That suicide remained a grievous, though nonfelonious, wrong is confirmed by the fact that colonial and early state legislatures and courts did not retreat from prohibiting assisting suicide.... And the prohibitions against suicide never contained exceptions for those who were near death....

The earliest American statute explicitly to outlaw assisting suicide was enacted in New York in 1828 ... and many of the new States and Territories followed New York's example.... In this century, the Model Penal Code also prohibited "aiding" suicide, prompting many States to enact or revise their assisted suicide bans. The Code's drafters observed that "the interests

in the sanctity of life that are represented by the criminal homicide laws are threatened by one who expresses a willingness to participate in taking the life of another, even though the act may be accomplished with the consent, or at the request, of the suicide victim."...

Though deeply rooted, the States' assisted suicide bans have in recent years been re-examined and, generally, reaffirmed. Because of advances in medicine and technology, Americans today are increasingly likely to die in institutions, from chronic illnesses.... Public concern and democratic action are therefore sharply focused on how best to protect dignity and independence at the end of life, with the result that there have been many significant changes in state laws and in the attitudes these laws reflect. Many States, for example, now permit "living wills," surrogate health care decision making, and the withdrawal or refusal of life sustaining medical treatment.... At the same time, however, voters and legislators continue for the most part to reaffirm their States' prohibitions on assisting suicide.

The Washington statute at issue in this case ... was enacted in 1975 as part of a revision of that State's criminal code. Four years later, Washington passed its Natural Death Act, which specifically stated that the "withholding or withdrawal of life sustaining treatment ... shall not, for any purpose, constitute a suicide" and that "nothing in this chapter shall be construed to condone, authorize, or approve mercy killing...." In 1991, Washington voters rejected a ballot initiative which, had it passed, would have permitted a form of physician assisted suicide. Washington then added a provision to the Natural Death Act expressly excluding physician assisted suicide.... Wash. Rev. Code § 70.122.100 (1994).

Attitudes toward suicide itself have changed since Bracton, but our laws have consistently condemned, and continue to prohibit, assisting suicide. Despite changes in medical technology and notwithstanding an increased emphasis on the importance of end of life decision making, we have not retreated from this prohibition. Against this backdrop of history, tradition, and practice, we now turn to respondents' constitutional claim.

II

The Due Process Clause guarantees more than fair process, and the "liberty" it protects includes more than the absence of physical restraint.... The Clause also provides heightened protection against government interference with certain fundamental rights and liberty interests.... In a long line of cases, we have held that, in addition to the specific freedoms protected by the Bill of Rights, the "liberty" specifically protected by the Due Process Clause includes the rights to marry, *Loving v. Virginia,* 388 U.S. 1 (1967); to have children, *Skinner v. Oklahoma ex rel. Williamson,* 316 U.S. 535 (1942); to direct the education and upbringing of one's children, *Meyer v. Nebraska,* 262 U.S. 390 (1923); *Pierce v. Society of Sisters,* 268 U.S. 510 (1925); to marital privacy, *Griswold v. Connecticut,* 381 U.S. 479 (1965); to use contraception, ... *Eisenstadt v. Baird,* 405 U.S. 438 (1972); to bodily integrity, *Rochin v. California,* 342 U.S. 165 (1952), and to abortion.... We have also assumed, and strongly suggested, that the Due Process Clause protects the traditional right to refuse unwanted life-saving medical treatment. *Cruzan,* 497 U.S., at 278–279.

But we "ha[ve] always been reluctant to expand the concept of substantive due process because guideposts for responsible decision making in this unchartered area are scarce and open ended."... By extending constitutional protection to an asserted right or liberty interest, we, to a great extent, place the matter outside the arena of public debate and legislative action. We must therefore "exercise the utmost care whenever we are asked to break new ground in this field," ... lest the liberty protected by the Due Process Clause be subtly transformed into the policy preferences of the members of this Court....

Our established method of substantive due process analysis has two primary features: First, we have regularly observed that the Due Process Clause specially protects those fundamental rights and liberties which are, objectively, "deeply rooted in this Nation's history and tradition," ... "so rooted in the traditions and conscience of our people as to be ranked as fundamental," and "implicit in the concept of ordered liberty," such that "neither liberty nor justice would exist if they were sacrificed."... Second, we have required in substantive due process cases a "careful description" of the asserted fundamental liberty interest.... Our Nation's history, legal traditions, and practices thus provide the crucial "guideposts for responsible decision making"... that direct and restrain our exposition of the Due Process Clause. As we stated recently ... the Fourteenth Amendment "forbids the government to infringe ... 'fundamental' liberty interests at all, no matter what process is provided, unless the infringement is narrowly tailored to serve a compelling state interest."... Justice Souter, relying on Justice Harlan's dissenting opinion in *Poe v. Ullman,* would largely abandon this restrained methodology, and instead ask "whether [Washington's] statute sets up one of those 'arbitrary impositions' or 'purposeless restraints' at odds with the Due Process Clause of the Fourteenth Amendment,"... (quoting *Poe* ... [1961]

[Harlan, J., dissenting]). In our view, however, the development of this Court's substantive due process jurisprudence, described briefly above ... has been a process whereby the outlines of the "liberty" specially protected by the Fourteenth Amendment—never fully clarified, to be sure, and perhaps not capable of being fully clarified—have at least been carefully refined by concrete examples involving fundamental rights found to be deeply rooted in our legal tradition. This approach tends to rein in the subjective elements that are necessarily present in due process judicial review. In addition, by establishing a threshold requirement— that a challenged state action implicate a fundamental right—before requiring more than a reasonable relation to a legitimate state interest to justify the action, it avoids the need for complex balancing of competing interests in every case.

Turning to the claim at issue here, the Court of Appeals stated that "properly analyzed, the first issue to be resolved is whether there is a liberty interest in determining the time and manner of one's death"... or, in other words, "is there a right to die?"... Similarly, respondents assert a "liberty to choose how to die" and a right to "control of one's final days"... and describe the asserted liberty as "the right to choose a humane, dignified death"... and "the liberty to shape death."... As noted above, we have a tradition of carefully formulating the interest at stake in substantive due process cases. For example, although *Cruzan* is often described as a "right to die" case ... we were, in fact, more precise: we assumed that the Constitution granted competent persons a "constitutionally protected right to refuse life-saving hydration and nutrition."... The Washington statute at issue in this case prohibits "aid[ing] another person to attempt suicide"... and, thus, the question before us is whether the "liberty" specially protected by the Due Process Clause includes a right to commit suicide which itself includes a right to assistance in doing so.

We now inquire whether this asserted right has any place in our Nation's traditions. Here, as discussed above ... we are confronted with a consistent and almost universal tradition that has long rejected the asserted right, and continues explicitly to reject it today, even for terminally ill, mentally competent adults. To hold for respondents, we would have to reverse centuries of legal doctrine and practice, and strike down the considered policy choice of almost every State....

Respondents contend, however, that the liberty interest they assert is consistent with this Court's substantive due process line of cases, if not with this Nation's history and practice. Pointing to *Casey* and *Cruzan,* respondents read our jurisprudence in this area as reflecting a general tradition of "self sovereignty"... and as teaching that the "liberty" protected by the Due Process Clause includes "basic and intimate exercises of personal autonomy."... According to respondents, our liberty jurisprudence, and the broad, individualistic principles it reflects, protects the "liberty of competent, terminally ill adults to make end of life decisions free of undue government interference."... The question presented in this case, however, is whether the protections of the Due Process Clause include a right to commit suicide with another's assistance. With this "careful description" of respondents' claim in mind, we turn to *Casey* and *Cruzan*.

Respondents contend that in *Cruzan* we "acknowledged that competent, dying persons have the right to direct the removal of life sustaining medical treatment and thus hasten death," ... and that "the constitutional principle behind recognizing the patient's liberty to direct the withdrawal of artificial life support applies at least as strongly to the choice to hasten impending death by consuming lethal medication."... Similarly, the Court of Appeals concluded that "*Cruzan*, by recognizing a liberty interest that includes the refusal of artificial provision of life sustaining food and water, necessarily recognize[d] a liberty interest in hastening one's own death."...

The right assumed in *Cruzan*, however, was not simply deduced from abstract concepts of personal autonomy. Given the common law rule that forced medication was a battery, and the long legal tradition protecting the decision to refuse unwanted medical treatment, our assumption was entirely consistent with this Nation's history and constitutional traditions. The decision to commit suicide with the assistance of another may be just as personal and profound as the decision to refuse unwanted medical treatment, but it has never enjoyed similar legal protection. Indeed, the two acts are widely and reasonably regarded as quite distinct.... In *Cruzan* itself, we recognize that most States outlawed assisted suicide—and even more do today—and we certainly gave no intimation that the right to refuse unwanted medical treatment could be somehow transmuted into a right to assistance in committing suicide....

Respondents also rely on *Casey*. There, the Court's opinion concluded that "the essential holding of *Roe v. Wade* should be retained and once again reaffirmed."... We held, first, that a woman has a right, before her fetus is viable, to an abortion "without undue interference from the State"; second, that States may restrict post-viability abortions, so long as exceptions are made to protect a woman's life and health; and third, that the State has legitimate interests throughout a pregnancy in protecting the health of the woman and the life of the unborn child.... In

reaching this conclusion, the opinion discussed in some detail this Court's substantive due process tradition of interpreting the Due Process Clause to protect certain fundamental rights and "personal decisions relating to marriage, procreation, contraception, family relationships, child rearing, and education," and noted that many of those rights and liberties "involv[e] the most intimate and personal choices a person may make in a lifetime."...

The Court of Appeals, like the District Court, found *Casey* "highly instructive" and "almost prescriptive" for determining "what liberty interest may inhere in a terminally ill person's choice to commit suicide."

"Like the decision of whether or not to have an abortion, the decision how and when to die is one of 'the most intimate and personal choices a person may make in a lifetime,' a choice 'central to personal dignity and autonomy.' "

By choosing this language, the Court's opinion in *Casey* described, in a general way and in light of our prior cases, those personal activities and decisions that this Court has identified as so deeply rooted in our history and traditions, or so fundamental to our concept of constitutionally ordered liberty, that they are protected by the Fourteenth Amendment.... That many of the rights and liberties protected by the Due Process Clause sound in personal autonomy does not warrant the sweeping conclusion that any and all important, intimate, and personal decisions are so protected ... and *Casey* did not suggest otherwise.

The history of the law's treatment of assisted suicide in this country has been and continues to be one of the rejection of nearly all efforts to permit it. That being the case, our decisions lead us to conclude that the asserted "right" to assistance in committing suicide is not a fundamental liberty interest protected by the Due Process Clause. The Constitution also requires, however, that Washington's assisted suicide ban be rationally related to legitimate government interests.... This requirement is unquestionably met here. As the court below recognized ... Washington's assisted suicide ban implicates a number of state interests....

First, Washington has an "unqualified interest in the preservation of human life."... The State's prohibition on assisted suicide, like all homicide laws, both reflects and advances its commitment to this interest....

Respondents admit that "the State has a real interest in preserving the lives of those who can still contribute to society and enjoy life."... The Court of Appeals also recognized Washington's interest in protecting life, but held that the "weight" of this interest depends on the "medical condition and the wishes of the person whose life is at stake."... Washington, however, has rejected this sliding scale approach and, through its assisted suicide ban, insists that all persons' lives, from beginning to end, regardless of physical or mental condition, are under the full protection of the law.... As we have previously affirmed, the States "may properly decline to make judgments about the 'quality' of life that a particular individual may enjoy."... This remains true, as *Cruzan* makes clear, even for those who are near death.

Relatedly, all admit that suicide is a serious public health problem, especially among persons in otherwise vulnerable groups.... The State has an interest in preventing suicide, and in studying, identifying, and treating its causes....

The State also has an interest in protecting the integrity and ethics of the medical profession. In contrast to the Court of Appeals' conclusion that "the integrity of the medical profession would [not] be threatened in any way by [physician assisted suicide]," ... the American Medical Association, like many other medical and physicians' groups, has concluded that "physician assisted suicide is fundamentally incompatible with the physician's role as healer." American Medical Association, Code of Ethics §2.211 (1994).... And physician assisted suicide could, it is argued, undermine the trust that is essential to the doctor patient relationship by blurring the time-honored line between healing and harming....

Next, the State has an interest in protecting vulnerable groups—including the poor, the elderly, and disabled persons—from abuse, neglect, and mistakes. The Court of Appeals dismissed the State's concern that disadvantaged persons might be pressured into physician assisted suicide as "ludicrous on its face." ... We have recognized, however, the real risk of subtle coercion and undue influence in end of life situations.... Similarly, the New York Task Force warned that "legalizing physician assisted suicide would pose profound risks to many individuals who are ill and vulnerable.... The risk of harm is greatest for the many individuals in our society whose autonomy and well being are already compromised by poverty, lack of access to good medical care, advanced age, or membership in a stigmatized social group."... If physician assisted suicide were permitted, many might resort to it to spare their families the substantial financial burden of end of life health care costs.

The State's interest here goes beyond protecting the vulnerable from coercion; it extends to protecting disabled and terminally ill people from prejudice, negative and inaccurate stereotypes, and "societal indifference."... The State's assisted suicide ban reflects and reinforces its policy that the lives of terminally ill, disabled, and elderly people must be no less valued than the lives of the young and healthy, and that a seriously disabled person's suicidal impulses should be interpreted and treated the same way as anyone else's....

Finally, the State may fear that permitting assisted suicide will start it down the path to voluntary and perhaps even involuntary euthanasia. The Court of Appeals struck down Washington's assisted suicide ban only "as applied to competent, terminally ill adults who wish to hasten their deaths by obtaining medication prescribed by their doctors."... Washington insists, however, that the impact of the court's decision will not and cannot be so limited.... If suicide is protected as a matter of constitutional right, it is argued, "every man and woman in the United States must enjoy it."... See *Kevorkian* ... 527 N. W. 2d, at 727–728, n. 41. The Court of Appeals' decision, and its expansive reasoning, provide ample support for the State's concerns. The court noted, for example, that the "decision of a duly appointed surrogate decision maker is for all legal purposes the decision of the patient himself," ... that "in some instances, the patient may be unable to self administer the drugs and ... administration by the physician ... may be the only way the patient may be able to receive them," ... and that not only physicians, but also family members and loved ones, will inevitably participate in assisting suicide.... Thus, it turns out that what is couched as a limited right to "physician-assisted suicide" is likely, in effect, a much broader license, which could prove extremely difficult to police and contain.... Washington's ban on assisting suicide prevents such erosion.

We need not weigh exactingly the relative strengths of these various interests. They are unquestionably important and legitimate, and Washington's ban on assisted suicide is at least reasonably related to their promotion and protection. We therefore hold that Wash. Rev. Code § 9A.36.060(1) (1994) does not violate the Fourteenth Amendment, either on its face or "as applied to competent, terminally ill adults who wish to hasten their deaths by obtaining medication prescribed by their doctors."

Justice Souter, concurring in the judgment
When the physicians claim that the Washington law deprives them of a right falling within the scope of liberty that the Fourteenth Amendment guarantees against denial without due process of law, they are ... [claiming] that the State has no substantively adequate justification for barring the assistance sought by the patient and sought to be offered by the physician. Thus, we are dealing with a claim to one of those rights sometimes described as rights of substantive due

process and sometimes as unenumerated rights, in view of the breadth and indeterminacy of the "due process" serving as the claim's textual basis. The doctors accordingly arouse the skepticism of those who find the Due Process Clause an unduly vague or oxymoronic warrant for judicial review of substantive state law, just as they also invoke two centuries of American constitutional practice in recognizing unenumerated, substantive limits on governmental action.... The persistence of substantive due process in our cases points to the legitimacy of the modern justification for such judicial review ... while the acknowledged failures of some of these cases point with caution to the difficulty raised by the present claim....

Respondents claim that a patient facing imminent death, who anticipates physical suffering and indignity, and is capable of responsible and voluntary choice, should have a right to a physician's assistance in providing counsel and drugs to be administered by the patient to end life promptly....

This liberty interest in bodily integrity was phrased in a general way by then Judge Cardozo when he said, "Every human being of adult years and sound mind has a right to determine what shall be done with his own body" in relation to his medical needs.... The familiar examples of this right derive from the common law of battery and include the right to be free from medical invasions into the body, ... as well as a right generally to resist enforced medication.... Thus "it is settled now ... that the Constitution places limits on a State's right to interfere with a person's most basic decisions about ... bodily integrity." ... Constitutional recognition of the right to bodily integrity underlies the assumed right, good against the State, to require physicians to terminate artificial life support, ... and the affirmative right to obtain medical intervention to cause abortion. See ... *Roe v. Wade....*

It is, indeed, in the abortion cases that the most telling recognitions of the importance of bodily integrity and the concomitant tradition of medical assistance have occurred. In *Roe v. Wade*, the plaintiff contended that the Texas statute making it criminal for any person to "procure an abortion," ... for a pregnant woman was unconstitutional insofar as it prevented her from "terminat[ing] her pregnancy by an abortion 'performed by a competent, licensed physician, under safe, clinical conditions,' " ... and in striking down the statute we stressed the importance of the relationship between patient and physician....

The analogies between the abortion cases and this one are several. Even though the State has a legitimate interest in discouraging abortion, the Court recognized a woman's right to a physician's counsel and care.... Like the decision to commit suicide, the decision to abort potential life can be made irresponsibly and under the influence of others, and yet the Court has held in the abortion cases that physicians are fit assistants. Without physician assistance in abortion, the woman's right would have too often amounted to nothing more than a right to self-mutilation, and without a physician to assist in the suicide of the dying, the patient's right will often be confined to crude methods of causing death, most shocking and painful to the decedent's survivors.

There is, finally, one more reason for claiming that a physician's assistance here would fall within the accepted tradition of medical care in our society, and the abortion cases are only the most obvious illustration of the further point. While the Court has held that the performance of abortion procedures can be restricted to physicians, the Court's opinion in *Roe* recognized the doctors' role in yet another way. For, in the course of holding that the decision to perform an abortion called for a physician's assistance, the Court recognized that the good physician is not just a mechanic of the human body whose services have no bearing on a person's moral choices, but one who does more than treat symptoms, one who ministers to the patient.... This idea of the physician as serving the whole person is a source of the high value traditionally placed on the medical relationship. Its value is surely as apparent here as in the abortion cases, for just as the decision about abortion is not directed to correcting some pathology, so the decision in which a dying patient seeks help is not so limited. The patients here sought not only an end to pain (which they might have had, although perhaps at the price of stupor) [but also] an end to their short remaining lives with a dignity that they believed would be denied them by powerful pain medication, as well as by their consciousness of dependency and helplessness as they approached death. In that period when the end is imminent, they said, the decision to end life is closest to decisions that are generally accepted as proper instances of exercising autonomy over one's own body, instances recognized under the Constitution and the State's own law, instances in which the help of physicians is accepted as falling within the traditional norm....

I take it that the basic concept of judicial review with its possible displacement of legislative judgment bars any finding that a legislature has acted arbitrarily when the following conditions are met: there is a serious factual controversy over the feasibility of recognizing the claimed right without at the same time making it impossible for the State to engage in an undoubtedly legitimate exercise of power; facts necessary to resolve the controversy are not readily ascertainable through the judicial process; but they are more readily subject to discovery through legislative fact finding and experimentation. It is assumed in this case, and must be, that a State's interest in protecting those unable to make responsible decisions and those who make no decisions at all entitles the State to bar aid to any but a knowing and responsible person intending suicide, and to prohibit euthanasia. How, and how far, a State should act in that interest are judgments for the State, but the legitimacy of its action to deny a physician the option to aid any but the knowing and responsible is beyond question....

The principal enquiry at the moment is into the Dutch experience, and I question whether an independent front line investigation into the facts of a foreign country's legal administration can be soundly undertaken through American courtroom litigation. While an extensive literature on any subject can raise the hopes for judicial understanding, the literature on this subject is only nascent. Since there is little experience directly bearing on the issue, the most that can be said is that whichever way the Court might rule today, events could overtake its assumptions, as experimentation in some jurisdictions confirmed or discredited the concerns about progression from assisted suicide to euthanasia.

Legislatures, on the other hand, have superior opportunities to obtain the facts necessary for a judgment about the present controversy. Not only do they have more flexible mechanisms for fact finding than the Judiciary, but their mechanisms include the power to experiment, moving forward and pulling back as facts emerge within their own jurisdictions. There is, indeed, good reason to suppose that in the absence of a judgment for respondents here, just such experimentation will be attempted in some of the States....

I do not decide here what the significance might be of legislative foot dragging in ascertaining the facts going to the State's argument that the right in question could not be confined as claimed. Sometimes a court may be bound to act regardless of the institu-

tional preferability of the political branches as forums for addressing constitutional claims.... Now, it is enough to say that our examination of legislative reasonableness should consider the fact that the Legislature of the State of Washington is no more obviously at fault than this Court is in being uncertain about what would happen if respondents prevailed today. We therefore have a clear question about which institution, a legislature or a court, is relatively more competent to deal with an emerging issue as to which facts currently unknown could be dispositive. The answer has to be, for the reasons already stated, that the legislative process is to be preferred. There is a closely related further reason as well.

One must bear in mind that the nature of the right claimed, if recognized as one constitutionally required, would differ in no essential way from other constitutional rights guaranteed by enumeration or derived from some more definite textual source than "due process." An unenumerated right should not therefore be recognized, with the effect of displacing the legislative ordering of things, without the assurance that its recognition would prove as durable as the recognition of those other rights differently derived. To recognize a right of lesser promise would simply create a constitutional regime too uncertain to bring with it the expectation of finality that is one of this Court's central obligations in making constitutional decisions....

Legislatures, however, are not so constrained. The experimentation that should be out of the question in constitutional adjudication displacing legislative judgments is entirely proper, as well as highly desirable, when the legislative power addresses an emerging issue like assisted suicide. The Court should accordingly stay its hand to allow reasonable legislative consideration. While I do not decide for all time that respondents' claim should not be recognized, I acknowledge the legislative institutional competence as the better one to deal with that claim at this time.

Case Questions

1. What was Dr. Glucksberg's argument in the U.S. Supreme Court?
2. On what grounds did Chief Justice Rehnquist justify his conclusion that Washington's statute did not violate the Due Process Clause?

Glucksberg Post script

Eleven years after the U.S. Supreme Court ruled in favor of the State of Washington in the *Glucksberg*

case, in 2008, Washington voters redefined the state's public policy regarding physician–assisted suicide by voting in favor of Initiative 1000. Oregon, in 1994 was the first state to enact a physician-assisted suicide statute, Washington became the second such state, and in May of 2013 Vermont's governor signed a bill into law making Vermont the third.

Montana's Supreme Court decided in the 2009 case of *Baxter v. Montana* that physician-assisted suicide was permissible in that state. The court ruled that there was no relevant statutory or case law prohibiting the practice. The Montana legislature, as of this writing, has not indicated whether it will maintain the status quo or enact legislation making the practice a crime.

INTERNET TIP

An edited version of the Montana Supreme Court's opinion in *Baker v. Montana* and excerpts from the concurring and dissenting opinions can be found with the Chapter I materials in the textbook's website. Future developments in Montana law regarding physician-assisted suicides will be posted on the textbook's website with the Chapter I materials.

VAGUENESS AND OVERBREADTH

One of our fundamental legal principles is that laws must be written with sufficient precision or they will fail substantive due process requirements. Courts will declare unconstitutional statutes and ordinances that are overly broad or too vague. **Vagueness** exists where legislation fails to control the police exercise of discretion and fails to provide citizens with fair notice of what the law prohibits. **Overbreadth** exists where a statute is insufficiently focused. Thus, a disorderly conduct statute would be overly broad if it includes within its scope conduct that is clearly criminal as well as conduct that is protected by the First Amendment.

INTERNET TIP

An interesting Supreme Court vagueness case, *Chicago v. Morales* (1999), can be found on the textbook's website. This case involves a constitutional challenge to a Chicago ordinance intended to help combat loitering by members of Chicago street gangs.

Procedural Due Process

American law is very much concerned with procedure and **procedural due process**. The underlying premise is that justice is more likely to result when correct procedures have been followed. All states and the federal government have extensive rules that govern criminal and civil litigation; these are subject to modification by federal and state legislative and judicial bodies. Although some rules are essentially arbitrary—for instance, one that requires a defendant to file an answer within twenty days of being served with a summons and complaint—other procedures are thought to be essential to due process and have been given constitutional protection. This latter category of rules promotes accurate fact-finding and fairness and is used in all jurisdictions in every case.

Procedural due process rules play a major role in criminal cases, placing limits on police investigative techniques and prosecutorial behavior, and outlining how criminal trials should be conducted.

Even when the Supreme Court has interpreted the Due Process Clause of the Fourteenth Amendment to require a procedural right, however, it sometimes permits states to deviate from practices followed in federal courts. Procedural due process, for example, guarantees criminal defendants who are subject to more than six months' incarceration upon conviction the right to a jury trial. A defendant who stands trial in a state court, however, may not receive the same type of jury trial as in a federal court. Due process has been interpreted to permit states to accept nonunanimous jury verdicts in criminal cases where a unanimous verdict would be required in a federal court. Similarly, states are not constitutionally mandated to provide twelve-member juries even though twelve jurors are required in federal court.

In civil cases, due process rules are less extensive. They ensure that the court has jurisdiction over the parties, that proper notice has been given to defendants, and that the parties have an equal opportunity to present evidence and argument to the decision maker. In both types of litigation, procedural due process rules help ensure that decisions are made in a fair and reasonable manner.

As mentioned earlier, however, accuracy and fairness are not the only considerations. Elaborate procedural requirements are costly in terms of time, money, and utility. When the Supreme Court decides that a procedural right is fundamental to due process, there are often financial costs imposed on government, society, and individual litigants. Due process requirements also can lengthen the time it takes to conclude litigation, adding to the existing backlogs in many jurisdictions. Courts therefore generally try to balance accuracy against its cost on a case-by-case basis. In criminal cases, the need for accurate decision making is paramount, and the requirements of due process are quite extensive.

It is important to emphasize that the Fifth and Fourteenth Amendment Due Process Clauses operate only as restraints on government. One of the consequences of this limitation is that private schools have considerably more procedural latitude than public schools. Private elementary and secondary schools can regulate what students wear, substantially restrict student expression and behavior, enforce a common moral code, and enforce rules that are so vague that they would not be constitutionally acceptable in a public school. If private schools contract with their students to provide due process, or if they violate public policy, commit torts, or act inequitably, courts have been increasingly willing to intervene. Over the years, there has been an expansion of the concept of "state action" and a closer relationship between private schools and government in the form of grants, scholarships, and research funds to institutions of higher education. Courts are beginning to require procedural due process in actions of those private colleges and universities that have such governmental involvement.

In recent years, state legislatures throughout the country have enacted controversial statutes intended to protect the public from future attacks by convicted sexual offenders. These statutes require convicted sexual offenders to register with one or more governmental agencies (often the police or state attorney general) and supply detailed personal information. Often these statutes are challenged on procedural due process grounds.

Introduction to *Melinda Speelman v. Bellingham Housing Authority*

The following case from the State of Washington was brought by a public housing resident. The resident, Melinda Speelman, and her family wanted to contest the housing authority's decision to terminate the financial support she relied upon to pay for her housing. She brought suit seeking a preliminary injunction (a court order that a judge can issue as an emergency measure to temporarily preserve the status quo between the parties until a full hearing addresses the merits of the underlying dispute). Ms. Speelman's petition for preliminary injunction was denied by the trial court, so she sought to overturn that decision in the state intermediate court of appeals.

Melinda Speelman v. Bellingham Housing Authority
273 P.3d 1035
Court of Appeals of Washington, Division One
April 9, 2012

Leach, C.J.
Melinda Speelman challenges the trial court's denial of her request for a preliminary injunction in her action contesting the termination of her family's Section 8 housing subsidy....

BHA is a public housing authority that administers the federal Section 8 Housing Choice Voucher Program in Whatcom County. This program provides housing assistance in the form of rental subsidies to eligible families. The United States Department of Housing and

Urban Development funds the Housing Choice Voucher Program. The governing statute requires BHA to adopt a conforming administrative plan....

BHA's administrative plan lists several "family obligations" that participants must accept when entering the Housing Choice Voucher Program. These obligations include (1) notifying BHA within 14 days if any family member no longer resides in the residence, (2) obtaining BHA approval of all occupants in the residence, and (3) alerting BHA within 14 days if the family is absent from the residence.... BHA may terminate assistance if a family fails to meet its obligations, is absent from the residence for more than 30 days without authorization, or allows persons who are not BHA approved to live in the residence. Before terminating a family's assistance, the administrative plan requires that BHA send a termination notice to the participant's home. The notice must inform the participant that he or she has the right to request a hearing within 14 days. BHA considers a mailed notice delivered unless it is returned to BHA clearly marked "undeliverable."

In February 2011, Speelman and her two minor children moved into Walton Place Two, a BHA-subsidized apartment in Bellingham.... At the time the family moved in, BHA knew that Speelman was on probation. In March, Speelman asked the sentencing court to revoke her probation because she could not pay monthly probation fees. The trial court did so and sentenced her to 75 days in jail.

Before beginning her sentence on April 28, Speelman arranged for Audry Larsen, her 19-year-old daughter, to care for Speelman's other children at the Walton Place Two apartment. Speelman did not obtain BHA's approval for Larsen to live in the apartment or notify BHA that she would be absent....

While Speelman was in jail, BHA's Bellingham police liaison, Officer Lowell English, investigated a complaint that Speelman's children were "running around the apartment complex at night."... When Officer English arrived at Speelman's apartment, he spoke to Larsen and her fiancé, Chris Kleman, who told Officer English that Speelman was not at the apartment because she was out of town visiting a hospitalized relative. After Officer English left Speelman's apartment, he ran background checks on Speelman, Larsen, and Kleman and discovered that Speelman was at that time confined in the Whatcom County Jail. Officer English also noticed that the police system listed Speelman's Walton Place Two apartment as Larsen's address.

On June 2, BHA sent a letter to Speelman's home address, notifying her that it would be terminating her housing choice voucher payments effective July 31. Citing BHA administrative plan provisions, the letter listed three reasons for the termination decision: (1) an unauthorized person was residing in Speelman's apartment, (2) Speelman had been absent from her apartment for more than 30 days because she was in jail, and (3) Speelman failed to alert the BHA that she would be absent.... The letter advised Speelman of her right to appeal BHA's decision by submitting a written request for a hearing within 14 days of the notice date. Although Speelman had given Larsen the key to her mailbox, Larsen did not open BHA's letter because Speelman had instructed her not to open any mail except that from the children's school.

On June 17, Speelman completed her sentence and returned to her apartment. There, she discovered BHA's termination notice. On June 23, seven days after the deadline, Speelman requested a hearing. BHA denied Speelman's request as untimely.... BHA sent Speelman a final termination notice on June 29 and reassigned the housing choice voucher funds to another family.

Speelman sued BHA in superior court under 42 U.S.C. § 1983, alleging substantive and procedural due process violations, and requesting declaratory and injunctive relief. Speelman also asked for a preliminary injunction requiring BHA to continue making housing assistance payments to her during the pendency of the lawsuit.

The trial court denied Speelman's motion for a preliminary injunction. In its oral ruling, it found "no due process violation whatsoever" and stated, "[A]ny loss of the appeal rights are solely and exclusively due to the circumstances of the plaintiff [and] entirely beyond the control of the defendant." The trial court also denied Speelman's motion for reconsideration....

... This court granted Speelman's petition for discretionary review and BHA's cross petition for discretionary review....

Speelman challenges the trial court's denial of her motion for a preliminary injunction. A party seeking a preliminary injunction must show (1) a clear legal or equitable right, (2) a well-grounded fear of immediate invasion of that right, and (3) the acts complained of have or will result in actual and substantial injury....

The first criterion requires a court to examine the likelihood that the moving party will prevail on the merits of its claim.... Speelman contends that BHA violated her constitutional right to procedural due process by providing insufficient notice of its termination decision.... "When a state seeks to deprive a person of a protected interest, procedural due process requires that an individual receive notice of the deprivation and an opportunity to be heard to guard against erroneous deprivation."... Due process does not require actual notice.... "Rather, ... due process requires the government to provide 'notice reasonably calculated, under all the circumstances, to apprise interested parties of the pendency of the action and afford them an opportunity to present their objections.'"...

Neither party disputes that Speelman has a constitutionally protected property interest in her housing choice voucher or that she was entitled to an opportunity to be heard. Instead, the dispute centers on the adequacy of the notice she received. Speelman contends that due process required BHA to send the termination notice to the Whatcom County Jail. We agree....

BHA's termination notice affirmatively shows that it knew Speelman was incarcerated when it sent the letter to her apartment. The letter states, "The head of household *has been in jail since 4/28/11*—unreported to the landlord and BHA." (Emphasis added.)... Even if BHA's policy is reasonably calculated to provide notice in normal circumstances, the special circumstances of this case triggered BHA's obligation to do something else. Because BHA knew at the time it sent the termination letter that Speelman would not receive it, this letter was not reasonably calculated under the circumstances to provide notice. It was constitutionally insufficient. A reasonably calculated action would have been to send the notice to the Whatcom County Jail in lieu of or in addition to sending it to Speelman's residence.

BHA argues that our Supreme Court's decision in *State v. Nelson* ... requires a different result. The State suspended Nelson's license to drive after he refused to take a breath test when stopped on suspicion of driving under the influence.... Nelson then spent several months at the King County North Rehabilitation Facility (NRF).... While there, he sent a letter to the Department of Licensing (DOL), asking how he could have his license reinstated.... More than two months later and while Nelson remained in custody, DOL revoked Nelson's license after determining that he was a habitual traffic offender. It sent the order of revocation to Nelson's home address.... The postal service returned the order of revocation unclaimed to DOL four days after Nelson's release.... A year later, Nelson was arrested and convicted for driving with a suspended or revoked driver's license.... He appealed on procedural due process grounds.... The court addressed whether DOL deprived Nelson of procedural due process when it sent the revocation notice only to Nelson's address of record and not to NRF, "where DOL knew that Nelson had *previously* been incarcerated."...

After considering the unique circumstances of the case, the court held that notice was adequate and affirmed Nelson's conviction.... In *Nelson*, ... "the State did not know that the notice sent to Nelson's address of record was ineffective until after the revocation

became operative."... The court reasoned Nelson's inquiry sent from NRF two months earlier did not put DOL on notice that Nelson would still be at NRF when it sent the revocation letter.... And because Nelson had already been released from NRF by the time DOL learned that notice had been ineffective, DOL did not have an obligation to take additional steps to provide notice. Based on these considerations, the court determined that notice had been reasonably calculated to inform Nelson of DOL's actions.

BHA cites three reasons why it believes this case is more like *Nelson*.... First, BHA claims that "there is nothing in the record indicating that BHA knew that Plaintiff was incarcerated on *June 2, 2011*, the date the BHA sent the Termination Notice." As previously noted, we disagree. The termination letter itself demonstrates that BHA had actual knowledge that Speelman was in jail at the time the letter was sent.

Second, BHA contends that it "did not have actual knowledge that notice would not reach Plaintiff personally" because it "did not know that Plaintiff [had] asked Ms. Larsen to simply stack her mail up without opening it." BHA's argument seems to imply that Speelman had an obligation to alert BHA that she had a different address or that she should have had her mail forwarded to the jail. But a party's ability to take steps to safeguard its interests does not relieve the State of its constitutional obligation."...

Third, BHA claims that "[a]dequate notice does not mean the BHA needs to verify that Plaintiff actually read the notice." We agree. Due process does not require actual notice. Speelman, however, does not contend otherwise; she simply contends that notice was not reasonably calculated to inform her of BHA's termination decision.

BHA's three arguments that *Nelson* should apply here are unconvincing....

BHA violated Speelman's procedural due process rights. Therefore, Speelman is likely to prevail on the merits of her claim. Speelman satisfies the first preliminary injunction factor. This, however, does not end our inquiry. Turning to the second and third criteria for the issuance of a preliminary injunction, Speelman must demonstrate that she has a well-grounded fear of immediate invasion of her asserted right and that BHA's actions have or will result in actual and substantial injury.

Here, Speelman asserts the right to due process before the government interferes with her property interest. She has shown a fear of immediate invasion of that right. Indeed, BHA has already interfered with that right by terminating her federal benefits after giving her defective notice, which effectively deprived her of an opportunity to be heard.

Speelman has also shown actual and substantial injury. Due to the failure of notice, she missed the deadline to appeal BHA's decision and now faces eviction without the benefit of a hearing. As the United States Supreme Court stated in *Goldberg v. Kelly*, ... the importance of a hearing in situations like this one is paramount:

"[T]he stakes are simply too high for the welfare recipient, and the possibility for honest error or irritable misjudgment too great, to allow termination of aid without giving the recipient a chance, if he so desires, to be fully informed of the case against him so that he may contest its basis and produce evidence in rebuttal."

Finally, ... both the parties and the public have an interest in ensuring that BHA administers its programs lawfully. Contrary to BHA's contention, Speelman is not asking for an exception to be applied to her case. She is asking that she be given the process due to her and everyone else in her situation. Therefore, the equities favor granting Speelman a preliminary injunction.

Speelman meets the above criteria for a preliminary injunction; the trial court should have granted her motion....

Because Speelman meets the preliminary injunction criteria, the trial court erred by denying Speelman's motion for a preliminary injunction. We reverse and remand for further proceedings consistent with this opinion.

Cox and Appelwick, JJ., concur.

Case Questions

1. Since the Bellingham Housing Authority sent the termination letter to Speelman's home, what was the procedural due process problem in this case?
2. According to the Washington Court of Appeals, was Speelman entitled to actual notice of the termination?
3. Due process protects life, liberty, and property. Which of these interests was infringed in this case?

CRIMINAL AND CIVIL LAW

The distinction between criminal and civil law is a very important concept in our legal system (see Figure 1.1). This text deals primarily with civil law. A civil suit involves a dispute between private individuals involving either a breach of an agreement or a breach of a duty imposed by law. A criminal action is brought by the government against an individual who allegedly has committed a crime. Crimes are classified as treason, felonies, and misdemeanors, depending on the punishment attached to the crime. **Treason** is a crime defined only by the Constitution, article III, section 3, clause 1. To commit treason—levying war against the United States, or adhering to or giving aid or comfort to its enemies—there must be an overt act and the intent to commit treason. A **felony** is a crime that is classified by statute in the place in which it is committed. That is, the severity of the punishment for a felony varies from place to place. A felony is generally regarded as being any criminal offense for which a defendant may be imprisoned for more than one year, or executed. One determines whether a crime is a felony according to the sentence that might lawfully be imposed, not according to the sentence actually ordered. Felonies do not include **misdemeanors,** offenses that generally are punishable by a maximum term of imprisonment of less than one year.

In a civil suit, the court attempts to remedy the dispute between individuals by determining their legal rights, awarding money damages to the injured party, or directing one party to perform or refrain from performing a specific act. Since a crime is an act against society, the criminal court punishes a guilty defendant by imposing a fine or imprisonment or both.

In a criminal prosecution, the rules of court procedure differ. In order to meet the burden of proof to find a person guilty of a crime, guilt must be proved beyond a reasonable doubt, a stricter standard than the preponderance of evidence usually required in a civil case.

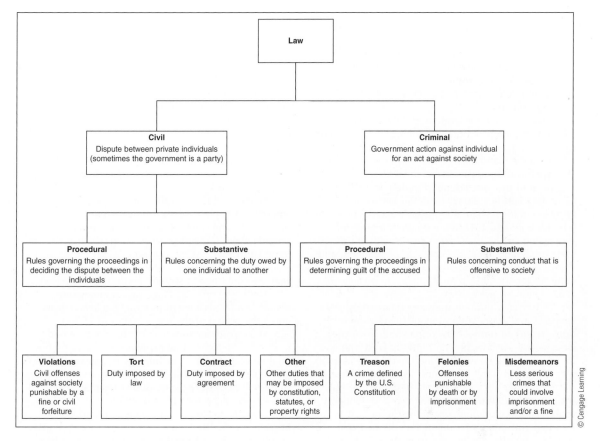

FIGURE 1.1 Criminal and Civil Law

As we will see in the next case, when the same act gives rise to both a criminal proceeding and a civil suit, the actions are completely independent of each other. *Katko v. Briney* involves a civil suit for damages brought against the victim of a criminal larceny by the person convicted of committing the crime.

Katko v. Briney
183 N.W.2d 657
Supreme Court of Iowa
February 9, 1971

Moore, Chief Justice

The primary issue presented here is whether an owner may protect personal property in an unoccupied boarded-up farmhouse against trespassers and thieves by a spring gun capable of inflicting death or serious injury.

We are not here concerned with a man's right to protect his home and members of his family.

Defendants' home was several miles from the scene of the incident to which we refer infra.

Plaintiff's action is for damages resulting from serious injury caused by a shot from a 20-gauge spring shotgun set by defendants in a bedroom of an old farmhouse, which had been uninhabited for several years. Plaintiff and his companion, Marvin McDonough, had broken and entered the house to find and steal old bottles and dated fruit jars, which they considered antiques. At defendants' request, plaintiff's action was tried to a jury consisting of residents of the community where defendants' property was located. The jury returned a verdict for plaintiff and against defendants for $20,000 actual and $10,000 punitive damages.

After careful consideration of defendants' motions for judgment notwithstanding the verdict and for a new trial, the experienced and capable trial judge overruled them and entered judgment on the verdict. Thus we have this appeal by defendants....

Most of the facts are not disputed. In 1957 defendant Bertha L. Briney inherited her parents' farmland in Mahaska and Monroe Counties. For about ten years, 1957 to 1967, there occurred a series of trespassing and housebreaking events with loss of some household items, the breaking of windows, and "messing up of the property in general." The latest occurred June 8, 1967, prior to the event on July 16, 1967, herein involved.

Defendants through the years boarded up the windows and doors in an attempt to stop the intrusions. They had posted "no trespass" signs on the land several years before 1967. The nearest one was 35 feet from the house. On June 11, 1967, defendants set a "shotgun trap" in the north bedroom. After Mr. Briney cleaned and oiled his 20-gauge shotgun, the power of which he was well aware, defendants took it to the old house where they secured it to an iron bed with the barrel pointed at the bedroom door. It was rigged with wire from the doorknob to the gun's trigger so that it would fire when the door was opened. Briney first pointed the gun so an intruder would be hit in the stomach but at Mrs. Briney's suggestion it was lowered to hit the legs. He admitted he did so "because I was mad and tired of being tormented" but "he did not intend to injure anyone." He gave no explanation of why he used a loaded shell and set it to hit a person already in the house. Tin was nailed over the bedroom window. The spring gun could not be seen from the outside. No warning of its presence was posted.

Plaintiff lived with his wife and worked regularly as a gasoline station attendant in Eddyville, seven miles from the old house. He had observed it for several years while hunting in the area and considered it as being abandoned. He knew it had long been uninhabited. In 1967 the area around the house was covered with high weeds. Prior to July 16, 1967 plaintiff and McDonough had been to the premises and found several old bottles and fruit jars, which they took and added to their collection of antiques. On the latter date about 9:30 P.M. they made a second trip to the Briney property. They entered the old house by removing a board from a porch window, which was without glass. While McDonough was looking around the kitchen area, plaintiff went to another part of the house. As he started to open the north bedroom door the shotgun went off, striking him in the right leg above the ankle bone. Much of his leg, including part of the tibia, was blown away. Only by McDonough's assistance was plaintiff able to get out of the house and after crawling some distance, he was put in his vehicle and rushed to a doctor and then to a hospital. He remained in the hospital 40 days.

Plaintiff's doctor testified he seriously considered amputation but eventually the healing process was successful. Some weeks after his release from the hospital plaintiff returned to work on crutches. He was required to keep the injured leg in a cast for approximately a year and wear a special brace for another year. He continued to suffer pain during this period.

There was undenied medical testimony that plaintiff had a permanent deformity, a loss of tissue, and a shortening of the leg.

The record discloses plaintiff to trial time had incurred $710 for medical expenses, $2056.85 for hospital service, $61.80 for orthopedic service and $750 as loss of earnings. In addition thereto the trial court submitted to the jury the question of damages for pain and suffering and for future disability.

Plaintiff testified he knew he had no right to break and enter the house with intent to steal bottles and fruit jars therefrom. He further testified he had entered a plea of guilty to larceny in the nighttime of property of less than $20 value from a private building. He stated he had been fined $50 and costs and paroled during good behavior from a 60-day jail sentence. Other than minor traffic charges, this was plaintiff's first brush with the law. On this civil case appeal, it is not our prerogative to review the disposition made of the criminal charge against him.

The main thrust of defendants' defense in the trial court and on this appeal is that "the law permits use of a spring gun in a dwelling or warehouse for the purpose of preventing the unlawful entry of a burglar or thief."... [T]he court referred to the early case history of the use of spring guns and stated under the law their use was prohibited except to prevent the commission of felonies of violence and where human life is in danger. The instruction included a statement that breaking and entering is not a felony of violence.

Instruction 5 stated: "You are hereby instructed that one may use reasonable force in the protection of his property, but such right is subject to the qualification that one may not use such means of force as will take human life or inflict great bodily injury. Such is the rule even though the injured party is a trespasser and is in violation of the law himself."

Instruction 6 stated: "An owner of premises is prohibited from willfully or intentionally injuring a trespasser by means of force that either takes life or inflicts great bodily injury; and therefore a person owning a premise is prohibited from setting out 'spring guns' and like dangerous devices which will likely take life or inflict great bodily injury, for the purpose of harming trespassers. The fact that the trespasser may be acting in violation of the law does not change the rule. The only time when such conduct of setting a 'spring gun' or a like dangerous device is justified would be when the trespasser was committing a felony of violence or a felony punishable by death, or where the trespasser was endangering human life by his act."

Instruction 7, to which defendants made no objection or exception, stated:

"To entitle the plaintiff to recover for compensatory damages, the burden of proof is upon him to establish by a preponderance of the evidence each and all of the following propositions:

"1. That defendants erected a shotgun trap in a vacant house on land owned by defendant, Bertha L. Briney, on or about June 11, 1967, which fact was known only by them, to protect household goods from trespassers and thieves.
"2. That the force used by defendants was in excess of that force reasonably necessary and which persons are entitled to use in the protection of their property.
"3. That plaintiff was injured and damaged and the amount thereof.
"4. That plaintiff's injuries and damages resulted directly from the discharge of the shotgun trap which was set and used by defendants."

The overwhelming weight of authority, both textbook and case law, supports the trial court's statement of the applicable principles of law.

Prosser on Torts, third edition, pages 116–118, states that:

[T]he law has always placed a higher value upon human safety than upon mere rights in property. [I]t is the accepted rule that there is no privilege to use any force calculated to cause death or serious bodily injury to repel the threat to land or chattels, unless there is also such a threat to the defendant's personal safety as to justify a self defense ... spring guns and other man-killing devices are not justifiable against a mere trespasser, or even a petty thief. They are privileged only against those upon whom the landowner, if he were present in person, would be free to inflict injury of the same kind.

Restatement of Torts, §85, page 180, states that:

the value of human life and limbs, not only to the individual concerned but also to society, so outweighs the interest of a possessor of land in excluding from it those whom he is not willing to admit thereto that a possessor of land has, as is stated in §79, no privilege to use force intended or likely to cause death or serious harm against another whom the possessor sees about to enter his premises or meddle with his chattel, unless the intrusion threatens death or serious bodily harm to the occupiers or users of the premises.... A possessor of land cannot do indirectly and by a mechanical device that which, were he present, he could not do immediately and in person. Therefore, he cannot gain a privilege to install, for the purpose of protecting his land from intrusions harmless to the lives and limbs of the occupiers or users of it, a mechanical device whose only purpose is to inflict death or serious harm upon such as may intrude, by giving notice of his intention to inflict, by mechanical means and indirectly, harm which he could not, even after request, inflict directly were he present....

In *Hooker v. Miller,* 37 Iowa 613, we held defendant vineyard owner liable for damages resulting from a spring gunshot although plaintiff was a trespasser and there to steal grapes. At pages 614, 615, this statement is made: "This court has held that a mere trespass against property other than a dwelling is not a sufficient justification to authorize the use of a deadly weapon by the owner in its defense; and that if death results in such a case it will be murder, though the killing be actually necessary to prevent the trespass."... At page 617 this court said: "Trespassers and other inconsiderable violators of the law are not to be visited by barbarous punishments or prevented by inhuman inflictions of bodily injuries."

The facts in *Allison v. Fiscus,* 156 Ohio 120, decided in 1951, are very similar to the case at bar. There plaintiff's right to damages was recognized for injuries received when he feloniously broke a door latch and started to enter defendant's warehouse with intent to steal. As he entered, a trap of two sticks of dynamite buried under the doorway by defendant owner was set off and plaintiff seriously injured. The court held the question whether a particular trap was justified as a use of reasonable and necessary force against a trespasser engaged in the commission of a felony should have been submitted to the jury. The Ohio Supreme Court recognized the plaintiff's right to recover punitive or exemplary damages in addition to compensatory damages....

In *United Zinc & Chemical Co. v. Britt*, 258 U.S. 268, 275, the Court states: "The liability for spring guns and mantraps arises from the fact that the defendant has ... expected the trespasser and prepared an injury that is no more justified than if he had held the gun and fired it."

In addition to civil liability many jurisdictions hold a landowner criminally liable for serious injuries or homicide caused by spring guns or other set devices....

In Wisconsin, Oregon and England the use of spring guns and similar devices is specifically made unlawful by statute....

The legal principles stated by the trial court in instructions 2, 5 and 6 are well established and supported by the authorities cited and quoted supra. There is no merit in defendants' objections and exceptions thereto. Defendants' various motions based on the same reasons stated in exceptions to instructions were properly overruled.

Plaintiff's claim and the jury's allowance of punitive damages, under the trial court's instructions relating thereto, were not at any time or in any manner challenged by defendants in the trial court as not allowable. We therefore are not presented with the problem of whether the $10,000 award should be allowed to stand.

We express no opinion as to whether punitive damages are allowable in this type of case. If defendants' attorneys wanted that issue decided, it was their duty to raise it in the trial court.

The rule is well established that we will not consider a contention not raised in the trial court. In other words, we are a court of review and will not consider a contention raised for the first time in this court....

Under our law punitive damages are not allowed as a matter of right. When malice is shown or when a defendant acted with wanton and reckless disregard of the rights of others, punitive damages may be allowed as punishment to the defendant and as a deterrent to others. Although not meant to compensate a plaintiff, the result is to increase his recovery. He is the fortuitous beneficiary of such an award simply because there is no one else to receive it.

The jury's findings of fact including a finding that defendants acted with malice and with wanton and reckless disregard, as required for an allowance of punitive or exemplary damages, are supported by substantial evidence. We are bound thereby.

This opinion is not to be taken or construed as authority that the allowance of punitive damages is or is not proper under circumstances such as exist here. We hold only that a question of law not having been properly raised cannot in this case be resolved.

Study and careful consideration of defendants' contentions on appeal reveal no reversible error.

Affirmed.

Larson, Justice, dissenting

I respectfully dissent, first because the majority wrongfully assumes that by installing a spring gun in the bedroom of their unoccupied house the defendants intended to shoot any intruder who attempted to enter the room. Under the record presented here, that was a fact question. Unless it is held that these property owners are liable for any injury to an intruder from such a device regardless of the intent with which it is installed, liability under these pleadings must rest on two definite issues of fact, i.e., did the defendants intend to shoot the invader, and if so, did they employ unnecessary and unreasonable force against him?

It is my feeling that the majority oversimplifies the impact of this case on the law, not only in this but other jurisdictions, and that it has not thought through all the ramifications of this holding.

There being no statutory provisions governing the right of an owner to defend his property by the use of a spring gun or other like device, or of a criminal invader to recover punitive damages when injured by such an instrumentality while breaking into the building of another, our interest and attention are directed to what should be the court determination of public policy in these matters. On both issues we are faced with a case of first impression. We should accept the task and clearly establish the law in this jurisdiction hereafter. I would hold there is no absolute liability for injury to a criminal intruder by setting up such a device on his property, and unless done with an intent to kill or seriously injure the intruder, I would absolve the owner from liability other than for negligence. I would also hold the court had no jurisdiction to allow punitive damages when the intruder was engaged in a serious criminal offense such as breaking and entering with intent to steal....

Case Questions

1. Suppose that, instead of a spring gun, the Brineys had unleashed on the premises a vicious watchdog that severely injured Katko's leg? Would the result have been different? What if the watchdog had been properly chained?
2. When may one set a spring gun and not be subject to liability? What can one legally do to protect property or life?
3. What do you think the consequences would have been if the dissenting judge's suggestions had become law?
4. A case involving breaking and entering and shooting a gun might appear to be a criminal matter. What factors make this a civil lawsuit?

EQUAL PROTECTION OF THE LAW

The **Equal Protection Clause** of the Fourteenth Amendment has been used to strike down legislation that was enacted for the purpose of discriminating against certain groupings of people (called "classifications" in legalese). The Jim Crow laws, used to discriminate against African Americans, are one notorious example of an invidious and legally impermissible classification scheme.

Earlier in this chapter, we learned about the U.S. Supreme Court's decision in the 1967 case of *Loving v. Virginia*. Virginia's miscegenation statute was found to violate substantive due process. We return to that case at this time because the Lovings had an additional ground for challenging the statute. They maintained that it also violated the Equal Protection Clause of the Fourteenth Amendment. The Supreme Court agreed. It ruled that the statute had deprived the Lovings of equal protection because "Virginia prohibit[ed] only interracial marriages involving white persons" and because there "is patently no legitimate overriding purpose independent of invidious racial discrimination which justifies this classification."

The Equal Protection Clause has been invoked to invalidate discriminatory classification schemes that are based on national origin, alienage, religion, and gender (in some situations).

TORT AND CONTRACT LAW

A person has a right to bring a civil action against another for a wrongful act or omission that causes injury to him or her. The basis of the suit is a violation of some duty owed to the injured person. This duty arises either from an agreement of the persons or by operation of the law.

Torts

Tort law establishes standards of conduct that all citizens must meet. A plaintiff sues in tort to recover money damages for injuries to his or her person, reputation, property, or business caused by a breach of a legal duty.

A tort is any wrongful act, not involving a breach of an agreement, for which a civil action may be maintained. The wrongful act can be intentional or unintentional. Intentional torts are based on the defendant's willful misconduct or intentional wrongdoing. This does not necessarily mean the defendant had a hostile intent, but only that he or she had a belief that a particular harmful result was substantially likely to follow. *Katko v. Briney* was such a case. When Briney rigged the spring gun, he did so believing that serious bodily injury was very likely to occur to any intruder who opened the door. Briney was civilly found to have violated the standard of care owed by a property owner to a trespasser such as Katko under the circumstances of that case. A person who commits an intentional tort also may be committing a criminal act, for which the government may bring criminal charges. As we saw in *Katko v. Briney,* the tort and criminal actions would be independent of each other.

An unintentional tort occurs when a person acts negligently. That is, he or she unintentionally fails to live up to the community's ideal of reasonable care. Every person has a legal duty to act toward other people as a reasonable and prudent person would have acted under the circumstances. Torts are discussed more fully in Chapter XI.

Contracts

A contract is a promissory agreement between two or more people that creates, modifies, or destroys a legally enforceable obligation. People voluntarily enter into a contract in order to create private duties for mutual advantage. Thus, under ordinary conditions, contractual terms are not imposed by law. There are exceptions to this rule; however, the essence of contract law is the enforcement of a promise voluntarily made.

Although contract law is more thoroughly discussed in Chapter X, it will be helpful to introduce it here. In the legal sense, the term **contract** does not mean the tangible document that contains evidence of an agreement. Rather, a contract is the legally enforceable agreement itself. There are three parts to every contract: **offer, acceptance,** and **consideration.** An offer is a communication of a promise, with a statement of what is expected in return. An offer is made with the intention of creating an enforceable legal obligation. Acceptance is the evidence of assent to the terms of the offer. Consideration is the inducement each party has to enter into an agreement. Only legally enforceable obligations are called contracts.

A person who fails to perform a contractual obligation has breached the contract. The plaintiff brings a suit in contract to obtain legal relief from the breaching party. The normal remedy for a breach of contract is monetary damages, although in appropriate circumstances, the breaching party may be ordered to perform his or her agreement.

Contracts may be oral, written, express (explicit terms), implied in fact (inferred from the person's actions), or implied in law. In *Suggs v. Norris,* which follows, the trial court permitted the jury to find an implied-in-law agreement from the facts of the case, even though there was no proof of an oral agreement or written document evidencing a contract.

Suggs v. Norris
364 S.E.2d 159
Court of Appeals of North Carolina
February 2, 1988

Wells, Judge

The overriding question presented by this appeal is whether public policy forbids the recovery by a plaintiff partner to an unmarried but cohabiting or meretricious relationship, from the other partner's estate, for services rendered to or benefits conferred upon the other partner through the plaintiff's work in the operation of a joint business when the business proceeds were utilized to enrich the estate of the deceased partner.

Defendant argues under her first three assignments of error that any agreement between plaintiff and the decedent providing compensation to plaintiff for her efforts in the raising and harvesting of produce was void as against public policy because it arose out of the couple's illegal cohabitation. While it is well settled that no recovery can be had under either a contractual or restitutionary (*quantum meruit*) theory arising out of a contract or circumstances which violate public policy ... defendant's application of the rule to the present case is misplaced.

This Court has made it clear that we do not approve of or endorse adulterous meretricious affairs, *Collins v. Davis,* 68 N.C. App. 588.... We made it clear in *Collins,* however, that cohabiting but unmarried individuals are capable of "entering into enforceable express or implied contracts for the purchase and improvement of houses, or for the loan and repayment of money."... Judge Phillips, writing for the majority, in *Collins* was careful to point out that if illicit sexual intercourse had provided the consideration for the contract or implied agreement, all claims arising therefrom, having been founded on illegal consideration, would then be unenforceable.

While our research has disclosed no other North Carolina cases which address this specific issue, we do find considerable guidance in the decisional law of other states. Most notable is Justice Tobriner's landmark decision in *Marvin v. Marvin,* 18 Cal.3d 660 ... (1976) which held that express contracts between unmarried cohabiting individuals are enforceable unless the same are based solely on sexual services....

The *Marvin* Court also held that an unmarried couple may, by words and conduct, create an implied-in-fact agreement regarding the disposition of their mutual properties and money as well as an implied agreement of partnership or joint venture.... Finally, the court endorsed the use of constructive trusts wherever appropriate and recovery in quantum meruit where the plaintiff can show that the services were rendered with an expectation of monetary compensation....

Other jurisdictions have fashioned and adhered to similar rules. In *Kinkenon v. Hue* [207 Neb. 698 (1981)], the Nebraska Supreme Court confirmed an earlier rule that while bargains made in whole or in part for consideration of sexual intercourse are illegal, any agreements not resting on such consideration, regardless of the marital status of the two individuals, are enforceable....

Likewise, the New Jersey Supreme Court held as enforceable an oral agreement between two adult unmarried partners where the agreement was not based "explicitly or inseparably" on sexual services. *Kozlowski v. Kozlowski* [80 N.J. 378 (1979)]. In *Fernandez v. Garza*, 88 Ariz. 214 (1960), the Arizona Supreme Court held that plaintiff's meretricious or unmarried cohabitation with decedent did not bar the enforcement of a partnership agreement wherein the parties agreed to share their property and profits equally and where such was not based upon sexual services as consideration....

We now make clear and adopt the rule that agreements regarding the finances and property of an unmarried but cohabiting couple, whether express or implied, are enforceable as long as sexual services or promises thereof do not provide the consideration for such agreements....

In the present case, the question is before this Court on an appeal of the trial court's denial of defendant's Motion for Judgment Notwithstanding the Verdict; therefore, our standard of review is whether the evidence, viewed in the light most favorable to plaintiff, is sufficient to support the jury verdict. *Wallace v. Evans,* [60 N.C. App. 145 (1982)]. Applying the foregoing standard, we find that plaintiff's evidence that she began work for the decedent in his produce business several years before she began cohabiting with him and that at the time she began work

she believed the two of them were "partners" in the business, was sufficient evidence for the jury to have inferred that plaintiff's work comprised a business relationship with decedent which was separate and independent from and of their cohabiting relationship. Therefore, the jury may have inferred that sexual services did not provide the consideration for plaintiff's claim. We therefore hold that plaintiff's claim for a *quantum meruit* recovery was not barred as being against public policy. Defendant's first three assignments of error are overruled.

Defendant next argues under assignments of error 4 and 5 that the trial court erred in submitting a *quantum meruit* recovery issue to the jury because any services rendered by plaintiff were either gratuitous or incidental to an illegal relationship. As we have already addressed the issue of illegality, we are concerned here only with the question of whether there existed sufficient evidence to submit the issue of recovery in *quantum meruit* to the jury.

The trial court placed the following issue regarding a quasi-contract or *quantum meruit* recovery before the jury:

Issue Four:

> Did DARLENE SUGGS render services to JUNIOR EARL NORRIS involving the raising, harvesting and sale of produce under such circumstances that the Estate of JUNIOR EARL NORRIS should be required to pay for them?
> ANSWER: Yes

Recovery on quantum meruit requires the establishment of an implied contract.... The contract may be one implied-in-fact where the conduct of the parties clearly indicates their intention to create a contract or it may be implied-in-law based on the restitutionary theory of quasi-contract, which operates to prevent unjust enrichment.... An implied-in-law theory required the plaintiff to establish that services were rendered and accepted between the two parties with the mutual understanding that plaintiff was to be compensated for her efforts.... Moreover, plaintiff's efforts must not have been gratuitous as is generally presumed where services are rendered between family or spousal members....

In the present case, the evidence clearly showed that the plaintiff had from 1973 until the death of the decedent in 1983 operated a produce route for and with the decedent. According to several witnesses' testimony, plaintiff had worked decedent's farm, disked and cultivated the soil, and harvested and marketed the produce. Plaintiff, working primarily without the decedent's aid, drove the produce to various markets over a 60-mile route. She handled all finances and deposited them in the couple's joint banking account. Finally, the evidence showed that the decedent, an alcoholic, depended almost entirely on plaintiff's work in the produce business and as well her care of him while he was ill. Because of plaintiff's efforts the couple had amassed seven vehicles valued at $20,000; some farm equipment valued at $4,000; $8,000 in cash in the account, and all debts which had attached to the farm when plaintiff began working with decedent in 1973 were paid—all due to plaintiff's efforts. Additionally, plaintiff testified that when she began work with the decedent in 1973 she believed they were partners and that she was entitled to share in one-half the profits.

The foregoing evidence clearly establishes a set of facts sufficient to have submitted a quasi-contractual issue to the jury and from which the jury could have inferred a mutual understanding between plaintiff and the decedent that she would be remunerated for her services. Plaintiff's efforts conferred many years of benefits on the decedent and the decedent, by all accounts, willingly accepted those benefits.

Because the evidence viewed in the light most favorable to plaintiff was clearly sufficient to permit the jury to find a mutual understanding between plaintiff and decedent that plaintiff's work in the produce business was not free of charge and because plaintiff's work in the produce business was not of the character usually found to be performed gratuitously … defendant's Motions for Directed Verdict and Judgment Notwithstanding the Verdict were properly denied.

No Error.

Case Questions

1. Darlene Suggs's suit against the estate of Junior E. Norris was based on what legal theories?
2. Under what circumstances does the court indicate that the contracts between unmarried but cohabiting persons would not be enforceable?
3. Why should a court be able to create a contract after a dispute arises for parties who never signed a binding contract?
4. Do you see any moral principles reflected in the court's opinion in this case?

CHAPTER SUMMARY

Chapter I began by raising a fundamental jurisprudential question, What is law? Many students who have not previously thought much about law are surprised to learn that there is no single universally accepted answer to the question and that the likely best answer is, It depends. After reading brief synopses of several differing philosophical schools, it becomes apparent why developing a consensus definition has proven to be so difficult. What followed next were a discussion of legal objectives that are common to both private and public law in this country, and a review of Anglo–American historical and cultural heritage with a focus on how these have contributed to law as we know it today. Because students using this textbook need immediately to begin developing the ability to read excerpts from judicial opinions, the chapter included a highly simplified overview of civil procedure. This overview was necessary preparation for students about to read their first case. Civil procedure is a topic that is covered in considerably more detail in Chapter V. The chapter continued with some additional comments on reading cases immediately prior to the first judicial opinion, *Miller v. Alabama*. An analysis of that case followed, along with a sample brief, both of which were intended to further help students learn how to read and understand judicial opinions in general, and the first case in particular. The chapter then turned to an overview of constitutional due process and equal protection, and a discussion of the differences between civil and criminal law. The chapter concluded with an explanation of the differences between tort and contract law.

CHAPTER QUESTIONS

1. Inmates in a state reformatory brought suit against the state department of corrections because corrections officials refused to permit certain persons to visit inmates. The inmates brought suit because receiving visitors is essential to inmates' morale and to maintaining contacts with their families. They argued that the state had established regulations to guide prison officials in making visitation decisions, thus the court should recognize that inmates have a constitutionally protected liberty right to a hearing whenever prison officials deny a visitation. Convening such a hearing would make it possible for inmates to determine whether prison officials had complied with the guidelines or had acted arbitrarily in denying a visitation. Should the inmates have a due process right to a hearing?

   Kentucky Department of Corrections v. Thompson, 490 U.S. 454 (1989)

2. Terry Foucha, a criminal defendant, was charged with aggravated burglary and a firearms offense. On October 12, 1984, Foucha was found not guilty by reason of insanity and was ordered committed to a mental institution until medically discharged or released pursuant to a court order. In March 1988, doctors evaluated Foucha and determined that he was "presently in remission from mental illness, [but] [w]e cannot certify that he would not constitute a menace to himself or to others if released." There was testimony from one doctor that Foucha had "an antisocial personality, a condition that is not a mental disease, and that is untreatable." Based on these opinions, the court ordered that Foucha remain in the mental institution because he posed a danger to himself as well as others. Under state law, a person who has been acquitted of criminal charges because of insanity but who is no longer insane can only be released from commitment if he can prove that he is not a danger to himself or to society. Does the statutory scheme violate Foucha's liberty rights under the Due Process Clause?

   Foucha v. Louisiana, 504 U.S. 71 (1992)

3. Rhode Island's legislature enacted laws that prevented liquor retailers from advertising the retail prices of their merchandise at sites other than their retail stores. It feared that allowing package stores to advertise their prices freely and honestly would lower the cost to consumers and increase the use of alcoholic beverages. 44 Liquormart, a liquor retailer, brought suit seeking a declaratory judgment on the grounds that Rhode Island's laws violated the store's First Amendment right to freedom of speech. The U.S. District Court made a finding of fact that Rhode Island's law had "no significant impact on levels of alcohol consumption" and concluded that the law was unconstitutional. The district judge's rationale was that the statute in question did not further the goal of reducing alcohol consumption, and further, that its restrictions on commercial freedom of speech were unnecessary and excessive. The U.S. Court of Appeals for the First Circuit reversed, however, and the U.S. Supreme Court granted certiorari. Do you believe that Rhode Island's statute violates the package store's First Amendment and due process right to engage in commercial speech?

   44 Liquormart, Inc. v. Rhode Island, 517 U.S. 484 (1996)

4. Margaret Gilleo is a homeowner in a St. Louis suburb. In December 1990, she placed a 24-by-36-inch sign on her lawn expressing opposition to Operation Desert Storm. She contacted police after her sign was stolen on one occasion and knocked down on another occasion. Police officials told Margaret that her signs were prohibited by city ordinance. Margaret unsuccessfully petitioned the city council for a variance and then filed suit. In her civil rights action, she maintained that the city ordinance violated her First Amendment right of freedom

of speech, which was applicable to the state through the Fourteenth Amendment Due Process Clause. The U.S. District Court agreed and enjoined the enforcement of the ordinance. Margaret then placed an 8½-by-11-inch sign in an upstairs window indicating her desire for "Peace in the Gulf." The city, in the meantime, repealed its original ordinance and replaced it with an ordinance that prohibited all signs that did not fit within ten authorized exemptions. The ordinance's preamble indicated that its purpose was to improve aesthetics and protect property values within the city. Margaret's peace sign did not fit within any of the authorized exemptions. She amended her complaint and challenged the new ordinance because it prohibited her from expressing her opposition to the war. The city defended by arguing that its ordinance was content neutral and its purposes justified the limited number of exemptions. It noted that alternative methods of communication, such as hand-held signs, pamphlets, flyers, etc., were permissible under the ordinance. How would you decide this case?

City of Ladue v. Gilleo, 512 U.S. 43 (1994)

5. Keen Umbehr was in the trash collection business. He had an exclusive contract with Wabaunsee County and six of the county's seven cities to collect the trash from 1985 to 1991. Throughout his term as the primary trash collector, he publicly criticized the county board and many of its policies, successfully sued the board for violating the state open meetings law, and tried, unsuccessfully, to be elected to the board. The board's members retaliated against Umbehr by voting to terminate his contract with the county. Umbehr, however, successfully negotiated new agreements with five of the six cities whose trash he had previously collected. In 1992, Umbehr sued the two county board members who had voted to terminate his contract. He alleged that his discharge–nonrenewal was in retaliation for having exercised his right to freedom of speech.

The U.S. District Court ruled that only public employees were protected by the First Amendment from retaliatory discharge. The U.S. Court of Appeals disagreed and reversed. Should independent contractors who have government contracts be protected by the Fourteenth Amendment's Due Process Clause from retaliatory contract discharges resulting from a contractor's exercise of speech? Should the well-known system of patronage, a practice followed by politicians of all stripes by which they reward their supporters with contracts and discharge those who are their political adversaries or who criticize their policies, take precedence over First Amendment considerations?

Board of County Commissioners, Wabaunsee County, Kansas v. Umbehr, 518 U.S. 668 (1996)

6. A Cincinnati, Ohio, ordinance makes it a criminal offense for "three or more persons to assemble, except at a public meeting of citizens, on any of the sidewalks, street corners, vacant lots, or mouths of alleys, and there conduct themselves in a manner annoying to persons passing by, or occupants of adjacent buildings." Coates, a student who became involved in a demonstration, was arrested and convicted for the violation of this ordinance. His argument on appeal was that the ordinance on its face violated the Fourteenth Amendment. Is this a valid contention?

Coates v. City of Cincinnati, 402 U.S. 611 (1971)

7. Fuentes purchased a stove and stereo from Firestone Tire and Rubber Company. Payment was to be made in monthly installments over a period of time. After two-thirds of the payments were made, Fuentes defaulted. Firestone filed an action for repossession and at the same time instructed the sheriff to seize the property pursuant to state law. The sheriff seized the property before Fuentes even knew of Firestone's suit for repossession. Fuentes claims that she was deprived of due process because her property was taken without notice or a hearing. What should the result be?

Fuentes v. Shevin, 407 U.S. 67 (1972)

8. Plaintiff brought a class action on behalf of all female welfare recipients residing in Connecticut and wishing divorces. She alleged that members of the class were prevented from bringing divorce suits by Connecticut statutes that required payment of court fees and costs of service of process as a condition precedent to access to the courts. Plaintiff contended that such statutes violate basic due process considerations. Is her argument valid?

    Boddie v. Connecticut, 401 U.S. 371 (1970)

9. Like many other states, Connecticut requires nonresidents of the state who are enrolled in the state university system to pay tuition and other fees at higher rates than residents of the state who are so enrolled. A Connecticut statute defined as a nonresident any unmarried student if his or her "legal address for any part of the one-year period immediately prior to [his or her] application for admission … was outside of Connecticut," or any married student if his or her "legal address at the time of his application for admission … was outside of Connecticut." The statute also provided that the "status of a student, as established at the time of [his or her] application for admission … shall be [his or her] status for the entire period of his attendance." Two University of Connecticut students who claimed to be residents of Connecticut were by the statute classified as nonresidents for tuition purposes. They claimed that the Due Process Clause does not permit Connecticut to deny an individual the opportunity to present evidence that he or she is a bona fide resident entitled to state rates and that they were being deprived of property without due process. Is this a valid argument?

    Vlandis v. Kline, 412 U.S. 441 (1973)

NOTES

1. Special recognition goes to Bruce D. Fisher and Edgar Bodenheimer. Students seeking more extensive treatment of this material should see Fisher, *Introduction to the Legal System* (St. Paul, MN: West Publishing Co., 1977); and Bodenheimer, *Jurisprudence* (Cambridge, MA: Harvard University Press, 1967).

2. J. G. Murphy and J. Coleman, *An Introduction to Jurisprudence* (Totowa, NJ: Rowman and Allenheld Publishers, 1984), p. 13.

3. Bodenheimer, p. 71; and Fisher, p. 7.

4. Bodenheimer, p. 72.

5. Examples are adverse possession, delivery of a deed, the concept of escheat, estate, the covenant of seisin, and the rule against restraints on alienation.

6. Property law addresses the notion that property equals rights, the rights of a finder vis-à-vis everyone but the true owner, the importance of delivery in the making of a gift, or the right of survivorship in joint tenancies.

7. The concepts of consideration, silence as acceptance, and the Statute of Frauds are addressed by contract law.

8. The Massachusetts legislature subsequently reenacted a mandatory seat belt law. An attempt to repeal this statute was unsuccessful.

9. G. Sabine, A *History of Political Theory,* 3d ed. (New York: Holt, Rinehart and Winston, 1961), pp. 681–684; and Bodenheimer, p. 85.

10. Bodenheimer, p. 84; and B. H. Levy, *Anglo-American Philosophy of Law* (New Brunswick, NJ: Transaction Publishers, 1991), pp. 19–23.

11. Bodenheimer, pp. 94, 99; and Levy, pp. 29–36.

12. Bodenheimer, p. 96; and Fisher, p. 11.

13. *Lochner v. New York,* 198 U.S. 45 (1905).

14. *Adair v. United States,* 208 U.S. 161 (1908).

15. B. Cardozo, *The Nature of Judicial Process* (New Haven, CT: Yale University Press, 1921), pp. 65–66.

16. R. Pound, "The Scope and Purpose of Sociological Jurisprudence," 24 *Harvard Law Review* 591 (1911).

17. Ibid., pp. 591–594.

18. Bodenheimer, p. 116.

19. K. Llewellyn, "A Realistic Jurisprudence—The Next Step," 30 *Columbia Law Review* 431 (1930) 453.

20. K. Llewellyn, *The Bramble Bush* (Oxford: Oxford University Press, 1930), p. 12.

21. D. Black, *Sociological Justice* (New York: Oxford University Press, 1989), p. 5.

22. Ibid., p. 21.

23. Ibid., pp. 24–25 and Chapter II, "Sociological Litigation."

24. Ibid., pp. 9–13, 21–22.

25. Ibid., p. 24–25, 95–96.

26. F. Marcham, *A History of England* (New York: Macmillan, 1937), p. 62.

27. G. Keeton, *The Norman Conquest and the Common Law* (London: Ernest Benn Limited, 1966), p. 14.

28. Ibid., p. 128; and Marcham, pp. 60–61.

29. T. F. F. Plucknett, *A Concise History of the Common Law* (Boston: Little, Brown and Co., 1956), p. 102.

30. Marcham, p. 62; and Plucknett, p. 144.

31. Keeton, p. 23.

32. F. Barlow, *The Feudal Kingdom* of England, 4th ed. (London: Longman, 1988), p. 51; P. Loyn, The *Making of the English Nation* (London: Thames & Hudson, 1991), p. 78; C. Brooke, *From Alfred to Henry III* (London: Norton, 1961), p. 78.

33. Plucknett, p. 139.

34. A. K. R. Kiralfy, *Potter's Historical Introduction to English Law,* 4th ed. (London: Sweet and Maxwell Ltd., 1962), p. 11.

35. Plucknett, p. 141; and Keeton, p. 13.

36. Marcham, p. 80.

37. Plucknett, p. 11; and Barlow, p. 81.

38. Marcham, p. 83.

39. Ibid., p. 86.

40. Ibid., p. 90; and Plucknett, p. 12.

41. Marcham, pp. 110–111.

42. Keeton, p. 160.

43. A. C. Baugh and T. Cable, *A History of the English Language*, 3d ed. (Englewood Cliffs, NJ: Prentice Hall, 1978), pp. 145, 148–149.

44. Brooke, pp. 160, 192.

45. Ibid., p. 156; and Plucknett, p. 14.

46. Marcham, p. 118; and Plucknett, p. 22.

47. Plucknett, p. 15.

48. Brooke, pp. 182–185; and Loyn, p. 128.

49. Marcham, pp. 156–157.

50. Plucknett, p. 103.

51. Keeton, p. 125.

52. Ibid., p. 201.

53. Loyn, p. 139.

54. Marcham, p. 131; and Plucknett, p. 355.

55. Marcham, p. 295.

56. Plucknett, p. 408.

57. Ibid., p. 357.

58. R. Walsh, A *History of Anglo-American Law* (Indianapolis, IN: Bobbs-Merrill Co., 1932), p. 65.

59. P. H. Winfield, *Chief Sources of English Legal History* (Cambridge, MA: Harvard University Press, 1925).

60. Plucknett, p. 259.

61. Ibid., pp. 280–281.

62. M. Grossberg, *Governing the Hearth* (Chapel Hill: University of North Carolina Press, 1985), p. 15.

63. Marcham, p. 295.

64. Plucknett, p. 178.

65. Ibid., p. 180.

66. Ibid., p. 280; and Marcham, p. 295.

67. Cardinal Wolsey was educated at Oxford, and Becket was educated at the Universities of Paris and Bologna. Brooke, p. 64.

68. Ibid.

69. D. Roebuck, *The Background of the Common Law*, 2d ed. (Oxford: Oxford University Press, 1990), p. 64; and Marcham, p. 295.

70. Plucknett, p. 688.

71. Ibid., p. 689; and Potter, pp. 581–584.

72. Potter, p. 280; and Plucknett, pp. 693–694.

73. Roebuck, p. 68.

74. E. Ward, "Mandatory Court-Annexed Alternative Dispute Resolution in the United States Federal Courts: Panacea or Pandemic?" 81 *St. John's Law Review* 77, 83 (2007).

75. Ibid, p. 87.

76. M. Galanter, "The Vanishing Trial: An Examination of Trials and Related Matters in Federal and State Courts," 1 *J. Empirical Legal Studies* 459, 463 (2004).

77. Loyn, p. 141; and Brooke, pp. 220–223.

78. Marcham, p. 143; and Brooke, p. 221.

79. Brooke, p. 223.

80. C. A. Miller, "The Forest of Due Process of Law: The American Constitutional Tradition," in J. R. Pennock and J. W. Chapman, *Due Process* (New York: New York University Press, 1977), p. 6.

81. Ibid.

82. Ibid., p. 9.

II

Ethics

CHAPTER OBJECTIVES

1. *Increase awareness of the connection between ethics and law.*
2. *Encourage students to understand why there are different ways of thinking about moral questions.*
3. *Build on themes addressed in the philosophy of law discussion in Chapter I (especially natural law, utilitarianism, and analytical positivism).*
4. *Encourage students to think about current highly controversial moral issues (such as same-sex marriage, abortion, physician-assisted suicide, medical marijuana, and capital punishment) from differing ethical perspectives.*

This chapter builds on themes introduced in the philosophy section of Chapter I. It shows readers why people need to be sensitive to ethical issues and illustrates some of the problems that arise when members of our complex and diverse society disagree as to the proper boundaries of ethics and law. Because of the limitations of space, it is only possible to give the reader a taste of the ways law and ethics intertwine. However, this discussion can expand interest and understanding and stimulate thinking about this rich and intricate subject.

All human beings face ethical challenges in their personal, professional, and public lives. Ethical questions permeate our society. In charting public policy, for example, legislators choose from among alternative courses of action as part of the lawmaking process. Similarly, when appellate judges construe constitutions and statutes and review the decisions of lower courts in contract and tort cases, they also make choices about public policy. Is it morally right for the Supreme Judicial Court of Maine to rule in a medical malpractice unintended pregnancy case that "a parent cannot be said to have been damaged by the birth and rearing of a healthy, normal child?"[1]

Is the Massachusetts legislature morally justified in enacting an extremely short statute of limitations for the commencement of skiers' personal injury actions against ski area operators, to the detriment of injured skiers?[2] Some states have enacted laws that permit health care professionals in certain circumstances to refuse to fill a customer's prescription if doing so would violate the professional's moral beliefs. Others have statutes that focus specifically on pharmacists, like the following law from South Dakota:

South Dakota Codified Laws 36-11-70.
Refusal to dispense medication.

No pharmacist may be required to dispense medication if there is reason to believe that the medication would be used to:

1. Cause an abortion; or
2. Destroy an unborn child as defined in subdivision 22-1-2(50A); or
3. Cause the death of any person by means of an assisted suicide, euthanasia, or mercy killing.

No such refusal to dispense medication pursuant to this section may be the basis for any claim for damages against the pharmacist or the pharmacy of the pharmacist or the basis for any disciplinary, recriminatory, or discriminatory action against the pharmacist.

Other states have statutes that immunize all health care professionals and their employers who refuse to provide health care that would violate the provider's conscience. These statutes typically bar such providers from criminal prosecutions, civil litigation, or administrative sanctions.

Should health care professionals be legally permitted to refuse to fulfill their patients'/customers' lawful requests because of the provider's deeply held moral beliefs? If so, do providers exercising

this legal right have any moral obligation to inform their potential customers of this fact?

Reasonable people can differ about whether the ethical judgments embodied in these legislative and judicial decisions should be legally sanctioned as the public policy of the state. It is no wonder that great public concern about the morality of governmental policies exists regarding such topics as capital punishment, abortion, assisted suicide, same-sex marriages, homosexuality, interracial adoptions, the rights of landowners versus environmental protection, the meaning of cruel and unusual punishment, and the right of indigents to appellate counsel in capital cases.

Introduction to *Gregg v. Georgia*

The following case is an example of an ethical debate over public policy. The petitioner was a convicted robber and murderer who was sentenced to death pursuant to a Georgia statute. He failed to convince the courts in Georgia to overturn his sentence, but he did successfully petition the U.S. Supreme Court for certiorari. In the case of *Gregg v. Georgia,* the Supreme Court justices debated the ethics and the legality of capital punishment. The case of *Gregg v. Georgia* was decided in 1976. In that case, seven justices ruled that Georgia's statute authorizing capital punishment was not inherently cruel and unusual under the Eighth and Fourteenth Amendments to the U.S. Constitution. The following excerpts from *Gregg* have been edited to focus on the argument about the morality of capital punishment. In the opinions below, you will find several references to an earlier case, *Furman v. Georgia. Furman* was a 1972 case in which the Supreme Court prohibited states from imposing the death penalty in an arbitrary manner. The justices wrote extensively on the ethical issue of capital punishment in *Furman,* and only summarized their views in *Gregg.* Because of limitations of space, *Gregg* has been excerpted below. However, you are encouraged to read the *Furman* case on the Internet.[3] You will better understand the following discussion of *Gregg* if you do so.

Gregg v. Georgia
428 U.S. 153
Supreme Court of the United States
July 2, 1976

Opinion of Justices Stewart, Powell, and Stevens.

C

... We now consider specifically whether the sentence of death for the crime of murder is a per se violation of the Eighth and Fourteenth Amendments to the Constitution. We note first that history and precedent strongly support a negative answer to this question.

The imposition of the death penalty for the crime of murder has a long history of acceptance both in the United States and in England. The common-law rule imposed a mandatory death sentence on all convicted murderers ... , And the penalty continued to be used into the 20th century by most American States, although the breadth of the common-law rule was diminished, initially by narrowing the class of murders to be punished by death and subsequently by widespread adoption of laws expressly granting juries the discretion to recommend mercy....

It is apparent from the text of the Constitution itself that the existence of capital punishment was accepted by the Framers. At the time the Eighth Amendment was ratified, capital punishment was a common sanction in every State. Indeed, the First Congress of the United States enacted legislation providing death as the penalty for specified crimes.... The Fifth Amendment, adopted at the same time as the Eighth, contemplated the continued existence of the capital sanction by imposing certain limits on the prosecution of capital cases:

> No person shall be held to answer for a capital, or otherwise infamous crime, unless on a presentment or indictment of a Grand Jury ... ; nor shall any person be subject for the same offense to be twice put in jeopardy of life or limb; ... nor be deprived of life, liberty, or property, without due process of law....

And the Fourteenth Amendment, adopted over three quarters of a century later, similarly contemplates the existence of the capital sanction in providing that no State shall deprive any person of "life, liberty, or property" without due process of law.

For nearly two centuries, this Court, repeatedly and often expressly, has recognized that capital punishment is not invalid per se....

... In *Trop v. Dulles* ... Mr. Chief Justice Warren, for himself and three other Justices, wrote:

Whatever the arguments may be against capital punishment, both on moral grounds and in terms of accomplishing the purposes of punishment ... the death penalty has been employed throughout our history, and, in a day when it is still widely accepted, it cannot be said to violate the constitutional concept of cruelty.

Four years ago, the petitioners in *Furman* ... predicated their argument primarily upon the asserted proposition that standards of decency had evolved to the point where capital punishment no longer could be tolerated. The petitioners in those cases said, in effect, that the evolutionary process had come to an end, and that standards of decency required that the Eighth Amendment be construed finally as prohibiting capital punishment for any crime regardless of its depravity and impact on society. This view was accepted by two Justices. Three other Justices were unwilling to go so far; focusing on the procedures by which convicted defendants were selected for the death penalty rather than on the actual punishment inflicted, they joined in the conclusion that the statutes before the Court were constitutionally invalid.

The petitioners in the capital cases before the Court today renew the "standards of decency" argument, but developments during the four years since *Furman* have undercut substantially the assumptions upon which their argument rested. Despite the continuing debate, dating back to the 19th century, over the morality and utility of capital punishment, it is now evident that a large proportion of American society continues to regard it as an appropriate and necessary criminal sanction.

The most marked indication of society's endorsement of the death penalty for murder is the legislative response to *Furman*. The legislatures of at least 35 States have enacted new statutes that provide for the death penalty for at least some crimes that result in the death of another person. And the Congress of the United States, in 1974, enacted a statute providing the death penalty for aircraft piracy that results in death. These recently adopted statutes have attempted to address the concerns expressed by the Court in *Furman* primarily (i) by specifying the factors to be weighed and the procedures to be followed in deciding when to impose a capital sentence, or (ii) by making the death penalty mandatory for specified crimes. But all of the post - *Furman* statutes make clear that capital punishment itself has not been rejected by the elected representatives of the people....

As we have seen, however, the Eighth Amendment demands more than that a challenged punishment be acceptable to contemporary society. The Court also must ask whether it comports with the basic concept of human dignity at the core of the Amendment.... Although we cannot "invalidate a category of penalties because we deem less severe penalties adequate to serve the ends of penology," ... the sanction imposed cannot be so totally without penological justification that it results in the gratuitous infliction of suffering....

The death penalty is said to serve two principal social purposes: retribution and deterrence of capital crimes by prospective offenders.

In part, capital punishment is an expression of society's moral outrage at particularly offensive conduct. This function may be unappealing to many, but it is essential in an ordered society that asks its citizens to rely on legal processes rather than self-help to vindicate their wrongs.

> The instinct for retribution is part of the nature of man, and channeling that instinct in the administration of criminal justice serves an important purpose in promoting the stability of a society governed by law. When people begin to believe that organized society is unwilling or unable to impose upon criminal offenders the punishment they 'deserve,' then there are sown the seeds of anarchy—of self-help, vigilante justice, and lynch law. *Furman v. Georgia* ... (STEWART, J., concurring).

> "Retribution is no longer the dominant objective of the criminal law," *Williams v. New York* ... but neither is it a forbidden objective nor one inconsistent with our respect for the dignity of men.... Indeed, the decision that capital punishment may be the appropriate sanction in extreme cases is an expression of the community's belief that certain crimes are themselves so grievous an affront to humanity that the only adequate response may be the penalty of death.

Statistical attempts to evaluate the worth of the death penalty as a deterrent to crimes by potential offenders have occasioned a great deal of debate. The results simply have been inconclusive....

... In sum, we cannot say that the judgment of the Georgia Legislature that capital punishment may be necessary in some cases is clearly wrong. Considerations

of federalism, as well as respect for the ability of a legislature to evaluate, in terms of its particular State, the moral consensus concerning the death penalty and its social utility as a sanction, require us to conclude, in the absence of more convincing evidence, that the infliction of death as a punishment for murder is not without justification and thus is not unconstitutionally severe....

We hold that the death penalty is not a form of punishment that may never be imposed, regardless of the circumstances of the offense, regardless of the character of the offender, and regardless of the procedure followed in reaching the decision to impose it.

Mr. Justice Brennan, dissenting.

... In *Furman v. Georgia*, ... I said:

> From the beginning of our Nation, the punishment of death has stirred acute public controversy. Although pragmatic arguments for and against the punishment have been frequently advanced, this longstanding and heated controversy cannot be explained solely as the result of differences over the practical wisdom of a particular government policy. At bottom, the battle has been waged on moral grounds. The country has debated whether a society for which the dignity of the individual is the supreme value can, without a fundamental inconsistency, follow the practice of deliberately putting some of its members to death. In the United States, as in other nations of the western world, 'the struggle about this punishment has been one between ancient and deeply rooted beliefs in retribution, atonement or vengeance on the one hand, and, on the other, beliefs in the personal value and dignity of the common man that were born of the democratic movement of the eighteenth century, as well as beliefs in the scientific approach to an understanding of the motive forces of human conduct, which are the result of the growth of the sciences of behavior during the nineteenth and twentieth centuries.' It is this essentially moral conflict that forms the backdrop for the past changes in and the present operation of our system of imposing death as a punishment for crime.

That continues to be my view. For the Clause forbidding cruel and unusual punishments under our constitutional system of government embodies in unique degree moral principles restraining the punishments that our civilized society may impose on those persons who transgress its laws. Thus, I too say: "For myself, I do not hesitate to assert the proposition that the only way the law has progressed from the days of the rack, the screw, and the wheel is the development of moral concepts, or, as stated by the Supreme Court ... the application of 'evolving standards of decency.'"...

This Court inescapably has the duty, as the ultimate arbiter of the meaning of our Constitution, to say whether, when individuals condemned to death stand before our Bar, "moral concepts" require us to hold that the law has progressed to the point where we should declare that the punishment of death, like punishments on the rack, the screw, and the wheel, is no longer morally tolerable in our civilized society. My opinion in *Furman v. Georgia* concluded that our civilization and the law had progressed to this point and that therefore the punishment of death, for whatever crime and under all circumstances, is "cruel and unusual" in violation of the Eighth and Fourteenth Amendments of the Constitution. I shall not again canvass the reasons that led to that conclusion. I emphasize only the foremost among the "moral concepts" recognized in our cases and inherent in the Clause is the primary moral principle that the State, even as it punishes, must treat its citizens in a manner consistent with their intrinsic worth as human beings— a punishment must not be so severe as to be degrading to human dignity. A judicial determination whether the punishment of death comports with human dignity is therefore not only permitted but compelled by the Clause....

I do not understand that the Court disagrees that "in comparison to all other punishments today ... the deliberate extinguishment of human life by the State is uniquely degrading to human dignity." ... For three of my Brethren hold today that mandatory infliction of the death penalty constitutes the penalty cruel and unusual punishment. I perceive no principled basis for this limitation. Death for whatever crime and under all circumstances "is truly an awesome punishment. The calculated killing of a human being by the State involves, by its very nature, a denial of the executed person's humanity.... An executed person has indeed 'lost the right to have rights.'" Death is not only an unusually severe punishment, unusual in its pain, in its finality, and in its enormity, but it serves no penal purpose more effectively than a less severe punishment; therefore the principle inherent in the Clause that prohibits pointless infliction of excessive punishment when less severe punishment can adequately achieve the same purposes invalidates the punishment....

The fatal constitutional infirmity in the punishment of death is that it treats "members of the human race as nonhumans, as objects to be toyed with and discarded. [It is] thus inconsistent with the fundamental premise of the Clause that even the vilest criminal remains a human being possessed of common human dignity." ... As such it is a penalty that "subjects the individual to a fate forbidden by the principle of civilized treatment guaranteed by the [Clause]." I therefore would hold, on that ground alone, that death is today a cruel and unusual punishment prohibited by the Clause. "Justice of this kind is obviously no less shocking than the crime itself, and the new 'official' murder, far from offering redress for the offense committed against society, adds instead a second defilement to the first."

I dissent from the judgments in ... *Gregg v. Georgia* ... *Proffitt v. Florida,* and ... *Jurek v. Texas,* insofar as each upholds the death sentences challenged in those cases. I would set aside the death sentences imposed in those cases as violative of the Eighth and Fourteenth Amendments.

Mr. Justice Marshall, dissenting.

In *Furman v. Georgia,* 408 U.S. 238, 314 (1972) (concurring opinion), I set forth at some length my views on the basic issue presented to the Court in these cases. The death penalty, I concluded, is a cruel and unusual punishment prohibited by the Eighth and Fourteenth Amendments. That continues to be my view....

In *Furman* I concluded that the death penalty is constitutionally invalid for two reasons. First, the death penalty is excessive.... And second, the American people, fully informed as to the purposes of the death penalty and its liabilities, would in my view reject it as morally unacceptable....

... Assuming ... that the post-*Furman* enactment of statutes authorizing the death penalty renders the prediction of the views of an informed citizenry an uncertain basis for a constitutional decision, the enactment of those statutes has no bearing whatsoever on the conclusion that the death penalty is unconstitutional because it is excessive. An excessive penalty is invalid under the Cruel and Unusual Punishments Clause "even though popular sentiment may favor" it.... The inquiry here, then, is simply whether the death penalty is necessary to accomplish the legitimate legislative purposes in punishment, or whether a less severe penalty—life imprisonment—would do as well....

The two purposes that sustain the death penalty as nonexcessive in the Court's view are general deterrence and retribution. In *Furman,* I canvassed the relevant data on the deterrent effect of capital punishment....

The available evidence, I concluded ... was convincing that "capital punishment is not necessary as a deterrent to crime in our society." ... The evidence I reviewed in *Furman* remains convincing, in my view, that "capital punishment is not necessary as a deterrent to crime in our society." ... The justification for the death penalty must be found elsewhere....

The other principal purpose said to be served by the death penalty is retribution. The notion that retribution ... can serve as a moral justification for the sanction of death finds credence in the opinion of my Brothers Stewart, Powell, and Stevens, and that of my Brother White.... It is this notion that I find to be the most disturbing aspect of today's unfortunate decisions.

The concept of retribution is a multifaceted one, and any discussion of its role in the criminal law must be undertaken with caution. On one level, it can be said that the notion of retribution or reprobation is the basis of our insistence that only those who have broken the law be punished, and in this sense the notion is quite obviously central to a just system of criminal sanctions. But our recognition that retribution plays a crucial role in determining who may be punished by no means requires approval of retribution as a general justification for punishment. It is the question whether retribution can provide a moral justification for punishment—in particular, capital punishment—that we must consider.

My Brothers Stewart, Powell, and Stevens offer the following explanation of the retributive justification for capital punishment:

'The instinct for retribution is part of the nature of man, and channeling that instinct in the administration of criminal justice serves an important purpose in promoting the stability of a society governed ... by law. When people begin to believe that organized society is unwilling or unable to impose upon criminal offenders the punishment they 'deserve,' then there are sown the seeds of anarchy—of self-help, vigilante justice, and lynch law.' ...

This statement is wholly inadequate to justify the death penalty. As my Brother Brennan stated in *Furman*, "There is no evidence whatever that utilization of imprisonment rather than death encourages private blood feuds and other disorders." ... It simply defies belief to suggest that the death penalty is necessary to prevent the American people from taking the law into their own hands.

In a related vein, it may be suggested that the expression of moral outrage through the imposition of the death penalty serves to reinforce basic moral values—that it marks some crimes as particularly offensive and therefore to be avoided. The argument is akin to a deterrence argument, but differs in that it contemplates the individual's shrinking from antisocial conduct, not because he fears punishment, but because he has been told in the strongest possible way that the conduct is wrong. This contention, like the previous one, provides no support for the death penalty. It is inconceivable that any individual concerned about conforming his conduct to what society says is "right" would fail to realize that murder is "wrong" if the penalty were simply life imprisonment.

The foregoing contentions—that society's expression of moral outrage through the imposition of the death penalty preempts the citizenry from taking the law into its own hands and reinforces moral values—are not retributive in the purest sense. They are essentially utilitarian in that they portray the death penalty as valuable because of its beneficial results. These justifications for the death penalty are inadequate because the penalty is, quite clearly I think, not necessary to the accomplishment of those results.

There remains for consideration, however, what might be termed the purely retributive justification for the death penalty—that the death penalty is appropriate, not because of its beneficial effect on society, but because the taking of the murderer's life is itself morally good. Some of the language of the opinion of my Brothers Stewart, Powell, and Stevens ... appears positively to embrace this notion of retribution for its own sake as a justification for capital punishment. They state:

The decision that capital punishment may be the appropriate sanction in extreme cases is an expression of the community's belief that certain crimes are themselves so grievous an affront to humanity that the only adequate response may be the penalty of death....

They then quote with approval from Lord Justice Denning's remarks before the British Royal Commission on Capital Punishment:

'The truth is that some crimes are so outrageous that society insists on adequate punishment, because the wrongdoer deserves it, irrespective of whether it is a deterrent or not.' ...

Of course, it may be that these statements are intended as no more than observations as to the popular demands that it is thought must be responded to in order to prevent anarchy. But the implication of the statements appears to me to be quite different, that society's judgment that the murderer "deserves" death must be respected not simply because the preservation of order requires it, but because it is appropriate that society make the judgment and carry it out. It is this latter notion, in particular, that I consider to be fundamentally at odds with the Eighth Amendment....

The mere fact that the community demands the murderer's life in return for the evil he has done cannot sustain the death penalty, for as Justices Stewart, Powell, and Stevens remind us, "the Eighth Amendment demands more than that a challenged punishment be acceptable to contemporary society." ... ; To be sustained under the Eighth Amendment, the death penalty must "compor[t] with the basic concept of human dignity at the core of the Amendment," ... the objective in imposing it must be "[consistent] with our respect for the dignity of [other] men." ... Under these standards, the taking of life "because the wrongdoer deserves it" surely must fall, for such a punishment has as its very basis the total denial of the wrongdoer's dignity and worth.

The death penalty, unnecessary to promote the goal of deterrence or to further any legitimate notion of retribution, is an excessive penalty forbidden by the Eighth and Fourteenth Amendments. I respectfully dissent from the Court's judgment upholding the sentences of death imposed upon the petitioners in these cases....

Case Questions

1. How does Justice Stewart justify his conclusion that capital punishment is a permissible form of punishment?
2. What is the moral principle that is the fundamental basis of Justice Brennan's dissent?
3. Does Justice Marshall believe that retribution provides a moral justification for capital punishment? Why or why not?
4. In your opinion, is the fact that capital punishment is popular with a majority of society a sufficient fact to decide the debate about whether the death penalty is cruel and unusual under the Eighth Amendment?

People also are affected by ethical considerations in their professional interactions with others. Although we may not realize it at the time, our actions and inactions at work and school are often interpreted by others as evidence of our personal values and character—who we are and what we stand for. A person whose behavior is consistent with moral principles is said to have integrity. It is common for people to try to create at least the illusion that they have integrity. Integrity is prized by employers, who try to avoid hiring persons known to lie, cheat, and steal. Many companies also try to avoid doing business with firms that are reputed to engage in fraudulent practices, who try to take unfair advantage of those with whom they contract, who negotiate in bad faith, or who are otherwise unscrupulous to their business partners. Students applying to professional schools quickly learn that integrity is important to members of admissions committees. Such committees generally require recommenders to include an evaluation of an applicant's character in their letters. People also are concerned about ethical behavior in their personal lives. They worry about whether a person with whom they have shared a confidence is trustworthy.

But it is often difficult to know the parameters of ethical behavior in particular situations. Is it ever permissible to break a promise not to tell? Are there any rules about lying? Who determines the rules? How are they enforced? Under what circumstances is it morally permissible to lie to a total stranger? A family member? A best friend? A business partner? When is it acceptable for other people to lie to you? What are the social and legal consequences of lying?[4]

In your role as a student you may have encountered situations in which you or some classmates have cheated on a test or paper. Have you ever seriously thought about the ethics of cheating? Is it always morally wrong for a student to cheat? Can circumstances make a difference? Does it make a difference if the teacher makes no effort to prevent dishonesty and virtually every other student in the class is cheating on a test or written assignment? Would it make a difference if you believed the teacher had been unfair to you on a previous assignment and cheating would enable you to get the final grade that you "really deserved"? If you observe classmates cheat, do you have any duty to tell the instructor? What would you think about some other student who did tell? What is the basis for your position?

Who makes the rules for you? Is it up to you to decide, your peer group, your parents, or other significant people in your life? Perhaps you look to religious leaders for guidance. Religious groups historically have assumed a major role in setting moral standards, and religious leaders frequently take firm positions on contemporary ethical issues. How can anyone tell who is "right"? Thomas Jefferson in the Declaration of Independence said, "We hold these truths to be self-evident...." Is that sufficient proof of the proposition that all people are created equal?

Philosophers have argued for centuries about the answers to questions such as those raised above. The following discussion will help to provide some background and structure for the discussion of the cases that follow.

ETHICS

Ethics, which is the study of morality, is one of the five traditional branches of study within philosophy, as can be seen in Figure 2.1. Ethicists are concerned with what makes conduct morally right or wrong and the essential nature of moral responsibility. They also investigate the application of ethical principles to the practice of professions such as law, medicine, and business.

We see in Figure 2.2 that ethical theories are often classified as being either metaethical or normative in their approach.[5]

Ethics	The study of morality
Metaphysics	The study of the nature of reality or being
Aesthetics	The study of beauty
Logic	The study of correct reasoning
Epistemology	The study of knowledge

FIGURE 2.1 Branches of Philosophy

Metaethics	Theoretical foundations of ethics
Normative ethics	Applied ethics

FIGURE 2.2 Ethics

Metaethical scholars have centered on defining ethical terms and developing theories. They have tended to focus on abstract topics, such as identifying the fundamental characteristics of moral behavior. These discussions have tended to be extremely theoretical and often have been criticized for not having many practical applications.[6] The following example is intended to raise philosophical questions about the essential nature of integrity under circumstances when it is acknowledged that all of the actors have engaged in "correct" actions.

Karen, Keisha, and Kelly

Assume that Karen is a "goody-goody" and always tries to do the "right" thing in order to comply with what she perceives to be her moral duty. Assume that Keisha also does the "right" thing, but does so at least in part for selfish reasons (being seen doing the right thing will make the newspapers and will be good for business). What if Kelly selectively does the "right" thing only when she feels a personal connection with some other person in need, under circumstances when she feels she can help without putting herself at risk? Does Karen have more integrity than Keisha or Kelly?

Normative ethicists have been more concerned with answering practical questions such as "Is killing in self-defense wrong?" or "What should a physician do when a patient dying of a terminal disease asks for assistance in committing suicide?" Modern ethicists primarily focus on normative moral issues rather than metaethical ones, although this tendency is of recent origin and primarily began in the 1970s.[7]

Philosophers disagree about whether ethical judgments about right and wrong can be conclusively proven.[8] Some have argued that ethical judgments can be scientifically proven. Others have rejected science and insisted that such judgments be based on natural law, sounding intuitive notions of right and wrong,[9] or based on the logical soundness of the reasons underlying the ethical judgment.[10]

Another area of disagreement involves where those making ethical judgments should focus their attention. Some philosophers believe that whether an action is "good" or "bad" can be determined only after an act has occurred, by examining the outcomes. Only by looking backward can the relative costs and benefits of an action be weighed and its worth assessed.[11]

Utilitarianism, which was discussed in Chapter I, is such a theory. Thus, from a utilitarian perspective, publicly and brutally caning one prisoner for a given criminal offense would be moral if it could be proven later that it has deterred thousands of others from engaging in that same offense.

Deontologists would reject a focus on aftermaths in favor of studying the role of moral duty. Immanuel Kant, for example, argued that, to be ethical, an actor's deeds should be evaluated based on the reasoning that led to the act.[12] Kant believed that intent mattered and that an ethical actor should be motivated only by a desire to comply with a universally accepted moral duty. He did not view actions motivated by feelings of love or sympathy or by the potential for personal gain as being thically principled.[13] Caning a convicted person could not be a moral act if it amounted to torture. **Egoists** had yet a different approach. They believed that individuals were ethically "right" to act in their own self-interest, without regard for the consequences to other people.[14] Many theorists have argued that conduct is moral only if it coincides with religious mandates such as the Ten Commandments or the Golden Rule. Society, however, has been unable to agree on any single, universally acceptable ethical theory. Serious disagreements exist about what constitutes ethical conduct in specific contexts. "Right" answers are not always obvious, and rules, interpretive opinions, and guidelines are needed to direct individuals toward "good" conduct.

Law and Morality

One of the unresolved debates revolves around what role law should play in making ethical rules. Should law supply the enforcement mechanism for enforcing moral norms? What should an ethical person do when confronted with "bad" laws? Should decisions about morality in some contexts be reserved to the individual?

Although law can contribute rules that embody moral norms, law in our democracy is not expected to play the primary role in promoting ethical behavior in society. Parents, churches, schools, youth organizations, athletic teams, and business, professional, and fraternal groups of all types are expected to fill the void. They often establish ethical codes, rules (such as those prohibiting "unsportsmanlike conduct" or "conduct unbecoming an officer"), and discipline and even expel members who violate their terms. A precise calculus of law's relationship to morality, however, remains elusive.

You may recall reading in Chapter I about the fundamental and unresolved disagreement between philosophers who are natural law adherents and those who are *analytical positivists* regarding the true nature of law. From the positivist point of view, laws are merely the rules that political superiors develop pursuant to duly established procedures that are imposed on the rest of the polity. Laws are viewed as being intrinsically neither good nor bad. They do establish norms of legal behavior, but such efforts sometimes amount to little more than arbitrary line drawing. Positivists would point out that law establishes a floor but not a ceiling. Individuals who satisfy their legal obligations always retain the right to self-impose additional restrictions on their conduct in order to satisfy a deeply felt moral duty. But law does not depend for its authority on an ad hoc assessment of whether the government ought to follow a different policy. It is clear, however, that defying the law can result in state-imposed sanctions. Assume, for example, that a taxpayer takes an unauthorized "deduction" off her income tax obligation and makes an equivalent dollar donation to a charity rather than to the Internal Revenue Service. The fact that her conscience tells her that it is self-evident that the U.S. government is morally wrong to spend our dollars on some disfavored program is unlikely to save her from criminal and civil sanctions.

In the following passage, Martin Luther King Jr. distinguishes between just and unjust laws and argues that immoral laws should be civilly disobeyed.

Letter from Birmingham Jail★

You express a great deal of anxiety over our willingness to break laws. This is certainly a legitimate concern. As we so diligently urge people to obey the Supreme Court's decision of 1954 outlawing segregation in the public schools, it is rather strange and paradoxical to find us consciously breaking laws. One may well ask, "How can you advocate breaking some laws and obeying others?" The answer is found in the fact that there are two types of laws: there are just and there are unjust laws....

... A just law is a man-made code that squares with the moral law or the law of God. An unjust law is a code that is out of harmony with the moral law. To put it in the terms of Saint Thomas Aquinas, an unjust law is a human law that is not rooted in eternal and natural law. Any law that uplifts human personality is just. Any law that degrades human personality is unjust. All segregation statutes are unjust because segregation distorts the soul and damages the personality. It gives the segregator a false sense of superiority, and the segregated a false sense of inferiority....

So segregation is not only politically, economically and sociologically unsound, but it is morally wrong and sinful....

... I submit that an individual who breaks a law that conscience tells him is unjust and willingly accepts the penalty by staying in jail to arouse the conscience of the community over its injustice, is in reality expressing the very highest respect for law....

We can never forget that everything Hitler did in Germany was "legal" and everything that Hungarian freedom fighters did in Hungary was "illegal." It was "illegal" to aid and comfort a Jew, in Hitler's Germany. But I am sure that if I had lived in Germany during that time I would have aided and comforted my Jewish brothers even though it was illegal....

Positive Law Rules

In our republic, the people are sovereign, but there is no law higher than the U.S. Constitution.[15] We have adopted the analytical positivist view that bills that have been enacted in conformity with constitutional requirements are the law. Individuals, for reasons of conscience, may defy these duly enacted laws, but they are lawfully subject to prosecution.

It is important to note, however, that political majorities in federal and state legislatures often enact statutes that reflect widely held moral beliefs in the electorate. Examples include the Civil Rights Act of 1964, the Americans with Disabilities Act, the Clean Air Act, the Clean Water Act, and the Sherman Act, to name just a few. Legislative bodies have also taken the ethical views of political minorities into consideration when drafting legislation. Congress, for example, exempted conscientious objectors from having to register with the Selective Service System. Similarly, Congress's 1998 omnibus spending bill contained a provision that permitted

★ *Letter from Birmingham Jail,* reprinted by arrangement with the Estate of Martin Luther King, Jr., c/o Writers House, Inc. as agent for the proprietor, New York, NY. Copyright © 1963 by Dr. Martin Luther King, Jr. Copyright renewed 1991 by Coretta Scott King.

doctors opposed to birth control to refuse on moral grounds to write prescriptions for contraceptives requested by federal employees.[16] But one need only look at Article I, Section 9, of the U.S. Constitution to see an example of political expediency taking precedence over moral considerations. In that article, antislavery founders compromised their moral principles in order to win ratification of the Constitution in southern states.

Federal and state judicial bodies also impart moral views when they construe constitutions and statutes. Examples include the U.S. Supreme Court's interpretations of the Fourteenth Amendment in *Lawrence v. Texas* (the right of two same-sex, consenting adults, while at home, to determine the nature of their sexual intimacy), *Loving v. Virginia* (an individual's right to marry a person of a different race), and *Moore v. City of East Cleveland* (in which the court broadened the meaning of the term "family"), three famous cases involving interpretations of the Due Process Clause, which are included elsewhere in this textbook.

It is obvious that moral rules and legal rules often overlap. Our criminal laws severely punish persons convicted of murder, rape, and robbery, and they ought to do so. Such acts simultaneously violate legal and moral principles. Tort law provides another example. Damages in negligence cases should be borne by the parties based on the extent to which each was responsible for the damages. Because this decision is, with some exceptions, based on the relative fault of the parties, it also can be argued both on teleological and on deontological grounds to be an ethical rule. We see another example of legal and ethical harmony in the *Iacomini* case (Chapter VII). In that case the court ruled that the law would permit a mechanic to claim an equitable lien against a motor vehicle that he had repaired, under circumstances when no other relief was possible. The court said that such a remedy was legally appropriate in proper circumstances to prevent unjust enrichment. The following materials raise interesting legal and moral questions about legal and moral duties as they relate to members of one's family.

Aiding and Abetting, Misprision, Informing, and the Family

Imagine how difficult it must be for a person who, after acquiring bits and pieces of information from various sources, ultimately concludes that a member of his or her family is probably involved in criminal activity. Suppose further that the crimes involved are a series of premeditated murders, and that the offender will probably be sentenced to the death penalty upon conviction of the charges. Assume further that you have to admit that, unless you inform authorities, other innocent persons may well become additional victims. Suppose a million-dollar cash award will be paid to the person who provides the information that ultimately leads to the conviction of the offender. What would you do if you were that family member? Would you tell authorities and run the risk of being viewed as being disloyal to your family? Would you stay silent and hope that nobody else is harmed?[17]

If you were writing a statute to prevent people from harboring fugitive felons, would you carve out an exception for people protecting members of their own families? Examine the following New Mexico statute from ethical and legal perspectives.

New Mexico Statutes Annotated 30–22–4. Harboring or Aiding a Felon.

Harboring or aiding a felon consists of any person, not standing in the relation of husband or wife, parent or grandparent, child or grandchild, brother or sister, by consanguinity or affinity, who knowingly conceals any offender or gives such offender any other aid, knowing that he has committed a felony, with the intent that he escape or avoid arrest, trial conviction or punishment. Whoever commits harboring or aiding a felon is guilty of a fourth degree felony. In a prosecution under this section it shall not be necessary to aver, or on the trial to prove, that the principal felon has been either arrested, prosecuted or tried.

Do you agree with the way the legislature defined the scope of the legal duty? Should the scope of the moral duty be the same as the scope of the legal duty?

The above statute has its roots in the common law crime of accessory after the fact. With the exceptions indicated above, it creates a legal duty on everyone else to refrain from helping a known felon escape apprehension by authorities. You can see how this statute was applied in the following case. Read the case and think about whether you agree with the opinion of the court majority or the dissenting judges. What is the basis for your choice?

State v. Mobbley
650 P.2d 841
Court of Appeals of New Mexico
August 3, 1982

Wood, Judge.

The criminal information charged that defendant did "knowingly aid Andrew Needham knowing that he had committed a felony with the intent that he escape arrest, trial, conviction and punishment.... The issue is whether the agreed upon facts are such that defendant may not be prosecuted for the offense of aiding a felon.

Defendant is married to Ricky Mobbley. Police officers went to a house and contacted defendant; they advised defendant that felony warrants had been issued for Ricky Mobbley and Andrew Needham. The officers asked defendant if "both were there." Defendant denied that the men were there, although she knew that both men were in the house. Hearing noises, the officers entered the house and discovered both men. Defendant could not have revealed Needham without also revealing her husband. The criminal charge was based on the failure to reveal Needham....

The power to define crimes is a legislative function....

Section 30–22–4, *supra,* applies to "any person, not standing in the relation of husband or wife, parent or grandparent, child or grandchild, brother or sister by consanguinity or affinity...." There is no claim that any of the exempted relationships applies as between defendant and Needham. As enacted by the Legislature, § 30–22–4, *supra,* applies to the agreed facts.

Defendant contends that such a result is contrary to legislative intent because statutes must be interpreted in accord with common sense and reason, and must be interpreted so as not to render the statute's application absurd or unreasonable.... We give two answers to this contention.

First, where the meaning of the statutory language is plain, and where the words used by the Legislature are free from ambiguity, there is no basis for interpreting the statute.... Section 30–22–4, *supra,* applies to "any person" not within the relationship exempted by the statute. Defendant is such a person.

Second, if we assume that the statute should be interpreted, our holding that § 30–22–4, *supra,* applies to the agreed facts accords with legislative intent. Statutes proscribing harboring or aiding a felon grew out of the common law of accessories after the fact. LaFave & Scott, Criminal Law § 66 (1972). However:

> At common law, only one class was excused from liability for being accessories after the fact. Wives did not become accessories by aiding their husbands. No other relationship, including that of husband to wife, would suffice. Today, close to half of the states have broadened the exemption to cover other close *relatives....* This broadening of the excemption [sic] may be justified on the ground that it is unrealistic to expect persons to be deterred from giving aid to their close *relations.* (Our emphasis.)

LaFave & Scott, *supra,* at 523–24.

New Mexico legislative history accords with the discussion in LaFave & Scott, *supra.* In 1875 New Mexico adopted the common law.... The present statute ... was a part of the Criminal Code enacted in 1963....

Limiting the exemptions in § 30–22–4, *supra,* to *relatives* named in that statute accords with the legislative intent as shown by legislative history. In light of the limited exemption at common law, and legislation limited to relatives, it is not absurd and not unreasonable to hold that if defendant aided Needham, § 30–22–4, *supra,* applies to that aid.

Except for one fact, there would have been no dispute as to the applicability of § 30–22–4, *supra.* That one fact is that defendant could not have revealed Needham without also revealing her husband. The statute does not exempt a defendant from prosecution when this fact situation arises; to judicially declare such an additional exemption would be to improperly add words to the statute.... Also, such a judicial declaration would be contrary to the rationale for this type of statute; it is unrealistic to expect persons to be deterred from giving aid to their close relations. LaFave & Scott, *supra.*

We recognize that defendant was placed in a dilemma; if she answered truthfully she revealed the presence of her husband; if she lied she took the chance of being prosecuted....

Defendant contends we should follow two Arkansas decisions which support her position.... We decline to do so. Our duty is to apply the New Mexico statute, not the Arkansas law of accomplices.

The order of the trial court, which dismissed the information, is reversed. The cause is remanded with instructions to reinstate the case on the trial court's docket.

It is so ordered....

Lopez, Judge (dissenting).

I respectfully dissent. The majority holds that the defendant can be charged with the offense of harboring or aiding Andrew Needham ... because she does not qualify under any of the exemptions listed in the statute with respect to Needham. It arrives at this holding in spite of the fact that the defendant could not have revealed the presence of Needham in the house without also revealing the presence of her husband. This holding negates the legislative intent of the statute to exempt a wife from being forced to turn in her husband. Under the majority ruling, the defen-

dant would have had to turn in Needham to escape being charged under § 30–22–4, which would have been tantamount to turning in her husband.

Whether the rationale underlying the legislative exemption is a recognition "that it is unrealistic to expect persons to be deterred from giving aid to their close relations," LaFave and Scott, Criminal Law § 66 (1972), or an acknowledgment of human frailty, Torcia, Wharton's Criminal Law § 35 (14th ed. 1978), that rationale is ignored by requiring a wife to turn in her husband if he is with another suspect. Such a result requires a proverbial splitting of analytic hairs by attributing the defendant's action, in denying that Needham was at the house, to an intent to aid Needham rather than her husband....

The practical effect of the majority opinion, which requires a wife to turn in her husband if he is with a co-suspect, is to deny the wife's exemption in § 30–22–4. The reasons for refusing to force a wife to inform on her husband are the same whether or not he is alone. The statute should not be construed so narrowly as to frustrate the legislative intent to exempt a wife from turning in her husband.... Although the court should not add to the provisions of a statute, it may do so to prevent an unreasonable result.... Given the wife's exemption from turning in her husband contained in § 30–22–4, it would be unreasonable to require her to do just that by revealing Needham.

For the foregoing reasons, I cannot agree that the defendant in this case can be charged under § 30–22–4 for refusing to tell the police that Needham was in the house. I would affirm the action of the trial court in dismissing the information against the defendant.

Case Questions

1. Given the wording of the statute, did the majority have any flexibility in applying this law to the facts of this case? Do you think that Andrew Needham's presence in the house with Ricky Mobbley *ought* to warrant application of this legal rule?
2. Do you believe the statute should be amended to exempt individuals in Pam Mobbley's predicament from prosecution?
3. What would you have done if you had been in Pam's situation? Why?

Misprision of a felony is another common law crime. It makes it criminal for a person to fail to tell authorities of the commission of a felony of which he or she has knowledge. The history and rationale for this crime are explained in the following excerpt from the case of *Holland v. State.* In *Holland,* the court had to decide whether misprision is a crime in Florida. At the

present time, the federal government (see Title 18, Section 4, United States Code) and the State of South Dakota (see Title 22-11-12) are the only American jurisdictions that can prosecute criminal misprision. Ironically, because federal prosecutors initiate misprision prosecutions in federal courts throughout the country, it is still deserving of academic attention.

Holland v. State of Florida
302 So.2d 806
Supreme Court of Florida
November 8, 1974

McNulty, Chief Judge.

... As far as we know or are able to determine, this is the first case in Florida involving the crime of misprision of felony....

As hereinabove noted, we chose to decide this case on the fundamental issue of whether misprision of felony is a crime in Florida.

In any case, we now get on to the merits of the question we decide today. We begin by pointing out that almost every state in the United States has adopted the Common Law of England to some extent. Many of these states have done so by constitutional or statutory provisions similar to ours. But the nearly universal interpretation of such provisions is that they adopt the common law of England only to the extent that such laws are consistent with the existing physical and social conditions in the country or in the given state.

To some degree Florida courts have discussed this principle in other contexts. In *Duval v. Thomas,* for example, our Supreme Court said:

> When grave doubt exists of a true common law doctrine ... we may ... exercise a 'broad discretion' taking 'into account the changes in our social and economic customs and present day conceptions of right and justice.' It is, to repeat, only when the common law is plain that we must observe it.

Moreover, our courts have not hesitated in other respects to reject anachronistic common law concepts.

Consonant with this, therefore, we think that the legislature in enacting § 775.01, *supra,* recognized this judicial precept and intended to grant our courts the discretion necessary to prevent blind adherence to those portions of the common law which are not suited to our present conditions, our public policy, our traditions or our sense of right and justice.

With the foregoing as a predicate, we now consider the history of the crime of misprision of felony and whether the reasons therefor have ceased to exist, if indeed they ever did exist, in this country. The origin of the crime is well described in 8 U. of Chi. L. Rev. 338, as follows:

> Misprision of felony as defined by Blackstone is merely one phase of the system of communal responsibility for the apprehension of criminals which received its original impetus from William I, under pressure of the need to protect the invading Normans in hostile country, and which endured up

to the Seventeenth Century in England. In order to secure vigilant prosecution of criminal conduct, the vill or hundred in which such conduct occurred was subject to fine, as was the tithing to which the criminal belonged, and every person who knew of the felony and failed to make report thereof was subject to punishment for misprision of felony. Compulsory membership in the tithing group, the obligation to pursue criminals when the hue and cry was raised, broad powers of private arrest, and the periodic visitations of the General Eyre for the purpose of penalizing laxity in regard to crime, are all suggestive of the administrative background against which misprision of felony developed. With the appearance of specialized and paid law enforcement officers, such as constables and justices of the peace in the Seventeenth Century, there was a movement away from strict communal responsibility, and a growing tendency to rely on professional police....

In short, the initial reason for the existence of misprision of felony as a crime at common law was to aid an alien, dictatorial sovereign in his forcible subjugation of England's inhabitants. Enforcement of the crime was summary, harsh and oppressive; and commentators note that most prosecutors in this country long ago recognized the inapplicability or obsolescence of the law and its harshness in their contemporary society by simply not charging people with that crime....

Many courts faced with this issue have also found, though with varying degrees of clarity, that the reasons for the proscription of this crime do not exist. Moreover, as early as 1822 in this country Chief Justice John Marshall states in *Marbury v. Brooks:*

> It may be the duty of a citizen to accuse every offender, and to proclaim every offense which comes to his knowledge; but the law which would punish him in every case, for not performing this duty, is too harsh for man....

We agree with Chief Justice Marshall ... that the crime of misprision of felony is wholly unsuited to American criminal law.... While it may be desirable, even essential, that we encourage citizens to "get involved" to help reduce crime, they ought not be adjudicated criminals themselves if they don't. The fear of such a consequence is a fear from which our traditional concepts of peace and quietude guarantee freedom. We cherish the right to mind our own business when our own best interests dictate.

Accordingly, we hold that misprision of felony has not been adopted into, and is not a part of, Florida substantive law.

Case Questions

1. The majority in *Holland* noted that American judges going back to the esteemed John Marshall have concluded that it is "un-American" for citizens to be criminally prosecuted for not reporting the commission of known felonies to the authorities. Is this position morally justifiable in your opinion?
2. Justice John Marshall is quoted in an 1822 case as follows: "It may be the duty of a citizen to accuse every offender, and to proclaim every offense which comes to his knowledge...." Do you think Marshall was referring to a moral duty, a legal duty, or both?

Good Samaritan Laws

Traditionally individuals have not been legally obligated to intervene to aid other persons in the absence of a judicially recognized duty owed to that person. Courts have recognized the existence of a duty where a special relationship exists. The special relationships generally fall within one of the following categories: (a) where a statutory duty exists (such as the obligation parents have to support their children), (b) where a contractual duty exists (lifeguards are employed to try to make rescues on the beach), or (c) where a common law duty exists (such as when an unrelated adult has voluntarily assumed primary responsibility for bringing food to an isolated, incapacitated, elderly neighbor and then stops without notifying authorities). In the absence of a legal duty to act, the law generally has left the decision as to whether or not to be a Good Samaritan up to each individual's conscience.

Many people feel that Americans today are less willing than in times past to play the role of Good Samaritan. But do bystanders, who have no special relationship to a person in need, have a moral obligation to intervene? Should they have a legal duty either to intervene or to inform authorities, if they can do so without placing themselves in jeopardy? Consider the 1997 Las Vegas case in which an eighteen-year-old young man enticed a seven-year-old girl into a ladies' room stall in a Las Vegas casino and sexually assaulted and murdered her.

The attacker had a male friend who allegedly watched some of the events in that stall and presumably knew that the little girl was in danger. The friend made no attempt to dissuade the attacker, save the girl, or tell authorities. He was not subject to prosecution under the laws of Nevada.

Should a person who is a passive observer, as in the above situation, be subjected to criminal prosecution for failing to act? The following Massachusetts statute was enacted in 1983 in response to a brutal rape at a tavern. This crime was the basis for the movie *The Accused*.

Massachusetts General Law Chapter 268, Section 40. Reports of Crimes to Law Enforcement Officials.

Whoever knows that another person is a victim of aggravated rape, rape, murder, manslaughter or armed robbery and is at the scene of said crime shall, to the extent that said person can do so without danger or peril to himself or others, report said crime to an appropriate law enforcement official as soon as reasonably practicable. Any person who violates this section shall be punished by a fine of not less than five hundred nor more than two thousand and five hundred dollars.

Why do you believe the Massachusetts legislature limited the scope of this duty to only these five crimes? Do you see any potential problems that may result because of this statute? Do you think that such laws will influence more bystanders to intervene? Should society enact legislation primarily to make a moral statement and put society on record as expecting citizens to act as members of a larger community? Do you agree with Lord Patrick Devlin that our society would disintegrate if we didn't criminalize immoral conduct? Devlin argues that such statutes encourage citizens to think similarly about questions of right and wrong, and that this helps to bind us together as a people.[18]

The following discussion focuses on the society's right to promote a common morality by enacting statutes that prohibit certain types of private sexual conduct between consenting adults.

Individual Choice Versus Social Control: Where Is the Line?

Members of our society often disagree about the extent to which the states are entitled to promote a "common morality" by criminalizing conduct that the proponents of such legislation believe to be morally offensive. When such statutes are enacted into law, those prosecuted for alleged violations often ask the courts to rule that the state has crossed an imprecise constitutional line separating the lawful exercise of the state's police power from the constitutionally protected privacy rights of individuals to engage in the prohibited conduct. State legislatures and supreme courts during the last forty years have confronted this issue with respect to the constitutionality of their respective deviant sexual intercourse statutes. Kentucky and Pennsylvania are examples, because their state supreme courts accepted the argument that it was up to individual adults to determine for themselves the nature of their voluntary, noncommercial, consensual, intimate relationships. The state, through the exercise of the police power, should not use the criminal law to "protect" such adults from themselves where the conduct in question doesn't harm any other person. The supreme courts in these states

declared statutes unconstitutional that made it a crime for consenting adults to engage in prohibited sexual conduct that the legislature deemed to be morally reprehensible.

The constitutional right of the federal and state legislatures to enact laws is discussed more thoroughly on pages 91–99; however, before reading *Lawrence v. Texas* it is necessary that readers know more about a legal concept known as the **police power.**

In general, the police power is a term that refers to each state's inherent right as a sovereign (autonomous) government to enact laws to protect the public's health, welfare, safety, and morals. You will recall that the states were in existence prior to the adoption of the U.S. Constitution, and that they had traditionally exercised broad lawmaking powers to protect the citizens of their states. Congress's right to legislate, however, has no such historical underpinning. Congress does not have the right to legislate based on the police power because it derives all its authority from powers granted in the federal constitution. Because the states retained their right to exercise the police power when the U.S. Constitution was adopted, they continue to enact laws pursuant to this right today.

Introduction to *Lawrence v. Texas*

The Texas legislature, in 1973, pursuant to the police power, repealed its laws that regulated non-commercial sexual conduct taking place in private between consenting, heterosexual adults. At the same time, however, the legislature enacted a statute making it a misdemeanor for same-sex adults to engage in identical conduct, classifying such conduct in such circumstances as "deviate sexual intercourse."

In *Lawrence v. Texas*, the U.S. Supreme Court had to determine whether the Texas deviant sexual intercourse statute's restrictions on the behavior of same-sex adults constituted a lawful exercise of the police power or a constitutionally invalid infringement of individual liberty rights.

John Geddes Lawrence v. Texas
539 U.S. 558
Supreme Court of the United States
June 26, 2003

Justice Kennedy delivered the opinion of the Court.

Liberty protects the person from unwarranted government intrusions into a dwelling or other private places. In our tradition the State is not omnipresent in the home. And there are other spheres of our lives and existence, outside the home, where the State should not be a dominant presence. Freedom extends beyond spatial bounds. Liberty presumes an autonomy of self that includes freedom of thought, belief, expression, and certain intimate conduct. The instant case involves liberty of the person both in its spatial and more transcendent dimensions.

I.

The question before the Court is the validity of a Texas statute making it a crime for two persons of the same sex to engage in certain intimate sexual conduct.

In Houston, Texas, officers of the Harris County Police Department were dispatched to a private residence in response to a reported weapons disturbance. They entered an apartment where one of the petitioners, John Geddes Lawrence, resided. The right of the police to enter does not seem to have been questioned. The officers observed Lawrence and another man, Tyron Garner, engaging in a sexual act. The two petitioners were arrested, held in custody overnight, and charged and convicted before a Justice of the Peace.

The complaints described their crime as "deviate sexual intercourse, namely anal sex, with a member of the same sex (man)."... The applicable state law is Tex. Penal Code Ann. §21.06(a) (2003). It provides: "A person commits an offense if he engages in deviate sexual intercourse with another individual of the same sex." The statute defines "[d]eviate sexual intercourse" as follows:

(A) "any contact between any part of the genitals of one person and the mouth or anus of another person; or

(B) the penetration of the genitals or the anus of another person with an object." 2 §21.01(1).

The petitioners exercised their right to a trial de novo in Harris County Criminal Court. They challenged the statute as a violation of the Equal Protection Clause of the Fourteenth Amendment and of a like provision of the Texas Constitution. Tex. Const., Art. 1,

§3a. Those contentions were rejected. The petitioners, having entered a plea of *nolo contendere*, were each fined $200 and assessed court costs of $141.25....

The Court of Appeals for the Texas Fourteenth District ... affirmed the convictions.... The majority opinion indicates that the Court of Appeals considered our decision in *Bowers v. Hardwick*, 478 U.S. 186 (1986), to be controlling on the federal due process aspect of the case. *Bowers* then being authoritative, this was proper.

We granted certiorari ... to consider three questions:

1. Whether Petitioners' criminal convictions under the Texas "Homosexual Conduct" law—which criminalizes sexual intimacy by same-sex couples, but not identical behavior by different-sex couples—violate the Fourteenth Amendment guarantee of equal protection of laws?

2. Whether Petitioners' criminal convictions for adult consensual sexual intimacy in the home violate their vital interests in liberty and privacy protected by the Due Process Clause of the Fourteenth Amendment?

3. Whether *Bowers v. Hardwick*, 478 U.S. 186 (1986) should be overruled?"...

The petitioners were adults at the time of the alleged offense. Their conduct was in private and consensual.

II.

We conclude the case should be resolved by determining whether the petitioners were free as adults to engage in the private conduct in the exercise of their liberty under the Due Process Clause of the Fourteenth Amendment to the Constitution. For this inquiry we deem it necessary to reconsider the Court's holding in *Bowers*. There are broad statements of the substantive reach of liberty under the Due Process Clause in earlier cases, ... but the most pertinent beginning point is our decision in *Griswold v. Connecticut,* 381 U.S. 479 (1965).

In *Griswold* the Court invalidated a state law prohibiting the use of drugs or devices of contraception and counseling or aiding and abetting the use of contraceptives. The Court described the protected interest as a right to privacy and placed emphasis on the marriage relation and the protected space of the marital bedroom....

After *Griswold* it was established that the right to make certain decisions regarding sexual conduct extends beyond the marital relationship. In *Eisenstadt v. Baird* ... (1972), the Court invalidated a law prohibiting the distribution of contraceptives to unmarried persons. The case was decided under the Equal Protection Clause ... but with respect to unmarried persons, the Court went on to state the fundamental proposition that the law impaired the exercise of their personal rights.... It quoted from the statement of the Court of Appeals finding the law to be in conflict with fundamental human rights, and it followed with this statement of its own:

> It is true that in *Griswold* the right of privacy in question inhered in the marital relationship.... If the right of privacy means anything, it is the right of the individual, married or single, to be free from unwarranted governmental intrusion into matters so fundamentally affecting a person as the decision whether to bear or beget a child....

The opinions in *Griswold* and *Eisenstadt* were part of the background for the decision in *Roe v. Wade* ... (1973). As is well known, the case involved a challenge to the Texas law prohibiting abortions, but the laws of other States were affected as well. Although the Court held the woman's rights were not absolute, her right to elect an abortion did have real and substantial protection as an exercise of her liberty under the Due Process Clause. The Court cited cases that protect spatial freedom and cases that go well beyond it. *Roe* recognized the right of a woman to make certain fundamental decisions affecting her destiny and confirmed once more that the protection of liberty under the Due Process Clause has a substantive dimension of fundamental significance in defining the rights of the person.

In *Carey v. Population Services Int'l* ... (1977), the Court confronted a New York law forbidding sale or distribution of contraceptive devices to persons younger than 16 years of age. Although there was no single opinion for the Court, the law was invalidated. Both *Eisenstadt* and *Carey*, as well as the holding and rationale in *Roe*, confirmed that the reasoning of *Griswold* could not be confined to the protection of rights of married adults. This was the state of the law with respect to some of the most relevant cases when the Court considered *Bowers v. Hardwick*.

The facts in *Bowers* had some similarities to the instant case. A police officer, whose right to enter seems not to have been in question, observed Hardwick, in his own bedroom, engaging in intimate sexual conduct with another adult male. The conduct was in violation of a Georgia statute making it a criminal offense to engage in sodomy. One difference between the two cases is that the Georgia statute prohibited the conduct whether or not the participants were of the same sex, while the Texas statute, as we have seen, applies only to participants of the same sex. Hardwick was not prosecuted, but he brought an action in federal court to declare the state statute invalid. He alleged he was a practicing homosexual and that the criminal prohibition violated rights guaranteed to him by the Constitution. The Court, in an opinion by Justice White, sustained the Georgia law....

The Court began its substantive discussion in *Bowers* as follows: "The issue presented is whether the Federal Constitution confers a fundamental right upon homosexuals to engage in sodomy and hence invalidates the laws of the many States that still make such conduct illegal and have done so for a very long time." ... That statement, we now conclude, discloses the Court's own failure to appreciate the extent of the liberty at stake. To say that the issue in *Bowers* was simply the right to engage in certain sexual conduct demeans the claim the individual put forward, just as it would demean a married couple were it to be said marriage is simply about the right to have sexual intercourse. The laws involved in *Bowers* and here are, to be sure, statutes that purport to do no more than prohibit a particular sexual act. Their penalties and purposes, though, have more far-reaching consequences, touching upon the most private human conduct, sexual behavior, and in the most private of places, the home. The statutes do seek to control a personal relationship that, whether or not entitled to formal recognition in the law, is within the liberty of persons to choose without being punished as criminals.

This, as a general rule, should counsel against attempts by the State, or a court, to define the meaning of the relationship or to set its boundaries absent injury to a person or abuse of an institution the law protects. It suffices for us to acknowledge that adults may choose to enter upon this relationship in the confines of their homes and their own private lives and still retain their dignity as free persons. When sexuality finds overt expression in intimate conduct with another person, the conduct can be but one element in a personal bond that is more enduring. The liberty protected by the Constitution allows homosexual persons the right to make this choice.

Having misapprehended the claim of liberty there presented to it, and thus stating the claim to be whether there is a fundamental right to engage in consensual sodomy, the *Bowers* Court said: "Proscriptions against that conduct have ancient roots." ... In academic writings, and in many of the scholarly amicus briefs filed to assist the Court in this case, there are fundamental criticisms of the historical premises relied upon by the majority and concurring opinions in *Bowers*.... We need not enter this debate in the attempt to reach a definitive historical judgment, but the following considerations counsel against adopting the definitive conclusions upon which *Bowers* placed such reliance.

At the outset it should be noted that this country has no longstanding history of laws directed at homosexual conduct as a distinct matter. Beginning in colonial times, prohibitions of sodomy derived from the English criminal laws passed in the first instance by the Reformation Parliament of 1533. The English prohibition was understood to include relations between men and women as well as relations between men and men.... Nineteenth-century commentators similarly read American sodomy, buggery, and crime-against-nature statutes as criminalizing certain relations between men and women and between men and men.... The absence of legal prohibitions focusing on homosexual conduct may be explained in part by noting that according to some scholars the concept of the homosexual as a distinct category of person did not emerge until the late 19th century.... Thus early American sodomy laws were not directed at homosexuals as such but instead sought to prohibit nonprocreative sexual activity more generally. This does not suggest approval of homosexual conduct. It does tend to show that this particular form of conduct was not thought of as a separate category from like conduct between heterosexual persons.

Laws prohibiting sodomy do not seem to have been enforced against consenting adults acting in private. A substantial number of sodomy prosecutions and convictions for which there are surviving records were for predatory acts against those who could not or did not consent, as in the case of a minor or the victim of an assault.... Instead of targeting relations between consenting adults in private, 19th-century sodomy prosecutions typically involved relations between men and minor girls or minor boys, relations between adults involving force, relations between adults implicating disparity in status, or relations between men and animals.

To the extent that there were any prosecutions for the acts in question, 19th-century evidence rules imposed a burden that would make a conviction more difficult to obtain even taking into account the problems always inherent in prosecuting consensual acts committed in private. Under then-prevailing standards, a man could not be convicted of sodomy based upon testimony of a consenting partner, because the partner was considered an accomplice. A partner's testimony,

however, was admissible if he or she had not consented to the act or was a minor, and therefore incapable of consent....

American laws targeting same-sex couples did not develop until the last third of the 20th century. The reported decisions concerning the prosecution of consensual, homosexual sodomy between adults for the years 1880–1995 are not always clear in the details, but a significant number involved conduct in a public place....

It was not until the 1970s that any State singled out same-sex relations for criminal prosecution, and only nine States have done so.... Over the course of the last decades, States with same-sex prohibitions have moved toward abolishing them. See, e.g., *Jegley v. Picado,* 349 Ark. 600 ... (2002); *Gryczan v. State,* 283 Mont. 433 ... (1997); *Campbell v. Sundquist,* 926 S. W. 2d 250 (Tenn. App. 1996); *Commonwealth v. Wasson,* 842 S. W. 2d 487 (Ky. 1992); see also 1993 Nev. Stats. p. 518 (repealing Nev. Rev. Stat. §201.193).

In summary, the historical grounds relied upon in *Bowers* are more complex than the majority opinion and the concurring opinion by Chief Justice Burger indicate. Their historical premises are not without doubt and, at the very least, are overstated.

It must be acknowledged, of course, that the Court in *Bowers* was making the broader point that for centuries powerful voices have condemned homosexual conduct as immoral. The condemnation has been shaped by religious beliefs, conceptions of right and acceptable behavior, and respect for the traditional family. For many persons these are not trivial concerns but profound and deep convictions accepted as ethical and moral principles to which they aspire and which thus determine the course of their lives. These considerations do not answer the question before us, however. The issue is whether the majority may use the power of the State to enforce these views on the whole society through operation of the criminal law. "Our obligation is to define the liberty of all, not to mandate our own moral code." ...

In all events we think that our laws and traditions in the past half century are of most relevance here. These references show an emerging awareness that liberty gives substantial protection to adult persons in deciding how to conduct their private lives in matters pertaining to sex. "History and tradition are the starting point but not in all cases the ending point of the substantive due process inquiry." ...

Two principal cases decided after *Bowers* cast its holding into even more doubt. In *Planned Parenthood of Southeastern Pa. v. Casey* ... (1992), the Court reaffirmed the substantive force of the liberty protected by the Due Process Clause. The *Casey* decision again confirmed that our laws and tradition afford constitutional protection to personal decisions relating to marriage, procreation, contraception, family relationships, child rearing, and education.... In explaining the respect the Constitution demands for the autonomy of the person in making these choices, we stated as follows:

> These matters, involving the most intimate and personal choices a person may make in a lifetime, choices central to personal dignity and autonomy, are central to the liberty protected by the Fourteenth Amendment. At the heart of liberty is the right to define one's own concept of existence, of meaning, of the universe, and of the mystery of human life. Beliefs about these matters could not define the attributes of personhood were they formed under compulsion of the State....

Persons in a homosexual relationship may seek autonomy for these purposes, just as heterosexual persons do. The decision in *Bowers* would deny them this right.

The second post-*Bowers* case of principal relevance is *Romer v. Evans* ... (1996). There the Court struck down class-based legislation directed at homosexuals as a violation of the Equal Protection Clause. *Romer* invalidated an amendment to Colorado's constitution which named as a solitary class persons who were homosexuals, lesbians, or bisexual either by "orientation, conduct, practices or relationships," ... (internal quotation marks omitted), and deprived them of protection under state antidiscrimination laws. We concluded that the provision was "born of animosity toward the class of persons affected" and further that it had no rational relation to a legitimate governmental purpose....

As an alternative argument in this case, counsel for the petitioners and some amici contend that *Romer* provides the basis for declaring the Texas statute invalid under the Equal Protection Clause. That is a tenable argument, but we conclude the instant case requires us to address whether *Bowers* itself has continuing validity. Were we to hold the statute invalid under the Equal Protection Clause some might question whether a prohibition would be valid if drawn differently, say, to prohibit the conduct both between same-sex and different-sex participants.

Equality of treatment and the due process right to demand respect for conduct protected by the substantive guarantee of liberty are linked in important respects, and a decision on the latter point advances both interests. If protected conduct is made criminal and the law which does so remains unexamined for its substantive validity, its stigma might remain even if it were not enforceable as drawn for equal protection reasons. When homosexual conduct is made criminal by the law of the State, that declaration in and of itself is an invitation to subject homosexual persons to discrimination both in the public and in the private spheres. The central holding of *Bowers* has been brought in question by this case, and it should be addressed. Its continuance as precedent demeans the lives of homosexual persons.

The stigma this criminal statute imposes, moreover, is not trivial. The offense, to be sure, is but a class C misdemeanor, a minor offense in the Texas legal system. Still, it remains a criminal offense with all that imports for the dignity of the persons charged. The petitioners will bear on their record the history of their criminal convictions. Just this Term we rejected various challenges to state laws requiring the registration of sex offenders.... We are advised that if Texas convicted an adult for private, consensual homosexual conduct under the statute here in question the convicted person would come within the registration laws of at least four States were he or she to be subject to their jurisdiction.... This underscores the consequential nature of the punishment and the state-sponsored condemnation attendant to the criminal prohibition. Furthermore, the Texas criminal conviction carries with it the other collateral consequences always following a conviction, such as notations on job application forms, to mention but one example.

The foundations of *Bowers* have sustained serious erosion from our recent decisions in *Casey* and *Romer*. When our precedent has been thus weakened, criticism from other sources is of greater significance. In the United States criticism of *Bowers* has been substantial and continuing, disapproving of its reasoning in all respects, not just as to its historical assumptions.... The courts of five different States [Arkansas, Georgia, Montana, Tennessee, and Kentucky] have declined to follow it....

The doctrine of *stare decisis* is essential to the respect accorded to the judgments of the Court and to the stability of the law. It is not, however, an inexorable command....

The rationale of *Bowers* does not withstand careful analysis. In his dissenting opinion in *Bowers* Justice Stevens came to these conclusions:

> Our prior cases make two propositions abundantly clear. First, the fact that the governing majority in a State has traditionally viewed a particular practice as immoral is not a sufficient reason for upholding a law prohibiting the practice; neither history nor tradition could save a law

prohibiting miscegenation from constitutional attack. Second, individual decisions by married persons, concerning the intimacies of their physical relationship, even when not intended to produce offspring, are a form of 'liberty' protected by the Due Process Clause of the Fourteenth Amendment. Moreover, this protection extends to intimate choices by unmarried as well as married persons....

Justice Stevens' analysis, in our view, should have been controlling in *Bowers* and should control here.

Bowers was not correct when it was decided, and it is not correct today. It ought not to remain binding precedent. *Bowers v. Hardwick* should be and now is overruled.

The present case does not involve minors. It does not involve persons who might be injured or coerced or who are situated in relationships where consent might not easily be refused. It does not involve public conduct or prostitution. It does not involve whether

the government must give formal recognition to any relationship that homosexual persons seek to enter. The case does involve two adults who, with full and mutual consent from each other, engaged in sexual practices common to a homosexual lifestyle. The petitioners are entitled to respect for their private lives. The State cannot demean their existence or control their destiny by making their private sexual conduct a crime. Their right to liberty under the Due Process Clause gives them the full right to engage in their conduct without intervention of the government. "It is a promise of the Constitution that there is a realm of personal liberty which the government may not enter."... The Texas statute furthers no legitimate state interest which can justify its intrusion into the personal and private life of the individual....

The judgment of the Court of Appeals for the Texas Fourteenth District is reversed, and the case is remanded for further proceedings not inconsistent with this opinion.

It is so ordered.

Case Questions

1. What did Justice Kennedy mean when he said in his opinion, "The Texas statute furthers no legitimate state interest which can justify its intrusion into the personal and private life of the individual"?
2. According to Justice Kennedy, what public policy objective that is impermissible under the Fourteenth Amendment was the State of Texas trying to accomplish through this criminal statute?
3. What conclusion does the U.S. Supreme Court reach?
4. Why does the Court say it reached this conclusion?

Business Ethics

Business managers often encounter ethical questions as they attempt to increase profits, lower costs, and secure and preserve markets in their never-ending quest to maximize earnings and the return that stockholders receive on their investments. One of the most interesting debates presently taking place in academic and professional circles involves ethical challenges to the traditional definition of the role of the corporation in society. The question—which encompasses both legal and ethical dimensions—is, Do corporations have ethical obligations beyond increasing stockholder equity? Do corporations, for example, have any ethical obligations to such other stakeholders as employees, suppliers, customers, and the community?[19]

To what extent should law attempt to influence business decision makers to expand their

perspectives and include in their calculus the concerns of a broad range of constituencies? Some authors argue that ethical managers are more likely to flourish where businesses view themselves as a "corporate community." In such an environment, it is suggested, the need to weigh and balance the corporate community's competing needs and interests will naturally lead policymakers to make ethical choices.[20]

Business people often employ lawyers to help them monitor legal developments in such highly relevant subject areas as contract, tort, property, and employment law. As you read this textbook you will become familiar with traditional common law doctrines such as privity of contract, caveat emptor, the preference traditionally shown to landlords over tenants, and the at-will employment doctrine. Implicit in these judicial doctrines are assumptions about what constitutes ethical business conduct. The trend in recent decades has been for legislatures and courts to use law as a catalyst for influencing companies to change or modify their business practices. Their apparent goal has been to encourage businesses to become more aware of the ethical implications and the societal consequences resulting from their business choices.

Between 1890 and 1914, Congress enacted a series of antitrust statutes to counter the perceived abuses of economic power by the dominant national monopolies of that era. The Sherman Act (1890), the Clayton Act (1914), and the Federal Trade Commission Act (1914) were intended to redress price discrimination and other monopolistic practices. Unethical business practices in the securities industry in the early 1930s led to the creation of the Securities and Exchange Commission. More recently, legal initiatives have produced implied warranty statutes, so-called lemon laws, strict liability in tort, state and federal environmental protection standards, and protections against discrimination in employment.

Legislatures and courts make decisions about the extent to which principles of fairness and equity apply in particular circumstances. For example, each state has laws that specify how the legislature believes financial responsibility should be apportioned between businesses and their unintentionally injured customers. And state judiciaries often have to decide whether one party to contract has crossed a theoretical line and "unconsciously" abused the freedom to contract. For example, courts are often asked to refuse to enforce contractual terms that release one party from liability for harming another party (a "release agreement"), where to do so would be substantively unfair. For example, a release agreement in a residential lease might be declared to be substantively unfair where a landlord in a very tight housing market only rents apartments to tenants who "voluntarily agree" that they cannot sue the landlord for negligence under any circumstances—even where the tenant is seriously injured and the landlord is 100% at fault. Customers being sued for breach of contract by a business often argue that they had signed a contract document that had been

drafted by lawyers working for the business, and that the terms of the agreement were one-sided, overreaching, and exclusively for the benefit of the business. Consumers often argue that the contract documents are also procedurally unfair in that they typically consist of a printed form with "take it or leave it" (nonnegotiable) terms that are often presented to the other party for signature at the last minute—contracts of adhesion. The consumer in the following case claimed that she was a victim of this type of abuse of the right to contract.

Introduction to *James and Heidi Glassford v. BrickKicker and GDM*

James and Heidi Glassford contracted with Brick-Kicker to inspect a home that the Glassfords were interested in buying. Unfortunately, these buyers concluded, after BrickKicker completed its inspection and submitted its report, that the inspector had been negligent in performing his duties. Prospective buyers rely on these reports when they decide whether to back out of or go forward with the purchase of an inspected dwelling. Approximately three years later, the Glassfords filed suit claiming that they would never have gone through with the purchase of the inspected dwelling had they been properly appraised of the house's defects. The trial court dismissed the plaintiff's complaint. The court decided to enforce two provisions of the contract, which had been written by lawyers working for BrickKicker. One clause required that disputes between customers and Brick-Kicker be decided by an arbitrator instead of in a court of law. Arbitration is frequently preferred by businesses because it is often less expensive than a court trial and it eliminates the possibility that the dispute might be decided by a jury (students can learn more about arbitration in Chapter XIV).

The trial judge also enforced a second clause that provided that the Glassfords would waive any rights to make claims against BrickKicker unless they gave the company notice of such claims within 90 days after the performance of the inspection—a requirement that was not met by the plaintiffs. The Glassfords appealed from the trial court's decision to the Vermont Supreme Court.

James and Heidi Glassford v. BrickKicker and GDM
35 A.3d 1044
Supreme Court of Vermont
November 4, 2011

Skoglund, J.

Plaintiffs James and Heidi Glassford, who brought suit to obtain compensation for an allegedly negligent home inspection, appeal the superior court's order granting summary judgment in favor of the home inspector based on the terms of a binding arbitration agreement in the parties' contract. In this appeal, we consider whether the superior court erred in rejecting plaintiffs' contention that the terms of the home inspection contract are unconscionable under the common law and unfair and deceptive under Vermont's Consumer Fraud Act....

In 2005, plaintiffs contracted to buy a house in Barre Town, contingent upon a satisfactory home inspection. After being given a list of home inspection companies, plaintiffs contacted the first name on the list, defendant GDM Home Services, Inc., a local franchisee of a national home inspection company called The BrickKicker (hereinafter collectively referred to as BrickKicker). On December 22, 2005, the date of the scheduled inspection, only Mrs. Glassford was present. Before beginning the inspection, the home inspector presented a contract for Mrs. Glassford to sign. She signed the contract and paid the $285 inspection fee.

The two-page contract was on a preprinted form drafted by BrickKicker. The back page of the contract contains ten numbered paragraphs in small print without headers. Paragraphs 5 and 6 in the middle of the back page state as follows:

> Client understands and agrees that it would be extremely difficult to determine the actual damages that may result from an inspector's failure to properly perform duties under this contract. As such, it is agreed that the liability of the Inspection Company arising out of this inspection and subsequent Property Inspection Report shall be limited to actual damages, or equal to the inspection fee charged, whichever is less. IT IS AGREED THAT THIS IS AN ADEQUATE LIQUIDATED DAMAGE AND IS IN NO WAY INTENDED AS A PENALTY, ADMISSION OF NEGLIGENCE OR DEFAULT SETTLEMENT. THE CLIENT UNDERSTANDS AND AGREES THAT ACTUAL DAMAGES, OR EQUAL TO THE INSPECTION FEE PAID, WHICHEVER IS LESS, IS THE CLIENT'S SOLE AND EXCLUSIVE REMEDY NO MATTER THE THEORY OF LIABILITY UPON WHICH THE CLIENT SEEKS RECOVERY....

> Any dispute, controversy, interpretation or claim for, but not limited to, breach of contract, any form of negligence, fraud or misrepresentation or any other theory of liability arising out of, from or related to this contract, the inspection or inspection report shall be submitted to final and binding arbitration under Rules and Procedures of the Expedited Arbitration of Home Inspection Disputes of Construction Arbitration Services, Inc.

Thus, the contract limited BrickKicker's liability to no more than the $285 charged for its inspection. This limitation effectively foreclosed arbitration because the "Rules and Procedures of the Expedited Arbitration of Home Inspection Disputes," which were not set forth in the contract presented for Mrs. Glassford to sign, required the party seeking arbitration to pay, among other things, an initial arbitration fee of $1350, $450 each day after the first day's hearing, and travel expenses for an arbitrator residing more than fifty miles from the arbitration site. In short, a homebuyer disputing BrickKicker's performance would have to pay, at minimum, a $1350 arbitration fee to recover no more than the $285 inspection fee.

The contract also required plaintiffs to pay BrickKicker's costs, attorney's fees, and insurance policy deductibles in any arbitration in which BrickKicker prevailed, but imposed no such reciprocal obligation on BrickKicker. Further, the contract provided that plaintiffs waived any and all claims against BrickKicker unless they gave BrickKicker notice of the claim "within 90 days from the date of the inspection or 30 days after taking possession of the property, whichever is later" and allowed BrickKicker to reinspect the property.

Following his inspection of plaintiffs' prospective home, BrickKicker's inspector produced a detailed report declaring the house to be "[a] nice new home in need of routine maintenance and observation." Plaintiffs bought the house for $230,500. According to their complaint, after moving in they found numerous defects which should have been discovered and reported by the inspector, and which, they claim, would have caused them to break the sales contract. Nearly three years later, in December 2008, plaintiffs brought suit against BrickKicker, alleging negligence in the home inspection.

BrickKicker moved to dismiss the suit, arguing that the complaint was barred by the contract's time-limit waiver and binding arbitration clause. Treating BrickKicker's motion as one for summary judgment, the court invited the parties to submit statements of undisputed fact and competing memoranda. Plaintiffs opposed BrickKicker's motion and attached a copy of the arbitration rules that the contract indicated would govern any arbitration proceedings. Plaintiffs argued that the arbitration fees required by the rules, combined with the contract's provision limiting liability, effectively insulated BrickKicker against any liability based on its services and assured that no arbitration proceeding would take place....

On July 2, 2009, the superior court [the trial court] dismissed the complaint, ruling that arbitration was the sole forum for plaintiffs to seek redress because the contract's arbitration clause was "utterly clear on its face."... The [trial] court did not address plaintiffs'... claims of unconscionability except to note that plaintiffs made "no claim that the arbitration clause itself is unconscionable" but instead directed "their 'unconscionability' arguments to other substantive terms of the contract such as the limitations on liability."

Plaintiffs moved for reconsideration, arguing, among other things, that the [trial] court ignored their claims that certain contract provisions were unconscionable under the common law ... , and that the arbitration clause was unenforceable due to the practical impossibility of arbitration, given that the arbitration fee exceeded any potential recovery under the liability cap in the contract. The [trial] court rejected these arguments....

In short, according to the [trial] court, plaintiffs failed to allege procedural unconscionability, which it deemed to be a necessary predicate to their unconscionability claim, and further failed to produce a record or legal authority to support their claim that the challenged contractual provisions were substantively unconscionable....

Plaintiffs appeal the dismissal of their suit....

For the reasons stated below, we find unconscionable the subject contract's illusory remedy for any claim for damages resulting from its provisions limiting liability to the inspection fee and requiring binding arbitration costs that would exceed the amount of the liability limit. Because the limited liability and arbitration provisions are interconnected in creating the substantively unconscionable illusory remedy, we strike both of them.... The superior court was mistaken in assuming that the presence of procedural unconscionability is required to void a contract based on it containing unconscionable terms.... In any event, we also

note significant elements of procedural unfairness in the contract, as described below.

The principal barrier in the contract to the possibility of any relief for plaintiffs is the provision limiting liability to the $285 inspection fee. Plaintiffs challenged this provision, among others, before the superior court....

Notwithstanding the trial court's statement suggesting otherwise, plaintiffs submitted a memorandum of law attacking the contract's limitation on liability, citing primarily this Court's decision in *Dalury v. S-K-I, Ltd.*... On appeal, plaintiffs renew their claim that the contract's limitation on liability is unconscionable, this time additionally relying upon decisions from other jurisdictions that are directly on point. See *Pitts v. Watkins*, ... (Miss. 2005) ... ; *Lucier v. Williams*, ... (N.J. Super. Ct. App. Div. 2004).... These cases are among the numerous decisions from around the country that have addressed allegedly unconscionable home inspection contracts. Typically, the challenged contracts contain provisions, as in the case before us, setting forth short notice requirements, limiting liability to the amount of the inspection fee, and compelling arbitration that would incur costs exceeding the liability limit.

Here, as noted, the contract's limitation on BrickKicker's liability creates a disingenuous arbitration remedy for plaintiffs. Even standing alone, limiting liability to $285 irrespective of the actual damages incurred by the customer would be, at minimum, highly suspect. But under this contract's governing arbitration rules, plaintiffs could not recover even the cost of the filing fee much less any compensatory damages.... Thus, the liability limit in the contract is a complete impediment to any effective remedy for the home inspector's negligence or even intentional tort. As a number of courts have held, a provision limiting liability to damages that are insignificant in comparison with a customer's actual loss is really an exculpatory clause insulating the home inspector from all liability....

Because the contract before us contains what are, in effect, exculpatory clauses in consumer transactions, we turn to *Dalury* ... for guidance. *Dalury* holds that exculpatory clauses are valid as long as they do not violate public policy. In determining whether exculpatory clauses violate public policy, we adopted the standards from *Tunkl v. Regents of University of California*... (Cal. 1963), as "relevant considerations."... The *Tunkl* standards provide that an exculpatory agreement is invalid if it exhibits some or all of the following characteristics:

It concerns a business of a type generally thought suitable for public regulation. The party seeking exculpation is engaged in performing a service of great importance to the public, which is often a matter of practical necessity for some members of the public. The party holds [it]self out as willing to perform this service for any member of the public who seeks it, or at least for any member coming within certain established standards. As a result of the essential nature of the service, in the economic setting of the transaction, the party invoking exculpation possesses a decisive advantage of bargaining strength against any member of the public who seeks [the party's] services. In exercising a superior bargaining power the party confronts the public with a standardized adhesion contract of exculpation, and makes no provision whereby a purchaser may pay additional reasonable fees and obtain protection against negligence. Finally, as a result of the transaction, the person or property of the purchaser is placed under the control of the seller, subject to the risk of carelessness by the seller or [the seller's] agents....

Although *Dalury* has distinctive facts and does not involve a home inspection contract, the factors that were central in that case are also present here. The record in this case indicates that GDM Home Services is a local franchisee of BrickKicker, a national home inspection corporation. Its services are generally open to the public, and plaintiffs chose it as one of three home inspection services referred by the seller's realtor. Although Vermont is one of a minority of states that have not regulated home inspection contractors, many states have adopted regulatory schemes. See http://www.homeinspector.org/stateregulations/default.aspx (detailing state home inspector regulation as of Oct. 25, 2011). Thus, home inspection contracting is clearly a "business of a type generally thought suitable for public regulation," the first of the *Tunkl* factors....

As in *Dalury*, a legitimate public interest arises "as a result of the seller's general invitation to the public to utilize the ... services in question."... Thus, as in *Dalury*, public policy requires consequences when home inspectors do not perform with due care. Only the inspectors are able to conform their services to their contractual obligations and the necessary quality. If the law immunizes them from liability for their negligence, it eliminates the greatest and most important incentive for proper performance.

The importance of home inspection services to consumers cannot be doubted, as explained in *Lucier*:

The foisting of a contract of this type in this setting on an inexperienced consumer clearly demonstrates a lack of fair dealing by the professional. The cost of homes in New Jersey is substantial. It has often been said that the purchase of a home is usually the largest investment a person will make in life. The purchase of a home is, for most people, a very infrequent occurrence, and a very major undertaking. People may buy a home once in a lifetime, or not very often. Home inspectors, on the other hand, conduct a volume operation. As a businessperson who possesses knowledge about and experience in the industry, [the inspector] is aware of the cost of repairing major defects. In fact, that is a major selling point of his service to residential buyers....

... [T]he home purchaser must "take the precautionary steps to properly assess that the price of the residence reflects its actual value."... Thus, a competent inspection is not only crucial to "negotiating the price for the residence," but it is normally required by the financing agency, which also relies upon it....

At the time of the home inspection, consumers have normally already decided to buy a house based on factors such as aesthetics and amenities, and "the only issue left is the integrity of the house."... The purpose of a home inspection "is to give a consumer a rational basis upon which to decline to enter into a contract to buy, to provide lawful grounds to be relieved from a contractual commitment to buy, or to offer a sound basis upon which to negotiate a lower price."... If home inspectors can exempt themselves from liability for their negligence, they could "walk through the house in five minutes, fabricate a report, and escape liability, without any consideration of the consequences of their conduct" on the homebuyer's decision involving hundreds of thousands of dollars.... Limiting the liability to the inspection fee does not provide a realistic incentive to act diligently, see *Lucier*, ... ("To be enforceable, the amount of the cap on a party's liability must be sufficient to provide a real incentive to act diligently."), particularly given the countervailing incentive to please the referring realtor by soft-pedaling the inspection and allowing the sale to go forward....

The importance of home inspection services also relates to the last of the *Tunkl* factors: whether, "as a result of the transaction, the person or property of the purchaser is placed under the control of the seller, subject to the risk of carelessness by the seller or his agents."... The affidavit of Heidi Glassford, who was primarily responsible for the house purchase, indicates that she is a high school graduate who has no expertise or experience in housing construction and had never before purchased a house. The purchase and sales agreement had a provision allowing plaintiffs to back out of the contract if the house inspection revealed defects. Thus, the house purchase depended upon an acceptable inspection report, and plaintiffs' right under the contract to decline to purchase a house with major defects as set forth in an inspection also depended on a competent housing inspection. In short, plaintiffs were entirely at the mercy of BrickKicker and without other means of protection if BrickKicker was careless in its housing inspection....

In addition to the substantive unconscionability, this case also has elements of procedural unconscionability, particularly with respect to the limited-liability clause, which is contained in boilerplate language without a separate heading in a contract of adhesion.... The front page of the contract describes the elements and limitations of the inspection, but does not contain any of the provisions about which plaintiffs complain—the arbitration requirement, the limit on liability, or the notice requirement and shortened limitation period. The customer's signature line is on the front so that the customer can sign without ever turning over the document. The reverse side of the page lists the "INSPECTION CONTRACT CONDITIONS." The conditions are in eleven separate paragraphs, generally in very small print and all without separate headers. The limited liability provision is in the middle of fine print in paragraphs five and six and is not identified by a header. Two sentences about the liability limit are in capital letters, but ... [o]nly the second expresses clearly that the customer's only remedy is damages, but subject to the liability limit.

... [T]he critical contractual provisions limiting the customers' liability and creating, in effect, an illusory arbitration remedy are set forth in fine print, unidentified, on the back page of a standard contract of adhesion.

For the reasons outlined above, we conclude that the contract's limited liability and binding arbitration provisions are unconscionable and thus unenforceable. Although the contract contains a boilerplate severability clause, we decline to strike only the limited liability provision, considering that both clauses operate together to effectively deny plaintiffs a forum to resolve their claims. Theoretically, we could sever just the limited liability provision and force plaintiffs to proceed to binding arbitration, recognizing that Vermont law favors arbitration.... But we decline to do so. BrickKicker should not benefit from a binding arbitration clause that is a major component of the scheme to offer plaintiffs an illusory remedy for any claims they might have against BrickKicker....

Reversed and remanded for further proceedings consistent with this opinion....

Case Questions

1. The trial court thought that this was not a difficult case. It was not the defendant's responsibility to make sure that the plaintiff read and understood the terms of the contract. She was not coerced into signing this agreement. In your opinion is the plaintiff more or less responsible for her own predicament than the defendant?
2. Can you make an argument from the utilitarian perspective that the Vermont Supreme Court was right to step in and override the contractual terms as it did in this case?
3. Can you make an argument from a natural law point of view that the plaintiff should have prevailed in this case?

Professional Ethics

We have learned that law is only one of society's resources for developing standards of ethical conduct. Professional associations also make significant contributions. It is common for persons in a trade or profession who share a common concern about competency, quality, and integrity to organize an association. Such an association typically will develop a code of ethics to which the members will subscribe. In this fashion, many of the dos and don'ts of a profession become codified, at least as far as the members are concerned. Theoretically, a member who fails to comply with the code will be expelled from membership. This process has the twin advantages of distinguishing the membership from predatory competitors and enabling the members to establish and maintain a positive image with consumers. Real estate brokers, undertakers, social workers, engineers, doctors, police chiefs, and lawyers, to name but a few, have formed associations, at least in part, to establish and maintain standards of ethical behavior for their memberships. In some of the regulated professions, membership in an association is required as a condition of licensure. This is true in the legal profession, where thirty states require attorneys to be dues-paying members of the state's bar association.[21]

The American Bar Association and many state bar associations have standing committees on ethics that issue advisory opinions at the request of members. These opinions are often highly respected and can be influential when used in conjunction with disciplinary proceedings. Bar associations also are heavily involved in developing proposed rules for consideration by the state supreme courts, and they often sponsor courses in continuing legal education for the benefit of the membership.

Ethics and Professional Responsibility Codes for Lawyers and Judges

The supreme court of each state is normally responsible for overseeing the practice of law within its jurisdiction. It fulfills this obligation in part by promulgating standards of professional conduct to protect the public from incompetent and/or unethical lawyers and from judges who prove to be unsuited or unfit to remain on the bench. Supreme courts also create administrative boards to investigate complaints and enforce rules, and increasingly require that all attorneys and judges participate in continuing legal education programs.

Typical codes of conduct for lawyers and judges will express concerns about competency, confidentiality, loyalty, honesty, candor, fairness, and avoiding conflicts of interest.

The West Virginia Supreme Court of Appeals, for example, has promulgated such codes of conduct for its lawyers and judges. It has established a special commission to investigate complaints against

judges and to "determine whether probable cause exists to formally charge a judge with a violation of the Code of Judicial Conduct."

The West Virginia Code of Judicial Conduct, in Canon 3E(1), prohibits any judge from participating in any proceeding where "the judge's impartiality might reasonably be questioned...."

West Virginia is one of thirty-nine states that elect rather than appoint some or all of their judges.

Judges everywhere appreciate that the only power they possess is the right to make decisions. They depend on the executive branch of government to enforce their orders and on the legislative branch of government to provide funding. Judges who are not fair and impartial threaten public support for the judiciary as an institution and potentially undermine respect for all other judges. It is unusual for a judge to refuse to voluntarily remove (in legal jargon, "recuse") himself or herself from a proceeding that fairly or unfairly involves circumstances that could be perceived as raising questions about whether that judge is biased or has a conflict of interest. It is even more rare for a sitting judge to deny three separate recusal motions brought by one of the parties to a highly publicized and contentious case, which is the issue in the following U.S. Supreme Court opinion.

Introduction to *Caperton v. Massey Coal Co.*

In our country, whenever it appears that a federal or state court trial has been fundamentally unfair for procedural reasons, an aggrieved party, after exhausting all other available sources of relief, has the right to petition the U.S. Supreme Court for a writ of certiorari. This is what happened in the case of *Caperton v. Massey Coal Co.* The U.S. Supreme Court granted certiorari and thereby agreed to decide this case, in part because the facts were so compelling. However, by accepting this case the Court was also reminding the lower courts, political operatives, and the country that the protections of the Due Process Clause can be invoked to remedy a procedural wrong, if it is necessary to the preservation of judicial integrity.

Hugh M. Caperton v. A. T. Massey Coal Company, Inc.
129 S. Ct. 2252
Supreme Court of the United States
June 8, 2009

Justice Kennedy delivered the opinion of the Court.
In this case, the Supreme Court of Appeals of West Virginia reversed a trial court judgment, which had entered a jury verdict of $50 million. Five justices heard the case, and the vote to reverse was 3 to 2. The question presented is whether the Due Process Clause of the Fourteenth Amendment was violated when one of the justices in the majority denied a recusal motion. The basis for the motion was that the justice had received campaign contributions in an extraordinary amount from, and through the efforts of, the board chairman and principal officer of the corporation found liable for the damages....

I.

In August 2002 a West Virginia jury returned a verdict that found respondents A. T. Massey Coal Co. and its affiliates (hereinafter Massey) liable for fraudulent misrepresentation, concealment, and tortious interference with existing contractual relations. The jury awarded petitioners Hugh Caperton, Harman Development Corp., Harman Mining Corp., and Sovereign Coal Sales (hereinafter Caperton) the sum of $50 million in compensatory and punitive damages.

In June 2004 the state trial court denied Massey's post-trial motions challenging the verdict and the damages award, finding that Massey "intentionally acted in utter disregard of [Caperton's] rights and ultimately destroyed [Caperton's] businesses.... In March 2005 the trial court denied Massey's motion for judgment as a matter of law.

Don Blankenship is Massey's chairman, chief executive officer, and president. After the verdict but before the appeal, West Virginia held its 2004 judicial elections. Knowing the Supreme Court of Appeals of West Virginia would consider the appeal in the case, Blankenship decided to support an attorney who sought to replace Justice McGraw. Justice McGraw was a candidate for reelection to that court. The attorney who sought to replace him was Brent Benjamin.

In addition to contributing the $1,000 statutory maximum to Benjamin's campaign committee, Blankenship donated almost $2.5 million to "And For The Sake Of The Kids," a political organization formed under 26 U. S. C. §527. The §527 organization opposed McGraw and supported Benjamin.... Blankenship's donations accounted for more than two-thirds of the total funds it raised.... This was not all. Blankenship

spent, in addition, just over $500,000 on independent expenditures—for direct mailings and letters soliciting donations as well as television and newspaper advertisements—" 'to support ... Brent Benjamin.'"...

To provide some perspective, Blankenship's $3 million in contributions were more than the total amount spent by all other Benjamin supporters and three times the amount spent by Benjamin's own committee....

Benjamin won. He received 382,036 votes (53.3 percent), and McGraw received 334,301 votes (46.7 percent)....

In October 2005, before Massey filed its petition for appeal in West Virginia's highest court, Caperton moved to disqualify now-Justice Benjamin under the Due Process Clause and the West Virginia Code of Judicial Conduct, based on the conflict caused by Blankenship's campaign involvement. Justice Benjamin denied the motion in April 2006.... In December 2006 Massey filed its petition for appeal to challenge the adverse jury verdict. The West Virginia Supreme Court of Appeals granted review.

In November 2007 that court [consisting of "then-Chief Justice Davis and joined by Justices Benjamin and Maynard"] reversed the $50 million verdict against Massey.... Justice Starcher dissented, stating that the "majority's opinion is morally and legally wrong...."

Caperton sought rehearing, and the parties moved for disqualification of three of the five justices who decided the appeal. Photos had surfaced of Justice Maynard vacationing with Blankenship in the French Riviera while the case was pending.... Justice Maynard granted Caperton's recusal motion. On the other side Justice Starcher granted Massey's recusal motion, apparently based on his public criticism of Blankenship's role in the 2004 elections. In his recusal memorandum Justice Starcher urged Justice Benjamin to recuse himself as well.... He noted that "Blankenship's bestowal of his personal wealth, political tactics, and 'friendship' have created a cancer in the affairs of this Court."... Justice Benjamin declined Justice Starcher's suggestion and denied Caperton's recusal motion.

The court granted rehearing. Justice Benjamin, now in the capacity of acting chief justice, selected Judges Cookman and Fox to replace the recused justices. Caperton moved a third time for disqualification.... Justice Benjamin again refused to withdraw, noting that the "push poll" was "neither credible nor sufficiently reliable to serve as the basis for an elected judge's disqualification."... In April 2008 a divided court again reversed the jury verdict, and again it was a 3-to-2 decision. Justice Davis filed a modified version of his prior opinion, repeating the two earlier holdings. She was joined by Justice Benjamin and Judge Fox. Justice Albright, joined by Judge Cookman, dissented: "Not only is the majority opinion unsupported by the facts and existing case law, but it is also fundamentally unfair. Sadly, justice was neither honored nor served by the majority...." The dissent also noted "genuine due process implications arising under federal law" with respect to Justice Benjamin's failure to recuse himself....

Four months later—a month after the petition for writ of certiorari was filed in this Court—Justice Benjamin filed a concurring opinion. He defended the merits of the majority opinion as well as his decision not to recuse. He rejected Caperton's challenge to his participation in the case under both the Due Process Clause and West Virginia law. Justice Benjamin reiterated that he had no "'direct, personal, substantial, pecuniary interest' in this case.'"

We granted certiorari. 555 U. S.__ (2008).

II.

It is axiomatic that "[a] fair trial in a fair tribunal is a basic requirement of due process."... The early and leading case on the subject is *Tumey* v. *Ohio,* 273 U. S. 510 (1927)....

To place the present case in proper context, two instances where the Court has required recusal merit further discussion.

A.

The first involved the emergence of local tribunals where a judge had a financial interest in the outcome of a case, although the interest was less than what would have been considered personal or direct at common law.

This was the problem addressed in *Tumey.* There, the mayor of a village had the authority to sit as a judge (with no jury) to try those accused of violating a state law prohibiting the possession of alcoholic beverages. Inherent in this structure were two potential conflicts. First, the mayor received a salary supplement for performing judicial duties, and the funds for that compensation derived from the fines assessed in a case. No fines were assessed upon acquittal. The mayor-judge thus received a salary supplement only if he convicted the defendant.... Second, sums from the criminal fines were deposited to the village's general treasury fund for village improvements and repairs....

The Court held that the Due Process Clause required disqualification "both because of [the mayor-judge's] direct pecuniary interest in the outcome, and because of

his official motive to convict and to graduate the fine to help the financial needs of the village."... It so held despite observing that "[t]here are doubtless mayors who would not allow such a consideration as $12 costs in each case to affect their judgment in it."... The Court articulated the controlling principle:

> Every procedure which would offer a possible temptation to the average man as a judge to forget the burden of proof required to convict the defendant, or which might lead him not to hold the balance nice, clear and true between the State and the accused, denies the latter due process of law....

The Court was thus concerned with more than the traditional common-law prohibition on direct pecuniary interest. It was also concerned with a more general concept of interests that tempt adjudicators to disregard neutrality....

B.

The second instance requiring recusal that was not discussed at common law emerged in the criminal contempt context, where a judge had no pecuniary interest in the case but was challenged because of a conflict arising from his participation in an earlier proceeding. This Court characterized that first proceeding (perhaps pejoratively) as a " 'one-man grand jury.' " *Murchison,* 349 U.S., at 133.... In that first proceeding, and as provided by state law, a judge examined witnesses to determine whether criminal charges should be brought. The judge called the two petitioners before him. One petitioner answered questions, but the judge found him untruthful and charged him with perjury. The second declined to answer on the ground that he did not have counsel with him, as state law seemed to permit. The judge charged him with contempt. The judge proceeded to try and convict both petitioners....

This Court set aside the convictions on grounds that the judge had a conflict of interest at the trial stage because of his earlier participation followed by his decision to charge them. The Due Process Clause required disqualification. The Court recited the general rule that "no man can be a judge in his own case," adding that "no man is permitted to try cases where he has an interest in the outcome."... It noted that the disqualifying criteria "cannot be defined with precision. Circumstances and relationships must be considered."... That is because "[a]s a practical matter it is difficult if not impossible for a judge to free himself from the influence of what took place in his 'grand-jury' secret session...."

The *Murchison* Court was careful to distinguish the circumstances and the relationship from those where the Constitution would not require recusal. It noted that the single-judge grand jury is "more a part of the accusatory process than an ordinary lay grand juror," and that "adjudication by a trial judge of a contempt committed in [a judge's] presence in open court cannot be likened to the proceedings here." *Id.*, at 137. The judge's prior relationship with the defendant, as well as the information acquired from the prior proceeding, was of critical import....

Again, the Court considered the specific circumstances presented by the case.... The inquiry is an objective one. The Court asks not whether the judge is actually, subjectively biased, but whether the average judge in his position is "likely" to be neutral, or whether there is an unconstitutional "potential for bias."

III.

Based on the principles described in these cases we turn to the issue before us. This problem arises in the context of judicial elections, a framework not presented in the precedents we have reviewed and discussed.

Caperton contends that Blankenship's pivotal role in getting Justice Benjamin elected created a constitutionally intolerable probability of actual bias. Though not a bribe or criminal influence, Justice Benjamin would nevertheless feel a debt of gratitude to Blankenship for his extraordinary efforts to get him elected. That temptation, Caperton claims, is as strong and inherent in human nature as was the conflict the Court confronted in *Tumey* ... when a mayor-judge (or the city) benefitted financially from a defendant's conviction, as well as the conflict identified in *Murchison* ... when a judge was the object of a defendant's contempt.

Justice Benjamin was careful to address the recusal motions and explain his reasons why, on his view of the controlling standard, disqualification was not in order.... We do not question his subjective findings of impartiality and propriety. Nor do we determine whether there was actual bias....

... [A] judge inquires into reasons that seem to be leading to a particular result. Precedent and *stare decisis* and the text and purpose of the law and the Constitution; logic and scholarship and experience and common sense; and fairness and disinterest and neutrality are among the factors at work. To bring coherence to the process, and to seek respect for the resulting judgment, judges often explain the reasons for their conclusions and rulings. There are instances when the introspection that often attends this process may reveal that what the judge had assumed to be a proper, controlling factor is not the real one at work. If the judge discovers that some personal bias or improper consideration seems to be the actuating cause of the decision or to be an influence so difficult to dispel a real possibility of undermining neutrality, the judge may think it necessary to consider withdrawing from the case.

The difficulties of inquiring into actual bias, and the fact that the inquiry is often a private one, simply underscore the need for objective rules.... [T]he Due Process Clause has been implemented by objective standards that do not require proof of actual bias.... In defining these standards the Court has asked whether, "under a realistic appraisal of psychological tendencies and human weakness," the interest "poses such a risk of actual bias or prejudgment that the practice must be forbidden if the guarantee of due process is to be adequately implemented."...

We turn to the influence at issue in this case. Not every campaign contribution by a litigant or attorney creates a probability of bias that requires a judge's recusal, but this is an exceptional case.... We conclude that there is a serious risk of actual bias—based on objective and reasonable perceptions—when a person with a personal stake in a particular case had a significant and disproportionate influence in placing the judge on the case by raising funds or directing the judge's election campaign when the case was pending or imminent. The inquiry centers on the contribution's relative size in comparison to the total amount of money contributed to the campaign, the total amount spent in the election, and the apparent effect such contribution had on the outcome of the election.

Applying this principle, we conclude that Blankenship's campaign efforts had a significant and disproportionate influence in placing Justice Benjamin on the case. Blankenship contributed some $3 million to unseat the incumbent and replace him with Benjamin....

Massey responds that Blankenship's support, while significant, did not cause Benjamin's victory. In the end the people of West Virginia elected him, and they did so based on many reasons other than Blankenship's efforts. Massey points out that every major state newspaper, but one, endorsed Benjamin.... It also contends that then-Justice McGraw cost himself the election by giving a speech during the campaign, a speech the opposition seized upon for its own advantage.... Justice Benjamin raised similar arguments....

Whether Blankenship's campaign contributions were a necessary and sufficient cause of Benjamin's victory is not the proper inquiry. Much like determining whether a judge is actually biased, proving what ultimately drives the electorate to choose a particular candidate is a difficult endeavor, not likely to lend itself to a certain conclusion. This is particularly true where, as here, no procedure for judicial factfinding exists and the sole trier of fact is the one accused of bias.... Blankenship's campaign contributions—in comparison to the total amount contributed to the campaign, as well as the total amount spent in the election—had a significant and disproportionate influence on the electoral outcome. And the risk that Blankenship's influence engendered actual bias is sufficiently substantial that it "must be forbidden if the guarantee of due process is to be adequately implemented...."

The temporal relationship between the campaign contributions, the justice's election, and the pendency of the case is also critical. It was reasonably foreseeable, when the campaign contributions were made, that the pending case would be before the newly elected justice. The $50 million adverse jury verdict had been entered before the election, and the Supreme Court of Appeals was the next step once the state trial court dealt with post-trial motions. So it became at once apparent that, absent recusal, Justice Benjamin would review a judgment that cost his biggest donor's company $50 million. Although there is no allegation of a *quid pro quo* agreement, the fact remains that Blankenship's extraordinary contributions were made at a time when he had a vested stake in the outcome. Just as no man is allowed to be a judge in his own cause, similar fears of bias can arise when—without the consent of the other parties—a man chooses the judge in his own cause. And applying this principle to the judicial election process, there was here a serious, objective risk of actual bias that required Justice Benjamin's recusal....

We find that Blankenship's significant and disproportionate influence—coupled with the temporal relationship between the election and the pending case —"offer a possible temptation to the average ... judge to ... lead him not to hold the balance nice, clear and true."... On these extreme facts the probability of actual bias rises to an unconstitutional level.

IV.

Our decision today addresses an extraordinary situation where the Constitution requires recusal.... Massey and its ... [advocates] predict that various adverse consequences will follow from recognizing a constitutional violation here—ranging from a flood of recusal motions to unnecessary interference with judicial elections. We disagree. The facts now before us are extreme by any measure. The parties point to no other instance involving judicial campaign contributions that presents a potential for bias comparable to the circumstances in this case.

It is true that extreme cases often test the bounds of established legal principles, and sometimes no administrable standard may be available to address the perceived wrong. But it is also true that extreme cases are more likely to cross constitutional limits, requiring this Court's intervention and formulation of objective standards. This is particularly true when due process is violated....

This Court's recusal cases are illustrative. In each case the Court dealt with extreme facts that created an unconstitutional probability of bias that " 'cannot be defined with precision.' "... Yet the Court articulated an objective standard to protect the parties' basic right to a fair trial in a fair tribunal. The Court was careful to distinguish the extreme facts of the cases before it from those interests that would not rise to a constitutional level.... In this case we do nothing more than what the Court has done before....

"Courts, in our system, elaborate principles of law in the course of resolving disputes. The power and the prerogative of a court to perform this function rest, in the end, upon the respect accorded to its judgments. The citizen's respect for judgments depends in turn upon the issuing court's absolute probity. Judicial integrity is, in consequence, a state interest of the highest order...."

"The Due Process Clause demarks only the outer boundaries of judicial disqualifications. Congress and the states, of course, remain free to impose more rigorous standards for judicial disqualification than those we find mandated here today...." Because the codes of judicial conduct provide more protection than due process requires, most disputes over disqualification will be resolved without resort to the Constitution. Application of the constitutional standard implicated in this case will thus be confined to rare instances.

The judgment of the Supreme Court of Appeals of West Virginia is reversed, and the case is remanded for further proceedings not inconsistent with this opinion.

It is so ordered.

Case Questions

1. The Supreme Court split 5–4 in deciding this case. What do you suppose were some of the concerns of the dissenting four justices?
2. What single fact was most important to you as you went about making up your own mind as to whether this case was correctly decided?
3. Does this case have any possible ethical implications that might have relevance for appointed judges?

Author's Comment

Interested readers can find Chief Justice Roberts's dissent online at the textbook's website. Another interesting case is also available on the website. In 2005, the Florida Supreme Court disciplined two attorneys because their television advertisement featured a pit bull with a spiked collar and their firm's telephone number: 1–800–PIT–BULL. This form of advertising, said the Florida Supreme Court, violated the Florida Rules of Professional Conduct. You can read an edited version of *The Florida Bar v. John Robert Pape* on this textbook's website.

Ethics and Professional Responsibility Codes for Paralegals

Lawyers, law firms, businesses, and governments have increasingly been hiring people as legal assistants or paralegals (hereafter called simply paralegals) to do work previously performed by licensed attorneys. The primary reason for this trend is the financial savings realized by having legal work performed by nonlawyers.

Paralegals today perform a wide variety of tasks, depending on their training, education, and experience. Because they are not licensed attorneys, they cannot represent clients in court, give legal advice, or sign pleadings. Subject to these limitations, the scope of a paralegal's duties is largely a matter of what the supervising attorney is willing to permit. Often this includes interviewing clients, conducting research, preparing drafts of documents, undertaking investigations, preparing affidavits, and collecting and organizing materials for hearings.

Legally, a supervising attorney is responsible for providing oversight and regulating his or her paralegal's work and conduct. There have been proposals that paralegals be subject to rules of professional responsibility established by each state's supreme court. This was proposed in New Jersey, but rejected by that state's supreme court.[22] Several states have established paralegal divisions within the state bar. One state that undertook this step in 1995 is New Mexico.

All three of the national paralegal associations—the National Federation of Paralegal Associations, the American Alliance of Paralegals, Inc., and the National Association of Legal Assistants—have recognized the need to provide paralegals with ethical guidelines, and each has promulgated a code of ethics to which its members subscribe. State and local paralegal organizations also promote ethical conduct within their memberships.

The New Mexico Supreme Court has been a leader in enhancing ethical conduct and professional responsibility on the part of paralegals. The court, through its "Rules Governing Paralegal Services," has helped to clarify the boundaries of the paralegal's role within that state. (Readers can see the complete text of the rules and commentary on the textbook's website.) The court also has recognized the importance of establishing general ethical guidelines for paralegals in its "Canons of Ethics" (see Figure 2.3).

Many states have defined what it means to be a paralegal and require people holding themselves out to be paralegals to have satisfied minimum standards with respect to education, certification, and/or experience. These laws usually prohibit paralegals from advertising or offering their services to consumers and require that all paralegal work be performed at the direction and under the supervision of a licensed attorney of that state. Such laws are intended to prevent paralegals from engaging in the unauthorized practice of law. Some states, notably California, require paralegals to complete mandatory continuing legal education courses periodically.

The American Bar Association also has a Standing Committee on Paralegals and has published "ABA Guidelines for the Approval of Paralegal Education Programs" and "ABA Model Guidelines for the Utilization of Paralegal Services."

It is the responsibility of every member of the Paralegal Division of the State Bar of New Mexico (hereinafter referred to as "Paralegal") to adhere strictly to the accepted standards of legal ethics. The Canons of Ethics set forth hereafter are adopted by the Paralegal Division of the State Bar of New Mexico as a general guide.

CANON 1. A Paralegal must not perform any of the duties that only attorneys may perform nor take any actions that attorneys may not take.

CANON 2. A Paralegal may perform any task which is properly delegated and supervised by an attorney, as long as the attorney is ultimately responsible to the client, maintains a direct relationship with the client, and assumes professional responsibility for the work product.

CANON 3. A Paralegal must not: (a) engage in, encourage, or contribute to any act which could constitute the unauthorized practice of law; and (b) establish attorney-client relationships, set fees, give legal opinions or advice or represent a client before a court or agency unless so authorized by that court or agency; and (c) engage in conduct or take any action which would assist or involve the attorney in a violation of professional ethics or give the appearance of professional impropriety.

CANON 4. A Paralegal must use discretion and professional judgment commensurate with knowledge and experience but must not render independent legal judgment in place of an attorney. The services of an attorney are essential in the public interest whenever such legal judgment is required.

CANON 5. A Paralegal must disclose his or her status as a Paralegal at the outset of any professional relationship with a client, attorney, a court or administrative agency or personnel thereof, or a member of the general public. A Paralegal must act prudently in determining the extent to which a client may be assisted without the presence of an attorney.

CANON 6. A Paralegal must strive to maintain integrity and a high degree of competency through education and training with respect to professional responsibility, local rules and practice, and through continuing education in substantive areas of law to better assist the legal profession in fulfilling its duty to provide legal service.

CANON 7. A Paralegal must protect the confidences of a client and must not violate any rule or statute now in effect or hereafter enacted controlling the doctrine of privileged communications between a client and an attorney.

CANON 8. A Paralegal must do all other things incidental, necessary, or expedient for the attainment of the ethics and responsibilities as defined by statute or rule of court.

CANON 9. A Paralegal's conduct is governed by the codes of professional responsibility and rules of professional conduct of the State Bar of New Mexico and the New Mexico Supreme Court. A member of the Paralegal Division of the State Bar of New Mexico shall be governed by the Rules Governing Paralegal Services (Rules 20-101 et seq. NMRA, as the same may be amended).

FIGURE 2.3   State Bar of New Mexico, Canon of Ethics for Paralegal Division

CHAPTER SUMMARY

Ethical questions permeate our society and are reflected in the laws enacted by our legislative bodies and the decisions of our judges and executive branch officials. Ethics is the study of morality and is a branch of the larger field of philosophy. Philosophers disagree about many things, including whether ethical judgments about right and wrong can be proven conclusively, whether "goodness or badness" is dependent on aftermaths, and whether there is such a thing as an "unjust" law. Because people differ in their moral beliefs, we have seen an ongoing ethical debate in this country as to where to draw the line between the right of individual choice and the right of society to promote a common morality. This chapter discussed codes of ethics and rules of professional responsibility. Readers also saw that establishing objective rules to govern complex ethical problems is often a difficult undertaking. We saw one contemporary example of this in conjunction with the financing of judicial elections in West Virginia. It is hard to draft objective rules that tell a sitting judge who has accepted campaign contributions precisely when recusal is required to ensure judicial impartiality and avoid the possibility of bias. Justice Kennedy explained that in some circumstances the likelihood of bias is clear and a constitutional remedy is re-

quired. Kennedy and a majority of Supreme Court justices believed *Caperton v. Massey* was such a case.

But in providing a new Due Process Clause–based remedy in *Caperton,* the Court essentially opened Pandora's Box. They made it likely that future U.S. Supreme Court justices will find it difficult to draw clear-cut ethical lines. Because many states require that judges be elected, judicial candidates have difficult decisions to make as they attempt to fund their campaigns without creating the appearance of being biased in favor of large donors and without compromising their impartiality should they be elected to office.

CHAPTER QUESTIONS

1. Michael and Patricia Sewak bought a house from Charles and Hope Lockhart. Prior to the sale, the Lockharts had employed a contractor for $12,000 to renovate their basement. Somehow, the main structural support that held up the house was removed during the renovations. Shortly after moving in, the Sewaks noticed that the kitchen floor was not level, that doors were not in alignment, and that the first and second floors were sagging. They hired a consultant, who investigated and determined that the support column was missing and that an illegal jack, found in the back of a heater closet, was used to provide the needed structural support. The consultant predicted that the absence of the structural column would ultimately result in the collapse of the house. The Sewaks filed suit, alleging fraud and a violation of the Pennsylvania Unfair Trade Practices and Consumer Protection Law (UTPCPL). The Sewaks maintained that the Lockharts should have informed them that the support column had been removed. The trial evidence, according to the appellate court, permitted the jury to find that the Lockharts not only had knowledge of the column's removal, but also took steps to conceal its replacement with the illegal jack, and that they had not obtained the proper building permits before undertaking the renovations.

Did the Lockharts act ethically in their dealings with the Sewaks? Should the law impose a legal duty on the Sewaks to investigate and discover the absence of the structural support column for themselves?

Sewak v. Lockhart, 699 A.2d 755 (1997)

2. Jonas Yoder and Wallace Miller, members of the Amish religion, withdrew their daughters, Frieda Yoder and Barbara Miller, from school after they had completed the eighth grade. This refusal violated a Wisconsin compulsory school attendance law that required Frieda and Barbara to be in school until their sixteenth birthdays. The U.S. Supreme Court ruled that the Amish parents had a constitutionally protected right to control the religious education of their children under the First and Fourteenth Amendments. The Court's majority concluded that to require the children to attend public high school would undermine fundamental Amish values and religious freedoms. Frieda and Barbara were not parties to the lawsuit, and there is no record as to their positions on the issue in this case. Given the Supreme Court's holding in *Wisconsin v. Yoder,* what posture should the law take in a situation where Amish children desire to attend high school over the objections of their parents?

Wisconsin v. Yoder, 406 U.S. 205 (1972)

3.   Raymond Dirks worked for a New York City broker–dealer firm. He specialized in analyzing insurance company investments. Dirks received a tip from Ronald Secrist, a former officer of Equity Funding of America (an insurance company), that Equity Funding had fraudulently overstated its assets. Dirks decided to investigate. Although neither Dirks nor his employer traded in Equity Funding shares, he told others in the securities industry about the tip, and soon thereafter Equity Funding's shares dropped precipitously in value. The Securities and Exchange Commission (SEC) investigated Dirk's role in disclosing the existence of the fraud and charged him with being a "tippee" who had aided and abetted violations of the Securities Act of 1933. This statute makes it illegal for persons with inside knowledge (nonpublic information) to take unfair advantage of a company's shareholders by trading in the affected securities before the news has become public. Can you make an argument supporting the conclusion that it was unethical for Dirks to share the information he obtained from Secrist with other people in the industry? Can you make an argument that Dirk's conduct was not unethical?

Dirks v. Securities and Exchange Commission, 463 U.S. 646 (1983)

4.   Three separate federal suits were brought by gay men and lesbians who had been discharged from their jobs. One plaintiff, a schoolteacher, alleged that his firing was because he wore an earring to school. The second suit was brought by two lesbians who alleged that they were terminated from their jobs because of their sexual orientation. The third suit was filed by three homosexual plaintiffs who alleged that they were in one case denied employment and in two cases fired from employment because their employer had a corporate policy of not employing homosexuals. The U.S. District Court dismissed the complaints on the grounds that Title VII does not protect employees from discharges based on effeminacy or homosexuality. The U.S. Court of Appeals affirmed the decision of the District Court. Does the fact that two federal courts ruled that the plaintiffs were not entitled to legal relief affect the ethical merits of their claims?

De Santis v. Pacific Tel. & Tel. Co., Inc., 608 F.2d 327 (1979)

5.   In many regions of the country, it is customary for schools to take a break for school vacations during February. Many families arrange their schedules so that families can take special trips to remote destinations. The airlines are beneficiaries of this tradition, and flights to popular vacation spots are often totally booked. In 1999, airline pilots involved in collective bargaining disputes with their employer engaged in a "sick-out" during the school vacation period. Analyze this scenario from the *egoist* perspective.

6.   The Massachusetts Supreme Judicial Court has interpreted a statute to require injured skiers who wish to sue ski area operators to give the operators notice of the skier's claims within 90 days of the injury and comply with a one-year statute of limitations. Failure to give timely notice of the claims will preclude bringing the suit at all. Both the court majority and the dissenting justices attributed these unusually short limitations to bringing actions to a legislative policy. Both concluded that the legislature evidently placed a higher value on the economic vitality of the Massachusetts ski industry than on the rights of injured skiers to seek recoveries in tort and contract from ski area operators. Analyze this case from a *utilitarian* perspective.

Atkins v. Jiminy Peak, Inc. 514 N.E.2d 850 (1987)

NOTES

1. See *Macomber v. Dillman* in Chapter VI.

2. *See Atkins v. Jiminy Peak, Inc., in* Chapter V.

3. You can find this case on the Internet. The case citation is *Furman v. Georgia,* 408 U.S. 238 (1972).

4. Telling a lie about a material fact while under oath is a crime called perjury. Theft by false pretense is another crime that is based on a fraudulent, actual, factual misrepresentation. In contracts, fraud in the formation of an agreement can result in rescission and an award of damages to the injured party.

5. R. N. Hancock, *Twentieth Century Ethics* (New York: Columbia University Press, 1974), p. 2.

6. An example is the debate about whether the concept we call "good" is composed of parts or is essentially indefinable. G. E. Moore, *Principia Ethica* (Cambridge, England: University Printing House, 1976) (1903).

7. J. Rachels, *The Elements of Moral Philosophy,* 2d ed. (New York: McGraw-Hill, 1986), pp. 8–14.

8. Hancock, p. 12.

9. Ibid., p. 12.

10. Rachels, pp. 12–24.

11. You will recall from Chapter I, for example, that utilitarians sought to produce the greatest good for the greatest number of people. This kind of calculation can only be undertaken by examining aftermaths.

12. Carol Gilligan and Jane Attanucci maintain that all people think about the morality of their relations with others from two perspectives. One perspective is based on a concern for treating people fairly, which they call the "justice perspective," and the other focuses on responding to persons who are in need, which they call the "care perspective." The authors suggested that males are more oriented toward concerns for "justice" and females toward "caring." See C. Gilligan et al., *Mapping the Moral Domain* (Cambridge, MA: Harvard University Graduate School of Education, 1988), Chapter IV.

13. I. Kant, *Groundwork of the Metaphysics of Morals* (1785), Chapter I. http://www.gutenberg.org/etext/5682

14. *Egoism* (Benedict Spinoza, 1632–1677): "The virtues that ethics seeks to inculcate are the qualities we require to have personally fulfilled lives." These, he said, included "courage, temperance, harmonious, cooperative and stable relations with others."

15. Under Article VI's Supremacy Clause, the federal Constitution is the ultimate authority as to matters arising under it, but the state constitutions are the ultimate authority as to matters that do not amount to federal questions.

16. *Boston Globe*, October 16, 1998, p. A17.

17. Note that these facts parallel the facts in the Unabomber case, and that Ted Kaczynski's brother did tell authorities of his suspicions, he did receive a large cash reward, and he gave it all to charity.

18. P. Devlin, "Morals and the Criminal Law," in *The Enforcement of Morals* (Oxford: Oxford University Press, 1965), pp. 9–10.

19. David Millon refers to this as a dispute between the "contractarians" and the "communitarians." See D. Millon, "Communitarians, Contractarians, and the Crisis in Corporate Law," 50 *Washington & Lee Law Review* 1373 (1993).

20. See J. Nesteruk, "Law, Virtue, and the Corporation," 33 *American Business Journal* 473 (1996).

21. For a brief and critical history of the development of bar associations, see H. Abadinsky, *Law and Justice* (Chicago: Nelson-Hall, 1991), p. 102.

22. The New Jersey Supreme Court in 1999 rejected its own Committee on Paralegal Education's recommendation that the state supreme court adopt "a court directed licensing system." The New Jersey high court indicated that it supported in principle "the creation of a Code of Conduct for Paralegals," but thought that this should be produced by "paralegals and attorneys and their respective associations." New Jersey Supreme Court Press Release of May 24, 1999.

III

Institutional Sources of American Law

CHAPTER OBJECTIVES

1. *Identify the primary sources of American law.*
2. *Summarize each source's formal role in the making of American law.*
3. *Explain important aspects of our federal form of government such as federal supremacy, the police power of the states, full faith and credit, and conflict-of-laws rules.*
4. *Explain the judicial doctrine known as stare decisis.*
5. *Describe the fundamental differences between civil law and common law legal systems.*

It is important to understand that the rules constituting American law derive from several authoritative sources. The most important of these are the federal and state constitutions; legislation produced at the federal, state, and local levels of government; decisions of federal and state courts; and regulations and adjudicatory rulings of federal, state, and local administrative agencies. In this chapter we preview each of these major sources of law and focus on the legislative and judicial branches of government.

COMMON LAW AND CIVIL LAW LEGAL SYSTEMS

From your reading of Chapter I, you have already seen how the English common law system developed over many centuries.[1] You know that as judges decided cases, rules slowly evolved and became recognized as judicial precedents, which began to be written down and followed. These practices made it possible for cases raising a particular issue to be decided in essentially the same way throughout England. With its emphasis on judge-made law, this approach differs markedly from the legal systems found in France, Germany, and Italy. Those countries follow a different approach, often referred to as the civil law system.[2]

Civil law systems are based upon detailed legislative codes rather than judicial precedents. Such a code is a comprehensive, authoritative collection of rules covering all the principal subjects of law. Civil law codes are often developed by academicians and then enacted by legislative bodies. They are based on philosophy, theory, and abstract principles. Civil law systems usually reject the use of precedent, dispense with juries in civil cases, and avoid complex rules of evidence. In civil law countries, judges are expected to base their decisions on the appropriate provisions of the relevant code, and they do not treat the decisions of other judges as authoritative sources.

The civil law tradition traces its roots to historically famous codes of law such as ancient Rome's **Corpus Juris Civilis** and France's **Code Napoleon.** At present, Europe, Central and South America, the Province of Quebec, and the former French colonies of Africa have adopted the civil law system.

Although the common law system has had much more impact on American law, the civil law system has been of increasing influence. For example, early nineteenth-century American legislatures wanted to replace the complex and ponderous system of common law pleading, and reformers campaigned in favor of replacing the traditional reliance on judge-made law with legislated codes. Today, codes of civil procedure regulate litigation in all federal and state courts. Many states have taken a similar approach with respect to probate law, criminal law, and commercial law. State legislatures in forty-nine states, for example, have adopted the Uniform Commercial Code to replace the common law with respect to the sale of goods. (Louisiana is the holdout.)

CONSTITUTIONS

The United States in its Constitution has adopted a federal form of government. Like the federal government, each of the fifty states is sovereign with a written constitution and legislative, executive, and judicial branches of government. The written constitution is the fundamental source of the rule of law within each jurisdiction. It creates a framework for the exercise of governmental power and allocates responsibility among the branches of government. It authorizes and restrains the exercise of governmental authority, protects fundamental rights, and provides an orderly vehicle for legal change. Laws and governmental actions that violate its terms are unconstitutional.

The U.S. Constitution grants certain powers to the federal government in Article I, such as the right to regulate interstate commerce, operate post offices, declare war, and coin money. The states, however, retain many important powers and can implement significant change by enacting statutes and by amending their state constitutions. A strength of our federal form of government is that states can innovate and experiment without having to obtain permission from other states. Nebraska's constitution, for example, provides for a unicameral legislature (the only state to do so); Oregon's laws provide persons who are terminally ill with the option of physician-assisted suicide; Vermont was the first state to legalize civil unions; and Massachusetts was the first state to issue marriage licenses to same-sex couples. Because of federalism, it is not unusual for states to provide their residents with greater substantive and procedural protections as a matter of state law than are required by the U.S. Constitution.

LEGISLATION

To maintain social harmony, society needs uniformly operating rules of conduct. The responsibility for determining the rules lies primarily with legislative bodies. The legislative branch creates law by enacting statutes. An examination of legislation reveals the problems and moods of the nation. Legislatures write history through the legislative process. There have been legislative reactions to almost all political, social, and business problems that have faced society. Laws have been passed in response to wars, depressions, civil rights problems, crime, and concern for cities and the environment. Checks and balances have been built into the system in order to prevent overreaction by the legislature and to promote wise and timely legislation.

The process of enacting statutes is lengthy and complex. At the federal level, it is a procedure that involves 535 persons in the House and Senate who represent the interests of their constituents, themselves, and the country. A proposed bill may encounter numerous obstacles. Mere approval by the legislative bodies does not ensure passage, for at both federal and state levels the executive branch has the power to veto a bill. Another check on legislation can come once a bill becomes law. At that point, the constitutionality of the legislative act may be challenged in court.

With the exception of bills for raising revenue, which must originate in the House (Article I, Section 7 of the Constitution), it makes no difference in which body a bill is introduced, because a statute must be approved by both houses of the legislature. However, the legislative process varies slightly between the Senate and House. If differences exist between the House and Senate versions of a bill, a joint conference committee meets to reconcile the conflicts and draft a compromise bill.

After a bill has been approved by both houses and certain formalities have been completed, it must be approved and signed by the president of the United States to become effective. If the president vetoes a bill—which rarely occurs—it does not become law unless the veto is overridden by a two-thirds vote of both houses.

Defeat of a bill is far more common than passage. More than 95 percent of all legislation introduced is defeated at some point. Still, much legislation *is* signed into law each year. Legislative death can result at any stage of the process, and from many sources. For legislation to be successful in passing, assignment to the proper committee is crucial. However, committees can be cruel. They may refuse to hold hearings. They may alter a bill completely. Or they may kill it outright. If a proposed statute survives the committee stage, the House Rules Committee or the Senate majority leader determines the bill's destiny. Once a bill reaches the floor of the House or Senate, irrelevant proposals—known as riders—may be added to it. Or drastic amendments can so alter it that it is defeated. The possibilities are almost endless.

The need for certainty and uniformity in the laws among the states is reflected in federal legislation and uniform state laws. A great degree of uniformity has been accomplished among the states on a number of matters. An important example is the **Uniform Commercial Code (UCC).** With increased interstate business operations, business firms pressured for uniform laws dealing with commercial transactions among states. Judges, law professors, and leading members of the bar drafted the UCC for adoption by the individual states. The UCC was first adopted by the Pennsylvania legislature in 1953, and it has now been adopted at least partially in all fifty states. The UCC covers sales and leasehold interests in goods, commercial paper, bank collection processes, letters of credit, bulk transfers, warehouse receipts, bills of lading, other documents of title, investment securities, and secured transactions.

The Role of Legislatures

Legislative bodies are organized in accordance with the provisions of the U.S. and state constitutions, and are entrusted with wide-ranging responsibilities and powers. These powers include enacting laws, raising taxes, conducting investigations, holding hearings, and determining how public money will be appropriated. Legislatures play a major role in determining public policy. It is widely understood,

Article I, Section 8 of the U.S. Constitution

The Congress shall have the power ...

3. To regulate commerce with foreign nations, and among the several states, and with the Indian tribes ...

F I G U R E 3.1   The Commerce Clause

however, that today's legislatures actually share policymaking duties with the executive and judicial branches and with administrative agencies.

The Federal Government's Power to Legislate

The federal government cannot exercise any authority that is not granted to it by the Constitution, either expressly or by implication. The U.S. Constitution, in Article I, Section 8, and in authorizing sections contained in various constitutional amendments, enumerates the powers granted to the Congress (see Figure 3.1 above). The powers that the Constitution delegates to the federal government are comprehensive and complete. They are limited only by the Constitution. The power to regulate interstate commerce is one of the most important of the expressly delegated powers.

From 1900 until 1937, the U.S. Supreme Court often followed a formalistic approach in its interpretations of the Commerce Clause. The justices severely limited the scope of this clause in a series of controversial cases. The Court, for example, rejected Congress's claim that Article I, Section 8, permitted the federal government to address problems resulting from indirect as well as direct impacts on interstate commerce,[3] and it defined interstate commerce very narrowly in cases in which Congress sought to regulate mining,[4] protect workers wishing to join labor unions,[5] and discourage the use of child labor in factories.[6]

The Supreme Court reversed its direction in 1937 and began to defer to Congress in cases where a rational connection existed between the legislation and commerce.

The Court often used the Necessary and Proper Clause in conjunction with the Commerce Clause to justify extensions of federal authority.[7] In one case it upheld a federal act that was jurisdictionally based on indirect effects on interstate commerce, and that authorized the use of injunctions against companies engaging in unfair labor practices,[8] and in a second case it upheld minimum wage legislation.[9] The continued viability of the "deferential" standard was called into question because of the Court's decision in *United States v. Lopez,* a case in which the U.S. Supreme Court ruled that Congress did not have authority under the Commerce Clause to enact the Gun-Free School Zones Act of 1990.

In 2012 the U.S, Supreme Court decided the case of *National Federation of Independent Business v. Kathleen Sebelius.* This case required the Court to determine whether Congress had the constitutional authority to establish an individual mandate within the Patient Protection and Affordable Care Act (ACA, although more popularly known as "Obamacare"). The government's position was that Congress had authority pursuant to the Constitution's Commerce and Necessary and Proper Clauses to statutorily mandate that individuals purchase health insurance policies. The Act did not excuse from participation individuals who did not want to participate in this program. Opponents of the legislation maintained that the government could not constitutionally mandate that someone had to purchase this insurance against his or her will.

The Supreme Court's associate justices were divided 4-4 on this issue. It was up to Chief Justice Roberts to cast the critical fifth vote, and he sided with the government. Although the Chief Justice agreed with Justices Ginsburg, Breyer, Sotomayor, and Kagan that Congress had constitutional authority to enact this mandate pursuant to the government's power to tax, he also agreed with the four dissenting justices (Justices Scalia, Kennedy, Thomas, and Alito) that there was no such authority under the Commerce and Necessary and Proper Clauses.

Chief Justice Roberts explained his reasoning in the excerpt from his opinion that follows this introduction. Because the Court found the Affordable Care Act to be constitutional and within Congress's power to tax, the discussion of the Commerce and Necessary and Proper Clauses was technically **dictum** (a judge's extraneous statement in an opinion that addresses legal issues unnecessary to deciding the case then before the court). The fact that five U.S. Supreme Court justices believe that Congress's powers to legislate based on the Commerce and Necessary and Proper Clauses should be limited does not have any direct legal significance and does not establish any legal precedent (a topic addressed later in this chapter). It will, however, have considerable informal significance beyond the judiciary and will influence the executive and legislative branches of the government and members of the bar. This opinion undoubtedly will encourage the filing of other lawsuits where one of the parties can claim that Congress has exceeded its constitutional authority.

The following edited excerpt is from Part III–A of Chief Justice Roberts's opinion in *National Federation of Independent Business v. Kathleen Sebelius.*

National Federation of Independent Business v. Kathleen Sebelius
567 U. S. ___ (2012)
Supreme Court of the United States
June 28, 2012

Chief Justice Roberts announced the judgment of the Court and delivered the opinion of the Court with respect to Parts I, II, and III–C, an opinion with respect to Part IV, in which Justice Breyer and Justice Kagan join, and an opinion with respect to Parts III–A, III–B, and III–D.

III

A
The Government's first argument is that the individual mandate is a valid exercise of Congress's power under the Commerce Clause and the Necessary and Proper Clause....

... By requiring that individuals purchase health insurance, the mandate prevents cost-shifting by those who would otherwise go without it. In addition, the mandate forces into the insurance risk pool more healthy individuals, whose premiums on average will be higher than their health care expenses. This allows insurers to subsidize the costs of covering the unhealthy individuals the reforms require them to accept. The Government claims that Congress has power under the Commerce and Necessary and Proper Clauses to enact this solution.

1
The Government contends that the individual mandate is within Congress's power because the failure to purchase insurance "has a substantial and deleterious effect on interstate commerce" by creating the cost-shifting problem.... The path of our Commerce Clause decisions has not always run smooth ..., but it is now well established that Congress has broad authority under the Clause. We have recognized, for example, that "[t]he power of Congress over interstate commerce is not confined to the regulation of commerce among the states," but extends to activities that "have a substantial effect on interstate commerce." ... Congress's power, moreover, is not limited to regulation of an activity that by itself substantially affects interstate commerce, but also extends to activities that do so only when aggregated with similar activities of others....

Given its expansive scope, it is no surprise that Congress has employed the commerce power in a wide variety of ways to address the pressing needs of the time. But Congress has never attempted to rely on that power to compel individuals not engaged in commerce to purchase an unwanted product.... Legislative novelty is not necessarily fatal; there is a first time for everything. But sometimes "the most telling indication of [a] severe constitutional problem ... is the lack of historical precedent" for Congress's action.... At the very least, we should "pause to consider the implications of the Government's arguments" when confronted with such new conceptions of federal power....

The Constitution grants Congress the power to "regulate Commerce." Art. I, §8, cl. 3 (emphasis added). The power to regulate commerce presupposes the existence of commercial activity to be regulated. If the power to "regulate" something included the power to create it, many of the provisions in the Constitution would be superfluous. For example, the Constitution gives Congress the power to "coin Money," in addition to the power to "regulate the Value thereof." ... And it gives Congress the power to "raise and support Armies" and to "provide and maintain a Navy," in addition to the power to "make Rules for the Government and Regulation of the land and naval Forces." ... If the power to regulate the armed forces or the value of money included the power to bring the subject of the regulation into existence, the specific grant of such powers would have been unnecessary. The language of the Constitution reflects the natural understanding that the power to regulate assumes there is already something to be regulated....

Our precedent also reflects this understanding. As expansive as our cases construing the scope of the commerce power have been, they all have one thing in common: They uniformly describe the power as reaching "activity." ... The individual mandate, however, does not regulate existing commercial activity. It instead compels individuals to become active in commerce by purchasing a product, on the ground that their failure to do so affects interstate commerce. Construing the Commerce Clause to permit Congress to regulate individuals precisely because they are doing nothing would open a new and potentially vast domain to congressional authority. Every day individuals do not do an infinite number of things. In some cases they decide not to do something; in others they simply fail to do it. Allowing Congress to justify federal regulation by pointing to the effect of inaction on commerce would bring countless decisions an individual could potentially make within the scope of federal regulation, and—under the Government's theory—empower Congress to make those decisions for him.

Applying the Government's logic to the familiar case of Wickard v. Filburn shows how far that logic would carry us from the notion of a government of limited powers. In Wickard, the Court famously upheld a federal penalty imposed on a farmer for growing wheat for consumption on his own farm.... That amount of wheat caused the farmer to exceed his quota under a program designed to support the price of wheat by limiting supply. The Court rejected the farmer's argument that growing wheat for home consumption was beyond the reach of the commerce power. It did so on the ground that the farmer's decision to grow wheat for his own use allowed him to avoid purchasing wheat in the market. That decision, when considered in the aggregate along with similar decisions of others, would have had a substantial effect on the interstate market for wheat....

Wickard has long been regarded as "perhaps the most far reaching example of Commerce Clause authority over intrastate activity," ... but the Government's theory in this case would go much further. Under Wickard it is within Congress's power to regulate the market for wheat by supporting its price. But price can be supported by increasing demand as well as by decreasing supply. The aggregated decisions of some consumers not to purchase wheat have a substantial effect on the price of wheat, just as decisions not to purchase health insurance have on the price of insurance. Congress can therefore command that those not buying wheat do so, just as it argues here that it may command that those not buying health insurance do so. The farmer in Wickard was at least actively engaged in the production of wheat, and the Government could regulate that activity because of its effect on commerce. The Government's theory here would effectively override that limitation, by establishing that individuals may be regulated under the Commerce Clause whenever enough of them are not doing something the Government would have them do.

Indeed, the Government's logic would justify a mandatory purchase to solve almost any problem.... To consider a different example in the health care market, many Americans do not eat a balanced diet. That group makes up a larger percentage of the total population than those without health insurance.... The failure of that group to have a healthy diet increases health care costs, to a greater extent than the failure of the uninsured to purchase insurance. See, e.g., Finkelstein, Trogdon, Cohen, & Dietz, Annual Medical Spending Attributable to Obesity: Payer- and Service-Specific Estimates, ... (detailing the "undeniable link between rising rates of obesity and rising medical spending," and estimating that "the annual medical burden of obesity has risen to almost 10 percent of all medical spending and could amount to $147 billion per year in 2008"). Those increased costs are borne in part by other Americans who must pay more, just as the uninsured shift costs to the insured.... Congress addressed the insurance problem by ordering everyone to buy insurance. Under the Government's theory, Congress could address the diet problem by ordering everyone to buy vegetables....

People, for reasons of their own, often fail to do things that would be good for them or good for society. Those failures—joined with the similar failures of others—can readily have a substantial effect on interstate commerce. Under the Government's logic, that authorizes Congress to use its commerce power to compel citizens to act as the Government would have them act.

That is not the country the Framers of our Constitution envisioned. James Madison explained that the Commerce Clause was "an addition which few oppose and from which no apprehensions are entertained." ... While Congress's authority under the Commerce

Clause has of course expanded with the growth of the national economy, our cases have "always recognized that the power to regulate commerce, though broad indeed, has limits." ... The Government's theory would erode those limits, permitting Congress to reach beyond the natural extent of its authority, "everywhere extending the sphere of its activity and drawing all power into its impetuous vortex." ... Congress already enjoys vast power to regulate much of what we do. Accepting the Government's theory would give Congress the same license to regulate what we do not do, fundamentally changing the relation between the citizen and the Federal Government....

To an economist, perhaps, there is no difference between activity and inactivity; both have measurable economic effects on commerce. But the distinction between doing something and doing nothing would not have been lost on the Framers, who were "practical statesmen," not metaphysical philosophers.... The Framers gave Congress the power to regulate commerce, not to compel it, and for over 200 years both our decisions and Congress's actions have reflected this understanding. There is no reason to depart from that understanding now.

The Government sees things differently. It argues that because sickness and injury are unpredictable but unavoidable, "the uninsured as a class are active in the market for health care, which they regularly seek and obtain." ... The individual mandate "merely regulates how individuals finance and pay for that active participation—requiring that they do so through insurance, rather than through attempted self-insurance with the back-stop of shifting costs to others."...

The Government repeats the phrase "active in the market for health care" throughout its brief, ... but that concept has no constitutional significance.... The phrase "active in the market" cannot obscure the fact that most of those regulated by the individual mandate are not currently engaged in any commercial activity involving health care, and that fact is fatal to the Government's effort to "regulate the uninsured as a class."... Our precedents recognize Congress's power to regulate "class[es] of activities," ... not classes of individuals, apart from any activity in which they are engaged....

The individual mandate's regulation of the uninsured as a class is, in fact, particularly divorced from any link to existing commercial activity. The mandate primarily affects healthy, often young adults who are less likely to need significant health care and have other priorities for spending their money. It is precisely because these individuals, as an actuarial class, incur relatively low health care costs that the mandate helps counter the effect of forcing insurance companies to cover others who impose greater costs than their premiums are allowed to reflect....

The Government, however, claims that this does not matter. The Government regards it as sufficient to trigger Congress's authority that almost all those who are uninsured will, at some unknown point in the future, engage in a health care transaction. Asserting that "[t]here is no temporal limitation in the Commerce Clause," the Government argues that because "[e]veryone subject to this regulation is in or will be in the health care market," they can be "regulated in advance."...

The proposition that Congress may dictate the conduct of an individual today because of prophesied future activity finds no support in our precedent. We have said that Congress can anticipate the effects on commerce of an economic activity. See, e.g., ... *Heart of Atlanta Motel, Inc. v. United States*, ... (1964) (prohibiting discrimination by hotel operators); *Katzenbach v. McClung*, ... (1964) (prohibiting discrimination by restaurant owners). But we have never permitted Congress to anticipate that activity itself in order to regulate individuals not currently engaged in commerce....

The Government argues that the individual mandate can be sustained ... because health insurance is a unique product. According to the Government, upholding the individual mandate would not justify mandatory purchases of items such as cars or broccoli because, as the Government puts it, "[h]ealth insurance is not purchased for its own sake like a car or broccoli; it is a means of financing health-care consumption and covering universal risks." ... But cars and broccoli are no more purchased for their "own sake" than health insurance. They are purchased to cover the need for transportation and food.

... The individual mandate forces individuals into commerce precisely because they elected to refrain from commercial activity. Such a law cannot be sustained under a clause authorizing Congress to "regulate Commerce."

2

The Government next contends that Congress has the power under the Necessary and Proper Clause to enact the individual mandate because the mandate is an "integral part of a comprehensive scheme of economic regulation"— the guaranteed-issue and community-rating insurance reforms.... Under this argument, it is not necessary to consider the effect that an individual's inactivity may have on interstate commerce; it is enough that Congress regulate commercial activity in a way that requires regulation of inactivity to be effective.

The power to "make all Laws which shall be necessary and proper for carrying into Execution" the powers enumerated in the Constitution, Art. I, §8, cl. 18, vests Congress with authority to enact provisions "incidental to the [enumerated] power, and conducive to its beneficial exercise,".... Although the Clause gives Congress authority to "legislate on that vast mass of incidental powers which must be involved in the constitution," it does not license the exercise of any "great substantive and independent power[s]" beyond those specifically enumerated.... Instead, the Clause is " 'merely a declaration, for the removal of all uncertainty, that the means of carrying into execution those [powers] otherwise granted are included in the grant.' "...

Applying these principles, the individual mandate cannot be sustained under the Necessary and Proper Clause as an essential component of the insurance reforms. Each of our prior cases upholding laws under that Clause involved exercises of authority derivative of, and in service to, a granted power.... The individual mandate, by contrast, vests Congress with the extraordinary ability to create the necessary predicate to the exercise of an enumerated power.

This is in no way an authority that is "narrow in scope,".... Rather, such a conception of the Necessary and Proper Clause would work a substantial expansion of federal authority. No longer would Congress be limited to regulating under the Commerce Clause those who by some preexisting activity bring themselves within the sphere of federal regulation. Instead, Congress could reach beyond the natural limit of its authority and draw within its regulatory scope those who otherwise would be outside of it. Even if the individual mandate is "necessary" to the Act's insurance reforms, such an expansion of federal power is not a "proper" means for making those reforms effective.

The Government relies primarily on our decision in *Gonzales v. Raich*. In *Raich*, we considered "comprehensive legislation to regulate the interstate market" in marijuana.... Certain individuals sought an exemption from that regulation on the ground that they engaged in only intrastate possession and consumption. We denied any exemption, on the ground that marijuana is a fungible commodity, so that any marijuana could be readily diverted into the interstate market. Congress's attempt to regulate the interstate market for marijuana would therefore have been substantially undercut if it could not also regulate intrastate possession and consumption.... Accordingly, we recognized that "Congress was acting well within its authority" under the Necessary and Proper Clause even though its "regulation ensnare[d] some purely intrastate activity." ... *Raich* thus did not involve the exercise of any "great substantive and independent power," ... of the sort at issue here. Instead, it concerned only the constitutionality of "individual applications of a concededly valid statutory scheme."...

Just as the individual mandate cannot be sustained as a law regulating the substantial effects of the failure to purchase health insurance, neither can it be upheld as a "necessary and proper" component of the insurance reforms. The commerce power thus does not authorize the mandate. Accord, ... (joint opinion of SCALIA, KENNEDY, THOMAS, and ALITO, JJ., dissenting).

Case Questions

1. Exactly what aspect of the ACA individual mandate requirement is impermissible under the Commerce Clause according to the Chief Justice?
2. Why does Chief Justice Roberts feel it so important to prohibit Congress from enacting legislation such as the ACA? What were his concerns?
3. Do you agree with the Chief Justice that "cars and broccoli are no more purchased for their 'own sake' than health insurance. They are purchased to cover the need for transportation and food"?

THE DEBATE OVER THE ACA, THE COMMERCE CLAUSE, AND BROCCOLI

A short summary of Justice Ginsburg's concurring and dissenting opinion, which was joined in by Justice Sotomayor and in part by Justices Breyer and Kagan (only as to the use of the Commerce Clause to require most individuals to purchase insurance). Justice Ginsburg disagreed with Chief Justice Roberts and Justices Kennedy, Scalia, Thomas, and Alito (her "opposing colleagues") over whether Congress had authority pursuant to the Commerce and Necessary and Proper Clauses to require most people to purchase health insurance when it enacted the ACA.

Justice Ginsburg began her opinion by using the term "the minimum coverage" requirement when referring to the ACA provision that obliges most people to purchase health insurance. She rejected Chief Justice Roberts's term, the "individual mandate." She also rejected her opposing colleagues' major argument, which was that Congress had no Commerce Clause authority to require people to purchase health insurance against their will. Justice Ginsburg argued that U.S. Supreme Court precedents had established Congress's broad authority to regulate interstate commerce. She commented that the "Chief Justice's crabbed reading of the Commerce Clause harks back to the era in which the Court routinely thwarted Congress's efforts to regulate the national economy in the interest of those who labor to sustain it." She emphasized the incredible size of the health care market and how likely it is that almost all those who live in this country at some point will need such services. The justice pointed out that an estimated 50 million people are without health insurance and that 60 percent of them will obtain health care for which they will be unable to pay—they will get a "free ride." She also cited data that showed that the medical care industry went uncompensated for $43 billion worth of care in 2008 and that this sum was passed along to everyone who does have health insurance.

Justice Ginsburg pointed out that the health care problem cannot be solved at the state level because no state can afford to have a health care system that is better than its neighbors' systems. No state wants to see an in-migration of uninsured people looking for health care unavailable to them in the state in which they currently reside. That, she said, would lead to "higher taxes and increased insurance costs" and would "encourage businesses and healthy individuals to leave the State."

The justice summarized the rationale for the ACA thusly:

> … Congress passed the minimum coverage provision as a key component of the ACA to address an economic and social problem that has plagued the Nation for decades: the large number of U. S. residents who are unable or unwilling to obtain health insurance. Whatever one thinks of the policy decision Congress made, it was Congress's prerogative to make it. Reviewed with appropriate deference, the minimum coverage provision, allied to the guaranteed-issue and community-rating prescriptions, should survive mea-

surement under the Commerce and Necessary and Proper Clauses.

According to Justice Ginsburg, "rather than evaluating the constitutionality of the minimum coverage provision in the manner established by our precedents, the Chief Justice relies on a newly minted constitutional doctrine. The commerce power does not, the Chief Justice announces, permit Congress to 'compe[l] individuals to become active in commerce by purchasing a product.'"

The Chief Justice expressed concern about congressional overreaching and postulated that Congress could use the Commerce Clause and the Necessary and Proper Clause to require individuals to eat broccoli so as to lessen the need for cost shifting to others. Justice Ginsburg answered this fear in footnote 9 of her opinion:

> The failure to purchase vegetables in the Chief Justice's hypothetical, then, is *not* what leads to higher health-care costs for others; rather, it is the failure of individuals to maintain a healthy diet, and the resulting obesity, that creates the cost-shifting problem…. Requiring individuals to purchase vegetables is thus several steps removed from solving the problem. The failure to obtain health insurance, by contrast, is the *immediate cause* of the cost-shifting Congress sought to address through the ACA…. Requiring individuals to obtain insurance attacks the source of the problem directly, in a single step.

An excerpt of the portion of the joint dissent authored by Justices Scalia, Kennedy, Thomas, and Alito that discusses the ACA's individual mandate.

> Article I, §8, of the Constitution gives Congress the power to "regulate Commerce … among the several States." The Individual Mandate in the Act commands that every "applicable individual shall for each month beginning after 2013 ensure that the individual, and any dependent of the individual who is an applicable individual, is covered under minimum essential

coverage."... If this provision "regulates" anything, it is the *failure* to maintain minimum essential coverage. One might argue that it regulates that failure by requiring it to be accompanied by payment of a penalty. But that failure—that abstention from commerce—is not "Commerce." To be sure, *purchasing* insurance *is* "Commerce"; but one does not regulate commerce that does not exist by compelling its existence.

In *Gibbons* v. *Ogden*, ... (1824), Chief Justice Marshall wrote that the power to regulate commerce is the power "to prescribe the rule by which commerce is to be governed." That understanding is consistent with the original meaning of "regulate" at the time of the Constitution's ratification, when "to regulate" meant "[t]o adjust by rule, method or established mode," 2 N. Webster, An American Dictionary of the English Language (1828); "[t]o adjust by rule or method," 2 S. Johnson, A Dictionary of the English Language (7th ed. 1785); "[t]o adjust, to direct according to rule," 2 J. Ash, New and Complete Dictionary of the English Language (1775)....

We do not doubt that the buying and selling of health insurance contracts is commerce generally subject to federal regulation. But when Congress provides that (nearly) all citizens must buy an insurance contract, it goes beyond "adjust[ing] by rule or method," ... or "direct[ing] according to rule," ... ; it directs the creation of commerce.

As to Justice Ginsburg's rejection of the broccoli analogy, the joint dissenters said:

> ... [Justice Ginsburg's] dissent dismisses the conclusion that the power to compel entry into the health-insurance market would include the power to compel entry into the ... new-car or broccoli markets. The latter purchasers, it says, "will be obliged to pay at the counter before receiving the vehicle or nourishment," whereas those refusing to purchase health-insurance will ultimately get treated anyway, at others' expense.... "[T]he unique attributes of the health-care market ... give rise to a significant free riding problem that does not occur in other markets." ... And "a vegetable-purchase mandate" (or a car-purchase mandate) is not "likely to have a substantial effect on the health-care costs" borne by other Americans.... Those differences make a very good argument by the dissent's own lights, since they show that the failure to purchase health insurance, unlike the failure to purchase cars or broccoli, creates a national, social-welfare problem that is (in the dissent's view) included among the unenumerated "problems" that the Constitution authorizes the Federal Government to solve. But those differences do not show that the failure to enter the health-insurance market, unlike the failure to buy cars and broccoli, is an *activity* that Congress can "regulate." (Of course one day the failure of some of the public to purchase American cars may endanger the existence of domestic automobile manufacturers; or the failure of some to eat broccoli may be found to deprive them of a newly discovered cancer fighting chemical which only that food contains, producing health-care costs that are a burden on the rest of us—in which case, under the theory of Justice Ginsburg's dissent, moving against those inactivities will also come within the Federal Government's unenumerated problem-solving powers.)

State Government's Power to Legislate

The authority that resides in every sovereignty to pass laws for its internal regulation and government is called **police power.** It is the power inherent in the state to pass reasonable laws necessary to preserve public health, welfare, safety, and morals.

The states, as sovereigns, were exercising the police power prior to the adoption of the federal Constitution, and they never delegated it to the federal government in that Constitution. In fact, the Constitution itself, in the Tenth Amendment, explicitly reserves to the states (or to the people) any power not delegated to the federal government. Although the police power exists without any express limitations in the U.S. Constitution, the federal and state constitutions set limits on its exercise.

The basis of the police power is the state's obligation to protect its citizens and provide for the safety and order of society. This yields a broad, comprehensive authority. The definition of crimes and the regulating of trades and professions are examples of this vast scope of power. A mandatory precondition to the exercise of police power is the existence of an ascertainable public need for a particular statute, and the statute must bear a real and substantial relation to the end that is sought. The possession and enjoyment of all rights may be limited under the police power, provided that it is reasonably exercised.

Limitations on the police power have never been drawn with exactness or determined by a general formula. The power may not be exercised for private purposes or for the exclusive benefit of a few. Its scope has been declared to be greater in emergency situations. Otherwise its exercise must be in the public interest, must be reasonable, and may not be repugnant to the rights implied or secured in the Constitution.

Powers delegated by the federal government and individual state constitutions also serve as a basis for state legislation. Any activity solely attributable to the sovereignty of the state may not be restrained by Congress.

Federal Supremacy

The U.S. Constitution divides powers between the federal government and the states. Certain powers are delegated to the federal government alone. Others are reserved to the states. Still others are exercised concurrently by both. The Tenth Amendment to the Constitution specifies that the "powers not delegated to the United States by the Constitution … are reserved to the states … or to the people." Unlike the federal power, which is granted, the state already has its power, unless expressly or implicitly denied by the state or federal constitutions. Each state has the power to govern its own affairs, except where the Constitution has withdrawn that power. The powers of both the federal and the state governments are to be exercised so as not to interfere with each other's exercise of power. Whenever there is a conflict, state laws must yield to federal acts to the extent of the conflict. This requirement is expressed by the **Supremacy Clause** in Article VI of the Constitution.

Under the Supremacy Clause, Congress can enact legislation that may supersede state authority and preempt state regulations. The preemption doctrine is based on the Supremacy Clause. Hence state laws that frustrate or are contrary to congressional objectives in a specific area are invalid. In considering state law, one takes into account the nature of the subject matter, any vital national interests that may be involved, the need for uniformity between state and federal laws, and the expressed or implied intent of Congress. It is necessary to determine whether Congress has sought to occupy a particular field to the exclusion of the states. All interests, both state and federal, must be examined.

Constitutionality of Statutes

The power to declare legislative acts unconstitutional is the province and the duty of the judiciary, even though there is no express constitutional grant of the power. It is generally presumed that all statutes are constitutional and that a statute will not be invalidated unless the party challenging it clearly shows that it is offensive to either a state or the federal constitution. When a court encounters legislation that it believes to be unconstitutional, it first tries to interpret the statute in a narrow way with what is called a limiting construction. An act of the legislature is declared invalid only as a last resort if it is clearly incompatible with a constitutional provision.

The right and power of the courts to declare whether the legislature has exceeded the constitutional limitations is one of the highest functions of the judiciary. The Supreme Court declared in *Marbury v. Madison,* 5 U.S. (1 Cranch) 137 (1803) that the judicial branch has the power to declare void an act of the legislature that conflicts with the Constitution. The issue of the supremacy of the U.S. Constitution, and the right of individuals to claim protection thereunder whenever they were aggrieved by application of a contrary statute, was decided in *Marbury.* Chief Justice John Marshall wrote the opinion for the Court, stating in part:

> The question, whether an act, repugnant to the Constitution, can become the law of the land, is a question deeply interesting to the United States; but, happily, not of an intricacy proportioned to its interest. It seems only necessary to recognize certain principles, supposed to have been long and well established, to decide it.
>
> That the people have an original right to establish, for their future government, such principles as, in their opinion, shall most conduce to their own happiness, is the basis on which the whole American fabric has been erected. The exercise of this original right is a very great exertion; nor can it, nor ought it, to be frequently repeated. The principles, therefore, so established, are deemed fundamental. And as the authority from which they proceed is supreme, and can seldom act, they are designated to be permanent.
>
> ... It is a proposition too plain to be contested, that the Constitution controls any legislative act repugnant to it; or that the legislature may alter the Constitution by an ordinary act.
>
> Between these alternatives there is no middle ground. The Constitution is either a superior paramount law, unchangeable by ordinary means, or it is on a level with ordinary legislative acts, and, like other acts, is alterable when the legislature shall please to alter it.
>
> If the former part of the alternative be true, then a legislative act, contrary to the Constitution, is not law; if the latter part be true, then written constitutions are absurd attempts, on the part of the people, to limit a power, in its own nature illimitable....
>
> It is, emphatically, the province and duty of the judicial department to say what the law is. Those who apply the rule to particular cases must of necessity expound and interpret that rule. If two laws conflict with each other, the courts must decide on the operation of each.
>
> So, if a law be in opposition to the Constitution; if both the law and the Constitution apply to a particular case, so that the court must either decide that case, conformable to the law, disregarding the Constitution, or conformable to the Constitution, disregarding the law; the court must determine which of the conflicting rules governs the case. This is of the very essence of judicial duty.
>
> If, then, the courts are to regard the Constitution—and the Constitution is superior to any ordinary act of the legislature—the Constitution, and not such ordinary act, must govern the case to which they both apply.

Ex Post Facto Laws and Bills of Attainder

Article I, Section 9 of the federal Constitution prohibits Congress from enacting **ex post facto** laws or **bills of attainder.** The state legislatures are likewise prohibited by Article I, Section 10. An ex post facto law is a law that makes acts criminal that were not criminal at the time they were committed. Statutes that classify a crime more severely than when committed, impose greater punishment, or make proof of guilt easier have also been held to be unconstitutional ex post facto laws. Such laws deprive an accused of a substantial right provided by the law that was in force at the time when the offense was committed.

The Ex Post Facto Clause restricts legislative power and does not apply to the judicial function. The doctrine applies exclusively to criminal or penal statutes. A law's ex post facto impact may not be avoided by disguising criminal punishment in a civil form. When a law imposes punishment for certain activity in both the past and the future, even though it is void for the punishment of past activity, it is valid insofar as the law acts prospectively. A law is not ex post facto if it "mitigates the rigor" of the law or simply reenacts the law in force when the crime was committed.

To determine if a legislative act unconstitutionally punishes past activity, courts examine the intent of the legislature. The court, after examining the text of the law and its legislative history, makes a determination as to whether an act that imposes a present disqualification is, in fact, merely the imposition of a punishment for a past event. The principle governing the inquiry is whether the aim of the legislature was to punish an individual for past activity, or whether a restriction on a person is merely incident to a valid regulation of a present situation, such as the appropriate qualifications for a profession.

A constitutionally prohibited bill of attainder involves the singling out of an individual or group for punishment. Bills of attainder are acts of a legislature that apply either to named individuals or to easily ascertainable members of a group in such a way as to impose punishments on them without a trial. For example, an act of Congress that made it a crime for a member of the Communist Party to serve as an officer of a labor union was held unconstitutional as a bill of attainder (*United States v. Brown*, 381 U.S. 437, 1965).

Statutory Construction

To declare what the law shall be is a legislative power; to declare what the law *is* is a judicial power. The courts are the appropriate body for construing acts of the legislature. Because courts decide only real controversies and not abstract or moot questions, a court does not construe statutory provisions unless doing so is required for the resolution of a case before it. A statute is open to construction only when the language used in the act is ambiguous and requires interpretation. Where the statutory language conveys a clear and definite meaning, there is no occasion to use rules of statutory interpretation.

Courts have developed rules of statutory construction to determine the meaning of legislative acts. For interpreting statutes, the legislative will is the all-important and controlling factor. In theory, the sole object of all rules for interpreting statutes is to discover the legislative intent; every other rule of construction is secondary.

It is the duty of the judiciary in construing criminal statutes to determine whether particular conduct falls within the intended prohibition of the statute. Criminal statutes are enforced by the court if worded so that they clearly convey the nature of the proscribed behavior. Legislation must be appropriately tailored to meet its objectives. Therefore it cannot be arbitrary, unreasonable, or capricious. A court will hold a statute void for vagueness if it does not give a person of ordinary intelligence fair notice that some contemplated conduct is forbidden by the act. The enforcement of a vague statute would encourage arbitrary and erratic arrests and convictions.

Penal statutes impose punishment for offenses committed against the state. They include all statutes that command or prohibit certain acts and establish penalties for their violation. Penal statutes are enacted for the benefit of the public. They should receive a fair and reasonable construction. The words used should be given the meaning commonly attributed to them. Criminal statutes are to be strictly construed, and doubts are to be resolved in favor of the accused. **Strict construction** means that the statute should not be enlarged by implication beyond the fair meaning of the language used. However, the statute should not be construed so as to defeat the obvious intention of the legislature.

A literal interpretation of statutory language can lead to unreasonable, unjust, or even absurd consequences. In such a case, a court is justified in adopting a construction that sustains the validity of the legislative act, rather than one that defeats it.

Courts do not have legislative authority and should avoid "judicial legislation." To depart from the meaning expressed by the words of the statute so as to alter it is not construction—it is legislative alteration. A statute should not be construed more broadly or given greater effect than its terms require. Nothing should be read into a statute that was not intended by the legislature. Courts, however, don't always adhere to the principle.

Statutes are to be read in the light of conditions at the time of their enactment. A new meaning is sometimes given to the words of an old statute because of changed conditions. The scope of a statute may appear to include conduct that did not exist when the statute was enacted—for example, certain activity related to technological progress. Such a case does not preclude the application of the statute thereto.

ADMINISTRATIVE AGENCIES

As we will see in more detail in Chapter XIII, legislative bodies often delegate some of their authority to governmental entities called agencies, boards, authorities, and commissions. Legislatures do this when they lack expertise in an area requiring constant oversight and specialized knowledge. Agencies such as the Environmental Protection Agency; the Securities and Exchange Commission; the boards that license doctors, attorneys, and barbers; and public housing authorities are other examples.

Legislative bodies often permit the agencies to exercise investigative and rulemaking powers. Administrative rules, if promulgated according to law, have the same force as statutes. Some agencies also are delegated authority to conduct adjudicatory hearings before administrative law judges who will determine whether agency rules have been violated.

Judicial Decision Making

The way people today think judges go about making decisions is about the same as it was in 1940. (See the legal realism discussion in Chapter I.)

In theory every judge in this country follows a two-step process when making a decision. The first step requires the judge to examine the facts of a case, research the relevant constitutional and statutory sources, look at the case law for legal precedents (if there are any), and consider any relevant historical practices and principles (such as judicial restraint), as well as philosophical notions of fairness and justice. In step two the judge relies on reasoning to arrive at a logical and fair decision.

Over time and with experience, some appellate court justices become linked with what are called "judicial philosophies." For example, some judges are "strict constructionists," in that they favor literal interpretations of statutes and constitutions. Other judges believe in "judicial restraint" and make it a point to carefully follow precedent and defer to the political branches of government. Judges who interpret constitutions and statutes to mean what they meant when they were originally created favor "original intent."

Biopsychological and Sociocultural Research

Academicians today, as in the past, have engaged in quantitative and qualitative research in an effort to identify other factors that might influence the judicial decision-making process. They study judicial voting patterns and try to learn about the various factors that influence judges.

It is unrealistic to attempt to produce a comprehensive list of the possible sociocultural factors that could influence judicial decisions because there are so many. But here some examples of factors that should be included. It is likely that education (all judges graduate from law school), religion, cultural and ethnic influences, socioeconomic status, and career path both prior to and subsequent to law school are important influences. Judges, like other people, associate with people around them. They have families and friends, join professional and social associations, are members of communities, and may have previous experience in government or may have held partisan offices. They also have opinions, which are often expressed in articles and speeches. These and other factors help to form a person's character and may influence his or her judgment.

Appellate judges, unlike trial court judges, are members of multijudge panels. And researchers often explore how groups of judges interact and influence each other. Some appellate judges establish voting patterns, which makes it possible to say that they tend vote as "members" of a block with respect to one or more types of cases. The members of a block generally dissent together and agree with one another when all of their votes are considered over time.

In recent decades prominent scholars have been focusing on judges as human beings whose "behavior is inescapably the product of both biopsychological and sociocultural influences."[10] The late Glendon Schubert, this textbook author's father, believed that the underlying biopsychological question was "how and why judges (like other human beings) learn, modify, remember (and forget), and sooner or later lose, their values...."[11] Through the use of statistical tools such as Guttman scaling, researchers are learning more about the extent to which biological factors such as gender, aging, and race influence judicial decision making.[12] Biopolitics, although a new subdiscipline within political science, may produce important research findings that help to influence judicial decision making in the future.

Doctrine of Stare Decisis

In this portion of the chapter, we will learn about the use of common law precedents and how judges determine which body of substantive law to apply when the facts of a case involve the laws of more than one state.

One of the most fundamental principles of the common law is the doctrine of **stare decisis.** A doctrine is a policy—in this case a judicial policy that guides courts in making decisions. The doctrine normally requires lower-level courts to follow the legal precedents that have been established by higher-level courts. Following precedent helps to promote uniformity and predictability in judicial decision making. All judges within a jurisdiction

are expected to apply a rule of law the same way until that rule is overturned by a higher court.

Literally, stare decisis means that a court will "stand by its decisions" or those of a higher court. This doctrine originated in England and was used in the colonies as the basis of their judicial decisions.

A decision on an issue of law by a court is followed in that jurisdiction by the same court or by a lower court in a future case presenting the same—or substantially the same—issue of law. A court is not bound by decisions of courts of other states, although such decisions may be considered in the decision-making process. A decision of the U.S. Supreme Court on a federal question is absolutely binding on state courts, as well as on lower federal courts. Similarly, a decision of a state court of final appeal on an issue of state law is followed by lower state courts and federal courts in the state dealing with that issue.

The doctrine of stare decisis promotes continuity, stability, justice, speed, economy, and adaptability within the law. It helps our legal system to provide guidelines so that people can anticipate legal consequences when they decide how to conduct their affairs. It promotes justice by establishing rules that enable many legal disputes to be concluded fairly. It eliminates the need for every proposition in every case to be subject to endless relitigation. Public faith in the judiciary is increased where legal rules are consistently applied and are the product of impersonal and reasoned judgment. In addition, the quality of the law decided on is improved, as more careful and thorough consideration is given to the legal questions than would be the case if the determinations affected only the case before the court.

Stare decisis is not a binding rule, and a court need not feel absolutely bound to follow previous cases. However, courts are not inclined to deviate from it, especially when the precedents have been treated as authoritative law for a long time. The number of decisions announced on a rule of law also has some bearing on the weight of the precedent. When a principle of law established by precedent is no longer appropriate because of changing economic, political, and social conditions, however, courts sometimes recognize this decay and overrule the precedent to reflect what is best for society.

The Holding of the Case

Under the doctrine of stare decisis, only a point of law necessarily decided in a reported judicial opinion is binding on other courts as precedent. A question of fact determined by a court has no binding effect on a subsequent case involving similar questions of fact. The facts of each case are recognized as being unique.

Those points of law decided by a court to resolve a legal controversy constitute the **holding** of the case. In other words, the court holds (determines) that a certain rule of law applies to the particular factual situation present in the case being decided and renders its decision accordingly.

Sometimes, in their opinions, courts make comments that are not necessary to support the decision. These extraneous judicial expressions are referred to as **dictum**. They have no value as precedent because they do not fit the facts of the case. The reason for drawing a distinction between holding and dictum is that only the issues before the court have been argued and fully considered. Even though dictum is not binding under the doctrine of stare decisis, it is often considered persuasive. Other judges and lawyers can determine what the decision makers are thinking and gain an indication of how the problem may be handled in the future.

It is the task of the lawyer and judge to find the decision or decisions that set the precedent for a particular factual situation. In court, lawyers argue about whether a prior case should or should not be recognized as controlling in a subsequent case.

The Ohio Supreme Court had to make such a decision in the following 1969 case. Did the prosecution violate Butler's federal due process rights when it used his voluntary, in-custody statement (which was obtained without prior *Miranda* warnings) to **impeach** his trial testimony? The U.S. Supreme Court had ruled in a 1954 case *(Walder v. United States)* that prosecutors could impeach a testifying defendant with illegally obtained evidence once the defendant had "opened the door" with false testimony. The U.S. Supreme Court's *Miranda v. Arizona* (1966) opinion seemed to suggest that constitutional due process prevented the government from using such statements for any purpose. In *Miranda,* however, the prosecution had used the defendant's statement to prove guilt, not to impeach the defendant's testimony. Butler's lawyer argued to the Ohio Supreme Court that (1) the language contained in *Miranda* applied to impeachment uses, (2) *Miranda* should be recognized as controlling, and (3) Butler's statement was inadmissible. The lawyers for the State of Ohio disagreed. They argued that (1) *Miranda* was not controlling, because Butler's facts were distinguishable from the facts in *Miranda,* (2) the *Walder* case was controlling, and (3) Butler's statement was admissible for purposes of impeachment.

State v. Butler
19 Ohio St. 2d 55, 249 N.E.2d 818
Supreme Court of Ohio
July 9, 1969

Schneider, Justice.
... The offense for which appellant was indicted, tried, and convicted occurred on August 30, 1964. He struck Annie Ruth Sullivan with a jack handle, causing an injury which resulted in loss of sight [in] her left eye. Appellant was apprehended and arrested by the Cincinnati police, and while in custody he was interrogated by police officers. Prior to the questioning, the police gave no explanation to appellant as to his rights to remain silent and have an attorney present. The interrogation was recorded and reduced to writing. Over objection by appellant's counsel, these questions and answers were repeated by the prosecutor at trial to impeach statements made by appellant during cross-examination.

Appellant appeared before the municipal court of Hamilton County on November 22, 1965. Probable cause was found and appellant was bound over to the

Hamilton County grand jury. Bond was set at $500, which appellant posted. The grand jury returned an indictment for the offense of "maiming." Appellant was arraigned and pleaded not guilty, after which the court appointed counsel. Trial was set. A jury was waived and appellant was found guilty by the court of the lesser included offense of aggravated assault. The court of appeals affirmed the judgment of conviction.

Appellant raises [the question in this appeal as to] whether, in cross-examination of a defendant the prosecutor may use prior inconsistent statements of the defendant, made to police without *Miranda* warnings, in order to impeach his credibility....

Appellant's ... contention is that the prosecution violated his Fifth Amendment right against self-incrimination by using statements of his which were made to police during in-custody interrogation with no warning of his right to silence or to counsel.... The United States Supreme Court ... in *Miranda v. Arizona* [1966] ... held there that the prosecution's use of statements of an accused, made to police without prior warnings of his rights to remain silent, to counsel and appointed counsel if indigent, was a violation of the accused's Fourteenth and Fifth Amendment right against self-incrimination....

The appellant took the stand and, on cross-examination by the prosecution, he made assertions as to the facts surrounding the crime. A recorded statement appellant made to a detective after arrest was then read to him to show a prior inconsistent statement. Counsel objected, but the court allowed the statement to be used as evidence to impeach the witness's credibility. Appellant contends that this use of the statements, made without cautionary warnings, violated his Fifth Amendment rights as defined by *Miranda v. Arizona, supra*....

We cannot agree. First, the statements used by the prosecution were not offered by the state as part of its direct case against appellant, but were offered on the issue of his credibility after he had been sworn and testified in his own defense. Second, the statements used by the prosecution were voluntary, no claim to the contrary having been made.

The distinction between admissibility of wrongfully obtained evidence to prove the state's case in chief and its use to impeach the credibility of a defendant who takes the stand was expressed in *Walder v. United States* [1954].... "It is one thing to say that the government cannot make an affirmative use of evidence unlawfully obtained. It is quite another to say that the defendant can turn the illegal method by which evidence in the Government's possession was obtained to his own advantage, and provide himself with a shield against contradiction of his untruths...."

Those words of Justice Frankfurter were uttered in regard to evidence inadmissible under the Fourth Amendment exclusionary rule. In the case of the Fifth Amendment, even greater reason exists to distinguish between statements of an accused used in the prosecution's direct case and used for impeachment in cross-examining the accused when he takes the stand. We must not lose sight of the words of the Fifth Amendment: " ... nor shall be compelled to be a witness against himself...." This is a privilege accorded an accused not to be compelled to testify, nor to have any prior statements used by the prosecution to prove his guilt. We cannot translate those words into a privilege to lie with impunity once he elects to take the stand to testify....

We do not believe that ... *Miranda* ... dictates a conclusion contrary to ours. In *Miranda,* the court indicated that statements of a defendant used to impeach his testimony at trial may not be used unless they were taken with full warnings and effective waiver. However, we note that in all four of the convictions reversed by the decision, statements of the accused, taken without cautionary warnings, were used by the prosecution as direct evidence of guilt in the case in chief.

We believe that the words of Chief Justice Marshall regarding the difference between holding and *dictum* are applicable here. "It is a maxim not to be disregarded, that general expressions, in every opinion, are to be taken in connection with the case in which those expressions are used. If they go beyond the case, they may be respected, but ought not to control the judgment in a subsequent suit when the very point is presented for decision. The reason of this maxim is obvious. The question actually before the court is investigated with care, and considered in its full extent. Other principles which may serve to illustrate it are considered in their relation to the case decided, but their possible bearing on all other cases is seldom completely investigated."...

The court, in *Miranda,* was not faced with the facts of this case. Thus, we do not consider ourselves bound by the *dictum* of *Miranda.*

The "linchpin" (as Mr. Justice Harlan put it ...) of *Miranda* is that police interrogation is destructive of human dignity and disrespectful of the inviolability of the human personality. In the instant case, the use of the interrogation to impeach the voluntary testimony of the accused is neither an assault on his dignity nor disrespectful of his personality. He elected to testify, and cannot complain that the state seeks to demonstrate the lack of truth in his testimony.

Finally, we emphasize that the statements used by the prosecution were voluntarily made. The decision in *Miranda* did not discard the distinction between voluntary and involuntary statements made by an accused and used by the prosecution.... Lack of cautionary warnings is one of the factors to consider in determining whether statements are voluntary or not. However, appellant here has never claimed that the statements used to impeach were involuntary. Thus, we assume they were voluntary, and hold that voluntary statements of an accused made to police without cautionary warnings are admissible on the issue of credibility after defendant has been sworn and testifies in his own defense....

Judgment affirmed.

Duncan, Justice, dissenting.

... The use of statements made by the defendant for impeachment without the warnings set forth in *Miranda v. Arizona* ... having been given, is reversible error.

In *Miranda*, Chief Justice Warren stated ...

The warnings required and the waiver necessary in accordance with our opinion today are, in the absence of a fully effective equivalent, prerequisites to the admissibility of *any statement made by a defendant.* No distinction can be drawn between statements which are direct confessions and statements which amount to 'admissions' of part or all of an offense. The privilege against self-incrimination protects the individual from being compelled to incriminate himself in any manner; it does not distinguish degrees of incrimination. Similarly, for precisely the same reason, *no distinction may be drawn between inculpatory*

statements and statements alleged to be merely 'exculpatory.' If a statement made were in fact truly exculpatory, it would, of course, never be used by the prosecution. *In fact, statements merely intended to be exculpatory by the defendant are often used to impeach his testimony at trial or to demonstrate untruths in the statement given under interrogation and thus to prove guilt by implication.* These statements are incriminating in any meaningful sense of the word and may not be used without the full warnings and effective waiver required for any other statement.... [Emphasis supplied.]

This *specific* reference to impeachment, I believe, forecloses the use of defendant's in-custody statement in the instant case.

The United States Court of Appeals for the Second Circuit ... arrived at a decision contrary to that arrived at by the majority in this case. Judge Bryan ... stated:

"These pronouncements by the Supreme Court may be technically *dictum.* But it is abundantly plain that the court intended to lay down a firm general rule with respect to the use of statements unconstitutionally obtained from a defendant in violation of *Miranda* standards. The rule prohibits the use of such statements whether inculpatory or exculpatory, whether bearing directly on guilt or on collateral matters only, and whether used on direct examination or for impeachment."...

I would reverse.

Case Questions

1. Explain the difference between holding and dictum.
2. Can the holding of a case be broader than the precedent relied on?
3. Why should dictum not be considered binding under the doctrine of stare decisis?
4. Was *Miranda* properly relied on by the majority in the *Butler* case?
5. If this same case had been decided by the United States Court of Appeals for the Second Circuit, would the decision have been different or the same? Why?

Requirements for a Precedent

Only a judicial opinion of the majority of a court on a point of law can have stare decisis effect. A dissent has no precedential value, nor does the fact that an appellate court is split make the majority's decision less of a precedent. When judges are equally divided as to the outcome of a particular

case, no precedent is created by that court. This is true even though the decision affirms the decision of the next-lower court.

In addition, in order to create precedent, the opinion must be reported. A decision by a court without a reported opinion does not have stare decisis effect. In the great majority of cases, no opinion is written. Appellate courts are responsible for practically all the reported opinions, although occasionally a trial judge will issue a written opinion relating to a case tried to the court. Trial judges do not write opinions in jury cases.

Once a reported judicial precedent-setting opinion is found, the effective date of that decision has to be determined. For this purpose, the date of the court decision, not the date of the events that gave rise to the suit, is crucial.

The Retroactive Versus Prospective Application Question

A court has the power to declare in its opinion whether a precedent-setting decision should have retroactive or prospective application. **Retroactive effect** means that the decision controls the legal consequences of some causes of action arising prior to the announcement of the decision. **Prospective effect** means that the new rule will only apply to cases subsequently coming before that court and the lower courts of the jurisdiction. Prior to the U.S. Supreme Court's 1993 decision in *Harper v. Virginia Dep't of Taxation,* the general rule in civil cases was that unless a precedent-setting court had expressly indicated otherwise, or unless special circumstances warranted the denial of retroactive application, an appellate

court decision was entitled to retroactive as well as prospective effect in all actions that were neither **res judicata** (i.e., had been previously decided) nor barred by a **statute of limitations** (meaning the plaintiff's lawsuit cannot go forward because of the plaintiff's failure to start the action within the period of time allowed for that purpose by state statute. (This topic is more thoroughly discussed in Chapter VI). This pre-*Harper* approach was based on the U.S. Supreme Court's decision in a 1971 case, *Chevron Oil Co. v. Huson.* The U.S. Supreme Court's decision in *Harper* prohibited federal courts from applying a decision prospectively. Each state then had to decide whether or not to continue following the *Chevron* approach. This was the question before the Montana Supreme Court in the 2004 case of *Dempsey v. Allstate Insurance Company.*

The following excerpt from the majority opinion in *Dempsey* provides an excellent summary of the evolution of the law as it relates to retroactivity. Readers may recall from Chapter I references to Sir William Blackstone as an important figure in the development of the common law and to the philosophical school known as legal realism. Notice how Justice Leaphart in the *Dempsey* opinion contrasts Blackstone's belief that judges "discover law" with the view of the legendary legal realist, Justice Oliver Wendell Holmes, that judges make law.

Dempsey v. Allstate Insurance Company
104 P.3d. 483
Supreme Court of Montana
December 30, 2004

Justice W. William Leaphart delivered the Opinion of the Court.
[The "Factual and Procedural Background" segment of this opinion has been omitted in order to focus on the court's discussion about whether decisions should apply prospectively.]

DISCUSSION
In 1971 the United States Supreme Court announced *Chevron Oil Co. v. Huson* (1971), 404 U.S. 97.... *Chevron* laid out a flexible three-factored test for whether a decision applies prospectively only. We adopted the *Chevron* test for questions of Montana law ... and subsequently applied it several times.... In the

meantime, the United States Supreme Court revisited the question of prospective application several times and eventually overruled *Chevron* in *Harper v. Virginia Dep't of Taxation* (1993)....

... [I]t appeared that we would follow the rule of the United States Supreme Court's *Harper* decision. However, subsequent decisions did not bear that out ... [as] we applied the *Chevron* test to determine whether prospective application was appropriate.... Given our long history of applying decisions prospectively we cannot ignore these recent decisions applying the *Chevron* test....
As we explain later in this opinion, the two lines of cases may be comfortably merged into a rule of

retroactivity in keeping with the last seventy years of this Court's jurisprudence....

A. A Brief History of Retroactivity

The retroactive/prospective distinction is relatively new to our common law tradition. In the days of Blackstone the law was understood as something that the courts applied, not something that they made. Accordingly, it made no sense for a court to comment on whether its ruling applied retroactively or not. Its ruling was simply the law as it is and always was ... ("[T]he Blackstonian model takes law as a timeless constant, always [optimistically] assuming the correctness of the current decision. Prior inconsistent decisions are and always were incorrect.")

This view, of course, is no longer even remotely fashionable in today's climate of legal realism and aversion to castles in the clouds. Justice Holmes, the great realist of his time, was one of the first to see past Blackstone and spy the retroactive/prospective distinction. In endorsing what we now call "retroactivity" he characterized common law adjudication not as a search for an entity separate from the courts, but as an act of creation, stating "[t]he law of a State does not become something outside of the state court and independent of it by being called the common law. Whatever it is called it is the law as declared by the state judges and nothing else." *Kuhn v. Fairmont Coal Co.* (1910) ... (Holmes, J., dissenting).

After flirting with the issue of prospective decisions in a handful of now defunct .... common law cases, the Court ruled in 1932 that a state supreme court does not violate the United States Constitution by giving a decision mere prospective effect. *Great N. Ry. Co. v. Sunburst Oil & Ref. Co.* (1932), ... ("A state in defining the limits of adherence to precedent may make a choice for itself between the principle of forward operations and that of relation backward.")....

After receiving the United States Supreme Court's blessing in *Great Northern* this Court used its power to prospectively apply its decisions when it saw fit.... The United States Supreme Court fully endorsed and justified its own use of prospective application in 1965 with *Linkletter v. Walker*.... In *Linkletter* the Warren Court was faced with an extraordinarily explosive issue. Four years before, [in] *Mapp v. Ohio* (1961) ... the Court had ruled that the exclusionary rule applies against the states. Linkletter argued that his conviction was obtained through evidence that should have been inadmissible under the exclusionary rule. Even though he was convicted and his case became final before the *Mapp* ruling, he reasoned that because the decisions of the United States

Supreme Court apply retroactively he must be granted habeas corpus relief....

If the Court had granted Linkletter's request, thousands of otherwise properly obtained convictions would have immediately become suspect. The Court found such retroactive application too great a disruption of the criminal justice system.... Also, applying *Mapp* to cases closed before its issuance would do nothing to further the policy behind the exclusionary rule—deterrence of unconstitutional police actions.

Therefore, after weighing these factors and others, the Court concluded it was prudent to rule that cases final before the *Mapp* decision were unaffected by it.

In 1971 the Court extended this flexible approach to civil cases in *Chevron Oil Co. v. Huson* (1971).... In applying a prior decision that had greatly changed the operation of statutes of limitations under the Outer Continental Shelf Lands Act, the Court adopted a version of the nonretroactivity test used in its criminal cases. In the context of criminal appeals, the three factors of the test were as follows:

> First, the decision to be applied nonretroactively must establish a new principle of law, either by overruling clear past precedent on which litigants may have relied or by deciding an issue of first impression whose resolution was not clearly foreshadowed. Second, it has been stressed that "we must ... weigh the merits and demerits in each case by looking to the prior history of the rule in question, its purpose and effect, and whether retrospective operation will further or retard its operation." Finally, we have weighed the inequity imposed by retroactive application, for "[w]here a decision of this Court could produce substantial inequitable results if applied retroactively, there is ample basis in our cases for avoiding the injustice or hardship by a holding of nonretroactivity." ... With this test in place the federal courts had flexibility to grant nonretroactive relief to litigants who had justifiably relied on old rules of law when there was no indication that the rule would change. Gone was any pretense that the law that the courts announce is the law as it has always been.

B. The Decline and Fall of Chevron

The United States Supreme Court's tolerance of prospective decisions did not last long. After indicating several times that it was not satisfied with current doctrine, the Court finally overruled itself in 1987, jettisoning the *Linkletter* approach.

Griffith v. Kentucky (1987).... The Court announced a new rule requiring that all criminal decisions apply retroactively to all cases "pending on direct review or not yet final." ... It reasoned that it was unfair to announce a new rule that would affect some defendants and not others merely because of the timing of their prosecutions....

It was only a matter of time before this approach to retroactivity in criminal cases found its way into the Court's civil jurisprudence.... [T]he Court announced [in *Harper v. Virginia Dep't of Taxation*, 509 U.S. 86 (1993)] that due to the inequities inherent in a flexible *Chevron* approach, federal rules of law may not be selectively applied prospectively....

After *Harper*, the *Chevron* test no longer had any applicability to interpretations of federal law, whether in federal or state court. The *Harper* decision is grounded in fairness and the arbitrariness of "temporal barriers," rather than a renewed embrace of Blackstone's theory of law "existing" independently of a court's decisions.

C. Revolt in the Provinces: Chevron Is Alive and Well in the State Courts
Chevron concerned a federal question, and thus only governed issues of federal law. Therefore, although the United States Supreme Court has rejected *Chevron*, the states are free to continue employing the *Chevron* criteria in deciding questions of retroactivity of state law. Prior to *Harper*, the *Chevron* approach proved popular in state courts....

The state courts' reactions to *Harper* have been decidedly mixed, with many expressing disagreement, if not open hostility. For example, the Supreme Court of New Hampshire voiced support for the rejection of *Chevron*.... However, inspired by Justice O'Connor's dissent in *Harper*, the court reserved for itself the authority to give new rules prospective effect, but that if a rule is applied retroactively to the parties before the court, it must be given uniform retroactive effect.... In contrast, the New Mexico Supreme Court took great issue with much of *Harper*, ... [constructing] a *presumption* in favor of retroactivity "in lieu of the hard-and-fast rule prescribed for federal cases in *Harper*."... Many states are uncomfortable with the harsh results that might follow if they abandon

Chevron and completely disallow prospective decisions.

D. Reserving Chevron as an Exception
Our precedent allows for a compromise between the powerful arguments of the *Harper* court and the compelling need for prospective application in limited circumstances....

We agree with the *Harper* court that limiting a rule of law to its prospective application creates an arbitrary distinction between litigants based merely on the timing of their claims. Interests of fairness are not served by drawing such a line, nor are interests of finality. In the interests of finality, the line should be drawn between claims that are final and those that are not (the line drawn in *Harper*).... We have already recognized the arbitrary nature of prospective decisions in the criminal context ... [and] ... in keeping with the United States Supreme Court's opinion in *Griffith*, we overruled all of our prior decisions which limited a new judicial rule of criminal procedure to prospective application....

We also understand, however, that what follows from civil litigation is different in kind from the consequences inherent in a criminal prosecution and conviction. On many occasions we have noted the disruption that a new rule of law can bring to existing contracts and to other legal relationships. Therefore today we reaffirm our general rule that "[w]e give retroactive effect to judicial decisions,".... We will, however, allow for an exception to that rule when faced with a truly compelling case for applying a new rule of law prospectively only.

The *Chevron* test is still viable as an exception to the rule of retroactivity. However, given that we wish prospective applications to be the exception, we will only invoke the *Chevron* exception when a party has satisfied *all three* of the *Chevron* factors....

Therefore, we conclude that, in keeping with our prior cases, all civil decisions of this court apply retroactively to cases pending on direct review or not yet final, unless all three of the *Chevron* factors are satisfied. For reasons of finality we also conclude that the retroactive effect of a decision does not apply ... to cases that became final or were settled prior to a decision's issuance....

Case Questions

1. Based on what you have read about the history of the rule of retroactivity, do you see any fundamental problems with the *Harper v. Virginia Department of Taxation* decision that could in the future threaten its survival as a precedent?

2.   Think about the positions advocated by Sir William Blackstone and Justice Oliver Wendell Holmes with respect to whether judges "discover law" or "make law." How would you characterize the decision-making process followed by the Montana Supreme Court in reaching its conclusions in *Dempsey*?

Do you believe that ethical considerations played any role in the Montana Supreme Court's decision not to follow exclusively the rule promulgated by the U.S. Supreme Court in *Harper v. Virginia Department of Taxation?*

Absence of Precedent

When judges are confronted by a novel fact situation, they must rely on their own sense of justice and philosophy of law. The public interest, tradition, prevailing customs, business usage, and moral standards are important considerations in the decision-making process. Judges encountering a case of first impression first look for guidance within the forum state. When precedent is lacking in the forum state, decisions of other state and federal courts, as well as English decisions, may be considered persuasive on the legal point at issue.

The trial court in the following case encountered a problem that was unique. The trial and appellate courts were required to make decisions without being able to benefit from the experience of others as reflected in statutory law and common law opinions. They had to create new law when life and death were at stake. Note that three of the seven members of the appellate court dissented.

Strunk v. Strunk
445 S.W.2d 145
Court of Appeals of Kentucky
September 26, 1969

Osborne, Judge.

The specific question involved upon this appeal is: Does a court of equity have power to permit a kidney to be removed from an incompetent ward of the state upon petition of his committee, who is also his mother, for the purpose of being transplanted into the body of his brother, who is dying of a fatal kidney disease? We are of the opinion it does.

The facts of the case are as follows: Arthur L. Strunk, 54 years of age, and Ava Strunk, 52 years of age, of Williamstown, Kentucky, are the parents of two sons. Tommy Strunk is 28 years of age, married, an employee of the Penn State Railroad and a part-time student at the University of Cincinnati. Tommy is now suffering from chronic glomerus nephritis, a fatal kidney disease. He is now being kept alive by frequent treatment on an artificial kidney, a procedure that cannot be continued much longer.

Jerry Strunk is 27 years of age, incompetent, and through proper legal proceedings has been committed to the Frankfort State Hospital and School, which is a state institution maintained for the feeble-minded. He has an IQ of approximately 35, which corresponds with the mental age of approximately six years. He is further handicapped by a speech defect, which makes it difficult for him to communicate with persons who are not well acquainted with him. When it was determined that Tommy, in order to survive, would have to have a kidney, the doctors considered the possibility of using a kidney from a cadaver if and when one became available, or one from a live donor if this could be made available. The entire family, his mother, father, and a number of collateral relatives, were tested. Because of incompatibility of blood type or tissue, none was medically acceptable as a live donor. As a last resort, Jerry was tested and found to be highly acceptable. This immediately presented the legal problem as to what, if anything, could be done by the family, especially the mother and the father, to procure a transplant from Jerry to Tommy. The mother as a committee petitioned the county court for authority to proceed with the operation. The court found that the operation was necessary, that under the peculiar circumstances of this case, it would not only be beneficial to Tommy but also beneficial to Jerry because Jerry was greatly dependent on Tommy, emotionally and psychologically, and that his well-being would be jeopardized more severely by the loss of his brother than by the removal of a kidney.

Appeal was taken to the Franklin Circuit Court where the chancellor reviewed the record, examined the testimony of the witnesses, and adopted the findings of the county court.

A psychiatrist, in attendance to Jerry, who testified in the case, stated in his opinion the death of Tommy under these circumstances would have "an extremely traumatic effect upon him [Jerry]."

The Department of Mental Health of this commonwealth has entered the case as *amicus curiae* and on the basis of its evaluation of the seriousness of the operation as opposed to the traumatic effect on Jerry as a result of the loss of Tommy, recommended to the court that Jerry be permitted to undergo the surgery. Its recommendations are as follows: "It is difficult for the mental defective to establish a firm sense of identity with another person. The acquisition of this necessary identity is dependent on a person whom one can conveniently accept as a model and who at the same time is sufficiently flexible to allow the defective to detach himself with reassurances of continuity. His need to be social is not so much the necessity of a formal and mechanical contact with other human beings as it is the necessity of a close intimacy with other men, the desirability of a real community of feeling, an urgent need for a unity of understanding. Purely mechanical and formal contact with other men does not offer any treatment for the behavior of a mental defective; only those who are able to communicate intimately are of value to hospital treatment in these cases. And this generally is a member of the family.

"In view of this knowledge, we now have particular interest in this case. Jerry Strunk, a mental defective, has emotions and reactions on a scale comparable to that of a normal person. He identifies with his brother Tom. Tom is his model, his tie with his family. Tom's life is vital to the continuity of Jerry's improvement at Frankfort State Hospital and School. The testimony of the hospital representative reflected the importance to Jerry of his visits with his family and the constant inquiries Jerry made about Tom's coming to see him. Jerry is aware he plays a role in the relief of this tension. We the Department of Mental Health must take all possible steps to prevent the occurrence of any guilt feelings Jerry would have if Tom were to die.

"The necessity of Tom's life to Jerry's treatment and eventual rehabilitation is clearer in view of the fact that Tom is his only living sibling and at the death of their parents, now in their fifties, Jerry will have no concerned, intimate communication so necessary to his stability and optimal functioning.

"The evidence shows that at the present level of medical knowledge, it is quite remote that Tom would be able to survive several cadaver transplants. Tom has a much better chance of survival if the kidney transplant from Jerry takes place."

Upon this appeal, we are faced with the fact that all members of the immediate family have recommended the transplant. The Department of Mental Health has likewise made its recommendation. The county court has given its approval. The circuit court has found that it would be to the best interest of the ward of the state that the procedure be carried out. Throughout the legal proceedings, Jerry has been represented by a guardian *ad litem,* who has continually questioned the power of the state to authorize the removal of an organ from the body of an incompetent who is a ward of the state. We are fully cognizant of the fact that the question before us is unique. Insofar as we have been able to learn, no similar set of facts has come before the highest court of any of the states of this nation or the federal courts. The English courts have apparently taken a broad view of the inherent power of the equity courts with regard to incompetents. *Ex parte Whitebread* (1816) ... holds that courts of equity have the inherent power to make provisions for a needy brother out of the estate of an incompetent.... The inherent rule in these cases is that the chancellor has the power to deal with the estate of the incompetent in the same manner as the incompetent would if he had his faculties. This rule has been extended to cover not only matters of property but also to cover the personal affairs of the incompetent....

The right to act for the incompetent in all cases has become recognized in this country as the doctrine of substituted judgment and is broad enough not only to cover property but also to cover all matters touching on the well-being of the ward....

The medical practice of transferring tissue from one part of the human body to another (autografting) and from one human being to another (homografting) is rapidly becoming a common clinical practice. In many cases, the transplants take as well when the tissue is dead as when it is alive. This has made practicable the establishment of tissue banks where such material can be stored for future use. Vascularized grafts of lungs, kidneys, and hearts are becoming increasingly common. These grafts must be of functioning, living cells with blood vessels remaining anatomically intact. The chance of success in the transfer of these organs is greatly increased when the donor and the donee are genetically related. It is recognized by all legal and medical authorities that several legal problems can arise as a result of the operative techniques of the transplant procedure....

The renal transplant is becoming the most common of the organ transplants. This is because the normal body has two functioning kidneys, one of which it can reasonably do without, thereby making it possible for one person to donate a kidney to another. Testimony in this record shows that there have been over 2,500 kidney transplants performed in the United States up to this date. The process can be effected under present techniques with minimal danger to both the donor and the donee....

Review of our case law leads us to believe that the power given to a committee under KRS 387.230 would not extend so far as to allow a committee to subject his ward to the serious surgical techniques here under consideration unless the life of his ward be in jeopardy. Nor do we believe the powers delegated to the county court by virtue of the above statutes would reach so far as to permit the procedure which we [are] dealing with here.

We are of the opinion that a chancery court does have sufficient inherent power to authorize the operation. The circuit court having found that the operative procedures are to the best interest of Jerry Strunk and this finding having been based on substantial evidence, we are of the opinion the judgment should be affirmed. We do not deem it significant that this case reached the circuit court by way of an appeal as opposed to a direct proceeding in that court.

Judgment affirmed.

Hill, C.J., Milliken, and Reed, JJ., concur.

Neikirk, Palmore, and Steinfeld, JJ., dissent.

Steinfeld, Judge, dissenting.

Apparently because of my indelible recollection of a government which, to the everlasting shame of its citizens, embarked on a program of genocide and experimentation with human bodies, I have been more troubled in reaching a decision in this case than in any other. My sympathies and emotions are torn between a compassion to aid an ailing young man and a duty to fully protect unfortunate members of society.

The opinion of the majority is predicated on the authority of an equity court to speak for one who cannot speak for himself. However, it is my opinion that in considering such right in this instance, we must first look to the power and authority vested in the committee, the appellee herein. KRS 387.060 and KRS 387.230 do nothing more than give the committee the power to take custody of the incompetent and the possession, care, and management of his property.

Courts have restricted the activities of the committee to that which is for the best interest of the incompetent.... The authority and duty have been to protect and maintain the ward, to secure that to which he is entitled and preserve that which he has....

The wishes of the members of the family or the desires of the guardian to be helpful to the apparent objects of the ward's bounty have not been a criterion. "A curator or guardian cannot dispose of his ward's property by donation, even though authorized to do so by the court on advice of a family meeting, unless a gift by the guardian is authorized by statute."... Two Kentucky cases decided many years ago reveal judicial policy. In *W. T. Sistrunk & Co. v. Navarra's Committee*, ... 105 S.W.2d 1039 (1937), this court held that a committee was without right to continue a business which the incompetent had operated prior to his having been declared a person of unsound mind. More analogous is *Baker v. Thomas*, ... 114 S.W.2d 1113 (1938), in which a man and woman had lived together out of wedlock. Two children were born to them. After the man was judged incompetent, his committee, acting for him, together with his paramour, instituted proceedings to adopt the two children. In rejecting the application and refusing to speak for the incompetent, the opinion stated: "The statute does not contemplate that the committee of a lunatic may exercise any other power than to have the possession, care, and management of the lunatic's or incompetent's estate."... The majority opinion is predicated on the finding of the circuit court that there will be psychological benefits to the ward but points out that the incompetent has the mentality of a six-year-old child. It is common knowledge beyond dispute that the loss of a close relative or a friend to a six-year-old child is not of major impact. Opinions concerning psychological trauma are at best most nebulous. Furthermore, there are no guarantees that the transplant will become a surgical success, it being well known that body rejection of transplanted organs is frequent. The life of the incompetent is not in danger, but the surgical procedure advocated creates some peril.

It is written in *Prince v. Massachusetts*, 321 U.S. 158 (1944), that "Parents may be free to become martyrs themselves. But it does not follow they are free, in identical circumstances, to make martyrs of their children before they have reached the age of full and legal distinction when they can make the choice for themselves." The ability to fully understand and consent is a prerequisite to the donation of a part of the human body....

Unquestionably, the attitudes and attempts of the committee and members of the family of the two young men whose critical problems now confront us are commendable, natural, and beyond reproach. However, they refer us to nothing indicating that they are privileged to authorize the removal of one of the kidneys of the incompetent for the purpose of donation, and they cite no statutory or other authority vesting such right in the courts. The proof shows that less compatible donors are available and that the kidney of a cadaver could be used, although the odds of operational success are not as great in such cases as they would be with the fully compatible donor brother.

I am unwilling to hold that the gates should be open to permit the removal of an organ from an incompetent for transplant, at least until such time as it is conclusively demonstrated that it will be of significant benefit to the incompetent. The evidence here does not rise to that pinnacle. To hold that committees, guardians, or courts have such awesome power, even in the persuasive case before us, could establish legal precedent, the dire result of which we cannot fathom. Regretfully I must say no.

Neikirk and Palmore, JJ., join with me in this dissent.

Case Questions

1. The Court of Appeals of Kentucky is the court of last resort in that state. The *Strunk* decision is now Kentucky law. Does the decision make mental institutions a storehouse of human bodies available for distribution to the more productive members of society whenever the state decides that someone's need outweighs the danger to the incompetent?
2. Which opinion, the majority or dissent, was more persuasive?
3. Where no legal cases have a direct bearing on the issue of a case, should the court turn to other disciplines for authority?

 What ethical considerations do you think convinced the dissenters in this case to oppose the operation on Jerry Strunk?

RECOGNIZING LAWS OF OTHER STATES

Every person within the territorial limits of a government is bound by its laws. However, it is well-recognized that law does not of its own force have any effect outside the territory of the sovereignty from which its authority is derived. Because each of the fifty states is an individual sovereignty that creates its own common and statutory law, there are often inconsistencies among the laws of the various states.

When the facts of a case under consideration have occurred in more than one state or country, and a court must make a choice between the laws of different states or nations, a **conflict–of–laws** issue is presented. Another type of conflict-of-laws problem exists where an event occurred in one state and the suit is brought in another state.

For example, a driver from Michigan might bring suit in Kentucky regarding an automobile collision in Ohio involving a driver from Kentucky. In this situation, the court must decide whether to apply its own substantive law, the law of the state in which the events occurred, or possibly the law of some other state.

Conflict-of-Laws Rules

Conflict-of-laws rules have been developed by each state to assist its courts in determining whether and when foreign substantive law (i.e., some other state's contract law, tort law, property law, etc.) should be given effect within the territory of the forum. Remember that a state court always follows its own procedural law, even when it decides to apply the substantive law of some other state. The rules afford some assurance that the same substantive law will be used to decide the case irrespective of where the suit is tried.

Tort Cases

The traditional approach in tort cases is to apply the law of the place where the wrong was committed— *lex loci delicti commissi.* The place of the wrong is where the last event necessary to make the actor liable takes place or where the person or thing harmed is situated at the time of the wrong. The following case exemplifies a trend that has been occurring in recent years. The Indiana Supreme Court used the *Hubbard* case to replace the traditional *lex loci delicti commissi* rule with the **significant relationship rule.** The significant relationship approach is more flexible than a rigid *lex loci* approach. A court following the significant relationship rule can apply the law of the place that has the most significant contacts with the incident or event in dispute.

Hubbard Manufacturing Co., Inc., v. Greeson
515 N.E.2d 1071
Supreme Court of Indiana
December 1, 1987

Shepard, Chief Justice.

The question is whether an Indiana court should apply Indiana tort law when both parties are residents of Indiana and the injury occurred in Illinois.

Plaintiff Elizabeth Greeson, an Indiana resident, filed a wrongful death action in Indiana against defendant Hubbard Manufacturing Co., Inc., an Indiana corporation. The defendant corporation built lift units for use in cleaning, repairing, and replacing streetlights.

On October 29, 1979, Donald Greeson, plaintiff's husband and also a resident of Indiana, happened to be working in Illinois maintaining street lights. He died that day while using a lift unit manufactured by Hubbard in Indiana.

Elizabeth Greeson's suit alleged that defective manufacture of Hubbard's lift unit caused her husband's death. When she raised the possibility that Illinois products-liability law should be applied to this case, Hubbard moved the trial court for a determination of the applicable law. The trial court found that Indiana had more significant contacts with the litigation but felt constrained to apply Illinois substantive law because the decedent's injury had been sustained there. The Court of Appeals expressed the opinion that Indiana law should apply but concluded that existing precedent required use of Illinois law....

We grant transfer to decide whether Indiana or Illinois law applies.

Greeson's complaint alleged two bases for her claim: "the defective and unreasonably dangerous condition of a lift type vehicle sold ... by the defendant" and "the negligence of the defendant." Both theories state a cause for liability based on Hubbard's manufacture of the vehicle in Indiana.

The differences in Indiana law and Illinois law are considerable. First, in Indiana a finding that the product represented an open and obvious danger would preclude recovery on the product liability claim ... to impress liability on manufacturers the defect must be hidden and not normally observable. Under Illinois law, the trier of fact may find product liability even if the danger is open and obvious.... Second, under Indiana law misuse would bar recovery.... In Illinois misuse merely reduces a plaintiff's award.... These differences are important enough to affect the outcome of the litigation.

Choosing the applicable substantive law for a given case is a decision made by the courts of the state in which the lawsuit is pending. An early basis for choosing law applicable to events transversing *(sic)* several states was to use the substantive law of the state "where the wrong is committed" regardless of where the plaintiff took his complaint seeking relief....

The historical choice-of-law rule for torts ... was *lex loci delicti commissi,* which applied the substantive law where the tort was committed. *Burns v. Grand Rapids and Indiana Railroad Co.* (1888).... The tort is said to have been committed in the state where the last event necessary to make an actor liable for the alleged wrong takes place.

Rigid application of the traditional rule to this case, however, would lead to an anomalous result. Had plaintiff Elizabeth Greeson filed suit in any bordering state the only forum which would not have applied the substantive law of Indiana is Indiana.... To avoid this inappropriate result, we look elsewhere for guidance.

Choice-of-law rules are fundamentally judge-made and designed to ensure the appropriate substantive law applies. In a large number of cases, the place of the tort will be significant and the place with the most contacts.... In such cases, the traditional rule serves well. A court should be allowed to evaluate other factors when the place of the tort is an insignificant contact. In those instances where the place of the tort bears little connection to the legal action, this Court will permit the consideration of other factors such as:

1. the place where the conduct causing the injury occurred;
2. the residence or place of business of the parties; and
3. the place where the relationship is centered.

Restatement (Second) of Conflicts of Laws § 145(2) (1971). These factors should be evaluated according to their relative importance to the particular issues being litigated.

The first step in applying this rule in the present case is to consider whether the place of the tort "bears little connection" to this legal action. The last event necessary to make *Hubbard* liable for the alleged tort took place in Illinois. The decedent was working in Illinois at the time of his death and the vehicle involved

in the fatal injuries was in Illinois. The coroner's inquest was held in Illinois, and the decedent's wife and son are receiving benefits under the Illinois Workmen's Compensation Laws. None of these facts relates to the wrongful death action filed against Hubbard. The place of the tort is insignificant to this suit.

After having determined that the place of the tort bears little connection to the legal action, the second step is to apply the additional factors. Applying these factors to this wrongful death action leads us to the same conclusion that the trial court drew: Indiana has the more significant relationship and contacts. The plaintiff's two theories of recovery relate to the manufacture of the lift in Indiana. Both parties are from Indiana; plaintiff Elizabeth Greeson is a resident of Indiana and defendant Hubbard is an Indiana corporation with its principal place of business in Indiana. The relationship between the deceased and Hubbard centered in Indiana. The deceased frequently visited defendant's plant in Indiana to discuss the repair and maintenance of the lift. Indiana law applies.

The Court of Appeals decision is vacated and the cause remanded to the trial court with instructions to apply Indiana law.

Case Questions

1. Under *lex loci delicti commissi*, how should a court determine where a tort was committed?
2. Why did the Indiana Supreme Court decide to replace the traditional *lex loci delicti commissi* approach?
3. What contacts were evaluated by the court in determining which state had a more significant relationship with the occurrence and with the parties?

Contract Cases

All states have developed their own conflict-of-laws rules for contractual disputes, which differ from the rules that apply to tort cases. In contractual disputes, depending on the facts involved and jurisdictional preferences, courts have historically applied the law of place in any of the following ways: (1) where the action was instituted (***lex fori***), (2) where the contract was to be performed (***lex loci solutionis***), (3) which law the parties intended to govern their agreement, (4) the law of the state where the last act necessary to complete the contract was done and which created a legal obligation (***lex loci contractus***), and (5) the law of the state that has the greatest concern with the event and the parties (**significant relationship rule**). A court may choose to follow

its own substantive law of contracts and will do so if the application of the foreign law would offend its public policy.

Courts often honor the law intended by the parties to be controlling. The state chosen usually has a substantial connection with the contract, but courts have held that no such connection is necessary if the parties intended that that state's laws govern the agreement. For example, automobile and house insurance contracts generally included a choice-of-law clause, usually a forum selected by the lawyers for the insurance company and "agreed to" by the insured. If a contract fails to include a choice-of-law clause, courts still may determine the parties' intent by examining the facts surrounding the contract.

One of the important developments in contract law has been the enactment by all states of at least some provisions of the Uniform Commercial Code (UCC). This code was created in order to enhance the uniformity of state laws regulating certain commercial transactions. The UCC does not apply to all types of contracts. It does not apply, for example, to employment contracts, services, or the sale of real property. With respect to conflicts of law, the UCC basically follows the significant relationship rule when parties to contracts have not specified a choice of law.

Full Faith and Credit

Prior to learning about full faith and credit, readers may find it helpful to reread the "Procedural Primer" that begins on page 12 of Chapter I. There can be found a simplified overview of civil procedure, a topic that will be explored in much greater detail in Chapter V.

When beginning a discussion of full faith and credit, it is important to emphasize that each state in the United States is a distinct sovereignty. In the absence of a federal constitutional requirement to the contrary, each state would be entitled to totally disregard the constitutions, statutes, records, and judgments of other states. Clearly, the refusal of some states to recognize and enforce the judgments issued by other states would deny justice to those who had taken their disputes to court. A judgment debtor, the party ordered in the judgment to pay money to the winner of the lawsuit (the "judgment creditor"), could flee to a state that refuses to recognize and enforce judgments from the issuing state, undermining public confidence in the law.

The authors of the U.S. Constitution anticipated this problem and addressed it in Article IV, Section 1, which provides that "full faith and credit shall be given in each state to the public acts, records, and judicial proceedings of every other state." Thus the Constitution requires the states to cooperate with each other and binds them together into one nation. As final judgments of each state are enforceable in every other state, irrespective of differences in substantive law and public policy, the full-faith-and-credit requirement also helps to preserve the legal differences that exist from state to state. There are some exceptions to the full-faith-and-credit requirement. For example, the requirement does not apply if the judgment-issuing court lacked jurisdiction over the subject matter or person or if the judgment was fraudulently obtained.

Another important benefit of the full-faith-and-credit requirement is that it puts teeth into the doctrine of res judicata. Once a valid judgment has been rendered on the merits in one jurisdiction, the claims adjudicated in that lawsuit cannot be relitigated by the same parties in some other jurisdiction.

A state can justifiably refuse to grant full faith and credit to another state's judgment under limited circumstances: for example, when the issuing court has failed to follow the mandates of the U.S. Constitution regarding due process of law. Full faith and credit can be denied when the issuing court did not have minimum contacts with the person of the judgment debtor, or when the judicial proceedings denied the judgment debtor the constitutionally required elements of notice and an opportunity for a hearing.

Article IV, Section 1 of the U.S. Constitution only requires that the states provide full faith and credit to other states. The federal Full Faith and Credit Act (28 U.S.C. Section 1738), however, also requires all federal courts to afford full faith and credit to state court judgments.

INTERNET TIP

You can read the excerpt from the federal Full Faith and Credit Act (28 U.S.C. Section 1738)), online at the textbook's website.

Although a properly authenticated judgment of an issuing state is presumptively valid and binding in all other states, it is not self-implementing. A judgment creditor who has to go to some other state to enforce a judgment will have to begin an action against the judgment debtor in the nonissuing state. Normally, the courts of the nonissuing state will then have to enforce the foreign judgment in the same manner as they would one of their own judgments, even if enforcing the judgment would contravene the enforcing state's public policy. This was the problem presented in the following case, in which three same-sex adoptive couples sought to overturn an Oklahoma statute that denied them recognition as the adoptive parents of their children. The parents of "E.D." sued to obtain a supplemental birth certificate, claiming that Oklahoma was obligated under the Full Faith and Credit Clause of the Constitution to recognize the judgment of adoption rendered by a California court.

Finstuen v. Crutcher
496 F.3d 1139
United States Court of Appeals, Tenth Circuit
August 3, 2007

Ebel, Circuit Judge.
Defendant-Appellant Dr. Mike Crutcher, sued in his official capacity as the Commissioner of Health (hereinafter referred to as "Oklahoma State Department of Health ('OSDH')") appeals a district court judgment that a state law barring recognition of adoptions by same-sex couples already finalized in another state is unconstitutional. OSDH also appeals the district court's order requiring it to issue a revised birth certificate for E.D., a Plaintiff-Appellee who was born in Oklahoma but adopted in California by a same-sex couple....

I
Three same-sex couples and their adopted children have challenged the following amendment to Oklahoma's statute governing the recognition of parent-child relationships that are created by out-of-state adoptions.
§ 7502-1.4. Foreign adoptions
A. The courts of this state shall recognize a decree, judgment, or final order creating the relationship of parent and child by adoption, issued by a court or other governmental authority with appropriate jurisdiction in a foreign country or in another state or territory of the United States. The rights and obligations of the parties as to matters within the jurisdiction of this state shall be determined as though the decree, judgment, or final order were issued by a court of this state. Except that, this state, any of its agencies, or any court of this state shall not recognize an adoption by more than one individual of the same sex from any other state or foreign jurisdiction.
Okla. Stat. tit. 10, § 7502-1.4(A) (the "adoption amendment").
Each of the three families has a different set of circumstances. Mr. Greg Hampel and Mr. Ed Swaya are residents of Washington, where they jointly adopted child V in 2002. V was born in Oklahoma, and...the men agreed to bring V to Oklahoma to visit her mother "from time to time."... However, they do not...have any ongoing interactions with the state of Oklahoma. After V's adoption, Mr. Hampel and Mr. Swaya requested that OSDH issue a new birth certificate for V. OSDH did so...but named only Mr. Hampel as V's parent. Mr. Hampel and Mr. Swaya contested that action, prompting OSDH to seek an opinion from the Oklahoma attorney general.... The attorney general opined that the U.S. Constitution's Full Faith and Credit Clause required Oklahoma to recognize any validly issued out-of-state adoption decree. OSDH subsequently issued V a new birth certificate naming both men as parents. The state legislature responded one month later by enacting the adoption amendment.

Lucy Doel and Jennifer Doel live with their adopted child E in Oklahoma. E was born in Oklahoma. Lucy Doel adopted E in California in January 2002. Jennifer Doel adopted E in California six months later.... OSDH issued E a supplemental birth certificate naming only Lucy Doel as her mother. The Doels have requested a revised birth certificate from OSDH that would acknowledge Jennifer Doel as E's parent, but OSDH denied the request.

Anne Magro and Heather Finstuen reside in Oklahoma with their two children. Ms. Magro gave birth to S and K in New Jersey in 1998. In 2000, Ms. Finstuen adopted S and K in New Jersey as a second parent, and New Jersey subsequently issued new birth certificates for S and K naming both women as their parents.

These three families brought suit against the state of Oklahoma seeking to enjoin enforcement of the adoption amendment, naming the governor, attorney general and commissioner of health in their official capacities. The Doels also requested a revised birth certificate naming both Lucy Doel and Jennifer Doel as E's parents.

On cross-motions for summary judgment, the district court found that Mr. Hampel, Mr. Swaya and their child V lacked standing to bring the action.... However, the district court granted summary judgment for the remaining plaintiffs, determining that they had standing and that the Oklahoma adoption amendment violated the Constitution's Full Faith and Credit, Equal Protection and Due Process Clauses.... The court enjoined enforcement of the amendment, and ordered that a new birth certificate be issued for E.D....

OSDH appeals from the district court's conclusion that the Doels and the Finstuen-Magro family have standing and its ruling that the adoption amendment is unconstitutional. The Oklahoma governor and attorney general did not appeal. In addition, Mr. Hampel, Mr. Swaya and their child V timely appeal from the denial of standing, and reassert their claim that the Oklahoma amendment violates their constitutional right to travel....

II

A. Jurisdiction
[The court's expansive discussion of standing, a topic examined in Chapter VI of this text, is omitted. The Court concluded that it could not decide the case brought by Hampel and Swaya (child V), primarily because this family had minimal connections with Oklahoma, and did "not establish the circumstances in which the non-recognition of the adoption would arise," and therefore lacked standing to sue. The court also found that Finstuen and Magro lacked standing. Magro was the children's birth mother and not an adoptive parent, and Finstuen, who was an adoptive mother, could point to "no encounter with any public or private official in which her authority as a parent was questioned." The court ruled that Lucy Doel and Jennifer Doel, the adoptive parents of child E.D., did have standing to maintain their suit.]

B. Full Faith and Credit Clause
Having established jurisdiction, we proceed to consider the merits of OSDH's appeal. The district court concluded that the adoption amendment was unconstitutional because the Full Faith and Credit Clause requires Oklahoma to recognize adoptions—including same-sex couples' adoptions—that are validly decreed in other states.... We affirm, because there is "no roving 'public policy exception' to the full faith and credit due *judgments*" ... and OSDH presents no relevant legal argument as to why the Doels' out-of-state adoption judgments should not be recognized under the Full Faith and Credit Clause.

The Constitution states that "Full Faith and Credit shall be given in each State to the public Acts, Records, and judicial Proceedings of every other State." U.S. Const. art. 4, § 1. The Supreme Court has often

explained the purpose and policies behind the Full Faith and Credit Clause.

The very purpose of the Full Faith and Credit Clause was to alter the status of the several states as independent foreign sovereignties, each free to ignore obligations created under the laws or by the judicial proceedings of the others, and to make them integral parts of a single nation throughout which a remedy upon a just obligation might be demanded as of right, irrespective of the state of its origin.

... The Clause is designed "to preserve rights acquired or confirmed under the public acts and judicial proceedings of one state by requiring recognition of their validity in other states."... The Clause "is one of the provisions incorporated into the Constitution by its framers for the purpose of transforming an aggregation of independent, sovereign States into a nation. If in its application local policy must at times be required to give way, such is part of the price of our federal system."... "To vest the power of determining the extraterritorial effect of a State's own laws and judgments in the State itself risks the very kind of parochial entrenchment on the interests of other States that it was the purpose of the Full Faith and Credit Clause and other provisions of Art. IV of the Constitution to prevent"....

In applying the Full Faith and Credit Clause, the Supreme Court has drawn a distinction between statutes and judgments.... Specifically, the Court has been clear that although the Full Faith and Credit Clause applies unequivocally to the judgments ... of sister states, it applies with less force to their statutory laws.... *Nevada v. Hall,* 440 U.S. 410 ... (1979).... However, with respect to final judgments entered in a sister state, it is clear there is no "public policy" exception to the Full Faith and Credit Clause:

Regarding judgments ... the full faith and credit obligation is exacting. A final judgment in one State, if rendered by a court with adjudicatory authority over the subject matter and persons governed by the judgment, qualifies for recognition throughout the land. For claim and issue preclusion (res judicata) purposes, in other words, the judgment of the rendering State gains nationwide force....

In numerous cases th[e] [Supreme] Court has held that credit must be given to the judgment of another state although the forum would not be required to entertain the suit on which the judgment was founded; that considerations of policy of the forum which would defeat a suit upon the original cause of action are not involved in a suit upon the judgment and are insufficient to defeat it.

OSDH stops short of arguing that the Full Faith and Credit Clause permits states to invoke a "policy exception," but contends that requiring Oklahoma to recognize an out-of-state adoption judgment would be tantamount to giving the sister state control over the effect of its judgment in Oklahoma....

Full faith and credit ... does not mean that States must adopt the practices of other States regarding the time, manner, and mechanisms for enforcing judgments. Enforcement measures do not travel with the sister state judgment as preclusive effects do; such measures remain subject to the even-handed control of forum law....

A California court made the decision, in its own state and under its own laws, as to whether Jennifer Doel could adopt child E. That decision is final. If Oklahoma had no statute providing for the issuance of supplementary birth certificates for adopted children, the Doels could not invoke the Full Faith and Credit Clause in asking Oklahoma for a new birth certificate. However, Oklahoma has such a statute — i.e., it already has the necessary "mechanism[] for enforcing [adoption] judgments."... The Doels merely ask Oklahoma to apply its own law to "enforce" their adoption order in an "even-handed" manner....

Oklahoma continues to exercise authority over the manner in which adoptive relationships should be enforced in Oklahoma and the rights and obligations in Oklahoma flowing from an adoptive relationship. And Oklahoma has spoken on that subject:

After the final decree of adoption is entered, the relation of parent and child and all the rights, duties, and other legal consequences of the natural relation of child and parent shall thereafter exist between the adopted child and the adoptive parents of the child and the kindred of the adoptive parents. From the date of the final decree of adoption, the child shall be entitled to inherit real and personal property from and

through the adoptive parents in accordance with the statutes of descent and distribution. The adoptive parents shall be entitled to inherit real and personal property from and through the child in accordance with said statutes.

After a final decree of adoption is entered, the biological parents of the adopted child, unless they are the adoptive parents or the spouse of an adoptive parent, shall be relieved of all parental responsibilities for said child and shall have no rights over the adopted child or to the property of the child by descent and distribution.... By way of illustration, the right of a parent in Oklahoma to authorize medical treatment for her minor child ... extends ... to adoptive parents as well. Whatever rights may be afforded to the Doels based on their status as parent and child, those rights flow from an application of Oklahoma law, not California law....

The rights that the Doels seek to enforce in Oklahoma are Oklahoma rights....

We hold today that final adoption orders and decrees are judgments that are entitled to recognition by all other states under the Full Faith and Credit Clause. Therefore, Oklahoma's adoption amendment is unconstitutional in its refusal to recognize final adoption orders of other states that permit adoption by same-sex couples. Because we affirm the district court on this basis, we do not reach the issues of whether the adoption amendment infringes on the Due Process or Equal Protection Clauses.

We reverse the district court's order in this matter to the extent it held that the Magro-Finstuen plaintiffs had standing and directed OSDH to issue new birth certificates for the Magro-Finstuen plaintiffs. The order and judgment of the district court in all other respects is affirmed.

Case Questions

1. Why did the authors of the Constitution create the Full Faith and Credit Clause?
2. Why did Oklahoma refuse to recognize the California judgment?

CHAPTER SUMMARY

In this chapter readers have learned that federal and state constitutions, statutes, judicial opinions, and administrative rules constitute the primary sources of American law. Summary explanations were provided as to how each primary source contributes to the making of American law.

The importance of the federal and state constitutions as the fundamental sources of the rule of law was emphasized. Because of the federal constitution, Congress's right to legislate is confined, and because it is limited, the state legislatures, as sovereigns, retained the constitutional right to pass laws pursuant to the police power. But where state laws directly conflict with a constitutionally enacted federal statute, the federal law is supreme.

There was a major emphasis in this chapter on judicial decision making and the important role of the doctrine of stare decisis. Laws can vary from state to state both procedurally and substantively. Federal and state laws also can differ. States, for example, can elect to provide a higher level of procedural protections than is required either under the U.S. Constitution or by federal statute. Last, we have seen that state choice-of-law rules provide methods for ensuring cooperation between states and that the Full Faith and Credit Clause of the U.S. Constitution helps to preserve differences between the states.

CHAPTER QUESTIONS

1. Elizabeth Fedorczyk slipped and fell in a bathtub in her cabin on board the M/V *Sovereign,* a cruise ship sailing in navigable waters. She brought a negligence suit against the ship's owners and operators in a state court in New Jersey. The defendants removed the case to the U.S. District Court for the District of New Jersey on the basis of diversity jurisdiction. Neither party addressed the admiralty issue in their pleadings. The trial court entered summary judgment in favor of the defendants. The plaintiffs appealed to the U.S. Court of Appeals. The appeals court, in order to rule on the appeal, had to determine whether it should apply admiralty law to this dispute or follow instead the substantive law of the state of New Jersey. Which option should the Court of Appeals choose, and why?

   Fedorczyk v. Caribbean Cruise Lines, LTD, No. 95-54622, U.S. Court of Appeals (3rd Circuit 1996)

2. Sludge, Inc., entered into a contract with XYZ, Inc., whereby Sludge was to build a building for XYZ in Detroit, Michigan, at the price of $1 million. Sludge was incorporated in Ohio; its principal place of business was in Chicago, Illinois. XYZ is a Delaware corporation with its home office in New York. The contract was negotiated primarily in Chicago but became effective when it was signed at XYZ's home office. There was a dispute concerning the agreement, and XYZ sued Sludge in a federal district court in Ohio. Which state law would govern the dispute if the court

follows (1) the *lex fori* approach, (2) the *lex loci contractus* approach, or (3) the *lex loci solutionis* approach?

3. Lorretta Klump, at the time a resident of Illinois, was injured in an automobile collision in which her vehicle was struck by a vehicle driven by Curt Eaves, also an Illinois resident. This incident occurred in Illinois. After the accident, Lorretta moved to North Carolina, where she retained a local attorney, J. David Duffus Jr., to represent her in a lawsuit she wanted to file in Illinois against Mr. Eaves. She subsequently moved back to Illinois, where she maintained regular contact with Attorney Duffus. Lorretta's doctor and her insurance carrier were both situated in Illinois. She filed a malpractice suit against Duffus when he failed to file her Illinois suit prior to the lapsing of the Illinois statute of limitations. The jury awarded a judgment in plaintiff's favor in the amount of $424,000. The defendants appealed on the grounds that the trial court did not have jurisdiction over them personally because his allegedly negligent acts occurred in North Carolina. Duffus maintained that, he could not be subject to personal jurisdiction in Illinois. Is Duffus correct? Why or why not?

   Klump v. Duffus, Jr., No. 90-C-3772, U.S. Court of Appeals (7th Circuit 1995)

4. Evian Waters of France, Inc., a New York corporation, was an importer of natural spring water from France. Evian contracted in 1987 with Valley Juice Limited, of Boston,

Massachusetts, to become Evian's exclusive New England distributor. Valley came to believe that Evian was violating its exclusivity rights in New England and alleged breach of contract and other claims in a suit it filed in Massachusetts state court. Evian, believing that Valley had not paid it for contract water it had delivered, filed suit in Connecticut. Both suits were removed to federal court on the basis of diversity jurisdiction, and the two suits were consolidated in the U.S. District Court for the District of Connecticut. The case was tried to a jury, which found in favor of Evian. Valley appealed to the U.S. Court of Appeals for the Second Circuit. Before reviewing the appellant's claims, the appeals court had to determine what state's law applied when two suits, which were initially filed in different states, were consolidated for trial, as in this case. Evian argued that a provision in its agreement with Valley provided that New York law should apply. Valley contended that if the states' laws conflict, Massachusetts law should apply. How should the court of appeals resolve this dispute?

Valley Juice Ltd., Inc. v. Evian Waters of France, Inc., Nos. 94-7813, 94-7817, 95-7709, U.S. Court of Appeals (2nd Circuit 1996)

5. On May 20, Arnie Walters's car crashed into a train owned and operated by the Regional Transit Authority at its crossing in Smithville. As a matter of law, the court found that the "Smithville crossing is extremely hazardous." On December 1 of that same year, Ole and Anna Hanson ran into an RTA train at the same crossing while George was driving them home from a party. Does the doctrine of stare decisis require that the court in *Hanson* accept the conclusion announced in the *Walters* case?

6. While en route to jury duty, Evans sustained a personal injury as a result of carelessness on the part of the county commissioners in permitting the concrete steps at the El Paso, Colorado, county courthouse to deteriorate. The lower court dismissed the complaint under the doctrine of governmental immunity. On appeal, the Supreme Court of Colorado, in its opinion dated March 22, 1971, decided to abolish governmental immunity for that state. The court stated, "Except as to the parties in this proceeding the ruling here shall be prospective only and shall be effective only as to causes of action arising after June 30, 1972." Why might a court make its decision effective as a precedent some fifteen months after the date of its decision?

Evans v. Board of County Commissioners, 174 Colo. 97, 482 P.2d 968 (1971)

7. P. Whitney, a West Virginia contractor, was under contract with the state of West Virginia to construct State Route 2 near East Steubenville, just across the border from Steubenville, Ohio. Because the area was very hilly, Whitney used high explosives, such as dynamite and nitroglycerin, to clear the way for the road. One particularly large blast damaged a storeroom of the Steubenville Plate and Window Glass Company, located across the border in Ohio. The damage was extensive, and most of the stored glass was broken and rendered unusable. Keeping in mind that the blasting was done in West Virginia and the damage occurred in Ohio, which state's law will govern the action brought in a West Virginia court by Steubenville Plate Glass against Whitney?

Dallas v. Whitney, 118 W. Va. 106 (1936)

NOTES

1. You might want to refresh your memory and review this material in conjunction with your current reading.

2. L. Fuller, *Anatomy of the Law* (New York: Praeger, 1968), p. 85.

3. *Schechter Poultry Corp. v. United States,* 295 U.S. 495 (1935).

4. *Carter v. Carter Coal Co.,* 298 U.S. 495 (1936).

5. *Adair v. United States,* 208 U.S. 161 (1908).

6. *Hammer v. Dagenhart,* 247 U.S. 251 (1981).

7. *Heart of Atlanta Motel, Inc. v. United States,* 379 U.S. 241 (1964).

8. *National Labor Relations Board v. Jones & Laughlin Steel Corp.,* 301 U.S. 1 (1937).

9. *West Coast Hotel v. Parrish,* 300 U.S. 379 (1937).

10. G. Schubert, *Evolutionary Politics* (Carbondale: Southern Illinois University Press, 1989), p. 225.

11. Ibid., p. 224.

12. K. L. Manning, B. A. Carroll, and R. A. Carp, "Does Age Matter? Judicial Decision Making in Age Discrimination Cases," 85 *Social Science Quarterly* 1, 1 (March 2004); J. Stribopoulos and M A. Yaha, "Does a Judge's Party of Appointment or Gender Matter to Case Outcomes?" 45 *Osgoode Hall Law Journal* 2, 55 (2007).

IV

The Judicial System

CHAPTER OBJECTIVES

1. *Understand the basic underlying common law heritage from England.*
2. *Describe how the federal and state court systems are organized.*
3. *Identify the functions of the trial and appellate courts.*
4. *Summarize the procedural differences between cases tried to juries and cases tried to judges.*
5. *Summarize the fundamental requirements for jurisdiction and venue in the federal and state judicial systems.*
6. *Describe when cases can be removed from state court to federal court.*
7. *Understand the policy reason underlying the Erie doctrine.*

COURTS

A court is a governmental body that is empowered to resolve disputes according to law. Courts are reactive institutions. They do not undertake to adjudicate disputes on their own initiative and can only act when someone files suit.

Courts are created in accordance with constitutional provisions and legislative acts. The legislative branch of the government usually has the right to establish and change courts, to regulate many of their procedures, and to limit their jurisdiction.

In the United States, we have a separate judicial system for each of the states, and yet another for the federal government. These systems vary in size and complexity, although they usually have hierarchical structures. Since federal and state judicial systems function simultaneously through-out the nation, conflicts can arise with respect to jurisdictional issues, substantive law, supremacy, and the finality of decisions.

Trial Courts

Courts are classified by function: there are trial courts and appellate courts. A trial court hears and decides controversies by determining facts and applying appropriate rules. The opposing parties to a dispute establish their positions by introducing evidence of the facts and by presenting arguments on the law.

The right of a trial by jury provides litigants with a choice of trying the case to a single judge or to a jury of peers. When a case is litigated before a judge instead of a jury, it is called a bench trial. The judge controls the entire trial and determines the outcome. In a jury trial, the decision-making functions are divided between the judge and the jury, which provides a safeguard of checks and balances. The judge rules on the admissibility of evidence, decides questions of law, and instructs the jury. The jury listens to the testimony, evaluates the evidence, and decides what facts have been proven. In many instances, the testimony of witnesses is contradictory. In such cases, the jury can determine the facts only after deciding which witnesses should be believed. It then applies the law to those facts in accordance with the judge's instructions. The judge supervises the entire process. This includes ruling on pretrial motions, supervising discovery, and conducting the trial, matters that are addressed in Chapter V.

When the jury's verdict is submitted, the jury decides who wins and what the recovery will be. Over half of the states permit a less-than-unanimous verdict in civil cases. The usual requirement in such states is five jurors in agreement out of six. Unless the parties stipulate otherwise, the rule in federal civil trials is that the jury verdict must be unanimous. The three types of verdicts in civil cases are a general verdict, a special verdict, and a combination of general and special verdicts, which is called a hybrid

verdict. Where the jury returns with a general verdict it indicates whether it finds for the plaintiff or for the defendant.

Where the law authorizes the jury to return with a special verdict, the jury answers specific questions related to the most important factual issues in the case. For example:

> We the jury ... find the following special verdict on the issues submitted to us:

> Issue 1: Was the defendant negligent? (Answer "yes" or "no.")

> Answer: _____

> If you answered "yes" as to Issue 1, then answer Issue 2.

> Issue 2: Was the negligence of the defendant a proximate cause of the plaintiff's injury? (Answer "yes" or "no.")

> Answer _____

> If you answered "yes" as to Issue 2, then answer Issue 3.

> Issue 3   etc....

A special verdict is used to focus the jury's attention on the evidence and the factual disputes in the case. It discourages jurors from determining the case's outcome by deciding which party they would like to see win the lawsuit. When the jury returns a special verdict, the judge applies the law to the jury's answers and reaches a final judgment.

It is often said that questions of fact are for the jury and questions of law are for the judge. A factual issue is presented when reasonable people could arrive at different conclusions in deciding what happened in an actual event. When an inference is so certain that all reasonable people must draw the same conclusion, it becomes a question of law for the judge. It is often difficult to make a distinction between questions of fact and questions of law.

There is no need for a trial (either to a jury or to the court) unless there is a factual dispute between the parties. If the parties agree about the facts, but disagree about the law, the judge can determine the applicable law and dispose of the case by motion for summary judgment.

A jury was traditionally composed of twelve people. Today, many jurisdictions have authorized six-person juries. Jurors are chosen from the community, and their qualifications are reviewed before they are accepted and seated. At trial, they make their decision in the privacy of the jury room.

Although federal and state constitutions guarantee the right to a trial by jury, there is some dispute about the effectiveness of the jury system. Jury trials take more time to conduct than bench trials and contribute to the congestion of court dockets. Jury trials also are expensive. Because jurors do not know how to evaluate evidence, rules of evidence and trial procedures have been developed so that they are exposed only to competent evidence and permissible argument. In a bench trial, many of these procedures and rules can be eliminated or relaxed.

In addition, juries are known to be very unpredictable and sometimes arbitrary, and add uncertainty to the adjudication process. Lawyers deal with this uncertainty by attempting to discover jurors' hidden tendencies, biases, and attitudes. More and more, trial attorneys employ jury research firms in big cases to help them select the jury and prepare and present their clients' cases. Attorneys who try such cases develop special skills and strategies to sway juries that would be inappropriate to use in a bench trial before an experienced judge.

One of the most important benefits of the jury system is that it allows citizens to participate in the legal process. A jury is supposed to represent a cross section of the public, whereas a judge does not. Despite the weaknesses of the jury system, it is not likely that the right to a trial by jury will be eliminated in the near future.

Appellate Courts

Appellate courts review the decisions of trial courts. Usually, an appeal can only be taken from a lower court's judgment. In the case of *Du Pont v. Christopher* (a case you can read in the textbook's appendix),

however, readers learn that some jurisdictions permit a limited interlocutory appeal to be made prior to a trial in some circumstances. That is, appellate review may be permitted to resolve a controlling question of law before the case itself is actually decided. In a civil action, any dissatisfied party generally may appeal to a higher court. In criminal cases, the defendant usually may appeal, but the prosecution generally may not.

The appellate court reviews the proceedings of the trial court to determine whether the trial court acted in accordance with the law, and whether the appellant properly preserved the error. This means that an attorney cannot observe error occurring in a trial court and do nothing. The attorney must inform the judge of the error and request specific relief. Failure to object results in a waiver of the right to raise the matter subsequently on appeal.

An appellate court bases its decision solely on the theories argued and evidence presented in the lower court. There are no witnesses or jurors at the appellate level. The appellate court does not retry the facts of the case, and no new arguments or proof is permitted. The appellate court reaches its decision by using only the record of the proceedings in the lower court, the written briefs filed by both parties to the appeal, and the parties' oral arguments given before the appellate judges. The record of the proceedings in the lower court includes the pleadings, pretrial papers, depositions, and a transcript of the trial proceedings and testimony.

STATE COURT SYSTEMS

The power to create courts is an attribute of every sovereignty. The various states of the United States have exercised this power either by constitutional provisions or by statutory enactments. The power to create courts includes the authority to organize them, including the establishment of judgeships, and to regulate their procedure and jurisdiction.

Although each of the states has developed its own unique structure, substantive law, rules, and procedures, there is an underlying common law heritage. In our nation's formative years Americans were greatly influenced by English structures, procedures, and substantive law. Yet from the earliest days, the states modified or replaced both substantive law and legal structures when necessary, and created new ones. Each of the various states was independently charged with dispensing justice in its courts. Each system had the capacity to adapt, reform, and experiment. From those early days down to the present, the states have borrowed from each other in order to improve the administration of justice.

Even though fifty-one judicial systems are available to resolve disputes, very few cases actually go to trial. Disputes are usually settled outside the courtroom on the basis of the lawyer's predictions of what would happen if the case were tried. Litigation is very expensive and time consuming, which encourages litigants to settle cases without a trial.

JURISDICTION

Jurisdiction is the power or authority of a court to determine the merits of a dispute and to grant relief. A court has jurisdiction when it has this power over the subject matter of the case (**subject-matter jurisdiction**), and over the persons of the plaintiff and defendant (**personal—*in personam*—jurisdiction)** or the property that is in dispute (***in rem* jurisdiction**). The court itself must determine whether it has jurisdiction over a controversy presented before it. This is true even if neither party questions the court's jurisdiction. Once a court has acquired jurisdiction, it keeps it throughout the case, even if a party changes domicile or removes property from the state. When more than one court has a basis for jurisdiction, the first to exercise it has exclusive jurisdiction until the case is concluded. Questions about jurisdiction should be resolved before the court concerns itself with other matters involved in the case.

The primary function of trial courts is to exercise original jurisdiction. This term refers to the court's power to take note of a suit at its beginning, try it, and pass judgment on the law and the facts of the controversy. In many states, trial courts also exercise appellate jurisdiction over decisions of courts of limited subject-matter jurisdiction.

Some state judicial systems provide that appeals from the decisions of trial courts go directly to the state's highest court (usually, but not always, called the supreme court). Many states, however, usually require review by an intermediate appellate court (often called a court of appeals) before the matter can be heard by the state's highest court. The state's highest court reviews appeals of major questions emanating from the lower state courts, and at the state level, its decision is final. A typical example of a state court system can be seen in Figure 4.1.

Subject-Matter Jurisdiction in State Court

Legislatures, in accordance with state constitutions, have the right to allocate the workload throughout the state's judicial system. This means that the legislature usually enacts statutes that define each court's subject-matter jurisdiction (the types of controversies that can be litigated in that court). The parties to a lawsuit cannot by consent confer subject-matter jurisdiction on a court.

Legislatures often create specialized trial courts, including the land court, probate court (which handles deceased persons' estates), juvenile court, environmental court, and housing court, to exercise original subject-matter jurisdiction over particular types of controversies. Subject-matter jurisdiction may also be limited by the dollar amount involved in the controversy, as in small claims court, or by territory, as in municipal courts. All these courts would be possessed of limited subject-matter jurisdiction.

Legislatures also create trial courts to exercise original subject-matter jurisdiction over all other controversies. These courts, which go by various names such as the court of common pleas, district court, superior court, circuit court, county court, or even—in New York State—the trial division of the supreme court, are classified as courts of general or residual jurisdiction.

Introduction to *Cheap Escape Co., Inc. v. Haddox LLC*

In the following case, the plaintiff–appellant filed suit in the Franklin County Municipal Court

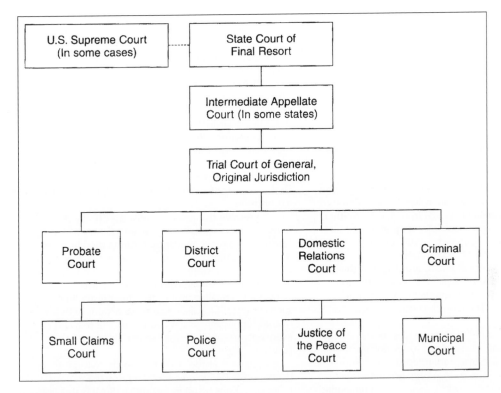

FIGURE 4.1 A State Court System

Source: Adapted from Arnold J. Goldman and William D. Sigismond, Business Law: Principles & Practices, 2d ed. Copyright © 1988 by Houghton Mifflin Company.

against the defendant–appellee for breach of contract and was awarded a default judgment when the defendant failed to answer the plaintiff's complaint. Approximately eleven months later, the defendant filed a motion asking the municipal court to vacate its own judgment, claiming that the court lacked subject-matter jurisdiction to rule in the case. The case was brought before the Ohio Supreme Court.

Notice how Judge Moyer's opinion refers to an Ohio court known as the Court of Common Pleas. The first court bearing this name was established in 1178 by England's King Henry II. Besides Ohio, courts of common pleas also exist in Delaware, Pennsylvania, and South Carolina. The Court of Common Pleas in Ohio is a court with general jurisdiction over civil and criminal matters.

Cheap Escape Co., Inc. v. Haddox, LLC
900 N.E.2d 601
Supreme Court of Ohio
December 11, 2008

Moyer, C. J.

I.
This appeal requires us to determine whether municipal courts have subject-matter jurisdiction over matters lacking connections to their geographical territories....

II.
Appellant, Cheap Escape Company, Inc., d.b.a. JB Dollar Stretcher ("Cheap Escape"), produces a magazine that features business advertisements. Haddox, L.L.C., a construction firm located in Summit County, entered into two contracts with Cheap Escape to run

ads in this magazine; appellee, Jeffrey L. Tessman, signed both agreements as a guarantor. The contracts provided that "in the event either party is in noncompliance with any provision of this Agreement the proper venue for litigation purposes will be in the Franklin County Municipal Court or Franklin County Common Pleas." The parties agree that the events relevant to these transactions occurred outside Franklin County and that the only connection to that forum arises from the forum-selection clauses in the contracts between them.

After Haddox allegedly defaulted on the agreements, Cheap Escape filed a breach-of-contract action against Haddox and Tessman in the Franklin County Municipal Court, seeking $1,984 in damages. Neither defendant filed a responsive pleading, and the municipal court eventually entered default judgment for Cheap Escape. Nearly 11 months later, Tessman moved to vacate the default judgment, arguing that the municipal court lacked subject-matter jurisdiction because none of the relevant events occurred in Franklin County.... The municipal court denied this motion.

Tessman appealed. The court of appeals ... held that the municipal court did not have subject-matter jurisdiction over the case, regardless of the forum-selection clause.... The court of appeals therefore reversed the municipal court's decision and remanded the case for dismissal....

III.

This case requires us to examine the limits of municipal court jurisdiction. Unfortunately, jurisdiction is a vague term.... Several distinct concepts, including territorial jurisdiction, monetary jurisdiction, personal jurisdiction, and subject-matter jurisdiction, must be demonstrated for a municipal court to be able to hear a specific case.

While the parties agree that the Franklin County Municipal Court had territorial jurisdiction [because the municipal court deciding the case was situated in Columbus Ohio, which is geographically within Franklin County], monetary jurisdiction [because the amount in dispute was less than the $15,000 monetary statutory ceiling for breach of contract cases], and personal jurisdiction in this case, they disagree sharply on the issue of municipal court subject-matter jurisdiction. "Subject-matter jurisdiction of a court connotes the power to hear and decide a case upon its merits" and "defines the competency of a court to render a valid judgment in a particular action." *Morrison v. Steiner* (1972)....

Unlike courts of common pleas [which in Ohio is the name given to what other states call the county

courts], which are created by the Ohio Constitution and have statewide subject-matter jurisdiction, ... municipal courts are statutorily created, ... and their subject-matter jurisdiction is set by statute.... R.C. 1901.18(A) provides the applicable law in this regard: "Except as otherwise provided in this division or section 1901.181 of the Revised Code, subject to the monetary jurisdiction of municipal courts as set forth in section 1901.17 of the Revised Code, a municipal court has original jurisdiction within its territory in all of the following actions or proceedings...." The list of enumerated actions includes breach-of-contract cases, which is the cause of action here....

To resolve this case, we must specifically determine what the phrase "original jurisdiction within its territory" means. Appellant interprets the phrase to mean that a municipal court has subject-matter jurisdiction over any statutorily prescribed action, regardless of where the underlying events occurred. Conversely, appellee argues that the phrase limits subject-matter jurisdiction to those actions with a territorial connection to the court (e.g., the relevant events occurred within the territorial limits of the court)....

Appellant argues that the words "within its territory" refer to "jurisdiction" and not the various types of actions listed in R.C. 1901.18(A)(1) through (12). Under this reading, R.C. 1901.18(A) grants a municipal court subject-matter jurisdiction to hear one of those actions if the court convenes within its geographical territory, regardless of whether the case has a territorial connection to the forum. Thus, appellant claims that the Franklin County Municipal Court had jurisdiction over this case because it was operating in Columbus, as required by R.C. 1901.02(A), even though the relevant events occurred in Summit County....

Appellee argues that this approach renders the phrase "within its territory" irrelevant and that R.C. 1901.18 should instead be read to give municipal courts subject-matter jurisdiction only over events having a territorial connection to the court. This interpretation requires us to read "within its territory" as referring to the types of actions that a municipal court may hear....

After reviewing these arguments and the plain text of R.C. 1901.18(A), we find the statute to be ambiguous.... It is simply unclear from the statutory language whether the General Assembly intended to limit municipal court subject-matter jurisdiction to territorial matters or to give municipal courts subject-matter jurisdiction over all matters suitable for municipal court review so long as the court sits within its territory when it disposes of a dispute. Both interpretations are reasonable....

To resolve this ambiguity, we must rely on additional methods of statutory interpretation. Because R.C. 1901.18 is part of a complex series of statutes related to jurisdiction, it is appropriate to review the statutes in pari materia.... Under this canon of construction, we read all statutes relating to the same general subject matter together and interpret them in a reasonable manner that "give[s] proper force and effect to each and all of the statutes."...

As noted above, appellant argues that "within its territory" means that a municipal court may hear any of the actions enumerated in R.C. 1901.18(A)(1) through (12) so long as it sits within its geographical territory....

Thus, appellant's interpretation would make the phrase "within its territory" in R.C. 1901.18 mere surplusage.... If the General Assembly had intended to merely repeat the provisions of these statutes, it could have incorporated them by reference ...

However, the General Assembly chose to use the unique phrase "original jurisdiction within its territory" in R.C. 1901.18, and we must afford those words some meaning. "It is axiomatic in statutory construction that words are not inserted into an act without some purpose."... Because "within its territory" does not refer to the areas in which a municipal court may sit, the only other logical way to read the phrase is as a limit on the types of actions that a court may hear.

Thus, the phrase "original jurisdiction within its territory in all of the following actions" means that a municipal court may hear only those matters listed in R.C. 1901.18(A)(1) through (12) that have a territorial connection to the court.

This reading makes sense in view of ... R.C. 1901.20 [which] provides that municipal courts have subject-matter jurisdiction in criminal matters only when the crime was committed "within its territory" or "within the limits of its territory." R.C. 1901.20(A)(1) and (B). We find no reason that the General Assembly would have granted municipal courts statewide subject-matter jurisdiction over civil matters but only territorial subject-matter jurisdiction over criminal matters. Further, the fact that the General Assembly used the words "within its territory" in both sections suggests that the phrase should carry the same meaning in both.

We therefore hold that R.C. 1901.18(A) limits municipal court subject-matter jurisdiction to actions or proceedings that have a territorial connection to the court. Because the parties admittedly did not have territorial connections to the Franklin County Municipal Court, the court lacked subject-matter jurisdiction in this matter. Although the parties entered into contracts with what appear to be valid forum-selection clauses, such clauses may be used only to choose from among venues that have subject-matter jurisdiction; litigants cannot vest a court with subject-matter jurisdiction by agreement....

Case Question

1. The parties to this case contractually agreed that in the event of a breach, suit could be brought in either the Franklin County Municipal Court or the Franklin County Court of Common Pleas. Why did the Ohio Supreme Court conclude that this contractual term could not be enforced?

Jurisdiction over the Person

The establishment of personal jurisdiction is constitutionally required for a court to impose binding liability on a person.

Imagine what would happen in our country if there were no jurisdictional limits on a state judicial system's ability to exercise personal jurisdiction over nonresidents. Every state would try to maximize its power, and total chaos would result. It was for this reason that jurisdictional rules were created: to prevent courts from deciding the merits of a case unless they have jurisdiction over the particular parties to the suit.

In the 1860s there were two methods of establishing a basis for jurisdiction over a person (in personam jurisdiction). The first involved showing that the party had been served within the boundaries of the state in which the lawsuit was filed (called the forum state) with a summons originating from within the forum state (see Figure 4.2).

STATE OF WISCONSIN   _____ Court   _____ County

_____, Plaintiff

v.   Summons File No. _____

_____, Defendant

The State of Wisconsin

To each person named above as a defendant:

You are hereby notified that the plaintiff named above has filed a lawsuit or other legal action against you. The complaint, which is attached, states the nature and basis of the legal action.

Within 45 days of receiving this summons, you must respond with a written answer, as that term is used in chapter 802 of the Wisconsin Statues, to the complaint. The court may reject or disregard an answer that does not follow the requirements of the statutes. The answer must be sent or delivered to the court, whose address is . . . . , and to . . . . , plaintiff's attorney, whose address is . . . . . You may have an attorney help or represent you.

If you do not provide a proper answer within 45 days, the court may grant judgment against you for the award of money or other legal action requested in the complaint, and you may lose your right to object to anything that is or may be incorrect in the complaint. A judgment may be enforced as provided by law. A judgment awarding money may become a lien against any real estate you own now or in the future, and may also be enforced by garnishment or seizure of property.

Dated: . . . . . . , 20 . . .

[signed] _____
                        Attorney for Plaintiff

Address: _____

FIGURE 4.2 State of Wisconsin Statutory Form of Summons Tort Actions [Sec. 801.095]

The constitutionality of this method was upheld by the U.S. Supreme Court in the 1990 case of *Burnham v. Superior Court*. The Court rejected Burnham's argument that basing personal jurisdiction on someone's mere presence within the forum state when served is unfair where minimum contacts between the person and the forum state do not exist. California, said the Court, was entitled to exercise personal jurisdiction over a nonresident from New Jersey who voluntarily traveled to California and was served with a California summons while he was in San Francisco for the weekend to visit his children.[1] The summons had nothing to do with his actions within California.[2]

A second traditional method of establishing personal jurisdiction not involving the existence of "sufficient minimum contacts" was based on consent. For example, a plaintiff implicitly consents to personal jurisdiction in a state when he or she files a lawsuit with a clerk of court. Defendants also can consent to personal jurisdiction in the following circumstances:

1. The defendant makes a general appearance in a case. If the defendant argues the substantive facts of the case, he or she is implicitly consenting to personal jurisdiction. Thus, a defendant wishing to challenge in personam jurisdiction must notify the court that she or he is making a special appearance for the limited purpose of contesting jurisdiction.

2. A nonresident defendant allegedly commits a tortious act within the forum state.

3. A nonresident drives a motor vehicle on the roads of the forum state and becomes involved in a collision. Under the laws of most states, the motorist impliedly appoints an official of the forum state to be his agent for receiving service of the plaintiff's summons arising from the accident.

Because nonresident defendants rarely consent to being sued and can avoid being served within the forum state by never going there, a new theory for jurisdiction was necessary. To remedy this problem, the U.S. Supreme Court developed its "sufficient minimum contacts" rule.

The sufficiency of the defendant's contacts with the forum state is determined by looking at the particular facts of each case. Sufficient minimum contacts, for example, exist in the state in which the defendant is domiciled. A person's domicile is the state in which the defendant has established his or her permanent home and to which the defendant returns after temporary absences. Factors such as where a person is licensed to drive, votes, and is employed are considered in determining domicile.

The consequences of not establishing personal jurisdiction are significant. Assume, for example, that a plaintiff has won a lawsuit and been awarded a judgment (the court document declaring the plaintiff the victor and specifying the remedy) entitling the plaintiff (now called the judgment creditor) to collect money damages from the defendant (now called the judgment debtor) and the judgment debtor fails to pay. If the trial court had proper personal jurisdiction over the defendant, the judgment creditor would be entitled to take the judgment to any state in which the judgment debtor owns property and there have it enforced. If the court issuing the judgment lacked in personam jurisdiction over the defendant, however, that judgment would be unenforceable.

Long-Arm Statutes

Every state has enacted what are called **long-arm statutes** (see Figure 4.3 below) that permit the exercise of personal jurisdiction over nonresident defendants who have had sufficient minimum contacts with the forum state. A long-arm statute allows the plaintiff to serve the forum state's summons on the defendant in some other state.

When a plaintiff successfully uses the long-arm statute, the defendant can be required to return to the forum state and defend the lawsuit. If the defendant fails to do so, he or she risks the entry of a default judgment.

Introduction to *Swoboda v. Hero Decks*

The parties in *Swoboda v. Hero Decks* disagreed about whether in personam jurisdiction existed over the defendant, Parody Productions. Parody, an Ohio company, offered playing cards for sale on its Internet website. Parody had no connections with Louisiana other than the operation of a

454.210. Personal jurisdiction of courts over nonresident—Process, how served—Venue

(1) As used in this section, "person" includes an individual, his executor, administrator, or other personal representative, or a corporation, partnership, association, or any other legal or commercial entity, who is a nonresident of this Commonwealth.

(2) (a) A court may exercise personal jurisdiction over a person who acts directly or by an agent, as to a claim arising from the person's:

    1. Transacting any business in this Commonwealth;

    2. Contracting to supply services or goods in this Commonwealth;

    3. Causing tortious injury by an act or omission in this Commonwealth;

    4. Causing tortious injury in this Commonwealth by an act or omission outside this Commonwealth if he regularly does or solicits business, or engages in any other persistent course of conduct, or derives substantial revenue from goods used or consumed or services rendered in this Commonwealth, provided that the tortious injury occurring in this Commonwealth arises out of the doing or soliciting of business or a persistent course of conduct or derivation of substantial revenue within the Commonwealth;

    5. Causing injury in this Commonwealth to any person by breach of warranty expressly or impliedly made in the sale of goods outside this Commonwealth when the seller knew such person would use, consume, or be affected by, the goods in this Commonwealth, if he also regularly does or solicits business, or engages in any other persistent course of conduct, or derives substantial revenue from goods used or consumed or services rendered in this Commonwealth;

    6. Having an interest in, using, or possessing real property in this Commonwealth, providing the claim arises from the interest in, use of, or possession of the real property, provided, however, that such in personam jurisdiction shall not be imposed on a nonresident who did not himself voluntarily institute the relationship, and did not knowingly perform, or fail to perform, the act or acts upon which jurisdiction is predicated;

    7. Contracting to insure any person, property, or risk located within this Commonwealth at the time of contracting;

    …

(3) (a) When personal jurisdiction is authorized by this section, service of process may be made on such person, or any agent of such person, in any county in this Commonwealth, where he may be found, or on the Secretary of State who, for this purpose, shall be deemed to be the statutory agent of such person;
    …

(4) When the exercise of personal jurisdiction is authorized by this section, any action or suit may be brought in the county wherein the plaintiff resides or where the cause of action or any part thereof arose.

(5) A court of this Commonwealth may exercise jurisdiction on any other basis authorized in the Kentucky Revised Statutes or by the Rules of Civil Procedure, notwithstanding this section.

FIGURE 4.3 Excerpt from Kentucky Long-Arm Statute, KRS 454.210.

website from which residents of any state could "interactively" purchase its products. The cards in question in this lawsuit included images of baseball players (one of whom was the plaintiff, Ronald Swoboda, a former member of the New York Mets Baseball Team). Swoboda claimed that Parody had used his likeness without his permission and filed suit in Louisiana. Swoboda's legal position in the trial court was that his attorney's online purchase from Parody of cards that contained Swoboda's likeness was enough of a connection between Louisiana and Parody to satisfy the minimum contacts requirements of the Due Process Clause. The trial court disagreed and ruled that the court lacked personal jurisdiction to decide the merits of the case. Swoboda then appealed the trial court's decision to the Louisiana intermediate court of appeals.

Ronald A. Swoboda v. Hero Decks, A Division of Parody Productions, LLC
36 So.3d 994
Court of Appeal of Louisiana, Fourth Circuit
March 31, 2010

Roland L. Belsome, Judge.

This Court is presented with the question of whether an internet merchandiser has established sufficient minimum contacts with Louisiana to be subjected to personal jurisdiction. For the following reasons, we affirm the trial court's finding that personal jurisdiction cannot be extended.

Parody Productions, LLC is a company that publishes novelty playing cards, which are sold over the internet. The product at issue for this appeal is referred to as the "Hero Decks" line which portrays well known players from a sports team's history. One such deck includes fifty-two (52) past and present players from the New York Mets baseball team. The plaintiff in this suit, Ronald Swoboda, is included in the New York Mets Hero Deck.

Mr. Swoboda claims that he has never given Parody permission to use his image. He further contends that through his attorney he sent Parody a cease and desist letter. Parody refused to stop selling cards featuring Mr. Swoboda's name and likeness. In response, Mr. Swoboda filed the instant lawsuit to enjoin Parody from the continued use of his name and likeness and for damages for violating his right to publicity, and, alternatively, damages for unjust enrichment. Subsequently, Parody filed exceptions of lack of personal jurisdiction.... The trial court sustained the exception [or objection] of lack of personal jurisdiction and this appeal followed.

... The party that seeks to invoke personal jurisdiction bears the burden of establishing such jurisdiction exists. This burden is satisfied upon a prima facie [legally adequate] showing that jurisdiction is appropriate.

Our authority to exercise jurisdiction over a non-resident defendant is granted under the Louisiana Long-arm Statute.... This authority is limited by the due process requirements of the Fourteenth Amendment.... The due process test was first established by the United States Supreme Court in *International Shoe Co. v. Washington*, 326 U.S. 310 ... (1945). Two prongs of the due process test must be satisfied before personal jurisdiction can be exercised.... First, the non-resident defendant must have "minimum contacts" with the forum state; and secondly, the exercise of personal jurisdiction in the forum state must not violate the basic notions of "fair play and substantial justice." When applying the test the quality and nature of the activity must be considered....

... Mr. Swoboda argues that because Parody maintains an interactive website that has allowed Louisiana residents to purchase the cards, ... jurisdiction is warranted.

In order for a plaintiff to satisfy its burden of proving minimum contacts with the forum state, there must be a showing that the defendant purposefully availed itself of the laws and protections of the forum state...

In general, questions of personal jurisdiction are factual determinations that must be weighed on a case by case basis. There are no clear-cut rules or a set jurisdictional formula that can be applied in determining whether personal jurisdiction conforms with the notion of "fair play and substantial justice."... To the contrary, "... any inquiry into fair play and substantial justice 'necessarily requires determinations in which few answers will be written in black and white.

The greys are dominant and even among them the shades are innumerable.' "... As relevant as that statement was at the time it was written, the world wide use of the internet has expanded the grey areas of personal jurisdiction.

The *Zippo* court employed a sliding scale approach to determine whether a website has minimum contacts with a forum state sufficient to invoke personal jurisdiction. *Zippo Mfg. Co. v. Zippo Dot Com, Inc....* The sliding scale categorizes the website's activities as passive or interactive.... Passive websites disseminate information and do not provide the minimum contacts that warrant the exercise of personal jurisdiction.... On the other side of the scale is the interactive website where business is clearly done through the website. Those websites typically have repeated contacts and transmissions and may also allow participants to enter into contracts. Under those circumstances personal jurisdiction is warranted.... However, when a website falls somewhere in the midrange of the scale and information is exchanged between the host and user, but not on an ongoing basis, the court must look to the extent of the interactivity and commercial nature of the exchange of information to determine whether personal jurisdiction should be exercised....

For instance, in *Quality Design & Constr. v. Tuff Coat Mfg., Inc.,* ... and later in *Crummey v. Morgan,* .... the Louisiana First Circuit Court of Appeal utilized the *Zippo* sliding scale approach as a guide for determining personal jurisdiction. In both cases the cause of action arose from an allegedly defective product purchased by a Louisiana citizen.

Tuff Coat manufactured a polyurethane coating for cement.... Tuff Coat's product, Ultra Tuff, was used in a Louisiana water park.... The pigment from the Ultra Tuff leaked and damaged the water purification system.... The construction company filed suit against Tuff Coat and Tuff Coat excepted on the grounds of personal jurisdiction.... Tuff Coat operated a website that provided a telephone number for ordering the products and a list of other Louisiana businesses that had used the products.... Tuff Coat argued that their website was purely informational and thus, passive.... The First Circuit, using the *Zippo* sliding scale, found that Tuff Coat's website was passive and even though Tuff Coat's products had been purchased by at least five Louisiana businesses, there was no purposeful availment "of Louisiana's law such

that it could expect to be hailed into a Louisiana court."...

The *Crummey* court was presented with a defendant that used a third-party website to advertise and sell a recreational vehicle.... The defendants and the vehicle were located in Texas.... The record indicated that Crummey found the vehicle online, had communicated with the seller over the telephone, and used telephone contact to place a deposit on the vehicle with a credit card.... The defendants offered to deliver the vehicle to Louisiana, but Mr. Crummey chose to travel to Texas to pick it up.... The transfer of ownership took place in Texas and Mr. Crummey took possession of the vehicle and began his drive back to Louisiana.... Prior to crossing the Texas–Louisiana border, the vehicle stopped running.... The defendants refused to submit a full refund for the vehicle and Mr. Crummey filed suit in Louisiana.... The defendants filed an exception of lack of personal jurisdiction....

Using the *Zippo* sliding scale and distinguishing the *Tuff Coat* decision, the First Circuit found that there were appropriate minimum contacts to exercise personal jurisdiction.... The *Crummey* court found that the repeated contact the defendant had with Louisiana beginning with the advertising of the vehicle over the internet, then the negotiations and the tender of money over the telephone supported its finding that the defendants had purposefully availed themselves to the laws and protections of Louisiana.... The court also noted that the defendants had delivered two other vehicles to buyers in Louisiana. In *dicta* the court raised its concern for online buyers who would have no recourse in their home state against sellers who misrepresent products and/or sell defective products....

Although the *Zippo* sliding scale is a useful guide when examining the extent to which websites are present in a forum state, it does not eliminate the necessity of this Court to independently review the relationship among the forum, the defendant, and the litigation when determining personal jurisdiction.... As an internet merchandiser, Parody sells playing cards on an interactive website that would fall midrange on the *Zippo* sliding scale. The record indicates that the playing cards can be purchased directly from the site. Other than the ability of Louisiana residents to access the website and purchase the merchandise, the record is void of any other contact Parody had with Louisiana. Once Parody refused to stop using Mr. Swoboda's likeness, his attorney purchased a deck of the Mets playing cards over the internet shortly before filing suit against Parody.

The pivotal question in this case is whether the plaintiff's counsel's purchase from this website or the mere ability of Louisiana citizens to access the merchandise from the website constitutes Parody purposefully availing itself of the benefits and laws of Louisiana for this cause of action. The United States Supreme Court has maintained that "the mere unilateral activity of those who claim some relationship with the nonresident defendant cannot satisfy the requirement of contact with the forum state."... Further, although the cause of action complained

of in the plaintiff's petition stems from Parody's manufacturing and selling of the playing cards, Mr. Swoboda's cause of action as plead in his petition arose prior to his attorney's purchase of the Mets cards in Louisiana. Thus, we find that the connexity between Parody's contact with Louisiana and Mr. Swoboda's cause of action are too attenuated to constitutionally exercise personal jurisdiction over Parody. Accordingly, under the facts and circumstances of this case, extending personal jurisdiction over Parody would not comport with the notions of fair play and substantial justice. Therefore, we affirm the trial court's ruling.

Affirmed.

Case Questions

1. Why did the Louisiana Court of Appeals conclude that the courts of that state did not have the right to exercise personal jurisdiction in this case?
2. In your opinion, might Swoboda be able to establish personal jurisdiction in Ohio?
3. What is your reaction to the decision in this case?

In Personam Jurisdiction over Corporations

Every corporation has been incorporated by one of the fifty states and is therefore subject to the in personam jurisdiction of that state's courts. A corporation also may consent to in personam jurisdiction in other states. Generally, a state will require that all corporations doing business within its borders register with it and appoint an in-state person or company as its agent. Many states also designate a state government official, often the secretary of state, as the default agent if no appointed agent can be found. The default agent will be authorized to receive service of process relating to litigation arising from an in-state business's presence and commercial activities conducted within that state. Soliciting orders, writing orders, and entering into contracts would establish a corporate presence that would be sufficient for in personam jurisdiction. The mere presence of corporate officers

within the forum state or the occasional shipping of orders into the forum is not sufficient for personal jurisdiction.

Jurisdiction over Property—In Rem Jurisdiction

A state has jurisdiction over property located within the state. The property may be real (land and buildings) or personal (clothes, cars, televisions, checking accounts, antique clocks, etc.). This is called *in rem* jurisdiction, or jurisdiction over things. An in personam decision imposes liability on a person and is personally binding. A decision in rem, however, is directed against the property itself and resolves disputes about property rights. A court can determine the rights to property that is physically located within the forum state, regardless of whether the court has personal jurisdiction over all interested individuals. For example, if two parties—one of whom is from out of state—dispute the ownership of a piece of land in Montana, the courts of Montana can determine ownership because it relates to property located within that state.

Procedural Due Process Requirements

In addition to establishing a basis for jurisdiction over the person or the property that is in dispute, a court must give proper notice to a defendant. The statutes of each jurisdiction often make distinctions between the types of notice required for in personam actions and in rem actions. This subject is covered in more detail in Chapter V.

Venue

Venue requirements determine the place where judicial authority should be exercised. Once personal jurisdiction has been established, a plaintiff has to litigate in a court that has subject-matter jurisdiction over the controversy and in a place that the legislature says is a permissible venue.

State legislatures enact venue statutes to distribute the judicial workload throughout the system. They often provide for venue in the county or district where the cause of action arose, the county or district in which the defendant resides, and the county or district in which the plaintiff resides. In cases where the venue requirements can be satisfied in more than one district, the plaintiff's choice usually will prevail.

Parties wishing to challenge venue must assert their objections promptly, or they may be waived. In both civil and criminal cases, venue may be considered improper for several reasons. A court may decline to hear a case for fear of local prejudice, for the convenience of litigants and witnesses, or in the interests of justice.

In a civil case, the most common reason given for a court to decline to exercise jurisdiction is that it believes the case can proceed more conveniently in another court. This is known as the doctrine of *forum non conveniens*. The doctrine is applied with discretion and caution. One frequent ground for

applying the doctrine occurs when the event that gave rise to the suit took place somewhere other than in the forum state. The difficulties of securing the attendance of out-of-state witnesses and applying foreign law may make decision making inconvenient. The court balances the conveniences between the forum court and another court and weighs the obstacles to a fair proceeding against the advantages.

INTERNET TIP

You can see an example of a venue statute and read *Massey v. Mandell,* a Michigan venue case, on the textbook's website.

THE FEDERAL COURT SYSTEM

Article III, Section 1 of the U.S. Constitution is the basis of our federal court system. It provides that "the judicial power of the United States shall be vested in one supreme court, and in such inferior courts as the Congress may, from time to time, ordain and establish." Congress first exercised this power by passing the Judiciary Act of 1789, which has been amended and supplemented many times in order to establish the various federal courts, as well as their jurisdiction and procedures.

The federal court system consists of the district courts, exercising general, original jurisdiction; the courts of appeals, exercising intermediate appellate jurisdiction; and the U.S. Supreme Court, sitting as the highest court for both federal and state cases involving federal questions. Federal courts of limited jurisdiction include the U.S. Court of Federal Claims, which decides nontort claims filed against the United States; the U.S. Tax Court, which reviews decisions of the secretary of the treasury with respect to certain provisions of the Internal Revenue Code; the U.S. Court of International Trade, which has jurisdiction over civil actions relating to embargoes on imports, customs duties, and revenues from imports or tonnage; the Federal Bankruptcy Court, which hears bankruptcy cases; and

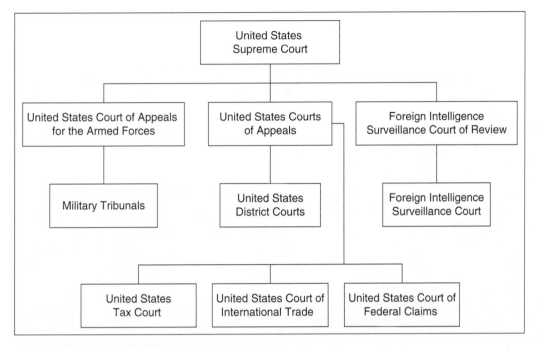

FIGURE 4.4 The Federal Court System

Source: Adapted from Arnold J. Goldman and William D. Sigismond, Business Law: Principles & Practices, 2d ed. Copyright © 1988 by Houghton Mifflin Company.

the Court of Appeals for the Armed Forces, which is a court of last resort in military criminal appeals. An organizational chart of the federal judiciary can be seen in Figure 4.4.

▶ THE U.S. DISTRICT COURTS

There are ninety-four federal district courts, with at least one in each state and territory in the United States. They are courts of original jurisdiction and serve as the trial court in the federal court system. The federal district courts are given limited subject-matter jurisdiction by the Constitution and by Congress. Article III provides that federal courts have jurisdiction over "all cases … arising under … the laws of the United States."

Because there are no federal common law crimes, all federal criminal actions must be based on federal statutes. In civil actions, Congress has authorized federal courts to exercise subject-matter jurisdiction in two categories of cases:

1. Federal question jurisdiction exists where the case involves claims based on the Constitution, laws, or treaties of the United States. Such claims would include suits by the United States and civil rights, patent, copyright, trademark, unfair competition, and admiralty suits.

2. Diversity of citizenship jurisdiction exists if a suit is between citizens of different states or between a citizen of a state and an alien, and if the amount in controversy exceeds $75,000 (the jurisdictional amount). Diversity jurisdiction provides qualifying plaintiffs with a choice of a federal or state forum for many types of civil actions. However, federal courts traditionally have declined to exercise diversity jurisdiction in divorce actions, child custody cases, and probate matters.

State citizenship is a key concept in diversity cases. For natural citizens, state citizenship is closely related to the establishment of a principal residence (domicile). Thus, a person who presently makes her home in Texas is a citizen of Texas. If she spends the summer working in Colorado and plans to return to Texas in September, she would still be a citizen of Texas.

Federal diversity jurisdiction requires that the diversity of citizenship be complete. This means that in a multiple-party suit, no one plaintiff and one defendant can be citizens of the same state. Thus, if a citizen of New York brings suit against two defendants, one a citizen of Wisconsin and one a citizen of Michigan, there would be total diversity of citizenship. A federal district court would have jurisdiction over the subject matter if the plaintiff were suing in good faith for over $75,000. If, however, one of the defendants were a citizen of New York, there would not be complete diversity of citizenship necessary for federal court jurisdiction and the plaintiff would be limited to bringing an action in an appropriate state court.

Congress has provided special citizenship rules for corporations. A corporation is considered a citizen in the state where it is incorporated, as well as in the state of its principal place of business. For example, a corporation incorporated in Delaware with its principal place of business in New York cannot sue or be sued by citizens of either of the two states in a diversity case in a federal district court.

Diversity jurisdiction avoids exposing the defendant to possible prejudice in the plaintiff's state court. Many argue against diversity jurisdiction, claiming that the fear of possible prejudice does not justify the expense of the huge diversity caseload in federal courts. See Figure 4.5 for data regarding civil cases brought in the U.S. District Courts from 2007 to 2011.

INTERNET TIP

It is unusual for Foreign Intelligence Surveillance Court opinions to be published in the Federal Reports. However both of the cases appealed by the government to the Foreign Intelligence Surveillance Court of Review, *In re: Sealed Case*, 310 F.3d 717 (2002), and *In re Directives*, 551 F.3d 1004 (2009), have been so reported. They can be found by searching for those citations online.

The Plaintiff's Choice of Forum

Various factors influence plaintiffs in their choice of a federal or state forum. One forum may be more attractive than another because it is closer and more convenient for the plaintiff. The plaintiff's attorney may be influenced by the reputation of the county or court in terms of the size of verdicts awarded there, by whether the forum is rural or urban, by socioeconomic factors, or by the reputations of the plaintiff and defendant within the forum. Plaintiffs may also be influenced to file in a federal forum if the federal procedural rules are more liberal than the corresponding state rules.

Introduction to *St. James Apartments, LLC v. Coinmach Corporation*

Coinmach, the defendant corporation, sought dismissal of a diversity suit on the grounds that the parties were not totally diverse. It alleged that it had citizenship in both New Jersey and Delaware and argued that the plaintiffs were also citizens of New Jersey, despite their claims of citizenship in Florida. If this were true, the federal court would have had to dismiss the case for lack of subject-matter jurisdiction.

St. James Apartments, LLC v. Coinmach Corporation
Civil Action No. 10-6778 (GEB)
United States District Court, D. New Jersey
July 13, 2011

MEMORANDUM OPINION

Garrett Brown Jr., District Judge.
This matter comes before the Court on the motion of Defendant Coinmach Corporation ("Defendant") to

dismiss the Complaint filed by Plaintiffs St. James Apartments, LLC, Hackensack Associates L.P., and Jasontown Apartments, LLC ("Plaintiffs") for lack of subject matter jurisdiction.... Plaintiffs oppose Defendant's motion....

Type of Case	Cases Commenced				
	2007	2008	2009	2010	2011
Total Cases	**257,507**	**267,257**	**276,397**	**282,895**	**289,252**
Constitutionality of State Statutes	277	254	273	329	333
Contract Actions, Total	33,939	34,172	35,634	31,109	32,306
Real Property Actions, Total	5,180	5,072	5,998	7,432	10,688
Tort Actions, Total	61,359	72,011	78,093	83,055	78,175
Personal Injury, Total	57,244	68,121	72,897	78,350	73,749
Personal Property Damage, Total	4,115	3,890	5,196	4,705	4,426
Civil Rights, Total	31,756	32,132	33,761	34,872	37,020
Voting	118	145	127	102	168
Employment	13,375	13,219	14,036	14,543	15,141
Housing & Accommodations	665	644	746	687	783
Welfare	27	48	71	58	52
ADA—Employment	1,041	1,095	1,195	1,522	1,768
ADA—Other	1,277	1,583	1,974	2,309	2,713
Environmental Matters	767	920	741	942	726
Deportation	115	130	91	61	53
Prisoner Petitions, Total	53,945	55,271	53,187	52,583	53,611
Motions to Vacate Sentence	5,896	6,352	5,771	5,858	6,260
Habeas Corpus—General	22,192	21,298	20,319	19,825	19,624
Habeas Corpus—Death Penalty	246	192	245	208	195
Prison Condition	7,309	7,610	7,540	8,107	8,609
Intellectual Property Rights, Total	10,783	9,592	8,365	8,966	9,940
Copyright	4,400	3,234	2,192	2,013	2,297
Patent	2,896	2,909	2,792	3,301	4,015
Trademark	3,487	3,449	3,381	3,652	3,628
Securities, Commodities, and Exchanges	1,394	1,637	1,674	1,397	1,402
Social Security Laws, Total	12,974	13,138	13,622	14,016	15,705
Disability Insurance	6,187	6,080	6,389	6,141	6,779
Supplemental Security Income	6,135	6,373	6,472	7,088	8,176
Retirement and Survivors Benefits	594	603	665	715	682

FIGURE 4.5 U.S. District Courts: Civil Cases Commenced 2007–2011

Source: Administrative Office of the United States Courts, *2011 Annual Report of the Director: Judicial Business of the United States Courts*. Washington, D.C.: U.S. Government Printing Office, 2012.

I. BACKGROUND

This case arises out of a dispute regarding the execution and validity of certain lease agreements between Plaintiffs and Defendant. Plaintiffs assert that federal jurisdiction under 28 U.S.C. § 1332 exists based upon their allegation that Plaintiffs and Defendant are citizens of different states (Florida for the Plaintiffs and Delaware and New Jersey for the Defendant), and the total amount in controversy exceeds $75,000. Defendant does not contest that it is a citizen of Delaware and New Jersey or that the amount in controversy

exceeds $75,000. In its present motion to dismiss, however, Defendant argues that Plaintiffs are actually citizens of New Jersey and have misrepresented their New Jersey citizenship in an attempt to manufacture diversity jurisdiction. Defendant bases this argument upon records that list a business address for Plaintiffs in New Jersey. It appears undisputed that Plaintiffs St. James Apartments, LLC and Jasontown Apartments, LLC are limited liability companies, and Plaintiff Hackensack Associates, L.P. is a limited partnership. It also appears undisputed that the sole member of all three Plaintiffs is James Nuckel ("Nuckel"). In response to Defendant's present motion, Nuckel argues that he is a domiciliary of Florida, and thus, that diversity jurisdiction is appropriate.

II. DISCUSSION

Subject matter jurisdiction is established under 28 U.S.C. § 1332 where the amount in controversy exceeds $75,000, and the controversy is between citizens of different states.... In establishing diversity of citizenship, the burden of proving, by preponderance of the evidence, that such jurisdiction is proper lies on the party claiming diversity.... Limited liability companies are considered citizens of each state in which their members are citizens, rather than their state of incorporation or the company's principal place of business....

An individual is considered a citizen of the state in which he is domiciled. "The domicile of an individual is his true, fixed and permanent home and place of habitation. It is the place to which, whenever he is absent, he has the intention of returning."... Courts consider numerous factors when determining an individual's domicile, including house of residence, payment of personal taxes, vehicle registration, place of business, and the exercise of political rights.... Obviously, ties to the community that cannot be easily formed or broken are afforded more weight than those easily established.... The party asserting diversity jurisdiction bears the burden of proving that their citizenship is diverse from that of the adverse party....

Here, the Court concludes that Plaintiffs have carried that burden through the certification of their managing partner, James Nuckel. In Nuckel's Certification ... he states that he and his immediate family reside in a primary residence in Florida.... Further, Nuckel states that his children attend school in Florida, his vehicle is registered in Florida, he is registered to vote in Florida, and he will be filing his income taxes as a Florida resident....

In contrast, Defendant has failed to successfully rebut Nuckel's assertion that he is a citizen of Florida, rather than New Jersey. It appears that Nuckel reported a New Jersey business address in order to register his business in New Jersey. Nuckel was given the option to provide a New Jersey business address or a place of residence for the managing partner in order to register as a New Jersey business entity.... Nuckel chose his New Jersey business address, rather than that of his Florida residence, in order to fill out the form. Defendant also alleges that Nuckel owns an "owner occupied" home in New Jersey. These two factual allegations alone, however, fail to persuade the Court that Nuckel is a New Jersey citizen when viewed in light of Nuckel's Certification.

Therefore, the Court concludes by a preponderance of the evidence presented that Nuckel is a Florida citizen. It is undisputed that Nuckel is the sole managing party of the three Plaintiffs. As such, Plaintiffs are deemed Florida for purposes of establishing diversity jurisdiction, and diversity jurisdiction is appropriate.

III. CONCLUSION

For the foregoing reason, Defendant's motion to dismiss the complaint for lack of subject matter jurisdiction will be denied. An appropriate form of order accompanies this memorandum opinion.

Case Questions

1. What factors did the court say it considered in determining where a party is domiciled (and therefore has citizenship for purposes of diversity jurisdiction in federal courts)?
2. Assume that a student who graduated from high school in Hawaii attends college in Oregon. What factors should influence the determination of where that student is domiciled?
3. Can you think of any policy reasons for the need for the federal courts to have subject-matter jurisdiction in diversity of citizenship cases, as these cases could be decided in state courts?

In Rem and In Personam Jurisdiction

In order for a district court to hear a civil case, it must have, in addition to jurisdiction over the subject matter, jurisdiction over the property in an in rem proceeding or over the person of the defendant in an in personam proceeding. Jurisdiction over the person is normally acquired by serving a summons within the territory. In an ordinary civil action, the summons may be properly served anywhere within the territorial limits of the state in which the district

Year	2007	2008	2009	2010	2011
Removals	30,282	30,065	30,161	31,341	34,190

FIGURE 4.6 Removal from State Courts to U.S. District Courts 2007–2011

Source: Administrative Office of the United States Courts, *2011 Annual Report of the Director: Judicial Business of the United States Courts*. Washington, D.C.: U.S. Government Printing Office, 2012.

court is located. A federal summons also may be served anywhere that a state summons could be served pursuant to the state's long-arm statute.

Venue in Federal Courts

Congress has provided that venue generally exists in the federal district where any defendant resides, if all defendants reside in the same state. It also exists where the claim arose or the property is located. If these choices are inappropriate, venue will exist in a diversity case in the federal district in which the defendant is subject to personal jurisdiction at the time the action is filed. In federal question cases, the alternative venue is the federal district in which any defendant can be found.[3]

A corporate defendant is subject to suit in any federal district in which it is subject to personal jurisdiction when the suit is filed.

Removal from State to Federal Courts (Removal Jurisdiction)

Except in those areas in which federal courts have exclusive jurisdiction, a suit does not have to be brought in a federal district court just because that court could exercise jurisdiction over the subject matter and over the person or property. A plaintiff may bring a dispute in any state or federal court that has jurisdiction.

A defendant sued in a state court may have a right to have the case removed to the federal district court. Any civil action brought in a state court that could originally have been filed in a district court is removable. Thus, removal jurisdiction is permissible where a federal question is raised or where the requirements for diversity of citizenship jurisdiction

are met. Where the basis of removal jurisdiction is diversity of citizenship, that basis must exist at the time of filing the original suit and also at the time of petitioning for removal. To initiate the removal process, the defendant must file notice of removal with the federal court within 30 days after service of the complaint. In recent years, U.S. District Court judges have approved the removal of approximately 31,000 cases per year from state to federal court (see Figure 4.6).

Introduction to *Abigail Frump v. Claire's Boutiques, Inc.*

The plaintiff in the following case, Abigail Frump, a minor, was detained by store security personnel in conjunction with an alleged theft while shopping at defendant's store with some friends. After the criminal charges against the plaintiff were dismissed, this civil action was brought against the defendant in state court in Missouri. The plaintiff estimated the damages as being in excess of $25,000 for each of three counts—false imprisonment, negligent supervision by store management, and malicious prosecution. She also sought an unspecified amount of punitive damages. The defendant responded by filing a removal motion in federal court alleging that the court had diversity subject-matter jurisdiction. The plaintiff opposed the removal motion and asked the federal judge to remand the matter to the Missouri state courts. She argued that as of the date of her motion for remand, the "known" damages in the case could not exceed $75,000.

You are about to read the U.S. District Court's ruling on the remand motion. In the memorandum opinion, the federal judge explains her ruling and the rationale that supports her conclusions.

Abigail Frump v. Claire's Boutiques, Inc.
Case No. 10-1106-CV-W-SWH
United States District Court, W.D. Missouri, Western Division
March 22, 2011

ORDER

Sarah Hays, Magistrate Judge.
This matter is before the Court on Plaintiff's Motion for Remand to State Court.... Defendant opposes the motion.... At issue is whether the amount in controversy requirement of 28 U.S.C. § 1332(a) is satisfied so that the Court may assert jurisdiction over the case or whether it must be remanded to state court....

I. BACKGROUND
On September 22, 2010, plaintiff filed a three count Petition in the Circuit Court of Jackson County, Missouri.... The Petition alleges that on or about April 18, 2009, plaintiff, a minor, was shopping at the Claire's store located at the Oak Park Mall in Overland Park, Kansas, and was accused of theft.... Plaintiff alleges that a Claire's employee would not let plaintiff and the girls she was with leave the store.... The Overland Park Police Department was called and plaintiff was issued a citation for theft as well as a citation directing that she not return to Oak Park Mall for one year. Plaintiff was later charged with a Class A Misdemeanor which was subsequently dismissed. Plaintiff alleges that numerous people were present who witnessed the event and who laughed and pointed at plaintiff.... The Petition alleges false imprisonment (Count I); negligent supervision (Count II); and malicious prosecution (Count III).... As a result of defendant's actions, plaintiff alleges she experienced mental suffering, injury to feelings, injury to reputation, embarrassment, humiliation, fear, indignity, disgrace, stress and loss of liberty.... For each count, plaintiff prays for actual damages in excess of $25,000, for reasonable punitive or exemplary damages against defendant, interest, attorney's fees, costs and for such other relief as the Court deems just and proper....

On November 5, 2010, defendant removed this case to federal court claiming jurisdiction is proper pursuant to 28 U.S.C. § 1332(a) because the parties are diverse and the amount in controversy, exclusive of interest and costs, exceeds $75,000.... Thereafter, plaintiff requested that the case be remanded to state court because "as of the day of filing this Motion for Remand, all known damages are less than $75,001."...

Defendant opposes the motion arguing that the petition clearly states damages which could exceed $75,000....

II. LEGAL STANDARDS FOR DETERMINING THE AMOUNT IN CONTROVERSY
A defendant may remove an action from state court to federal court if the action is within the court's original jurisdiction.... Here, defendant removed the case on the basis of diversity jurisdiction. Diversity jurisdiction exists where there is (1) complete diversity of citizenship and (2) the amount in controversy exceeds the jurisdictional minimum of $75,000, exclusive of interest and costs.... In this case, there is no dispute that there is complete diversity of citizenship between the parties.... The issue is whether the amount in controversy exceeds the $75,000 statutory requirement.

The starting point for analyzing whether the jurisdictional limit is satisfied is the Supreme Court's decision in *St. Paul Mercury Indemnity Co. v. Red Cab Co.*, ... (1938):

The rule governing dismissal for want of jurisdiction in cases brought in the federal court is that, unless the law gives a different rule, the sum claimed by the plaintiff controls if the claim is apparently made in good faith. It must appear to a legal certainty that the claim is really for less than the jurisdictional amount to justify dismissal. The inability of plaintiff to recover an amount adequate to give the court jurisdiction does not show his bad faith or oust the jurisdiction. Nor does the fact that the complaint discloses the existence of a valid defense to the claim. But if, from the face of the pleadings, it is apparent, to a legal certainty, that the plaintiff cannot recover the amount claimed or if, from the proofs, the court is satisfied to a like certainty that the plaintiff never was entitled to recover that amount, and that his claim was therefore colorable for the purpose of conferring jurisdiction, the suit will be dismissed. Events occurring subsequent to the institution of suit which reduce the amount recoverable below the statutory limit do not oust jurisdiction.... (the general federal rule is to decide the amount in controversy from the complaint itself). Following this directive, numerous courts have held that "when the amount in controversy claimed in the plaintiff's state court complaint exceeds $75,000, the complaint generally is determinative of the amount in controversy for purposes of federal jurisdiction upon removal."...

If, after the removal of an action to federal court, the plaintiff seeks a remand to state court, the defendant bears the burden of establishing federal jurisdiction by a preponderance of the evidence.... Any doubt about the court's removal jurisdiction should be resolved in favor of a remand to state court....

A. Determining the Amount of Compensatory Damages

Plaintiff alleges that her petition does nothing more than set forth the jurisdictional requirement for circuit court jurisdiction, and thus, defendant has not demonstrated that the federal jurisdictional amount requirement has been satisfied.... Rule 55.05 of the Missouri Rules of Civil Procedure prohibits pleading a specific dollar amount in tort actions except as is necessary to determine the proper jurisdictional authority. The Missouri pleading rules further require that every filing be signed [by] at least one attorney of record.... The signature is the attorney's representation to the court that the claim is not presented for an improper purpose, that the claims are warranted by existing law and that the allegations have evidentiary support or are likely to have evidentiary support after a reasonable opportunity for further investigation.... Thus, while counsel may have been required to plead that the claim involved an amount either above or below the $25,000 amount which divides circuit from associate circuit jurisdiction, the decision to plead damages in excess of $25,000 is counsel's representation of the value of the case, based upon counsel's knowledge at the time the petition was filed, and cannot be ignored.

Plaintiff has three claims against defendant, each seeking an amount in excess of $25,000 for actual damages and, in addition, punitive damages, costs and attorney's fees. When separate claims are brought by a sole plaintiff against a sole defendant, as in this case, the totality of the claims is the determining jurisdictional factor rather than the damages set forth in each claim....

However, when aggregating claims to determine if more than $75,000 is at issue, the court may not aggregate claims that merely assert different theories of recovery for the same damages....

In the circumstances of this case, the claims for false imprisonment ... and malicious prosecution ... can clearly be aggregated as each claim has an independent basis for damages. These claims are not merely different theories of recovery for the same damages. Each claim relies on different facts and the damages sought arise out of different actions taken at different time periods. The false imprisonment claim arises out of events occurring at the store on April 18, 2009, when plaintiff alleges she was called back into the store and was not allowed to leave for a period of at least ninety minutes following which she was required to provide information and be photographed by both the Overland Park Police Department and mall

security.... The malicious prosecution claim arises out of the misdemeanor charges that were ultimately dismissed.... Other courts have allowed plaintiffs to recover separate damages for false imprisonment and malicious prosecution claims....

While Missouri courts have recognized a cause of action for negligent supervision, ... it would appear that this would provide an alternative theory on which to recover the same damages sought under the false imprisonment and, possibly, the malicious prosecution claims. Thus, based on the face of the Petition, plaintiff has alleged actual damages in excess of $25,000 for each count, which damages may be aggregated as to at least two of the counts, for a total claim in excess of $50,000 in actual damages.

B. Determining the Amount of Punitive Damages

In addition to the claims for actual damages, plaintiff claims punitive damages under each theory of recovery. Punitive damages are included in determining the amount in controversy, unless it is apparent to a legal certainty that punitive damages may not be recovered.... The court explained this general principle in Miller v. Progressive Casualty Insurance Co. ... (M.D. Pa. Apr. 17, 2008):

> In calculating the jurisdictional amount, "[c]laims for punitive damages may be aggregated with claims for compensatory damages unless the former are 'patently frivolous and without foundation.'"... Such claims "are per se 'patently frivolous and without foundation' if they are unavailable as a matter of state substantive law."... If a plaintiff has authority under state law to seek punitive damages, however, the claim "will generally satisfy the amount in controversy requirement because it cannot be stated to a legal certainty that the value of the plaintiff's claim is below the statutory minimum."...

Causes of action for malicious prosecution and false arrest or imprisonment are intentional torts supporting the submission of punitive damages on these claims.... The issue then is how to value plaintiff's punitive damage claims for the purpose of determining whether the jurisdictional amount requirement is met....

The Supreme Court has been reluctant to establish a concrete constitutional limit on the ratio between harm, or potential harm, to a plaintiff and a punitive damage award. However, the Court has commented that: "few awards exceeding a single-digit ratio between punitive and compensatory damages, to a significant degree, will satisfy due process."...

In the circumstances of this case, plaintiff has pled the existence of compensatory damages in excess of $25,000 as to each of the counts of the petition. For jurisdictional purposes, the Court has treated the petition as stating two causes of action for independent damages for total compensatory damages in an amount in excess of $50,000. Thus, an award of punitive damages, on even one of these counts, in an amount of $25,000 would establish the requisite amount in controversy. Moreover, a punitive damage award of $25,000, a ratio of 1 to 1, would be well within the constitutional ratio accepted by other courts. Accordingly, the Court finds that when the compensatory and punitive damages, as pled in the petition, are aggregated, the amount in controversy requirement for federal diversity jurisdiction has been satisfied....

III. CONCLUSION
For the reasons set forth herein, it is ORDERED that Plaintiff's Motion for Remand to State Court ... is denied.

Case Questions

1. What is the general federal rule in a diversity case as to how judges should decide whether the amount in controversy exceeds $75,000?
2. Under what circumstances should a U.S. District Court judge in a diversity case conclude that the plaintiff's allegations as to the amount in controversy should be rejected?
3. Assume that the defendant in a diversity action has removed the case to federal court and that the plaintiff wants the federal court to remand the matter back to the state court. Assume also that the parties disagree as to whether the amount in controversy exceeds $75,000. Which party has the burden of proving the existence of federal jurisdiction?

The *Erie* Doctrine

In adjudicating state matters, a federal court is guided by a judicial policy known as the *Erie* doctrine. In the 1938 landmark case of *Erie Railroad Company v. Tompkins,* 304 U.S. 64, the U.S. Supreme Court decided that federal questions are governed by federal law. In other cases, however, the substantive law that should generally be applied in federal courts is the law of the state. The law of the state was defined as including judicial decisions as well as statutory law. In addition, no federal general common law governs state matters. A federal district court is bound by the statutes and precedents of the state in which it sits.

This restriction prevents a federal court and a state court from reaching different results on the same issue of state law.

The ***Erie* doctrine**, which goes to the heart of relations between the state and federal courts, is one of the most important judicial policies ever adopted by the U.S. Supreme Court. Many of the civil cases brought subsequent to this landmark case have been affected by the decision.

Where state and federal procedural rules differ, the *Erie* doctrine does not normally apply. Federal courts do not generally apply state procedural rules. Instead, the Federal Rules of Civil Procedure apply in federal courts unless they would significantly affect a litigant's substantive rights, encourage forum shopping, or promote a discriminatory application of the law. The Federal Rules of Civil Procedure were not designed to have any effect upon the rules of decision.

It is important to remember that the *Erie* doctrine does require that federal judges apply the same conflict-of-law rule that would be applied in the courts of the state in which the federal court is situated. In the following case, a U.S. District Court sitting in Indiana had to determine whether it should apply Indiana law or that of California in reaching its decision.

INTERNET TIP

Interested readers will find an excellent case that illustrates the *Erie* doctrine, *Carson v. National Bank,* on the textbook's website. This case was "retired" in the ninth edition after initially appearing in the second edition of the textbook, twenty-eight years ago. It can be found with other "Retired Cases."

Readers may recall reading the Chapter III conflict-of-law case from Indiana of *Hubbard Manufacturing Co. v. Greeson*. In that 1987 case the Indiana Supreme Court decided to apply the significant relationship rule in tort cases where a conflict of law issue is raised but the place where the tort was committed was an unimportant fact in the case.

We see that precedent followed in the next 2001 federal appeals case, which illustrates the working of the *Erie* doctrine.

The U.S. District Court sitting in Indiana, at the request of Yamaha Motor Corporation, granted Yamaha's motion for summary judgment, thereby declaring Yamaha the prevailing party in this lawsuit. Summary judgment is granted only if no genuine issues of material fact exist.. This pretrial motion is not granted if important facts are in dispute between the parties, because it would deprive them of their right to a trial.

The key issue at trial and on appeal was whether Indiana or California law should be applied to this product liability case. Yamaha argued that Indiana law should be applied, and Charles and April Land maintained that California law should control. As we learned in Chapter III, the outcome of disputes as to which state's law should be applied in a case depends on the **conflict-of-laws rule** (also known as **choice-of-law rule**) that has been adopted in the forum state. The District Court, following the principles of the *Erie* doctrine, concluded after applying Indiana's choice-of-law rule that Indiana law should apply. It determined that an Indiana statute required that product liability suits like this one be brought within ten years of the date when *the product was first purchased from the manufacturer (here, Yamaha)*. Therefore, said the District Court, inasmuch as the Lands had not started their suit within that time period, there was no way that they could prevail at trial. Yamaha, the court concluded, was entitled to summary judgment. The Lands subsequently appealed to the Seventh Circuit, arguing that the District Court had wrongfully applied Indiana law instead of California law.

Charles and April Land v. Yamaha Motor Corporation
272 F.3d 514
U.S. Court of Appeals for the Seventh Circuit
December 10, 2001

Flaum, Chief Judge.

The district court granted summary judgment in favor of defendants Yamaha Motor Corporation, U.S.A. ("YMUS") and Yamaha Motor Co., Ltd. ("YMC"), holding plaintiffs Charles and April Land's product liability suit [was] barred by the Indiana Statute of [Limitations]....

When appellant Charles Land, an Indiana resident, attempted to start a Yamaha WaveRunner Model WR500G on Heritage Lake in Indiana on June 25, 1998, the vehicle exploded and caused Land permanent back injury. The plaintiffs contend that the WaveRunner was defective in design: it allowed fuel fumes to accumulate in the hull of the boat, posing serious risk of fire upon ignition.... For purposes of the summary judgment motion, the district court assumed that the plaintiffs could prove their product liability claim on the merits. That is, it assumed that when the Wave Runner left the possession and control of the defendants, it was in a defective condition unreasonably dangerous to anticipated users. Furthermore, it is undisputed that the Lands filed suit on December 23, 1999, and that both the injury and the filing of the suit occurred more than ten years after the WaveRunner was delivered to Wallace Richardson, the first user.

The Indiana Statute of Repose provides in relevant part that product liability actions must be commenced within ten years after the delivery of the product to the initial user or consumer. YMC, a Japanese corporation with its principal place of business in Japan, designed, manufactured, and tested the WaveRunner in Japan. It petitioned for an exemption from the United States Coast Guard's requirement that every vehicle like the WaveRunner have a fan to ventilate fuel fumes out of the hull of the boat. YMUS knew of the test results, and, according to the Lands, gave false information to the Coast Guard as to the known danger of the WaveRunner design in order to keep its exemption from the fan requirement. YMUS, which maintains its principal place of business in California, participated in developing the WaveRunner and imported it to the United States. YMUS, while it has no office in Indiana, is authorized and does business in the state. On July 7, 1987, YMUS sold and shipped the vehicle to a boating store in Kentucky. On July 28, 1987, Wallace Richardson, an Indiana resident, purchased the WaveRunner.

Larry Bush, another Indiana resident, subsequently bought the WaveRunner in 1989 or 1990. Bush was the registered owner when the WaveRunner caused Land's injury. From the time of Bush's purchase, the boat was registered, garaged, and serviced in Indiana.

Between 1988 and 1998, 24 other WaveRunners were reported to have exploded. YMUS twice recalled certain models of WaveRunners for modifications to reduce the likelihood of fuel leakage. It never recalled the WR500 series....

Appellants argue that although they did not commence their action until well over ten years after delivery to the initial user, their case is not barred because ... California law, which includes no statute of repose, governs the action....

We review a grant of summary judgment de novo [i.e., take a fresh look at the evidence], construing the evidence in the light most favorable to the nonmoving party.... Summary judgment is appropriate if there is no genuine issue as to any material fact and the moving party is entitled to judgment as a matter of law....

Choice of Law

A federal court sitting in diversity jurisdiction must apply the substantive law of the state in which it sits, 304 U.S. 64 ... (1938).... The *Erie* doctrine extends to choice-of-law principles and requires the court to apply the conflicts rules of the forum state.... Therefore, the district court properly applied the choice-of-law rule of Indiana.

Indiana applies a two-step conflicts analysis. *Hubbard Mfg. v. Greeson* (Ind. 1987). First, the court must determine if the place where the last event necessary to make the defendant liable—that is, the place of the injury—is insignificant.... If it is not, the law of that state applies.... Only if the court finds that the place of injury is insignificant does it move to step two which requires the court to consider "other factors such as: 1) the place where the conduct causing the injury occurred; 2) the residence or place of business of the parties; and 3) the place where the relationship is centered."... In the instant case, we, like the district court, arrive at the inevitable conclusion that the place of the injury—Indiana—is not insignificant. Therefore, we apply Indiana law and need not address the second prong in Indiana's choice-of-law analysis....

Charles Land was injured while operating the WaveRunner in Indiana. He was a resident of Indiana, the owner of the boat was a resident of Indiana, and

the boat had been garaged and serviced in Indiana for a decade before it caused Land's injury. No evidence exists in the record that the WaveRunner was ever used outside of Indiana. It was not mere fortuity that the injury occurred in Indiana, as the Lands suggest by comparing this choice-of-law determination with those involving pass-through automobile or airplane accidents in which the place of the injury is given little weight, and the argument that Indiana's contacts have little or no relevance to the legal action simply cannot withstand scrutiny. Therefore, our analysis of Indiana choice-of-law policy must end with step one.

The Lands argue that California, where YMUS was incorporated and where the defendant's tortious conduct occurred, has greater relevance. Maybe so.... This analysis belongs in step two of the Indiana conflicts policy, however, which we cannot reach. Some states use the "most significant relationship" approach suggested by the Restatement (Second) of Conflict of Laws. If Indiana did so, we would skip step one of our analysis and instead "isolate the pertinent issue, examine each state's connection to the occurrence, identify the governmental policies espoused by each state relevant to the issue, and proclaim applicable the law of the state with the superior interest."... That case might have a different outcome from the one at hand. Indiana does not adhere to the most significant relationship analysis, however, and the Supreme Court of Indiana has not signaled that it intends to overrule *Hubbard*. Although *Hubbard* does note some discomfort with the rigid place of injury, or *lex loci delicti*, approach, it still adheres to an analysis that uses the place of injury as a baseline.... If the place of injury is not insignificant, we must apply its law regardless of the greater interest another state may have. The Lands propose an approach whereby the law of the place of the tortious conduct is controlling in product liability cases. The state of Indiana has given us no indication that it intends to change its choice-of-law policy to reach such a result, and we decline to make that policy decision for it. Indiana's contacts to this case are not insignificant. Therefore, its law, including the Statute of Repose, applies.

Because Indiana law governs this case and because the Indiana Statute of Repose bars product liability actions that, like this one, are brought more than ten years after delivery of the product to the initial user or consumer, we find that the district court properly granted summary judgment in favor of the defendants. We AFFIRM.

Case Questions

1. What was the basis for federal jurisdiction in this case?
2. Since the case was heard in federal court, why didn't the judge apply the law as generally applied in the nation, rather than the law of Indiana?

THE THIRTEEN U.S. COURTS OF APPEALS

The United States has been divided by Congress into eleven circuits (clusters of states), and a court of appeals has been assigned to each circuit. A court of appeals also has been established for the District of Columbia. In 1982, Congress created a new court of appeals with broad territorial jurisdiction and with very specialized subject-matter jurisdiction. This court is called the Court of Appeals for the Federal Circuit. Its job is to review appeals from the U.S. District Courts throughout the nation in such areas as patent, trademark, and copyright cases; cases in which the United States is the defendant; and cases appealed from the U.S. Court of International Trade and the U.S. Court of Federal Claims. Figure 4.7 shows the boundaries of the thirteen circuits.

These appellate courts hear appeals on questions of law from decisions of the federal district courts in their circuits and review findings of federal administrative agencies. For most litigants, they are the ultimate appellate tribunals of the federal system. Appeal to these courts is a matter of right, not discretion, so long as proper procedures are followed.

When attorneys wish to appeal decisions of lower tribunals, they must follow such procedures to get the cases before a court of appeals. Notice of appeal must be filed within 30 days from the entry of judgment (60 days when the United States or an

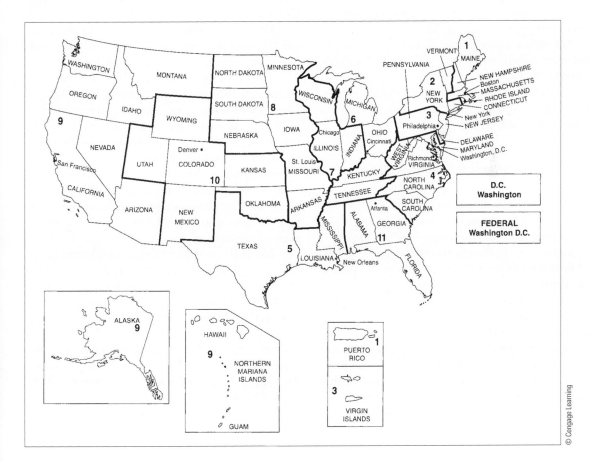

FIGURE 4.7 The Thirteen Federal Judicial Circuits

© Cengage Learning

	2008	2009	2010	2011
Cases Filed	61,104	67,740	55,992	55,126
Cases Terminated	59,096	60,508	59,526	57,357

F I G U R E 4.8 U.S. Courts of Appeals: Appeals Commenced and Terminated during Forty-Eight-Month Period Ending September 30, 2011

Source: Administrative Office of the United States Courts, *Annual Report of the Director: Judicial Business of the United States Courts.* Washington, D.C.: U.S. Government Printing Office, 2010 and 2011.

officer or agent thereof is a party). A cost bond (in civil cases) may be required to ensure payment of the costs of the appeal. Both the record on appeal and a brief must be filed.

Attorneys then must persuade the judges that the lower tribunals committed errors that resulted in injustices to their clients. On appeal, the court of appeals does not substitute its judgment for that of the lower tribunal's finding of fact. It does reverse the lower court's decision if that decision was clearly erroneous as a matter of law. See Figure 4.8 for statistical information regarding cases filed and terminated by U.S. Courts of Appeals between 2008 and 2011.

THE U.S. SUPREME COURT

The U.S. Supreme Court has existed since 1789. Today the court consists of a chief justice and eight associate justices. It exercises both appellate and original jurisdiction. Its chief function is to act as the last and final court of review over all cases in the federal system and some cases in the state systems.

Supreme Court review is not a matter of right. A party wishing to have its case reviewed by the Supreme Court (called a petitioner) is required by statute to file a petition for a writ of certiorari with the court. The other party, called the respondent, will have the right to oppose the granting of the writ. The Court grants certiorari only where special and important reasons exist for so doing. If four or

more justices are in favor of granting the petition, the writ issues and the case is accepted. The Court thus controls its docket, reserving its time and efforts for the cases that seem to the justices to deserve consideration. Figure 4.9 contains data regarding petitions for certiorari granted by the U.S. Supreme Court in 2000, 2004, 2008, and 2011.

The U.S. Supreme Court is the only court specifically created in the Constitution. All other federal courts are statutorily created by the Congress. The Constitution provides for the Court's original jurisdiction. (Original jurisdiction is the power to take note of a suit at its beginning, try it, and pass judgment on the law and the facts of the controversy.) The Constitution has given the Court the power to perform the function of trial court in cases affecting ambassadors, public ministers, and consuls, and in controversies in which a state is a party. Usually the power is not exclusive, nor is the Court required to hear all cases over which it has original jurisdiction.

Article III authorizes Congress to determine the Court's appellate jurisdiction. A history-making example occurred in 1983 when Congress enacted the Military Justice Act. This act conferred jurisdiction on the Supreme Court to directly review designated categories of appeals from the Court of Military Appeals. These appeals are brought to the Court pursuant to the writ of certiorari procedure. This marked the first time in the history of the United States that any Article III court was authorized to review the decisions of military courts.

Certiorari Granted	October 1, 1999–Sept. 30, 2000	October 1, 2003–Sept. 30, 2004	October 1, 2007–Sept. 30, 2008	October 1, 2010–Sept. 30, 2011
Total	99	104	259	122
Criminal	12	16	170	42
U.S. Civil	29	28	22	12
Private Civil	51	54	50	58
Administrative Appeals	7	6	17	10

FIGURE 4.9 Petitions for Review of Certiorari Granted by the U.S. Supreme Court

Source: Administrative Office of the United States Courts, *Annual Reports of the Director: Judicial Business of the United States Courts.* Washington, D.C.: U.S. Government Printing Office, 2001, 2005, 2009, 2012.

THE FOREIGN INTELLIGENCE SURVEILLANCE COURTS

The U. S. Supreme Court is undoubtedly the best-known federal court, and at the opposite end of the continuum are probably the least-known federal courts, the Foreign Intelligence Surveillance Court (FISC) and the Foreign Intelligence Surveillance Court of Review (FISCR). The FISC and FISCR were established in 1978 in the aftermath of a Senate Select Committee's groundbreaking and comprehensive study of the federal government's domestic intelligence operations over the preceding four decades. The Committee, which was appointed in 1975, was headed by the late U.S. Senator Frank Church. After an extensive investigation, the Church Committee concluded that "domestic intelligence activity has threatened and undermined the constitutional rights of Americans to free speech, association and privacy. It has done so primarily because the constitutional system for checking abuse of power has not been applied."[4]

Among the many Church Committee recommendations was one urging the Congress to "… turn its attention to legislating restraints upon intelligence activities which may endanger the constitutional rights of Americans." Congress responded in 1978 by enacting the Foreign Intelligence Surveillance Act (FISA). The legislation centralized the federal government's surveillance activities and provided for judicial oversight of the surveillance process. Pursuant to this legislation, Congress established the FISC and FISCR to protect Americans from executive branch abuses such as had happened in the past, and required that government obtain warrants from the FISC.

Congress decided not to require that federal officers investigating domestic espionage and terrorism comply with the same warrant requirements that apply in all other criminal prosecutions. Instead it established separate and less stringent requirements for national security operations. For example, prior to the enactment of the FISA Amendments Act (FAA) in 2008, the government was required to satisfy the FISC that there was probable cause to believe that the person to be monitored (the target) was either directly or indirectly connected to a "foreign power," and that the target could be found within the premises that were to be monitored.

Congress, however, decided to expand the government's ability to conduct monitoring activities, reduced the FISC's oversight responsibilities, and eliminated the previous requirements that required specificity and particularization as to individual targets.[5]

The Chief Justice of the United States appoints the eleven members of the Foreign Intelligence

Action Taken	2008	2009	2010	2011
New applications submitted to FISC	2,081	1,376	1,579	1,745
Applications approved by FISC	2,080	1,320	1,506	1,674
Applications denied by FISC	1	1	0	0
Applications modified by FISC	2	1 entirely 1 partially	14	30
Applications wilhdrawn prior to FISC ruling and not resubmitted for approval	0	8	5	2

FIGURE 4.10 Foreign Intelligence Surveillance Court: Applications Submitted, Approved, Denied, Substantively Modified, and Withdrawn Prior to Court Ruling and Not Resubmitted

Source: U.S. Department of Justice, Annual Reports to the Congress for 2008, 2009, 2010, and 2011, as required by Sections 1807 and 1862 of the Foreign Intelligence Surveillance Act of 1978.

Surveillance Court and chooses one of these appointees to be the chief judge. The judges serve nonrenewable seven-year terms.

FISC proceedings are closed, and only Department of Justice (DOJ) lawyers are present at hearings. The DOJ attorneys try to persuade the FISC judges to approve the issuance of surveillance warrants. The FISC, which conducts its business in secret, can approve an electronic surveillance upon Justice Department certification that "a significant purpose" of the investigation is to obtain foreign intelligence. It should be noted that what constitutes a "significant purpose" is undefined.

The FISCR has three federal judges, all of whom are appointed by the Chief Justice. These judges serve nonrenewable seven-year terms. It is interesting to note that no cases were appealed to the FISCR from 1978, when the court was established, through 2001. Since 2001, the government appealed for the first time in 2002 (In re: Sealed Case, 310 F.3d 717), and a second time in 2008 (In re Directives, 551 F.3d 1004).

Under FISA, in the most unlikely event that the DOJ loses in both the FISC and the FISCR, the government still can seek review in the U.S. Supreme Court. See Figure 4.10 for data regarding applications for warrants brought in the FISC from 2008 to 2011.

CHAPTER SUMMARY

In this chapter readers have learned how federal and state court systems are organized and about the different functions of trial and appellate courts. Explanations also were provided as to the procedural differences between jury trials and bench trials. The fundamental requirements for subject-matter and personal jurisdiction in federal and state courts were summarized, and the importance of venue was explained. Students also learned the circumstances under which cases can be removed from state court to federal court and why federal trial courts need to be concerned about the Erie doctrine.

CHAPTER QUESTIONS

1. Bensusan Restaurant Corporation owns and operates a popular, large New York City jazz club called "The Blue Note." Richard King owns and has operated a small cabaret, also called "The Blue Note," in Columbia, Missouri, since 1980. King's establishment features live music

and attracts its customers from central Missouri. In 1996, King decided to establish a website for the purpose of advertising his cabaret. King included a disclaimer on his website in which he gave a plug to Bensusan's club and made it clear that the two businesses were unrelated. He later modified this disclaimer by making it even more explicit and said that his "cyberspot was created to provide information for Columbia, Missouri area individuals only."

Bensusan brought suit in the U.S. District Court for the Southern District of New York against King seeking monetary damages and injunctive relief. The plaintiff maintained that King had infringed on his federally protected trademark by calling his cabaret "The Blue Note." King moved to dismiss the complaint for lack of personal jurisdiction. He contended that he had neither engaged in business within New York nor committed any act sufficient to confer in personam jurisdiction over him by New York. The U.S. District Court agreed with King, and the case was appealed to the U.S. Court of Appeals for the Second Circuit. Should the Second Circuit affirm or reverse the District Court? Why?

Bensusan Restaurant Corporation v. Richard B. King, Docket No. 96-9344, 126 F.3d 25, U.S. Court of Appeals (2nd Circuit 1997)

2. Dorothy Hooks brought a class action suit against Associated Financial Services, Inc., and others for breach of contract, fraud, and conspiracy. In her complaint, Hooks stipulated for the members of the class that the plaintiffs would waive both the right to recover more than $49,000 in damages and any right to recover punitive damages. The defendant nevertheless sought removal predicated on diversity of citizenship jurisdiction. Should the U.S. District Court grant the plaintiff's petition to remand this case back to the state courts?

Hooks v. Associated Financial Services Company, Inc. et al., 966 F. Supp. 1098 (1997)

3. David Singer was injured when his automobile was struck by an uninsured motorist. David was insured against this type of accident up to a policy limit of $30,000 by State Farm Mutual Automobile Insurance Company. When State Farm stalled on paying on his insurance claim, David filed suit in state court, alleging breach of contract and breach of good faith and fair dealing. David did not demand any specified amount of money damages in his complaint because state law prohibited him from doing so. State Farm filed a removal petition in U.S. District Court, alleging that the federal court had subject-matter jurisdiction based on diversity of citizenship. The defendant alleged that damages existed in excess of $50,000 (the jurisdictional amount at the time the suit was filed). Has the defendant followed the correct procedure, under these circumstances, for establishing the existence of the jurisdictional amount? How should the U.S. Court of Appeals for the Ninth Circuit rule?

Singer v. State Farm, No. 95-55441, 116 F.3d 373, U.S. Court of Appeals (9th Circuit 1997)

4. Sludge Inc., a Wisconsin corporation, has a website in Wisconsin in which it advertises its wares. This website is accessible in every state in the nation. Can a Colorado corporation that believes Sludge has infringed on its trademarks successfully establish a basis for in personam jurisdiction if suit is brought in a Colorado court? Should it make a difference if the website had generated several thousand messages, as well as 500 contacts, and 10 percent of its sales from Colorado? What argument would you make in favor of jurisdiction over Sludge? What argument would you make in opposition to jurisdiction over Sludge?

5. Mr. and Mrs. Woodson instituted a product liability action in an Oklahoma state court to recover for personal injuries sustained in Oklahoma in an accident involving a car that they had bought in New York while they were New York residents. The Woodsons were driving the car through Oklahoma at the time of the accident. The defendants were the car retailer and its wholesaler, both New York corporations, who did no business in Oklahoma. The defendants entered a special

appearance, claiming that the Oklahoma state court did not have personal jurisdiction. Would there be enough "minimum contacts" between the defendants and the forum state for the forum state to have personal jurisdiction over the defendants?

World-Wide Volkswagen Corp. v. Woodson, 444 U.S. 286 (1980)

6. In this hypothetical diversity of citizenship case, federal law requires complete diversity of citizenship between plaintiffs and defendants and an amount in controversy greater than $75,000 in order for federal courts to entertain jurisdiction of an action. Tom Jones and Leonard Woodrock were deep-shaft coal miners in West Virginia, although Leonard lived across the border in Kentucky. Tom purchased a new Eureka, a National Motors car, from Pappy's Auto Sales, a local firm. National Motors Corporation is a large auto manufacturer with its main factory in Indiana, and is incorporated in Kentucky. When Tom was driving Leonard home from the mine, the Eureka's steering wheel inexplicably locked. The car hurtled down a 100-foot embankment and came to rest against a tree. The Eureka, which cost $17,100, was a total loss. Tom and Leonard suffered damages of $58,000 apiece for personal injuries. Can Tom sue National Motors for damages in a federal court? Why? Can Leonard? Can Leonard and Tom join their claims and sue National Motors in federal court?

7. National Mutual Insurance Company is a District of Columbia corporation. It brought a diversity action in the U.S. District Court for the District of Maryland against Tidewater Transfer Company, a Virginia corporation doing business in Maryland. National Mutual contends that, for diversity purposes, a D.C. resident may file suit against the resident of a state. Tidewater Transfer disagrees. What should be taken into consideration in deciding whether the District of Columbia can, for diversity purposes, be regarded as a state?

National Mutual Insurance v. Tidewater Transfer Co., 337 U.S. 582 (1949)

8. Several Arizona citizens brought a diversity suit in a federal district court against Harsh Building Company, an Oregon corporation. All parties involved in the suit stipulated that the defendant had its principal place of business in Oregon. During the trial, evidence showed that the only real business activity of Harsh Building Co. was owning and operating the Phoenix apartment complex that was the subject of the suit. The plaintiffs lost the suit. On appeal, they claimed that the District Court did not have jurisdiction because of lack of diversity of citizenship. Did the plaintiffs waive their right to challenge jurisdiction?

Bialac v. Harsh Building Co., 463 F.2d 1185 (9th Cir. 1972)

9. Colin Cody, a Connecticut resident, invested $200,000 in the common stock of Phillips Company, a firm that installs video gambling machines in Louisiana casinos. Cody brought suit against the defendant, Kevin Ward, a resident of California, alleging that Ward had used an Internet website called "Money Talk" to perpetrate a fraud on potential investors. The gist of Cody's complaint was that Ward had engaged in false and fraudulent misrepresentations about the Phillips Company's impending financial prospects. Cody claimed to have made decisions about whether to buy and hold Phillips stock in partial reliance on Ward's misrepresentations on the Internet and in telephone calls made by Ward that encouraged Cody to buy and hold Phillips stock. Cody further claimed that the Phillips stock was essentially worthless. Ward sought to dismiss the complaint, alleging that he could not be sued in Connecticut because there were insufficient grounds for personal jurisdiction. Cody maintains that a defendant who orally or in writing causes information to enter Connecticut by wire is committing a tortious act within Connecticut and is subject to suit pursuant to the Connecticut long-arm statute. Do you believe that Ward has committed a tortious act within the forum state that would satisfy the requirements of the long-arm statute? Do you

believe that there is a constitutional basis for Connecticut to exercise in personam jurisdiction over Ward?

Cody v. Ward, 954 F.Supp 43 (D. Conn. 1997)

10. The Stars' Desert Inn Hotel filed suit against Richard Hwang, a citizen of Taiwan, to collect on a $1,885,000 gambling debt. Stars unsuccessfully tried to serve Hwang on six occasions at a guarded and gated housing complex in Beverly Hills. The process server, after verifying with the guard that Hwang was inside, left the summons and complaint with the gate attendant. Hwang moved to quash the service. Was Hwang properly served?

Stars' Desert Inn Hotel & Country Club v. Hwang, 105 F.3d 521 (9th Cir. 1997)

NOTES

1. In personam jurisdiction generally will not be recognized where someone is duped into entering the state for the purpose of making service. *Townsend v. Smith* 3 N.W. 439 (1879) and *Jacobs/Kahan & Co. v. Marsh* 740 F.2d 587 (7th Cir. 1984). Similarly, a person who enters a state to challenge jurisdiction cannot be validly served. *Stewart v. Ramsay* 242 U.S. 128 (1916).

2. *Burnham v. Superior Court*, 495 U.S. 604 (1990).

3. 28 U.S.C. §1391.

4. Senate Select Committee Report on Governmental Operations with Respect to Intelligence Operations, Part IV, Conclusions and Recommendations, p. 290.

5. See Gerard E. Lynch's concurring opinion in the denial of rehearing en banc in *Amnesty International, USA v. Clapper* 667 F.3d 163 (2d Cir. 2011).

V

Civil Procedure

CHAPTER OBJECTIVES

1. *Understand the importance of procedure in our civil legal system.*
2. *Describe the basic steps of the civil litigation process.*
3. *Identify the functions of the complaint, answer, and reply.*
4. *Explain the use of pretrial motions to dismiss and for summary judgment.*
5. *Summarize modern discovery tools and their use.*
6. *Describe the procedural steps in the conduct of a trial.*

Courts are a passive adjudicator of disputes and neither initiate nor encourage litigation. The court system does nothing until one of the parties has called on it through appropriate procedures. Detailed procedural rules create the process that is used to decide the merits of a dispute. At the beginning of the process, these rules explain what a plaintiff must do to start a lawsuit and how the plaintiff can assert a legal claim against a defendant. Defendants are similarly told how to raise defenses and claims once they have been notified of a suit. Procedural rules govern what documents must be prepared, what each must contain, and how they should be presented to the court and the defendant. Once the lawsuit has been initiated, procedures govern how the parties discover relevant information and evidence, especially when it is in the possession of one's opponent. Rules also govern the conduct of trials, any enforcement procedures necessary after trial, the conduct of appeals, and the imposition of sanctions on rule violators. The principal objective of procedural law is to give the parties to a dispute an equal and fair opportunity to present their cases to a nonprejudiced and convenient tribunal. If procedural rules are correctly drafted and implemented, both parties to the dispute should feel that they have been fairly treated.

Although all procedures must satisfy constitutional due process requirements, the state and federal governments, as separate sovereigns, have promulgated separate rules of civil procedure that govern the litigation process in their respective forums. This means, for example, that Oregon lawyers have to learn two sets of procedural rules. If they are litigating in the state courts of Oregon, they comply with the *Oregon Rules of Civil Procedure,* and when litigating in the U.S. District Court for the District of Oregon, they follow the provisions of the *Federal Rules of Civil Procedure* (FRCP).

The purpose of this chapter is to explain the procedures that govern a civil suit from the time a litigant decides to sue until final court judgment. Indispensable to an understanding of these systems is a familiarity with the various stages and terms that are encountered in a civil proceeding.

PROCEEDINGS BEFORE A CIVIL TRIAL

The first step in civil litigation involves a triggering event that injures the plaintiff or damages his or her property (see Figure 5.1). The second step usually involves the plaintiff selecting an attorney. It is important to understand that, in general, each party pays for his or her attorney's fee irrespective of who ultimately prevails in the substantive dispute. This is subject to exceptions where statutory law provides otherwise and where common law judicial doctrines permit the court to order the loser to pay the winner's attorney fees.

Hiring a Lawyer

The period between the event that gives rise to the suit (the triggering event) and the filing of a complaint is known as the **informal discovery period.**

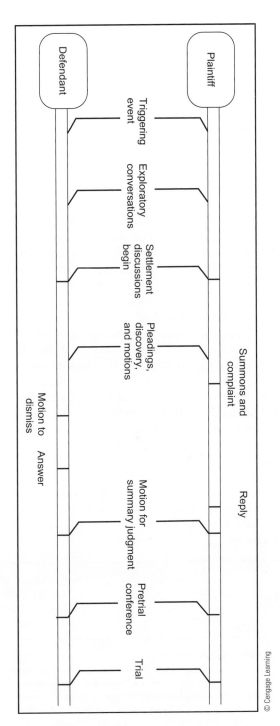

FIGURE 5.1 Proceedings before a Civil Trial

© Cengage Learning

The court has neither knowledge of nor interest in the plaintiff's cause of action against the defendant.

During this time, the plaintiff contacts an attorney and describes the circumstances that led to the injury. The attorney discusses in general terms the legal alternatives available and usually asks for an opportunity to conduct an independent investigation to assess the value of the claim. This meeting is known as an exploratory conversation. At this point, the plaintiff and the attorney are not contractually bound to each other.

After the exploratory conversation and further investigation, the plaintiff meets again with the attorney to determine which course of action should be taken. The attorney presents an evaluation of the case in terms of the remedies available, the probability of achieving a favorable verdict, and the nature and probability of the award likely to be granted. At this point, the plaintiff retains the attorney as a representative in the judicial proceedings that are likely to follow.

Attorney's fees may be determined in several ways. Attorneys may charge the client by the hour. They may contract with the client to take a specified percentage of the money collected as compensation, pursuant to what is called a **contingent fee agreement.** If no money is recovered for the client, an attorney is not entitled to any fee. However, the client will still be responsible for expenses. An attorney may be on a retainer, in which case the client pays the attorney an agreed-upon sum of money to handle all of or specified portions of a client's legal problems for a specified period of time such as a year. Last, an attorney may charge a flat rate for certain routine services.

After the plaintiff officially retains his or her lawyer, the attorney normally contacts the defendant. This information puts the defendant on notice that the plaintiff is preparing to seek an adjudicative settlement of the claim. If the defendant has not already retained an attorney, this is the time to do so. The attorneys confer, with or without their clients, to discuss a reasonable settlement. These discussions are referred to as **settlement conferences.** If they prove unsuccessful, the judicial machinery is set in motion.

Clients always have the right to discharge their lawyers at any time, with or without cause. Readers will see in the next case, however, that discharged attorneys may still be entitled to compensation from their former clients.

Virginia Atkinson and James Howell, the lawyers in the next case, entered into a contingent fee contract with Joy Salmon. After Salmon discharged them, they sued, requesting that the court award them a **quantum meruit** recovery ("as much as they deserved"). The lawyers, at the client's request, had engaged in legal work prior to their discharge date. Because of their discharge, they argued, the terms of the contingency fee agreement no longer applied. Under these circumstances, they asserted, their former client should have to pay them immediately a reasonable sum for the work they had completed on her behalf. The case was tried to a jury, which found in favor of the attorneys in the amount of $7,200. The client argued that the attorneys were not entitled to recover any fees. The Arkansas Supreme Court was called upon to decide.

Joy Salmon v. Virginia Atkinson
137 S.W.3d 383
Supreme Court of Arkansas
December 11, 2003

Donald L. Corbin, Justice.
This case involves an issue of first impression: Whether an attorney who enters into a contingent-fee contract with a client and is later discharged by the client may bring an action for a quantum meruit fee prior to the resolution of the former client's lawsuit. Appellant Joy Salmon contends that the discharged attorney's cause of action does not accrue unless and until the client is successful in recovering an award. She thus contends that the Pulaski County Circuit Court erred in awarding Appellees Virginia Atkinson and James Howell legal fees in the amount of $7,200 for work they performed in representing Appellant prior to date that she discharged them....

The essential facts are not disputed. In June 2000, Appellant hired Appellees to pursue a claim for damages against the estate of George Brown. Appellant had lived with Brown for some time prior to his death and had cared for him as his nurse. Additionally, Appellant believed that she was married to Brown and, as his widow, she wanted to pursue a claim against Brown's estate. Appellees agreed to take Appellant's case on a contingency basis, in which Appellees would receive fifty percent of any recovery awarded to Appellant, plus costs and expenses. The contingent-fee contract was entered into on June 19, 2000, and it provided in pertinent part: "It is understood that in the event of no recovery, no fee shall be charged by Atkinson Law Offices."

Appellees then began to work on Appellant's case. They interviewed multiple witnesses, researched Appellant's claim of marriage to Brown, researched the general law, and negotiated with the estate's attorneys…. Based on their investigation and research, Appellees drew up a petition for Appellant to file in the probate case. Sometime in late July, they presented the petition to Appellant for her signature. Appellant indicated that she wanted to think about filing the claim, and she took the petition with her. The next communication Appellees received from Appellant was a letter, dated August 1, informing them that their services were no longer required.

Thereafter, in a letter dated August 21, 2000, Appellees informed Appellant that she had abrogated the June 19 contract without justification and that, therefore, she was required to pay Appellees for their services from June 19 to July 31. The letter reflects in part: "In investigation of your claims, legal research, and negotiation with the estate we expended 48 hours. At our customary billing rate of $150 per hour, the total fee payable at this time is $7,200." The letter also informed Appellant that the last date for which she could file her claim against Brown's estate was September 1, 2000. The record reflects that on September 1, 2000, Appellant filed a petition against the estate, *pro se.*

On May 10, 2001, Appellees filed suit against Appellant in circuit court, seeking recovery in quantum meruit for work they had performed on Appellant's case prior to the date that she discharged them. Following a trial on December 3, 2002, the jury returned a verdict in favor of Appellees. Thereafter, Appellant filed a motion for judgment notwithstanding the verdict (JNOV), arguing that because the contingent-fee contract specifically provided that no fee would be charged unless there was a recovery, and because there had not yet been any recovery, the jury verdict was not supported by substantial evidence. The trial court denied that motion on December 17, 2002. The judgment was also entered of record on that date. On January 2, 2003, Appellant filed a motion for new trial and a renewed motion for JNOV. The trial court denied

those motions on February 4, 2003. Appellant then filed a notice of appeal on February 28, 2003.

On appeal, Appellant argues that allowing Appellees to collect a quantum meruit fee directly conflicts with the language of the contract providing that no fee would be charged in the event that Appellant did not recover on her probate claim. Thus, she asserts that because she has not yet recovered on her claim, it was error to award a fee to Appellees. She contends further that the award of fees to Appellees under the circumstances impaired her absolute right, as the client, to discharge Appellees and terminate their services.

As stated above, the issue of when a discharged attorney's cause of action for a quantum meruit fee accrues is one of first impression in this court. However, this court has consistently held that a discharged attorney may be paid for the reasonable value of his or her services notwithstanding that the parties originally entered into a contingent-fee contract…. The plain rationale behind this rule is that where the attorney has conferred a benefit upon the client, *i.e.,* legal services and advice, the client is responsible to pay such reasonable fees.

The question in this case is not whether the discharged attorney may recover a quantum meruit fee, but whether recovery of such a fee is dependent upon the contingency originally agreed to in the contract, *i.e.,* the successful prosecution of the client's case. There is a split amongst the states on this issue. Some states adhere to the "California rule," which provides that the discharged attorney's cause of action does not accrue unless and until the occurrence of the stated contingency…. Under this rule, a discharged attorney is barred from receiving any fee if the client does not recover on the underlying matter. This is true even if the attorney was discharged without cause.

Other states subscribe to the "New York rule," which provides that the discharged attorney's cause of action accrues immediately upon discharge and is not dependent upon the former client's recovery…. The courts that subscribe to this rule do so primarily for two reasons. First, they reason that when the client terminates the contingent-fee contract by discharging the attorney, the contract ceases to exist and the contingency term, *i.e.,* whether the attorney wins the client's case, is no longer operative. As the New York Court of Appeals explained: "Either [the contract] wholly stands or totally falls."… Because the contract is terminated, the client can no longer use the contract's term to prevent the discharged attorney from recovering a fee in quantum meruit. "A client cannot terminate the agreement and then resurrect the contingency term when the discharged attorney files a fee claim."…

The second primary reason that courts subscribe to the "New York rule" is that they believe that forcing the discharged attorney to wait on the occurrence of the contingency is unfair in that it goes beyond what the parties contemplated in the contract. The New York Court of Appeals said it best:

> The value of one attorney's services is not measured by the result attained by another. This one did not contract for his contingent compensation on the hypothesis of success or failure by some other member of the bar.... In making their agreement, the parties may be deemed to have estimated this lawyer's pecuniary merit according to his own character, temperament, energy, zeal, education, knowledge and experience which are the important factors contributing to his professional status and constituting in a large degree, when viewed in relation to the volume of work performed and the result accomplished, a fair standard for gauging the value of services as prudent counsel and skillful advocate....

An additional reason for holding that a discharged attorney does not have to wait on the occurrence of the contingency is that the attorney is not claiming under the contingent-fee contract. The Illinois Supreme Court explained:

> Quantum meruit is based on the implied promise of a recipient of services to pay for those services which are of value to him. The recipient would be unjustly enriched if he were able to retain the services without paying for them. The claimant's recovery here should not be linked to a contract contingency when his recovery is not based upon the contract, but upon quantum meruit....

We believe that the "New York rule" is the better rule. Applying that rule to the facts of this case, we hold that the trial court did not err in awarding a quantum meruit fee to Appellees. The undisputed evidence showed that Appellant hired Appellees to pursue a claim against the estate of George Brown. She entered into a contingency-fee agreement, whereby she agreed to pay Appellees fifty percent of any recovery they obtained for her, plus costs and expenses. For the next six weeks or so, Appellees performed work on Appellant's case, which involved interviewing multiple witnesses, performing document research and general legal research, negotiating with the estate's attorneys, and, finally, preparing a petition for Appellant to file in the probate matter.

Appellees reviewed the prepared petition with Appellant and presented it to her for her signature. She declined to sign the petition at that time, indicating that she wanted to think about it. She then took the petition with her. The next communication Appellees had with Appellant was a letter in which Appellant discharged them without explanation....

Based on the foregoing evidence, we hold that Appellees' cause of action to recover reasonable attorney's fees, under the theory of quantum meruit, accrued immediately upon their being discharged by Appellant. While we are mindful of the client's right to discharge his or her attorney at any time, we do not believe that our holding in this case in any way impairs that right. To the contrary, this court has previously determined that the client's right to discharge the attorney is not compromised by allowing the discharged attorney to recover in quantum meruit.... We thus affirm the trial court's judgment.

Case Questions

1. How do contracts between attorneys and their clients differ from other contracts?
2. List the pros and cons of contingent fees.
3. Should a court uphold a contingent fee contract between attorney and client that prohibits a settlement by the client?

 Assume Attorney Smith orally contracted to represent a client in a real estate transaction and had performed satisfactorily for six months. Assume further that the client, who had been completely satisfied with Smith's work until this point, discharged him from employment without legal cause after learning that Attorney Brown would perform the remaining legal work for 30 percent less than the client was currently obligated to pay Smith. Should an attorney who is discharged without cause be compensated by his client pursuant to the oral agreement or only for the reasonable value of the services rendered?

The Pleadings

The pleading stage begins after the client has chosen a lawyer and decides to bring suit. The role of pleadings in Anglo-American law goes back to the earliest days of the English common law system and writ system.[1] In the twelfth century, persons wishing to litigate in the royal courts had to purchase an original writ (such as the Writ of Right) from the king or chancellor in order to establish the court's jurisdiction. Each writ specified the procedures and substantive law to be followed in deciding the dispute.[2] The writ would often require the plaintiff to make an oral recitation (a **pleading**) in which the claims would be stated, after which the defendant would be entitled to respond orally. In this way the parties would inform the court of the nature of the dispute.[3] In time, the practice of oral pleadings was replaced with written documents, and the common law and equitable pleading process became very complex, overly technical, cumbersome, and long.

In 1848, New York merged the common law and equity courts and replaced its writ system with a newly enacted Code of Civil Procedure. Thus began a reform movement that swept the country and produced modern code pleading at the state level. The popularity of code pleading convinced Congress to enact the Rules Enabling Act in 1934, which led to the development and adoption in 1938 of the Federal Rules of Civil Procedure.

Today's pleadings are written documents and consist of the plaintiff's **complaint,** the defendant's **answer,** and, rarely, the plaintiff's **reply.** The complaint is a document in which the plaintiff alleges jurisdiction, sets forth facts that establish the existence of a legal claim that entitles the plaintiff to relief from the defendant, and demands relief. Figure 5.2 provides a sample of a federal complaint. The complaint is filed with the court and served on the defendant.

The answer is a responsive pleading in which the defendant makes admissions or denials, asserts legal defenses, and raises counterclaims. Figure 5.3 provides a sample of a federal answer.

Admissions help to narrow the number of facts that are in dispute. The plaintiff will not have to prove facts at the trial that have been admitted by the defendant in the answer. A denial in the answer, however, creates a factual issue that must be proven at trial. Defendants often will plead one or more **affirmative defenses** in the answer. Each defense will consist of facts that the defendant contends may bar the plaintiff from recovery. The defendant may also make a claim for relief against the plaintiff by raising a **counterclaim** in the answer. A counterclaim is appropriate when the defendant has a **cause of action** against a plaintiff arising out of essentially the same set of events that gave rise to the plaintiff's claim. For example, assume that P observes D fishing without permission on P's land and tells D to vacate. If P kicks D in the back as D leaves the property, P is committing a battery against D. P could bring suit against D for trespass, and D could counterclaim against P for the battery. P could file a pleading called the **reply** to the defendant's counterclaim. In this reply, the plaintiff may admit, deny, or raise defenses against the factual allegations raised in the counterclaim.

The pleadings are somewhat less important under modern rules of civil procedure, because the current procedural rules provide each side of a dispute with the right to engage in extensive discovery. This means that litigants have a variety of available tools for obtaining relevant evidence of which the opponent has knowledge or which is in the possession of the opponent.

Methods of Service

The complaint is usually served on the defendant at the same time as the **writ of summons**. (Readers saw an example of a summons in Chapter IV; see Figure 4.2.) A summons warns the defendant that a default judgment can be awarded unless the defendant responds with an answer within a stated period of time (often between 20 and 45 days).[4]

Some jurisdictions require that the summons must be served on the defendant within a statutorily specified period of time so that the defendant has notice of the suit and can take defensive action. The summons has to be served on a defendant being

UNITED STATES DISTRICT COURT
. . . . District of . . . .

. . . . Plaintiff :
                                  :

                        :   Civil Action No. . . . .
             V.   :   COMPLAINT
. . . . Defendant :

                        :   JURY TRIAL DEMANDED

This is a civil action seeking damages under the laws of the State of . . . . . . for injuries to the person of the plaintiff, and to her automobile, caused by the defendant's negligent and/or willful, wanton, or reckless conduct.

1. The court has jurisdiction of this matter by virtue of the fact that the plaintiff is a citizen of the State of . . . . . , and the defendant, ... is a citizen of the State of . . . . . . and the amount in controversy exceeds $75,000 exclusive of interest and costs.

2. This suit is brought pursuant to Section . . . . . . of the Revised Statutes.

3. The plaintiff . . . . is, and at all times material to this action was, a resident of the City of . . . . , State of . . . .

4. The defendant, ... is, and at all times material to this action was, a resident of the City of . . . . , State of . . . .

5. At all times hereinafter mentioned, plaintiff was in the exercise of all due care and caution for her own safety and the safety of others.

6. On January . . . . 20 . . . . at or about . . . . P.M., plaintiff . . . . was operating her automobile in a northerly direction along United States Route . . . . at or about . . . . miles north of . . . .

7. On January . . . . 20 . . . . at or about . . . . P.M., defendant was operating her motor automobile in a southerly direction along United States Route . . . . at or about . . . . miles north of . . . .

8. At that date and time, defendant, ... , negligently operated her vehicle in one or more of the following ways:

    a. Improperly failed to give a signal of her intention to make a turn.

    b. Negligently made an improper left-handed turn, without yielding the right-of-way to traffic coming in the opposite direction.

    c. Negligently failed to yield the right-of-way.

    d. Operated her vehicle on the wrong side of the road.

    e. Negligently failed to keep said vehicle under proper control.

    f. Operated her vehicle in a negligent manner.

    g. Negligently failed to stop her vehicle when danger to the plaintiff was imminent.

9. As a result of one or more of the acts or omissions complained of, the vehicle driven by . . . . . . was caused violently to collide with the vehicle driven by . . . . . .

10. As a direct and proximate result thereof, the plaintiff suffered painful, severe and permanent injuries, loss of income, and has incurred, and will continue to incur expenses for medical care and further was caused to expend the sum of $ . . . . to repair the damages to her automobile caused by the accident.

    WHEREFORE, plaintiff prays for judgment against the defendant, ... in the sum of dollars ($ . . . .) plus costs.

    Plaintiff requests a jury trial.

                                    . . . .
                                    Attorney for Plaintiff
                                    Office and P.O. Address
                                    . . . .

FIGURE 5.2 Complaint Document

UNITED STATES DISTRICT COURT
. . . . District of . . . .

. . . . Plaintiff   :
                                 :   Civil Action No. . . . .
                V.   :   ANSWER
                                 :
. . . . Defendant   :
                                 :   JURY TRIAL DEMANDED

Now comes the defendant in the above-captioned action and gives the following answers to the plaintiff's complaint:

1. Denies the allegations of paragraphs 1 and 2 of the complaint.
2. Admits the allegations of paragraphs 3 and 4 of the complaint.
3. Denies the allegations of paragraphs 5 through 10 of the complaint.

<u>FIRST AFFIRMATIVE DEFENSE</u>

This court lacks subject matter jurisdiction as the amount in controversy does not exceed $75,000, exclusive of interest and cost.

<u>SECOND AFFIRMATIVE DEFENSE</u>

Plaintiff was guilty of negligence which was a contributing cause of the accident in that the plaintiff was negligently operating her automobile at the time that same collided with defendant's automobile. The plaintiff is therefore barred from recovery.

WHEREFORE, the defendant demands that the plaintiff's complaint be dismissed and that the costs of this action be awarded the defendant.

Defendant claims a trial by jury.

. . . .
Attorney for Defendant
Office and P.O. Address
. . . .
. . . .

F I G U R E 5.3 Answer

sued in federal court within 120 days after the plaintiff files the case. In Wisconsin it is 90 days and in California it is within 60 days. The defendant's right to have notice is constitutionally guaranteed by the state and federal due process clauses. Several methods to serve the summons can be found in the statute books of each state. These requirements must be precisely followed, and service in in personam actions may differ from service in in rem actions. Clearly, the most desirable method is to deliver the summons personally to the defendant.

The summons, sometimes called **process,** is generally served by a process server or sheriff.

The federal rules reward defendants who voluntarily waive their right to be formally served with process. These defendants are allowed sixty days, instead of just twenty days, to respond to the complaint. The benefit to plaintiffs is in not having to pay someone to serve the summons and complaint. Defendants who refuse to honor a requested waiver of service can be required to pay the service costs unless they can show good cause for the refusal.

In addition to having the summons personally served on a defendant, many states permit service by certified mail or registered mail, return receipt requested. This method is increasingly preferred because it is inexpensive and generally effective.

When **personal service** of a summons and the complaint to a defendant is not possible, the law often permits what is called **substituted service.** This method involves mailing the summons and complaint to the defendant by certified mail and leaving these documents at the defendant's home with a person who resides there and who is of "suitable age and discretion." Traditionally this means someone age fourteen or over. If the plaintiff is suing a corporation, the statutes usually authorize the use of substituted service on a designated agent or even a state official such as the secretary of state or the commissioner of insurance. The agent or official then sends a copy of the documents to the corporation. In some circumstances, the statutes provide for **constructive service**, which means publishing the notice of summons in the legal announcements section of newspapers. Traditionally the law has required that the summons be published for three weeks.

A defendant who has been properly served with a summons and complaint **defaults** by failing to file a written answer in a timely manner. The court can then award judgment to the plaintiff for the sum of money or other legal relief that was demanded in the complaint. In a default judgment, the defendant loses the right to object to anything that is incorrect in the complaint.

The following case illustrates how important it is to correctly name the party being sued in the summons and complaint. This mistake proved to be fatal because it meant the trial court had no personal jurisdiction.

Robert Johnson v. Cintas Corporation & United Healthcare
811 N.W.2d 756
Supreme Court of Wisconsin
Decided March 27, 2012

Annette Kingsland Ziegler, J.

This is a review of a published decision of the court of appeals, *Johnson v. Cintas Corp. No. 2*, ... that reversed a default judgment entered by the Kenosha County Circuit Court ... in favor of Robert Johnson (Johnson) and against Cintas Corporation No. 2 (Cintas No. 2). Because Johnson's summons and complaint did not name Cintas No. 2 as a defendant and instead named Cintas Corporation (Cintas), the parent corporation of Cintas No. 2, the court of appeals concluded that the circuit court lacked personal jurisdiction over Cintas No. 2, and therefore, the default judgment is void. Accordingly, the court of appeals reversed the default judgment and remanded the cause to the circuit court for further proceedings.

On appeal to this court, Johnson argues that the circuit court had personal jurisdiction over Cintas No. 2 because, despite not being named in the summons and complaint, Cintas No. 2 was served with the summons and complaint and was not prejudiced by Johnson's error. Alternatively, Johnson contends that his pleadings ought to be construed as only technically defective on the grounds that Cintas No. 2 held itself out as Cintas....

II. STANDARD OF REVIEW

In this case, the circuit court granted Johnson's motion to reconsider the court's order vacating the default judgment against Cintas No. 2. The determination of whether to vacate a default judgment is within the circuit court's sound discretion.... We will not disturb the circuit court's discretionary determination to reconsider its order vacating the default judgment unless the court erroneously exercised its discretion....

III. ANALYSIS

Wisconsin Stat. ch. 801 governs civil procedure as it relates to the commencement of an action. Wisconsin Stat. § 801.02(1) provides, in relevant part, that "a civil action in which a personal judgment is sought is commenced as to any defendant when a summons and a complaint naming the person as defendant are filed with the court," provided that the defendant is served with an authenticated copy of the summons and complaint within 90 days after filing.... A Wisconsin court obtains personal jurisdiction over a defendant by proper service of a summons upon the defendant.... Wisconsin Stat. § 801.09 lists the required contents of a summons. Relevant to this case, a summons must contain, *inter alia*, "the names and addresses of the parties to the action, plaintiff and defendant." § 801.09(1).

A summons serves two purposes. First, a summons provides notice to the defendant that an action has been commenced against the defendant.... Indeed, notice that apprises a party of the pendency of an action against it and affords the opportunity to present objections is regarded as "[a]n elementary and fundamental requirement of due process."... Second, consistent with Wis. Stat. §§ 801.05 and 801.11, a summons confers personal jurisdiction on a court over the defendant served....

Given that a defendant's constitutional right to due process is at stake, "Wisconsin requires strict compliance with its rules of statutory service, even though the consequences may appear to be harsh." ... In particular, "[t]he service of a summons in a manner prescribed by statute is a condition precedent to a valid exercise of personal jurisdiction,"... as any action taken by a court over a defendant not properly served is a deprivation of that defendant's constitutional protection.... Significantly, a defendant's actual notice of an action is not alone enough to confer personal jurisdiction upon the court; rather, "[s]ervice must be made in accordance with the manner prescribed by statute."...

In keeping with the above rule, our courts have recognized a distinction between service that is fundamentally defective, such that the court lacks personal jurisdiction over the defendant in the first instance, and service that is merely technically defective.... If the defect is fundamental, then the court lacks personal jurisdiction over the defendant, regardless of whether or not the defect prejudiced the defendant.... If the defect is technical, however, then the court has personal jurisdiction over the defendant only if the complainant can show that the defect did not prejudice the defendant.... The burden rests on the complainant to show that service was not defective or, if service was defective, that the defect was merely technical and did not prejudice the defendant....

... Johnson urges us to conclude that the circuit court appropriately reconsidered its order vacating the default judgment against Cintas No. 2.... [He] maintains that he merely misnamed Cintas No. 2 as Cintas in his summons and complaint, and therefore, his pleadings were only technically defective. He argues that the defect did not prejudice Cintas No. 2 because, pursuant to the circuit court's finding, Cintas No. 2 was served with the summons and complaint. We disagree.

We conclude that the circuit court erred as a matter of law when it reconsidered its order vacating the default judgment against Cintas No. 2. Johnson's failure to name Cintas No. 2 as a defendant in his summons and complaint, contrary to Wis. Stat.

§§ 801.02(1) and 801.09(1), constituted a fundamental defect that deprived the circuit court of personal jurisdiction over Cintas No. 2, regardless of whether or not the defect prejudiced Cintas No. 2. Because the circuit court lacked personal jurisdiction over Cintas No. 2, the default judgment entered against Cintas No. 2 is void.

This case is resolved by a straightforward application of the above-stated law.... [A] complainant's failure to name a defendant in the summons and complaint in accordance with Wis. Stat. §§ 801.02(1) and 801.09(1) constitutes a fundamental defect that precludes personal jurisdiction over that defendant, regardless of whether or not the defect prejudiced the defendant.... Here, it is undisputed that Johnson named Cintas, not Cintas No. 2, in his summons and complaint. Cintas No. 2, as a wholly owned subsidiary of Cintas, is a legal entity that exists independently of Cintas.... Johnson's failure to name Cintas No. 2 in his summons and complaint constituted a fundamental defect that precluded the circuit court of personal jurisdiction over Cintas No. 2, regardless of whether or not the defect prejudiced Cintas No. 2. For that reason, it is irrelevant that Johnson served his summons and complaint upon the registered agent for Cintas No. 2 and Cintas No. 2 therefore might have had knowledge that it was meant to be a party....

As far as the law is concerned, Cintas No. 2 was "a stranger to the court."...

Johnson does not quarrel with the fact that his summons and complaint named the wrong party, Cintas, and that the party he intended to sue, Cintas No. 2, is an independent legal entity. Instead, Johnson maintains that when the party intended to be sued is the entity served, as Cintas No. 2 was in this case, the distinction between a fundamental and technical defect should not depend upon the mere "happenstance" of whether the misnomer in the summons and complaint corresponds to another, existing legal entity. So long as the right party is the entity served, Johnson contends, the purpose of the summons is fulfilled. According to Johnson, this court's decision in *Ness* [v. *Digital Dial Communications, Inc.*, 596 N.W.2d 365 (1999)] ... "stands for the proposition that when a plaintiff has served the party he or she intended to sue, a misnomer is subject to correction, without reserving the defendant, even if the misnomer corresponds to the actual name of someone else."

While Johnson's argument may seem appealing on the surface, it lacks support in the law. To begin with ... a summons that does not name the party intended to be sued fails, as a matter of law, to give notice to that party that an action has been commenced against it.... That the named party happens to have a name that closely resembles the name of the party intended to be sued is simply not enough.... In any event, Johnson's argument rests on the false premise that a summons' only purpose is to provide notice to the defendant that an action has been commenced against it. As set forth above, a summons serves a second and equally significant purpose of conferring personal jurisdiction on a court over the defendant served. This court has made clear that "actual notice alone is not enough to confer jurisdiction upon the court. Service must be made in accordance with the manner prescribed by statute." ...

Finally, Johnson contends that even if we conclude that his failure to name Cintas No. 2 constituted a fundamental defect, we ought to nevertheless construe his pleadings as only technically defective on the grounds that Cintas No. 2 held itself out as Cintas.... Again, we decline Johnson's invitation for the simple reason that his argument is without support in the law.... While the circuit court made findings related to the manner in which Cintas No. 2 held itself out to the public and to Johnson specifically, the facts remain that Johnson named Cintas instead of Cintas No. 2 in his summons and complaint, and our courts recognize Cintas No. 2 as a legal entity that exists independently of its parent corporation. Therefore, the court lacked personal jurisdiction over Cintas No. 2 in the first instance, irrespective of whether Johnson was under the impression that he was suing the right entity or whether Johnson served the right entity. As we have explained, Wisconsin requires plaintiffs to strictly comply with our rules of statutory service "even though the consequences may appear to be harsh."... It is worth mentioning that the DFI [Wisconsin Department of Financial Institutions] records, accessible online to the public unambiguously reveal that Cintas is not a registered corporation in Wisconsin. In any case, if Johnson remained unsure of which entity to name, Cintas or Cintas No. 2, it would have been a simple and routine matter to name them both.

IV. CONCLUSION

We conclude that service in this case was fundamentally defective because Johnson failed to name Cintas No. 2 as a defendant in his summons and complaint, contrary to Wis. Stat. §§ 801.02(1) and 801.09(1). Therefore, the circuit court lacked personal jurisdiction over Cintas No. 2, regardless of whether or not the defect prejudiced Cintas No. 2 and regardless of the manner in which Cintas No. 2 held itself out to the public or to Johnson specifically. Because the circuit court lacked personal jurisdiction over Cintas No. 2, the default judgment entered against Cintas No. 2 is void.

Case Questions

1. According to the Wisconsin Supreme Court, the service of the summons serves what two purposes?
2. Why wasn't the plaintiff's mistake easily correctable as a mere technical violation given that Cintas 2 had actual notice of the suit?

Pretrial Motions

The second stage of the litigation process involves decisions about whether motions should be filed prior to trial. Sometimes a defendant's lawyer, after receiving the plaintiff's complaint, will decide to challenge the complaint because of legal insufficiency. For example, the complaint might be poorly drafted and so vague that the defendant can't understand what is being alleged, whether the venue might be wrong, or whether there might be some problem with service. In such situations the attorney may choose to file a **motion to dismiss** (sometimes also called a **demurrer** or a "12(b) motion" in some jurisdictions) prior to preparing the answer. A motion to dismiss is often used by a defendant to challenge perceived defects in the plaintiff's complaint. Common grounds for this motion include the lack of subject-matter jurisdiction or in personam jurisdiction, improper or inadequate service of the summons, and failure to state a claim upon which relief can be granted. The motion to dismiss is decided by a judge, and jurisdictions differ about permitting the attorneys to argue orally the merits of the motion. If the judge grants the motion, the plaintiff often will try to cure any defect by amending the complaint. If the judge denies the motion, the defendant normally will submit an answer. Alleged defects in the answer and reply also can be raised through a motion to dismiss or an equivalent motion used for that purpose in a particular jurisdiction.

The motion for summary judgment can be made by either or both parties. As we saw in Chapter I, this motion is intended to dispose of controversies when no genuine issues of material fact exist, or when the facts necessary to prove the other party's case are not provable. The motion is supported with proof in the form of affidavits and depositions. This proof is used to illustrate that there is no need to conduct a trial because there is no factual dispute between the parties. The party opposing the motion will present affidavits and depositions to prove the existence of contested issues of fact. Such proof also may be used to show the impossibility of certain facts alleged by an opposing party. For example, a complaint might accuse a defendant of various counts of negligence in operating a car. However, if the defendant was in jail that day, it could be proved that he or she could not possibly have committed the acts in question. The defendant in this instance would move for a summary judgment. Motions for summary judgment are disfavored by courts because, when granted, a party is denied a trial.

Summary judgment should not be granted if there is a genuine issue of material fact because it would deprive the parties of their right to a trial.

Discovery and Pretrial Conference

To prevent surprise at the trial, each party is provided with tools of **discovery** before trial in order to identify the relevant facts concerning the case. Discovery is based on the premise that, prior to a civil action, each party is entitled to information in the possession of others. This includes the identity and location of persons, the existence and location of documents, known facts, and opinions of experts.

There is a distinction between the right to obtain discovery and the right to use in court the statements or information that is the product of discovery. The restrictions that are made concerning the admissibility in court of the product of discovery are discussed later in the chapter. The requirements for discovery are as follows: the information sought cannot be privileged, it must be relevant, it cannot be the "work product" of an attorney, and if a physical or mental examination is required, good cause must be shown.

The most common tools of discovery are oral depositions, written interrogatories to parties, production of documents, physical and mental examinations, and requests for admissions. In an **oral deposition,** a witness is examined under oath outside court before a person legally authorized to conduct depositions (usually a court reporter or, if the deposition is being videotaped, a video technician who is similarly authorized by law). The party wishing the deposition must give notice to the opposing party to the suit, so that party's attorney may be present to cross-examine the witness. The questioning of the witness at an oral deposition is thus much the same as it would be in a courtroom. **Written interrogatories** to the parties are lists of questions that must be answered in writing and under oath. Interrogatories are submitted only to the parties to the case, not to witnesses. Because the rules of discovery can differ in federal and state courts, lawyers may take this into consideration in making a choice of forum. A state court, for example, might only permit an attorney to ask a party to answer thirty questions by written interrogatories, whereas fifty questions might be permissible under the federal rules.

One party to the suit may compel the **production of documents** or things in the possession of the other party for inspection. When the mental or physical condition of a party is at issue, a court may order the party to submit to a **mental examination** or **physical examination** by a physician or psychologist. Finally, one party may send to the other party a **request for admissions or denials** as to certain specified facts or as to the genuineness of certain documents. If no reply is made to such a request, the matters are considered admitted for the purpose of the suit.

All discovery except for physical examinations can be done without a court order. In case of noncompliance, the discovering party may request a court order to compel compliance. Failure to comply with the court order may result in imposition of the sanctions provided in the discovery statute.

Discovery may begin after the filing of the complaint, but usually commences after the answer is filed and continues until trial. In addition, a **pretrial conference** may be called by the judge to discuss the issues of the case. A judge and the two opposing lawyers discuss and evaluate the controversy informally. They consider the simplification and sharpening of the issues, the admissions and disclosure of facts, possible amendments to the pleadings, the limitation of the number of witnesses, the possibility of reaching an out-of-court settlement, and any other matters that may aid in the speedy and just disposition of the action.

The importance of discovery cannot be overestimated. Discovery results in the disclosure of unknown facts and reveals the strengths and weaknesses of each side's proof, and is an educational process for the lawyers and their clients. Each side is, in sports terminology, "scouting" their opponent and learning what they plan to prove and how they intend to do it if the case goes to trial. Justice is not supposed to be determined based on surprise witnesses, trickery, and deceit. Discovery allows the parties to identify the core issues; pin witnesses down so they can't easily change their views at trial; determine witness credibility, especially in the case of experts; and clarify where impeachment and cross-examination will be effective.

Lawyers who fail to comply with discovery rules can gain an outcome-determinative tactical advantage over their opponents when a case comes to trial. When this occurs, the injured party has the right to ask for judicial intervention and seek the imposition of sanctions against the offending party.

The court in the next case has to determine how heavily to sanction a defenday who destroyed information that should have been disclosed to the plaintiff pursuant to the rules of discovery. Notice the defense attorney's ethical obligation to reveal his own client's violations of the discovery rules.

Rajesh Idnani et al. v. Venus Capital Management, Inc.
No. SUCV201001280BLS2
Commonwealth of Massachusetts Superior Court, Suffolk, SS.
November 30, 2011

MEMORANDUM
Sanders, Janet L., J.
This case is the latest chapter in a long-running dispute between the parties concerning management fees and ownership interests in certain hedge funds operated by the defendants. After prevailing in an arbitration,... plaintiffs brought this action, contending that defendants had engaged in fraudulent and otherwise wrongful conduct intended to deprive them of obtaining the benefit of that arbitration award. Plaintiffs now contend that the defendants have intentionally destroyed evidence and seek sanctions, including default judgment....

BACKGROUND
Many of the facts relating to the instant motion are undisputed. This case was filed in March 2010. Pursuant to a scheduling order of this Court ... the parties were to complete document discovery by May 1, 2011, with other fact discovery to be completed by September 30, 2011. In order to respond to the document requests, defendants and their prior counsel, McDermott Will & Emory, retained Evidox Corporation, a Boston-based firm providing e-discovery services. From August 2010 through the spring of 2011, Evidox collected, processed, and searched a large volume of electronic files made available to it by defendants. In the meantime, defense counsel advised his clients both in writing and orally of the need to preserve all records.

In April 2011, Evidox made arrangements to come to the offices of the defendant Venus Capital Management ("Venus") for the purpose of collecting hard copy files. The plan was to scan the files into an electronic database so that the information could then be electronically searched. Within days of the date on which Evidox was scheduled to retrieve the hard copy documents, Venus's Chief Executive Officer, defendant Vikas Mehrotra, took it upon himself to review the documents first and to discard whatever he determined not to be relevant to the litigation. This decision was in direct violation of the instructions he had received from his own counsel. Moreover, this Court does not credit Mehrotra's claim that this was part of some "regular cleanup" or was undertaken to free up storage space.

Enlisting the assistance of Venus Chief Operating Officer Vikas Chawla, Mehrotra cleaned out four and a half 36-inch file cabinets and three or four standard sized file cabinet drawers between 4:00 and 5:30 p.m., after regular trading hours. That translates into a total of between 18,720 pages and 51,600 pages of material. No copies were made and no record was kept of what was thrown out. In sworn testimony, Mehrotra stated that many of these materials had nothing to do with the instant litigation: for example, he disposed of research reports on certain Chinese companies from 2004, brochures from industry conferences, and old telephone directories. He admitted, however, that the documents discarded did include printouts of "screen shots" of online account statements for various Venus funds, vendor invoices, and credit card statements. These documents conceivably fell within the scope of outstanding document requests from the plaintiffs.

When this came to the attention of defense counsel Anthony Bongiorno, he conducted his own investigation and determined that the Canons of Professional Conduct required him to disclose this to the Court and opposing counsel. At a hearing held on July 7, 2011, Bongiorno informed this Court that his investigation had determined that in fact his clients had destroyed documents which were responsive to the pending Rule 34 requests of plaintiffs. Bongiorno withdrew from the case, with new counsel entering an appearance. After some period of discovery relating to the spoliation issue, plaintiffs filed the instant motion.

DISCUSSION

The principles of law that this Court applies to resolve plaintiffs' motion are well established. Once a litigant knows or reasonably should know that evidence might be relevant to a possible legal action, the law imposes on that litigant a duty to preserve such evidence.... Where that duty has been breached, whether negligently or intentionally, sanctions are appropriate, with the court given considerable discretion to craft a remedy that will address the "precise unfairness that would otherwise result."... As a general rule, the judge should impose the least severe sanction necessary to remedy the prejudice to the nonspoliating party.... In determining which sanction to impose upon a finding of spoliation of evidences the court should take into account the wilfulness of the conduct in question together with the danger and the extent of any prejudice to the party deprived of the evidence.

Here, there is no question that the conduct was wilful. Mehrotra was aware of his duty to preserve records, including hard copies of documents, when he made the decision to destroy thousands of pages of materials. His explanation for this—that it was part of a routine "cleanup"—is not credible in light of the timing: the destruction occurred within days of Evidox's appointment to come to Venus's offices to view the materials for itself. There is also no real dispute that the documents destroyed included materials which fell within the scope of plaintiffs' pending Rule 34 requests and were therefore relevant. That Mehrotra may have believed (as he testified) that most of the information contained in these documents could be found elsewhere in documents that were stored electronically does not make these documents any less relevant. Moreover, the discarded documents may well have included handwriting or notes which would not be maintained in electronic form. Mehrotra has never attempted to put together a list of what was destroyed, so this Court (and the plaintiffs) have only his word to go on. That he decided to take the action that he did even after being specifically told by his attorney to retain records itself suggests that he may have had something to hide.

Whether there are alternative sources for the information and how important the documents would have been to the plaintiffs, however, are both key considerations in determining the level of prejudice. With regard to credit card statements and vendor invoices, defendants contend that all such expenses would have been scanned and then emailed to Venus accounting staff at Catamaran in India. Thus, the information is either among the e-discovery already produced to the plaintiffs or can be obtained directly from Catamaran.... As to the screen shots of the account statements, any trading activity would also appear (according to the defendants) in at least three other electronic versions. Again, this electronic information has been or will be produced. To date, the defendants appeared to have been fully cooperative in turning over all electronic discovery, placing no restrictions on Evidox and producing more than 1.4 million pages of responsive documents in electronic format. Finally, plaintiffs' counsel conceded at the hearing that plaintiffs already have substantial evidence to show that defendants intentionally closed down one hedge fund and opened another using the identical investment strategy in order to cheat the plaintiffs out of the fees they had won in the arbitration. Indeed, the smoking gun (if there is one) consists of various emails to and from Venus investors in 2008 that have already been produced to plaintiffs. Accordingly, the material which was destroyed would not appear to go to the heart of the plaintiffs' case.

That being said, this Court concludes that Mehrotra's conduct cannot go unsanctioned. Although the prejudice to plaintiffs is not so strong as to justify default, there is certainly a potential that some relevant information has been irretrievably lost, and could have been of some benefit to plaintiffs' case. More important, the conduct was intentional and given the circumstances, in bad faith. The judicial system depends in large part on the integrity of those who participate in it. Whenever relevant evidence is destroyed, that has a "pernicious effect on the truth finding function of our court." ... Also, this kind of conduct imposes significant costs on opposing counsel and requires the expenditure of judicial resources. It should not go unpunished.

Accordingly, it is hereby ORDERED that:

1. Defendants shall pay all attorneys fees and costs incurred by plaintiffs in connection with this motion. Plaintiffs shall serve on defendants within fourteen days a motion seeking a specific amount, accompanied by an affidavit detailing such costs and expenses. Defendants may respond within ten days thereafter, with the papers filed in the manner provided by Superior Court Rule 9A.

2. At trial of the plaintiffs' claims, the Court will permit plaintiffs to introduce evidence of Mehrotra's conduct as set forth herein. The Court will instruct the jury that it may infer from that conduct that additional relevant materials existed and were not produced as a result of Mehrotra's conduct, and that such materials would have provided evidence of facts supportive of plaintiff's claims.

Case Questions

1. What should a party do when an opponent fails to follow the rules of civil procedure with respect to discovery?
2. The media often depict courtroom lawyers using surprise witnesses and evidence. In reality, thorough discovery usually destroys any possibility of surprise. Is this good or bad?
3. All discovery in general, and e-discovery in particular, is very expensive. One party frequently will be able to afford significantly more discovery than his or her opponent. Do you see any fundamental problems relating to discovery that might result from such a discrepancy?

 How do the discovery rules seek to encourage ethical conduct in the context of the adversarial process of litigation?

CIVIL TRIALS

A trial is a legal procedure that is available to parties who have been otherwise unwilling or unable to resolve their differences through negotiations, settlement offers, and even mediation attempts. Trials involve the staging of a confrontation between the plaintiff and the defendant as contradicting witnesses, and arguments collide in a courtroom in accordance with procedural and evidentiary rules. The trial process may, as a result of appeals or new trials, take many years, but it will ultimately result either in a dismissal of the complaint or in a judgment.

In some cases, parties waive a jury trial, preferring to try their case before a judge. (This is called a **bench trial.**) Bench trials can be scheduled more quickly, and they take less time to conclude because the procedures associated with the jury are eliminated. Bench trials also cost the parties and taxpayers less money than jury trials.

The right to a federal jury trial is provided by the Seventh Amendment to the U.S. Constitution to parties involved in a common law civil action. There is no federal right to have a jury decide equitable claims. The right to a jury trial in the state judicial system is determined by state law and may not exist for some types of actions, such as equitable claims and small claims cases. Federal rules permit parties to stipulate to less than twelve jurors, and local court rules often provide for six.

The judge is responsible for making sure that (1) the jury is properly selected in a jury trial, (2) due process requirements for a fair trial are satisfied, (3) proper rulings are made with respect to the admissibility of evidence, (4) the rules of procedure are followed by the parties, and (5) the judgment is awarded in accordance with law.

Selection of the Jury

The procedure discussed here applies only to jury trials (see Figure 5.4). Jurors are selected at random from a fair cross section of the community and summoned to the courthouse for jury duty.[5] After a case has been assigned to a court, the judge calls in a group of prospective jurors, who take their seats in the jury box. A **voir dire** (literally, "to speak the truth") examination is conducted to determine each juror's qualifications for jury duty under the appropriate statute and any grounds for a challenge for cause or information on which to base a peremptory challenge. A **challenge for cause** may be based on prejudice or bias. A juror's relationship, business involvement, or other close connection with one of the parties or attorneys also may be considered cause for replacing a juror. Attorneys for both sides may make as many challenges for cause as they wish, and it is within the judge's sound discretion to replace a juror for cause. In addition to the challenges for cause, each party is given a limited number of **peremptory challenges** that may be exercised for any reason other than race *(Baton v. Kentucky,* 476 U.S. 79 [1986]) or gender *(J. E. B. v. Alabama* ex rel. T.B., 511 U.S. 127 [1994]).

Opening Statements and Examination of Witnesses

After a jury has been selected and sworn, the trial begins with an opening statement by the plaintiff's attorney. The opening statement explains the case in general, including the attorney's legal theories and what he or she intends to prove. The defendant's lawyer also may present at this time an opening statement introducing legal theories of the case

and the facts the defense intends to prove, or reserve the right to make such a statement prior to presenting the defendant's case-in-chief.

In order to win the case, the plaintiff must prove the disputed allegations of the complaint by presenting evidence. Witnesses and exhibits are produced by both parties to the suit. If witnesses do not voluntarily appear to testify, they may be ordered by means of a **subpoena** (see Figure 5.5) to appear in court. A **subpoena duces tecum** ("subpoena to bring with you") issued by the court commands a witness to produce a document that is in his or her possession. If witnesses refuse to appear, to testify, or to produce required documents, or if they perform any act that disrupts the judicial proceedings, they may be punished for contempt of court.

Judges have much discretion with respect to the order of production of evidence. Normally, a plaintiff's attorney presents the plaintiff's case first. The attorney presents witnesses, documents, and other evidence, and rests the case when he or she decides that enough evidence has been produced to substantiate the allegations. Defendant's lawyer then presents the defendant's case in the same manner. When the defense is finished, the plaintiff's attorney may introduce additional witnesses and exhibits in rebuttal of the defense's case. If new matters are brought out by the rebuttal, the defendant may introduce evidence in surrebuttal, limited to answering the new matters.

Both attorneys introduce their own witnesses and question them. This is called **direct examination**. The opposing attorney **cross-examines** the witnesses after the direct examination is completed. Attorneys may conduct **redirect examinations** of their own witnesses following the cross-examinations. Attorneys generally may not ask their own witnesses leading questions (except for preliminary questions to introduce a witness or questions to a hostile witness). A **leading question** is one that suggests the answer to the witness. For instance, suppose an attorney asks, "You've never seen this gun before, have you?" That lawyer is almost telling the witness to answer no. Leading questions are permissible on cross-examination because they promote the purpose of cross-examination: testing the credibility of witnesses. Upon cross-examination, for example, an attorney

© Cengage Learning

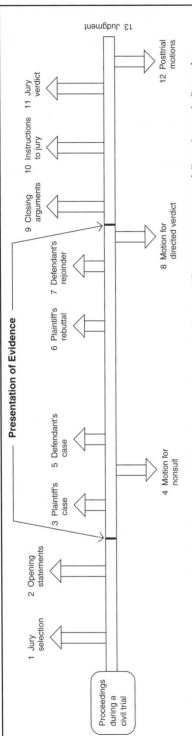

Presentation of Evidence

1 Jury selection
2 Opening statements
3 Plaintiff's case
4 Motion for nonsuit
5 Defendant's case
6 Plaintiff's rebuttal
7 Defendant's rejoinder
8 Motion for directed verdict
9 Closing arguments
10 Instructions to jury
11 Jury verdict
12 Posttrial motions
13 Judgment

Proceedings during a civil trial

1   Prospective jurors are questioned by attorneys and judge. A prospective juror is dismissed if an attorney successfully makes a challenge for cause or exercises a peremptory challenge.

2   Attorneys explain facts of case in general to judge and jury. Plaintiff's attorney's opening argument usually precedes defendant's.

3   Plaintiff's attorney presents witnesses, documents, and other evidence to substantiate allegations in complaint.

4   Defendant's attorney moves for an involuntary dismissal (motion for nonsuit) if it is felt that plaintiff failed to prove allegations. If judge agrees, motion is granted and plaintiff loses. If judge disagrees, motion is denied and trial continues.

5   Defendant's attorney presents witnesses, documents, and other evidence to rebut plaintiff's case.

6   Plaintiff's attorney presents evidence to rebut evidence brought out during presentation of defendant's case.

7   Defendant's attorney presents evidence to rebut any new matters brought out during plaintiff's rebuttal.

8   After both parties rest their case, either or both parties may move for a directed verdict. If judge feels that reasonable persons could not disagree that the moving party should win, judge grants motion. If motion is granted, moving party wins and trial is over. If motion is denied, trial continues.

9   Both attorneys sum up evidence for jury. They suggest how the jury should resolve specific disputed items. Plaintiff's attorney argues first, but may reserve time to rebut defendant's attorney's closing argument.

10 Judge explains substantive law to jury, and tells how it should be applied to facts. Both attorneys may suggest specific instructions to judge, but final instructions are left to judge's discretion.

11 After deliberation, jury returns either a general or special verdict or both. A general verdict is simply a declaration of winner and amount of recovery. A special verdict answers specific factual questions requested by judge.

12 After jury returns its verdict, either or both parties may move to have verdict set aside by filing a motion for a new trial or a motion for a judgment notwithstanding verdict of jury or relief from judgment. If the judge denies the motion, judge renders judgment in accordance with jury verdict.

13 By rendering judgment, judge declares who prevailed at trial and amount of recovery. If losing party does not voluntarily pay prescribed amount, winning party can force payment by obtaining an order of execution.

F I G U R E 5.4 Proceedings during a Civil Trial

UNITED STATES DISTRICT COURT
FOR THE . . . . . DISTRICT OF . . . . .
. . . . DIVISION

. . . .
Plaintiff,

v.   Civil Action No. . . . .

. . . .
Defendant.

To: . . . . *[name and address of witness]*
   You are commanded to appear in the United States District Court for
the . . . . District of . . . ., at . . . . in the City of . . . .,
State of . . . . . on the . . . . . day of . . . . ., 20 . . . . . at . . . . . o'clock
. . . . .M. to testify on behalf of . . . . . in the above pending action.
Dated . . . . ., 20 . . . . . .
[Name and address of attorney]

[Signature and title of clerk]

[Seal]

FIGURE 5.5   Subpoena—For Attendance of Witness [FRCP 45(a)]

could ask a witness the following question: "Isn't it true, Mr. Smith, that you are a firearms expert?"

RULES OF EVIDENCE

Since 1975, federal trials have been conducted pursuant to the Federal Rules of Evidence (FRE). Although each state is entitled to promulgate its own rules, most states have chosen to adopt the federal rules as their "state rules." Rules of evidence apply to jury and nonjury trials, although they are applied less strictly in the latter. Many of the so-called rules are actually more like policy statements because many provide judges with considerable discretion in their application. Trial judges use the rules to control the admissibility of evidence, and their decisions are generally upheld on appeal

unless there has been a clear abuse of discretion. Judges will instruct jurors to disregard evidence that has been improperly presented to them, but it is difficult to evaluate the effect that this excluded evidence has on the jurors' decision-making process. Once jurors have heard testimony, they may not be able to simply forget what they have seen and heard. In some situations, the judge may conclude that significant prejudice has occurred and that instructing the jury is an inadequate remedy. When this occurs, a mistrial will be declared.

Relevance and Materiality

Evidence, whether it be testimony, demonstrative evidence (such as photographs, charts, and graphs), or physical evidence, is admissible only if it is **relevant.** That is, it must logically tend to prove or disprove some issue of consequence that is in dispute at the trial. Irrelevant evidence confuses the jury, wastes court time, and is often prejudicial. Relevancy is sometimes confused with materiality, which has to do with the probative value of evidence. **Probative evidence** tends to prove something of importance to the case. Relevant evidence that has "significant" probative value is **material.** Evidence that is either immaterial or irrelevant should be excluded.

Competency

Evidence must be **competent** (legally adequate) to be admissible. Competency is a broad concept. To be competent, witnesses have to take an oath or affirm that they will testify truthfully. A nonexpert witness is limited to testimony about what he or she has heard or seen firsthand (i.e., to facts); the opinions and conclusions of such a witness are "incompetent."

As fact finder, the jury must draw its own conclusions from the evidence. However, where special expertise is required to evaluate a fact situation, a jury may not be competent to form an opinion. In that case, a person with special training, knowledge, or expertise may be called to testify as an expert witness. Doctors, for example, are frequently called as expert witnesses in personal injury cases. The qualifications and expertise of such expert witnesses must be established to the court's satisfaction before their opinions are admissible.

The Best Evidence Rule

The **best evidence rule** requires that, unless they are unobtainable, original documents rather than copies be introduced into evidence. Even when the original writing is unobtainable, secondary evidence of the contents is admissible only if the unavailability is not the fault of the party seeking to introduce the evidence. In this situation, the best available alternative proof must be presented. For example, a photocopy of a writing is preferred over oral testimony as to its contents.

The Hearsay Rule

The **hearsay evidence rule** excludes witness testimony that proceeds not from the personal knowledge of the witness but instead from the repetition of what was said or written outside court by another person, and is offered for the purpose of establishing the truth of what was written or said. The person who made the out-of-court statement may have been lying, joking, or speaking carelessly. The witness reporting the statement in court may have a poor memory. This exclusionary rule guarantees the opportunity to cross-examine the person who made the out-of-court statement and prevents highly unreliable evidence from being considered.

The hearsay rule contains many exceptions. The **spontaneous declarations exception** (in legalese called *res gestae*) permits courts to admit in court testimony by the witness about spontaneous declarations made by another person who is not in court, where the declarations were uttered simultaneously with the occurrence of an act. The basis for the admission is the belief that a statement made instinctively at the time of an event, without the opportunity for formulation of a statement favorable to one's own cause, is likely to be truthful.

INTERNET TIP

Readers wishing to read an interesting case involving the admissibility of hearsay evidence will want to read *Barbara Harris v. Toys"R"Us* on the textbook's website. In this case, a children's motorized vehicle weighing ten pounds was alleged to have fallen from the middle shelf of a three-tiered commercial shelving unit in a Toys"R"Us store. The falling vehicle allegedly struck customer Barbara Harris on her head while she was shopping, knocking her to the floor and causing her injury.

Communicative Privileges

The general rule is that all persons who can provide relevant, competent, and material information that would help the fact finder search for the truth are required to testify at trial. But the law also provides some exceptions where certain communications, for reasons of public policy, are recognized by constitutional provision, statute, judicial decision, or rule of evidence as being privileged. Privileges exist for reasons of public policy. Where a **privilege** (i.e., a **privileged communication**) exists, a person benefitted by the privilege (called the **holder**) is entitled to refuse to testify or to block some other person from testifying as a witness. Because privileges permit the withholding of important evidence at trial, they are disfavored by courts. This means that privileges are narrowly construed and only recognized when the facts clearly demonstrate that the interest being protected by the privilege would be threatened if the testimony were to be given.

Probably the best-known privilege is the privilege against self-incrimination, which is provided for in the Fifth and Fourteenth Amendments to the U.S. Constitution. This privilege permits individuals to refuse to disclose information (in most circumstances) that might expose them to a criminal prosecution. (This is the privilege against self-incrimination that is protected by the *Miranda* warnings.[6])

Traditionally the law has recognized two types of privileges that are intended to protect spousal relationships and the institution of marriage: the marital testimonial privilege and the confidential marital communications privilege. The marital testimonial privilege permits one spouse to refuse to testify in a criminal case in which the other spouse is the defendant. The nonaccused spouse is the holder of this privilege and decides whether to testify or claim this privilege. The confidential marital communications privilege prevents a spouse or former spouse from being forced to testify involuntarily in any proceeding, whether criminal or civil, against the other spouse about the content of a private marital communication between the two. Either type of marital privilege usually can be waived and does not apply to cases in which the spouses clearly have adverse interests (such as in spousal battery, divorce, or child neglect, abuse, or support cases). In cases like these, permitting the spouse's testimony is essential to the action, and there is no intact intimate marital relationship interest to protect. Many states no longer recognize the testimonial privilege, and states differ as to the exact requirements for the confidential marital communications privilege.

The wife of the appellant in the next case claimed the marital testimonial privilege and refused to testify against her criminally accused husband. The prosecution used statements the wife had voluntarily given to the police and a nurse as evidence at the preliminary hearing (a pre-trial evidentiary hearing in a criminal case). The use of these statements in this manner to convict the husband was appealed to the Utah Supreme Court.

State of Utah v. Travis Dee Timmermann
2009 UT 58
Supreme Court of Utah
September 4, 2009

Durham, Chief Justice.

INTRODUCTION

Travis Timmerman was charged with attempted rape, forcible sexual abuse, and assault. At the preliminary hearing, the victim, Mrs. Timmerman, invoked her spousal privilege not to testify against her husband. The State then introduced into evidence Mrs. Timmerman's previous statements to the police and to a sexual assault nurse. With those statements, the magistrate bound Mr. Timmerman over for trial. Mr. Timmerman subsequently filed a motion to quash the bindover.

The district court denied the motion and held that the admission of Mrs. Timmerman's statements did not violate Mr. Timmerman's constitutional rights or Mrs. Timmerman's spousal testimonial privilege. Mr. Timmerman now appeals the district court's denial of his motion. We are asked to consider whether the Confrontation Clauses of the United States Constitution and Utah Constitution apply to preliminary hearings and whether the spousal testimonial privilege embodied in the Utah Constitution applies to a spouse's voluntary, out-of-court statements. We affirm the trial court.

BACKGROUND

During the early morning hours of June 30, 2007, the Timmermans' neighbor heard a woman screaming "Stop it!" and "Help me!" The neighbor thought the screams came from the Timmermans' house. Around 7:00 a.m., the neighbor notified the police. Officer McLelland responded and spoke with Mrs. Timmerman. During their conversation, Officer McLelland observed bruises on her arms and face. He asked Mrs. Timmerman to fill out a witness statement. In her three-page statement, Mrs. Timmerman wrote that Mr. Timmerman repeatedly hit her and tried to force her to have ... intercourse.

Another police officer, Detective Harding, interviewed Mrs. Timmerman and asked her to submit to a sexual assault examination at the hospital. When Mrs. Timmerman arrived at the hospital, a sexual assault nurse examined her and filled out a Sexual Assault Nurse Examination (SANE) report. In the report, the nurse cataloged Mrs. Timmerman's bruises and her statements that Mr. Timmerman hit her and tried to have forced sex with her.

Mr. Timmerman was charged with attempted rape, a first-degree felony; forcible sexual abuse, a second-degree felony; and assault, a class B misdemeanor.... At the preliminary hearing, the State called Mrs. Timmerman as a witness, but she invoked her spousal privilege not to testify against her husband. Instead, Officer McLelland and Detective Harding testified for the State, and the State introduced Mrs. Timmerman's witness statement and SANE report. Mr. Timmerman objected to the admission of the statement and the report on the grounds that they violated Mrs. Timmerman's spousal privilege and Mr. Timmerman's confrontation rights under the federal and state constitutions. The magistrate admitted both documents and bound Mr. Timmerman over for trial.

In his motion to quash the bindover before the district court, Mr. Timmerman argued that his confrontation rights under the federal and state constitutions were violated because he could not cross-examine Mrs. Timmerman at the preliminary hearing regarding her out-of-court statements. He also argued that the magistrate had ignored Mrs. Timmerman's spousal privilege when he admitted her out-of-court statements into evidence. Without Mrs. Timmerman's statements, there was insufficient evidence to bind Mr. Timmerman over for trial on the attempted rape charge. The district court held that confrontation rights under the federal and state constitutions do not apply to preliminary hearings and that

out-of-court statements made by spouses to third parties are not excluded under the spousal testimonial privilege.

Mr. Timmerman subsequently filed this interlocutory appeal....

ANALYSIS

Mr. Timmerman argues that the right to confrontation in preliminary hearings is guaranteed by the Sixth Amendment of the United States Constitution and by article 1, section 12 of the Utah Constitution. He also argues that the spousal testimonial privilege found in the Utah Constitution prevents the use of out-of-court, voluntary statements.

[Note: Part I of this opinion which contains the Court's discussion of the right to confrontation has been omitted to focus readers on the spousal privilege discussion.]

II. THE TRIAL COURT PROPERLY DENIED THE MOTION TO QUASH BECAUSE THE CONSTITUTIONAL SPOUSAL TESTIMONIAL PRIVILEGE APPLIES ONLY TO COMPELLED, IN-COURT TESTIMONY

Mr. Timmerman argues that the trial court erred when it allowed Mrs. Timmerman's out-of-court statements into evidence even though Mrs. Timmerman invoked her spousal privilege not to testify against her husband. Utah recognizes two different spousal privileges: the spousal testimonial privilege and the spousal communications privilege. The spousal testimonial privilege is defined in article I, section 12 of the Utah Constitution: "[A] wife shall not be compelled to testify against her husband, nor a husband against his wife." The Utah Rules of Evidence codifies the privilege in rule 502(a). In contrast, the spousal communications privilege, as codified in Utah Code section 78B-1-137 and Rule 502(b) of the Utah Rules of Evidence, protects confidential communications between spouses during their marriage. However, the accused spouse cannot invoke the spousal communications privilege if the accused spouse is charged with a crime.... Mr. Timmerman argues that the privileges were violated, but since Mr. Timmerman is accused of a crime against his spouse, he cannot invoke the spousal communications privilege.... Hence, only the spousal testimonial privilege is at issue here.

Mr. Timmerman argues that Mrs. Timmerman's out-of-court statements were improperly admitted after she invoked her spousal testimonial privilege....

Article I, section 12 of the Utah Constitution provides, "[A] wife shall not be compelled to testify against her husband." In examining the language of the privilege, we recognize that a privilege should be "strictly construed in accordance with its object,"… because of its "undesirable effect of excluding relevant evidence."… Because a privilege withholds "relevant information from the factfinder, it applies only where necessary to achieve its purpose."…

The purpose of the spousal testimonial privilege is to foster "the harmony and sanctity of the marriage relationship."… If spouses were forced to testify against each other, then "the testifying spouse would be placed in the unenviable position of either committing perjury or testifying to matters that are detrimental to his or her spouse, which could clearly lead to marital strife."…

Construing the privilege strictly, according to its plain language and in light of its purpose, we interpret the spousal testimonial privilege to apply only to compelled testimony, or in other words, involuntary, in-court testimony. We believe this narrow interpretation of the privilege will not serve to exclude relevant testimony or extend the privilege beyond its narrow purpose. Further, admitting an out-of-court statement into evidence does not force one spouse to testify against the other or tempt the testifying spouse to commit perjury.

Criticism of the spousal testimonial privilege further bolsters this narrow interpretation. The privilege enables "abusers to silence their victims" and makes the testifying spouse "vulnerable to coercion from the defendant-spouse and his lawyer." Amanda H. Frost, Updating the Marital Privileges: A Witness-Centered Rationale, 14 Wis. Women's L.J. 1, 34 (1999). Similarly, the Advisory Committee of the Utah Rules of Evidence is convinced that the justifications for the spousal testimonial privilege are insufficient: "[The privilege] does not promote marital felicity, is based on the outmoded concept that the husband and wife are one, and causes suppression of relevant evidence." … The Advisory Committee recommends that only the spousal communications privilege be preserved and the spousal testimonial privilege be repealed. However, such a change is dependent on a constitutional amendment to article I, section 12 that would remove the spousal testimonial privilege.

In this case, the introduction of Mrs. Timmerman's statements into evidence at the preliminary hearing did not violate her spousal testimonial privilege, which protects a spouse from giving involuntary, in-court statements. Mrs. Timmerman was not forced to testify at the preliminary hearing. She invoked her privilege and was dismissed from the witness stand. In lieu of her in-court testimony, the State introduced Mrs. Timmerman's witness statement and her statements in the SANE report. Mrs. Timmerman made those statements voluntarily. She was not forced to attend a sexual assault examination or write a witness statement. Because the statements were neither compelled nor in court, the spousal testimonial privilege does not apply.

We also note that barring the statements would not comport with the justifications for the privilege. Whatever degree of marital harmony that previously existed between the Timmermans was most likely absent when Mrs. Timmerman voluntarily gave her statements to the police and to the sexual assault nurse. Blocking her statements from admission into evidence at the preliminary hearing would promote excluding relevant evidence more than it would promote marital harmony. Furthermore, Mrs. Timmerman was not placed in a position where she had to choose either to perjure herself or harm her husband because she was not forced to testify in court…

Because the spousal testimonial privilege does not apply to the voluntary, out-of-court statements given to the police and to the sexual assault nurse, the trial court properly held that the spousal testimonial privilege was not violated and denied the motion to quash the bindover… We therefore affirm.

Associate Chief Justice Durrant, Justice Wilkins, Justice Parrish, and Justice Nehring concur in Chief Justice Durham's opinion.

Case Questions

1. This case illustrates how recognition of a spousal immunity can result in the exclusion of evidence. In this case, the prosecution was able to introduce the victim/wife's statement in lieu of having her testify at trial. Given that the public policy in Utah is to recognize spousal immunity, should the wife/victim have been "advised of her rights" by the police or hospital personnel prior to giving a statement to the police or to the SANE nurse?
2. Chief Justice Durham's opinion points out that one of the spousal immunities has been heavily criticized as bad public policy. Do you believe that there is any continuing need for the recognition of either spousal privilege? Explain and defend your position.

INTERNET TIP

Due to the complexity of the marital privilege, interested readers are invited to read the Florida case of *Dennis and Mary Hill v. State of Florida*. This is a criminal case involving confidential communications between husband and wife as well as the psychotherapist–patient privilege, both of which are also recognized under Florida law. You can read this case on the textbook's website.

Also on the website is the Wisconsin statute containing that state's attorney–client privilege rule, as well *Raymond Binkley v. Georgette Allen*, a case in which the appellant claimed that the physician–patient privilege permitted her to refuse to disclose during discovery information relating to her use of prescribed medications.

Other privileges involving confidential communications include the doctor–patient privilege and the attorney–client privilege. The doctor–patient privilege applies to confidential information provided by a patient to a doctor for the purpose of treatment. The attorney–client privilege, the oldest common law privilege, protects confidential communications between lawyers and their clients and thereby encourages clients to speak frankly with their lawyers. The privilege applies to all communications between a client and his or her lawyer relating to professional representation. In addition, the attorney's work product, including all matters considered to be part of the preparation of a case, is privileged. These privileges can be waived by the client for whose protection they are intended.

The privilege on communications to clergy protects a parishioner who has divulged confidential information to a member of the clergy while seeking spiritual guidance. If the parishioner reveals confidential information to a member of the clergy who is acting in his or her professional religious capacity, this communication can be excluded from evidence at trial as privileged. The modern version of this privilege has very imprecise boundaries, which may become more clear with the evolution of the case law.

Trial Motions

If, after the plaintiff's attorney presents plaintiff's case, the defendant's attorney believes that the plaintiff was unable to substantiate the essential allegations adequately, the defendant may make a **motion to dismiss**.[7] The judge grants the motion only if a reasonable person could not find in favor of the plaintiff after considering the evidence most favorable to the plaintiff. If the motion is granted, the case is over and the plaintiff loses.

If the motion to dismiss is denied or not made at all, the defendant's lawyer then presents the defendant's case and tries to disprove the plaintiff's evidence or substantiate the defendant's arguments. Witnesses and exhibits are presented, following the same procedure as the plaintiff's direct examination followed by cross-examination. After the defendant rests his or her case, the plaintiff then may produce evidence to rebut the defendant's evidence.

At the end of the presentation of evidence, but before the issues are submitted to the jury, either or both parties may make a motion for a **directed verdict**. The motion is granted for the party making the motion if the judge decides that the case is perfectly clear and that reasonable people could not disagree on the result. If the motion is granted, the moving party wins the dispute without the jury deciding the case. If no motion for a directed verdict is made, or if one is made and denied, the case is submitted to the jury.

Jury Verdict and Posttrial Motions

Both parties' attorneys have an opportunity to make oral arguments to the jury summarizing their cases. The judge then instructs the members of the jury as to how they should proceed. Although jurors deliberate in private, certain restrictions must be observed to avoid possible grounds for setting aside the verdict. These include prohibitions on juror misconduct, such as drunkenness; the use of unauthorized evidence, such as secretly visiting the scene of an accident; or disregarding the judge's instructions, such as discussing the merits of the case over lunch with a friend.

After the verdict has been rendered, a party not satisfied with it may move for judgment notwithstanding the verdict, a new trial, or relief from judgment. A **motion for judgment notwithstanding the verdict (JNOV)** is granted when the judge decides that reasonable people could not have reached the verdict that the jury has reached. A **motion for a new trial** before a new jury may be granted by a judge for a variety of reasons, including excessive or grossly inadequate damages, newly discovered evidence, a questionable jury verdict, errors in the production of evidence, or simply the interest of justice. A **motion for relief from judgment** is granted if the judge finds a clerical error in the judgment, newly discovered evidence, or fraud that induced the judgment.

Additur and Remittitur

On occasion, juries award money damages that are, in the view of the trial or appellate courts, inadequate as a matter of law.

When a jury's award is grossly insufficient, a prevailing party in state court is often entitled to ask the trial court to award the plaintiff an additional sum of money (called **additur**). If the trial court agrees, it will specify an additional amount for the defendant to pay the plaintiff. In that event, the defendant can agree to pay the additur; refuse to pay, in which case the trial court will order a new trial on damages; or appeal to a higher court. Federal judges cannot award additur because of the Seventh Amendment, which provides that "no fact tried by a jury shall be otherwise reexamined … than according to the rules of the common law." This means that no federal judge can award money damages in an amount above the sum awarded by the jury.

Both state and federal judges, with the consent of the plaintiff, can reduce unreasonably high jury verdicts. When a jury finds for the plaintiff and the money damage award is grossly excessive, the defendant is entitled to ask the trial and appellate courts to reduce the size of the award by ordering a **remittitur.** If the trial court awards a remittitur, the plaintiff is given three choices: the plaintiff can accept the reduced sum that was determined by the court; refuse to remit any of the jury's award, in which case the trial court will order a new trial on damages; or appeal to a higher court.

Introduction to *Tammy Lou Fontenot v. Taser International, Inc.*

The deceased in this wrongful death case was named Darryl Turner, a seventeen-year-old male who had been employed by a grocery store as a bagger. The incident that concluded with his death began when Turner refused to peacefully leave the store premises after he was fired from his job for "insubordination." The youth began engaging in disruptive and threatening behavior that caused the store to call police. The responding police officers twice resorted to the use of an electrical device commonly known as a Taser to deliver electrical shocks to Turner's body while taking him into custody. Turner fell while being shocked and could not be revived.

The plaintiff in this case was Tammy Lou Fontenot, the person charged with administrating Turner's estate. She filed suit against the City of Charlotte and Taser International seeking money damages for the alleged wrongful death of Darryl Turner. Although the City of Charlotte settled with the plaintiff for $625,000, the claim against Taser was tried to a jury. The jury found for the plaintiff and awarded damages of $10 million. Taser filed posttrial motions asking for JNOV and a new trial or remittitur. The trial judge denied JNOV but agreed with the defendant that remittitur was required. The judge filed his order in March of 2012 and unfortunately miscalculated the amount of the remittitur. The parties brought this to the court's attention and the judge issued a revised version of his order that corrected his original mistake.

What follows is a heavily edited excerpt of the revised order that focuses on the judge's rulings on the JNOV and remittitur portions of defendant's motion.

Tammy Lou Fontenot v. Taser International, Inc.
3:10-cv-125-RJC-DCK
U.S. District Court, Western District of North Carolina, Charlotte Division
April 20, 2012

Robert J. Conrad, Jr., Chief United States District Judge.

ORDER
THIS MATTER comes before the Court on Plaintiff Tammy Lou Fontenot's ("Plaintiff") Declaration, ... and Defendant's response....

Plaintiff's Declaration took exception to the ... Court's discounting methodology used in calculating the present monetary value of the decedent, Darryl Turner, to his parents....

TASER's argument ... indicate[s] its agreement with Plaintiff's requested formula. The statutory annuity table that TASER offers uses the same formula that Plaintiff asks the Court to use.... Therefore, the Court will use the parties' agreed formula and a 1% real interest rate as the discount rate....

As Justice Frankfurter observed, "[w]isdom too often never comes, and so one ought not to reject it merely because it comes late.... Therefore, the Court has amended its March 27 [2012] Order and enters this Order in its place....

II. LEGAL STANDARD
TASER moves for a JNOV pursuant to Federal Rule of Civil Procedure 50(b), for a new trial pursuant to Rule 59(a), or, in the alternative, remittitur of the jury's $10 million verdict....

A. JNOV
"When evaluating a Rule 50(b) motion, the court does not weigh the evidence or consider the credibility of the witnesses, but must grant the motion where it finds that 'substantial evidence does not support the jury's findings.' "... A Rule 50(b) motion must be granted "if a reasonable jury could reach only one conclusion based on the evidence or if the verdict in favor of the non-moving party would necessarily be based upon speculation and conjecture."... Thus, "[i]f reasonable minds could differ, [the court] must affirm the jury's verdict."...

B. New Trial
Under Rule 59(a), ... a district court may set aside the jury's verdict and grant a new trial only if "(1) the verdict is against the clear weight of the evidence, or (2) is based upon evidence which is false, or (3) will result in a miscarriage of justice even though there may be substantial evidence which would prevent the direction of a verdict." ... In considering a Rule 59 motion, courts may make credibility judgments in determining the clear weight of the evidence....

C. Remittitur
As an alternative to ordering a new trial, a court may order a remittitur. "Remittitur, which is used in connection with Fed. R. Civ. P. 59(a), 'is a process, dating back to 1822, by which the trial court orders a new trial unless the plaintiff accepts a reduction in an excessive jury award.' "... "There is no specific provision for remittitur under the Federal Rules of Civil Procedure, but it is well established that a remittitur should be ordered when a jury award will result in a miscarriage of justice."... "The decision as to whether damages are excessive and should be subject to remittitur is 'entrusted to the sound discretion of the district court.' "...

III. ANALYSIS
TASER makes a number of arguments in support of its Motion. First, TASER argues that JNOV should be entered because (a) Plaintiff failed to show that TASER's conduct was a proximate cause of Turner's death and (b) Turner was contributorily negligent.... Second, TASER contends that it is entitled to a new trial because "the jury verdict stems from an incomplete and inaccurate view of the law, liability evidence, and damages evidence that deprived TASER of a fair trial, and is otherwise against the weight of the evidence."... Finally, in the alternative, TASER argues that the jury was impermissibly motivated by passion or prejudice in awarding the "extraordinary $10 million verdict" and moves the Court for a remittitur.... The Court will address these arguments in turn.

A. Rule 50 JNOV

1. Contributory negligence
Before trial, on July 5, 2011, Plaintiff moved the Court to exclude evidence and argument regarding contributory negligence .... TASER's motion must be DENIED.

2. Causation

TASER moves the Court to overturn the jury's verdict due to a failure of proof on causation....

After listening to Plaintiff's and TASER's causation experts, the jury decided that TASER's product, used as directed, caused Turner's death. This Court will not displace that factual finding. There was substantial evidence before the jury to support its finding of ... causation. Therefore, TASER's motion must be DENIED on this issue.

3. Failure to warn

TASER argues that Plaintiff failed to show that TASER should have known of the inadequacy of its warnings at the time of sale or at least by the time of Turner's death....

Plaintiff presented substantial evidence that TASER's warning was inadequate and that its failure to provide a reasonable warning was an actual and proximate cause of Turner's death. Therefore, TASER's motion must be DENIED on this issue

B. Rule 59(a) New Trial

TASER moves for a new trial under Rule 59(a), or, in the alternative, for a remittitur of the jury's verdict. "On a Rule 59(a) motion, a district court may set aside the jury's verdict and grant a new trial only if '(1) the verdict is against the clear weight of the evidence, or (2) is based upon evidence which is false, or (3) will result in a miscarriage of justice even though there may be substantial evidence which would prevent the direction of a verdict.' "... In considering a Rule 59 motion, "courts may make credibility judgments in determining the clear weight of the evidence."...

... TASER has not shown that the verdict is against the clear weight of the evidence, is based on false evidence, or will result in a miscarriage of justice. Thus, the Court will not grant a new trial. The Court will, however, grant TASER's motion for remittitur because the jury's award was excessive....

The Court's finding that the jury award was excessive does not require a new trial. The "Fourth Circuit has held that, to receive a new trial on liability and damages, the jury verdict must be made excessive by 'passion and prejudice springing from indulgence, in the jury room, in such feelings, [that] may not be cured by a remittitur, but only a new trial.' "...

Here, with the exception of its own conclusory assertions, TASER has presented no evidence that the verdict was solely the result of the jury's passion or prejudice. "[W]ithout additional evidence of passion and prejudice by the jury, an excessive verdict alone is insufficient to require a new trial." ... Nor are the issues of liability and damages so interconnected as to prevent a fair determination of damages apart from evidence of liability. The Court finds that the jury's verdict as to liability was reasonable, as stated above, and the jury's damages award can be fairly addressed by an order of remittitur.

C. Remittitur

"[A] remittitur, used in connection with Federal Rule of Civil Procedure 59(a), is the established method by which a trial judge can review a jury award for excessiveness."... Remittitur is a process "by which the trial court orders a new trial unless the plaintiff accepts a reduction in an excessive jury award."... "Indeed, if a court finds that a jury award is excessive, it is the court's duty to require a remittitur or order a new trial."... In deciding whether a jury's award is excessive, a federal court sitting in diversity looks to substantive state law....

In North Carolina wrongful death actions, damages are available for medical expenses, the decedent's pain and suffering, funeral expenses, the present monetary value of the decedent to his beneficiaries, punitive damages and nominal damages.... Here, Turner's pain and suffering and punitive damages were not at issue.... Beyond modest funeral and medical expenses, ... this case concerned primarily pecuniary damages under N.C. GEN. STAT. § 28A-18-2(b)(4):

> (4) The present monetary value of the decedent to the persons entitled to receive the damages recovered, including but not limited to compensation for the loss of the reasonably expected; ...
> b. Services, protection, care and assistance of the decedent, whether voluntary or obligatory, to the persons entitled to the damages recovered,
> c. Society, companionship, comfort, guidance, kindly offices and advice of the decedent to the persons entitled to the damages recovered.

... North Carolina courts agree that "[t]he first step to determine the damages recoverable under paragraph (4) is to identify the particular persons who are entitled to receive the damages recovered."... Turner died unmarried and childless so his beneficiaries under the wrongful death statute were his parents.... In ascertaining the amount of damages recoverable under section (b)(4), only the losses suffered by those who are going to share in the recovery may be taken into account....

... [T]his Court should consider how close Turner was to his beneficiaries in evaluating damages:

> If the persons entitled to the damages recovered were collateral relatives whose contacts with the decedent were casual and infrequent, there may be no basis for the recovery of any significant amount under paragraph (4)....

TASER argues that Turner was not close with his parents, stating:

> Evidence supporting damages was modest. Turner lived with his grandparents rather than either of his divorced parents. He occasionally stayed with his father. He periodically assisted his mother....

The evidence presented at trial, however, painted a different picture. Turner's grandparents lived next door to his mother and Turner frequently went between the two homes, babysitting five nights per week for his younger siblings at his mother's house and staying at his grandparents' house on the other nights. Contrary to TASER's assertion that Turner "occasionally" stayed with his father, Turner lived with his father for a year when he was 15 and 16 years old. Turner's "periodic" assistance to his mother included extensive babysitting services, running errands, and providing invaluable assistance during her diabetic episodes. As demonstrated by the trial testimony, Turner enjoyed a close familial relationship with his parents which could be the basis for the recovery of a significant amount....

1. The Jury's analysis of North Carolina case law

... It is in the jury's discretion to determine a decedent's worth to his beneficiaries.... Plaintiff put on significant evidence of Turner's high worth. Indeed, Plaintiff called six witnesses to testify about Turner's habits, character and relations with his next of kin. TASER could have put on witnesses to testify about Turner's alleged low worth, or cross-examined Plaintiff's witnesses to elicit contrary evidence, but chose not to.

During the trial, Turner was portrayed as a "very promising" 17-year-old who graduated first in his high school class at age 16, was a model Food Lion employee, aspired to attend college, and babysat his much younger siblings five nights per week while his mother worked evenings. Turner was described as dependable, trustworthy, outgoing and friendly. Based on this evidence, the jury could have found great worth to Turner's life and this Court will exercise the proper deference to the jury's evaluation.

2. Evidence supporting damages under N.C. GEN. STAT. § 28A-18-2(b)(4)

TASER argues that the evidence supporting damages under N.C. GEN. STAT. §28A-18-2(b)(4) was insufficient to support the jury's verdict. The Court finds that, to some extent, TASER is correct on this point. The evidence as to damages was relatively thin. That being said, making the permitted credibility determinations, ... the Court finds that Turner's parents were credible witnesses on the issue of Turner's value to them. Turner's parents's testimony, corroborated by the testimony of his girlfriend, grandmother and Food Lion supervisor, established that Turner's life had significant worth and that his death caused great loss to his parents. The jury's $10 million damages award, however, was excessive. For this reason, the Court will remit the verdict....

3. Assessment of damages

"The present monetary value of the decedent to the persons entitled to receive the damages recovered will usually defy any precise mathematical computation."... "Therefore, the assessment of damages must, to a large extent, be left to the good sense and fair judgment of the jury—subject, of course, to the discretionary power of the judge to set its verdict aside when, in his opinion, equity and justice so require."... Damages are never presumed; the plaintiff must satisfy the jury by the greater weight of the evidence of the existence of damages and of facts which will furnish some basis for a reasonable assessment.... "[T]he damages in any wrongful death action are to some extent uncertain and speculative. A jury may indulge in such speculation where it is necessary and there are sufficient facts to support speculation."... When juries make awards that are statutorily allowed, "the role of the trial judge is 'to determine whether the jury's verdict is within the confines set by state law, and to determine, by reference to federal standards developed under Rule 59, whether a new trial or remittitur should be ordered.'" ... Whether a jury award is excessive is a question of law....

The Court finds that there was sufficient evidence presented at trial for the jury to find that Turner's present monetary value to his parents was significant. The jury's $10 million damages award, however, was excessive even according to Plaintiff's own assessment. Plaintiff argued that the jury should consider each parent's loss equivalent to $1,000 or $2,000 per week for forty years.... Plaintiff then took the $2,000 figure and argued that this would come out to $2 to $4 million per parent and requested a verdict somewhere between $4 and $8 million total.... But Plaintiff did not suggest how the jury might discount this total lifetime loss to present value. The jury's verdict suggests that it did not reduce its figure to present value.

The damages are to be reduced to the highest amount the jury could have properly awarded.... In so reducing the jury's verdict, the Court has kept in mind "proper deference to the finality and sanctity of the jury's findings." The Court also appreciates that any measure of the worth of a human being is incapable of mathematical precision and can only ever be an approximation based on the evidence

The Court finds that the jury was clearly convinced of Plaintiff's case and believed Turner to be worth a substantial amount to his parents. Therefore, the Court finds that a figure toward the high end of Plaintiff's estimation is appropriate and uses $7.5 million as its estimate of the highest value the jury could have determined Turner to be worth to his parents over their projected final forty years....

This amount must be reduced to its present value. As far back as 1912, the North Carolina Supreme Court cautioned that "no special formula has yet been prescribed as alike applicable to all cases and as one that should be used in trials."... Therefore, the Court's present value calculation is only one illustration of how a reasonable jury could have reduced its estimation of Turner's parents' loss to present value.

Plaintiff has argued for a one percent discount value in its post-trial briefing.... This is a very optimistic, defense-friendly discount rate as the United States Treasury's current thirty-year constant maturity rate is only 3.38 percent while inflation is expected to approach 3 percent, leading to a 0.38% real interest rate.... Using this discount rate to reduce a forty-year annuity ... to its present value, yields a $6,156,503.65 award.

Plaintiff has already received $625,000, ... from its settlement with the City of Charlotte and $40,000 ... from Food Lion's workers compensation award. North Carolina law provides that these amounts diminish Plaintiff's claim against TASER.... Therefore, the Court will remit Plaintiff's verdict to $5,491,503.65.

IV. CONCLUSION

IT IS, THEREFORE, ORDERED that TASER's Motion for Rule 50 JNOV, Rule 59 New Trial, or Remittitur, (Doc. No. 141), is GRANTED in part and DENIED in part. The Court will DENY the portions of TASER's Motion seeking judgment notwithstanding the verdict and new trial, but will GRANT the portion of TASER's motion seeking remittitur. The Court hereby remits the jury's verdict from $10 million to $5,491,503.65. Plaintiff shall have 30 days from the entry of this Order to either accept or reject the remitted damages award. Should Plaintiff choose to reject the remittitur, the Court will order a new trial.... See *Hetzel v. Prince William Cnty.*, 523 U.S. 208, 210 (1998) (ordering a remittitur without the option of a new trial violates a plaintiff's Seventh Amendment right to a jury trial). Should Plaintiff accept the remitted damages award, judgment shall issue in the amount of $5,491,503.65.

Case Questions

1. What is the purpose of remittitur?
2. What decision did the court's order require the plaintiff to make?
3. What factors can you think of that would influence the plaintiff in making that decision?

INTERNET TIP

Students wishing to read an additur case, *Ruben Dilone v. Anchor Glass Container Corporation,* or another remittitur case, *Bunch v. King County Department of Youth Services,* can find these cases on the textbook's website.

Judgment and Execution

The trial process concludes with the award of a **judgment.** The judgment determines the rights of the disputing parties and decides what relief is awarded (if any). A judgment is awarded after the trial court has ruled on posttrial motions. Appeals are made from the court's entry of judgment. Either party (or both) may appeal from a trial court's judgment to an appellate court.

A person who wins a judgment is called a **judgment creditor,** and the person who is ordered to pay is called a **judgment debtor.** Many times the judgment debtor will comply with the terms of the judgment and deliver property or pay a specified sum of money to the judgment creditor. If necessary, however, the judgment creditor can enforce the judgment by obtaining a **writ of execution** from the clerk of court where the judgment is filed. The writ will be directed to the sheriff who can then seize the judgment debtor's nonexempt personal property and sell it to satisfy the judgment. An example of a statute exempting specified property from seizure can be seen in Figure 5.6. The statute authorizing judicial sale includes safeguards to prevent abuse of the defendant's rights.

Alternatively, the plaintiff may have a **lien (a legally enforceable claim)** placed against the judgment debtor's real property.[8] It is created when the clerk of courts records the judgment (officially informing interested persons of the existence of the lien). The judgment debtor's property cannot be transferred until the lien is satisfied. This often means that when the judgment debtor's property is sold, part of the sale proceeds is paid to the judgment creditor to satisfy the lien. **Garnishment** is another remedy for judgment creditors. It is a process that results in the debtor's employer being ordered to deduct a percentage of the debtor's earnings from each paycheck. These payments are first credited against the debt and then forwarded to the judgment creditor.

Vermont Statutes Annotated § 2740.
GOODS AND CHATTELS; EXEMPTIONS FROM

The goods or chattels of a debtor may be taken and sold on execution, except the following articles, which shall be exempt from attachment and execution, unless turned out to the officer to be taken on the attachment or execution, by the debtor:

(1) the debtor's interest, not to exceed $2,500.00 in aggregate value, in a motor vehicle or motor vehicles;

(2) the debtor's interest, not to exceed $5,000.00 in aggregate value, in professional or trade books or tools of the profession or trade of the debtor or a dependent of the debtor;

(3) a wedding ring;

(4) the debtor's interest, not to exceed $500.00 in aggregate value, in other jewelry held primarily for the personal, family or household use of the debtor or a dependent of the debtor;

(5) the debtor's interest, not to exceed $2,500.00 in aggregate value, in household furnishings, goods or appliances, books, wearing apparel, animals, crops or musical instruments that are held primarily for the personal, family or household use of the debtor or a dependent of the debtor;

(6) growing crops, not to exceed $5,000.00 in aggregate value;

(7) the debtor's aggregate interest in any property, not to exceed $400.00 in value, plus up to $7,000.00 of any unused amount of the exemptions provided under subdivisions (1), (2), (4), (5) and (6) of this section;

(8) one cooking stove, appliances needed for heating, one refrigerator, one freezer, one water heater, sewing machines;

(9) ten cords of firewood, five tons of coals or 500 gallons of oil;

(10) 500 gallons of bottled gas;

(11) one cow, two goats, 10 sheep, 10 chickens, and feed sufficient to keep the cow, goats, sheep or chickens through one winter;

(12) three swarms of bees and their hives with their produce in honey;

(13) one yoke of oxen or steers or two horses kept and used for team work;

(14) two harnesses, two halters, two chains, one plow, and one ox yoke;

(15) the debtor's interest, not to exceed $700.00 in value, in bank deposits or deposit accounts of the debtor;

(continued)

F I G U R E 5.6 Vermont Statute Exempting Goods and Chattels from Execution

(16) the debtor's interest in self-directed retirement accounts of the debtor, including all pensions, all proceeds of and payments under annuity policies or plans, all individual retirement accounts, all Keogh plans, all simplified employee pension plans, and all other plans qualified under sections 401, 403, 408, 408A or 457 of the Internal Revenue Code. However, an individual retirement account, Keogh plan, simplified employee pension plan, or other qualified plan, except a Roth IRA, is only exempt to the extent that contributions thereto were deductible or excludable from federal income taxation at the time of contribution, plus interest, dividends or other earnings that have accrued on those contributions, plus any growth in value of the assets held in the plan or account and acquired with those contributions. A Roth IRA is exempt to the extent that contributions thereto did not exceed the contribution limits set forth in section 408A of the Internal Revenue Code, plus interest, dividends or other earnings on the Roth IRA from such contributions, plus any growth in value of the assets held in the Roth IRA acquired with those contributions. No contribution to a self-directed plan or account shall be exempt if made less than one calendar year from the date of filing for bankruptcy, whether voluntarily or involuntarily. Exemptions under this subdivision shall not exceed $5,000.00 for the purpose of attachment of assets by the office of child support pursuant to 15 V.S.A. § 799;

(17) professionally prescribed health aids for the debtor or a dependent of the debtor;

(18) any unmatured life insurance contract owned by the debtor, other than a credit life insurance contract;

(19) property traceable to or the debtor's right to receive, to the extent reasonably necessary for the support of the debtor and any dependents of the debtor:

    (A) Social Security benefits;

    (B) veteran's benefits;

    (C) disability or illness benefits;

    (D) alimony, support or separate maintenance;

    (E) compensation awarded under a crime victim's reparation law;

    (F) compensation for personal bodily injury, pain and suffering or actual pecuniary loss of the debtor or an individual on whom the debtor is dependent;

    (G) compensation for the wrongful death of an individual on whom the debtor was dependent;

    (H) payment under a life insurance contract that insured the life of an individual on whom the debtor was dependent on the date of that individual's death;

    (I) compensation for loss of future earnings of the debtor or an individual on whom the debtor was or is dependent;

    (J) payments under a pension, annuity, profit-sharing, stock bonus, or similar plan or contract on account of death, disability, illness, or retirement from or termination of employment.

CHAPTER SUMMARY

Chapter V introduced readers to the importance of procedure in our civil legal system. Although civil procedure varies somewhat within the fifty-two court systems in this country (federal, state, and District of Columbia), all jurisdictions have adopted rules of civil procedure that serve as the road map for civil litigation. These rules tell attorneys how to move successfully through each stage of the litigation process. Fair procedures are essential to achieving just outcomes.

The basic steps of the litigation process were discussed. The chapter began with a discussion of what lawyers do after being retained by a client contemplating litigation. This was followed by a discussion about the role of the pleadings. Here readers learned about the complaint, answer, and reply. The requirements for serving the summons and consequences of defective service also were discussed.

The use of the pretrial motion to dismiss (for lack of subject-matter jurisdiction or in personam jurisdiction, improper or inadequate service of the summons, or failure to state a claim upon which relief can be granted) and the motion for summary judgment (which is used to dispose of cases not needing to be tried, such as where no genuine issues of material fact exist) were explained.

Readers also were shown how modern discovery provides attorneys with various tools to identify the relevant facts in the case, especially those in the possession of the opposing party.

The procedural steps in the conduct of a trial also were discussed, starting with the selection of a jury and including, the opening statements of the attorneys, the presentation of evidence, the rules of evidence, legal privileges, trial motions (such as the motions to dismiss and for JNOV), and the closing arguments of the attorneys.

The chapter concluded with explanations of the jury verdict, the award of a judgment, posttrial motions (for JNOV, remittitur, additur, and a new trial), and how a judgment can be enforced.

CHAPTER QUESTIONS

1. Richmond was convicted of sexually assaulting Krell, a woman with whom, according to the evidence , he had been in an "intimate relationship." In the aftermath of the alleged criminal act, Richmond had contacted a priest, Father Dick Osing, who was also a "part-time unlicensed marriage and family counselor." Richmond and Osing had conversed privately at an Episcopal church at which Osing was a priest. Father Osing testified at trial for the prosecution and disclosed the contents of the private discussion between Richmond and himself. Richmond appealed his conviction for sexual assault in the second degree on the grounds that Father Osing's testimony should have been excluded at the trial because of the privilege on communications with clergy. The facts showed that Richmond had contacted Father Osing for "advice on his relationship with Krell." Do you think the clergy privilege should apply?

   John M. Richmond v. State of Iowa, 97-954 Supreme Court of Iowa (1999)

2. The Stars' Desert Inn Hotel ("Stars") filed suit against Richard Hwang, a citizen of Taiwan, to collect on a $1,885,000 gambling debt. The parties were unable to cooperate in scheduling a date for taking defendant Hwang's deposition.

The court, aware of the scheduling problem, entered an order requiring that the deposition be taken no later than November 29, 1994. Stars requested that Hwang provide at least two dates prior to the deadline when he would be available to be deposed. When Hwang failed to respond to this request, Stars set the date for November 23. Hwang's lawyers responded on November 21 with a proposal that Hwang be deposed in Taiwan prior to November 29. Stars rejected this proposal and filed a motion asking the court to strike Hwang's answer and enter a default judgment in favor of the plaintiff. Hwang's attorneys explained that their client was not cooperating with them and that he refused to be deposed in Nevada. The court imposed a $2,100 fine against Hwang and ordered him either to be deposed in Nevada or to prepay the plaintiff's expenses (estimated by the plaintiff to be between $20,000 and $40,000) for taking the deposition in Taiwan no later than February 10, 1995. Hwang failed to pay the fine, asserted that the plaintiff's estimate of the costs of taking the deposition in Taiwan were excessive, and refused to comply with either option contained in the court's order. The plaintiff again requested that the court impose the sanctions. Should the court strike the answer and award a default judgment to the plaintiff in the amount of $1,885,000 (plus interest, costs, attorney's fees, and post-judgment interest)? Are there any less drastic steps that should be taken before such a severe sanction is imposed?

Stars' Desert Inn Hotel & Country Club v. Hwang, 105 F.3d 521 (9th Cir. 1997)

3. Colm Nolan and others brought suit against two City of Yonkers police officers and the City of Yonkers, New York, for alleged brutality and false arrest. The plaintiff's process server alleged that he had served the police officer defendants at police headquarters (rather than at their place of residence), and also mailed copies of the summons and complaint to each officer at police headquarters. New York law provides that a summons can be delivered to "the actual place of business of the person to be served and by mailing a copy to the person to be served at his actual place of business." One defendant admitted receiving a copy of the summons and complaint at his police mailbox; the second officer denied ever receiving either document at police headquarters. Neither officer suffered any prejudice, because both police officer defendants did receive the summons and complaint and both filed answers in a timely manner. Rule 4 of the Federal Rules of Civil Procedure permits service "pursuant to the law of the state in which the district court is located." The two police officers asked the court to dismiss the complaint for lack of personal jurisdiction. Was the service at police headquarters sufficient to confer in personam jurisdiction over these defendants?

Nolan v. City of Yonkers, 168 F.R.D. 140 (S.D.N.Y. 1996)

4. A car driven by James Murphy struck a boy and injured him. Immediately after the accident, according to the boy's mother, Murphy told her "that he was sorry, that he hoped her son wasn't hurt. He said he had to call on a customer and was in a bit of a hurry to get home." At trial, Murphy denied telling the boy's mother that he was involved in his employment at the time of the accident. It was shown, however, that part of his normal duties for his employer, Ace Auto Parts Company, included making calls on customers in his car. Can the plaintiff have the mother testify about Murphy's statement as being a spontaneous exclamation?

5. Carolyn McSwain was driving a vehicle owned by John Denham in New York City on November 5, 1994. In the vehicle with McSwain were John Denham's mother, Ollie Denham, and John's child, Raesine. All the people in this vehicle were residents of Covington County, Mississippi. This vehicle was in a collision with a commuter van owned by Rockaway Commuter Line and driven by Sylvan Collard. Rockaway was a New York corporation with no significant contacts with Mississippi. As a result of this collision, McSwain and Raesine were injured, and Ollie Denham died. On November 4, 1997, John Denham sued McSwain, Rockaway, and Collard in Smith County, Mississippi, for wrongfully causing the death of Ollie and for causing Raesine's injuries. Denham sent process to Rockaway by certified mail in November of 1997. Rockaway waited almost twenty-one months before filing an answer to Rockaway's complaint on August 27, 1999. The answer raised as a defense the lack of personal jurisdiction, improper service of process, and a motion for change of venue from Smith County to New York City. Rockaway's motion to dismiss was denied by the trial court, but Rockaway's petition for interlocutory appeal was granted by the Mississippi Supreme Court. Did Smith County have personal jurisdiction over Rockaway? Did Rockaway waive its lack of personal jurisdiction defense by not filing its answer in a timely manner?

Rockaway Commuter Line, Inc. v. Denham, 897 So. 2d 156 (2004)

6. James Duke filed a suit against Pacific Telephone & Telegraph Company (PT&T) and two of its employees for invasion of privacy through unauthorized wiretapping.

Duke claimed that defendant's employees bugged his telephone line without his knowledge or consent. Through the use of the bugging devices, defendants acquired information that they communicated to the police department, resulting in his arrest. Although the charges were dismissed, he was discharged from his job. As part of the plaintiff's discovery, oral depositions were taken of the defendant's employees who installed the listening device. These employees refused to answer (1) questions relating to the procedure used in making unauthorized tapes of phone conversations (training of personnel, equipment, authority among employees), (2) questions relating to the deponents' knowledge of the illegality of unauthorized monitoring, (3) questions relating to a possible working relationship between the police and PT&T, and (4) questions relating to the monitoring of telephone conversations of subscribers other than the plaintiff. The defendant claimed that these questions were irrelevant to the litigation and therefore not proper matters for discovery. Do you agree?

Pacific Telephone & Telegraph Co. v. Superior Court, 2 Cal. 3d 161, 465 P.2d 854, 84 Cal. Rptr. 718 (1970)

7. W. R. Reeves filed suit under the Federal Employers Liability Act against his employer, Central of Georgia Railway Company, seeking damages he allegedly suffered when the train on which he was working derailed near Griffin, Georgia. The liability of the defendant railroad was established at trial, and the issue of damages remained to be fixed. Several physicians testified regarding the injuries received by Reeves. Reeves also testified. On the witness stand, he said that an examining physician had told him that he would be unable to work because of a weakness in his right arm, a dead place on his arm, stiffness in his neck, and nerve trouble in his back. Did the trial court err in allowing Reeves to give this testimony?

Central of Georgia Ry. Co. v. Reeves, 257 So. 2d 839 (Ga. 1972)

8. On December 10, 1962, Rosch obtained a judgment against Kelly from the superior court of Orange County, California. The California Code permits execution of a judgment only within ten years after entry of a judgment. If this is not done, the judgment may be enforced only by leave of court, after notice to the judgment debtors, accompanied by an affidavit setting forth the reasons for the failure to proceed earlier. The plaintiff made no attempt to enforce the judgment in California before Kelly moved to Texas in 1970. On February 15, 1974, the plaintiff attempted to execute on the California judgment in Texas. Do you think that the Texas court should have to allow execution under the Full Faith and Credit Clause?

Rosch v. Kelly, 527 F.2d 871 (5th Cir. 1976)

NOTES

1. T. F. F. Plucknett, *A Concise History of the Common Laws*, 5th ed. (Boston: Little, Brown and Co., 1956), p. 408.

2. Ibid., pp. 408-409

3. Ibid., p. 400

4. The Federal Rules of Civil Procedure have significantly altered the service requirement in federal court. Rule 4(d) requires plaintiffs to send a copy of the complaint and a request for waiver of service to the defendant. A defendant who signs the waiver of service is allowed sixty days from the date of the notice to file an answer. A defendant who fails to sign the waiver and cannot prove good cause for this refusal can be required to pay the plaintiff's costs and attorney fees associated with going to court to obtain enforcement.

5. Jurors generally are selected from rosters containing lists of taxpayers, licensed drivers, or registered voters.

6. The U.S. Supreme Court's decision in *Miranda v. Arizona* is addressed within the custodial interrogation topic in Chapter VIII of this textbook.

7. The name varies for the motion made at the conclusion of the plaintiff's case-in-chief to challenge the legal sufficiency of the evidence. In some jurisdictions it is called a *motion to dismiss*, in others a *motion for directed verdict*, and in a few, a *motion for nonsuit*.

8. *Real property* is a term referring to the interest or rights that a person has to land and things permanently attached to land (fixtures). This topic is discussed more thoroughly in Chapter XII.

VI

Limitations in Obtaining Relief

CHAPTER OBJECTIVES

1. *Understand how constitutions, statutes, and judicial doctrines play a role in deciding which cases can be decided in the public courts.*

2. *Explain the case-or-controversy requirement.*

3. *Summarize what can make a case nonjusticiable.*

4. *Describe how statutes of limitations and the equitable doctrine of laches limit plaintiffs.*

5. *Explain the conditions that must be met for a claim to be barred by the claim preclusion–res judicata doctrine.*

6. *Understand why immunities exist and how they work.*

People with grievances have a variety of options for obtaining relief. Nonjudicial alternatives such as mediation and arbitration, for example, are discussed in Chapter XIV. Access to the public courts, however, is not available to every litigant who would like to have a dispute decided there. We have already seen in Chapter IV, for example, that jurisdictional requirements prevent or limit courts from deciding many cases. In this chapter we learn about other constitutional, statutory, and common law limitations that have been created to determine if suits should be litigated in the public courts.

In some lawsuits courts are asked to provide legal answers to theoretical questions. These suits generally will be dismissed for failure to state a "case or controversy." Cases also can be dismissed for inappropriateness. This occurs, for example, when a plaintiff sues prematurely, takes "too long" to initiate litigation, or tries to relitigate a matter that had been previously decided in a prior suit. Similarly, courts don't want to waste time on cases where the parties are not truly adversarial (such as where **collusion** exists and one party is financing and controlling both sides of the litigation) or where the person bringing the suit has no personal stake in the litigation (such as where the plaintiff is suing on behalf of a friend who is reluctant to sue).

Later in the chapter we will learn that, in some circumstances, the public interest requires that certain defendants receive **immunity** (preferential protection) from lawsuits. Immunities historically have been granted to governments and certain public officials. In some jurisdictions immunities also limit lawsuits between family members.

CASE-OR-CONTROVERSY REQUIREMENT

To be within the federal judicial power, a matter must be a "case" or "controversy" as required by Article III, Section 2, of the U.S. Constitution. The parties to a lawsuit filed in federal court must truly be adversaries. The U.S. Supreme Court has always construed the **case-or-controversy requirement** as precluding the federal courts from advising the other branches of the government or anyone else.

Assume that a police chief has devised a new search-and-seizure strategy for identifying and apprehending terrorists. Assume further that the chief, wishing to know whether this strategy, if implemented, would violate the Fourth Amendment's "reasonableness" clause regarding searches and seizures, sends a letter posing the question to the U.S. Supreme Court. Will the court answer the question? No, it will not. The police chief is asking for a legal opinion. The question posed is based on a set of assumed facts. The facts are limited and entirely hypothetical, and there are no true adversaries here. The entire matter is premature. The case-or-controversy requirement would be satisfied, however, if the police chief were to implement the strategy, seize evidence, and make an arrest that resulted in a criminal prosecution. In that circumstance, were the case ultimately to reach the U.S. Supreme Court, the justices would have jurisdiction. The parties would truly be adverse, and the constitutional issues before the Court for decision would be real and not hypothetical.

Many state constitutions follow the federal approach and do not permit state courts to render advisory opinions. Their executive and legislative branches only may seek advice from the state attorney general. However, the constitutions of some states specifically permit the state supreme court to issue advisory opinions to government officials concerning certain matters of law. In this capacity, the court acts only as an adviser; its opinion does not have the effect of a judicial decision.

JUSTICIABILITY—A MATTER OF STANDING, RIPENESS, AND RES JUDICATA

Only cases that are **justiciable** can be decided by courts on their merits. To be justiciable, a case must be well suited for judicial determination. Courts use judicial doctrines (policies) such as standing, ripeness, and res judicata to weed out cases that lack justiciability. One of the cornerstones of our judicial system is the notion that the parties to a lawsuit must be true adversaries. The underlying assumption is that the best way to determine the truth and do justice in a lawsuit is to require disputing parties to use their full faculties against each other in court. Their interests must collide, and they must be seeking different relief. The ripeness and standing doctrines help courts preserve this essential aspect of the litigation process.

The concepts of ripeness and standing, although distinguishable, are similar and can overlap. A **ripeness** inquiry focuses on whether a case has developed sufficiently to be before a court for adjudication. A challenge to a party's **standing** differs in that it focuses on whether the plaintiff who filed the lawsuit is the right person or entity to be bringing this particular claim before the court.

A lawsuit is not ripe for adjudication, and is therefore nonjusticiable, if it has been filed prematurely. The adversary system works best when the litigants' positions are definite, distinct, and unambiguously adverse. In such a situation, the consequences of ruling for or against each party are more apparent. Where the full facts of a case are unknown or obscured, making a decision becomes much more difficult because the decision maker in such situations has to make too many assumptions in order to reach a well-reasoned conclusion. A just outcome is more likely if more certainty is required.

To have standing, a plaintiff must have a legally sufficient personal interest in the dispute and must be adversely affected by the defendant's conduct (i.e., injured in fact). With a few notable exceptions (such as for parents of minor children and guardians of incompetents), one person cannot sue to recover on behalf of another person who has been legally injured. Most people actually refuse to bring lawsuits against individuals they have a legal right to sue. They choose not to take legal action because the persons who have caused them harm are their friends, relatives, neighbors, or acquaintances. The standing requirement ensures that the injured person is in control of the decision to sue, prevents undesired and unnecessary suits, and prevents people who have marginal or derivative interests from filing multiple suits.

Introduction to *Hollingsworth v. Perry*

Kristin Perry wanted to marry her same-sex partner, Sandra Stier, in California. Paul Katami similarly wanted to marry his same-sex partner, Jeffery Zarrillo. The two couples were refused a marriage license based on a 2008 California constitutional amendment, Proposition 8, that banned same-sex marriage in that state. Both couples filed suit in federal court claiming that California's Proposition 8 violated their rights under the Due Process and Equal Protection Clauses of the U.S. Constitution. Normally when a state statute or a state constitutional provision is challenged, the state attorney general will appear in court and defend the state and state officials who are named in the complaint. That did not happen in this case. California officials refused to defend Proposition 8, and this resulted in the district court allowing the organization that initiated Proposition 8, ProtectMarriage, to defend the constitutionality of the amendment. The district court found in favor of the plaintiffs and ruled that

Proposition 8 was unconstitutional, and the defendants (now called the appellants) appealed to the U.S. Court of Appeals for the Ninth Circuit. Once again California officials refused to defend the constitutional provision. The Ninth Circuit then asked the California Supreme Court to determine who should defend Proposition 8. California's highest court said that the organization that initiated Proposition 8, ProtectMarriage, should continue to defend. That is what happened. Dennis Hollingsworth, a member of ProtectMarriage, became the lead appellant. The Ninth Circuit ultimately affirmed the district court, and ProtectMarriage (now called the *petitioners*) then successfully petitioned the U.S. Supreme Court for certiorari. The two same-sex couples (who were the appellees in the court of appeals), were now the *respondents*.

The Hollingsworth case is very unusual. It presented the U.S. Supreme Court with options. Because the federal trial and appellate courts had ruled California's Proposition 8 to be unconstitutional, the Supreme Court could have used this case to signal its intent to overturn not only the California constitutional amendment, but all the statutes and constitutional provisions enacted in recent years by various states that prohibit same-sex marriages…[1]

Another option for the Court would be to decide that it did not wish to review the matter after all. Even though certiorari had been granted, the Court could have decided that it had made a mistake by granting cert. This would require the justices to dismiss the case on the grounds that certiorari had been "improvidently granted." If they had chosen this option the Ninth Circuit's decision affirming that Proposition 8 was unconstitutional would stand, and the respondents–appellees—the two same-sex couples in this case—would have been able to marry in California. Allowing the Ninth Circuit decision to stand also would invalidate the laws on marriage in other states within the Ninth Circuit's jurisdiction that banned same-sex marriage, but would not have affected any state laws outside the Ninth Circuit's jurisdiction.[2]

The Court, however, chose a third option. It decided not to decide the constitutional question, but instead to dismiss the case on technical grounds, finding that ProtectMarriage lacked standing to substitute for the State of California in defending the state constitution. This decision permitted each state to continue to define marriage, and concluded the California case in a way that allowed the same-sex parties to marry (because the Ninth Circuit's decision was now the final ruling). Thus although the same-sex couples litigated this case all the way to the Supreme Court, they ultimately received no decision from that Court on their claims. Nevertheless, the couples prevailed in fact, because they were able to marry in California due to a legal technicality—their opponents, ProtectMarriage, lacked standing.

Dennis Hollingsworth v. Kristin M. Perry,
570 U.S. ____
Supreme Court of the United States
June 26, 2013

Chief Justice Roberts delivered the opinion of the Court.

The public is currently engaged in an active political debate over whether same-sex couples should be allowed to marry. That question has also given rise to litigation. In this case, petitioners, who oppose same-sex marriage, ask us to decide whether the Equal Protection Clause "prohibits the State of California from defining marriage as the union of a man and a woman."... Respondents, same-sex couples who wish to marry, view the issue in somewhat different terms: For them, it is whether California—having previously recognized the right of same-sex couples to marry—may reverse that decision through a referendum.

Federal courts have authority under the Constitution to answer such questions only if necessary to do so in the course of deciding an actual "case" or "controversy." As used in the Constitution, those words do not include every sort of dispute, but only those "historically viewed as capable of resolution through the judicial process."... This is an essential limit on our power: It ensures that we act as judges, and do not engage in policymaking properly left to elected representatives.

For there to be such a case or controversy, it is not enough that the party invoking the power of the court have a keen interest in the issue. That party must also have "standing," which requires, among other things, that it have suffered a concrete and particularized injury. Because we find that petitioners do not have standing, we have no authority to decide this case on the merits, and neither did the Ninth Circuit.

I

In 2008, the California Supreme Court held that limiting the official designation of marriage to opposite-sex couples violated the equal protection clause of the California Constitution.... Later that year, California voters passed the ballot initiative at the center of this dispute, known as Proposition 8. That proposition amended the California Constitution to provide that "[o]nly marriage between a man and a woman is valid or recognized in California."... Shortly thereafter, the California Supreme Court rejected a procedural challenge to the amendment, and held that the Proposition was properly enacted under California law....

... Under California law, same-sex couples have a right to enter into relationships recognized by the State as "domestic partnerships," which carry "the same rights, protections, and benefits, and shall be subject to the same responsibilities, obligations, and duties under law...as are granted to and imposed upon spouses."... In *In re Marriage Cases*, the California Supreme Court concluded that the California Constitution further guarantees same-sex couples "all of the constitutionally based incidents of marriage," including the right to have that marriage "officially recognized" as such by the State.... Proposition 8, the court explained in *Strauss*, left those rights largely undisturbed, reserving only "the official designation of the term 'marriage' for the union of opposite-sex couples as a matter of state constitutional law."...

Respondents, two same-sex couples who wish to marry, filed suit in federal court, challenging Proposition 8 under the Due Process and Equal Protection Clauses of the Fourteenth Amendment to the Federal Constitution. The complaint named as defendants California's Governor, attorney general, and various other state and local officials responsible for enforcing California's marriage laws. Those officials refused to defend the law, although they have continued to enforce it throughout this litigation. The District Court allowed petitioners—the official proponents of the initiative— ... to intervene to defend it. After a 12-day bench trial, the District Court declared Proposition 8 unconstitutional, permanently enjoining the California officials named as defendants from enforcing the law, and "directing the official defendants that all persons under their control or supervision" shall not enforce it....

Those officials elected not to appeal the District Court order. When petitioners did, the Ninth Circuit asked them to address "why this appeal should not be dismissed for lack of Article III standing."... After briefing and argument, the Ninth Circuit certified a question to the California Supreme Court:

> Whether under Article II, Section 8 of the California Constitution, or otherwise under California law, the official proponents of an initiative measure possess either a particularized interest in the initiative's validity or the authority to assert the State's interest in the initiative's validity, which would enable them to defend the constitutionality of the initiative upon its adoption or appeal a judgment invalidating the initiative, when the public officials charged with that duty refuse to do so....

The California Supreme Court agreed to decide the certified question, and answered in the affirmative. Without addressing whether the proponents have a particularized interest of their own in an initiative's validity, the court concluded that "[i]n a postelection challenge to a voter-approved initiative measure, the official proponents of the initiative are authorized under California law to appear and assert the state's interest in the initiative's validity and to appeal a judgment invalidating the measure when the public officials who ordinarily defend the measure or appeal such a judgment decline to do so."...

Relying on that answer, the Ninth Circuit concluded that petitioners had standing under federal law to defend the constitutionality of Proposition 8. California, it reasoned, " 'has standing to defend the constitutionality of its [laws],' " and States have the "prerogative, as independent sovereigns, to decide for themselves who may assert their interests."...

On the merits, the Ninth Circuit affirmed the District Court.... Proposition 8, in the court's view, violated the Equal Protection Clause because it served no purpose "but to impose on gays and lesbians, through the public law, a majority's private disapproval of them and their relationships."...

We granted certiorari to review that determination, and directed that the parties also brief and argue "Whether petitioners have standing under Article III, §2, of the Constitution in this case."...

II

Article III of the Constitution confines the judicial power of federal courts to deciding actual "Cases" or "Controversies." §2. One essential aspect of this requirement is that any person invoking the power of a federal court must demonstrate standing to do so....

In other words, for a federal court to have authority under the Constitution to settle a dispute, the party before it must seek a remedy for a personal and tangible harm. "The presence of a disagreement, however sharp and acrimonious it may be, is insufficient by itself to meet Art. III's requirements."...

The doctrine of standing, we recently explained, "serves to prevent the judicial process from being used to usurp the powers of the political branches."... In light of this "overriding and time-honored concern about keeping the Judiciary's power within its proper constitutional sphere, we must put aside the natural urge to proceed directly to the merits of [an] important dispute and to 'settle' it for the sake of convenience and efficiency."...

Most standing cases consider whether a plaintiff has satisfied the requirement when filing suit, but Article III demands that an "actual controversy" persist throughout all stages of litigation.... We therefore must decide whether petitioners had standing to appeal the District Court's order.

... After the District Court declared Proposition 8 unconstitutional and enjoined the state officials named as defendants from enforcing it, however ... [r]espondents no longer had any injury to redress—they had won—and the state officials chose not to appeal.

The only individuals who sought to appeal that order were petitioners, who had intervened in the District Court.... To have standing, a litigant must seek relief for an injury that affects him in a "personal and individual way."... He must possess a "direct stake in the outcome" of the case.... Here, however, petitioners had no "direct stake" in the outcome of their appeal. Their only interest in having the District Court order reversed was to vindicate the constitutional validity of a generally applicable California law....

Petitioners argue that the California Constitution and its election laws give them a " 'unique,' 'special,' and 'distinct' role in the initiative process—one 'involving both authority and responsibilities that differ from other supporters of the measure.' "... True enough—but only when it comes to the process of enacting the law. Upon submitting the proposed initiative to the attorney general, petitioners became the official "proponents" of Proposition 8.... As such, they were responsible for collecting the signatures required to qualify the measure for the ballot.... After those signatures were collected, the proponents alone had the right to file the measure with election officials to put it on the ballot.... Petitioners also possessed control over the arguments in favor of the initiative that would appear in California's ballot pamphlets....

But once Proposition 8 was approved by the voters, the measure became "a duly enacted constitutional amendment or statute."... Petitioners have no role—special or otherwise—in the enforcement of Proposition 8.... They therefore have no "personal stake" in defending its enforcement that is distinguishable from the general interest of every citizen of California....

Article III standing "is not to be placed in the hands of 'concerned bystanders,' who will use it simply as a 'vehicle for the vindication of value interests.' "... No matter how deeply committed petitioners may be to upholding Proposition 8 or how "zealous [their] advocacy,"... that is not a "particularized" interest sufficient to create a case or controversy under Article III....

III

A

Without a judicially cognizable interest of their own, petitioners attempt to invoke that of someone else. They assert that even if they have no cognizable interest in appealing the District Court's judgment, the State of California does, and they may assert that interest on the State's behalf. It is, however, a "fundamental restriction on our authority" that "[i]n the ordinary course, a litigant must assert his or her own legal rights and interests, and cannot rest a claim to relief on the legal rights or interests of third parties."... There are "certain, limited exceptions" to that rule.... But even when we have allowed litigants to assert the interests of others, the litigants themselves still "must have suffered an injury in fact, thus giving [them] a sufficiently concrete interest in the outcome of the issue in dispute."...

For the reasons we have explained, petitioners have ... not suffered an injury in fact, and therefore would ordinarily have no standing to assert the State's interests.

B

Petitioners contend that this case is different, because the California Supreme Court has determined that they are "authorized under California law to appear and assert the state's interest" in the validity of Proposition 8.... The court below agreed: "All a federal court need determine is that the state has suffered a harm sufficient to confer standing and that the party seeking to invoke the jurisdiction of the court is authorized by the state to represent its interest in remedying that harm."...

... Petitioners here hold no office and have always participated in this litigation solely as private parties.

[None of the] ... cases relied upon by the dissent ... comes close to establishing that mere authorization to represent a third party's interests is sufficient to confer Article III standing on private parties with no injury of their own....

The dissent highlights the discretion exercised by special prosecutors appointed by federal courts to pursue contempt charges.... Such prosecutors do enjoy a degree of independence in carrying out their appointed role, but no one would suppose that they are not subject to the ultimate authority of the court that appointed them....

C

... Petitioners argue that, by virtue of the California Supreme Court's decision, they are authorized to act " 'as agents of the people' of California."... But that Court never described petitioners as "agents of the people," or of anyone else.... All that the California Supreme Court decision stands for is that, so far as California is concerned, petitioners may argue in defense of Proposition 8. This "does not mean that the proponents become de facto public officials"; the authority they enjoy is "simply the authority to participate as parties in a court action and to assert legal arguments in defense of the state's interest in the validity of the initiative measure."... That interest is by definition a generalized one, and it is precisely because proponents assert such an interest that they lack standing under our precedents....

Neither the California Supreme Court nor the Ninth Circuit ever described the proponents as agents of the State, and they plainly do not qualify as such.

IV

The dissent eloquently recounts the California Supreme Court's reasons for deciding that state law authorizes petitioners to defend Proposition 8.... We do not "disrespect" or "disparage" those reasons.... Nor do we question California's sovereign right to maintain an initiative process, or the right of initiative proponents to defend their initiatives in California courts, where Article III does not apply. But as the dissent acknowledges, ... standing in federal court is a question of federal law, not state law. And no matter its reasons, the fact that a State thinks a private party should have standing to seek relief for a generalized grievance cannot override our settled law to the contrary.

The Article III requirement that a party invoking the jurisdiction of a federal court seek relief for a personal, particularized injury serves vital interests going to the role of the Judiciary in our system of separated powers. "Refusing to entertain generalized grievances ensures that...courts exercise power that is judicial in nature,"... and ensures that the Federal Judiciary respects "the proper—and properly limited—role of the courts in a democratic society,"... States cannot alter that role simply by issuing to private parties who otherwise lack standing a ticket to the federal courthouse....

We have never before upheld the standing of a private party to defend the constitutionality of a state statute when state officials have chosen not to. We decline to do so for the first time here.

Because petitioners have not satisfied their burden to demonstrate standing to appeal the judgment of the District Court, the Ninth Circuit was without jurisdiction to consider the appeal. The judgment of the Ninth Circuit is vacated, and the case is remanded with instructions to dismiss the appeal for lack of jurisdiction.

It is so ordered.

Case Questions

1. What must a plaintiff demonstrate to establish standing?
2. Why do federal courts have a special concern about standing?
3. Why did the U.S. Supreme Court reject the substitution of Hollingsworth and ProtectMarriage as a party?

Students wishing to read a federal case focusing on both standing and ripeness can read *Thomas v. Anchorage Equal Rights Commission,* 220 F.3d 1134, on the textbook's website.

MOOTNESS

Moot cases are outside the judicial power because there is no case or controversy. Mootness is an aspect of ripeness, in that there is no reason to try a case unless there has been some direct adverse effect on some party. Deciding when a case is moot is sometimes difficult. An actual controversy must not only exist at the date the action was filed, but also exist at the appellate stage. Courts recognize an exception to the mootness rule when an issue is capable of repetition. If a defendant is "free to return to his or her old ways," the public interest in determining the legality of the practices will prevent mootness.

Introduction to *Chafin v. Chafin*

Jeffrey Chafin, an American, and Lynne Hales, a citizen of the United Kingdom, were married in 2006. They became the parents of a daughter, E.C. Lynne had legal custody of this child after Jeffrey sued her for divorce in an Alabama court in 2010. E.C. was placed in the custody of her father in February of 2011, because Lynne, who had been arrested for domestic abuse, was deported back to the United Kingdom.

Lynne returned to the United States a few months later and filed suit in federal district court pursuant to the International Child Abduction Remedies Act (ICARA). ICARA was enacted by Congress in 1988 (42 U.S.C. 11601), in order to comply with treaty obligations established by the Hague Convention on the Civil Aspects of Child Abductions. ICARA has forty-five articles. Excerpts are presented below from three of these articles that explain ICARA's objectives relevant to the *Chafin* case.

Article 1

The objects of the present Convention are to secure the prompt return of children wrongfully removed to or retained in any Contracting State and … to ensure that rights of custody and of access under the law of one Contracting State are effectively respected in the other Contracting States.…

Article 3

The removal or the retention of a child is to be considered wrongful where … it is in breach of rights of custody attributed to a person, an institution or any other body, either jointly or alone, under the law of the State in which the child was habitually resident immediately before the removal or retention and … at the time of removal or retention those rights were actually exercised, either jointly or alone, or would have been so exercised but for the removal or retention.…

Article 12

Where a child has been wrongfully removed or retained in terms of Article 3 and, at the date of the commencement of the proceedings before the judicial or administrative authority of the Contracting State where the child is, a period of less than one year has elapsed from the date of the wrongful removal or retention, the authority concerned shall order the return of the child forthwith....

A U.S. District Court judge, after conducting a bench trial, ruled that pursuant to ICARA, E.C. should be returned to the United Kingdom. Within hours of that decision, Lynne and E.C. were on their way back to Scotland. Thereafter, Lynne suc-

cessfully petitioned a Scottish court to grant her custody of E.C. and to issue an injunction forbidding Jeffrey from removing their daughter back to the United States.

Jeffrey also was moving ahead with both his state and federal suits. He was unsuccessful in his appeal of the district court's decision to the Eleventh Circuit Court of Appeals. That court concluded that the case was moot and ordered the district court to dismiss his suit. Jeffrey had no better luck in the Alabama courts. That state's trial court dismissed the case and the Alabama intermediate court of appeals affirmed. Jeffrey was successful, however, with his petition to the United States Supreme Court for a writ of certiorari. The Court reached a unanimous decision in this case. An edited version of the court's opinion follows.

Jeffrey Lee Chafin v. Lynne Hales Chafin
568 U.S. _____
Supreme Court of the United States
February 19, 2013

Chief Justice Roberts delivered the opinion of the Court.
The Hague Convention on the Civil Aspects of International Child Abduction generally requires courts in the United States to order children returned to their countries of habitual residence, if the courts find that the children have been wrongfully removed to or retained in the United States. The question is whether, after a child is returned pursuant to such an order, any appeal of the order is moot.

I

A
The Hague Conference on Private International Law adopted the Hague Convention on the Civil Aspects of International Child Abduction in 1980.... In 1988, the United States ratified the treaty and passed implementing legislation, known as the International Child Abduction Remedies Act (ICARA)....

Eighty-nine nations are party to the Convention as of this writing.... In the 2009 fiscal year, 324 children removed to or retained in other countries were returned to the United States under the Convention, while 154 children removed to or retained in the United States were returned to their countries of habitual residence....

B
Petitioner Jeffrey Lee Chafin is a citizen of the United States and a sergeant first class in the U. S. Army. While stationed in Germany in 2006, he married respondent Lynne Hales Chafin, a citizen of the United Kingdom. Their daughter E. C. was born the following year.

Later in 2007, Mr. Chafin was deployed to Afghanistan, and Ms. Chafin took E. C. to Scotland. Mr. Chafin was eventually transferred to Huntsville, Alabama, and in February 2010, Ms. Chafin traveled to Alabama with E. C. Soon thereafter, however, Mr. Chafin filed for divorce and for child custody in Alabama state court. Towards the end of the year, Ms. Chafin was arrested for domestic violence, an incident that alerted U. S. Citizenship and Immigration Services to the fact that she had overstayed her visa. She was deported in February 2011, and E. C. remained in Mr. Chafin's care for several more months.

In May 2011, Ms. Chafin initiated this case in the U. S. District Court for the Northern District of Alabama. She filed a petition under the Convention and ICARA seeking an order for E. C.'s return to Scotland. On October 11 and 12, 2011, the District Court held a bench trial. Upon the close of arguments, the court ruled in favor of Ms. Chafin, concluding that E. C.'s country of habitual residence was Scotland and granting the petition for return. Mr. Chafin immediately moved for a stay pending appeal, but the court denied his request. Within hours, Ms. Chafin left the country with E. C., headed for Scotland. By December 2011, she had initiated custody proceedings there. The Scottish court soon granted her interim custody and a preliminary injunction, prohibiting Mr. Chafin from removing E. C. from Scotland. In the meantime, Mr. Chafin had appealed the District Court order to the Court of Appeals for the Eleventh Circuit.

In February 2012, the Eleventh Circuit dismissed Mr. Chafin's appeal as moot … [and] remanded this case to the District Court with instructions to dismiss the suit as moot and vacate its order.

On remand, the District Court did so, and also ordered Mr. Chafin to pay Ms. Chafin over $94,000 in court costs, attorney's fees, and travel expenses. Meanwhile, the Alabama state court had dismissed the child custody proceeding initiated by Mr. Chafin for lack of jurisdiction. The Alabama Court of Civil Appeals affirmed, relying in part on the U. S. District Court's finding that the child's habitual residence was not Alabama, but Scotland.

We granted certiorari….

II

Article III of the Constitution restricts the power of federal courts to "Cases" and "Controversies." Accordingly, "[t]o invoke the jurisdiction of a federal court, a litigant must have suffered, or be threatened with, an actual injury traceable to the defendant and likely to be redressed by a favorable judicial decision."… Federal courts may not "decide questions that cannot affect the rights of litigants in the case before them" or give "opinion[s] advising what the law would be upon a hypothetical state of facts."… The "case-or-controversy requirement subsists through all stages of federal judicial proceedings, trial and appellate."… "[I]t is not enough that a dispute was very much alive when suit was filed"; the parties must "continue to have a 'personal stake' " in the ultimate disposition of the lawsuit….

There is thus no case or controversy, and a suit becomes moot, "when the issues presented are no longer 'live' or the parties lack a legally cognizable interest in the outcome."… But a case "becomes moot only when it is impossible for a court to grant any effectual relief whatever to the prevailing party."… "As long as the parties have a concrete interest, however small, in the outcome of the litigation, the case is not moot."…

III

This dispute is still very much alive. Mr. Chafin continues to contend that his daughter's country of habitual residence is the United States, while Ms. Chafin maintains that E. C.'s home is in Scotland. Mr. Chafin also argues that even if E. C.'s habitual residence was Scotland, she should not have been returned because the Convention's defenses to return apply. Mr. Chafin seeks custody of E. C., and wants to pursue that relief in the United States, while Ms. Chafin is pursuing that right for herself in Scotland. And Mr. Chafin wants the orders that he pay Ms. Chafin over $94,000 vacated, while Ms. Chafin asserts the money is rightfully owed.

On many levels, the Chafins continue to vigorously contest the question of where their daughter will be raised. This is not a case where a decision would address "a hypothetical state of facts."… And there is not the slightest doubt that there continues to exist between the parties "that concrete adverseness which sharpens the presentation of issues."…

A

At this point in the ongoing dispute, Mr. Chafin seeks reversal of the District Court determination that E. C.'s habitual residence was Scotland and, if that determination is reversed, an order that E. C. be returned to the United States (or "re-return," as the parties have put it). In short, Mr. Chafin is asking for typical appellate relief: that the Court of Appeals reverse the District Court and that the District Court undo what it has done…. The question is whether such relief would be effectual in this case.

Ms. Chafin argues that this case is moot because the District Court lacks the authority to issue a re-return order either under the Convention or pursuant to its inherent equitable powers. But that argument—which goes to the meaning of the Convention and the legal availability of a certain kind of relief—confuses mootness with the merits…. In *Powell v. McCormack*, … (1969), this Court … explained, "this argument … confuses mootness with whether [the plaintiff] has established a right to recover …, a question which it is inappropriate to treat at this stage of the litigation."… Mr. Chafin's claim for re-return—under the Convention itself or according to general equitable principles—cannot be dismissed as so implausible that it is insufficient to preserve jurisdiction, … and his prospects of success are therefore not pertinent to the mootness inquiry.

As to the effectiveness of any relief, Ms. Chafin asserts that even if the habitual residence ruling were reversed and the District Court were to issue a re-return order, that relief would be ineffectual because Scotland would simply ignore it…. But even if Scotland were to ignore a U. S. re-return order, or decline to assist in enforcing it, this case would not be moot. The U. S. courts continue to have personal jurisdiction over Ms. Chafin, may command her to take action even outside the United States, and may back up any such command with sanctions…. No law of physics prevents E. C.'s return from

Scotland, ... and Ms. Chafin might decide to comply with an order against her and return E. C. to the United States.... After all, the consequence of compliance presumably would not be relinquishment of custody rights, but simply custody proceedings in a different forum.

Enforcement of the order may be uncertain if Ms. Chafin chooses to defy it, but such uncertainty does not typically render cases moot. Courts often adjudicate disputes where the practical impact of any decision is not assured. For example, courts issue default judgments against defendants who failed to appear or participate in the proceedings and therefore seem less likely to comply.... Courts also decide cases against foreign nations, whose choices to respect final rulings are not guaranteed.... And we have heard the Government's appeal from the reversal of a conviction, even though the defendants had been deported, reducing the practical impact of any decision; we concluded that the case was not moot because the defendants might "re-enter this country on their own" and encounter the consequences of our ruling....

So too here. A re-return order may not result in the return of E. C. to the United States, just as an order that an insolvent defendant pay $100 million may not make the plaintiff rich. But it cannot be said that the parties here have no "concrete interest" in whether Mr. Chafin secures a re-return order.... "[H]owever small" that concrete interest may be due to potential difficulties in enforcement, it is not simply a matter of academic debate, and is enough to save this case from mootness....

IV

Ms. Chafin is correct to emphasize that both the Hague Convention and ICARA stress the importance of the prompt return of children wrongfully removed or retained. We are also sympathetic to the concern that shuttling children back and forth between parents and across international borders may be detrimental to those children. But courts can achieve the ends of the Convention and ICARA—and protect the well-being of the affected children—through the familiar judicial tools of expediting proceedings and granting stays where appropriate. There is no need to manipulate constitutional doctrine and hold these cases moot. Indeed, doing so may very well undermine the goals

of the treaty and harm the children it is meant to protect.

If these cases were to become moot upon return, courts would be more likely to grant stays as a matter of course, to prevent the loss of any right to appeal.... In cases in which a stay would not be granted but for the prospect of mootness, a child would lose precious months when she could have been readjusting to life in her country of habitual residence, even though the appeal had little chance of success. Such routine stays due to mootness would be likely but would conflict with the Convention's mandate of prompt return to a child's country of habitual residence.

Routine stays could also increase the number of appeals. Currently, only about 15% of Hague Convention cases are appealed.... If losing parents were effectively guaranteed a stay, it seems likely that more would appeal, a scenario that would undermine the goal of prompt return and the best interests of children who should in fact be returned. A mootness holding here might also encourage flight in future Hague Convention cases, as prevailing parents try to flee the jurisdiction to moot the case....

Importantly, whether at the district or appellate court level, courts can and should take steps to decide these cases as expeditiously as possible, for the sake of the children who find themselves in such an unfortunate situation. Many courts already do so.... Cases in American courts often take over two years from filing to resolution; for a six-year-old such as E. C., that is one-third of her lifetime. Expedition will help minimize the extent to which uncertainty adds to the challenges confronting both parents and child....

The Hague Convention mandates the prompt return of children to their countries of habitual residence. But such return does not render this case moot; there is a live dispute between the parties over where their child will be raised, and there is a possibility of effectual relief for the prevailing parent. The courts below therefore continue to have jurisdiction to adjudicate the merits of the parties' respective claims.

The judgment of the United States Court of Appeals for the Eleventh Circuit is vacated, and the case is remanded for further proceedings consistent with this opinion.

It is so ordered.

Case Questions

1. Why is the ICARA important to this case?
2. Ms. Chafin argued successfully to the Eleventh Circuit Court of Appeals that her ex-husband's appeal should be dismissed as moot. What was her reasoning?
3. Why did the U.S. Supreme Court reverse the lower appellate court?
4. Where did the U.S. Supreme Court's decision leave the parties?

POLITICAL QUESTIONS

Because of the constitutional separation of powers, the Supreme Court has long recognized a **political-question doctrine.** It provides that the judicial branch is not entitled to decide questions that more properly should be decided by the executive and legislative branches of the federal government. U.S. Supreme Court Justice Scalia explained this doctrine in his plurality opinion in *Richard Vieth v. Robert C. Jubelirer,* 541 U.S. 267, p. 275 (2004):

> As Chief Justice Marshall proclaimed two centuries ago, "It is emphatically the province and duty of the judicial department to say what the law is." *Marbury v. Madison* … (1803). Sometimes, however, the law is that the judicial department has no business entertaining the claim of unlawfulness—because the question is entrusted to one of the political branches or involves no judicially enforceable rights.… See, e.g., *Nixon v. United States,* … (1993) (challenge to procedures used in Senate impeachment proceedings); *Pacific States Telephone & Telegraph Co. v. Oregon,* … (1912) (claims arising under the Guaranty Clause of Article IV, §4). Such questions are said to be "nonjusticiable," or "political questions."

The federal constitution allocates separate governmental power to the legislative, executive, and judicial branches. As members of the judicial branch of government, the courts exercise judicial powers. As the political departments, the executive and legislative branches are entrusted with certain functions, such as conducting foreign relations, making treaties, or submitting our country to the jurisdiction of international courts. Such issues fall outside the jurisdiction of the courts. Courts classify an issue as justiciable or as a nonjusticiable political question on a case-by-case basis.

INTERNET TIP

Students wishing to read an interesting case in which the political-question doctrine is thoroughly discussed will find *Schneider v. Kissinger* on the textbook's website. The plaintiffs in *Schneider* sought to sue former Secretary of State Henry Kissinger and other prominent governmental officials over the U.S. government's actions in Chile during the Nixon administration. This case was decided in 2005 by the U.S. Court of Appeals for the District of Columbia and certiorari was denied by the U.S. Supreme Court in 2006.

THE ACT-OF-STATE DOCTRINE

The judicially created **act-of-state doctrine** provides that American courts should not determine the validity of public acts committed by a foreign sovereign within its own territory. This doctrine's roots go back to England in 1674. The doctrine is pragmatic: it prevents our courts from making pronouncements about matters over which they have no power. Judicial rulings about such matters could significantly interfere with the conduct of foreign policy—a matter that the Constitution assigns to the political branches of government. The Constitution does not require the act-of-state doctrine; rather, the doctrine is based on the relationships among the three branches of the federal government.

Assume, for example, that a foreign dictator confiscates a warehouse containing merchandise belonging to an American corporation. The American corporation subsequently files suit in an American court to challenge the foreign nation's laws and procedures, alleging that the dictator did not have a valid right to confiscate the merchandise. The American court can apply the act-of-state doctrine and refuse to make any pronouncements about the foreign nation's laws or procedures. The law presumes the public acts of a foreign sovereign within its own territory to be valid.

STATUTE OF LIMITATIONS

There is a time period, established by the legislature, within which an action must be brought upon claims or rights to be enforced. This law is known as the **statute of limitations**. (See Figure 6.1.) The statute of limitations compels the exercise of a right of action within a reasonable time, so that the opposing party has a fair opportunity to defend and will not be surprised by the assertion of a stale

| | Contract | | | | Tort | | | | | | | | | | | |
| | | | | | Negligence | | | Intentional Torts | | | | | | | | |
	Breach of Sales Contract	Breach of Warranty	Oral	Written	Personal Injury	Wrongful Death	Medical Malpractice	Assault and Battery	Fraud and Deceit	Libel	Slander	Trespass	Damage to Personal Property	Conversion	False Imprisonment	Malicious Prosecution
Alabama	4	4	6	6	1	2	2	6	2	1	1	6	1	6	6	1
Alaska	4	4	6	6	2	2	2	2	2	2	2	6	6	6	2	2
Arizona	4	4	3	6	2	2	2	2	3	1	1	2	2	2	1	1
Arkansas	4	4	3	5	3	3	2	1	5	3	1	3	3	3	1	5
California	4	4	2	4	1	1	3	1	3	1	1	3	3	3	1	1
Colorado	4	4	3	3	2	2	2	1	1	1	1	2	2	3	1	2
Connecticut	4	4	3	6	2	2	2	3	3	2	2	3	3	3	3	3
Delaware	4	4	3	3	2	2	2	2	3	2	2	3	2	3	2	2
District of Columbia	4	4	3	3	3	1	3	1	3	1	1	3	3	3	1	1
Florida	4	4	4	5	4	2	2	4	4	2	2	4	4	4	4	4
Georgia	4	4	4	6	2	2	2	2	4	1	1	4	4	4	2	2
Hawaii	4	4	6	6	2	2	2	2	6	2	2	2	2	6	6	6
Idaho	4	4	4	5	2	2	2	2	3	2	2	3	3	3	2	4
Illinois	4	4	5	10	2	2	2	2	5	1	1	5	5	5	2	2
Indiana	4	4	6	10	2	2	2	2	6	2	2	6	2	6	2	2
Iowa	5	5	5	10	2	2	2	2	5	2	2	5	5	5	2	2
Kansas	4	4	3	5	2	2	2	1	2	1	1	2	2	2	1	1
Kentucky	4	4	5	15	1	1	1	1	5	1	1	5	2	2	1	1
Louisiana	10	1	10	10	1	1	1	1	1	1	1	1	1	1	1	1
Maine	4	4	6	6	6	2	2	2	6	2	2	6	6	6	2	6
Maryland	4	4	3	3	3	3	3	1	3	1	1	3	3	3	3	3
Massachusetts	4	4	6	6	3	3	3	3	3	3	3	3	3	3	3	3
Michigan	4	4	6	6	3	3	2	2	6	1	1	3	3	3	2	2
Minnesota	4	4	6	6	6	3	2	2	6	2	2	6	6	6	2	2
Mississippi	6	6	3	6	6	2	2	1	6	1	1	6	6	6	1	1
Missouri	4	4	5	10	5	3	2	2	5	2	2	5	5	5	2	5
Montana	4	4	5	8	3	3	3	2	2	2	2	2	2	2	2	5
Nebraska	4	4	4	5	4	2	2	1	4	1	1	4	4	4	1	1
Nevada	4	4	4	6	2	2	2	2	3	2	2	3	3	3	2	2
New Hampshire	4	4	3	3	3	3	2	3	3	3	3	3	3	3	3	3
New Jersey	4	4	6	6	2	2	2	2	6	1	1	6	6	6	2	2

F I G U R E 6.1 Statutes of Limitations for Civil Actions (in Years)

| | Contract | | | | Tort | | | | | | | | | | | |
| | | | | | Negligence | | | Intentional Torts | | | | | | | | |
	Breach of Sales Contract	Breach of Warranty	Oral	Written	Personal Injury	Wrongful Death	Medical Malpractice	Assault and Battery	Fraud and Deceit	Libel	Slander	Trespass	Damage to Personal Property	Conversion	False Imprisonment	Malicious Prosecution
New Mexico	4	4	4	6	3	3	3	3	4	3	3	4	4	4	3	3
New York	4	4	6	6	3	2	2½	1	6	1	1	3	3	3	1	1
North Carolina	4	4	3	3	3	2	3	1	3	1	1	3	3	3	1	3
North Dakota	4	4	6	6	6	2	2	2	6	2	2	6	6	6	2	6
Ohio	4	4	6	15	2	2	1	1	4	1	1	4	2	4	1	1
Oklahoma	5	5	3	5	2	2	2	1	2	1	1	2	2	2	1	1
Oregon	4	4	6	6	2	3	2	2	2	1	1	6	6	6	2	2
Pennsylvania	4	4	4	4	2	2	2	2	2	1	1	2	2	2	2	2
Rhode Island	4	4	10	10	3	2	3	10	10	10	1	10	10	10	3	10
South Carolina	6	6	6	6	6	6	3	2	6	2	2	6	6	6	2	6
South Dakota	4	4	6	6	3	3	2	2	6	2	2	6	6	6	2	6
Tennessee	4	4	6	6	1	1	1	1	3	1	½	3	3	3	1	1
Texas	4	4	2	4	2	2	2	2	2	1	1	2	2	2	2	1
Utah	4	4	4	6	4	2	2	1	3	1	1	3	3	3	1	1
Vermont	4	4	6	6	3	2	3	3	6	3	3	6	3	6	3	3
Virginia	4	4	3	5	2	2	2	2	1	1	1	5	5	5	2	1
Washington	4	4	3	6	3	3	3	2	3	2	2	3	3	3	2	3
West Virginia	4	4	5	10	2	2	2	2	2	1	1	2	2	2	1	1
Wisconsin	6	6	6	6	3	3	3	2	6	2	2	6	6	6	2	6
Wyoming	4	4	8	10	4	2	2	1	4	1	1	4	4	4	1	1

F I G U R E 6.1 Statutes of Limitations for Civil Actions (in Years) (*Continued*)

© Cengage Learning

claim after evidence has been lost or destroyed. With the lapse of time, memories fade and witnesses may die or move. The prospects for impartial and comprehensive fact-finding diminish.

The statutory time period begins to run immediately on the accrual of the cause of action, that is, when the plaintiff's right to institute a suit arises. If the plaintiff brings the suit after the statutory period has run, the defendant may plead the statute of limitations as a defense. Although jurisdictions have differing definitions, a cause of action generally can be said to exist when the defendant breaches some legally recognized duty owed to the plaintiff and thereby causes some type of legally recognized injury to the plaintiff.

Generally, once the statute of limitations begins to run, it continues to run until the time period is exhausted. However, many statutes of limitation contain a "saving clause" listing conditions and events that "toll" (suspend) the running of the statute. The occurrence of one of these conditions also may extend the limitations period for a prescribed period of time. In personal injury cases, for example, the statute may start to run from the date of the injury or from the date when the injury is discoverable, depending on the jurisdiction. Conditions that may serve to toll the running of the statute or extend the time period include infancy, insanity, imprisonment, court orders, war, and fraudulent concealment of a cause of action by a trustee or other fiduciary. The statute of limitations often starts to run in medical malpractice cases on the day that the doctor or patient stops the prescribed treatment or on the day that the patient becomes aware (or should have become aware) of the malpractice and

subsequent injury. The commencement of an action almost universally tolls the running of the statute of limitations. Thus, once an action is commenced on a claim within the statutory time period, it does not matter if judgment is ultimately rendered after the period of limitations has expired.

In the following case the interests of consumers were pitted against the economic welfare of an important industry (and a major regional employer) within the state. The state legislature used the statute of limitations and a 90-day notification requirement to further the economic interests of the state's ski industry at the expense of consumers.

Marybeth Atkins v. Jiminy Peak, Inc.
514 N.E.2d 850
Massachusetts Supreme Judicial Court
November 5, 1987

O'Connor, Justice.

This case presents the question whether an action by an injured skier against a ski area operator is governed by the one-year limitation of actions provision of G.L.c. 143, §71P, where the plaintiff's theories of recovery are negligence and breach of warranty, as well as breach of contract, in the renting of defective ski equipment.

In her original complaint, filed on December 5, 1984, the plaintiff alleged that on March 20, 1982, she sustained serious injuries while skiing at the defendant's ski resort, and that those injuries were caused by defective ski equipment she had rented from the rental facility on the premises. She further alleged that the defendant had not inspected or adjusted the equipment, and this failure amounted to negligence and breach of contract. In an amended complaint filed on February 14, 1986, the plaintiff added counts alleging that the defendant had breached warranties of merchantability and fitness for a particular purpose.

The defendant moved for summary judgment on the ground that the plaintiff's action was barred by the statute of limitations. A judge of the Superior Court granted the motion, and the plaintiff appealed. We transferred the case to this court on our own motion, and now affirm.

The statute we must interpret, G.L.c. 143, §71P, imposes a one-year limitation on actions "against a ski area operator for injury to a skier." There is no contention that the defendant is not a "ski area operator," or that this action is not "for injury to a skier." The text of the statute, then, seems fully to support the decision of the Superior Court judge. The plaintiff

argues, however, that the statute should be construed as governing only actions based on a defendant ski area operator's violation of those duties prescribed by G.L.c.143, §71N. Section 71N requires that ski areas be maintained and operated in a reasonably safe manner, and prescribes methods by which skiers must be warned about the presence of equipment and vehicles on slopes and trails. The plaintiff thus contends that the statute does not bar her lawsuit because her action does not assert a violation of §71N but rather was brought against the defendant solely in its capacity as a lessor of ski equipment. We do not interpret the statute in this limited way. Rather, we conclude that the one-year limitation in §71P applies to all personal injury actions brought by skiers against ski area operators arising out of skiing injuries.

If the Legislature had intended that the one-year limitation apply only to actions alleging breach of a ski area operator's duties under §71N, it easily could have employed language to that effect instead of the sweeping terms contained in the statute. Nothing in §71P suggests that its reach is so limited.

The plaintiff contends that there is no sound basis for applying the one-year limitation to her action, because if she "had rented skis from an independently operated ski rental shop which leased space in the Defendant's base lodge, such an independent rental shop could not defend against the Plaintiff's action by relying upon Section 71P." Hence, she argues, it makes no sense to afford special protection to lessors of ski equipment who happen also to be ski operators. We assume for purposes of this case that the plaintiff's assertion that §71P would not apply to an independent ski rental shop is correct. But we cannot say that, in enacting §71P, the Legislature could not reasonably have decided that ski area operators require more protection than do other sectors of the ski industry. "Personal injury claims by skiers ... may be myriad in number, run a whole range of harm, and constitute a constant drain on the ski industry."... The Legislature appears to have concluded that, in view of this perceived threat to the economic stability of owners and operators of ski areas, not shared by those who simply rent ski equipment, a short period for the commencement of skiers' personal injury actions against ski operators, regardless of the fault alleged, is in the public interest....

Because §71P applies to the plaintiff's action, the Superior Court judge correctly concluded that the plaintiff's action was time barred.

Judgment affirmed.

Liacos, J. (dissenting, with whom Wilkins and Abrams, JJ., join).

I respectfully dissent. The court's interpretation of G.L.c. 143, §71P (1986 ed.), is too broad. The general purpose of G.L.c. 143, §§71H–71S (1986 ed.), is to set the terms of responsibility for ski area operators and skiers in a sport which has inherent risks of injury or even death. This legislative intent to protect ski area operators was designed, as the court indicates, not only to decrease the economic threat to the ski industry, but also to enhance the safety of skiers.

An examination of the whole statutory scheme reveals, however, that the Legislature did not intend to protect the ski area operators from claims for all harm which occurs in connection with skiing accidents, regardless of where the negligence that caused the harm takes place. Indeed, this court decided not long ago that G.L.c. 143, §71P, on which it relies to rule adversely on this plaintiff's claim, did not apply to wrongful death actions arising from injuries on the ski slope. *Grass v. Catamount Dev. Corp.,* 390 Mass. 551 (1983) (O'Connor, J.). The court now ignores the wisdom of its own words in *Grass,* supra at 553: "Had the Legislature intended that G.L.c. 143, §71P, should apply to claims for wrongful death as well as to claims for injuries not resulting in death, we believe it would have done so expressly."... Here, however, the court extends the protective provisions of §71P to ordinary commercial activity simply because it occurred at the base of a ski area and was conducted by the operator of the ski slope. No such intent can be perceived in this statute. To the contrary, the statute clearly manifests an intent to promote safety on ski slopes by regulating, through the creation of a recreational tramway board and otherwise, the operation of tramways, chair lifts, "J bars," "T bars," and the like (§§71H–71M).The statute defines the duties both of ski area operators and skiers (§§71K–71O).

In §71O, liability of ski area operators for ski slope accidents is sharply limited: "A skier skiing down hill shall have the duty to avoid any collision with any other skier, person or object on the hill below him, and, except as otherwise provided in this chapter, the responsibility for collisions by any skier *with any other skier or person shall be solely that of the skier or person involved and not that of the operator,* and the responsibility for the collision with an obstruction, man-made or otherwise, shall be solely that of the skier and not that of the operator, provided that such obstruction is properly marked pursuant to the regulations promulgated by the board" (emphasis supplied). Clearly, then, the statutory scheme is designed not only to enhance the safety of skiers, but also to limit the liability of a ski area operator for his negligent activities which cause injuries (but not deaths, see *Grass,* supra) on the ski slopes. It is in this context that the court ought to consider the additional protection of a ninety-day notice requirement, as well as the short statute of limitations of one year found in §71P.

General Laws c. 143, §71P, imposes a ninety-day notice requirement and a one-year statute of limitations on a party who brings suit against a ski area operator. The imposition in §71P of the ninety-day notice requirement as a condition precedent to recovery confirms, I think, my view that this statute is designed only to protect the ski area operator as to claims arising from conditions on the ski slope. But there is an even stronger argument against the court's position—that is in the very language of the statute. A "[s]ki area operator" is defined in G.L.c. 143, §71I(6), as "the owner or operator of a ski area." In the same subsection, a "[s]ki area" is defined as: "[A]ll of the slopes and trails under the control of the ski area operator, including cross-country ski areas, slopes and trails, and any recreational tramway in operation on any such slopes or trails administered or operated as a single enterprise *but shall not include base lodges, motor vehicle parking lots and other portions of ski areas used by skiers when not actually engaged in the sport of skiing*" (emphasis supplied).

The alleged negligence and breach of warranty that occurred in this case happened in the rental shop in the base lodge area. It was there that the defendant rented allegedly defective equipment to the plaintiff and failed to check and to adjust that equipment. The injury was not due to ungroomed snow or exposed rocks or any condition on the slopes or trails under the control of the ski area operator. Rather, the injury allegedly was the result of a transaction in the rental shop, not of a defect on the slope. The rental shop is an area excluded from the purview of G.L.c. 143, §71P, and thus the ninety-day notice requirement and the one-year statute of limitations do not apply.

The Legislature intended to separate the many functions of a ski area operator so as to focus on the business of operating ski slopes and trails. The statute does not apply where the alleged negligent behavior occurs when the ski area operator is acting as a restaurateur, barkeeper, parking lot owner, souvenir vendor, or, as is the case here, rental agent. For this reason, I would reverse the judgment of the Superior Court.

Case Questions

1. Marybeth Atkins severely broke her leg while using skis and ski bindings rented from a shop at a ski resort. The shop was owned and operated by the owners of the resort. What argument did Atkins make to the court in an effort to avoid the one-year statute of limitations?
2. Do you agree with the dissenters, who feel that the negligent action that caused the harm occurred in the rental shop (an area not covered by the statute), or with the majority, who feel that the accident occurred on the slopes (an area covered by the statute)?

The state supreme court stated in its opinion that "The Legislature appears to have concluded that ... a short period for the commencement of skiers' personal injury actions against ski operators ... was in the public interest." It denied recovery to a plaintiff who alleged that she was seriously injured as a result of the defendant's negligence in fitting her with defective ski equipment at its on-premises rental facility. Do you see any utilitarian aspects in the making of public policy in this instance?

EQUITABLE DOCTRINE OF LACHES

You may recall Chapter I's discussion of the emergence in England, and subsequently in this country, of courts of equity, and that although a few states continue to maintain separate equitable courts, most states have merged these courts into a single judicial system. In these merged systems, judges often are authorized to exercise the powers of a common law judge as well as the powers of a chancellor in equity. Which "hat" the judge wears is determined by the remedy sought by the plaintiff. Readers will learn about both legal and equitable remedies in Chapter VII, which is entirely devoted to that topic. But for now it is sufficient to know that when a plaintiff requests the court to award an equitable remedy such as an injunction (a court order mandating or prohibiting specified conduct), the court may resort to equitable doctrines in reaching a decision.

One of the traditional equitable doctrines is called **laches.** This doctrine can be used in some circumstances to deny a plaintiff an equitable remedy. One such context involves plaintiffs who unjustifiably procrastinate when it comes to serving the defendant with a summons. Laches can be used to deny equitable relief if the delay is unreasonable and has unfairly prejudiced (legally harmed) the defendant. Consider the following hypothetical case: Assume that a plaintiff has brought a tort action against a defendant and is seeking money damages. Assume further that in her complaint this plaintiff, in addition to the money damages, has asked for equitable remedies such as a declaratory judgment and an injunction. Also assume that the statute of limitations gives the plaintiff ten years within which to file her suit and that she waits eight years before serving the defendant with the summons and complaint. Under these circumstances, the defendant might argue that the plaintiff should be denied equitable relief because of laches. The defendant could support this argument with proof that he suffered legal harm because of the plaintiff's unreasonable delay in bringing suit. The prejudice might occur if, due to the delay, previously available documentary evidence essential to the defendant's case has been irretrievably lost or destroyed. Prejudice also might result if a previously available important potential witness has died, has disappeared, or recently has been adjudicated to be incompetent because of dementia. This proof of prejudice would enable the defendant to argue that the plaintiff should be limited to her common law remedies.

INTERNET TIP

Students wishing to read a court decision that illustrates the doctrine of laches can read *SMDFUND, Inc. v. Fort Wayne–Allen County Airport Authority* on the textbook's website.

CLAIM PRECLUSION–RES JUDICATA

Many jurisdictions now use the term **claim preclusion** when referring to the judicial doctrine traditionally known as **res judicata.** This doctrine, by either name, provides that a final decision by a competent court on a lawsuit's merits concludes the litigation of the parties and constitutes a bar (a legal barrier) to a new suit. Irrespective of whether a a plaintiff wins his or her lawsuit, the claims that he or she made (and could have made, but didn't) merge into the judgment and are extinguished. Thus no subsequent suit can be maintained against the same defendant based on the same claim. This is known as the principle of **bar and merger.** Once a claim has been judicially decided, it is finally decided. The loser may not bring a new suit against the winner for the same claim in any court. The loser's remedy is to appeal the decision of the lower court to a higher court.

The doctrine reduces litigation and prevents harassment of or hardship on an individual who otherwise could be sued multiple times (and perhaps in multiple jurisdictions) for the same cause of action. In addition, once the parties realize that they have only one chance to win, they will make their best effort.

For claim preclusion–res judicata to apply, two conditions must be met. First, there must be an identity of parties. Identity means that parties to a successive lawsuit are the same as, or in **privity** with, the parties to the original suit. Privity exists, for example, when there is a relationship between two people that allows one not directly involved in the case to take the place of the one who is a party. Thus if a person dies during litigation, the executor of the estate may take the deceased person's place in the lawsuit. Privity exists between the person who dies and the executor, so that as far as this litigation is concerned, they are the same person.

Second, there must be an identity of claims. In other words, for claim preclusion–res judicata to bar the suit, the claim—or cause of action—in the first case must be essentially the same the second time the litigation is attempted. For instance, if *A* sues *B* for breach of contract and loses, res judicata prohibits any further action on that same contract by *A* and *B* (except for appeal). However, *A* could sue *B* for the breach of a different contract, because that would be a different cause of action.

In 1982, adjacent neighbors Donald Czyzewski and Paul Harvey went to court over a land dispute. Although both parties were mutually mistaken about the true location of the boundary line that separated their two properties, Czyzewski filed suit against Harvey because Harvey had dug a ditch along what they believed to be the property line. Czyzewski claimed that the ditch had caused erosion on his land and had damaged his fence. After Harvey agreed to plant grass seed to prevent erosion and to pay Czyzewski $1,500, this lawsuit was dismissed. Czyzewski subsequently sold his property to Lawrence Kruckenberg. Kruckenberg was unaware of the 1982 lawsuit. In 2000 Kruckenberg had his land surveyed and discovered that the presumed boundary line was incorrect. The survey indicated that Kruckenberg actually owned a 16-foot strip that both he and Harvey believed to be part of Harvey's parcel. Kruckenberg filed suit against Harvey after Harvey cut down some trees in the disputed strip, contrary to Kruckenberg's wishes. Kruckenberg thereafter sued for trespass and a judicial determination of his rights to the 16-foot strip. The trial and intermediate appellate courts ruled in favor of Harvey, and Kruckenberg appealed to the Wisconsin Supreme Court.

When reading this opinion, you will find that the state supreme court refers to Czyzewski as "plaintiff's predecessor in title." This refers to the fact that Kruckenberg purchased the parcel of land from Czyzewski and was deeded all of Czyzewski's rights to that parcel. Because their interests in the land were identical, there existed between the two what is called a "privity of estate."

The problem confronting the Wisconsin Supreme Court was that the facts appeared to support the application of the claim-preclusion doctrine. Czyzewski, back in 1982, could have and probably should have included in his complaint a request for a judicial determination of the boundary line between the two parcels. He didn't, the trial court dismissed the case, and the parties' mutual misunderstanding about the location of the boundary line was left unnoticed.

Because a mechanical application of the claim-preclusion doctrine would have led to an unfair result, the Wisconsin Supreme Court refused to apply this doctrine in that manner. The chief justice of that court explains why not in the following opinion.

Lawrence A. Kruckenberg v. Paul S. Harvey
685 N.W.2d 844
Supreme Court of Wisconsin
April 14, 2005

Shirley S. Abrahamson, Chief Justice.
This is a review of a published decision of the court of appeals affirming a judgment and order of the Circuit Court for Green Lake County....

The issue presented is whether the doctrine of claim preclusion bars the plaintiff's action. The prior action brought by the plaintiff's predecessor in title against the defendant was for failing to provide lateral support; the defendant had dug a ditch. The prior action ended in a judgment of dismissal on the merits. The plaintiff's present action against the defendant is for trespass and conversion (the cutting and taking of trees) and for a declaratory judgment regarding the location of the boundary line between the plaintiff's and defendant's land....

For purposes of deciding how to apply the doctrine of claim preclusion to the present case, we set forth the following facts derived from the record on the motion for summary judgment.

The question of claim preclusion in the present case arises from a lawsuit brought by Donald A. Czyzewski, the plaintiff's predecessor in title, against the defendant in 1982. According to the 1982 complaint, the defendant dug a ditch along the northern boundary of his property, altering the topography and natural watershed, causing Czyzewski's soils and trees to collapse, causing the line fence to collapse ... and causing the water level of Czyzewski's pond to subside.

Czyzewski's 1982 complaint alleged that the defendant breached a duty of lateral support and a duty to maintain a line fence and that his conduct was contrary to Wisconsin Statutes ... §§844.01-.21, relating to physical injury to or interference with real property; §101.111 relating to protection of adjoining property and buildings during excavation; and chapter 90 relating to fences. For the alleged violations, Czyzewski requested: (1) restoration of the line fence, (2) restoration of the eroded portion of his property, (3) restoration of the water level, and (4) $10,000.

The defendant's answer to the 1982 complaint admitted that the defendant and Czyzewski owned adjoining parcels and that the defendant had dug the ditch along the northern boundary of his property. The defendant denied all other allegations of the complaint.

On April 6, 1983, on stipulation of the parties, the circuit court entered an order dismissing the Czyzewski suit on its merits. The defendant agreed to pay Czyzewski $1,500 and plant rye grass along the drainage ditch to prevent erosion.

Czyzewski's sale of his parcel to the plaintiff was completed after the 1982 lawsuit was dismissed, and the plaintiff claims he did not know about the lawsuit.

The plaintiff had his land surveyed in 2000 and learned that the "line fence" was not on the boundary line; the fence was 16 feet north of his property's southern boundary. In other words, the survey showed that the plaintiff's property included a strip of about 16 feet wide that was previously thought to belong to the defendant and on which the defendant had dug a ditch.

Peace between the parties was disturbed in "late winter and early spring of 2001" when the defendant decided to harvest some trees on the south side of the fence; according to the 2000 survey, the trees were on the plaintiff's property. The plaintiff asked the defendant not to cut the trees.

After the defendant removed the trees, the plaintiff, armed with his new survey, sued the defendant for trespass and conversion (cutting and taking the trees), failure to provide lateral support (failing to plant rye grass continually to prevent erosion), and a declaratory judgment regarding the location of the boundary line between their properties. The defendant denied many of the allegations of the complaint....

The circuit court granted summary judgment in the defendant's favor and dismissed the action. The circuit court ruled that the plaintiff could not challenge the location of the line fence as not being the boundary line because of the doctrine of claim preclusion. The circuit court found that the line fence was an issue in the 1982 lawsuit and in effect placed the boundary line at the line fence. The circuit court also ruled that the issue of lateral support was litigated in 1982 and that the doctrine of issue preclusion therefore barred this count....

A divided court of appeals affirmed the circuit court's judgment of dismissal, also on the ground that the lawsuit was barred by the doctrine of claim preclusion....

This court reviews a grant of summary judgment using the same methodology as the circuit court.... A motion for summary judgment will be granted "if the pleadings, depositions, answers to interrogatories, and admissions on file, together with the affidavits, if any, show that there is no genuine issue as to any material fact and that the moving party is entitled to a judgment as a matter of law."... In the present case no genuine issue of material fact exists.

The only question presented is one of law, namely whether the defendant is entitled to judgment on the ground of claim preclusion. This court determines this question of law independently of the circuit court and court of appeals, benefitting from their analyses.... To decide this case we must determine the application of the doctrine of claim preclusion....

The doctrine of claim preclusion provides that a final judgment on the merits in one action bars parties from relitigating any claim that arises out of the same relevant facts, transactions, or occurrences.... When the doctrine of claim preclusion is applied, a final judgment on the merits will ordinarily bar all matters "'which were litigated or which might have been litigated in the former proceedings.' "...

Claim preclusion thus provides an effective and useful means to establish and fix the rights of individuals, to relieve parties of the cost and vexation of multiple lawsuits, to conserve judicial resources, to prevent inconsistent decisions, and to encourage reliance on adjudication.... The doctrine of claim preclusion recognizes that "endless litigation leads to chaos; that certainty in legal relations must be maintained; that after a party has had his day in court, justice, expediency, and the preservation of the public tranquillity requires that the matter be at an end."...

In Wisconsin, the doctrine of claim preclusion has three elements:

"(1) identity between the parties or their privies in the prior and present suits;
(2) prior litigation resulted in a final judgment on the merits by a court with jurisdiction; and
(3) identity of the causes of action in the two suits..."

In effect, the doctrine of claim preclusion determines whether matters undecided in a prior lawsuit fall within the bounds of that prior judgment....

The parties do not dispute, and we agree, that the first two elements of claim preclusion have been satisfied in the case at bar. The identities of the parties or their privies are the same in the present and the prior suits. The plaintiff was the successor in interest to the property owned by Czyzewski, and the two are in privity for the purposes of claim preclusion.... The 1982 litigation resulted in a final judgment on the merits by a court with jurisdiction, satisfying the second element of claim preclusion.... The parties' disagreement focuses on the third element of the doctrine of claim preclusion, namely, the requirement that there be an identity of the causes of action or claims in the two suits.

Wisconsin has adopted the "transactional approach" set forth in the Restatement (Second) of Judgments to determine whether there is an identity of the claims between two suits.... Under the doctrine of claim preclusion, a valid and final judgment in an action extinguishes all rights to remedies against a defendant with respect to all or any part of the transaction, or series of connected transactions, out of which the action arose.... The transactional approach is not capable of a "mathematically precise definition,"... and determining what factual grouping constitutes a "transaction" is not always easy. The Restatement (Second) of Judgments §24 (2) (1982) explains that the transactional approach makes the determination pragmatically, considering such factors as whether the facts are related in time, space, origin, or motivation. Section 24 (2) provides as follows:

(2) What factual grouping constitutes a "transaction", and what groupings constitute a "series", are to be determined pragmatically, giving weight to such considerations as whether the facts are related in time, space, origin, or motivation, whether they form a convenient trial unit, and whether their treatment as a unit conforms to the parties' expectations or business understanding or usage.

The goal in the transactional approach is to see a claim in factual terms and to make a claim coterminous with the transaction, regardless of the claimant's substantive theories or forms of relief, regardless of the primary rights invaded, and regardless of the evidence needed to support the theories or rights.... Under the transactional approach, the legal theories, remedies sought, and evidence used may be different between the first and second actions.... The concept of a transaction connotes a common nucleus of operative facts....

The transactional approach to claim preclusion reflects "the expectation that parties who are given the capacity to present their 'entire controversies' shall in fact do so."... One text states that the pragmatic approach that seems most consistent with modern procedural philosophy "looks to see if the claim asserted in the second action should have been presented for decision in the earlier action, taking into account practical considerations relating mainly to trial convenience and fairness."…

At first blush the events giving rise to the two actions (1982 and 2001) do not appear part of the same transaction, as they are separated by time, space, origin, and motivation. The 1982 suit was prompted when the defendant dug a ditch and allegedly caused Czyzewski to claim erosion to his property and damage to the line fence. The 2001 suit was prompted when the defendant cut trees; this time the plaintiff claimed trespass on his property and sought a declaratory judgment concerning the location of the boundary line between the properties.

Because the trees were not cut until 2001, obviously neither Czyzewski nor the plaintiff could have brought a claim for tree cutting and taking (trespass and conversion) in 1982. The plaintiff reasons that the 2001 claim is therefore not part of the same transaction as the 1982 claim, and he should not be barred by the doctrine of claim preclusion.

The plaintiff makes a good point, but he overlooks that the aggregate operative facts in both the 1982 and 2001 claims are the same, namely the defendant's conduct in relation to the location of the boundary line. The facts necessary to establish the location of the boundary line between the plaintiff's and defendant's properties were in existence in 1982.

Czyzewski's 1982 claims and judgment depended on who owned the property south of the line fence upon which the ditch had been dug. Czyzewski's 1982 claim was that the defendant dug a ditch on the defendant's property, injuring Czyzewski's property by removing lateral support…. In 1982, both parties were mistaken about the location of the boundary line and the ownership of the property upon which the defendant had acted when he dug the ditch.

Similarly, the plaintiff's 2001 claims depend on who owned the property south of the line fence upon which the defendant cut trees. The plaintiff's 2001 claim is that the defendant cut trees on the plaintiff's property, an action that constitutes trespass and conversion.

Even though the 1982 litigation did not determine the boundary line, the two lawsuits have such a measure of identity of claims that a judgment in the second in favor of the plaintiff would appear to impair the rights or interests established in the first judgment.

The plaintiff's 2001 action might well be precluded under the well-settled claim preclusion analysis. We need not decide that difficult question, however, because even if claim preclusion were to apply here, we conclude that the plaintiff's 2001 lawsuit should proceed under a narrow exception to the doctrine of claim preclusion.

The parties' current dispute over the common boundary line illustrates that claim preclusion in the present case presents the "classic struggle between the need for clear, simple, and rigid law and the desire for its sensitive application."… Claim preclusion is a harsh doctrine; it necessarily results in preclusion of some claims that should go forward and it may fail to preclude some claims that should not continue….

Judicial formulation of the doctrine of claim preclusion should seek to minimize the over-inclusion of the doctrine through exceptions that are narrow in scope…. This court has previously stated that "[e]xceptions to the doctrine of claim preclusion, confined within proper limits, are 'central to the fair administration of the doctrine.' "

Exceptions to the doctrine of claim preclusion are rare, but in certain types of cases "the policy reasons for allowing an exception override the policy reasons for applying the general rule."…

Recognizing these truths, the Restatement (Second) of Judgments describes exceptions to the doctrine of claim preclusion. The present case falls within the "special circumstances" exception set forth in §26(1)(f), … which reads as follows:

> When any of the following circumstances exists, the general rule of §24 does not apply to extinguish the claim, and part or all of the claim subsists as a possible basis for a second action by the plaintiff against the defendant:…
> (f) It is clearly and convincingly shown that the policies favoring preclusion of a second action are overcome for an extraordinary reason, such as the apparent invalidity of a continuing restraint or condition having a vital relation to personal liberty or the failure of the prior litigation to yield a coherent disposition of the controversy.

We apply Restatement (Second) of Judgments §26(1) (f) in the present case. We conclude that in the present case the policies favoring preclusion are overcome for an "extraordinary reason," namely, "the failure of the prior litigation to yield a coherent disposition of the controversy."…

The exception we adopt is as follows: When an action between parties or their privies does not explicitly determine the location of a boundary line, the doctrine of claim preclusion will not bar a future declaratory judgment action to determine the proper location of the boundary line.

The narrowly drawn exception we adopt today serves important policy considerations.

First, strict application of the doctrine of claim preclusion in the present case may result in over-litigation in cases involving real property disputes.... Faced with the prospect that they will forever be fore-closed from having boundary lines judicially deter-mined in the future if they fail to litigate the issue in even the most simple lawsuit involving real property, parties will litigate the issue, even when it is appar-ently not in dispute.

There is no shortage of everyday situations that may implicate the location of a boundary line. The plaintiff's counsel mentioned just a few at oral argu-ment: a pet strays onto a neighbor's property; a child throws his or her ball into the neighbor's flowerbed; trees overhang the neighbor's shed; guests at a party wander onto the neighbor's property. If any of these situations results in a final judgment on the merits without a determination of the boundary line, the parties (and their privies) would, under the defen-dant's theory of the present case, forever be pre-cluded from determining the location of the boundary line....

Second, strict application of the doctrine of claim preclusion in the present case may discourage individuals from promptly settling lawsuits relating to real property. Parties may fear that without adequate discovery, any stipulated dis-missal on the merits could terminate rights or claims they had yet to even discover were potentially implicated.

Lastly, strict application of the doctrine of claim preclusion in the present case places process over truth. The boundary line is important to the parties in the present litigation and future owners of the properties and should be decided on the merits once and for all. Allowing litigation about the boundary line will pro-duce a final judgment that definitively settles the issue and can be recorded to put the public on notice. The legal system should, in the present case, be more con-cerned with deciding the location of the boundary line

than with strictly applying the doctrine of claim preclusion.

The parties in the 1982 action believed the boundary line was at the line fence. A survey in 2000 showed the line fence was not on the boundary line. Neither the parties to the present litigation, nor their predecessors in title, have ever litigated the location of the boundary line. The boundary line can be deter-mined in the present case, without repeating prior litigation.

Claim preclusion is grounded on a desire to maintain reliable and predictable legal relationships. Public policy seeks to ensure that real estate titles are secure and marketable, and therefore the doc-trine of claim preclusion ordinarily will apply in property cases. But the strict application of the doc-trine of claim preclusion in the present case creates uncertainty. The policies favoring preclusion of the 2001 action are overcome, because the 1982 action, in the words of Restatement (Second) of Judgments, "failed to yield a coherent disposition of the con-troversy" ... and "has left the parties not in a state of repose but in an unstable and intolerable condition."...

We hold that barring the declaratory judgment action (and the trespass and conversion action) to determine the location of the boundary line, when that line has not been previously litigated, undermines the policies that are at the foundation of the doctrine of claim preclusion. The unique nature of a claim to identify the location of a boundary line warrants this narrow exception.

We therefore conclude that important policy concerns exist that favor creation of a narrowly drawn exception in the present case, namely that when a prior action between the parties or their privies does not explicitly determine the location of a boundary line between the properties, the doctrine of claim preclusion will not bar a later declaratory judgment action to determine the location of the boundary line....

Accordingly, we reverse the decision of the court of appeals and remand the cause to the circuit court for proceedings not inconsistent with this decision.

By the Court. The decision of the court of appeals is reversed and the cause remanded.

Case Questions

1. What must a defendant prove in order to establish a claim preclusion res judicata defense?
2. How did the Wisconsin Supreme Court avoid applying the claim preclusion res judicata doctrine in a mechanical way to the facts of this case?
3. What rationale was given by the Wisconsin Supreme Court for its decision in this case?

IMMUNITY FROM LEGAL ACTION

The law provides immunity from tort liability when to do so is thought to be in the best interest of the public. Immunities are an exception to the general rule that a remedy must be provided for every wrong, and they are not favored by courts. They make the right of the individual to redress a private wrong subservient to what the law recognizes as a greater public good. Immunity does not mean that the conduct is not tortious in character, but only that for policy reasons the law denies liability resulting from the tort. Today, many courts are willing to abolish or limit an immunity when it becomes apparent that the public is not actually deriving any benefit from its existence.

Sovereign Immunity

It is a basic principle of common law that no sovereign may be sued without its express consent. This concept is referred to as the doctrine of **sovereign immunity.** When a person sues the government, the person is actually suing the taxpayers and him- or herself, because any judgment is paid for out of public revenues. The payment of judgments would require the expenditure of funds raised to provide services to the public.

The doctrine of governmental immunity from liability originated in the English notion that "the monarch can do no wrong." (Ironically, although most U.S. jurisdictions have retained the doctrine, England has repudiated it.) Congress consented to be sued in contract cases in the 1887 Tucker Act. In 1946 the federal government passed the Federal Tort Claims Act, in which the U.S. government waived its immunity from tort liability. It permitted suits against the federal government in federal courts for negligent or wrongful acts committed by its employees within the scope of their employment. Liability is based on the applicable local tort law. Thus the government may be sued in its capacity as a landlord and as a possessor of land, as well as for negligent acts and omissions (concepts explained in Chapter XI). Immunity was not waived for all acts of federal employees, however. Acts within the discretionary function of a federal employee or acts of military and naval forces in time

of war are examples of situations in which immunity has not been waived. In addition, members of the armed forces who have suffered a service-related injury due to governmental negligence are denied the right to sue. Permitting such suits has been thought to undermine military discipline. State governments and officially recognized Native American tribes also are entitled to claim sovereign immunity.

Introduction to *Miller v. Right*

The *Miller* case gives readers a glimpse into a very complex and controversial subject—the sovereignty rights of Native Americans. One of the over 500 Native American tribes officially recognized by the federal government is the Puyallup Tribe from Pierce County in the State of Washington.

This tribe entered into a treaty with the United States government back in 1854 when Washington was still a territory, and then as now claims sovereignty rights. Overall, the federal and state governmental responses to the sovereignty aspirations of Native Hawaiians and Native American Indians have been dismal. This case provides readers with a contemporary example of an issue whose roots both predate the founding of our nation and in all likelihood will continue for the foreseeable future.

This case focuses on whether the Tribe waived its claim of sovereign immunity in 2005 when it contracted with the state as to the taxation rate that purchasers of cigarettes would have to pay for cigarettes purchased on tribal lands. The most important benefit accruing to the state was the Tribe's commitment to require purchasers on tribal lands to pay the same amount of tax as would off-reservation purchasers throughout Washington. The primary benefit to the Tribe was the state's agreement that the Tribe would retain 70% and the state would receive 30% of all tax money collected from on-reservation cigarette purchases.

Plaintiff Matheson, a Tribe member, operated a store on tribal land from which he sold cigarettes to both tribal members and nonmembers. His two co-plaintiffs, Miller and Lanphere, were non-Indian customers who bought cigarettes at his store.

Matheson filed suit in a state trial court in 2005 believing that it was illegal for the Tribe and the state to enter into a contract that provided for identical taxation rates on tribal and nontribal lands within Washington—he argued that this was an unlawful restraint of trade. He wanted to be able to sell cigarettes on tribal lands at a lower price than could off-reservation vendors. The trial judge, however, dismissed the case, concluding that the suit was barred because of the Tribe's sovereign immunity. Matheson was unsuccessful in 2007 when he appealed to the state intermediate court of appeals. That court affirmed the trial court.

Matheson and Lanphere filed a second lawsuit in Puyallup Tribal Court in 2006, which was dismissed by the Tribal Trial Court on sovereign immunity grounds. The Tribal Court of Appeals affirmed the Tribal Trial Court's decision.

The plaintiffs then filed a third suit in U.S. District Court. That court dismissed the suit, concluding that the Tribe was immune from suit and that the matter also was res judicata.

Plaintiffs then appealed the District Court's decision to the U.S. Court of Appeals, which handed down the following opinion.

Daniel T. Miller v. Chad Wright
No. 11-35850
United States Court of Appeals, Ninth Circuit
November 13, 2012

Rawlinson, Circuit Judge.

Opinion
This is the latest iteration of cigarette vendors' challenge to taxes imposed by virtue of the authority vested in an Indian tribe. Appellants Daniel T. Miller (Miller), Amber Lanphere (Lanphere), and Paul M. Matheson (Matheson) appeal the district court's dismissal of their antitrust action against appellees Herman Dillon (Dillon), Chad Wright (Wright) and the Puyallup Tribe (the Tribe). The district court dismissed the action for lack of subject matter jurisdiction in light of the tribe's sovereign immunity.... We have jurisdiction pursuant to 28 U.S.C. §1291, and we affirm the district court.

I. Background

A. Allegations of Matheson, Miller, and Lanphere
Matheson is an enrolled Puyallup Indian who owns a retail store that sells cigarettes. Matheson's store is located within the Puyallup Indian Reservation. The Tribe operates retail stores in the same vicinity.

Miller is a non-Indian, non-resident of the reservation who purchased cigarettes from Matheson. As a result of the Tribe's cigarette tax, the price Miller paid for a carton of cigarettes included a $30.00 fee. This $30.00 fee stemmed from the cigarette tax contract between the State of Washington and the Tribe. The price also included a $5 fee for the benefit of Washington's public health fund. Washington requires collection of the $5 fee to comply with provisions of the Master Settlement Agreement (MSA), a settlement between the tobacco industry and numerous states, including Washington....

Miller seeks a refund of these fees and a permanent injunction against their future collection.

Lanphere is also a non-Indian, non-resident of the reservation who purchased cigarettes from Matheson's store. Like Miller, the price Lanphere paid included the tribe's cigarette tax and the health fund fee....

B. The Tribe
Chad Wright "is or was the Tax Enforcement Officer of the Puyallup Tribe" and Chief Executive Officer of the Tribe's store located near Matheson's. Herman Dillon, Sr., is the tribal chairman of the Puyallup Tribe.

The Puyallup Tribe entered into a compact with the State of Washington whereby the Tribe agreed that tribal retailers would purchase only from Washington State Tobacco Wholesalers or state certified wholesalers. Likewise, the Tribe agreed to require retailers to charge a cigarette tax equal to the amount of the tax that would otherwise be imposed by the state. The Tribe's agreement with the state provides that "[r]esponsibility for enforcement of the terms of this agreement shall be shared by the State and the Tribe...." The agreement also provides for mediation.

C. Miller's, Lanphere's, and Matheson's Allegations Before the District Court
Miller, Lanphere, and Matheson alleged that the Tribe forces them "to pay more for the cigarettes by adding illegal charges and restricting [Matheson's] purchases at wholesale to wholesalers who charge more...." Their complaint sought an injunction, a declaratory judgment, damages, and a refund of fees paid as a result of the charges imposed by the Tribe.

D. The District Court's Dismissal Order
The district court granted the Tribe's motion to dismiss, explaining that Miller, Lanphere, and Matheson "failed [to meet their] burden of showing that sovereign immunity has been waived and that [the district court] has jurisdiction to hear the matter."

Miller, Lanphere, and Matheson timely appealed.

II. Standards of Review
We review *de novo* a district court's dismissal for lack of subject matter jurisdiction....

III. Discussion

A. Sovereign Immunity
1. Waiver of tribal sovereign immunity
Miller, Lanphere, and Matheson argue that the Tribe implicitly waived its sovereign immunity by agreeing to dispute resolution procedures and by ceding its authority to Washington State when entering into the cigarette tax contract.

"Tribal sovereign immunity protects Indian tribes from suit absent express authorization by Congress or clear waiver by the tribe. This immunity applies to the tribe's commercial as well as governmental activities...."

a. The cigarette tax contract
The nature of the cigarette tax contract between the Tribe and the State of Washington does not reflect a waiver of tribal sovereign immunity simply by entering into the contract....

b. The dispute resolution clause
The Supreme Court has held that agreeing to an arbitration clause may establish a clear waiver of sovereign immunity.... We have described the [U.S. Supreme Court's] ruling in *C&L [Enters., Inc. v. Citizen Band Potawatomi Indian Tribe of Okla.,]* as one in which the Court relied on two provisions of a contract between a tribe and a construction company to find sufficient evidence of a clear waiver of tribal sovereign immunity: (1) a clause stating that all contractual disputes should be resolved according to American Arbitration Association Rules and providing for enforcement of the arbitrator's award in accordance with applicable law in any court having jurisdiction thereof; and (2) a choice-of-law clause consenting to the law of the project location, Oklahoma. The referenced arbitration rules provided that parties to these rules shall be deemed to have consented to enforcement of the award in federal and state court....

The inclusion of a mediation provision to resolve disputes between the State of Washington and the Tribe does not evidence a clear and explicit waiver of immunity. As a preliminary matter, mediation generally is not binding and does not reflect an intent to submit to adjudication by a non-tribal entity.... Moreover, the CTC [cigarette tax contract with the State of Washington] in this case did not contain any of the provisions, including subjecting itself to the jurisdiction of the state.... The Tribe did not waive its sovereign immunity when it executed the CTC....

2. Abrogation of tribal sovereign immunity
Miller, Lanphere, and Matheson contend that tribal immunity is preempted by federal antitrust laws. The Tribe counters that federal antitrust law does not apply to Indian tribes. Abrogation of tribal immunity by Congress "must be unequivocally expressed in explicit legislation. Abrogation of tribal sovereign immunity may not be implied."...

... [F]ederal antitrust laws are not intended to apply to Indian tribes. This conclusion forecloses the argument that federal antitrust law is of general applicability vis-à-vis the Tribe.... Because Miller, Lanphere, and Matheson failed to successfully challenge the Tribe's sovereign immunity, we affirm the district court's holding that it lacked subject matter jurisdiction to adjudicate the claims asserted against the Tribe.

3. Immunity of tribal officials
Miller, Lanphere, and Matheson argue that the tribal officials are not covered by tribal sovereign immunity because they assess unconstitutional taxes. The Tribe counters that the officials act in their official capacity when they collect the Tribe's taxes, which the officials have the authority to impose.

A suit against the Tribe and its officials "in their official capacities is a suit against the tribe [and] is barred by tribal sovereign immunity unless that immunity has been abrogated or waived.".... "Tribal sovereign immunity extends to tribal officials when acting in their official capacity and within the scope of their authority.... [A] plaintiff cannot circumvent tribal immunity by the simple expedient of naming an officer of the Tribe as a defendant, rather than the sovereign entity...."

As the district court found, the tribal officials are protected by the Tribe's sovereign immunity because they were acting pursuant to the Tribe's authority. "The power to tax transactions occurring on trust lands and significantly involving a tribe or its members is a fundamental attribute of sovereignty which the tribes retain unless divested of it by federal law or necessary implication of their dependent status." *Washington v. Confederated Tribes of Colville Indian Reservation*, 447 U.S. 134, 152 (1980).

The Tribe's sovereign immunity thus extends to its officials who were acting in their official capacities and within the scope of their authority when they taxed transactions occurring on the reservation.... Moreover, to the extent the complaint seeks monetary relief, such claims are barred.... We therefore reject Miller's, Lanphere's, and Matheson's attempt to circumvent tribal immunity by naming tribal officials as defendants....

In the alternative, the district court also correctly concluded that res judicata bars this action. "Res judicata, also known as claim preclusion, applies only where there is (1) an identity of claims, (2) a final judgment on the merits, and (3) privity between parties...."

Res judicata bars this action. Like the suits in state court and tribal court, the claims in this case involve allegedly unlawful cigarette taxes arising from the sales at Matheson's store on the Puyallup reservation. There is thus an identity of claims. See *Turtle Island*, 673 F.3d at 917-18. Likewise, the state and tribal courts reached final judgments and Miller is in privity [the

parties are essentially the same] with Lanphere and Matheson given the substantial commonality of their interests....

IV. Conclusion
As we have described, this action fails for four reasons. First, the Tribe has not waived its tribal sovereign immunity. Neither the cigarette tax contract nor the dispute resolution clause in the contract constitutes a waiver by the Tribe. Second, contrary to Miller's, Lanphere's, and Matheson's argument, federal antitrust law does not abrogate tribal sovereign immunity. Third, the Tribe's sovereign immunity extends to the tribal officials who were acting in their official capacities and pursuant to the Tribe's authority. Fourth, the district court correctly held that res judicata bars this action in light of the prior litigation in state and tribal courts.

AFFIRMED.

Case Questions

1. Why did the Ninth Circuit reject the argument that the Tribe had waived its sovereign immunity?
2. Why was this case barred by res judicata?

INTERNET TIP

Interested readers can learn more about the Puyallup Tribe online at www.puyallup-tribe.com. There you can read a copy of the 1845 Treaty and the Tribal Constitution.

Author's Commentary on Sovereign Immunity

Courts have made a distinction between governmental and proprietary functions. When a public entity is involved in a governmental function, it is generally immune from tort liability. When the government engages in activity that is usually carried out by private individuals or that is commercial in character, it is involved in a proprietary function, and the cloak of immunity is lost. For example, a state is not immune when it provides a service that a private company may perform, such as providing electricity.

Courts currently favor limiting or abolishing sovereign immunity. Their rationale is the availability of liability insurance and the perceived inequity of denying relief to a deserving claimant. Many legislatures

have replaced blanket sovereign immunity with tort claims acts that limit governmental liability. For example, legislators can reduce exposure to suit by restricting recoveries to the limits of insurance policies or by establishing ceilings on maximum recoveries (often ranging from $25,000 to $100,000). Many states continue to immunize discretionary functions and acts.

Immunity of Governmental Officials

As described in the previous section, executive, legislative, and judicial officers are afforded **governmental immunity** when the act is within the scope of their authority and in the discharge of their official duties. Immunity increases the likelihood that government officials will act impartially and fearlessly in carrying out their public duties. Thus, it is in the public interest to shield responsible government officers from harassment or ill-founded damage suits based on acts they committed in the exercise of their official responsibilities. Prosecutors, for example, enjoy immunity when they decide for the public who should be criminally prosecuted. Public defenders, however, are not immunized, because their clients are private citizens and not the general public.

This immunity applies only when public officers are performing discretionary acts in conjunction with official functions. Officials are not immune from liability for tortious conduct when they exceed their lawful authority and invade the constitutional rights of others. They are legally responsible for their personal torts.

Some argue that granting immunity to officials does not protect individual citizens from harm resulting from oppressive or malicious conduct on the part of public officers. A governmental official may in some jurisdictions lose this protection by acting maliciously or for an improper purpose, rather than honestly or in good faith.

High-level executive, legislative, and judicial officials with discretionary functions enjoy more immunity than do lower-level officials. Judges, for example, are afforded absolute immunity when they exercise judicial powers, regardless of their motives or good faith. But judges are not entitled to absolute immunity from civil suit for their nonjudicial acts.

Police officers, however, are only entitled to qualified immunity from suit because of the discretionary nature of police work and the difficulty of expecting officers to make instant determinations as to how the constitution should be interpreted. The qualified immunity defense is unavailable if the illegality of the officer's constitutionally impermissible conduct has been previously well established and would be clearly understood as such by a properly trained officer.

INTERNET TIP

Interested readers can learn more about qualified immunity and policing by reading the case of *Solomon v. Auburn Hills Police Department*, a 2004 case decided by the U.S. Court of Appeals for the Sixth Circuit. Search for 389 F.3d 167.

Immunity among Family Members

American courts traditionally have recognized two types of immunities among family members: interspousal and parental immunity.

Under the common law doctrine of **interspousal immunity**, husbands and wives were immune from liability for negligence and intentional torts perpetrated against their spouses. In part this policy was a byproduct of the old-fashioned common law notion that husbands and wives were legally one and the same. But adherents also argued that interspousal immunity was necessary because tort actions between spouses would be harmful to marriages and would disrupt the peace and harmony of the home. They claimed that allowing husbands and wives to sue one another would lead to collusion and fraud. During the twentieth century, reformers successfully argued that married persons and unmarried persons should have equivalent legal rights and remedies. Today, only Louisiana continues to adhere in whole to the common law approach. Some states partially retain this immunity. In Georgia, for example, the immunity is limited to personal injury claims, and the immunity will not be recognized if the marital relationship has deteriorated to the point that the spouses are "married" in name only, or where it is likely that the spouses are perpetrating a fraud or engaging in collusion.

Author's Commentary

In the late 1920s the author's great-grandfather, August Schubert, while negligently driving one of his company's cars on company business, struck a vehicle in which his wife, Jessie, the author's great-grandmother, was a passenger. Jessie was injured as a result of this collision. Prior to 1937, New York recognized interspousal immunity in tort cases. Thus Jessie was not permitted to sue her husband in tort for the damages she sustained resulting from his bad driving. But Jessie (and her lawyers) decided to sue August's company and compel it to pay for her damages. Jessie claimed that the company was financially responsible for the tortious conduct of its employee—her husband, August. Although the company had not directly caused the harm to Jessie, her lawyers successfully argued that the business was still financially responsible for her injury because of a legal doctrine known as *respondeat superior*. Before readers learn about the case it is necessary to explain briefly in general terms the doctrine Jessie relied upon in her suit.

Respondeat Superior

Respondeat superior is an ancient doctrine. The famous American U.S. Supreme Court Justice Oliver Wendell Holmes traced its origin back to the reign of Edward I of England (1272–1307).[3] This doctrine evolved over the centuries. It essentially permits an injured plaintiff, under certain conditions, to hold a company financially responsible for an employee's negligence and intentional torts. Basically, the plaintiff has to prove that the person committed a tort, and that the tortious conduct causing the plaintiff's injury was committed by an employee of the company to be sued, and not by an independent contractor. The plaintiff also has to prove that the tortious conduct occurred while the employee was acting within the scope of his or her employment. For example, if an employee drives a company car for a personal, nonbusiness reason, say to the grocery store, and commits a tort in the parking lot, the employee's personal errand would have amounted to unauthorized travel as far as the employer is concerned. An employer is not vicariously liable for an employee's torts that involve unauthorized travel or other nonbusiness-related conduct.

There are three primary arguments by those who favor this doctrine. The first is that the companies are to some extent responsible. They recruit, select, train, and supervise each employee, and therefore have the ability to affect how carefully and safely an employee performs his or her job.

The second argument is that the doctrine makes sense as good public policy. Somebody has to pay for the injured person's damages. Of the three alternatives—the injured victim, the employee, or the employer—making employers pay, it is argued, is the best option. Employers are more likely than their employees to have the ability to pay. Companies can purchase liability insurance, deduct the cost of the premium on their tax returns, and recoup some of cost from their customers as one of the overhead costs of operating a business.

Lastly, placing the burden on employers also creates an incentive for them to promote safe conduct by their employees.

Respondeat superior applies at both the state and the federal levels of government. As previously mentioned in the discussion of sovereign immunity, the Federal Tort Claims Act provides that the federal government can be sued for tortious conduct committed by federal employees who were acting within the scope of their employment.

Back to the Lawsuit—*Jessie Schubert v. August Schubert Wagon Company,* 164 N.E. 42 (1928)

The company unsuccessfully argued to the trial court that because spousal immunity barred Jessie from suing her husband directly in tort, it made no sense to allow her to do the same thing by suing his company. The company then appealed to New York's highest court, the Court of Appeals. The Court of Appeals agreed with the trial court that Jessie's respondeat superior claim had nothing to do with the spousal immunity relationship. The trial court had properly applied the law to the facts and ruled in her favor. The Court of Appeals opinion was written by Chief Judge Benjamin Cardozo, who in 1932 was nominated by President Hoover, and unanimously confirmed as an associate justice of the U. S. Supreme Court. Cardozo's opinion in the *Schubert* case was widely quoted in similar cases throughout the country and played a role in convincing other states to adopt similar policies. It also helped to undermine the continued vitality of spousal immunity in the state of New York.

August Schubert grew up in Oneida, New York and, like his father, became a blacksmith. During the 1880s, August (whom everyone called Gus) and two of his brothers started building wagons and carriages in Oneida. August was 25 and Jessie Winona 23 when they married in 1889. They became the parents of two boys. August was an innovator and was granted several patents relating to wagons and carriages. Although the businesses prospered and grew over the years, they did not survive the Great Depression. August was 64 in

1928 when the Court of Appeals of New York handed down its decision in the *Schubert* case, and he died three years later in 1931. Jessie and August had been husband and wife for 42 years. Jessie lived to be 82 and died in 1948. August was highly thought of by his family and descendants who, for three consecutive generations, have given some of their sons the middle name of August.

AUTHOR'S NOTE ——————————————

Interested readers can read Judge Cardozo's opinion in *Jessie Schubert v. August Schubert Wagon Company,* 164 N.E. 42 (1928), in the textbook's appendix.

Parental immunity was created to prohibit unemancipated minor children from suing their parents for negligence or intentional torts. This immunity was first recognized in 1891 by the Mississippi Supreme Court.[4] The New Hampshire Supreme Court explained in a 1930 case that the "disability of a child to sue the parent for any injury negligently inflicted by the latter upon the former while a minor is not absolute, but is imposed for the protection of family control and harmony, and exists only where the suit, or the prospect of a suit, might disturb the family relations."[5]

Courts in many states were reluctant to intrude into the parental right and obligation to determine how their children are raised. They also thought it in society's interest to prohibit unemancipated minor children from maintaining actions for negligence or intentional torts against their parents. At common law, children remained minors until they reached the age of twenty-one. Today, legislation has reduced this age to eighteen. Many courts believed that subjecting the parent to suit by the child might interfere with domestic harmony, deplete family funds at the expense of the other family members, encourage fraud or collusion, and interfere with the discipline and control of children.

The plaintiff in the next case, Lamoni K. Riordan, was a five-year-old boy who accompanied his father to land owned by the Church of Jesus Christ of Latter-Day Saints. The church had instructed Lamoni's father, Ken, a church employee, to cut the grass at this location. Ken, while carrying out this assignment, accidently backed a riding lawnmower over Lamoni's foot. The damage resulted in the partial amputation of Lamoni's foot.

Lamoni filed suit against the church that employed his father. At the time of the accident, Missouri still recognized parental immunity, thereby making it impossible for the child to sue his father in tort. He claimed that because of the doctrine of respondeat superior the church was legally responsible for the injury to his foot.

Lamoni K. Riordan v. Presiding Bishop, Latter-Day Saints
416 F.3d 825
United States Court of Appeals, Eighth Circuit
August 5, 2005

Riley, Circuit Judge.

A jury awarded Lamoni Riordan (Lamoni) over $1.18 million in damages on his claims against the Corporation of the Presiding Bishop of The Church of Jesus Christ of Latter-Day Saints (CPB) for injuries Lamoni sustained when his father, Ken Riordan (Ken), a CPB employee, was operating a riding lawnmower in reverse and backed over Lamoni's foot. CPB appeals, arguing Ken's parental immunity shielded CPB from liability, and the district court ... erroneously submitted both a *respondeat superior* and a direct negligence claim to the jury.... We affirm *in toto.*

I. Background

On April 13, 1985, five-year-old Lamoni was injured in an accident involving a riding lawnmower operated by Ken while Ken was mowing at a CPB-owned facility. Because of the accident, Lamoni's foot was partially amputated. Lamoni filed suit against CPB on February 15, 2002, in Missouri state court, claiming ... CPB was liable for Ken's negligence under the doctrine of *respondeat superior,* ... and ... CPB negligently failed to train and supervise its employees properly. CPB removed the case to the federal district court.

The district court denied CPB's motion for summary judgment ... [and] concluded Lamoni could bring both the *respondeat superior* and direct negligence claims at trial....

CPB appeals....

II. Discussion

Exercising diversity jurisdiction, we interpret Missouri law.... We review the district court's interpretation of Missouri law ... attempting to forecast how the Missouri Supreme Court would decide the issues presented....

A. Respondeat Superior Claim

... CPB claims the district court erred in submitting Lamoni's *respondeat superior* claim to the jury. CPB also contends applying parental immunity to bar Lamoni's claims is necessary to prevent collusion between Lamoni and Ken.

Although the Missouri Supreme Court has ... [abolished] parental immunity, the doctrine still applies to causes of action accrued before December 19, 1991.... The parties stipulated "[p]arental immunity applies to this case and, therefore, Plaintiff's parents, Kenneth and Pearl Riordan, cannot be joined as parties to this action." We find no reason to disagree. Thus, we examine whether Ken's parental immunity shields CPB from liability.

The Missouri Supreme Court has recognized the close and analogous connection between parental immunity and spousal immunity.... Missouri adopted parental immunity on "the belief that allowing children to sue their parents would disturb the unity and harmony of the family."... Spousal immunity also had underpinnings in notions of family unity and harmony.... In the absence of authority on the applicability of parental immunity in situations like that presented here, it is appropriate for us to consider Missouri courts' rulings on spousal immunity.

In *Mullally v. Langenberg Brothers Grain Co.* ... (1936), the defendant contended, because a wife could not maintain an action against her husband for damages arising from injuries caused by the husband's negligence, the husband's employer enjoyed ... immunity against the wife's *respondeat superior* claim against the employer. After noting two lines of authority on this question, the Missouri Supreme Court concluded "legal principle and public policy [dictate] the wife has a right of action against the husband's employer."... The court quoted extensively from the reasoning in *[Jessie] Schubert v. August Schubert Wagon Co.* ... : "The disability of wife or husband to maintain an action against the other for injuries to the person is not a disability to maintain a like action against the other's principal or master...." [Quoting *Schubert.*] "The statement sometimes made that it is derivative and secondary ... means this, and nothing more: That at times the fault of the actor will fix the quality of the act. Illegality established, liability ensues."... (quoting *Schubert.*) The court reasoned, "A trespass, negligent or willful, upon the person of a wife, does not cease to be an unlawful act, though the law exempts the husband from liability for the damage. Others may not hide behind the skirts of his immunity." *Id.* (quoting *Schubert.*)

According to the Restatement (Second) of Agency, in an action against a principal based on an agent's conduct during the course of the agent's employment, "[t]he principal has no defense because of the fact that ... the agent had an immunity from civil liability as to the act." Restatement (Second) of Agency §217 (1958). These immunities include those "resulting from the relation of parent and child and of husband and wife".... Moreover, "[s]ince the Restatement, ... the trend has been strongly to enforce the liability of the [employer]"....

We believe the Missouri Supreme Court, if confronted with this appeal, would conclude parental immunity does not bar Lamoni's *respondeat superior* claim against CPB. We forecast the Missouri Supreme Court would adopt the majority view, i.e., "the holding that the immunity of a parent is a personal immunity, and it does not, therefore, protect a third party who is liable for the tort." ... Accordingly, the district court did not err in so holding.

CPB also argues application of the parental immunity doctrine is necessary to protect it from collusion between Ken and Lamoni....

... [O]ur review of the record does not convince us collusion occurred.... Witnesses testified at trial Ken blamed himself for the accident from the moment it occurred, admitted the injury was his fault, and stated he did not realize Lamoni was behind him as he mowed. In his deposition, Ken acknowledged mowing in reverse was more dangerous. During trial, Ken recounted the events surrounding the accident. Although Ken did not state he blamed himself, his testimony clearly demonstrates he accepted the blame for the accident, again acknowledging the danger involved in mowing in reverse.... [W]hatever collusion CPB claims occurred certainly was insufficient to warrant application of the now-abrogated parental immunity doctrine to bar Lamoni's *respondeat superior* claim against CPB.

B. Direct Negligence Claim

CPB argues the court erred in submitting to the jury Lamoni's direct negligence claim based on negligent supervision. CPB contends this claim is inextricably in- tertwined with the *respondeat superior* claim and is barred by parental immunity, and CPB claims Ken's own negligence was an intervening cause of the injury....

In this case, Ken's negligence resulted from CPB's negligent failure to train or supervise him properly. CPB's failure to train and supervise Ken properly caused Ken to operate the mower negligently.... The jury ver- dict establishes not only the negligence and causation, but the foreseeability of the failure to train and super- vise leading directly to the injury.... The district court did not err in submitting both claims to the jury....

III. Conclusion
We affirm in all respects.

Case Questions

1. What was the traditional rationale for recognizing parental immunity?
2. Why did the U.S. Court of Appeals look to a New York case on spousal immunity to help it decide a Missouri case involving parental immunity?

Author Commentary

The parental immunity doctrine has been signifi- cantly eroded in the United States. According to one source "at least twenty-four states now have either abrogated the doctrine of parental immunity altogether or have held that as a general rule, a parent may be liable to a child for injuries caused by the parent's negligence."[6] It should be empha- sized that all states permit the criminal prosecution of parents for child abuse and neglect. Moreover, states that still immunize parents in tort create one or more exceptions for special situations such as where a parent has sexually abused his or her child.

AUTHOR'S NOTE

Students wishing to read a case in which the state su- preme court creates an exception to the doctrine of pa- rental immunity so that children can sue their parents for sexual abuse can read *Hurst v. Capitell* on the textbook's website.

Immunity through Contract

In addition to the immunities imposed by law, par- ties can create their own immunities by agreeing not to sue referred to as **immunity through con- tract**). Because public policy favors freedom of contract, such agreements may be legally enforce- able. However, courts often enforce immunity clauses reluctantly. An immunity provision in a contract usually is construed against the party assert- ing the contract and is held invalid if the contract is against public policy or is a result of unfair negotia- tions. Factors that the court considers in determin- ing whether to enforce the agreement are the subject matter involved, the clause itself, the rela- tion of the parties, and the relative bargaining power of the parties.

A basic tenet of freedom of contract is that both parties are free to negotiate the terms of the con- tract. As a result, the contract should reflect a real and voluntary meeting of the minds. Therefore the equality of bargaining power is an important consid- eration for courts in determining unfair negotiations. Different courts may accord different degrees of importance to such elements as superior bargaining power, a lack of meaningful choice by one party, take-it-or-leave-it propositions, or exploitation by one party of another's known weaknesses.

In the following case, thieves successfully stole jewels valued at over $1 million from three safe deposit boxes rented by jewelers from a branch of the Firstar Bank. Two of the jewelers had pur- chased insurance to protect themselves from inci- dents such as this and collected as provided in their policies from Jewelers Mutual Insurance Company. The insurance company in turn sought to recover from Firstar Bank. The bank, although admitting negligence, claimed that it was contractually immune under the circumstances of this case and refused to pay. The question was tried and appealed and ultimately was decided by the Illinois Supreme Court.

Jewelers Mutual Insurance Co. v. Firstar Bank III.
820 N.E.2d 411
Supreme Court of Illinois
November 18, 2004

Justice Thomas delivered the opinion of the court.
At issue is whether the exculpatory clause in defendant Firstar Bank's safety deposit box rental agreement is enforceable under the facts of this case....

Background
More than $1 million worth of loose diamonds and jewelry was stolen from three safety deposit boxes that defendant leased to jewel dealers at one of its Chicago branches. The safety deposit box lease ... agreement contained the following paragraph:

> 1. It is understood that said bank has no posses-sion or custody of, nor control over, the contents of said safe and that the lessee assumes all risks in connection with the depositing of such con-tents, that the sum mentioned is for the rental of said safe alone, and that there shall be no liabil-ity on the part of said bank, for loss of, or injury to, the contents of said box from any cause whatever unless lessee and said bank enter into a special agreement in writing to that effect, in which case such additional charges shall be made by said bank as the value of contents of said safe, and the liability assumed on account thereof may justify. The liability of said bank is limited to the exercise of ordinary care to pre-vent the opening of said safe by any person not authorized and such opening by any person not authorized shall not be inferable from loss of any of its contents.

None of the dealers had entered into the "special agreement" referenced in the first sentence of this paragraph (hereinafter, the exculpatory clause). Two of the dealers, Annaco Corporation and Irving M. Ringel, Inc., had the contents of their boxes insured by plaintiff Jewelers Mutual Insurance Company. The third dealer, Bachu Vaidya, was uninsured. Jewelers Mutual paid losses totaling $887,400.37 to Annaco and Ringel and then brought [suit] ... against defendant. The complaint alleged breach of contract and negligence. Vaidya also separately sued defendant and sought recovery under the same theories. In its answer in both cases, defendant admitted that it had to some extent been negligent and had breached the agreement as alleged by plaintiff.

Relying on the exculpatory clause, defendant moved for and was granted summary judgment in both cases.... Plaintiffs appealed, and the two cases were consolidated on appeal.

The appellate court affirmed the dismissal of the negligence count in Vaidya's case.... However, the court reversed the summary judgment in favor of defendant in both cases on the breach of contract counts, holding that the exculpatory clause was unen-forceable. The court gave two reasons for finding the clause unenforceable. First, that the contract was ambiguous because the first sentence of paragraph one provided that "there shall be no liability," while the second sentence said that the "liability of said bank is limited to the exercise of ordinary care."... The court held that the ambiguity had to be resolved against defendant because it drafted the contract.... The court stated that defendant had admitted that it allowed unauthorized access to the safety deposit boxes in both cases, and therefore the court granted in part Jewelers Mutual's motion for summary judgment and directed the entry of partial summary judgment for Vaidya. The court remanded for proof of damages....

Presiding Justice McBride dissented from the reversal of summary judgment for defendant. She disagreed with the majority's conclusion that the contract was ambiguous. She believed that the two sentences in paragraph one could be reconciled by reading the second sentence as referring to the "special agreement" mentioned in the first sentence.... In other words, the paragraph means that defendant has no liability for any loss whatso-ever, unless the parties enter into the special agree-ment referenced in the first sentence. If they do, then defendant's liability is limited to the exercise of ordinary care to prevent unauthorized access to the box.... Finally, she did not believe that the exculpa-tory clause was void as against public policy because safety deposit companies are not generally insurers of the safety of the box contents.... We allowed defendant's petition for leave to appeal....

Analysis

Summary judgment is proper where the pleadings, affidavits, depositions, admissions, and exhibits on file, when viewed in the light most favorable to the non-moving, reveal that there is no issue as to any material fact and that the movant is entitled to judgment as a matter of law....

We review summary judgment orders *de novo*....

Defendant first argues that the court erred in finding paragraph one ambiguous. According to defendant, although this provision could have been drafted better, its meaning is clear. Defendant contends that the word "liability" is used two different ways in the first and second sentences. In the first sentence, it refers to the amount of damages for which defendant can be held responsible. In the second sentence, the word "liability" addresses the standard of care. Thus, the second sentence means that defendant has a duty to exercise ordinary care to prevent the unauthorized opening of the box, but the first sentence limits the amount of damages that can be collected for a breach of that duty. At oral argument, defendant clarified that its position was that the only damages that a customer could recover if defendant breaches its duty of care would be a return of the rental fee. Defendant argues that this interpretation takes into account the commercial setting in which the parties contracted and also fairly allocates the liability to the party who elected to bear the risk of loss. Here, none of the parties entered into the special agreement referenced in the first sentence to insure the contents of the box. Defendant argues that Annaco Corporation and Irving M. Ringel, Inc., insured the contents of the boxes with Jewelers Mutual and thus elected that Jewelers Mutual would bear the risk of loss. Vaidya did not purchase insurance and thus chose to bear the risk of loss himself.

We disagree with defendant's argument. First, the first sentence of paragraph one is simply not a limitation of damages clause. That sentence provides that the customer assumes all risks of depositing the contents of the box with defendant and that there "shall be no liability on the part of said bank, for loss of, or injury to, the contents of said box from any cause whatever." The clause does not say that, in the event of a breach, the plaintiff's damages are limited to a return of the rental fee. Rather, it is a general exculpatory clause purporting to exculpate defendant from all liability for loss of or damage to the contents of the box. In the very next sentence, however,

defendant assumes one particular liability: it must exercise ordinary care to prevent the unauthorized opening of the box. We do not believe that the clauses can be reconciled in the manner suggested by defendant.

Further, defendant's invocation of insurance law "risk of loss" concepts is a red herring. The issue in this case is not a dispute between insurance companies over who bore the risk of loss. The issues are whether defendant breached the contract it entered into with plaintiffs and whether defendant can exculpate itself from all liability for breach of an express obligation assumed in the contract.

The construction placed on paragraph one by the dissenting justice in the appellate court must also be rejected. The dissent argued that the second sentence referred to defendant's liability in the event that the parties entered into the "special agreement" listed in clause one. This obviously cannot be the case because the first sentence provides, in part, that there is "no liability on the part of said bank, for loss of, or injury to, the contents of said box from any cause whatever unless lessee and said bank enter into a special agreement in writing to that effect."... In other words, there is no liability for loss of or injury to the contents of the box from any cause whatsoever unless the parties enter into an agreement that there will be liability on the part of the bank for loss of, or injury to, the contents of the box from any cause whatsoever. If the parties entered into such an agreement, defendant's liability would not be limited to a failure to exercise ordinary care to keep unauthorized persons out of the box. Rather, defendant would become a general insurer of the contents of the box. Thus, the two sentences cannot be reconciled in the manner suggested by the appellate court dissent.

We believe that paragraph one of the lease agreement is ambiguous and that its two sentences are conflicting. In the first sentence, defendant disclaims liability for any loss whatsoever. In the second sentence, defendant assumes one particular liability. It must exercise ordinary care to prevent unauthorized persons from accessing the box. Defendant argues that, if we find this paragraph ambiguous, then the resolution of its meaning is a question of fact and the case cannot be decided on a motion for summary judgment.... Defendant thus contends that, if we find an ambiguity, we must remand the case to the fact finder to resolve the ambiguity.

We disagree.

Whatever the meaning of the exculpatory clause, it clearly cannot be applied to a situation in which defendant is alleged to have breached its duty to exercise ordinary care to prevent unauthorized persons from opening the box. This is a specific duty that defendant assumed in the contract, and it formed the heart of the parties' agreement. A party cannot promise to act in a certain manner in one portion of a contract and then exculpate itself from liability for breach of that very promise in another part of the contract.... Here, plaintiffs have received nothing in return for their rental fee if they cannot hold defendant to its contractual obligation to exercise ordinary care to prevent unauthorized persons from accessing their safety deposit boxes.

This same conclusion was reached by the Florida District Court of Appeal in *Sniffen v. Century National Bank of Broward,* ... (Fla. App. 1979). In that case, the safety deposit box rental agreement was similar to the one here in that it contained two conflicting provisions. One was a general, broad exculpatory clause denying liability for any loss: "It is expressly understood ... that in making this lease the Bank ... shall not be liable for loss or damage to, the contents of said box, caused by burglary, fire or any cause whatsoever, but that the entire risk of such of loss or damage is assumed by the lessee."... In the second provision, the bank assumed a duty to prevent unauthorized access: "No person other than the renter or approved deputy named in the books of Bank ... shall have access to the safe."... The plaintiff alleged that the bank breached this agreement when it allowed an authorized person, his ex-wife, to access his safety deposit box. She removed over $250,000 worth of bearer bonds and other valuables. The trial judge dismissed the complaint on the ground that the exculpatory clause barred plaintiff's action....

The Florida District Court of Appeal reversed, holding that, "whatever the possible effect of the exculpatory clause in other situations ... it is clear that it cannot be employed, as it was below, to negate the specific contractual undertaking to restrict access to the vault."... The *Sniffen* court further elaborated on how this principle applies to safety deposit box rental agreements:

> It should be emphasized that ... an acceptance of the bank's position in this case would render the agreement between the parties entirely nugatory. If a safety deposit customer cannot enforce the bank's undertaking to preclude unauthorized

persons from entry to his box which is the very heart of the relationship and the only real reason that such a facility is used at all, ... it is obvious that he will have received nothing whatever in return for his rental fee. The authorities are unanimous in indicating that no such drastic effect may properly be attributed to contractual provisions such as those involved here....

We agree with the *Sniffen* court's analysis. In this contract, in exchange for plaintiff's rental fee, defendant assumed the obligation to exercise ordinary care to prevent unauthorized access to the safety deposit box. Having assumed this duty, defendant cannot exculpate itself from liability for a breach of that duty. Accepting defendant's argument would mean that, if defendant routinely breached these safety deposit box rental agreements by handing the keys to anyone who came in off the street and asked for them, it would have no liability to its customers except to give them their rental fee back. It is safe to assume that, if defendant explained the agreement this way in the contract, defendant would not have many safety deposit box customers.

Defendant's response to *Sniffen* is two-fold. First, defendant argues that it is distinguishable because it involved an exculpatory clause that conflicted with another provision of the contract, while the contract in the case before us contains no such conflict. This is clearly incorrect. The contract here contains the same conflict as the contract in *Sniffen:* a general exculpatory clause absolving the bank for all liability from any loss whatsoever, and an express obligation to prevent unauthorized opening of the box.... Second, defendant argues that *Sniffen* was distinguished in Federal Deposit Insurance Corp.... Defendant is correct, but that does not help defendant....

We hold that the exculpatory provision is not applicable to an allegation that defendant breached its duty to exercise ordinary care to prevent unauthorized access to the box....

We affirm the appellate court's judgment reversing the summary judgment for defendant, entering summary judgment for plaintiffs, and remanding for proof of damages.

Affirmed.

Case Questions

1. What was the bank attempting to do in its contract with its safety box customers?
2. Why did the Illinois Supreme Court conclude that this exculpatory clause was unenforceable?

AUTHOR'S NOTE

Students may be interested in reading the case of *Gimple v. Host Enterprises, Inc.,* in the retired cases section of the textbook's website. The *Gimple* case debuted in this textbook in the fourth edition in 1989. It is a case in which an exculpatory clause contained in a bicycle rental agreement was enforced, despite the fact that the rental bike had bad brakes.

CHAPTER SUMMARY

Chapter VI began with a discussion of the "case-or-controversy" requirement. This requirement, which is based in the federal constitution, prevents federal courts from providing mere advisory opinions to the legislative and executive branches. The chapter then discussed the umbrella concept known as "justiciability." The court will only decide cases that are well suited to be decided by means of the judicial process. Various judicial doctrines have been developed that are used to exclude disputes that do not lend themselves to judicial determination. Examples included the "standing," "ripeness," "mootness," "political-question," and "act-of-state" judicial doctrines. Readers also learned about statutes of limitations, which are legislatively created time limits within which plaintiffs must exercise their right to sue. A plaintiff who fails to bring an action within the specified period of time forfeits the right to sue, though, in some circumstances, that time period can be extended. The chapter also included a discussion of the equitable doctrine of laches. If a plaintiff is suing for an equi-

table remedy and the defendant sustains legal injury due to the plaintiff's unreasonable delay in bringing the action, the court may refuse to award the plaintiff any equitable relief because of the doctrine of laches. Next, the chapter addressed the judicial doctrine traditionally known as res judicata and, more recently, as claim preclusion. This doctrine prevents the same parties from relitigating the same claims in a second lawsuit. If a judgment has been awarded, generally any claims that were decided or could and should have been litigated in that first action are included in the judgment. Last, the chapter examined some of the more common types of legal immunities from tort liability. Most legal immunities exist to protect some important public interest. This principle is explained in the discussions of sovereign immunity, immunities granted to governmental officials, and intrafamily immunities. The chapter concluded with a discussion of immunities that are created by contract, and when courts will and will not enforce exculpatory clauses.

CHAPTER QUESTIONS

1. The city of Jacksonville, Florida, sought to increase the percentage of municipal contracts awarded to minority business enterprises (MBEs) and enacted an ordinance containing a 10 percent set-aside. Members of the Association of General Contractors brought suit against the city because they thought the set-aside program impermissibly favored one race over another. Such a race-based classification

system in the awarding of municipal construction contracts, they contended, violated the Equal Protection Clause of the Fourteenth Amendment. The trial court granted summary judgment in favor of the contractors' association; however, the U.S. Court of Appeals for the Eleventh Circuit vacated the judgment on the grounds that the contractors lacked standing to sue. The appeals court concluded that the contractors' association had "not demonstrated that, but for the program, any member would have bid successfully for any of the contracts." After the U.S. Supreme Court granted the contractors' association's petition for a writ of certiorari, the city repealed its MBE ordinance and enacted a second ordinance that was very similar in that it provided for contractual set-asides favoring women and black contractors. Is this case moot, inasmuch as the ordinance complained about has been repealed?

Association of General Contractors v. City of Jacksonville, 508 U.S. 656 (1993)

2. Assume the same facts as in question 1. Assume further that the city argued in the Supreme Court that the contractors' association lacked standing in that no member of the association alleged that he or she would have been awarded a city contract but for the set-aside ordinance. Did the contractors' association have standing to sue? Why? Why not?

Association of General Contractors v. City of Jacksonville, 508 U.S. 656 (1993)

3. Paula Piper was a public defender assigned to defend William Aramy. Prior to William's trial, Paula told the judges she thought William was crazy. Bail was set and William was placed in a mental institution. Paula failed to tell William how he could arrange bail. Claiming that his prolonged stay in the mental institution was caused by Paula's negligence, William sued Paula for malpractice. Paula claims that her position as an officer of the court gives her the defense of judicial immunity. Who wins? Why?

4. On February 1, 1999, John Smith bought a car for $10,000. He paid $1,000 down and signed a promissory note for $9,000, due in three years. Assume that the note was never paid and that the applicable statute of limitations is five years. The plaintiff could wait until what date to bring a civil suit for nonpayment of the note?

5. The Endangered Species Act of 1973 authorizes citizens to bring suits against the government to protect threatened wildlife and plant life. When the U.S. Fish and Wildlife Service decided to restrict the amount of water released from an irrigation project along the Oregon–Washington border, Oregon ranchers brought suit against the federal government. The ranchers maintained that their businesses would be severely damaged as a result of this decision. They also alleged that the government had not used the "best scientific and commercial data available," as required by the federal statute. The U.S. Court of Appeals for the Ninth Circuit ruled that the ranchers did not have standing because the statute only provided for citizen suits brought on behalf of endangered species. Should citizens who believe that the government has been overly pro-environment and insufficiently sensitive to the economic consequences of environmental protection have standing to sue the government?

Bennett v. Spear, 520 U.S. 154 (1997)

6. In 1942, Congress amended the Nationality Act of 1940 to make it easier for noncitizens who had fought in World War II and who had been honorably discharged from the U.S. Armed Services to become American citizens. The 1942 Act specifically provided that the noncitizen servicemen could complete naturalization before a designated immigration and naturalization officer and while outside the borders of the United States. This procedure was in lieu of requiring the applicant to come to the United States and appear before a U.S. District Court judge. In August 1945, the U.S. vice consul in Manila was designated by the Immigration and Naturalization Service (INS) to perform this responsibility. The government of the Philippines, concerned that too many of its nationals would take advantage of this law, soon prevailed on the United States to restrict this opportunity. The U.S. attorney general responded by revoking the vice consul's authority to process citizenship applications from October 1945 until October 1946.

Congress also proceeded to limit the window of opportunity to those who filed petitions by December 1946. Filipino war veterans brought suit, contending that they were entitled to become citizens under the amended Nationality Act. The INS responded by asserting that the plaintiffs' claims were nonjusticiable because they were political questions. Should the political-question doctrine apply in cases such as this?

Pangilinan v. Immigration and Naturalization Service, 796 F.2d 1091, U.S. Court of Appeals (9th Circuit 1986)

7. Judge Stump, a judge of a circuit court in Indiana (a court of general jurisdiction), approved a mother's petition to have her "somewhat retarded" 15-year-old daughter sterilized. The judge approved the mother's petition the same day, without a hearing and without notice to the daughter or appointment of a guardian ad litem. The operation was performed on Linda Sparkman, but she was told that she was having her appendix removed. A few years later, after Sparkman married and discovered that she had been sterilized, she and her husband brought suit against Judge Stump. Should Judge Stump be immune under the circumstances?

Stump v. Sparkman, 435 U.S. 349 (1978)

NOTES

1. However, on the same day, June 26, 2013, that the U.S. Supreme Court issued its ruling in Hollingsworth, the Court also ruled on another case, U.S. v. Windsor. In Windsor the Court held that a provision in a1996 federal statute known as the Defense of Marriage Act (DOMA) was unconstitutional where it denied federal benefits to same-sex married couples that were made available to heterosexual married couples. By finding that this provision of DOMA was unconstitutional, the U.S. Supreme Court upheld the concept that defining marriage remained a matter of states' rights. It was not a subject to be determined by federal statute. Hence if a state permitted same-sex marriage, the federal government had to recognize a same-sex married couple as being entitled to the same benefits as a heterosexual married couple. See the discussion of this case in Chapter IX.

2. The U.S. Ninth Circuit Court covers the states of California, Oregon, Washington, Montana, Idaho, Nevada, Arizona, Alaska, and Hawaii, plus the territories of Guam and the Northern Mariana Islands. All of these states and territories except the State of Washington have imposed some degree of statutory or constitutional ban on same-sex marriage.

3. *Hewlett v. George,* 9 So. 885 (1891).

4. *Lloyd Dunlap v. Dunlap*, 150 A. 905 (1930).

5. R. N. Heath, "The Parental Immunity Doctrine: Is Insurer Bad Faith an Exception or Should the Doctrine Be Abolished," 83 *The Florida Bar Journal* 9, 58 (October 2009).

6. Oliver Wendell Holmes and Harold Joseph Laski, *Collected Legal Papers* (New York: Harcourt Brace and Howe, 1920), pp. 65–69.

VII

Judicial Remedies

CHAPTER OBJECTIVES

1. *Explain the important differences between equitable and common law relief.*
2. *Describe the function of each remedy.*
3. *Understand what an equitable maxim is and how it is used.*
4. *Identify and explain the three classes of injunctions.*
5. *Explain how compensatory, punitive, nominal, and liquidated damages differ.*

Before addressing the power of the court to award various types of relief, we should establish that courts do not have a monopoly on resolving private disputes. Many disputes within families, for example, are settled without resort to the judiciary by grandparents, parents, or an older sibling. Other peacemakers include religious leaders, coaches, teachers, and other respected persons. Arbitrators, mediators, and private courts also offer disputants alternative procedures for resolving disagreements without involving the public court systems.

Some readers would better understand remedies if they took a few minutes to review the material in Chapter I regarding the development of the English common law and equitable courts. If readers also take another look at Article III, Section 2, of the U.S. Constitution and the Seventh Amendment, they will see that notions of law and equity are specifically mentioned within the text of our Constitution. Lastly, reviewing this historical material will remind readers of the reasons for the traditional rule that a plaintiff who has an adequate legal remedy is not entitled to equitable relief.

We now turn to a discussion of judicial remedies. Once a person has established a substantive right through judicial procedures, the court will award relief. Judicial relief can assume many different forms, called remedies (see Figure 7.1). The most

© Cengage Learning

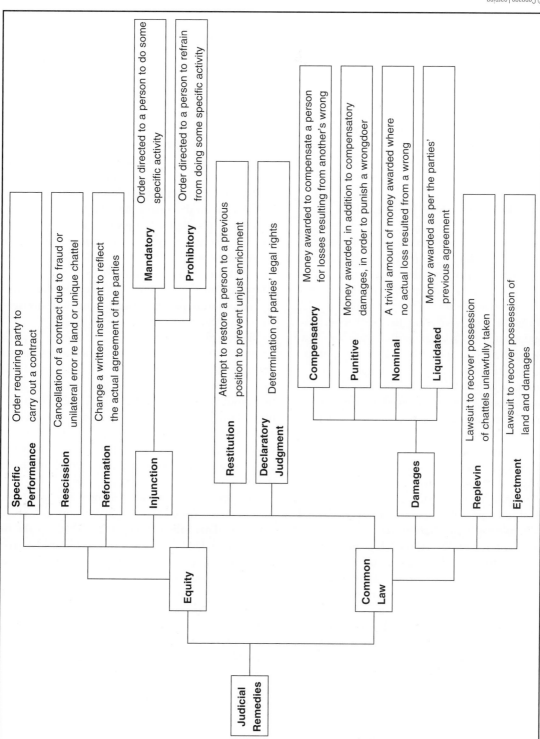

FIGURE 7.1 Judicial Remedies

common remedy is awarding money damages in the form of compensatory damages and, where permissible, punitive damages. Additional remedies include injunctive relief (requiring someone to do or refrain from doing something), restitution (restoring a person to a previous position to prevent unjust enrichment), declaratory judgment (a judicial determination of the parties' rights), and reformation (judicially rewriting a written instrument to reflect the real agreement of the parties).

COMMON LAW REMEDIES

Common law remedies generally are limited to the court's determination of some legal right and the award of money damages. There are some exceptions. For example, when parties want the court's opinion concerning their legal rights but are not seeking damages or injunctive relief, they seek a declaratory judgment. In addition, the common law remedies of ejectment and replevin both seek restitution. An **ejectment** occurs when a trespasser secures full possession of the land and the owner brings an action to regain possession, as well as damages for the unlawful retention of possession. Usually this process involves a title dispute between plaintiff and defendant, and the ejectment action settles this dispute. **Replevin** is an action used to recover possession of personal property wrongfully taken. Once the action is brought, the goods are seized from the defendant after proper notice has been given and held until title has been determined.

Usually, however, a common law court grants relief in the form of damages, a sum of money awarded as compensation for an injury sustained as the consequence of either a tortious act or a breach of a legal obligation. Damages are classified as compensatory, punitive, nominal, and liquidated.

Compensatory Damages

Compensatory damages are awarded to compensate the plaintiff for pecuniary losses that have resulted from the defendant's tortious conduct or breach of contract. Although the permissible damage elements vary by jurisdiction, they typically include awards for loss of time or money, bodily pain and suffering, permanent disabilities or disfigurement, injury to reputation, and mental anguish. Future losses are also recoverable; however, compensation is not allowed for consequences that are remote, indirect, or uncertain (i.e., where speculative).

Damages usually are limited to those reasonably foreseeable by the defendant as a result of the breach. Assume that two plaintiffs have a contract to buy some equipment needed to open their new business, and a defendant breaches by nondelivery. If the plaintiffs sue for lost profits from the delay in opening because they have to procure alternative goods, they would probably not recover, because the defendant could not have foreseen this without knowing that the opening depended on the delivery. Also, future profits are very difficult to measure with any degree of certainty.

In awarding compensatory damages, the court's objective is to put the plaintiff in the same financial position as existed before the commission of the tort or, in a contract case, in the financial position that would have resulted had the promise been fulfilled. In the absence of circumstances giving rise to an allowance of punitive damages, the law will not put the injured party in a better position than the person would have been in had the wrong not been done.

A person who is injured must use whatever means are reasonable to avoid or minimize damages. This rule is called by most the **rule of mitigation** (and by others the **avoidable-harm doctrine**). It prevents recovery for damages that could have been foreseen and avoided by reasonable effort without undue risk, expense, or humiliation. For example, P sues to recover the loss of a crop, because D removed some rails from P's fence, and as a result, cattle escaped and destroyed the crop. Since P, knowing the rails were missing, did not repair the fence, only the cost of repairing the fence is recoverable, because the loss of the crop could have been avoided.

When the defendant's misconduct causes damages but also operates directly to confer some benefit on the plaintiff, then the plaintiff's damage claim may be diminished by the amount of the benefit conferred. This policy is called the **benefit rule.** For example, a trespasser digs on plaintiff's land, but the digging works to drain swampy areas and improves the value. The plaintiff may recover for the trespass and any damage it caused, but the defendant gets a credit for the value of the benefit conferred. However, this credit exists only for clear benefits and not for those that are remote and uncertain. Problems arise in deciding what constitutes a benefit and what standard to measure it by.

Compensatory damages may be categorized as either general or special. This distinction is very important to lawyers because general damages do not have to be specifically pleaded, whereas special damages must be listed in the pleadings. **General damages** are those that are the natural and necessary result of the wrongful act or omission, and thus can normally be expected to accompany the injury. Pain and suffering, mental anguish, and the loss of enjoyment of life are damages that occur so frequently in the tort of battery that they do not have to be specifically pleaded. **Special damages** are awarded for injuries that arise from special circumstances of the wrong. A plaintiff in a battery case, for example, would have to plead specifically such special damages as medical and hospital expenses, loss of earnings, and a diminished ability to work.

Putting a dollar value on the plaintiff's loss for the purpose of compensation often becomes a difficult task. Because the amount of damages is a factual question and decisions on factual issues do not create precedent, previous case decisions are not binding. The amount of damages is decided by a jury, unless a jury trial has been waived.

The next case involves a plaintiff who seeks to recover a variety of damages for medical malpractice. The court rules that the state's public policy prohibits her from recovering for all that she claims. The concurrence contains a discussion of the benefits rule and the rule requiring the mitigation of damages.

Macomber v. Dillman
505 A.2d 810
Supreme Judicial Court of Maine
February 27, 1986

Glassman, Justice.

In April of 1984, the plaintiffs, Roxanne and Steven Macomber, filed a complaint against the defendants, Carter F. Dillman and the Webber Hospital Association. The complaint alleged, *inter alia,* that as a proximate result of the defendants' negligent and careless failure to comply with the standard of care of medical practice in the performance of a tubal ligation on Roxanne for the purpose of permanent sterilization, Roxanne was not permanently sterilized and had conceived and given birth to a child, Maize. Although the plaintiffs did not allege in their complaint that Maize is a healthy, normal child, they did not allege otherwise, and the parties have agreed to these facts. Plaintiffs sought damages from defendants "including, but not limited to, the cost of raising and educating Maize May Macomber, the medical and other expenses of the pregnancy and childbirth, the medical and other expenses of a subsequent hysterectomy for purposes of sterilization, lost wages, loss of consortium, the medical and other expenses of the unsuccessful tubal liga-

tion, permanent physical impairment to Roxanne Macomber resulting from bearing Maize May, her sixth child, and physical and mental pain and suffering resulting [therefrom]."

Defendants filed motions for dismissal or summary judgment on the grounds that the plaintiffs by their complaint failed to state a claim for which relief could be granted and could not recover damages for the cost of rearing and educating a healthy, normal child. After hearing, the Superior Court entered its order denying the defendants' motions and adopting the analysis that should the plaintiffs prevail they would be entitled to recover "all reasonable, foreseeable, and proximately caused damages, including the expenses of child rearing." The court refused to rule on whether damages so recoverable by plaintiffs "should be offset by benefits" of parenthood.

On a joint motion of the parties, the Superior Court reported the case to this court thereby posing the following questions of law: (1) Did the Superior Court by its order properly deny the defendants' motion to dismiss the plaintiffs' complaint for failure to state a claim against the defendants for which relief can be granted? (2) Did the Superior Court by its order properly set forth the damages that the plaintiffs could recover should they prevail in their action against the defendants?

We first address the question of whether the plaintiffs have by their complaint stated a claim against the defendants. Contrary to the defendants' contention, the plaintiffs' action does not represent a new cause of action in the state of Maine. "Since the early days of the common law a cause of action in tort has been recognized to exist when the negligence of one person is the proximate cause of damage to another person."... When a plaintiff claims he has suffered a personal injury as the result of medical mistreatment, his remedy lies in a complaint for negligence.... The necessary elements of a cause of action for negligence are a duty owed, a breach of that duty proximately causing the plaintiff's injuries and resulting damages.... Applying these principles to the allegations in the plaintiffs' complaint, it is clear that the necessary elements of a cause of action in negligence have been set forth against the defendants.

We next consider whether the Superior Court correctly established the scope of recoverable damages. We are aware that the courts which have considered this type of case have not reached a consensus as to damages, if any, that may be recoverable....

We hold for reasons of public policy that a parent cannot be said to have been damaged or injured by the birth and rearing of a healthy, normal child. Accordingly, we limit the recovery of damages, where applicable, to the hospital and medical expenses incurred for the sterilization procedures and pregnancy, the pain and suffering connected with the pregnancy and the loss of earnings by the mother during that time. Our ruling today is limited to the facts of this case, involving a failed sterilization procedure resulting in the birth of a healthy, normal child.

We also must address whether the plaintiff, Steven Macomber, may recover for loss of consortium of his wife, Roxanne. For centuries courts have recognized a husband's right to recover damages for the loss of consortium when a tortious injury to his wife detrimentally affects the spousal relationship.... Because his wife's cause of action is for negligence, Steven Macomber may recover proven damages for loss of consortium.

The entry is:

The order of the Superior Court is modified to limit the scope of recoverable damages, and as so modified, affirmed. Remanded to the Superior Court for further proceedings consistent with the opinion herein.

McKusik, Nichols, and Roberts, J.J., concurring. Scolnik, Justice, concurring in part and dissenting in part.
Although I concur that a cause of action exists for medical malpractice in the performance of a tubal ligation, I am unable to agree with the Court's judicially imposed limitation on the damages that are recoverable. The Court reasons that in no circumstances can a parent be said to have been damaged by the birth and rearing of a healthy, normal child. This rationale, however, is not only plainly inconsistent with the Court's recognition of a cause of action but also totally ignores the fact that many individuals undergo sterilization for the very purpose of avoiding such a birth. Moreover, the Court's opinion is an unwarranted departure from the fundamental principle of tort law that once a breach of duty has been established, the tortfeasor is liable for all foreseeable damages that proximately result from his acts. I dissent because, in my view, the jury should be permitted to consider awarding damages for child rearing costs.

By finding that a parent is not harmed by the birth of a healthy child, the Court's opinion is logically inconsistent. In the first part of its opinion, the Court applies traditional tort principles to recognize a cause of action for negligence resulting in an unwanted conception and subsequent birth of a normal, healthy child. Although the opinion is noticeably silent as to what the required harm is to support the cause of action ... the Court has in effect concluded that the birth of a normal child is recognized as an injury that is directly attributable to the health-care provider's negligence. In the second part of its opinion, however, the Court states that based on unarticulated reasons of public policy, the birth of a normal, healthy child cannot be said to constitute an injury to the parents. As a result, the Court limits the damages that a parent can recover to the hospital and medical expenses incurred for the sterilization procedure and the pregnancy, the pain and suffering connected with the pregnancy and the loss of earnings sustained by the mother during that time. If, however, the birth of a child does not constitute an injury, no basis exists for any award of damages. Damages for "pain and suffering" and medical expenses incidental to childbirth cannot be recoverable if the birth itself is not an injury. Similarly, if the parent is to be compensated for the loss of earnings that result from the pregnancy, should she not equally be compensated for the identical loss following the birth of the child? The Court's opinion fails to reconcile these obvious inconsistencies.

Not only is the Court's opinion internally inconsistent, but its stated rationale to support an artificial limitation on the scope of recoverable damages ignores reality. To hold that a parent cannot be said to have been damaged or injured by the birth and rearing of a normal, healthy child is plainly to overlook the fact that many married couples, such as the plaintiffs, engage in contraceptive practices and undergo sterilization operations for the very purpose of avoiding the birth of [a] child. Many of these couples resort to such conception avoidance measures because, in their particular circumstances, the physical or financial hardships in raising another child are too burdensome. Far from supporting the view that the birth of a child is in all situations a benefit, the social reality is that, for many, an unplanned and unwanted child can be a clear detriment.... "[W]hen a couple has chosen not to have children, or not to have any more children, the suggestion arises that for them, at least, the birth of a child would not be a net benefit."... This is not to say that there are not many benefits associated with the raising of a child. The point is that it is unrealistic universally to proclaim that the joy and the companionship a parent receives from a healthy child always outweigh the costs and difficulties of rearing that child. As one judge explained:

> A couple privileged to be bringing home the combined income of a dual professional household may well be able to sustain and cherish an unexpected child. But I am not sure the child's smile would be the most memorable characteristic to an indigent couple, where the husband underwent a vasectomy or the wife underwent a sterilization procedure, not because they did not desire a child, but rather because they faced the stark realization that they could not afford to feed an additional person, much less clothe, educate and support a child when that couple had trouble supporting one another. The choice is not always giving up personal amenities in order to buy a gift for the baby; the choice may only be to stretch necessities beyond the breaking point to provide for a child that the couple had purposely set out to avoid having....

I know of no instance where we have strayed from the common law principle that a tortfeasor is liable for every foreseeable injury proximately caused by his negligent act and we should avoid doing so here. The Court states that public policy dictates the result it reaches without explaining the source from which it was derived or the foundation on which it rests. This is not a case where change is required in the common law, without legislative help, because of a conflict between an outdated judicially crafted policy and contemporary legal philosophy.... In fact, I am sure that the Court realizes that substantial disagreement exists among the courts as to whether a parent is harmed by the birth of an unexpected child. This fact coupled with the empirical reality that many individuals choose to forego parenthood for economic or other reasons demonstrates that the Court's unexplicated judicial declaration of public policy is unwarranted....

In my view, it is the duty of this Court to follow public policy, not to formulate it, absent a clear expression of public opinion. Moreover, it has always been the public policy of this State to provide relief to those injured by tortfeasors and to allow for compensation for damages caused by their acts. To deprive the plaintiffs in this case of the opportunity to recover compensation for all their damages contravenes this basic policy. Any limitation on the scope of recoverable damages in such cases is best left to the Legislature where the opportunity for wide ranging debate and public participation is far greater than in the Law Court....

Rather than to rely on unstated notions of public policy, the better approach to determine what damages may be recoverable is to apply traditional common-law rules. It is certainly foreseeable that a medical health professional's failure properly to perform a tubal ligation will result in the birth of an unplanned child. As a result of the tortfeasor's act, the parents, who had chosen not to have a child, find themselves unexpectedly burdened both physically and financially. They seek damages not because they do not love and desire to keep the child, but because the direct and foreseeable consequences of the health-care provider's negligence has [sic] forced burdens on them that they sought and had a right to avoid.

In assessing damages for child rearing costs, I would follow those jurisdictions that have adopted the "benefit rule" of the Restatement (Second) of Torts §920 (1979).... The benefit rule recognizes that various tangible and intangible benefits accrue to the parents of the unplanned child and therefore to prevent unjust enrichment, their benefits should be weighed by the factfinder in determining damages associated with the raising of the unexpected child. The rule provides that "[w]hen the defendant's tortious conduct has caused harm to the plaintiff or to his property and in so doing has conferred a special benefit to the interest of the plaintiff that was harmed, the value of the benefit conferred is considered in mitigation of damages, to the extent that this is equitable."... The assessment of damages, if any, should focus on the specific interests of the parents that were actually impaired by the physician's negligence. An important factor in making that determination would be the reason that sterilization was sought, whether it was economic, genetic, therapeutic or otherwise.... The advantages of this approach were succinctly stated by the Arizona Supreme Court.

> By allowing the jury to consider the future costs, both pecuniary and non-pecuniary, of rearing and educating the child, we permit it to consider all the elements of damage on which the parents may present evidence. By permitting the jury to consider the reason for the procedure and to assess and offset the pecuniary and non-pecuniary benefits which will inure to the parents by reason of their relationship to the child, we allow the jury to discount those damages, thus reducing speculation and permitting the verdict to be based upon the facts as they actually exist in each of the unforeseeable variety of situations which may come before the court. We think this by far the better rule. The blindfold on the figure of justice is a shield from partiality, not from reality....

Although the benefit rule approach requires the jury to mitigate primarily economic damages by weighing them against primarily noneconomic factors, I reject the view that such a process is "an exercise in prophecy, an undertaking not within the specialty of our factfinders."... The calculation of the benefits a parent could expect to receive from the child is no

more difficult than similar computations of damages in wrongful death actions, for extended loss of consortium or for pain and suffering....

As a final note, the parents should not be forced to mitigate their damages by resorting to abortion or to adoption. A doctrine of mitigation of damages known as the avoidable consequences rule requires only that reasonable measures be taken.... Most courts that have considered the matter have held, as a matter of law, neither course of action would be reasonable.... I agree. The tortfeasor takes the injured party as he finds him and has no right to insist that the victims of his negligence have the emotional and mental make-up of a woman who is willing to undergo an abortion or offer her child for adoption. Moreover, the parents should not be precluded from recovering damages because they select the most desirable alternative and raise the child. Accordingly, the avoidable consequences rule is not relevant to the issue of the recovery of child rearing expenses.

Damages recoverable under the cause of action recognized today by this Court should not be limited by unstated notions of public policy so as arbitrarily to limit recovery of proximately caused and foreseeable damages. I recognize that this is an extremely difficult case but I find no public policy declaring that physicians should be partially immunized from the consequences of a negligently performed sterilization operation nor declaring that the birth of a healthy child is in all circumstances a blessing to the parents. Accordingly, I see no justification for supporting a departure from the traditional rules that apply to tort damages.

I would affirm, without modification, the order of the Superior Court and permit the recovery of the potential costs of rearing the child.

Case Questions

1. Why does the court majority hold that the parents could recover damages for hospital and medical expenses, pain, and suffering connected with the unwanted pregnancy, the loss of earnings by the mother during the pregnancy, and loss of consortium, but denies a recovery for the cost of rearing and educating a healthy, normal child?
2. The dissenting justice argues that the majority opinion is inconsistent. Explain the inconsistencies.
3. After carefully reading the majority and dissenting opinions, how would you rule?

 Do you agree with the court that "a parent cannot be said to have been damaged or injured by the birth and rearing of a healthy, normal child"?

Liquidated Damages

Parties may agree, in advance, about the amount to be paid as compensation for loss in the event of a breach of contract. **Liquidated damages** are the stipulated sum contained in such an agreement. An example can be seen in the *Campbell Soup* case (page 243), where Campbell's contract with the Wentz brothers included a provision for damages of $50 per acre if the contract were breached. If the court determines that the amount stipulated in the agreement is a punishment used to prevent a breach rather than an estimate of actual damages, it will deem that sum a penalty and refuse to enforce it. Traditionally, the court upholds a liquidated damages clause only when (1) the damages in case of breach are uncertain or difficult to compute, (2) the parties have agreed in advance to liquidate the damages, and (3) the amount agreed on is reasonable and not disproportionate to the probable loss. Another form of liquidated damages results when money is deposited to guarantee against future damages. Some courts require plaintiffs to prove some actual loss before the liquidated damage clause is triggered.

Occasionally, a plaintiff who has suffered no actual damages can recover substantial liquidated damages; however, this occurs only rarely.

Introduction to *Steve James v. Rodney Fenske*

The nine employee–plaintiffs in this case claimed that their employer wrongfully denied them earned wages–overtime compensation in violation of the Fair Labor Standards Act (FLSA). After a jury trial in federal district court that lasted six days, the jury returned a verdict for the employees. According to the statute, the sum to which each plaintiff was entitled was at a minimum the amount of money that had been wrongfully withheld.

The plaintiffs then filed a motion to obtain a court order awarding them liquidated damages. This additional award was specifically provided for in the FLSA where an employer had willfully deprived the employees of their just compensation. What follows is the district court judge's decision on this motion.

Steve James v. Rodney Fenske
Civil Action No. 10-cv-02591-WJM-CBS
United States District Court, D. Colorado
September 26, 2012

ORDER GRANTING PLAINTIFFS' MOTION FOR LIQUIDATED DAMAGES AND DIRECTING CLERK TO ENTER JUDGMENT

William J. Martínez, District Judge.
... Before the Court is Plaintiffs' Motion for Liquidated Damages ("Motion").... The FLSA provides that "any employer who violates [the minimum wage or overtime provisions] shall be liable to the employee or employees affected in the amount of their unpaid minimum wages, or their unpaid overtime compensation, as the case may be, and in an additional equal amount as liquidated damages."... This additional compensation is "not a penalty exacted by the law, but rather compensation to the employee occasioned by the delay in receiving wages due caused by the employer's violation of the FLSA."... "The purpose for the award of liquidated damages is the reality that the retention of a workman's pay may well result in damages too obscure and difficult of proof for estimate other than by liquidated damages."...

To avoid paying liquidated damages, an employer may typically "show" to the satisfaction of the court that the act or omission giving rise to such action was in good faith and that he had reasonable grounds for believing that his act or omission was not a violation of the FLSA."... However, when the jury has found that the employer acted willfully, "the Seventh Amendment right to a jury trial prohibits the district court from reaching a contrary conclusion."... In this case, the jury found that Defendants' violation of the FLSA was willful.... Thus, the Court cannot find that Defendants acted in good faith or had reasonable grounds for believing that their actions did not violate the FLSA. Plaintiffs are therefore entitled to liquidated damages on the jury's verdict....

Accordingly, Plaintiffs' Motion for Liquidated Damages ... is GRANTED. The Clerk shall enter judgment in favor of each Plaintiff in the following amount:

Steve James:	$10726.88
Aaron D'Mize:	$ 9059.60
Antonio Labato:	$12320.62
Charles King:	$10665.88
Arin Hart:	$ 9378.86

George Whittington:	$2814.20
Amy Reyes:	$1501.52
Delfino Ortega:	$7540.28
Kevin Moore:	$2069.88

In addition to the compensatory damages awarded above, Plaintiffs are entitled to post-judgment interest at the statutory rate.... Any issues related to attorney's fees and costs will be dealt with post-judgment upon motion of the parties.

Case Questions

1. Why might "the retention of a workman's pay ... result in damages too obscure and difficult of proof" and necessitate the award of liquidated damages?
2. How can an employer prove that liquidated damaged should not be imposed by the court?
3. The court said that the Seventh Amendment right to a jury trial made it obligatory that liquidated damages be awarded to the plaintiff. Why? You can find the answer by reading the Seventh Amendment in this textbook's appendix.

Nominal Damages

If a defendant breaches a legal duty owed to the plaintiff and injures that person, compensatory damages may be awarded. The compensatory damages are measured by the amount of the loss. **Nominal damages** are awarded when there has been a breach of an agreement or an invasion of a right but there is no evidence of any specific harm. This occurs, for example, if a person trespasses on your land but causes no actual harm. In such a situation, the plaintiff would only be entitled to a judgment for a trivial amount, such as $1 or $50. The judge awards this token sum to vindicate the plaintiff's claim or to establish a legal right. Nominal damages also are awarded when a plaintiff proves breach of duty and harm but neglects to prove the value of the loss. They are likewise allowable when the defendant's invasion of the plaintiff's rights produces a benefit.

Courts award nominal damages because a judgment for money damages is the only way a common law court can establish the validity of the plaintiff's claim. Students should be careful not to confuse nominal charges with small compensatory damage awards, which are awarded when the actual loss was minor.

Punitive Damages

Damages also can be awarded to punish defendants for their conduct and to deter others from similar conduct. These are called **punitive damages** or **exemplary damages,** and are awarded to the plaintiff beyond the compensatory amount. They are additional damages for a civil wrong and are not imposed as a substitute for criminal punishment. Punitive damages are awarded to plaintiffs to deter defendants from repeating their conduct, and to deter others from following their example. An award of punitive damages also may include an award of attorney's fees, although this varies by jurisdiction.

Such an award is appropriate only when a defendant has engaged in aggravated, wanton, reckless, malicious, or oppressive conduct. This includes all acts done with an evil disposition or a wrong and unlawful motive, or the willful doing of an injurious act without a lawful excuse. Punitive damages generally are available only for intentional torts and for some statutory wrongs. The reason courts generally refuse to award punitive damages where defendants have acted negligently is that such persons did not intend to cause the harmful result that ensued. A person cannot be deterred from causing harms that were never intended in the first place.

Some of the actions that may result in punitive damage awards are copyright and trademark infringement, corporate crimes such as antitrust violations, insurers not paying compensation as required by their policies, employers wrongfully discharging employees, libel and slander, wrongful death, trespass, conversion, battery, securities fraud, and negligence actions that involve wanton and willful misconduct. Traditionally, punitive damages have not been awarded in contract cases, even in situations in which there has been a malicious breach. Some jurisdictions have modified this rule in some situations: if a breach of contract is accompanied by a malicious tort, exemplary damages will be awarded for the tort.

The facts in the next case, *Martin v. Glass,* have been summarized in order to enhance understanding and to conserve space.

Introduction to *Martin v. Glass*

Angeline Glass, the plaintiff, alleged that the defendant, Robert L. Martin, had intentionally trespassed at least three times on her property while logging on her neighbor's land in September of 2008. She claimed that there were 52 stumps where the unauthorized logging had occurred, and that Martin had cut her hardwood trees, some of which were very old. Glass filed suit to obtain compensatory and punitive damages. Martin denied intentionally trespassing on the land and maintained that he had only cut seven trees, which were mostly pines.

The case was tried by a judge sitting without a jury, who ruled that Martin had intentionally trespassed, and found for the plaintiff in the amount of $25,000. Martin claimed that the $25,000 award was "excessive," and the court agreed, reducing the award to $15,000.

Martin appealed again to the state intermediate court of appeals.

Robert L. Martin v. Angeline Caudell Glass
84 So. 3d 131
Court of Civil Appeals of Alabama
November 4, 2011

Pittman, Judge.

... Martin timely appealed ... and ... argues that the trial court erred in awarding Glass more than nominal damages because, he says, by neglecting to present evidence of the difference between the value of her property immediately before and immediately after the trespass, Glass failed to establish her entitlement to damages. In *Ford* [*v. Sellers* ... (1952)], our supreme court held:

> [I]n a count for damages for trespass ... the damages recoverable are for injury to the lands and not for the value of the timber.... "[T]he mere fact that it is alleged in the complaint that timber was cut, injured, and removed from the land does not constitute a claim for damages as for the value of the timber," that being "a mere description of the nature and character of the trespass to the land."

... "([T]he measure of damages for trespass when trees have been cut is the difference between the value of the land before the cutting and the value of

the land immediately after the cutting"). Glass argues that Martin has not preserved for review the issue that her failure to present evidence of the value of her property before and after the trespass means that she is not entitled to more than nominal damages because, she says, Martin did not object to her testimony regarding damages or otherwise bring the issue to the attention of the trial court.

... Martin contends that he preserved the issue by filing a post-judgment motion challenging the damages award as excessive....

We conclude that ... the trial court's damages award in this case can be upheld on the basis that, unlike the plaintiff in *Loper,* Glass sought (and the trial court apparently found that the evidence established a basis for awarding) punitive damages. "Once actual damages, even nominal damages, are established, punitive damages may be awarded if it is a proper case to do so."...

Punitive damages are ... available to a plaintiff in a trespass action, even if only nominal damages are awarded, "if the trespass is attended by rudeness, wantonness, recklessness or an insulting manner or is accompanied by circumstances of fraud and malice, oppression, aggravation, or gross negligence."...

In the present case, the trial court's amended judgment reflects that, in awarding damages, it considered Martin's "culpability." In its initial judgment, the trial court found that "[Martin's] trespass continued to occur even after warning and protest by [Glass]." That continued trespass after warning and protest warrants the award of punitive damages can be deduced from the fact that a "[f]ormer [criminal statute, Ala. Code 1975,] §13-2-100, [pertaining to] trespass after warning, [penalized] '(a)ny person who, *without legal cause or good excuse*, enter[ed] ... on the premises of another, after having been warned within six months preceding not to do so.' "... Our caselaw has recognized that the wantonness necessary for the imposition of punitive damages as to a civil trespass claim "is shown by mere 'knowledge on the part of the defendant[] of the invasion of the plaintiffs rights.' "...

In *Calvert & Marsh Coal Co. v. Pass*, the court noted "that the word 'wanton' when used in an action for trespass is not governed by the same rules as when used in a negligence action."... In a trespass action, the court held, wantonness "means simply an invasion of the plaintiffs' premises with knowledge of the violation of plaintiffs' rights."...

Because the evidence supports a conclusion that Martin's trespass was wanton, the trial court was authorized to award punitive damages in addition to nominal damages.... This court may not reverse a trial court's damages award unless it is "palpably wrong, ... without supporting evidence, or ... manifestly unjust."... "[U]nless the amount awarded is so excessive as to indicate prejudice or passion, such an award will not be reversed."... The record indicates no reason to conclude that the damages award was the result of prejudice or passion.

The judgment of the Shelby Circuit Court is affirmed.

AFFIRMED.

Thomas, J., concurs. Thompson, P.J., and Bryan and Moore, JJ., concur in the result, without writings....

Case Questions

1. Why do courts generally refuse to award punitive damages where the defendant has been negligent?
2. According to the court, what must an Alabama plaintiff in a trespass prove in order to establish the right to be awarded punitive damages in that state?

EQUITABLE REMEDIES

An **equitable remedy** would have been awarded by a court of equity before the merger of the equity and common law courts. Today, most courts in the United States are empowered to grant both equitable and legal relief as required to achieve justice. However, the availability of equitable remedies is a matter for judges, and not juries. Traditionally, courts only grant equitable remedies when the common law remedies are inadequate.

Injunctions

An injunction is an equitable remedy in the form of a judicial order directing the defendant to act or refrain from acting in a specified way. An order compelling one to do an act is called a **mandatory injunction**, whereas one prohibiting an act is called a **prohibitory injunction.** An injunction may be enforced by the contempt power of a court, and a defendant may be fined, sent to jail, or deprived of the right to litigate issues if he or she disobeys an injunction. This order must be obeyed until it is reversed, even if it is issued erroneously or the court lacks jurisdiction.

Injunctions may be divided into three classes: (1) permanent, (2) preliminary or interlocutory, and (3) temporary restraining orders. A permanent injunction is a decree issued after a full opportunity to present evidence. It is permanent only in the sense that it is supposed to be a final solution to a dispute. It may still be modified or dissolved later. A preliminary or interlocutory injunction is granted as an emergency measure before a full hearing is held. There must be notice to the defendant and a hearing, usually informal. This remedy is generally limited to situations in which there is a serious need to preserve the status quo until the parties' rights have finally been decided. Thus a preliminary injunction continues only until a further order of the court is issued.

The **temporary restraining order,** known as a **TRO,** is an **ex parte-injunction.** This means that it is granted without notice to the defendant. The trial judge has heard only the plaintiff's side of the case. Because of the potential for abuse, certain procedures protect a defendant. A TRO may not be granted unless irreparable harm would result and there is no time for notice and a hearing. There must be clear evidence on the merits of the case. The court should look at any damage to the defendant that would be noncompensable in money if the plaintiff's relief is later shown to be improper. This consideration must be balanced with the plaintiff's harm if the TRO is not granted. Factors weigh more heavily against the plaintiff, since there is no notice to defendant.

Certain classes of cases are not considered proper subject matter for injunctions. In general, an injunction is not issued to stop a criminal prosecution or to prevent crimes. However, this policy has been modified in recent years by regulatory statutes and civil rights statutes. Injunctions are usually not proper in defamation cases because they would intrude on the defendant's constitutional right of free speech and would be considered prior restraint.

INTERNET TIP

The case of *Harper v. Poway Unified School District,* which follows, was decided by a panel of three judges assigned to the U.S. Court of Appeals for the Ninth Circuit. Two judges concluded that the federal district court's decision not to enjoin the school district should be affirmed. The third judge, Judge Kozinski, disagreed and wrote a lengthy, thought-provoking dissenting opinion. Judge Kozinski was greatly concerned about the adequacy of the proof and the potential implications of the majority's decision for the legitimate exercise of First Amendment freedoms by high school students.

Students who read both opinions will notice how judges on both sides of the debate engaged in a balancing of the interests and the harm, which is a hallmark of equity courts. An edited version of Judge Kozinski's dissent can be read on the textbook's website.

Introduction to *Harper v. Poway Unified School District*

In 2004 Tyler Chase Harper was a high school sophomore attending a school that had experienced conflict over the issue of sexual orientation. In the preceding school year, 2003, the administration of the school, in conjunction with students who had formed a group called the Gay-Straight Alliance, organized what was called a "Day of Silence," purportedly for the purpose of promoting tolerance between gay and straight students. This first "Day of Silence" was followed shortly thereafter by a "Straight-Pride Day," which was loosely sponsored by an opposing group of students. There were incidents involving name-calling; the wearing of special T-shirts, some of which displayed disparaging statements; and at least one physical confrontation in which the principal had to separate students.

When the Gay-Straight Alliance sought to sponsor a second "Day of Silence" in 2004, the school administration insisted that some planning be undertaken to prevent a repetition of the altercations and confrontations that had occurred in 2003.

On April 21, 2004, the date for the 2004 "Day of Silence," Chase wore a T-shirt to school that contained statements on both the front and the back that disparaged homosexuality. The following day he wore the same shirt to school, but this time the message on the shirt's front was slightly altered. One of Chase's teachers noticed the shirt, unsuccessfully requested that Chase remove it, and referred Chase to the principal's office for violating the dress code. The vice principal talked to Chase and explained the purported purpose of the "Day of Silence," and said that he could return to class only if he changed his shirt. A similar scenario followed when Chase met with the school principal. When Chase asked to be suspended, the principal declined. Chase spent the remainder of the school day in the office doing homework and then went home. Chase was not sanctioned in any way for not having attended classes on that day.

Forty-two days later, Chase filed suit in federal court claiming that the school had violated his First Amendment rights to freedom of speech and religion, as well as rights protected by the Equal Protection and Due Process Clauses under the federal Constitution and the California Civil Code. The

school asked the trial court to dismiss the suit, and Chase asked the court for a preliminary injunction prohibiting the school from violating his constitutionally protected rights.

The District Court dismissed Chase's due process, equal protection, and civil code claims, and dismissed his damage claim against the school district because of the district's qualified immunity. The court refused to dismiss the First Amendment claims. The judge also denied Chase's preliminary injunction request, which decision he appealed to the U.S. Court of Appeals for the Ninth Circuit.

Tyler Chase Harper v. Poway Unified School District
445 F.3d 1166
U.S. Court of Appeals for the Ninth Circuit
April 20, 2006, as amended May 31, 2006

Reinhardt, Circuit Judge.
May a public high school prohibit students from wearing T-shirts with messages that condemn and denigrate other students on the basis of their sexual orientation? Appellant ... [who] was ordered not to wear [such] a T-shirt to school ... appeals the district court's order denying his motion for a preliminary injunction....

IV. Standard and Scope of Review
For a district court to grant a preliminary injunction, the moving party must demonstrate either "(1) a combination of probable success on the merits and the possibility of irreparable harm; or (2) that serious questions are raised and the balance of hardships tips in its favor."... "Each of these two formulations requires an examination of both the potential merits of the asserted claims and the harm or hardships faced by the parties."... "These two alternatives represent extremes of a single continuum, rather than two separate tests...." Accordingly, "the greater the relative hardship to the moving party, the less probability of success must be shown."...

We review a district court's grant or denial of a preliminary injunction for abuse of discretion.... Where, as here, the appellant does not dispute the district court's factual findings, we are required to determine "whether the court employed the appropriate legal standards governing the issuance of a preliminary injunction and whether the district court correctly apprehended the law with respect to the underlying issues in the case."...

V. Analysis

1. Freedom of Speech Claim
The district court concluded that Harper failed to demonstrate a likelihood of success on the merits of his claim that the School violated his First Amendment right to free speech because, under *Tinker v. Des Moines Indep. Cmty. Sch. Dist.,* the evidence in the record was sufficient to permit the school officials to "reasonably ... forecast substantial disruption of or material interference with school activities."...

a. Student speech
Under *Tinker* Public schools are places where impressionable young persons spend much of their time while growing up. They do so in order to receive what society hopes will be a fair and full education—an education without which they will almost certainly fail in later life, likely sooner rather than later.... The public school, with its free education, is the key to our democracy.... Almost all young Americans attend public schools....

The courts have construed the First Amendment as applied to public schools in a manner that attempts to strike a balance between the free speech rights of students and the special need to maintain a safe, secure and effective learning environment.... Although public school students do not "shed their constitutional rights to freedom of speech or expression at the schoolhouse gate," ... the Supreme Court has declared that "the First Amendment rights of students in public schools are not automatically coextensive with the rights of adults in other settings, and must be applied in light of the special characteristics of the school environment."... Thus, while Harper's shirt embodies the very sort of political speech that would be afforded First Amendment protection outside of the public school setting, his rights in the case before us must be determined "in light of [those] special characteristics."...

This court has identified "three distinct areas of student speech," each of which is governed by different Supreme Court precedent: (1) vulgar, lewd, obscene, and plainly offensive speech ... (2) school-sponsored speech ... and (3) all other speech....

In *Tinker,* the Supreme Court confirmed a student's right to free speech in public schools.... In balancing that right against the state interest in maintaining an ordered and effective public education system, however, the Court declared that a student's speech rights could be curtailed under two circumstances. First, a school may regulate student speech that would "impinge upon the rights of other students."... Second, a school may prohibit student speech that would result in "substantial disruption of or material interference with school activities."...

In *Tinker,* the Supreme Court held that public schools may restrict student speech which "intrudes upon ... the rights of other students" or "collides with the rights of other students to be secure and to be let alone." ... Harper argues that *Tinker's* reference to the "rights of other students" should be construed narrowly to involve only circumstances in which a student's right to be free from direct physical confrontation is infringed.... Harper contends that ... a student must be physically accosted in order to have his rights infringed.

... The law does not support Harper's argument. This court has explained that vulgar, lewd, obscene, indecent, and plainly offensive speech "by definition ..., may well 'impinge upon the rights of other students,'" even if the speaker does not directly accost individual students with his remarks.... So too may other speech capable of causing psychological injury....

We conclude that Harper's wearing of his T-shirt "collides with the rights of other students" in the most fundamental way.... Public school students who may be injured by verbal assaults on the basis of a core identifying characteristic such as race, religion, or sexual orientation have a right to be free from such attacks while on school campuses. As *Tinker* clearly states, students have the right to "be secure and to be let alone."... Being secure involves not only freedom from physical assaults but from psychological attacks that cause young people to question their self-worth and their rightful place in society.... The "right to be let alone" has been recognized by the Supreme Court,

of course, as " 'the most comprehensive of rights and the right most valued by civilized men.' " ... Although name-calling is ordinarily protected outside the school context, "students cannot hide behind the First Amendment to protect their 'right' to abuse and intimidate other students at school."...

Speech that attacks high school students who are members of minority groups that have historically been oppressed, subjected to verbal and physical abuse, and made to feel inferior, serves to injure and intimidate them, as well as to damage their sense of security and interfere with their opportunity to learn.... The demeaning of young gay and lesbian students in a school environment is detrimental not only to their psychological health and well-being, but also to their educational development. Indeed, studies demonstrate that "academic underachievement, truancy, and dropout are prevalent among homosexual youth and are the probable consequences of violence and verbal and physical abuse at school." ... [I]t is well established that attacks on students on the basis of their sexual orientation are harmful not only to the students' health and welfare, but also to their educational performance and their ultimate potential for success in life.

Those who administer our public educational institutions need not tolerate verbal assaults that may destroy the self-esteem of our most vulnerable teenagers and interfere with their educational development.... To the contrary, the School had a valid and lawful basis for restricting Harper's wearing of his T-shirt on the ground that his conduct was injurious to gay and lesbian students and interfered with their right to learn....

We consider here only whether schools may prohibit the wearing of T-shirts on high school campuses and in high school classes that flaunt demeaning slogans, phrases or aphorisms relating to a core characteristic of particularly vulnerable students and that may cause them significant injury. We do not believe that the schools are forbidden to regulate such conduct....

In his declaration in the district court, the school principal justified his actions on the basis that "any shirt which is worn on campus which speaks in a derogatory manner towards an individual or group of individuals is not healthy for young people...." If, by this, the principal meant that all such shirts may be banned under *Tinker,* we do not agree. T-shirts proclaiming "Young Republicans Suck" or "Young Democrats Suck," for example, may not be very civil but they would certainly not be sufficiently damaging to the individual or the educational process to warrant a limitation on the wearer's First Amendment rights.

Similarly, T-shirts that denigrate the President, his administration, or his policies, or otherwise invite political disagreement or debate, including debates over the war in Iraq, would not fall within the "rights of others" *Tinker* prong....

Although we hold that the School's restriction of Harper's right to carry messages on his T-shirt was permissible under *Tinker,* we reaffirm the importance of preserving student speech about controversial issues generally and protecting the bedrock principle that students "may not be confined to the expression of those sentiments that are officially approved." ... Limitations on student speech must be narrow, and applied with sensitivity and for reasons that are consistent with the fundamental First Amendment mandate. Accordingly, we limit our holding to instances of derogatory and injurious remarks directed at students' minority status such as race, religion, and sexual orientation.... Moreover, our decision is based not only on the type and degree of injury the speech involved causes to impressionable young people, but on the locale in which it takes place.... Thus, it is limited to conduct that occurs in public high schools (and in elementary schools). As young students acquire more strength and maturity, and specifically as they reach college age, they become adequately equipped emotionally and intellectually to deal with the type of verbal assaults that may be prohibited during their earlier years. Accordingly, we do not condone the use in public colleges or other public institutions of higher learning of restrictions similar to those permitted here.

Finally, we emphasize that the School's actions here were no more than necessary to prevent the intrusion on the rights of other students. Aside from prohibiting the wearing of the shirt, the School did not take the additional step of punishing the speaker: Harper was not suspended from school nor was the incident made a part of his disciplinary record.

Under the circumstances present here, we conclude that ... the district court did not abuse its discretion in finding that Harper failed to demonstrate a likelihood of success on the merits of his free speech claim....

b. Viewpoint discrimination
In reaching our decision that Harper may lawfully be prohibited from wearing his T-shirt, we reject his argument that the School's action constituted impermissible viewpoint discrimination. The government is generally prohibited from regulating speech "when the specific motivating ideology or the opinion or perspective of the speaker is the rationale for the restriction."... However, as the district court correctly pointed out, speech in the public schools is not always governed by the same rules that apply in other circumstances.... Indeed, the Court in *Tinker* held that a school may prohibit student speech, even if the consequence is viewpoint discrimination, if the speech violates the rights of other students or is materially disruptive....

The dissent claims that although the School may have been justified in banning discussion of the subject of sexual orientation altogether, it cannot "gag only those who oppose the Day of Silence."... As we have explained, however, although *Tinker* does not allow schools to restrict the non-invasive, non-disruptive expression of political viewpoints, it does permit school authorities to restrict "one particular opinion" if the expression would "impinge upon the rights of other students" or substantially disrupt school activities.... Accordingly, a school may permit students to discuss a particular subject without being required to allow them to launch injurious verbal assaults that intrude upon the rights of other students. "A school need not tolerate student speech that is inconsistent with its basic educational mission, even though the government could not censor similar speech outside the school."... Part of a school's "basic educational mission" is the inculcation of "fundamental values of habits and manners of civility essential to a democratic society."... For this reason, public schools may permit, and even encourage, discussions of tolerance, equality and democracy without being required to provide equal time for student or other speech espousing intolerance, bigotry or hatred. As we have explained ... because a school sponsors a "Day of Religious Tolerance," it need not permit its students to wear T-shirts reading, "Jews Are Christ-Killers" or "All Muslims Are Evil Doers."... In sum, a school has the right to teach civic responsibility and tolerance as part of its basic educational mission; it need not as a quid pro quo permit hateful and injurious speech that runs counter to that mission....

2. Free Exercise of Religion Claim
Harper ... asserts that his wearing of the T-shirt was "motivated by sincerely held religious beliefs" regarding homosexuality ... and that the School "punished" him for expressing them, or otherwise burdened the exercise of those views. Additionally, Harper argues that the School "attempted to change" his religious views and that this effort violated both the Free Exercise Clause and the Establishment Clause.

The Free Exercise Clause of the First Amendment provides that Congress shall make no law "prohibiting the free exercise" of religion.... The Clause prohibits the government from "compelling affirmation of religious belief, punishing the expression of religious doctrines it believes to be false, imposing special disabilities on the basis of religious views or religious status, or lending its power to one or the other side in controversies over religious authority or dogma."...

We seriously doubt that there is "a fair probability or a likelihood" that Harper's claim that a companion right—free speech—has been violated will succeed on the merits.... The record simply does not demonstrate that the School's restriction regarding Harper's T-shirt imposed a substantial burden upon the free exercise of Harper's religious beliefs. There is no evidence that the School "compelled affirmation of a repugnant belief," "penalized or discriminated against [Harper] because [he] holds religious views abhorrent to the authorities," or "conditioned the availability of benefits upon [Harper's] willingness to violate a cardinal principle of [his] religious faith." ... Nor did the School "lend its power to one or the other side in controversies over religious authority or dogma," or "punish the expression of religious doctrines it believes to be false."...

Schools may prohibit students and others from disrupting the educational process or causing physical or psychological injury to young people entrusted to their care, whatever the motivations or beliefs of those engaged in such conduct. Indeed, the state's interest in doing so is compelling....

Accordingly, we affirm the district court's decision that Harper was not entitled to a preliminary injunction on the basis of his free exercise claim.

3. Establishment Clause Claim

Finally, we consider the district court's conclusion that Harper did not demonstrate a likelihood of success on the merits of his claim that the School violated the Establishment Clause by attempting to "coerce" him into changing his religious beliefs that "homosexuality is harmful to both those who practice it and the community at large."...

Government conduct does not violate the Establishment Clause when (1) it has a secular purpose, (2) its principal and primary effect neither advances nor inhibits religion, and (3) it does not foster excessive government entanglement in religion.... It is ... clear from the record that the primary effect of the School's banning of the T-shirt was not to advance or inhibit religion but to protect and preserve the educational environment and the rights of other members of the student body....

VI. Conclusion

We hold that the district court did not abuse its discretion in denying the preliminary injunction. Harper failed to demonstrate that he will likely prevail on the merits of his free speech, free exercise of religion, or establishment of religion claims. In fact, such future success on Harper's part is highly unlikely, given the legal principles discussed in this opinion. The Free Speech Clause permits public schools to restrict student speech that intrudes upon the rights of other students. Injurious speech that may be so limited is not immune from regulation simply because it reflects the speaker's religious views. Accordingly, we affirm the district court's denial of Harper's motion for a preliminary injunction.

Affirmed; Remanded for further proceedings consistent with this opinion.

Case Questions

1. How did the court of appeals go about determining whether the injunction should have been granted by the district court judge?
2. Why did the Ninth Circuit panel affirm the trial court?
3. If you were writing an opinion in this case, would you agree with the panel majority?

Reformation and Rescission

The equitable remedy of **reformation** is granted when a written agreement fails to express accurately the parties' agreement because of mistake, fraud, or the drafter's ambiguous language. Its purpose is to rectify or reform a written instrument in order that it may express the real agreement or intention of the parties.

The equitable remedy of **rescission** is granted when one of the parties consents to a contract because of duress, undue influence, fraud, or innocent misrepresentation, or when either or both of the parties made a mistake concerning the contract. Rescission means the court cancels the agreement. If a court orders rescission, each party normally has to return any property or money received from the other party in performance of the agreement (**restitution**). This topic, with an illustrative case (*Carter v. Matthews*), is addressed in Chapter X.

The following case involves a contractor who was the successful bidder on a public construction contract. The contractor made a unilateral error in computing his bid and subsequently brought suit seeking the equitable remedy of reformation. The appellate court majority ruled that the plaintiff was not entitled to reformation. The dissenting judge disagreed on the basis of the defendant's inequitable conduct. The majority opinion also discusses the equitable remedy of rescission and explains why the plaintiff has waived any claim to that remedy.

Department of Transportation v. Ronlee, Inc.
518 So. 2d 1326
District Court of Appeal of Florida, Third District
December 22, 1987

Per Curiam.

The threshold question presented is whether the successful bidder for a government road construction contract is entitled to reformation of the contract to increase the price by $317,463 based on a unilateral mistake, after the competing bids are all opened, where the new contract price would still be lower than the second lowest bid.

The Department of Transportation (DOT) solicited bids pursuant to section 337.11, Florida Statutes (1985), for the construction of an interchange at the intersection of State Road 826 and Interstate 75 in Hialeah. On December 7, 1983, DOT declared Ronlee, Inc. the apparent low bidder with a bid of $15,799,197.90. The second lowest bid exceeded Ronlee's bid by $610,148.

On February 13, 1984, DOT entered into a contract with Ronlee to construct the project based on the bid, and on March 7, 1984, gave Ronlee notice to proceed with the project. Five days later, Ronlee advised DOT that the bid contained a "stupid mistake" in the amount of $317,463. The letter alleged an error with respect to the unit price for concrete culverts which occurred when an employee of Ronlee erroneously transcribed a phone quote of $525 for each culvert as $5.25 each. By letter dated March 21, 1984, DOT informed Ronlee that it was aware of the apparently unbalanced unit price for the concrete culverts, but that it was unable, as a matter of state policy, to permit an increase in the contract price.

Nevertheless, on March 22, 1984, having made no effort to withdraw the bid, Ronlee began construction of the project. Twenty-one months later, with the project seventy-five percent completed, Ronlee filed suit against DOT seeking reformation of the contract. Both sides moved for a summary judgment, agreeing that the material facts were not in dispute. Ronlee's motion for summary judgment was granted, the trial court holding that DOT's silence about Ronlee's apparent error in price calculations constituted inequi-

table conduct and that reformation of the contract would not undermine the competitive bidding process. In addition to the $317,463, the court awarded Ronlee $60,000 in prejudgment interest and costs. We reverse.

Where a contractor makes a unilateral error in formulating his bid for a public contract, the remedy is rescission of the contract.... Florida courts have permitted a contractor to *withdraw* a bid on a public contract, subject to certain equitable conditions. In *State Board of Control v. Clutter Construction Corp.* ... a contractor was permitted to withdraw a bid on a showing of the following equitable factors: (1) the bidder acted in good faith in submitting the bid; (2) in preparing the bid there was an error of such magnitude that enforcement of the bid would work severe hardship upon the bidder; (3) the error was not a result of gross negligence or willful inattention; (4) the error was discovered and communicated to the public body, *along with a request for permission to withdraw the bid,* before acceptance.

No reported Florida decision has permitted reformation by belated request of a bid contract for a public project in order to make it profitable to the contractor. *Graham v. Clyde* ... is the only case presented by the parties where reformation was even sought as relief for a mistaken bid. There a building contractor was low bidder on a proposal to construct a public school building and was awarded the contract. The following day he notified public officials that he had made a mistake of $5,000 in computing items in his bid and asked to be relieved of his obligation to perform according to the contract terms. He offered to perform the contract for $5,000 more, which was still less than the next low bidder. The circuit court did not grant a reformation but did rescind the contract and enjoined the school board from attempting to enforce it.

The Florida Supreme Court, citing a number of cases from other jurisdictions, reversed, holding that unilateral errors are not generally relieved and that there was no equitable basis for relief. In an opinion by Justice Terrell the court stated the reason for the firm rule:

> If errors of this nature can be relieved in equity, our system of competitive bidding on such contracts would in effect be placed in jeopardy and there would be no stability whatever to it. It would encourage careless, slipshod bidding in some cases and would afford a pretext for the dishonest bidder to prey on the public.... After the bid is accepted, the bidder is bound by his error and is expected to bear the consequence of it....

The prevailing view is that reformation is not the appropriate form of relief for unilateral mistakes in public contract bids where the bidder is negligent.... The reason for not permitting reformation of bid contracts for public projects based on unilateral mistake is the same in other jurisdictions—to prevent collusive schemes between bidders, or between bidders and awarding officials, or multiple claims from contractors asserting mistake and claiming inequity at taxpayers' expense....

A written instrument may be reformed where it fails to express the intention of the parties as a result of mutual mistake, or unilateral mistake accompanied by inequitable conduct by the other party.... Because the mistake in this instance was admittedly unilateral, in order to obtain reformation of the contract, Ronlee was obligated to show by clear and convincing evidence that DOT's conduct in not calling Ronlee's attention to a possible error in the bid tabulations was fraudulent or otherwise inequitable.... That burden was not carried. The Department's failure to call Ronlee's attention to the error in calculation was of no consequence since Ronlee discovered its own error shortly after the Department learned of the miscalculation.

Competitive bidding statutes are enacted to protect the public and should be construed to avoid circumvention.... A government unit is not required to act for the protection of a contractor's interest; it is entitled to the bargain obtained in accepting the lowest responsible bid and is under no obligation to examine bids to ascertain errors and to inform bidders accordingly.... Absent an obligation to do so, failure of the government in this case to call the bidder's attention to a relatively minor two percent error in its calculations, after the bids were opened, was not such fraud or imposition as would entitle the bidder to reformation of the contract.

Further, Ronlee forfeited any right it may have had to reformation or rescission. It had knowledge of its own mistake at least ten days before commencement of construction. Ronlee's conduct in performing according to the terms of the agreement for twenty-one months instead of seeking to withdraw the bid, after DOT had advised that it could not administratively correct the error, effected a waiver of rights. *See Farnham v. Blount* ... (any unreasonable or unnecessary delay by a party seeking to cancel an instrument based on fraud or other sufficient cause will be construed as a waiver or ratification)....

Reversed and remanded with instructions to enter judgment for the Department of Transportation.

Hendry and Ferguson, JJ., concur. Schwartz, Chief Judge, dissenting

With respect, I must dissent. The majority does not say that the record shows and the trial judge found just the inequitable conduct by the DOT which, under principles it acknowledges, renders reformation an entirely appropriate remedy; although the DOT was aware of the mistake when the bids were opened and well before construction commenced, it deliberately failed to inform the contractor of this fact. The final judgment under review contains, among others, the following, essentially undisputed determinations:

> (e) The Defendant acknowledged receipt of notice, *prior* to commencement of construction, of the existence of the error and further acknowledged that the Plaintiff's bid "error was unintentional" and "resulted from inexperienced personnel" generating a simple mathematical error by misplacing a decimal point and "not comprehending the reasonableness of the money figures being used." (Exhibit D to Plaintiff's Motion).

> (f) Indeed, the Defendant even admitted that *prior* to the Plaintiff's March 12, 1984 notification to the Defendant, the Defendant had already been "aware of the apparent unbalanced unit price of the item of Class II Concrete Culverts" (Exhibits D and C to Plaintiff's Motion; Plaintiff's Motion at 5–6, 9). Exhibit C, a December 19, 1983 computer print-out (entitled "summary of bids") produced by Defendant during discovery, demonstrates that the "apparent unbalanced unit price" with respect to the bids "opened at Tallahassee, Florida on December 7, 1983" was known to Defendant promptly upon examination of the bids.

> 3. The Court is therefore of the view that plaintiff has proved inequitable conduct by the Defendant by clear and convincing proof. Clearly,

the Defendant was aware, or certainly should have been aware, that the unit item bid price for 400–2–1 Class II Concrete Culverts was one hundred (100) times less than the nearest unit price for the same item. However, the Defendant chose wrongfully to remain silent as to the existence of this error and, further, refused to act equitably after the Plaintiff had discovered the error and promptly acted to notify the Defendant of the error.

On this basis, the trial court held:

4. While the Court is not unmindful of the fact that competitive bidding statutes should be construed to avoid circumvention, under the unique facts of the case *sub judice,* the integrity of the competitive bidding process will not be undermined with the granting of contract reformation. Where, as here, the differential between the mistaken bid and the second lowest bid exceeds the amount of the error sought to be reformed, no frustration or harm to beneficial purpose can fairly be demonstrated.

I entirely agree.

It is undisputed that, through a simple mistake in decimal point transcription, Ronlee was out and the DOT was in over $300,000 in material expenses. Short of reliance on the well-known playground maxim about keepers and weepers, there is no reason why the state should be entitled to retain this found money. Under ordinary reformation law, the combination of a

unilateral mistake and inequitable conduct fully justifies that relief … and no bases exist or are advanced for the application of a different rule merely because a process of competitive bidding is involved. Since the correction of the mistake would still bring the appellee under the next highest bid, no administratively difficult process of rebidding would be required and none of the purported horribles—"collusive schemes between bidders, or between bidders and awarding officials, or multiple claims from contractors asserting mistake and claiming inequity at taxpayers' expense" … are even arguably implicated.... I would not refuse to reach a just result here because of the mechanical application of an unsupportable rule or out of a necessarily unjustified fear that someone may in the future misapply our holding in a materially different situation.

The very salutary Florida rule of unilateral mistake—which represents a minority view on the question … —is that the courts will relieve one of the consequences of such an error and the opposite party should be deprived of any consequent windfall whenever there is neither a detrimental reliance upon the mistake nor an inexcusable lack of due care which led to its commission.... Neither is present in this case. While the law of our state says otherwise, the majority has permitted DOT successfully to play "gotcha" with Ronlee's money. The state, perhaps even more and certainly no less than a private party, should not be permitted to do so....

I would affirm.

Case Questions

1. Why did the trial court grant the plaintiff's summary judgment motion and order reformation in this case?
2. What is the difference between reformation and rescission of a contract?
3. Could Ronlee have rescinded the contract?

 What ethical consideration motivated Chief Judge Schwartz to dissent in this case?

Court of Conscience

In equity's early period, chancellors were almost always members of the clergy attempting to attain justice between parties to a dispute. A court of equity has always been considered to be a court of con-science in which natural justice and moral rights take priority over precedent. For example, a chancellor may decline to grant a plaintiff relief because of the plaintiff's wrongdoing in connection with the dispute. A chancellor may also decline to enforce a contract clause that is too unfair or one-sided. Such a clause would be declared to be **unconscionable.** To enforce it by granting equitable remedies would "shock the conscience of the court."

In the two cases that follow, the plaintiffs–appellants acted inequitably. Why did the courts in these cases decide that equitable relief was inappropriate?

Campbell Soup Company v. Wentz
172 F.2d 80
U.S. Court of Appeals, Third Circuit
December 23, 1948

Goodrich, Circuit Judge.

These are appeals from judgments of the District Court denying equitable relief to the buyer under a contract for the sale of carrots....

The transactions which raise the issues may be briefly summarized. On June 21, 1947, Campbell Soup Company (Campbell), a New Jersey corporation, entered into a written contract with George B. Wentz and Harry T. Wentz, who are Pennsylvania farmers, for delivery by the Wentzes to Campbell of *all* the Chantenay red-cored carrots to be grown on fifteen acres of the Wentz farm during the 1947 season.... The contract provides ... for delivery of the carrots at the Campbell plant in Camden, New Jersey. The prices specified in the contract ranged from $23 to $30 per ton according to the time of delivery. The contract price for January 1948 was $30 a ton.

The Wentzes harvested approximately 100 tons of carrots from the fifteen acres covered by the contract. Early in January, 1948, they told a Campbell representative that they would not deliver their carrots at the contract price. The market price at that time was at least $90 per ton, and Chantenay red-cored carrots were virtually unobtainable.

On January 9, 1948, Campbell, suspecting that [defendant] was selling it[s] "contract carrots," refused to purchase any more, and instituted these suits against the Wentz brothers ... to enjoin further sale of the contract carrots to others, and to compel specific performance of the contract. The trial court denied equitable relief. We agree with the result reached, but on a different ground from that relied upon by the District Court.... A party may have specific performance of a contract for the sale of chattels if the legal remedy is inadequate. Inadequacy of the legal remedy is necessarily a matter to be determined by an examination of the facts in each particular instance.

We think that on the question of adequacy of the legal remedy the case is one appropriate for specific performance. It was expressly found that at the time of the trial it was "virtually impossible to obtain Chantenay carrots in the open market." This Chantenay carrot is one which the plaintiff uses in large quantities, furnishing the seed to the growers with whom it makes contracts. It was not claimed that in nutritive value it is any better than other types of carrots. Its blunt shape makes it easier to handle in processing. And its color and texture differ from other varieties. The color is brighter than other carrots.... It did appear that the plaintiff uses carrots in fifteen of its twenty-one soups. It also appeared that it uses these Chantenay carrots diced in some of them and that the appearance is uniform. The preservation of uniformity in appearance in a food article marketed throughout the country and sold under the manufacturer's name is a matter of considerable commercial significance and one which is properly considered in determining whether a substitute ingredient is just as good as the original.

The trial court concluded that the plaintiff had failed to establish that the carrots, "judged by objective standards," are unique goods. This we think is not a pure fact conclusion like a finding that Chantenay carrots are of uniform color. It is either a conclusion of law or of mixed fact and law and we are bound to exercise our independent judgment upon it. That the test for specific performance is not necessarily "objective" is shown by the many cases in which equity has given it to enforce contracts for articles—family heirlooms and the like—the value of which was personal to the plaintiff.

Judged by the general standards applicable to determining the adequacy of the legal remedy we think that on this point the case is a proper one for equitable relief. There is considerable authority, old and new, showing liberality in the granting of an equitable remedy. We see no reason why a court should be reluctant to grant specific relief when it can be given without supervision of the court or other time-consuming processes against one who has deliberately broken his agreement. Here the goods of the special type contracted for were unavailable on the open market, the plaintiff had contracted for them long ahead in anticipation of its needs, and had built up a general reputation for its products as part of which reputation uniform appearance was important. We think if this were all that was involved in the case, specific performance should have been granted.

The reason that we shall affirm instead of reversing with an order for specific performance is found in the contract itself. We think it is too hard a bargain and too one-sided an agreement to entitle the plaintiff to relief in a court of conscience. For each individual grower the agreement is made by filling in names and quantity and price on a printed form furnished by the buyer. This form has quite obviously been drawn by skillful draftsmen with the buyer's interests in mind.

Paragraph 2 provides for the manner of delivery. Carrots are to have their stalks cut off and be in clean sanitary bags or other containers approved by Campbell. This paragraph concludes with a statement that Campbell's determination of conformance with specifications shall be conclusive.

The defendants attack this provision as unconscionable. We do not think that it is, standing by itself. We think that the provision is comparable to the promise to perform to the satisfaction of another and that Campbell would be held liable if it refused carrots which did in fact conform to the specifications.

The next paragraph allows Campbell to refuse carrots in excess of twelve tons to the acre. The next contains a covenant by the grower that he will not sell carrots to anyone else except the carrots rejected by Campbell nor will he permit anyone else to grow carrots on his land. Paragraph 10 provides liquidated damages to the extent of $50 per acre for any breach by the grower. There is no provision for liquidated or any other damages for breach of contract by Campbell.

The provision of the contract which we think is the hardest is paragraph 9.... It will be noted that Campbell is excused from accepting carrots under certain circumstances. But even under such circumstances, the grower, while he cannot say Campbell is liable for failure to take the carrots, is not permitted to sell them elsewhere unless Campbell agrees. This is the kind of provision which the late Francis H. Bohlen would call "carrying a good joke too far." What the grower may do with his product under the circumstances set out is not clear. He has covenanted not to store it anywhere except on his own farm and also not to sell to anybody else.

We are not suggesting that the contract is illegal. Nor are we suggesting any excuse for the grower in this case who has deliberately broken an agreement entered into with Campbell. We do think, however, that a party who has offered and succeeded in getting an agreement as tough as this one is should not come to a chancellor and ask court help in the enforcement of its terms. That equity does not enforce unconscionable bargains is too well established to require elaborate citation.

The plaintiff argues that the provisions of the contract are separable. We agree that they are, but do not think that decisions separating out certain provisions from illegal contracts are in point here. As already said, we do not suggest that this contract is illegal. All we say is that the sum total of its provisions drives too hard a bargain for a court of conscience to assist....

The judgments will be affirmed.

Case Questions

1. If the plaintiff had sued for damages, would the result of the suit have been different?
2. Campbell Soup Company lost this case in its attempt to get equitable relief. May it now sue for money damages?
3. If the contract between Campbell Soup Company and Wentz were not unconscionable, would specific performance of the contract be an appropriate remedy? What is necessary before specific performance will be granted?

   Why did the court hold the contract to be unconscionable and therefore unenforceable in equity?

Equitable Maxims

Instead of using rules of law in reaching decisions, courts of equity use *equitable maxims,* which are short statements that contain the gist of much equity law. These maxims were developed over the years (with no agreement as to the number or order) and today are used as guides in the decision-making process in disputes in equity. The following are some of the equitable maxims:

Equity does not suffer a wrong to be without a remedy.

Equity regards substance rather than form.

Equality is equity.

Equity regards as done that which should be done.

Equity follows the law.

Equity acts in personam rather than in rem.

Whoever seeks equity must do equity.

Whoever comes into equity must do so with clean hands.

Delay resulting in a prejudicial change defeats equity (laches).

Isbell v. Brighton Area Schools
500 N.W.2d 748
Court of Appeals of Michigan
April 5, 1993

Taylor, Judge.
Defendants appeal as of right a December 1990 order denying defendants' motion for summary disposition and granting plaintiff's motion for summary disposition, both brought pursuant to MCR 2.116(C)(10). We reverse.

During each semester of the 1988–89 school year, plaintiff's senior year at Brighton High School, plaintiff was absent without excuse on more than six occasions. She was denied course credit under the school's attendance policy, and was ultimately denied a diploma.

Plaintiff sued defendants alleging constitutional, contract, and tort theories, and also raising equitable claims. The trial court ruled that plaintiff lacked an adequate remedy at law and was entitled to equitable relief (issuance of a diploma) because the school attendance policy was unreasonable. Accordingly, the trial court granted plaintiff's (and denied defendants') motion for summary disposition.

Because we conclude that plaintiff is barred from equitable relief by the clean hands doctrine, we need not and do not reach the question whether defendants' attendance policy was reasonable.

One who seeks the aid of equity must come in with clean hands. This maxim is an integral part of any action in equity, and is designed to preserve the integrity of the judiciary. The ... Court [has] described the clean hands doctrine as "a self-imposed ordinance that closes the doors of a court of equity to one

tainted with inequitableness or bad faith relative to the matter in which he seeks relief, however improper may have been the behavior of the defendant. That doctrine is rooted in the historical concept of the court of equity as a vehicle for affirmatively enforcing the requirements of conscience and good faith. This presupposes a refusal on its part to be "the abettor of iniquity."...

Plaintiff admittedly forged excuse notes, so she does not have clean hands. In determining whether the plaintiffs come before this Court with clean hands, the primary factor to be considered is whether the plaintiffs sought to mislead or deceive the other party, not whether that party relied upon plaintiff's misrepresentations.... Thus, it is plaintiff's deceit, not defendants' reliance on the forged notes, that determines whether the clean hands doctrine should be applied. As Justice Cooley wrote:

[I]f there are any indications of overreaching or unfairness on [equity plaintiff's] part, the court will refuse to entertain his case, and turn him over to the usual remedies.

We find that the clean hands doctrine applies to prevent plaintiff from securing the relief she requests. In view of our resolution of this matter, we do not reach the other issues raised.

Reversed.

Case Questions

1.   Why did the trial court believe that the plaintiff was entitled to an equitable remedy?
2.   Why did the appellate court reverse the trial court?

What is the practical significance of the equitable maxim called the *clean-hands doctrine*?

Specific Performance

Specific performance is an equitable remedy that is identified with breaches of contract. The plaintiff brings suit to obtain a court order that requires the defendant to fulfill his or her contractual obligations. Specific performance will only be granted where there is a valid contract.[1] It is enforced through the use of the contempt power.

Like all equitable relief, specific performance is limited to situations in which there is no adequate remedy at common law. This means that under the particular circumstances of the case, the plaintiff can establish that a breach of contract action for money damages is inadequate. We saw an example of this in the *Campbell* case. Campbell wanted the court to order the Wentz brothers to live up to their contractual obligations to deliver Chantenay carrots to Campbell. Campbell argued that requiring the Wentz brothers to pay Campbell $50 per acre in liquidated damages for breach of contract was an inadequate remedy. Campbell contended that it couldn't go out on the open market and purchase Chantenay carrots from another seller. There was no alternative source of supply.

Specific performance is usually applied in situations involving contracts for the sale of land and unique goods. Common law relief is often inadequate for unique goods, because one cannot take money damages and go out and purchase the same item. A similar item might be purchased, but that is not what the parties had bargained. The buyer had an agreement to purchase a particular, unique property item. Thus, if a seller and buyer have contracted for the sale of real estate, a painting, a sculpture, an antique car, or a baseball card collection, money damages are just not a substitute for the item. The Chantenay carrot was unique for Campbell soup. It was the only carrot that would work in the machinery. Consumers of Campbell soups were accustomed to that particular carrot's firmness, consistency, color, and taste.

A plaintiff must have substantially performed, or be ready to perform, his or her obligations under the contract in order to be entitled to specific performance. This is referred to as a **condition precedent** for specific performance.

In addition, equity courts are concerned with practicality. For example, an equitable court generally will not order one person to fulfill a personal service contract and perform work for another. Such a decree would be tantamount to involuntary servitude. It is also impractical for a court to require one person to work for another. Such an order could involve the court in a never-ending series of employer–employee spats.

A defendant can assert various equitable defenses in response to a plaintiff's claim for specific performance. These include (1) unclean hands, (2) hardship, and (3) laches. Hardship involves sharp practices where the contractual terms are entirely one-sided and where there is a gross inadequacy of consideration. Hardship exists because one party is attempting to take unfair advantage of the other party. Laches, as we saw in Chapter VI, is an equitable defense that is used to deny equitable relief where a plaintiff's unreasonable delay in bringing the action has caused prejudicial harm to the defendant. This defense is similar to the common law defense of statute of limitations. The equitable defense of laches does not involve any specific period of time.

Contracts for the sale of goods are governed by the Uniform Commercial Code (UCC).[2] The UCC provides buyers with a right to specific performance in Section 2-716, and sellers with an equivalent remedy in Section 2-709.

In *Bloch v. Hillel Torah North Suburban Day School*, Helen Bloch's parents brought suit to obtain a court order for specific performance of a contract to prevent the expulsion of their grade-school child from a private Jewish school.

Bloch v. Hillel Torah North Suburban Day School
426 N.E.2d 976
Appellate Court of Illinois, First District, Third Division
September 9, 1981

McNamara, Justice.
Plaintiffs appeal from an order of the trial court granting summary judgment in favor of defendant Hillel Torah North Suburban Day School. Helen Bloch is a grade school child who was expelled from defendant, a private Jewish school, at mid-year in 1980. Her parents brought this action seeking to enjoin expulsion and for specific performance of defendant's contract to educate Helen.

The complaint alleged that defendant arbitrarily and in bad faith breached its contract, and that Helen's expulsion was motivated by defendant's disapproval of plaintiff's leadership role in combating an epidemic of head lice at the school. The complaint also alleged that the school uniquely corresponded exactly to the religious commitments desired by plaintiffs. Defendant's answer stated that Helen was expelled, pursuant to school regulations, for excessive tardiness and absences. The parties also disputed the duration of the contractual obligation to educate. Defendant contended that the contract was to endure only for a school year since tuition for only that period of time was accepted by it. Plaintiffs maintained that the contract, as implied by custom and usage, was to endure for eight years, the first year's tuition creating irrevocable option contracts for the subsequent school years, provided that Helen conformed to defendant's rules.

After the trial court denied plaintiff's request for a preliminary injunction, both sides moved for summary judgment. The trial court denied plaintiff's motion and granted the motion of the defendant. In the same order, the trial court gave plaintiffs leave to file an amended complaint for money damages.

Whether a court will exercise its jurisdiction to order specific performance of a valid contract is a matter within the sound discretion of the court and dependent upon the facts of each case.... Where the contract is one which establishes a personal relationship calling for the rendition of personal services, the proper remedy for a breach is generally not specific performance but rather an action for money damages.... The reasons for denying specific performance in such a case are as follows: the remedy at law is adequate; enforcement and supervision of the order of specific performance may be problematic and could result in protracted litigation; and the concept of compelling the continuance of a personal relationship to which one of the parties is resistant is repugnant as a form of involuntary servitude....

Applying these principles to the present case, we believe that the trial court properly granted summary judgment in favor of defendant. It is beyond dispute that the relationship between a grade school and a student is one highly personal in nature. Similarly, it is apparent that performance of such a contract requires a rendition of a variety of personal services. Although we are cognizant of the difficulties in duplicating the personal services offered by one school, particularly one like defendant, we are even more aware of the difficulties pervasive in compelling the continuation of a relationship between a young child and a private school which openly resists that relationship. In such a case, we believe the trial court exercises sound judgment in ruling that plaintiffs are best left to their remedy for damages....

Illinois law recognizes the availability of a remedy for monetary damages for a private school's wrongful expulsion of a student in violation of its contract.... And especially, where, as here, the issue involves a personal relationship between a grade school and a young child, we believe plaintiffs are best left to a remedy for damages for breach of contract.

For the reasons stated, the judgment of the circuit court of Cook County is affirmed, and the cause is remanded for further proceedings permitting plaintiffs to file an amended complaint for money damages.

Affirmed and remanded.

Rizzi, P. J., and McGillicuddy, J., concur.

Case Questions

1.   What problems might have been encountered had the court ordered specific performance?
2.   In what types of cases would specific performance be granted?

Restitution

The remedy of restitution is in some situations an equitable remedy and in other cases a common law remedy. **Restitution** means restoration to the plaintiff of property in the possession of the defendant. The purpose of restitution is to prevent unjust enrichment, which means that a person should not be allowed to profit or be enriched inequitably at another's expense. Thus a person is permitted recovery when another has received a benefit and retention of it would be unjust.

The restoration may be *in specie,* in which a specific item is recovered by the plaintiff from the defendant. In many situations, an *in specie* recovery is impossible or impractical. In such instances, the remedy might have to be "substitutionary," whereby the defendant is ordered to return to the plaintiff as restitution the dollar value of any benefit he or she has received. If so, the amount is determined by the defendant's gain, not by the plaintiff's

loss, as in the case of money damages. So if D takes P's car, worth $4,000, and sells it to someone else at $8,000, D may be liable to make restitution to P for the full amount of $8,000. P never had $8,000, only a car worth half as much, but is still entitled to the total amount. If there was cash in the glove compartment, P would be entitled to recover that also.

The following case discusses restitution in both the common law and equitable contexts. The court first determines whether the plaintiff was entitled to a statutory mechanics lien or a common law lien. It is only after ruling the plaintiff ineligible for a lien under the common law that the court turns to equity. The balancing of interests and harm to produce a just result is clearly evidenced here. Observe how damages are computed in an unjust enrichment case. The court said the mechanic's recovery would be limited to the difference in a vehicle's value before and after it was repaired, and he would not receive damages reflecting his hourly rate.

Iacomini v. Liberty Mutual Insurance Company
497 A.2d 854
Supreme Court of New Hampshire
August 7, 1985

Douglas, Justice.
The issue presented in this case is whether a party may subject an owner's interest in an automobile to a lien for repair and storage charges, without the owner's knowledge, acquiescence, or consent. We hold that no common law or statutory lien may be created under such circumstances but that equitable relief for unjust enrichment may be appropriate.

On August 10, 1983, the plaintiff, Richard Iacomini, d/b/a Motor Craft of Raymond, contracted with one Theodore Zadlo for the towing, storage, and repair of a 1977 Mercedes Benz 450-SL. Mr. Zadlo represented himself to be the owner of the car and presented the plaintiff with a New Hampshire registration

certificate for the car bearing Zadlo's name. In fact, the car did not belong to Mr. Zadlo but had been stolen in 1981 from a car lot in New Jersey. The defendant, Liberty Mutual Insurance Company, had earlier fulfilled its policy obligations by reimbursing the owner of the stolen car $22,000. It thereby had gained title to the vehicle.

Extensive damage was done to the car after its theft, and Zadlo brought the car to Mr. Iacomini for the purpose of repairing this damage. The plaintiff kept the car at his garage, where he disassembled it in order to give a repair estimate. He apparently never fully reassembled it. Mr. Zadlo periodically returned to the plaintiff's garage to check the status of the repair work.

In October 1983, the Raymond Police Department notified the plaintiff that the Mercedes was a stolen car and also notified Liberty Mutual of the location of the car. Mr. Iacomini at that point moved the vehicle from the lot to the inside of his garage where it remained for the next several months. Liberty Mutual contacted the plaintiff soon after it learned of the vehicle's location to arrange its pick-up. The plaintiff refused to relinquish the car until he had been reimbursed for repair and storage fees.

... Liberty Mutual instituted a replevin action ... seeking return of the car.... On the basis of facts presented at a hearing ... in the replevin action, the Court ... found that the plaintiff (defendant in that action) did not have a valid statutory lien since the vehicle was brought to the plaintiff by one other than the owner. The court then ordered Mr. Iacomini to make the vehicle available forthwith to Liberty Mutual with the proviso that Liberty Mutual retain the vehicle in its possession and ownership for a period of at least ninety days in order to allow Mr. Iacomini the opportunity to file an action against Liberty Mutual relating to repairs.

The plaintiff petitioned for an *ex parte* attachment ... claiming approximately $10,000, most of which was for storage fees.... [T]he same court entered judgment in Liberty Mutual's favor finding that "the plaintiff was not authorized or instructed by the legal or equitable owner of the automobile to perform any repair work on the vehicle." On either the day before, or the day of, the hearing ... the plaintiff filed a Motion to Specify Claim to include an action for unjust enrichment. Liberty Mutual objected to the plaintiff's attempt to amend his cause of action at that date, and the court denied the motion. It also denied the plaintiff's requests for findings that the value of the car had been enhanced by the plaintiff and that denial of the plaintiff's claim would result in unjust enrichment. This appeal followed.

The law generally recognizes three types of liens: statutory, common law, and equitable.... The statutes provide as follows:

For Storage. Any person who maintains a public garage, public or private airport or hangar, or trailer court for the parking, storage or care of motor vehicles or aircraft or house trailers brought to his premises or placed in his care *by or with the consent of the legal or equitable owner* shall have a lien upon said motor vehicle or aircraft or house trailer, so long as the same shall remain in his possession, for proper charges due him for the parking, storage or care of the same....

For Labor. Any person who shall, by himself or others, perform labor, furnish materials, or

expend money, in repairing, refitting or equipping any motor vehicle or aircraft, *under a contract expressed or implied with the legal or equitable owner,* shall have a lien upon such motor vehicle or aircraft, so long as the same shall remain in his possession, until the charges for such repairs, materials, or accessories, or money so used or expended have been paid....

"[I]n the case of a statutory lien, the specified requisites must be strictly observed."... By the language of the statute, no lien may be created on an automobile as to the owner without the owner's knowledge, acquiescence, or consent. Under the present circumstances, where the repairman contracted with the possessor of a stolen vehicle for the repair of the car, it is difficult to imagine how the owner could have consented to, or acquiesced in, the repair of the vehicle. The owner in this case had no idea even where the car was located. Whether the plaintiff was reasonable in believing Mr. Zadlo to be the true owner is irrelevant to whether a contract existed between him and Liberty Mutual.

Prior to the passage of a statute on the subject of mechanics' liens, ... "there existed here and elsewhere a lien at common law in favor of anyone who upon request expended labor and materials upon another's property." ... The statutory lien does not supplant, but supplements, the common law mechanic's lien, so that we must also look to the rights of the plaintiff under the common law....

As with the statutory liens, common law liens on property for repair costs could be created only by the owner or by a person authorized by him. "By common law, every person, who employs labor and skill upon the goods of another, *at the request of the owner,* without a special contract, is entitled to retain the goods until a proper recompense is made." ... New Hampshire common law is consistent with the common law of other jurisdictions which also require the owner's consent or acquiescence before a lien may be established on the property of the owner....

The necessity of the owner's consent is consistent with the contractual relationship between the lienor and the lienee which underlies the establishment of a lien.... As discussed previously, no such contractual relationship may be inferred where a possessor of a stolen vehicle turns it over to a garageman for repairs; accordingly, no lien is created against the owner. This is the correct result under the common law even though hardships may result to a good faith repairman. "There are many hard cases ... of honest and innocent persons, who have been obliged to surrender goods to the true owners without remedy.... But these are hazards to which persons in business are continually exposed." ... Of course, the repairman would always have a cause of action against the third party who contracted with him for repairs without the owner's consent.

Although the facts of this case do not establish either a statutory or common law lien, the plaintiff may be entitled to restitution under principles of equity. An equitable lien may be imposed to prevent unjust enrichment in an owner whose property was improved, for the increased value of the property.... "In the absence of a contractual agreement, a trial court may require an individual to make restitution for

unjust enrichment if he has received a benefit which would be unconscionable to retain."... The trial court must determine whether the facts and equities of a particular case warrant such a remedy....

We here note that "when a court assesses damages in an unjust enrichment case, the focus is not upon the cost to the plaintiff, but rather it is upon the value of what was actually received by the defendants."... In this case, the damages would thus be the difference between the value of the vehicle before and after the plaintiff worked on it, regardless of its worth when stolen.

Reversed and remanded.

Case Questions

1. Why should the defendant insurance company be required to pay the plaintiff repairman for services that the plaintiff performed without the defendant's knowledge or consent?
2. What is an equitable lien? How does it work?
3. How does a judge determine the amount of an award in an unjust enrichment case?

Declaratory Judgment

When someone seeks a judicial determination of the rights and obligations of the parties, that person is seeking the remedy of **declaratory judgment.** The court determines what the law is, or the constitutionality or the meaning of the law. For example, if a legislative body passes a statute making your business activity illegal, you could continue to operate the business and be arrested. You also could try to prevent the enforcement of the law by seeking a declaratory judgment. This action asks a court to determine whether the statute in question is constitutional. Because a judge granting declaratory judgment does not issue any orders telling anyone to act or refrain from acting, people who are seeking declaratory relief often ask for injunctive relief as well.

Declaratory judgment is considered by some courts to be an equitable remedy and by other courts to be a legal remedy.

Jury Trial

Cases are set for a jury trial only if a right to jury trial exists and one or both of the parties properly assert this right. For the most part, trial by jury is a constitutional right. The Seventh Amendment to the U.S. Constitution guarantees litigants in federal court a jury trial in suits at common law, and most state constitutions make similar provisions. However, there is no constitutional right to a jury trial in equity cases because jury trials were not a part of chancery procedure.

Parties in most U.S. courts may join common law and equitable remedies in the same action without giving up their right to a jury trial. A jury decides the legal issues, and the judge decides the equitable issues.

INTERNET TIP

State v. Yelsen Land Company is a case in which the parties were seeking both equitable and legal relief. The state objected to being denied a jury trial with respect to issues that were inherently legal. Students can read this case on the textbook's website.

CHAPTER SUMMARY

Students were reminded to refresh their memories with respect to the historical characteristics of the law courts and equitable courts in England because their differences continue to have significance today. It is always important when discussing remedies to remember that equitable remedies are not available to a party who has adequate remedies available at law. It was emphasized that the primary common law remedy is the award of money damages. When a plaintiff establishes that the defendant has committed a tort or breached a contract, the remedy most requested is the award of money damages. Although there are some exceptions, it is generally true that a plaintiff in a tort or contract case is entitled to have a jury decide whether money damages should be awarded. The four types of money damages—compensatory, punitive, nominal, and liquidated—were explained.

The use of the equitable remedy of injunction was explained, with particular attention paid to each of the three classes: permanent, preliminary (interlocutory), and temporary restraining orders. The three equitable remedies that apply to contract cases—reformation, rescission, and specific performance—were explained, as were the two remedies that have roots in both equity and law—restitution and declaratory judgment. The traditional role of equity as a "court of conscience" also was explained. A plaintiff, for example, may have suffered injury at the defendant's hands, but if the plaintiff also has acted inequitably, a judge may decide to deny the plaintiff any remedy in equity. This concept is reflected in two of the equitable maxims set out on page 245, which provide that "whoever seeks equity must do equity" and "whoever comes into equity must do so with clean hands."

CHAPTER QUESTIONS

1. The federal Food and Drug Administration (FDA), after warning Lane Labs on multiple occasions that it was marketing three of its products without having obtained necessary FDA approval, filed suit for a permanent injunction. The FDA alleged that the three Lane Lab products in question were advertised to the public as remedies for cancer, HIV, and AIDS, and none were properly branded or approved. The FDA's amended complaint requested injunctive relief and an order of restitution for consumers. The District Court judge granted the FDA's summary judgment motion, permanently enjoined Lane Labs, and ordered restitution. Lane Labs appealed to the U.S. Court of Appeals for the Third Circuit, maintaining that the Federal Food, Drug and Cosmetic Act (FDCA) only permitted the FDA to obtain injunctive relief in cases such as this, and did not authorize district courts to order restitution. Assume that there is no statutory provision authorizing federal judges to issue an order of restitution in FDA cases. Assume you are a judge having to decide this question. Based on your knowledge of the history of remedies, how should the court rule?

   U.S. v. Lane Labs-USA Inc., 427 F.3d 219 (2005)

2. The plaintiff rented a Halloween costume to Sharp for $20. The rental agreement included a liquidated damages clause, which stated, "an amount equal to one-half the rental fee will be charged for each day the costume is returned late." Sharp returned the costume seventy-nine days late, and the plaintiff sued in small claims court. At a hearing before a referee, the plaintiff testified that he had lost one rental during the seventy-nine days. The referee awarded the plaintiff $500, noting that the plaintiff's complaint sought only that amount. Sharp filed objections to the referee's report, and the matter was brought to the trial court. It entered judgment against Sharp for $400. The case was appealed to the state intermediate appellate

court. Should the appellate court affirm the trial court?

Lakewood Creative Costumers v. Sharp, 509 N.E.2d 77 (1986)

3. Richard and Darlene Parker leased an apartment from Sun Ridge Investors for $465 per month. The lease provided that the Parkers would be charged a $25 late fee if the rent was not paid by the third day of the month, and $5 per day for each additional day until the account was paid in full. The Parkers were late in making their February 1995 rental payment, for which the landlord assessed the monthly and per diem late fees. The Parkers made their subsequent monthly rental payments in a timely manner, but the landlord, after informing the Parkers, applied their payments to the amount that was past due. The Parkers refused to pay the $5 per diem fee. Sun Ridge brought suit in state court seeking the right to forcibly enter and repossess the apartment and $330 in past due rent. The trial court granted judgment to the landlord, and the Parkers unsuccessfully appealed to the intermediate court of appeals. The Parkers appealed to the Supreme Court of Oklahoma. The landlord argued that the per diem fees were additional rent, but the Parkers contended the fees amounted to an unenforceable penalty. Should the Oklahoma Supreme Court affirm or reverse the lower court? Explain your reasoning.

Sun Ridge Investors, Ltd v. Parker, 956 P.2d 876 (1998)

4. El Paso Gas Company transports natural gas through pipelines to points throughout the country. TransAmerican is a natural gas producer. The two companies and their predecessors negotiated various contracts during the 1970s and 1980s. TransAmerican brought suit in 1988 against El Paso when the parties were unable to resolve several disagreements about their respective contractual rights and duties. The trial court entered judgment in favor of TransAmerican. While El Paso's appeal was pending, the parties negotiated a settlement agreement that resulted in the termination of all litigation by both sides, the payment of compensation to TransAmerican by El Paso, and a restructuring of their relationship. The agreement also included a choice of forum clause, which provided that a party, in the event of a breach, would have to bring suit in the Delaware Court of Chancery. In 1993, TransAmerican filed suit against El Paso, in Texas, alleging, among other claims, breach of the settlement contract. El Paso responded by filing suit against TransAmerican in the Delaware Court of Chancery. The Delaware Chancery Court dismissed the petition on the grounds that it did not have jurisdiction, and the Delaware Supreme Court agreed. What was the fundamental problem that caused the court to rule that it did not have subject-matter jurisdiction?

El Paso Natural Gas Company v. TransAmerican Natural Gas Company, 669 A.2d 36 (1995)

5. Plaintiff Whalen discovered upon his return from a trip that an anonymous caller had left a message on his answering machine to the effect that his dog had been found roaming at large, had been given poison, and would die within 24 hours unless the dog were treated immediately. Whalen took the dog to the veterinarian, who examined the animal and concluded that the dog had not ingested poison. Whalen filed suit for damages against Isaacs (the anonymous caller) for intentional infliction of emotional distress, believing that the story about the dog poisoning was a hoax. Under Georgia law, the question as to whether the facts supporting the plaintiff's claim are sufficiently outrageous to constitute the tort of intentional infliction of emotional distress is decided by the trial judge. Both parties moved for summary judgment. The plaintiff's evidence primarily consisted of incidents of conduct in which the defendant demonstrated hostility toward the plaintiff's dog when it was unleashed and allowed to run onto the defendant's property. The defendant, in a deposition, admitted making the telephone call, but

explained that he was acting as a Good Samaritan and made the call to help save the life of the dog. The defendant further claimed that he was only relaying what he had been told about the dog by an unknown bicyclist. Which party should be awarded judgment? Why?

Whalen v. Isaacs, 504 S.E.2d 214 (1998)

6. Chris Titchenal, the plaintiff, and Diane Dexter, the defendant, both women, were in an intimate relationship from 1985 until they broke up in 1994. Their home, cars, and bank accounts were jointly owned, and they had jointly acted as caretakers to Dexter's adopted daughter Sarah (who was named Sarah Ruth Dexter-Titchenal). The plaintiff had not sought to adopt the child jointly. Titchenal alleged that she was a de facto parent and had provided 65 percent of Sarah's care prior to the demise of her personal relationship with Dexter. Titchenal brought suit when Dexter severely cut off Titchenal's visitation opportunities with Sarah. The trial court granted Dexter's motion to dismiss the plaintiff's suit, because it concluded that Titchenal had no common law, statutory, constitutional, or compelling public-policy right to visitation with Sarah. Titchenal appealed, contending that the trial court had equitable jurisdiction, in the best interest of the child, to grant "non-traditional" family members visitation rights where a parent-like situation existed, as in this instance. Do you agree with the trial court and the Vermont Supreme Court that equity has no jurisdiction in this case?

Titchenal v. Dexter, 693 A.2d 682 (1997)

NOTES

1. You can learn about the requirements of a valid contract by reading the brief discussion in Chapter I or the more detailed presentation in Chapter X. In general, a valid contract must be clear, the terms must be reasonably certain, and there must have been an agreement between competent parties, supported by consideration, that does not contravene principles of law and that, in some circumstances, must be in writing.

2. Please see the discussion on the Uniform Commercial Code in Chapter X and in the glossary.

VIII

Criminal Law and Procedure

CHAPTER OBJECTIVES

1. *Understand the sources of American criminal law.*
2. *Describe the different classifications of crimes.*
3. *Explain how the federal Constitution limits the imposition of criminal liability and punishment.*
4. *Understand and describe the basic components of a criminal offense.*
5. *Understand each of the justification and excuse defenses and how they differ.*
6. *Explain a defendant's rights to counsel under the Sixth and Fourteenth Amendments.*
7. *Understand why the Supreme Court came to require the Miranda warnings.*
8. *Describe why the Supreme Court created the exclusionary rule.*
9. *Describe the procedural steps in a typical criminal trial.*

This chapter introduces students to some of the fundamental principles of criminal law and criminal procedure. Each of these subjects is a course in itself; in one chapter it is only possible to examine some of the major issues associated with each topic, and even then the discussion has to be limited.

CRIMINAL LAW

William Blackstone, an English judge and author of *Commentaries on the Laws of England* (1765–1769), defined a crime as a wrong committed against the public,[1] a definition that is today still widely recognized as appropriate. Because the general public is injured when a crime is committed, as well as the person who was

254

the perpetrator's targeted victim, the government and not the victim is responsible for deciding whether to initiate a criminal prosecution. It is the government's responsibility, and not the victim's, to investigate, prosecute, and punish those found by the courts to be criminally responsible. This public character of criminal prosecutions means that, irrespective of the targeted victim's financial condition, the government has an obligation to pay all the costs of investigating and litigating the action. If the accused is convicted and sentenced to incarceration, state-funded correctional institutions will become involved. If the court imposes a sentence of probation, probation officers will be assigned to supervise the probationer at public expense.

Civil remedies, burdens of proof, and court procedures differ significantly from those in criminal cases. Readers might benefit from reviewing Figure 1.2 in Chapter I. Because the actions that are defined as criminal also are recognized as violations of the civil law, it is not uncommon for the victims in criminal cases to maintain separate civil suits against their attackers.

Sources of American Criminal Law

You will recall from the discussion in Chapter I that the colonists along the Eastern Seaboard of North America were very influenced by the English common law. This diminished because of public opposition to things English.[2] Many of the states that abolished common law crimes converted most of them into statutes.[3] Although these "American" statutes deviated in some respects from the common law, they retained significant aspects of that heritage. Some states continue to recognize common law crimes without statutes, and both federal and state judges are sometimes influenced by the common law when interpreting the meaning of criminal statutes.

In the twentieth century, the legislative branch has replaced the judiciary as the dominant criminal law policymaker. The inventions of automobiles, fax machines, copying machines, airplanes, computers, and the Internet and the growth of sophisticated

banking–finance companies and the securities industry produced as a byproduct new and previously unforeseen criminal opportunities. Legislative bodies responded by enacting prodigious numbers of new criminal laws. Some of these laws were well thought out; others were enacted on a piecemeal basis to appease voters without sufficient attention to detail or to appropriate constitutional limitations such as vagueness and overbreadth.

The complexities of modern society and the common law's imprecision led reformers, among them the drafters of the influential Model Penal Code, to call for the abolition of common law crimes. Today, most states define criminal offenses only through statutes, an approach that is consistent with federal law. In 1812, the U.S. Supreme Court decided that Article I, Section 8, of the U.S. Constitution does not include among the enumerated powers the power to adopt the common law. Thus, all federal crimes have to be statutory.

Classification of Crimes

The common law classified crimes as either *mala in se* or *mala prohibita*. *Mala in se* crimes were offenses that were intrinsically bad, such as murder, rape, arson, and theft. Acts that were criminal only because the law defined them as such were classified as *mala prohibita*. A second way of categorizing crimes is in terms of the harm they cause to society. Today, state statutes are often organized so that crimes of a particular type are clustered: for example, crimes against persons (rape, kidnapping, battery, murder, etc.); crimes against property (larceny, robbery, burglary, arson, etc.); and crimes against government (contempt, perjury, bribery, etc.).

Crimes also can be classified as felonies and misdemeanors, and the distinction between the two is essentially a decision of each state's legislature. In some states, felonies are crimes resulting in sentences that are served in state prisons, and misdemeanors are offenses resulting in sentences that are served in county jails. Other jurisdictions provide that crimes authorizing sentences of incarceration of over one year are felonies, whereas those authorizing sentences of one year or less are misdemeanors. The distinction between misdemeanor and felonious theft is usually based on the value of the stolen article. Felony thresholds in theft cases range from $20 in South Carolina to $2,000 in Pennsylvania. In recent years, other classification schemes have gained popularity: for example, white-collar crime (tax evasion, insider trading, kickbacks, defrauding governmental agencies, etc.); and victimless crimes (smoking marijuana, loitering, consensual sodomy, etc.). Other crimes have been reclassified: for example, driving while intoxicated, a misdemeanor twenty years ago, is today a felony.

Constitutional Limitations on Criminalization

The Constitution limits the imposition of criminal liability and criminal punishments. A criminal statute, for example, must be reasonably precise, since one that is too vague or overly broad violates substantive due process.

Article I, Sections 9 and 10 of the Constitution prohibit federal and state legislative bodies from enacting **ex post facto laws**—laws that make acts criminal that were not criminal at the time they were committed. Statutes that make a crime greater than when committed, impose greater punishment, or make proof of guilt easier also have been held to be unconstitutional ex post facto laws. A law is not ex post facto if it "mitigates the rigor" of the law or simply reenacts the law in force when the crime was done. The Ex Post Facto Clause restricts only legislative power and does not apply to the judiciary. In addition, the doctrine applies exclusively to penal statutes, whether civil or criminal in form (see *Hiss v. Hampton*, 338 F. Supp. 1141 [1972]).

The Constitution also prohibits **bills of attainder**—acts of a legislature that apply either to named individuals or to easily ascertainable members of a group in such a way as to impose punishments on them without a trial. In *United States v. Brown*, 381 U.S. 437 (1965), for example, an act of Congress that made it a crime for a member of the Communist Party to serve as an officer of a labor union was held unconstitutional as a bill of attainder by the U.S. Supreme Court.

Although no specific provision in the federal Constitution guarantees a general right of personal privacy, the U.S. Supreme Court has recognized that a limited privacy right is implicit in the due process guarantees of life, liberty, and property in the Fourth and Fifth Amendments, and in the First, Ninth, and Fourteenth Amendments. The Court also has recognized that certain fundamental liberties are inherent in the concept of ordered liberty as reflected in our nation's history and tradition and has selected them for special protection. These rights include personal intimacies relating to the family, marriage, motherhood, procreation, and child rearing. The Court also has recognized that a person's home is entitled to special privacy protection. For example, it has been more exacting in assessing the reasonableness of warrantless searches and seizures under the Fourth Amendment that are conducted within a suspect's home.

The limited constitutionally recognized right of privacy is not absolute and is subject to limitations when the government's interest in protecting society becomes dominant. However, a statute affecting a fundamental constitutional right will be subjected to strict and exacting scrutiny, and the statute will fail to pass constitutional muster unless the state proves a compelling need for the law and shows that its goals cannot be accomplished by less restrictive means. If a challenged statute does *not* affect a fundamental constitutional right, the law will be upheld if it is neither arbitrary nor discriminatory, and if it bears a rational relation to a legitimate legislative purpose—protecting the public health, welfare, safety, or morals. A state can satisfy this rational basis test if it can show that there is some conceivable reason for finding such a rational relationship.

The Equal Protection Clause of the Fourteenth Amendment provides that "No state shall ... deny to any person within its jurisdiction the equal protection of the laws." This clause was included in the Fourth Amendment in the aftermath of the Civil War for the purpose of securing freedom for black people. On its face, the clause might seem to guarantee individuals as well as groups not only the equal application of the laws, but also equal outcomes. The Supreme Court has rejected such an expansive interpretation and has ruled that the

Equal Protection Clause only requires that the laws be applied equally and leaves issues associated with the existence of unequal outcomes to the political branches of government.

The Supreme Court has ruled that classification schemes are inherently suspect if they are based on race, national origin, or alienage, or if they hamper the exercise of fundamental personal rights. When an inherently suspect classification scheme is challenged in court on equal protection grounds, it is subject to "strict scrutiny." This means that the classification scheme will be overturned unless the government can demonstrate that its discriminatory impact is narrowed as much as possible and that the remaining discrimination is necessary to achieve a "compelling" governmental interest.

Discriminatory classifications that are neither suspect nor based on gender will be sustained only if they are rationally related to a legitimate governmental interest. When a challenged classification scheme involves gender, the Supreme Court applies a special rule. In these cases, the discriminatory scheme must bear a "substantial relationship" to "important governmental objectives."[4]

Although the Equal Protection Clause rarely has been relied upon to strike down criminal statutes, it has played a small but important role in preventing legislatures from defining crimes in ways that target groups on the basis of race and gender. Examples of criminal statutes that were overturned by the Supreme Court on equal protection grounds include a Massachusetts statute that made it a crime for unmarried adults to use birth control[5] and an Oklahoma statute that allowed females 18 years or older to consume beer containing 3.2 percent alcohol, while withholding this right from males until they were 21 years of age.[6]

The Imposition of Punishment

It is a principle of U.S. law that people convicted of crimes receive only punishments that have been provided by law. Also, legislative bodies are limited in the types of sentences they can provide by the Eighth Amendment's protection against the imposition of cruel and unusual punishments.

The Supreme Court has interpreted this provision as preventing the use of "barbaric punishments as well as sentences that are disproportionate to the crime committed." The meaning of "barbaric punishment" has been the subject of much discussion in the debate over capital punishment. The majority of the Supreme Court has consistently rejected arguments that imposition of capital punishment is barbaric, emphasizing that capital punishment was known to the common law and was accepted in this country at the time the Eighth Amendment was adopted. At this time 38 states have enacted statutes providing for the death penalty.

Since 2002, the Supreme Court has reversed course on two capital punishment issues previously decided in 1989. In *Atkins v. Virginia,* 536 U.S. 304 (2002), the Court, by a 6–3 margin, reversed its ruling in *Penry v. Lynaugh,* 492 U.S. 302 (1989), which had permitted the execution of mentally retarded offenders. In *Roper v. Simmons,* 543 U.S. 551 (2005), the Court, by a 5–4 margin, reversed its ruling in *Stanford v. Kentucky,* 492 U.S. 361, which had permitted states to execute offenders who were as young as 16 years old. The justices ruled in *Roper* that the Eighth and Fourteenth Amendments prohibited the imposition of capital punishment on criminal offenders who were less than 18 years of age when their crimes were committed.

The Eighth Amendment's proportionality requirement can be traced to the Virginia Declaration of Rights (1775), the English Bill of Rights (1689), the Statute of Westminster (1275), and even the Magna Carta (1215). The Supreme Court in the past has used this principle to strike down sentences imposed pursuant to (1) a statute authorizing a jail sentence for drug addiction (because it is cruel and unusual punishment to incarcerate a person for being ill), (2) a statute authorizing the death penalty for rapists, and (3) a statute authorizing a sentence of life imprisonment without parole for a recidivist who wrote a $100 check on a nonexistant account. In the aftermath of the Supreme Court's decision in *Harmelin v. Michigan,* 501 U.S. 957 (1991), the constitutional importance of proportionality in sentencing decisions, especially in noncapital cases, is very much unresolved.

THE BASIC COMPONENTS
OF A CRIMINAL OFFENSE

Criminal offenses traditionally consist of the following basic components: (1) the wrongful act, (2) the guilty mind, (3) the concurrence of act and intent, and (4) in some crimes, causation. To obtain a conviction in a criminal case, the government has to establish each of these components beyond a reasonable doubt. Because criminal defendants are presumed innocent of the charges made against them, the prosecution is required to rebut that presumption with evidence that is probative of guilt. The prosecution always presents its evidence of guilt (its **case-in-chief**) at the beginning of the trial. Prosecutors have to offer at least a minimum amount of evidence of guilt as to every fact that must be proven to obtain a conviction (the **prima facie case**).

Whether the prosecutor has established a prima facie case is determined by the trial judge after the prosecution "rests" its case-in-chief (i.e., has finished presenting evidence of guilt). At this point the defense will make a motion for acquittal (also known as a motion for directed verdict). The trial judge will deny the motion if the prosecution's case-in-chief is legally sufficient (i.e., the state has established a prima facie case). The judge will grant the motion, however, if the prosecution's case-in-chief is legally inadequate. If the motion is granted, the trial is ended and the defendant is acquitted.

The Wrongful Act

The wrongful act, or *actus reus,* is most easily defined by example. The wrongful act of larceny includes an unlawful taking and carrying away of another person's property. The wrongful act in a battery is the unjustified, offensive, or harmful touching of another person. The law makes a distinction between acts that are classified as voluntary, and those that result from reflexive acts, epileptic seizures, or hypnotic suggestion (see the Model Penal Code in Figure 8.1). A voluntary act occurs when the accused causes his or her body to move in a manner that produces prohibited conduct.

Introduction to *Kansas v. Dinh Loc Ta*

The defendant in the next case, Dinh Loc Ta, was accused of having lewdly touched or fondled two little girls (one child was two years old and the other was three). The prosecution alleged that Ta after first introducing himself to the mothers and while in their presence, had touched the girls, on their faces, legs, hands, and hair outside a movie theater. The defendant, who readily admitted to law enforcement that he desired to have sex with children, was arrested, prosecuted, and convicted by a jury of "aggravated indecent liberties with a child." He was sentenced to concurrent terms of life imprisonment with a minimum 25 years of incarceration.

Ta appealed to the state supreme court, claiming that the trial court should have granted his motion for acquittal, which had been made after the prosecution had rested its case-in-chief. The prosecution, Ta maintained, had not established a prima facie case because it had not proven the commission of any criminal act as required by law. The Kansas Supreme Court's decision follows.

State of Kansas v. Dinh Loc Ta
No. 104241
Supreme Court of the State of Kansas
December 28, 2012

Luckert, Judge.

Facts and Procedural Background
... The charges arose on July 19, 2009, when Ta approached and touched two young girls who were playing outside a Wichita movie theater. The girls, who were 2 and 3 years old respectively, were with their mothers. Just before Ta approached the group, one of the mothers placed her daughter, who was the older child, on a bench and then sat on an adjoining bench with the other mother and younger child.

According to Ta's testimony, he approached the group, introduced himself, and then began talking to the older child. He testified that he told the child she was cute and asked her name. When the child did not respond, Ta held out his hand to her and she tentatively stuck out her hand. He then released her hand and touched her leg because there "was some kind of dirt in the grass so I brush[ed] it off." Ta further testified that when the child did not say anything, he touched her face and her hair.

The older child's mother testified that Ta approached the group and introduced himself to the adults. He then approached her daughter and asked the child her name. When the child did not answer, Ta pulled the child's hair away from the front of her face and tucked it behind her ear. He then began to rub his fingertips up and down the child's arm in what the mother agreed could be described as a very brief, "comforting pat." She did not see Ta touch her daughter's leg.

The younger child's mother testified that Ta approached the older child and moved her hair back while "kind of caressing her face." He then rubbed up and down on the older child's upper leg. She did not see Ta touch the older child on the arm before she picked up the child and began to walk toward the theater.

Ta then approached the younger child. Ta testified that he noticed the girl was not enjoying the day and because she was sitting with her head down, he rubbed her knee and said "hi" to her and told her his name "just to get her to look up, but she didn't look up…. [T]hen I … touch[ed] her face and her hair and her chin, and I ask[ed] her what's wrong and I didn't get any response from her." When he decided the younger child did not want to talk, he walked away, according to his testimony before the jury.

The older child's mother, who was sitting next to the younger child, told the jury, "He grabbed [the younger child's] arm and was feeling on it." He then walked away. She picked up the younger child and walked toward the theater.

The younger child's mother, who had picked up the older child before Ta approached the younger child, testified she heard Ta ask her daughter her name and age. The younger child did not respond. The mother did not see Ta touch her daughter.

The mother of the older child, who worked at the theater, approached her boss and told him what had happened. She testified, "[H]e said that if [Ta came] up to them again he'd call the cops, and then we took matters in our hands and we called the cops ourselves." When the law enforcement officer arrived, the mothers reported that a man had touched their daughters' legs and faces and "they believed he was trying to molest the kids." The officer decided to do a

brief interview of Ta "because at that point I didn't know if we had a violation of anything."

The officer first asked Ta some general questions. Ta then "kind of went into advising that he had a problem, that he wanted to go speak with a doctor and then stated that he felt that he was a danger." When the officer asked Ta to explain what he meant, Ta "advised that he wanted to have sex with children. Then he stated that he was having a difficult time controlling his urges and they were becoming stronger, and then he repeated that he wanted to have sex with kids and that he feels that he's a danger." During follow-up questioning, the officer asked Ta whether "touching their legs … satisf[ied] your sexual desires or did you feel the need for more?" Ta replied that "he wanted to have sex with them." The officer explained that all the statements Ta made about having sex with children were hypothetical, Ta did not admit that it was something that he did or had done. In fact, "[h]e said he never had sex with children."

The officer took Ta into custody. Subsequently, Ta made several statements in which he reiterated that he had strong urges to have sex with small children. A video of some of these statements, including some sexually explicit and vulgar statements he made while by himself in a conference room, were played to the jury.

At trial, Ta did not dispute that there was substantial evidence to establish his intent but insisted there was no evidence that he had committed a lewd touching. Based on this argument, Ta moved for judgment of acquittal at the close of the State's evidence and again after the verdict. The trial judge denied both motions and let stand the jury convictions of two counts of aggravated indecent liberties with a child in violation of K.S.A. 21-3504(a)(3)(A).

The judge … imposed concurrent terms of life imprisonment with a mandatory minimum sentence of 25 years. Ta timely appeals his convictions….

Analysis
On appeal, Ta raises two arguments regarding the trial judge's denial of his motions for judgment of acquittal. First, Ta contends the judge applied the wrong standard when it ruled on the motions. Second, Ta contends there is insufficient evidence of a violation of K.S.A. 21-3504(a)(3)(A), which provides that aggravated indecent liberties with a child is engaging in "[a]ny lewd fondling or touching of the person of either the child or the offender, done or submitted to with the intent to arouse or to satisfy the sexual desires of either the child or the offender, or both." As at trial, Ta does not dispute that there is overwhelming evidence of his intent, but he continues to argue the

State failed to present evidence of a lewd fondling or touching....

(1) Standard and Standard of Review
... Ta argues ... the trial judge was obligated to examine whether there was evidence to establish each element of the crime beyond a reasonable doubt. Ta argues it was predictable that a reasonable jury would find him guilty because the theme of the State's case was that his illicit thoughts proved his guilt of the crimes....

The State's melding of the elements also led the trial judge to commit error, according to Ta. He argues the judge, in denying the motions for judgment of acquittal, single mindedly focused on Ta's intent and not his actions.... According to Ta, ... the trial judge— like the State and the jury—focused on the overwhelming evidence of intent and failed to examine the separate element of whether the touching was a lewd fondling or touching defined by the statute.

As Ta notes, "the Due Process Clause of the Fourteenth Amendment requires proof beyond a reasonable doubt of each element of the crime charged.... "[B]oth a culpable *mens rea* and a criminal *actus reus* are generally required for an offense to occur." *United States v. Apfelbaum*, 445 U.S. 115 ....

Further, due process requires the factfinder to "'rationally apply [the proof-beyond-a-reasonable-doubt] standard to the facts in evidence.'"... *Jackson v. Virginia*, 443 U.S. 307 ... (1979). Hence, when a defendant challenges the sufficiency of the evidence through a motion for judgment of acquittal, a court must examine the evidence in the light most favorable to the prosecution and determine if a juror could rationally apply the evidence and find proof beyond a reasonable doubt of each element of the charged crime....

If there is not sufficient evidence of each element of a charged crime, ... a court "shall order the entry of judgment of acquittal...." An appellate court applies the same standard....

Hence, the trial judge ... had an independent duty to determine if the evidence, when viewed in that light, was sufficient to establish that Ta had committed the required *actus reus*, which is lewd fondling or touching of a child younger than 14 years of age, while possessing the required *mens rea*, which is the intent to arouse or satisfy sexual desires.... If the evidence was insufficient as to either element, the trial judge was required to grant the motion for judgment of acquittal.

This brings us to an analysis of the definition of a "lewd fondling or touching," an assessment of whether there was sufficient evidence of a lewd act in this case, and whether, as Ta argues, the trial judge improperly relied on evidence of Ta's mental state to determine there was sufficient evidence of lewd fondling or touching.

The Evidence of a Lewd Act was Insufficient
The State ... argues the trial judge correctly considered the totality of the circumstances, which necessarily included Ta's state of mind.... For support, the State cites *State v. Rutherford*, ... and *State v. Stout*, ... and the Pattern Instructions for Kansas (PIK) defining the term "lewd fondling or touching,"...

Although neither the *Rutherford* nor *Stout* courts explicitly considered the defendant's intent, the State argues intent [is] ... an appropriate consideration because it is incorporated into the definition of "lewd fondling or touching" found in PIK. As stated in PIK Crim. 3d 53.00, that instruction provides:

> [Lewd fondling or touching means] fondling or touching in a manner which tends to undermine the morals of the victim, which is so clearly offensive as to outrage the moral senses of a reasonable person, and which is done with the specific intent to arouse or satisfy the sexual desires of either the victim or the offender or both. Lewd fondling or touching does not require contact with the sex organ of one or the other....

This definition is taken from this court's decision in *State v. Wells*, 223 Kan. 94, 97-98, 573 P.2d 580 (1977)....

... [T]he Wells court stated:

> In our judgment the words in the statute, "lewd fondling or touching" of the person of either the child or the offender, should be construed to require the [S]tate to prove a fondling or touching in a manner which tends to undermine the morals of the child, which is so clearly offensive as to outrage the moral senses of a reasonable person, *and which is done with the specific intent to arouse or to satisfy the sexual desires of either the child or the offender or both.* (Emphasis added.) *Wells*, 223 Kan. at 98....

On close reading of the *Wells* decision, we conclude the *Wells* court mislabeled its summary as a definition of one element of the crime of indecent liberties with a child— the element of a "lewd fondling or touching"—when the court was actually restating both elements of the crime in commonly understood terms.... This mislabeling is made apparent by a reading of the *Wells* court's prior discussion of the definition of "lewd" because in that more expanded discussion the court defined the criminal act element by looking at the definition of lewd and determining the element was aimed at an act that tends to undermine the morals of the child and which is so clearly offensive as to outrage the moral senses of a reasonable person. Intent was not a part of the discussion....

Additionally, in cases where this court determined a touching was lewd, the focus was placed on whether there was evidence of an act that undermined the morals of a child and was clearly offensive to the morals of a reasonable person....

We have also cautioned against collapsing the separate elements of a lewd touching and an intent to arouse into one element....

Here, the trial judge's findings similarly collapsed the two elements into one, and the State perpetuates this error on appeal by arguing the strong evidence of intent is proof Ta's acts were lewd. This interpretation of the law reverts to the crime found to be unconstitutionally vague ... it makes any fondling or touching a violation of the statute as long as the act is performed with a lewd intent. To avoid this constitutional infirmity, there must be evidence that the act was lewd, and this element should not be dependent upon the subjective intent of a defendant.

To hold otherwise would allow punishment for impure, criminal thoughts, and it is a fundamental principle that "the law does not punish criminal thoughts." *United States v. Shabani*, 513 U.S. 10.... Both a criminal act, an *actus reus*, and a culpable mental state, a *mens rea*, are required for the offense to occur....

In summary, a defendant's mental state should not be used to define or determine whether a touching is lewd. We, therefore, clarify *Wells* and hold that whether a touching is lewd should be determined by considering the common meaning of the term "lewd,"

that is whether a touching is "sexually unchaste or licentious; suggestive of or tending to moral looseness; inciting to sensual desire or imagination; indecent, obscene, or salacious."... In considering if a touching meets this definition, a factfinder should consider whether the touching "tends to undermine the morals of a child [and] ... is so clearly offensive to outrage the moral senses of a reasonable person."... Any contrary language in *Wells* is overruled.

In the present case, viewing the evidence in the light most favorable to the State, the State presented evidence that Ta caressed the children's faces, hair, arms, and legs. This type of touching, when considered without regard to surrounding circumstances, was not lewd. When considered in the surrounding circumstances, as it should be, the fact that Ta was a stranger who approached small children and who was undaunted by the reaction to his touching makes the touching awkward and strange to the point the mothers were understandably uneasy. Nevertheless, the touches were not indecent, obscene, salacious, unchaste, or licentious.... Nor did the touches tend to undermine the morals of the children or outrage the moral sense of a reasonable person. Thus, the State failed to establish sufficient evidence to support the element of lewd fondling or touching.

Accordingly, because the State failed to present evidence that Ta engaged in any lewd fondling or touching of the two children, we reverse Ta's convictions for aggravated indecent liberties with a child.

Consequently, we need not address Ta's other allegations of trial and sentencing error.

Reversed.

Case Questions

1. What, according to the Kansas Supreme Court, is the *actus reus* for the crime of "aggravated indecent liberties with a child"?
2. What did the state supreme court say was the constitutional standard that a trial court should employ when ruling on a motion to acquit?
3. Why was the trial court overruled?

Special Rules

When the law recognizes the existence of a legal duty, the failure to act is equivalent to a criminal act. The duty to act can be imposed by statute (filing income tax returns, making child support payments, registering with selective service, registering firearms), by contract (such as that between parents and a day-

care center), as a result of one's status (parent–child, husband–wife), or because one has assumed a responsibility (voluntarily assuming responsibility for providing food to a person under disability).

Another exception to the requirement of a physical act is recognized in possession offenses in which the law treats the fact of possession as the equivalent of

---

MODEL PENAL CODE*
Official Draft, 1985

Copyright 1985 by The American Law Institute.
Reprinted with the permission of The American Law Institute.

Section 2.01.   Requirement of Voluntary Act; Omission as Basis of Liability; Possession as an Act

(1) A person is not guilty of an offense unless his liability is based on conduct which includes a voluntary act or the omission to perform an act of which he is physically capable.

(2) The following are not voluntary acts within the meaning of this Section:

   (a)   a reflex or convulsion;

   (b)   a bodily movement during unconsciousness or sleep;

   (c)   conduct during hypnosis or resulting from hypnotic suggestion;

   (d)   a bodily movement that otherwise is not a product of the effort or determination of the actor, either conscious or habitual.

(3) Liability for the commission of an offense may not be based on an omission unaccompanied by action unless:

   (a)   the omission is expressly made sufficient by the law defining the offense; or

   (b)   a duty to perform the omitted act is otherwise imposed by law.

(4) Possession is an act, within the meaning of this Section, if the possessor knowingly procured or received the thing possessed or was aware of his control thereof for a sufficient period to have been able to terminate his possession.

*A collection of suggestions for reforming American criminal law, the Model Penal Code was prepared by a private association of professors, lawyers, and judges called the American Law Institute. Over two-thirds of the states have adopted at least some of its provisions and hundreds of courts have been influenced by its suggestions.

F I G U R E 8.1 Model Penal Code Section 2.01

Source: Copyright 1985 by The American Law Institute. Reprinted with the permission of The American Law Institute.

---

a wrongful act. For example, a person found with a controlled substance in his jacket pocket is not actually engaging in any physical act. Possession can be actual, as when the accused is found with the contraband on his or her person, or constructive, as when the contraband is not on the suspect's person but is under the suspect's dominion and control.

Status Crimes

The Supreme Court has emphasized the importance of the wrongful act requirement in its decisions relating to status crimes, ruling that legislatures cannot make the status of "being without visible means of support" or "being ill as a result of narcotic addiction" into a crime. Selling a controlled substance can be made criminal because it involves a voluntary act. The condition of being an addict, however, is a status.

The Criminal State of Mind

The second requirement of a criminal offense (subject to a few exceptions) is that an alleged criminal offender must possess a criminal state of mind (**mens rea**) at the time of the commission of the wrongful act. This is called the concurrence of a wrongful act with a wrongful state of mind. Concurrence is required because some people who commit wrongful acts do not have a wrongful state of mind. For example, if the student sitting next to you mistakenly picks up your copy of a textbook, instead of her copy, and leaves the classroom, there has been a wrongful act but no wrongful intent. Although it is theoretically easy to make this distinction between accidental and criminal acts, it is often difficult to prove that a person acted with *mens rea,* and prosecutors often have to prove *mens rea* indirectly and circumstantially. In addition, judges routinely instruct jurors that the law permits them to find that a defendant intended the natural and probable consequences of his or her deliberate acts. This instruction is based on human experience: most people go about their daily affairs intending to do the things they choose to do.

In the United States, *mala in se* offenses require proof of criminal intent. *Mala prohibita* offenses may require criminal intent (in possession of a controlled substance, for instance), or they may involve no proof of intent at all (as in traffic offenses or sales of illegal intoxicating beverages to minors).

There are two major approaches to *mens rea,* one formed by the traditional common law approach, the other by the Model Penal Code. The common law approach recognizes three categories of intent: general intent, specific intent, and criminal negligence. **General-intent crimes** include serious offenses such as rape and arson and less serious offenses such as trespass and simple battery. For conviction of a general-intent crime, the prosecution has to prove that the accused intended to commit the *actus reus.* The common law permitted the trier of fact to infer a wrongful state of mind from proof that the actor voluntarily did a wrongful act. Thus a person who punches another person in anger (without any lawful justification or excuse) may be found to have possessed general criminal intent.

A **specific-intent crime** requires proof of the commission of an *actus reus,* plus a specified level of knowledge or an additional intent, such as an intent to commit a felony. A person who possesses a controlled substance (the *actus reus*) and who at the time of the possession has an intent to sell (an additional specified level of intent beyond the commission of the *actus reus*) has committed a specific-intent crime.

Criminal negligence results from unconscious risk creation. For example, a driver who unconsciously takes his or her eyes off the road to take care of a crying infant is in fact creating risks for other drivers and pedestrians. Thus if the driver's unreasonable conduct created substantial and unjustifiable risks of harm, and if she or he did not act the way a reasonable person would have acted under similar circumstances, the driver would have been acting negligently.

The defendant in the following case was charged and convicted of the specific-intent crime of robbery. He appealed his conviction on the ground that he did not have specific intent—the intent to permanently deprive the true owner of his property.

State v. Gordon
321 A.2d 352
Supreme Judicial Court of Maine
June 17, 1974

Wernick, Justice.

An indictment returned (on June 27, 1972) by a Cumberland County Grand Jury to the Superior Court charged defendant, Richard John Gordon, with having committed the crime of "armed robbery" in violation of 17 M.R.S.A. §3401-A. A separate indictment accused defendant of having, with intention to kill, assaulted a police officer, one Harold Stultz. Defendant was arraigned and pleaded not guilty to each charge. Upon motion by the State, and over defendant's objection, the residing Justice ordered a single trial on the two indictments. The trial was before a jury. On the "assault" the jury was unable to reach a verdict and as to that charge a mistrial was declared. The jury found defendant guilty of "armed robbery." From the judgment of conviction entered on the verdict defendant has appealed, assigning ten claims of error.

We deny the appeal.

The jury was justified in finding the following facts.

One Edwin Strode and defendant had escaped in Vermont from the custody of the authorities who had been holding them on a misdemeanor charge. In the escape defendant and Strode had acquired two hand guns and also a blue station wagon in which they had fled from Vermont through New Hampshire into Maine. Near Standish, Maine, the station wagon showed signs of engine trouble, and defendant and Strode began to look for another vehicle. They came to the yard of one Franklin Prout. In the yard was Prout's 1966 maroon Chevelle and defendant, who was operating the station wagon, drove it parallel to the Prout Chevelle. Observing that the keys were in the Chevelle, Strode left the station wagon and entered the Chevelle. At this time Prout came out of his house into the yard. Strode pointed a gun at him, and the defendant and Strode then told Prout that they needed his automobile, were going to take it but they "would take care of it and see he [Prout] got it back as soon as possible." With defendant operating the station wagon and Strode the Chevelle, defendant and Strode left the yard and proceeded in the direction of Westbrook. Subsequently, the station wagon was abandoned in a sand pit, and defendant and Strode continued their flight in the Chevelle. A spectacular series of events followed— including the alleged assault (with intent to kill) upon Westbrook police officer Stultz, a shoot-out on Main Street in Westbrook, and a high speed police chase, during which the Chevelle was driven off the road in the vicinity of the Maine Medical Center in Portland where it was abandoned, Strode and defendant having commandeered another automobile to resume their flight. Ultimately, both the defendant and Strode were apprehended, defendant having been arrested on the day following the police chase in the vicinity of the State Police Barracks in Scarborough....

...[D]efendant maintains that the evidence clearly established that (1) defendant and Strode had told Prout that they "would take care of ... [the automobile] and see [that] he [Prout] got it back as soon as possible" and (2) defendant intended only a temporary use of Prout's Chevelle. Defendant argues that the evidence thus fails to warrant a conclusion beyond a reasonable doubt that defendant had the specific intent requisite for "robbery." (Hereinafter, reference to the "specific intent" necessary for "robbery" signifies the "specific intent" incorporated into "robbery" as embracing "larceny.")

Although defendant is correct that robbery is a crime requiring a particular specific intent ... defendant wrongly apprehends its substantive content.

A summarizing statement appearing in defendant's brief most clearly exposes his misconception of the law. Acknowledging that on all of the evidence the jury could properly

> "... have inferred ... that [defendant and Strode] ... intended to get away from the authorities by going to New York or elsewhere *where they would abandon* the car ..." (emphasis supplied)

defendant concludes that, nevertheless, the State had failed to prove the necessary specific intent because it is

> "... entirely irrational to conclude ... that the defendant himself intended at the time he and Strode took the car, *to keep the car in their possession for any length of time.*" (emphasis supplied)

Here, defendant reveals that he conceives as an essential element of the specific intent requisite for "robbery" that the wrongdoer must intend: (1) an advantageous relationship between himself and the property wrongfully taken, and (2) that such relationship be permanent rather than temporary.

Defendant's view is erroneous. The law evaluates the "animus furandi" of "robbery" in terms of the detriment projected to the legally protected interests of the owner rather than the benefits intended to accrue to the wrongdoer from his invasion of the rights of the owner....

... [M]any of the earlier decisions reveal language disagreements, as well as conflicts as to substance, concerning whether a defendant can be guilty of "robbery" without specifically intending a gain to himself (whether permanent or temporary), so-called "lucri causa." In the more recent cases, there is overwhelming consensus that "lucri causa" is not necessary....

We now decide, in confirmatory clarification of the law of Maine, that "lucri causa" is not an essential element of the "animus furandi" of "robbery." ... [T]he specific intent requisite for "robbery" is defined solely in terms of the injury projected to the interests of the property owner: — specific intent "to deprive permanently the owner of his property."...

The instant question thus becomes: on the hypothesis, arguendo, that defendant here actually intended to use the Prout automobile "only temporarily" (as he would need it to achieve a successful flight from the authorities), is defendant correct in his fundamental contention that this, *in itself,* negates, *as a matter of law,* specific intent of defendant to deprive permanently the owner of his property? We answer that defendant's claim is erroneous.

Concretely illustrative of the point that a wrongdoer may intend to use wrongfully taken property "only temporarily" and yet, without contradiction, intend that the owner be deprived of his property permanently is the case of a defendant who proposes to use the property only for a short time and then to destroy it. At the opposite pole, and excluding (as a matter of law) specific intent to deprive permanently the owner of his property, is the case of a defendant who intends to make a temporary use of the property and then by his own act to return the property to its owner. Between these two extremes can lie various situations in which the legal characterization of the wrongdoer's intention, as assessed by the criterion of whether it is a specific intent to deprive permanently the owner of his property, will be more or less clear and raise legal problems of varying difficulty.

In these intermediate situations a general guiding principle may be developed through recognition that a "taking" of property is *by definition* "temporary" only if the possession, or control, effected by the taking is relinquished. Hence, measured by the correct criterion of the impact upon the interests of the owner, the wrongdoer's "animus furandi" is fully explored for its true legal significance only if the investigation of the wrongdoer's state of mind extends beyond his anticipated *retention* of possession and includes an inquiry into his contemplated manner of *relinquishing* possession, or control, of the property wrongfully taken.

On this approach, it has been held that when a defendant takes the tools of another person with intent to use them temporarily and then to leave them wherever it may be that he finishes with his work, the fact-finder is justified in the conclusion that defendant had specific intent to deprive the owner permanently of his property....

Similarly, it has been decided that a defendant who wrongfully takes the property of another intending to use it for a short time and then to relinquish possession, or control, in a manner leaving to chance whether the owner recovers his property is correctly held specifically to intend that the owner be deprived permanently of his property.

The rationale underlying these decisions is that to negate, as a matter of law, the existence of specific intent to deprive permanently the owner of his property, a wrongful taker of the property of another

must have in mind not only that his retention of possession, or control, will be "temporary" but also that when he will relinquish the possession, or control, he will do it in some manner (whatever, particularly, it will be) he regards as having affirmative tendency toward getting the property returned to its owner. In the absence of such thinking by the defendant, his state of mind is fairly characterized as *indifference* should the owner *never* recover his property; and such indifference by a wrongdoer who is the moving force separating an owner from his property is appropriately regarded as his "willingness" that the owner *never* regain his property. In this sense, the wrongdoer may appropriately be held to entertain specific intent that the deprivation to the owner be permanent....

On this basis, the evidence in the present case clearly presented a jury question as to defendant's specific intent. Although defendant may have stated to the owner, Prout, that defendant

> "would take care of ... [the automobile] and see [that] ... [Prout] got it back as soon as possible,"

defendant himself testified that

> "[i]n my mind it was just to get out of the area.... Just get out of the area and leave the car and get under cover somewhere."

This idea to "leave the car" and "get under cover somewhere" existed in defendant's mind as part of an uncertainty about where it would happen. Because defendant was "... sort of desperate during the whole day," he had not "really formulated any plans about destination."

Such testimony of defendant, together with other evidence that defendant had already utterly abandoned another vehicle (the station wagon) in desperation, plainly warranted a jury conclusion that defendant's facilely uttered statements to Prout were empty words, and it was defendant's true state of mind to use Prout's Chevelle and abandon it in whatever manner might happen to meet the circumstantial exigencies of defendant's predicament— without defendant's having any thought that the relinquishment of the possession was to be in a manner having some affirmative tendency to help in the owner's recovery of his property. On this finding the jury was warranted in a conclusion that defendant was indifferent should the owner, Prout, *never* have back his automobile and, therefore, had specific intent that the owner be deprived permanently of his property.

Appeal denied.

Case Questions

1. What must a wrongful taker of property do to avoid legal responsibility for having specific intent to deprive the owner permanently of his property?
2. Does a wrongful taker of property have specific intent if the taker does not intend to keep the property for any particular period of time?

The Model Penal Code recognizes four categories of criminal intent. To be criminally culpable, a person must act purposely, knowingly, recklessly, or negligently (see Figure 8.2).

A person acts purposely when he or she has a conscious desire to produce a prohibited result or harm, such as when one person strikes another in order to injure the other person.

A person acts knowingly when he or she is aware that a prohibited result or harm is very likely to occur, but nevertheless does not consciously intend the specific consequences that result from the act. If a person sets a building on fire, the person may be aware that it is very likely that people inside will be injured, and yet hopes that the people escape and that only the building is burned.

A person acts recklessly when he or she consciously disregards the welfare of others and creates a significant and unjustifiable risk. The risk has to be one that no law-abiding person would have consciously undertaken or created. A driver acts recklessly if he or she consciously takes his or her eyes off the road to take care of a crying infant, is aware that this conduct creates risks for other drivers and pedestrians, and is willing to expose others to jeopardy. As seen in the common law approach, negligence involves unconscious risk creation. A driver acts negligently if he or she unconsciously takes his or her eyes off the road to take care of a crying infant. The driver is unreasonably creating significant risks to other drivers and pedestrians and is not driving as a reasonable person would under similar circumstances.

Strict Liability

In strict liability offenses there is no requirement that there be a concurrence between the criminal act and criminal intent. In such offenses, the offender poses a generalized threat to society at large. Examples include a speeding driver, a manufacturer who fails to comply with pure food and drug rules, and a liquor-store owner who sells alcohol to minors. With respect to such *mala prohibita* offenses, the legislature may provide that the offender is strictly liable. The prosecution need only prove the *actus reus* to convict the accused; there is no intent element.

Causation

There are some criminal offenses that require proof that the defendant's conduct caused a given result. In a homicide case, for example, the prosecution must prove that the defendant's conduct caused death. To be convicted of an assault, the defendant's actions must have caused the victim to fear an impending battery. In a battery, the defendant's conduct must have caused a harmful or offensive touching. In contrast, offenses such as perjury, reckless driving, larceny, and burglary criminalize conduct irrespective of whether any actual harm results.

The prosecution must establish causation beyond a reasonable doubt whenever it is an element of a crime. A key to establishing causation is the legal concept of *proximate cause*. Criminal liability only attaches to conduct that is determined to be the **proximate cause (legal cause)** of the harmful result. This includes both direct and indirect causation. Often the legal cause is the direct cause of harm. If the defendant strikes the victim with his fist and injures him, the defendant is the direct cause of the injury. If the defendant sets in motion a chain of events that eventually results in harm, the defendant may be the indirect cause of the harm.

Proximate cause is a flexible concept. It permits fact finders to sort through various factual causes and determine who should be found to be legally responsible for the result. In addition, an accused is

MODEL PENAL CODE
Official Draft, 1985

Copyright 1985 by The American Law Institute.
Reprinted with the permission of The American Law Institute.

Section 2.02   General Requirements of Culpability

*   *   *

(2) *Kinds of Culpability Defined.*

(a) *Purposely.*

A person acts purposely with respect to a material element of an offense when:

(i)   if the element involves the nature of his conduct or a result thereof, it is his conscious object to engage in conduct of that nature or to cause such a result; and

(ii)   if the element involves the attendant circumstances, he is aware of the existence of such circumstances or he believes or hopes that they exist.

(b) *Knowingly.*

A person acts knowingly with respect to a material element of an offense when:

(i)   if the element involves the nature of his conduct or the attendant circumstances, he is aware that his conduct is of that nature or that such circumstances exist; and

(ii)   if the element involves a result of his conduct, he is aware that it is practically certain that his conduct will cause such a result.

(c) *Recklessly.*

A person acts recklessly with respect to a material element of an offense when he consciously disregards a substantial and unjustifiable risk that the material element exists or will result from his conduct. The risk must be of such a nature and degree that, considering the nature and purpose of the actor's conduct and the circumstances known to him, its disregard involves a gross deviation from the standard of conduct that a law-abiding person would observe in the actor's situation.

(d) *Negligently.*

A person acts negligently with respect to a material element of an offense when he should be aware of a substantial and unjustifiable risk that the material element exists or will result from his conduct. The risk must be of such a nature and degree that the actor's failure to perceive it, considering the nature and purpose of his conduct and the circumstances known to him, involves a gross deviation from the standard of care that a reasonable person would observe in the actor's situation.

F I G U R E 8.2 Model Penal Code Section 2.2

Source: Copyright 1985 by The American Law Institute. Reprinted with the permission of The American Law Institute.

only responsible for the reasonably foreseeable consequences that follow from his or her acts. The law provides, for example, that an accused is not responsible for consequences that follow the intervention of a new, and independent, causal force. The next case, *Commonwealth v. Berggren,* illustrates the legal principle that an accused is only responsible for consequences that are reasonably foreseeable.

Commonwealth v. Berggren
496 N.E.2d 660
Supreme Judicial Court of Massachusetts
August 26, 1986

Lynch, Justice.

The defendant is awaiting trial before a jury of six in the Barnstable Division of the District Court on a complaint charging him with motor vehicle homicide by negligent operation of a motor vehicle so as to endanger public safety (G.L. c. 90, §24G(b) [1984 ed.]). The District Court judge granted the joint motion to "report an issue" to the Appeals Court pursuant to Mass. R. Crim. P. 34, 378 Mass. 905 (1979). We transferred the report here on our own motion.

We summarize the stipulated facts. On March 29, 1983, about 8:28 P.M., Patrolman Michael Aselton of the Barnstable police department was on radar duty at Old Stage Road in Centerville. He saw the defendant's motorcycle speed by him and commenced pursuit in a marked police cruiser with activated warning devices. The defendant "realized a cruiser was behind him but did not stop because he was 'in fear of his license.'" The pursuit lasted roughly six miles through residential, commercial and rural areas. At one point, the defendant had gained a 100-yard lead and crossed an intersection, continuing north. The patrolman's cruiser approached the intersection at about "76 m.p.h. minimal" and passed over a crown in the roadway which caused the patrolman to brake. The wheels locked and the cruiser slid 170 yards, hitting a tree. Patrolman Aselton died as a result of the impact. The defendant had no idea of the accident which had occurred behind him. "No other vehicles were in any way involved in the causation of the accident." The stipulation further states that the decision to terminate a high-speed chase "is to be made by the officer's commanding officer." No such decision to terminate the pursuit had been made at the time of the accident. The Barnstable police department determined that patrolman Aselton died in the line of duty.

We understand the report to raise the question whether the stipulated facts would be sufficient to support a conviction of motor vehicle homicide by negligent operation under G.L. c. 90, §24G(b). We hold that it is.

A finding of ordinary negligence suffices to establish a violation of §24G.

The Appeals Court has observed: "It would seem to follow that if the jury's task is to find ordinary negligence, then the appropriate principles of causation to apply are those which have been explicated in a large body of decisions and texts treating the subject in the context of the law of torts."...

The defendant argues, however, that the "causation theory properly applied in criminal cases is not that of proximate cause."... If this theory has any application in this Commonwealth ... it does not apply to a charge of negligent vehicular homicide. We adopt instead the suggestion of the Appeals Court and conclude that the appropriate standard of causation to be applied in a negligent vehicular homicide case under §24G is that employed in tort law.

The defendant essentially contends that since he was one hundred yards ahead of the patrolman's cruiser and was unaware of the accident, his conduct cannot be viewed as directly traceable to the resulting death of the patrolman. The defendant, however, was speeding on a motorcycle at night on roads which his attorney at oral argument before this court characterized as "winding" and "narrow." He knew the patrolman was following him, but intentionally did not stop and continued on at high speed for six miles. From the fact that the defendant was "in fear of his license," it may reasonably be inferred that he was aware that he had committed at least one motor vehicle violation. Under these circumstances, the defendant's acts were hardly a remote link in the chain of events leading to the patrolman's death.... The officer's pursuit was certainly foreseeable, as was, tragically, the likelihood of serious injury or death to the defendant himself, to the patrolman, or to some third party. The patrolman's death resulted from the "natural and continuous sequence" of events caused by the defendant's actions....

We conclude that the proper standard of causation for this offense is the standard of proximate cause enunciated in the law of torts. We further conclude that, should the jury find the facts as stipulated in the instant case, and should the only contested element of the offense of motor vehicle homicide by negligent operation be that of causation, these facts would support a conviction under G.L. c.90, §24G(b).

Report answered

Case Questions

1. Explain the difference between factual and legal causation, based on the facts of this case.
2. Do you agree with Massachusetts that Berggren should be legally responsible for the officer's death?

 Berggren claims to have been unaware of the collision involving the officer's cruiser and the tree, and he insists that he never intended that the officer die. Do you think that *moral* culpability (as opposed to *legal* culpability) should be determined by looking primarily at the collision and the officer's death (the outcome), or should it be determined primarily by Berggren's intentions and what he knew about the facts prior to the officer's death?

Inchoate Crime

The criminal law recognizes society's need to protect itself from those people who have taken some preliminary steps leading to a criminal act, but who have not yet completed their intended criminal objectives. Thus the law defines as criminal the preparatory activities of solicitation, attempt, and conspiracy and refers to them as **inchoate crimes**.

Solicitation is a specific-intent crime committed by a person who asks, hires, or encourages another to commit a crime. It makes no difference whether the solicited person accepts the offer; the solicitation itself constitutes the *actus reus* for this offense. All jurisdictions treat solicitations to commit a felony as a crime, and some jurisdictions also criminalize solicitations to commit a misdemeanor.

The crime of **attempt** is committed by a person who has the intent to commit a substantive criminal offense and does an act that tends to corroborate the intent, under circumstances that do not result in the completion of the substantive crime. For example, assume that person *Y* intends to commit armed robbery of a bank. *Y* dresses in clothing that disguises his appearance, wears a police scanner on his belt, carries a revolver in his coat pocket, wears gloves, and drives to a bank. *Y* approaches the front door with one hand in his pocket and the other over his face. When he attempts to open the front door, he discovers that the door is locked and that it is just after the bank's closing time. *Y* quickly returns to his car, leaves the bank, and is subsequently apprehended by police. *Y* had specific intent to rob the bank, and took many substantial steps to realize that intent; however, he was unable to complete the crime because of his poor timing. *Y* has committed the crime of attempted robbery.

The crime of **conspiracy** is committed when two or more people combine to commit a criminal act. The essential *actus reus* of conspiracy is the agreement to commit a criminal act, coupled with the commission of some overt act by one or more of the coconspirators that tends to implement the agreement. The prosecution can prove the existence of an unlawful agreement either expressly or inferentially. The crime of conspiracy is designed to protect society from group criminality. Organized groups bent on criminal activity pose a greater threat to the public than do the isolated acts of individuals. Conspiracy is a separate crime and, unlike attempt, does not merge into the completed substantive offense. Thus a person can be prosecuted both for murder and for conspiracy to murder. If a member of the conspiracy wants to abandon the joint enterprise, he or she must notify every other coconspirator. Conspiracy is a powerful prosecutorial weapon.

The Racketeer Influenced and Corrupt Organization Act

In 1970, the federal government enacted a criminal statute called the Racketeer Influenced and Corrupt Organization Act (RICO). This statute and its state counterparts have been very important weapons in combating organized criminal activity such as drug trafficking, the theft and fencing of property, syndicated gambling, and extortion. A very broad statute, RICO applies to all people and organizations, whether public or private. It focuses on patterns of racketeering activity, the use of money obtained from racketeering to acquire legitimate businesses, and the collection of unlawful debt. The act defines racketeering activity as involving eight state crimes and twenty-four federal offenses called the predicate acts. A person who has committed two or more of the predicate acts within a ten-year period has engaged in a pattern of racketeering activity. People convicted under RICO can be required to forfeit property acquired with money obtained through racketeering and punished with fines and up to twenty years' incarceration. Civil penalties, including the award of treble damages, also can be imposed.

INTERNET TIP

An interesting RICO case involving members of the Outlaws Motorcycle Club who allegedly participated in a drug distribution enterprise can be found on the textbook's website. The case of *U.S. v. Lawson* was decided in 2008 by the U.S. Court of Appeals for the Sixth Circuit.

Vicarious Liability

Criminal law recognizes two conditions under which individuals and groups can be held criminally liable for actions committed by other people. Employers can be held responsible for the acts of their employees that occur within the course and scope of employment. For example, if a bartender illegally sells liquor to minors, the bartender's employer (as well as the bartender) can be prosecuted. Vicarious liability helps to impress on employers the importance of insisting that employees comply with legal requirements. However, an employer can be held vicariously liable only for a strict liability offense. Legislators, when creating a strict liability offense, declare conduct that is not intrinsically (i.e., deliberately) "bad" to be an offense and dispense with the proof of the *mens rea* requirement for reasons of public policy. For example, prosecutors do not have to prove *mens rea* at the trial of a person accused of driving 40 m.p.h. in a school zone where the posted limit is 15 m.p.h., because it is necessary to protect children and it would be too easy for drivers to avoid conviction if proof of *mens rea* were required. Because of the unique nature of strict liability offenses, a person (e.g., an employer) convicted vicariously can be subject only to a fine or forfeiture.

Corporations also can be held vicariously responsible for criminal acts committed by authorized corporate employees who have acted on behalf of the company to enhance corporate profits. For example, a corporate CEO who engages in criminal conduct can be prosecuted just like any other person. But additional charges also can be brought against the corporation itself in order to hold it vicariously liable for the CEO's criminal acts.

INTERNET TIP

Corporations even can be convicted of committing homicides. A trucking company was found guilty by a jury and convicted of the homicide of a police officer in a controversial 2006 Massachusetts case. The truck's driver, whose vehicle lacked a working backup alarm, struck an officer situated in the truck driver's "blind spot." The trucking company was charged with violating the state's vehicular homicide statute. The conviction was appealed to the state's highest court, which affirmed. The majority and dissenting opinions in the case of *Commonwealth vs. Todesca Corporation* can be read on the textbook's website.

Prosecutors usually bring criminal charges against corporations for reasons of deterrence. If a corporation's culture has become corrupted, merely prosecuting the individuals involved is sometimes not enough. Corporations have much to lose if prosecuted and convicted of criminal conduct. They risk public embarrassment, damage to the company's reputation and goodwill, and the devaluation of its stock. The punishment options for corporations are limited, however. The law permits the imposition of fines, but these are often inadequate in size, and it is obvious that corporations cannot go to jail.

Defenses

Defense attorneys often file pretrial motions that ask the trial court to suppress evidence that the accused alleges was obtained improperly by the police. For example, they might allege that the police did not comply with the requirements of *Miranda v. Arizona* when they interrogated the defendant or violated the requirements of the Fourth Amendment when they conducted a search of the defendant's home. The court will conduct a hearing on the motion, at which it hears testimony as to the facts and makes a ruling. If the defense is successful, the court will exclude improperly obtained evidence from the trial.

Because of the constitutional presumption of innocence, criminal defendants are not required to prove anything at trial. If the government cannot prove the defendant's guilt beyond a reasonable doubt with its own evidence, the law provides that the accused is not guilty.

One defense strategy is, therefore, to establish reasonable doubt exclusively through the use of the government's own witnesses. It is possible to challenge the credibility of prosecution witnesses on the grounds that their testimony is unbelievable. The defense attorney, for example, may be able to show through cross-examination that a prosecution witness was too far away to have clearly seen what he or she testified to having observed, to be biased against the defendant, or to not really be certain as to the identity of the attacker as was suggested on direct examination. If the defense believes at trial that the prosecution's evidence is insufficient to establish elements of the crime, the defense attorney can move to dismiss, and it is always possible to defend by arguing that the level of *mens rea* required for conviction was not proven or that the prosecution in some other respect has failed to carry its burden of proving the defendant's guilt beyond a reasonable doubt.

Sometimes an accused can call witnesses to testify that the defendant was somewhere other than at the scene of the crime on the date and time that the offense allegedly occurred—thereby raising an **alibi defense.** Rarely, an accused will present a **good-character defense.** For example, a defendant who is charged with a crime of violence could introduce reputation or opinion testimony that the defendant is nonviolent and peace loving. From this evidence the defense attorney could argue that the defendant's character is so sterling that she would never have committed the crime with which she was charged.

The law gradually began to recognize that in some situations it would be unfair to impose criminal responsibility on a defendant who admits to having committed an *actus reus* because of the presence of factors that legitimately mitigated, justified, or excused the defendant's conduct. These special circumstances came to be known as *affirmative defenses* or *excuse defenses* (see section on these defenses below). The defendant always bears the burden of production with respect to affirmative defenses. Unless the defense affirmatively introduces some evidence tending to establish such a defense, the court will refuse to give the corresponding affirmative defense instruction to the jury. Because affirmative defenses do not negate any element of the crime(s) charged by the government, states are constitutionally permitted to decide for themselves whether the defendant should bear the burden of persuasion with respect to affirmative defenses. Some states require the prosecution to disprove affirmative defenses beyond a reasonable doubt. But many other jurisdictions refuse that burden and require that the defendant carry the burden. When that occurs, the defendant has to persuade the judge (in a bench trial) or the jury that the claimed affirmative defense has been proven by a preponderance of the evidence and that the defendant's conduct was either justified or excused. Jurisdictions differ as to the availability of particular defenses and as to their definitions. Affirmative defenses are often further subdivided into justification defenses and excuse defenses.

Justification defenses Criminal laws are often written in general terms and without limitations and exceptions. It is understood that exceptions will be made, on a case-by-case basis, where it becomes apparent that a defendant was justified in his or her actions given the then-existing circumstances. Recognized **justification defenses** often include self-defense, defense of others, defense of property, necessity–choice-of-evils, and duress–coercion. In each of these defenses, the accused admits to having committed the act that is alleged by the prosecution; however, in each instance the accused claims to have acted correctly.

The law recognizes an individual is justified in defending his or her person and property, and in defending others. A person is entitled to use reasonable force in self-defense, to protect him- or herself from death or serious bodily harm. Obviously the amount of force that can be used in defense depends on the type of force being used by the attacker. An attack that threatens neither death nor serious bodily harm does not warrant the use of deadly force in defense. When the attack has been repelled, the defender does not have the right to continue using force to obtain revenge. Although the common law required one to "retreat to the wall" before using deadly force in self-defense, the modern rule permits a person to remain on his or her property and to use reasonable force (including the reasonable use of deadly force in defense of others who are entitled to act in self-

defense). However, as we saw in *Katko v. Briney*, in Chapter I, it is never justifiable to use force that could cause death or serious bodily injury solely in defense of property. Necessity (also known as the choice-of-evils defense) traces its lineage to the English common law. Over time it became apparent that in some limited circumstances, committing a criminal act would actually result in a less harmful outcome than would occur were the accused to adhere strictly to the requirements of the law. To be successful with this defense, the accused must be able to establish that there was no reasonable, legal alternative to violating the law. That was the critical question addressed in the following case.

United States v. Juan Donaldo Perdomo-Espana
522 F.3d 983
United States Court of Appeals, Ninth Circuit
April 14, 2008

Gould, Circuit Judge.

Juan Perdomo-Espana ("Perdomo") appeals his jury conviction for one count of illegal entry into the United States as a deported alien in violation of 8 U.S.C. §1326. In this opinion, we consider whether the defense of necessity that Perdomo advanced must be tested under an objective or subjective standard....

I

In the early morning hours of March 21, 2006, a United States border patrol officer found Perdomo and four others hiding in brush near the United States-Mexican border. Perdomo was wearing dark clothes. Upon discovery, Perdomo admitted that he is a Mexican citizen with no documents to allow him to enter or to remain in the United States. He was found with $598 (USD) and 155 Mexican pesos on his person. Perdomo was arrested and taken to a nearby border patrol station, where he was questioned and fingerprinted.... Immigration records revealed that he had twice previously been deported and had not subsequently applied for reentry.

At trial, Perdomo testified that he had illegally entered the United States for fear of his life. Perdomo stated that in 2000, while in a United States federal prison, he had a stroke precipitated by a high blood sugar level associated with Type 2 diabetes, and thereafter he was treated with insulin injections. Upon his release from prison, Perdomo was given a small insulin supply and was removed to Mexico on

March 7, 2006, where his insulin supply soon ran out. While in Tijuana, Perdomo purchased varying kinds of replenishing insulin, but none of the insulin was sufficiently effective, and his blood sugar level began to rise.

According to Perdomo, shortly before the border patrol caught him, he tried to enter the United States via the pedestrian lane at a nearby port of entry, but was turned away despite telling the officers of his need for diabetic-related treatment. Perdomo claims that his blood sugar level soon thereafter rose to 480, the level it had reached when he suffered his diabetes-induced stroke. Perdomo asserted that he then attempted to cross clandestinely into the United States.

Perdomo testified that he entered the United States fearing for his life because of his high blood sugar levels, and did not intend to remain. He believed he was in desperate need of medical treatment which was unavailable in Mexico. Perdomo testified that he did not go to any hospital, church, or the police in Tijuana because he believed that he would not be able to secure the needed treatment in Tijuana, despite the money he carried. According to Perdomo, a person had to be dying on the street to gain medical attention there.

During questioning that took place about four to five hours after his initial capture, Perdomo told a border patrol agent for the first time that he is a Type 2 diabetic and that he had been hospitalized for two weeks in the last six months because of his diabetes....

After questioning, Perdomo was taken to an emergency room, where his blood sugar level was recorded as 340. The emergency room physician who treated Perdomo, Dr. Vincent Knauf, characterized this glucose level as a "severe elevation." However, Dr. Knauf concluded that, in his opinion, Perdomo was not facing serious or imminent risk of bodily harm at that time; although he needed longer-term care, Perdomo was classified as a "non-urgent" patient....

During pre-trial hearings, Perdomo requested to present a necessity defense, which the government moved to preclude. Reserving its final ruling until after the presentation of evidence at trial, the district court allowed Perdomo to testify before the jury about why he had entered the country.

At the conclusion of evidence, Perdomo again requested that the jury be instructed on his proffered defense of necessity. The district court declined to give the requested instruction, reasoning that Perdomo showed no "threat of imminent harm," and that it was "incredulous to suggest that Mexico doesn't have clinics, doctors, [or] hospitals that could manage people who are in need of treatment," especially given that Perdomo "had $600 on him at the time." The district court, instead, instructed the jury that the "theory of the defense" was that Perdomo had come to the United States for medical care. After the jury found Perdomo guilty, Perdomo moved for a new trial, which the district court denied. Perdomo appeals the district court's denial of his request for a necessity defense jury instruction.

II

... [W]e review de novo the legal question whether the necessity defense requires an objective inquiry. Once we have resolved that legal question, we review for abuse of discretion whether there is a sufficient factual basis for Perdomo's proffered jury instruction.

III

A defendant is entitled to have the jury instructed on his or her theory of defense, as long as that theory has support in the law and some foundation in the evidence.... A defendant "has the right to have a jury resolve disputed factual issues. However, where the evidence, even if believed, does not establish all of the elements of a defense, ... the trial judge need not submit the defense to the jury." ... "[It] is well established that a criminal defendant is entitled to have a jury instruction on any defense which provides a legal defense to the charge against him and which has some foundation in the evidence, even though the evidence may be weak, insufficient, inconsistent, or of doubtful credibility. In the necessity context, the proper inquiry is whether the evidence offered by a defendant, if

taken as true, is sufficient as a matter of law to support the defense."...

[T]he defense of necessity, or choice of evils, traditionally covered the situation where physical forces beyond [an] actor's control rendered illegal conduct the lesser of two evils.... In recent years, our case law has expanded the scope of the defense. We have held that a defendant may present a defense of necessity to the jury as long as the defendant "establish[es] that a reasonable jury could conclude: (1) that he was faced with a choice of evils and chose the lesser evil; (2) that he acted to prevent imminent harm; (3) that he reasonably anticipated a causal relation between his conduct and the harm to be avoided; and (4) that there were no other legal alternatives to violating the law."

A defendant must prove each of these elements to present a viable necessity defense....

Perdomo's principal argument is that these elements require a subjective analysis and that the relevant inquiry is thus into his state of mind—i.e., his allegedly genuine fear of the likely, dire medical consequences that he would have faced if he did not illegally reenter the United States. By contrast, the government asserts that the inquiry is an objective one. We agree with the government.

A careful reading of our cases on the subject reveals that we assess a defendant's proffered necessity defense through an objective framework.... In *United States v. Schoon* ... (9th Cir.1992), we applied an objective standard in assessing the fourth element of a necessity defense.... We stated that "the law implies a reasonableness requirement in judging whether legal alternatives exist."...

Embedded in our recognition that a person who seeks to benefit from a justification defense must act reasonably is the principle that justification defenses necessarily must be analyzed objectively. *Schoon* echoed this principle:

Necessity is, essentially, a utilitarian defense. It therefore justifies criminal acts taken to avert a greater harm, maximizing social welfare by allowing a crime to be committed where the social benefits of the crime outweigh the social costs of failing to commit the crime.... The law could not function were people allowed to rely on their *subjective* beliefs and value judgments in determining which harms justified the taking of criminal action.

... The latter statement follows logically from the former statement; after all, if the necessity defense were entirely subjective, then allowing a defendant to benefit from it would only advance the common good when the defendant's subjective beliefs were in alignment with an objective perspective.

More recently in [*United States v.*] *Arellano-Rivera,* we upheld the district court's preclusion of a defendant's proffered necessity defense, reasoning that the defendant had failed to show that he had no legal alternatives other than illegally reentering the United States.... We denied the defendant's appeal, notwithstanding his speculation that the Attorney General would have denied the defendant's application for reentry based on his advanced medical condition; the defendant's subjective belief that this legal alternative was unavailable to him was insufficient to sustain his necessity defense....

We therefore hold that the test for entitlement to a defense of necessity is objective. The defendant must establish that a reasonable jury could conclude that (1) he was faced with a choice of evils and reasonably chose the lesser evil; (2) he reasonably acted to prevent imminent harm; (3) he reasonably anticipated a causal relation between his conduct and the harm to be avoided; and (4) he reasonably believed there were no other legal alternatives to violating the law.... It is not enough, as Perdomo argues, that the defendant had a subjective but unreasonable belief as to each of these elements. Instead, the defendant's belief must be reasonable, as judged from an objective point of view.

IV

Applying an objective standard to Perdomo's case, his argument that he was entitled to a jury instruction on the necessity defense fails on several bases. Dr. Knauf concluded that Perdomo was in no immediately dire medical condition when he was treated in the emergency room soon after crossing the border; thus Perdomo's crossing was not averting any objective, imminent harm, causing his defense to fail on the second element. Additionally, Dr. Knauf testified that there are multiple clinics in Tijuana where Perdomo could have obtained medical treatment, particularly with the money he had, and that, even assuming that his medical condition had been dire, a saline injection would have been the fastest effective means of bringing Perdomo's condition under control; thus there objectively were legal alternatives to violating the law, causing Perdomo's defense to fail on the fourth prong. Moreover, from an objective perspective, Perdomo's tactic of hiding in bushes, in dark clothing, and in a remote area, trying to escape border patrol's detection, likely thwarted rather than advanced the speedy receipt of medical treatment, meaning that the defense fails on the third prong as well.

Failure on any one of these three bases, let alone all three, was sufficient to support the district court's determination that Perdomo did not present adequate evidence to establish a prima facie case of the necessity defense. Our case law is clear that a trial judge may decline to allow evidence of a necessity defense where the defendant fails to present a prima facie case.... See, e.g., *Arellano-Rivera,* ... "Where the evidence, even if believed, does not establish all of the elements of a defense, ... the trial judge need not submit the defense to the jury." ... All the more so, then, a trial court may preclude a jury instruction after having heard evidence at trial that collectively presents an insufficient factual foundation to establish the defense as a matter of law.

Perdomo was not entitled to a jury instruction regarding necessity in this case because the defense lacked a necessary foundation in evidence. Even if Perdomo's testimony were believed, he did not establish all of the elements of the defense of necessity.... The district court properly analyzed Perdomo's case under an objective framework and did not abuse its discretion when it denied Perdomo's requested jury instruction.

Affirmed.

Case Questions

1. What must a defendant do to be entitled to a jury instruction on the defense of necessity?
2. What is the difference between an objective and a subjective test? Why was that distinction important in this case?

Affirmative or excuse defenses In **affirmative defenses,** also called **excuse defenses,** the defendant admits to having acted unlawfully, but argues that no criminal responsibility should be imposed, given the particular circumstances accompanying the act. Examples of this type of affirmative defense include duress, insanity, and involuntary intoxication.

A person who commits a criminal act only because he or she was presently being threatened with death or serious bodily injury may assert the defense called duress–coercion. This defense is based on the theory that the person who committed the criminal act was not exercising free will. Most states do not allow the use of this defense in murder cases. In addition, coercion is difficult to establish. It fails, as we see in the next case, if there was a reasonable alternative to committing the crime, such as running away or contacting the police.

United States v. Scott
901 F.2d 871
U.S. Court of Appeals, Tenth Circuit
April 20, 1990

Seay, District Judge.

Appellant, Bill Lee Scott, was found guilty by a jury and convicted of one count of conspiracy to manufacture methamphetamine in violation of 21 U.S.C. §2, and one count of manufacturing methamphetamine in violation of 21 U.S.C. §841(a)(1), and 18 U.S.C. §2. Scott appeals his convictions contending that he was denied a fair trial when the district court refused to instruct the jury on the defense of coercion. We disagree, and therefore affirm the judgment of the district court.

I

Between the middle of August 1987, and the early part of January 1988, Scott made approximately six trips to Scientific Chemical, a chemical supply company in Humble, Texas. Scott made these trips at the request of co-defendant Mark Morrow. These trips resulted in Scott purchasing various quantities of precursor chemicals and laboratory paraphernalia from Scientific Chemical. Some trips resulted in Scott taking possession of the items purchased, other trips resulted in the items being shipped to designated points to be picked up and delivered at a future date. These chemicals and laboratory items were purchased to supply methamphetamine laboratories operated by Morrow in New Mexico with the assistance of Silas Rivera and co-defendants George Tannehill, Jerry Stokes, and Robert Stokes.

Scott first became acquainted with Morrow when Morrow helped him move from Portales, New Mexico, to Truth or Consequences, New Mexico, in late July or early August 1987.... Shortly thereafter, Morrow became aware that Scott was going to Houston, Texas, to sell some mercury and Morrow asked Scott if he could pick up some items from Scientific Chemical.... Scott made the trip to Scientific Chemical and purchased the items Morrow requested.... Scott subsequently made approximately five other trips to Scientific Chemical at Morrow's request to purchase various quantities of precursor chemicals and assorted labware.... During the course of one trip on August 31,

1987, Scott was stopped by Drug Enforcement Administration agents after he had purchased chemicals from Scientific Chemical.... The agents seized the chemicals Scott had purchased as well as $10,800 in U.S. currency and a fully loaded .38 Smith and Wesson.... Scott was not arrested at that time.... Scott, however, was subsequently indicted along with the codefendants after the seizure of large quantities of methamphetamine and precursor chemicals from a laboratory site in Portales in January 1988.

At trial Scott claimed that his purchase of the chemicals and labware on behalf of Morrow was the result of a well-established fear that Morrow would kill him or members of his family if he did not act as Morrow had directed. Scott further claimed that he did not have any reasonable opportunity to escape the harm threatened by Morrow. To support this defense of coercion Scott testified on his own behalf as to the nature and circumstances of the threats. Scott testified that approximately one month after the August 31, 1987, trip Morrow called him at his home in Truth or Consequences and talked him into a meeting in Houston to "get that straightened out." It was Scott's contention that Morrow might not have believed that the money and chemicals had been seized and that Morrow might have thought that he had merely kept the money....

After the trip to Houston and Scientific Chemical to confirm Scott's story about the seizure of the chemicals and cash, Morrow contacted Scott at Scott's daughter's house in Portales to have Scott make another trip to Scientific Chemical to make another purchase.... After Scott declined to make another trip, Morrow responded by stating that Scott would not want something to happen to his daughter or her house.... Scott thereafter made the trip for Morrow....

Approximately one week later, Morrow again came by Scott's daughter's house and wanted Scott to make another trip.... At some point during this discussion they decided to go for a ride in separate vehicles.... After traveling some distance, they both stopped their vehicles and pulled off to the side of the road.... Morrow pulled out a machine gun and two banana clips and emptied the clips at bottles and rocks.... Morrow stated "you wouldn't want to be in front of that thing would you?" and "you wouldn't want any of your family in front of that, would you?"... Scott responded negatively to Morrow's statements and thereafter made another trip to Scientific Chemical for Morrow.... On another occasion, Scott testified that Morrow threatened him by stating that he had better haul the chemicals if he knew what was good for him....

Scott testified that Morrow not only knew his adult daughter living in Portales, but that he knew his wife and another daughter who were living in Truth or Consequences and that Morrow had been to the residence in Truth or Consequences.... Scott testified that he made these trips for Morrow because he feared for the safety of his family in light of the confrontations he had with Morrow.... Scott stated he had no doubt that Morrow would have carried out his threats.... Scott was aware of information linking Morrow to various murders.... Scott further testified that he did not go to the police with any of this information concerning Morrow because he had gone to them before on other matters and they did nothing.... Further, Scott believed that Morrow had been paying a DEA agent in Lubbock, Texas, for information regarding investigations....

On cross-examination Scott testified that all of Morrow's threats were verbal, ... that he saw Morrow only a few times between August 1987 and January 1988, ... that he had an acquaintance by the name of Bill King who was a retired California Highway Patrolman living in Truth or Consequences, ... and that he could have found a law enforcement official to whom he could have reported the actions of Morrow....

II

A coercion or duress defense requires the establishment of three elements: (1) an immediate threat of death or serious bodily injury, (2) a well-grounded fear that the threat will be carried out, and (3) no reasonable opportunity to escape the threatened harm....

Scott proffered a coercion instruction to the district court in conformity with the above elements. Scott ... contended that the testimony before the court concerning coercion was sufficient to raise an issue for the jury and that a coercion instruction should be given. The district court found that Scott had failed to meet his threshold burden as to all three elements of a coercion defense. Accordingly, the district court refused to give an instruction on the defense of coercion.

Scott contends that the district court committed reversible error by substituting its judgment as to the weight of his coercion defense rather than allowing the jury to decide the issue. Scott maintains that he presented sufficient evidence to place in issue the defense of coercion and that it was error for the district court to usurp the role of the jury in weighing the evidence. We disagree and find that the district court acted properly in requiring Scott to satisfy a threshold showing of a coercion defense, and in finding the evidence insufficient to warrant the giving of a coercion instruction. In doing so, we find the evidence clearly lacking as to the third element for a coercion defense—absence of any reasonable opportunity to escape the threatened harm.

Only after a defendant has properly raised a coercion defense is he entitled to an instruction requiring the prosecution to prove beyond a reasonable doubt that he was not acting under coercion when he performed the act or acts charged....

The evidence introduced must be sufficient as to *all* elements of the coercion defense before the court will instruct the jury as to such defense.... If the evidence is lacking as to any element of the coercion defense the trial court may properly disallow the defense as a matter of law and refuse to instruct the jury as to coercion.... Consequently, a defendant who fails to present sufficient evidence to raise a triable issue of fact concerning the absence of any reasonable opportunity to escape the threatened harm is not entitled to an instruction on the defense of coercion....

The evidence in this case as to Scott's ability to escape the threatened harm wholly failed to approach the level necessary for the giving of a coercion instruction. Scott's involvement with Morrow covered a period of time in excess of one hundred twenty-five days. Scott's personal contact with Morrow was extremely limited during this time. Scott had countless opportunities to contact law enforcement authorities or escape the perceived threats by Morrow during this time. Scott made no attempt to contact law enforcement officials regarding Morrow's activities. In fact, Scott even failed to take advantage of his acquaintance, King, a retired law enforcement official, to seek his assistance in connection with Morrow's threats and activities. Scott's failure to avail himself of the readily accessible alternative of contacting law enforcement officials is persuasive evidence of the hollow nature of Scott's claimed coercion defense.... Clearly, the record establishes that Scott had at his disposal a reasonable legal alternative to undertaking the acts on behalf of Morrow....

Morrow did not accompany Scott when he made the purchases nor was there any evidence that Scott was under surveillance by Morrow. In fact, Scott's contact with Morrow was limited and he admitted he saw Morrow only a few times during the course of his involvement on behalf of Morrow between August 1987 and January 1988. Based on all of these circumstances, the district court was correct in finding that Scott had failed to establish that he had no reasonable opportunity to escape the threatened harm by Morrow.

III

In conclusion, we find that Scott failed to present sufficient evidence to establish that he had no reasonable opportunity to escape the harm threatened by Morrow. Accordingly, the district court properly refused to instruct the jury as to the defense of coercion. We affirm the judgment of the district court.

Case Questions

1. What must a defendant do to be entitled to a jury instruction on the defense of coercion?
2. Given the facts of this case, why did the trial court refuse to give the instruction?

The law also recognizes that occasionally police officers induce innocent people to commit crimes. When this occurs, the person so induced can raise an affirmative defense called entrapment. If an officer provides a person who is previously disposed to commit a criminal act with the opportunity to do so, that is not entrapment. If, however, an officer placed the notion of criminal wrongdoing in the defendant's mind, and that person was previously indisposed to commit the act, entrapment has occurred, and the charges will be dismissed. In entrapment cases, the defendant admits to having committed a criminal act, but the law relieves him or her of criminal responsibility in order to deter police officers from resorting to this tactic in the future.

Intoxication is frequently recognized as a defense in limited circumstances. Most jurisdictions distinguish between voluntary and involuntary intoxication. Most do not recognize voluntary intoxication as a defense to general intent crimes, and some do not recognize it at all—Hawaii is one example. In many states, however, a person who commits a specific intent crime while voluntarily intoxicated may have a defense if the intoxication is quite severe. In those jurisdictions a defendant cannot be convicted of a specific intent crime if the intoxication was so severe that the person was incapable of forming specific intent. Involuntary intoxication, however, completely relieves a defendant of all criminal responsibility. This could occur, for example, when a defendant inadvertently ingests incompatible medicines.

Insanity is one of the least used and most controversial defenses. A defendant who claims insanity admits to having committed the act, but denies criminal responsibility for that act. Because insanity is a legal and not a medical term, jurisdictions use different tests to define insanity. The **M'Naghten Rule** specifies that a defendant is not guilty if he or she had a diseased mind at the time of the act and was unable to distinguish right from wrong or was unaware of the nature and quality of his or her act due to a diseased mind. The **irresistible-impulse test** specifies that a defendant is not guilty if he or she knows that an act is wrong and is aware of the nature and quality of the act, but cannot refrain from committing the act. The Model Penal Code specifies that a defendant is not criminally responsible if the defendant's conduct is due to either mental disease or defect, and if the defendant lacked substantial capacity to understand its criminality or comply with legal requirements. The states of Idaho, Utah, and Montana do not recognize insanity as a defense.

CRIMINAL PROCEDURE

Criminal procedure is that area of the law that deals with the administration of criminal justice, from the initial investigation of a crime and the arrest of a suspect, through trial, sentence, and release.

The goal of criminal justice is to protect society from antisocial activity without sacrificing individual rights, justice, and fair play. The procedures used to apprehend and prosecute alleged criminal offenders must comply with the requirements of the law. One objective of using an adversarial system involving prosecutors and defense attorneys is to ensure that procedural justice is accorded the defendant. The judge umpires this confrontation and tries to ensure that both parties receive a fair trial—one that accords with the requirements of the substantive and procedural law. The judge or jury determines the guilt or innocence of the accused by properly evaluating the facts presented in open court. Ideally, the truth emerges from adversarial proceedings conducted in a manner consistent with constitutional guarantees. (See Figure 8.3.)

The constitutional limitations on the way governmental officials procedurally go about investigating criminal offenses and prosecuting alleged criminal offenders are primarily contained in the very general statements of the Fourth, Fifth, Sixth, Eighth, and Fourteenth Amendments to the U.S. Constitution. The U.S. Supreme Court, as well as the other federal and state courts, has played a significant role in determining what these amendments actually mean in practice. Does the Constitution mandate that arrested persons who are indigent be provided a court-appointed attorney? Does the Constitution require that twelve-person juries be convened in criminal cases, or are six-person juries sufficient? Do defendants have a constitutional right to be convicted beyond a reasonable doubt by a unanimous jury, or can a guilty verdict be received that is supported by nine out of twelve jurors?

PROCEEDINGS PRIOR TO TRIAL

A criminal trial occurs only after several preliminary stages have been completed. Although there are some jurisdictional variations in the way these stages occur, some generalizations can be made. The "typical" criminal prosecution originates with a police investigation of a crime that has been reported to officers or that officers have discovered through their own initiative. This investigation establishes if there really was a crime committed and, if so, determines the identity and whereabouts of the offender. In their investigations, officers are limited by federal and state constitutional and statutory law: (1) they are only permitted to make arrests if they have sufficient evidence to constitute probable cause; (2) they also are limited in conducting searches and making seizures; and (3) they are limited in the way they conduct custodial interrogations and lineups. The failure to follow correct procedures in the preliminary stages of a criminal case can result in the suppression of evidence and the dismissal of the charges filed against the accused. Violations of a defendant's constitutional rights also can result in a civil or criminal lawsuit against the responsible police officers.

Arrest

An arrest occurs when an officer takes someone into custody for the purpose of holding that person to answer a criminal charge. The arrest must be made in a reasonable manner, and the force employed must be reasonable in proportion to the circumstances and conduct of the party being arrested. The traditional rule was that police officers could make arrests in felonies based on probable cause, but officers were required to observe the commission of a misdemeanor offense in order to make a valid arrest. Today, many states have repealed the in-presence requirement and permit officers to make arrests for both misdemeanors and felonies based on probable cause. Probable cause means that the arresting officer has a well-grounded belief that the individual being arrested has committed, or is committing, an offense.

If police officers intend to make a routine felony arrest in a suspect's home, the U.S. Supreme Court has interpreted the U.S. Constitution as requiring that the officers first obtain an arrest warrant. An arrest warrant is an order issued by a judge, magistrate, or other judicial officer commanding the arresting officer to take an individual into custody and to bring the person before the court to answer criminal charges. Before the court will issue a warrant, a complaint containing the name of the

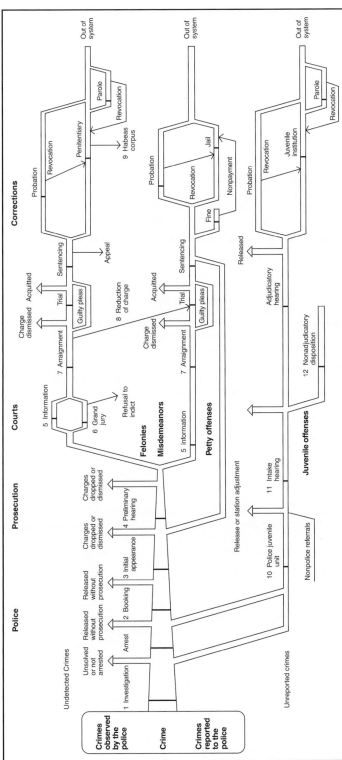

1 May continue until trial.
2 Administrative record of arrest. First step, temporary release on bail, may be available.
3 Before magistrate, commissioner, or justice of peace. Formal notice of charge, advice of rights. Bail set. Summary trials for petty offenses usually conducted here without further processing.
4 Preliminary testing of evidence against defendant. Charge may be reduced. No separate preliminary hearing for misdemeanors in some systems.
5 Charge filed by prosecutor on basis of information submitted by police or citizens. Alternative to grand jury indictment; often used in felonies, almost always in misdemeanors.
6 Review whether government evidence is sufficient to justify trial. Some states have no grand jury system; others seldom use it.
7 Appearance for plea: defendant elects trial by judge or jury (if available); counsel for indigent usually appointed here.
8 Charge may be reduced at any time before trial in return for guilty plea or for other reasons.
9 Challenge on constitutional grounds to legality of detention. May be sought at any point in process.
10 Police often hold informal hearings and dismiss or adjust many cases without further processing.
11 Probation officer decides desirability of further court action.
12 Welfare agency, social services, counseling, medical care, and the like. for cases where adjudicatory handling not needed.

A simple yet comprehensive view of the movement of cases through the criminal justice system. Procedures in individual jurisdictions may vary from pattern shown here. Differing widths of lines indicate relative volumes of cases disposed of at various points in system, but these are only suggestive, since no nationwide data of the sort exist.

F I G U R E 8.3   General View of the Criminal Justice System accused, or a description of the accused, must be filed. The complaint must be supported by affidavits and contain a description of the offense and the surrounding circumstances. A warrant is then issued if the court magistrate decides that (1) the evidence supports the belief that (2) probable cause exists to believe that (3) a crime has been committed and that (4) the suspect is the probable culprit. Many times, the complaining party does not have firsthand information and is relying on hearsay. The warrant may still be issued if the court believes that there is substantial basis for crediting it.

Some policing agencies, such as the FBI, make a large number of arrests based on warrants. Most arrests, however, are made without a warrant, as illustrated in the following *Draper* case. This case also explains what constitutes probable cause to arrest.

Draper v. United States
358 U.S. 307
Supreme Court of the United States
January 26, 1959

Mr. Justice Whittaker delivered the opinion of the Court.
The evidence offered at the hearing on the motion to suppress was not substantially disputed. It established that one Marsh, a federal narcotic agent with 29 years' experience, was stationed at Denver; that one Hereford had been engaged as a "special employee" of the Bureau of Narcotics at Denver for about six months, and from time to time gave information to Marsh regarding violations of the narcotic laws, for which Hereford was paid small sums of money, and that Marsh had always found the information given by Hereford to be accurate and reliable. On September 3, 1956, Hereford told Marsh that James Draper (petitioner) recently had taken up abode at a stated address in Denver and "was peddling narcotics to several addicts" in that city. Four days later, on September 7, Hereford told Marsh "that Draper had gone to Chicago the day before [September 6] by train [and] that he was going to bring back three ounces of heroin [and] that he would return to Denver either on the morning of the 8th of September or the morning of the 9th of September also by train." Hereford also gave Marsh a detailed physical description of Draper and of the clothing he was wearing, and said that he would be carrying "a tan zipper bag" and habitually "walked real fast."

On the morning of September 8, Marsh and a Denver police officer went to the Denver Union Station and kept watch over all incoming trains from Chicago, but they did not see anyone fitting the description that Hereford had given. Repeating the process on the morning of September 9, they saw a person, having the exact physical attributes and wearing the precise clothing described by Hereford, alight from an incoming Chicago train and start walking "fast" toward the exit. He was carrying a tan zipper bag in his right hand and the left was thrust in his raincoat pocket. Marsh, accompanied by the police officer, overtook, stopped and arrested him. They then searched him and found the two "envelopes containing heroin" clutched in his left hand in his raincoat pocket, and found the syringe in the tan zipper bag. Marsh then took him (petitioner) into custody. Hereford died four days after the arrest and therefore did not testify at the hearing on the motion.... [T]he Narcotic Control Act of 1956 ... provides in pertinent part:

> The Commissioner ... and agents, of the Bureau of Narcotics ... may— ...
> (2) Make arrests without warrant for violations of any law of the United States relating to narcotic drugs ... where the violation is committed in the presence of the person making the arrest or where such person had reasonable grounds to believe that the person to be arrested has committed or is committing such a violation.

The crucial question for us then is whether knowledge of the related facts and circumstances gave Marsh "probable cause" within the meaning of the Fourth Amendment, and "reasonable grounds" ... to believe that petitioner had committed or was committing a violation of the narcotic laws. If it did, the arrest, though without warrant, was lawful....

Petitioner ... contends (1) that the information given by Hereford to Marsh was "hearsay" and, because hearsay is not legally competent evidence in a criminal trial, could not legally have been considered, but should have been put out of mind by Marsh in assessing whether he had "probable cause" and "reasonable grounds" to arrest petitioner without a warrant, and (2) that, even if hearsay could lawfully have been considered, Marsh's information should be held insufficient to show "probable cause" and "reasonable grounds" to believe that petitioner had violated or was violating the narcotic laws and to justify his arrest without a warrant.

Considering the first contention, we find petitioner entirely in error. *Brinegar v. United States,* 338 U.S. 160 ... has settled the question the other way. There, in a similar situation, the convict contended "that the factors relating to inadmissibility of the evidence [for] *purposes of proving guilt at the trial,* deprive[d] the evidence as a whole of sufficiency to show probable cause for the search...." But this Court, rejecting that contention, said: "[T]he so-called distinction places a wholly unwarranted emphasis upon the criterion of admissibility in evidence, to prove the accused's guilt, of facts relied upon to show probable cause. The emphasis, we think, goes much too far in confusing and disregarding the difference between what is required to prove guilt in a criminal case and what is required to show probable cause for arrest or search. It approaches requiring (if it does not in practical effect require) proof sufficient to establish guilt in order to substantiate the existence of probable cause. There is a large difference between the two things to be proved [guilt and probable cause], as well as between the tribunals which determine them, and therefore a like difference in the *quanta* and modes of proof required to establish them."...

Nor can we agree with petitioner's second contention that Marsh's information was insufficient to show probable cause and reasonable grounds to believe that petitioner had violated or was violating the narcotic laws and to justify his arrest without a warrant. The information given to narcotic agent Marsh by "special employee" Hereford may have been hearsay to Marsh, but coming from one employed for that purpose and whose information had always been found accurate and reliable, it is clear that Marsh would have been derelict in his duties had he not pursued it. And when, in pursuing that information, he saw a man, having the exact physical attributes and wearing the precise clothing and carrying the tan zipper bag that Hereford had described, alight from one of the very trains from the very place stated by Hereford and start to walk at a "fast" pace toward the station exit, Marsh had personally verified every facet of the information given him by Hereford except whether the petitioner had accomplished his mission and had the three ounces of heroin on his person or in his bag. And surely, with every other bit of Hereford's information being thus personally verified, Marsh had "reasonable grounds" to believe that the remaining unverified bit of Hereford's information—that Draper would have the heroin with him—was likewise true.

"In dealing with probable cause ... as the very name implies, we deal with probabilities. These are not technical; they are the factual and practical considerations of everyday life on which reasonable and prudent men, not legal technicians, act." *Brinegar v. United States.* Probable cause exists where "the facts and circumstances within ... [the arresting officer's] knowledge and of which they had reasonably trustworthy information [are] sufficient in themselves to warrant a man of reasonable caution in the belief that" an offense has been or is being committed....

We believe that, under the facts and circumstances here, Marsh had probable cause and reasonable grounds to believe that petitioner was committing a violation of the laws of the United States relating to narcotic drugs at the time he arrested him. The arrest was therefore lawful, and the subsequent search and seizure, having been made incident to that lawful arrest, were likewise valid. It follows that petitioner's motion to suppress was properly denied and that the seized heroin was competent evidence lawfully received at the trial.

Affirmed.

Case Questions

1. Why did the Supreme Court allow hearsay evidence to be used to establish probable cause, when it would have been inadmissible at trial?
2. Do you believe that an officer who has time to obtain an arrest warrant should have to do so in lieu of making a warrantless arrest in a public place?

Custodial Interrogation

Part of the criminal investigative procedure involves questioning suspects with the aim of obtaining confessions and disclosures of crimes.

The privilege against self-incrimination applies to this questioning done outside the courtroom as well as at the trial. In general, only statements that are voluntarily made by a suspect are admissible.

That is, statements must be the product of free and rational choice. The statements cannot be the result of promises, threats, inducements, or physical abuse. However, the U.S. Supreme Court has ruled that confessions that are neither voluntary nor intelligently made can in some instances be admissible if the coercion amounts to "harmless error."

In the case of *Miranda v. Arizona,* 384 U.S. 436 (1966), the Supreme Court required that people being interrogated while in police custody (i.e., people subjected to **custodial interrogation**) must first be informed in clear and unequivocal language that they have the right to remain silent, that anything they say can and will be used against them in court, that they have the right to consult with a lawyer and to have a lawyer with them during interrogation, and that they have the right to an appointed lawyer to represent them if they are indigent.

Police officers who take a person into custody and who do not ask this person any questions are not violating the person's *Miranda* rights because there is no interrogation. Similarly, if police officers ask incriminating questions of a person who is standing on the sidewalk outside the police station and the person is not explicitly or implicitly in police custody, there is again no *Miranda* violation.

For a violation of *Miranda* to exist both police custody and interrogation must have occurred.

In general, courts will suppress statements obtained by police as a result of custodial interrogation from an accused person who was not given the *Miranda* warnings. That means the prosecution is not allowed to introduce those statements at trial as part of its case-in-chief to prove the defendant's guilt.

Introduction to *Vermont v. Tran*

As we will see in the next case, it can be difficult to determine what constitutes a custodial interrogation. Hieu Tran was questioned for about an hour in a police vehicle outside his home in conjunction with an assault and attempted robbery investigation. Tran was not given his *Miranda* warnings at any time, and he made incriminating statements that the prosecution could use as evidence as part of its case-in-chief at trial. Tran's motion to suppress the incriminating statements was granted by the trial court. This ruling was appealed to the Vermont Supreme Court by the state, which contended that no warnings were required because the statements were made voluntarily.

State of Vermont v. Hieu Tran
2012 VT 104
Supreme Court of Vermont
December 21, 2012

Skoglund, J.

... Defendant was charged with assault and attempted robbery.... Defendant filed a motion to suppress statements he made to police during an interview in March 2011. Defendant claimed that the statements were made in violation of his rights under the Fifth Amendment of the Federal Constitution and Chapter I, Article 10 of the Vermont Constitution because police conducted a custodial interrogation without providing defendant with the necessary *Miranda* warnings. The court held a hearing on the motion in August 2011. At the hearing, the only witness was one of the police detectives who interviewed defendant. In addition, a recording and transcript of the police interview were admitted.

At the suppression hearing, the detective described the following facts concerning the

investigation and the challenged interview. In the early afternoon of March 23, two police detectives drove in an unmarked police car to defendant's residence to question him about his possible involvement in an assault and robbery that had occurred a couple of days earlier.

Prior to the interview, police had already compiled information regarding the assault and robbery from the victim, the victim's friend who was present at the scene, and a person in the neighborhood who witnessed the altercation. The investigation started when police were dispatched to an emergency room where a man was being treated for an assault, which required stitches on his hand. The information from the man led detectives to the place where the incident occurred. After speaking with a witness at the scene and the injured man's friend, police understood that the assault occurred during a drug transaction. Two perpetrators were involved, and one carried a gun. The victim's friend identified defendant as the suspect without a gun. Police recovered a baseball cap from the scene that reportedly belonged to defendant.

When the detectives arrived at defendant's residence, defendant's mother indicated that he was not at home and she was going to pick him up. Police followed her car when she left to get defendant. When defendant arrived back at home, police again went to the door and defendant came out onto the porch. Police asked defendant to meet in their car. The detective testified that he decided to conduct the interview in the police car to be more comfortable and to afford some privacy from defendant's mother and brother, who were at home. Defendant entered the front passenger seat. The officer could not remember if defendant or the other detective had shut the front door. The door remained unlocked during the interview. The detective testified he did not tell defendant that he was not free to leave, but on cross-examination agreed he did not tell defendant that he was free to leave. One detective sat in the driver's seat, and the other sat in the back seat. Both questioned defendant.

At the beginning of the interview, the detectives told defendant that they had spoken to the victim and other witnesses, that they knew something had happened and there was a fight, and that they wanted defendant to have a chance to explain his side of the story. The detectives asked defendant how the drug deal was set up. Defendant explained that the victim had initiated it by calling him. The detectives told defendant that they "already have the answers to some questions" and "know how it went down and where it went down and all of that stuff." In response to questions about the gun, defendant stated that the gun was fake and plastic. At one point, one detective directed defendant not to play with his cell phone during the interview. The detectives explained to defendant that he could be charged with armed robbery even if he was not holding the gun because he was there and part of the deal. Defendant made little response to the questioning, stating that he did not have anything to say, and did not know or remember what happened. At one point, he admitted that he was there, and again stated the gun was not real. He admitted he lost his hat at the scene.

The detective testified that prior to the interview, he believed there was probable cause to arrest defendant. The interview was recorded and lasted for about one hour. At the end of the interview, defendant was arrested.

The court made brief oral findings on the record. The court found that the circumstances of the questioning created a police-dominated atmosphere. The court found several factors demonstrated that defendant was in custody at the time of the interview and not free to leave. First, the court found it significant that prior to the interview, police had enough information to arrest defendant and were, in fact, planning to arrest defendant at the close of the interview. The court emphasized that defendant would not have felt free to leave insofar as he was young, and had been told by police that they had information linking him to the assault and robbery. Finally, the court pointed to the physical conditions of the interrogation: two officers questioning defendant in a small space—a police car—for one hour.

The court subsequently denied the State's motion to reconsider the suppression decision. The State then moved for permission to appeal.... The trial court granted the motion, and this Court accepted the State's appeal.

On appeal, the State argues that the court's order was error because the court erroneously considered the detective's subjective belief in defendant's guilt and defendant's subjective characteristics like his age. The State argues there was no custody because a reasonable person would have felt free to leave....

In the landmark decision of *Miranda v. Arizona*, the U.S. Supreme Court held that to adequately protect Fifth Amendment rights police are required to advise suspects of their rights to remain silent and to have an attorney present prior to any custodial interrogation.... "Suspects not in custody are not entitled to *Miranda* warnings."... The custody determination involves an objective test based on "'the totality of the circumstances.'"... The key inquiry is whether "'a reasonable person would believe he or she were free to leave or to refuse to answer police questioning.'"... In the absence of a formal arrest, the critical question is whether law enforcement officials acted or spoke in a manner that conveyed the message that they would not permit the individual to leave....

In *State v. Muntean*, 2010 VT 88, ... we identified several factors to consider in making the custody determination. These include: (1) the location of the interview; (2) the interviewer's communication to the suspect of his belief in the suspect's guilt; (3) whether the suspect arrives at the interview voluntarily; and (4) "whether the police told the suspect that he was free to terminate the interview at any point and leave." *Muntean* listed other indicators of custody including: the extent to which the suspect was confronted with evidence of guilt; whether and to what degree the suspect's freedom of movement was restrained; whether the police used deceptive techniques in conducting the interview; the degree to which the suspect was isolated from the outside world; the duration of the interview; whether the police officers were armed; and the number of police officers present during the interview.... We cautioned that the list was not exhaustive and that the totality of the circumstances should be considered.

Applying this analysis to the unchallenged facts, we conclude that police engaged in a custodial interview of defendant without providing the necessary *Miranda* warnings.

We begin with the most important factor— whether police informed defendant that he was free to leave. "Numerous courts have held that such disclosure is significant in determining whether a reasonable person would have felt at liberty to terminate a police interview."... ("[T]he absence of police advisement that the suspect is not under formal arrest, or that the suspect is at liberty to decline to answer questions, has been identified as an important indicium of the existence of a custodial setting."). That is why custody is usually not found when police assure a defendant that he is not under arrest, and is free to terminate the questioning and leave.... Here, officers did not inform defendant he was free to leave or that he was not under arrest. This fact strongly indicates a custodial setting.

In addition, the content of the questioning created a custodial atmosphere because throughout the interview the detectives repeatedly confronted defendant with evidence of his guilt.... The detective who testified at the suppression hearing stated that he believed there was probable cause to arrest defendant prior to the interview and that he intended to arrest defendant at that time. The detectives communicated this belief to defendant explaining they knew he was involved in the crime and confronting defendant with the existing evidence they had of his guilt. They emphasized that they had spoken with the victim and his friend, had interviewed witnesses in the neighborhood, and had identified defendant as one of the suspects. They also stated they knew there was a gun involved. They communicated that defendant could be arrested for armed robbery—a serious offense—based on that evidence. In fact, they did arrest defendant at the close of the interview. See *[United States v.] Griffin* ... (explaining that arrest at termination of interview is "objective evidence which tends to support the reasonableness of [the defendant's] subjective belief that he was in custody from the inception of the encounter and that his arrest was imminent").

This type of repeated accusatory questioning created the kind of "'coercive environment'" indicative of police custody.... While the detective's subjective belief in defendant's guilt is not necessarily relevant, it

becomes so when communicated to the suspect because it affects the person's objective belief in whether he or she is free to leave.... "A reasonable person would not feel at liberty to terminate a police interview after being confronted with such evidence, as a 'reasonable person understands that the police ordinarily will not set free a suspect when there is evidence strongly suggesting that the person is guilty of a serious crime.'" *Muntean*, 2010 VT 88.... Here, from the outset, the police presented defendant with evidence that: defendant was present during the drug deal and the robbery; a gun was used in the crime; and defendant could be arrested for his involvement.

Finally, other aspects of the questioning are indicative of a police-dominated atmosphere. Defendant did not voluntarily initiate contact with police, but spoke with the detectives after they sought him out, waited for him to come home, and placed him inside a police car. Inside the car, defendant was in a small space with two officers in close proximity, who both questioned him at length for an hour. All of these facts—the initiation of contact by police, the location, the number of officers, and the length of the interview—are indicia of custody....

Questioning of a suspect in a cruiser will not always support a finding of custody.... In this case, however, the facts describe a situation in which defendant would not have felt free to leave. Here, two detectives came to defendant's house and asked him to get in the police cruiser. They deliberately chose to conduct the interview in the cruiser, rather than in the home, thus separating defendant from the familiar setting of his home and his family.... During the interview, police directed defendant not to use his cell phone, further cutting him off from contact with others and asserting their authority....

The State ... argues that the trial court erroneously considered the officer's subjective belief in defendant's guilt and defendant's age of nineteen years, a subjective characteristic. The State contends that since defendant was an adult his age was irrelevant because the proper inquiry is whether a reasonable person would believe he or she was free to leave.... We do not reach this question because we do not rely on defendant's young age in our analysis of whether defendant was in custody. As to the consideration of the officer's subjective belief in defendant's guilt, we conclude there was no error. This belief was relevant because it was communicated to defendant during the questioning.

Finally, the State argues ... that even if defendant was in custody later in the interview, custody did not arise until the detectives began to confront defendant with evidence of his guilt, and that his incriminating statements made early in the interview should not be suppressed. We are not persuaded. From the outset of the questioning, there were indicia of custody and police dominance over defendant. He was directed into the cruiser; not informed that he was free to leave or to terminate the interview; told that they had gathered information/evidence from the victim of the assault, his friend, and other witnesses; and told that the police already knew what had happened in the assault. Certainly, later in the interview the detectives more precisely laid out the evidence against defendant and concretely told defendant that there was sufficient evidence to arrest him. We cannot say, however, that under the totality of the circumstances, defendant's statements even at the beginning of the interview were made in response to mere questioning rather than the product of a custodial interrogation.

We conclude that defendant was in custody and entitled to *Miranda* warnings, and because such warnings were not provided, defendant's statements made during the March interview must be suppressed.

Affirmed.

Case Questions

1. Imagine that you were a police officer determining whether and, if so, when to administer *Miranda* warnings in this case. In your opinion, how useful would the "custodial interrogation" benchmark be in your decision-making process?

2. The court ruled 3–2 to affirm. Do you agree with the three judges who concluded that warnings were required early on, or with the two judges who believed that warnings were only required toward the end of the interrogation process?

Author's Comment

In the *Tran* decision, the two dissenting justices concluded that no *Miranda* warnings were required until "the detectives assert[ed] … control over defendant by curtailing his cell phone and advising they could arrest him." These justices would only have suppressed Tran's statements made subsequent to this point in time. They "respectfully dissent[ed], however, from the majority's position that *Miranda* warnings were required before any facts objectively suggested that not only was defendant not immediately free to go, but that he was also likely to be kept under formal arrest."

Searches and Seizures

Examinations of a person or premises are conducted by officers of the law in order to find stolen property or other evidence of guilt to be used by the prosecutor in a criminal action. With some exceptions, a warrant must be obtained by an officer before making a search. (See Figure 8.4.)

As in the case of an arrest warrant, the Fourth Amendment requires probable cause for searches and seizures. Although the Fourth Amendment does not prescribe the forms by which probable cause must be established, evidence of probable cause has traditionally been presented to a magistrate in a written application for warrant supported by oath or affirmation, filed by someone who has personal information concerning items to be seized. Today it is increasingly common for statutes to provide for telephonic search warrants, as seen in Figure 8.5.

A valid warrant must be specific and sufficiently descriptive. An officer conducting a search is prohibited from going outside the limits set by the warrant.

Courts prefer that searches and seizures are undertaken pursuant to warrants. The warrant process permits a neutral and detached magistrate, in lieu of police officers, to determine if probable cause exists to support a requested search and seizure. But the Supreme Court has recognized that warrantless searches or seizures are constitutionally reasonable in some circumstances. In an introductory chapter, it is not possible to explain each of the circumstances in which an exception to the warrant requirement has been recognized. However, the most common of these recognized exceptions can be found in Figure 8.6. Interested students can look

---

SEARCH WARRANT

To . . . . *[specify official or officials authorized to execute warrant]:*
    Affidavit having been made before me by . . . . *[affiant]* that he has
reason to believe that on the . . . . . [person of *or* premises known as]
. . . . *[state name of suspect or specify exact address, including
apartment or room number, if any, and give description of premises],* in
the City of . . . . , State of . . . . , in the . . . . District of
. . . . , there is now being concealed certain property, namely,
. . . . *[specify, such as* certain dies, hubs, molds and plates, fitted
and intended to be used for the manufacture of counterfeit coins of the
United States, in violation of . . . . *(cite statute)],* and as I am satisfied
that there is probable cause to believe that the property so described is
being concealed on the . . . . [person *or* premises] above . . . .
[named *or* described], and that grounds for issuance of a search warrant
exist,
    You are hereby commanded to search within . . . . [ten] days from
this date the . . . . [person *or* place] named for the property specified,
serving this warrant and making the search . . . . [in the daytime *or* at any
time in the day or night], and if the property be found there to seize
it, leaving a copy of this warrant and a receipt for the property taken, and
prepare a written inventory of the property seized, and promptly return
this warrant and bring the property before me, as required by law.
Dated . . . . , 20. . . . .

[Signature and title]

F I G U R E 8.4   Sample Search Warrant [Federal Rules of Criminal Procedure 41(c)]

up the cases on the Internet or at the library using the case names and corresponding citations.

The Exclusionary Rule

In 1914, the U.S. Supreme Court ruled in the *Weeks* case that the Fourth Amendment prevented the use of evidence obtained from an illegal search and seizure in federal prosecutions. This **exclusionary rule** was incorporated into the Fourteenth Amendment's Due Process Clause and made binding on the states in the 1961 case of *Mapp v. Ohio* (367 U.S. 643). Although illegally obtained evidence may not be used by the government to prove the defendant's guilt, such evidence may be used to contradict (impeach) a defendant's trial testimony,

thus showing that the defendant's testimony may be untruthful.

The exclusionary rule has been quite controversial, because it suppresses evidence that—since the jury is not allowed to hear this evidence—can lead to a failed prosecution. In recent decades, the rule has been severely limited by Supreme Court decisions. Procedural hurdles to its use have been established and judicial doctrines created to narrow the circumstances in which it can be used. When a recognized exception applies, the evidence still can be admitted as evidence of guilt, despite the violation of the Fourth Amendment. Examples are the **independent-source exception** (when an untainted source of evidence unrelated to the illegal search and seizure is shown to exist) and the

968.12 Search warrant

(a) *General rule.* A search warrant may be based upon sworn oral testimony communicated to the judge by telephone, radio or other means of electronic communication, under the procedure prescribed in this subsection.

(b) *Application.* The person who is requesting the warrant shall prepare a duplicate original warrant and read the duplicate original warrant, verbatim, to the judge. The judge shall enter, verbatim, what is read on the original warrant. The judge may direct that the warrant be modified.

(c) *Issuance.* If the judge determines that there is probable cause for the warrant, the judge shall order the issuance of a warrant by directing the person requesting the warrant to sign the judge's name on the duplicate original warrant. In addition, the person shall sign his or her own name on the duplicate original warrant. The judge shall immediately sign the original warrant and enter on the face of the original warrant the exact time when the warrant was ordered to be issued. The finding of probable cause for a warrant upon oral testimony shall be based on the same kind of evidence as is sufficient for a warrant upon affidavit.

(d) *Recording and certification of testimony.* When a caller informs the judge that the purpose of the call is to request a warrant, the judge shall place under oath each person whose testimony forms a basis of the application and each person applying for the warrant. The judge or requesting person shall arrange for all sworn testimony to be recorded either by a stenographic reporter or by means of a voice recording device. The judge shall have the record transcribed. The transcript, certified as accurate by the judge or reporter, as appropriate, shall be filed with the court. If the testimony was recorded by means of a voice recording device, the judge shall also file the original recording with the court.

FIGURE 8.5 Excerpt from the Wisconsin Search Warrant Statute [968.12]

Exception	Case	Citation
Abandoned Property	*California v. Greenwood*	486 U.S. 35
Booking Searches	*Illinois v. Lafeyette*	462 U.S. 640
Consent Searches	*Schnecloth v. Bustamonte*	412 U.S. 218
Hot Pursuit	*Warden v. Hayden*	387 U.S. 294
Open Fields	*Oliver v. United States*	466 U.S. 170
	United States v. Dunn	480 U.S. 294
Plain View	*Arizona v. Hicks*	480 U.S. 321
Mobile Vehicles	*Carroll v. United States*	267 U.S. 132
	Chambers v. Maroney	399 U.S. 42
	Ross v. Moffit	417 U.S. 600
	California v. Acevedo	500 U.S. 386
Incident to Arrest	*Chimel v. California*	395 U.S. 752
	United States v. Robinson	414 U.S. 218
	Maryland v. Buie	494 U.S. 325
Vehicle Inventories	*South Dakota v. Opperman*	428 U.S. 364
	Colorado v. Bertine	479 U.S. 367

© Cengage Learning

FIGURE 8.6 Some Common Exceptions to the Search Warrant Requirement

good-faith exception (which applies if the police acted reasonably in relying on what subsequently turned out to be a defective warrant in obtaining evidence).

Introduction to *Missouri v. McNeely*

Tyler McNeely, the respondent in this case, was suspected by police of driving while intoxicated. Although McNeely had twice refused to consent to breath and blood tests, the arresting officer requested that a hospital technician perform a blood-alcohol test, which required that blood be drawn from McNeely. The arresting officer chose not to procure a search warrant prior to the taking of the blood sample. The defendant was subsequently charged with DWI ("driving while intoxicated," as the crime is called under Missouri law).

Missouri claimed that the taking of blood in DWI cases was permitted as an exception to the warrant requirement under existing U.S. Supreme Court decisions. The exemption was needed, Missouri said, because the alcohol in an accused person's blood dissipates over time and from the police point of view constituted vanishing evidence. This fact, said the State, created an emergency need for police officers, in all DWI cases, to obtain blood-alcohol evidence from nonconsenting drivers. The State also argued that this long-established exigency exception to the warrant requirement was a "per se rule" (an inflexible, inherent right, and independent of factual differences in particular cases). The trial

court disagreed and granted a defense motion to suppress the results of the blood test. It ruled that there was no emergency present in this case that would excuse the officer from the normal requirement that a search warrant be obtained prior to the nonconsensual taking of respondent's blood.

The state unsuccessfully appealed the trial court's ruling to the Missouri Supreme Court. That court rejected the State's per se–rule argument, concluding that what constitutes an emergency should be determined after examining the "totality of the circumstances" on a case-by-case basis. The U.S. Supreme Court agreed to decide whether this warrantless, nonconsensual blood taking was a reasonable search under the Fourth Amendment

Justice Sotomayor's majority opinion was joined by Justices Ginsburg, Kagan, Kennedy, and Scalia. Justice Sotomayor's opinion consisted of four sections plus two paragraphs (in which she announced the holding and judgment of the court). The sections were designated as I, II-A, -B, -C, III, and IV. Because Justice Kennedy did not agree with Justice Sotomayor's opinion in sections I-C and III, these segments were not part of the opinion of the Court and have been omitted from the excerpt of the case that follows. Justice Sotomayor in the omitted segments explained why she believed the totality-of-the-circumstances test was a better approach than the per se rule, and she defended her position that warrants should be required in nonemergency circumstances where the police want to have blood withdrawn from a nonconsenting person.

Missouri v. Tyler G. McNeely
_____ U.S. _____
Supreme Court of the United States
April 17, 2013

Justice Sotomayor announced the judgment of the Court and delivered the opinion of the Court with respect to Parts I, II-A, II-B, and IV.
In *Schmerber v. California*, 384 U. S. 757 (1966), this Court upheld a warrantless blood test of an individual arrested for driving under the influence of alcohol because the officer "might reasonably have believed that he was confronted with an emergency, in which the delay necessary to obtain a warrant, under the cir-

cumstances, threatened the destruction of evidence."... The question presented here is whether the natural metabolization of alcohol in the bloodstream presents a per se exigency that justifies an exception to the Fourth Amendment's warrant requirement for nonconsensual blood testing in all drunk-driving cases. We conclude that it does not, and we hold, consistent with general Fourth Amendment principles, that exigency in this context must be determined case by case based on the totality of the circumstances.

I

While on highway patrol at approximately 2:08 a.m., a Missouri police officer stopped Tyler McNeely's truck after observing it exceed the posted speed limit and repeatedly cross the centerline. The officer noticed several signs that McNeely was intoxicated, including McNeely's bloodshot eyes, his slurred speech, and the smell of alcohol on his breath. McNeely acknowledged to the officer that he had consumed "a couple of beers" at a bar ... and he appeared unsteady on his feet when he exited the truck. After McNeely performed poorly on a battery of field-sobriety tests and declined to use a portable breath-test device to measure his blood alcohol concentration (BAC), the officer placed him under arrest.

The officer began to transport McNeely to the station house. But when McNeely indicated that he would again refuse to provide a breath sample, the officer changed course and took McNeely to a nearby hospital for blood testing. The officer did not attempt to secure a warrant. Upon arrival at the hospital, the officer asked McNeely whether he would consent to a blood test. Reading from a standard implied consent form, the officer explained to McNeely that under state law refusal to submit voluntarily to the test would lead to the immediate revocation of his driver's license for one year and could be used against him in a future prosecution.... McNeely nonetheless refused. The officer then directed a hospital lab technician to take a blood sample, and the sample was secured at approximately 2:35 a.m. Subsequent laboratory testing measured McNeely's BAC at 0.154 percent, which was well above the legal limit of 0.08 percent....

McNeely was charged with driving while intoxicated (DWI), in violation of §577.010.... He moved to suppress the results of the blood test, arguing in relevant part that, under the circumstances, taking his blood for chemical testing without first obtaining a search warrant violated his rights under the Fourth Amendment. The trial court agreed. It concluded that the exigency exception to the warrant requirement did not apply because, apart from the fact that "[a]s in all cases involving intoxication, [McNeely's] blood alcohol was being metabolized by his liver," there were no circumstances suggesting the officer faced an emergency in which he could not practicably obtain a warrant....

The Missouri Supreme Court affirmed....

We granted certiorari to resolve a split of authority on the question whether the natural dissipation of

alcohol in the bloodstream establishes a per se exigency that suffices on its own to justify an exception to the warrant requirement for nonconsensual blood testing in drunk-driving investigations.... We now affirm.

II

A

The Fourth Amendment provides in relevant part that "[t]he right of the people to be secure in their persons, houses, papers, and effects, against unreasonable searches and seizures, shall not be violated, and no Warrants shall issue, but upon probable cause." Our cases have held that a warrantless search of the person is reasonable only if it falls within a recognized exception.... That principle applies to the type of search at issue in this case, which involved a compelled physical intrusion beneath McNeely's skin and into his veins to obtain a sample of his blood for use as evidence in a criminal investigation. Such an invasion of bodily integrity implicates an individual's "most personal and deep-rooted expectations of privacy."...

We first considered the Fourth Amendment restrictions on such searches in *Schmerber*, where, as in this case, a blood sample was drawn from a defendant suspected of driving while under the influence of alcohol.... Noting that "[s]earch warrants are ordinarily required for searches of dwellings," we reasoned that "absent an emergency, no less could be required where intrusions into the human body are concerned," even when the search was conducted following a lawful arrest.... We explained that the importance of requiring authorization by a "'neutral and detached magistrate'" before allowing a law enforcement officer to "invade another's body in search of evidence of guilt is indisputable and great."...

As noted, the warrant requirement is subject to exceptions. "One well-recognized exception," and the one at issue in this case, "applies when the exigencies of the situation make the needs of law enforcement so compelling that a warrantless search is objectively reasonable under the Fourth Amendment."... A variety of circumstances may give rise to an exigency sufficient to justify a warrantless search, including law enforcement's need to provide emergency assistance to an occupant of a home ... engage in "hot pursuit" of a fleeing suspect, ... or enter a burning building to put out a fire and investigate its cause.... As is relevant here, we have also recognized that in some circumstances law enforcement officers may conduct a search without a warrant to prevent the imminent destruction of evidence.... While these contexts do not necessarily involve equivalent dangers, in each a warrantless search is potentially reasonable because "there is compelling need for official action and no time to secure a warrant."...

To determine whether a law enforcement officer faced an emergency that justified acting without a warrant, this Court looks to the totality of circumstances.... We apply this "finely tuned approach" to Fourth Amendment reasonableness in this context because the police action at issue lacks "the traditional justification that ... a warrant ... provides."... Absent that established justification, "the fact-specific nature of the reasonableness inquiry,"... demands that we evaluate each case of alleged exigency based "on its own facts and circumstances."...

Our decision in *Schmerber* applied this totality of the circumstances approach. In that case, the petitioner had suffered injuries in an automobile accident and was taken to the hospital.... While he was there receiving treatment, a police officer arrested the petitioner for driving while under the influence of alcohol and ordered a blood test over his objection.... After explaining that the warrant requirement applied generally to searches that intrude into the human body, we concluded that the warrantless blood test "in the present case" was nonetheless permissible because the officer "might reasonably have believed that he was confronted with an emergency, in which the delay necessary to obtain a warrant, under the circumstances, threatened 'the destruction of evidence.'"...

In support of that conclusion, we observed that evidence could have been lost because "the percentage of alcohol in the blood begins to diminish shortly after drinking stops, as the body functions to eliminate it from the system."... We added that "[p]articularly in a case such as this, where time had to be taken to bring the accused to a hospital and to investigate the scene of the accident, there was no time to seek out a magistrate and secure a warrant."... "Given these special facts," we found that it was appropriate for the police to act without a warrant.... We further held that the blood test at issue was a reasonable way to recover the evidence because it was highly effective, "involve[d] virtually no risk, trauma, or pain," and was conducted in a reasonable fashion "by a physician in a hospital environment according to accepted medical practices." ... And in conclusion, we noted that our judgment that there had been no Fourth Amendment violation was strictly based "on the facts of the present record."...

Thus, our analysis in *Schmerber* fits comfortably within our case law applying the exigent circumstances exception. In finding the warrantless blood test reasonable in *Schmerber*, we considered all of the facts

and circumstances of the particular case and carefully based our holding on those specific facts.

B
The State properly recognizes that the reasonableness of a warrantless search under the exigency exception to the warrant requirement must be evaluated based on the totality of the circumstances.... But the State nevertheless seeks a per se rule for blood testing in drunk-driving cases. The State contends that whenever an officer has probable cause to believe an individual has been driving under the influence of alcohol, exigent circumstances will necessarily exist because BAC evidence is inherently evanescent. As a result, the State claims that so long as the officer has probable cause and the blood test is conducted in a reasonable manner, it is categorically reasonable for law enforcement to obtain the blood sample without a warrant.

It is true that as a result of the human body's natural metabolic processes, the alcohol level in a person's blood begins to dissipate once the alcohol is fully absorbed and continues to decline until the alcohol is eliminated....

But it does not follow that we should depart from careful case-by-case assessment of exigency and adopt the categorical rule proposed by the State and its amici. In those drunk-driving investigations where police officers can reasonably obtain a warrant before a blood sample can be drawn without significantly undermining the efficacy of the search, the Fourth Amendment mandates that they do so.... We do not doubt that some circumstances will make obtaining a warrant impractical such that the dissipation of alcohol from the bloodstream will support an exigency justifying a properly conducted warrantless blood test. That, however, is a reason to decide each case on its facts, as we did in *Schmerber*, not to accept the "considerable overgeneralization" that a per se rule would reflect....

The context of blood testing is different in critical respects from other destruction-of-evidence cases in which the police are truly confronted with a "'now or never'" situation.... In contrast to, for example, circumstances in which the suspect has control over easily disposable evidence ... BAC evidence from a drunk-driving suspect naturally dissipates over time in a gradual and relatively predictable manner. Moreover, because a police officer must typically transport a drunk-driving suspect to a medical facility and obtain the assistance of someone with appropriate medical training before conducting a blood test, some delay between the time of the arrest or accident and the time of the test is inevitable regardless of whether police officers are required to obtain a warrant....

Consider, for example, a situation in which the warrant process will not significantly increase the delay before the blood test is conducted because an officer can take steps to secure a warrant while the suspect is being transported to a medical facility by another officer. In such a circumstance, there would be no plausible justification for an exception to the warrant requirement.

The State's proposed per se rule also fails to account for advances in the 47 years since *Schmerber* was decided that allow for the more expeditious processing of warrant applications, particularly in contexts like drunk-driving investigations where the evidence offered to establish probable cause is simple. The Federal Rules of Criminal Procedure ... now allows a federal magistrate judge to consider "information communicated by telephone or other reliable electronic means."... States have also innovated. Well over a majority of States allow police officers or prosecutors to apply for search warrants remotely through various means, including telephonic or radio communication, electronic communication such as e-mail, and video conferencing....

We by no means claim that telecommunications innovations have, will, or should eliminate all delay from the warrant-application process. Warrants inevitably take some time for police officers or prosecutors to complete and for magistrate judges to review. Telephonic and electronic warrants may still require officers to follow time-consuming formalities designed to create an adequate record, such as preparing a duplicate warrant before calling the magistrate judge. See Fed. Rule Crim. Proc. 4.1(b)(3). And improvements in communications technology do not guarantee that a magistrate judge will be available when an officer needs a warrant after making a late-night arrest. But technological developments that enable police officers to secure warrants more quickly, and do so without undermining the neutral magistrate judge's essential role as a check on police discretion, are relevant to an assessment of exigency. That is particularly so in this context, where BAC evidence is lost gradually and relatively predictably....

Of course, there are important countervailing concerns. While experts can work backwards from the BAC at the time the sample was taken to determine the BAC at the time of the alleged offense, longer intervals may raise questions about the accuracy of the calculation. For that reason, exigent circumstances justifying a warrantless blood sample may arise in the regular course of law enforcement due to delays from the warrant application process. But adopting the State's per se approach would improperly ignore the current and future technological developments in warrant procedures, and might well diminish the

incentive for jurisdictions "to pursue progressive approaches to warrant acquisition that preserve the protections afforded by the warrant while meeting the legitimate interests of law enforcement."...

In short, while the natural dissipation of alcohol in the blood may support a finding of exigency in a specific case, as it did in *Schmerber*, it does not do so categorically. Whether a warrantless blood test of a drunk-driving suspect is reasonable must be determined case by case based on the totality of the circumstances.

IV

The State argued before this Court that the fact that alcohol is naturally metabolized by the human body creates an exigent circumstance in every case. The State did not argue that there were exigent circumstances in this particular case because a warrant could not have been obtained within a reasonable amount of time. In his testimony before the trial court, the arresting officer did not identify any other factors that would suggest he faced an emergency or unusual delay in securing a warrant.... He explained that he elected to forgo a warrant application in this case only because he believed it was not legally necessary to obtain a warrant.... Based on this testimony, the trial court concluded that there was no exigency and specifically found that, although the arrest took place in the middle of the night, "a prosecutor was readily available to apply for a search warrant and a judge was readily available to issue a warrant."...

Here and in its own courts the State based its case on an insistence that a driver who declines to submit to testing after being arrested for driving under the influence of alcohol is always subject to a nonconsensual blood test without any precondition for a warrant. That is incorrect....

... The relevant factors in determining whether a warrantless search is reasonable, including the practical problems of obtaining a warrant within a timeframe that still preserves the opportunity to obtain reliable evidence, will no doubt vary depending upon the circumstances in the case.

Because this case was argued on the broad proposition that drunk-driving cases present a per se exigency, the arguments and the record do not provide the Court with an adequate analytic framework for a detailed discussion of all the relevant factors that can be taken into account in determining the reasonableness of acting without a warrant. It suffices to say that the metabolization of alcohol in the bloodstream and the ensuing loss of evidence are among the factors that must be considered in deciding whether a warrant is required. No doubt, given the large number of arrests for this offense in different jurisdictions nationwide, cases will arise when anticipated delays in obtaining a warrant will justify a blood test without judicial authorization, for in every case the law must be concerned that evidence is being destroyed. But that inquiry ought not to be pursued here where the question is not properly before this Court. Having rejected the sole argument presented to us challenging the Missouri Supreme Court's decision, we affirm its judgment....

We hold that in drunk-driving investigations, the natural dissipation of alcohol in the bloodstream does not constitute an exigency in every case sufficient to justify conducting a blood test without a warrant.

The judgment of the Missouri Supreme Court is affirmed.

It is so ordered.

Case Questions

1. What are the pros and cons of the per se rule and the totality-of-the-evidence approach as they relate to this case?
2. Which approach did you find more persuasive in this case?

Investigatory Detentions (Stop-and-Frisk)

The requirement that police officers have probable cause to arrest makes it difficult for them to investigate individuals whose conduct has aroused their suspicions. The Supreme Court was asked in 1968 to balance police investigative needs against citizen privacy rights in the famous case of *Terry v. Ohio.* In *Terry,* the Supreme Court ruled that it was reasonable under the Fourth Amendment for police officers to make brief seizures (a "stop") of individuals based on reasonable suspicion, and, in appropriate circumstances, to make limited searches of the individuals for weapons (a "frisk"). Such a procedure is referred to as a **stop-and-frisk.** The court interpreted the Fourth Amendment as permitting officers to detain suspiciously acting individuals so that the officers could determine their identity and question them about their behavior. However, police officers must be able to articulate the specific facts and circumstances that created a reasonable suspicion in their minds that criminal activity has been, is being, or is about to be committed.

Further, the Supreme Court has ruled that officers who can articulate facts and circumstances that suggest that the stopped individual is armed have a right to make a "frisk." The frisk is less than a full search and consists of the pat down of the outer clothing of a stopped individual in order to locate weapons that might be used against the officer. If an officer, while conducting the pat down, feels an object that could be a weapon, the officer is entitled to reach inside the clothing and take the object. If a seized object or weapon is lawfully possessed, it must be returned upon the conclusion of the investigatory detention. If the weapon is unlawfully possessed, it can be seized and used in a criminal prosecution.

Stop-and-frisk is a very controversial investigative technique in many communities. Police frequently are accused of making stops of individuals based on factors such as race, age, and choice of friends, rather than on actual evidence of impending criminal activity. Officers also are accused of making investigative stops and frisks for the purpose of conducting exploratory searches for evidence.

In the next case, Illinois State Trooper Craig Graham's narcotics detection dog sniffed around Roy Caballes's car while he was being stopped for speeding by Trooper Daniel Gillette. The dog alerted to drugs, and the officers discovered marijuana in the trunk. The U.S. Supreme Court granted certiorari to determine "whether the Fourth Amendment requires reasonable, articulable suspicion to justify using a drug-detection dog to sniff a vehicle during a legitimate traffic stop."

Illinois v. Roy I. Caballes
543 U.S. 405
Supreme Court of the United States
January 24, 2005

Justice Stevens delivered the opinion of the Court.

Illinois State Trooper Daniel Gillette stopped respondent for speeding on an interstate highway. When Gillette radioed the police dispatcher to report the stop, a second trooper, Craig Graham, a member of the Illinois State Police Drug Interdiction Team, overheard the transmission and immediately headed for the scene with his narcotics-detection dog. When they arrived, respondent's car was on the shoulder of the road and respondent was in Gillette's vehicle. While Gillette was in the process of writing a warning ticket, Graham walked his dog around respondent's car. The dog alerted at the trunk. Based on that alert, the officers searched the trunk, found marijuana, and arrested respondent. The entire incident lasted less than 10 minutes.

Respondent was convicted of a narcotics offense and sentenced to 12 years' imprisonment and a $256,136 fine. The trial judge denied his motion to suppress the seized evidence and to quash his arrest. He held that the officers had not unnecessarily prolonged the stop and that the dog alert was sufficiently reliable to provide probable cause to conduct the search. Although the Appellate Court affirmed, the Illinois Supreme Court reversed, concluding that because the canine sniff was performed without any "'specific and articulable facts'" to suggest drug activity, the use of the dog "unjustifiably enlarg[ed] the scope of a routine traffic stop into a drug investigation."…

The question on which we granted certiorari … is narrow: "Whether the Fourth Amendment requires reasonable, articulable suspicion to justify using a drug-detection dog to sniff a vehicle during a legitimate traffic stop."… Thus, we proceed on the assumption that the officer conducting the dog sniff had no information about respondent except that he had been stopped for speeding; accordingly, we have omitted any reference to facts about respondent that might have triggered a modicum of suspicion.

Here, the initial seizure of respondent when he was stopped on the highway was based on probable cause, and was concededly lawful. It is nevertheless clear that a seizure that is lawful at its inception can violate the Fourth Amendment if its manner of execution unreasonably infringes interests protected by the Constitution…. A seizure that is justified solely by the interest in issuing a warning ticket to the driver can become unlawful if it is prolonged beyond the time reasonably required to complete that mission. In an earlier case involving a dog sniff that occurred during an unreasonably prolonged traffic stop, the Illinois Supreme Court held that use of the dog and the subsequent discovery of contraband were the product of an unconstitutional seizure…. We may assume that a similar result would be warranted in this case if the dog sniff had been conducted while respondent was being unlawfully detained.

In the state-court proceedings, however, the judges carefully reviewed the details of Officer Gillette's conversations with respondent and the precise timing of his radio transmissions to the dispatcher to determine whether he had improperly extended the duration of the stop to enable the dog sniff to occur. We have not recounted those details because we accept the state court's conclusion that the duration of the stop in this case was entirely justified by the traffic offense and the ordinary inquiries incident to such a stop.

Despite this conclusion, the Illinois Supreme Court held that the initially lawful traffic stop became an unlawful seizure solely as a result of the canine sniff that occurred outside respondent's stopped car. That is, the court characterized the dog sniff as the cause rather than the consequence of a constitutional violation. In its view, the use of the dog converted the citizen-police encounter from a lawful traffic stop into a drug investigation, and because the shift in purpose was not supported by any reasonable suspicion that respondent possessed narcotics, it was unlawful. In our view, conducting a dog sniff would not change the character of a traffic stop that is lawful at its inception and otherwise executed in a reasonable manner, unless the dog sniff itself infringed respondent's constitutionally protected interest in privacy. Our cases hold that it did not.

Official conduct that does not "compromise any legitimate interest in privacy" is not a search subject to the Fourth Amendment…. We have held that any interest in possessing contraband cannot be deemed "legitimate," and thus, governmental conduct that only reveals the possession of contraband "compromises no legitimate privacy interest."… This is because the expectation "that certain facts will not come to the attention of the authorities" is not the same as an interest in "privacy that society is prepared to consider reasonable."... In *United States v. Place* ... (1983), we treated a canine sniff by a well-trained narcotics-detection dog as "sui generis" because it "discloses only the presence or absence of narcotics, a contraband item."... Respondent likewise concedes that "drug sniffs are designed, and if properly conducted are generally likely, to reveal only the presence of contraband."... Although respondent argues that the error rates, particularly the existence of false positives, call into question the premise that drug-detection dogs alert only to contraband, the record contains no evidence or findings that support his argument. Moreover, respondent does not suggest that an erroneous alert, in and of itself, reveals any legitimate private information, and, in this case, the trial judge found that the dog sniff was sufficiently reliable to establish probable cause to conduct a full-blown search of the trunk.

Accordingly, the use of a well-trained narcotics-detection dog—one that "does not expose noncontraband items that otherwise would remain hidden from public view," ... —during a lawful traffic stop, generally does not implicate legitimate privacy interests. In this case, the dog sniff was performed on the exterior of respondent's car while he was lawfully seized for a traffic violation. Any intrusion on respondent's privacy expectations does not rise to the level of a constitutionally cognizable infringement.

This conclusion is entirely consistent with our recent decision that the use of a thermal-imaging device to detect the growth of marijuana in a home constituted an unlawful search. *Kyllo v. United States* ... (2001). Critical to that decision was the fact that the device was capable of detecting lawful activity—in that case, intimate details in a home, such as "at what hour each night the lady of the house takes her daily sauna and bath."... The legitimate expectation that information about perfectly lawful activity will remain private is categorically distinguishable from respondent's hopes or expectations concerning the nondetection of contraband in the trunk of his car. A dog sniff conducted during a concededly lawful traffic stop that reveals no information other than the location of a substance that no individual has any right to possess does not violate the Fourth Amendment.

The judgment of the Illinois Supreme Court is vacated, and the case is remanded for further proceedings not inconsistent with this opinion.

It is so ordered.

Case Questions

1. Why did the Illinois Supreme Court suppress the marijuana found by Trooper Gillette in the trunk of Roy Caballes's car?
2. Why did the U.S. Supreme Court vacate the Illinois Supreme Court's judgment?
3. Do you think that police officers could use the Supreme Court's ruling in this case to justify the use of dog sniffs of people and luggage on buses, boats, and trains and in public parks? How far do you think they could go before crossing the line and infringing on a reasonable expectation of privacy?

Bail

Although the U.S. Constitution does not guarantee criminal defendants the right to **bail,** at the present time bail is authorized for all criminally accused persons except those charged with capital offenses (crimes for which punishment may be death). There is also much constitutional debate about whether legislatures can classify certain other non-capital offenses as nonbailable.

Under the traditional money bail system, the judge sets bail to ensure the defendant's attendance in court and obedience to the court's orders and judgment. The accused is released after he or she deposits with a clerk cash, a bond, or a secured pledge in the amount of bail set by the judge. In 1951 the U.S. Supreme Court declared that the Eighth Amendment prevents federal judges and magistrates from setting bail at a figure higher than an amount reasonably calculated to ensure the defendant's appearance at trial. However, the Eighth Amendment's prohibition against excessive bail has been interpreted to apply only to the federal government and has not been incorporated into the Fourteenth Amendment. Thus it is not binding on the states.

During the early 1960s there was considerable dissatisfaction with the money bail system in this country because it discriminated against low-income people. Reform legislation was enacted in many states. The bail reform statutes make it easier for criminally accused people to obtain their release, since judges are required to use the least restrictive option that would ensure that the accused appeared for trial. In most cases, courts require that a surety bond or property be posted as collateral in order for the defendant to be released from custody. In appropriate cases, however, a defendant can be released on his or her own recognizance (also called a signature bond). This type of bond is an unsecured promise to appear when required, which means the defendant doesn't have to post any money.

A judge or magistrate can impose appropriate limitations on the accused's right to travel, as well as his or her contacts with other people. Such laws permit judges to base their decisions on the defendant's offense, family roots, and employment history.

The court can revoke bail if the accused fails to appear in court as ordered, is found in possession of a firearm, fails to maintain employment, or disregards the limitations of the bail order.

Public fear about crimes committed by individuals out on bail resulted in the enactment of legislation authorizing preventive detention in the Bail Reform Act of 1984. Under these laws, people can be denied bail who are accused of serious crimes and are thought to be dangerous. The targeted crimes include violent crimes, offenses punishable by life imprisonment, and drug-related crimes punishable by a term of incarceration exceeding ten years. At a hearing a court determines if the accused is likely to flee and if judicially imposed bail conditions would reasonably protect the public safety. In appropriate cases the court is authorized to deny bail and detain the accused until trial.

The Right to an Attorney

As said earlier, a defendant has an unqualified right to the assistance of retained counsel at all formal stages of a criminal case. An indigent defendant is entitled to a court-appointed attorney under much more limited circumstances. An indigent who is subjected to custodial interrogation by the police is entitled to an appointed attorney in order to protect the Fifth Amendment privilege against self-incrimination. His or her Sixth Amendment right to counsel does not arise until after adversarial judicial proceedings have begun—and the government has formally initiated criminal proceedings against a defendant—usually, unless waived, after the defendant's initial appearance in court.

The Supreme Court has ruled that an indigent defendant cannot be sentenced to a term of incarceration for a criminal offense unless appointed counsel was afforded to the defendant at all "critical stages" of a prosecution. Postindictment lineups for identification purposes, initial appearances, and preliminary hearings, as well as trials and sentencing hearings, are examples of such critical stages. Finally, the Court has recognized that indigents convicted of criminal offenses who want to appeal the trial court's judgment only have a Fourteenth Amendment right to appointed counsel for purposes of a first appeal.

The importance of a nonindigent Missouri defendant's right to be represented by the attorney of his or her choosing (if he or she is paying the bill) was reemphasized in the case of *U.S. v. Gonzalez-Lopez*. The defendant in this case, Cuauhtemoc Gonzalez-Lopez, was accused in federal district court of conspiracy to distribute more than 100 kilograms of marijuana. He rejected the lawyer hired by his parents (Fahle) and hired a California attorney named Low who was not licensed to practice law in Missouri. The district court judge initially permitted Low to represent Gonzalez-Lopez, pro hac vice ("for this case only"), but subsequently revoked this privilege. Gonzalez-Lopez still wanted Low to be his lawyer and so informed Fahle, who was allowed to withdraw by the judge. Low made repeated attempts to be permitted to appear pro hac vice, all to no avail. With the trial approaching, Gonzalez-Lopez, while still preferring Low, agreed to be represented by an attorney named Dickhaus. The case was tried to a jury, which convicted the defendant. The defendant appealed the district court's refusal to permit him the counsel of his choice, and the federal court of appeals ruled in his favor, reversed his conviction, and ordered a new trial. The U.S. Department of Justice then successfully petitioned the U.S. Supreme Court for certiorari. The government argued in the Supreme Court that, although it agreed that Gonzalez-Lopez should have been permitted to be represented by Low, this was a "harmless error"—it was a trivial mistake that

had no bearing on the outcome of the trial. They argued that Gonzalez-Lopez had been effectively represented by Attorney Dickhaus. The government concluded that the appeals court was wrong to have ordered that the conviction be reversed and the case retried. The Supreme Court explains its decision in the case below. This opinion has been extensively edited because of limitations of space.

United States v. Cuauhtemoc Gonzalez-Lopez
548 U.S. 140
Supreme Court of the United States
June 26, 2006

Justice Scalia delivered the opinion of the Court.
We must decide whether a trial court's erroneous deprivation of a criminal defendant's choice of counsel entitles him to a reversal of his conviction....

II
The Sixth Amendment provides that "in all criminal prosecutions, the accused shall enjoy the right ... to have the Assistance of Counsel for his defence." We have previously held that an element of this right is the right of a defendant who does not require appointed counsel to choose who will represent him. The Government here agrees ... that "the Sixth Amendment guarantees the defendant the right to be represented by an otherwise qualified attorney whom that defendant can afford to hire, or who is willing to represent the defendant even though he is without funds."... [T]he Government does not dispute the Eighth Circuit's conclusion in this case that the District Court erroneously deprived respondent of his counsel of choice.

III
Having concluded, in light of the Government's concession of erroneous deprivation, that the trial court violated respondent's Sixth Amendment right to counsel of choice, we must consider whether this error is subject to review for harmlessness. In *Arizona v. Fulminante* ... we divided constitutional errors into two classes. The first we called "trial error," because the errors "occurred during presentation of the case to the jury" and their effect may "be quantitatively assessed in the context of other evidence presented in order to determine whether [they were] harmless beyond a reasonable doubt."... These include "most constitutional errors."... The second class of constitutional error we called "structural defects." These "defy analysis by 'harmless-error' standards" because they

"affect the framework within which the trial proceeds," and are not "simply an error in the trial process itself."... Such errors include the denial of counsel ... , the denial of the right of self-representation, ... the denial of the right to public trial, ... and the denial of the right to trial by jury by the giving of a defective reasonable-doubt instruction.... We have little trouble concluding that erroneous deprivation of the right to counsel of choice, "with consequences that are necessarily unquantifiable and indeterminate, unquestionably qualifies as 'structural error.'"... Different attorneys will pursue different strategies with regard to investigation and discovery, development of the theory of defense, selection of the jury, presentation of the witnesses, and style of witness examination and jury argument. And the choice of attorney will affect whether and on what terms the defendant cooperates with the prosecution, plea bargains, or decides instead to go to trial. In light of these myriad aspects of representation, the erroneous denial of counsel bears directly on the "framework within which the trial proceeds" ... or indeed on whether it proceeds at all. It is impossible to know what different choices the rejected counsel would have made, and then to quantify the impact of those different choices on the outcome of the proceedings. Many counseled decisions, including those involving plea bargains and cooperation with the government, do not even concern the conduct of the trial at all. Harmless-error analysis in such a context would be a speculative inquiry into what might have occurred in an alternate universe.

... To determine the effect of wrongful denial of choice of counsel, however, we would not be looking for mistakes committed by the actual counsel, but for differences in the defense that would have been made by the rejected counsel—in matters ranging from questions asked on voir dire and cross-examination to such intangibles as argument style and relationship with the prosecutors. We would have to speculate upon what matters the rejected counsel would have handled differently—or indeed, would have handled the same but with the benefit of a more jury-pleasing courtroom style or a longstanding relationship of trust with the prosecutors. And then we would have to speculate upon what effect those different choices or different intangibles might have had. The difficulties of conducting the two assessments of prejudice are not remotely comparable....

IV
Nothing we have said today casts any doubt or places any qualification upon our previous holdings that limit the right to counsel of choice and recognize the authority of trial courts to establish criteria for admitting lawyers to argue before them. As the dissent too discusses, ... the right to counsel of choice does not extend to defendants who require counsel to be appointed for them.... Nor may a defendant insist on representation by a person who is not a member of the bar.... We have recognized a trial court's wide latitude in balancing the right to counsel of choice against the needs of fairness, ... and against the demands of its calendar.... The court has, moreover, an "independent interest in ensuring that criminal trials are conducted within the ethical standards of the profession and that legal proceedings appear fair to all who observe them."... None of these limitations on the right to choose one's counsel is relevant here. This is not a case about a court's power to enforce rules or adhere to practices that determine which attorneys may appear before it, or to make scheduling and other decisions that effectively exclude a defendant's first choice of counsel. However broad a court's discretion may be ... the District Court here erred when it denied respondent his choice of counsel. Accepting that premise, we hold that the error violated respondent's Sixth Amendment right to counsel of choice and that this violation is not subject to harmless-error analysis.

The judgment of the Court of Appeals is affirmed, and the case is remanded for further proceedings consistent with this opinion.

It is so ordered.

Case Questions

1. What did the government argue before the Supreme Court?
2. Why did the Supreme Court majority reject this argument?
3. This case was resolved in the Supreme Court on a 5–4 vote because the justices found it to be a very close question. If you were a justice, how would you have voted, and why?

Lineups

The police conduct **lineups** before witnesses for the purpose of identifying a suspect. When formal charges are pending, an accused may not be in a lineup before witnesses for identification unless the accused and accused's counsel have been notified in advance. In addition, the lineup may not be conducted unless counsel is present, so that the defendant's counsel is not deprived of the right to effectively challenge the lineup procedures and any identifications that result. It is interesting to note that the U.S. Supreme Court has not required the presence of an attorney where an array of photographs is used in lieu of an actual lineup. Unlike a lineup, a photo array is not a trial-like confrontation that requires the presence of the accused.

Preliminary Hearing and Grand Jury

In order to weed out groundless or unsupported criminal charges before trial, a preliminary hearing is conducted or a grand jury is convened. In a **preliminary hearing,** the court examines the facts superficially to determine whether there is a strong enough case to hold the arrestee for further proceedings. The prosecution presents evidence before the court, without a jury, in order to determine if there is probable cause. The accused has a right to be present at the preliminary hearing, to cross-examine prosecution witnesses, and to present evidence. If there is no chance of conviction because of lack of evidence, the court dismisses the charges.

A **grand jury,** composed of people selected at random from the list of registered voters, decides whether there is reason to believe an accused has committed an offense, not whether the person is guilty or innocent. Thus, it determines whether a person should be brought to trial. The decision is based on evidence heard during a secret criminal investigation attended by representatives of the state and witnesses. The grand jury has the right to subpoena witnesses and documents for its investigation. The accused has no right to be present at the proceedings. A grand jury returns an indictment (an accusation in writing) to the court if it believes that the evidence warrants a prosecution. (See Figure 8.7.)

For prosecutions involving crimes against the United States, the Fifth Amendment provides that all prosecution for infamous crimes (an offense carrying a term of imprisonment in excess of one year) must be commenced by a grand jury indictment. Virtually all states provide for a preliminary hearing for charges involving a felony. Approximately half of the states require a grand jury indictment, while the remainder use a bill of information (a formal charging document prepared by the prosecutor and filed with the court).

Arraignment

An **arraignment** follows a grand jury indictment or the judge's finding of probable cause at a preliminary hearing. At arraignments, accused people are advised of the formal charges against them as required by the Sixth Amendment. The description of the charges must be sufficiently clear so that the defendant may be able to enter an intelligent plea. The accused also are asked whether they understand the charges and whether they have an attorney. The court appoints counsel if the accused cannot afford an attorney. Finally, a trial date is set at the arraignment. Defendants and their counsel must be given adequate opportunity to prepare for trial.

UNITED STATES DISTRICT COURT
FOR THE . . . . . . DISTRICT OF . . . . . .
. . . . DIVISION

United States of America,
    Plaintiff,
      v.
_____)
  Defendant.

Crim. No. . . . .
(. . . . .–USC § . . . .

INDICTMENT

The grand jury charges:
  On or about the . . . . . . day of . . . . . . , 20 . . . . , in the . . . . . . District of . . . . , ... *[defendant]* . . . . *[state essential facts constituting offense charged],* in violation of . . . . USC § . . . . Dated . . . . , 20. . . . .

A True Bill.

[Signature],
Foreman

. . . . ,
United States Attorney.

FIGURE 8.7 Sample Indictment [Federal Rules of Criminal Procedure 7(c)]

The defendant is called on to enter a plea at the arraignment. This plea may be guilty, **nolo contendere,** or not guilty. The plea of guilty is entered in the great majority of situations; it is simply a confession of guilt. The plea of *nolo contendere* ("no contest") is the same as a guilty plea, except that it cannot be used later against the accused as an admission. It is a confession only for the purposes of the criminal prosecution and does not bind the defendant in a civil suit for the same wrong. When the defendant pleads not guilty, the prosecution has the burden of proving him or her guilty beyond a reasonable doubt at the trial.

Plea bargaining is the process by which the accused agrees to enter a plea of guilty, often to a lesser offense, in exchange for a promise by the prosecuting attorney to recommend either a relatively light sentence or a dismissal of part of the charges. The judge does not have to accept the prosecutor's recommendations and will explain this to the defendant before accepting a negotiated plea.

THE CRIMINAL TRIAL

Every person who is charged with a crime has a constitutional right to a trial. In this way a defendant has the opportunity to confront and cross-examine the witnesses against him or her, testify and present evidence and arguments as a defense against the charges, have the assistance of an attorney in most cases, and take full advantage of the rights and protections afforded all people accused of crimes under the Constitution. Trial procedures are essentially the same in criminal and civil trials. The people of the state—as represented by a public prosecutor—are the plaintiffs, and must present legally sufficient evidence of the defendant's criminal culpability with respect to each element of the crime, or the judge will dismiss the charges and terminate the trial. A criminal defendant, unlike a civil defendant, has a constitutional right not to testify at trial. This privilege often is waived by defendants, however, because they wish to explain their version of the facts to the jury, or to the judge in a bench trial. Every criminal defendant (and every

juvenile charged with a criminal offense) is additionally protected by the constitutional due process requirement that the prosecution prove guilt beyond a reasonable doubt in order to be entitled to a judgment of conviction.[7]

The Sixth and Fourteenth Amendments guarantee criminally accused people many important rights, including notice of the charges, trial by jury, a speedy and public trial, and representation by counsel. Also protected by these amendments are the rights to present witnesses and evidence and to cross-examine opposing witnesses.

Trial by Jury

Accused people have a constitutional right to have their guilt or innocence decided by a jury composed of people representing a cross section of their community (this right to a jury trial does not extend to offenses traditionally characterized as petty offenses). The jury trial right is a safeguard for defendants who have concerns about whether they would receive a fair trial were the case to be tried only to a judge.

Unless a jury trial is waived, the jury is selected at the beginning of the trial. The number of jurors ranges from six to twelve, depending on state law. A unanimous decision is not required for conviction in all states. However, twelve jurors are required in federal criminal courts, and a unanimous decision is necessary for a conviction. If a jury cannot agree on a verdict, it is called a hung jury, and the judge dismisses the charges. In this situation, the prosecutor may retry the defendant before a new jury.

If a defendant pleads guilty, there are no questions of fact for a jury to decide, and the judge will proceed to the sentencing phase.

Fair and Public Trial and Cross-Examination

The right to be confronted by their accusers in an adversary proceeding protects accused people from being convicted by testimony given in their absence without the opportunity of cross-examination. The defendant also has a right to a public trial. This constitutional right prevents courts from becoming instruments of persecution through secret action.

The right is not unlimited, however. It is subject to the judge's broad power and duty to preserve order and decorum in the courtroom. Judges may limit the number of spectators in order to prevent overcrowding or to prevent disturbances. Judges also have the power to impose sanctions on participants and observers for acts that hinder or obstruct the court in administering justice.

Right to a Speedy Trial

The accused's right to a speedy trial is interpreted as meaning that the trial should take place as soon as possible without depriving the parties of a reasonable period of time for preparation. This right, applicable to both state and federal courts, protects an accused from prolonged imprisonment prior to trial, prevents long delay that could impair the defense of an accused person through the loss of evidence, and prevents or minimizes public suspicion and anxiety connected with an accused who is yet untried.

The right to speedy trial attaches when the prosecution begins, either by indictment or by the actual restraints imposed by arrest. How much time must elapse to result in an unconstitutional delay varies with the circumstances. The accused has the burden of showing that the delay was the fault of the state and that it resulted in prejudice.

The Prosecutor's Role

The sovereignty has the duty of prosecuting those who commit crimes; its attorney for this purpose is the prosecutor. As trial lawyer for the sovereignty, the prosecutor has extensive resources for investigation and preparation. The prosecutor is not at liberty to distort or misuse this information, and must disclose information that tends to relieve the accused of guilt. Any conduct of a prosecutor or judge that hinders the fairness of a trial to the extent that the outcome is adversely affected violates the defendant's right to due process.

Sentencing

Following conviction or a guilty plea, the judge determines the sentence that will be imposed on the convicted defendant in accordance with the laws of that particular jurisdiction. The sentencing options, depending on the sentencing structure of the jurisdiction, usually include, incarceration, incarceration with work release privileges, house arrest, fines, community service, restitution, and probation. A convicted person has the right to challenge the constitutionality of his or her sentence by arguing that it is cruel and unusual and in violation of the Eighth Amendment, or that it violates the Equal Protection Clause of the Fourteenth Amendment.

Appeal

The federal and state constitutions guarantee defendants a fair trial, but not an error-free trial. In the federal and state judicial systems, appellate courts determine if significant errors that warrant correction were committed by lower courts. The U.S. Constitution does not require states to provide for appellate review, although all defendants who enter a plea of not guilty are granted at least one appeal. The states differ in the number of discretionary appeals that are made available. A defendant who appeals has to exhaust all appellate opportunities at the state level and raise a federal question before petitioning the U.S. Supreme Court for a writ of certiorari. A person convicted of a crime in a federal district court can obtain review in the U.S. Court of Appeals, and then petition the U.S. Supreme Court for certiorari.

The prosecution is prohibited by the Fifth Amendment's double-jeopardy clause, and by due process, from appealing a court's entry of a judgment of acquittal based on a jury verdict or on the insufficiency of the evidence. Statutes, however, may permit the prosecution to appeal (1) pretrial court orders suppressing evidence, (2) a trial judge's refusal to enter judgment on the jury's guilty verdict and the entry instead of judgment for the defendant (JNOV), (3) where the sentencing judge abused his or her discretion and imposed an "inadequate" sentence, and (4) from a judgment of acquittal, for the sole purpose of clarifying the law.

Habeas Corpus

The writ of **habeas corpus** (Latin for "you have the body") is used to test the legality of a person's detention by government. It is frequently used by prisoners who have been unsuccessful in directly appealing their convictions and who are serving sentences of imprisonment. The writ of habeas corpus was recognized in Article 1, Section 9 of the U.S. Constitution. Congress extended the common law writ to federal prisoners in the Judiciary Act of 1789, and to state prisoners in 1867. In 1948 Congress replaced the common law practices defining prisoners' use of the writ with legislation, and the U.S. Supreme Court expanded its scope during the 1960s and 1970s.

Federal habeas corpus has much strategic importance because it permits convicted people, whether convicted in a federal or state court, to seek collateral review of their sentences in a federal court. The habeas process permits local federal district courts to "take a second look" at the functioning of state judicial systems. There have been times when Congress essentially deferred to the judiciary as to the substantive scope of this writ, and access to habeas corpus expanded when the Supreme Court felt it desirable to exercise more oversight over states. In 1976, however, the Supreme Court decided that the federal judiciary was being flooded with federal habeas petitions filed by prisoners in state prisons for drug offenses who wanted to challenge the constitutionality of police searches and seizures that led to their convictions. Because these petitioners' claims had already been fully litigated in state courts (albeit unsuccessfully), the Court's majority concluded that there was no reason for continued federal oversight in these cases. The justices announced, in the case of *Stone v. Powell,* 428 U.S. 465 (1976), that district courts no longer could review Fourth Amendment claims by way of habeas corpus if "the state has provided an opportunity for full and fair litigation of a Fourth Amendment Claim." This ruling meant that unless the U.S. Supreme Court granted a certiorari petition after a Fourth Amendment claim had been fully litigated in the state courts, the federal judiciary had essentially closed the door to such claims. It is interesting to note that the Court has not adopted a similar strategy with respect to habeas corpus petitions based on the Fifth and Sixth Amendments.

In 1996 the Antiterrorism and Effective Death Penalty Act of 1996 (AEDPA) was enacted. This federal statute greatly limited the scope of federal habeas corpus review in capital punishment cases and was enacted by members of Congress who believed that the writ was being abused by desperate defendants seeking to postpone their execution dates.

Readers will see in the next case how statutory high hurdles can limit the ability of federal courts to "undo" fundamental constitutional mistakes committed by state courts in noncapital cases.

Introduction to *Batchelor v. Cain*

Marshall Batchelor, the defendant in the following case, was prosecuted for the commission of an armed robbery. Batchelor entered a plea of not guilty.

Because he was indigent, the trial court appointed an attorney to represent him. The defendant, however, wanted to exercise his constitutionally protected right to represent himself (i.e., to appear in court "pro se"). The U.S. Supreme Court recognized such a right in 1975 in the case of *Faretta v. California,* concluding that self-representation was a right protected by the Sixth and Fourteenth Amendments to the U.S. Constitution.

Several months prior to the scheduled date of his trial, on October 14, 1999, Batchelor personally drafted and filed a written motion in which he asked the court to dismiss the appointed counsel and recognize his right to conduct his own defense. The court didn't grant a hearing on this motion until February 7, 2000, at which time the motion was denied. Batchelor drafted and filed an essentially identical second written pro se motion with the court on November 29, 2000, which was also the first day of his trial. The court took the position that this purportedly "new motion" wasn't really "new," as it had been heard and denied previously.

The defendant was convicted of armed robbery by a jury, which means that this case had been "adjudicated on its merits," a necessary prerequisite before Batchelor could exhaust his appeal rights at the state court level and eventually could seek federal habeas corpus relief. The sentence was 60 years in state prison.

Batchelor, still acting on his own behalf, prepared the documents and brief necessary to appeal and filed them with the appropriate state appellate court in a timely manner. This appeal was considered by a three-judge panel, which ruled 2–1 in Batchelor's favor. The panel concluded that the trial court had violated Batchelor's *Faretta* rights to self-representation. The state successfully petitioned for a rehearing of the appeal before a five-judge panel (two judges were added to the first panel) and this second panel ruled 3–2 in favor of the state. Batchelor's certiorari petition was denied by the Louisiana Supreme Court, and after exhausting all other postconviction remedies at the state level, Batchelor turned to the federal courts for relief.

Batchelor successfully petitioned the U.S. District Court for the Western District of Louisiana for a writ of habeas corpus, and the state appealed that ruling to the U.S. Court of Appeals for the Fifth Circuit. The following excerpt is from Judge Dennis's opinion for the Fifth Circuit.

Marshall Batchelor v. Burl Cain, Warden
682 F.3d 400
U.S. Court of Appeals, Fifth Circuit
May 29, 2012

Dennis, Circuit Judge.

II

We review the district court's conclusions of law de novo.... We "may affirm a district court's decision on any basis supported by the record."... Here, although the district court concluded that the writ may issue because the state appellate court's decision "was an unreasonable application of Federal law" ... we affirm the grant of habeas relief on the basis that the state appellate court's decision "was based on an unreasonable determination of the facts" ...

The Antiterrorism and Effective Death Penalty Act of 1996 (AEDPA) prevents a federal court from granting habeas relief to a state prisoner

> with respect to any claim that was adjudicated on the merits in State court proceedings unless the adjudication of the claim — (1) resulted in a decision that was contrary to, or involved an unreasonable application of, clearly established Federal law, as determined by the Supreme Court of the United States; or (2) resulted in a decision that was based on an unreasonable determination of the facts in light of the evidence presented in the State court proceeding.

28 U.S.C. §2254(d). Under §2254(d)(2), "[i]t is not enough to show that a state court's decision was incorrect or erroneous. [Rather, a] petitioner must show that the decision was objectively unreasonable" ... requiring "the petitioner [to] show that 'a reasonable factfinder *must* conclude' that the state court's determination of the facts was unreasonable."... Additionally ... "a determination of a factual issue made by a State court shall be presumed to be correct," and that presumption must be rebutted "by clear and convincing evidence."...

Under AEDPA, we review "the last reasoned state court decision."... Here, we review the state appellate court's rejection of Batchelor's claim that the trial court violated his right to self-representation when it denied his *Faretta* motion at the February 7, 2000 hearing.

Finally, the denial of the right to self-representation constitutes a structural error that is not subject to harmless error review and instead requires automatic reversal. *McKaskle v. Wiggins*, 465 U.S. 168 ... (1984) ("Since the right of self-representation is a right that when exercised usually increases the likelihood of a trial outcome unfavorable to the defendant, its denial is not amenable to 'harmless error' analysis. The right is either respected or denied; its deprivation cannot be harmless."); see *United States v. Gonzalez-Lopez*, 548 U.S. 140....

III

In *Faretta* [*v. California*] the Supreme Court announced that the right of a criminal defendant to represent himself at trial is implicit in the structure of the Sixth

Amendment, and applies to state court proceedings through the Fourteenth Amendment. ... The Court determined that this right was violated where, "weeks before trial, Faretta clearly and unequivocally declared to the judge that he wanted to represent himself and did not want counsel," and Faretta's request was nonetheless denied by the trial court.

... The Court explained:

> It is undeniable that in most criminal prosecutions defendants could better defend with counsel's guidance than by their own unskilled efforts. But where the defendant will not voluntarily accept representation by counsel, the potential advantage of a lawyer's training and experience can be realized, if at all, only imperfectly.... Although a defendant need not himself have the skill and experience of a lawyer in order competently and intelligently to choose self-representation, he should be made aware of the dangers and disadvantages of self-representation, so that the record will establish that "he knows what he is doing and his choice is made with eyes open."

... Additionally, the Court stated that "a State may—even over objection by the accused—appoint a 'standby counsel' to aid the accused if and when the accused requests help, and to be available to represent the accused in the event that termination of the defendant's self-representation is necessary."... In *McKaskle* [v. Wiggins, 465 U.S. 168 (1984)], the Court reaffirmed that appointment of standby counsel—whether at the defendant's request or over the defendant's objection—is consistent with the exercise of the right to self-representation....

> Even if defendant requests to represent himself, ... the right may be waived through defendant's subsequent conduct indicating he is vacillating on the issue or has abandoned his request altogether.... A waiver may be found if it reasonably appears to the court that defendant has abandoned his initial request to represent himself....

Batchelor argues—as he did on direct appeal in state court—that he clearly, unequivocally, and timely moved to represent himself on October 14, 1999, and that the state trial court violated his right to self-representation by erroneously denying that motion at the February 7, 2000 pretrial hearing on the basis that Batchelor's appointed counsel was "well capable of mounting a defense on [his] behalf." The state contends that §2254(d) prohibits the federal courts from granting Batchelor relief because the state appellate

court reasonably found that Batchelor implicitly waived his October 13, 1999 *Faretta* request prior to its denial.

Whether Batchelor abandoned his *Faretta* motion and thereby waived his right to represent himself is a question of fact.... Our review of the state court record provides clear and convincing evidence that Batchelor's conduct was in no way inconsistent with his formal and unequivocal request to represent himself with the assistance of standby counsel.... We conclude that the state court's ultimate decision was based on an unreasonable determination that Batchelor waived his initial *Faretta* request....

A

The record admits of no doubt that Batchelor's October 14, 1999 "Motion for Dismissal of Counsel" constituted a "clear[] and unequivocal[] declar[ation] that he wanted to represent himself and did not want counsel."...

B

Instead, the state contends that two events establish a reasonable basis upon which the state appellate court could have implicitly found that Batchelor waived his right to represent himself after filing his October 14, 1999 *Faretta* motion: first, Batchelor's statement to the trial court at the attempted arraignment that same day that he preferred not to enter a plea "unless I have a presence of counsel"; and, second, the discussion of Batchelor's *Faretta* motion at the February 7, 2000 hearing. We examine the state court records of these exchanges and conclude that the state court could not reasonably have found a waiver....

... Batchelor's unwillingness to plead on October 14, 1999 without the "presence of counsel" was entirely consistent with his request, made in his motion, that the court appoint standby counsel while allowing him to proceed pro se.... Indeed, the Court in *McKaskle* repeatedly referred to the "presence" of standby counsel ... and itself used the terms "counsel" and "standby counsel" interchangeably....

The state argues that Batchelor failed to reiterate his *Faretta* request when the trial court asked if he had anything to say. However, Batchelor was not required, in order to avoid waiver, to add anything to the straightforward request that he had already made plain in writing. It was the trial court, and not Batchelor, which failed to respond properly to the discussion of the *Faretta* motion. Under *Faretta*, the trial court should have initiated a colloquy in which it made Batchelor "aware of the dangers and disadvantages of self-representation, so that the record w[ould] establish that he kn[ew] what he [was] doing and his choice [was] made with eyes open."... The trial court's failure to conduct the required *Faretta* colloquy is an indication only of the trial court's error. That the appropriate colloquy did not occur cannot be construed as an indication of vacillation by Batchelor. In any event, while the trial court's stated rationale for denying Batchelor's self-representation request was certainly erroneous under *Faretta* ... there is no indication that the court misunderstood the nature of Batchelor's clear request.... Thus, as at his appearance on October 14, 1999, Batchelor did nothing inconsistent with his *Faretta* request at the February 7, 2000 hearing....

The state advances no other factual basis for a finding that Batchelor abandoned or vacillated in his request, and our review of the record reveals none. Accordingly, we conclude that Batchelor has met his burden of rebutting by clear and convincing evidence the presumptive correctness afforded the state appellate court's implicit factual determination that Batchelor equivocated or abandoned his motion....

3.
We conclude that the state appellate court's adjudication of Batchelor's *Faretta* claim resulted in a decision based on an objectively unreasonable factual determination.... While "it is possible [for a] state court [to] err[] with respect to one factual finding under

§2254(e)(1)" and yet for "its determination of facts resulting in its decision in the case [to be] reasonable... under §2254(d)(2), he waiver issue is determinative in light of the state's concession that the state trial court did in fact deny Batchelor's *Faretta* request at the February 7, 2000 hearing. As the record admits of no basis for a finding that Batchelor waived his request to represent himself prior to its erroneous denial by the district court at that hearing, the only reasonable factual determination would have been that Batchelor did not waive his request.... Therefore, we conclude that the state appellate court's decision that Batchelor was not impermissibly denied the right to represent himself was based on an objectively unreasonable determination of the facts....

IV
In sum, we conclude that the trial court violated Batchelor's Sixth Amendment right to represent himself by erroneously denying a clear and unequivocal assertion of that right.... We further conclude that Batchelor has demonstrated by clear and convincing evidence that the state appellate court's implicit finding that he waived his *Faretta* request was erroneous ... and that the state appellate court's denial of Batchelor's claim on direct appeal resulted from an unreasonable determination of the facts in light of the evidence in the state court record....

Accordingly, we AFFIRM the district court's grant of habeas relief.

Case Questions

1. Batchelor was a state prisoner and the merits of his case had been fully adjudicated by the state trial and appellate courts in Louisiana. What was the AEDPA basis for the federal court's jurisdictional right to consider this habeas corpus application?
2. What were the two most important mistakes made by the trial judge in this case?
3. What was the most important factual error made by the appellate court that influenced the federal district court and the Fifth Circuit to rule in favor of Batchellor?
4. The District Court, which had ruled in favor of Batchelor, initially ordered that Batchelor's conviction be vacated and that he be released from custody unless the state granted him a new trial within 120 days of the date of the Judgment. This order was stayed on September 14, 2010, by U.S. District Judge Robert G. James at the request of the state, pending the outcome of the state's appeal to the Fifth Circuit. Judge James explained why he granted the stay:

   In ruling on Batchelor's habeas petition, this court specifically found that the evidence at trial was sufficient to convict Batchelor of an armed robbery which caused great bodily harm to the victim.... Although Batchelor is entitled to a new trial on the basis of the denial of the right to self-representation, the Court cannot say that he is the victim of an otherwise wrongful conviction....

   Assume that the State of Louisiana grants Batchelor a new trial, that he defends himself, that he is convicted, and that he is resentenced. In your opinion would such an outcome make this entire legal odyssey merely an expensive, meaningless exercise in futility?

CHAPTER SUMMARY

This chapter has provided readers with a "taste" of what criminal law and criminal procedure are all about. Readers began with an introduction to the sources of American criminal law and the way the common law influenced American thinking. Other themes included how the law-making role of legislatures evolved and came to replace the judiciary as the dominant policy-maker, and how the Model Penal Code has greatly influenced the modern development of criminal law. Criminal law classifications such as *mala in se, mala prohibita,* felony, and misdemeanor were explained, as were the constitutional limitations on the imposition of criminal liability and criminal punishments.

The focus then shifted to learning about the basic components of a criminal offense: the wrongful act, the guilty mind, the concurrence of act and intent, and, in some crimes, causation. This was followed by an overview of the inchoate crimes: solicitation, attempt, and conspiracy, which society relies upon to protect itself from people who have taken some steps toward, but have not yet completed, their intended criminal objectives. The criminal law portion of the chapter concluded with a discussion of some of the common recognized defenses, including affirmative defenses that can mitigate, justify, or excuse a defendant's conduct.

The next discussion focused on criminal procedure, which is the administrative process society has established for determining whether a crime has been committed and whether the person or persons accused are guilty of the crime. The way that constitutional provisions limit this process—in particular the Fourth, Fifth, Sixth, Eighth, and Fourteenth Amendments—was explained.

Next was an overview of several procedural stages that occur prior to the commencement of a criminal trial. These included the requirements for a valid arrest, custodial interrogations of suspects *(Miranda* rights), searches and seizures, and investigative detentions (stop-and-frisk). Other topics discussed included bail and the right to an attorney. The pretrial segment concluded with explanations of the preliminary hearing, the role of the grand jury, and what happens at an arraignment. This was followed by an overview of the criminal trial and the defendant's rights to a trial by jury, to a fair and public trial, to cross-examine witnesses, and to a speedy trial. The chapter concluded with discussions of the prosecutor's role, sentencing, and a defendant's right to appeal and to petition for a writ of habeas corpus.

CHAPTER QUESTIONS

1. Holmes was convicted and received a death sentence for murdering, beating, raping, and robbing an eighty-six-year-old woman. Although his convictions and sentence were affirmed on appeal by the state courts, he was granted a new trial upon postconviction review. Holmes sought at the new trial to introduce evidence that the victim's attacker was another man named White.

    The trial court excluded Holmes's evidence that White had perpetrated the crime. The state supreme court affirmed the trial court, ruling "where there is strong evidence of an appellant's guilt, especially where there is strong forensic evidence, the proffered evidence about a third party's alleged guilt does not raise a reasonable inference as to the appellant's own innocence." Holmes successfully petitioned for a writ of certiorari. He argued to the U.S. Supreme Court that he had a constitutionally protected right to introduce proof that White had committed the attack on the victim, even if the introduction of forensic evidence would "strongly support a guilty verdict." Was the state supreme court correct? *Holmes v. South Carolina, 126 S. Ct. 1727 (2006)*

2. Brandon, a driver, was lawfully stopped by Colorado state police officers for speeding. Besides Brandon, there were two passengers in the vehicle—one male and one female. When the officer asked Brandon to produce evidence that he had the right to operate the vehicle, Brandon only produced an identification card. The officer then contacted his dispatcher to determine if Brandon was a licensed driver. While waiting for the dispatcher's response, the officer asked Brandon and the passengers questions as to their destination and the purpose of their trip. The officer became suspicious when Brandon's and the passengers' answers were inconsistent. The dispatcher then notified the officer that Brandon was licensed in California.

   The officer then asked for and was given permission to search the car by the vehicle's owner, the female passenger. Brandon, however, refused to consent to a search. The officer then put a police dog into the car, and after the dog alerted to the presence of cocaine, it was seized, and Brandon was arrested. Brandon was convicted of possession of a controlled substance. He unsuccessfully moved to suppress the evidence of the cocaine. The trial court ruled that the female passenger had consented to the search that led to the discovery of the cocaine. The defendant then appealed to the state court of appeals. Should the appellate court reverse the trial court and suppress the evidence of cocaine?

   State of Colorado v. Brandon, 03CA1176 (2005)

3. James Brogan was unexpectedly visited one evening at his home by federal investigators. The officers had records indicating that Brogan had received cash payments from a company whose employees were members of a union in which Brogan was an officer. Such an act would have violated federal bribery statutes. The officers asked Brogan if he had received any cash or gifts from the company. Brogan answered "no." Brogan was charged with violating federal bribery laws and with lying to a federal officer who was in the course of performing his or her duty to investigate criminal activity, as prohibited by 18 U.S.C. §1001. Do you see any potential for the possible abuse of prosecutorial discretion if persons in Brogan's situation can be convicted of a federal felony for untruthfully answering an incriminating question posed by federal officers in the course of an investigation?

   Brogan v. United States, 96-1579 522 U.S. 398 (1998)

4. Kalb County Police Officer Richardson stopped a motorist named Brown for driving without using his headlights while it was raining, because he suspected that Brown might be DUI. Brown explained to the officer that he was not aware the lights were not on. When the officer asked Brown to produce his operator's license and evidence of insurance, Brown began a search for the requested documentation. While looking for the documents, Brown pulled an object out of one of his front pockets that the officer described as a "piece of paper" approximately one to two inches in diameter. When the paper fell in between Brown's legs onto the car seat, Brown immediately closed his legs. The officer asked Brown, "What are you trying to hide?" The trial testimony is silent as to Brown's reply. Officer Richardson then asked Brown to exit the car; however, Brown did not comply. He continued looking in the car for the documents until they were finally found. Brown appeared nervous and shaky while poking around the car. This made Richardson suspicious that Brown was attempting to hide something. After Brown produced the documents, Officer Richardson asked him to step out of the car. Brown was given a *Terry* investigative pat down, which produced neither weapons nor contraband, and he was then placed, without formal arrest, inside of Richardson's locked patrol car. The officer then proceeded to enter Brown's car to look for the piece of paper. Richardson found

it, in plain view, on the car seat. This search disclosed the existence of several small plastic bags, which were subsequently identified from field tests to contain rock cocaine. Brown was then arrested for possession of cocaine. The officer did not know that anything was in the piece of paper at the time he conducted his search, and he did not see the cocaine in the paper until the officer subjected it to close examination. Did Officer Richardson have probable cause to make a warrantless search of Brown's car?

Brown v. State of Georgia, 504 S.E.2d 443 (1998)

5. Hillsborough County, New Hampshire, installed a teleconferencing system between the Nashua District Court and the Nashua Police Station. This system made it unnecessary to have police officers physically transport arrested persons to the courthouse for purposes of arraignment and setting bail. This procedure was intended to conserve time as well as money, and was approved by the state supreme court. Jay Larose and two other people were arraigned using this system, and bail was set, but they were unable to make bail. They subsequently petitioned for a writ of habeas corpus. The petitioners argued that this high-tech approach to arraignments violated their due process rights under the state and federal constitutions. They also maintained that the teleconferencing procedure violated a state statute, which required that arrested persons "shall be taken before a district or municipal court without unreasonable delay, but not exceeding 24 hours, Sundays and holidays excepted, to answer for the offense." What due process rights could the petitioners have claimed were infringed upon, based on these facts? How might the state respond to the claimed infringement of the statutory right?

Larose v. Hillsborough County, 702 A.2d 326 (1997)

6. Bajakajian tried to take $357,000 in cash out of the United States without completing the necessary paperwork. After his conviction, the federal government asked the court to order that the entire sum be forfeited, as called for by the federal statute. Would this punitive forfeiture violate the requirements of the excessive fines clause of the Eighth Amendment?

United States v. Bajakajian, 96-1487 524. U.S. 321 (1998)

7. The Edmonds Police Department received an anonymous tip contained in a mailed note that Robert Young was growing marijuana in his house. A police detective went to the address. He noted that the windows of the house were always covered, bright lights never could be seen inside, and there was no apparent odor of marijuana detectable from the public sidewalk. The detective obtained records of Young's electric power consumption and believed it to be unusually high—a factor that his prior experience suggested to him was consistent with the cultivation of marijuana. The detective contacted the federal DEA, which supplied an agent trained in the use of infrared thermal detection equipment. This equipment, when used at night, can detect manmade heat sources. Young's house was subjected to thermal surveillance, and the results suggested a pattern consistent with the growth of marijuana; the downstairs, for example, was warmer than the upstairs portion of the house. The detective used this information to establish probable cause for the issuance of a search warrant. Officers executing the search warrant found marijuana within the house, and Young was arrested and charged with possession of marijuana with intent to manufacture or deliver. Young sought to suppress the evidence on the grounds that the infrared surveillance of his home constituted an infringement of his rights under the Fourth Amendment to the U.S. Constitution, and a corresponding right under the Washington State Constitution. Do you believe the suppression motion should be granted?

State of Washington v. Young, 867 P.2d 593 (1994)

NOTES

1. G. Jones, *The Sovereignty of the Law* (Toronto: University of Toronto Press, 1973), pp. 189–191.

2. B. Schwartz, *The Law in America* (New York: McGraw-Hill, 1974), p. 9.

3. Ibid, pp. 12–18, 72, 73.

4. *Craig v. Boren,* 429 U.S. 197 (1976).

5. *Eisenstadt v. Baird,* 405 U.S. 438 (1972).

6. *Craig v. Boren,* 429 U.S. 197 (1976).

7. *In re Winship,* 379 U.S. 358 (1970).

IX

Family Law

CHAPTER OBJECTIVES

1. *Understand the antecedents of American family law.*
2. *Describe differing configurations of a family.*
3. *Explain legal obligations that parents have vis-à-vis their children.*
4. *Understand how spousal relationships end.*
5. *Describe the basic stages of the adoption process.*
6. *Explain the two approaches to the division of property in divorce.*

People today conceptualize the family's role in society very differently than they did in seventeenth-century America. Back then, the economy was primarily agrarian. The family unit was responsible for providing care for all its members from the cradle to the grave. There was no social security for the old or unemployment security for those out of work. The family was responsible for performing functions within the home that today are often provided by others outside the home. For example, there were no public schools to educate the young, no day-care centers, no hospitals to care for the sick, and no nursing homes to care for the elderly. Even religious instruction had to be provided by families within the home until churches could be established.[1] In the past, it was common for families to be larger than is typical today. It took many people to take care of the domestic tasks and work the farms. Uneducated children were not as mobile and had fewer opportunities to leave the family home and town. They were also subject to parental discipline for longer periods of time than is the case today.

The traditional notion of family also has evolved significantly from what it was over the last fifty years. Increasingly, children are being raised by single and same-sex parents. Back in 1980 less than 20% of children younger than 18 years of age lived with a single parent; that number had increased to almost 30% by 2008.[2] And a recent U.S. Census Bureau study estimated that 19% of children are living in households inhabited by same-sex couples.[3] Instead of working on a farm, today's parents often work outside the home. They sometimes commute long distances to their jobs. It is the norm in two-parent families for both parents to work in order to make ends meet. Families today are often unable to provide care for elder family members.[4] Today's children, as they grow into adolescence in the digital age, become increasingly more mobile and become functionally independent much sooner than in the past, and parents often find themselves having less ability to exercise influence and control.[5]

These changes in families have been accompanied by changes in society's legal expectations about family life.[6] **Family law,** also called **domestic-relations law,** has been recognized as a legal subfield only since the early 1900s.[7] Despite the law's tardiness in formally recognizing family law, legal institutions have long been concerned with the rights and responsibilities of family members.

One of the most enduring features of the Western tradition is the deference shown by the law to family self-governance, also called *family autonomy.*[8] This deference was recognized in Roman law[9] and was subsequently incorporated into Anglo-Saxon law;[10] canon law (the law applied in the English ecclesiastical courts, which historically handled domestic relations cases);[11] and the common law.[12]

Also dating from the time of the Roman emperors, however, is the legal recognition that society, through government, has a legitimate right to prevent the maltreatment and abuse of family members.[13] One example of this interest is the existence of laws in every state prohibiting child abuse and neglect. As the U.S. Supreme Court explained, governments today are expected to intervene to prevent "harm to the physical or mental health of [a] child...."[14]

These two legal principles, which accompanied the English immigrants who settled the Eastern Seaboard of North America, were widely accepted, although they were modified to meet the particular needs of each colony.[15]

In colonial America, the family was the most important unit of society. It was essential to preserving public order and producing economic stability.[16] After the Revolutionary War, the structure of the family was weakened by the ready availability of land, the shortage of labor, and the ease with which individuals could migrate.[17] Independence also brought a greater appreciation for the rights of individuals within the family and a corresponding decline in the outmoded view of a father's traditional rights (see Figure 9.1).[18] This trend has continued to the present time, and today mothers and fathers have equal rights and responsibilities.

Given the complexity of family law, the differences in the laws of the 50 states, and the limitations of available space, this chapter can provide only an introductory overview of the topic. This discussion focuses on how families are created, the nature of the rights and responsibilities of family members,

---

From *Chapman v. Mitchell,* 44 A.2d 392, 393 (1945)

" . . . the plaintiff [husband] is the master of his household. He is the managing head, with control and power to preserve the family relation, to protect its members and to guide their conduct. He has the obligation and responsibility of supporting, maintaining, and protecting the family and the correlative right to exclude intruders and unwanted visitors from the home despite the whims of the wife."

F I G U R E 9.1 The Role of the Father—An Old-Fashioned View how family relationships are terminated, and emerging issues such as the evolving dispute about the nature of the family.[19]

WHAT IS A FAMILY?

Although it is apparent that a **family** always includes people in a relationship, major disagreements exist about the precise meaning of the term. There is no single universally accepted legal definition of *family*. The word is generally defined in operational terms by statute within a particular context (i.e., for purposes of specifying who is entitled to particular benefits).

Traditionally, the family has been based on kinship and defined as the "customary legal relationship established by birth, marriage, or adoption."[20] This definition has been challenged recently on the ground that it is too rigid. Critics argue that even if they are unmarried, "two adult lifetime partners whose relationship is long term and characterized by an emotional and financial commitment and interdependence"[21] should receive the same rights and benefits as those who have been married. Anthropologists such as Collier, Rosaldo, and Yanagisako have favored such a functional approach. They think of families as "spheres of human relationships" that "hold property, provide care and welfare, and attend particularly to the young—a sphere conceptualized as a realm of love and intimacy," as contrasted with other more "impersonal" relationships.[22]

The legal definition of family becomes important because special rights, benefits, and privileges favor family membership. Some of these benefits are intangible, such as the societal approval that accompanies birth, marriage, and to some extent adoption. Another example is the sense of identity that family members have as to who they are and how they fit into the larger society.[23] Many other benefits are more tangible. Federal law, for example, favors married taxpayers who file jointly, and it provides social security benefits to family members in some circumstances. State legislatures also provide economic and noneconomic benefits favoring

family members. Although states differ greatly as to the nature and scope of the benefits provided, they often include housing rights, homestead acts that protect some family property from creditors, statutory provisions that determine inheritance rights in the event a family member dies without leaving a will, mutual spousal support obligations, evidentiary privileges that prohibit adverse spousal testimony and that protect private spousal communications, and limited tort immunities. Some employers, who can afford to do so, favor families. Employee fringe-benefit packages may provide family members with health and life insurance programs and 401k plans, as well as family leave and educational benefits.

Strong families perform essential tasks and help to create social and economic stability.[24] The family unit is expected to produce children and care for their needs. This includes raising children who will grow into responsible, well-adjusted, educated, and employable adults. Family members are expected to care for each other from "cradle to grave," especially in times of crisis. When families do not or cannot meet the most basic responsibilities, they have to be met at public expense.

In the following case, the City of East Cleveland sought to enforce a housing ordinance that restricted the occupancy of a dwelling unit to a single family. The ordinance defined "family" so restrictively that it was criminal for a grandmother to live under the same roof with one of her grandsons. As written, the law prohibited a grandmother, her adult son, and his child, Dale Jr., and another grandson, John (who was a first cousin of Dale Jr.), from living as a family. John had moved to his grandmother's house after the death of his mother. The grandmother, Inez Moore, was criminally charged, convicted of the crime, and sentenced to serve a jail term of five days and pay a $25 fine. Mrs. Moore appealed her conviction because she believed the statute violated her rights under the Due Process Clause of the Fourteenth Amendment. Notice the Supreme Court's sympathy for the concept of the extended family, as well as the roles played by race, culture, and economics in defining the nature of a family.

Moore v. City of East Cleveland, Ohio
431 U.S. 494
Supreme Court of the United States
May 31, 1977

Mr. Justice Powell announced the judgment of the Court, and delivered an opinion in which Mr. Justice Brennan, Mr. Justice Marshall, and Mr. Justice Blackmun joined.

East Cleveland's housing ordinance, like many throughout the country, limits occupancy of a dwelling unit to members of a single family.... But the ordinance contains an unusual and complicated definitional section that recognizes as a "family" only a few categories of related individuals.... Because her family, living together in her home, fits none of those categories, appellant stands convicted of a criminal offense. The question in this case is whether the ordinance violates the Due Process Clause of the Fourteenth Amendment.

I

Appellant, Mrs. Inez Moore, lives in her East Cleveland home together with her son, Dale Moore, Sr., and her two grandsons, Dale, Jr., and John Moore, Jr. The two boys are first cousins rather than brothers; we are told that John came to live with his grandmother and with the elder and younger Dale Moores after his mother's death.

In early 1973, Mrs. Moore received a notice of violation from the city, stating that John was an "illegal occupant" and directing her to comply with the ordinance. When she failed to remove him from her home, the city filed a criminal charge. Mrs. Moore moved to dismiss, claiming that the ordinance was constitutionally invalid on its face. Her motion was overruled, and upon conviction she was sentenced to five days in jail and a $25 fine. The Ohio Court of Appeals affirmed after giving full consideration to her constitutional claims, and the Ohio Supreme Court denied review....

II

The city argues that our decision in *Village of Belle Terre v. Boraas,* 416 U.S. 1, 94 (1974), requires us to sustain the ordinance attacked here.

But one overriding factor sets this case apart from *Belle Terre.* The ordinance there affected only unrelated individuals. It expressly allowed all who were related by "blood, adoption, or marriage" to live together, and in sustaining the ordinance we were careful to note that it promoted "family needs" and "family values."... East Cleveland, in contrast, has chosen to regulate the occupancy of its housing by slicing deeply into the family itself. This is no mere incidental result of the ordinance. On its face it selects certain categories of relatives who may live together and declares that others may not. In particular, it makes a crime of a grandmother's choice to live with her grandson in circumstances like those presented here.

When a city undertakes such intrusive regulation of the family ... the usual judicial deference to the legislature is inappropriate. "This Court has long recognized that freedom of personal choice in matters of marriage and family life is one of the liberties protected by the Due Process Clause of the Fourteenth Amendment." *Cleveland Board of Education v. LaFleur,* 414 U.S. 632 ... (1974).... But when the government intrudes on choices concerning family living arrangements, this Court must examine carefully the importance of the governmental interests advanced and the extent to which they are served by the challenged regulation....

When thus examined, this ordinance cannot survive. The city seeks to justify it as a means of preventing overcrowding, minimizing traffic and parking congestion, and avoiding an undue financial burden on East Cleveland's school system. Although these are legitimate goals, the ordinance before us serves them marginally, at best. For example, the ordinance permits any family consisting only of husband, wife, and unmarried children to live together, even if the family contains a half dozen licensed drivers, each with his or her own car. At the same time it forbids an adult brother and sister to share a household, even if both faithfully use public transportation. The ordinance would permit a grandmother to live with a single dependent son and children, even if his school-age children number a dozen, yet it forces Mrs. Moore to find another dwelling for her grandson John, simply because of the presence of his uncle and cousin in the same household. We need not labor the point. Section 1341.08 has but a tenuous relation to alleviation of the conditions mentioned by the city.

III

The city would distinguish the cases based on *Meyer* and *Pierce.* It points out that none of them "gives grandmothers any fundamental rights with respect to grandsons,"... and suggests that any constitutional right to live together as a family extends only to the nuclear family—essentially a couple and their dependent children.

To be sure, these cases did not expressly consider the family relationship presented here. They were immediately concerned with freedom of choice with respect to childbearing, e.g., *LaFleur, Roe v. Wade, Griswold, supra,* or with the rights of parents to the custody and companionship of their own children, *Stanley v. Illinois, supra,* or traditional parental authority in matters of child rearing and education. *Yoder, Ginsberg, Pierce, Meyer, supra.* But unless we close our eyes to the basic reasons why certain rights associated with the family have been accorded shelter under the Fourteenth Amendment's Due Process Clause, we cannot avoid applying the force and rationale of these precedents to the family choice involved in this case....

Appropriate limits on substantive due process come not from drawing arbitrary lines but rather from careful "respect for the teachings of history [and] solid recognition of the basic values that underlie our society."

Our decisions establish that the Constitution protects the sanctity of the family precisely because the institution of the family is deeply rooted in this Nation's history and tradition. It is through the family that we inculcate and pass down many of our most cherished values, moral and cultural.

Ours is by no means a tradition limited to respect for the bonds uniting the members of the nuclear family. The tradition of uncles, aunts, cousins, and especially grandparents sharing a household along with parents and children has roots equally venerable and equally deserving of constitutional recognition. Over the years millions of our citizens have grown up in just such an environment, and most, surely, have profited from it. Even if conditions of modern society have brought about a decline in extended family households, they have not erased the accumulated wisdom of civilization, gained over the centuries and honored throughout our history, that supports a larger conception of the family. Out of choice, necessity, or a sense of family responsibility, it has been common for close relatives to draw together and participate in the duties and the satisfactions of a common home. Decisions concerning child rearing, which *Yoder, Meyer, Pierce* and other cases have recognized as entitled to constitutional protection, long have been shared with grandparents or other relatives who occupy the same household—indeed who may take on major responsibility for the rearing of the children. Especially in times of adversity, such as the death of a spouse or economic

need, the broader family has tended to come together for mutual sustenance and to maintain or rebuild a secure home life. This is apparently what happened here.

Whether or not such a household is established because of personal tragedy, the choice of relatives in this degree of kinship to live together may not lightly be denied by the State. *Pierce* struck down an Oregon law requiring all children to attend the State's public schools, holding that the Constitution "excludes any general power of the State to standardize its children by forcing them to accept instruction from public teachers only." ... By the same token the Constitution prevents East Cleveland from standardizing its children—and its adults—by forcing all to live in certain narrowly defined family patterns.

Reversed.

**Mr. Justice Brennan, with whom
Mr. Justice Marshall joins, concurring.**

I join the plurality's opinion. I agree that the Constitution is not powerless to prevent East Cleveland from prosecuting as a criminal and jailing a 63-year-old grandmother for refusing to expel from her home her now 10-year-old grandson who has lived with her and been brought up by her since his mother's death when he was less than a year old. I do not question that a municipality may constitutionally zone to alleviate noise and traffic congestion and to prevent overcrowded and unsafe living conditions, in short to enact reasonable land-use restrictions in furtherance of the legitimate objectives East Cleveland claims for its ordinance. But the zoning power is not a license for local communities to enact senseless and arbitrary restrictions which cut deeply into private areas of protected family life. East Cleveland may not constitutionally define "family" as essentially confined to parents and the parents' own children. The plurality's opinion conclusively demonstrates that classifying family patterns in this eccentric way is not a rational means of achieving the ends East Cleveland claims for its ordinance, and further that the ordinance unconstitutionally abridges the "freedom of personal choice in matters of ... family life [that] is one of the liberties protected by the Due Process Clause of the Fourteenth Amendment."... I write only to underscore the cultural myopia of the arbitrary boundary drawn by the East Cleveland ordinance in the light of the tradition of the American home that has been a feature of our society since our beginning as a Nation—the "tradition" in the plurality's words, "of uncles, aunts, cousins, and especially grandparents sharing a household along with parents and children."...

... The line drawn by this ordinance displays a depressing insensitivity toward the economic and emotional needs of a very large part of our society.

In today's America, the "nuclear family" is the pattern so often found in much of white suburbia.... The Constitution cannot be interpreted, however, to tolerate the imposition by government upon the rest of us of white suburbia's preference in patterns of family living. The "extended family" that provided generations of early Americans with social services and economic and emotional support in times of hardship, and was the beachhead for successive waves of immigrants who populated our cities, remains not merely still a pervasive living pattern, but under the goad of brutal economic necessity, a prominent pattern—virtually a means of survival—for large numbers of the poor and deprived minorities of our society. For them, compelled pooling of scant resources requires compelled sharing of a household.

The "extended" form is especially familiar among black families. We may suppose that this reflects the truism that black citizens, like generations of white immigrants before them, have been victims of economic and other disadvantages that would worsen if they were compelled to abandon extended, for nuclear, living patterns....

I do not wish to be understood as implying that East Cleveland's enforcement of its ordinance is motivated by a racially discriminatory purpose: The record of this case would not support that implication. But the prominence of other than nuclear families among ethnic and racial minority groups, including our black citizens, surely demonstrates that the "extended family" pattern remains a vital tenet of our society. It suffices that in prohibiting this pattern of family living as a means of achieving its objectives, appellee city has chosen a device that deeply intrudes into family asso-ciational rights that historically have been central, and today remain central, to a large proportion of our population.... Indeed, *Village of Belle Terre v. Boraas,* 416 U.S. 1 ... (1974), the case primarily relied upon by the appellee, actually supports the Court's decision. The Belle Terre ordinance barred only unrelated individuals from constituting a family in a single-family zone. The village took special care in its brief to emphasize that its ordinance did not in any manner inhibit the choice of related individuals to constitute a family, whether in the "nuclear" or "extended" form. This was because the village perceived that choice as one it was constitutionally powerless to inhibit. Its brief stated: "Whether it be the extended family of a more leisurely age or the nuclear family of today the role of the family in raising and training successive generations of the species makes it more important, we dare say, than any other social or legal institution.... If any freedom not specifically mentioned in the Bill of Rights enjoys a 'preferred position' in the law it is most certainly the family." ... The cited decisions recognized, as the plurality recognizes today, that the choice of the "extended family" pattern is within the "freedom of personal choice in matters of ... family life [that] is one of the liberties protected by the Due Process Clause of the Fourteenth Amendment."...

Mr. Justice Stevens, concurring in the judgment.
In my judgment the critical question presented by this case is whether East Cleveland's housing ordinance is a permissible restriction on appellant's right to use her own property as she sees fit....

There appears to be no precedent for an ordinance which excludes any of an owner's relatives from the group of persons who may occupy his residence on a permanent basis. Nor does there appear to be any justification for such a restriction on an owner's use of his property. The city has failed totally to explain the need for a rule which would allow a homeowner to have two children live with her if they are brothers, but not if they are cousins. Since this ordinance has not been shown to have any "substantial relation to the public health, safety, morals, or general welfare" of the city of East Cleveland, and since it cuts so deeply into a fundamental right normally associated with the ownership of residential property—that of an owner to decide who may reside on his or her property ... East Cleveland's unprecedented ordinance constitutes a taking of property without due process and without just compensation. For these reasons, I concur in the Court's judgment.

Case Questions

1. What is the Supreme Court plurality's underlying criticism of the City of East Cleveland ordinance?
2. This case involves due process, a concept discussed in Chapter I. How does due process apply in this instance?
3. Why does Justice Stevens write a concurring opinion?

Justice Powell's plurality opinion links the legal meaning of substantive due process to moral values and the institution of the family. What is Powell's point?

CREATING FAMILY RELATIONSHIPS

An individual's family relationships are primarily created through marriage, the formation of a civil union–domestic partnership, and parenthood through birth, adoption, or (to a much lesser extent) foster-care placements. Each of these relationships is examined in turn.

Marriage

When two people decide to marry, they are voluntarily seeking to enter into a number of relationships involving personal, economic, social, religious, and legal considerations. It is often said that marriage is a contract, and to an extent that is true, but it is unlike other civil contracts because of the extent of governmental regulation. In 1888 the U.S. Supreme Court noted that "[other] contracts may be modified, restricted, or enlarged, or entirely released upon the consent of the parties. Not so with marriage. The relation once formed, the law steps in and holds the parties to various obligations and liabilities. It is an institution, in the maintenance of which in its purity the public is deeply interested, for it is the foundation of the family and of society, without which there would be neither civilization nor progress."[25]

The States' Power to Regulate Marriage

Marriage is regulated by the states, and each state determines who may marry, the duties and obligations of marriage, and how marriages are terminated. Although eligibility requirements for marriage differ from state to state, they generally include minimum age thresholds, monogamy (it is illegal to marry someone who is already married), competency (neither party can be mentally incompetent), and prohibitions on marriage between close relatives.

Parties seeking to marry must be acting voluntarily. They indicate their consent to the marriage by jointly applying for a license. Issuance of the license certifies that the applicants have complied with the relevant marriage eligibility requirements. Although states have broad rights to regulate marriage, there are constitutional limitations on this power. This was demonstrated in 1967 in a case argued before the U.S. Supreme Court involving a Virginia criminal statute prohibiting interracial marriages. In the case of *Loving v. Virginia,* the Supreme Court was asked to determine whether such a statute was constitutionally permissible under the Fourteenth Amendment's Due Process and Equal Protection Clauses. The Court ruled that the "freedom to marry a person of another race resides with the individual and cannot be infringed by the state."

Loving v. Commonwealth of Virginia
388 U.S. 1
Supreme Court of the United States
June 12, 1967

Mr. Chief Justice Warren delivered the opinion of the Court.

This case presents a constitutional question never addressed by this Court: whether a statutory scheme adopted by the State of Virginia to prevent marriages between persons solely on the basis of racial classifications violates the Equal Protection and Due Process Clauses of the Fourteenth Amendment. For reasons which seem to us to reflect the central meaning of those constitutional commands, we conclude that these statutes cannot stand consistently with the Fourteenth Amendment.

In June 1958, two residents of Virginia, Mildred Jeter, a Negro woman, and Richard Loving, a white man, were married in the District of Columbia pursuant to its laws. Shortly after their marriage, the Lovings returned to Virginia and established their marital abode in Caroline County. At the October Term, 1958, of the Circuit Court of Caroline County, a grand jury issued an indictment charging the Lovings with violating Virginia's ban on interracial marriages. On January 6, 1959, the Lovings pleaded guilty to the charge and were sentenced to one year in jail; however, the trial judge suspended the sentence for a period of 25 years on the condition that the Lovings leave the State and not return to Virginia together for 25 years. He stated in an opinion that:

> Almighty God created the races white, black, yellow, malay and red, and he placed them on separate continents. And but for the interference with his arrangement there would be no cause for such marriages. The fact that he separated the races shows that he did not intend for the races to mix.

After their convictions, the Lovings took up residence in the District of Columbia. On November 6, 1963, they filed a motion in the state trial court to vacate the judgment and set aside the sentence on the ground that the statutes which they had violated were repugnant to the Fourteenth Amendment. The motion not having been decided by October 28, 1964, the Lovings instituted a class action in the United States District Court for the Eastern District of Virginia requesting that a three-judge court be convened to declare the Virginia antimiscegenation statutes unconstitutional and to enjoin state officials from enforcing their convictions. On January 22, 1965, the state trial judge denied the motion to vacate the sentences, and the Lovings perfected an appeal to the Supreme Court of Appeals of Virginia. On February 11, 1965, the three-judge District Court continued the case to allow the Lovings to present their constitutional claims to the highest state court.

The Supreme Court of Appeals upheld the constitutionality of the antimiscegenation statutes and, after modifying the sentence, affirmed the conviction. The Lovings appealed this decision.... The two statutes under which appellants were convicted and sentenced are part of a comprehensive statutory scheme aimed at prohibiting and punishing interracial marriages. The Lovings were convicted of violating § 20–58 of the Virginia Code:

> *Leaving State to evade law.*—If any white person and colored person shall go out of this State, for the purpose of being married, and with the

intention of returning, and be married out of it, and afterwards return to and reside in it, cohabiting as man and wife, they shall be punished as provided in § 20–59.

Section 20–59, which defines the penalty for miscegenation, provides:

> *Punishment for marriage.*—If any white person intermarry with a colored person, or any colored person intermarry with a white person, he shall be guilty of a felony and shall be punished by confinement in the penitentiary for not less than one nor more than five years.

... The Lovings have never disputed in the course of this litigation that Mrs. Loving is a "colored person" or that Mr. Loving is a "white person" within the meanings given those terms by the Virginia statutes.

Virginia is now one of 16 States which prohibit and punish marriages on the basis of racial classifications. Penalties for miscegenation arose as an incident to slavery and have been common in Virginia since the colonial period. The present statutory scheme dates from the adoption of the Racial Integrity Act of 1924, passed during the period of extreme nativism which followed the end of the First World War. The central features of this Act, and current Virginia law, are the absolute prohibition of a "white person" marrying other than another "white person," a prohibition against issuing marriage licenses until the issuing official is satisfied that the applicants' statements as to their race are correct, certificates of "racial composition" to be kept by both local and state registrars, and the carrying forward of earlier prohibitions against racial intermarriage.

I.

In upholding the constitutionality of these provisions in the decision below, the Supreme Court of Appeals of Virginia referred to its 1955 decision in *Naim v. Naim* ... as stating the reasons supporting the validity of these laws. In *Naim,* the state court concluded that the State's legitimate purposes were "to preserve the racial integrity of its citizens," and to prevent "the corruption of blood," "a mongrel breed of citizens," and "the obliteration of racial pride," obviously an endorsement of the doctrine of White Supremacy.... The court also reasoned that marriage has traditionally been subject to state regulation without federal intervention, and, consequently, the regulation of marriage should be left to exclusive state control by the Tenth Amendment.

While the state court is no doubt correct in asserting that marriage is a social relation subject to the State's police power ... the State does not contend in its argument before this Court that its powers to regulate marriage are unlimited notwithstanding the commands of the Fourteenth Amendment.... Instead, the State argues that the meaning of the Equal Protection Clause, as illuminated by the statements of the Framers, is only that state penal laws containing an interracial element as part of the definition of the offense must apply equally to whites and Negroes in the sense that members of each race are punished to the same degree. Thus, the State contends that, because its miscegenation statutes punish equally both the white and the Negro participants in an interracial marriage, these statutes, despite their reliance on racial classifications, do not constitute an invidious discrimination based upon race. The second argument advanced by the State assumes the validity of its equal application theory. The argument is that, if the Equal Protection Clause does not outlaw miscegenation statutes because of their reliance on racial classifications, the question of constitutionality would thus become whether there was any rational basis for a State to treat interracial marriages differently from other marriages. On this question, the State argues, the scientific evidence is substantially in doubt and, consequently, this Court should defer to the wisdom of the state legislature in adopting its policy of discouraging interracial marriages.

Because we reject the notion that the mere "equal application" of a statute containing racial classifications is enough to remove the classifications from the Fourteenth Amendment's proscription of all invidious racial discriminations, we do not accept the State's contention that these statutes should be upheld if there is any possible basis for concluding that they serve a rational purpose.... In the case at bar, we deal with statutes containing racial classifications, and the fact of equal application does not immunize the statute from the very heavy burden of justification which the Fourteenth Amendment has traditionally required of state statutes drawn according to race.... There can be no question but that Virginia's miscegenation statutes rest solely upon distinctions drawn according to race. The statutes proscribe generally accepted conduct if engaged in by members of different races. Over the years, this Court has consistently repudiated "[d]istinctions between

citizens solely because of their ancestry" as being "odious to a free people whose institutions are founded upon the doctrine of equality." ... At the very least, the Equal Protection Clause demands that racial classifications, especially suspect in criminal statutes, be subjected to the "most rigid scrutiny," ... and, if they are ever to be upheld, they must be shown to be necessary to the accomplishment of some permissible state objective, independent of the racial discrimination which it was the object of the Fourteenth Amendment to eliminate. Indeed, two members of this Court have already stated that they "cannot conceive of a valid legislative purpose ... which makes the color of a person's skin the test of whether his conduct is a criminal offense." ...

There is patently no legitimate overriding purpose independent of invidious racial discrimination which justifies this classification. The fact that Virginia prohibits only interracial marriages involving white persons demonstrates that the racial classifications must stand on their own justification, as measures designed to maintain White Supremacy. We have consistently denied the constitutionality of measures which restrict the rights of citizens on account of race. There can be no doubt that restricting the freedom to marry solely because of racial classifications violates the central meaning of the Equal Protection Clause.

These statutes also deprive the Lovings of liberty without due process of law in violation of the Due Process Clause of the Fourteenth Amendment. The freedom to marry has long been recognized as one of the vital personal rights essential to the orderly pursuit of happiness by free men.

Marriage is one of the "basic civil rights of man," fundamental to our very existence and survival.... To deny this fundamental freedom on so unsupportable a basis as the racial classifications embodied in these statutes, classifications so directly subversive of the principle of equality at the heart of the Fourteenth Amendment, is surely to deprive all the State's citizens of liberty without due process of law. The Fourteenth Amendment requires that the freedom of choice to marry not be restricted by invidious racial discriminations. Under our Constitution, the freedom to marry or not marry a person of another race resides with the individual and cannot be infringed by the State.

These convictions must be reversed. It is so ordered. Reversed.

Case Questions

1. Virginia argued to the Supreme Court that its miscegenation statute did not constitute an invidious classification scheme based on race. What was the basis for this position?

2. What response did the Supreme Court make to Virginia's restrictions on an individual's right to decide whether to marry a person of another race?
3. Do you see any merit to the argument often made today that statutes that restrict marriage to heterosexual couples deny same-sex couples wishing to marry the equal protection of the law?

 When *Loving v. Virginia* arrived at the U.S. Supreme Court, Virginia and fifteen other states had statutes on the books that made it a crime for blacks and whites to intermarry. These statutes, called *antimiscegenation laws,* were common in former slave states, and had existed in Virginia since colonial times. The justices of the U.S. Supreme Court declared, "There is patently no legitimate overriding purpose independent of invidious racial discrimination which justifies this classification." Which ethical tradition is most reflected in the Court's opinion in this case? The answer can be found on page 2.

The Ongoing Dispute over the Definition of Marriage

At the present time, Americans profoundly disagree about whether same-sex couples have the same right to become married as do heterosexual couples. This disagreement is reflected in the contradictory positions taken by the state governments. It also illustrates one of the benefits of the federal form of government: the flexibility afforded each state to establish its own public policy—subject, of course, to the requirements of the U.S. Constitution. It is interesting to see how the same-sex marriage movement has slowly but steadily taken hold in this country's northeastern states. It is also overwhelmingly clear, however, that most states favor limiting marriage to heterosexual relationships.

As of this writing, twelve states permit same-sex marriages (see Figure 9.2). Opponents of same-sex marriages have responded at both the federal and the state levels to ban such marriages by statute and constitutional amendment.

The Federal Government's Position—The Defense of Marriage Act

The federal **Defense of Marriage Act (DOMA)** was signed into law by President Clinton in 1996. This statute defined the term "effect," a term used in the U.S. Constitution's Full Faith and Credit Clause, as not requiring any state, against its will, to recognize same-sex marriages as valid. Because of the Supreme Court's decision in the Windsor case, which you are about to read, the federal government has announced that as of September 16, 2013 it will recognize all validly married couples as being entitled to the same federal tax benefits irrespective of the sexual orientation of the marital partners and irrespective of the state laws of the state in which the marital partners reside. All valid marriages will from that date on be treated equally.

The question about DOMA's constitutionality was decided by the U.S. Supreme Court in 2013, in the case of *United States v. Edith S. Windsor.* The Court had to decide whether Section 3 of the Act, which restricts federal benefits to heterosexual marriages, violated the Fifth Amendment by denying legally married same-sex couples the equal protection of the laws.

Introduction to *United States v. Edith S. Windsor*

The U.S. Supreme Court had to decide two issues in *United States v. Windsor.* The first question involved whether the petitioners had standing, a topic we first saw in the Chapter VI case of

Year	State
2004	Massachusetts
2008	Connecticut
2009	Vermont and Iowa
2010	New Hampshire
2011	New York
2012	Maine and Washington
2013	Maryland, Rhode Island, Delaware, and Minnesota

© Cengage Learning 2015

F I G U R E   9.2 States that have legalized same-sex marriages

Hollingsworth v. Perry. (That was the case challenging the constitutionality of California's Proposition 8). The second issue was whether the federal Defense of Marriage Act (DOMA) was unconstitutional.

The problems with standing in *Hollingsworth* and *Windsor* are similar. In each case the governmental officials who would normally defend the challenged statute refused to do so because they agreed with the respondents that the statutes were unconstitutional. In *Hollingsworth*, the U.S. Supreme Court ruled that the nongovernmental petitioners did not have standing. In *Windsor*, the Court ruled that members of Congress who collectively wanted to defend the statute in court (the group was called the Bipartisan Legal Advisory Group), did have standing. Because of space limitations and the need to focus on the constitutionality issue, the U.S. Supreme Court's discussion of the standing issue in part II of the majority opinion of *Windsor* has been omitted.

Edith Windsor and Thea Spyer were a same-sex couple for over 40 years. They were married in 2007 in Canada, where same-sex marriages were legal, because they could not be issued marriage licenses in New York. But New York did recognize Canadian marriages as valid and Edith and Thea were considered to be legally married and entitled to all marital benefits under state law. Thea, who was a millionaire, died in 2009, leaving her entire estate to Edith. Had Edith's deceased spouse been a man instead of a woman, Edith would not have had to pay federal inheritance taxes. But under DOMA, the estate tax exemption for surviving spouses was not available to same-sex couples. Edith had to pay the Internal Revenue Service $363,053. Edith proceeded to sue the United States for a refund, claiming that DOMA's §3 was unconstitutional in that it unfairly singled out legally married same-sex couples for "differential treatment compared to other similarly situated couples without justification." She prevailed in the U.S. District Court and in U.S. Court of Appeals for the Second Circuit. The U.S. Supreme Court granted certiorari.

United States v. Edith S. Windsor
570 U.S. _____
Supreme Court of the United States
June 26, 2013

Justice Kennedy delivered the opinion of the Court.
Two women then resident in New York were married in a lawful ceremony in Ontario, Canada, in 2007. Edith Windsor and Thea Spyer returned to their home in New York City. When Spyer died in 2009, she left her entire estate to Windsor. Windsor sought to claim the estate tax exemption for surviving spouses. She was barred from doing so, however, by a federal law, the Defense of Marriage Act, which excludes a same-sex partner from the definition of "spouse" as that term is used in federal statutes. Windsor paid the taxes but filed suit to challenge the constitutionality of this provision. The United States District Court and the Court of Appeals ruled that this portion of the statute is unconstitutional and ordered the United States to pay Windsor a refund. This Court granted certiorari and now affirms the judgment in Windsor's favor.

I.
In 1996, as some States were beginning to consider the concept of same-sex marriage . . . and before any State had acted to permit it, Congress enacted the Defense of Marriage Act (DOMA).... DOMA contains two operative sections: Section 2, which has not been challenged here, allows States to refuse to recognize same-sex marriages performed under the laws of other States....

Section 3 is at issue here. It amends the Dictionary Act in Title 1, §7, of the United States Code to provide a fed eral definition of "marriage" and "spouse." Section 3 of DOMA provides as follows:

> In determining the meaning of any Act of Congress, or of any ruling, regulation, or interpretation of the various administrative bureaus and agencies of the United States, the word "marriage" means only a legal union between one man and one woman as husband and wife, and the word 'spouse' refers only to a person of the opposite sex who is a husband or a wife....

... The enactment's comprehensive definition of marriage for purposes of all federal statutes and other regulations or directives covered by its terms, however, does control over 1,000 federal laws in which marital or spousal status is addressed as a matter of federal law....

Edith Windsor and Thea Spyer met in New York City in 1963 and began a long-term relationship. Windsor and Spyer registered as domestic partners when New York City gave that right to same-sex couples in 1993. Concerned about Spyer's health, the couple made the 2007 trip to Canada for their marriage, but they continued to reside in New York City. The State of New York deems their Ontario marriage to be a valid one....

Spyer died in February 2009, and left her entire estate to Windsor. Because DOMA denies federal recognition to same-sex spouses, Windsor did not qualify for the marital exemption from the federal estate tax, which excludes from taxation "any interest in property which passes or has passed from the decedent to his surviving spouse.". . . Windsor paid $363,053 in estate taxes and sought a refund. The Internal Revenue Service denied the refund, concluding that, under DOMA, Windsor was not a "surviving spouse." Windsor commenced this refund suit in the United States District Court for the Southern District of New York. She contended that DOMA violates the guarantee of equal protection, as applied to the Federal Government through the Fifth Amendment.

While the tax refund suit was pending, the Attorney General of the United States notified the Speaker of the House of Representatives, ... that the Department of Justice would no longer defend the constitutionality of DOMA's §3....

Although "the President ... instructed the Department [of Justice] not to defend the statute in Windsor," he also decided "that Section 3 will continue to be enforced by the Executive Branch" and that the United States had an "interest in providing Congress a full and fair opportunity to participate in the litigation of those cases.". . . The stated rationale for this dual-track procedure (determination of unconstitutionality coupled with ongoing enforcement) was to "recogniz[e] the judiciary as the final arbiter of the constitutional claims raised.". . .

In response ... the Bipartisan Legal Advisory Group (BLAG) of the House of Representatives voted to intervene in the litigation to defend the constitutionality of §3 of DOMA. The Department of Justice did not oppose limited intervention by BLAG.... The District Court ... grant[ed] intervention by BLAG as an interested party....

On the merits of the tax refund suit, the District Court ruled against the United States. It held that §3 of DOMA is unconstitutional and ordered the Treasury to refund the tax with interest.... [T]he Court of Appeals for the Second Circuit affirmed the District Court's judgment.... The United States has not complied with

the judgment. Windsor has not received her refund, and the Ex ecutive Branch continues to enforce §3 of DOMA....

II
[The Court's determination that BLAG had standing to maintain it's appeals has been omitted because of space limitations.]

III
When at first Windsor and Spyer longed to marry, neither New York nor any other State granted them that right. After waiting some years, in 2007 they traveled to Ontario to be married there. It seems fair to conclude that, until recent years, many citizens had not even considered the possibility that two persons of the same sex might aspire to occupy the same status and dignity as that of a man and woman in lawful marriage. For marriage between a man and a woman no doubt had been thought of by most people as essential to the very definition of that term and to its role and function throughout the history of civilization. That belief, for many who long have held it, became even more urgent, more cherished when challenged. For others, however, came the beginnings of a new perspective, a new insight. Accordingly some States concluded that same-sex marriage ought to be given recognition and validity in the law for those same-sex couples who wish to define themselves by their commitment to each other....

Slowly at first and then in rapid course, the laws of New York came to acknowledge the urgency of this issue for same-sex couples who wanted to affirm their commitment to one another before their children, their family, their friends, and their community. And so New York recognized same-sex marriages performed elsewhere; and then it later amended its own marriage laws to permit same-sex marriage. New York, in common with, as of this writing, 11 other States and the District of Columbia, decided that same-sex couples should have the right to marry.... After a statewide deliberative process that enabled its citizens to discuss and weigh arguments for and against same- sex marriage, New York acted to enlarge the definition of marriage to correct what its citizens and elected representatives perceived to be an injustice that they had not earlier known or understood....

Against this background of lawful same-sex marriage in some States, the design, purpose, and effect of DOMA should be considered as the beginning point in deciding whether it is valid under the Constitution. By history and tradition the definition and regulation of marriage ... has been treated as being within the authority and realm of the separate States. Yet it is further established that Congress, in enacting discrete statutes, can make determinations that bear on marital rights and privileges....

... [P]recedents involving congressional statutes which affect marriages and family status ... illustrate this point. In addressing the interaction of state domestic relations and federal immigration law Congress determined that marriages "entered into for the purpose of procuring an alien's admission [to the United States] as an immigrant" will not qualify the noncitizen for that status, even if the noncitizen's marriage is valid and proper for state-law purposes.... And in establishing income-based criteria for Social Security benefits, Congress decided that although state law would determine in general who qualifies as an applicant's spouse, common-law marriages also should be recognized, regardless of any particular State's view on these relationships....

Though these discrete examples establish the constitutionality of limited federal laws that regulate the meaning of marriage in order to further federal policy, DOMA has a far greater reach; for it enacts a directive applicable to over 1,000 federal statutes and the whole realm of federal regulations. And its operation is directed to a class of persons that the laws of New York, and of 11 other States, have sought to protect....

In order to assess the validity of that intervention it is necessary to discuss the extent of the state power and authority over marriage as a matter of history and tradition. State laws defining and regulating marriage, of course, must respect the constitutional rights of persons, see, e.g., *Loving v. Virginia*, 388 U. S. 1 (1967); but, subject to those guarantees, "regulation of domestic relations" is "an area that has long been regarded as a virtually exclusive province of the States."...

The significance of state responsibilities for the definition and regulation of marriage dates to the Nation's beginning; for "when the Constitution was adopted the common understanding was that the domestic relations of husband and wife and parent and child were matters reserved to the States."... Marriage laws vary in some respects from State to State. For example, the required minimum age is 16 in Vermont, but only 13 in New Hampshire.... Likewise the permissible degree of consanguinity can vary (most States permit first cousins to marry, but a handful—such as Iowa and Washington ... prohibit the practice)....

Against this background DOMA rejects the long-established precept that the incidents, benefits, and obligations of marriage are uniform for all married couples within each State, though they may vary, subject to constitutional guarantees, from one State to the next. Despite these considerations, it is unnecessary to decide whether this federal intrusion on state power is a violation of the Constitution because it disrupts the federal balance. The State's power in defining the marital relation is of central relevance in this case quite apart from principles of federalism. Here the State's decision to give this class of persons the right to marry conferred upon them a dignity and status of immense import. When the State used its historic and essential authority to define the marital relation in this way, its role and its power in making the decision enhanced the recognition, dignity, and protection of the class in their own community. DOMA, because of its reach and extent, departs from this history and tradition of reliance on state law to define marriage....

The Federal Government uses this state-defined class for the opposite purpose—to impose restrictions and disabilities. That result requires this Court now to address whether the resulting injury and indignity is a deprivation of an essential part of the liberty protected by the Fifth Amendment. What the State of New York treats as alike the federal law deems unlike by a law designed to injure the same class the State seeks to protect.

In acting first to recognize and then to allow same-sex marriages, New York was responding "to the initiative of those who [sought] a voice in shaping the destiny of their own times.".... These actions were without doubt a proper exercise of its sovereign authority within our federal system, all in the way that the Framers of the Constitution intended. The dynamics of state government in the federal system are to allow the formation of consensus respecting the way the members of a discrete community treat each other in their daily contact and constant interaction with each other.

... Private, consensual sexual intimacy between two adult persons of the same sex may not be punished by the State, and it can form "but one element in a personal bond that is more enduring."... By its recognition of the validity of same-sex marriages performed in other jurisdictions and then by authorizing same-sex unions and same-sex marriages, New York sought to give further protection and dignity to that bond. For same-sex couples who wished to be married, the State acted to give their lawful conduct a lawful status. This status is a far-reaching legal acknowledgment of the intimate relationship between two people, a relationship deemed by the State worthy of dignity in the community equal with all other marriages. It reflects both the community's considered perspective on the historical roots of the institution of marriage and its evolving understanding of the meaning of equality.

IV

DOMA seeks to injure the very class New York seeks to protect. By doing so it violates basic due process and equal protection principles applicable to the Federal Government.... The Constitution's guarantee of equality "must at the very least mean that a bare congressional desire to harm a politically unpopular group cannot" justify disparate treatment of that group.... DOMA cannot survive under these principles. The responsibility of the States for the regulation of domestic relations is an important indicator of the substantial societal impact the State's classifications have in the daily lives and customs of its people. DOMA's unusual deviation from the usual tradition of recognizing and accepting state definitions of marriage here operates to deprive same-sex couples of the benefits and responsibilities that come with the federal recognition of their marriages. This is strong evidence of a law having the purpose and effect of disapproval of that class. The avowed purpose and practical effect of the law here in question are to impose a disadvantage, a separate status, and so a stigma upon all who enter into same-sex marriages made lawful by the unquestioned authority of the States.

The history of DOMA's enactment and its own text demonstrate that interference with the equal dignity of same-sex marriages, a dignity conferred by the States in the exercise of their sovereign power, was more than an incidental effect of the federal statute. It was its essence. The House Report announced its conclusion that "it is both appropriate and necessary for Congress to do what it can to defend the institution of traditional heterosexual marriage.... The House concluded that DOMA expresses "both moral disapproval of homosexuality, and a moral conviction that heterosexuality better comports with traditional (especially Judeo-Christian) morality.". . . The stated purpose of the law was to promote an "interest in protecting the traditional moral teachings reflected in heterosexual-only marriage laws.". . . Were there any doubt of this far-reaching purpose, the title of the Act confirms it: The Defense of Marriage.

... The Act's demonstrated purpose is to ensure that if any State decides to recognize same-sex marriages, those unions will be treated as second-class marriages for purposes of federal law. This raises a most serious question under the Constitution's Fifth Amendment.

DOMA's operation in practice confirms this purpose. When New York adopted a law to permit same-sex marriage, it sought to eliminate inequality; but DOMA frustrates that objective through a system-wide enactment with no identified connection to any particular area of federal law. DOMA writes inequality into the entire United States Code. The particular case at hand concerns the estate tax, but DOMA is more than a simple determination of what should or should

not be allowed as an estate tax refund. Among the over 1,000 statutes and numerous federal regulations that DOMA controls are laws pertaining to Social Security, housing, taxes, criminal sanctions, copyright, and veterans' benefits.

... By creating two contradictory marriage regimes within the same State, DOMA forces same-sex couples to live as married for the purpose of state law but unmarried for the purpose of federal law, thus diminishing the stability and predictability of basic personal relations the State has found it proper to acknowledge and protect. By this dynamic DOMA undermines both the public and private significance of state-sanctioned same-sex marriages; for it tells those couples, and all the world, that their otherwise valid marriages are unworthy of federal recognition. This places same-sex couples in an unstable position of being in a second-tier marriage. The differentiation demeans the couple, whose moral and sexual choices the Constitution protects ... and whose relationship the State has sought to dignify. And it humiliates tens of thousands of children now being raised by same-sex couples. The law in question makes it even more difficult for the children to understand the integrity and closeness of their own family and its concord with other families in their community and in their daily lives.

Under DOMA, same-sex married couples have their lives burdened, by reason of government decree, in visible and public ways. By its great reach, DOMA touches many aspects of married and family life, from the mundane to the profound. It prevents same-sex married couples from obtaining government health-care benefits they would otherwise receive.... It deprives them of the Bankruptcy Code's special protections for domestic-support obligations.... It forces them to follow a complicated procedure to file their state and federal taxes jointly.... It prohibits them from being buried together in veterans' cemeteries. National Cemetery Administration Directive....

For certain married couples, DOMA's unequal effects are even more serious.... DOMA ... brings financial harm to children of same-sex couples. It raises the cost of health care for families by taxing health benefits provided by employers to their workers' same-sex spouses.... And it denies or reduces benefits allowed to families upon the loss of a spouse and parent, benefits that are an integral part of family security . . . (benefits available to a surviving spouse caring for the couple's child)....

DOMA divests married same-sex couples of the duties and responsibilities that are an essential part of married life and that they in most cases would be honored to accept were DOMA not in force. For instance, because it is expected that spouses will support each other as they pursue educational opportunities, federal law takes into consideration a spouse's income in calculating a student's fed- eral financial aid eligibility.... Same-sex married couples are exempt from this requirement. The same is true with respect to federal ethics rules. Federal executive and agency officials are prohibited from "participat[ing] personally and substantially" in matters as to which they or their spouses have a financial interest.... A similar statute prohibits Senators, Senate employees, and their spouses from accepting high-value gifts from certain sources ... and another mandates detailed financial disclosures by numerous high-ranking officials and their spouses.... Under DOMA, however, these Government-integrity rules do not apply to same-sex spouses....

The power the Constitution grants it also restrains. And though Congress has great authority to design laws to fit its own conception of sound national policy, it cannot deny the liberty protected by the Due Process Clause of the Fifth Amendment.

What has been explained to this point should more than suffice to establish that the principal purpose and the necessary effect of this law are to demean those persons who are in a lawful same-sex marriage. This requires the Court to hold, as it now does, that DOMA is unconstitutional as a deprivation of the liberty of the person protected by the Fifth Amendment of the Constitution.

The liberty protected by the Fifth Amendment's Due Process Clause contains within it the prohibition against denying to any person the equal protection of the laws.... While the Fifth Amendment itself withdraws from Government the power to degrade or demean in the way this law does, the equal protection guarantee of the Fourteenth Amendment makes that Fifth Amendment right all the more specific and all the better understood and preserved.

The class to which DOMA directs its restrictions and restraints are those persons who are joined in same-sex marriages made lawful by the State. DOMA singles out a class of persons deemed by a State entitled to recognition and protection to enhance their own liberty. It imposes a disability on the class by refusing to acknowledge a status the State finds to be dignified and proper. DOMA instructs all federal officials, and indeed all persons with whom same-sex couples interact, including their own children, that their marriage is less worthy than the marriages of others. The federal statute is invalid, for no legitimate purpose overcomes the purpose and effect to disparage and to injure those whom the State, by its marriage laws, sought to protect in personhood and dignity. By seeking to displace this protection and treating those persons as living in marriages less respected than others, the federal statute is in violation of the Fifth Amendment. This opinion and its holding are confined to those lawful marriages.

The judgment of the Court of Appeals for the Second Circuit is affirmed.

It is so ordered.

Case Questions

1. Which protected personal interest in the Due Process Clause was denied to Windsor?
2. The Court limits its holding to same-sex marriages that are lawful? What do you think that means?

The State's Responses—Statutes and Constitutional Amendments

At present, the states overwhelmingly oppose the legalization of same-sex marriages. As of this writing thirty-five states have enacted copy-cat "state Defense of Marriage" statutes or prohibit same-sex marriages in their state constitutions.

Although the U.S. Supreme Court granted certiorari in *Hollingsworth v. Perry*, a suit in which two same-sex couples directly challenged the constitutionality of California's Proposition 8, the Court refused to rule on the merits of that claim because the justices concluded that the petitioner, (Hollingsworth), lacked standing. However, because both of the lower courts that had ruled on the merits were in agreement that Proposition 8 was unconstitutional, that decision became the final decision in the case. Thus California became one of 13th states to legalize same-sex marriages. Readers can find an edited version of the Hollingsworth case (as it relates to standing) in Chapter 6 of the text.

Marriage Solemnization Ceremonies

States generally require that persons intending to marry solemnize their union with either a civil or a religious ceremony. The solemnization ceremony provides tangible and public evidence that a marriage has occurred. It demonstrates that the parties mutually desire to marry and have satisfied all legal requirements.[26]

Common Law Marriages

Some jurisdictions recognize privately created, informal marriages by agreement that dispense with licenses and solemnization ceremonies. They are called **common law marriages**.

Although each state that recognizes such marriages has its own particular requirements, most require that the parties be of age and unmarried. Most important, the parties must have established the relationship of husband and wife, live together as a married couple, and present themselves to the world as being married. Living together, jointly owning property, and having a child are insufficient acts, in themselves, to establish a common law marriage. States that still recognize common law marriages include Montana, Iowa, Alabama, Colorado, Rhode Island, South Carolina, Utah, Texas, and Kansas.

Adoption

Informal adoptions existed in this country from its earliest days, and into the 1860s orphans often were apprenticed to masters or worked on farms and plantations as indentured servants in exchange for their room and board, and in many instances transportation from Europe to North America.[27] Adoption, which was unknown to the common law, first came into existence in 1851, when Massachusetts enacted the first adoption statute.[28]

Although modern statutes permit the adoption of adults, subject to some exceptions,[29] most adoptions involve children. **Adoption** is both a social and a legal process by which the rights and duties accompanying the parent–child relationship are transferred from birth parents to adoptive parents. State adoption statutes were originally intended primarily to help qualified childless couples "normalize" their marriages,[30] but today the statutes encourage adoption in part to provide families for many abandoned, abused, deserted, neglected, or unwanted children, who might otherwise need to be supported at public expense. Adoptions can be classified as either independent or agency placements. In **agency adoptions,** the birth parents consent to the termination of their parental rights and surrender the child to an adoption agency that selects the adoptive parent(s) and places the child. An **independent adoption** takes place when the birth parent(s) themselves interview prospective adoptive parents and make a selection without agency involvement. Some states prohibit independent adoptions and require that agencies participate in the process.

Becoming an adoptive parent is highly regulated, and the procedures vary by state and by the type of adoption. It often makes a difference whether the adoption involves an agency or is independent, is between relatives, or is of an adult. In adoptions between related persons, for example, where a stepparent wishes to adopt his or her spouse's child, the investigative process is often simplified or eliminated. In an independent adoption, the nature and scope of any investigation are left up to the birth parent(s). They interview prospective adoptive parents and place the child without agency participation. When a public or private agency licensed by the state places a child for adoption, the law usually requires close scrutiny. Adoptive parents who are unrelated to an adopted child are carefully investigated to determine whether the placement is suitable and in the best interests of the child. This investigation is often very detailed and probes most areas of an applicant's life. The probe results in a report that includes information on the applicant's race, age, marital status, and financial condition; the "adequacy of the home environment"; and information about very personal matters such as religious preferences, current romantic interests, and sexual orientation.[31]

Matching

The investigative process makes it possible for agencies to rank prospective adoptive parents in terms of how closely they match the agency's conception of the ideal family for the child. Those who most closely fit the profile are often matched with the most "desirable" adoptees.[32] Petitioners who are married generally rank higher than those who are unmarried, younger applicants rank higher than older, able bodied higher than disabled, and heterosexuals higher than homosexuals.[33]

Interracial adoption has long been a topic heavily laden with emotion. Most of the fury arises when whites seek to adopt nonwhite children. Questions are frequently raised about whether white adoptive parents have the ability to develop fully a nonwhite child's racial identity and appreciation for the richness of his or her culture.[34]

Congress, however, declared the nation's public policy as to interracial adoption in 1994 when it enacted the **Multiethnic Placement Act (MEPA)** of 1994, and again in 1996 when it amended MEPA by enacting the **Interethnic Adoption Provisions (IEP)**. The two acts are generally known as the MEPA–IEP; these laws essentially do the following:

1. Prohibit adoption agencies that receive federal funds from using an aspiring adoptive or foster parent's race, color, or national origin against him or her for purposes of denying such parent the placement of a child.

2. Make it illegal to delay or deny a child an adoptive or foster-care placement because of his or her race, color, or national origin.

The MEPA–IEP intends that placement decisions be made on a case-by-case basis, and cultural needs cannot routinely be used to prevent white adoptive parents, for example, from adopting nonwhite children. Congress's intent could not be more clear, because it included a provision in the IEP repealing language in the original MEPA that expressly permitted agencies to consider a "child's cultural, ethnic, and racial background and the capacity of the prospective foster or adoptive parents to meet the needs of a child from this background" in the making of placement decisions. Many states had to amend their adoption statutes in order to comply with the MEPA–IEP. An example of a post-MEPA–IEP state adoption statute can be seen in Figure 9.3. Notice how the Arkansas statute prohibits discrimination on the basis of race, color, or national origin; creates legal preferences favoring adult relatives over nonrelatives; and authorizes religious matching.

Despite Congress's clear definition of public policy, it is difficult to determine in practice the extent to which the law is being followed. How can prospective white adoptive parents, who have been told that because of the child's cultural needs they will not be permitted to adopt a nonwhite child, know whether this justification is merely a pretext for invidious racial discrimination? It is likely that categorical discrimination in which placements are based on legally impermissible factors still occurs. Similarly, discrimination in placements based on religion, education levels, and socioeconomic status may continue to exist.

The U.S. Supreme Court has strongly indicated that government should remain neutral in religious matters[35] and has supported parental choice regarding the religious upbringing of children. But the Court has not attempted to answer, as a general proposition, whether religious matching is in the best interest of adoptive children. (See Figure 9.3.)

As we have just seen, state statutes sometimes express a preference that adoptive parents be of the same religion as the adoptee or birth parent(s). Should adoptive parents who are of mixed religions, who adhere to obscure faiths, or who are atheists be legally disadvantaged in placement decisions?[36] Should adoptive parents have the right to choose the religion of their adoptive child, or must they raise the child in the faith chosen by the birth parents? Does it matter whether the adoptive child's religion differs from that of the other members of the adoptive family?[37] Questions like these are easy to ask, but they raise policy issues that are difficult to resolve.

Another area of current controversy involves the placement of adoptees with gay and lesbian adoptive parents. The stated reasons for rejecting

---

9-9-102. Religious preference — Removal of barriers to inter-ethnic adoption — Preference to relative caregivers for a child in foster care.

(a) In all custodial placements by the Department of Human Services in foster care or adoption, the court shall give preferential consideration to an adult relative over a nonrelated caregiver, provided that the relative caregiver meets all relevant child protection standards and it is in the best interest of the child to be placed with the relative caregiver.

(b) If the genetic parent or parents of the child express a preference for placing the child in a foster home or an adoptive home of the same or a similar religious background to that of the genetic parent or parents, the court shall place the child with a family that meets the genetic parent's religious preference, or if a family is not available, to a family of a different religious background that is knowledgeable and appreciative of the child's religious background.

(c) The court shall not deny a petition for adoption on the basis of race, color, or national origin of the adoptive parent or the child involved.

F I G U R E 9.3   Arkansas Code Section 9-9-102

gays and lesbians as adoptive parents are often based on the perceived incompatibility of the " 'gay life-style' with social mores and on a fear that an adoptive child would be exposed to an increased risk of contracting AIDS."[38] Where no statutes prevent them, gay–lesbian adoptions are theoretically permitted, at least for the most-difficult-to-place children.[39] However, the preference of agencies for married couples is sometimes used as a convenient justification for opposing placements that are really rejected because the adoptive parents are gays or lesbians. Some states have resorted to a backdoor strategy to prevent gay or lesbian adoptions. Utah and Mississippi, for example, simultaneously prohibit same-sex marriages and require adoptive parents to be married.

Florida's statute, which until recently explicitly prohibited all "homosexuals" from adopting, was recently overturned by a state court, as we will see in the following case.

Florida Department of Children and Families v. X.X.G. & N.R.G.
45 So. 3d 79
District Court of Appeal of Florida, Third District
September 22, 2010

Cope, J.

This is an appeal of a final judgment of adoption, under which F.G. became the adoptive father of two boys, X.X.G. and N.R.G. (collectively, "the children"). The trial court found, and all parties agree, that F.G. is a fit parent and that the adoption is in the best interest of the children.

The question in the case is whether the adoption should have been denied because F.G. is a homosexual. Under Florida law, a homosexual person is allowed to be a foster parent. F.G. has successfully served as a foster parent for the children since 2004. However,

Florida law states, "No person eligible to adopt under this statute [the Florida Adoption Act] may adopt if that person is a homosexual." § 63.042(3), Fla. Stat. (2006). According to the judgment, "Florida is the only remaining state to expressly ban all gay adoptions without exception." ... Judge Cindy Lederman, after lengthy hearings, concluded that there is no rational basis for the statute. We agree and affirm the final judgment of adoption....

We begin with three observations. First, there does not appear to be any disagreement between the parties regarding the facts of the case.... Second, the parties agree that the father is a fit parent and that the adoption is in the best interest of the children.... Third, the Department of Children and Families ["Department"] "agrees that gay people and heterosexuals make equally good parents."...

II

Turning now to the facts of this case, in 2004 the Department removed X.X.G., then four years old, and N.R.G., then four months old, from their home based on allegations of abandonment and neglect. The Department contacted F.G., a licensed foster caregiver, and asked him to accept the children on a temporary basis until a more permanent placement could be found....

The children arrived with medical problems and other needs. X.X.G. arrived wearing a dirty adult-sized t-shirt and sneakers four sizes too small. Both children were suffering from ringworm and the four-month-old suffered from an untreated ear infection. X.X.G., the four-year-old, did not speak and his main concern was changing, feeding and caring for his baby brother.

The children thrived in F.G.'s household. "It is clear to this Court that [F.G.] is an exceptional parent to [X.X.G. and N.R.G.] who have healed in his care and are now thriving."...

Because of the natural parents' neglect of the two children, the Department filed a petition for termination of the natural parents' parental rights. In 2006, that petition was granted and the natural parents' parental rights were terminated. X.X.G. and N.R.G. became available for adoption.

F.G. applied to adopt the children. The Center for Family and Child Enrichment, Inc. ("The Family Center"), a private nonprofit corporation, had been monitoring the two boys during foster care and was assigned the duty of evaluating F.G.'s ability to provide a satisfactory adoptive placement.... The Family Center reported that F.G.'s home presented a suitable environment and that he met all the criteria required to adopt the two boys. The parties stipulated that F.G. provides a safe, healthy, stable and nurturing home for the children meeting their physical, emotional, social and educational needs. The Family Center recommended against the application, though, because F.G. is a homosexual and is prohibited from adopting children under subsection 63.042(3), Florida Statutes. The Department denied the application on that basis. The Department acknowledged that it would have approved the application if it had not been for the statute.

In 2007, F.G. filed a petition in the circuit court to adopt the children. F.G. asked the court to find subsection 63.042(3) unconstitutional because it violates his rights to equal protection, privacy, and due process. Independent counsel acting on behalf of the children asserted that the children's rights to equal protection and due process had also been violated. The Department filed a motion to dismiss, but the court only dismissed the privacy claim.

Trial began on October 1, 2008, and continued for four days....

The trial court rendered a 53-page judgment declaring subsection 63.042(3) unconstitutional and granting the petition for adoption. The trial court found, among other things, that the statute violates the equal protection rights of F.G. and the children that are guaranteed by Article I, Section 2 of the Florida Constitution.

The Department has appealed.

III

The Department contends that the trial court erred by finding subsection 63.042(3) unconstitutional. The Department argues that there is a rational basis for the statute and that the trial court misinterpreted the law.

Under the Florida Constitution, each individual person has a right to equal protection of the laws. The constitutional provision states, in part:

> SECTION 2. Basic rights.
> All natural persons, female and male alike, are equal before the law and have inalienable rights, among which are the right to enjoy and defend life and liberty, to pursue happiness, to be rewarded for industry, and to acquire, possess and protect property.... Art. I, § 2, Fla. Const.

F.G. successfully argued in the trial court that the statute treated him unequally in violation of the constitutional provision because the statute creates an absolute prohibition on adoption by homosexual persons, while allowing all other persons—including those with criminal histories or histories of substance abuse—to be considered on a case-by-case basis.

When this case was pending in the trial court, the parties and trial court agreed that this case does not involve a fundamental right or suspect class, so the case was decided under the rational basis test. That being so, we have considered this appeal only under that test....

Under the rational basis test, "a court must uphold a statute if the classification bears a rational relationship to a legitimate governmental objective."... The classification must be "based on a real difference which is reasonably related to the subject and purpose of the regulation."...

IV

We next consider how the adoption statute works. The statute requires that there be individual studies which the judge must consider in order to decide whether the proposed adoption is in the best interest of the child....

There must be a favorable preliminary home study ... followed by a final home investigation "to ascertain whether the adoptive home is a suitable home for the minor and whether the proposed adoption is in the best interest of the minor."... "The report of the investigation must contain an evaluation of the placement with a recommendation on the granting of the petition for adoption and any other information the court requires regarding the petitioner or the minor."... This process includes a family social and medical history, in-home visits with the minor and minor's proposed adoptive parent or parents and gathering any other information which may be relevant to the suitability of the intended adoptive home.... If the trial judge concludes that the adoption is in the best interest of the person to be adopted, the Court enters the judgment of adoption....

Simply put, the statute calls for an individual, case-by-case evaluation to determine if the proposed adoption is in the best interest of the child. Except for homosexual persons, there is no automatic, categorical exclusion of anyone from consideration for adoption.

For example, "[a]doption applicants who have previous verified findings of abuse, neglect or abandonment of a child are subject to a special review before they can be approved to adopt, but are not automatically disqualified from adopting."... For a child who was privately placed (not placed by the Department or Department's agent), there is no categorical exclusion for adoption by a person with a prior criminal history, although a special review is involved.... Where the placement is through the Department, a very serious criminal history is disqualifying.... There is a five-year preclusion if there is a prior history for assault, battery, or a drug crime ... and no preclusion for other felonies.

Florida law specifies that a person cannot be "prohibited from adopting solely because such person possesses a physical disability or handicap, unless it is determined by the court or adoption entity that such disability or handicap renders such person incapable of serving as an effective parent."... An individual who is HIV-positive but healthy and able to care for a child is not excluded if, after having a physical, a doctor determines that the applicant is healthy and that the child is not going to go through another loss.... There

is a special review, but no categorical exclusion, for an applicant "with serious or chronic medical conditions that could predictably compromise ... the ability to provide the physical, emotional, social and economic support necessary for a child to thrive."... "No person shall be denied the opportunity to become an adoptive parent on the basis of race, color or national origin." Fla. Admin. Code R. 65C-16.005(1).

A single adult is specifically allowed to adopt.... Florida "makes over a third of its adoptive placements with single adults."... "The percentage of adoptions of dependent children in Florida that were by single parents for the year 2006 was 34.47 %."...

The Department or its agents "have placed children in the permanent care of foster parents known by [the Department] and/or its agents to be lesbians or gay men."... Homosexual persons "are not prohibited by any state law or regulation from being legal guardians of children in Florida."... The Department or its agents have placed children in the care, including permanent care, of legal guardians known by the Department and/or its agents to be lesbians or gay men, and ceased Department supervision....

However, the Florida Adoption Act categorically excludes a homosexual person from adopting. The question is whether there is a rational basis for the difference in treatment.

V

Given a total ban on adoption by homosexual persons, one might expect that this reflected a legislative judgment that homosexual persons are, as a group, unfit to be parents.

No one in this case has made, or even hinted at, any such argument. To the contrary, the parties agree "that gay people and heterosexuals make equally good parents."... Thus in this case no one attempts to justify the prohibition on homosexual adoption on any theory that homosexual persons are unfit to be parents.

Instead, the Department argues that there is a rational basis for the prohibition on homosexual adoption because children will have better role models, and face less discrimination, if they are placed in non-homosexual households, preferably with a husband and wife as the parents. But that is not what the statute does.

It is difficult to see any rational basis in utilizing homosexual persons as foster parents or guardians on a temporary or permanent basis, while imposing a blanket prohibition on adoption by those same persons. The Department contends, however, that the basis for this distinction can be found in the social science evidence.

VI

The trial court heard extensive expert testimony in this case....

The court concluded as follows:

... These reports and studies find that there are no differences in the parenting of homosexuals or the adjustment of their children.... As a result, based on the robust nature of the evidence available in the field, this Court is satisfied that the issue is so far beyond dispute that it would be irrational to hold otherwise; the best interests of children are not preserved by prohibiting homosexual adoption....

VIII

... In conclusion on the equal protection issue, the legislature is allowed to make classifications when it enacts statutes.... As a general proposition, a classification "will be upheld even if another classification or no classification might appear more reasonable."... The classifications must, however, be "based on a real difference which is reasonably related to the subject and purpose of the regulation."... "The reason for the equal protection clause was to assure that there would be no second class citizens."...

Under Florida law, homosexual persons are allowed to serve as foster parents or guardians but are barred from being considered for adoptive parents. All other persons are eligible to be considered case-by-case to be adoptive parents, but not homosexual persons—even where, as here, the adoptive parent is a fit parent and the adoption is in the best interest of the children.

The Department has argued that evidence produced by its experts and F.G.'s experts supports a distinction wherein homosexual persons may serve as foster parents or guardians, but not adoptive parents. Respectfully, the portions of the record cited by the Department do not support the Department's position. We conclude that there is no rational basis for the statute.

IX

The trial court held that the statute violated the equal protection rights of the children in addition to violating the equal protection rights of F.G. Because we affirm the judgment on account of the violation of F.G.'s equal protection rights, we need not reach the claim of violation of the children's equal protection rights.

... Because we affirm the declaration of unconstitutionality on the ground that there is an equal protection violation under the Florida Constitution, we need not reach the trial court's alternative holding.

X

We affirm the judgment of adoption, which holds subsection 63.042(3), Florida Statutes, violates the equal protection provision found in article I, section 2, of the Florida Constitution....

Case Questions

1. The trial court found that there were two equal-protection violations in this case—what were they?
2. Why did the appellate court only rule on one of these claims?
3. What was the basis for the appellate court's conclusion that F.G.'s equal protection right had been infringed by Florida?

Case Update

The State of Florida did not appeal the decision in this case to the Florida Supreme Court.

Voluntary and Involuntary Adoption

Adoptions may be classified as voluntary or involuntary. Involuntary adoptions occur after a court has formally terminated the parental rights of the birth parent(s) on grounds such as abuse, abandonment, or neglect. In such a situation, an agency is generally responsible for placement. If the adoption is voluntary, the birth parent(s) consent to the termination of their parental rights and surrender the child either to an agency for placement or to adoptive parents of their choosing.

The Adoption Petition

The adoption process starts with the filing of a petition for adoption by the adoptive parents and the serving of a summons on all affected parties (the child, the agency, birth parents, guardian, etc.). In voluntary adoptions, care must be taken to account for all relevant parties, and obtaining the consent of necessary third parties is a major consideration. When both birth parents have an intact marriage, they must jointly consent to a proposed adoption of their child. If the parents are not married to each other, and both the noncustodial and custodial parents have taken an active role in fulfilling parental obligations, each has the right to withhold or grant consent to the adoption of their child.

The birth parents and adoptive parents are not the only individuals who have legal interests in adoptions. An adoptee, if over a specified age (often twelve or fourteen), has a right to refuse to be adopted. Additionally, grandparents may have legally enforceable visitation rights even after the birth father's parental rights have been terminated. We will see more about this topic later on in this chapter when addressing child custody and visitation rights after a divorce.

In addition to providing notice to affected individuals, the petition for adoption will indicate whether the parental rights have been voluntarily or involuntarily terminated and will allege that the adoption is in the best interests of the child.

INTERNET TIP

Readers can find online at the textbook's website an edited version of *Lehr v. Robertson,* a case in which the U.S. Supreme Court ruled that no consent to adopt is required from a noncustodial parent who has only sporadically visited and supported his child, and who otherwise has shown little or no interest in functioning as a parent.

Interim Orders

After the adoption petition has been filed, the parties properly served, and all necessary consents obtained, the court usually will issue interim orders. In voluntary adoptions the court will order the birth parents' rights terminated and grant the adoptive

parents temporary legal custody of the child, pending issuance of the final decree. A hearing then can be scheduled to take testimony about whether the final decree of adoption should be approved by the court. State statutes usually require that the adoptive parents have temporary custody of the adopted child for a statutorily determined minimum period of time so that the court will have evidence that the adoptive parents and child are making a successful adjustment. This waiting period usually is waived in adoptions by relatives. After the waiting time has passed, the court will enter a final decree declaring that the adopted person is now the child of the petitioner(s), and a new birth certificate will be issued to reflect this change.[40]

Confidentiality and Privacy Considerations in Adoptions

One of the most important decisions in adoptions is the extent to which, if at all, the adoptive parent(s) and the birth parent(s) share identification information with one another. This decision as to whether the adoption will be "open," "closed," or something in between has great significance to all involved parties. Whether the adopted child will be able to learn the identity of the birth parents varies from state to state. In recent years, there has been some movement away from permanently sealing such information. Today, although many states maintain the confidentiality of adoption records, the trend is toward more openness.[41] Almost all states have established some type of registry system whereby consenting birth parents and their subsequently adopted children can mutually indicate a desire for contact.[42] Adoptees frequently wish to learn more about their birth parents, not only out of curiosity, but also to gain information about their parents' medical histories.

INTERNET TIP

Readers interested in learning more about state laws regarding open and closed adoptions should visit the following website: http://www.childwelfare.gov/systemwide/laws_policies/statutes/cooperative.cfm

---

Foster Care

According to U.S. Department of Health and Human Services, preliminary estimates based on fiscal year 2008 **Adoption and Foster Care Analysis and Reporting System (AFCARS)** data indicate that 463,000 children are currently in foster care in the United States.[43] Some parents voluntarily place their children in foster care for a brief time. Most foster placements, however, result from court intervention because of alleged child abuse or neglect.[44] Once a court determines that a child is abused or neglected, it next determines whether foster care is the most appropriate disposition under the circumstances. In many situations, foster care provides temporary care for children while the biological parents work to fulfill the requirements of a case plan. The objective in such situations is reunification of the family, once caseworkers have helped the family to work out its problems. If the birth parents address the problems that gave rise to the judicial intervention in the first place, the child will generally be returned to the parents. If the parents are uncooperative or fail to complete the intervention plan, the court may decide ultimately that it is in the best interests of the child to terminate the parental rights and place the child for adoption.

According to preliminary estimates that were based on fiscal year 2008 AFCARS data, 19 percent of the foster children leaving the foster-care system in 2008 were adopted, and over 60 percent were ordered returned to their birth parents or other relatives.[45] State governments license foster homes, and federal and state resources financially support foster children. The foster-care system has been criticized in the past as underfunded, overwhelmed with cases, and staffed by persons who are not trained as social workers.[46]

Congress took action to improve this situation when it enacted the Adoption and Safe Families Act of 1997. This legislation created financial incentives and performance expectations for states in an effort to speed up the adoption process and increase the number of children placed for adoption.

Critics have complained that federal financial support to the states has been insufficient, especially since the states have moved increasing numbers of children from the foster-care system into adoption placements. In September 2009, however, the U.S. Department of Health and Human Services announced an Adoptive Incentives Program through which it was awarding $35 million to thirty-eight states for the express purpose of increasing the adoption of children currently in foster care. Special incentives rewarded states that were able to move qualifying special needs children and children who are nine years old or older from foster homes to adoptive families.[47]

FAMILY RELATIONS IN ONGOING FAMILIES

Where families are intact, the law recognizes that spouses and children assume obligations to each other and are entitled to certain rights and benefits. Some of these rights, benefits, and obligations are economic and others are noneconomic.

Spousal-Property Rights

Although modern marriages are essentially partnerships, historically husbands and wives were legally considered to be a single unit with the husbands holding the preferred status as head of the household.[48] Before the enactment of married-women's property statutes in the 1800s, wives generally did not own property in their own names. Upon marriage, a wife's property was controlled by her husband. An exception was created by equitable courts that allowed fathers to establish trusts for their daughters. This device was used to keep family assets out of the control of sons-in-law, but few women from the lower and middle classes were the beneficiaries of such arrangements. A husband, while benefiting from his preferred status as head of the household, also was legally obligated to provide economic support for his wife. The term traditionally associated with this responsibility for support is *necessaries,* usually defined to include food, clothing, shelter, and medical care.[49] In earlier times this obligation only applied to husbands; however, it is now shared by both spouses.

Courts were initially resistant to statutory reforms expanding women's property rights and often construed them very narrowly.[50] Today, in common-law title states, married women have essentially achieved legal equality. Each spouse retains title to property owned prior to marriage, has the separate right to his or her own earnings, and has title to property acquired separately during marriage. The judge in **common-law title** jurisdictions is charged with "equitably" distributing the property between the spouses. This means that fairness, and not equality, is the goal. The court considers each spouse's contributions to the marriage, financial circumstances, and all other relevant factors when determining what constitutes a fair apportionment of the marital assets.

In **community-property states** (see Figure 9.4), each spouse is legally entitled to a percentage of what the state defines as community property, which will vary by jurisdiction. Although states differ, community property usually is defined as including the earnings of both spouses, and property rights acquired with those earnings during the marriage. State statutes, however, usually exclude from community property rights acquired prior to marriage and spousal inheritances and gifts received during the marriage. These are classified as separate property. Community-property states differ on whether earnings from separate property should be treated as community property.

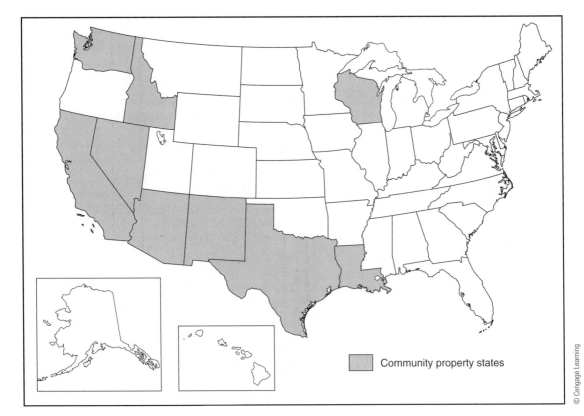

Community property states

© Cengage Learning

F I G U R E   9.4   Community Property States

Decision Making within Traditional Families

The U.S. Supreme Court has reinforced family autonomy by ruling that married couples have the right to make decisions regarding the use of birth control[51] and whether they will become parents. If they do, it is they who will decide how many children they will have and how those children will be raised.[52] This right to raise children includes decisions about the nature and extent of their education and their religious upbringing.

Spouses also have great latitude in deciding how their households will operate. Decisions about who is responsible for particular household chores, about how recreational time is used, and about having children and child rearing are often jointly made. Of course, a woman's decision to obtain an abortion early in a pregnancy can be made unilaterally—without regard to the wishes of the putative father. A married woman also has the right to retain her own surname, if she chooses.

Because of **spousal privileges** contained within state and federal rules of evidence, a spouse may refuse to testify against his or her spouse in a criminal trial and may also refuse to testify about confidential communications that occurred between spouses during their marriage.

INTERNET TIP

Parents traditionally have exercised primary responsibility for determining the religious upbringing of their children. In *Yoder v. Wisconsin,* Amish parents were prosecuted by the State of Wisconsin for violating a compulsory school-attendance law. These parents withdrew their children from the public schools after they had completed the eighth grade. The parents appealed their convictions and claimed that the law infringed on their constitutionally protected right to determine the religious development of their children. You can read the U.S. Supreme Court's decision in this case on the textbook's website.

Family Status and the Obligation to Minor Children

Historically, parents have been legally responsible for the financial costs of providing their children with food, clothing, shelter, medical care, and education. This duty exists irrespective of whether the parents are married, divorced, separated, living together, or living apart. The breach of this duty is treated by most states as a criminal offense and also can result in civil actions for nonsupport and child neglect. The government is most eager to identify and locate "deadbeat parents" and to hold them financially accountable for their children so that the public doesn't have to bear these costs.

The exact nature and extent of the parental support obligation varies, and depends on the child's needs as well as on each parent's financial condition. Though all states require that parents fulfill support obligations, some have gone so far as to require stepparents[53] and grandparents[54] to provide child support. When marriages break up, a court usually will require the noncustodial parent to pay child support until the child attains the **age of majority** (each state specifies the age at which a minor legally becomes an adult. At present, most states set the age as eighteen, but in three states it is twenty-one), marries, becomes **emancipated,**[55] or dies. Even after a child reaches the age of majority, parents often have a continuing support obligation if their offspring are disabled or haven't completed high school, or if such an obligation exists pursuant to a separation agreement.

One of the areas of recent conflict relates to a parent's duty to pay for a child's college education, an expense that usually isn't due until after the child has passed the age of majority. Although parents in intact families have no legal duty to fund college educations for their children, as we see in the next case, some courts have ruled that a parent's support obligation can include funding their child's college education.

In re Gilmore
803 A.2d 601
Supreme Court of New Hampshire
July 24, 2002

Dalianis, J.

The respondent, William E. Gilmore, Jr., appeals an order of the Superior Court ... requiring him to pay certain monthly expenses towards his adult child's college education. We reverse and remand.

The record supports the following facts. The parties were divorced in 1991. At the time of their divorce, the parties had two minor children. In the divorce decree the respondent was ordered to pay, among other obligations, "the entire expense of any private schooling or college for the two girls."

By July 2000, the parties' daughter Lindsey was an adult who was commuting to college while living with the petitioner, Nancy J. Gilmore. In September 2000, the petitioner filed a motion requesting that the respondent be ordered to continue paying child support for Lindsey while she attended college.

On November 22, 2000, the trial court dismissed the petitioner's request for child support but ordered the respondent to pay what it characterized as "reasonable college expenses" for Lindsey, including expenses for room and board while she lived at home with the petitioner, as follows:

Tuition, fees and books:	As required
Allowance, as previously established:	$200 per month
Room:	$532 per month
Gas:	$140 per month
Car insurance, repairs, and registration:	$146 per month
Medical and dental expenses:	$ 75 per month
Clothing and shoes:	$200 per month
Food:	$350 per month

The respondent filed a motion for reconsideration and clarification arguing, among other things, that the court did not have jurisdiction to order him to pay for items such as clothing, shoes and an allowance because they are not educational expenses, and that he should not be responsible for Lindsey's educational expenses when she was not in school. The court agreed that the

respondent was not responsible for paying Lindsey an allowance, and that he was responsible for her educational expenses only during the months she was attending college, but otherwise denied the respondent's motion.

On appeal, the respondent argues that the court erred in ordering him to pay for such items as transportation, insurance, medical coverage, clothing, and shoes because they are not educational expenses. He also argues that the court erred in requiring payments for Lindsey's room and board to be made to the petitioner.

We afford broad discretion to the trial court in divorce matters, and will not disturb the trial court's rulings regarding child support absent an unsustainable exercise of discretion or an error of law.... The party challenging the court's order has the burden of showing that the order was "improper and unfair." *Hunneyman v. Hunneyman* ... (1978).... RSA 458:17, I (1992) (amended 1993) provides that:

> In all cases where there shall be a decree of divorce or nullity, the court shall make such further decree in relation to the support, education, and custody of the children as shall be most conducive to their benefit and may order a reasonable provision for their support and education.

Generally, a parent's obligation to pay child support ceases when the child turns eighteen years old or graduates from high school, whichever is later.... Both this court and the legislature, however, have recognized the superior court's jurisdiction to order divorced parents, consistent with their means, to contribute toward the educational expenses of their adult children.... The respondent does not dispute the court's authority to order him to provide for Lindsey's educational expenses. He contends, however, that the court erred when it ordered him to pay for, among other things, transportation costs, medical expenses and clothing. He argues that these expenses are tantamount to child support, which he is no longer obligated to pay. The petitioner counters that the trial court's order was proper because RSA 458:20 allows the court to order the respondent to provide for Lindsey's support, maintenance and general welfare while she attends college. We disagree. RSA 458:20, in pertinent part, provides:

> In a proceeding under this chapter, the court may set aside a portion of the property of the parties in a separate fund or trust ... for a child of the parties, who is 18 years of age or older, if the child is in college....

This provision gives the trial court authority, when dividing the property of divorcing parties, to order a portion of that property to be placed into a separate educational trust fund for a child who is both in college and at least eighteen years old.

A divorced parent's support obligation does not automatically terminate when a child reaches eighteen years of age.... However, the nature of that support varies depending upon the circumstances and needs of the child.... RSA 458:35-c does not place a time limit on a parent's obligation to pay for reasonable college expenses.... This is so because "jurisdiction to award education expenses is not limited as a matter of law to jurisdiction over minors."...

The issue before us, which is one of first impression, is what constitutes "educational expenses." A number of jurisdictions that have addressed the issue have construed educational expenses to be only those costs directly related to attending college, such as tuition, room and board, and related fees.... We agree and hold that "educational expenses" are those expenses that are directly related to the child's college education. Such expenses, therefore, include tuition, books, room, board and other directly related fees.

To define "educational expenses" more broadly would essentially require the respondent to pay for Lindsey's general support and maintenance, which would, in this case, conflict with RSA 458:35-c because the petitioner's request for a continuation of child support was dismissed. Consequently, the superior court erred in including amounts for transportation (gas, maintenance and registration), medical and dental coverage, clothing and shoes in its order....

Moreover, with respect to room and board, we hold that the respondent is not required to pay an amount greater than he would be required to pay if the child resided on campus in college housing. If he is currently paying more than the cost of college housing, then the court must modify its order accordingly. In addition, payments for room and board must ordinarily be made, if Lindsey resides in campus housing, directly to the college, or, if she lives off campus, directly to Lindsey to defray reasonable expenses for "room and board."

We, therefore, reverse the trial court's decision and remand for further proceedings consistent with this opinion.

Case Questions

1. Should a child's aptitude for college-level work be considered in cases such as this?
2. Should the obligation to pay for educational expenses include some of the cost of studying abroad?

Noneconomic Obligations

Parents' noneconomic obligations include nurturing and controlling their children, seeing that they attend school, and protecting them from abuse and neglect. Authorities can intervene if parents fail to perform these duties. Although parents generally have the right to make decisions on their child's behalf about religious training and educational and medical needs, this right is limited. When a child's life is threatened, for example, and the parents' religious beliefs prevent them from seeking necessary medical care, the state often will intervene and ensure that the child receives treatment.

Children also have obligations, the single most important of which is to obey their parents. When children perpetually defy their parents, a judicial **CHINS** (child-in-need-of-supervision) proceeding may be instituted. Many states also statutorily require adult children to provide their parents with necessaries in the event that the parents become unable to provide for themselves.[56]

Parental Immunity from Suit by Child

As we saw in Chapter VI, parents traditionally have been protected by immunity from suits brought by their children for negligence and intentional torts. Over the last thirty years, however, many states have created exceptions to this immunity and have permitted suits in cases of child abuse, neglect, serious batteries, and the negligent operation of automobiles. Today, most states have either abolished the immunity or severely limited its use.

ENDING SPOUSAL RELATIONSHIPS

Spousal relationships can be ended through the legal actions of annulment and divorce, and they can be judicially altered by legal separation.

Annulment

An action to **annul** is appropriate when a marriage partner seeks to prove that no valid marriage ever existed. Thus the plaintiff is not seeking to terminate a valid marriage, but rather to have a court declare that no valid marriage ever occurred. Annulments were historically important, especially during periods when divorces were difficult to obtain. Obtaining an annulment of a marriage was very useful because it could end the spousal relationship without branding either party as being "divorced," and thus enable each party to remarry. Today, with the advent of no-fault divorce, actions for annulment are much less popular, except among those who for religious reasons prefer to end a marriage legally without going through a divorce.

Although each state has its own grounds for annulments, common reasons include bigamy (where a person who is already married marries yet again); incest (where a person marries someone who is a close blood relative, contrary to law); mental incompetence (such as where the parties were intoxicated at the time of the ceremony);[57] fraud (such as where one party

misrepresents a willingness to engage in sexual relations and have children);[58] coercion; and one or both parties being underage at the time of the marriage.

Because of the serious potential consequences of an annulment, particularly to property rights, many states have declared the children born to parents whose marriage has been annulled to be legitimate.[59] These states provide by statute that child support and custody matters will be determined in the same way as in divorce cases.[60] Many state courts award temporary alimony and some award permanent alimony to dependent spouses.[61] Each party to an annulment recovers the property held prior to the marriage and is considered a co-owner of property acquired during the marriage.

Legal Separation

Many states have statutorily recognized an action for **legal separation,** also called a **divorce *a mensa et thoro*** (Latin for "from table and bed," or, more colloquially, "from bed and board").[62] The divorce *a mensa et thoro,* which also is called in some places a *limited divorce* and in others a *legal separation*, can be granted when lawfully married parties have actually separated and when adequate grounds for a legal separation have been shown. Although states differ on what constitutes sufficient grounds, common reasons include irreconcilable differences, adultery, desertion, cruelty, and nonsupport. If a court grants a legal separation, the parties remain married to each other but live apart. A criminal action can be brought if one spouse interferes with the other spouse's privacy. Unlike a final divorce, neither party to a legal separation is free to remarry. The court, after considering the financial conditions of each party, can require one spouse to support the other and can determine child custody. States differ about whether a property division should occur. During the legal separation, the possibility of reconciliation still exists, as does the option to proceed with a final divorce. The separation period allows the estranged parties to try to work out their difficulties while living apart.

Divorce–Dissolution

From the perspective of the early twenty-first century, it is difficult to understand the degree to which contemporary expectations of marriage differ from those of our ancestors. Historically, absolute divorce under Anglo-American law was very difficult to obtain. In New York, for example, the legislature had to approve each divorce until 1787, when courts became statutorily authorized to grant divorces in cases of adultery. This was New York's only ground for a lawful divorce until 1966![63] In nineteenth-century America it was assumed that persons were married for life.[64] In 1900, women lived an average of only 48 years,[65] so people were married for shorter periods of time. The social, legal, and economic circumstances of that era encouraged husbands and wives to remain formally married despite the existence of dysfunctional relationships and irreparable differences between the parties. Today, people live longer lives and have more choices.[66] There are fewer pressures on people to marry in the first place, and the miserably married are less likely to remain in intolerable relationships.[67] The availability of birth control permits people to be sexually active without conceiving children. Single parenting is common and is no longer considered unusual. Women have more economic opportunities than they did in 1950. The social stigma of being thirty and divorced or unmarried has greatly diminished. People who marry today do so primarily for companionship,[68] a need that can bring people together but also can cause them to follow different paths as their lives evolve with time.

This social transformation has gradually produced legal changes as well. Although many states had liberalized their divorce laws more than New York had by the early 1960s, divorces generally were limited—at least theoretically—to plaintiffs who proved that their spouses had engaged in adultery, cruelty (sometimes interpreted very liberally), or desertion.[69] The fact that a married couple had irreconcilable differences and was married in name only was not a sufficient basis under the law for a divorce. The fault-based approach was antidivorce and existed because of widely held fears about the social consequences to families and society that would result from what was feared might become divorce on demand. States began liberalizing their laws to meet public insistence that the divorce laws be reformed. Divorces took too long to complete—they often required long waiting periods before becoming final. During the waiting period it was unlawful for people to remarry.[70] To get around such restrictions, people often went to Nevada to obtain what were called "quickie divorces," because that state required only a six-week waiting period.[71] Reformers pressed for change, urging lawmakers to focus on the marriage relationship itself and to recognize that the adversarial process of proving fault was making a bad situation worse. It was damaging the parties and making the process of ending a marriage more difficult and painful than it ought to be. It encouraged collusion and caused some parties to perjure themselves, "admitting" things they had not done, just in order to qualify for a divorce.[72] In California, proponents of reform carefully drafted and quietly pursued the legislative process[73] and were rewarded with enactment of the nation's first "no-fault" divorce law, which took effect on January 1, 1970.[74] Once that dam was broken, all states adopted some form of no-fault divorce; the last state acted in 1985.[75] Today, in many states the plaintiff can choose to proceed either on a no-fault basis or on the traditional fault basis. Proving fault can sometimes be advantageous if it makes it possible to avoid the waiting period that some states require before a divorce becomes final. Furthermore, in some jurisdictions proving fault can affect alimony and child-custody decisions. Although state no-fault laws differ, a plaintiff usually has to prove marital breakdown and prove that the parties have been living separately for a statutorily determined minimum period of time. In most states, a divorce can be granted despite the respondent's objection.[76] As a result of the philosophical changes that have occurred in recent years, the term *divorce* is increasingly being replaced with the more neutral term *dissolution,* which denotes the legal ending of the marital relationship.

Same-sex couples who legally marry are often in a legal quandary if their relationship doesn't work out and the parties decide to divorce. This is especially true if the divorcing couple files for divorce in a state that doesn't recognize the couple as having been married. The courts in many states take the position that they do not have jurisdiction to grant a divorce to people who could not become lawfully married in that state. All divorcing couples have the need to disentangle their relationship both emotionally, financially, and socially. They have to apportion their respective responsibilities and obligations. They will need to have a legal conclusion of their marriage that is ratified in court. This process is often difficult, but it is especially so for same-sex couples, who often live in a state that does not recognize same-sex unions, get married in another state that does legalize same-sex marriages, and may well end up living in a third state that will not grant them a divorce.

Introduction to *Jessica Port v. Virginia Anne Cowan*

At the time the following case was decided, Maryland law prohibited same-sex marriages. In 2008 Jessica Port and Virginia Cowan, a same-sex couple residing in Washington, D.C., were legally married in San Francisco, California. Two years later they decided to divorce. Port, at that time a Maryland resident, filed suit for divorce in that state. The trial court ruled that same-sex marriages and divorces were "not valid" in Maryland, and Port and Cowan appealed to the highest court in that state, the Maryland Court of Appeals (established in 1776).

Jessica Port v. Virginia Anne Cowan
44 A.3d 970
Court of Appeals of Maryland
May 18, 2012

Opinion by Harrell, J.
Appellant, Jessica Port, and Appellee, Virginia Anne Cowan ... [b]eing aggrieved equally ... filed appeals timely, asking why an out-of-state, same-sex marriage, valid when and where performed, was not cognizable in Maryland for purposes of the application of its domestic divorce laws....

I. FACTUAL AND PROCEDURAL HISTORY
... The trial judge reasoned solely that the "same sex marriage in which the parties hereto participated is not valid pursuant to Maryland law.... [T]o recognize the alleged marriage would be contrary to the public policy of Maryland."
.... Despite being opposing parties technically, Port and Cowan agree that their California marriage should be recognized in Maryland for purposes of the application of Maryland's divorce laws, and a divorce granted. Prior to the intermediate appellate court deciding the appeal, we issued, on our initiative, a writ of certiorari....

II. QUESTION PRESENTED
Port and Cowan present in their respective appeals the same, single question for our consideration: "Must the Circuit Court grant a divorce to two people of the same sex who were validly married in another jurisdiction and who otherwise meet the criteria for divorce under Maryland law?"....

The parties posit that an affirmative response by us to their question is compelled by proper application of the principles of the common-law doctrine of comity. They argue alternatively that the Circuit Court's failure to recognize their marriage violated their equal protection and due process rights, contained within Article 24 of the Maryland Declaration of Rights. No one appeared before us, in writing or in person, to argue that we should affirm the Circuit Court's judgment.... Because we resolve this appeal on the non-constitutional ground of comity, we shall not reach the parties' equal protection and due process arguments.... (... the Court of Appeals will not reach a constitutional issue when a case may be decided on a non-constitutional ground).

III. DISCUSSION
... § 2-201 of the Family Law Article provides (now and at the time the Circuit Court decided this case) that "[o]nly a marriage between a man and a woman is valid in this State."... In 2007, we concluded that this prohibition on domestic same-sex marriage did not violate Articles 24 and 46 of the Maryland Declaration

of Rights.... Thus, Maryland will recognize a marriage solemnized within its boundaries if it is between a man and a woman only....

... [W]e are asked whether a valid out-of-state, same-sex marriage may be recognized in this State, for purposes of a domestic divorce action. Courts deciding whether a foreign marriage is valid in this State, for purposes of divorce or otherwise, employ the common-law doctrine of comity, not principally our domestic marriage laws....

A. The Doctrine of Comity

Under the doctrine of comity, long applied in our State, Maryland courts "will give effect to laws and judicial decisions of another state or jurisdiction, not as a matter of obligation but out of deference and respect."... When considering a foreign marriage specifically, Maryland courts follow the choice-of-law rule of lex loci celebrationis ... applying the substantive law of the place where the contract of marriage was formed.

Generally, Maryland courts will honor foreign marriages as long as the marriage was valid in the state where performed.... There are two exceptions to this rule: the foreign marriage may not be "repugnant" to Maryland public policy and may not be prohibited expressly by the General Assembly....

Maryland recognizes liberally foreign marriages, even those marriages that may be prohibited from being formed if conducted in this State. Research ... failed to reveal a case, decided by this Court, voiding a valid out-of-state marriage that was prohibited from being formed in Maryland.... Liberal recognition of out-of-state marriages promotes "uniformity in the recognition of the marital status, so that persons legally married according to the laws of one state will not be held to be living in adultery in another State, and that children begotten in lawful wedlock in one State will not be held illegitimate in another."...

B. Applying Lex Loci Celebrationis to the Parties' Valid Foreign Same-Sex Marriage

... The parties' California same-sex marriage is valid. Therefore, in order for their marriage to be valid for purposes of whether Maryland will adjudicate its dissolution, it must not run afoul of either exception to lex loci celebrationis: that is, it cannot be prohibited by statute or "repugnant" to the public policies of Maryland. For the following reasons, Port's and Cowan's entitlement, on this record, to a Maryland divorce from their California same-sex marriage is not prohibited, as a matter of law and on this record, by these exceptions....

Regarding the statutory prohibition exception, Family Law Article § 2-201 does not forbid expressly valid-where-formed foreign same-sex marriages. The plain wording of § 2-201 provides that "[o]nly a marriage between a man and a woman is valid in this State." It does not preclude from recognition same-sex marriages solemnized validly in another jurisdiction, only those sought-to-be, or actually, performed in Maryland. To preclude the former from being valid, the statute in question must express a clear mandate voiding such marriages and abrogating the common law.... Moreover, we note that same-sex marriages are not listed in Family Law Article § 2-202 as among those marriages considered void.

Other states intending to prevent recognition of valid foreign same-sex marriages have done so expressly and clearly, rather than by implication, subtlety, or indirection. For example, the Pennsylvania Code provides, "A marriage between persons of the same sex which was entered into in another state or foreign jurisdiction, even if valid where entered into, shall be void in this Commonwealth."... The language of § 2-201, by comparison, fails to void for present purposes valid foreign same-sex marriages.

On at least eight occasions, the Maryland General Assembly failed to amend § 2-201 to preclude valid out-of-state same-sex marriages from being recognized in Maryland.... Similar amendments have failed to become law on at least seven other occasions, by our count.... This pattern permits an inference, which we take, that the General Assembly intended the doctrine of comity regarding foreign same-sex marriages to remain the proper analysis to employ here....

We conclude also that the parties' same-sex marriage is not "repugnant" to Maryland "public policy," as that term is understood properly in applying the doctrine of comity in modern times. Admittedly, "public policy" is an amorphous legal concept.... It is agreed, however, that wherever found and identified, that public policy prohibits generally conduct that injures or tends to injure the public good....

With regard to the second exception to lex loci celebrationis, recognizing valid foreign same-sex marriages is consistent actually with Maryland public policy. Prior to the Attorney General's opinion surmising that this Court would recognize foreign same-sex marriages (valid where entered), the General Assembly enacted several laws that protect and support same-sex couples, as alluded to earlier in this opinion. An array of statutes prohibit public or private discrimination based on sexual orientation in the areas of employment, public accommodations, leasing commercial property, and housing....

After the Attorney General published his opinion in 2010, the State of Maryland expressed a panoply of policies recognizing explicitly out-of-state same-sex marriages.... The Department of Budget and Management changed its paid-leave and employee-benefit policies to include same-sex spouses of eligible State employees.... The Board of Regents of the University System of Maryland, for purposes of tuition remission and other policies, redefined spouse to be "consistent with the advice given by the Office of the Attorney General."... Finally, the Department of Health and Mental Hygiene changed its procedure so that a female same-sex spouse (who did not give birth) can be listed as a parent without having to obtain a court order....

A number of other states with similar comity principles and relevant domestic marriage laws to those of Maryland have recognized foreign same-sex marriages for purposes of their domestic divorce laws....

Some states have elected not to recognize valid foreign same-sex marriages for purposes of domestic divorce proceedings....

IV. CONCLUSION

Under the principles of the doctrine of comity applied in our State, Maryland courts will withhold recognition of a valid foreign marriage only if that marriage is "repugnant" to State public policy. This threshold, a high bar, has not been met yet; e.g., no still viable decision by this Court has deemed a valid foreign marriage to be "repugnant," despite being void or punishable as a misdemeanor or more serious crime were it performed in Maryland. The present case will be treated no differently. A valid out-of-state same-sex marriage should be treated by Maryland courts as worthy of divorce, according to the applicable statutes, reported cases, and court rules of this State.

JUDGMENT OF THE CIRCUIT COURT FOR PRINCE GEORGE'S COUNTY REVERSED; CASE REMANDED TO THAT COURT WITH DIRECTION TO GRANT A FINAL DIVORCE TO THE PARTIES....

Case Questions

1. At the time this case was decided Maryland law prohibited same-sex couples from marrying. Given that fact, why did Maryland's highest court rule that this same-sex couple was entitled to obtain a Maryland divorce?
2. How persuasive did you find the Court's rationale for its decision?

Case Postscript

The State of Maryland legalized same-sex marriages in November of 2012 when voters approved an initiative that went into effect on January 1, 2013.

Jurisdictional and Procedural Considerations

You will recall the discussions of in personam and in rem jurisdiction in Chapter IV, and of civil procedure in Chapter V. Because terminating a marriage often involves some interesting jurisdictional problems and specialized procedures, it is important briefly to revisit these topics as they relate to divorce.

Jurisdiction

If it is determined that a court has granted a divorce, awarded alimony, or determined custody of a child without having jurisdiction, the court's action is void and without effect. Furthermore, this jurisdictional deficiency would make the court's judgment ineligible for full faith and credit in other states. Although constitutional due process often permits the termination of a marriage on the basis of in rem jurisdiction, a court must have in personam jurisdiction over a person who is to be required to make alimony and child support payments. Thus, a court has jurisdiction to grant a divorce decree where at least one marital party has lived within the forum state long enough to satisfy that state's residency requirement. The residency requirement demonstrates a substantial connection with the forum state and helps to establish the in rem notion that the marriage itself (the *res*) is physically located within the forum state.

If the plaintiff seeks to have a court decree alimony or order child support in addition to terminating the marriage, however, in rem jurisdiction is insufficient, and the minimum contacts requirement of in personam jurisdiction must be satisfied.

Procedure

Many states statutorily permit a court to issue temporary support orders once a divorce action is initiated. This order may temporarily require one party to pay for an economically dependent spouse's necessaries, determine child custody and support, and determine who is responsible for paying which debts. This order is limited and is intended only to enable both parties to meet their living expenses while the action is pending. These issues are not permanently decided until the divorce and related claims have been acted on and a final judgment and order are entered in the case. Although laypeople generally use the term **divorce** to refer to the entire process of concluding and reordering a couple's marital, parental, and economic relationships, this is actually a misnomer. It is common in many states for each of the divorce-related claims to be decided in segments rather than in one long trial. This approach is called **bifurcation,** and it means that child custody, alimony, property division, and marriage dissolution are taken up separately by the court.

Procedural requirements in a divorce action generally vary with the type and complexity of the claims that must be resolved. Thus a contested divorce generally will be more procedurally cumbersome than an uncontested action, and a no-fault action will often be less procedurally complex than a fault-based action. In some states, cooperating parties can privately negotiate a separation agreement that reflects their mutual decision about how property should be divided, the amounts and types of support to be paid, and even proposals about child custody. If the terms of this contract are not unconscionable, the laws of the state can make this agreement binding on the court except as it relates to child custody provisions. In some states, parties to no-fault divorces who have no children and no substantial assets can end their marriages in a matter of minutes.

Allocation of Financial Obligations

When people divorce, in addition to terminating their marital relationship, there is a need to untangle their financial affairs so that each spouse can function independently. This involves determining whether alimony and child support will be paid and allocating the marital assets and liabilities. In some cases the parties are able to resolve these matters amicably by themselves. They also may benefit from the assistance of a mediator or arbitrator (see Chapter XIV for more about these options). Where the parties are unable to reach agreement, a judge must ultimately make the decision.

Court-Ordered Alimony

Virtually all states permit a court to require an economically strong spouse to pay financial support to an economically dependent spouse where it is necessary and appropriate. This payment, which is discretionary with the court, is often referred to as **alimony,** although it is also called *spousal support.*[77] Some jurisdictions deny it to any spouse whose marriage ended as a result of that person's marital fault.

One form of spousal support is called *permanent alimony* because it continues until the recipient dies or is remarried. This form of alimony is intended to compensate an economically dependent wife who was married in another era, when homemaking was commonly viewed as a career and when it was reasonable to expect that one's husband would provide support for life. Someone who invested many years taking care of her home and her family, rather than working outside the home, is granted alimony when her marriage is terminated so that she receives economic justice. This form of alimony is on the decline, because public policy today favors sexual equality and because women today generally have the skills and education necessary to get a job and to be self-supporting.

Another type of spousal support, called *rehabilitative alimony,* is awarded for a specified period of years and is intended to provide funds so that the recipient can obtain education or training that will strengthen the person's job prospects. In deciding whether to grant rehabilitative alimony, a court takes into consideration many factors, including the payor's earning capacity; the dependent spouse's health status, work history, and present and future prospects for employment; and the likelihood that the person will take advantage of training and educational opportunities.

A court can order that alimony be paid either in a lump sum or periodically, usually on a monthly basis. If conditions materially change over time, either party can petition for modification. The payor, for example, might seek a reduction because of ill health and unemployment and the fact that the recipient, though not remarried, is cohabiting with another partner and has less financial need. The recipient, for example, might argue for an increase to offset inflation's impact on purchasing power and the recipient's need to pay for necessary medical treatment.

Enforcing payment of alimony is very problematic, because courts are reluctant to incarcerate defaulters (how can they earn money while in jail?), and because it is often too expensive for recipients to use the normal remedies available for enforcing civil judgments. (These remedies were discussed in Chapter V.)

Child Custody and Child Support

The general responsibility of parents to support their children was previously addressed in this chapter. The current discussion focuses on child custody and support in the context of a divorce, annulment, or temporary separation.

Although parents can negotiate an agreement and resolve many issues, they can only recommend whether the court should grant custody to both parents (**joint custody**) or grant custody to only one parent. Although the court has the responsibility to protect children, it usually will incorporate into the final judgment the custodial arrangements that have been agreed to by the parents, if the arrangements are reasonable and appropriate. The court's decision is of great importance because of the custodial parent's sole right to make important decisions regarding a child's upbringing. Although judges historically have granted custody of young children to their mothers,[78] most states have discarded the "tender-years doctrine," at least as a rigid rule, in response to increasing challenges from fathers during the 1970s.[79] The "best-interest-of-the-child" rule, preferred-custody statutes (that favor the primary caretaker), and joint custody have become the most widely accepted standards for determining custody.[80] The "best-interest-of-the-child" rule requires judges to show no gender preference and to act in the best interest of each child. When making this decision, the courts consider such matters as each parent's ability to provide—and interest in providing—the child with love, a good home, food, clothing, medical care, and education. Inquiry will be made into the stability of each parent's employment and whether the employment is compatible with the child's needs. Courts also look for instances of parental misconduct (such as substance abuse and sexually and morally questionable behavior),[81] continuity of care, and a sound moral foundation for the child. Figure 9.5 (on page 346) shows one state's list of factors to be considered when making custody determinations.

The following case demonstrates the difficulty of applying the "best-interest-of-the-child" rule. Notice how issues of employment, educational and professional accomplishment, and parental bonding bear on the determination of custody.

Shannon Blakely v. Brandon Blakely
218 P.3d 253
Supreme Court of Wyoming
October 20, 2009

Hill, Justice.
Shannon Blakely (Mother) appeals from her divorce decree, contending that the district court abused its discretion when it awarded Brandon Blakely (Father) primary residential custody of the parties' two sons, while the half-brother remained in Mother's custody....

ISSUE

Mother states the single issue as follows:

Whether the District Court erred when it awarded primary residential custody of the parties' two minor children to [Father]?

FACTS

The parties to this action married on January 7, 2003. Mother brought a son, CS, into the marriage, and at the time of the marriage, Mother was pregnant with the couple's first son, CB, who was born in May of 2003. The couple's second son, EB, was born in August of 2005. During the relationship, the family lived in Buffalo, but Father often worked out of town.

The couple separated in October of 2005, with Mother leaving the home and taking all three boys with her. In June of 2007, Mother officially moved to Gillette with the three boys—by this time Mother was engaged to another man and expecting her fourth son, who was born in September of 2007. Father, meanwhile, continued to exercise visitation with his two sons.

Mother filed for divorce in August of 2007, and both parties requested temporary custody, which the district court awarded to Father on January 25, 2008. The case was tried on July 11, 2008, and at the close of evidence, the court made findings on the record. Ultimately, the court awarded primary residential custody to Father, with visitation to Mother. Mother appeals that decision.

STANDARD OF REVIEW

We have stated before that "[c]ustody, visitation, child support, and alimony are all committed to the sound discretion of the district court."...

This Court has consistently recognized the broad discretion enjoyed by a district court in child custody matters. We will not interfere with the district court's custody determination absent procedural error or a clear abuse of discretion. In determining whether an abuse of discretion has occurred, our primary consideration is the reasonableness of the district court's decision in light of the evidence presented. We view the evidence in the light most favorable to the district court's determination, affording every favorable inference to the prevailing party and omitting from our consideration the conflicting evidence....

DISCUSSION

Mother claims on appeal that in its decision giving primary residential custody to Father, the district court did not "give the welfare and needs of the children paramount consideration." Mother insists that the evidence presented at trial indicated that she was the more appropriate party to have primary residential custody. Essentially, Mother asks us to reweigh the evidence considered by the district court when she points to, and analyzes in detail, each of the statutory factors that guide a custody determination....

Father contends that the court's decision is supported by the evidence and was a proper exercise of discretion—and, as evidenced by the court's oral ruling, the court thoroughly evaluated the evidence along with the statutory factors.

As we have consistently articulated, "This Court ... does not reweigh evidence. Instead, we view the facts in the light most favorable to the prevailing party."... In child custody determinations, the district court must base its decision on the factors articulated in §20-2-201(a), which provides:

(a) In granting a divorce, separation or annulment of a marriage or upon the establishment of paternity pursuant to W.S. 14-2-401 through 14-2-907, the court may make by decree or order any disposition of the children that appears most expedient and in the best interests of the children. In determining the best interests of the child, the court shall consider, but is not limited to, the following factors:

(i) The quality of the relationship each child has with each parent;

(ii) The ability of each parent to provide adequate care for each child throughout each period of responsibility, including arranging for each child's care by others as needed;

(iii) The relative competency and fitness of each parent;

(iv) Each parent's willingness to accept all responsibilities of parenting, including a willingness to accept care for each child at specified times and to relinquish care to the other parent at specified times;

(v) How the parents and each child can best maintain and strengthen a relationship with each other;

(vi) How the parents and each child interact and communicate with each other and how such interaction and communication may be improved;

(vii) The ability and willingness of each parent to allow the other to provide care without intrusion, respect the other parent's rights and responsibilities, including the right to privacy;

(viii) Geographic distance between the parents' residences;

(ix) The current physical and mental ability of each parent to care for each child;

(x) Any other factors the court deems necessary and relevant.

No single factor is determinative.... In fact, depending on the case, different factors will present a greater need for emphasis. The one constant is that the resolution must be in the best interests of the children in that particular family....

With these principles in mind, we turn to the facts of the instant case. The record is clear that each parent had a good relationship with the children. The court stated in its oral findings, "... these are two good parents. They both love their children and want the best for their children." Indeed, each party appears to be more than able to handle the care of the children, and the record contains evidence favorable to each party.

For instance, Mother lives in a four-bedroom, two-bath home on two and a half acres, and is a stay-at-home mom. And even though Father works full-time, he is very responsible regarding daycare and has that "all lined out," according to the district court. The court found both parents to be on equal footing regarding maintaining and strengthening relationships with each other. The court also found to be a positive feature of both parents "the support of their extended families." The phrase "equal footing" was also applied regarding how the parents and each child interact and communicate with each other, as well as the ability and willingness of each parent to allow the other to provide care without intrusion, respecting the other parent's rights and responsibilities, including the right to privacy. By and large, the court found the parents to be on "equal footing" on most of the factors it considered.

Nevertheless, Mother points to a factor in particular that she believes weighs in her favor—that giving custody of EB and CB to Father splits up the four brothers. This Court has addressed the issue of separating siblings:

[G]enerally speaking the separating of siblings through custody awards to different parents is not preferred. Keeping siblings together in the same household is considered the better practice. However, this court clarified that the effect

of separating siblings from each other is just one of several factors courts consider in determining the primary issue—the best interests of the children....

The district court addressed this very issue at length on the record:

All right. Another factor I want to take up, under factor 10, which is the general factor that may influence the Court decision is the subject of the half siblings, because it is very important.

... I want the record to reflect I have taken into account the value of half-siblings being raised under the same roof, and I recognize that value....

I am also going to note that right at this moment, that dad has indicated that he has no problem in affording access of these two boys, [CB] and [EB] to their half siblings, and I take that representation at face value.

I want you to know, sir, that if that does not happen, that this Court is going to consider that to be a material and substantial change in circumstances, that could conceivably justify a change in custody later on so that should influence you in the right direction here. These boys need to have a full, deep, and long relationship with their half-siblings. And there is no reason why you and their mother cannot arrange that, particularly when you have the support of your extended families behind you.

The court concluded that it was in the children's overall best interests that Father be awarded custody. Furthermore, the court's oral findings were sufficiently detailed so as to provide an adequate basis for its ultimate determination awarding Father custody of the two boys, effectively separating them from their brothers for much of the time.

Because this was such a close case, we would like to again emphasize:

"The law affords wide discretion to the district court when fashioning custody and visitation provisions for the best interests of the children."... We recognize such discretion encompasses one of the most difficult and demanding tasks assigned to a trial judge.... Ultimately, the "goal to be achieved is a reasonable balance of the rights and affections of each of the parents, with paramount consideration being given to the welfare and needs of the children...."

Certainly, reasonable minds could reach different conclusions about which parent's custody would be in the best interests of the children....

Seldom if ever does a divorce court have a choice between a parent who is all good on one side and a parent who is all bad on the other side. The matter of awarding custody is a comparative proposition wherein the court exercises its best judgment and discretion and awards custody to one parent or to the other, according to what the court thinks is for the best interest and welfare of the children.

... Here, even the district court admitted this was a close, tough case. This Court will accede to the district court's determination of the admissibility of evidence unless the court clearly abused its discretion.... The burden is on the party asserting an abuse of discretion to establish such an abuse.... In this instance, Mother has failed to meet the applicable burden and because the record includes sufficient evidence to support the district court's decision, we can find no abuse of discretion in the district court's award of custody to Father.

CONCLUSION
The district court did not err when it awarded Father primary residential custody of his two sons. This Court can find no abuse of discretion by the district court, and, accordingly, we affirm its decision.

Case Questions

1. Are you satisfied with the Wyoming Supreme Court's reasoning for affirming the trial court's decision?
2. Do you think there is a better way, in cases as close on the merits as this one, to arrive at a just decision as to which parent should have primary physical custody?

 From your perspective, how should a court ethically decide which parent should be awarded primary physical placement if the court cannot say that the child's interests are better served by either parent, because the parents are equally desirable?

Grandparental Visitation

The question as to what rights, if any, grandparents should have to visit their grandchildren has provoked considerable legislation and litigation throughout the country. In a case decided by the U.S. Supreme Court in 2002, *Troxel v. Granville*, 530 U.S. 57, a trial court in Washington, pursuant to a state statute, granted grandparents named Troxel visitation rights with their deceased son's minor children. The children's mother disagreed with the amount of visitation granted by the trial court and appealed to the Washington Supreme Court. That court, believing that the statute was overly broad, concluded that it violated the federal Constitution. Although the Troxels successfully

petitioned the U.S. Supreme Court for a writ of certiorari, the justices agreed with the Washington Supreme Court and affirmed its decision.

In the aftermath of the *Troxel* decision, many state legislatures redrafted their statutes to accommodate the Supreme Court's concerns. They sought to create a framework for balancing the rights of parents to determine how children should be raised, and with whom they should associate, against denying children and their grandparents—where appropriate and in the best interest of the children—the right to maintain an existing relationship, even if the parent(s) and grandparents are antagonistic toward one another. Pennsylvania's current statute can be seen in Figure 9.5.

Pennsylvania Statute—Factors to consider when awarding custody

(a) Factors. — In ordering any form of custody, the court shall determine the best interest of the child by considering all relevant factors, giving weighted consideration to those factors which affect the safety of the child, including the following:

(1) Which party is more likely to encourage and permit frequent and continuing contact between the child and another party.

(2) The present and past abuse committed by a party or member of the party's household, whether there is a continued risk of harm to the child or an abused party and which party can better provide adequate physical safeguards and supervision of the child.

(3) The parental duties performed by each party on behalf of the child.

(4) The need for stability and continuity in the child's education, family life and community life.

(5) The availability of extended family.

(6) The child's sibling relationships.

(7) The well-reasoned preference of the child, based on the child's maturity and judgment.

(8) The attempts of a parent to turn the child against the other parent, except in cases of domestic violence where reasonable safety measures are necessary to protect the child from harm.

(9) Which party is more likely to maintain a loving, stable, consistent and nurturing relationship with the child adequate for the child's emotional needs.

(10) Which party is more likely to attend to the daily physical, emotional, developmental, educational and special needs of the child.

(11) The proximity of the residences of the parties.

(12) Each party's availability to care for the child or ability to make appropriate child-care arrangements.

(13) The level of conflict between the parties and the willingness and ability of the parties to cooperate with one another. A party's effort to protect a child from abuse by another party is not evidence of unwillingness or inability to cooperate with that party.

(14) The history of drug or alcohol abuse of a party or member of a party's household.

(15) The mental and physical condition of a party or member of a party's household.

(16) Any other relevant factor.

(b) Gender neutral. — In making a determination under subsection (a), no party shall receive preference based upon gender in any award granted under this chapter.

(c) Grandparents and great-grandparents. —

(1) In ordering partial physical custody or supervised physical custody to a party who has standing under section 5325(1) or (2) (relating to standing for partial physical custody and supervised physical custody), the court shall consider the following:

(i) the amount of personal contact between the child and the party prior to the filing of the action;

(ii) whether the award interferes with any parent-child relationship; and

(iii) whether the award is in the best interest of the child.

(2) In ordering partial physical custody or supervised physical custody to a parent's parent or grandparent who has standing under section 5325(3), the court shall consider whether the award:

(i) interferes with any parent-child relationship; and

(ii) is in the best interest of the child.

FIGURE 9.5   23 Pa. C.S.A. § 5328.—Factors to Consider When Awarding Custody

In the Matter of the Adoption of: ADA and SSA, CJ v. SA
132 P.3d 196
Supreme Court of Wyoming
April 20, 2006

Kite, Justice.

CJ is the stepfather of ADA and SSA (the children), and SA is their biological father. Stepfather petitioned the district court to adopt the children without father's consent because father had failed to provide adequate child support for the children. The district court denied the petition, finding stepfather failed to prove by clear and convincing evidence that father willfully failed to pay child support....

FACTS

The children's mother and father were divorced in 2001, and the divorce decree awarded custody of the children to mother and ordered father to pay $527.46 per month in child support. Mother married stepfather in January 2003, and stepfather assumed responsibility for supporting the children. Father did not comply with his child support obligation; consequently, on February 2, 2004, stepfather filed a petition to adopt the children without father's consent pursuant to Wyo. Stat. Ann. § 1-22-110.

The district court held a hearing on stepfather's petition. Father admitted he had not paid child support in accordance with the order but argued his failure was not willful.... [T]he district court concluded father's failure to pay child support was not willful and, consequently, denied stepfather's petition. Stepfather appealed....

DISCUSSION

Stepfather claims the district court abused its discretion by denying his petition to adopt the children without father's consent. A petition for adoption without parental consent may be granted by the district court if the elements outlined in Wyo. Stat. Ann. § 1-22-110 are satisfied.... Wyo. Stat. Ann. § 1-22-110 states, in pertinent part:

(a) In addition to the exceptions contained in W.S. 1-22-108, the adoption of a child may be ordered without the written consent of a parent or the putative father if the court finds ... that the putative father or the nonconsenting parent or parents have: ...

(iv) Willfully failed to contribute to the support of the child for a period of one (1) year im-mediately prior to the filing of the petition to adopt and has failed to bring the support obligation current within sixty (60) days after service of the petition to adopt; or ...

(ix) Willfully failed to pay a total dollar amount of at least seventy percent (70 percent) of the court-ordered support for a period of two (2) years or more and has failed to bring the support obligation one hundred percent (100 percent) current within sixty (60) days after service of the petition to adopt.

The petition stated the adoption should be allowed without father's permission ... because father had will-fully failed to pay a total dollar amount of at least seventy percent of the court-ordered support for a period of two years or more. However, the district court's order denying the petition focused on Wyo. Stat. Ann. § 1-22-110(a)(iv), which allows adoption without the parent's consent if the parent has "willfully failed to contribute to the support of the child for a period of one (1) year immediately prior to the filing of the petition to adopt and has failed to bring the support obligation current within sixty (60) days after service of the petition to adopt." ... Our inquiry, therefore, focuses on the willful-ness element and not on the amount of support father did or did not pay.

We have explained the importance of the willful-ness requirement as follows:

Clearly, by inclusion of the modifying term "will-fully" the statute draws a distinction, as it must, between the parent who though financially able to pay his court-ordered child support is unwilling to do so, and the parent who though willing to pay his court-ordered child support is financially unable to do so. "A natural parent's failure to support his or her child does not obviate the ne-cessity of the parent's consent to the child's adoption, where the parent's financial condition is such that he or she is unable to support the child." 2 Am.Jur.2d Adoption § 88 (1974).

Moreover, this court has defined willfully in the context of Wyo. Stat. Ann. § 1-22-110 as "intentionally, knowingly, purposely, voluntarily, consciously, deliber-ately, and without justifiable excuse, as distinguished from carelessly, inadvertently, accidentally, negligently, heedlessly or thoughtlessly."...

... Father acknowledged he was aware of his child support obligation and did not pay it on a regular basis. He claimed he was unable to consistently pay child support because he had difficulty finding employment ... and he had been incarcerated intermittently on a number of different charges....

Stepfather argues father's actions were willful because his behavior led to his incarceration which prevented him from earning the money to pay child support. We have directly addressed the issue of whether a non-consenting parent's failure to pay child support because he is incarcerated is sufficient to establish willfulness.... We [have] said ... "Incarceration, standing alone, does not provide the direct intent necessary to constitute willful failure to pay under the pertinent statute."... Instead, "the focus must remain on the parent's intent and ability to pay. The courts should look at whether the parent has demonstrated, through whatever financial means available to him, that the parent has not forgotten his statutory obligation to his child."... When a parent is incarcerated, "the proper inquiry to address ... is whether the natural parent intentionally incapacitated himself for the purpose of avoiding the duty imposed by law; if so then imprisonment may constitute justification for dispensing with his consent in the adoption proceeding...." There is no evidence in this record which indicates father willfully committed any crimes in order to have himself incarcerated so he could avoid his child support obligation. Thus, his incarceration, by itself, does not justify a finding of willfulness.

Of course, even when a parent is incarcerated, he must pay child support if he has the means to do so. "A parent must always pay child support according to his or her financial ability."... The record indicates father was incarcerated off and on over a period of several years; however, neither the actual dates of his imprisonment nor the total amount of time he spent in jail is shown in the record. Furthermore, stepfather did not present any evidence as to whether father earned wages while incarcerated.... Thus, we do not know if he had the ability to pay any child support while he was incarcerated....

Father testified, when he was not in jail, he attempted to find work in order to earn the funds to pay child support, but was not able to find consistent work in Uinta County. He identified two construction companies for which he had worked as a truck driver and stated, without contradiction, his child support was paid while he was working. Father also testified he had attempted to find work through "the union" and with "the rigs," but was unsuccessful. After he was unable to secure other employment, he said he started his own business with the hopes of earning a living. At the time of the hearing, the business apparently had not yet yielded any earnings. Father testified he was living with friends because he could not afford his own residence....

The determination of whether father's failure to pay child support was willful involves disputed factual issues; consequently, it was within the district court's province to weigh the evidence and judge the credibility of the witnesses.... Evidence exists in the record supporting father's contention he did not have the means to pay his child support because he had difficulty earning a living and had been incarcerated....

Stepfather also argues the record shows father chose to spend his money on drugs and/or alcohol instead of paying his child support obligation. The record does contain evidence suggesting father's use of intoxicating substances contributed to his difficulties....

Obviously, if a parent has money with which to buy drugs or alcohol and chooses to do so rather than pay child support, an argument could be made that the failure to pay child support was willful.... However, it is important to focus on the proper query when evaluating such an argument. As explained by the Montana Supreme Court when reviewing a lower court's termination of a mother's parental rights:

> [A parent's] admitted drug addiction alone cannot serve as clear and convincing evidence that she had the means to contribute to her children's support. The relevant inquiry is whether she obtained funds which could have been used for the support of the children which, instead, she chose to spend on drugs....

In the case at bar, there was no evidence concerning the extent of father's drug or alcohol use or the actual amount of money he spent on such substances. More importantly, the record does not show father had funds available to him to buy drugs and/or alcohol instead of paying child support.

As we have said before, the right of parents to associate with their children is fundamental, and due process requires we stringently guard this important right. Stepfather was charged with proving, by clear and convincing evidence, father willfully disregarded his child support obligation. The district court concluded he did not meet that onerous burden. Although father's efforts to pay his child support certainly cannot be characterized as model and may have, at times, been willful, stepfather must prove that fact with clear and convincing evidence, and this record does not contain such evidence. When there is a failure of proof, we cannot conclude the district court's denial of the petition for adoption was an abuse of discretion. Affirmed.

Case Questions

1. What was the stepfather's claim in the intermediate appellate court?
2. What did the appellate court decide?
3. What rationale did the Wyoming Supreme Court give for its decision?

Preferred-Custody Statutes

Preferred–custody statutes were enacted because it was uncertain whether judges had sufficient reliable information to predict accurately what would be in a child's best interest.[82] Some states require that preference be given to a child's primary caretaker, when the primary caretaker can be established. Such an approach has the advantage of not favoring either gender, and it provides the child with continuity and stability in the parenting role. When the statutory preference is for joint custody, public policy provides that even though the marital relationship between the parents has ended, their parenting roles and responsibilities will continue as before. Both parents will share decision making in regard to their child's upbringing. Joint custody produces no winners and losers of a custody battle. The parents continue to share a family, but not a marriage.[83] When joint custody works, the child benefits from the active involvement of both a mother and a father. But it works only where divorcing parents are willing and able to separate their marital and parental relationships and act cooperatively to benefit their child.[84]

Once a court has determined that one parent should have custody, the noncustodial parent normally will be awarded visitation rights. It is important to encourage the noncustodial parent to continue to play an active role in the child's life. Sometimes the custodial parent wants to relocate, which would have the effect of curtailing the visitation opportunities of the noncustodial spouse. Courts are divided on what standard to apply when the parents disagree about making such a move.[85] Although the initial custody determination can be modified at a future date if material changes in the child's circumstances prove harmful, courts are reluctant to unsettle a child unless compelling reasons are shown.

Child Support

Although parents have the right to formally and informally break up with one another, they cannot divorce their minor children. Thus parents generally will be required to support their children until they reach the age of majority. In some special circumstances, however, the support obligation continues even beyond that date. We focus now on the special circumstances that can arise in conjunction with a divorce.

When a marriage that involves children is terminated, the court will examine the earning capacity of each parent and the needs of each child, determine who has custody, and determine each parent's support obligation. Every state has some guidelines to help judges make this determination. Generally, when custody has been awarded to one parent, the noncustodial parent will be ordered to make support payments. This parent is legally required to make the payments irrespective of side issues such as whether the custodial parent has violated the noncustodial parent's visitation rights or whether the custodial parent is spending the support payment money for other purposes than the children. Although child support is awarded to provide for the needs of the child, courts disagree about the exact meaning of that term. It certainly includes a child's necessaries, and there are cases in which noncustodial parents have been required to pay for their children's college educations.[86] Nevertheless, child support has a theoretically different purpose from that of alimony and property awards, which are intended to benefit a spouse.

When parents divorce, remarry, and establish second families, their support obligation to their first family continues, and many states require that the children from the first family receive priority over the children in the second family. Some states are moving away from this traditional approach and are structuring child support so that it benefits both families.[87] As was previously indicated, states differ about whether stepparents have a support liability for stepchildren.

As is the case with alimony, either party can petition for modification of the support order when there is a substantial change of circumstances.

Property Division

As we saw earlier in this chapter, when people divorce, the property they have accumulated during their marriage is apportioned between them. It is common for married people to own a house, cars, and other tangible personal property concurrently, and to have joint accounts at the bank. If they have been married for a long time, they probably will have accumulated much property. States address the distribution problem differently, depending on whether they follow the common law equitable-distribution approach or the community-property approach.

Common Law Equitable-Distribution Approach

In most states, what is known as **equitable distribution** has replaced the traditional common-law approach to determining property rights. Under the common law, the person who had title to property owned it, and generally this meant the husband. When lawmakers and judges began to look upon marriage as an economic partnership, property acquired during marriage was perceived in different terms. This new perspective produced reforms intended to result in the more equitable distribution of property to each of the divorcing parties. Though not all states that adopt equitable distribution classify property, many do. In those states, property is classified as *separate property* or as *marital property*. **Marital property** is nonseparate property acquired during the marriage and is subject to an equitable distribution by a judge. **Separate property,** that which was owned individually by one or the other spouse prior to the marriage or was received as a gift or inheritance, is not subject to distribution.

Obviously, the legal definition of property is crucial to any distribution scheme. Many states now treat pensions in which the ownership rights have matured (vested) and medical insurance benefits also as subject to distribution.

Though not all states agree with the holding in the following case, it is looked upon as a landmark decision. In the *O'Brien* case, the court declared that a spouse who has made significant contributions to her husband's medical education and licensing as a doctor was entitled to a property interest in his license at the time of their divorce.

O'Brien v. O'Brien
489 N.E.2d 712
Court of Appeals of New York
December 26, 1985

Simons, Judge.

In this divorce action, the parties' only asset of any consequence is the husband's newly acquired license to practice medicine. The principal issue presented is whether that license, acquired during their marriage, is marital property subject to equitable distribution under Domestic Relations Law § 236(B)(5). Supreme Court held that it was and accordingly made a distributive award in defendant's favor. It also granted defendant maintenance arrears, expert witness fees and attorneys' fees.... On appeal to the Appellate Division, a majority of that court held that plaintiff's medical license is not marital property and that defendant was not entitled to an award for the expert witness fees. It modified the judgment and remitted the case to Supreme Court for further proceedings, specifically for a determination of maintenance and a rehabilitative award.... The matter is before us by leave of the Appellate Division.

We now hold that plaintiff's medical license constitutes "marital property" within the meaning of Domestic Relations Law § 236(B)(1)(c) and that it is therefore subject to equitable distribution pursuant to subdivision 5 of that part....

I

Plaintiff and defendant married on April 3, 1971. At the time both were employed as teachers at the same private school. Defendant had a bachelor's degree and a temporary teaching certificate but required 18 months of postgraduate classes at an approximate cost of $3,000, excluding living expenses, to obtain permanent certification in New York. She claimed, and the trial court found, that she had relinquished the opportunity to obtain permanent certification while plaintiff pursued his education. At the time of the marriage, plaintiff had completed only three and one-half years of college but shortly afterward he returned to school at night to earn his bachelor's degree and to complete sufficient premedical courses and enter medical school. In September 1973 the parties moved to Guadalajara, Mexico, where plaintiff became a full-time medical student. While he pursued his studies defendant held several teaching and tutorial positions and contributed her earnings to their

joint expenses. The parties returned to New York in December 1976 so that plaintiff could complete the last two semesters of medical school and internship training here. After they returned, defendant resumed her former teaching position and she remained in it at the time this action was commenced. Plaintiff was licensed to practice medicine in October 1980. He commenced this action for divorce two months later. At the time of trial, he was a resident in general surgery.

During the marriage both parties contributed to paying the living and educational expenses and they received additional help from both of their families. They disagreed on the amounts of their respective contributions but it is undisputed that in addition to performing household work and managing the family finances defendant was gainfully employed throughout the marriage, that she contributed all of her earnings to their living and educational expenses and that her financial contributions exceeded those of plaintiff. The trial court found that she had contributed 76 percent of the parties' income exclusive of a $10,000 student loan obtained by defendant. Finding that plaintiff's medical degree and license are marital property, the court received evidence of its value and ordered a distributive award to defendant. Defendant presented expert testimony that the present value of plaintiff's medical license was $472,000. Her expert testified that he arrived at this figure by comparing the average income of a college graduate and that of a general surgeon between 1985, when plaintiff's residency would end, and 2012, when he would reach age 65. After considering Federal income taxes, an inflation rate of 10 percent and a real interest rate of 3 percent he capitalized the difference in average earnings and reduced the amount to present value. He also gave his opinion that the present value of defendant's contribution to plaintiff's medical education was $103,390. Plaintiff offered no expert testimony on the subject.

The court, after considering the lifestyle that plaintiff would enjoy from the enhanced earning potential his medical license would bring and defendant's contributions and efforts toward attainment of it, made a distributive award to her of $188,800, representing 40 percent of the value of the license, and ordered it paid in 11 annual installments of various amounts beginning November 1, 1982 and ending November 1, 1992. The court also directed plaintiff to maintain a life insurance policy on his life for defendant's benefit for the unpaid balance of the award and it ordered plaintiff to pay defendant's counsel fees of $7,000 and her expert witness fee of $1,000. It did not award defendant maintenance.

A divided Appellate Division ... concluded that a professional license acquired during marriage is not marital property subject to distribution. It therefore modified the judgment by striking the trial court's determination that it is and by striking the provision ordering payment of the expert witness for evaluating the license and remitted the case for further proceedings....

II

The Equitable Distribution Law contemplates only two classes of property: marital property and separate property (Domestic Relations Law § 236[B][1][c], [d]). The former, which is subject to equitable distribution, is defined broadly as "*all* property acquired by either or both spouses during the marriage and before the execution of a separation agreement or the commencement of a matrimonial action, *regardless of the form in which title is held*" (Domestic Relations Law § 236[B][1][c] [emphasis added]; see § 236 [B][5][b], [c]). Plaintiff does not contend that his license is excluded from distribution because it is separate property; rather, he claims that it is not property at all but represents a personal attainment in acquiring knowledge. He rests his argument on decisions in similar cases from other jurisdictions and on his view that a license does not satisfy common-law concepts of property. Neither contention is controlling because decisions in other States rely principally on their own statutes, and the legislative history underlying them, and because the New York Legislature deliberately went beyond traditional property concepts when it formulated the Equitable Distribution Law.... Instead, our statute recognizes that spouses have an equitable claim to things of value arising out of the marital relationship and classifies them as subject to distribution by focusing on the marital status of the parties at the time of acquisition. Those things acquired during marriage and subject to distribution have been classified as "marital property" although, as one commentator has observed, they hardly fall within the traditional property concepts because there is no common-law property interest remotely resembling

marital property. "It is a statutory creature, is of no meaning whatsoever during the normal course of a marriage and arises full-grown, like Athena, upon the signing of a separation agreement or the commencement of a matrimonial action. [Thus] [i]t is hardly surprising, and not at all relevant, that traditional common-law property concepts do not fit in parsing the meaning of 'marital property.' "... Having classified the "property" subject to distribution, the Legislature did not attempt to go further and define it but left it to the courts to determine what interests come within the terms of section 236(B)(1)(c). We made such a determination in *Majauskas v. Majauskas* ... 463 N.E.2d 15, holding there that vested but unmatured pension rights are marital property subject to equitable distribution. Because pension benefits are not specifically identified as marital property in the statute, we looked to the express reference to pension rights contained in section 236(B)(5)(d)(4), which deals with equitable distribution of marital property, to other provisions of the equitable distribution statute and to the legislative intent behind its enactment to determine whether pension rights are marital property or separate property. A similar analysis is appropriate here and leads to the conclusion that marital property encompasses a license to practice medicine to the extent that the license is acquired during marriage.

Section 236 provides that in making an equitable distribution of marital property, "the court shall consider: ... (6) any equitable claim to, interest in, or direct or indirect contribution made to the acquisition of such marital property by the party not having title, including joint efforts or expenditures and contributions and services as a spouse, parent, wage earner and homemaker, and *to the career or career potential* of the other party [and] ... (9) the impossibility or difficulty of evaluating any component asset or any interest in a business, corporation or *profession*" (Domestic Relations Law § 236-[B][5][d][6], [9] [emphasis added]). Where equitable distribution of marital property is appropriate but "the distribution of an interest in a business, corporation or *profession* would be contrary to law" the court shall make a distributive award in lieu of an actual distribution of the property (Domestic Relations Law § 236[B][5][e] [emphasis added]). The words mean exactly what they say: that an interest in a profession or professional career potential is marital property which may be represented by direct or indirect contributions of the non-title-holding spouse, including financial contributions and nonfinancial contributions made by caring for the home and family.

The history which preceded enactment of the statute confirms this interpretation. Reform of section 236 was advocated because experience had proven that application of the traditional common-law title theory of property had caused inequities upon dissolution of a marriage. The Legislature replaced the existing system with equitable distribution of marital property, an entirely new theory which considered all the circumstances of the case and of the respective parties to the marriage.... Equitable distribution was based on the premise that a marriage is, among other things, an economic partnership to which both parties contribute as spouse, parent, wage earner or homemaker.... Consistent with this purpose, and implicit in the statutory scheme as a whole, is the view that upon dissolution of the marriage there should be a winding up of the parties' economic affairs and a severance of their economic ties by an equitable distribution of the marital assets. Thus, the concept of alimony, which often served as a means of lifetime support and dependence for one spouse upon the other long after the marriage was over, was replaced with the concept of maintenance which seeks to allow "the recipient spouse an opportunity to achieve [economic] independence."...

The determination that a professional license is marital property is also consistent with the conceptual base upon which the statute rests. As this case demonstrates, few undertakings during a marriage better qualify as the type of joint effort that the statute's economic partnership theory is intended to address than contributions toward one spouse's acquisition of a professional license. Working spouses are often required to contribute substantial income as wage earners, sacrifice their own educational or career goals and opportunities for child rearing, perform the bulk of household duties and responsibilities and forego the acquisition of marital assets that could have been accumulated if the professional spouse had been employed rather than occupied with the study and training necessary to acquire a professional license. In this case, nearly all of the parties' nine-year marriage was devoted to the acquisition of plaintiff's medical license and defendant played a major role in that project. She worked continuously during the marriage and contributed all of her earnings to their joint effort, she sacrificed her own educational and career opportunities, and she traveled with plaintiff to Mexico for three and one-half years while he attended medical school there. The Legislature has decided, by its explicit reference in the statute to the contributions of one spouse to the other's profession

or career ... that these contributions represent investments in the economic partnership of the marriage and that the product of the parties' joint efforts, the professional license, should be considered marital property.

The majority at the Appellate Division held that the cited statutory provisions do not refer to the license held by a professional who has yet to establish a practice but only to a going professional practice.... There is no reason in law or logic to restrict the plain language of the statute to existing practices, however, for it is of little consequence in making an award of marital property, except for the purpose of evaluation, whether the professional spouse has already established a practice or whether he or she has yet to do so. An established practice merely represents the exercise of the privileges conferred upon the professional spouse by the license and the income flowing from that practice represents the receipt of the enhanced earning capacity that licensure allows. That being so, it would be unfair not to consider the license a marital asset.

Plaintiff's principal argument, adopted by the majority below, is that a professional license is not marital property because it does not fit within the traditional view of property as something which has an exchange value on the open market and is capable of sale, assignment or transfer. The position does not withstand analysis for at least two reasons. First, as we have observed, it ignores the fact that whether a professional license constitutes marital property is to be judged by the language of the statute which created this new species of property previously unknown at common law or under prior statutes. Thus, whether the license fits within traditional property concepts is of no consequence. Second, it is an overstatement to assert that a professional license could not be considered property even outside the context of section 236(B). A professional license is a valuable property right, reflected in the money, effort and lost opportunity for employment expended in its acquisition, and also in the enhanced earning capacity it affords its holder, which may not be revoked without due process of law.... That a professional license has no market value is irrelevant. Obviously, a license may not be alienated as may other property and for that reason the working spouse's interest in it is limited. The Legislature has recognized that limitation, however, and has provided for an award in lieu of its actual distribution....

Plaintiff also contends that alternative remedies should be employed, such as an award of rehabilitative maintenance or reimbursement for direct financial con-tributions.... The statute does not expressly authorize retrospective maintenance or rehabilitative awards and we have no occasion to decide in this case whether the authority to do so may ever be implied from its provi-sions.... It is sufficient to observe that normally a work-ing spouse should not be restricted to that relief because to do so frustrates the purposes underlying the Equitable Distribution Law. Limiting a working spouse to a maintenance award, either general or rehabilita-tive, not only is contrary to the economic partnership concept underlying the statute but also retains the uncertain and inequitable economic ties of dependence that the Legislature sought to extinguish by equitable distribution. Maintenance is subject to termination upon the recipient's remarriage and a working spouse may never receive adequate consideration for his or her contribution and may even be penalized for the deci-sion to remarry if that is the only method of compen-sating the contribution. As one court said so well, "[t]he function of equitable distribution is to recognize that when a marriage ends, each of the spouses, based on the totality of the contributions made to it, has a stake in and right to a share of the marital assets accumulated while it endured, not because that share is needed, but because those assets represent the capital product of what was essentially a partnership entity" *(Wood v. Wood,* ... 465 N.Y. S.3d 475). The Legislature stated its intention to eliminate such inequities by providing that a supporting spouse's "direct or indirect contribution" be recognized, considered and rewarded (Domestic Re-lations Law § 236 [B][5][d][6]).

Turning to the question of valuation, it has been suggested that even if a professional license is con-sidered marital property, the working spouse is enti-tled only to reimbursement of his or her direct financial contributions.... If the license is marital property, then the working spouse is entitled to an equitable portion of it, not a return of funds advanced. Its value is the enhanced earning capacity it affords the holder and although fixing the present

value of that enhanced earning capacity may present problems, the problems are not insurmountable. Cer-tainly they are no more difficult than computing tort damages for wrongful death or diminished earning capacity resulting from injury and they differ only in degree from the problems presented when valuing a professional practice for purposes of a distributive award, something the courts have not hesitated to do.... The trial court retains the flexibility and discre-tion to structure the distributive award equitably, taking into consideration factors such as the working spouse's need for immediate payment, the licensed spouse's current ability to pay and the income tax consequences of prolonging the period of payment ... and, once it has received evidence of the present value of the license and the working spouse's contri-butions toward its acquisition and considered the re-maining factors mandated by the statute ... it may then make an appropriate distribution of the marital property including a distributive award for the pro-fessional license if such an award is warranted. When other marital assets are of sufficient value to provide for the supporting spouse's equitable portion of the marital property, including his or her contributions to the acquisition of the professional license, however, the court retains the discretion to distribute these other marital assets or to make a distributive award in lieu of an actual distribution of the value of the pro-fessional spouse's license....

III

... Accordingly, in view of our holding that plaintiff's license to practice medicine is marital property, the order of the Appellate Division should be modified, with costs to defendant, by reinstating the judgment and the case remitted to the Appellate Division for determination of the facts, including the exercise of that court's discretion (CPLR 5613), and, as so modified, affirmed.

Case Questions

1. When Loretta O'Brien sued her husband Michael for divorce, what claim did she make with respect to the marital property of the couple?
2. What was the basis of her claim?
3. How does the court define marital property in this case?

 What moral principles are reflected in the New York equitable-distribution statute?

Determining Fairness

For a distribution to be fair, the court must identify, classify, and determine the value of each spouse's assets—or their detriment, in the case of debts. The court must also consider the circumstances and needs of the parties, the length of their marriage, their marital standard of living, their contributions to the marriage, and other similar factors. Although it is possible to take such matters to trial and have them decided by a judge, it is often faster—and the parties have more control over the outcome—if they negotiate a property settlement in lieu of fighting it out in court. Property dispute battles can be very expensive. Appraisals and expensive expert witnesses are required to establish the value of assets. Litigation costs also can increase dramatically and diminish the assets ultimately available for distribution. Judges frequently incorporate a negotiated agreement that equitably allocates marital assets and debts into the final judgment.

Community-Property Approach

The states of Louisiana, Texas, California, New Mexico, Arizona, Nevada, Washington, Idaho, and Wisconsin statutorily treat all property that is not separate property and that was acquired during the marriage presumptively as community property that belongs equally to both spouses. Under this approach, it doesn't matter who worked and earned the money for a purchase, or who purchased the property. Both spouses have the right to make management decisions regarding community property (such as whether it is leased, loaned, invested, etc.). If the parties wish to alter the community-property presumption, they may do so by agreement, by gift, and by commingling separate and community assets so that separate property loses its character (such as the merger of a separate stamp collection with a community collection, or the deposit of birthday money into the community checking account). In the event of a divorce, the court in a community-property state makes an equitable division of all community property to each spouse.

The Decree

Irrespective of whether the issues are negotiated or litigated, at the end of the process the court issues a judgment that dissolves the marriage, distributes the property, and determines claims for alimony, child custody, and child support. The attorneys for the now-divorced parties then assist their respective clients to implement the orders. Property must be exchanged, ownership rights transferred, money transferred, debts paid, insurance policies obtained, pension rights transferred, and other details wrapped up.

CHAPTER SUMMARY

Chapter IX began with a discussion of the family and its historical roles, as well as its place in contemporary America. Emphasis was given to the many tangible and intangible benefits that accrue to family members, but are otherwise unavailable to nonfamily members. The discussion then shifted to the ways in which family relationships are created—through marriage or the formation of civil unions–domestic partnerships, by becoming a parent as a result of the birth of one's child, by adoption, and, to a limited extent, as a consequence of becoming a foster parent. The essential nature of each of these statutes was discussed and each process was explained.

The chapter concluded with an overview of how spousal relationships are legally ended—by way of annulment, legal separation, and divorce–dissolution. The discussion focused on how the divorcing couple's financial affairs are separated so that each spouse is able to function independently, and on decisions as to alimony, child custody and child support, and the distribution of property.

CHAPTER QUESTIONS

1. Andrea Moorhead was abandoned by her birth mother, a crack-cocaine user who had tested positive for venereal disease, shortly after birth. Andrea was placed with foster parents when she was nine days old. The foster parents, Melva and Robert Dearth, sought to adopt Andrea when she was ten months old. The county's Children Service Bureau (CSB) opposed this proposed adoption. The Dearths alleged that CSB's decision was predicated on the fact that they were white and Andrea was black. They proved that they lived in an interracial neighborhood, that they attended an interracial church, and that their two children attended an interracial school. They had a stable marriage and financial standing. The Dearths filed a motion for review of this administrative decision in the Common Pleas Court. They requested that CSB's custody be terminated and that permanent custody of Andrea be granted to them. The court denied the Dearths' motion. The Dearths appealed. The appeals court found that there was clear evidence that CSB had a documented policy of placing black children with white adoptive parents only when no black parent could be found. Under Ohio law, adoption placements are to be made in the "best interests of the child." To what extent can adoption agencies such as CSB consider factors such as race and culture in determining adoption procedures? Under the law, can the racial factor outweigh all other considerations?

   In re Moorhead, 600 N.E.2d 778 (1991)

2. Charles Collins and Bethany Guggenheim began living together in 1977. They were not married to each other. Bethany was recently divorced and had two children from the prior marriage. As part of the property settlement, she had received title to a sixty-eight-acre farm, and Charles, Bethany, and the children moved there in 1979. They intended to restore the circa 1740 farmhouse. Charles and Bethany jointly became liable for and made payments on a bank mortgage loan, insurance, and property taxes. They maintained a joint checking account to pay for joint expenses as well as individual checking accounts. They jointly purchased a tractor and other equipment, Charles paying two-thirds of the cost and Bethany one-third. Charles also invested $8,000 of his money in additional equipment and improvements for the farm. For several years they jointly operated a small business that made no profit. Despite Charles's contributions, the title to the farm remained at all times with Bethany. The parties experienced personal difficulties, and when they could not reconcile their differences, they permanently separated in 1986. During their cohabitation period, Charles contributed approximately $55,000 and Bethany $44,500 to the farm. Charles filed suit against Bethany. He claimed that fairness required either that Bethany and he should share title to the farm as tenants in common, or that he should receive an equitable distribution of the property acquired during the period of cohabitation. Charles did not allege that Bethany had breached any contract or engaged in any type of misconduct. The trial

court dismissed the complaint. What action should a court take in a situation such as this, where unmarried, cohabiting people go their separate ways?

Collins v. Guggenheim, 631 N.E.2d 1016 (1994)

3. James Ellam filed suit for divorce against his wife, Ann, on the ground that they had been living separately and apart. Ann counterclaimed against James for desertion. The facts reveal that James moved out of the marital home on July 5, 1972, because of severe marital discord. He moved back to his mother's home in a nearby city, where he slept, kept his clothes, and ate some of his meals. For the next eighteen months, James had an unusual weekday routine. His mother would drive James early in the morning from her home to the marital home so that James could see his dog, check on the house, take his car out of the garage, and go to work, much as he had done before he and Ann "separated." At the end of the day, James would drive to the marital residence, put the car back in the garage, play with the dog, talk with his wife until she went to bed, and watch television until 12:30 A.M., when his mother would pick him up and take him "home." On weekends, James would do chores at the marital home and even socialize with his wife (although the parties had terminated their sexual relationship). James lived this way because he claimed to love his wife and especially the dog, he wanted to maintain the marital home properly, and he did not want the neighbors to know about his marital problems. New Jersey law provides that persons who have lived separate and apart for a statutory period of time may be granted a divorce. Should the trial court have granted a divorce on the grounds that James and Ann had satisfied the statutory requirements by living "separate and apart in different habitations," as permitted under New Jersey law?

Ellam v. Ellam, 333 A.2d 577 (1975)

4. The state statute provides as follows: "The expenses of the family ... are chargeable upon the property of both husband and wife, or either of them, and in relation thereto they may be sued jointly or separately."... Should a husband be financially obligated to pay the legal costs resulting from his wife's appeal of criminal convictions?

State v. Clark, 563 P.2d 1253 (1977)

5. Oregon law provides for "no-fault" divorces. Marie and Max Dunn had been married for 20 years when Marie filed for divorce. After Marie presented evidence of irremediable and irreconcilable differences between herself and her husband, the trial court entered a decree dissolving the marriage. The court also awarded Marie custody of their two minor children, and set alimony at $200 per month. Max appealed to the Oregon Court of Appeals on the ground that the trial court's decree was premature and was not supported by adequate proof. Max argued that the court acted without considering the views of both parties to the marriage. The appellate court interpreted the Oregon statute to require only that the trial court determine whether the existing difference "reasonably appears to the court to be in the mind of the petitioner an irreconcilable one, and based on that difference ... whether or not ... the breakdown of that particular marriage is irremediable." What public policy arguments can you identify related to the facts in the above case that would favor "no-fault" divorces? What arguments could be brought to bear against them?

Dunn v. Dunn, 511 P.2d 427 (1973)

6. Sixteen-year-old Colleen provided day care for twelve-year-old Shane. The two began a sexual relationship that resulted in Colleen giving birth to a child when the mother and father were seventeen and thirteen years old, respectively. Although Shane was a victim of child abuse himself, a Kansas district court judge

ordered him to pay $50 child support per month and found him financially responsible for over $7,000 in other assistance provided to the mother and baby in conjunction with the childbirth. Shane filed an appeal arguing that since he could not legally consent to sexual

relations with Colleen, he should not be legally obligated to pay child support.

What public policies are in conflict in this case? How do you think the Kansas Supreme Court ruled and why?

State ex rel. Hermesmann v. Seyer, 847 P.2d 1273 (1993)

NOTES

1. J. Demos, "A Little Commonwealth: Family Life in Plymouth," in *Family and State,* ed. L. Houlgate (Totowa, NJ: Rowman & Littlefield, 1988), pp. 30-31.

2. *Statistical Abstract of the United States: 2012,* Table 1337: Single-Parent Households: 1980 to 2009.

3. U.S. Census Bureau, *American Community Survey Briefs: Same-Sex Couple Households* (Issued September 2011), Table I: Distribution of Same-Sex Couple Households by States Grouped by Legal Recognition of Same-Sex Couple Marriages and Unions: 2010, and Table 2: Couple Households with Children: 2010.

4. B. Yorburg, *The Changing Family* (New York: Columbia University Press, 1973), p. 94.

5. D. Castle, "Early Emancipation Statutes: Should They Protect Parents as Well as Children?" 20 *Family Law Quarterly* 363 (Fall 1986).

6. H. Jacob, *Silent Revolution* (Chicago: University of Chicago Press, 1988) p. 1.

7. M. Grossberg, *Governing the Hearth* (Chapel Hill: University of North Carolina Press, 1985), p. 3.

8. L. Houlgate, *Family and State* (Totowa, NJ: Rowman & Littlefield, 1988).

9. E. Pound, "Individual Interests in Domestic Relations," 14 *Michigan Law Review* 177, 179–181 (1916).

10. L. Wardle, C. Blakeseley, and J. Parker, *Contemporary Family Law* (Deerfield, IL: Clark Boardman Callaghan, 1988), Sec. 1:02.

11. E. Jenks, *A Short History of English Law,* 2d rev. ed. (Boston: Little, Brown & Co., 1922), n. 24 at 20–22.

12. Wardle, Blakeseley, and Parker, Sec. 1:02.

13. Ibid., Sec. 1:03.

14. *Wisconsin v. Yoder,* 406 U.S. 205, 229–230 (1972).

15. P. C. Hoffer, *Law and People in Colonial America* (Baltimore: Johns Hopkins University Press, 1982).

16. Grossberg, pp. 3–4.

17. Ibid., p. 5.

18. Ibid., p. 6.

19. R. Melton, "Evolving Definition of 'Family,'" 1990–1991 *Journal of Family Law* 504.

20. *Braschi v. Stahl Association,* 543 N.E.2d 49, 58 (1989).

21. Ibid., pp. 53–54.

22. J. Collier, M. Rosaldo, and S. Yanagisako, "Is There a Family? New Anthropological Views," in *Rethinking the Family: Some Feminist Questions,* ed. B. Thorne and M. Yalon (New York: Longman, 1982), pp. 25–39.

23. M. Farmer, *The Family* (London: Longmans, Green and Co., 1970), p. 17.

24. H. D. Krause, *Family Law in a Nutshell,* 2d ed. (St. Paul, MN: West Publishing, 1986), pp. 31–32.

25. *Maynard v. Hill,* 125 U.S. 211 (1888).

26. Wardle, Blakeseley, and Parker, Sec. 3:02.

27. National Commission for Adoption, *Adoption Factbook* 18 (Alexandria, VA, 1989), p. 18.

28. J. Evall, "Sexual Orientation and Adoptive Matching," 24 *Family Law Quarterly* 349 (1991).

29. Some states require that a petitioner be older than the person to be adopted by at least ten years or more, whereas others require that the adoptee not be related to the petitioner. Some states also refuse to allow an adult petitioner to adopt another adult who happens to be the petitioner's homosexual partner, where the parties may be trying to use the adoption law to circumvent the marriage, contract, and probate laws.

30. Krause, p. 163.

31. E. Bartholet, *Family Bonds* (Boston: Houghton Mifflin, 1993), p. 66.

32. Ibid., p. 71.

33. Ibid., pp. 70–72.

34. L. Schwartz, "Religious Matching for Adoption: Unraveling the Interests Behind the 'Best Interests' Standard," 25 *Family Law Quarterly* 2 (Summer 1991).

35. *Wisconsin,* 406 U.S. at 229–230.

36. Ibid., p. 189.

37. Ibid.

38. Evall, pp. 356–357.

39. Ibid., pp. 354-355.

40. Bartholet, p. 48.

41. Ibid., p. 55.

42. Ibid., p. 56.

43. Adoption and Foster Care Analysis and Reporting System (AFCARS), *Interim FY 2008 Estimates as of October 2009,* U.S. Dept. of Health and Human Services.

44. A. Hardin, ed., *Foster Children in the Courts,* Foster Care Project, National Legal Resource Center for Child Advocacy and Protection (Chicago: American Bar Association, 1983), p. 70.

45. *Foster Care Fact Sheet* (New York, NY, Evan B. Donaldson Adoption Institute, 2002).

46. American Public Welfare Association, as quoted in *Newsweek,* April 25, 1994, p. 55.

47. HHS Press Release of September 14, 2009, "HHS Awards $35 Million to States for Increasing Adoptions." http://www.hhs.gov/news/press/2009pres/09/20090914a.html

48. Jacob, p. 1.

49. States differ as to exactly what level of support must be provided. Some states define necessaries to be essentially the most basic needs, whereas other states are more generous in their construction of that term.

50. C. Hused, "Married Woman's Property Law 1800–1850," 71 *Georgetown Law Journal* 1359, n. 4 at 1400 (1983). Also see *Thompson v. Thompson,* 218 U.S. 611 (1910).

51. *Griswold v. Connecticut,* 381 U.S. 479 (1965).

52. *Wisconsin,* 406 U.S. at 229–230.

53. See Kentucky Revised Statutes Sec. 205.310, South Dakota Codified Laws Annotated Sec. 25-7-8, and Washington Revised Code Sec. 26.16.205. See also *M. H. B. v. H. T. B.,* 498 A.2d 775 (1985).

54. See Alaska Statutes Sec. 47.25.250, Iowa Code Sec. 252.5, *Estate of Hines,* 573 P.2d 1260 (1978), and Wisconsin Statutes Annotated Sec. 940.27.

55. The following information on emancipation is taken from http://www.nolo.com/legal-encyclopedia/emancipation-of-minors-32237.html:

A minor who is "emancipated" assumes most adult responsibilities before reaching the age of majority (usually 18). Emancipated minors are no longer considered to be under the care and control of parents—

instead, they take responsibility for their own care....

If a young person under the age of majority is emancipated, the parent or guardian no longer has any say over the minor's life. An emancipated minor can keep earnings from a job, decide where to live, make his or her own medical decisions, and more....

Eligibility can vary depending on state laws, but usually minors can obtain emancipation from parents or legal guardians by:

1. getting married

2. joining the military, or

3. obtaining a court's permission....

States differ as to the emancipation of minors. Some states have statutes that specify the circumstances and judges in all states rule on petitions for emancipation, making decisions on a case-by-case basis after taking into consideration the best interests of the minor. The following website contains statutory references for each state: http://www.law.cornell.edu/wex/table_emancipation

56. See Alaska Statutes Sec. 25.20.030 and Oregon Revised Statutes Sec. 109.010.

57. See *Mahan v. Mahan,* 88 So. 2d 545 (1956).

58. See *Heup v. Heup,* 172 N.W.2d 334 (1969).

59. Maryland Annotated Code Article 16, Sec. 27.

60. New Hampshire Revised Statutes Annotated Sec. 458:17 and Minnesota Statutes Sec. 518.57.

61. 4 *American Jurisprudence* 2d, 513.

62. *Posner v. Posner,* 233 So. 2d 381 (1970).

63. Jacob, p. 30.

64. Ibid., p. 4.

65. U.S. Bureau of the Census, *Historical Statistics of the United States, Colonial Times to 1957* (Washington, DC: U.S. Bureau of the Census, 1960), p. 25.

66. This is not to suggest that the amount of choice is equally distributed throughout society and is not affected by considerations of race, gender, and socioeconomic status.

67. It is important to emphasize that, in all eras, some spouses and parents have deserted their partners and families without bothering with legal formalities. Note also that the primary victims have been women who devoted their lives to their families and homes and who were often left destitute and with children. This has contributed to what is often referred to as the feminization of poverty.

68. Jacob, p. 251.

69. Ibid., p. 47.

70. Ibid., pp. 46-47.

71. Ibid., p. 34.

72. Walter Wadlington, "Divorce Without Fault Without Perjury," 52 *Virginia Law Review,* 32, 40 (1966).

73. Jacob, pp. 60-61.

74. Ibid., p. 59.

75. Ibid., p. 80.

76. *Hagerty v. Hagerty,* 281 N.W.2d 386 (1979).

77. Doris J. Freed, and Timothy B. Walker, "Family Law in the Fifty States: An Overview," 24 *Family Law Review* 309, 355 (1991).

78. Andrew I. Shepard. "Taking Children Seriously: Promoting Cooperative Custody After Divorce," 64 *Texas Law Review* 687 (1985).

79. S. Quinn, "Fathers Cry for Custody," *Juris Doctor* 42 (May 1976).

80. R. Cochran Jr., "Reconciling the Primary Caretaker Preference, and Joint Custody Preference and the Case-by-Case Rule," in *Joint Custody and Shared Parenting,* ed. Jay Folberg (New York: Guilford Press, 1991), pp. 218–219.

81. J. Goldstein, A. Freud, and A. Solnit, *Beyond the Best Interests of the Child* (New York: Free Press, 1970), pp. 107–109.

82. Cochran, p. 222.

83. M. Elkin, Joint Custody: In the Best Interest of the Family in *Joint Custody and Shared Parenting,* ed. Jay Folberg (New York: Guilford Press, 1991), pp. 12–13.

84. Ibid., p. 13.

85. See *Gruber v. Gruber,* 583 A.2d 434 (1990), and *In re Miroballi,* 589 N.E.2d 565 (1992), for cases supporting a parent's right to relocate. See *Plowman v. Plowman,* 597 A.2d 701 (1991), for a contrary opinion.

86. See *Fortenberry v. Fortenberry,* 338 S.E.2d 342 (1985), *Toomey v. Toomey,* 636 S.W.2d 313 (1982), and *Neudecker v. Neudecker,* 577 N.E.2d 960 (1991).

87. Krause, p. 211.

X

Contracts

CHAPTER OBJECTIVES

1. *Understand the origins of the modern contract action.*
2. *Identify and explain the essential requirements of an enforceable contract.*
3. *Explain how contracts are classified in terms of validity and enforceability.*
4. *Identify and explain the legal and equitable remedies available to an injured party when a contract is breached.*
5. *Understand how contractual rights and duties are transferred.*

Before exploring the roots of modern American contract law, readers should pause and think about what life would be like if contract law didn't exist. How many times do you go on the Internet or enter a store to make a purchase? Maybe you are buying electronics or booking a flight, cruise, or vacation. Perhaps you have purchased a used car from a dealer, or health or auto insurance, or you have placed an order with a bakery for a birthday cake. What all of these illustrations have in common is that you, the purchaser, are relying on promises of performance oftentimes made by complete strangers with whom you have had no prior dealings. The promises may turn out to be false or fraudulent, the performance incomplete or unsatisfactory. But you will not have any legal remedy unless the seller's promises were made under circumstances that, under contract law, entitle you to legal protection. This chapter introduces readers to many of the rules that define the types of promises that are and are not entitled to legal protection.

A BRIEF HISTORY OF AMERICAN CONTRACT LAW

It has taken centuries for American contract law to evolve to its present form. The modern contract action can be traced to the English common-law writs of debt, detinue, and covenant, which were created in the twelfth and thirteenth centuries.[1] The **writ of debt** was used to collect a specific sum of money owed. **Detinue** was used against one who had possession of another's personal property and refused to return it when requested by the true owner. **Covenant** was initially used to enforce agreements relating to land (especially leases).[2] Later it was employed to enforce written agreements under seal.[3] Gradually, these writs were supplemented by the common law **writ of trespass,** which included trespass to land, assaults, batteries, the taking of goods, and false imprisonment. Each of these acts involved a tortfeasor who directly caused injury to the victim by force and arms, and thereby violated the King's peace.

In 1285, Parliament enacted the Statute of Westminster, which authorized the chancery to create a new writ, called **trespass on the case,** to address private wrongs that fell outside the traditional boundaries of trespass.[4] *Case,* as it came to be called, could remedy injuries that resulted from the defendant's failure to perform a professional duty that in turn resulted in harm to the plaintiff. Thus case would be appropriate where *A*'s property was damaged while entrusted to *B*, as a result of *B*'s failure to exercise proper skill or care.[5] These early writs were based on property rights and were not based on modern contractual notions such as offer, acceptance, and consideration.

In the fifteenth and sixteenth centuries, some breaches of duty (called *undertakings*) that had been included within the writ of trespass on the case evolved into a new writ called **assumpsit.**[6] For example, in one early case a ferry operator was sued in assumpsit for improperly loading his boat such that the plaintiff's mare drowned while crossing the Humber River.[7] By the early 1500s, a plaintiff could also sue in assumpsit for nonfeasance (failure to perform a promise).[8] During the 1560s, plaintiffs bringing assumpsit actions generally were required to allege that undertakings were supported by **consideration** (the "this for that" inducement that motivates the parties to reach an agreement).[9] Consideration grew in importance, and in the 1700s chancellors began refusing to order specific performance if they thought the consideration inadequate.[10] This development made the enforceability of contracts uncertain because judges could invalidate agreements reached by the parties and could prevent the parties from making their own bargains.

Assumpsit was the principal "contract" action until the early 1800s, when economic changes and widespread dissatisfaction with the technical requirements and expense of common law pleading resulted in an erosion of the common law approach.[11] The 1800s brought a significant shift in thinking: away from the old writs and toward the emerging new substantive action, called contract, which included all types of obligations. Contributing to the demise of assumpsit was the old-fashioned notion that courts had a responsibility to ensure that contracting parties received equivalent value from their bargains.[12] It became apparent that commercial prosperity required that courts protect the parties' expectation damages (the return the respective parties each had been promised in an agreement by the other party).[13] When the courts responded to these changes and demands, contract law rapidly developed. New York's replacement of the writ system in 1848 with its newly enacted Code of Civil Procedure established a trend toward modern code pleading that swept the nation.[14]

By 1850, American courts had accepted the notion that contracts are based on the reciprocal promises of the parties.[15] As courts became increasingly willing to enforce private agreements, they began to recognize the customs of each trade, profession, and business, rather than general customs. The courts often would disregard existing legal requirements in favor of the rules created by the contracting parties. This fragmentation of law was bad for business. The absence of a widely accepted code of contract rules resulted in unpredictability and uncertainty in American society, the economy, and the courts. This caused business firms to press for uniform laws dealing with commercial transactions among states.

In the 1890s, the American Bar Association established the National Conference of Commissioners on Uniform State Laws to encourage states to enact uniform legislation. The Uniform Sales Act and the Negotiable Instruments Law were two products of this movement. During this era, Samuel Williston and Arthur Corbin wrote widely accepted treatises on the law of contracts. Then, in 1928, an esteemed group of lawyers, judges and law professors, collectively associated with the American Law Institute, developed and published the Restatement of Contracts, a proposed code of contract rules that was grounded in the common law.

In 1942, the American Law Institute and the American Bar Association sponsored a project to develop a **Uniform Commercial Code (UCC),** which was completed in 1952. In 1953, Pennsylvania was the first state to adopt the UCC. The code covers sales, commercial paper, bank collection processes, letters of credit, bulk transfers, warehouse receipts, bills of lading and other documents of title, investment securities, and secured transactions. The UCC governs only sales of (and contracts to sell) goods, defined as movables (personal property having tangible form). It does not cover transactions involving realty, services, or the sale of intangibles. If a contract involves a mixed goods–services sale (for example, application of a hair product as part of a beauty treatment), the courts tend to apply the UCC only if the sale-of-goods aspect dominates the transaction. The UCC has been adopted at least partially in all 50 states and is the legislation that has had the largest impact on the law of contracts.

NATURE AND CLASSIFICATION OF CONTRACTS

A **contract** is a legally enforceable agreement containing one or more promises. Not every promise is a contract—only those promises enforceable by law. Although the word *contract* is often used when referring to a written document that contains the terms of the contract, in the legal sense the word *contract* does not mean the tangible document, but rather the legally enforceable agreement itself.

In order to establish an enforceable contract, there must be (1) an agreement (2) between competent parties (3) based on genuine assent of the parties (4) supported by consideration (5) that does not contravene principles of law and (6) that is in writing (in certain circumstances). Each of these requirements is discussed in detail in this chapter.

An **agreement** is an expression of the parties' willingness to be bound to the terms of the contract. Usually, one party offers a proposal, and the other agrees to the terms by accepting it. Both parties to the contract must be **competent.** Some people—because of age or mental disability—are not competent and thus do not have, from the legal standpoint, the capacity to bind themselves contractually. **Genuine assent** of both parties is also necessary. It is presumed to exist unless one of the parties is induced to agree because of misrepresentation, fraud, duress, undue influence, or mistake.

Consideration on the part of both parties is an essential element of a contract. One party's promise (or consideration) must be bargained for and given in exchange for the other's act or promise (his consideration). The bargain cannot involve something that is prohibited by law or that is against the best interests of society. And, finally, certain contracts, to be enforceable, must be evidenced in writing.

Common law is the primary source of the law of contracts. Many statutes affect contracts, especially specific types of contracts such as employment and insurance agreements. But the overwhelming body of contractual principles is embodied in court decisions.

Valid, Void, Voidable, and Unenforceable Contracts

Contracts can be classified in terms of validity and enforceability. A **valid contract** is a binding and enforceable agreement that meets all the necessary contractual requirements. A contract is said to be valid and enforceable when a person is entitled to judicial relief in case of breach by the other party.

A **void contract** means no contract, because no legal obligation has been created. When an agreement lacks a necessary contractual element—such as consideration—the agreement is without legal effect, and therefore is void.

A **voidable contract** exists when one of the parties can elect to avoid an obligation created by a contract because of the manner in which the contract was brought about. For example, someone who has been induced to make a contract by fraud or duress may be able to avoid the obligation created by the contract. Contracts made by those who are not of legal age also are voidable, at the option of the party lacking legal capacity. A voidable contract is not wholly lacking in legal effect because not all the parties can legally avoid their duties under it. This means that a party who has capacity can be required to fulfill all contractual obligations owed to an opposite party who lacks capacity, if the party lacking capacity elects not to void the deal and fully performs all obligations. A contract is **unenforceable** (as opposed to *void* or *voidable*) when a defense to the enforceability of the contract is present. For example, a court will not enforce an agreement that must be reduced to writing if a sufficient writing cannot be produced. Also, when a party wanting to enforce a contract waits beyond the time period prescribed by law to bring the court action (statute of limitations), the contract is unenforceable.

Bilateral and Unilateral Contracts

All contracts involve at least two parties. **Bilateral contracts** consist simply of mutual promises by each party to do some future act. The promises need not be express on both sides; one of the promises could be implied from the surrounding circumstances.

A **unilateral contract** results when one party makes a promise in exchange for another person performing an act or refraining from doing something. For example, assume that someone wants to buy an item owned by another for $100. If the buyer promises to pay the owner $100 for the item if and when the owner conveys legal title and possession to the buyer, a unilateral contract is created. It is a *promise* in exchange for an *act*. The contract comes into existence when the act of conveying title and possession is performed. If, however, the buyer promises to pay $100 in exchange for the owner's *promise* to convey title and possession of the item, a bilateral contract results. A *bilateral* contract comes into existence when mutual promises are made.

AGREEMENT

In order for a contract to be formed, there must be mutual agreement between two or more competent parties, who must manifest their intent to be bound to definite terms. The agreement usually is reached by one party making an offer and the other—expressly or impliedly—accepting the terms of the offer.

The intention of the parties is the primary factor determining the nature of the contract. This is ascertained not just from the words used by the parties, but also from the entire situation, including the acts and conduct of the parties. In determining the intent of the parties, the courts generally use an objective rather than a subjective test. In an objective test, the question would be "What would a reasonable person in the position of party *A* think was meant by the words, conduct, or both of party *B*?" If a subjective test were used, the question would be "What did party *A* actually mean by certain expressions?" For example, suppose that one of the parties is not serious about creating a legal obligation, but the other party has no way of knowing this. Under the objective test, a contract still would be created.

In law, invitations to social events lack contractual intention and, when accepted, do not give rise to a binding contract. For example, when two people agree to have dinner together or to go to a baseball game together, each usually feels a moral obligation to fulfill his or her promise. Neither, however, expects to be legally bound by the agreement. An agreement also lacks contractual intent when a party's assent to it is made in obvious anger, excitement, or jest. This is true even when the parties' expressions, if taken literally as stated, would amount to mutual assent. Sometimes it is not obvious that a proposal is made in anger, excitement, or jest. Under the objective test, the surrounding circumstances and context of the expressions would be examined to determine what a reasonably prudent person would believe.

Offer

An **offer** is a proposal to make a contract. It is a promise conditional on a return promise, act, or forbearance being given by the offeree. The return promise, act, or forbearance is acceptance of the offer.

A legally effective offer must be (1) a definite proposal (2) made with the intent to contract and (3) communicated to the offeree. The terms of the offer, on acceptance, become the terms of the contract. An offer must be definite and certain, so that when the offeree accepts, both parties understand the obligations they have created.

It is important to distinguish between a definite proposal, which is an offer, and a solicitation of an offer. A willingness to make or receive an offer is not itself an offer, but an invitation to negotiate. For example, the question "Would you be interested in buying my television set for $100?" is considered an invitation to negotiate. A "yes" response would not create a contract, since there was no definite proposal made (form of payment, when due, etc.).

For an offer to be effective, it need not be made to one specific named person. It can be made to the general public, in the form of an advertisement. These may be circulars, quotation sheets, displays, and announcements in publications. However, the publication of the fact that an item is for sale, along with its price, is usually an invitation to negotiate, not an offer.

Termination of an Offer

The **offeree** (the person to whom the offer is made) can bind the **offeror** (the person who makes the offer) to his or her proposal for the duration of the offer—the time from the moment an offer is effectively communicated to the offeree until it is terminated. An offer can be terminated by (1) revocation by the offeror (if the revocation is made before the offeree accepts), (2) lapse of time, (3) subsequent illegality, (4) destruction of the subject matter, (5) death or lack of capacity, (6) rejection, or (7) because the offeree makes a counteroffer.

An offeror has the power to terminate the offer by revocation at any time before it is accepted. Even when an offeror promises to hold an offer open for a certain period of time, the offeror can revoke the offer before that time, unless consideration is given to hold the offer open. For example, if a seller promises in an offer to give the offeree one week to accept the offer, the seller still retains the power to withdraw the offer at any time.

A contract whereby an offeror is bound to hold an offer open for a period of time is called an **option**. In an option contract, consideration is necessary in return for the promise to hold the offer open. For example, if the offeree pays the offeror $10 to hold an offer open for ten days, the offeror does not have the power to withdraw the offer before the ten-day period is up.

If an offer stipulates how long it will remain open, it automatically terminates with the expiration of that period of time. When an offer does not stipulate a time period within which it may be accepted, it is then effective for a "reasonable" length of time.

An offer to enter into an agreement forbidden by law is ineffective and void, even if the offer was legal when made. If the subject matter of an offer is destroyed, the offer is automatically terminated because of impossibility. (For example, if a painter contracts to paint the owner's garage, but before the painter can commence the work, the garage is totally destroyed by a tornado, the agreement would be terminated due to an unforeseeable natural disaster.)

An offer is terminated prior to acceptance by the death of either the offeror or the offeree. Adjudication of insanity prior to acceptance usually has the same effect as death in terminating an offer. The termination is effective automatically, without any need for the terminating party to give notice. For example, if a person offers to sell an item at a stated price, but dies before the offer is accepted, there can be no contract, because one of the parties died before a meeting of the minds took place. If the offeree had accepted the offer before the death, however, there would have been a meeting of minds, and the offeror's estate would be responsible under the contract.

An offer is also terminated by a rejection or a counteroffer. When an offeree does not intend to accept an offer and so informs the offeror, the offer is said to have been terminated by rejection. If the offeree responds to an offer by making another proposal, the proposal constitutes a counteroffer and terminates the original offer. For example, if an offer is made to sell merchandise for $300 and the offeree offers to buy this merchandise for $250, the offeree has rejected the original offer by making a counteroffer. However, an *inquiry,* or a request for additional terms by the offeree, is not a counteroffer and does not terminate the offer. Thus, if the offeree had asked whether the offeror would consider reducing the price to $250, this inquiry would not terminate the original offer.

Acceptance

An **acceptance** is the agreement of the offeree (the person to whom an offer has been made) to be bound by the terms of the offer. There is no meeting of the minds until the offeree has consented to the proposition contained in the offer. In order for an acceptance to be effective in creating a contract, there must be (1) an unconditional consent (2) to an open offer (3) by the offeree only and (4) communicated to the offeror. In addition, there must be some act of manifestation of the intention to contract. This can be in the form of (1) silence or inaction, (2) a promise, (3) an act or forbearance from an act, or (4) any other manner specifically stipulated in the offer.

In most situations, silence or inaction on the part of the offeree does not constitute acceptance. When a person receives goods or services expecting that they will have to be paid for, the act of receiving the goods or services constitutes acceptance of the offer. An offeror is usually not permitted to word the offer in such a way that silence or inaction of the offeree constitutes acceptance. However, silence or inaction *can* do so in situations in which this method of dealing has been established by agreement between the parties or by prior dealings of the parties.

In an offer to enter into a bilateral contract, the offeree must communicate acceptance in the form of a promise to the offeror. The offeror must be made aware, by the express or implied promise, that a contract has been formed. An offer to enter into a unilateral contract requires an acceptance in the form of an act. A mere promise to perform the act is not an effective acceptance.

The offeror has the power to specify the means and methods of acceptance, and the acceptance must comply with those requirements. For example, an oral acceptance of an offer that called for a written acceptance would be ineffective. If nothing is stated, a reasonable means or method of acceptance is effective. An offer can provide that the acceptance is effective only on the completion of specified formalities. In such a situation, all these formalities must be complied with in order to have an effective acceptance.

At common law, an acceptance must be a "mirror image" of the offer. If it changes the terms of an offer in any way, it acts only as a counteroffer and has no effect as an acceptance. Under the UCC (Section 2-207), an acceptance that adds some new or different terms to a contract involving the sale of goods does create a contract. The new terms are treated as proposals that must be accepted separately.

Introduction to *Cea v. Hoffman*

The appellants in this case, Al and Laura Cea, wanted to have a modular log home erected on property they owned in California. They signed a purchase agreement with ATC (American Timber-Craft, LLC) and Roger Hoffmann to build this structure, and paid the builders $172,116 as a down payment. Thereafter, ATC had financial troubles and arranged for Modular Manufacturing, LLC, Investors Collaborative, LLC, and Roger Hoffman (the appellees) to purchase some of ATC's assets. Consequently, the appellees purchased some of ATC's assets and in return acquired ATC's contractual rights and duties with respect to the construction of the Ceas' log home. Negotiations between the parties broke down, and the Ceas filed suit. The trial court granted summary judgment to the builders, and the Ceas appealed to the Utah Court of Appeals.

Al Cea and Laura Cea v. Roger Hoffman
276 P.3d 1178
Court of Appeals of Utah
April 5, 2012

Voros, Associate Presiding Judge.

... This case arises from the Ceas' unsuccessful attempt to purchase a modular log home and have it delivered to their property in California. In June 2006, the Ceas entered into a purchase agreement with American TimberCraft, LLC (ATC), a Utah limited liability company. Pursuant to that agreement, the Ceas made a down payment of $172,116—half the total purchase price—to ATC. ATC incurred financial difficulties and never began construction of the home. In November 2006, ATC signed an agreement with Modular in which Modular "acquir[ed] from ATC its work in progress and pending orders along with all related deposits and down payments," including the Ceas' $172,116.

Six months later, Modular sent the Ceas a letter (the Modular Letter) explaining that ATC had "ceased operations," "liquidated all company assets," and was "no longer capable of completing or performing on its contract with [the Ceas]." However, the Modular Letter added, "all is not lost." Modular had acquired ATC's assets and proposed two options.

The first option was for Modular to complete the Ceas' log home:

> Although Modular did not purchase [ATC] itself[,] as part of the asset acquisitions[,] Modular agreed to complete all work in progress, including orders for which deposits have been taken (even if no physical work has commenced). Therefore if you had an order with [ATC], Modular has agreed to complete the work on your home for the previously agreed price, even though it did not acquire your actual contract from [ATC].... If you decide that you would like to proceed, enter into a new contract and have your home completed, there are some minor modifications to terms and payment schedules. However the specifications for the home itself will not change nor will the price.

The second option was for Modular to refund the Ceas' deposit:

> At this point in time we (as [Modular]) will be issuing new contracts for your home construction (regardless of what stage of construction it may be in) in order to complete and give you the assurance of a valid contract for performance. In lieu of a new contract we will be willing to pay you whatever deposits or payments you made to [ATC] for your home should you decide that you would prefer to cancel and just walk away.

... The Ceas responded with a letter (the First Cea Letter) purporting to accept Modular's proposal to build and deliver the home. However, the Ceas sought to change the specifications and place of delivery of the home and sought additional terms not offered by Modular, including a new delivery date:

> Please prepare a new contract for us showing the $172,116 paid in thr[ough] June 7, 2006. We wish to delete the garage. Also, please reflect the 5% of total contract to be retained by us and paid upon final setting ... of log shell.
> [W]e are changing the location of the job, our frustration with this project has taken a great toll on us in more ways than you can imagine. We ... will take delivery on a new parcel ... [and] we will obtain all necessary permits....
> We hope and expect our new delivery date for this shell to be on or before July 31, 2007.

Modular did not respond to the First Cea Letter. One week later, the Ceas sent a second letter (the Second Cea Letter) purporting to accept Modular's proposal to refund their deposit:

> Upon further consideration, we respectfully request that, in accordance with your December letter, you refund the $172,116 we have paid as a deposit on our log home.
> Please send a check at your earliest convenience.... This has been a very difficult

decision for us, but we don't believe your company can deliver a log home to us in any reasonable time frame.

Modular did not respond to the Second Cea Letter, nor did it refund the Ceas' deposit. Accordingly, in February 2008, the Ceas sued a number of defendants, including Modular, Investors, Hoffman, and ATC. The Ceas alleged (1) breach of contract for failure to build and deliver their home or, alternatively, for failing to refund the Ceas' deposit; (2) fraud or intentional misrepresentation; and (3) negligent or reckless misrepresentation. These causes of action all arose out of the Modular Letter....

Appellees successfully moved for summary judgment. The trial court ruled that Hoffman "is not personally liable for the actions of Modular" because "Hoffman never made any personal representations to the Ceas and that any action by Hoffman was limited to his capacity as a representative of [Modular]." It further ruled that Investors "is not personally liable for the actions of Modular" because Investors "never made any representations to the Ceas, and that any action by Investors was limited to its capacity as a representative of Modular." Finally, the court ruled that Modular and the Ceas never formed a binding contract and that Modular made no fraudulent or negligent misrepresentations. The Ceas appealed.

Issues and Standards of Review
The Ceas assert three principal claims of error. First, they contend that summary judgment should not have been granted, because discovery was not complete. Next, they contend that a genuine issue of material fact exists as to whether Hoffman is personally liable for his role in making distributions from Modular while Modular was insolvent. Finally, they contend that a genuine issue of law exists as to whether the Ceas and Modular formed a contract....

Analysis
[Claims I and II were decided against the Ceas on technical grounds.]

III. Contract Claims
The Ceas contend that the trial court erred by ruling as a matter of law that the Modular Letter was not an offer, that neither the First nor Second Cea Letter was an acceptance, and that no consideration existed for a contract. As we understand their argument, the Ceas maintain that the Modular Letter contained two alternative offers: (1) an offer to complete ATC's agreed performance, and (2) an offer to refund the Ceas' deposit. The Ceas argue that the First Cea Letter

constituted a valid acceptance of the offer to complete performance. Alternatively, the Ceas argue that the Second Cea Letter constituted a valid acceptance of the offer to refund their deposit.

Generally, formation of a contract requires an offer, an acceptance, and consideration.... An offer is a " 'manifestation of willingness to enter into a bargain, so made as to justify another person in understanding that his assent to the bargain is invited and will conclude it.' "... "For an offer to be one that would create a valid and binding contract, its terms must be definite and unambiguous."... The obligations of the parties must be "set forth with sufficient definiteness that [the contract] can be performed."... [S]ee Williston on Contracts § 4.21, at 644 (4th ed.) (discussing the definiteness of offers and noting that "[a] lack of definiteness in an agreement may concern the time of performance, the price to be paid, work to be done, property to be transferred, or miscellaneous stipulations to the agreement"). "The terms of a contract are reasonably certain if they provide a basis for determining the existence of a breach and for giving an appropriate remedy." Restatement (Second) of Contracts § 33(2). An offer (other than an option contract) may be withdrawn at any time before acceptance....

"An acceptance is a manifestation of assent to an offer, such that an objective, reasonable person is justified in understanding that a fully enforceable contract has been made.".... It "must unconditionally assent to all material terms presented in the offer, including price and method of performance, or it is a rejection of the offer."... "An offeree's proposal of different terms from those of the offer constitutes a counteroffer, and no contract arises unless the original offeror accepts it unconditionally."... 1 Corbin on Contracts § 3.27 (1993) ("Any expression of assent that changes the terms of the offer in any material respect may be operative as a counter-offer."). Generally, a counteroffer "operates as a rejection of the original offer." 1 Williston on Contracts § 5.3, at 908 (4th ed.).... The offeree's power to accept the original offer is thereby terminated. See Burton, 557 P.2d at 149. However, "[i]f the original offeror accepts the counteroffer before it is withdrawn, a binding contract is created."...

"Consideration is present when there is an act or promise given in exchange for the other party's promise."... "Thus, 'there is consideration whenever a promisor receives a benefit or where [a] promisee suffers a detriment, however slight.' "...

The proponent of the contract "has the burden of showing that an offer and acceptance were more probable than not."... Whether a contract exists between parties is ordinarily a question of law, reviewed for correctness.... Here, Appellees contend that the essential facts are undisputed. Although the Ceas frame the issue as one of fact—and disputed fact at that—they also argue that, given the existing factual picture, "a binding contractual relationship exists between these parties." We thus consider the question before us to be whether the undisputed facts show that the parties formed a contract under the foregoing principles of contract formation.

We first consider whether the parties formed a contract for the completion of construction. The Ceas challenge the trial court's ruling that the Modular Letter did not operate as an offer to complete construction due to the indefinite and uncertain nature of the contractual terms. However, we agree with Modular that, even if the Modular Letter operated as an offer, the First Cea Letter constituted a counteroffer and thus a rejection. As Modular notes, the First Cea letter sought to change material terms, including the specifications of the home, the location of delivery, and the time for completion of performance. The First Cea Letter was, therefore, a counteroffer that Modular did not accept. Accordingly, we affirm the trial court's ruling that the Ceas and Modular did not enter into a contract for Modular to complete construction and delivery of the home.

We next consider whether the parties formed a contract for the return of the Ceas' $172,116 deposit. Again, the trial court ruled that the Modular Letter was too indefinite and uncertain in its terms to operate as an offer. Modular likewise asserts that the Modular Letter was too indefinite to constitute a valid offer to refund the Ceas' deposit, because it was made in the context of a letter that had alternatives and options, indicating that the parties had not determined a course and were merely negotiating. We disagree.

The Modular Letter states that the Ceas may receive their deposit back instead of continuing with the construction and delivery of their home: "In lieu of a new contract we will be willing to pay you whatever deposits or payments you have made to ATC for your home should you decide that you would prefer to cancel and just walk away." It therefore expresses assent on behalf of Modular to refund the Ceas' deposit and it empowers the Ceas to accept that refund, end its relationship with Modular, "and walk away." Further, both parties were aware of the precise amount the Ceas had deposited, $172,116. The Modular Letter was therefore an effective offer to refund the deposit.

As noted above, the First Cea Letter included a counteroffer to Modular's proposal to complete construction. However, by not accepting that counteroffer, Modular left the Ceas free to withdraw it, which they effectively did in the Second Cea Letter. The Second Cea Letter also operated as an acceptance of Modular's offer to refund the deposit. That letter clearly states, "Upon further consideration, we respectfully request that, in accordance with your December letter, you refund the $172,116 we have paid as a deposit on our log home." Nothing suggests that "the parties had not come to an agreement on the essential terms of the contract."...

However, Modular contends that the First Cea Letter, by countering and thus rejecting the offer to build and deliver the home, also effectively rejected the offer to refund the Ceas' $172,116 deposit. In more general terms, Modular argues that where an offeree receives two mutually exclusive offers, a counteroffer to the first offer rejects not only the first offer, but the second as well....

In simple terms, Modular said, "We have your $172,116. Do you want us to return the money or finish the job?" By counteroffering—and then withdrawing their counteroffer before Modular accepted it—the Ceas replied, in effect, "We don't want you to finish the job." The unstated implication of this reply was not "so just go ahead and keep our money"; it was, if anything, "so just go ahead and refund our money." Accordingly, the First Cea Letter did not reject Modular's refund offer, and the Second Cea Letter accepted it.

Finally, the Ceas contend that the trial court erred in ruling as a matter of law that the agreement was not supported by consideration. Modular conceded at oral argument that, assuming the Modular Letter operated as an offer to refund the Ceas' deposit and the Second Cea Letter operated as an acceptance of that offer, the resulting agreement was supported by adequate consideration....

Consequently, we hold that the trial court erred in ruling as a matter of law that no contract was formed between Modular and the Ceas with respect to the return of the Ceas' $172,116 deposit. We conclude that the undisputed record facts, together with Modular's concession on appeal, demonstrate that a contract was formed between the Ceas and Modular for the return of the Ceas' $172,116 deposit....

Conclusion

We conclude as a matter of law that Modular and the Ceas formed a contract for the return of the Ceas' $172,116 deposit, and we thus reverse the ruling of the trial court on this point. In all other respects, we affirm the ruling of the trial court. The case is remanded for further proceedings consistent with this opinion.

Case Questions

1. Would you classify this contract as being unilateral or bilateral? Explain.
2. According to the Court of Appeals, did the Ceas and Modular enter into a contract for the construction of the log home? Explain.
3. Why did the Court of Appeals conclude that the parties had contracted for the return of the down payment?

INTERNET TIP

Students can read a contract formation case entitled *Beaman Pontiac v. Gill* on the textbook's website. This case involves an oral, bilateral contract, and the opinion discusses issues involving the Uniform Commercial Code, the mailbox rule,[16] and the existence of consideration.

REALITY OF CONSENT

Genuine assent to be bound by a contract is not present when one of the parties' consent is obtained through duress, undue influence, fraud, or innocent misrepresentation, or when either of the parties, or both, made a mistake concerning the contract. Such contracts usually are voidable, and the injured party has the right to elect to avoid or affirm the agreement. (These defenses against the enforceability of a contract also can be used against other legal documents, such as wills, trust agreements, and completed gifts.)

An injured party who wishes to avoid or rescind a contract should act promptly. Silence beyond a reasonable length of time may be deemed an implied ratification. An injured party who elects to rescind a contract is entitled to **restitution**—the return of any property or money given in performance of the contract. The injured party also must return any property or money received through the contract.

Duress

Freedom of will of both parties to a contract is absolutely necessary. When one of the parties' wills is overcome because of duress, the agreement is voidable. **Duress** is any unlawful constraint exercised on people that forces their consent to an agreement that they would not otherwise have made. Unlike those situations in which people act as a result of fraud, innocent misrepresentation, or mistake, a person acting under duress does so knowingly. Three elements are necessary for duress to exist: (1) coercion (2) causing a loss of free will and (3) resulting in a consent to be bound by a contract.

Any form of constraint *improperly* exercised in order to get another's consent to contract is sufficient for coercion. Exercise of pressure to contract is not enough; it must be exercised wrongfully. Thus, advice, suggestion, or persuasion is not recognized as coercive. Likewise, causing a person to fear embarrassment or annoyance usually does not constitute duress. In order to amount to coercion, the constraint must entail threatened injury or force. For duress to exist, the person must enter into the agreement while under the influence of this threat.

The threat need not necessarily be to the person or the property of the contracting party. For example, a threat to injure the child of a contracting party could amount to duress. A threat of criminal prosecution gives rise to duress when fear overcomes judgment and deprives the person of the exercise of free will. Making a threat to sue, however—with the honest belief that it may be successful—is not using duress. For example, assume that an employee embezzles an undetermined amount of money from an employer. The employer estimates that the theft amounts to about $5,000 and threatens to bring a civil suit for damages unless the employee pays $5,000. Even though the employee takes the threat seriously and pays the $5,000, no duress exists. If the employer were to threaten to bring criminal charges under the same circumstances, however, duress would be present.

Economic distress or business compulsion may be grounds for duress. The surrounding circumstances of the business setting and the relative bargaining positions of the contracting parties are examined in order to determine whether duress is present.

Undue Influence

Undue influence occurs when the will of a dominant person is imposed on and substituted for that of another person, and the substitution is done in an unlawful fashion, resulting in an unfair agreement. Usually, undue influence is found when there is (1) a confidential relationship that is used to create (2) an unfair bargain.

In determining whether a confidential relationship exists, all the surrounding circumstances are examined to find out whether one of the parties dominates the other to the extent that the other is dependent on him or her. Family relationships, such as husband–wife or parent–child, often give rise to confidential relationships. Some relationships involving a special trust—such as trustee–beneficiary or attorney–client—entail a confidential relationship. Sometimes confidential relationships are created between business associates, neighbors, or friends. A person who is mentally weak—because of sickness, old age, or distress—may not be capable of resisting the dominant party's influence.

Whenever there is dominance in a confidential relationship, the court must determine whether the contract was equitable and voluntary. A contract is not invalid simply because there is a confidential relationship. A contract is voidable if one abuses the confidence in a relationship in order to obtain personal gain by substituting one's own will or interest for that of another. Whether the weaker party has had the benefit of independent advice is an important factor in determining fairness in contractual dealings. A legitimate suggestion or persuasion may influence someone, but it is not undue influence; nor, usually, is an appeal to the party's affections. When methods go beyond mere persuasion and prevent a person from acting freely, undue influence is present.

Fraud

The term **fraud** covers all intentional acts of deception used by one individual to gain an advantage over another. The essential elements of actionable fraud are (1) the misstatement of a material fact (2) made with knowledge of its falsity or in reckless disregard of its truth or falsity (3) with the intention to deceive (4) that induces reliance by the other party and (5) that results or will result in injury to the other party.

For fraud, misstatements must be of a fact, a *fact* being something that existed in the past or exists at present. The misstated fact must be material. The often-used definition of a **material fact** is a fact without which the contract would not have been entered into. The speaker, when making the statement of fact, must know that it is false. The stating party must have the intention to deceive, and thereby to induce the other party to enter into the contract.

The deceived party's reliance on the misstatement must be justified and reasonable. A party wishing to rescind a contract need not show actual damages resulting from the fraud. However, a party wishing to sue for damages in addition to rescission must prove that actual damage has been sustained. Assume, for example, that Carlotta purchases a dog from Enrique based on his statements that the dog is a purebred with a pedigree from the American Kennel Club. Carlotta can rescind the contract, return the dog, and recover the purchase price from Enrique if she later discovers that the dog actually is a crossbreed. Carlotta also may be able to recover restitution for the dog's medical care, food, and supplies, based on the principles of equity (Carlotta would be entitled to a sum equal to the amount Enrique was benefited because of the fact that Carlotta had assumed full responsibility for the dog's care).

Misrepresentation

Misrepresentation occurs when a party to a contract misrepresents a material fact, even if unknowingly, and the other party relies on and is misled by the falsehood. If a contract is induced by misrepresentation, the deceived party has the right of rescission. Fraud and misrepresentation are quite similar. However, the intent to deceive is the primary distinction between fraudulent and nonfraudulent misrepresentation. Rescission and restitution are available for both, although damages are not obtainable in cases of misrepresentation.

Mistake

Sometimes one or both of the parties to a contract unintentionally misunderstand material facts. If ignorance is of a fact that is material to the contract, a **mistake of fact** exists, and the contract may be voidable. Although a mistake of material fact related to the contract is sufficient for relief, a mistake of law is not.[17] In addition, the mistake must refer to a past or present material fact as of the time that the contract was formed, and not to a future possibility.

When one enters into a plain and unambiguous contract, one cannot avoid the obligation created by proving that its terms were misunderstood. Carelessness, poor judgment, lack of wisdom, and a mistake as to the true value of an item contracted for are not grounds for relief. Relief based on mistake may not be had simply because one party to a speculative contract expected it to turn out differently.

The court in the following case ordered rescission of an executed agreement and restitution because the parties to the contract made a mutual mistake.

Carter v. Matthews
701 S.W.2d 374
Supreme Court of Arkansas
January 13, 1986

Newbern, Justice.

This is a real estate sale case in which the chancellor granted rescission in favor of the appellant on the ground of mutual mistake but did not award the money damages she claimed. The damages she sought were for her expenses in constructing improvements that subsequently had to be removed from the land. The appellant claims it was error for the chancellor to have found she did not rely on misrepresentations made by the appellees through their real estate agent, and thus it was error to refuse her damages for fraud plus costs and an attorney fee. On cross-appeal, the appellees contend the only possible basis for the rescission was fraud, not mistake, and the chancellor erred in granting rescission once he had found there was no reliance by the appellant on any active or constructive misrepresentations of the appellees. We find the chancellor was correct on all counts, and thus we affirm on both appeal and cross-appeal.

1. Rescission

The chancellor found that conversations between the appellant and the appellees' agent showed that both parties were under the mistaken impression that the low, flat portion of land in question was suitable for building permanent structures such as a barn, horse corral and fencing. In fact, however, the area where the appellant attempted to build a barn and corral and which she wanted to use as pasture for horses was subject to severe and frequent flooding. The chancellor held there was thus a mutual mistake of fact making rescission proper. While there was evidence the appellees had known of one instance of severe flooding on the land, the evidence did not show they knew it was prone to the frequent and extensive flooding which turned out to be the case.

Other matters not known to the parties were that the low portion of the land, about two-thirds of the total acreage, is in the 100-year floodplain and that a Pulaski County ordinance ... requires a seller of land lying in the floodplain to inform the buyer of that fact no later than ten days before closing the transaction. The county planning ordinance also requires that no structures be built in the floodplain. If the chancellor's decision had been to permit rescission because of the parties' lack of knowledge of these items, we would have had before us the question whether the mistake was one of law rather than fact and thus perhaps irremediable....

While the chancellor mentions these items, his basis for rescission was the mutual lack of knowledge about the extent of the flooding, and misunderstanding of the suitability of the property, as a matter of fact, for the buyer's purposes which were known to both parties. We sustain his finding that there was a mutual mistake of fact. A mutual mistake of fact as to a material element of a contract is an appropriate basis for rescission....

2. Damages for Fraud
The chancellor refused to allow the appellant any damages for the loss she sustained with respect to the improvements she had placed in the floodplain. He found the appellant had made an independent investigation of the propensity of the property to become flooded and had ascertained, erroneously, that the property was not in the floodplain. Thus, in spite of the legal duty on the part of the appellees to tell the appellant that the land was in the floodplain, and what might have been the resultant constructive fraud upon failure to inform her, he held that fraud may not be the basis of a damages award absent reliance on the misrepresentation. For the same reason the chancellor refused to base his decision on any alleged fraud resulting from the appellees' failure to tell the appellant what they may have known about the land's propensity to flood. He was correct. An essential element of an action for deceit is reliance by the plaintiff on the defendant's misrepresentation.... In view of the strong evidence, including her own testimony, that the appellant made her own investigation as to whether the land flooded, the extent to which a creek running through the land was in the floodplain, and the feasibility of bridging the creek above the floodplain, we can hardly say the chancellor's factual determination that the appellant did not rely on the failure of the appellees to give her information known to them or which they had a duty to disclose to her under the ordinance was clearly erroneous....

When rescission is based on mutual mistake rather than fraud, the recoveries of the parties are limited to their restitutionary interests.... As the appellant could show no benefit conferred on the appellees from her attempted improvements on the land, she was entitled to no recovery in excess of the return of the purchase price, which was awarded to her by the chancellor, as well as cancellation of her note and mortgage....

Affirmed.

Case Questions

1. The plaintiff–appellant in this case went to court seeking rescission as well as damages. What, exactly, is the remedy called rescission?
2. Why did the chancellor agree to grant rescission? What was the rationale behind this ruling?
3. Why did the chancellor refuse to allow the appellant any damages for fraud?
4. What recovery was made by the appellant?

CONSIDERATION

Consideration is simply that which is bargained for and given in exchange for another's promise. Each party to a contract has a motive or price that induces the party to enter into the obligation. This cause or inducement is called *consideration*. Consideration usually consists of an act or a promise to do an act. **Forbearance** or a promise to forbear also may constitute consideration. Forbearance is refraining from doing an act or giving up a right.

A person must bargain specifically for the promise, act, or forbearance in order for it to constitute consideration. A promise is usually binding only when consideration is given in exchange. If a person promises to give another person $100 without asking for anything in return, this is a promise to make a gift, and it is unenforceable by the person to whom the gift was promised, since the promise lacked consideration. If, however, the **promisee** (the person to whom a promise is made) had promised to convey a television set in return for the promise to convey $100, the promise to give $100 would have been supported by consideration and therefore would be enforceable. Although a promise to make a gift is not enforceable, a person who has received a gift is not required to return it for lack of consideration.

Consideration must be legally sufficient, which means that the consideration for the promise must be either a detriment to the promisee or a legal benefit to the **promisor** (the person making the promise). In most situations, both exist. **Benefit** in the legal sense means the receipt by the promisor of some legal right to which the person had not previously been entitled. **Legal detriment** is the taking on of a legal obligation or the doing of something or the giving up of a legal right by the promisee.

Assume that an uncle promises to pay a niece $1,000 if she enrolls in and graduates from an accredited college or university. If the niece graduates from an accredited college, she is entitled to the $1,000. The promisee–niece did something she was not legally obligated to do, so the promise was supported by legally sufficient consideration. The legal detriment of the niece certainly did not amount to actual detriment. It can hardly be said that the uncle received any tangible benefit either—although seeing the niece achieve in this way obviously was valuable to him and could have comforted him as well.

Consideration should not be confused with a condition. A condition is an event the happening of which qualifies the duty to perform a promise. A promise to give a person $100 if the person comes to your home merely to pick it up is a promise to make a gift on the condition that the person picks up the money. A promisee who shows up is not legally entitled to the $100.[18]

When one party to an agreement makes what appears at first glance to be a promise but when on examination no real promise is made, this situation is called an **illusory promise.** A contract is not entered into when one of the parties makes an illusory promise, because there is no consideration. For example, a promise to work for an employer at an agreed rate for as long as the promisor wishes to work is an illusory promise. The promisor is really promising nothing and cannot be bound to do anything.

A court will not concern itself with the terms of a contract as long as the parties have capacity and there has been genuine assent to the terms.

Whether the bargain was a fair exchange is for the parties to decide when they enter into the agreement. Consideration need not have a pecuniary or money value. If a mother promises her son $100 if he does not drink or smoke until he reaches the age of twenty-one, there is no pecuniary value to the abstinence; yet it is valid consideration.

It is not necessary to state the consideration on the face of the document when an agreement is put in writing. It may be orally agreed on or implied. Although the recital of consideration is not final proof that consideration exists, it is evidence of consideration that is *prima facie,* or sufficient on its face. Evidence that no consideration existed will, however, overcome the presumption that the recital creates. And a statement of consideration in an instrument does not create consideration where it was never really intended or given.

If a promise is too vague or uncertain concerning time or subject matter, it will not amount to consideration. If a promise is obviously impossible to perform, it is not sufficient consideration for a return promise. When a promise is capable of being performed, even though improbable or absurd, it is consideration.

Consideration must be bargained for and given in exchange for a promise. Past consideration is not consideration. If a person performs a service for another without the other's knowledge, and later the recipient of the service promises to pay for it, the promise is not binding, since the promise to pay was not supported by consideration. A promise to do what one is already legally obligated to do cannot ordinarily constitute consideration. For example, a promise by a father to pay child support payments that are already an existing legal obligation determined by a court will not constitute consideration. Similarly, consideration is lacking when a promise is made to refrain from doing what one has no legal right to do.

Introduction to *Brown v. King*

The facts in the following case have been summarized so that you can concentrate on learning about the importance of "consideration" in contract formation.

After Josephine Hopkins died, her estate decided to sell two adjacent parcels of land located in a wealthy neighborhood. One parcel was on Richwood Avenue and had a house on it, and the other was vacant land on LeBlond Avenue.

Joel and Sandra King, the defendants in the case, decided to buy the Richwood property. Joel King also decided to join with architect Gene Barber to buy the LeBlond Avenue land. Joel King and Barber negotiated an agreement providing that at the closing on the LeBlond parcel, Joel would promise to relinquish his rights in the LeBlond site to Barber in exchange for Barber's promise to deed a specified 10′ by 80′ portion of the LeBlond site to Joel for $1. Joel wanted to make sure that his parcel would be large enough to comply with zoning setback requirements.

Barber submitted two offers to the estate. Barber and Joel King made the first offer, and Barber and M. Ray Brown made the second offer. King was not an offeror on the second offer. Because no attorneys were involved in the LeBlond Avenue transaction, there were procedural irregularities. The estate, for example, accepted both offers and accepted earnest money from both purchasers. The second offer involving Barber and Brown closed.

The Kings made renovations to the existing house and put on a new addition. Barber and Brown built themselves a new house on the LeBlond parcel and put up a fence along the boundary line between their tract and the Kings' tract. The Kings took offense because the fence was erected on land that the Kings believed to be within "their" 10′ by 80′ strip. The Kings argued in the ensuing lawsuit that Barber and Brown had breached the contract. The trial court, however, granted summary judgment in favor of Barber and Brown after ruling that the agreement with Joel King was unenforceable due to a lack of sufficient consideration. The Kings appealed.

Brown v. King
869 N.E.2d 35
Court of Appeals of Ohio
December 29, 2006

Mark P. Painter, Judge.
This case involves neighbors and the ownership of a 10-foot-by-80-foot strip of land between their properties. The trial court granted summary judgment, holding that there was no consideration to support a contract requiring transfer of the strip....

II. Consideration
In their first assignment of error, the Kings argue that the trial court erred in granting summary judgment for Barber and Brown....

The elements of a contract include an offer, an acceptance, contractual capacity, consideration (the bargained-for legal benefit or detriment), a manifestation of mutual assent, and legality of object and of consideration.... The issue in the present case is whether there was consideration for the contract.

The Ohio Supreme Court has long recognized the rule that a contract is not binding unless it is supported by consideration. Consideration may consist of either a detriment to the promisee or a benefit to the promisor. A benefit may consist of some right, interest, or profit accruing to the promisor, while a detriment may consist of some forbearance, loss, or responsibility given, suffered, or undertaken by the promisee....

In the present case, the contract between Joel King and Barber was supported by consideration. Joel King had a valid contract with Barber to purchase the LeBlond parcel. The estate signed both offers and accepted $1,000 in earnest money. Thus, the contract where Joel King agreed to release all his rights to the LeBlond property in exchange for Barber's transferring a strip of land at the rear of the parcel was valid. The detriment to the promisee (Joel King) was his surrender of his property rights secured by the purchase contract. The surrendering of these rights in exchange for the rear strip of land was a contract supported by consideration.

And when "a contract is clear and unambiguous, then its interpretation is a matter of law and there is no issue of fact to be determined."...

There were no material facts in dispute. The Kings contracted for the rear strip of land and provided consideration by surrendering their remaining property rights in the LeBlond parcel. Thus, the trial court erred by granting summary judgment for Barber and Brown. Summary judgment should have been granted to the Kings because the contract provided them with the property rights to that rear strip. The Kings' first assignment of error is sustained.

Accordingly, we reverse the trial court's grant of summary judgment in favor of Barber and Brown and remand this case so the trial court can enter summary judgment in favor of Joel and Sandra King.

Judgment reversed and cause remanded....

Case Questions

1. Was the contract between Joel King and Barber bilateral or unilateral?
2. What was bargained for and given in exchange by each party?

INTERNET TIP

Readers will find another consideration case, *Labriola v. Pollard Group, Inc.,* included with the online materials for Chapter X. In that case, the Washington Supreme Court decided whether a restrictive covenant clause in an employment contract (a provision that an ex-employee not open a business or accept employment in a job that competes with the former employer) was supported by sufficient consideration.

CAPACITY

In order to create a contract that is legally binding and enforceable, the parties must have the legal **capacity to contract.** Not all parties have the same legal capacity to enter into a contract, however. Full contractual capacity is present when a person is of legal age and is not otherwise so impaired as to be substantially incapable of making decisions for him- or herself.

It is presumed that all parties to an agreement have full legal capacity to contract. Therefore, any party seeking to base a claim or a defense on incapacity has the burden of proof with respect to that issue. The principal classes given some degree of special protection on their contracts because of their incapacity are (1) minors, (2) people with mental disabilities or defects, and (3) intoxicated people.

Minors

At common law, people remained minors until they reached the age of twenty-one. Generally, present legislation has reduced this age to eighteen. The law pertaining to minors entering into contracts formerly held that those contracts were void. That law now has been almost universally changed, and such contracts are held to be voidable. This law applies not only to contracts, but also to transactions such as sales.

The law grants minors this right in order to protect them from their lack of judgment and experience, limited willpower, and presumed immaturity. A contract between an adult and a minor is voidable only by the minor; the adult must fulfill the obligation, unless the minor decides to avoid the contract. Ordinarily, parents are not liable for contracts entered into by their minor children.

Adults contract with minors at their own peril. Thus, an adult party frequently will refuse to contract with or sell to minors because minors are incapable of giving legal assurance that they will not avoid the contract.

Transactions a Minor Cannot Avoid

Through legislation, many states have limited minors' ability to avoid contracts. For instance, many states provide that a contract with a college or university is binding. A purchase of life insurance also has been held to bind a minor. Some statutes take away the right of minors to avoid contracts after they are married. Most states hold that a minor engaging in a business and operating in the same manner as a person having legal capacity will not be permitted to set aside contracts arising from that business or employment. Court decisions or statutes have established this law in order to prevent minors from using the shield of minority to avoid business contracts.

Minors are liable for the reasonable value (not the contract price) of any necessary they purchase, whether goods or services, if they accept and make use of it. The reasonable value of the necessaries, rather than their contract price, is specified to protect them against the possibility that the other party to the agreement has taken advantage of them by overcharging them. If the necessaries have not yet been accepted or received, the minor may disaffirm the contract without liability.

In general, the term **necessaries** includes whatever is needed for a minor's subsistence as measured by age, status, condition in life, and so on. These include food, lodging, education, clothing, and medical services. Objects used for recreation or entertainment and ordinary contracts relating to the property or business of the minor are not classified as necessaries.

Disaffirmance of Contract

Minors may avoid both **executed** (completed) and **executory** (incomplete) contracts at any time during their minority. They also may disaffirm a contract within a reasonable period of time after they attain their majority. In this way, former minors have a reasonable time in which to evaluate transactions made during their infancy. What constitutes a reasonable time depends on the nature of the property involved and the surrounding circumstances. As long as minors do not disaffirm their contracts, they are bound by the terms. They cannot refuse to carry out their part of an agreement, while at the same time requiring the adult party to perform.

Disaffirmance of a contract by a minor may be made by any expression of an intention to repudiate the contract. Disaffirmance need not be verbal or written. If a minor performs an act inconsistent with the continuing validity of a contract, that is considered a disaffirmance. For example, if a minor sells property to Gaskins and later, on reaching majority, sells the same property to Ginger, the second sale to Ginger would be considered a disaffirmance of the contract with Gaskins.

Minors may disaffirm wholly executory contracts, that is, contracts that neither party has performed. In addition, if only the minor has performed, he or she may disaffirm and recover the money or property paid or transferred to an adult. A conflict arises, however, if the contract is wholly executed or if only the adult has performed and the minor has spent what he or she has received and therefore cannot make restitution. As a general rule, minors must return whatever they have in their possession of the consideration under the contract; if the consideration has been destroyed, they may nevertheless disaffirm the contract and recover the consideration they have given. For example, suppose Weldon, a minor, purchases an automobile and has an accident that demolishes the car. She may obtain a full refund by disaffirming the contract; moreover, she will not be liable for the damage to the car.

A few states, however, hold that if the contract is advantageous to the minor and if the adult has been fair in every respect, the contract cannot be disaffirmed unless the minor returns the consideration. In the preceding example, the minor would have to replace the reasonable value of the damaged automobile before she could disaffirm the contract and receive the consideration she gave for the automobile. These states also take into account the depreciation of the property while in the possession of the minor.

Some states have enacted statutes that prevent minors from disaffirming contracts if they have fraudulently misrepresented their age. Generally, however, the fact that minors have misrepresented their age in order to secure a contract that they otherwise could not have obtained will not later prevent them from disaffirming that contract on the basis of their minority. Most courts will hold minors liable for any resulting damage to, or deterioration of, property they received under the contract. Minors also generally are liable for their torts; consequently, in most states, the other party to the contract could recover in a tort action for deceit. In any case, the other party to the contract may avoid it because of the minor's fraud.

Ratification

Although minors may disaffirm or avoid their contracts before reaching their majority, they cannot effectively ratify or approve their contracts until they have attained their majority. **Ratification** may consist of any expression or action that indicates an intention to be bound by the contract, and may come from the actions of a minor who has now reached majority. For example, if a minor acquires property under a contract and, after reaching majority, makes use of or sells the property, he or she will be deemed to have ratified the contract.

People with Mental Disabilities or Defects

A person must have the **mental competence** to enter into a valid contract. A person is said to be incapable of contracting due to mental disabilities or defects when that individual does not understand the nature and consequences of his or her act at the time of entering into an agreement. In such cases, the person lacks capacity and his or her contracts are either void or voidable.

The contracts of a person who has been judicially declared insane by a court are void. Such a person will have a judicially appointed guardian who is under a duty to transact all business for him or her.

The contracts of people who have not been judicially declared mentally incompetent are generally voidable. Although such people may not ratify or disaffirm a contract during their temporary insanity, they may do so once they regain their sanity. However, if the contract is executed and the sane party to the contract acts in good faith, not knowing that the other party is temporarily insane, most courts refuse to allow the temporarily insane person the right to avoid the contract, unless the consideration that has been received can be returned. On the other hand, if the sane party knows that the other party is mentally incompetent, the contract is voidable at the option of the insane person.

As in the case of minors, the party possessing capacity to contract has no right to disaffirm a contract merely because the insane party has the right to do so. The rule in regard to necessaries purchased by temporarily insane persons is the same as in the case of minors.

Intoxication

If persons enter into a contract when they are so intoxicated that they do not know at the time that they are executing a contract, the contract is voidable at their option. The position of the intoxicated person is therefore much the same as that of the temporarily insane person.

ILLEGALITY

A contract is said to be an **illegal agreement** when either its formation or its performance is criminal, tortious, or contrary to public policy. When an agreement is illegal, courts will not allow either party to sue for performance of the contract. The court will literally "leave the parties where it finds them." Generally, if one of the parties has performed, that person can recover neither the value of the performance nor any property or goods transferred to the other party. There are three exceptions to this rule, however.

First, if the law that the agreement violates is intended for the protection of one of the parties, that party may seek relief. For example, both federal and state statutes require that a corporation follow certain procedures before offering stocks and bonds for sale to the public. It is illegal to sell such securities without having complied with the legal requirements. People who have purchased securities from a corporation that has not complied with the law may obtain a refund of the purchase price if they desire to do so.

Second, when the parties are not equally at fault, the one less at fault is granted relief when the public interest is advanced by doing so.[19] This rule is applied to illegal agreements that are induced by undue influence, duress, or fraud. In such cases, the courts do not regard the defrauded or coerced party as being an actual participant in the wrong and will therefore allow restitution.

A third exception occurs within very strict limits. A person who repents before actually having performed any illegal part of an illegal contract may rescind the contract and obtain restitution.

For example, suppose James and Ricardo wager on the outcome of a baseball game. Each gives $500 to Smith, the stakeholder, who agrees to give $1,000 to the winner. Prior to the game, either James or Ricardo could recover $500 from Smith through legal action, since the execution of the illegal agreement would not yet have occurred.

If the objectives of an agreement are illegal, the agreement is illegal and unenforceable, even though the parties were not aware, when they arrived at their agreement, that it was illegal.

On the other hand, as a general rule, even if one party to an agreement knows that the other party intends to use the subject matter of the contract for illegal purposes, this fact will not make the agreement illegal unless the illegal purpose involves a serious crime. For example, suppose Sara lends money to Roja, at a legal interest rate, knowing Roja is going to use the money to gamble illegally. After Roja loses her money, she refuses to repay Sara on the grounds that the agreement was illegal. Sara can recover her money through court action, even though she knew Roja was going to gamble illegally with the money she lent her.

Contracts against Public Policy

A contract provision is contrary to public policy if it is injurious to the interest of the public, contradicts some established interests of society, violates a statute, or tends to interfere with the public health, safety, or general welfare. The term **contrary to public policy** is vague and variable; it changes as our social, economic, and political climates change. One example is the illegal lobbying agreement, an agreement by which one party uses bribery, threats of a loss of votes, or any other improper means to procure or prevent the adoption of particular legislation by a lawmaking body, such as Congress or a state legislature. Such agreements are clearly contrary to the public interest, since they interfere with the workings of the democratic process. They are both illegal and void.

The court in the following case ruled that Connecticut's public policy was violated by a "Waiver, Defense, Indemnity and Hold Harmless Agreement, and Release of Liability" that was intended to shield a ski resort operator from liability for its own negligent conduct.

Gregory D. Hanks v. Powder Ridge Restaurant Corp.
885 A.2d 734
Supreme Court of Connecticut
November 29, 2005

Sullivan, C. J.
This appeal ... arises out of a complaint filed by the plaintiff, Gregory D. Hanks, against the defendants, Powder Ridge Restaurant Corporation and White Water Mountain Resorts of Connecticut, Inc., doing business as Powder Ridge Ski Resort, seeking compensatory damages for injuries the plaintiff sustained while snowtubing at the defendants' facility. The trial court rendered summary judgment in favor of the defendants....

The record reveals the following factual and procedural history. The defendants operate a facility in Middlefield, known as Powder Ridge, at which the public, in exchange for a fee, is invited to ski, snowboard and snowtube. On February 16, 2003, the plaintiff brought his three children and another child to Powder Ridge to snowtube. Neither the plaintiff nor the four children had ever snowtubed at Powder Ridge, but the snowtubing run was open to the public generally, regardless of prior snowtubing experience, with the restriction that only persons at least six years

old or forty-four inches tall were eligible to participate. Further, in order to snowtube at Powder Ridge, patrons were required to sign a "Waiver, Defense, Indemnity and Hold Harmless Agreement, and Release of Liability" (agreement). The plaintiff read and signed the agreement on behalf of himself and the four children. While snowtubing, the plaintiff's right foot became caught between his snow tube and the man-made bank of the snowtubing run, resulting in serious injuries that required multiple surgeries to repair.

Thereafter, the plaintiff filed the present negligence action against the defendants....

The defendants, in their answer to the complaint, denied the plaintiff's allegations of negligence and asserted two special defenses. Specifically, the defendants alleged that the plaintiff's injuries were caused by his own negligence and that the agreement relieved the defendants of liability, "even if the accident was due to the negligence of the defendants." Thereafter, the defendants moved for summary judgment, claiming that the agreement barred the plaintiff's negligence claim as a matter of law. The trial court agreed and rendered summary judgment in favor of the defendants.... Specifically, the trial court determined ... that the plaintiff, by signing the agreement, unambiguously had released the defendants from liability for their allegedly negligent conduct. Thereafter, the plaintiff moved to reargue the motion for summary judgment. The trial court denied the plaintiff's motion and this appeal followed.

The plaintiff raises two claims on appeal. First, the plaintiff claims that the trial court improperly concluded that the agreement clearly and expressly releases the defendants from liability for negligence. Specifically, the plaintiff contends that a person of ordinary intelligence reasonably would not have believed that, by signing the agreement, he or she was releasing the defendants from liability for personal injuries caused by negligence and, therefore...the agreement does not bar the plaintiff's negligence claim. Second, the plaintiff claims that the agreement is unenforceable because it violates public policy. Specifically, the plaintiff contends that a recreational operator cannot, consistent with public policy, release itself from liability for its own negligent conduct where, as in the present case, the operator offers its services to the public generally, for a fee, and requires patrons to sign a standardized exculpatory agreement as a condition of participation....

I

We first address the plaintiff's claim that the agreement does not expressly release the defendants from liability for personal injuries incurred as a result of their own negligence.... Specifically, the plaintiff maintains that an ordinary person of reasonable intelligence would not understand that, by signing the agreement, he or she was releasing the defendants from liability for future negligence. We disagree.... We conclude that the trial court properly determined that the agreement in the present matter expressly purports to release the defendants from liability for their future negligence and, accordingly, satisfies the standard set forth by this court....

II

We next address ... whether the enforcement of a well drafted exculpatory agreement purporting to release a snowtube operator from prospective liability for personal injuries sustained as a result of the operator's negligent conduct violates public policy....

Although it is well established "that parties are free to contract for whatever terms on which they may agree" ... it is equally well established "that contracts that violate public policy are unenforceable."

As previously noted, "the law does not favor contract provisions which relieve a person from his own negligence."... This is because exculpatory provisions undermine the policy considerations governing our tort system. "The fundamental policy purposes of the tort compensation system [are] compensation of innocent parties, shifting the loss to responsible parties or distributing it among appropriate entities, and deterrence of wrongful conduct.... It is sometimes said that compensation for losses is the primary function of tort law ... [but it] is perhaps more accurate to describe the primary function as one of determining when compensation [is] required.... An equally compelling function of the tort system is the prophylactic factor of preventing future harm.... The courts are concerned not only with compensation of the victim, but with admonition of the wrongdoer."... Thus, it is consistent with public policy "to posit the risk of negligence upon the actor" and, if this policy is to be abandoned, "it has generally been to allow or require that the risk shift to another party better or equally able to bear it, not to shift the risk to the weak bargainer."...

Having reviewed the various methods for determining whether exculpatory agreements violate public policy, we conclude ... that "no definition of the concept of public interest can be contained within the four corners of a formula."... Accordingly, we agree with the Supreme Courts of Maryland and Vermont that "the ultimate determination of what constitutes the public interest must be made considering the totality of the circumstances of any given case against the backdrop of current societal expectations."...

We now turn to the merits of the plaintiff's claim. The defendants are in the business of providing snowtubing services to the public generally, regardless of prior snowtubing experience, with the minimal restriction that only persons at least six years old or forty-four inches tall are eligible to participate. Given the virtually unrestricted access of the public to Powder Ridge, a reasonable person would presume that the defendants were offering a recreational activity that the whole family could enjoy safely....

The societal expectation that family oriented recreational activities will be reasonably safe is even more important where, as in the present matter, patrons are under the care and control of the recreational operator as a result of an economic transaction. The plaintiff, in exchange for a fee, was permitted access to the defendants' snowtubing runs and was provided with snowtubing gear. As a result of this transaction, the plaintiff was under the care and control of the defendants and, thus, was subject to the risk of the defendants' carelessness. Specifically, the defendants designed and maintained the snowtubing run and, therefore, controlled the steepness of the incline, the condition of the snow and the method of slowing down or stopping patrons. Further, the defendants provided the plaintiff with the requisite snowtubing supplies and, therefore, controlled the size and quality of the snow tube as well as the provision of any necessary protective gear. Accordingly, the plaintiff voluntarily relinquished control to the defendants with the reasonable expectation of an exciting, but reasonably safe, snowtubing experience.

Moreover, the plaintiff lacked the knowledge, experience and authority to discern whether, much less ensure that, the defendants' snowtubing runs were maintained in a reasonably safe condition.... [The] defendants ... have the expertise and opportunity to foresee and control hazards, and to guard against the negligence of their agents and employees. They alone can properly maintain and inspect their premises, and train their employees in risk management. They alone can insure against risks and effectively spread the costs of insurance among their thousands of customers. Skiers, on the other hand, are not in a position to discover and correct risks of harm, and they cannot insure against the ski area's negligence.

"If the defendants were permitted to obtain broad waivers of their liability, an important incentive for ski areas to manage risk would be removed, with the public bearing the cost of the resulting injuries.... It is illogical, in these circumstances, to undermine the public policy underlying business invitee law and allow skiers to bear risks they have no ability or right to control." The concerns expressed by the court in *Dalury* [*v. S-K-I, Ltd.*] are equally applicable to the context of snowtubing, and we agree that it is illogical to permit snowtubers, and the public generally, to bear the costs of risks that they have no ability or right to control. Further, the agreement at issue was a standardized adhesion contract offered to the plaintiff on a "take it or leave it" basis. The "most salient feature [of adhesion contracts] is that they are not subject to the normal bargaining processes of ordinary contracts."... [S]ee also Black's Law Dictionary (7th Ed. 1999) (defining adhesion contract as "[a] standard form contract prepared by one party, to be signed by the party in a weaker position, [usually] a consumer, who has little choice about the terms"). Not only was the plaintiff unable to negotiate the terms of the agreement, but the defendants also

did not offer him the option of procuring protection against negligence at an additional reasonable cost. See Restatement (Third), Torts, Apportionment of Liability 2, comment (e), p. 21 (2000) (factor relevant to enforcement of contractual limit on liability is "whether the party seeking exculpation was willing to provide greater protection against tortious conduct for a reasonable, additional fee"). Moreover, the defendants did not inform prospective snowtubers prior to their arrival at Powder Ridge that they would have to waive important common-law rights as a condition of participation. Thus, the plaintiff, who traveled to Powder Ridge in anticipation of snowtubing that day, was faced with the dilemma of either signing the defendants' proffered waiver of prospective liability or forgoing completely the opportunity to snowtube at Powder Ridge. Under the present factual circumstances, it would ignore reality to conclude that the plaintiff wielded the same bargaining power as the defendants....

In the present case, the defendants held themselves out as a provider of a healthy, fun, family activity. After the plaintiff and his family arrived at Powder Ridge eager to participate in the activity, however, the defendants informed the plaintiff that, not only would they be immune from claims arising from the inherent risks of the activity, but they would not be responsible for injuries resulting from their own carelessness and negligence in the operation of the snowtubing facility. We recognize that the plaintiff had the option of walking away. We cannot say, however, that the defendants had no bargaining advantage under these circumstances.

For the foregoing reasons, we conclude that the agreement in the present matter affects the public interest adversely and, therefore, is unenforceable because it violates public policy.... Accordingly, the trial court improperly rendered summary judgment in favor of the defendants.

The defendants and the dissent point out that our conclusion represents the "distinct minority view."... We acknowledge that most states uphold adhesion contracts releasing recreational operators from prospective liability for personal injuries caused by their own negligent conduct. Put simply, we disagree with these decisions for the reasons already explained in this opinion....

The judgment is reversed and the case is remanded for further proceedings according to law.

Case Questions

1. Why did the Connecticut Supreme Court refuse to enforce the contractual immunity agreement?
2. Do you agree with the Connecticut Supreme Court's argument that the ski resort could purchase liability insurance against negligence and pass the cost on to its patrons, thus making sure that injured patrons are able to obtain compensation for injuries sustained at the ski resort?

Agreements to Commit Serious Crimes

An agreement is illegal and therefore void when it calls for the commission of any act that constitutes a serious crime. Agreements to commit murder, robbery, arson, burglary, and assault are obvious examples, but less obvious violations are also subject to the rule, depending on the jurisdiction.

Agreements to Commit Civil Wrongs

An agreement that calls for the commission of a civil wrong is also illegal and void. Examples are agreements to slander a third person, to defraud another, to damage another's goods, or to infringe upon another's trademark or patent.

A contract that calls for the performance of an act or the rendering of a service may be illegal for one of two reasons. (1) The act or service itself may be illegal (**illegal per se**), and thus any contract involving this act or service is illegal. Prostitution is a good example. (2) Certain other service contracts are not illegal per se, but may be illegal if the party performing or contracting to perform the service is not legally entitled to do so. This latter condition refers to the fact that a license is required before a person is entitled to perform certain functions for others. For example, doctors, dentists, lawyers, architects, surveyors, real estate brokers, and others rendering specialized professional services must be licensed by the appropriate body before entering into contracts with the general public.

All the states have enacted regulatory statutes concerning the practice of various professions and the performance of business and other activities. However, these statutes are not uniform in their working or in their scope. Many of the statutes specifically provide that all agreements that violate them shall be void and unenforceable. When such a provision is lacking, the court will look to the intent of the statute. If the court is of the opinion that a statute was enacted for the protection of the public, it will hold that agreements in violation of the statute are void. If, however, the court concludes that the particular statute was intended solely to raise revenue, then it will hold that contracts entered in violation of the statute are legal and enforceable.

A contract that has for its purpose the restraint of trade and nothing more is illegal and void. A contract to monopolize trade, to suppress competition, or not to compete in business, therefore, cannot be enforced, because the sole purpose of the agreement would be to eliminate competition. A contract that aims at establishing a monopoly not only is unenforceable, but also renders the parties to the agreement subject to indictment for the commission of a crime.

When a business is sold, it is commonly stated in a contract that the seller shall not go into the same or similar business again within a certain geographic area, or for a certain period of time, or both. In early times, such agreements were held void since they deprived the public of the service of the person who agreed not to compete, reduced competition, and exposed the public to monopoly. Gradually, the law began to recognize the validity of such restrictive provisions. To the modern courts, the question is whether, under the circumstances, the restriction imposed upon one party is reasonable, or whether the restriction is more extensive than is required to protect the other party. A similar situation arises when employees agree not to compete with their employers should they leave their jobs.

In the following case, the North Carolina Court of Appeals was asked to determine the validity of a postemployment noncompetition clause, which had been signed by a former employee at the time of his employment by Carolina Pride Carwash, Inc.

Carolina Pride Carwash, Inc. v. Tim Kendrick
C0A04-451
Court of Appeals of North Carolina
September 20, 2005

Calabria, Judge.

Tim Kendrick ("defendant") appeals from summary judgment entered in favor of Carolina Pride Carwash, Inc. ("Carolina Pride") for breach of an employment contract. We reverse and remand for entry of summary judgment in favor of defendant.

Carolina Pride is a car wash maintenance provider and distributor of car wash equipment and supplies. Carolina Pride employs approximately forty-five people and operates in North Carolina, South Carolina, and the southern half of Virginia, east of the Blue Ridge Parkway. In late 1999, Carolina Pride was negotiating for the purchase of PDQ Carolina ("PDQ"), a car wash equipment distributor, where defendant was employed as a service technician earning approximately $15.00 per hour. On 20 December 1999, defendant met with the president of Carolina Pride and entered into an employment contract. The contract provided that Carolina Pride would pay defendant $500.00 after signing, employ him beginning in January 2000 as a service technician at $15.00 per hour, and pay him a $1,000.00 bonus after one year of employment. The sixth and seventh provisions of the contract contained a covenant not to compete and a provision for liquidated damages:

> SIXTH: [Defendant] hereby agrees and guarantees to [Carolina Pride], that during the term of this contract and for three years after termination of this contract, [defendant] will not on his own account or as agent, employee or servant of any other person, firm or corporation engage in or become financially interested in the same line of business or any other line of business which could reasonably be considered as being in competition with [Carolina Pride] within North Carolina, South Carolina, or Virginia to-wit: Carwash sales and service of equipment, supplies, parts and any and all related merchandise; and further, that during this period, [defendant] will not directly or indirectly or by aid to others, do anything which would tend to divert from [Carolina Pride] any trade or business with any customer with whom [defendant] has made contracts or associations during the period of time in which he is employed by [Carolina Pride].

> SEVENTH: That in the event [defendant] violates the provision of the preceding paragraphs, then [Carolina Pride] shall be entitled to liquidated damages in the amount of $50,000.00 to be paid by [defendant] to [Carolina Pride].

In March 2000, defendant started employment as a technician with Carolina Pride and served customers predominantly in North Carolina and occasionally in South Carolina. The following year, in 2001, defendant left Carolina Pride's employ and took a position with Water Works Management Company, L.L.C. ("Water Works") as manager of repair, maintenance, and supply for several of their car wash facilities in Greensboro, Mt. Airy, Elkin, and Boone.

In January 2002, Carolina Pride filed suit alleging defendant interfered with its customer relationships in violation of the covenant not to compete. In the spring of 2002, Water Works discharged defendant due to Carolina Pride's lawsuit. Defendant answered Carolina Pride's complaint and included counterclaims for the following: (1) fraud; (2) negligent misrepresentation; (3) unfair and deceptive trade practices; and (4) wrongful or tortious interference with business relations.

Both defendant and Carolina Pride subsequently moved for summary judgment, and on 17 October 2003, the trial court granted Carolina Pride's motion based on defendant's alleged breach of the covenant not to compete. In addition, the trial court ordered that defendant pay $50,000.00 in liquidated damages.

Defendant assigns error to the trial court's denial of his motion for summary judgment and grant of Carolina Pride's motion for summary judgment. Defendant argues the covenant not to compete was unenforceable as a matter of law because the time and territorial restrictions of the covenant were unreasonable. We agree, under these facts, that the time and territorial restrictions were greater than reasonably necessary to protect Carolina Pride's legitimate interests....

> [A] covenant not to compete is valid and enforceable if it is "(1) in writing; (2) reasonable as to terms, time, and territory; (3) made a part of the employment contract; (4) based on valuable consideration; and (5) not against public policy."... "Although either the time or the territory restriction, standing alone, may be reasonable, the combined effect of the two may be unreasonable. A longer period of time is acceptable where the geographic restriction is relatively small, and vice versa."...

A central purpose of a covenant not to compete is the protection of an employer's customer relationships.... Therefore, to prove that a covenant's territorial restriction is reasonable, "an employer must ... show where its customers are located and that the geographic scope of the covenant is necessary to maintain those customer relationships."... "Furthermore, in determining the reasonableness of [a] territorial restriction, when the primary concern is the employee's knowledge of customers, the territory should only be limited to areas in which the employee made contacts during the period of his employment."... "If the territory is too broad, 'the entire covenant fails since equity will neither enforce nor reform an overreaching and unreasonable covenant.' "...

In the instant case, the covenant not to compete applied to all areas of North Carolina, South Carolina, and Virginia for a term of three years. However, the president of Carolina Pride testified that Carolina Pride's territory included North Carolina, South Carolina, and "the lower half of Virginia east of the Blue Ridge Parkway." Therefore, by including all of Virginia, the territorial restriction of the covenant encompassed a greater region than necessary to protect Carolina

Pride's legitimate interest in maintaining its customer relationships. Moreover, while employed by Carolina Pride, defendant only contacted customers in North and South Carolina but never in Virginia. Therefore, the covenant was unreasonable not only for encompassing a greater region than necessary but also for encompassing any portion of Virginia because defendant never contacted customers in that state while employed by Carolina Pride.

Additionally, although the covenant's three-year time period may be valid standing alone, it was unreasonable in this case when coupled with the unnecessarily broad territorial restriction.

Accordingly, we hold the covenant not to compete was unenforceable as a matter of law, and the trial court erred by entering summary judgment for Carolina Pride and failing to enter summary judgment for defendant with respect to Carolina Pride's breach of contract claim. We likewise reverse that portion of the trial court's order requiring defendant to pay liquidated damages and remand the case to the trial court for further proceedings not inconsistent with this opinion.

Reversed and remanded.

Case Questions

1. List some specific employment examples where a postemployment noncompetition agreement would be enforceable.
2. Why did the North Carolina Court of Appeals refuse to enforce the noncompete covenant?

WRITING

Every state has statutes requiring that certain contracts be in writing to be enforceable. Called the **statute of frauds,** these statutes are based on "An Act for the Prevention of Frauds and Perjuries," passed by the English Parliament in 1677. Statutes of frauds traditionally govern six kinds of contracts: (1) an agreement by an executor or administrator of the estate of a deceased person to answer personally for the debt of a decedent, (2) an agreement made in consideration of marriage, (3) an agreement to answer for the debt of another, (4) an agreement that cannot be performed in one year, (5) an agreement for the sale of an interest in real property, and (6) an agreement for the sale of goods above a certain dollar amount.

The writing required by the statute need not be in any special form or use any special language. Usually, the terms that must be shown on the face of the writing include the names of the parties, the terms and conditions of the contract, the consideration, a reasonably certain description of the subject matter of the contract, and the signature of the party—or the party's agent—against whom enforcement is sought. These terms need not be on one piece of paper but may be on several pieces of paper, provided that their relation or connection with each other appears on their face by the physical attachment of the papers to each other or by reference from one writing to the other. At least one, if not all, of the papers must be signed by the party against whom enforcement is sought. (The requirements differ for memorandums involving the sale of goods.)

Agreement by Executor or Administrator

A promise by an executor or administrator of a deceased person's estate to answer personally for the debt of the decedent is within the statute and must be in writing to be enforced. In order for the statute to operate, the executor's promise must be to pay out of the executor's own personal assets; a promise to pay a debt out of the assets of a decedent's estate is not required to be in writing.

Agreement in Consideration of Marriage

Agreements made in consideration of marriage are to be in writing. Mutual promises to marry are not within the statute, since the consideration is the exchanged promise, not the marriage itself. However, promises made to a prospective spouse or third party with marriage as the consideration are within the statute. For example, a promise by one prospective spouse to convey property to the other, provided the marriage is entered into, is required to be in writing. Similarly, if a third party—say, a rich relative—promises to pay a certain sum of money to a prospective spouse if a marriage is entered into, the promise will be unenforceable unless it is in writing.

INTERNET TIP

The case of *In re Marriage of DewBerry* involves the statute of frauds. In this case the appellate court had to rule on whether an oral prenuptial agreement that all income acquired by either spouse be strictly considered to be separate property was unenforceable under the statute of frauds as an agreement in consideration of marriage. Readers will find this case included with the online Chapter X materials.

Agreement to Answer for the Debt of Another

Agreements to answer for the debt or default of another are unenforceable unless in writing. The rationale for this provision is that the guarantor or surety has received none of the benefits for which the debt was incurred and therefore should be bound only by the exact terms of the promise. For example, Bob desires to purchase a new law text on credit. The bookstore is unsure as to Bob's ability to pay, so Bob brings in his friend, Ellen, who says, "If Bob does not pay for the text, I will." In effect, the promise is that the bookstore must first try to collect from Bob, who is primarily liable. After it has exhausted all possibilities of collecting from him, then it may come to Ellen to receive payment. Ellen is therefore secondarily liable. Ellen has promised to answer for Bob's debt even though she will not receive the benefit of the new law text; therefore, her agreement must be in writing to be enforceable.

This situation must be distinguished from those in which the promise to answer for the debt of another is an original promise; that is, the promisor's objective is to be primarily liable. For example, Bob wants to purchase a new law text. When he takes the book to the cashier, his friend Ellen steps in and says, "Give him the book. I will pay for it." Ellen has made an original promise to the bookstore with the objective of becoming primarily liable. Such a promise need not be in writing to be enforceable.

Sometimes it is difficult to ascertain whether the purpose of the promisor is to become primarily liable or secondarily liable. In resolving the issue, courts will sometimes use the **leading object rule.** This rule looks not only to the promise itself, but also to the individual for whose benefit the promise was made. The logic of the rule is that if the leading object of the promise is the personal benefit of the promisor, then the promisor must have intended to become primarily liable. In such a case, the promise will be deemed to be original and need not be in writing to be enforced.

INTERNET TIP

Readers can find the case of *Douglas D. Owens v. Leonard Goldammer* on the textbook's website. It is a 2002 Missouri appellate court opinion about whether a promisor's alleged oral agreement to pay another's debt was within or outside the scope of the statute of frauds.

Agreements Not to Be Performed in One Year

Most statutes require contracts to be in writing if they cannot be performed within one year from the time the contract is formed. This determination is made by referring to the intentions of the parties, to the nature of the performance, and to the terms of the contract itself. For example, if Jack agrees to build a house for Betty, the question is whether the contract is capable of being performed within one year. Houses can be built in one year. Therefore, this agreement need not be in writing even if Jack actually takes more than one year to build the house.

It is important to remember that the mere *possibility* that the contract could be performed within one year is enough to make the statute inapplicable regardless of how long performance actually took.

Agreement Conveying an Interest in Real Property

The statute of frauds generally renders unenforceable oral agreements conveying interests in real estate. There are primarily two issues in determining whether the statute of frauds applies in this context. The first is, What constitutes an interest in real estate? The second is, Does the agreement contemplate the transfer of any title, ownership, or possession of real property? Both must be involved to bring the statute into effect. Real property has commonly been held to include land, leaseholds, easements, standing timber, and, under certain conditions, improvements and fixtures attached to the land.

Sale of Goods

Generally, a contract for the sale of goods for the price of $500 or more is not enforceable unless there is some writing to serve as evidence that a contract has been entered into. An informal or incomplete writing will be sufficient to satisfy the UCC statute of frauds, providing that it (1) indicates that a contract between the parties was entered into, (2) is signed by the party against whom enforcement is sought, and (3) contains a statement of the quantity of goods sold. The price, time and place of delivery, quality of the goods, and warranties may be omitted without invalidating the writing, as the UCC permits these terms to be shown by outside evidence, custom and usage, and prior dealings between the parties. Thus, substantially fewer provisions must be included in a writing that will conform to the UCC statute of frauds than are necessary in a writing that evidences one of the other types of contracts governed by the statute of frauds. Under the UCC, the contract will be enforced only as to the quantity of goods shown in the writing (UCC § 2-201 [1]).

Introduction to *Nicolaos Terzis v. Pompano Paint and Body Repair, Inc.*

Nicolaos Terzis alleged that the defendant had breached an oral contract both had entered into in 2008 that required the plaintiff to make monthly payments of $100 and required the defendant to safely store the plaintiff's $175,000 boat. The boat was placed in storage, and the plaintiff paid $100 monthly until the boat was stolen on June 9, 2009. Only the hull of the boat was recovered by the sheriff, and the plaintiff sold that to an interested buyer for $36,000. The plaintiff then filed suit against the defendant to recover the amount necessary to reimburse him for the value of the unrecovered portion of the boat and its equipment. The trial court ruled that the oral contract was invalid and granted the defendant's motion to dismiss, and the plaintiff appealed.

Nicolaos Terzis v. Pompano Paint and Body Repair, Inc.
No. 4D11-2155 and No. 4D11-4939
District Court of Appeal of the State of Florida Fourth District
December 19, 2012

Gerber, J.

We conclude the court erred in finding, at the motion to dismiss stage, that the oral contract violated the statute of frauds. The statute of frauds provides, in pertinent part:

> No action shall be brought ... whereby to charge the defendant upon any special promise to answer for the debt, default or miscarriage of another person ... or upon any agreement that is not to be performed within the space of 1 year from the making thereof ... unless the agreement or promise upon which such action shall be brought, or some note or memorandum thereof shall be in writing and signed by the party to be charged therewith....

§ 725.01, Fla. Stat. (2008). Case law interpreting the statute of frauds further has held that "when no time is agreed on for the complete performance of the contract, if from the object to be accomplished by it and the surrounding circumstances, it clearly appears that the parties intended that it should extend for a longer period than a year, it is within the statute of frauds....

However, "[t]he general rule is that an oral contract for an indefinite time is not barred by the Statute of Frauds. Only if a contract could not possibly be performed within one year would it fall within the statute."... Moreover, "full performance by one party to the contract works to remove an oral agreement from the purview of the statute of frauds."...

Here, the plaintiff's third amended complaint did not allege the parties agreed on any time for the complete performance of the oral contract or that the parties intended that it should extend for a longer period than a year. Instead, the reasonable inferences arising from the complaint suggest that the oral contract was for an indefinite time and could be performed within one year.... Further, the plaintiff alleged that he fully performed the contract by paying the defendant on a month-to-month basis to store and secure his boat. Thus, the oral contract fell outside the purview of the statute of frauds....

Seeking to avoid reversal, the defendant argues that the court's order dismissing the complaint ... was correct for the other reasons argued in the motion to dismiss.... According to the defendant, the contract

lacked consideration, the third amended complaint failed to state a cause of action for breach of contract, and the plaintiff lacked standing because he sold the boat's hull and recovered $36,000 in mitigating his loss.

We disagree with all three arguments. First, the contract was supported by consideration. In order for a contract to be supported by consideration, "[i]t is not necessary that a benefit should accrue to the person making the promise. It is sufficient that something of value flows from the person to whom it is made, or that [the person] suffers some prejudice or inconvenience and that the promise is the inducement to the transaction."... Here, something of value flowed from the plaintiff, who suffered prejudice based on the defendant's promise. As alleged in the third amended complaint, the plaintiff paid the defendant $100 per month, in exchange for the defendant's promise to store the plaintiff's boat and keep it free from damage or theft. The plaintiff was prejudiced when the defendant allegedly allowed the boat to be stolen from its storage facility.

Second, the third amended complaint stated a cause of action for breach of contract. "The elements of a breach of contract action are: (1) a valid contract; (2) a material breach; and (3) damages."... Here, the plaintiff alleged those elements. He alleged the existence of a valid contract whereby he paid the defendant $100 per month to store his boat and keep it free from damage or theft. He alleged that the defendant materially breached the contract by allowing the boat to be stolen from the defendant's storage facility. Lastly, he alleged damages measured by the lost value of the boat's original condition minus the amount which he recovered by selling the hull before he filed suit. Thus, the plaintiff alleged sufficient ultimate facts to show that he is entitled to relief....

Third, the plaintiff had standing. "To satisfy the requirement of standing ... individuals must allege some threatened or actual injury resulting from the putatively illegal action."... Here, the plaintiff alleged an actual injury resulting from the putatively illegal action. Specifically, the plaintiff alleged that the defendant breached its contract to keep his boat free from damage or theft, which caused him damages....

Because we reverse the circuit court's order granting the defendant's motion to dismiss ... we also reverse the court's order awarding the defendant attorney's fees pursuant to section 57.105(1), Florida Statutes (2010).

Reversed and remanded for proceedings consistent with this opinion.

Case Questions

1. Why did the appellate court sustain this oral contract, given the fact that there was no evidence of an agreement between the parties as to when the contractual term was to expire?
2. According to the appellate court, what was the consideration that supported the oral contract?

Parol-Evidence Rule

After contracting parties have successfully negotiated a contract, they often sign a written document that contains what they intend to be a definitive and complete statement of the agreed-upon terms (in legalese this means that all terms are **fully integrated**). Courts usually will presume that a fully integrated writing is accurate. Therefore, under the **parol-evidence rule,** evidence of alleged prior oral or written agreements or terms not contained in the written document will be inadmissible if offered to change the terms of the document.

There are several exceptions to the parol-evidence rule. The parol-evidence rule, for example, would not apply where the contracting parties have prepared only a partial memorandum or other incomplete writing. (In legalese the terms of an incomplete agreement are only **partially integrated.**) An agreement that is only partially integrated is only intended to be a final and complete statement with respect to the terms actually addressed in the memorandum. Unaddressed terms, in this circumstance, often can be proven extrinsically. Other recognized exceptions exist where parol evidence is used to prove fraud or the absence of consideration in the formation of a contract, and where it helps to explain the meaning of ambiguous words.

Introduction to *Wind Wire v. Finney*

The plaintiffs in the next case, Roger and Patricia Finney, alleged that a company that was trying to sell them a wind turbine had engaged in fraud. The Finneys claimed that fraudulent representations both oral and in a brochure had convinced them to contract with the defendant for the purchase and installation of a wind turbine. The plaintiffs sued. The judge at the bench trial found in favor of the plaintiffs and the defendant appealed. One of the defendant–appellant's arguments was that the trial court had wrongfully allowed the brochure to be received into evidence. The defendant claimed that the written contract contained an integration clause (also often referred to as a "zipper clause" because it limits the agreement to the terms explicitly contained within the document. This clause and the parol-evidence rule, said the defendant, prohibited the trial court from relying upon extrinsic evidence (the brochure which contained allegedly fraudulent promises) when determining whether fraud had occurred.

Wind Wire, LLC v. Roger Finney and Patricia Finney
977 N.E.2d 401
Court of Appeals of Indiana
October 17, 2012

Bradford, Judge.

Appellant-Defendant Wind Wire LLC appeals the trial court's judgment that it fraudulently induced Appellees-Plaintiffs Roger and Patricia Finney to execute a contract for the purchase and installation of a residential wind turbine and that it breached that contract's implied warranty of fitness for a particular purpose....

Facts and Procedural History

The trial court based its judgment on these specific findings of fact. At some point prior to May 14, 2008, the Finneys received a copy of a Wind Wire advertising brochure that had been left in their mailbox by a Wind Wire representative. The brochure described the cost savings to be realized through the use of energy producing wind turbines and included the following representations:

> WIND-WIRE provides the average household the means to harness the wind at a feasible cost for a savings of approximately 75% to 100% of current electric service. With a savings of approximately $160 plus per month and a payoff span of 3-4 years you would control 75% to 100% of your electric supply utilizing nature and doing your small part for the ecology? (sic)
>
> If you could invest in a system that would not only increase the value of your property but could generate an average of 700K wh [sic] per hour could you do it? WIND-WIRE will show how the homeowner can receive a substantial refund on their (sic) taxes for the installation of the system, saving the homeowner even more money....

Wind Wire produced the brochure as an advertising tool to induce people to contract with Wind Wire for the purchase and installation of wind turbines, and it conceded at trial that a reasonable person would rely on the information contained in the brochure. Intrigued by the brochure's representations, the Finneys contacted Wind Wire and later met with Wind Wire representatives to discuss the installation of a wind turbine on the Finneys' property.

While meeting with Wind Wire, Mr. Finney declared that the Finneys wanted to install a turbine to save money on their electric bill. In response to Mr. Finney's statement, Wind Wire representative Glen Smith affirmed the cost savings representations contained in Wind Wire's brochure. At trial, however, Wind Wire could not recall the name or location of the customer alleged in the brochure to have generated an average of 700 kWh through the use of its wind turbine. Moreover, at the time Wind Wire placed the brochure in the Finneys' mailbox, it did not know the average wind speed in the town where the Finneys' property is located.

Smith also told the Finneys that Wind Wire was highly qualified, had been in the wind turbine business for awhile, and had installed two turbines at a bank in Mishawaka. Based on these representations, the Finneys believed Wind Wire's representatives to be qualified and knowledgeable. However, the extent of Smith's formal training was a one-hour "webinar"; he had no experience with wind turbines prior to undertaking the business of selling and installing them.

Wind Wire also told the Finneys that the company supplying their electric service, AEP, would purchase the excess energy produced by their wind turbine. As intended by Wind Wire, Mr. Finney understood this to mean that AEP would issue him a check for those periods in which his energy production exceeded his energy consumption. AEP, however, does not issue checks to its customers for this reason. Moreover, Wind Wire failed to inform the Finneys that, in order to measure the production of excess energy, their wind turbine would require a type of electrical meter other than the typical residential meter with which their wind turbine was equipped.

Wind Wire's representatives further told the Finneys that installation of a wind turbine would entitle them to a tax credit, the amount of which was described in terms of a percentage of the purchase price. In fact, the credit was fixed at $900.00 for the Finneys. Wind Wire created the impression that the amount of the Finneys' tax credit would be greater.

On May 14, 2008, in reliance on the representations contained in the brochure and the statements made by Wind Wire representatives during their meeting with the Finneys, the Finneys executed a contract with Wind Wire for the purchase and installation of a wind turbine. The wind turbine was not erected on the Finneys' property until October 2008, and it did not begin producing electrical power until September 2009. Since that time, the Finneys' wind turbine has produced no excess power and has had no effect on their electric bills. The wind turbine actually consumes energy while it sits idle. Based on the cost of electricity from AEP, it would not be possible for the Finneys' wind turbine to pay for itself in three to four years. AEP represents that it typically takes twenty-five years for a wind turbine to pay for itself. Moreover, in the approximately one year since its installation on the Finneys' property, the wind turbine has produced a total of only 134.2 kWh. According to AEP, even if the wind turbine were running continuously at maximum capacity, it would create only 1100-1200 kWh and produce, at most, a utility savings of $155 per month.

In July 2010 a Wind Wire representative met with representatives of Southwest Wind Power ("SWP"), the manufacturer of the wind turbines Wind Wire installs, to address problems with such installations. SWP had received customer complaints directed at Wind Wire and was concerned about customer expectations of energy production associated with Wind Wire's installation of SWP wind turbines. SWP questioned Wind Wire about its customers' experiences, specifically inquiring as to how Wind Wire arrived at the energy production data it was advertising. SWP was especially concerned about Wind Wire's marketing materials and its ability to service its customers adequately. Ultimately, SWP placed Wind Wire on a sixty-day suspension and admonished Wind Wire not to "share extraordinary production levels of previous customers with potential customers during the sales process."... SWP further placed Wind Wire on six months probation due to concerns with Wind Wire's marketing materials and customer satisfaction.

On August 9, 2010, the Finneys filed a complaint in St. Joseph Superior Court, alleging, among other things, breach of contract, breach of implied warranty of fitness for a particular purpose, and fraud. Relevant to these claims, the Finneys' contract with Wind Wire contained the following integration clause:

It is understood that this Agreement and any documents which are attached hereto or referenced herein constitute the intire [sic] agreement between the parties and all other agreements, represenstion [sic], promises, inducements, statements, and understandings, prior to and contemporaneous with this Agreement, written or oral, are suspended by this Agreement.

... The contract also included the following paragraph regarding warranties:

IF PURCHASER MAKES ALL PAYMENTS WHEN DUE, SELLER AND THE MANUFACTURER OF CERTAIN OF THE MATERIAL BEING SUPPLIED BY SELLER WILL PROVIDE PURCHASER WITH SPECIFICATE [sic] WARRANTIES. SELLER MAKES NO OTHER WARRANTIES, EXPRESS OR IMPLIED, OR MERCHANTABILITY OR FITNESS FOR A PARTICULAR PURPOSE WITH RESEPCT [sic] TO THE GOODS COVERED BY THIS CONTRACT....

On January 17, 2012, after a bench trial, the trial court entered judgment in favor of the Finneys. Specifically, the trial court concluded:

Wind Wire has breached [the contract] by failing to provide [the Finneys] the warranties referenced in paragraph 15....
[Wind Wire] has breached the implied warranty that the turbine at issue was fit for the particular purpose for which [the Finneys] purchased it.
[Wind Wire] fraudulently induced [the Finneys] to execute the contract by knowingly and falsely misrepresenting its experience and

expertise, knowingly and falsely misrepresenting the cost savings [the Finneys] would enjoy as a result of the installation of the wind turbine at issue, and by having made such representations, fully aware of their falsity, for the purpose of inducing [the Finneys] to contract with Wind Wire for the purchase and installation of a wind turbine....

The trial court determined that the Finneys suffered damages "at least in the amount of $14,500.00" and that they "are entitled to treble damages due to [Wind Wire's] fraudulent conduct."... The court also awarded the Finneys reasonable attorneys fees, for a total judgment of "$54,893.00 plus the costs of this action."...

Discussion and Decision

I. Integration Clause and Disclaimer

Wind Wire argues that the trial court erred in finding fraud in the inducement. The elements of fraud are "(1) a material representation of [...] facts which (2) was false, (3) was made with knowledge or reckless ignorance of its falsity, (4) was made with the intent to deceive, (5) was rightfully relied upon by the complaining party, and (6) proximately caused injury to the complaining party."... Wind Wire claims the Finneys are precluded from satisfying the fifth element—justifiable reliance—because its contract with the Finneys contained an integration clause that disclaimed reliance on any prior representations. We restate this issue as whether the trial court committed clear error by applying the wrong legal standard.

In the appellate review of claims tried without a jury, the findings and judgment are not to be set aside unless clearly erroneous, and due regard is to be given to the trial court's ability to assess the credibility of the witnesses. A judgment will be clearly erroneous when there is "no evidence supporting the findings or the findings fail to support the judgment," and when the trial court applies the wrong legal standard to properly found facts. While findings of fact are reviewed under the clearly erroneous standard, appellate courts do not defer to conclusions of law, which are reviewed de novo....

"An integration clause of a contract is to be considered as any other contract provision to determine the intention of the parties and to determine if that which they intended to contract is fully expressed in the four corners of the writing."... "Generally, where parties have reduced an agreement to writing and have stated in an integration clause that the written document embodies the complete agreement between the parties, the parol evidence rule prohibits courts from considering extrinsic evidence for the purpose of varying or adding to the terms of the written contract."... "An exception to the parol evidence rule applies, however, in the case of fraud in the inducement, where a party was 'induced' through fraudulent representations to enter a contract."...

Wind Wire contends the fraudulent inducement exception to the parol evidence rule only applies if the alleged misrepresentation specifically " 'induced or produced the execution of the disclaimer,' " as opposed to the signing of the contract generally.... Although Wind Wire accurately quotes our decision in *Circle Ctr. Dev. Co.*, the proposition upon which it relies has a broader application. "In both *Prall* and *Circle Ctr. Dev. Co.* we acknowledged that a party could overcome the effect of an integration clause if it could show it had a right to rely on the alleged misrepresentations and did in fact rely on them in executing the release and/or integration clause."... Moreover, our decision in *Circle Ctr. Dev. Co.* did not overrule the requirement that the weight given to a contract's integration clause be decided on a case-by-case basis.... (" 'Whether one has the right to rely depends largely on the facts of the case.' ").

We conclude that the trial court did not apply the wrong legal standard and, therefore, that its judgment is not clearly erroneous. We note that Wind Wire makes no claim in its Appellant's Brief that the evidence does not support the trial court's findings of fact or that these findings fail to support the court's conclusions of law. The trial court's judgment on this issue is affirmed.

II. Warranty of Fitness for a Particular Purpose
Having affirmed the trial court's judgment on fraud in the inducement, we need not reach Wind Wire's second argument that the court erred in finding breach of the implied warranty of fitness for a particular purpose. As Wind Wire correctly highlights in its reply brief, "the breach of warranty did not form the basis of [the trial court's] decision" or the resulting calculation of damages.... "Rather, the decision was based entirely on the finding of fraud."... Any error pertaining to this issue is, therefore, harmless.

The judgment of the trial court is affirmed.

ROBB, C.J., and BAKER, J., concur.

Case Questions

1. Why was the proof of fraud so important to the Finneys' case?
2. How are Indiana judges supposed to consider cases involving contracts containing zipper clauses?

ASPECTS OF CONTRACT PERFORMANCE

When parties enter into a contract, they generally expect that each side will fully perform in the manner called for in the agreement. Often, however, problems arise and full performance does not occur, as in the following examples.

Accord and Satisfaction

One party may agree to take something less than full performance to satisfy the agreement. For example, suppose that *A* asks *B* to pay a debt for services rendered and *B* states that he is too poor to pay the full amount. *A* may agree to accept payment for only half of the debt. In this situation, the parties have worked out an **accord and satisfaction.** An **accord** is the offer of something different from what was due under the original contract. The **satisfaction** is the agreement to take what is offered. Since the law favors a compromise, courts try to uphold any good-faith modification agreement.

Anticipatory Repudiation

Suppose that *A*, who is one party to a contract, clearly manifests that she will not perform at the scheduled time. This is called **anticipatory repudiation.** The other party, *B*, has a choice at common law. *B* may either sue immediately or ignore *A*'s repudiation and wait for the day of performance. If *B* waits, *A* may change her mind and still perform according to the original contract. Under

UCC Section 2-610, the injured party may not wait until the day of performance. *B* may wait for a change of mind only for a commercially reasonable period of time after repudiation before taking action.

Warranties

A **warranty** is a contractual obligation that sets a standard by which performance of the contract is measured. If the warranties are created by the parties to the contract, they are *express*. Under UCC Section 2-313, express warranties exist whenever a seller affirms facts or describes goods, makes a promise about the goods, or displays a sample model.

If warranties are imposed by law, they are *implied*. There are two types of **implied warranties** under UCC sections 2-314 and 2-315. (1) When a merchant sells goods that are reputed to be fit for the ordinary purpose for which they are intended and are of average quality and properly labeled and packaged, the merchant is bound by an **implied warranty of merchantability.** (2) When the seller has reason to know some particular (nonordinary) purpose for which the buyer has relied on the seller's skill or judgment in making a selection of the type of product to buy, the seller is bound by an **implied warranty of fitness for a particular purpose.**

Implied warranties may be disclaimed by a conspicuous disclaimer statement that the goods are being sold "as is." Once an express warranty is created, however, it cannot be disclaimed, and any attempt to do so is void. The Magnuson–Moss Federal Warranty Act is an act requiring that written warranties for consumer products be categorized as "full" or "limited," so that consumers know what type of warranty protection they are getting. In addition, under this Act, a consumer may sue under both the federal and the state warranties to recover actual damages.

Originally, a warranty was enforceable only by purchasers, but the trend has been to extend the warranty to nonbuyers (such as recipients of gifts) who have been injured by the defective product.

Discharge, Rescission, and Novation

A **discharge** from a duty to perform occurs because of objective impossibility, by operation of law, or by agreement. To illustrate, one party may die or become physically incapable of performing, a statute may be passed that prevents a party from performing, or a duty to perform may be discharged in bankruptcy. Parties can also agree to end their contractual relationship through a rescission. In a **rescission** each party gives up its right to performance from the other; this constitutes sufficient consideration for the discharge. A **novation** occurs when a promisee agrees to release the original promisor from a duty and enters into a new agreement with another party to obtain the desired performance.

Transfers of Duties and Rights

Sometimes one of the original parties to a contract decides to transfer its rights or duties to some third person who was not originally a party to the agreement. The transfer of *rights* is called an **assignment,** and the transfer of *duties* is called a **delegation.** An assignor assigns his or her rights to an assignee. For example, a creditor (the **assignor**) may decide to transfer to a finance company (the **assignee**) her right to collect money owed by a debtor.

In another example, Smith may contract with a builder to construct a garage next to her house using the *turnkey* method of construction (this means that the developer finances and builds the garage and receives payment when it is completed). The builder would negotiate a bank loan to finance the project, and the bank probably would negotiate a requirement that the contractor transfer his payment rights to the bank as security for the loan. A right is not assignable if it significantly affects the corresponding duty associated with that right. Thus, Smith probably would not be permitted to assign her right (to have the builder construct a garage on a particular site) to her sister who lives 20 miles away, since the added distance would be a significant detriment to the building contractor if he had to build a garage on the sister's property rather than Smith's.

A person contractually obligated to perform a duty often may delegate that duty to a third person. If Smith contracts with a painter to paint her new garage, the painter could delegate that duty to other painters. A party cannot delegate a duty if there is a personal component involved such that the duty can be performed only by the party to the original agreement. For example, the personal component exists when a person contracts with a famous photographer to take her portrait. The photographer in this situation would not be permitted to delegate the duty to just any other photographer.

An assignee is legally responsible for any claims that were originally available against the assignor. Thus, the debtor would be entitled to raise the same defenses (such as capacity, duress, illegality,

or mistake) against the finance agency that would be available against the creditor. The rules are similarly strict regarding the delegation of a duty. Smith's originally contracted painter (painter #1) would be responsible if the painter to whom he delegated the painting duty (painter #2) performed inadequately. If Smith agrees to a novation, however, painter #1 would be relieved of his duty to perform, and painter #2 would be substituted.

Statutory provisions generally require that some assignments be in writing. Statutes also prohibit contractual restrictions on most assignments of rights. The following case illustrates what happens when one original contracting party assigns rights and delegates duties over the objection of the other contracting party.

Macke Company v. Pizza of Gaithersburg, Inc.
270 A.2d 645
Court of Appeals of Maryland
November 10, 1970

Singley, Judge.
The appellees and defendants below, Pizza of Gaithersburg, Inc.; Pizzeria, Inc.; The Pizza Pie Corp., Inc. and Pizza Oven, Inc., four corporations under the common ownership of Sidney Ansell, Thomas S. Sherwood and Eugene Early and the same individuals as partners or proprietors (the Pizza Shops) operated at six locations in Montgomery and Prince George's Counties. The appellees had arranged to have installed in each of their locations cold drink vending machines owned by Virginia Coffee Service, Inc., and on 30 December 1966, this arrangement was formalized at five of the locations, by contracts for terms of one year, automatically renewable for a like term in the absence of 30 days' written notice. A similar contract for the sixth location, operated by Pizza of Gaithersburg, Inc., was entered into on 25 July 1967.

On 30 December 1967, Virginia's assets were purchased by The Macke Company (Macke) and the six contracts were assigned to Macke by Virginia. In January, 1968, the Pizza Shops attempted to terminate the five contracts having the December anniversary date, and in February the contract which had the July anniversary date.

Macke brought suit in the Circuit Court for Montgomery County against each of the Pizza Shops for damages for breach of contract. From judgments for the defendants, Macke has appealed.

The lower court based the result which it reached on two grounds: first, that the Pizza Shops, when they contracted with Virginia, relied on its skill, judgment and reputation, which made impossible a delegation of Virginia's duties to Macke; and second, that the damages claimed could not be shown with reasonable certainty. These conclusions are challenged by Macke.

In the absence of a contrary provision—and there was none here—rights and duties under an executory bilateral contract may be assigned and delegated, subject to the exception that duties under a contract to provide personal services may never be delegated, nor rights be assigned under a contract where *delectus personae* [*delectus personae* means choice of person] was an ingredient of the bargain....

The six machines were placed on the appellees' premises under a printed "Agreement-Contract" which identified the "customer," gave its place of business, described the vending machine, and then provided:

TERMS

1. The Company will install on the Customer's premises the above listed equipment in good operating order and stocked with merchandise.

2. The location of this equipment will be such as to permit accessibility to persons desiring use of same. This equipment shall remain the

property of the Company and shall not be moved from the location at which installed, except by the Company.

3. For equipment requiring electricity and water, the Customer is responsible for electrical receptacle and water outlet within ten (10) feet of the equipment location. The Customer is also responsible to supply the Electrical Power and Water needed.

4. The Customer will exercise every effort to protect this equipment from abuse or damage.

5. The Company will be responsible for all licenses and taxes on the equipment and sale of products.

6. This Agreement-Contract is for a term of one (1) year from the date indicated herein and will be automatically renewed for a like period, unless thirty (30) day written notice is given by either party to terminate service.

7. Commission on monthly sales will be paid by the Company to the Customer at the following rate:....

The rate provided in each of the agreements was "30 percent of Gross Receipts to $300.00 monthly[,] 35 percent over [$]300.00," except for the agreement with Pizza of Gaithersburg, Inc., which called for "40 percent of Gross Receipts."

... We cannot regard the agreements as contracts for personal services. They were either a license or concession granted Virginia by the appellees, or a lease of a portion of the appellees' premises, with Virginia agreeing to pay a percentage of gross sales as a license or concession fee or as rent, ... and were assignable by Virginia unless they imposed on Virginia duties of a personal or unique character which could not be delegated.... [T]he agreements with Virginia were silent as to the details of the working arrangements and contained only a provision requiring Virginia to

"install ... the above listed equipment and ... maintain the equipment in good operating order and stocked with merchandise."... Moreover, the difference between the service the Pizza Shops happened to be getting from Virginia and what they expected to get from Macke did not mount up to such a material change in the performance of obligations under the agreements as would justify the appellees' refusal to recognize the assignment.... Modern authorities ... hold that, absent provision to the contrary, a duty may be delegated, as distinguished from a right which can be assigned, and that the promisee cannot rescind, if the quality of the performance remains materially the same.

Restatement, Contracts § 160(3) (1932) reads, in part:

> Performance or offer of performance by a person delegated has the same legal effect as performance or offer of performance by the person named in the contract, unless, "(a) performance by the person delegated varies or would vary materially from performance by the person named in the contract as the one to perform, and there has been no ... assent to the delegation."...

In cases involving the sale of goods, the Restatement rule respecting delegation of duties has been amplified by Uniform Commercial Code § 2-210(5), Maryland Code (1957, 1964 Repl. Vol.) Art 95B §2-210(5), which permits a promisee to demand ... assurances from the party to whom duties have been delegated....

As we see it, the delegation of duty by Virginia to Macke was entirely permissible under the terms of the agreements....

Judgment reversed as to liability; judgment entered for appellant for costs, on appeal and below; case remanded for a new trial on the question of damages.

Case Questions

1. When Virginia Coffee Service sold its assets to Macke Company, what rights did it assign?
2. What duties were delegated?

Contracts for the Benefit of Third Parties

In some situations, the parties contract with a clear understanding that the agreement is intended to benefit some other, noncontracting person. For example, a son and daughter might contract with a carpenter to repair the back stairs at their elderly mother's house. In another case, a woman might have accidentally damaged a neighbor's fence and agreed to have the fence repaired. The woman might want to discharge this obligation by contracting with a carpenter to repair the damage.

The third person in the first example (the mother) is classified as a **donee beneficiary,** and the third person in the second example (the neighbor) is classified as a **creditor beneficiary**. American law generally permits donee beneficiaries and creditor beneficiaries to sue for breach of contract. The third party's right to sue, however, only exists if that party's rights have *vested,* that is, have matured to the point of being legally enforceable. Jurisdictions generally choose one of the following three rules to decide when rights vest: (1) rights vest when the contract is formed, (2) rights vest when the beneficiary acquires knowledge about the contract, or (3) rights vest when the beneficiary relies on the contract and changes his or her position.

INTERNET TIP

Readers can read a New York appellate court opinion in a case in which the deceased plaintiff's estate claimed that she was an intended third-party beneficiary in a contract between her landlord and a contractor. *Castorino v. Unifast Building Products* can be found on the textbook's website.

The Duty to Perform and Breach of Contract

Many agreements include conditions precedent and conditions subsequent that may affect a party's duty to perform. A **condition precedent** exists when some specified event must occur before a duty to perform becomes operative (i.e., obtain a mortgage at a specified rate of interest before the buyer has a duty to close on a purchase of real estate). A **condition subsequent** exists when a specified event occurs that discharges the parties from their duties.[20]

A breach of contract occurs when a party fails to perform a duty, or inadequately performs what he or she has promised. A breach of contract is a material breach if the nonperforming party totally or substantially fails to perform. Thus, a material breach has occurred if a homeowner contracts with a painter to paint a house with two coats of primer and one finish coat, and the painter quits after painting one coat of primer. The homeowner has not received the substantial benefit of his or her bargain.

In the next case, an exterminating company was found to have breached its contract with a homeowner through inadequate performance of its duty.

Clarkson v. Orkin Exterminating Co., Inc.
761 F.2d 189
U.S. Court of Appeals, Fourth Circuit
May 9, 1985

Haynsworth, Senior Circuit Judge.
A jury awarded the plaintiff damages on three separate claims. She claimed breach of a contract to inspect for termites and to treat again if necessary. There was a claim of fraud and of a violation of South Carolina's Unfair Trade Practices Act. § 39–0(a), Code of Laws of South Carolina, 1976.

There was adequate proof that Orkin broke its contract, though an improper measure of damages was applied. There is no evidence in the record, however, to support the finding of fraud or a violation of the Unfair Trade Practices Act. Hence, we reverse in part and affirm in part, but remand the contract claim for an appropriate assessment of damages.

I
In 1976 Mrs. Clarkson purchased a house. Orkin had contracted with her predecessor in title to retreat the house in the event that a termite problem developed. Orkin also promised, for a fee, to inspect the house yearly and, if necessary, retreat it for termites before certifying that the house remained free of termites.

In early 1983, Mrs. Clarkson offered her home for sale. When prospective purchasers noticed evidence of termite infestation, Mrs. Clarkson called Orkin and requested that they inspect the house. Orkin complied with her request and issued a report that the house was free of termites. The report also mentioned the presence of a moisture problem, which had been reported to Mrs. Clarkson on several earlier occasions but which remained uncorrected. For the moisture problem, Orkin had unsuccessfully attempted to sell a protective chemical treatment to Mrs. Clarkson.

The day after Orkin's 1983 inspection, Mrs. Clarkson had the house inspected by the representative of another exterminating company. He found two termite tunnels and damage from water. He attributed the water damage to a drainage problem and expressed the opinion that the water damage would progress unless there were alterations to a porch to prevent drainage of water into the basement.

After a contractor had made the necessary repairs and the recommended alterations, Mrs. Clarkson sought to have Orkin reimburse her for her entire cost of the reconstruction work. She also asked that Orkin reinspect the house and certify that the house was free of termite infestation. Orkin refused both requests.

A jury awarded Mrs. Clarkson $613.47 on the breach of contract claim, $551 on the Unfair Trade Practices Act Claim and $1,148 actual damages and $5,000 punitive damages on the fraud claim. The district judge concluded that the Unfair Trade Practices Act claim was a willful one and tripled the award on that claim and ordered Orkin to pay the plaintiff's attorneys' fees.

II

As proof of a violation of the South Carolina Unfair Trade Practices Act, Mrs. Clarkson points (1) to the fact that Orkin certified in 1983 that the house was free of termites when significant infestation was visible, and (2) the fact that Orkin on several occasions had attempted, though unsuccessfully, to sell to Mrs. Clarkson a "moisture problem treatment package" that would not have been an adequate corrective of an improper drainage problem.

It is abundantly clear that in its 1983 inspection Orkin's representative failed to discover termite infestation which was present and visible. This, however, does not establish a violation of the South Carolina Unfair Trade Practices Act. It shows no more than that Orkin's representative was negligent or incompetent. Mrs. Clarkson had not directed his

attention to the area where the infestation was present, though she did direct the attention of the other exterminator to that area....

III

There is enough to support a finding of contract violation. Orkin failed to retreat the house when a termite infestation was present, and it refused Mrs. Clarkson's subsequent request that it reinspect and spray the house after the repairs had been made.

There is no claim that Mrs. Clarkson lost an opportunity to sell the house because of the termite problem. What she claimed was the cost of repairs and alterations. On the breach of contract claim, the jury assessed the damaged at $613.47, which was precisely the cost to Mrs. Clarkson of replacing the wood damaged by the termites. In effect, the jury converted Orkin's retreatment contract into a repair contract.

Orkin offers its customers alternatives. It will promise and guarantee to provide retreatment if there is a later termite infestation. For a higher fee, it will promise and guarantee to effect necessary repairs after a termite infestation has occurred. Mrs. Clarkson's predecessor in title, and she, elected to take the lower option. In Orkin's guarantee to Mrs. Clarkson, there is an express recital of her waiver and release of Orkin from any liability for damage to the structure occasioned by termites. Mrs. Clarkson cannot now claim the benefits of a repair guarantee she chose not to purchase.

Mrs. Clarkson was entitled to a proper performance by Orkin of its contract, which was to inspect and treat again if an infestation was found. That promise was not properly performed, and Mrs. Clarkson is entitled to any damage she suffered by reason of that non-performance. Since she knew of the termite infestation one day after Orkin failed to detect it, her damage would apparently be limited to the cost of inspection by the other exterminator plus the cost of any retreatment she may have procured.

While we agree that the evidence supports a finding of a breach of contract, we remand that claim for further proceedings on damages as may be consistent with this opinion. Judgment in the plaintiff's favor on the unfair trade practice and fraud claims is reversed.

Reversed in part; Affirmed in part, and remanded.

Case Questions

1. In what way did Orkin breach its duty?
2. Why did the court remand the breach of contract claim for further proceedings?

REMEDIES FOR BREACH OF CONTRACT

An injured party who has established a breach of contract is entitled to turn to a court for legal or equitable relief, as discussed in Chapter VII.

Common Law Remedies

In most cases of breach, the injured party is awarded money damages, which can be compensatory, nominal, or liquidated (topics that were previously explained in Chapter VII).

The following case involves breach of contract claims between homeowners and a building contractor. The homeowners discharged the contractor because of defective work. The contractor filed suit against the homeowners to recover damages. The Maine Supreme Court vacated the trial court's judgment on the homeowners' counterclaim because of errors in the jury instructions regarding damages.

Anuszewski v. Jurevic
566 A.2d 742
Supreme Judicial Court of Maine
November 28, 1989

Clifford, Justice.
Defendants and counterclaim plaintiffs Richard and Judy Jurevic appeal from a judgment entered after a jury trial in Superior Court.... Because we conclude that the court improperly limited the jury's consideration of damages claimed by the Jurevics, we vacate the judgment on the counterclaim.

In early 1987, the Jurevics contracted with the plaintiff, Robert E. Anuszewski, a contractor doing business as Pine Tree Post & Beam, for Anuszewski to construct a home for the Jurevics in Kennebunkport. The home was to be completed by June 1, 1987, at a cost of $134,000, and the contract called for the Jurevics to make periodic progress payments. The home was only about fifty percent complete on June 1, 1987. In January, 1988, the Jurevics discharged Anuszewski. In March, 1988, Anuszewski brought an action against the Jurevics to recover $39,590. The $39,500 represented, alternatively, the unpaid part of the contract price, or the value of the labor and materials provided by Anuszewski for which he had not been paid. The Jurevics filed a counterclaim.

At trial, the Jurevics presented evidence that the construction work was defective and testimony in the form of an expert opinion as to the total cost to correct the defects and to complete the house. The testimony indicated that this cost would include a general contractor markup of fifty percent added to the actual cost of the work to be done for overhead and profit, and that this was a usual and customary practice of the industry. The Jurevics also claimed damages for rental and other incidental expenses caused by Anuszewski's delay in completing the house. The court, however, prohibited the Jurevics from presenting evidence of delay damages beyond January 5, 1988, the date the Jurevics terminated the contract with Anuszewski.

At the conclusion of the evidence, the court, in its jury instructions, precluded the jury from considering the general contractor's markup as follows:

[I]f you find that the Jurevics are entitled to recover damages from Mr. Anuszewski for completion of the work not done or for repairing work not performed in a workmanlike manner, any amount of damages that you award must be the cost of doing that work by the various workmen without any markup to a general contractor, such as was testified to by [the Jurevics' expert witness].

The jury returned a verdict awarding Anuszewski damages of $25,000 on his complaint and awarding $22,000 to the Jurevics on their counterclaim. This appeal by the Jurevics followed the denial of their motions for a mistrial, or in the alternative, for a new trial, and for additur.

We find merit in the Jurevics' contention that the court impermissibly restricted the jury's consideration of the full amount of damages that they were entitled to recover. The purpose of contract damages is to place the injured parties in the position they would have been in but for the breach, by awarding the value of the promised performance.... Those damages for breach of a construction contract are measured by either the difference in value between the performance promised and the performance rendered, or the amount reasonably required to remedy the defect.... The amount reasonably required to remedy the defect may be measured by the actual cost of necessary repairs.... Those costs may be proven by the presentation of expert testimony, as the Jurevics did here....

The court correctly instructed the jury that the Jurevics' measure of recovery for incomplete or defective work was "the amount reasonably required to remedy the defect" as specifically measured by the actual cost of repair.... The court went on, however, to instruct the jury that the cost of repair was to be considered "without any markup to a general contractor." This instruction was given despite testimony from an expert witness that the actual cost to remedy the incomplete and defective construction work of Anuszewski would include a general contractor markup for overhead and profit, and that such a markup was customary and usual in the construction business. Although Anuszewski defends the court's instruction, he did not argue at trial, nor does he now, that the Jurevics were not entitled to have the jury consider their claim that it was reasonable for them to hire a general contractor to supervise the repairs and completion of the house. If the jury concluded that it

would be reasonable for the Jurevics to hire a substitute general contractor to supervise the repairs and completion, but was precluded by the court's instruction from considering the award of damages for the reasonable cost of the substitute contractor's overhead, for which the evidence suggests they would be charged as a matter of routine, then the Jurevics could be deprived of full recovery in their breach of contract claim. They would not be placed in the same position they would have been had Anuszewski performed the contract....

In breach of contract cases we have upheld repair or replacement damage awards of the amount required to bring a home into compliance with the contract.... In addition, we have affirmed the computation of indebtedness owed a builder by a homeowner that included a contractor's overhead and profit.... We see no reason to exclude reasonable and customary profit and overhead of a contractor from the cost of repairs to remedy defects in a breach of contract case.

The entry is:

Judgment on the complaint affirmed. Judgment on the counterclaim vacated.

Remanded to the Superior Court for further proceedings consistent with the opinion herein.

Case Questions

1. According to the Jurevics, what error was committed by the trial judge?
2. What is a counterclaim?

Equitable Remedies

If money damages are deemed to be an inadequate remedy, the court may be persuaded to grant equitable relief. The discussion in Chapter VII addresses the most common forms of equitable relief in breach of contract cases (injunctions, restitution after the court has granted rescission, and specific performance).

UCC Remedies for Breach of Contract for the Sale of Goods

The Uniform Commercial Code provides special rules for breaches of contract involving the sale of

goods. For example, if a seller breaches his or her contract to deliver goods, the buyer is entitled to (1) rescind the contract, (2) sue for damages, and (3) obtain restitution for any payments made. If the goods are unique—such as rare artwork—or are custom-made, a court may order specific performance. Replevin also is permitted in some situations. If a buyer breaches a sales contract by not accepting delivery of goods, or wrongfully revokes a prior acceptance, the injured seller is entitled to (1) cancel the contract, (2) stop delivery of goods, and (3) recover money damages from the buyer.

CHAPTER SUMMARY

The contracts chapter began with a historical review of the common law antecedents of modern contract law. Included in this overview were the writs of debt, detinue, covenant, trespass, trespass on the case, and assumpsit, as well as the eventual replacement of the writ system with modern code pleading and the development of uniform legislation, such as the Uniform Commercial Code (UCC). Readers then learned that contracts are classified in terms of validity (valid, void, voidable), enforceability, and whether they are bilateral or unilateral. The discussion then turned to an examination of each of the essential requirements of an enforceable contract: (1) an agreement (2) between competent parties (3) based on genuine assent of the parties (4) supported by consideration (5) that does not contravene principles of law and (6) that must be in writing in certain circumstances. Attention also was given to several aspects of contract performance, such as accord and satisfaction, anticipatory repudiation, warranties, discharge, rescission, and novation, and to the transfers of rights and duties to other persons who were not parties to the original agreement. The chapter concluded with a brief return visit to the topic of remedies, which was earlier addressed in Chapter VII.

CHAPTER QUESTIONS

1. Paul Searle, a former basketball player at St. Joseph's College, brought suit against the college, the basketball coach, and the trainer for breach of contract and negligence. Searle alleged that he had sustained basketball-related injuries to his knees and that St. Joseph's had orally contracted to reimburse him for his basketball-related medical costs. Searle asserted in his complaint that the college had promised to pay his medical expenses if he continued to play for the team. His proof was a statement that the coach had approached Searle's parents after a game and expressed a willingness to pay for all of the medical bills. Given the above factual record, does Searle have a contract with St. Joseph's College?

   Searle v. Trustees of St. Joseph's College, 695 A.2d 1206 (1997)

2. S. Allen Schreiber, having tired of receiving unsolicited phone calls from telemarketers in general, received such a call on November 29, 1989, from Olan Mills, a national family portrait chain. Schreiber promptly sent a "Dear Telemarketer" letter to the defendant.

   Dear Telemarketer:

   Today, you called us attempting to sell us a product or a service. We have no interest in the product or service that you are selling. Please don't call us again. Please remove us from your telemarketing list and notify the provider of the list to also remove our name and number since we do not appreciate receiving telemarketing phone calls.

   We rely on the availability of our phone lines, which have been installed for our convenience and not for the convenience of telemarketers. We pay for these phone lines and instruments. You do not. Please don't tie up our phone lines.

   Should we receive any more calls from you or from anyone connected with your firm of a telemarketing nature, we will consider that you have entered into a contract with us for our listening services and that you have made those calls to us and expect us to listen to your message on a "for-hire" basis.

   If we receive any additional telemarketing phone calls from you, you will be invoiced in accordance with our rates, which are $100.00 per hour or fraction thereof, with a $100 minimum charge. Payment will be due on a net seven (7) day basis.

Late payment charge of 1-½% per month or fraction thereof on the unpaid balance subject to a minimum late charge of $ 9.00 per invoice per month or fraction thereof will be billed if payment is not made as outlined above. This is an annual percentage rate of 18%. In addition, should it become necessary for us to institute collection activities, all costs in connection therewith including, but not limited to, attorney fees will also be due and collectible.

Olan Mill representatives made two additional calls, which resulted in the present breach of contract suit. Did Olan Mills enter into an enforceable contract with Schreiber?

Schreiber v. Olan Mills, 627 A.2d 806 (1993)

3. George and Mary Jane Graham were driving in a car insured by State Farm when they were forced off the road by an unidentified motorist. The Grahams' vehicle struck a telephone pole and both occupants were injured. When the Grahams were unable to reach an agreement with their insurer, State Farm, regarding the amount they should be paid pursuant to the uninsured motorist provisions of their automobile insurance policy, they filed suit against State Farm. State Farm responded with a motion for summary judgment on the grounds that the policy called for binding arbitration in lieu of litigation in the event of such a dispute. The Grahams did not know about the arbitration clause at the time they paid the first premium. State Farm pointed out that the Grahams, after receiving a copy of the policy, never complained about the arbitration clause at any time during the following two years. The Grahams responded that this was a "take-it-or-leave-it" situation, under which they actually had no opportunity to "leave it" because they were denied the information necessary to make a decision at the time they enrolled with State Farm. The court, they contended, should not compel them to arbitrate their claim. They pointed out that this contract was drafted by the insurance company's lawyers, and that the terms were written

in a one-sided manner, permitting the powerful insurance company to take advantage of weaker insureds such as the Grahams. Delaware public policy favors the use of arbitration to resolve disputes in situations such as this. Should the court enforce the arbitration clause?

Graham v. State Farm Mutual Co., 565 A.2d 908 (1989)

4. Mr. Lucy and Mr. Zehmer were talking at a restaurant. After a couple of drinks, Lucy asked Zehmer if he had sold the Ferguson farm. Zehmer replied that he had not and did not want to sell it. Lucy said, "I bet you wouldn't take $50,000 cash for that farm," and Zehmer replied, "You haven't got $50,000 cash." Lucy said, "I can get it." Zehmer said Lucy might form a company and get it, "but you haven't got $50,000 to pay me tonight." Lucy asked him if he would put it in writing that he would sell him this farm. Zehmer then wrote on the back of a pad, "I agree to sell the Ferguson Place to W. O. Lucy for $50,000 cash." Lucy said, "All right, get your wife to sign it." Zehmer subsequently went to his wife and said, "You want to put your name to this?" She said no, but he said in an undertone, "It is nothing but a joke," and she signed it. At that time, Zehmer was not too drunk to make a valid contract. Lucy came up with the $50,000; however, the Zehmers refused to convey legal title to the property, and Lucy sued for specific performance. What defense would the Zehmers use in the suit? Who should win the suit?

Lucy v. Zehmer, 196 Va. 493, 84 S.E.2d 516 (1954)

5. National Beverages, Inc., offered to the public prizes to be awarded in a contest known as "Pepsi-Cola Streator-Chevrolet Sweepstakes." The first prize was a Chevrolet Corvair. No order of drawing was announced prior to the close of the contest. After the close of the contest, just prior to the drawing, a sign was displayed stating the order of drawing. The first tickets drawn would receive twelve cases of Pepsi-Cola, and the last ticket drawn would receive the automobile. Walters's ticket was the first ticket to be

drawn from the barrel. She claims that her number, being the first qualified number drawn, entitles her to the first prize, the Chevrolet Corvair. She bases her claim on the wording of the offer, which listed the automobile as the first prize. She accepted the offer by entering the contest. Is Walters entitled to the automobile?

Walters v. National Beverages, Inc., 18 Utah 2d 301, 422 P.2d 524 (1967)

6. Green signed a roofing contract with Clay Tile, agent for Ever-Tite Roofing Company, to have a new roof put on his house. The agreement stated that this contract was subject to Ever-Tite's approval and that the agreement would become binding upon written notice of acceptance or commencement of work. Nine days later, Clay Tile loaded up his truck and drove to Green's house, only to find that someone else was already doing the job. Ever-Tite wishes to sue on the contract for damages. Was Green's offer to Ever-Tite accepted before the offer was revoked?

Ever-Tite Roofing Corporation v. Green, 83 So. 2d 449 (La. App. 1955)

7. Workers agreed to work aboard a canning ship during the salmon canning season. The contract, signed individually by each worker, was to last for the length of time it took to sail from San Francisco, California, to Pyramid Harbor, Alaska, and back. Each worker was to receive a stated compensation. They arrived in Alaska at the height of the fishing and canning season. Knowing that every day's delay would be financially disastrous and that it would be impossible to find workers to replace them, the workers refused to work unless they were given substantial wage increases. The owner of the canning ship acceded to their demands. When the ship returned to San Francisco, the owner paid them in accordance with the original agreement. The workers now bring suit to recover the additional amounts due under the second agreement. Will the contract be upheld?

Alaska Packers Association v. Domenico, 117 F. 99 (9th Cir. 1902)

8. A little girl found a pretty stone about the size of a canary bird's egg. She had no idea what it was, so she took it to a jeweler, who eventually bought it from her for a dollar, although he, too, did not know what it was. The stone turned out to be an uncut diamond worth $10,000. The girl tendered back the $1 purchase price and sued to have the sale voided on the basis of mutual mistake. Should mutual mistake be a basis for recovery?

Wood v. Boynton, 64 Wis. 265, 25 N.W. 42 (1885)

9. William E. Story agreed orally with his nephew that if he would refrain from drinking liquor, using tobacco, swearing, and playing cards or billiards for money until he became twenty-one years old, then he, Story, would pay his nephew $5,000 when the nephew reached age twenty-one. The nephew fully performed his part of the agreement. But when the nephew reached age twenty-one, his uncle stated that he had earned the $5,000 and that he would keep it at interest for his nephew. Twelve years later, Story died, and his nephew brought an action to recover the $5,000 plus interest. Was there sufficient consideration to create a contract?

Hamer v. Sidway, 124 N.Y. 538, 27 N.E. 256 (1891)

NOTES

1. W. Walsh, *A History of Anglo-American Law* (Indianapolis, IN: Bobbs-Merrill Company, 1932), p. 339; A. W. B. Simpson, *A History of the Common Law of Contract* (Oxford, England: Clarendon Press, 1975), pp. 12, 53; A. K. R. Kiralfy, *Potter's Historical Introduction to English Law* (London: Sweet and Maxwell Ltd., 1962), pp. 452–457.

2. Kiralfy, p. 456.

3. Ibid., pp. 456–457.

4. Ibid., pp. 305–307; Walsh, p. 344.

5. Walsh, p. 342.

6. Simpson, p. 199; Walsh, p. 344.

7. Simpson, p. 210; Kiralfy, p. 461; Walsh, p. 341.

8. Walsh, p. 340; Simpson, p. 224; T. F. F. Plucknett, *A Concise History of the Common Law* (Boston: Little, Brown, 1956), p. 639.

9. Walsh, pp. 345, 351; Simpson, p. 406; Plucknett, pp. 649–656.

10. Kiralfy, p. 626.

11. B. Schwartz, *The Law in America* (New York: McGraw-Hill, 1974), pp. 59–62; W. E. Nelson, *Americanization of the Common Law* (Cambridge, MA: Harvard University Press, 1975), p. 86.

12. M. Horwitz, *The Transformation of American Law, 1780–1860* (Cambridge, MA: Harvard University Press, 1977), pp. 164–180; Nelson, p. 154.

13. Horwitz, pp. 167, 173.

14. Schwartz, p. 72; Nelson, p. 86.

15. Horwitz, p. 185.

16. The "mailbox rule" is a default rule that applies when the offeror does not specify when acceptance is effective in the offer. Thus if the offer is otherwise silent, acceptance occurs when the offeree places an envelope containing a writing that indicates acceptance and that is properly addressed, with first class postage paid, into the U.S. Mail.

17. A *mistake of law* occurs, for example, if a person drives into a state park without paying the entrance fee, mistakenly believing that in spite of the park entrance sign they saw to the contrary, they didn't have a legal obligation to pay. In this situation a *unilateral contract* has been formed in which the driver *accepts* the state park department's *offer* of admittance to the park in exchange for payment of a fee. The fact that the driver is mistaken about the law requiring payment of the fee does not relieve the driver of the obligation to pay once he or she has driven into the park.

18. However, requiring someone to come to your home *and visit with you* for an hour might constitute valid consideration.

19. Stanley, while married to Rosalie, received a gift of twenty acres of land. When his marriage seemed to be in trouble, he and his brother, Thomas, agreed that Stanley would transfer the twenty acres to Thomas and that after Stanley's divorce was final, Thomas would transfer it back to Stanley. After the divorce was finalized, Thomas reneged on his promise and was sued for breach of contract by Stanley. The trial court concluded that the brothers were defrauding both Rosalie and the family court judge in the divorce proceedings by trying to hide an asset from the court in violation of state law. The trial court dismissed the complaint. Stanley appealed. The court of appeals affirmed the trial court, pointing out that both divorcing parties have a statutory duty to disclose their real estate holdings and all assets to the family court. The appellate court noted that Stanley planned the scam and drafted the contract and the deed "with the intent to evade his statutory obligation." This, said the court, showed that Stanley's guilt was much greater than that of his brother. The court explained "the general rule is that both at law and in equity, a court will not aid either party to an illegal agreement … [and] leaves the parties where it finds them…. Because the court does not reward the perpetrator of a fraud upon the court, we affirm the trial court's decision to void the contract and permit the parcel to be titled in Thomas' name." *Jezeski v. Jezeski*, 763 N.W.2d 176 (2008).

20. For example, a trash-hauling company agrees to discharge a customer from her contractual obligation to make monthly payments for a year if the customer moves at least 30 miles from her current location. The monthly payments cease when the *condition subsequent* occurs, that is when the customer moves 30 miles or more away from her current location.

XI

The Law of Torts

CHAPTER OBJECTIVES

1. *Understand the historical origins of the modern tort action.*
2. *Identify the three types of civil wrongs that comprise modern tort law.*
3. *Explain the essential functions of tort law.*
4. *Understand how the named intentional torts differ.*
5. *Understand the elements that a plaintiff must prove to establish negligence.*
6. *Explain how comparative negligence states determine the payment of damages.*
7. *Understand and explain the concept of strict liability in tort.*

A tort is a civil wrong, other than a breach of contract, for which courts provide a remedy in the form of an action for damages. Tort law seeks to provide reimbursement to members of society who suffer losses because of the dangerous or unreasonable conduct of others. Each of the fifty states determines its own tort law, which is divided into the following three categories: intentional torts, negligence, and strict liability.

You may recall from Figure 1.1 "Criminal and Civil Law" and the accompanying discussion in Chapter I that that there are important differences between criminal law and tort law. It was there emphasized that criminal prosecutions are brought by the government to convict and then punish offenders who have committed crimes and thereby harmed society as a whole. You should also remember that the Constitution provides defendants in criminal cases with procedural protections that are unavailable in civil litigation. Nevertheless, it is possible for criminal defendants to be sued civilly irrespective of the criminal trial's outcome.

HISTORICAL EVOLUTION OF AMERICAN TORT LAW

The word **tort** (meaning "wrong") is one of many Norman words that became a part of the English and American legal lexicon. American tort law evolved from the writs of trespass[1] and trespass on the case.[2] Trespass covered a variety of acts, which included trespass to land, assaults, batteries, the taking of goods, and false imprisonment. Each of the acts involved a **tortfeasor** directly causing injury to a victim. By the end of Henry III's reign (1272), it was commonplace for plaintiffs to use trespass to recover money damages for personal injuries.[3] In 1285, Parliament enacted the Statute of Westminster,[4] which authorized the chancery to create new writs to address wrongs that fell outside the boundaries of trespass. Because the new writs were designed to remedy the factual circumstances of a particular case, they were called trespass actions on the case (also called "actions on the case"). From trespass on the case came our contemporary concept of negligence.

One of the major drawbacks of the writ system was that it lacked any comprehensive underlying theoretical base. In the 1800s, as the writ system was being replaced with more modern forms of pleading, American law professors and judges began to develop a basic theory for tort law based on fault.

FUNCTIONS OF TORT LAW

Tort law establishes standards of conduct for all members of society. It defines as civil wrongs these antisocial behaviors: the failure to exercise reasonable care (negligence); intentional interference with one's person, reputation, or property (intentional torts); and in some circumstances, liability without fault (strict liability). Tort law deters people from engaging in behavior patterns that the law does not condone and compensates victims for their civil injuries. It is thus a vehicle by which an injured person can attempt to shift the costs of harm to another person. Tort law is not static; courts can create new causes of action to remedy an injustice. Thus, the argument that a claim is novel does not prevent a court from granting relief when it becomes clear that the law should protect the plaintiff's rights.

Because the plaintiffs in tort cases are usually seeking money damages, tort actions that are not settled prior to trial generally are tried to juries. See Table 11.1.

INTENTIONAL TORTS

Intentional torts are based on willful misconduct or intentional wrongs. A tortfeasor who intentionally invades a protected interest of another, under circumstances for which there is no lawful justification or excuse, is legally and morally "at fault." The intent is not necessarily a hostile intent or even a desire to do serious harm. A person acts intentionally if he or she has a conscious desire to produce consequences the law recognizes as tortious. A person who has no conscious desire to cause the consequences, but is aware that the consequences are highly likely to follow, also can be found to have acted intentionally.

Assault

Assault is an intentional tort because as a general proposition, every person should have the right to live his or her life without being placed in reasonable fear of an intentional, imminent, unconsented, harmful, or offensive touching by another person. Assaults occur where the targeted person's anxiety is the product of the actor's threatening conduct, such as stalking. The law also recognizes that an assault has occurred where a targeted person's fear is the product of the actor's unsuccessful attempt to hit the target with a punch or a thrown object. Mere words alone, however, usually will not constitute

Case type	Number of tort trials	Percentage disposed of by	
		Jury Trial	Bench Trial
All tort trials	16,398	90.0	10.0
Medical malpractice	2,449	98.7	1.3
Professional malpractice	150	60.0	40.0
Asbestos product liability	87	95.4	4.6
Premises liability	1,863	93.8	6.2
Other product liability	268	92.5	7.5
Automobile accident	9,431	92.2	7.8
Animal attack	138	80.6	19.4
Intentional tort	725	78.2	21.8
Other/unknown tort	664	71.5	28.5
Slander/libel	187	64.2	35.8
False arrest/imprisonment	58	63.8	36.2
Conversion	378	46.3	53.7

F I G U R E   11.1   Tort Cases Disposed of by Bench or Jury Trial in State Courts, by Case Type, 2005

Source: U.S. Department of Justice, *Bureau of Justice Statistics Bulletin,* NCJ 228129 (November 2009), Table 1.

an assault, no matter how threatening or abusive they may be. Once an actor has committed an assault, the tort has been committed. An actor cannot, through the abandonment of further assaultive conduct, avoid civil liability for assaultive conduct already committed against a target.

Battery

In the intentional tort called battery, the tortfeasor has violated the target's right to be free from harmful or offensive touchings by another. A **battery** is defined as an unpermitted, unprivileged, intentional contact with another's person. This tort includes contact that is actually harmful, as well as conduct that is merely offensive. The standard used to determine offensiveness is not whether a particular plaintiff is offended, but whether an ordinary person who is not unusually sensitive in the matter of dignity would be offended. It is not essential that the plaintiff be conscious of the contact at the time it occurs.

Assault or battery may occur without the other, but usually both result from the same occurrence. As a result of an assault and battery—as well as other intentional torts—the injured party may bring a civil suit for damages and, as has been previously discussed, also seek a criminal prosecution for the same act.

The following case illustrates the intentional torts of assault, battery, and invasion of privacy.

Estate of Berthiaume v. Pratt, M.D.
365 A.2d 792
Supreme Judicial Court of Maine
November 10, 1976

Pomeroy, Justice.

The appellant, as administratrix, based her claim of right to damages on an alleged invasion of her late husband's "right to privacy" and on an alleged assault and battery of him. At the close of the evidence produced at trial, a justice of the Superior Court granted defendant's motion for a directed verdict. Appellant's seasonable appeal brings the case to this court.

The appellee is a physician and surgeon practicing in Waterville, Maine. It was established at trial without contradiction that the deceased, Henry Berthiaume, was suffering from a cancer of his larynx. Appellee, an otolaryngologist, had treated him twice surgically. A laryngectomy was performed; and later, because of a tumor which had appeared in his neck, a radical neck dissection on one side was done. No complaint is made with respect to the surgical interventions.

During the period appellee was serving Mr. Berthiaume as a surgeon, many photographs of Berthiaume had been taken by appellee or under his direction. The jury was told that the sole use to which these photographs were to be put was to make the medical record for the appellee's use....

Although at no time did the appellee receive any written consent for taking of photographs from Berthiaume or any members of his family, it was appellee's testimony that Berthiaume had always consented to having such photographs made.

At all times material hereto, Mr. Berthiaume was a patient of a physician other than the appellee. Such other physician had referred the patient to appellee for surgery. On September 2, 1970, appellee saw the patient for the last time for the purpose of treatment or diagnosis. The incident which gave rise to this lawsuit occurred on September 23, 1970. It was also on that day Mr. Berthiaume died.

Although appellee disputed the evidence appellant produced at trial in many material respects, the jury could have concluded from the evidence that shortly before Mr. Berthiaume died on the 23rd, the appellee and a nurse appeared in his hospital room. In the presence of Mrs. Berthiaume and a visitor of the patient in the next bed, either Dr. Pratt or the nurse, at his direction, raised the dying Mr. Berthiaume's head and placed some blue operating room toweling under his head and beside him on the bed. The appellee testified that this blue toweling was placed there for the purpose of obtaining a color contrast for the photographs which he proposed to take. He then proceeded to take several photographs of Mr. Berthiaume.

The jury could have concluded from the testimony that Mr. Berthiaume protested the taking of pictures by raising a clenched fist and moving his head in an attempt to remove his head from the camera's range. The appellee himself testified that before taking the pictures he had been told by Mrs. Berthiaume when he talked with her in the corridor before entering the room that she "didn't think that Henry wanted his picture taken."

It is the raising of the deceased's head in order to put the operating room towels under and around him that appellant claims was an assault and battery. It is the taking of the pictures of the dying Mr. Berthiaume that appellant claims constituted the actionable invasion of Mr. Berthiaume's right to privacy....

The law of privacy addresses the invasion of four distinct interests of the individual.... [T]he four different interests, taken as a whole, represent an individual's right "to be let alone." These four kinds of invasion are (1) intrusion upon the plaintiff's physical and mental solitude or seclusion; (2) public disclosure of private facts; (3) publicity which places the plaintiff in a false light in the public eye; [and] (4) appropriation for the defendant's benefit or advantage of the plaintiff's name or likeness....

> As it has appeared in the cases thus far decided, it is not one tort, but a complex of four. To date the law of privacy comprises four distinct kinds of invasion of four different interests of the plaintiff, which are tied together by the common name, but otherwise have almost nothing in common except that each represents an interference with the right of the plaintiff "to be let alone."...
>
> Taking them in order—intrusion, disclosure, false light, and appropriation—the first and second require the invasion of something secret, secluded or private pertaining to the plaintiff; the third and fourth do not. The second and third depend upon publicity, while the first does not, nor does the fourth, although it usually involves it. The third requires falsity or fiction; the other three do not. The fourth involves a use for the defendant's advantage, which is not true of the rest....

All cases so far decided on the point agree that the plaintiff need not plead or prove special damages. Punitive damages can be awarded on the same basis as in other torts where a wrongful motive or state of mind appears ... but not in cases where the defendant has acted innocently as, for example, in the mistaken but good faith belief that the plaintiff has given his consent....

In this case we are concerned only with a claimed intrusion upon the plaintiff's intestate's physical and mental solitude or seclusion. The jury had a right to conclude from the evidence that plaintiff's intestate was dying. It could have concluded he desired not to be photographed in his hospital bed in such condition and that he manifested such desire by his physical motions. The jury should have been instructed, if it found these facts, that the taking of pictures without decedent's consent or over his objection was an invasion of his legally protected right to privacy, which invasion was an actionable tort for which money damages could be recovered.

Instead, a directed verdict for the defendant was entered, obviously premised on the presiding justice's announced incorrect conclusion that the taking of pictures without consent did not constitute an invasion of privacy and the further erroneous conclusion that no tort was committed in the absence of "proof they [the photographs] were published."

Another claimed basis for appellant's assertion that a right to recover damages was demonstrated by the evidence is the allegations in her complaint sounding in the tort of assault and battery. The presiding justice announced as his conclusion that consent to a battery is implied from the existence of a physician-patient relationship....

Nothing suggests that the appellee's visit to plaintiff's intestate's room on the day of the alleged invasion of privacy was for any purpose relating to the *treatment* of the patient. Appellee acknowledges that his sole purpose in going to the Berthiaume hospital room and the taking of pictures was to conclude the making of a photographic record to complete appellee's record of the case. From the evidence, then, it is apparent that the jury had a right to conclude that the physician-patient relationship once existing between Dr. Pratt and Henry Berthiaume, the deceased, had terminated.

As to the claimed assault and battery, on the state of the evidence, the jury should have been permitted to consider the evidence and return a verdict in accordance with its fact-finding. It should have been instructed that consent to a touching of the body of a patient may be implied from the patient's consent to enter into a physician-patient relationship whenever such touching is reasonably necessary for the diagnosis and treatment of the patient's ailments while the physician-patient relationship continues. Quite obviously also, there would be no actionable assault and battery if the touching was expressly consented to. Absent express consent by the patient or one authorized to give consent on the patient's behalf, or absent consent implied from the circumstances, including the physician-patient relationship, the touching of the patient in the manner described by the evidence in this case would constitute assault and battery if it was part of an undertaking which, in legal effect, was an invasion of the plaintiff's intestate's "right to be let alone."...

We recognize the benefit to the science of medicine which comes from the making of photographs of the treatment and of medical abnormalities found in patients....

The court [also] recognizes that an individual has the right to decide whether that which is his shall be given to the public and not only to restrict and limit but also to withhold absolutely his talents, property, or other subjects of the right of privacy from all dissemination....

Because there were unresolved, disputed questions of fact, which, if decided by the fact finder in favor of the plaintiff, would have justified a verdict for the plaintiff, it was reversible error to have directed a verdict for the defendant.... New trial ordered.

Case Questions

1. Battery is unpermitted, unprivileged, intentional contact with another's person. In a physician–patient relationship, how does a physician receive consent to touch the body of a patient?
2. Could there have been a battery if Dr. Pratt had used rubber gloves in handling Mr. Berthiaume's head in preparation for the pictures? Could there have been a battery if Dr. Pratt had raised Mr. Berthiaume's head by cranking the hospital bed?
3. Could there have been an assault if Mr. Berthiaume was unconscious at the time Dr. Pratt raised his head and placed the blue operating towel under his head?

4. Are plaintiffs able to recover anything in suits for battery if they are unable to prove any actual physical injury?

 Does Dr. Pratt have a moral duty to comply with his patient's request? Does acting morally benefit Dr. Pratt?

Conversion

Conversion is an intentional tort that allows owners of tangible personal property (concepts discussed in Chapter XII) to regain possession of their property from other persons who have dispossessed the rightful owners. Any unauthorized act that deprives an owner of possession of his or her tangible personal property is conversion. There may be liability for the intentional tort of conversion even when the defendant acted innocently. For example, *D*, an auctioneer, receives a valuable painting from *X*, reasonably believing that *X* owns it. *D* sells the painting for *X*, but it turns out that *P* owns the painting. *D* is liable to *P* for conversion, even though the mistake is honest and reasonable.

Conversion may be accomplished in a number of ways—for example, if a defendant refuses to return goods to the owner or destroys or alters the goods. Even the use of the chattel may suffice. If you lend your car to a dealer to sell and the dealer drives the car once on business for a few miles, it would probably not be conversion. However, conversion would result if the dealer drives it for 2,000 miles.

Because conversion is considered a forced sale, the defendant must pay the full value, not merely the amount of the actual harm. However, courts consider several factors in determining whether defendant's interference with plaintiff's property is sufficient to require defendant to pay its entire value. These include dominion (complete ownership and actual control), good faith, harm, and inconvenience.

Introduction to *Henson v. Reddin*

Wesley Henson and Joseph Brophy were co-owners of Discount Industrial Coating, Inc. One of the company's assets was a truck trailer that housed a clogged-up, nonfunctioning spraying machine, which at one time was used to spray polyurethane on surfaces such as truck-bed liners. This machine was parked at the site of the business.

When Henson decided to sell his interest in the company, in December of 2006, Allen Reddin indicated that he would like to buy the polyurethane machine and fix it up. Reddin spent $4,561.52 of his own money on parts, which he used to repair the machine.

In January 2007, Henson moved the truck and its spraying machine—which included parts that belonged to Reddin and had been installed on the machine by Reddin—to an undisclosed location. Henson neither returned the parts to Reddin nor reimbursed him for his expenditures on these parts.

Reddin filed suit claiming that Henson had converted the parts.

Wesley Henson v. Allen Reddin
358 S.W.3d 428
Court of Appeals of Texas, Fort Worth
January 5, 2012

Sue Walker, Justice.

I. Introduction
We address two issues in this appeal: whether the evidence is legally and factually sufficient to establish that

Appellant Wesley Henson converted parts belonging to Appellee Allen Reddin and whether Reddin's evidence of conversion damages is legally and factually sufficient to support the trial court's judgment awarding Reddin $4,561.52 in damages....

II. Factual and Procedural Background

... Overview

The dispute between Henson and Reddin centered on a polyurethane machine used to spray truck bed liners, insulation, "or whatever you want to spray with it."... The polyurethane machine was permanently mounted inside an enclosed gooseneck trailer that had "Discount Industrial Coating, Incorporated" ... emblazoned on it.... The polyurethane machine had not been used for a while, so it had become clogged and was not in working order. Henson owned a one-half interest in Discount Industrial Coating, Inc.; Joseph Brophy owned the other one-half interest.

Henson decided that he wanted to sell his one-half interest in the company, and Reddin let Henson know that he was interested in purchasing the polyurethane machine if he could get it in working order. Reddin purchased parts and began working on the polyurethane machine in an attempt to get it in working order. After Reddin had purchased parts and had added them to the polyurethane machine, Henson moved the trailer in which the polyurethane machine was located. Henson did not return any parts to Reddin and did not disclose the location of the polyurethane machine....

... The Lawsuit

Reddin sued Henson in the justice court asserting a conversion claim and a money had and received claim. Henson failed to appear, and Reddin obtained a default judgment for $4,457—the amount he paid for the parts, plus court costs—against Henson. Henson appealed the judgment to the county court at law ... and Henson ... moved for summary judgment on Reddin's conversion claim and on his money had and received claim. The county court at law denied summary judgment on the conversion claim ... and ... the conversion claim was tried to the court.

After hearing the testimony from Reddin, Henson, and Brophy, the county court at law signed a judgment for Reddin in the amount of $5,419.46—$4,561.52 in damages plus $857.94 in prejudgment interest. The trial court made the following findings of fact:

1. On or about December 2006, Defendant Wesley Henson became interested in selling either his share of Defendant Discount Industrial Coating, Inc., or a machine that was an asset of that corporation.
2. On or about December 2006, Plaintiff became interested in purchasing either the business interest or the machine.
3. The machine was not in working order.
4. On or about December 2006 and January 2007, Plaintiff purchased certain items of equipment and tools for the purpose of repairing the machine and estimating its value.
5. The items and tools included a kit of foam, a transfer pump, a fusion gun, and assorted hoses, hereinafter called the "property."
6. Plaintiff purchased the property on the open market from retailers for the amount of $4,561.52.
7. The value of such items in Wise County, Texas, at that time was $4,561.52.
8. At the time of the events described below, Plaintiff Allen Reddin was the owner of the property.
9. In early January, 2007, Defendant Henson took a trailer containing the property and held it away from Plaintiff, which had the effect of destroying the property for its intended use.
10. By January 15, 2007, Defendant Henson unlawfully assumed and exercised control over the property to the exclusion of Plaintiff Reddin's rights as an owner.
11. Defendant Henson refused to return the property to Plaintiff Reddin after Plaintiff Reddin demanded the return of the property from Defendant Henson personally and through Defendant Henson's business associate.
12. Plaintiff Reddin originally filed suit in this cause on March 13, 2007.

The trial court also made the following conclusions of law:

1. Defendant Wesley Henson individually converted the property belonging to Plaintiff Allen Reddin.
2. Defendant Henson is individually liable to Plaintiff Reddin for actual damages in the amount of $4,561.52, and for prejudgment interest in the amount of $857.94.
3. The indebtedness of Defendant Henson to Plaintiff Reddin bears interest at the rate of 5.00% from December 16, 2010 until paid....

III. Standards of Review

Findings of fact entered in a case tried to the court have the same force and dignity as a jury's answers to jury questions.... The trial court's findings of fact are reviewable for legal and factual sufficiency of the evidence to support them by the same standards that are applied in reviewing evidence supporting a jury's answer....

IV. Sufficiency Analyses

A. Claim for Conversion
In his first issue, Henson argues that the evidence is legally and factually insufficient to establish that he converted any property belonging to Reddin; Henson argues that the evidence is legally and factually insufficient to establish that he knew at the time he removed the trailer that he was taking Reddin's property.

Conversion is the unauthorized and wrongful assumption and exercise of dominion and control over the personal property of another to the exclusion of, or inconsistent with, the owner's rights.... To establish a claim for conversion of personal property, a plaintiff must prove that (1) he owned or had legal possession of the property or entitlement to possession; (2) the defendant unlawfully and without authorization assumed and exercised dominion and control over the property to the exclusion of, or inconsistent with, the plaintiff's rights as an owner; (3) the plaintiff demanded return of the property; and (4) the defendant refused to return the property.... Acting with good faith or innocence is not a defense to conversion....

Here, as set forth above, the trial court found that Reddin had "purchased certain items of equipment and tools for the purpose of repairing the machine and estimating its value"; that Henson had taken "a trailer containing the property and [had] held it away from [Reddin], which had the effect of destroying the property for its intended use"; that "Henson unlawfully [had] assumed and [had] exercised control over the property to the exclusion of Plaintiff Reddin's rights as an owner"; and that "Defendant Henson [had] refused to return the property to Plaintiff Reddin after Plaintiff Reddin [had] demanded the return of the property from Defendant Henson personally and through Defendant Henson's business associate." The record supports these findings....

The testimony at trial established that Reddin was attempting to get the polyurethane machine in working order, that Reddin had purchased parts for the machine, that Reddin had installed the parts on the machine, and that Henson thereafter moved the trailer in which the machine was mounted. Reddin testified that he had called Henson numerous times, attempting to retrieve the parts, but Henson did not answer; the one time that Henson answered, he refused Reddin's request. Viewing the evidence favorable to the trial

court's findings, as we must, and disregarding the evidence to the contrary because a reasonable factfinder could do so based on a credibility determination, the evidence is legally sufficient to support the trial court's findings supporting each element of conversion of Reddin's property by Henson....

In considering the factual sufficiency of the evidence to support the trial court's findings, we consider Henson's testimony that is contrary to the findings. Henson testified that he did not know until after he moved the trailer that Reddin had parts on it. But even if Henson did not know about Reddin's parts until after the trailer was moved, his innocence is no defense to conversion.... Additionally, although the record contains conflicting testimony regarding Henson's refusal to return Reddin's parts to him—Henson claimed he offered to let Reddin call and come get the parts, while Reddin testified that Henson would not return his calls and refused to permit him to come get the parts—the trial court is the sole judge of the credibility of the witnesses and is to resolve any inconsistencies in their testimony.... Considering and weighing all of the evidence in the record pertinent to that finding, including that Henson's delay in authorizing the retrieval of the property that had the effect of destroying the parts, the credible evidence supporting the finding is not so weak, or so contrary to the overwhelming weight of all the evidence, that the finding should be set aside and a new trial ordered.... We overrule Henson's first issue challenging the legal and factual sufficiency of the evidence to show that a conversion took place.

B. Damages
In his second issue, Henson argues that the evidence is legally and factually insufficient to support the judgment's damage award. Henson contends that the only evidence in the record concerning damages consisted of Reddin's receipts for the property. Henson argues that while this evidence establishes the purchase price of the property, it wholly fails to establish the fair market value of the property, which Henson contends is the sole measure of damages for conversion.

Generally, the measure of damages in a conversion case is the fair market value of the property converted at the time of the conversion, with legal interest. Fair market value has been defined as the price that the property would bring when it is offered for sale by one who desires, but is not obliged to sell, and is bought by one who is under no necessity of buying it.... A property owner may testify about the market value of his property if his testimony shows that he is familiar with the market value and his opinion is based on that market value....

However, when converted property has no readily ascertainable fair market value, the measure of damages is the actual value of the property to the owner at the time of its loss.... In such circumstances, the purchase price is probative of actual value.... The original cost in the market and the manner and time and place of its use, the appearance before and after the alleged injury, and the relative usefulness and physical condition may be offered into evidence to establish conversion damages....

Testimony and evidence regarding purchase price, however, standing alone, is not factually sufficient to support a fair-market-value damages award or an actual-value damages award.... When converted property has no readily ascertainable fair market value, the measure of damages is the actual value of the property to the owner at the time of its loss and evidence of purchase price constitutes a starting point for determining actual damages.... From that starting point, amounts are subtracted for wear and tear, depreciation, etc....

Here, Reddin offered receipts for the parts into evidence and testified as to the purchase price of the parts that he had installed on the polyurethane machine. The receipts document that all of the parts were purchased within two to three weeks of the date they were installed on the polyurethane machine. The receipts indicate that M & M Insulation purchased the parts; Reddin testified that M & M Insulation was Brophy's company and that he, Reddin, had actually paid for the parts. Reddin said that he purchased them through Brophy's company because "I get my stuff cheaper through his account. I didn't have an account with companies that he's got."

Reddin also testified that the parts were worthless after the conversion because they had been ruined by the resin crystallizing in the polyurethane machine. The evidence conclusively establishes that the new parts were installed on the polyurethane machine on a Friday and that Henson moved the trailer with the machine mounted in it either one or two days after the new parts were installed; when Reddin and Brophy returned to work on the machine on Monday, it was gone.

Considering the evidence favorable to the trial court's finding that Reddin purchased the parts for $4,561.52 and its finding that the value of the parts in Wise County, Texas, at the time was $4,561.52, legally sufficient evidence exists to support these findings. Reddin testified to the purchase price of the parts and provided receipts documenting the prices; the parts were purchased within a few weeks of the date they were installed on the polyurethane machine and were on the machine only one or two days before they were converted. This evidence is legally sufficient to support the trial court's award of $4,561.52 in damages to Reddin under either an actual value or a fair market value measure of damages.... We therefore overrule the portion of Henson's second issue challenging the legal sufficiency of the evidence to support the damages award....

We overrule the portion of Henson's second issue challenging the factual sufficiency of the evidence to support the damages award.

V. Conclusion
Having overruled both of Henson's issues, we affirm the trial court's judgment.

Case Questions

1. What facts, according to Reddin, supported his claim that Henson had committed conversion?
2. What was Henson's version of the facts in the trial court as to the return of the parts, and why wasn't this defense more important to the appellate court?
3. Why did the appellate court rule as it did as to the damages?

Trespass to Land

Trespass is an intentional tort that protects a lawful owner–occupier's rights to exclusive possession of his or her real property. It occurs when someone makes an unauthorized entry on the land of another. Trespasses to land can occur through either a direct or an indirect entry. A direct entry would occur when one person walks on another person's land without permission. An indirect entry would occur when one person throws an object on another's land or causes it to flood with water or other fluids.

The law's protection of the exclusive possession of land is not limited to the surface of real property.

It extends below the surface as well as above it. Thus, a public utility that runs a pipe below the surface of a landowner's property without obtaining an easement or consent can commit a trespass. Similarly, overhanging structures, telephone wires, and even shooting across land have been held to be violations of owners' rights to the airspace above their land. Although the extent of such rights is still in the process of determination, the legal trend is for landowners to have rights to as much of the airspace that is immediately above or beneath their property as they can effectively occupy or use.[5]

Trespass also may occur to personal property, but most interference with the possession of personal property would be considered conversion rather than trespass.

Introduction to *Ivancic v. Olmstead*

The plaintiff in the following case brought suit in trespass after sustaining serious injury when an overhanging limb fell from the defendant's maple tree onto the plaintiff's driveway and struck the plaintiff.

Ivancic v. Olmstead
488 N.E.2d 72
Court of Appeals of New York
November 26, 1985

Jasen, Judge.
At issue on this appeal is whether plaintiff, who seeks to recover for injuries sustained when an overhanging limb from a neighbor's maple tree fell and struck him, established a prima facie case of negligence and whether Trial Term erred, as a matter of law, in refusing to submit to the jury the cause of action sounding in common-law trespass.

Plaintiff was working on his truck in the driveway of his parents' home located in the Village of Fultonville, New York. Since 1970, defendant has owned and lived on the property adjoining to the west. A large maple tree stood on defendant's land near the border with plaintiff's parents' property. Branches from the tree had extended over the adjoining property. During a heavy windstorm on September 26, 1980, an overhanging limb from the tree fell and struck plaintiff, causing him serious injuries. As a result, plaintiff commenced this action, interposing causes of action in negligence and common-law trespass.

At trial, the court declined to charge the jury on the common-law trespass cause of action or on the doctrine of *res ipsa loquitur,* submitting the case solely on the theory of negligence. The jury rendered a verdict in favor of the plaintiff in the sum of $3,500. Both parties moved to set aside the verdict, the plaintiff upon the ground of inadequacy, and the defendant upon the ground that the verdict was against the weight of the evidence. The court ultimately ... ordered a new trial on the issues of both liability and damages.

Upon cross appeals, the Appellate Division reversed, on the law, and dismissed the complaint. The court reasoned that no competent evidence was presented upon which it could properly be concluded that defendant had constructive notice of the alleged defective condition of the tree. The Appellate Division did not address the correctness of the trial court's ruling in declining to charge the jury on the common-law trespass cause of action....

Considering first the negligence cause of action, it is established that no liability attaches to a landowner whose tree falls outside of his premises and injures another unless there exists actual or constructive knowledge of the defective condition of the tree....

Inasmuch as plaintiff makes no claim that defendant had actual knowledge of the defective nature of the tree, it is necessary to consider whether there was sufficient competent evidence for a jury to conclude that defendant had constructive notice. We conclude, as did the Appellate Division, that plaintiff offered no competent evidence from which it could be properly found that defendant had constructive notice of the alleged defective condition of the tree. Not one of the witnesses who had observed the tree prior to the fall of the limb testified as to observing so much as a withering or dead leaf, barren branch, discoloration, or any of the indicia of disease which would alert an observer to the possibility that the tree or one of its branches was decayed or defective.

At least as to adjoining landowners, the concept of constructive notice with respect to liability for falling trees is that there is no duty to consistently and constantly check all trees for nonvisible decay. Rather, the manifestation of said decay must be readily observable in order to require a landowner to take reasonable steps to prevent harm.... The testimony of plaintiff's expert provides no evidence from which the jury could conclude that defendant should reasonably have realized that a potentially dangerous condition existed. Plaintiff's expert never saw the tree until the morning of the trial when all that remained of the tree was an eight-foot stump. He surmised from this observation and from some photographs of the tree that water had invaded the tree through a "limb hole" in the tree, thus causing decay and a crack occurring below. However, the expert did indicate that the limb hole was about eight feet high and located in the crotch of the tree which would have made it difficult, if not impossible, to see upon reasonable inspection. Although there may have been evidence that would have alerted an expert, upon close observation, that the tree was diseased, no evidence exists that would put a reasonable landowner on notice of any defective condition of the tree. Thus, the fact that defendant landowner testified that she did not inspect the tree for over 10 years is irrelevant. On the evidence presented, even if she were to have inspected the tree, no indicia of decay or disease put her on notice of a defective condition so as to trigger her duty as a landowner to take reasonable steps to prevent the potential harm.

Since the evidence adduced at trial failed to set forth any reasonable basis upon which notice of the tree's defective condition could be imputed to defendant ... we agree with the view of the Appellate Division that plaintiff failed to establish a prima facie case of negligence.

Turning to plaintiff's claim of error by the trial court in declining to submit to the jury the cause of action sounding in common-law trespass, we conclude that there was no error. The scope of the common-law tort has been delineated in *Phillips v. Sun Oil Co. ...* 121 N.E.2d 249, wherein this court held: "while the trespasser, to be liable, need not intend or expect the damaging consequences of his intrusion, he must intend the act which amounts to or produces the unlawful invasion, and the intrusion must at least be the immediate or inevitable consequence of what he willfully does, or which he does so negligently as to amount to willfulness." In this case, there is evidence that defendant did not plant the tree, and the mere fact that defendant allowed what appeared to be a healthy tree to grow naturally and cross over into plaintiff's parents' property airspace, cannot be viewed as an intentional act so as to constitute trespass....

Accordingly, the order of the Appellate Division should be affirmed, with costs.

Case Questions

1. The trial court and the appellate court concluded that the plaintiff was not entitled to an instruction with respect to common-law trespass. Why was the instruction refused?
2. Why was the plaintiff's negligence claim rejected?
3. Why should a plaintiff be entitled to recover for a trespass under circumstances where no actual harm has been shown?

Malicious Prosecution

Malicious prosecution is an intentional tort that provides targeted individuals with civil remedies against persons who have filed groundless complaints against the target that result in the target's criminal prosecution. Many states have extended the definition of this tort to permit such suits against individuals who initiate groundless civil actions. The plaintiff in a malicious prosecution case must prove that the defendant maliciously and without probable cause instituted a criminal or civil complaint against the target which resulted in a prosecution or lawsuit, which then resulted in a decision favorable to the target. The target

also must establish that he or she suffered legal injury as a result of the groundless charges. Merely threatening to bring a lawsuit against the target is not enough to result in civil liability for malicious prosecution.

In a criminal case, the prosecutor is absolutely immune from malicious prosecution suits. In addition, plea bargaining does not suffice to meet the favorable decision criterion.

False Imprisonment

False imprisonment is an intentional tort that provides targeted individuals with civil remedies against those who unlawfully deprive them of their freedom of movement. Plaintiffs must prove that they were intentionally and unlawfully detained against their will for an unreasonable period of time. The detention need not be in a jail. It may also take place in a mental institution, hospital, restaurant, hotel, store, or car. Most courts have held that plaintiffs must be aware of their confinement while suffering it, or if not, then they must suffer some type of actual harm.

The plaintiffs in the following case claimed that they were the victims of false imprisonment by Wal–Mart security personnel.

Kim Gallegly Wesson v. Wal-Mart Stores East, L.P.
38 So. 3d 746
Court of Civil Appeals of Alabama
December 4, 2009

Thomas, Judge.

On July 13, 2004, at about 9:30 a.m., Kim Gallegly Wesson and her four children went to the Pell City Wal-Mart discount department store, operated by Wal-Mart Stores East, L.P. ("Wal-Mart"), to have the tires on Wesson's automobile rotated and balanced. Wesson left her automobile at the tire and lube express department ("TLE department") for the service to be performed. Wesson had assumed that the service would take 20–30 minutes, so she and her children walked around the Wal-Mart store awaiting the completion of the service to her automobile. When the automobile was not ready in about 30 minutes, Wesson decided to take her children, who were hungry and requesting breakfast, to the McDonald's fast-food restaurant located inside the store. After finishing breakfast, Wesson checked again to see if her automobile service had been completed; it had not. Wesson and her children proceeded to the pharmacy department of the store, where Wesson dropped off one of her two prescriptions for refilling at the pharmacy counter. Wesson and the children then went to the electronics department of the store, where Wesson purchased additional minutes for her prepaid cellular telephone. When a third check on the status of her automobile yielded further waiting, Wesson dropped off her second prescription at the pharmacy counter for refilling. Wesson then decided to shop for groceries for the family's trip to Florida.

Once Wesson had completed her grocery shopping, she returned to the pharmacy department to retrieve her prescriptions. By this time, the pharmacy associate, Jennifer Vincent, had notified Kyle Jack, the in-store loss prevention associate, that Wesson would be picking up prescriptions from the pharmacy. Because Wal-Mart's policy allows customers to pay for most prescriptions at any check-out counter, the store has a computer system that keeps track of the time and place of the payment to ensure that all prescriptions picked up from the pharmacy department are ultimately paid for. Wesson's name had appeared on a list of persons who had not paid for prescriptions picked up from the pharmacy department on at least two other occasions, resulting in her placement on a "watch list" of sorts.

Once Wesson arrived at the pharmacy department to retrieve her prescriptions, Wesson said that an announcement came over the loudspeaker to inform her that her automobile service was completed. Wesson informed the pharmacy associate that she would pay for her prescriptions when she checked out her groceries and paid for her car service. Vincent gave Wesson both of her prescriptions; Wesson owed money on both prescriptions. Wesson and her children left the pharmacy department and returned to the TLE department; they were followed by Jack. Once she reached the check-out counter at the TLE department, Wesson proceeded to place her grocery items on the counter and to check out. Wesson did not, however, place her prescriptions on the counter to check out. Once she had paid for her groceries and car service, Wesson and her children left the store.

Tara Swain, the associate who checked out Wesson's groceries at the TLE department, testified that she had asked Wesson whether she wanted to pay for her prescriptions. Swain said that Wesson indicated that she had paid for the prescriptions already. Jack testified that he had seen Swain motion toward the child-seat portion of the cart, in which the prescriptions, Wesson's purse, and some of the children's dolls or toys sat, as she completed checking out Wesson's grocery items. Although he said that he did not hear Swain's exact question or Wesson's first answer to that question, Jack said that he moved closer to Wesson and heard her refer to the items in the child-seat portion of the cart as being her personal items. Jack said that he saw Wesson leave the store without paying for the prescriptions, so he followed her outside to apprehend her.

Once she reached the parking lot, Wesson and her children began to place her purchases into the automobile. Jack and another associate, Nathan Nichols, approached Wesson while she unloaded her groceries. Jack addressed Wesson by name and, according to Wesson, said: "Excuse me, but I don't think you paid for those prescriptions." Wesson said that she admitted that she had not, in fact, paid for the prescriptions.

According to Wesson, Jack told her that she needed to come back inside to fill out some forms and that she would be allowed to pay for the prescriptions. Wesson and her children returned to the store with Jack and the other associate. Once inside the store, Jack led Wesson and her children to the loss-prevention office in the front of the store, where, according to Wesson, Jack locked the door to the office. Wesson said that Jack asked for her driver's license and Social Security number and that he gave her several papers to sign. Wesson admitted that she did not read the papers that Jack gave her to sign other than to notice that the Wal-Mart logo appeared on them. Wesson said that, at that time, she still believed that she was simply going to have to pay for her prescriptions.

However, according to Wesson, once Jack secured her signature on the forms, he raised his voice and told her that she would be trespassing if she ever came back into a Wal-Mart store. She said that Jack accused her of stealing from the store "all the time" and told her, in front of her children, that she would be going to jail. Wesson said that Jack informed her that he had notified the police. Wesson said that she tried to reason with Jack, telling him that she had simply forgotten to pay and that she just wanted to settle the matter by paying for her prescriptions. Wesson further testified that Jack had told her that it did not matter to him whether she was guilty of theft under the law but that his job was loss prevention and that her leaving without paying for the items was a loss to Wal-Mart. Three Pell City police officers responded to Jack's earlier telephone call; they took Wesson into custody when they arrived.

Jack secured a warrant for theft of property in the third degree against Wesson. Wal-Mart then prosecuted Wesson in the municipal court. After a trial, the action was "dismissed by agreement," according to a notation on the case-action-summary sheet of the municipal-court criminal case. That document also indicates that Wesson paid court costs.

Wesson sued Wal-Mart and Jack, asserting claims of malicious prosecution and false imprisonment arising from the events of July 13, 2004, and the resulting criminal prosecution. Wal-Mart and Jack moved for a summary judgment, which Wesson opposed. As exhibits to their motion for a summary judgment, Wal-Mart and Jack submitted Wesson's deposition, Jack's deposition, the trial transcript of the criminal prosecution of Wesson, and the case-action-summary sheet of the municipal-court criminal action. Wal-Mart and Jack argued in their summary-judgment motion that Wesson could not establish the elements of a malicious-prosecution claim or a false-imprisonment claim. The trial court entered a summary judgment in favor of Wal-Mart and Jack. After her postjudgment motion was denied, Wesson appealed to the Alabama Supreme Court, which transferred the appeal to this court, pursuant to Ala. Code 1975, §12-2-7(6).

On appeal, Wesson challenges the summary judgment in favor of Wal-Mart and Jack because, she says, genuine issues of material fact preclude the entry of a summary judgment. She specifically argues that she can establish the elements of her ... false-imprisonment claim. We disagree....

Turning now to the false-imprisonment claim, we note that ... [p]ursuant to Ala. Code 1975, §15-10-14(a) and (c), both a merchant and its employee are immune from claims of false imprisonment instituted by a person detained on the suspicion of shoplifting, provided that the merchant or its employee had probable cause for believing that the person detained was attempting to shoplift. Those sections provide:

> (a) A peace officer, a merchant or a merchant's employee who has probable cause for believing that goods held for sale by the merchant have been unlawfully taken by a person and that he can recover them by taking the person into custody may, for the purpose of attempting to effect such recovery, take the person into custody and detain him in a reasonable manner for a reasonable length of time. Such taking into custody and detention by a peace officer, merchant or merchant's employee shall not render such police officer, merchant or merchant's employee criminally or civilly liable for false arrest, false imprisonment or unlawful detention....
>
> (c) A merchant or a merchant's employee who causes such arrest as provided for in subsection (a) of this section of a person for larceny of goods held for sale shall not be criminally or civilly liable for false arrest or false imprisonment where the merchant or merchant's employee has probable cause for believing that the person arrested committed larceny of goods held for sale....

... Jack had probable cause to suspect Wesson had purposefully failed to pay for her prescriptions based on the information he had available to him at the time of Wesson's detention. Wesson admits that she left the Wal-Mart store without paying for her prescriptions.

Jack had information compiled by Wal-Mart indicating that Wesson had left the store without paying for her prescriptions on at least two other occasions, and Jack observed Wesson leaving the store on July 13, 2004, after having two opportunities to pay for her prescriptions. Because there existed probable cause to detain Wesson, Wal-Mart and Jack are immune from Wesson's false-imprisonment claim.

Because we have determined that Wesson failed to establish that Wal-Mart and Jack did not have probable cause to institute criminal proceedings against Wesson for theft of the prescriptions, we affirm the summary judgment in Wal-Mart's and Jack's favor on the malicious-prosecution claim. Likewise, because of the existence of probable cause for Wesson's detention, we affirm the summary judgment in favor of Wal-Mart and Jack on the false-imprisonment claim because, under §15-10-14 (a) and (c), they are immune from that claim.

AFFIRMED.

Case Questions

1. Explain your position as to whether you believe that Wal-Mart employees had probable cause to detain Wesson for shoplifting given that the criminal case against her was dismissed.
2. Although the immunity statute protects merchants from shoplifters, does it make any allowance for the detention of customers? Should forgetful elders, shoppers who are absent minded or confused, parents preoccupied with keeping track of their children, or people who for other reasons are not adequately focused on the legalities of their conduct be subject to detention by store security to the same extent as professional shoplifters?

Defamation

Defamation is an intentional tort that is based on the policy that people should be able to enjoy their good names. This tort provides targeted individuals with remedies against persons who intentionally make malicious statements that injure the target's character, fame, or reputation. A publication is defamatory if it tends to lower a person in others' esteem. Language that is merely annoying cannot be defamatory. Generally, the truth of the statement is a complete defense in a suit for defamation because true statements are not considered to be malicious.

Libel and slander are both forms of defamation. **Libel** is defamation expressed by print, writing, signs, pictures, and in the absence of statutory provisions to the contrary, radio and television broadcasts. **Slander** involves spoken words that have been heard by someone other than the target.

The law treats some defamatory expressions as slanderous or libelous per se. Examples of **slander per se** or **libel per se** include falsely accusing another of committing a crime of moral turpitude (rape, murder, or selling narcotics); false accusations that another person has contracted a morally offensive communicative disease (such as leprosy, syphilis, gonorrhea, or AIDS), or defamatory expressions that interfere with another person's trade, business, or profession (saying that a banker is dishonest or that a doctor is a "quack"). In defamation cases, the law requires that special damages such as loss of job, loss of customers, or loss of credit be proven before the plaintiff can recover general damages, such as loss of reputation.[6] However, a plaintiff who proves slander per se is not required to prove special damages because such expressions are almost certain to harm the plaintiff's reputation and produce economic loss. Not having to prove special damages is very helpful to the plaintiff because they are difficult to prove. The defendant usually can lessen the amount of damages awarded by publishing a retraction.

Introduction to *Ryan v. Fox Television*

A Chicago television station alleged that Circuit Court Judge James Ryan (and three other judges) did not spend as much time at the courthouse as they should according to established circuit court policy. Ryan and the others were accused of leaving work too early. The television station reported the findings of its "investigation" in a series of four segments, which were telecast on four successive days in May 2010. An internal judicial inquiry by the state supreme court resulted in disciplinary action being taken against the accused judges.

Judge Ryan responded with a civil suit against the television station and other organizations that participated in the station's "investigation." Ryan claimed that he had been defamed, that his privacy rights had been violated, and that he was the victim of intentional infliction of emotional distress.

The defendants responded by asking the circuit court judge to dismiss the case, claiming that they were immune from suit under Illinois law. Their claim of immunity was based on an anti-SLAPP statute called the Citizen Participation Act (CPA). SLAPP is shorthand for *Strategic Lawsuit Against Public Participation*. The Illinois legislature and many other state legislatures have enacted statutes like the CPA in order to shield defendants from liability resulting from bogus lawsuits brought by plaintiffs— often companies or institutions that want to silence consumers or members of the public who are criticizing their operations, products, and the like. Their objective is to intimidate individuals into not exercising their First Amendment rights. These laws also seek to ensure that important information that would be of interest to the general public is not suppressed by persons who don't speak because they fear retaliatory lawsuits.

The defendants argued that this suit met the definition of a SLAPP. The defendants offered evidence that they were exercising their First Amendment rights and they presented evidence that plausibly supported the conclusion that the plaintiff's motivation in his suit was retaliation. When the defendant in a defamation suit asserts that the plaintiff is engaging in a SLAPP, the court has to hold a hearing. The hearing will consist of a two-step process. First, the court will determine whether the elements of a SLAPP are present. If that hurdle is crossed, the court will then consider whether the plaintiff's evidence supports the conclusion that the plaintiff is likely to prevail on the merits. The circuit court in this case denied the defendants' motion, ruling more than once in favor of Judge Ryan. The defendants did eventually appeal the circuit court's decision to the state intermediate court of appeals.

Readers know that most of the cases in this textbook involve appeals made after the conclusion of a trial. But sometimes the law permits a pretrial appeal. The appeal that occurs in our next case, *Ryan v. Fox Television Stations, Inc.*, is a pretrial appeal, which in legal jargon is called an **interlocutory appeal.**

James Ryan v. Fox Television Stations, Inc.
2012 IL App (1st) 120005
Appellate Court of Illinois First District, Fifth Division
October 23, 2012

Justice Connors.

In 2010, WFLD Fox News Chicago aired an investigative report on the working hours of judges in the circuit court of Cook County. The report presented information suggesting that at least four judges, one of whom was identified as plaintiff James Ryan, had been neglecting their official duties by leaving courthouses well before the end of the business day, contrary to the stated policy of the chief judge of the circuit court. The report prompted an inquiry from the supreme court and caused the chief judge of the circuit court to discipline the judges involved by transferring them to other duties. Plaintiff filed this lawsuit against

defendants, which in its current form alleges defamation, false-light invasion of privacy, intentional infliction of emotional distress, and invasion of privacy by intrusion upon seclusion. Defendants moved to dismiss the complaint on the ground that it is a "Strategic Lawsuit Against Public Participation" (SLAPP), which is barred under the Citizen Participation Act.... The circuit court denied the motion....

The investigative report originally aired in installments over four nights starting on May 24, 2010. The report was a collaborative effort between WFLD, which is owned by some of the defendants, and defendant Better Government Association, Inc., a nonprofit advocacy group. (The remaining individual defendants were involved in some aspect of the investigation or the presentation of the report.) The report's first installment detailed the basic findings of the investigation. According to the report, unofficial logs prepared by the Cook County sheriff's office revealed that a large number of courtrooms in the Daley Center were not open during business hours, which normally ran until 4 p.m. Investigators confirmed this finding by independently surveying the courtrooms during business hours. By means of hidden cameras, the investigators also confirmed that a number of judges were leaving before the end of business hours. In one of the most explosive portions of the report, a reporter found one judge sunbathing outside of her home at around 2 p.m. on a workday. After being confronted by the reporter, the judge argued that she had left the courthouse early that day only because she had completed her call and had nothing further to do.

The report also contained a segment specifically regarding plaintiff. The report stated, "We caught him leaving the courthouse early three times. On a rainy October day, he was home by 1:18 p.m. He never returned our calls." This statement was accompanied by images of a car parked in the driveway of a house. The report named two other judges who had allegedly been seen leaving before the end of business hours. The report also included statements by defendant Andy Shaw to the effect that judges should be required to punch in and out of courthouses in order to ensure that they are working during business hours.

The report's second installment focused on an analysis of the costs to taxpayers of the Cook County judicial system, including judicial salaries and benefits, and it also included reactions to the investigation from members of the judiciary and the public. The report also examined various methods of disciplining and supervising judges....

At the conclusion of this installment, Robinson announced that the previous night's installment contained an error regarding the evidence against plaintiff. Robinson stated:

> Last night's story, by the way, identified Judge Jim Ryan [i.e., plaintiff] as one of the judges leaving work early. We watched [plaintiff] leaving the courthouse and said he went home. But the house and the car we showed actually belonged to a neighbor. Our bad. While we saw the judge leave work early, we really don't know where he went. We do apologize for that mistake.

The report's third segment focused on the Illinois Supreme Court's reaction to the previous two

segments. Joe Tybor, the court's press secretary, stated that the judges' alleged behavior was "totally unacceptable and, in the court's mind, cannot be tolerated." Tybor also indicated that the supreme court planned to discuss the situation with Tim Evans, the chief judge of the circuit court, and other supervising judges in order to further investigate the situation and decide on corrective measures. Chief Judge Evans stated that he intended to take action if shown some evidence of wrongdoing by the judges involved.

The next day, May 27, 2010, plaintiff filed the original complaint in this case, alleging a single count of defamation. (The complaint was amended about a year later to include the other three counts now at issue.) The complaint centered on the report's claim during its first installment (which Robinson conceded was incorrect during the second installment) that plaintiff was at home with his car parked in the driveway prior to 4 p.m. on a workday. Plaintiff asked for damages of $7 million.

The fourth and final installment of the report aired the following night, May 28, 2010. This report detailed the fallout from the investigation. According to the report, Chief Judge Evans reassigned all of the judges involved to different duties and arranged for the judges to receive "mentoring" from other, veteran judges. The report explained that, because judges are elected, reassignment is one of the few supervisory tools that the chief judge can use to discipline judges....

The sole issue on appeal is whether plaintiff's suit should be dismissed because it is barred under the Act....

In 2007, the legislature enacted the Citizen Participation Act in order to combat the rise of what have been termed "Strategic Lawsuits Against Public Participation," commonly called SLAPPs. A SLAPP is a meritless lawsuit that is used to retaliate against a defendant for attempting to participate in government by exercising some first amendment right such as the right to free speech or the right to petition.... "Plaintiffs in SLAPP suits do not intend to win but rather to chill a defendant's speech or protest activity and discourage opposition by others through delay, expense, and distraction.... While the case is being litigated in the courts, however, defendants are forced to expend funds on litigation costs and attorney fees and may be discouraged from continuing their protest activities."...

The traditional SLAPP paradigm involves a large and powerful corporation or entity that sues an individual or grassroots political organization for defamation, intentional interference with economic advantage, or some other similar tort.... One of the most socially damaging aspects of SLAPPs is the fact that although plaintiffs nearly always lose … the defendants in such cases can be financially devastated by the costs of defending the suit or deterred into silence by the threat of the enormous monetary damages demanded by the plaintiffs.... In response to this problem, nearly 30 states have adopted anti-SLAPP legislation that allows for "expedited judicial review, summary dismissal, and recovery of attorney fees for the party who has been 'SLAPPed.' "…

In Illinois, the legislature declared four public policy goals for the Act:

> It is in the public interest and it is the purpose of this Act to [1] strike a balance between the rights of persons to file lawsuits for injury and the constitutional rights of persons to petition, speak freely, associate freely, and otherwise participate in government; [2] to protect and encourage public participation in government to the maximum extent permitted by law; [3] to establish an efficient process for identification and adjudication of SLAPPs; and [4] to provide for attorney's fees and costs to prevailing movants....

The legislature further declared that the Act "shall be construed liberally to effectuate its purposes and intent fully."…

As can be seen from the legislature's public policy statement, the Act seeks not only to protect individuals from meritless, retaliatory SLAPPs but also to allow plaintiffs who have legitimately been wronged to receive compensation. But this laudable goal runs almost immediately into the most intractable problem associated with SLAPPs: they are very hard to distinguish from normal lawsuits.... A SLAPP is often identifiable by its lack of merit and because it is filed against defendants who are exercising their first amendment rights, but this does not mean that all lawsuits that lack merit or that implicate first amendment activities are SLAPPs.

To help overcome this problem, the legislature established a standard for invoking immunity under the Act. Section 15 states:

> This Act applies to any motion to dispose of a claim in a judicial proceeding on the grounds that the claim is based on, relates to, or is in response to any act or acts of the moving party in furtherance of the moving party's rights of petition, speech, association, or to otherwise participate in government.
>
> Acts in furtherance of the constitutional rights to petition, speech, association, and participation in government are immune from liability,

regardless of intent or purpose, except when not genuinely aimed at procuring favorable government action, result, or outcome."…

Section 20(c) further mandates that the circuit court "shall grant the motion and dismiss the judicial claim unless the court finds that the responding party has produced clear and convincing evidence that the acts of the moving party are not immunized from, or are not in furtherance of acts immunized from, liability by this Act."…

The trouble with the standard as written, however, is that if it is applied to the letter then the Act would mandate dismissal of every lawsuit that implicated a defendant's first amendment activities regardless of whether the plaintiff's claims were meritorious or not, essentially creating absolute immunity for torts committed while exercising first amendment rights....

… [T]he threshold step in analyzing a motion to dismiss based on the Act is to "first determine whether the suit is the type of suit the Act was intended to address."… [A] lawsuit may only be dismissed due to immunity under the Act if:

> (1) the defendants' acts were in furtherance of their right to petition, speak, associate, or otherwise participate in government to obtain favorable government action; (2) the plaintiffs' claims are solely based on, related to, or in response to the defendants' "acts in furtherance"; and (3) the plaintiffs fail to produce clear and convincing evidence that the defendants' acts were not genuinely aimed at solely procuring favorable government action....

It is indisputable that defendants' actions in this case satisfy the first prong of the test. The investigatory report that defendants produced uncovered questionable activity by members of the judiciary in the performance of their official duties. Defendants communicated the findings of their investigation to the public and to members of local and state government via a televised newscast. Perhaps most importantly, the report sought comment from the Illinois Supreme Court and Chief Judge Evans on the investigation's findings and urged them to take action. Such activity is well within the scope of the Act, and in fact the investigatory report at issue here is an excellent example of the kind of activity that the legislature sought to protect, as shown by the Act's own language. The legislature noted in the Act's public policy statement that "[t]he information, reports, opinions, claims, arguments, and other expressions provided by citizens are vital to effective law enforcement, the operation of government ... and the continuation of representative democracy.

Yet merely because defendants' activities are the kind that the Act is designed to protect does not necessarily mean that plaintiff's lawsuit is a SLAPP and is therefore subject to dismissal under the Act. The next step in the analysis is to determine whether plaintiff's claim is "solely based on" defendants' protected acts.... This prong of the analysis is the central issue in this case.

To satisfy its burden under this prong of the test, a movant ... must affirmatively demonstrate that the nonmovant's claim is a SLAPP within the meaning of the Act, that is, that the claim is meritless and was filed in retaliation against the movant's protected activities in order to deter the movant from further engaging in those activities....

... Plaintiff filed his original complaint less than three days after the initial segment of the report aired. Although such a short amount of time is not necessarily dispositive evidence of retaliatory intent, it is a probative fact. But when we also consider the fact that plaintiff filed the lawsuit before the fourth segment aired, the inference that plaintiff intended his lawsuit to deter defendants from further publicizing their investigation's findings becomes much more plausible.

Further, there is the type of relief requested by plaintiff. The original complaint contained a single defamation claim and demanded compensatory damages of $7 million, as well as reserving the right to also demand unspecified punitive damages. Demanding damages in the millions for alleged defamation is a classic SLAPP scenario.... Moreover, the amended complaint included three additional counts that each also asked for compensatory damages of $7 million, making the total compensatory demand $28 million. Based on the nature of plaintiff's alleged injuries, it is difficult to see how such a high demand can be factually justified....

Plaintiff argues that the reason he filed his lawsuit so quickly was because of defendants' claim in the first installment of the report, which incorrectly stated that plaintiff was at his home early on a workday, and because defendants continued to air footage of plaintiff (which was accompanied by allegedly defamatory voiceovers) in advertisements and teasers for the remaining installments of the report. This argument has several problems. First, the defendants aired a correction during the second installment of the report, apparently after plaintiff contacted defendants and advised them of the error. Yet this occurred at least two days before plaintiff filed this lawsuit, which raises the question of why a lawsuit was necessary to obtain a correction that plaintiff had already received.

Second, plaintiff's original complaint demanded only money damages. If plaintiff's purpose in filing the lawsuit so quickly was to prevent further harm to his reputation, then we cannot see how a demand for $7 million rather than an injunction would resolve the problem in a way that does not involve intimidating defendants into silence.

Given the timing of the complaint and the speed with which it was filed, the high damages demand, and the type of relief requested, we must conclude that defendants have shown evidence of retaliatory intent.... But even though defendants have presented evidence of retaliatory intent, that alone does not make the lawsuit a SLAPP because a SLAPP is also "by definition, meritless."... Defendants must also present evidence that plaintiff's claims lack merit, but they have failed to do so here.... [T]he supreme court made clear ... that the movant (which is defendants in this situation), bears the burden of demonstrating that the nonmovant's claims are a meritless, retaliatory SLAPP.... In order to satisfy their burden, defendants must show that there are undisputed facts that demonstrate plaintiff's claim is meritless....

The only evidence that defendants have offered that could conceivably be proof that plaintiff's claims lack merit relates to the defamation count and to a lesser extent the false light count. Plaintiff's main contention in these counts is that the report's claim that he left work early and went home on several days is false. Defendants countered this allegation with logbooks from the sheriff's office that recorded the hours during which plaintiff's courtroom was open during April 2010. The logs showed that plaintiff's courtroom was usually empty by 2 p.m. Defendants argue that plaintiff's defamation claim is therefore meritless because these logs show that the report was substantially true....

The problem with this evidence is that it does not prove that the report's allegation that plaintiff left work early and went home on a number of days is substantially true. Indeed, it is undisputed that defendants retracted the report's central allegation that plaintiff was at home during the workday on October 9, 2009. Nor does the fact that plaintiff's courtroom was empty after 2 p.m. on certain days prove that he left work and went home. Judges work in their private chambers as well as their courtrooms, and many judges serve on committees in their official capacities or are otherwise involved in the legal community. A judge's official duties do not require a constant presence in the courtroom itself at all times, or even in the courthouse. Substantial truth is an affirmative defense ... that requires a defendant to show that "the 'gist' or 'sting' of the defamatory material is true."... The gist of the report was that plaintiff was neglecting his official duties because he habitually left the courthouse and went home during business hours, but the sheriff's logs prove only that plaintiff was not in his courtroom at certain times.

Had defendants offered undisputed evidence that the report's claims that plaintiff was neglecting his duties by going home during working hours were actually true, then this might be a different case. Unlike substantial truth, which is an affirmative defense, falsity is an essential element in a defamation claim.... But defendants have not offered any similar evidence in this case. Indeed, it is undisputed that

defendants retracted the report's claim that plaintiff was at home on October 9, 2009, and conceded that although they had seen defendant leave the courthouse they did not know where he went....

In sum, although defendants presented sufficient evidence that they engaged in protected activities and that plaintiff's claims were retaliatory, they failed to show that plaintiff's claims are meritless and are therefore a SLAPP. Defendants have consequently not carried their burden under the Act and the circuit court was correct to deny defendant's motion to dismiss.

Affirmed.

Case Questions

1. Why did the appellate court conclude that the plaintiff's lawsuit did not amount to a SLAPP?
2. What do you think the defendants will do in the aftermath of this decision?

INTERNET TIP

Readers should read the thought-provoking 2009 slander case of *Williams v. Tharp* on the textbook's website. The case's two plaintiffs were on their way back after an uneventful trip to a neighborhood pizza shop, where they had purchased a carryout pizza. They were utterly unprepared for what was about to transpire. Upon arriving at their intended destination, the home of one plaintiff, the two were apprehended at gunpoint by police officers. With their neighbors and family members looking on, the plaintiffs were ordered down on their knees, handcuffed, and detained for a prolonged period of time. They were utterly unaware of what was going on and why. It turned out that one of the pizza store employees, a delivery driver, who had been present when the pizza was purchased, thought that he had seen one of the plaintiffs with a handgun in the shop. This information was relayed to police and ultimately was the reason the police intervened and apprehended the plaintiffs. It turned out that the pizza delivery driver had been mistaken about the handgun. The plaintiffs sued the pizza shop and delivery driver for false imprisonment and defamation (slander per se). The case ultimately was decided by the state supreme court, which ruled 3–2 against the plaintiffs. Both of the judges who voted in favor of the plaintiffs wrote very interesting dissenting opinions in this case. Excerpts from the majority opinion and both dissents are included with the online materials for Chapter XI on the textbook's website.

Interference with Contract Relations

The underlying policy reason behind the intentional tort called interference with contract relations is the desire to strengthen our economy by promoting the stability of contracts. Strengthening the economy is important to the welfare of all Americans.

The intentional tort of **interference with contract relations** takes place when a noncontracting party or third person wrongfully interferes with the contract relations between two or more contracting parties. (See Chapter X for a discussion of contracts.) The tort of interference includes all intentional invasions of contract relations, including any act injuring a person or destroying property that interferes with the performance of a contract. For example, this tort occurs when someone wrongfully prevents an employee from working for an employer or prevents a tenant from paying rent to the landlord.

In order to maintain an action against a third person for interference, the plaintiff must prove that the defendant maliciously and substantially interfered with the performance of a valid and enforceable contract. The motive or purpose of the interfering party is an important factor in determining liability.

Infliction of Emotional Distress

The intentional tort called **infliction of emotional distress** evolved out of the need to recognize that every person has a right to not be subjected intentionally and recklessly to severe emotional distress caused by some other person's outrageous conduct. A person has a cause of action for infliction of emotional distress when the conduct of the defendant is serious in nature and causes anguish in the plaintiff's mind. Because it is difficult to prove mental anguish and to place a dollar amount on that injury, early cases allowed recovery for emotional distress only when it was accompanied by some other tort, such as assault, battery, or false imprisonment. Today, the infliction of emotional distress generally is considered to be a stand-alone intentional tort.[7]

Recovery for emotional distress is allowed only in situations involving extreme misconduct—for example, telling a wife the made-up story that her husband shot himself in the head. Mental worry, distress, grief, and mortification are elements of mental suffering for which an injured person can be awarded damages. Damages are not available for mere annoyance, disappointment, or hurt feelings. For example, the plaintiffs in a 2013 case claimed that they had suffered emotional distress resulting from a big gasoline leak that contaminated the aquifer from which they got their water. They argued they were entitled to money damages because of their fear of contracting cancer and the "distress" resulting from their fear that their property would decline in value. The court ruled against the plaintiffs because they had not proven their claims clearly and convincingly.[8]

Invasion of Privacy

The law recognizes one's right to be free from unwarranted publicity and, in general, one's right to be left alone. If one person invades the right of another to withhold self and property from public scrutiny, the invading party can be held liable in tort for invasion of the right of privacy. A suit for **invasion of privacy** may involve publicity that places the plaintiff in a false light, intrudes into the plaintiff's private life, discloses embarrassing private facts, or uses the plaintiff's name or likeness for the defendant's gain. Generally, the motives of the defendant are unimportant.

The standard used to measure any type of invasion of privacy is that the effect must be highly offensive to a reasonable person. For example, if a frustrated creditor puts up a notice in a store window stating that a named debtor owes money, this is an invasion of the debtor's privacy.

Technological developments in information storage and communications have subjected the intimacies of everyone's private lives to exploitation. The law protects individuals against this type of encroachment. A person who has become a public figure has less protection, however, because society has a right to information of legitimate public interest.

Although invasion of privacy and defamation are similar, they are distinct intentional torts, and both may be included in a plaintiff's complaint. The difference between a right of privacy and a right to freedom from defamation is that the former is concerned with one's peace of mind, whereas the latter is concerned with one's reputation or character. Unlike defamation, truth is generally not a defense for invasion of privacy,

INTERNET TIP

Readers can read on the textbook's website the case of *Elli Lake v. Wal-Mart Stores, Inc.,* 582 N.W.2d 231. This is a 1998 case in which the Minnesota Supreme Court explains why it decided to recognize only three of the four types of activities that commonly are included in the tort of invasion of privacy.

NEGLIGENCE

The law recognizes a duty or obligation to conform to a certain standard of conduct for the protection of others against unreasonable risk of harm. If the person fails to conform to the required standard, and that failure causes damage or loss, the injured party has a cause of action for **negligence.** Negligence is the unintentional failure to live up to the community's ideal of reasonable care; it is not based on moral fault. The fact that defendants may have suffered losses of their own through their negligent acts does not render them any less liable for plaintiffs' injuries.

An infinite variety of possible situations makes the determination of an exact set of rules for negligent conduct impossible. Conduct that might be considered prudent in one situation may be deemed negligent in another, depending on such factors as the person's physical attributes, age, and knowledge; the person to whom the duty was owed; and the situation at the time. If the defendant could not reasonably foresee any injury as the result of a certain conduct, there is no negligence and no liability.

The elements necessary for a cause of action for the tort of negligence are: (1) a duty or standard of care recognized by law, (2) a breach of the duty or failure to exercise the requisite care, and (3) the occurrence of harm proximately caused by the breach of duty. No cause of action in negligence is recognized if any of these elements are absent from the proof.

The plaintiff has the burden of proving, through the presentation of evidence, that the defendant was negligent. Unless the evidence is such that it can reasonably lead to but one conclusion, negligence is primarily a question of fact for the jury. A jury must decide whether the defendant acted as a reasonably prudent person would have under the circumstances—that is, a person having the same information, experience, physique, and professional skill. This standard makes no allowance for a person less intelligent than average.

Children are not held to the same standard as adults. A child must conform merely to the conduct of a reasonable person of like age, intelligence, and experience under like circumstances. This standard is subjective and holds a less intelligent child to what a similar child would do.

Malpractice

The term **malpractice** is a nonlegal term for professional negligence. Professional negligence takes different forms in different fields. Attorney negligence would include drafting a will but failing to see that it is properly attested; failing to file an answer in a timely manner on behalf of a client, with the result that the opposing party wins by default; and failing to file suit prior to the running of the statute of limitations, thus barring the client's claim. Accountant negligence would occur if a client paid for an audit but the accountant failed to discover that the client's employees were engaging in embezzlement, exposing the client to postaudit losses that could have been prevented. The case of *Macomber v. Dillman* (Chapter VII) is an example of medical malpractice. In that case, a surgeon improperly performed a tubal ligations, and the plaintiff subsequently gave birth to a child.

Plaintiffs in malpractice cases allege that the professional specifically breached a contractual duty (if the suit is in contract) or that the professional breached a duty of care imposed by law (if the suit is in tort). Professionals have a higher degree of knowledge, skills, or experience than a reasonable person and are required to use that capacity. They are generally required to act as would a reasonably skilled, prudent, competent, and experienced member of the profession in good standing within that state. Negligence in this area usually may be shown only by the use of expert testimony.

Duty of Care

There can be no actionable negligence without legal duty. Common law duty is found by courts when the kind of relationship that exists between the parties to a dispute requires the legal recognition of a duty of care. Legislative acts also may prescribe standards of conduct required of a reasonable person. It may be argued that a reasonable person would obey statutes such as traffic laws, ordinances, and regulations of administrative bodies.

In the case of legislative acts, plaintiffs must establish that they are within the limited class of individuals intended to be protected by the statute. In addition, the harm suffered must be of the kind that the statute was intended to prevent. Often the class of people intended to be protected may be very broad. For example, regulations requiring the labeling of certain poisons are for the protection of anyone who may come in contact with the bottle.

Many traffic laws are meant to protect other people on the highway. Once it is decided that a statute is applicable, most courts hold that an unexcused violation is conclusive as to the issue of negligence. In other words, it is **negligence per se,** and the issue of negligence does not go to the jury. However, some courts hold that the violation of such a statute is only evidence of negligence, which the jury may accept or reject as it sees fit.

Common law provides that one should guard against that which a reasonably prudent person would anticipate as likely to injure another. Damages for an injury are not recoverable if it was not foreseen or could not have been foreseen or anticipated. It is not necessary that one anticipate the precise injury sustained, however.

Courts do not ignore the common practices of society in determining the duty or whether due care was exercised in a particular situation. The scope of the duty of care that a person owes depends on the relationship of the parties. For example, those who lack capacity, the young, and the inexperienced are entitled to a degree of care proportionate to their relative ability to care for themselves given their age, mental condition, and experience.

As a general rule, the law does not impose the duty to aid or protect another. However, a duty *is* imposed where there is a special relationship between the parties—for example, parents must go to the aid of their children, and employers must render protection to their employees. In addition, if one puts another in peril, that person must render aid. A person can also assume a duty through contract where the duty would not otherwise exist. Although persons seeing another in distress have no obligation to be Good Samaritans, if they choose to do so, they incur the duty of exercising ordinary care. Some states have changed this common law duty by passing Good Samaritan statutes that state that those administering emergency care are liable only if the acts performed constitute willful or wanton misconduct.

Introduction to *Wright v. House of Imports, Inc.*

This is a "slip-and-fall" tort case in which there was some confusion as to whether the case should be considered to be a common-law negligence case or a negligence per se action. The trial court found in favor of the plaintiff, the intermediate court of appeals reversed, and the plaintiff appealed to the state supreme court.

Benjamin Wright, Jr. v. House of Imports, Inc.
381 S.W.3d 209
Supreme Court of Kentucky
September 20, 2012

Opinion of the Court by Justice SCOTT.
A Jefferson Circuit Court jury awarded Appellant, Benjamin Wright, Jr., $120,863.75 in his simple negligence action against Appellee, House of Imports, after he fell down a set of stairs at the retailer's business establishment. The Court of Appeals reversed and remanded for a new trial, holding that the trial court committed palpable error in permitting expert testimony of building code violations without instructing the jury as to the applicability of the code....

I. Background
Wright visited House of Imports to buy a pair of shoes on August 31, 2007. He selected a pair and ascended three stairs to an elevated level of the store where the cash register was located. He paid for the shoes and proceeded to exit the building. As he placed his foot on the top step of the elevated level, he slipped and, fell down the stairs to the first level of the store, suffering serious injuries as a result.

Thereafter, Wright filed a common-law negligence cause of action against House of Imports alleging that the retailer negligently maintained its business premises in a dangerous and defective condition, causing him to fall and suffer personal injuries. The case was tried to a jury which, under Kentucky's comparative fault principles, assigned 25% of the fault to Wright and 75% of the fault to House of Imports. The jury further found that Wright suffered $75,000 in pain and suffering in addition to his $86,151.56 in medical expenses. Based on the jury's apportionment of fault, the trial court awarded Wright $120,863.67.

At trial, Wright introduced the expert testimony of engineer and board-certified safety professional John Schroering, who testified that the stairs at House of Imports violated several of the Kentucky Building Code's safety standards.... [T]he Court of Appeals reversed, finding that the trial court's failure to instruct the jury on the applicability of the Code left the jury " 'to decide for itself what, if any, was its relevance and legal effect' " ... and constituted palpable error....

II. Analysis

The precise issue before us is whether a trial court errs when it admits expert testimony concerning building code violations without instructing the jury as to the applicability of the code; and, if so, whether the trial court in this case committed palpable error in doing so....

Turning to our analysis, we note first that this is a common-law negligence case—not a negligence per se case. A common-law negligence claim requires proof of (1) a duty owed by the defendant to the plaintiff, (2) breach of that duty, (3) injury to the plaintiff, and (4) legal causation between the defendant's breach and the plaintiff's injury.... The standard of care applicable to a common-law negligence action is that of ordinary care—that is, "such care as a reasonably prudent person would exercise under the circumstances."...

Negligence per se, on the other hand, " 'is a negligence claim with a statutory [or regulatory] standard of care substituted for the common-law standard of care.' "... KRS [Kentucky Revised Statute] 446.070 codifies the doctrine of negligence per se, and provides: "A person injured by the violation of any statute may recover from the offender such damages as he sustained by reason of the violation, although a penalty or forfeiture is imposed for such violation."

Because Wright brought a common-law negligence action against House of Imports, and not a negligence per se claim alleging statutory or regulatory violations, the testimony ... offered regarding the statutory duties imposed by the building code (and the alleged breaches of those duties) was irrelevant—that is, it did not "fit" a fact in issue.... The trial court therefore erred in permitting ... [testimony] about alleged violations of the building code.

We cannot, however, conclude that it rises to the level of "palpable" error. Although the Court of Appeals determined that the trial court erred in failing to instruct the jury as to the applicability of the building code, the allegedly fatal instructions were tendered by House of Imports.... When a trial court adopts a party's proposed jury instructions, that party cannot be heard to complain that its "substantial rights" have been affected by said instructions, nor that a "manifest injustice has resulted from the error."... This has been the law of this Commonwealth for decades....

III. Conclusion

In conclusion, we find no palpable error in the trial court's decision to admit expert testimony of building code violations without a concomitant jury instruction as to the applicability of the code. We therefore reverse the judgment of the Court of Appeals and reinstate that of the trial court.

Case Questions

1. Why did the Kentucky Supreme Court conclude that the "ordinary care" duty was applicable in this case rather than negligence per se?
2. Why did Kentucky's highest court overrule the intermediate court of appeals in this case and restore the judgment of the trial court?

 This case involves an alleged violation of the rule of general application in misfeasance cases that one has a legal duty to exercise ordinary care to prevent others from being injured as a result of one's conduct. How would Immanuel Kant probably react to this legal duty of ordinary care?

Liability Rules for Specialized Activities

The ordinary principles of negligence do not govern property owners' liability to those entering their premises. For example, the duty the property owner owes to a trespasser is less than the duty the property owner owes to the general public under the ordinary principles of negligence.[9] The special rules regarding liability of the possessor of land stem from the English tradition of high regard for land and from the dominance and prestige of the English landowning class. In the eighteenth and nineteenth centuries, owners of land were considered sovereigns within their own boundaries and were privileged to do what they pleased within their domains. The unrestricted use of land was favored over human welfare. Visitors were classified as invitees, licensees, or trespassers. Although English law has since rejected these distinctions, they remain part of the U.S. common law.

An **invitee** is either a **public invitee** or a **business visitor (business invitee).** A public invitee is a member of the public who enters land for the purpose for which the land is held open to the public—for example, where a visitor enters a bank and goes into a meeting room that the bank makes available at no cost to civic clubs, for the purpose of attending the club's monthly meeting. The club was meeting in this room in response to the bank's public invitation for civic groups to hold such meetings on its premises.[10]

A business visitor (also called a business invitee) enters land for a purpose directly or indirectly connected with business dealings with the possessor of the land. Thus, plumbers, electricians, trash collectors, and letter carriers are classified as business invitees. Invitees are given the greatest protection by the courts. A landowner owes the invitee a duty to exercise ordinary care under the usual principles of negligence liability, and must exercise reasonable care to make the premises safe. This preferred status applies only to the area of invitation.

One who enters or remains on land by virtue of the possessor's implied or express consent is a **licensee** —for example, door-to-door salespeople or social guests. In addition, police officers and firefighters are usually classified as licensees, because they often come on premises unexpectedly and it would not be fair to hold possessors to the standard of care applicable to invitees. Licensees ordinarily must accept the premises as they find them and look out for their own welfare. This is based on the principle that land occupiers cannot be expected to exercise a higher degree of care for licensees than they would for themselves. A possessor

of land generally owes the licensee only the duty to refrain from willful or wanton misconduct; however, the courts have developed some exceptions to this rule. With respect to active operations, for example, the possessor of land is subject to liability to licensees for injury caused by failure to exercise reasonable care for their safety. What might constitute activities dangerous to licensees depends on the court's interpretation, and knowledge of the nature of the activities normally precludes recovery by the licensee. Generally, the possessor of land is under a duty to give warning of known dangers.

A **trespasser** is one who enters and remains on the land of another without the possessor's express or implied consent. Licensees or invitees may become trespassers if they venture into an area where they are not invited or expected to venture, or remain on the premises for an unreasonable period of time. Generally, possessors of land are not liable to trespassers for physical harm caused by the owners' failure either to exercise reasonable care to make their land safe for the trespasser's reception or to carry on the owners' activities so as not to endanger them. The only duty that is owed to a trespasser by an occupier of land is to refrain from willful or wanton misconduct. However, a duty of reasonable care is owed to an adult trespasser whose presence has been discovered or who habitually intrudes on a limited area. Reasonable care is also owed to the child trespasser whose presence is foreseeable (for example, erecting a child-proof fence around a backyard swimming pool).

Many have questioned the legal and moral justification of a rule that determines the legal protection of a person's life and limb according to this classification scheme. Although courts have been reluctant to abandon the land occupier's preferred position set forth by history and precedent, some courts have replaced the common law distinction with ordinary principles of negligence to govern occupiers' liability to those entering their premises.

The following case is from North Dakota, a state that has abandoned the common law distinctions. The defendants in *Schmidt v. Gateway Community Fellowship* were sponsors of an outdoor automotive show that was being held in a shopping mall parking lot. The defendants persuaded the trial court that they were immune from suit under the state's recreational use immunity law, and the court granted them summary judgment. The plaintiff, who had injured her ankle while attending the show, appealed to the state supreme court. She maintained that the trial court's conclusion was erroneous in that these defendants were not entitled to protection under the recreational immunity statute.

Schmidt v. Gateway Community Fellowship
2010 ND 69
Supreme Court of North Dakota
April 8, 2010

Kapsner, Justice.

Jacqueline and Randall Schmidt appeal from a summary judgment dismissing their personal injury action against Gateway Community Fellowship and North Bismarck Associates II after the district court decided Gateway Community Fellowship and North Bismarck Associates II were entitled to recreational use immunity because Jacqueline Schmidt entered a parking lot at a shopping mall for recreational purposes and she was not charged to enter the premises. The Schmidts argue there are factual issues about whether Jacqueline Schmidt entered the premises for recreational purposes and whether there was a charge for her entry to the premises....

I.

The Schmidts alleged Jacqueline Schmidt injured her right ankle on September 14, 2002, when she stepped in a hole in a paved parking lot on the north side of Gateway Mall shopping center in Bismarck while attending an outdoor automotive show and skateboarding exhibition sponsored by Gateway Community Fellowship, a non-profit church affiliated with the Church of God. At the time, Gateway Community Fellowship leased space for church services inside Gateway Mall from North Bismarck Associates II, the mall owner.

On September 14, 2002, Gateway Community Fellowship sponsored an outdoor automotive show and skateboarding exhibition, the "Impact Auto Explosion," on a paved lot on the north side of Gateway Mall from 10 a.m. to 4 p.m., which was during the mall's regular Saturday business hours.... The public was not charged an admission fee for entry to the exhibition, but Gateway Community Fellowship procured exhibition sponsors to defray costs. Additionally, the automotive show included several contests, and Gateway Community Fellowship charged car owners a registration fee to enter the contests.... The ... mall manager for North Bismarck Associates II directed Gateway Community Fellowship to hold the exhibition ... on the parking lot on the north side of Gateway Mall to increase visibility from Century Avenue in Bismarck. North Bismarck Associates II did not separately charge Gateway Community Fellowship for use of the parking lot.... The parking lot on the north side of Gateway Mall had been part of a lumberyard of a previous mall tenant, and the area had holes and depressions in the concrete from the removal of posts that had formed part of an enclosure around the lumberyard. According to North Bismarck Associates II, the area of the parking lot used for the 2002 exhibition usually was roped off to be less accessible by the public.

On September 14, 2002, Jacqueline Schmidt and her son were driving by ... when they saw activity in the parking lot north of ... Gateway Mall, and they stopped at the exhibition. According to Jacqueline Schmidt, they decided "it would be fun. They had skateboarders, and they had music, and it was a nice day out.... We were enjoying ourselves. We were watching the skateboarders. We were looking around, looking at the vehicles. It was a pleasant day out. It was very nice out, and we were just enjoying spending time together, looking at the activities."

Jacqueline Schmidt and her son were not charged an admission fee for entry to the property or to the exhibition. According to her, she severely injured her right ankle as she walked across the parking lot and stepped in a posthole from the prior tenant's lumberyard.

The Schmidts sued Gateway Community Fellowship and North Bismarck Associates II, alleging they negligently and carelessly failed to eliminate the holes in the parking lot or to warn exhibition attendees about the holes and were liable for the hazardous condition on the premises. Gateway Community Fellowship and North Bismarck Associates II separately answered, denying they were negligent and claiming the Schmidts' action was barred by recreational use immunity under N.D.C.C. ch. 53-08. Gateway Community Fellowship and North Bismarck Associates II separately moved for summary judgment, arguing they were entitled to recreational use immunity ... because the premises were used for recreational purposes and Jacqueline Schmidt was not charged to enter the premises.

The district court granted summary judgment, concluding Gateway Community Fellowship and North Bismarck Associates II were entitled to recreational use immunity, because Jacqueline Schmidt entered the land for the recreational purpose of enjoying the exhibition with her son and she was not charged to enter the premises. The court also decided the statutory provisions for recreational use immunity were not unconstitutional as applied to the Schmidts' action.

II.

Summary judgment is a procedural device for promptly resolving a controversy on the merits without a trial if there are no genuine issues of material fact or inferences that reasonably can be drawn from undisputed facts, or if the only issues to be resolved are questions of law....

III.

Under North Dakota law for premises liability, general negligence principles govern a landowner's duty of care to persons who are not trespassers on the premises.... See *O'Leary v. Coenen* ... (N.D. 1977) (abandoning common-law categories of licensee and invitee for premises liability and retaining standard that owner owes no duty to trespasser except to refrain from harming trespasser in willful and wanton manner). Thus, a landowner or occupier of premises generally owes a duty to lawful entrants to exercise reasonable care to maintain the property in a reasonably safe condition in view of all the circumstances, including the likelihood of injury to another, the seriousness of injury, and the burden of avoiding the risk....

Under that formulation, an owner or possessor of commercial property owes a duty to lawful entrants to exercise reasonable care to maintain the property in a reasonably safe condition in view of all the circumstances, including the likelihood of injury to another, the seriousness of injury, and the burden of avoiding the risk... 1 Premises Liability Law and Practice, at §4.01[2][a] (explaining owner or possessor of commercial property must warn entrants of all known dangers, must inspect premises to discover hidden dangers, and must provide proper warning of known dangers); 62 Am. Jur. 2d Premises Liability, §§435, 439 (2005) (discussing commercial property owner's duty to customers and potential customers in shopping centers and malls). Similarly, a church or religious institution generally owes the same duty of care to lawful entrants on its premises....

In 1965, the Legislature enacted recreational use immunity statutes to encourage landowners to open their land for recreational purposes by giving them immunity from suit under certain circumstances.

Under N.D.C.C. §53-08-02, "an owner of land owes no duty of care to keep the premises safe for entry or use by others for recreational purposes, or to give any warning of a dangerous condition, use, structure, or activity on such premises to persons entering for such purposes." Section 53-08-03, N.D.C.C., also provides:

> Subject to the provisions of section 53-08-05, an owner of land who either directly or indirectly invites or permits without charge any person to use such property for recreational purposes does not thereby:
>
> 1. Extend any assurance that the premises are safe for any purpose;
> 2. Confer upon such persons the legal status of an invitee or licensee to whom a duty of care is owed; or
> 3. Assume responsibility for or incur liability for any injury to person or property caused by an act or omission of such persons....

... In 1995 ... the Legislature amended the definition of "recreational purposes" to its present form to cover "all recreational activities."...

IV.

The Schmidts argue the district court did not view the evidence in the light most favorable to them and erred in finding, as a matter of law, that Jacqueline Schmidt's use of the land was recreational in character and that there was no charge for her to enter the land. They argue the court erred in failing to weigh the business purposes of Gateway Community Fellowship and North Bismarck Associates II in having the exhibition on the dangerous parking lot. They claim Gateway Community Fellowship's purpose was to increase membership, including tithing, and North Bismarck Associate's purpose was to increase foot traffic for its Gateway Mall tenants.... The Schmidts ... also assert a factual issue exists in this case because, although Gateway Community Fellowship did not directly charge Jacqueline Schmidt to enter the exhibition, it procured sponsors for the exhibition and charged contestants a registration fee to enter the contests in the automotive show....

A common thread under our case law interpreting the recreational use immunity statutes is that the intent of both the owner and the user are relevant to the analysis and that the location and nature of the injured person's conduct when the injury occurs are also relevant.... Other jurisdictions have acknowledged that cases involving claims of recreational use immunity involve fact-driven inquiries in which nonrecreational uses or purposes may be mixed with recreational uses or purposes....

In *Auman v. School Distr. of Stanley-Boyd,* 2001 WI 125 ... the Wisconsin Supreme Court said the line between recreational and nonrecreational purposes was an intensely fact-driven inquiry and reiterated the test for resolving the issue:

> Although the injured person's subjective assessment of the activity is pertinent, it is not controlling. A court must consider the nature of the property, the nature of the owner's activity, and the reason the injured person is on the property. A court should consider the totality of circumstances surrounding the activity, including the intrinsic nature, purpose, and consequences of the activity. A court should apply a reasonable person standard to determine whether the person entered the property to engage in a recreational activity.

Under N.D.C.C. ch. 53-08 and our caselaw interpreting those provisions, we decline to construe our recreational use statutes to necessarily provide a commercial landowner immunity where there is a recreational and commercial component to the landowner's operation. We conclude the rationale and balancing test ... provide persuasive authority for construing our statutes and assessing mixed use cases. We hold that [the *Auman*] balancing test applies to our recreational use immunity statutes in mixed use cases and that inquiry generally involves resolution of factual issues unless the facts are such that reasonable minds could not differ.

... We conclude the facts in this case are not such that reasonable persons could reach one conclusion and there are disputed factual issues about whether North Bismarck Associates II and Gateway Community Fellowship are entitled to recreational use immunity. We therefore conclude resolution of the issue by summary judgment was inappropriate and a remand is necessary for the trier of fact to apply the balancing test to this mixed-use case....

We reverse the summary judgment and remand for proceedings consistent with this opinion.

Case Questions

1. What would it mean to these parties if ultimately on **remand** (i.e., when the case returns to the trial court for a jury trial), the North Dakota trial or appellate courts concluded that the trial court's original ruling on summary judgment was correct and that the plaintiff was engaging in a recreational activity when attending the auto show in the mall parking lot?
2. The North Dakota Supreme Court felt that the record was insufficient to permit the trial court to decide this case by summary judgment. Assume that the facts revealed upon remand indicate that the auto show contained some elements that were essentially recreational and other elements that were commercial. Which party do you think should ultimately win the lawsuit? Why?

INTERNET TIP

Readers will find *Benejam v. Detroit Tigers, Inc.,* on the textbook's website, a case in which a state intermediate appellate court concluded that the Tigers had a limited duty to make their stadium reasonably safe for fans.

Proximate Cause

One of the elements that must be proven to establish negligence is **causation.**[11] The plaintiff must prove that there is a reasonable connection between the negligent act of the defendant and the damage suffered by the plaintiff. For tort liability, however, proof of factual causation is not enough. Tort liability depends on the existence of **proximate cause.** Proximate cause means legal cause and consists of two elements: (1) causation in fact, and (2) foreseeability. A plaintiff must prove that his or her injuries were the actual or factual result of the defendant's actions. **Causation in fact** may be established directly or indirectly. Courts usually use a "but-for" test to establish causation in fact: but for the defendant's negligence, the plaintiff's injuries would not have occurred. This test is an extremely broad one and could have far-reaching results.

Every event has many contributing causes, even though some may be very remote. The defendant is not relieved from liability merely because other causes have contributed to the result. In many situations, application of the "but-for" test will identify several persons who could be placed on a causation continuum. The question before the court in a negligence case is whether the conduct has been so significant and important a cause that the defendant should be legally responsible. For example, in a nighttime automobile accident, the fact that one of the drivers worked late at the office would be a factual cause of the collision. If she hadn't worked late, she wouldn't have been at the location of the accident. But this cause should not be recognized as a legal cause of the collision. Because cause demands that some boundary be set for the consequences of an act, proximate cause (causation in fact plus foreseeability), rather than causation in fact alone, is used to determine liability.

The second element of proximate cause is **foreseeability.** An individual is only responsible for those consequences that are reasonably foreseeable, and will be relieved of liability for injuries that are not reasonably related to the negligent conduct. To illustrate, a driver drives his car carelessly and collides with another car, causing it to explode. Four blocks away, a nurse carrying a baby is startled by the explosion and drops the infant. It is doubtful if any court would hold the driver liable to the infant, even though the driver was negligent and was the factual cause of the infant's injury. The baby's injury is so far removed from the driver that it would be unfair to hold the driver liable. The driver could not reasonably have foreseen the injury sustained by the infant. In other words, the driving would not be the proximate cause of the injury.

If there is more than one cause for a single injury, liability is possible if each action by itself would have been sufficient to cause the harm without the other. If there are **joint tortfeasors** of a single injury, each possible tortfeasor's actions must be examined to see if the acts were so closely related to the damage to have proximately caused the plaintiff's injury.

INTERNET TIP

Readers visiting the textbook's web site will find there the 2002 Texas case of *McClure v. Roch*, a case that discusses the distinction between invitees and licensees, proximate cause, and foreseeability.

Contributory-Negligence and Assumption-of-Risk Defenses

Even after a plaintiff has proved that a defendant was negligent and that the negligence was the proximate cause of his or her injury, some states permit the defendant to counter by proving a defense. Contributory negligence and assumption of risk are two such defenses.

Contributory negligence is a defense that exists when injured persons proximately contributed to their injuries by their own negligence. This defense is based on the theory that the plaintiff is held to the same standard of care as the defendant: that is, that of a reasonable person under like circumstances. When proven, contributory negligence will usually bar any recovery by the plaintiff.

To illustrate, D-1 is driving his car and P is his passenger. Both are injured in a collision with D-2's car. If both cars were driven negligently, D-1 could not recover from D-2 because his own negligence contributed to his own injuries. Yet P could recover from both D-1 and D-2, because they were both joint tortfeasors in causing P's injuries. The burden of proving contributory negligence is on the defendant.

The defense of **assumption of risk** exists when the plaintiff had knowledge of the risk and made the free choice of exposing himself or herself to it. Assumption of risk may be express or implied. In an express assumption of risk, the plaintiff expressly agrees in advance that the defendant has no duty to care for him or her, and is not liable for what otherwise would be negligent conduct. For example, parents often expressly assume the risk of personal injury to their children in conjunction with youth soccer, basketball, and baseball programs. Where the assumption of risk is implied, consent is manifested by the plaintiff's continued presence after he or she has become aware of the danger involved. The plaintiff impliedly consents to take his or her chances concerning the defendant's negligence. For example, baseball fans who sit in unscreened seats at the ballpark know that balls and even bats may strike them; they implicitly agree to take a chance of being injured in this manner.

INTERNET TIP

North Carolina is one of the six states that continue to follow the contributory negligence–assumption of risk approach. Readers can find *Carolyn Alford v. Wanda E. Lowery*, a North Carolina case that illustrates how contributory negligence works, on the textbook's website.

Comparative Negligence

In states that allow the *contributory-negligence* defense, the entire loss is placed on the plaintiff even when both the plaintiff and the defendant are contributorily negligent. For this reason, most states now determine the amount of damage by comparing the negligence of the plaintiff with that of the defendant. Under this doctrine of **comparative negligence,** a negligent plaintiff may be able to recover a portion of the cost of an injury.

In negligence cases, comparative negligence divides the damages between the parties by reducing the plaintiff's damages in proportion to the extent of that person's contributory fault. The trier of fact in a case assigns a percentage of the total fault to the plaintiff, and the plaintiff's total damages are usually reduced by that percentage. For example, a plaintiff who was considered to be 40 percent at fault by the trier of fact would recover $1,200 if the total damages were determined to be $2,000.

Introduction to *Baker v. East Coast Properties, Inc.*

Plaintiff Alfred Baker is legally blind and is afflicted with many medical issues, including diabetes and Parkinson's disease. He has difficulty walking and frequently falls. At the time he sustained the injury that was the subject of this lawsuit, Baker rented an apartment that was specifically designed for people with medical problems like his. He sued his landlord for injuries he allegedly received when agents of the landlord entered his apartment and triggered an alarm, startling the sleeping Baker. Baker alleged that he was injured when he fell trying to get to the door. The landlord's defense was that its entry was not the proximate cause of Baker's injuries, and it moved for summary judgment. What follows is the trial court's ruling on the summary judgment motion.

Alfred L. Baker v. East Coast Properties, Inc.
C.A. No. N09C-11-144 MMJ
Superior Court of Delaware
November 15, 2011

Johnston, J.
Plaintiff Alfred Baker ("Baker") rented an apartment in Greenwood Acres Apartments ("Greenwood Acres") from Defendant East Coast Properties, Inc. ("East Coast"). Baker brought suit, claiming that he sustained injuries as a result of negligence on the part of East Coast. Baker contends that East Coast's unannounced and unauthorized entry into his apartment triggered an audible self-installed alarm attached to his front door. According to Baker, the sound of the alarm

startled him awake, causing him to get out of bed and subsequently fall as he attempted to get to the front door.

East Coast moves for summary judgment against Baker, arguing that it was not reasonably foreseeable that East Coast's entry into Baker's apartment would result in Baker falling and sustaining injuries. East Coast further argues that even if its actions were negligent, Baker's installation of the alarms constitutes an intervening and superseding cause....

Factual Background

The following facts are set forth in the light most favorable to Baker, as the non-moving party. Baker rented an apartment in Greenwood Acres from East Coast, owner and landlord of the apartment complex. Greenwood Acres provides housing specifically for the elderly and those with ambulatory difficulties. Baker, himself, is legally blind and suffers from numerous health problems, including COPD, diabetes ... , prostate cancer, and low back pain. Baker has also been diagnosed with Parkinson's disease. As a result of his Parkinson's disease, Baker exhibits ambulatory dysfunction which causes him to fall down frequently because his knees buckle.

Since moving to Greenwood Acres in 2000, Baker claimed that maintenance personnel employed by East Coast repeatedly had entered his apartment without permission. During one of these unauthorized visits, Baker claimed that his cable box had been stolen. As a result of the numerous unauthorized entries into his apartment, Baker purchased and installed an audible motion-sensitive alarm to hang on the interior front doorknob. When activated, the alarm would sound only if the door was opened.... Therefore, according to Baker, he would only set the alarm if he was home so that he could be alerted when someone entered his apartment.

On March 13, 2009, at approximately 9:00 a.m., Louis Desposito ("Desposito"), East Coast's maintenance man, arrived outside Baker's apartment. Desposito, who was accompanied by a fire technician from Simplex Grinnell, planned to conduct maintenance and inspections of the complex's fire suppression system, including equipment in Baker's unit. Baker contends that he never received oral or written notice that maintenance personnel would need to access his unit.

The parties dispute whether Desposito knocked on the door or rang the door bell before using the master key to enter Baker's unit. Viewing the facts in the light most favorable to Baker, however, the Court will assume that Desposito's entry in Baker's apartment was unannounced and unauthorized. As Desposito unlocked Baker's front door and opened it, the alarms immediately sounded.... According to Baker, he was startled awake by the sound of the alarm and jumped out of bed to see who was in his apartment. Baker took about three steps and fell to the ground when his legs gave way. As a result of the fall, Baker claimed to have sustained head and neck injuries. Baker managed to get back on his feet and proceeded to the front door to see who was attempting to enter his apartment....

Discussion

Common-Law Negligence

In order to establish a prima facie case of negligence, the plaintiff must show that the defendant's negligent act or omission breached a duty of care owed to plaintiff in a way that proximately caused plaintiff injury.... "Summary judgment can be appropriate in a negligence action if [the] [p]laintiff[] fail[s] to establish the elements of negligence by a preponderance of the evidence."...

Here, in determining whether summary judgment is appropriate, the Court's inquiry must focus on two issues: (1) whether East Coast breached any duty it owed to Baker; and (2) if so, whether its breach was the proximate cause of Baker's injuries.

Duty and Breach

Under Delaware law, one's "duty of care" is measured in terms of reasonableness.... One has a duty to act as a reasonably prudent person would act.... In defining the parameters of one's duty, the Court has incorporated the principle of foreseeability.... The duty encompasses protecting against reasonably foreseeable events....

Here, the relevant inquiry is whether it was reasonably foreseeable that East Coast's conduct—that is, East Coast's allegedly unauthorized and unannounced entry into Baker's apartment—would result in Baker's injuries. Absent a finding that such a result was reasonably foreseeable, East Coast cannot be said to have breached any duty to Baker under the circumstances.

East Coast argues that it was not reasonably foreseeable that Desposito's "knocking on the door and ringing [Baker's] doorbell for several minutes and opening his door yelling 'maintenance', would result in Baker's self-installed alarms going off, startling him awake, resulting in his attempt to walk when he was not physically capable to do so." Therefore, East Coast contends that it owed no duty to Baker under these circumstances.

Baker disputes East Coast's account of events, claiming that Desposito neither knocked on the door nor rang the doorbell. Instead, Baker claims that without authorization or announcement, Desposito entered Baker's apartment, triggered the alarm and caused injury by startling Baker. According to Baker, because East Coast was aware of his ambulatory difficulties as well as his prior complaints regarding unauthorized intrusions into his apartment, it was reasonably foreseeable that Baker may be injured due to East Coast's unannounced entry.

Intervening and Superseding Causation

Although a question of fact exists as to the manner of East Coast's entry into Baker's apartment, the Court need not resolve this factual dispute. Even if the Court were to find that East Coast's entry was unauthorized and unannounced, Baker has failed to establish that the injuries he sustained were proximately caused by East Coast's conduct.

Delaware applies the traditional "but for" definition of proximate cause.... Proximate cause is that which "brings about or produces, or helps to bring about or produce the injury and damage, and but for which the injury would not have occurred."... In other words, proximate cause exists if "a natural and continuous sequence, unbroken by any efficient intervening cause, produces the injury and without which the result would not have occurred."...

The mere occurrence of an intervening cause, however, does not automatically relieve the original tortfeasor of liability.... In determining whether the chain of causation stemming from the original tortious conduct is broken, the relevant inquiry is whether the intervening act was reasonably foreseen or reasonably anticipated by the original tortfeasor.... If the intervening act was not reasonably foreseeable, then the act constitutes a superseding cause and the initial tortfeasor is relieved of liability....

East Coast argues that Baker's actions constitute an intervening cause that supersedes any alleged negligent conduct by East Coast. According to East Coast, Baker's installation of the alarm on his front door was neither anticipated nor reasonably foreseeable by East Coast. Baker's own conduct, East Coast contends, was the sole proximate cause of Baker's injuries.

In response, Baker claims that East Coast's negligence—that is, East Coast's unauthorized and unannounced entry into his apartment—was the proximate cause of his injuries.

At his deposition, Baker acknowledged that the sole reason he fell was because he was startled out of bed by the sound of the alarm. The alarm operated precisely as Baker intended. When the door opened, the alarm sounded. According to Baker, when the alarm sounded, "it woke [him] up and startled [him]." In response to the sound of the alarm, Baker testified that he "jumped out of bed, made about three steps and fell" because his "legs gave way."

The Court finds that Baker's act of installing the alarm on the front door was neither reasonably foreseeable nor reasonably anticipated by East Coast. Baker testified that he saw no reason to inform East Coast that he had installed the alarm on the front door.

Viewing the facts in the light most favorable to Baker, the Court finds that the sounding of the alarm constitutes an intervening cause which relieves East Coast of liability. While it is undisputed that the alarm would not have sounded but for East Coast's entry into the apartment, it was the audible sound emitted from the alarm that directly caused Baker's injuries. It was not reasonably foreseeable that Baker would install a device that would cause him to panic to such an extent that he would forget that he was unable to walk without assistance. Therefore, the causal chain of liability stemming from any negligence on behalf of East Coast was effectively broken by Baker's intervening and superseding act.

Comparative Negligence
Even absent the intervening and superseding cause, the Court finds that Baker's own contributory negligence bars his recovery. Under Delaware's comparative negligence law, a plaintiff cannot recover if he acted more negligently than the defendant.... In other words, "if the plaintiff's contributory negligence is 51% or greater, it is an absolute bar to recovery according to the Delaware statute."... However, "if the plaintiff's contributory negligence is 50% or less, the plaintiff is permitted to recover, although the recovery is reduced proportionally."... Summary judgment may be granted in favor [of] the defendant if the trial judge determines that "no reasonable juror could find that the plaintiff's negligence did not exceed the defendant's."...

At his deposition, Baker acknowledged that his ambulatory dysfunction, a side effect of his Parkinson's disease, posed significant problems with his ability to stand and walk. According to Baker, he would fall frequently as a result of his condition. Baker was keenly aware of the physical limitations caused by his Parkinson's.

The Court finds, as a matter of law based on undisputed facts, that Baker's contributory negligence—installing the alarm without notice to East Coast, which caused him to jump up out of bed and take "three steps" despite the fact that he suffered from physical limitations which prevented him from walking without assistance—is greater than any negligence allegedly committed by East Coast.

Conclusion
Baker has failed to establish a prima facie case of negligence on the part of East Coast. Having considered the facts in the light most favorable to the non-moving party, the Court finds that the alarm, installed by Baker, constitutes an intervening and superseding cause which relieves East Coast of liability. The Court is cognizant of the fact that but for East Coast's entry into the apartment, the alarm would not have been triggered. However, the Court finds, as Baker conceded, that the sound emitted from the self-installed alarm (of which East Coast had no notice) directly caused Baker's injuries.

Additionally, the Court finds as a matter of law based on undisputed facts, that Baker's contributory negligence —installing the alarm and attempting to walk without assistance despite his physical limitations—exceeds any negligence of East Coast. Therefore, pursuant to Delaware's comparative negligence statute, Baker is barred from recovery.

THEREFORE, East Coast's Motion for Summary Judgment is hereby GRANTED....
IT IS SO ORDERED.
The Honorable Mary M. Johnston

Case Questions

1. Do you agree with the court with respect to proximate causation in this case?
2. Why did the court rule in favor of the defendant?
3. Based on what you have read, do you agree with the court that no reasonable juror could find that the defendant was more negligent than the plaintiff?

Negligence and Product Liability

Plaintiffs can recover in negligence by proving that a manufacturer's conduct violated the reasonable person standard and proximately caused injury. The manufacturer's allegedly tortious conduct could relate to any aspect of product design, manufacturing, quality control, packaging, or warnings.

In product liability suits, it is often difficult to prove the defendant's act or omission that caused the plaintiff's injury. Thus, in the interests of justice, courts developed the doctrine of **res ipsa loquitur** ("the thing speaks for itself"). This doctrine permits plaintiffs to prove negligence circumstantially if the following facts are proved: (1) the defendant had exclusive control over the allegedly defective product during manufacture; (2) under normal circumstances, the plaintiff would not have been injured by the product if the defendant had exercised ordinary care; and (3) the plaintiff's conduct did not contribute significantly to the accident. From the proved facts, the law permits the jurors to infer a fact for which there is no direct, explicit proof—the defendant's negligent act or omission. The trial judge will instruct the jurors that the law permits them to consider the inferred fact as well as the proved facts in deciding whether the defendant was negligent.

Duty to Warn

The following case illustrates typical problems associated with law suits in which the plaintiff alleges a negligent failure to warn. A manufacturer's duty to warn consumers depends on the nature of the product. Warnings are unnecessary for products that are obviously dangerous to everyone (knives, saws, and firearms). However, for products that may contain hazards that are not obvious, manufacturers have a duty to warn if the average person would not have known about a safety hazard. If the plaintiff is knowledgeable about the hazard that the warning would have addressed, the manufacturer's negligent failure to warn would not have proximately caused the plaintiff's injuries. Thus in such cases the extent of the plaintiff's actual knowledge of and familiarity with the hazard and the product are relevant to the issue of causation.

Laaperi v. Sears Roebuck & Co., Inc.
787 F.2d 726
U.S. Court of Appeals, First Circuit
March 31, 1986

Campbell, Chief Judge.
This is an appeal from jury verdicts totaling $1.8 million entered in a product liability suit against defendants Sears, Roebuck & Co. and Pittway Corporation. The actions were brought by Albin Laaperi as administrator of the estates of his three sons, all of whom were killed in a fire in their home in December 1976, and as father and next friend of his daughter, Janet, who was injured

in the fire. Plaintiff's theory of recovery was that defendants had a duty to warn plaintiff that a smoke detector powered by house current, manufactured by Pittway, and sold to Laaperi by Sears might not operate in the event of an electrical fire caused by a short circuit. Defendants contend on appeal that the district court erred in denying their motions for directed verdict and judgment notwithstanding the verdict; that the admission into evidence of purportedly undisclosed expert testimony violated Fed. R. Civ. P. 26(e); and that the award of $750,000 for injuries to Janet Laaperi was excessive and improper. We affirm the judgments in favor of plaintiff in his capacity as administrator of the estates of his three sons, but vacate the judgment in favor of Janet Laaperi, and remand for a new trial limited to the issue of her damages.

In March 1976, plaintiff Albin Laaperi purchased a smoke detector from Sears. The detector, manufactured by the Pittway Corporation, was designed to be powered by AC (electrical) current. Laaperi installed the detector himself in one of the two upstairs bedrooms in his home.

Early in the morning of December 27, 1976, a fire broke out in the Laaperi home. The three boys in one of the upstairs bedrooms were killed in the blaze. Laaperi's 13-year-old daughter, Janet, who was sleeping in the other upstairs bedroom, received burns over 12 percent of her body and was hospitalized for three weeks.

The uncontroverted testimony at trial was that the smoke detector did not sound an alarm on the night of the fire. The cause of the fire was later found to be a short circuit in an electrical cord that was located in a cedar closet in the boys' bedroom. The Laaperi home had two separate electrical circuits in the upstairs bedrooms: one that provided electricity to the outlets and one that powered the lighting fixtures. The smoke detector had been connected to the outlet circuit, which was the circuit that shorted and cut off. Because the circuit was shorted, the AC-operated smoke detector received no power on the night of the fire. Therefore, although the detector itself was in no sense defective (indeed, after the fire the charred detector was tested and found to be operable), no alarm sounded.

Laaperi brought this diversity action against defendants Sears and Pittway, asserting negligent design, negligent manufacture, breach of warranty, and negligent failure to warn of inherent dangers. The parties agreed that the applicable law is that of Massachusetts. Before the claims went to the jury, verdicts were directed in favor of the defendants on all theories of liability other than failure to warn.

Laaperi's claim under the failure to warn theory was that he was unaware of the danger that the very short circuit which might ignite a fire in his home could, at the same time, incapacitate the smoke detector. He contended that had he been warned of this danger, he would have purchased a battery-powered smoke detector as a backup or taken some other precaution, such as wiring the detector to a circuit of its own, in order better to protect his family in the event of an electrical fire.

The jury returned verdicts in favor of Laaperi in all four actions on the failure to warn claim. The jury assessed damages in the amount of $350,000 in each of the three actions brought on behalf of the deceased sons, and $750,000 in the action brought on behalf of Janet Laaperi. The defendants' motions for directed verdict and judgment notwithstanding the verdict were denied and defendants appealed.

Defendants contend that the district court erred in denying their motions for directed verdict and judgment n.o.v. First, they claim that they had no duty to warn that the smoke detector might not work in the event of some electrical fires. Second, they maintain that even if they had such a duty, there was insufficient evidence on the record to show that the failure to warn proximately caused plaintiff's damages. We address these arguments in turn.

A. Duty to Warn

We must look, of course, to Massachusetts law. While we have found no cases with similar facts in Massachusetts (or elsewhere), we conclude that on this record a jury would be entitled to find that defendants had a duty to warn. In Massachusetts, a manufacturer[*] can be found liable to a user of the product if the user is injured due to the failure of the manufacturer to exercise reasonable care in warning potential users of hazards associated with use of the product....

The manufacturer can be held liable even if the product does exactly what it is supposed to do, if it does not warn of the potential dangers inherent in the way a product is designed. It is not necessary that the product be negligently designed or manufactured; the failure to warn of hazards associated with foreseeable uses of a product is itself negligence, and if that negligence proximately results in a plaintiff's injuries, the plaintiff may recover....

---

[*]Defendants make no argument that the duty of Sears is any different from that of Pittway, the actual manufacturer. In the present case, Sears advertised the smoke detector as a "Sears Early One Fire Alarm." Pittway Corp. was not mentioned anywhere in these advertisements or in the 12-page owner's manual packaged with the detector. Where a seller puts out a product manufactured by another as its own, the seller is subject to the same liability as though it were the manufacturer....

The sole purpose of a smoke detector is to alert occupants of a building to the presence of fire. The failure to warn of inherent nonobvious limitations of a smoke detector, or of non-obvious circumstances in which a detector will not function, can, we believe, "create an unreasonable risk of harm in that the inhabitants of a structure may be lulled into an unjustified sense of safety and fail to be forewarned of the existence of a fire."... In the present case, the defendants failed to warn purchasers that a short circuit which causes an electrical fire may also render the smoke detector useless in the very situation in which it is expected to provide protection: in the early stages of a fire. We believe that whether such a failure to warn was negligent was a question for the jury.

To be sure, it was the fire, not the smoke detector per se, that actually killed and injured plaintiff's children. But as the Second Circuit recently held, the manufacturer of a smoke detector may be liable when, due to its negligence, the device fails to work:

Although a defect must be a substantial factor in causing a plaintiff's injuries, it is clear that a "manufacturer's liability for injuries proximately caused by these defects should not be limited to [situations] in which the defect causes the accident, but should extend to situations in which the defect caused injuries over and above that which would have occurred from the accident, but for the defective design."

It is true that, unlike the above, there was no defect of design or manufacture in this case. But there was evidence from which it could be inferred that the absence of a warning enhanced the harm resulting from the fire. Plaintiff testified that if he had realized that a short circuit that caused an electrical fire might at the same time disable the smoke detector, he would have purchased a back-up battery-powered detector or wired the detector in question into an isolated circuit, thus minimizing the danger that a fire-causing short circuit would render the detector inoperative. We find, therefore, a sufficient connection between the children's deaths and injury and the absence of any warning.

Defendants contend that the district court nevertheless erred in denying their motions because, they claim, the danger that an electrical fire will incapacitate an electric-powered smoke detector is obvious. They point out that anyone purchasing a device powered by house electrical current will necessarily realize that if the current goes off for any reason, the device will not work.

In Massachusetts, as elsewhere, a failure to warn amounts to negligence only where the supplier of the good known to be dangerous for its intended use "has no reason to believe that those for whose use the

chattel is supplied will realize its dangerous condition."...

Where the risks of the product are discernible by casual inspection, such as the danger that a knife can cut, or a stove burn, the consumer is in just as good a position as the manufacturer to gauge the dangers associated with the product, and nothing is gained by shifting to the manufacturer the duty to warn. Thus, a manufacturer is not required to warn that placing one's hand into the blades of a potato chopper will cause injury, ... that permitting a three-year-old child to ride on the running board of a moving tractor risks injury to the child, ... or that firing a BB gun at another at close range can injure or kill.... If a manufacturer had to warn consumers against every such obvious danger inherent in a product, "[t]he list of obvious practices warned against would be so long, it would fill a volume."...

Defendants ask us to declare that the risk that an electrical fire could incapacitate an AC-powered smoke detector is so obvious that the average consumer would not benefit from a warning. This is not a trivial argument; in earlier—some might say sounder—days, we might have accepted it....

Our sense of the current state of the tort law in Massachusetts and most other jurisdictions, however, leads us to conclude that, today, the matter before us poses a jury question; that "obviousness" in a situation such as this would be treated by the Massachusetts courts as presenting a question of fact, not of law. To be sure, it would be obvious to anyone that an electrical outage would cause this smoke detector to fail. But the average purchaser might not comprehend the specific danger that a fire-causing electrical problem can simultaneously knock out the circuit into which a smoke detector is wired, causing the detector to fail at the very moment it is needed. Thus, while the failure of a detector to function as the result of an electrical malfunction due, say, to a broken power line or a neighborhood power outage would, we think, be obvious as a matter of law, the failure that occurred here, being associated with the very risk—fire—for which the device was purchased, was not, or so a jury could find.

... We think that the issue of obviousness to the average consumer of the danger of a fire-related power outage was one for the jury, not the court, to determine. In the present case, the jury was specifically instructed that if it found this danger to be obvious it should hold for the defendants. It failed to do so.

B. Causation
While, as just discussed, the danger the detector would fail in these circumstances was not so obvious as to eliminate, as a matter of law, any need to warn, we must also consider whether Laaperi's specialized

electrical knowledge constituted a bar to his own recovery…. [P]laintiff's specialized knowledge is immaterial to whether defendants had a duty to warn, since that duty is defined by the knowledge of the average purchaser. But plaintiff's expertise *is* relevant to whether defendants' failure to warn caused plaintiff's damages. Even though defendants may have been required to provide a warning, plaintiff may not recover if it can be shown that because of his above-average knowledge, he already appreciated the very danger the warning would have described. In such event there would be no connection between the negligent failure to warn and plaintiff's damages.

Defendants here presented considerable evidence suggesting that Laaperi, who was something of an electrical handyman, knew of the danger and still took no precautions. Laaperi, however, offered evidence that he did not know of the danger, and that he would have guarded against it had he been warned….

Self-serving as this testimony was, the jury was free to credit it. In reviewing the denial of a motion for directed verdict or judgment n.o.v., we are obliged to view the evidence in the light most favorable to the verdict winner…. In light of this standard, we cannot say that the district court erred in denying defendants' motions for directed verdict and judgment n.o.v., for the jury could have believed Laaperi's testimony in the colloquy quoted above, among other evidence, and concluded that had he been properly warned, Laaperi would have instituted different fire detection methods in his home to protect his family against the danger that his smoke detector would be rendered useless in the event of a fire-related power outage.

IV.

… Considering Janet's injuries alone, apart from the horrible nature of her brothers' deaths, we find the award of $750,000 was so grossly disproportionate to the injuries of Janet Laaperi as to be unconscionable. It is therefore vacated.

The judgments in favor of Albin Laaperi in his capacity as administrator of the estates of his three sons are affirmed. In the action on behalf of Janet Laaperi, the verdict of the jury is set aside, the judgment of the district court vacated, and the cause remanded to that court for a new trial limited to the issue of damages.

So ordered.

Case Questions

1. What warning should the defendants arguably have given the plaintiffs under the facts of this case?
2. Would the outcome in this case have been different if Albin Laaperi were a licensed electrician?

 What would utilitarians think of the doctrine of res ipsa loquitur?

Imputed Negligence

Although people are always responsible for their own acts, one may be held liable for the negligence of another by reason of some relationship existing between two parties. This is termed **imputed negligence,** or vicarious liability.

Imputed negligence results when one person (the agent) acts for or represents another (the principal) by the latter's authority and to accomplish the latter's ends. A common example is the liability of employers for the torts that employees commit in the scope of their employment.

One should take a liberal view of the scope-of-employment concept, because the basis for vicarious liability is the desire to include in operational costs the inevitable losses to third persons incident to carrying on an enterprise, and thus distribute the burden among those benefited by the enterprise. Generally, an employee would not be within the scope of employment (1) if the employee is en route to or from home, (2) if the employee is on an undertaking of his own, (3) if the act is prohibited by the employer, or (4) if the act is an unauthorized delegation by the employer (in which case the employer would be directly liable).

One generally is not vicariously liable for the negligent act of an independent contractor. **Independent contractors** are those who contract to do work according to their own methods and are not subject to the control of employers, except with respect to the results. The right of control over the manner in which the work is done is the main consideration in determining whether one employed is an independent contractor or an agent. However, there are certain exceptions to this non-liability; for example, an employer who is negligent in hiring a contractor or who assigns a nondelegable duty may be directly liable.

Modified No-Fault Liability Statutes

As readers saw in Figure 11.1, automobile collision suits account for most of the tort claims filed in the United States. Responding to widespread dissatisfaction with the delay and expense in litigation of traffic accident cases, some states have enacted **modified no-fault liability statutes** in an attempt to correct the injustices and inadequacies of the fault system in automobile accident cases. Under a modified no-fault liability statute, an injured person normally has no right to file suit to recover money damages for personal injuries and lost wages below a statutorily specified threshold. Instead, the injured party is compensated by his or her own insurance company. The amount of compensation paid is determined by dollar ceilings specified in the injured person's insurance policy. All "no-fault" states, however, permit lawsuits for damages where the injured person has been seriously injured. States differ as to how they determine when this threshold is crossed. The goal of the statutes is to reduce the cost of automobile insurance by saving litigation costs, including attorneys' fees, and by allowing little or no recovery for the pain and suffering and emotional stress for a no-fault automobile accident.

STRICT LIABILITY

In addition to intentional torts and negligence, there is a third type of tort called strict liability or absolute liability. This imposes liability on defendants without requiring any proof of lack of due care. Under the early common law, people were held strictly liable for trespass and trespass on the case without regard to their intentions and whether they exercised reasonable care. Although the breadth of strict liability diminished with the emergence of negligence and intentional torts, **strict liability in tort** is applied in cases involving what the common law recognized as abnormally dangerous activities and, more recently, in certain product liability cases.

Abnormally Dangerous Activities

One who is involved in abnormally dangerous activities is legally responsible for harmful consequences that are proximately caused. The possessor of a dangerous instrumentality is an insurer of the safety of others who are foreseeably within the danger zone. Because of jurisdictional differences, it is impossible to formulate a general definition or complete listing of all dangerous instrumentalities. However, poisons, toxic chemicals, explosives, and vicious animals are examples of items that have been found to fall into this category.

INTERNET TIP

Readers can see an example involving strict liability and a dangerous animal in the case of *Westberry v. Blackwell,* which can be found with the Chapter XI materials on the textbook's website.

Strict Liability and Product Liability

A purchaser of tangible personal property may have a right to recover from the manufacturer for injuries caused by product defects. Product defects include defects in design, manufacturing defects, and warning defects. A person who has been injured by a product defect may be able to recover based on strict liability, as well as on breach of warranty (see discussion in Chapter X) and negligence (see earlier discussion in this chapter).

The application of strict liability in product liability cases occurred because of dissatisfaction with the negligence and warranty remedies. It was very difficult for average consumers to determine whether

> **§ 402A.Special Liability of Seller of Product for Physical Harm to User or Consumer**
>
> (1) One who sells any product in a defective condition unreasonably dangerous to the user or consumer or to his property is subject to liability for physical harm thereby caused to the ultimate user or consumer, or to his property, if
>
> (a) the seller is engaged in the business of selling such a product, and
>
> (b) it is expected to and does reach the user or consumer without substantial change in the condition in which it is sold.
>
> (2) The rule stated in Subsection (1) applies although
>
> (a) the seller has exercised all possible care in the preparation and sale of his product, and
>
> (b) the user or consumer has not bought the product from or entered into any contractual relation with the seller.

F I G U R E 11.2 Section 402A of the Restatement (Second) of Torts

Source: Copyright © 1965 by The American Law Institute. Reprinted with the permission of The American Law Institute.

manufacturers, wholesalers, or retailers of defective goods were responsible for their injuries. Also, the traditional requirement of privity limited the manufacturer's liability in tort and warranty actions to the person who purchased the defective product, often the wholesaler or retailer. Reformers argued that too often consumers assumed the full cost of the losses. They believed that it would be more just and economically wise to shift the cost of injuries to manufacturers, since manufacturers could purchase insurance and could distribute the costs of the premiums among those who purchased their products.

In contrast to breach of warranty and negligence remedies, which focus on the manufacturer's conduct, modern strict liability focuses on the product itself. A plaintiff who relies on strict liability has to prove that the product was unreasonably dangerous and defective and that the defect proximately caused the injury (although the unreasonably dangerous requirement is disregarded by some courts).

INTERNET TIP

Leichtamer v. American Motors Corporation is a strict liability case involving a Jeep CJ-7 that pitched over while being driven, killing two people and injuring two others. The plaintiffs brought suit, claiming a design defect was responsible for their injuries. The Ohio Supreme Court refers to Section 402A of the Restatement of Torts (see Figure 11.2) in this case and adopts it as part of Ohio law. You can read this case on the textbook's website.

TORT LAW—ADDITIONAL CONSIDERATIONS

Tort Reform

The hotly contested battle over tort reform continues to rage on, with "reformers" seeking to limit plaintiffs' venue choices; increase the immunities available to physicians, pharmacists, and physician assistants; reduce the liability of pharmaceutical manufacturers in product liability cases; and cap noneconomic and punitive damages. Many advocates of reform insist that trial-attorney greed is at the core of the problem. Others maintain that without tort reform it will be impossible to reduce the seemingly unstoppable increases in health costs.

Reform opponents point to reports that thousands of people die annually in the United States because of medical errors.[12] They argue that reforms ultimately seek to arbitrarily deny injured people the just recovery they are entitled to because of the circumstances and the nature and extent of their injuries. They point out that the damage awards are large only in cases in which the injuries are horrific and the tortfeasor's liability is great. They also argue that corporations must be held fully accountable for their tortious acts, or they will not have any economic incentive to act in the public's interest.

The battle has played out at the state level: thirty-five states have enacted laws intended to lessen recoveries, especially in medical malpractice cases.[13] Reform proposals typically eliminate joint and several liability, limit a plaintiff's choice of venues, cap noneconomic damages, shorten statute of limitations periods, and cap punitive damages.

Joint and Several Liability

Under the common law, if Sarah, Jose, and Soyinni commit a tort at the same time and are at fault, liability for the entire harm is imposed on each of the tortfeasors jointly and individually. This is termed **joint and several liability.** This means that the judgment creditors could recover one-third from each judgment debtor or the entire judgment from one defendant, at the option of the judgment creditor. This common law approach favors plaintiffs. It allows a judgment creditor to collect the entire judgment from the tortfeasor that has the "deepest pockets." This unfortunate person then has to go to court and seek "contribution" from the other tortfeasors (assuming they are neither bankrupt nor otherwise judgment-proof).[14] Reformers favor modifying the rule so that a judgment debtor who has been found to be only 10 percent liable is not required to pay for 100 percent of the judgment. Virginia is one of the states that still follow the common law rule. The Virginia statute establishing joint and several liability can be seen in Figure 11.3. Most states, however, have made modifications to the common law approach.

INTERNET TIP

Minnesota is one of the states that have modified the common law rule regarding joint and several liability. Readers will find Minnesota's apportionment of damages statute included with the Chapter XI materials on the textbook's website. Readers are encouraged to look at both the Virginia statute (Figure 11.3) and the Minnesota statute, and notice how they differ.

A judgment against one of several joint wrongdoers shall not bar the prosecution of an action against any or all the others, but the injured party may bring separate actions against the wrongdoers and proceed to judgment in each, or, if sued jointly, he may proceed to judgment against them successively until judgment has been rendered against, or the cause has been otherwise disposed of as to, all of the defendants, and no bar shall arise as to any of them by reason of a judgment against another, or others, until the judgment has been satisfied. If there be a judgment against one or more joint wrongdoers, the full satisfaction of such judgment accepted as such by the plaintiff shall be a discharge of all joint wrongdoers, except as to the costs; provided, however, this section shall have no effect on the right of contribution between joint wrongdoers as set out in § 8.01-34.

FIGURE 11.3 Va. Code Ann. §8.01-443. Joint Wrongdoers; Effect of Judgment Against One

Limitations on Venue Choice

Reformers allege that plaintiffs' lawyers are taking advantage of jurisdictions that permit forum shopping. In recent years, certain counties in some states have developed a reputation for consistently awarding large verdicts and have been designated "tort hellholes" by reform advocates.[15] Reformers suggest that plaintiffs be limited to filing suit in the county of the state in which the tort occurred.

Caps on Noneconomic Damages

Many states have tried to lower jury awards by statutorily establishing ceilings on recoveries for noneconomic damages such as pain and suffering, loss of consortium, and loss of enjoyment of life (**hedonic damages**). Proponents of "tort reform" often urge lawmakers to establish financial "caps" on the amount of damages a successful tort plaintiff can receive. The rationale generally given is that doctors cannot afford to pay the cost of malpractice insurance premiums, and establishing ceilings on damage awards will reduce the overall cost of medical care.

Introduction to *Atlanta Oculoplastic Surgery, P.C. v. Nestlehutt*

The following case from Georgia illustrates how this very controversial issue can generate institutional conflict between state legislatures and state supreme courts.

Atlanta Oculoplastic Surgery, P.C. v. Nestlehutt
691 S.E.2d 218
Supreme Court of Georgia
March 22, 2010

Hunstein, Chief Justice.

This case requires us to assess the constitutionality of OCGA §51-13-1, which limits awards of noneconomic damages in medical malpractice cases to a predetermined amount. The trial court held that the statute violates the Georgia Constitution by encroaching on the right to a jury trial.... In January 2006, Harvey P. Cole, M.D., of Atlanta Oculoplastic Surgery, d/b/a Oculus, performed ... laser resurfacing and a full facelift on appellee Betty Nestlehutt. In the weeks after the surgery, complications arose, resulting in Nestlehutt's permanent disfigurement. Nestlehutt, along with her husband, sued Oculus for medical malpractice. The case proceeded to trial, ending in a mistrial. On retrial, the jury returned a verdict of $1,265,000, comprised of $115,000 for past and future medical expenses; $900,000 in noneconomic damages for Ms. Nestlehutt's pain and suffering; and $250,000 for Mr. Nestlehutt's loss of consortium. Appellees then moved to have OCGA §51-13-1, which would have reduced the jury's noneconomic damages award by $800,000 to the statutory limit of $350,000, declared unconstitutional. The trial court granted the motion and thereupon entered judgment for appellees in the full amount awarded by the jury. Oculus moved for a new trial, which was denied, and this appeal ensued.

1. In relevant part, OCGA §51-13-1 provides:

In any verdict returned or judgment entered in a medical malpractice action, including an action for wrongful death, against one or more health care providers, the total amount recoverable by a claimant for noneconomic damages in such action shall be limited to an amount not to exceed $350,000.00, regardless of the number of defendant health care providers against whom the claim is asserted or the number of separate causes of action on which the claim is based.

... "Noneconomic damages" is defined as

damages for physical and emotional pain, discomfort, anxiety, hardship, distress, suffering, inconvenience, physical impairment, mental anguish, disfigurement, loss of enjoyment of life, loss of society and companionship, loss of consortium, injury to reputation, and all other nonpecuniary losses of any kind or nature.

... In addition to capping noneconomic damages against health care providers ... the statute also limits noneconomic damages awards against a single medical facility to $350,000; limits such awards to $700,000 for actions against more than one medical facility; and limits such awards to $1,050,000 for actions against multiple health care providers and medical facilities....

Enacted as part of a broad legislative package known as the Tort Reform Act of 2005, the damages caps were intended to help address what the General Assembly determined to be a "crisis affecting the provision and quality of health care services in this state."... Specifically, the Legislature found that health care providers and facilities were being negatively affected by diminishing access to and increasing costs of procuring liability insurance, and that these problems in the liability insurance market bore the potential to reduce Georgia citizens' access to health care services, thus degrading their health and well-being.... The provisions of the Tort Reform Act were therefore intended by the Legislature to "promote predictability and improvement in the provision of quality health care services and the resolution of health care liability claims and ... thereby assist in promoting the provision of health care liability insurance by insurance providers."...

2. We examine first the trial court's holding that the noneconomic damages cap violates our state Constitution's guarantee of the right to trial by jury.

Duly enacted statutes enjoy a presumption of constitutionality. A trial court must uphold a statute unless the party seeking to nullify it shows that it "manifestly infringes upon a constitutional provision or violates the rights of the people." The constitutionality of a statute presents a question of law. Accordingly, we review a trial court's holding regarding the constitutionality of a statute de novo....

The Georgia Constitution states plainly that "[t]he right to trial by jury shall remain inviolate."... It is well established that Article I, Section I, Paragraph XI (a) "guarantees the right to a jury trial only with respect to cases as to which there existed a right to jury trial at common law or by statute at the time of the adoption of the Georgia Constitution in 1798.... Prior to adoption of the 1798 Constitution, the General Assembly had adopted the common law of England and all statutes in force as of 1776 as the law of Georgia.... Thus, the initial step in our analysis must necessarily be an examination of the right to jury trial under late eighteenth century English common law.... See *Rouse v. State* ... (1848) (referring to Blackstone, "whose commentaries constituted the law of this State, before and since the Revolution," as authoritative on jury trial right as of 1798)....

(a) The antecedents of the modern medical malpractice action trace back to the 14th century.

The first recorded case in England on the civil [liability] of a physician was an action brought before the Kings Bench in 1374 against a surgeon by the name of J. Mort involving the treatment of a wounded hand. The physician was held not liable because of a legal technicality, but the court clearly enunciated the rule that if negligence is proved in such a case the law will provide a remedy.

... By the mid-18th century, the concept of "mala praxis" [malpractice] was sufficiently established in legal theory as to constitute one of five classes of "private wrongs" described by Sir William Blackstone in his Commentaries.... The concept took root in early American common law, the earliest reported medical negligence case in America dating to 1794.... Given the clear existence of medical negligence claims as of the adoption of the Georgia Constitution of 1798, we have no difficulty concluding that such claims are encompassed within the right to jury trial ... under Art. I, Sec. I, Par. XI (a). This conclusion is bolstered by the fact that medical negligence claims appear in Georgia's earliest systematically reported case law ... , and the fact that the tort of medical malpractice was included in Georgia's earliest Code. See Code of 1861, §2915 (effective Jan. 1, 1863)....

As with all torts, the determination of damages rests "peculiarly within the province of the jury."... Because the amount of damages sustained by a plaintiff is ordinarily an issue of fact, this has been the rule from the beginning of trial by jury.... Hence, "[t]he right to a jury trial includes the right to have a jury determine the amount of ... damages, if any, awarded to the [plaintiff]."...

Noneconomic damages have long been recognized as an element of total damages in tort cases, including those involving medical negligence.... Based on the foregoing, we conclude that at the time of the adoption of our Constitution of 1798, there did exist the common-law right to a jury trial for claims involving the negligence of a health care provider, with an attendant right to the award of the full measure of damages, including noneconomic damages, as determined by the jury.

(b) We next examine whether the noneconomic damages caps in OCGA §51-12-1 unconstitutionally infringe on this right. By requiring the court to reduce a noneconomic damages award determined by a jury that exceeds the statutory limit, OCGA §51-13-1 clearly nullifies the jury's findings of fact regarding damages and thereby undermines the jury's basic function.... Consequently, we are compelled to conclude that the caps infringe on a party's constitutional right, as embodied in Article I, Section I, Paragraph XI (a), to a jury determination as to noneconomic damages.... The fact that OCGA §51-13-1 permits full recovery of noneconomic damages up to the significant amount of $350,000 cannot save the statute from constitutional attack. "[I]f the legislature may constitutionally cap recovery at [$350,000], there is no discernible reason why it could not cap the recovery at some other figure, perhaps $50,000, or $1,000, or even $1."... The very existence of the caps, in any amount, is violative of the right to trial by jury....

Though we agree with the general principle ... that the Legislature has authority to modify or abrogate the common law, we do not agree with the notion that this general authority empowers the Legislature to abrogate constitutional rights that may inhere in common-law causes of action.... Likewise, while we have held that the Legislature generally has the authority to define, limit, and modify available legal remedies ... the exercise of such authority simply cannot stand when the resulting legislation violates the constitutional right to jury trial.

Nor does ... the existence of statutes authorizing double or treble damages attest to the validity of the caps on noneconomic damages. While it is questionable whether any cause of action involving an award thereof would constitute an analogue to a 1798 common-law cause of action so as to trigger the right to jury trial in the first place ... to the extent the right to jury trial did attach, treble damages do not in any way nullify the jury's damages award but rather merely operate upon and thus affirm the integrity of that award....

In sum, based on the foregoing, we conclude that the noneconomic damages caps in OCGA §51-13-1 violate the right to a jury trial as guaranteed under the Georgia Constitution....

3. "The general rule is that an unconstitutional statute is wholly void and of no force and effect from the date it was enacted."...

In this case, we do not find that the ... factors militate in favor of deviation from the general rule of retroactivity....

4. We find no abuse of the trial court's discretion in granting appellees' motion to exclude certain evidence, because that ruling was necessitated by the trial court's earlier grant of appellant's motion in limine.... As to appellant's claim that the evidence was relevant to establishing the bias of appellee's expert witness, the record establishes that the trial court's ruling in no manner precluded appellant from attempting to show the witnes[s]' bias through cross-examination or other means. Accordingly, this enumeration lacks merit.

For the foregoing reasons, we affirm the judgment of the trial court.

Judgment affirmed....

Case Questions

1. Why did the Georgia Supreme Court feel it necessary to examine English legal precedents going back as far as 1374 in order to decide a case before it for decision in 2010?
2. Why did the Georgia Supreme Court conclude that the statute was unconstitutional?

Statutes of Limitations

Legislatures often attempt to limit a potential defendant's exposure to tort liability by shortening the statute of limitations. Although this proposal is intended to benefit defendants, it does so at the expense of injured plaintiffs, who will be denied the opportunity for their day in court if they fail to file their suits in a timely manner.

Caps on Punitive Damages

Many states have abolished punitive damages unless such awards are specifically permitted by statute. Increasingly, states require that punitive damages be proven clearly and convincingly rather than by a preponderance of the evidence, and others require bifurcated trials for punitive damages. Reformers urge legislatures to impose dollar ceilings on punitive damage awards in medical malpractice and product liability cases. According to U.S. Bureau of Justice Statistics data, only 3 percent of tort plaintiffs were awarded punitive damages in 2005.[16]

CHAPTER SUMMARY

The chapter began with brief discussions of the historical development of the modern tort action and the functions of tort law in contemporary America. This was followed with an overview of intentional torts in general and discussions and cases focusing on such intentional torts as assault, battery, conversion, trespass to land, malicious prosecution, false imprisonment, defamation, interference with contract relations, infliction of mental distress, and invasion of privacy. The focus then shifted to negligence. The elements of a negligence claim were discussed, with an emphasis on the "duty of care" and "proximate cause" requirements. The workings of the comparative negligence approach, which involves an apportionment of fault between the plaintiff and defendant, was explained and illustrated in accompanying cases. The third type of tort, strict liability for abnormally dangerous activities and product defects, was then addressed. The chapter concluded with a brief overview of tort reform.

CHAPTER QUESTIONS

1. Jack McMahon and his wife, Angelina, decided to take a break from driving and stopped at a Mobil minimart for a take-out coffee. Angelina took the plastic lid off the Styrofoam cup as Jack resumed driving. She spilled coffee on her lap while trying to pour some of the coffee into another cup, and suffered second- and third-degree burns. Angelina experienced considerable pain for several months, and sustained scarring on one of her thighs and on her abdomen. The McMahons settled their claims against the manufacturers of the cup and lid, but brought suit against the manufacturer of the coffee-making machine, the Bunn-O-Matic Corporation. The plaintiffs alleged that the machine was defective because it brewed the coffee at too high a temperature, 179 degrees Fahrenheit (the industry average is between 175 and 185), and that the heat caused the cup to deteriorate. They also claimed that Bunn was negligent in failing to warn customers about the magnitude of the injuries (second- and third-degree burns) that could result from spilled coffee at this temperature. Did Bunn, in your opinion, have a legal duty to give plaintiffs the requested warnings?

   McMahon v. Bunn-O-Matic Corp., 150 F.3d 651 (7th Cir. 1998)

2. Patrick Reddell and Derek Johnson, both eighteen years of age, wanted to take part in a BB gun war "game." They agreed not to fire their weapons above the waist and that their BB guns would be pumped no more than three times, thereby limiting the force of the BBs' impact when striking the other person. They also promised each other only to fire a BB gun when the other person was "in the open." While participating in this activity, Johnson shot Reddell in the eye, causing seriously impaired vision. Reddell sued Johnson for gross negligence and for recklessly aiming his weapon above the waist. Johnson answered by denying liability and asserting the defenses of assumption of risk and contributory negligence. Both parties

   then filed motions for summary judgment. How should the trial judge rule on the motions?

   Reddell v. Johnson, 942 P.2d 200 (1997)

3. Shannon Jackson was injured while driving her car on a farm-to-market road when her vehicle hit and killed a horse named Tiny that was standing in the road. The force of the collision severely damaged her vehicle. Jackson brought a negligence suit against Tiny's owner, Naomi Gibbs, for failing to prevent Tiny from wandering onto the road. Gibbs defended by saying she owed Jackson no duty on a farm-to-market road that was within a "free-range" area. The trial court rejected the defense, and a jury found the defendant negligent and liable for damages of $7,000. The state intermediate appeals court affirmed the trial court, ruling that although there was no statutory duty to keep Tiny off the road, the court recognized a common law duty "to keep domestic livestock from roaming at large on public roads." This was a case of first impression before the state supreme court. Texas courts prior to this case had rejected the English common-law rule imposing a duty on the owner of a domestic animal to prevent it from trespassing on a neighbor's property. English common law imposed no corresponding duty to keep an animal from wandering onto a public road unless the animal had "vicious propensities." In light of the above, Texas law generally permitted healthy, nonvicious animals to roam freely, a condition associated with "free-range" jurisdictions. An exception to the free-range law was statutorily recognized where a "local stock law" was enacted to keep animals off of a state highway. What arguments might be made supporting and opposing the new common-law rule recognized by the intermediate court of appeals?

   Gibbs v. Jackson, 97-0961, Supreme Court of Texas (1998)

4. The plaintiff became ill in the defendant's store. The defendant undertook to render medical aid

to the plaintiff, keeping the plaintiff in an infirmary for six hours without medical care. It was determined that when the plaintiff finally received proper medical care, the extended lapse of time had seriously aggravated the plaintiff's illness. Discuss what action, if any, the plaintiff has.

Zelenka v. Gimbel Bros., Inc., 287 N.Y.S. 134 (1935)

5. Plaintiff came into defendant's grocery store and purchased some cigarettes. He then asked if the store had any empty boxes he could use. The defendant instructed the plaintiff that he could find some in the back room and told the plaintiff to help himself. Plaintiff entered the room, which was dark. While searching for a light switch, the plaintiff fell into an open stairwell and was injured. What is the status of the plaintiff (invitee, licensee, trespasser)? How will the status affect the plaintiff's ability to recover from the defendant, if at all? Do you think the fact that the defendant is operating a business should affect his duty?

    Whelan v. Van Natta Grocery, 382 S.W.2d 205 (Ky. 1964)

6. Plaintiff's decedent was killed when the roof of the defendant's foundry fell in on him. Plaintiff alleges that the defendant failed to make proper repairs to the roof, and that such neglect of the defendant caused the roof to collapse. The defendant claims, however, that the roof collapsed during a violent storm, and that, even though the roof was in disrepair, the high winds caused the roof to fall. What issue is raised, and how would you resolve it?

    Kimble v. Mackintosh Hemphill Co., 59 A.2d 68 (1948)

7. The plaintiff's decedent, who had been drinking, was crossing Broadway when he was negligently struck by one of defendant's cabs. As a result of the accident, the plaintiff's decedent, the victim, was thrown about twenty feet, his thigh was broken, and his knee was injured. He immediately became unconscious and was rushed to a hospital, where he died of delirium tremens (a disease characterized by violent shaking, often induced by excessive alcohol consumption). Defendant argued that the deceased's alcoholism might have caused delirium tremens and death at a later date, even if defendant had not injured him. What is the main issue presented here? Who should prevail and why?

    McCahill v. N.Y. Transportation Co., 94 N.E. 616 (1911)

8. Plaintiff, while a spectator at a professional hockey game, is struck in the face by a puck. The defendant shot the puck attempting to score a goal, but shot too high, causing the puck to go into the spectator area. Plaintiff brings suit, and defendant claims assumption of risk. Who prevails? Suppose the defendant had been angry at crowd reaction and intentionally shot the puck into the crowd. Would the outcome change?

9. Clay Fruit, a life insurance salesman, was required to attend a business convention conducted by his employer. The convention included social as well as business events, and Fruit was encouraged to mix freely with out-of-state agents in order to learn as much as possible about sales techniques. One evening, after all scheduled business and social events had concluded, Fruit drove to a nearby bar and restaurant, looking for some out-of-state colleagues. Finding none, he drove back toward his hotel. On the journey back, he negligently struck the automobile of the plaintiff, causing serious injuries to plaintiff's legs. Was Fruit in the course and scope of his employment at the time of the accident? From whom will the plaintiff be able to recover?

    Fruit v. Schreiner, 502 P.2d 133 (Alaska 1972)

NOTES

1. T. F. F. Plucknett, *A Concise History of the Common Law* (Boston: Little, Brown and Co., 1956), p. 372.

2. A. K. R. Kiralfy, *Potter's Historical Introduction to English Law*, 4th ed. (London: Sweet and Maxwell Ltd., 1962), pp. 376–377.

3. R. Walsh, *A History of Anglo-American Law* (Indianapolis: Bobbs-Merrill Co., 1932), p. 323.

4. Kiralfy, pp. 305–307; Walsh, p. 344.

5. Maryland plaintiffs sued Exxon Mobil after an estimated 26,00 gallons of gasoline leaked out of underground storage containers and allegedly contaminated the water supply. Some of the plaintiffs, who were unable at that time to detect any presently existing contamination (the "non-detect" Appellees), claimed that Exxon had committed a trespass. They argued that their property had been injured to an unknown exent by the leak and this had created the "potential for future detected contamination." Maryland's Court of Appeals (the state's highest court) rejected the claim. The court said:

   An action for trespass may lie "[w]hen a defendant interferes with a plaintiff's interest in the exclusive possession of the land by entering or causing something to enter the land."... Thus, recovery for trespass requires that the defendant must have entered or caused something harmful or noxious to enter onto the plaintiff's land.... Here, the non-detect Appellees failed to demonstrate any physical intrusion of their land. General contamination of an aquifer that may or may not reach a given Appellee's property at an undetermined point in the future is not sufficient to prove invasion of property. Thus, the non-detect Appellees could not recover, at the time of trial, damages for diminution in value of property based on a theory of

   trespass. *Exxon Mobil Corporation v. Albright,* No. 15 (Md. filed Feb. 26, 2013).

6. More discussion about the different types of damages can be found in Chapter VII.

7. *Note:* Most states also recognize the tort of *negligent* infliction of emotional distress, though proof of damages may be more stringent.

8. *Exxon Mobil Corporation v. Albright,* No. 15 (Md. filed Feb. 26, 2013).

9. Rental tenants and other authorized occupants of property (in legalese,, *lawful occupiers*) also have about the same protection against liability to trespassers as property owners.

10. *Mckinnon v. Wash. Fed. Sav. & Loan Ass'n,* 68 Wash. 2d 644 (1966).

11. As was explained in Chapter VIII the element of *causation* also must be proved in some, but not all, criminal cases and in some strict liability cases in tort, as well as in tort negligence cases.

12. "A Tragic Error," *Newsweek* (March 3, 2003), p. 22.

13. "Ohio's Tort Reform Law Hasn't Lowered Health-Care Costs," *The Plain Dealer* (March 20, 2010), http://www.cleveland.com/open/index.ssf/2010/03/ohios_tort_reform_law_hasnt_lo.html

14. As a practical matter, lawsuits seeking money damages generally are not brought against individuals who have no bank accounts, real property, insurance policies, or jobs. It doesn't make sense for plaintiffs to invest money in litigating a claim against a defendant who does not have the assets to satisfy a judgment—such a defendant is said to be "judgment-proof."

15. "Tort Reform Advances in Mississippi (for Starters)," *National Law Journal* A1, A10–A11 (February 3, 2003).

16. U.S. Department of Justice, *Bureau of Justice Statistics Bulletin,* NCJ 228129 (November 2009), p. 6.

XII

Property

CHAPTER OBJECTIVES

1. *Understand the historical origins of property law.*
2. *Explain the true meaning of the term* property.
3. *Identify two ways in which property is classified.*
4. *Understand the importance of intellectual property rights.*
5. *Identify the primary ways that government takes and limits the exercise of private property rights.*
6. *Understand the basic concept of an estate in land.*
7. *Explain the differences between easements and licenses.*
8. *Identify the different ways personal property can be acquired.*
9. *Understand the essential elements of a bailment.*

Property refers to a person's ownership rights to things and to a person's interests in things owned by someone else. Property includes the rights to possess, use, and dispose of things. These may be tangible objects, such as a car, book, or item of clothing, or they may be intangible—the technology in a camera, a song, or the right of publicity. Although many people refer to the objects themselves as property, *property.* actually refers only to ownership rights and interests.

HISTORICAL DEVELOPMENT OF THE REGULATION OF REAL PROPERTY

When we discuss property law, we must remember that the English common law greatly influenced legal thinking in the prerevolutionary colonies and in the new American states.[1]

Private property was thought to be essential to individual liberty, a proposition advanced by the English philosopher John Locke (1632–1704). Locke was a "natural law" philosopher who argued that before the creation of governments, people existed in a natural state in which they had total control over their life, liberty, and property. He reasoned that people who established governments retained these inalienable rights and were entitled to resist any government that failed to respect them. Locke's emphasis on the inviolability of private property was reflected in the decisions of colonial legislatures, judges, and political leaders.[2] Although American law was significantly influenced by the common law, most colonies were willing to take a different path when solutions provided by common law seemed inappropriate. The Puritans in New England, for example, refused to follow a rule of English common law (which was accepted in southern colonies[3]) that prevented a husband from conveying land without his wife's consent. They believed this was a bad social policy because it treated husbands and wives as individuals with separate legal interests rather than as a single, unified entity. They changed the law to allow husbands to make unilateral decisions for the family regarding the sale of real property.[4]

Before the industrial revolution, the economies of America and England were primarily based on agriculture. England's industrial revolution began with the rise of the textile industry in the 1700s. At this time most economic and political power was held by large landowners such as the church, monarchy, military, and landed gentry.[5] There, as in colonial America, the law recognized property owners as having absolute dominion over their land.[6] But no one could use his or her land in a manner that caused injury to any other landowner.

For example, a landowner could not divert the natural flow of a navigable river or stream in order to establish a mill if it created a detriment to another landowner.[7] The fact that economic and social benefits would result from the operation of a new mill was of no consequence.[8] Legal attitudes toward property began to change as America became industrialized in the 1800s and moved toward a market economy. After the Civil War, courts began to recognize that encouraging competition and economic development benefitted the public.[9] When one landowner's property use conflicted with another's, the courts balanced the nature of the infringement against its socially desirable economic benefits, and the developers usually prevailed.[10] This legal preference for development continued throughout the nineteenth and into the twentieth century. Although it produced new technology, new products, and an expanding economy, it also resulted in environmental pollution, the exploitation of workers, hazardous work environments, and labor–management conflict. These conditions resulted in legislative reform efforts throughout the century designed to protect society. Around 1900, the U.S. Supreme Court began to strike down state laws that interfered with employer–employee contracts with respect to wages, hours, and working conditions.[11] The Court concluded that these laws exceeded the state's legislative power because they infringed upon the individual's constitutionally protected due process liberty interest in freedom of contract.

Since the 1930s, the individual's property rights in land have declined as legislatures have acted to protect society from irresponsible and harmful uses of private property. Today, for example, zoning laws regulate land use and building codes regulate building construction. Environmental laws prohibit landowners from filling in wetlands and control the discharge of pollutants into the air, ground, and water.

As environmental regulations have increased in number, they have affected an increasing number of landowners. A heated ongoing national debate has resulted between supporters and opponents of the legal status quo. Opponents have charged that the existing legislation and case law are excessively anti-development and that government agencies are overzealous in enforcing environmental protection regulations. Environmental protection, they conclude, is often achieved without regard for the legitimate rights of landowners. Supporters of current environmental policies maintain that removing the regulations will produce a precipitous decline in habitat for endangered species and, in many instances, will ultimately lead to extinction. They also argue that backsliding from current standards will produce serious environmental hazards to the public's air, water, and land resources. In the 1990s, however, the Congress, many state legislatures, and federal and state courts began questioning whether our nation's environmental laws properly balanced society's dual interests in protecting the environment and private property rights. We examine this question in more detail later in this chapter when we discuss takings and eminent domain.

CLASSIFICATIONS OF PROPERTY

Property can be classified as realty, personalty (tangible or intangible), or fixtures. Property interests also can be classified as either contingent or vested. These distinctions matter. Tax rates, for example, often differ for realty, fixtures, and personalty. A second example is the determination of what body of law will be used to determine title. Thus, the common law of each state governs title to real property, whereas the Uniform Commercial Code often governs personalty.[12]

Real property, or **realty**, includes land and things that are attached permanently to land. It is distinguishable from personal property in that real property is immovable.

Personal property, also called personalty, can be classified as either tangible or intangible. **Tangible personal property** consists of physical objects that are neither realty nor fixtures, such as a book, a boat, or a piece of furniture. (*Fixtures* are defined below.) **Intangible personal property** is personalty that has no physical form. Ownership of intangible property is usually evidenced by some type of legal document that sets forth the ownership rights.

For example, a bank account is intangible personal property. A person who deposits money into the account receives from the bank intangible rights equal to the amount of the deposit plus interest (if it is an interest-bearing account). The deposit receipt and bank statement are evidence of the holder's title and right to possession of the funds contained in the account. Money, stocks, and bonds are considered to be intangible property because they are paper substitutes for certain ownership rights. Trademarks, patents, and copyrights are also intangible personal property, as are the intangible rights, duties, and obligations arising out of the ownership of physical objects. Thus personal property includes not only a physical or representative object, but also the right to own, use, sell, or dispose of it as provided by law.

Items of personal property are often the subject of both tangible and intangible property rights. For example, suppose that you buy a digital camera, the design and technology of which are protected by federal patents. Although you have acquired a piece of tangible personal property that you can use to take pictures, and you can give it as a gift or otherwise dispose of it in any legal manner, the law will recognize that you do not have all the rights vis-à-vis the camera. The patent holders, for example, have intangible property rights in the camera's technology. The purchaser does not have any such rights and therefore cannot sell duplicates of the product or the technology without permission. Thus the patent holders and the purchaser have concurrent property rights in the camera.

A **fixture** is a category of property between realty and personalty. For example, a dishwasher, which is classified as personalty when it is purchased at an appliance store, becomes a fixture when it is permanently built into the buyer's kitchen. These distinctions are based on practical considerations; for example, tax rates may differ for realty, fixtures, and personalty.

Lastly, property rights are classified in terms of when they become fully effective. A property right is said to be a **contingent property right** when some future event must occur for the right to become **vested** (fully effective). For example, employers often require that employees work for a company for a specified period of time before their vacation and pension rights mature. Once pension rights vest, they belong to the employees even if the employees subsequently leave the company.

TRADEMARKS, PATENTS, AND COPYRIGHTS

When one normally thinks of personal property, one generally thinks in terms of tangible property—the rights to things that have a physical existence. However, some of the most valuable property rights have no physical attributes. One who owns **intellectual property** rights (the rights to trademarks, patents, and copyrights) owns intangible personal property.

Trademarks

The distinctive Nike "Swoosh" is a **trademark** of the Nike Corporation. The company affixes this mark to its many products in order to distinguish them from those of competitors. Customers learn to associate trademarks with quality and style attributes—a matter of great importance to manufacturers and retailers. The name of a type of product, such as "microwave" or "DVD," cannot be a trademark. Sometimes, however, a company's trademark becomes recognized by the public as the name of the product itself and loses its legal status as a trademark. "Aspirin," "thermos," and "escalator" are examples of trademarks that lost their trademark status because they became words used for the product category. The Coca-Cola Company works diligently to ensure that the term *Coke* does not lose its status as a trademark by becoming a synonym for "soft drink." Similarly, the Xerox Corporation is most concerned that its trademark *Xerox* does not become a synonym for "photocopy." Trademarks to be used in interstate commerce are required to be registered with the U.S. Department of Commerce's Patent and Trademark Office, pursuant to the Lanham Act of 1946.

An infringement of a trademark occurs, for example, when an infringing mark is so similar to a well-established mark that it is likely to confuse, deceive, or mislead customers into believing that they are doing business with the more established company.

Federal and state statutes create causes of action for trademark infringement. The Lanham Act of 1946 and the Trademark Law Revision Act of 1988 are the principal federal statutes. At the state level, statutes authorize causes of action for trademark infringement and the common law also provides a basis for such suits. Successful plaintiffs can obtain treble damages, injunctive relief, an award of the defendant's profits, damages, costs, and attorney's fees in exceptional cases.

Introduction to *In re The Boston Beer Company Ltd. Partnership*

The plaintiff in the following case sought to trademark the words "The Best Beer in America" and appealed the Trademark Trial and Appeal Board's decision to reject the proposed trademark application.

In re The Boston Beer Company Ltd. Partnership
198 F.3d 1370
U.S. Court of Appeals, Federal Circuit
December 7, 1999

Mayer, Chief Judge.
The Boston Beer Company Limited Partnership ("Boston Beer") appeals from a decision of the U.S. Patent and Trademark Office Trademark Trial and Appeal Board affirming the final rejection of trademark application Serial No. 74/464,118 seeking to register "The Best Beer In America" on the principal register....

BACKGROUND
On November 30, 1993, the Boston Beer Company filed an application to register "The Best Beer In America"

on the principal register for "beverages, namely beer and ale," in Class 32. Boston Beer claimed use since 1985 and asserted that the words sought to be registered have acquired distinctiveness under 15 U.S.C. §§1052(f). Boston Beer claimed secondary meaning based on annual advertising expenditures in excess of ten million dollars and annual sales under the mark of approximately eighty-five million dollars. Specifically, Boston Beer spent about two million dollars on promotions and promotional items which included the phrase "The Best Beer in America."

In support of its claims, Boston Beer submitted an affidavit of its founder and co-president, James Koch, asserting that the words sought to be registered had developed secondary meaning as a source-indicator for its goods by virtue of extensive promotion and sales of beer under the mark since June 1985. It also submitted an advertisement for a competitor's product, Rolling Rock Bock beer, which included an invitation to sample "the beer that bested 'The Best Beer in America,'" as evidence that Rolling Rock regards "The Best Beer in America" as Boston Beer's trademark. The examining attorney rejected the proposed mark as merely descriptive and cited articles retrieved from the NEXIS database showing the proposed mark used by Boston Beer and others as a laudatory phrase to refer to superior beers produced by a number of different brewers. All of the beers mentioned had either won comparison competitions or had been touted as the best in America by their makers or others. Boston Beer responded by submitting articles showing its use of the proposed mark to refer to its product and in promoting its beer as a winner of the annual beer competition in Denver. Additionally, it argued that if marks such as "Best Products" and "American Airlines" can be registered even though they are also used descriptively, then the proposed mark should be similarly registered. The examining attorney issued a final refusal to register under 15 U.S.C. §§1052(e)(1), holding that Boston Beer had failed to establish that the mark had become distinctive.

Boston Beer filed a notice of appeal and attached further exhibits to its appeal brief. The application was remanded to the examiner on his request for consideration of the new evidence. Another office action was issued denying registration for lack of distinctiveness which noted that the phrase sought to be registered was selected and used after Boston Beer received awards at the Great American Beer Festival. The board then allowed Boston Beer to file a supplemental brief. Action on the appeal was suspended and the board remanded the application.

The examiner concluded that the proposed mark is the name of a genus of goods, namely "beers brewed in America that have won taste competitions or were judged best in taste tests," and included printouts from the Boston Beer Internet web site to show that it had adopted the proposed mark after it had won such competitions. He therefore issued an office action rejecting the proposed mark as generic and thus incapable of registration. Boston Beer submitted a second supplemental brief to respond to the genericness rejection. After the examiner filed his appeal brief, Boston Beer filed a third supplemental brief arguing against genericness and moved to strike portions of the examiner's brief. Boston Beer argued that the examiner was limited to responding to the issues raised in the second supplemental brief, namely genericness, and could not address descriptiveness and acquired distinctiveness. Boston Beer argued that its proposed mark was not generic because there was no single category at the Great American Beer Festival and thus no "best beer in America" award. The board rejected the motion to strike.

The board found the proposed mark to be merely descriptive because it is only laudatory and "simply a claim of superiority, i.e., trade puffery."... The proposed mark was found not to be generic because the examiner's characterization of the genus or class of goods as "'beers brewed in America which have won taste competitions or were judged best in taste tests' stretches the limits of our language and is inconsistent with common usage."... The board held, however, that the proposed mark inherently cannot function as a trademark because such "claims of superiority should be freely available to all competitors in any given field to refer to their products or services."... Finally, the board said that "even if [it] were to find this expression to be capable of identifying applicant's beer and distinguishing it from beer made or sold by others, [the board] also would find, in view of the very high degree of descriptiveness which inheres in these words, that applicant has failed to establish secondary meaning in them as an identification of source."... This appeal followed.

DISCUSSION

We review the board's legal conclusions, such as its interpretation of the Lanham Act, 15 U.S.C. §§1051-1127, de novo. We uphold the board's factual findings unless they are arbitrary, capricious, an abuse of discretion, or unsupported by substantial evidence....

"Marks that are merely laudatory and descriptive of the alleged merit of a product are also regarded as being descriptive.... Self-laudatory or puffing marks are regarded as a condensed form of describing the character or quality of the goods." 2 J. Thomas McCarthy, *McCarthy on Trademarks and Unfair Competition* §§11:17 (4th ed. 1996) (internal quotations omitted). "If the mark is merely descriptive it may nevertheless acquire distinctiveness or secondary meaning and be registrable under Section 1052(f), although ... the greater the degree of descriptiveness the term has, the heavier the burden to prove it has attained secondary meaning."... To acquire secondary meaning, section 1052(f) requires that the mark must have become "distinctive of the applicant's goods." 15 U.S.C. §§1052(f) (1994).

Boston Beer provided evidence of advertising expenditures, an affidavit from its co-president, and an advertisement from a competitor. It argues that the use of the mark by others was either referring to Boston Beer's products or merely descriptive of the goods of others and was not used as a trademark. This argument is unavailing. The examples of use of the phrase by others in its descriptive form support the board's conclusion that the mark had not acquired distinctiveness. Therefore, on the facts of this case, and considering the highly descriptive nature of the proposed mark, Boston Beer has not met its burden to show that the proposed mark has acquired secondary meaning.

Boston Beer does not dispute that "The Best Beer in America" is a generally laudatory phrase. We have held that laudation does not per se prevent a mark from being registrable.... As Boston Beer correctly notes, there is an assortment of generally laudatory terms that serve as trademarks. But that is not invariably true; the specific facts of the case control.... As in this case, a phrase or slogan can be so highly laudatory and descriptive as to be incapable of acquiring distinctiveness as a trademark. The proposed mark is a common, laudatory advertising phrase which is merely descriptive of Boston Beer's goods. Indeed, it is so highly laudatory and descriptive of the qualities of its product that the slogan does not and could not function as a trademark to distinguish Boston Beer's goods and serve as an indication of origin. The record shows that "The Best Beer in America" is a common phrase used descriptively by others before and concurrently with Boston Beer's use, and is nothing more than a claim of superiority. Because the board's conclusion of non-registrability is supported by substantial evidence, is not arbitrary and capricious, and is not an abuse of discretion, we agree that "The Best Beer in America" is incapable of registration as a trademark....

Accordingly, the decision of the board is affirmed....

Case Questions

1. Why did the Court of Appeals affirm the examiner and refuse to grant the trademark?
2. The Court of Appeals referred to a provision in the Lanham Act that permits recognition of a mark if the proposed mark has acquired a secondary meaning. What do you think that means?

Patents

A **patent** is a grant of rights to an inventor from the government. The inventor, or owner of the rights, has the exclusive right to make, use, license others to use, and sell an invention for a period of years (20 years for most inventions, 14 years for design patents). After the term of years has expired, the invention goes into the public domain. Patents are only granted for inventions that are beneficial, are original, and involve ingenuity. Patents are granted for new machines, methods, and uses and for improvements to existing inventions. Patents are also granted for genetically engineered plants.

Copyrights

A **copyright** is the exclusive legal right to reproduce, adapt, publish, sell, perform, display, or distribute the matter and form of something such as a literary, musical, or artistic work. Authors of literary pieces, musical compositions, dramatic works, photographs, graphic works of various types, video and audio recordings, and computer software can acquire federal legal protection against most unauthorized uses by placing a prescribed copyright notice on publicly disseminated copies of the work. An owner or author of a copyrighted work is required to register with the Copyright Office in

Washington, DC, prior to bringing suit for copyright infringement.

Congress enacted its first copyright statute in 1790, and that statute provided authors with exclusive rights to their works for two 14-year periods. Although the law has been amended many times, in recent decades substantial revisions occurred in 1978 and 1998. In 1978, Congress abolished common law copyrights and federalized the copyright process. In 1998, Congress extended the copyright protection for works created in 1978 and thereafter to 70 years after the death of the author. Proponents argue that extending the length of U.S. copyright protections brings the United States in line with similar provisions in existing international conventions. Opponents content that a creator's copyright protections were intended by the founders to be limited. Even the most profitable

works should ultimately make their way into the public domain (where anyone can freely use them without having to pay royalties).

The constitutionality of this statute was upheld by the U.S. Supreme Court in the 2003 case of *Eldred v. Ashcroft*. The Court ruled that Congress had legal authority to extend the terms of copyright protections as provided in the statute.

Introduction to *BMG Music v. Cecilia Gonzalez*

The appellant in the following copyright case was sued by BMG Music for downloading music. She appealed the trial court's decision to grant summary judgment in favor of BMG to the U.S. Court of Appeals for the Seventh Circuit, claiming that her conduct should have been recognized by the trial court as "fair use" under the copyright statute.

BMG Music v. Cecilia Gonzalez
430 F.3d 888
U.S. Court of Appeals for the Seventh Circuit
December 9, 2005

Easterbrook, Circuit Judge.

Last June the Supreme Court held in *MGM Studios, Inc. v. Grokster, Ltd.* ... (2005), that a distributed file-sharing system is engaged in contributory copyright infringement when its principal object is the dissemination of copyrighted material. The foundation of this holding is a belief that people who post or download music files are primary infringers....

In this appeal Cecilia Gonzalez, who downloaded copyrighted music through the Kazaa file-sharing network, ... contends that her activities were fair use rather than infringement. The district court disagreed and granted summary judgment for the copyright proprietors (to which we refer collectively as BMG Music).... The court enjoined Gonzalez from further infringement and awarded $22,500 in damages....

A "fair use" of copyrighted material is not infringement. Gonzalez insists that she was engaged in fair use ... or at least that a material dispute entitles her to a trial. It is undisputed, however, that she downloaded more than 1,370 copyrighted songs during a few weeks and kept them on her computer until

she was caught. Her position is that she was just sampling music to determine what she liked enough to buy at retail. Because this suit was resolved on summary judgment, we must assume that Gonzalez is telling the truth when she says that she owned compact discs containing some of the songs before she downloaded them and that she purchased others later. She concedes, however, that she has never owned legitimate copies of 30 songs that she downloaded. (How many of the remainder she owned is disputed.)

Instead of erasing songs that she decided not to buy, she retained them. It is these 30 songs about which there is no dispute concerning ownership that formed the basis of the damages award.... The files that Gonzalez obtained ... were posted in violation of copyright law; there was no license covering a single transmission or hearing—and, to repeat, Gonzalez kept the copies....

[Title 17 U.S Code] Section 107 provides that when considering a defense of fair use the court must take into account "(1) the purpose and character of the use, including whether such use is of a commercial nature or is for nonprofit educational purposes; (2) the nature of the copyrighted work; (3) the amount and substantiality of the portion used in relation to the copyrighted work as a whole; and (4) the effect of the use upon the potential market for or value of the copyrighted work."

Gonzalez was not engaged in a nonprofit use; she downloaded (and kept) whole copyrighted songs (for which, as with poetry, copying of more than a couplet or two is deemed excessive); and she did this despite the fact that these works often are sold per song as well as per album. This leads her to concentrate on the fourth consideration: "the effect of the use upon the potential market for or value of the copyrighted work."

As she tells the tale, downloading on a try-before-you-buy basis is good advertising for copyright proprietors, expanding the value of their inventory. The Supreme Court thought otherwise in *Grokster,* with considerable empirical support. As file sharing has increased over the last four years, the sales of recorded music have dropped by approximately 30%. Perhaps other economic factors contributed, but the events likely are related. Music downloaded for free from the Internet is a close substitute for purchased music; many people are bound to keep the downloaded files without buying originals. That is exactly what Gonzalez did for at least 30 songs. It is no surprise, therefore, that the only appellate decision on point has held that downloading copyrighted songs cannot be defended as fair use, whether or not the recipient plans to buy songs she likes well enough to spring for....

Although BMG Music sought damages for only the 30 songs that Gonzalez concedes she has never purchased, all 1,000+ of her downloads violated the statute. All created copies of an entire work. All undermined the means by which authors seek to profit. Gonzalez proceeds as if the authors' only interest were in selling compact discs containing collections of works. Not so; there is also a market in ways to introduce potential consumers to music.

Think of radio. Authors and publishers collect royalties on the broadcast of recorded music, even though these broadcasts may boost sales.... Downloads from peer-to-peer networks such as Kazaa compete with licensed broadcasts and hence undermine the income available to authors. This is true even if a particular person never buys recorded media.... Many radio stations stream their content over the Internet, paying a fee for the right to do so. Gonzalez could have listened to this streaming music to sample songs for purchase; had she done so, the authors would have received royalties from the broadcasters (and reduced the risk that files saved to disk would diminish the urge to pay for the music in the end).

Licensed Internet sellers, such as the iTunes Music Store, offer samples—but again they pay authors a fee for the right to do so, and the teasers are just a portion of the original. Other intermediaries (not only Yahoo! Music Unlimited and Real Rhapsody but also the revived Napster, with a new business model) offer licensed access to large collections of music; customers may rent the whole library by the month or year, sample them all, and purchase any songs they want to keep. New technologies, such as SNOCAP, enable authorized trials over peer-to-peer systems....

Authorized previews share the feature of evanescence: if a listener decides not to buy (or stops paying the rental fee), no copy remains behind. With all of these means available to consumers who want to choose where to spend their money, downloading full copies of copyrighted material without compensation to authors cannot be deemed "fair use." Copyright law lets authors make their own decisions about how best to promote their works; copiers such as Gonzalez cannot ask courts (and juries) to second-guess the market and call wholesale copying "fair use" if they think that authors err in understanding their own economic interests or that Congress erred in granting authors the rights in the copyright statute. Nor can she defend by observing that other persons were greater offenders; Gonzalez's theme that she obtained "only 30" (or "only 1,300") copyrighted songs is no more relevant than a thief's contention that he shoplifted "only 30" compact discs, planning to listen to them at home and pay later for any he liked.

BMG Music elected to seek statutory damages under 17 U.S.C. §504(c)(1) instead of proving actual injury. This section provides that the author's entitlement, per infringed work, is "a sum of not less than $750 or more than $30,000 as the court considers just." But if an "infringer sustains the burden of proving, and the court finds, that such infringer was not aware and had no reason to believe that his or her acts constituted an infringement of copyright, the court in its discretion may reduce the award of statutory damages to a sum of not less than $200."... Gonzalez asked the district court to reduce the award under this proviso, but the judge concluded that §402(d) bars any reduction in the minimum award. This subsection provides: "If a notice of copyright in the form and position specified by this section appears on the published phonorecord or phonorecords to which a defendant in a copyright infringement suit had access, then no weight shall be given to such a defendant's interposition of a defense based on innocent infringement in mitigation of actual or statutory damages." It is undisputed that BMG Music gave copyright notice as required—"on the surface of the phonorecord, or on the phonorecord label or container."... It is likewise undisputed that Gonzalez had "access" to records and compact disks bearing the proper notice. She downloaded data rather than discs, and the data lacked copyright notices, but the statutory question is whether "access" to legitimate works was available rather than whether infringers earlier in the chain attached copyright notices to the pirated works. Gonzalez readily could

have learned, had she inquired, that the music was under copyright.

As for the injunction: Gonzalez contends that this should be vacated because she has learned her lesson, has dropped her broadband access to the Internet, and is unlikely to download copyrighted material again. A private party's discontinuation of unlawful conduct does not make the dispute moot, however. An injunction remains appropriate to ensure that the misconduct does not recur as soon as the case ends.... The district court did not abuse its discretion in awarding prospective relief.

Affirmed.

Case Questions

1. What was the basis for Gonzalez's appeal?
2. How did the U.S. Court of Appeals for the Seventh Circuit respond to Gonzalez's claim?

Fixtures are often the subject of both tangible and intangible property rights. For example, suppose that you buy a camera, the design of which is protected by a valid federal patent. Although you have acquired a piece of tangible personal property that you can use and dispose of in any legal manner, the law will recognize that you do not have all the right vis-à-vis the camera. The patent holder, for example, has intangible property rights in the camera's technology that prevent a purchaser from selling duplicates of the product or the technology without permission. Thus, both the patent holder and the purchaser have property rights to the same object.

Property Ownership

Property can be owned in several different forms, including severalty ownership, concurrent ownership, and community property (i.e., marital property in a community property state). **Severalty ownership** exists when property is owned by one person. **Concurrent ownership** exists when property is held simultaneously by more than one person. This can occur in one of three ways—joint tenancy, tenancy in common, and tenancy by the entirety.[13]

In **joint tenancy**, each joint tenant takes an equal, undivided interest in the ownership of property from the same source and at the same time (i.e., from the same conveyance of the property, such as a son and daughter jointly inheriting a house from their deceased parent). Each joint tenant also has an undivided right of survivorship. Thus in a joint tenancy involving three tenants, the entire tenancy passes to the two survivors upon the death of the third and bypasses the deceased person's will and heirs. **Tenancy in common** is similar to a joint tenancy; however, there is no automatic passing of the deceased's rights to the surviving tenants. Instead, the deceased's rights pass according to the will. Tenancies in common can be sold, inherited, and given as a gift. **Tenancy by the entirety** can exist only between legally married husbands and wives and can be ended only through death, divorce, or mutual consent. Upon the death of one of the tenants, title passes to the surviving spouse. If a divorce occurs, the tenancy is converted into a tenancy in common.

The following case requires that the court determine whether a brother and sister hold title to real property as tenants in common or whether the brother holds title as the severalty owner.

In re Estate of Clayton Gulledge
637 A.2d 1278
District of Columbia Court of Appeals
April 4, 1996

Schelb, Associate Justice.

The issue ... is whether the unilateral transfer by one of two joint tenants of his interest to a third party, without the consent of the other joint tenant, converts the joint tenancy into a tenancy in common. We hold that it does.

I

The dispositive facts are undisputed. Clayton and Margie Gulledge owned a house at 532 Somerset Place, N.W. (the Somerset property) as tenants by the entirety. They had three children—Bernis Gulledge, Johnsie Walker, and Marion Watkins. Margie Gulledge died in 1970. Clayton Gulledge remarried the following year, but his second marriage was apparently unsuccessful.

In order to avert the possible loss, in any divorce proceedings, of the Somerset property, Bernis Gulledge advanced to his father the funds necessary to satisfy the second Mrs. Gulledge's financial demands. In exchange, Clayton Gulledge created a joint tenancy in the Somerset property, naming Bernis and himself as joint tenants. Bernis evidently expected that his father would predecease him, and that the right of survivorship which is the essence of a joint tenancy would enable him to acquire the entire property upon his father's death.

In 1988, however, Clayton Gulledge conveyed his interest in the Somerset property to his daughter, Marion Watkins, "in fee simple tenants in common." In 1991, Clayton Gulledge died, and he was survived by his three children. Bernis Gulledge died in 1993 and Johnsie B. Walker died in 1994. In the now consolidated proceedings relating to the estates of Clayton Gulledge, Bernis Gulledge, and Johnsie Walker, appellant Deborah Walker, Bernis' personal representative, claims that when Clayton died, Bernis, as the surviving joint tenant, became the sole owner of the Somerset property. Ms. Watkins, on the other hand, contends that Clayton Gulledge's earlier conveyance of his interest to her severed the joint tenancy, thereby destroying Clayton's right of survivorship, and that Ms. Watkins and Bernis became tenants in common. The trial court agreed with Ms. Watkins....

II

The parties agree that Clayton Gulledge's interest in the joint tenancy was alienable. They disagree only as to the nature of the interest which Clayton transferred to Ms. Watkins. The Estate of Bernis Gulledge (the Estate) argues that an owner cannot convey to a third party a greater interest than his own ... and that because Clayton Gulledge's interest was subject to Bernis' right of survivorship, the interest which Ms. Watkins received from Clayton must be similarly restricted. Ms. Watkins contends, on the other hand, that Clayton's conveyance to her converted the joint tenancy into a tenancy in common by operation of law, and that she received from Clayton an undivided one-half interest in the property.

The question whether a joint tenant severs a joint tenancy by ultimately conveying his interest to a third party without the consent of the other joint tenant has not been squarely decided in the District of Columbia. The issue is one of law, and our review is therefore de novo.... The applicable rule in a large majority of jurisdictions is that either party to a joint tenancy may sever that tenancy by unilaterally disposing of his interest, that the consent of the other tenant is not required, and that the transfer converts the estate into a tenancy in common...

Although no decision by a court in this jurisdiction is directly on point, the discussion of joint tenancy that can be found in District of Columbia cases is consistent with the majority approach. In *Harrington v. Emmerman* ... the court explained that "Joint tenancy cannot exist unless there be present unity of interest, title, time *and possession* that is to say, the interests must be identical, they must accrue by the same conveyance, they must commence at the same time and the estate must be held by the same undivided possession." (Emphasis added.) The interests of Bernis Gulledge and Marion Watkins were not created by the same conveyance, nor did they commence at the same time; the conveyance to Ms. Watkins thus destroyed the unities of title and time....

In *Coleman v. Jackson* ... the court held that where a marriage was invalid, the deed purporting to convey property to the couple as tenants by the entireties created a joint tenancy instead. Contrasting the two types of estates, the court pointed out that "[o]f course, joint tenancy lacks the feature of inalienability which tenancy by the entireties possesses.... [I]nalienability is an incident only of estates by the entireties...."

In *In re Estate of Wall*, the court restated the principle of *Coleman* and distinguished a tenancy by the entireties from a joint tenancy upon the ground that a tenancy by the entireties creates a "unilateral indestructible right of survivorship," while a joint tenancy does not. The court further stated that "survivorship incidental to joint tenancy differs because it may be frustrated ... by alienation or subjection to debts of a cotenant's undivided share or by compulsory partition."

Although the foregoing authorities do not conclusively settle the question before us, they provide no support for the notion that this court should reject the majority rule. Moreover, "[b]ecause District of Columbia law is derived from Maryland law, decisions of the Court of Appeals of Maryland, and particularly those relating to the law of property, are accorded the most respectful consideration by our courts.... Under Maryland law, the transfer of an interest in a joint tenancy

by either joint tenant will sever the joint tenancy and cause the share conveyed to become property held as tenants in common with the other cotenants."... We adopt the same rule here.

For the foregoing reasons, we conclude that when Clayton Gulledge conveyed his interest to Ms. Watkins, she and Bernis Gulledge both became owners of an undivided one-half interest in the property as tenants in common. Upon Bernis' death, his estate replaced Bernis as a tenant in common with Ms. Watkins. Accordingly, the trial court correctly held that Ms. Watkins and the Estate of Bernis Gulledge are tenants in common, and that each holds an undivided half interest in the Somerset property.

Affirmed.

Case Questions

1. What was the nature of the interest that Clayton transferred to his daughter, Marion Watkins?
2. Why didn't Bernis become the severalty owner of the Somerset property upon Clayton's death?
3. How was it possible for Clayton to create a joint tenancy in the property, with himself and his son Bernis as joint tenants?

Community Property

Community property is recognized by the states of Arizona, California, Idaho, Louisiana, Nevada, New Mexico, Texas, Washington, and Wisconsin. In community property states, each spouse is legally entitled to a percentage of what the state defines as community property, and this varies by jurisdiction. Although states differ, community property is usually defined as including the earnings of both spouses, and property rights acquired with those earnings during the marriage. State statutes, however, usually exclude from community property rights acquired individually by one or the other spouse prior to marriage, spousal inheritances, and gifts to the individual spouse received during the marriage. These are classified as separate property. Community property states differ on whether earnings from separately owned property should be treated as community property.

Title

Title refers to ownership rights in property. For example, when a student purchases a textbook

from a bookstore, he or she is purchasing the seller's title to the book. This means that the bookstore is selling all its rights in the book to the student. The bookstore will provide the purchaser with a receipt (bill of sale) to evidence the purchase of these rights and the transfer of ownership. If the student purchased the textbook from a thief, however, the student would not obtain title to the book. The larceny victim would still have the title, and the thief would be an unlawful possessor.[14]

A student who has purchased title to a textbook has many rights vis-à-vis that object. The student may decide to loan possessory rights to the book temporarily to another student. The student also has the right to decide whether to dispose of the book after completion of the course. For instance, the student might decide to make a gift of the book, sell his or her rights in the book to another student, or sell it back to the bookstore.

A bookstore does not have to produce a written document to establish its ownership when it sells a textbook to a student. However, the law does require the use of title documents to provide evidence of title for some property items. A seller of a motor vehicle, for example, must have a valid title document from the state to transfer ownership rights to the purchaser, and purchases of land require a title document called a **deed.**

GOVERNMENT'S RIGHT TO REGULATE AND TAKE PRIVATE PROPERTY

State government bears the primary responsibility for defining and limiting the exercise of private property rights through the **police power.** The police power refers to the authority of state legislatures to enact laws regulating and restraining private rights and occupations for the promotion of the public health, welfare, safety, and morals. The police power of the states is not a grant derived from a written constitution; the federal Constitution assumes the preexistence of the police power, and the Tenth Amendment reserves to the states any power not delegated to the federal government in Article I. Limitations on the police power have never been drawn with precision or determined by a general formula. But the Fifth and Fourteenth Amendments' Due Process Clauses require that state actions based on the police power be exercised in the public interest, be reasonable, and be consistent with the rights implied or secured by the Constitution. Government uses of the police power with respect to property are promulgated as environmental protection laws, administrative regulations (such as environmental rules), legislation (zoning, eminent domain, taxation), and tort law (for example, nuisance suits). See Figure 12.1 for an overview of the government's role in regulating private property.

Environmental Laws and Natural Resources Regulations: The Northern Spotted Owl Case

Historically, landowners have opposed governmental restrictions that prevent them from developing their land and harvesting its natural resources. In states where logging is big business and a major source of employment, limitations on commercial logging on privately owned timberland are very controversial. Environmentalists counter that it is essential that there be some legal regulation of commercial development on private property. They argue that the cumulative effect of decisions made independently by individual private landowners can produce destruction of critical habitat and cause already endangered species to become extinct.

This problem gained national prominence in 2006 when environmentalists in Washington sought to prevent small private landowners from logging portions of their forest land that threaten the Northern Spotted Owl's habitat. The triggering event was a federal lawsuit brought by the Seattle and Kittitas Audubon Societies against the Weyerhaeuser Company and state officials for allegedly violating the Endangered Species Protection Act. The plaintiffs wanted to prevent further destruction of owl habitat on Weyerhaeuser land and on other privately held forest timberland. They sought declaratory and injunctive relief, and a hearing was held over the granting of a temporary injunction that would prevent any new logging within the targeted forest areas pending the conclusion of the litigation. The plaintiffs explained to the court that they feared that state officials would, if not enjoined, allow private landowners to engage in logging activities that could harm owls present within owl habitat located on their timberland properties. The plaintiffs identified by location 266 owl habitat administrative zones called "owl circles" that they believed warranted legal protection from logging pending the resolution of the suit. Four of the "owl circles" were located on Weyerhaeuser property, with the remaining 262 situated on other privately owned sites. The district court agreed with the plaintiffs with respect to the Weyerhaeuser owl circles and issued the injunction. But the court refused to enjoin the state, concluding that the plaintiffs' proof was legally insufficient to support an injunction. The plaintiffs had only provided evidence that owls were actually present in 44 of the 262 owl circles. Also lacking was proof as to how much owl habitat actually existed in any of the 262 administrative zones. The only

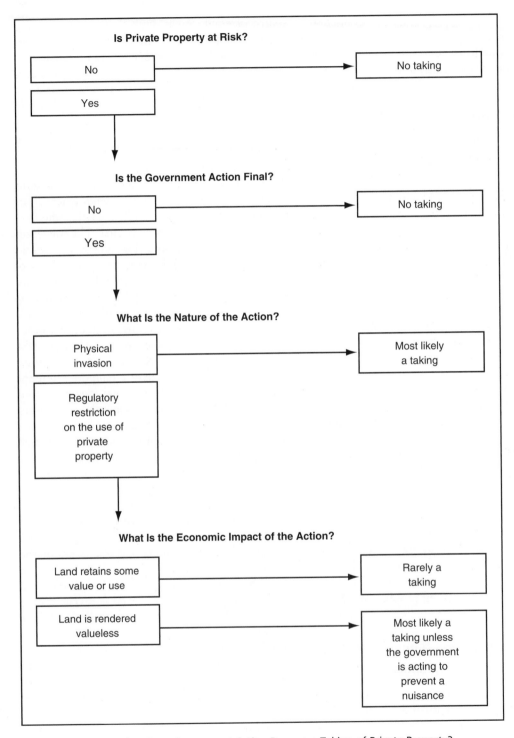

F I G U R E   12.1   When Does Government Action Become a Taking of Private Property?

Source: Kathleen C. Zimmerman and David Abelson, "Takings Law: A Guide to Government, Property, and the Constitution," Copyright © 1993 by The Land & Water Fund of the Rockies, Inc.

habitat-specific evidence presented was limited to the four owl circles on Weyerhaeuser land.[15]

The district judge's rulings on the injunctions may have caused the parties to rethink the wisdom of resolving their differences in a judicial forum. The plaintiffs may have concluded that the cost of obtaining the missing data, paying the costs of a trial, and litigating this and other similar cases in the future just did not make economic sense. What is certain is that in July 2008 the parties jointly announced that they had reached a settlement. Although not all of the settlement terms were revealed, the parties reported that they had agreed to work collaboratively as members of a "policy working group," and to scientifically determine the best strategies for identifying, improving, and preserving spotted owl habitat that is located on privately owned land. Weyerhaeuser also agreed to protect the four owl circles on its land.

In 2010, the working group initiated a "pilot project" for eastern Washington that focuses on protecting owl habitat located on privately held land that is frequently subject to forest fires.

The federal government, recognizing the need to encourage small owners of forestland to participate voluntarily in protecting endangered species habitat, has attempted to address some of the landowners' concerns. Because many private owners of timberland fear governmental land restrictions, they find it necessary to discourage the presence of an endangered species on their forested land. Having recognized the fear, and wishing to overcome this disincentive, the U.S. Fish and Wildlife Service (FWS) developed a "Safe Harbor Agreements" program. Under this program, the FWS can negotiate agreements with private landowners to encourage them to manage their private property actively in ways that benefit endangered species. The landowners benefit from these agreements because the government provides them with written "assurances." The government, in essence, promises that landowners who help in building and retaining habitat as specified in the agreement will not be subjected to enhanced levels of land regulation in the future. These agreements also can include provisions allowing a landowner to alter an endangered habitat in specified ways (including some logging), if in the end there is a "net conservation benefit" to the endangered species.

Zoning

State legislatures originally authorized local governments to enact **zoning ordinances** to promote public health and safety by separating housing districts from incompatible commercial and industrial uses. Today, zoning ordinances also preserve a community's historically significant landmarks and neighborhoods and restrict adult entertainment. State and local environmental protection agencies often resort to zoning ordinances in deciding whether to grant licenses to land developers where a proposed land use threatens wetlands or natural habitat, or increases air or water pollution. Zoning ordinances can be very controversial, such as when they prohibit trailer parks or require that structures and lots be large (and therefore often unaffordable to low-income people). In the family law chapter (Chapter XI), you can see another example of restrictive zoning. In that 1977 case decided by the U.S. Supreme Court, entitled *Moore v. City of East Cleveland*, governmental authorities unsuccessfully sought to use a zoning ordinance to prohibit a grandmother from living with her two grandchildren.

Eminent Domain

The government can take private property for a public purpose over the objection of a landowner, pursuant to what is called the power of **eminent domain.** The Fifth Amendment's Takings Clause provides that whenever the federal government takes property to benefit the public, it must pay just compensation. This constitutional control on government has been incorporated into the Fourteenth Amendment and also is binding on the states. The Takings Clause protects individual private property rights by ensuring that taxpayers, rather than targeted private individuals, pay for public benefits.

Government obtains title to private land through condemnation proceedings in which a court ensures that statutory and constitutional requirements are satisfied. In a related proceeding, a court will determine the fair-market value of the land that will be paid to the property owner.

The U.S. Supreme Court has been unsuccessful to date in precisely establishing what constitutes a "taking." It has, however, recognized that takings can assume different forms. One obvious example is where the government takes title to land for the purpose of building a public highway. Other takings, however, are less obvious. The Supreme Court found in 1946 that a taking had occurred where low-flying military aircraft created so much noise while flying over a chicken farm that the farm went out of business.[16] The Court ruled that under these circumstances the government had exploited and in effect taken airspace above it for a flight path (a public purpose), to the commercial detriment of the farmer. The farmer, said the Court, was entitled to compensation.

In a 1978 case, the U.S. Supreme Court had to rule on whether New York City, as part of a historic landmarks preservation program, could impose limitations on the development or redevelopment of historic sites such as Grand Central Station. The city wanted to prevent the construction of a large office building above the station. To the developer, the restrictions imposed by the Landmark Preservation Law amounted to a taking of private property (the airspace above the station) for a public purpose, for which compensation was due. The Court ruled in favor of the city, largely because the law served a public purpose (improving the quality of life for all New Yorkers) and provided the developer with a reasonable economic return on investment.

Historically, landowners have argued that they should be compensated when their property values fall as a result of governmental restrictions that prevent them from commercially developing their land and its natural resources. Defenders maintained that such regulations were necessary because the cumulative effect of the individual actions of private landowners would likely result in endangered species becoming extinct. Legislative initiatives designed to protect the environment, and preserve aesthetic and cultural landmarks, generally have been upheld by the Supreme Court.

The Controversial Decision in the *Kelo* Case

The U.S. Supreme Court's 2005 decision in *Susette Kelo v. City of New London,* 545 U.S. 469, attracted national attention and considerable outrage throughout the nation. The case arose out of an attempt by the state of Connecticut and the city of New London to revitalize an "economically distressed" area of New London. The proponent of the redevelopment plan—a private developer of commercial property—sought to use the power of eminent domain to acquire the title to parcels owned by persons who rejected the city's offers to buy them out. Susette Kelo was one of the owners unwilling to sell to the private developer. Those favoring the plan argued that this development would create jobs, improve New London's image, strengthen its tax base and generally enhance its downtown and waterfront areas.

Susette Kelo claimed that the Takings Clause prohibited New London from acquiring her residential property by way of eminent domain and then conveying it to another private owner in order to implement an economic development plan. The justices disagreed over whether to commit the federal judiciary to using the Fifth Amendment's Takings Clause to establish national standards with respect to the potentially endless battles between developers and landowners. The Supreme Court ruled 5–4 that the states should have this responsibility.

Justice Stevens, for the majority, explained that the Takings Clause only required that a condemned parcel be used for a "public purpose," where the taking of the private property occurred pursuant to a "carefully considered development plan." In *Kelo,* Stevens argued that Susette Kelo's house had been taken by eminent domain as part of a comprehensive economic development plan, which had been authorized specifically by Connecticut statute. Justice Stevens acknowledged that many states might believe the federal "public purpose" standard to be too low, and he rejected imposing a "one-size-fits-all" approach on the country. He basically left it up to the states to decide for themselves what standard should apply, explaining it this way:

> We emphasize that nothing in our opinion precludes any State from placing further restrictions on its exercise of the takings power. Indeed, many States already impose "public use" requirements that are stricter than the federal baseline. Some of these requirements have been established as a matter of state constitutional law ... while others are expressed in state eminent domain statutes that carefully limit the grounds upon which takings may be exercised.... As the submissions of the parties and their amici make clear, the necessity and wisdom of using eminent domain to promote economic development are certainly matters of legitimate public debate.... This Court's authority, however, extends only to determining whether the City's proposed condemnations are for a "public use" within the meaning of the Fifth Amendment to the Federal Constitution....
> (*Kelo,* 545 U.S. 469 at 489.)

Justic O'Connor, in a dissent in *Kelo,* disagreed, saying:

> Today the Court abandons this long-held, basic limitation on government power. Under the banner of economic development, all private property is now vulnerable to being taken and transferred to another private owner, so long as it might be upgraded—*i.e.,* given to an owner who will use it in a way that the legislature deems more beneficial to the public—in the process. To reason, as the Court does, that the incidental public benefits resulting from the subsequent ordinary use of private property render economic development takings "for public use" is to wash out any distinction between private and public use of property—and thereby effectively to delete the words "for public use" from the Takings Clause of the Fifth Amendment.
> (*Kelo,* 545 U.S. 469 at 494.)

Kelo v. New London—The Aftermath

The public reaction to the *Kelo* decision was loud and negative. Within one year, over half of the states took action by statute or constitutional amendment and increased the restrictions on the use of eminent domain. That number has increased to over 40 states.

Unfortunately for the citizens of New London, the comprehensive development plan to revitalize their city just wasn't to be. The developer was unable to arrange the necessary funding and Pfizer, the pharmaceutical giant that was expected to lead in the economic revitalization of the city, moved out of New London along with over 1,000 jobs. So the bottom line is this: what used to be on the site is gone, what was supposed to replace it isn't, and that is tragic.

INTERNET TIP

Readers can find an edited version of the majority opinion in *Kelo v. New London,* and Justice O'Connor's thought-provoking dissent, with the Chapter XII materials on the textbook's website.

Introduction to *Kaur v. New York State Urban Development Corporation*

We have seen how the U.S. Supreme Court in *Kelo* has effectively transferred the complicated battles that routinely occur in economic-development takings cases to the states. The federal courts will no longer play an active supervisory role over the states in such cases. Each state will have to establish rules as to what is required for a proposed development project to qualify for governmental support via the exercise of the state's power of eminent domain. States will differ as to how the conflicting interests of those preferring economic development are balanced vis-à-vis the preservation of private property rights. It will be interesting to see whether state courts decide these disputes on a case-by-case basis or, following the U.S. Supreme Court's lead, essentially defer these decisions to state legislatures and administrative agencies.

In our next case, *Kaur v. New York State Urban Development Corporation,* we see how New York's highest court addressed this dilemma. The petitioners in *Kaur* owned gas stations and storage facilities in West Harlem, New York City. Unfortunately for them, their businesses were located on 17 acres of land that Columbia University wanted to acquire for a "new urban campus."

Columbia's development team began its campaign to garner governmental support for its new campus project in 2001, when it approached New York City's Economic Development Commission (EDC). The city became interested in Columbia's proposal and over the course of the next few years funded two separate studies of the West Harlem neighborhoood. One was an economic study, and the second focused on the structural integrity of existing buildings, sanitation and infrastructure issues, and the neighborhood's prospects for increased levels of private investment and improved future growth. Both of the firms conducting the research reported that the neighborhood was "blighted."

Columbia began purchasing as much property within the targeted area as possible and successfully acquired slightly over half of the necessary properties. But the Kaurs and other neighborhood business owners (the petitioners) refused Columbia's entreaties to sell.

Project supporters, believing that it would be necessary for some parcels to be acquired via eminent domain, began discussions with New York State's Empire State Development Corporation (ESDC). The ESDC is a public benefit corporation created by the New York legislature to help finance economic and job development throughout the state of New York. The ESDC was created as a hybrid entity (i.e., partly governmental and partly private). This meant it could get around limitations in the New York Constitution that presented hurdles to developers. The ESDC, for example, could issue bonds for which the state was not responsible and could circumvent the debt limitation provisions in the state constitution. Most important, it was statutorily authorized to exercise the state's sovereign power of eminent domain to achieve the agency's public-purpose objectives.

Discussions involving Columbia and the city and state economic development officials progressed

rapidly during 2004–2007, and the ESDC commissioned its own "status of the neighborhood" report (the AKRF report). That report concluded, as did the preceding ones, that the neighborhood was "blighted." The New York City Council then agreed to zoning changes in the targeted development area to accommodate Columbia's project, and the ESDC declared that it supported going ahead with the project.

Columbia's proposal was comprehensive and included an extensive package of benefits intended to improve and enrich the lives of neighborhood residents and dislocated businesses. These included an affordable-housing fund, a demonstration community school (involving Columbia's famous Teacher's College), lawyers to advise neighbors about landlord–tenant law, a hiring preference for "qualified local residents," job opportunities that would pay a "living wage," additional help for displaced neighborhood businesses, job training, scholarships, community access to the new swimming pool, and much, much more.

The small-business owners who were unwilling to sell to Columbia were organizing an opposition to the planned development. They were also preparing for the legal battles to come. In 2008 the owners successfully used the Freedom of Information Law (FOIL) to obtain important and sometimes revealing documents that the respondents had not wanted disclosed. In fact, the ESDC only disclosed some of the requested documents after a trial court's order requiring such disclosure was affirmed by a New York intermediate court of appeals.

The business owners then requested that the intermediate appellate court review the ESDC's determination that eminent domain should be used to take their property. They objected to the taking of their property against their will in this manner so that another private property owner, Columbia University, could build its new campus.

The matter was reviewed by a panel of five judges assigned to the Appellate Division of the Supreme Court of New York, First Department. That court ruled 3-2 for the petitioners and ordered that the ESDC's determination be annulled. Judge Catterson wrote in his opinion for the Court:

> Justice O'Connor's admonition [in *Kelo*] is equally true in this case in that "[a]ny property may now be taken for the benefit of another private party, but the fallout from this decision will not be random. The beneficiaries are likely to be those citizens with disproportionate influence and power in the political process, including large corporations and development firms. As for the victims, the government now has license to transfer property from those with fewer resources to those with more. The Founders cannot have intended this perverse result."…
> (*In re Kaur v. NY State Urban Dev. Corp.*, 72 A.D.3d 1 [1st Dept 2009].)

The ESDC appealed the Appellate Division of the Supreme Court of New York's decision to New York's highest court, the Court of Appeals of New York.

Kaur v. New York State Urban Development Corp.
933 N.E.2d 721
Court of Appeals of New York
June 24, 2010

Ciparick, J.

In this appeal, we are called upon to determine whether respondent's exercise of its power of eminent domain to acquire petitioners' property for the development of a new Columbia University campus was supported by a sufficient public use, benefit or purpose….

I

Petitioners in this proceeding are the owners of different commercial establishments located in the West Harlem neighborhood of Manhattan. Petitioners Parminder Kaur and Amanjit Kaur own a gasoline service station located on West 125th Street. Petitioners Tuck-It-Away, Inc., Tuck-It-Away Bridgeport, Inc., Tuck-It-Away at 133rd Street, Inc., and Tuck-It-Away Associates, L.P. (collectively TIA) own storage facilities located on Broadway and on West 131st and West 125th Streets. Petitioner P.G. Singh Enterprises, LLP also owns a gasoline service station located on West 125th Street….

II

Petitioners' main argument on this appeal is that the Project approved by ESDC is unconstitutional because the condemnation is not for the purpose of putting properties to "public use" within the meaning of article I, §7(a) of the N.Y. Constitution, which provides that "[p]rivate property shall not be taken for public use without just compensation." First, petitioners vociferously contend that ESDC's blight findings were made in bad faith and the Project only serves the private interests of Columbia. ESDC counters that the duly approved Project qualifies as a "land use improvement project" within the meaning of the Urban Development Corporation Act and that the Appellate Division plurality erred as a matter of law when it conducted a de novo review of the administrative record and concluded that the Project site was not blighted….

In *Matter of Goldstein*, we reaffirmed the longstanding doctrine that the role of the Judiciary is limited in reviewing findings of blight in eminent domain proceedings…. [T]he determinations of blight and public purpose are the province of the Legislature, and are entitled to deference by the Judiciary….

> Indeed, we observed that "[t]he Constitution accords government broad power to take and clear substandard and insanitary areas for redevelopment. In so doing, it commensurately deprives the Judiciary of grounds to interfere with the exercise."… These principles are based on a consistent body of law that goes back over 50 years…. Thus, a court may only substitute its own judgment for that of the legislative body authorizing the project when such judgment is irrational or baseless….

Applying this standard of review, as we must, we now look to the relevant statute. The UDC Act provides that, in the case of land use improvement projects, ESDC must find:

> (1) That the area in which the project is to be located is a substandard or insanitary area, or is in danger of becoming a substandard or insanitary area and tends to impair or arrest the sound growth and development of the municipality;

(2) That the project consists of a plan or undertaking for the clearance, replanning, reconstruction and rehabilitation of such area and for recreational and other facilities incidental or appurtenant thereto;

(3) That the plan or undertaking affords maximum opportunity for participation by private enterprise, consistent with the sound needs of the municipality as a whole....

The term "substandard or insanitary area" is defined as "a slum, blighted, deteriorated or deteriorating area, or an area which has a blighting influence on the surrounding area."... Here, the two reports prepared by ESDC consultants—consisting of a voluminous compilation of documents and photographs of property conditions—arrive at the conclusion that the area of the Project site is blighted. Just as in *Matter of Goldstein*, "all that is at issue is a reasonable difference of opinion as to whether the area in question is in fact substandard and insanitary," which is "not a sufficient predicate ... to supplant [ESDC's] determination."...

Thus, given our precedent, the de novo review of the record undertaken by the plurality of the Appellate Division was improper. On the "record upon which the ESDC determination was based and by which we are bound" ... it cannot be said that ESDC's finding of blight was irrational or baseless. Indeed, ESDC considered a wide range of factors including the physical, economic, engineering and environmental conditions at the Project site. Its decision was not based on any one of these factors, but on the Project site conditions as a whole. Accordingly, since there is record support "extensively documented photographically and otherwise on a lot-by-lot basis"... for ESDC's determination that the Project site was blighted, the Appellate Division plurality erred when it substituted its view for that of the legislatively designated agency.

III

Despite the objective data utilized by ESDC in its finding of blight, petitioners conclusorily assert that ESDC acted in "bad faith" and with pretext when it arrived at its determination.... Petitioners and the plurality at the Appellate Division particularly take umbrage at ESDC's decision to hire AKRF to conduct a neighborhood conditions study because Columbia had previously engaged AKRF to prepare its EIS. Here, the record does not support petitioners' contention that the study conducted by AKRF was compromised simply because it separately prepared an EIS on behalf of Columbia.

Moreover, ESDC—as a measure of caution and in response to criticism of its choice to retain AKRF—hired a second consulting firm, Earth Tech, to conduct review of the Project site. This company arrived at conclusions similar to AKRF's. Contrary to petitioners' assertions, Earth Tech did not merely review and rubber-stamp AKRF's study, but conducted its own independent research and gathered separate data and photographs of the area before arriving at its own conclusions. Further, unlike AKRF, Earth Tech had never previously been affiliated with or employed by Columbia. Simply put, petitioners' argument that ESDC acted in "bad faith" or pretextually is unsubstantiated by the record.

IV

In addition to attacking the neighborhood blight studies and ESDC's determination based on those studies, petitioners also challenge the constitutionality of the statutory term "substandard or insanitary area."... They argue that we should find this term void for vagueness. This contention is likewise unpersuasive....

It has long been settled that "civil as well as penal statutes can be tested for vagueness under the due process clause."... Due process requires that a statute be sufficiently definite "so that individuals of ordinary intelligence are not forced to guess at the meaning of statutory terms."... In the context of eminent domain cases, we have held that ... blight is an elastic concept that does not call for an inflexible, one-size-fits-all definition.... Rather, blight or "substandard or insanitary areas," as we held in Matter of Goldstein and Yonkers Community Dev. Agency, must be viewed on a case-by-case basis. Accordingly, because the UDC Act provides adequate meaning to the term "substandard or insanitary area," we reject petitioners' argument that the statute is unconstitutionally vague on its face.

V

On appeal to the Appellate Division, petitioners argued that there were no findings of blight in the Project site prior to Columbia's acquisition of property there.... This argument is unsupported by the record.... Earth Tech found that, since 1961, the neighborhood has suffered from a long-standing lack of investment interest. Thus, since there is record support that the Project site was blighted before Columbia began to acquire property in the area, the issue is beyond our further review.

We also conclude that ESDC properly qualified this Project, in the alternative, as a "civic project" within the meaning of the UDC Act.... A civic project is defined as "[a] project or that portion of a multi-purpose project designed and intended for the purpose of providing facilities for educational, cultural, recreational, community, municipal, public service or other civic purposes."...

The plurality at the Appellate Division held that the expansion of a private university does not qualify as a "civic purpose." This conclusion does not have statutory support. Indeed, there is nothing in the statutory language limiting a proposed educational project to public educational institutions. In fact, the UDC Act encourages participation in projects by private entities.... Thus, there is no reason to depart from the plain meaning of the word "education" by limiting the term to public institutions.

Moreover, consonant with the policy articulated in the UDC Act, ESDC has a history of participation in civic projects involving private entities. The most recent example of a civic project is the Atlantic Yards project, which authorized a private entity to construct and operate an arena for the Nets professional basketball franchise.... The petitioners in that case argued that the project did not qualify as a "civic project" because the arena would be used by a professional basketball team and operated by a private profit-making entity. In rejecting that argument, the Appellate Division explained "that a sports arena, even one privately operated for profit, may serve a public purpose."...

The proposed Project here is at least as compelling in its civic dimension as the private development.... Unlike the Nets basketball franchise, Columbia University, though private, operates as a nonprofit educational corporation. Thus, the concern that a private enterprise will be profiting through eminent domain is not present. Rather, the purpose of the Project is unquestionably to promote education and academic research while providing public benefits to the local community. Indeed, the advancement of higher education is the quintessential example of a "civic purpose."... It is fundamental that education and the expansion of knowledge are pivotal government interests. The indisputably public purpose of education is particularly vital for New York City and the State to maintain their respective statuses as global centers of higher education and academic research. To that end, the Project plan includes the construction of facilities dedicated to research and the expansion of laboratories, libraries and student housing.

In addition to these new educational facilities, the Project will bestow numerous other significant civic benefits to the public. For example, the Project calls for the development of approximately two acres of gateless, publicly accessible park-like and landscaped space as well as an open-air market zone along 12th Avenue. Other civic benefits include upgrades in transit infrastructure and a financial commitment to West Harlem Piers Park. Moreover, this Project is projected to stimulate job growth in the local area. In addition to hiring 14,000 people for construction at the Project site, Columbia estimates that it will accommodate 6,000 permanent employees once the Project is completed. In sum, there can be no doubt that the Project approved by ESDC—which provides for the expansion of Columbia's educational facilities and countless public benefits to the surrounding neighborhood, including cultural, recreational and job development benefits—qualifies as a "civic project" under the UDC Act.

VII

Petitioners finally contend that they were denied procedural due process when ESDC both failed to turn over certain documents during the administrative process pursuant to their FOIL request and closed the record prior to completion of the FOIL litigation. Because ESDC did not withhold any documents that formed part of the administrative record ... we ... reject this argument as lacking merit....

It is well settled that procedural due process in the context of an agency determination requires that the agency provide an opportunity to be heard in a meaningful manner at a meaningful time.... In this case, petitioners had an opportunity to comment on the proposed Project in a meaningful manner—both orally and through written submissions—and at a meaningful time—well before ESDC issued its findings and determination to acquire petitioners' property by eminent domain.

It should be emphasized that prior to the ESDC determination, petitioners had unfettered access to over 8,000 pages of documents including ... the AKRF and Earth Tech neighborhood conditions studies. All of these documents were available to the public during the comment period.... Indeed, petitioners' substantial opportunity to be heard is reflected in their extensive written submissions after the completion of the two-day public hearing. As a result, ESDC prepared 75 pages of detailed responses to petitioners' comments and duly considered their submissions before rendering its final findings and determination....

In sum, we give deference to the findings and determination of the ESDC that the Project qualifies as both a land use improvement project and ... a civic project serving a public purpose under the UDC Act. We further conclude that petitioners were not deprived of procedural due process.

Accordingly, the order of the Appellate Division should be reversed, with costs, and the petitions should be dismissed.

Case Questions

1. What, according to New York's highest court, did the intermediate court of appeals do wrong?
2. How would you characterize the way New York has balanced the competing interests of small-business owners and those favoring economic development taking?
3. What are your thoughts about the public policy implications of this decision?

Author's Comment

In November 2009, seven months before it decided *Kaur,* the Court of Appeals of New York decided *Goldstein v. Urban Development Corporation,* a case that raised many of the same issues that were addressed in *Kaur.* In *Goldstein,* New York's highest court approved the use of eminent domain to take previously existing, lesser-value residential and commercial properties in Brooklyn in conjunction with the Atlantic Yards development project. That project, which is expected to take 25 years to complete, involved constructing over a dozen residential and commercial high-rises, as well as the construction of the recently completed Barclay's Center, the new home of the Brooklyn Nets NBA basketball team.

The developers of the Brooklyn project, much like the West Harlem and New London developers, promised that the neighborhood would benefit from affordable housing and job opportunities in future years, if the project is fully completed.

INTERNET TIP

Readers will find the details about the promises made by Columbia University to West Harlem by searching on the Internet for "West Harlem Community Benefits Agreement" (May 18, 2009).

Also on the Internet is a 2009 brochure produced by the private property advocacy group Institute for Justice called "Building Empires, Destroying Homes: Eminent Domain Abuse in New York." This document identifies many other economic development takings in projects throughout the Empire State.

Taxation

A property owner usually is required to pay taxes to the government based on the value and use of the property. Failure to pay these taxes can result in the filing of a lien and eventually in the public taking of the property to satisfy the taxes. Government frequently uses tax concessions to encourage property uses it favors.

Nuisance

A **nuisance** exists when an owner's use of his or her property unreasonably infringes on other persons' use and enjoyment of their property rights. Nuisances are classified as public, private, or both. A **public nuisance** exists when a given use of land poses a generalized threat to the public. It is redressed by criminal prosecution and injunctive relief. Examples of public nuisances include houses of prostitution, actions affecting the public health (such as water and air pollution), crack houses, and dance halls. A **private nuisance** is a tort that requires proof of an injury that is distinct from that suffered by the general public. (It differs from trespass because the offensive activity does not occur on the victim's property.) A party injured by a private nuisance can obtain both damages and injunctive relief.

Introduction to *Evans v. Lochmere Recreation Club, Inc.*

Hugh and Jackie Evans claimed that the conduct of the defendant, Lochmere Recreation Club, interfered with their right to the enjoyment and use of their property, and constituted a private nuisance. They appealed from a trial court's decision to dismiss their complaint for failing to state a claim on which relief could be granted.

Hugh K. Evans v. Lochmere Recreation Club, Inc.
627 S.E.2d 340
Court of Appeals of North Carolina
March 21, 2006

Bryant, Judge.

Hugh K. Evans and Jackie Evans (plaintiffs) appeal from an order entered 27 April 2005 dismissing their claims against Lochmere Recreation Club, Inc. (defendant)....

FACTS & PROCEDURAL HISTORY

In 1994, plaintiff Hugh Evans (Evans) filed suit against MacGregor Development Co. (MacGregor) and Lochmere Swim & Tennis Club, Inc. (LSTC), claiming the noise from the speakers and crowds located at the Swim Club interfered with the use and enjoyment of his property. At trial, a jury found in favor of Evans and awarded him $50,000.00 in compensatory damages and $135,000.00 in punitive damages. The trial court further granted a permanent injunction and restraining order against MacGregor and LSTC instructing them to take measures, such as repositioning their speakers, to reduce the noise encroachment on plaintiff's property. This final judgment was affirmed on appeal.... In 1998 defendant Lochmere Recreation Club acquired the property from LSTC.

Plaintiffs initiated the instant civil action against defendant on 22 December 2004, alleging that between May and September of each year from 1998–2004, defendant operated their swim and tennis club in a manner that created a nuisance. Plaintiff's complaint listed several different ways in which plaintiffs assert that defendant caused an unreasonable interference with the enjoyment of their home.... On 13 January 2005, defendant moved to dismiss plaintiffs' complaint....

Defendant's motion was heard on 5 April 2005.... On 27 April 2005, the trial court granted defendant's motion to dismiss.... Plaintiffs appeal.

Plaintiffs argue that the trial court erred in dismissing their claim for private nuisance....

STANDARD OF REVIEW

"The system of notice pleading affords a sufficiently liberal construction of complaints so that few fail to survive a motion to dismiss."... In considering a Rule 12(b)(6) motion to dismiss, the trial court must determine whether the factual allegations in the complaint state a claim for relief.... A plaintiff must state the "substantive elements of a legally recognized claim" in order to survive a Rule 12(b)(6) motion to dismiss.... To support a complaint for private nuisance, a plaintiff must allege "sufficient facts from which it may be determined what liability forming conduct is being complained of and what injury plaintiffs have suffered."... When hearing a motion to dismiss, the trial court must take the complaint's allegations as true and determine whether they are " 'sufficient to state a claim upon which relief may be granted under some legal theory.' "...

SUFFICIENCY OF COMPLAINT

"[A] private nuisance exists in a legal sense when one makes an improper use of his own property and in that way injures the land or some incorporeal right of one's neighbor."... In their complaint plaintiffs alleged several specific actions which would support a private nuisance claim against defendant, including that defendant "has used amplified sound from speakers aimed directly at [plaintiffs'] premises" and that when the public address system is used, "it can be clearly heard in plaintiffs' home even with all plaintiffs' doors and windows closed and their television playing."... As the complaint is to be liberally construed, we find it is sufficient on its face to "provide defendant sufficient notice of the conduct on which the claim is based to enable defendant to respond and prepare for trial" and "states enough ... to satisfy the substantive elements" of a private nuisance claim against defendant....

Affirmed in part, reversed in part, and remanded for further proceedings on plaintiffs' claim for private nuisance....

Case Questions

1. What does the court mean when it says that the complaint is to be liberally construed?
2. What is required to change a private nuisance into a public nuisance?

REAL PROPERTY

The laws that govern real property in America have their origins in medieval England. Under feudal law all land was derived from the king; thus it was possible for someone to own an estate in land but not the actual land itself. Estates were classified according to their duration, a practice that continues in American law today.

Estates in Land

The word *estate* is derived from the Latin word for *status*. An **estate in land,** therefore, is the amount of interest a person has in land. Some estates in land can be inherited. A person who holds an estate in what is known as **fee simple** can pass his or her interest on to heirs. This represents the maximum ownership right to land that is permissible by law. A person who has an estate in land for the duration of his or her life has a **life estate** in land. Life estates cannot be passed on to heirs.

A person who leases real property has only a possessory interest in land, called a **leasehold.** Leaseholds allow tenants to hold **possessory interests** in real property—i.e., the right to occupy or control, as opposed to the ownership interest of the titleholder, who holds the estate in land—for a month, a year, or even at will.

A landowner has the right to minerals that exist beneath the surface of the land. Landowners also have the right to control and use the airspace above their land. Governmental regulations regarding the height of buildings, as well as engineering limitations that are associated with a particular property, often limit the exercise of this right.

Easements

Easements and licenses are interests in land that do not amount to an estate but affect the owner's use of land. An **easement** is a nonpossessory property right in land; it is one person's right to use another person's land. For example, *B* might grant *A* an easement that permits her to use a private road on *B*'s property. Because *B* continues to own the land, *B* can grant similar easements to persons *C* and *D*. *B* can grant these additional easements without having to obtain permission from *A,* because *A* lacks possessory rights on *B*'s land. Easements often are classified as affirmative or negative. An affirmative easement would exist where landowner *A* conveys to *B* the right to lay a pipeline across *A*'s land. A negative easement would exist where *A* conveys part of her land to *B* and retains an easement that forbids *B* to burn trash or plant trees within five yards of *A*'s property line.

An easement also may be created by eminent domain. In such a case, the landowner is constitutionally entitled to receive just compensation. Easements often are created by deed, and usually have to be in writing to be legally enforceable. They can be limited to a specific term or event, or they can be of infinite duration. It is commonly said that easements "run with the land," meaning that the burden or benefit of the easement is transferred with the land to the subsequent owners.

Licenses

A **license** is a temporary grant of authority to do specified things on the land of another, for example, hunt or fish. A license can be oral because it is not an actual estate in land and therefore is not subject to the statute of frauds (see Chapter X). Licenses can generally be revoked at will.

Covenants

To protect themselves from sellers who don't have title, purchasers of land often require the seller to make certain promises in the deed, called **covenants.** The grantor's covenants ensure that he or she has possessory rights to the premises and that the title is good and is free of encumbrances. The grantor will further promise to defend this title against the claims and demands of other people.

Other covenants that affect land use are those that run with the land (i.e., are binding on the current owner and all future owners). Historically, restrictive covenants have discriminated against people because of race, religion, or national origin. Today such covenants are illegal and contrary to public policy and would not be enforced in any court. Courts will, in appropriate cases, enforce nondiscriminatory covenants that run with the land and that create contractual rights in property. Although easements have traditionally been used to affect land use, lawyers began to resort to covenants to augment the kind of restrictions sellers could require of purchasers beyond the scope of easements. A baker, for example, might be willing to sell an adjacent lot that he owns; however, he might protect his business by requiring the purchaser to covenant that the premises conveyed will not be used for the operation or maintenance of a bakery, lunchroom, or restaurant.

Covenants that run with the land are regulated closely by courts because they restrict the use of property. For a covenant to run with the land and bind successive landowners, the original grantor and grantee must have intended that the restrictions on the covenant go with the land. In addition, a close, direct relationship known as **privity of estate** must exist between a grantor and a grantee. The privity requirement is satisfied, for example, when land developer *A* deeds part of her land to *B*, and *B* covenants not to put up a fence on *B*'s land without *A*'s written approval. Finally, covenants must "touch and concern" land; they may not be promises that are personal and unrelated to land. Successors in interest to the original grantor and grantee will be bound by the terms of a properly created covenant that runs with the land.

Adverse Possession

A person who has no lawful right of possession can obtain title to another's land by complying with the rules for **adverse possession** (also known as an **easement by prescription**). The law requires property owners to ensure that no one else uses the land without permission, and a person who fails to use or protect his or her land for many years may one day lose title to an adverse possessor. In order to obtain title by adverse possession, the adverse possessor must take actual possession of the land; the possession must be hostile (without the consent of the owner); the possession must be adverse (against the owner's interest); the possession must be open and notorious (obvious and knowable to anyone who is interested); and the possession must be continuous for a statutorily determined period of time, often 20 years. A successful adverse possessor cannot sell the land until he or she has a marketable title (clear ownership of the land). To obtain a marketable title, the adverse possessor has to file what is called a **quiet title action.** If the court rules in favor of the adverse possessor, he or she will have a clear title to the land.

Introduction to *Steuck v. Easley*

The defendant–appellant in the next case, Dr. Newell Easley, appealed a trial judge's decision that Easley's neighbors to the east, Peter and Barbara Steuck, had acquired title to 17 acres of Easley's land by adverse possession. The Steucks had purchased their property from Dale Daggett in 2001, who had in turn purchased this parcel in 1974 from Gordon Daniels. The Daniels–Daggett–Steuck property was adjacent to an essentially undeveloped 17-acre parcel that Easley purchased in 1987. The Steucks (referred to as the plaintiffs in the court's opinion) filed suit claiming that they had acquired title to the 17 acres through adverse possession. They offered as proof the testimony of their predecessors in title (Daggett and Daniels). Daggett and Daniels testified that while they were owners of the property now owned by the Steucks, they had hunted on the 17 acres. When their years of hunting were added to the Steucks' possession, it added up to 29 consecutive years on that parcel. Both maintained that throughout that 29-year period they had been unaware that the land belonged to Easley.

The question before the intermediate court of appeals was: Were the hunters adverse possessors or merely trespassers?

Steuck v. Easley
2009 AP 757
Court of Appeals of Wisconsin, District IV
May 13, 2010

Vergeront, J

This adverse possession claim concerns approximately seventeen acres of undeveloped land in a larger tract of several hundred acres primarily used for hunting by the titleholder, Newell Easley…. Easley appeals the circuit court's determination that the plaintiffs established title to the disputed area by adverse possession….

BACKGROUND

Easley owns at least 360 acres of undeveloped land in the Township of Shields, Marquette County. He uses his land primarily for hunting and also for activities such as gathering firewood, picking apples, and hiking on the hiking trails. He has set aside some of his land as a sanctuary for the purpose of managing, growing and protecting a deer herd….

The complaint alleges that the use of the disputed area by the plaintiffs' predecessors in title for more than twenty years has established ownership by adverse possession as provided in Wis. Stat. §893.25….

At the trial to the court, Dale Daggett, the plaintiffs' predecessor in title, testified that when he purchased the property in 2001, he believed he owned the disputed area and he treated it as his. He bow hunted there in the fall of 2003; he went four-wheeling there three or four times in 2003 and a couple times in 2004; he took friends to walk there; and he cleared brush off a trail. He never saw anyone else in that area….

Easley testified that he and one or more of his family and friends are on his land approximately 180 days per year. They do not hunt in the sanctuary, which includes the disputed area. He goes into the disputed area once or twice a year and tries to observe it from a distance because walking through it defeats the purpose of a sanctuary. He never noticed persons trespassing in the disputed area nor saw anything that caused him to believe someone was doing something of a permanent nature. No one in his family or his hunting group gave him any indication there was hunting or other activities going on in the disputed area. He did see two tree stands in the area, but they were very old, and he was sure they had been there for many years prior to his purchase of the property.

The court concluded that the plaintiffs had established title by adverse possession to the disputed area and entered judgment granting full right and title to that property to the plaintiffs….

DISCUSSION

On appeal Easley contends: (1) the circuit court disregarded the presumption in favor of the titleholder and improperly placed the burden on him to prove he had taken measures to keep people off his property; (2) the evidence is insufficient to establish adverse possession when the correct legal standard is applied; and (3) the evidence is insufficient to show he acquiesced to the man-made ditch as the boundary between his property in Lot 6 and the plaintiffs' property….

I. Adverse Possession under WIS. STAT. §893.25

Pursuant to WIS. STAT. §893.25(2)(a) and (b), real estate is possessed adversely only if "the person possessing it, in connection with his or her predecessors in interest, is in actual continued occupation under claim of title, exclusive of any other right," and "[o]nly to the extent that it is actually occupied." In addition, the property must be "protected by a substantial enclosure" or "usually cultivated or improved." §893.25(2)(b). Pursuant to §893.25(1), the adverse possession must be uninterrupted for twenty years….

In order to constitute adverse possession, "the use of the land must be open, notorious, visible, exclusive, hostile and continuous, such as would apprise a reasonably diligent landowner and the public that the possessor claims the land as his own."… "Hostile" in this context does not mean a deliberate and unfriendly animus; rather, the law presumes the element of hostile intent if the other requirements of open, notorious, continuous, and exclusive use are satisfied…. "Both … the fact of possession and its real adverse character" must be sufficiently open and obvious to "apprize the true owner … in the exercise of reasonable diligence of the fact and of an intention to usurp the possession of that which in law is his own."… The size and nature of the disputed area are relevant in deciding if the use is sufficient to apprise the true owner of an adverse claim….

The party seeking to claim title by adverse possession bears the burden of proving the elements by clear and positive evidence…. The evidence must be strictly construed against the claimant and all reasonable presumptions must be made in favor of the true owner…. One of these presumptions is that "actual possession is subordinate to the right of [the true] owner."…

We consider first Easley's assertion that the circuit court ignored the presumption in favor of the titleholder and improperly placed the burden on him. Easley points to the court's several references to Easley's failure, until 2006, to post no-trespassing signs on the eastern boundary of the disputed area to keep out people entering from the plaintiffs' property. The court contrasted Easley's failure to take "anti-trespasser actions" regarding the disputed area with his posting of the rest of his property and his concern with trespassers on the rest of his property. The court also apparently found it significant that there was no trail cut from the lower portion of Lot 6 into the disputed area.

The circuit court acknowledged that a titleholder need not use his or her land at all in order to retain title and that the burden was on the plaintiffs to prove adverse possession. However, we agree with Easley that certain of the court's findings and comments appear to require that Easley prove efforts to keep trespassers out, to post his land, and to patrol it. We clarify here that this is not the law. The elements of adverse possession are directed to the claimant's use of the land, and the claimant has the burden to prove those elements by clear and positive evidence.... If the claimant's use gives the titleholder reasonable notice that the claimant is asserting ownership and the titleholder does nothing, that failure to respond may result in losing title. However, in the absence of such use by the claimant, the titleholder is not obligated to do anything in order to retain title....

We next examine whether the facts as found by the circuit court are sufficient to fulfill the legal standard that the use of the disputed area by Daggett and Daniels was open, notorious, visible, exclusive, hostile, and continuous. The circuit court determined that the regular use of the disputed area for hunting in the various annual hunting seasons by Daggett and Daniels and their friends, the dirt road and trail, and the deer stands should have been noticed by anyone who claimed title to the disputed area. The exclusivity of this use, in the circuit court's opinion, was demonstrated by an incident Daniels described, occurring in approximately 1998, in which he cut down a tree in the disputed area because a tree stand that did not belong to him or his friends was in the tree. The use was continuous, the court determined, because it occurred regularly according to the seasonal nature of hunting.

For the following reasons, we conclude the regular use of the disputed area for hunting, the deer stands, and the dirt road and trail do not constitute open, notorious, visible, exclusive and hostile use. Because of this conclusion, we do not discuss the requirement of continuous use.

There was no finding that Easley ever met Daniels, Daggett or their friends hunting in the disputed area. The circuit court found that Easley could have and should have heard the gunshots during spring and fall gun seasons. We do not agree that the sound of gunshots gives a reasonably diligent titleholder notice of adverse possession. Even assuming that the shots come from the titleholder's property and not from someone else's property beyond, the gunshots would have been consistent with trespassers. As for the deer stands, the testimony was that they were portable deer stands, some kept in place all year. Even if visible, the deer stands, too, are consistent with trespassers. The dirt road and the trail continuing on to the lake are consistent with an easement to the lake rather than adverse possession of the seventeen acres....

We also do not agree that Daniels' act of cutting down a tree on one occasion because it held someone else's tree stand showed Easley and the public that Daniels was attempting to keep others out of the disputed area. Given the nature and size of the disputed area, this is not reasonable notice of an exclusive claim by another. Notably, neither Daggett nor Daniels posted the disputed area, which would have been notice to Easley that someone else claimed it....

The circuit court and the plaintiffs rely on the statement in *Burkhardt* [*v. Smith* ... (1962)] ... that "actual occupancy" for purposes of adverse possession is "the ordinary use of which the land is capable and such as an owner would make of it."... The circuit court reasoned, and the plaintiffs argue on appeal, that the "highest and best use" of the disputed area was hunting, and the plaintiffs' predecessors used the area for hunting just as much as a true owner would or could. However, the quoted sentence from *Burkhardt* is followed by the italicized sentence:

Actual occupancy is not limited to structural encroachment which is common but is not the only physical characteristic of possession. Actual occupancy means the ordinary use of which the land is capable and such as an owner would make of it. *Any actual visible means, which gives notice of exclusion from the property to the true owner or to the public and of the defendant's domination over it, is sufficient....*

In other words, although the use need be only the ordinary use an owner would make of it, the use must also be open, notorious, visible, exclusive, and hostile (as well as continuous)....

The necessary implication of a determination of adverse possession based on the facts here is that a titleholder of large areas of hunting land must either fence or post his or her lands and be diligent about keeping trespassers off in order to avoid the risk of losing title. This result is ... not supported in this case by evidence that satisfies the legal standard for adverse possession with the presumption favoring the titleholder and the burden properly allocated to the plaintiffs.

The next issue we take up is that of the substantial enclosure requirement in WIS. STAT. §893.25(2)(b)1.... Although we could conclude our discussion of adverse possession without addressing this issue, we choose to address it. Doing so will provide a more complete analysis of the adverse possession arguments of the parties and will be useful in addressing their arguments on acquiescence.

The purpose of the substantial enclosure requirement is to alert a reasonable person to the possibility of a border dispute.... "The boundaries may be artificial in part and natural in part if the circumstances are such as to clearly indicate that the inclosure, partly artificial and partly natural, marks the boundaries of the adverse occupancy."... In addition, the enclosure "must be of a substantial character in the sense of being appropriate and effective to reasonably fit the premises for some use to which they are adapted."... However, the enclosure need not actually prevent others from entering....

Given the configuration of the disputed area and the location of the lake, the issue of a substantial enclosure in this case focuses on the southern boundary of the disputed area. As noted above, the court found that there was a substantial enclosure of the disputed property on the south, consisting of the swampy area and a man-made drainage ditch that runs approximately 200 feet from that swampy area to the eastern boundary of Lot 6....

With respect to the swampy area, a natural, swampy area on a titleholder's property does not provide reasonable notice that someone else is or may be claiming title to land on the other side. Therefore, the fact that the swampy area may make it harder to access the disputed area from the southern portion of Lot 6 than from the plaintiffs' property is irrelevant to the issue of a substantial enclosure. This difficulty of natural access does not contribute to providing notice to the Lot 6 titleholder that the owner of the property to the east is or may be claiming ownership of a part of Lot 6.

With respect to the man-made drainage ditch ... this ditch does not alert a reasonable titleholder of Lot 6 that someone else is or might be claiming land on the north side of the ditch in Lot 6. The ditch had already been on Lot 6 for at least three decades when Easley purchased it....

We conclude the evidence does not establish that Daggett's and Daniels' use of the disputed area was open, notorious, visible, exclusive, and hostile, and also does not establish that the disputed area was protected by a substantial enclosure as required by WIS. STAT. §893.25(2)(b)1.

II. Acquiescence

The parties dispute whether the plaintiffs have established adverse possession by showing that Easley acquiesced for twenty years to the man-made ditch as the northern boundary line of his property in Lot 6. As we explain below, it is not clear whether the doctrine of acquiescence remains a distinct means of proving adverse possession when, as here, there is no issue concerning the twenty-year time period. However, whatever the precise relationship between adverse possession and the doctrine of acquiescence, we conclude the evidence does not establish acquiescence.

As already noted, the "hostile" requirement of adverse possession does not refer to a particular state of mind on the part of the claimant.... However, the law at one time did require a hostile intent—knowledge that the land was owned by another and the intent to dispossess the true owner.... The result was that "one who occupied part of his neighbor's land, due to an honest mistake as to the location of his boundary" could never establish adverse possession.... Thus, courts developed the doctrine of acquiescence under which, even though a hostile intent was absent, a party could acquire land by adverse possession if the true owner acquiesced in such possession for twenty years.... More specifically, "acquiescence by adjoining owners in the location of a fence as establishing the common boundary line of their respective properties was conclusive as to the location of such line" where the fence had stood in the same location for more than twenty years....

With the focus now on the acts of possession rather than on the subjective intent of the parties, it would appear that the elements of adverse possession—actual occupancy that is open, notorious, visible, exclusive, hostile, and continuous, plus a substantial enclosure—can be established with the evidence that has sufficed under the case law to show occupancy up to a fence line for twenty years, without the need for specific proof of acquiescence by the titleholder....

If we assume the doctrine of acquiescence remains a distinct means of proving adverse possession where there is no dispute regarding the twenty-year requirement, that assumption does not aid the plaintiffs. The cases on which the plaintiffs rely ... all involve visible activities such as gardening, planting, farming or building up to a fence or fence line for twenty years without objection from the titleholder. The visible nature of the activity together with the commonly understood purpose of a fence to define property lines forms the basis for the reasonable inference that the titleholder's lack of objection constitutes acquiescence to that boundary line....

We have already concluded that the activity of the plaintiffs' predecessors in the disputed area was not open and visible. We have also concluded that the swampy area and man-made ditch do not provide reasonable notice to the titleholder of a potential adverse claim. Even if we assume a fence is not essential to the acquiescence doctrine, the boundary must be physically defined in some equivalent way that makes it reasonable to infer the titleholder understood it as the boundary. The swampy area and man-made ditch do not meet this standard....

Accordingly, we conclude the plaintiffs have not established adverse possession under the doctrine of acquiescence, assuming this doctrine remains a distinct means of establishing adverse possession.

CONCLUSION
We conclude the plaintiffs have not established adverse possession of the disputed area. We therefore reverse and remand for further proceedings consistent with this opinion.

Case Questions

1. What was the decision of the trial court?
2. Why did Easley appeal?
3. What decision was made by the Wisconsin Court of Appeals? How did the court explain its decision?

INTERNET TIP

Judge Dykman dissented in the *Easley* case, saying, "I believe that the majority has re-weighed the evidence, focused on evidence it finds more persuasive than the evidence relied on by the trial court, and therefore is able to reach a conclusion contrary to that of the trial court." Readers can find this dissent included with the Chapter XII materials on the textbook's website.

The Recording System

The **recording system** gives purchasers of land notice of claims against real property. It also helps resolve questions of priority if, for example, a seller deeds land to one person and then deeds the same land to a second person. In every county there is a governmental office called the registry of deeds, usually located in the county courthouse. There the registrar of deeds maintains an index of documents relating to all real property transactions. These include deeds, easements, options, and mortgages. The recording system permits buyers of real property to evaluate the quality of the seller's title. In addition, the purchaser's attorney or a bank's attorney may obtain a document called a title abstract or an insurance company's agreement to insure the title. The abstract is a report that summarizes all the recorded claims that affect the seller's title. If a dispute

arises between competing claimants, the recording statutes help the courts resolve whom the law will recognize as having title to the property.

PERSONAL PROPERTY

There are many ways by which title to personal property is acquired. These include purchase, creation, capture, accession, finding, confusion, gift, and inheritance. In addition, one person may acquire the personal property of another, though not the title to that property, through bailment.

Purchase

The purchase or sale of goods is the most common means of obtaining or conveying ownership rights to personal property. Most purchases involve an exchange of money for the ownership rights to goods. This is a contractual relationship and is governed by the Uniform Commercial Code.

Creation

A person who manufactures products out of raw materials through physical or mental labor has title to the items created. Thus, a person who builds a boat, writes a song, makes a quilt, or develops a software program will have title to that item. A person who is employed to produce something, however, will not have title; ownership rights will belong to the employer.

Capture

A person who acquires previously unowned property has title to the items captured. For example, a person who catches fish on the high seas has title by way of **capture.** Such captures usually require the purchase of a fishing or hunting license. This license authorizes the holder to take title by way of capture according to established regulations that, for example, define the size of the daily catch and determine the season of the year when capture of the particular species covered under the license is permitted.

Accession

A person can take title to additions that occur to his or her property because of natural increases. This means that the owner of animals has title to the offspring by way of **accession.** Similarly, the owner of a savings account has title to the interest that is earned on that account by way of accession.

Finding

A finder of lost property has title that is good against everyone except the true owner. Some states provide that a finder of a lost item above some designated dollar value has a duty to turn the item over to an agency (often the police) for a period of time. If the true owner fails to claim the item, the finder takes title, and the true owner's ownership rights are severed. A finder has a duty to make reasonable efforts to locate the true owner, although no expenses must be incurred to satisfy this obligation. As will be explained below, lost property differs from mislaid and abandoned property. If you inadvertently leave your jacket in a classroom after a class, you have mislaid it.

As we see in the next case, a finder who is a trespasser acquires neither possessory nor ownership rights.

Favorite v. Miller
407 A.2d 974
Supreme Court of Connecticut
December 12, 1978

Bogdanski, Associate Justice.
On July 9, 1776, a band of patriots, hearing news of the Declaration of Independence, toppled the equestrian statue of King George III, which was located in Bowling Green Park in lower Manhattan, New York. The statue, of gilded lead, was then hacked apart and the pieces ferried over Long Island Sound and loaded onto wagons at Norwalk, Connecticut, to be hauled some fifty miles northward to Oliver Wolcott's bullet-molding foundry in Litchfield, there to be cast into bullets. On the journey to Litchfield, the wagoners halted at Wilton, Connecticut, and while the patriots were imbibing, the loyalists managed to steal back pieces of the statue. The wagonload of the pieces lifted by the Tories was scattered about in the area of the Davis Swamp in Wilton and fragments of the statue have continued to turn up in that area since that time.

Although the above events have been dramatized in the intervening years, the unquestioned historical facts are: (1) the destruction of the statue; (2) cartage of the pieces to the Wolcott Foundry; (3) the pause at Wilton where part of the load was scattered over the Wilton area by loyalists; and (4) repeated discoveries of fragments over the last century.

In 1972, the defendant, Louis Miller, determined that a part of the statue might be located within property owned by the plaintiffs. On October 16 he entered the area of the Davis Swamp owned by the plaintiffs although he knew it to be private property. With the aid of a metal detector, he discovered a statuary fragment fifteen inches square and weighing twenty pounds which was embedded ten inches below the soil. He dug up this fragment and removed it from the plaintiffs' property. The plaintiffs did not learn that a piece of the statue of King George III had been found on their property until they read about it in the newspaper, long after it had been removed.

In due course, the piece of the statue made its way back to New York City, where the defendant agreed to sell it to the Museum of the City of New York for $5500. The museum continues to hold it pending resolution of this controversy.

In March of 1973, the plaintiffs instituted this action to have the fragment returned to them and the case was submitted to the court on a stipulation of facts. The trial court found the issues for the plaintiffs, from which judgment the defendant appealed to this court. The sole issue presented on appeal is whether the claim of the defendant, as finder, is superior to that of the plaintiffs, as owners of the land upon which the historic fragment was discovered.

Traditionally, when questions have arisen concerning the rights of the finder as against the person upon whose land the property was found, the resolution has turned upon the characterization given the property. Typically, if the property was found to be "lost" or "abandoned," the finder would prevail, whereas if the property was characterized as "mislaid," the owner or occupier of the land would prevail.

Lost property has traditionally been defined as involving an involuntary parting, i.e., where there is no intent on the part of the loser to part with the ownership of the property.

Abandonment, in turn, has been defined as the voluntary relinquishment of ownership of property without reference to any particular person or purpose; i.e., a "throwing away" of the property concerned … while mislaid property is defined as that which is intentionally placed by the owner where he can obtain custody of it, but afterwards forgotten.

It should be noted that the classification of property as "lost," "abandoned," or "mislaid" requires that a court determine the intent or mental state of the unknown party who at some time in the past parted with the ownership or control of the property.

The trial court in this case applied the traditional approach and ruled in favor of the landowners on the ground that the piece of the statue found by Miller was "mislaid." The factual basis for that conclusion is set out in the finding, where the court found that "the loyalists did not wish to have the pieces [in their possession] during the turmoil surrounding the Revolutionary War and hid them in a place where they could resort to them [after the war], but forgot where they put them."

The defendant contends that the finding was made without evidence and that the court's conclusion "is legally impossible now after 200 years with no living claimants to the fragment and the secret of its

burial having died with them." While we cannot agree that the court's conclusion was legally impossible, we do agree that any conclusion as to the mental state of persons engaged in events which occurred over two hundred years ago would be of a conjectural nature and as such does not furnish an adequate basis for determining rights of twentieth-century claimants.

The defendant argues further that his rights in the statue are superior to those of anyone except the true owner (i.e., the British government). He presses this claim on the ground that the law has traditionally favored the finder as against all but the true owner, and that because his efforts brought the statue to light, he should be allowed to reap the benefits of his discovery. In his brief, he asserts: "As with archeologists forever probing and unearthing the past, to guide man for the betterment of those to follow, explorers like Miller deserve encouragement, and reward, in their selfless pursuit of the hidden, the unknown."

There are, however, some difficulties with the defendant's position. The first concerns the defendant's characterization of himself as a selfless seeker after knowledge. The facts in the record do not support such a conclusion. The defendant admitted that he was in the business of selling metal detectors and that he has used his success in finding the statue as advertising to boost his sales of such metal detectors, and that the advertising has been financially rewarding. Further, there is the fact that he signed a contract with the City Museum of New York for the sale of the statuary piece and that he stands to profit thereby.

Moreover, even if we assume his motive to be that of historical research alone, that fact will not justify his entering upon the property of another without permission. It is unquestioned that in today's world even archeologists must obtain permission from owners of property and the government of the country involved before they can conduct their explorations. Similarly, mountaineers must apply for permits, sometimes years in advance of their proposed expeditions. On a more familiar level, backpackers and hikers must often obtain permits before being allowed access to certain of our national parks and forests, even though that land is public and not private. Similarly, hunters and fishermen wishing to enter upon private property must first obtain the permission of the owner before they embark upon their respective pursuits.

Although few cases are to be found in this area of the law, one line of cases which have dealt with this issue has held that except where the trespass is trivial or merely technical, the fact that the finder is trespassing is sufficient to deprive him of his normal preference over the owner of the place where the property was found. The presumption in such cases is that possession of the article found is in the owner of the land and that the finder acquires no rights to the article found.

The defendant, by his own admission, knew that he was trespassing when he entered upon the property of the plaintiffs. He admitted that he was told by Gertrude Merwyn, the librarian of the Wilton Historical Society, *before* he went into the Davis Swamp area, that the land was privately owned and that Mrs. Merwyn recommended that he call the owners, whom she named, and obtain permission before he began his explorations. He also admitted that when he later told Mrs. Merwyn about his discovery, she again suggested that he contact the owners of the property, but that he failed to do so.

In the stipulation of facts submitted to the court, the defendant admitted entering the Davis Swamp property "with the belief that part of the 'King George Statue' ... might be located within said property and

with the intention of removing [the] same if located." The defendant has also admitted that the piece of the statue which he found was embedded in the ground ten inches below the surface and that it was necessary for him to excavate in order to take possession of his find.

In light of those undisputed facts the defendant's trespass was neither technical nor trivial. We conclude that the fact that the property found was embedded in the earth and the fact that the defendant was a trespasser are sufficient to defeat any claim to the property which the defendant might otherwise have had as a finder.

Where the trial court reaches a correct decision but on mistaken grounds, this court has repeatedly sustained the trial court's action if proper grounds exist to support it. The present case falls within the ambit of that principle of law and we affirm the decision of the court below.

There is no error.

Case Questions

1. On what grounds did the trial court hold for the plaintiff?
2. Why did the Supreme Court of Connecticut disagree with the lower court's reasoning?

 Why, in your opinion, should anyone be expected to act "ethically," unless it is in the person's self-interest to do so?

Confusion

Confusion of goods involves the blending or intermingling of **fungible goods**—goods of a similar character that may be exchanged or substituted for one another; for example, wheat, corn, lima beans, or currency (money). Once similar items are mingled, it is impossible to separate the original owner's money or crops from those of others. In such cases each depositor owns an equivalent tonnage or number of bushels of the crop in an elevator or an equivalent dollar amount on deposit with a bank.

Gift

A person who has title to an item can make a gift by voluntarily transferring all rights in the item to another. A person making a gift is called a **donor,**

and the recipient of the gift is called a **donee.** The donor has to have **donative intent**—this means that he or she wants to relinquish all property rights and expects nothing tangible in return. The law requires that a donor make an actual or constructive delivery of the item. This means that if the donor is making a gift of a car, for example, the donor must bring the car to the donee (actual delivery) or present the car keys to the donee (constructive delivery). The donee must accept for a valid gift to occur.

Introduction to *Campbell v. Robinson*

The parties in this case showed great animosity toward one another after the cancellation of their engagement. Matthew Campbell sued seeking, among other things, a court order declaring him to have title to the ring he had given Ashley

Robinson. Matthew also wanted compensation, alleging that after the breakup he had asked Ashley to return the ring and that she had not done so in a timely manner. Ashley responded in kind. She counterclaimed, alleging that Matthew had breached his promise to marry her, for which she was entitled to money damages. She sought additional compensation from Matthew, for her wedding-related expenditures, for the mental anguish he had caused her, and for allegedly having injured her health.

The case was tried to a jury, and about the only thing that Ashley and Matthew could agree on was that he had given her the ring.

Ashley testified that Matthew was responsible for breaking the engagement, but Matthew testified that it was a mutual decision. Matthew testified that he had asked Ashley to return the ring. Ashley claimed that he had told her that she could keep it—despite the fact that they had "broken up."

The trial court ruled that the party not at fault for the breakup was entitled to the ring, further ruled that Ashley would be entitled to money damages if Matthew had "breached the promise to marry," and denied Matthew's other claims.

Both parties asked the court to grant directed verdicts, and both were unsuccessful.

The jury was instructed accordingly to the rulings explained above.

Although the jury found that Matthew had cancelled the engagement (which would mean that Ashley would have title to the ring), it also found that Ashley was not entitled to any damages. Both parties moved for judgment notwithstanding the verdict (JNOV) and for a new trial, and these motions all were denied by the court.

Both parties appealed to the state intermediate court of appeals. You will see as you read Judge Thomas's opinion that the appellate court disagreed with the trial court's assertion that determining which party was at fault for the cancellation of the engagement was the controlling issue in terms of who should have title to the ring. The appellate court asserted that the law of gifts should determine that outcome.

Matthew Campbell v. Ashley Robinson
726 S.E.2d 221
Court of Appeals of South Carolina
May 9, 2012

Thomas, J.
These cross appeals arise out of a broken engagement between Matthew Campbell and Ashley Robinson....

FACTS AND PROCEDURAL HISTORY
Campbell proposed and presented a ring to Robinson in December 2005. In a spring 2006 phone conversation, they agreed to postpone the wedding. The engagement was later cancelled, and a dispute ensued over ownership of the ring.

ISSUES ON APPEAL

1. Did the trial court err in denying Campbell's motion for directed verdict on Robinson's breach of promise to marry action?
2. Did the trial court err in denying Campbell's motions for directed verdict and JNOV on his claims?

3. Did the trial court err in overruling Campbell's objections to the jury charge and verdict form?
4. Did the trial court err in denying Robinson's post-trial motions for her breach of promise to marry action?

CAMPBELL's APPEAL

I. The Action for Breach of Promise to Marry
Campbell argues the trial court erred in denying his motion for directed verdict on Robinson's breach of promise to marry action because South Carolina courts no longer recognize the claim.... We disagree.

Certain heart balm actions similar to breach of promise to marry claims have been abolished.... However, promise to marry actions have not been expressly abolished, and we may not overrule supreme court precedent.... Consequently, we affirm the denial of Campbell's directed verdict motion.

II. Directed Verdict and JNOV

Campbell contends the trial court erred in denying his motions for directed verdict and JNOV because the trial court hinged ownership of the ring upon who was at fault in the engagement's cancellation. We agree that fault does not determine ownership of the ring but affirm the denial of Campbell's motions....

An engagement ring by its very nature is a symbol of the donor's continuing devotion to the donee. Once an engagement is cancelled, the ring no longer holds that significance.... Thus, if a party presents evidence a ring was given in contemplation of marriage, the ring is an engagement ring. As an engagement ring, the gift is impliedly conditioned upon the marriage ... taking place. Until the condition underlying the gift is fulfilled, the attempted gift is unenforceable and must be returned to the donor upon the donor's request....

The person challenging the assertions that the ring is an engagement ring and therefore impliedly conditioned upon marriage has the burden of presenting evidence to overcome those assertions. This burden may be satisfied by presenting evidence showing that the ring was not given in contemplation of marriage—it was not an engagement ring—or was not conditioned upon the marriage. If the parties do not dispute that the ring was originally an engagement ring conditioned upon the marriage, the burden may also be satisfied by presenting evidence establishing the ring subsequently became the challenger's property....

Jurisdictions differ on whether ownership of an engagement ring may be based upon fault in the breakup. Courts that do consider fault generally reason that it is unfair for a person to retain the fruit of a broken promise.... In contrast, courts with a "no-fault" approach often base their decision upon the abolishment of heart balm actions, adoption of no-fault divorce, desire to limit courtroom dramatics, and reduction of the difficulty in determining the issue of what constitutes fault in the decline of a relationship.

We hold that the consideration of fault has no place in determining ownership of an engagement ring. Generally, gift law will dictate who has the legal right to the ring.

... [N]o legal standard exists by which a fact finder can adjudge culpability or fault in a prenuptial breakup.... ("What is fault or the unjustifiable calling off of an engagement?... [S]hould courts be asked to determine which of the following grounds for breaking an engagement is fault or justified? (1) The parties have nothing in common; (2) one party cannot stand prospective in-laws; (3) a minor child of one of the parties is hostile to and will not accept the other party; (4) an adult child of one of the parties will not accept the other party; (5) the parties' pets do not get along;

(6) a party was too hasty in proposing or accepting the proposal; (7) the engagement was a rebound situation which is now regretted; (8) one party has untidy habits that irritate the other; or (9) the parties have religious differences. The list could be endless.") ... ("What fact justifies the breaking of an engagement? The absence of a sense of humor? Differing musical tastes? Differing political views?... They must be approached with intelligent care and should not happen without a decent assurance of success. When either party lacks that assurance, for whatever reason, the engagement should be broken. No justification is needed. Either party may act. Fault, impossible to fix, does not count.").

South Carolina's use of fault in dividing property within the family court's jurisdiction does not mandate the use of the fault approach for determining ownership of engagement rings when the marriage fails to occur. When the family court apportions property based upon fault, the parties in the dispute have a special statutory right in the subject property.... Outside of property apportionment during a divorce, that statutory right does not exist....

... Two of the main purposes of an engagement are to prepare the couple for marriage and test the permanency of their compatibility. In some circumstances, the fault approach may penalize a party who innocently recognizes the couple's incompatibility....

Robinson explicitly characterizes the ring as an engagement ring. However, she has presented evidence that the ring was converted into an absolute gift by testifying Campbell told her to keep the ring after the engagement was cancelled. Because Campbell disputes this contention, the evidence conflicts as to whether the ring was conditioned upon marriage. See *Worrell v. Lathan* ... (noting that a gift is complete when there is "a donative intent to transfer title to the property, a delivery by the donor, and an acceptance by the donee.")... [S]ee also *Smith v. Johnson* ... (holding that "delivery" need not be "manual" but, "so far as the donor can make it so," must only be "some act which indicates a relinquishment of possession and dominion on the part of the donor in behalf of the donee.")... Accordingly, ownership of the ring was a jury issue, and a directed verdict on Campbell's claims for declaratory judgment and claim and delivery were not warranted.

We also affirm the trial court's denial of Campbell's motions for directed verdict and JNOV on his restitution claim. Restitution is an equitable remedy sought to prevent unjust enrichment.... Thus, "the plaintiff must show: (1) that he conferred a nongratuitous benefit on the defendant; (2) that the defendant realized some value from the benefit; and (3) that it would be inequitable for the defendant to retain the benefit without paying the plaintiff its value."... To be conferred nongratuitously, the plaintiff must confer the benefit either "(1) at the defendant's request or (2) in circumstances where the plaintiff reasonably relies on the defendant to pay for the benefit and the defendant understands or ought to understand that the plaintiff expects compensation and looks to him for payment."...

Here, the record does not contain evidence Campbell presented the ring to Robinson at her request. Nor does the record contain evidence Campbell permitted Robinson to keep the ring at her request or that he reasonably relied upon her to pay for the ring. Thus, Campbell was not entitled to a directed verdict or JNOV on his restitution claim.

III. Verdict Form and Jury Charge

Campbell claims the trial court erred in denying his motion for a new trial absolute because the verdict form and jury charge were erroneous. In light of our rulings above, we agree....

Here, the trial court provided an erroneous jury charge and verdict form. The evidence presented a jury issue of whether the ring was a conditional or absolute gift. While the charge instructed the jury that the gift was conditional, it did not explain that the gift could become absolute. Moreover, the jury charge and verdict form hinged ownership of the ring upon fault in the breakup.

The focus on fault in the jury charge and verdict form undoubtedly affected the verdict. Fault was the only question posed to the jury to determine ownership of the ring, and the jury's finding on the question was adverse to Campbell. Thus, his actions for declaratory judgment and claim and delivery were prejudiced by the jury charge and verdict form. He is entitled to a new trial on those claims....

ROBINSON's APPEAL

Robinson argues the trial court erred in declining to grant her JNOV to award her damages ... and a new trial as to damages because the jury's verdict was inconsistent....

We affirm....

CONCLUSION

For the aforementioned reasons, we affirm the issues as they relate to Campbell's action for restitution and Robinson's action for breach of promise to marry. We reverse and remand for a new trial on Campbell's actions for declaratory judgment and claim and delivery.

Case Questions

1. According to the appellate court, what errors were committed at trial by the trial court?
2. Why was ownership of the ring an issue for the jury?

Inheritance

A person can acquire property from the estate of a deceased person. This is called an inheritance. When a person making a will—a **testator** (man) or **testatrix** (woman)—makes a bequest of property, the title to the item will be transferred from a deceased's estate. If the person died without a will (**intestate**), property is transferred according to a statutory plan enacted by the state legislature (called a **statute of descent**).

BAILMENT

A **bailment** relationship exists when one person (called the **bailor**) delivers personal property to another person (called the **bailee**) without conveying title. Although the possession of the object is transferred in a bailment, the bailor intends to recover possession of the bailed object, and thus does not part with the title. When a person borrows, loans, or rents a DVD, or leaves one's lawn mower or car for repair—for example, a bailment is created.

Some bailments primarily benefit only one person, either the bailee or the bailor. These are called gratuitous bailments. For example, the bailee primarily benefits when he or she borrows a lawn mower from a neighbor. Other bailments primarily benefit the bailor, for example, when he or she asks to leave a motor vehicle in the bailee's garage for a month. Some bailments are mutually beneficial, such as when the bailor leaves shoes for repair at a shoe repair shop or takes clothes to the dry cleaners.

Some bailments are created by contract, such as when a person rents a car from a car rental company. Other bailments are created by a delivery and acceptance of the object, such as when one student loans a textbook to another student. Here there is no contract, because there is no consideration.

All types of bailments involve rights and obligations. In a mutual benefit bailment, the bailee has the duty to exercise reasonable care toward the bailed object. The bailee is not allowed to use the bailed object for his benefit, but may work on the object for the benefit of the bailor. The bailor's duties include paying the bailee and warning the bailee of any hidden dangers associated with the bailed object.

With a gratuitous bailment for the benefit of the bailor, the bailee must exercise at least slight care and store the bailed object in the agreed-upon manner. There is no compensation or quid pro quo involved.

With respect to a bailment for the benefit of the bailee, a bailee must exercise a high degree of care. Since the bailor is acting solely out of friendship and is not receiving any benefit, and the bailee is allowed to use the bailed object without charge, the bailee must use the bailed object in the proper manner and return it in good condition when the bailment period ends. The bailee is responsible in negligence for any damages caused to the bailed object. As we see in the next case, the bailor can end the bailment period at any time and ask for the return of the bailed object.

Introduction to *Dinnes v. Martin*

Norma Dinnes inherited some of her late grandmother's furniture, a china doll, and a sewing machine when her grandmother died in Iowa. Norma, although appreciative, had a problem—she had no place to store the inherited items. So she was happy to accept her Uncle Lewis Martin's kind offer to store these items for her at no cost at his farm, which also was located in Iowa. The inherited property was subsequently stored in a "cottage" located on the premises of the Martin farm. Norma's items were intermingled within the cottage with personal property belonging to the Martins. Over the course of the next thirty years Norma periodically visited the Martins at the farm and looked in the cottage at her property, and things seemed to be fine. The last visit was in 2005.

Her aunt, Lewis Martin's wife, died in 2006, and her Uncle Lewis died in 2009. Norma did not take any action with respect to her inherited property until 2010, when she filed a claim for $18,000 in conjunction with the probate of her uncle's estate. Norma's claim was rejected by the executor of the uncle's estate who explained that "The items stored by [Lewis, the uncle,] were placed in a small cottage … and much of that property has been damaged and destroyed by rainfall and by wild animals during the past thirty years." The executor then asked the probate court to dismiss Norma's claim.

Dinnes v. Martin
817 N.W.2d 31
Court of Appeals of Iowa
April 25, 2012

Doyle, J.
Norma Dinnes appeals the probate court's denial of her bailment claim against the estate of Lewis R. Martin. She contends her property stored by the decedent was damaged and lost due to the decedent's negligence. She requested return of her damaged property and monetary damages for repairs and replacement of her lost property….

I. BACKGROUND FACTS AND PROCEEDINGS
Norma Dinnes's grandmother passed away in 1975. Thereafter, Norma inherited several pieces

of her grandmother's furniture, as well as a china doll and a sewing machine. At the time of her grandmother's death, Norma lived out of state and did not have a place to store her inherited property.

Lewis and Virginia Martin, Norma's uncle and his wife, owned a farm in Marshall County, Iowa. Virginia enjoyed antiques, and she refinished furniture. The Martins' farm had outbuildings, including one referred to as "the cottage" and one referred to as "the milking parlor." Virginia stored her own antiques and furniture in the cottage.

The Martins had a close relationship with Norma, and they volunteered to store her inherited property in the cottage. Norma was aware Virginia stored her antiques there and that their property would be commingled. Norma accepted their offer, and Norma's father, John Dinnes, moved the property into the cottage. The Martins never charged Norma for storing her property nor did they use her property.

Norma visited the Martins over the years, and she checked on her property when she was there. Norma admitted the last time she saw her property at the Martins' farm was in approximately 2005, thirty years after the Martins volunteered to store the property. She admitted the cottage was full of furniture and she could not see all of her property, but the items she did see were in satisfactory condition. She believed her property was being cared for in the same manner as Virginia's property.

Virginia died in January 2006. Norma did not file a claim in Virginia's estate, nor did she request her property be returned to her at that time. Lewis died three years later in August 2009. After filing a petition for probate of Lewis's will in September 2009, the Martins' son, Robert Martin, was named the executor of Lewis's estate as proposed in Lewis's will.

In January 2010, Norma filed a claim against the estate for $18,000 "based upon property held by executor of estate." The estate denied her claim stating, among other things: "The items stored by [Lewis] were placed in a small cottage ... and much of that property has been damaged and destroyed by rainfall and by wild animals during the past thirty years." The estate then filed a motion to dismiss Norma's claim.

The parties reached an agreement to allow Norma to inspect property in the estate to determine if any of the property belonged to her, and the trial scheduled for May 2010 was cancelled. However, the parties were unable to reach an agreement thereafter. Norma resisted the estate's motion to dismiss and affirmatively stated the Martins "entered into a voluntary agreement in 1975 to allow storage of personal property belonging to [Norma] creating a legal bailment between family ... without monetary consideration." Norma asserted Lewis refused financial compensation from her, "indicating his appreciation for her visits and medical advice."

Trial began in August 2010 before district court judge Michael Moon. Robert testified his mother and his sister had kept property in the cottage and their property was intermingled with Norma's property. He further testified that the cottage's condition had deteriorated over the years; part of the roof had collapsed, and there were holes in the walls that allowed wildlife in. Robert testified that much of the property

in the cottage was covered in raccoon feces and damaged from wildlife and water. After Lewis's death, Robert moved the salvageable items in the cottage to the milking parlor and disposed of the rest.

Robert testified Norma spent little time with Lewis after Virginia died. He testified Lewis was concerned about Norma's items deteriorating, but Robert himself did not contact Norma. Although he identified two cabinets and a dresser that belonged to Norma, due to the commingling of the property, he did not know what remaining property belonged to Norma or his mother. For instance, Norma asserted that four hardback chairs she inherited were placed in storage at the Martins' farm. Robert found thirty-five different hardback chairs. Norma asserted a claim to a sewing machine; Robert found three sewing machines in the milking parlor. Robert testified he and his siblings did not trust Norma and believed she would claim property that was not hers and deprive the estate of assets.

Norma conversely testified that she kept in contact with the Martins and regularly asked about her property. She stated she was told by Virginia and Martin her property was fine, she did not need to compensate them, and she did not need to pick the items up. She testified Lewis had told her the cottage's roof was leaking and he and his grandchildren moved her property to the milking parlor. She testified she volunteered to pay for the roof repairs, but Lewis refused. She testified that had she known of the deteriorating and damaged condition of her property, she would have moved her items from the Martins' farm.

John, Norma's father, testified that Norma inherited property from his mother, and he and his brother Fred placed the items in the cottage. He testified he would know which items were his mother's if he saw them again. The court then requested John to go out to the Martins' farm and look over the antiques to determine what had belonged to his mother. On the record, the court stated:

If John could ... go through those items and then these other three, the dresser and the two cabinets, we're going to get those back.... [W]e have to get that stuff picked up and moved out of there together with whatever John identifies that's [Norma's]."

Robert agreed that was fair, and Judge Moon entered an order for John to go out the farm and identify the items. The judge encouraged the parties to cooperate in allowing Norma to remove her property from the Martins' farm so the issues could be narrowed. The parties were to report back to the court.

John identified two more pieces of furniture as belonging to his mother, a bed frame with headboard and a dining table. Other items listed by Norma that

Robert thought could possibly be in the milking parlor, such as the sewing machine and hardwood chairs, were determined by John not to belong to his mother. The remaining items claimed by Norma, such as the china doll, were not found at the Martins' farm.

The parties attempted to make arrangements for Norma to pick up her property, but ultimately could not reach an agreement. In September 2010, Norma asked for further proceedings to set a time for delivery of the property and for damages for the cost of repairs and replacement of the damaged property. Additionally, Norma filed a motion to amend the amount of her claim from $18,000 to $27,255.

Trial resumed in February 2011 before district court judge Carl Baker. The transcript from the first day of trial in August was admitted into evidence. The parties again testified similarly as before. Norma had new estimates on the value of her property from visiting antique shops and reviewing antique books.

The court denied Norma's claim. Noting the parties were in agreement that a bailment relationship had been created, the court found Lewis was a gratuitous bailee and the damage and loss of Norma's property "was not due to a violation of the standard of care to be met by [Lewis]." Robert was not ordered to return the five items identified as Norma's property at the Martins' farm.

Thereafter, Norma filed a motion to amend or enlarge the court's findings and conclusions.... She requested her property be returned and the estate be ordered to pay her $27,255 for the diminished value of the five recovered items and $17,422 for the missing items. The estate resisted, and the district court denied her motion.

Norma now appeals....

II. SCOPE AND STANDARDS OF REVIEW
Our review of law actions is for correction of errors at law....

III. DISCUSSION
On appeal, Norma contends the district court erred in his application of law to the facts.... She ... contends the court erred "by not finding Robert liable under Iowa Code [section] 633.158 [(2011)] or constructive bailment law."...

A. Duty of Care
... Here, the parties agree that a bailment was established.

A bailment denotes delivery of personalty by one person [the bailor] to another [the bailee], for a specific purpose beneficial to bailee or bailor or both, upon a contract, express or implied, that the conditions shall be faithfully executed and the personalty returned to bailor, or duly accounted for when the specific purpose of the bailment shall have been accomplished, or kept by the bailee until claimed by the bailor.... A bailment "can also arise by operation of law when justice requires. Thus, when a person comes into lawful possession of personal property of another without an underlying agreement, the possessor may become a constructive bailee."... Generally, "the bailment contract is governed by the same rules of law that govern other contracts." 8A Am.Jur.2d Bailments §29, at 553 (2009)....

There are three types of bailments: (1) those for the sole benefit of the bailor, known as a gratuitous bailment; (2) those for the sole benefit of the bailee; and (3) those for the mutual benefit ... of both.... In a meld of contract and tort law ... our case law concerning bailment relationships holds that the type of bailment established determines the degree of care the bailee is required to exercise in caring for the bailor's property while it is in their possession....

A bailment for the mutual benefit of the parties arises when an individual takes the personal property of another into his or her care or custody in exchange for some monetary payment or other benefit. Such a bailment occurs whenever both parties to the bailment contract receive some benefit flowing from the transaction.... Where the bailment is for mutual benefit, the fact the property was damaged while in the bailee's possession creates a presumption the damage is due to the bailee's lack of care.... This presumption, along with proof of the amount of loss, establishes a prima facie case for the bailor.... The bailee must then rebut the presumption "by showing the damage occurred through something consistent with due care on his part...."

This is not the case for a gratuitous bailment where "the bailee receives no compensation, as when one borrows a friend's car." Black's Law Dictionary 137 (7th ed. 1999).... "There is inherent justice in the requirement that one who undertakes to perform a duty gratuitously should not be under the same measure of obligation as one who enters upon the same undertaking for pay...."

The general doctrine, as stated by text writers and in judicial decisions, is that gratuitous bailees of another's property are not responsible for its loss, unless guilty of gross negligence in its keeping. But gross negligence in such cases is nothing more than a failure to bestow the care which the property in its situation demands. The omission of the reasonable care required is the negligence which creates the liability; and whether this existed is a question of fact for the jury to determine, or by the court where a jury is waived.... A gratuitous bailee is "not responsible simply because the [bailor's] property was lost."...

B. Type of Bailment

Norma ... argues the district court erred in not finding the bailment relationship was constructive or one for mutual benefit of the parties.... Here, the district court found:

> Norma left the property on the Martin farm for over [thirty-five] years. She rarely checked on the condition of the property. Norma knew the property had been moved from the cottage to the milking parlor in order to avoid water damage. Norma did not instruct Lewis on how to care for her property....
>
> Norma never used the furniture she inherited.... Norma knew that the property was stored in buildings on the Martins' farm. They were older buildings which were not in good condition. Norma's property was stored with property owned by Virginia Martin in the same buildings.

Additionally, the court found:

> It is clear that Lewis Martin did not receive any compensation for storing Norma's property over the [thirty-five]-year period it was on his farm in the cottage or milk parlor. Lewis never used

Norma's property. The property was stored on the Martin farm because Norma did not have adequate storage space elsewhere.

We find the district court's factual findings are supported by substantial evidence. We agree with the district court's conclusion that "[t]he evidence supports the conclusion that Norma was the sole beneficiary of this bailment agreement and that Lewis Martin was therefore a gratuitous bailee." We find the court correctly stated the standard of care required in gratuitous bailments—gross negligence, and whether gross negligence existed in this case was a question of fact for the court, the trier of fact, to determine. The court determined the damage to and disappearance of Norma's property was not due to a violation of the standard of care to be met by Lewis Martin. We find no error in this determination. However, because the parties agree the relationship was a bailment, Robert should return the property determined to be Norma's to her....

IV. CONCLUSION

We agree with the district court's denial of Norma's claim for damages for lost and damaged property, and affirm upon that issue. However, there is no dispute the estate has in its possession five items that belong to Norma. She requested the items be returned. We remand for an order providing for the return of Norma's property to her.

Case Questions

1. What type of bailment was this?
2. Why did the court conclude that Norma was entitled to the return of any property that remained at the farm?

CHAPTER SUMMARY

The chapter began with a historical overview of real property law and a discussion of how property is classified. Intellectual property—the law of trademarks, patents, and copyrights—was next. Readers also learned about the common forms of property ownership—severalty, joint tenancies, tenancies in common, and tenancies by the entireties. The

discussion then turned to the controversial U.S. Supreme Court case of *Kelo v. New London,* and what happened in the aftermath of that decision. Special emphasis was given to the government's use of the power of eminent domain to transfer property from one private owner to another. The section on real property followed, where students learned about estates in land, easements, licenses, covenants, adverse possession, and the recording system.

The discussion of personal property included eight different ways in which personal property is acquired: purchase, creation, capture, accession, finding, confusion, gift, and inheritance. The chapter concluded with an overview of the law of bailments.

CHAPTER QUESTIONS

1. Jackson Chapel Church believed it had ownership rights over a small parcel of land that the church's neighbors, the Mobleys, had begun to develop. The church filed suit seeking ejectment, declaratory judgment, and injunctive relief. The trial court ruled that the church was entitled to a portion of the disputed parcel because it had acquired title by adverse possession. The portion not used by the church still belonged to the Mobleys. The Mobleys appealed to the Georgia Supreme Court. They claimed that their remote predecessor in title, while building on a small portion of the parcel decades ago, had a paper title to the entire parcel. They argued that this gave them the right to possess constructively the entire parcel, despite the trial court's adverse possession ruling in favor of the church. Should the appellate court affirm or reverse the trial court's adverse possession ruling regarding the portion of the Mobleys' parcel that had been used continuously for over 100 years by the church.

   Mobley v. Jackson Chapel Church, 636 S.E.2d 535 (2006)

2. C/R TV, Inc. is a cable television company that sought to provide its services to a private housing subdivision (Shannondale). The subdivision had contracted with Mid-Atlantic Cable Services, Inc., one of C/R's competitors, to provide exclusive cable services to Shannondale. C/R, however, believed it had a lawful right to string cable on existing telephone poles in the subdivision, pursuant to a 1972 licensing agreement with Potomac Edison. Shannondale had granted easements to Potomac Edison for electrical and telephone services in most of the subdivision in 1955 and in part of the development in 1991. The

   Shannondale president threatened a trespass action against C/R TV when he learned that the company had installed over six miles of cable wiring in the subdivision. C/R TV responded by bringing a declaratory judgment action against Shannondale. The trial judge ruled in favor of Shannondale, concluding that the 1955 easements were not "sufficiently broad to provide for television cable facilities." The trial court did rule that the part of the subdivision covered by the 1991 easements could be serviced by the plaintiff. C/R TV appealed. Should the 1955 easements, which were granted to Potomac Edison "for the purpose of installation, erection, maintenance, repair and operation of electric transmission and distribution pole lines, and electric service lines, with telephone lines thereon," be interpreted so as to permit Potomac Edison's licensee the right to install cable-television wiring over Shannondale's objections?

   C/R TV, Inc. v. Shannondale, Inc., 27 F.3d (1994)

3. Tracy Price took her English bulldog to Dr. Nancy Brown, a veterinarian, for surgery, which was performed on August 30, 1991. When Tracy visited her dog the next evening at the veterinary hospital, the animal appeared groggy and was panting heavily. Tracy requested that the dog be monitored all day and night and was assured that this would be done. The dog died on the morning of September 1. Tracy filed suit on May 4, 1993. She claimed that she had entrusted her dog to Dr. Brown based on Brown's assurances that appropriate surgery would be performed and the dog returned to her in a healthy condition.

Tracy demanded damages in the amount of $1,200, the fair market value of the animal. She claimed that her dog had been entrusted to the veterinarian for surgical treatment and that it had died while in the doctor's care as a result of the doctor's negligence. Has Tracy stated a cause of action for breach of a bailment agreement?

Price v. Brown, 680 A.2d 1149 (1996)

4. The Kingsmen, a rock band formed in 1958, recorded a rock classic entitled "Louie Louie." The band members contracted with Spector Records in 1968, which provided that the band would receive 9 percent of the future licensing fees and profits generated by the song. Spector subsequently assigned its rights under the agreement to Gusto Records and G.M.L., Inc. In 1993, the Kingsmen sued Gusto, G.M.L., and Highland Music for rescission of the contract and back royalties calculated from the date that the suit was filed. They sought rescission because that would result in the restoration of their title to and possession of the master. The band alleged that the defendants and their predecessors in title had for thirty years failed to pay the band its contracted share of royalties. The defendants argued that the action was barred by the four-year statute of limitations, and that the plaintiffs were not entitled to income produced pursuant to licenses that predated the rescission. The trial court ruled in favor of the Kingsmen. The defendants appealed to the U.S. Court of Appeals (9th Circuit). Should the Kingsmen prevail on appeal?

Peterson v. Highland Music, Nos. 95-56393, 97-55597, and 97-55599 (1998)

5. Hiram Hoeltzer, a professional art restorer, sought declaratory relief to quiet title to a large mural that once was affixed to the walls of the Stamford High School. This mural had been painted as part of the Works Progress Administration (WPA) in 1934. Workers removed the mural when the high school was renovated in the summer of 1970. They cut it into thirty pieces and placed it on top of a heap of construction debris, adjacent to a Dumpster. This was done despite oral and written requests from school officials that the mural be taken down and preserved. A 1970 graduate of Stamford High, recognizing the value of the mural, placed the mural pieces into his car and took them home. The student took the mural to Karel Yasko, a federal official responsible for supervising the restoration of WPA artwork. Yasko suggested that the mural be taken to Hiram Hoeltzer. In 1980, city officials and other interested people began contacting Hoeltzer about the mural. In 1986, the city formally wrote to Hoeltzer and claimed title. Hoeltzer, however, who had retained possession of the mural for ten years, claimed that he was the rightful owner of the mural. Who has legal title to the mural? Why?

Hoeltzer v. City of Stamford, Conn., 722 F. Supp. 1106 (1989)

6. Leonard and Bernard Kapiloff are stamp collectors. In 1976, they purchased two sets of stamps worth $150,400. Robert Ganter found the stamps in a dresser he had purchased for $30 in a used furniture store in 1979 or 1980. Ganter had taken the stamps to an auction house, and they were listed for sale in a nationally distributed catalogue that was read by the Kapiloff brothers. The brothers contacted Ganter and demanded the return of the stamps. Ganter refused. The brothers then contacted the FBI, which took physical possession of the stamps. The brothers then brought a replevin action against Ganter for the stamps and asked the court for a declaratory judgment that they were the true owners of the stamps. The person who originally sold the brothers the stamps supported the brothers' allegations that the stamps Ganter found were the same stamps that had belonged to the Kapiloffs. Who is the owner of the stamps?

Ganter v. Kapiloff, 516 A.2d 611 (1986)

7. The case of *Clevenger v. Peterson Construction Company* turned on the question of whether

forty-four mobile trailers should be classified as personal property or fixtures. The trailers had axles, although they were without hitches or wheels. They were positioned on concrete blocks and not on permanent foundations, and were connected to utilities with flexible hoses. Which classification is more appropriate?

Clevenger v. Peterson Construction Company, Inc., 542 P.2d 470 (1975)

8. The District of Columbia enacted an ordinance that made it unlawful for any hotel to exclude any licensed taxicab driver from picking up passengers at hotel taxicab stands. The Washington Hilton did not have to operate a taxicab stand on its property but elected to do so for the convenience of its guests. The hotel was dissatisfied with the quality of service provided by some of the taxicab drivers and with the cleanliness of some of their vehicles. The hotel wanted to discriminate against some taxis in favor of others. It wanted to require cab drivers to obtain permits and pay an annual fee to use the hotel's taxicab stand. The city's attorney was consulted about these plans and ruled that they violated the Taxicab Act. Does this ordinance constitute a taking of the hotel's property by the District?

Hilton Washington Corporation v. District of Columbia, 777 F.2d 47 (1985)

9. Terry Bohn presented Tommie Louise Lowe with a ring in 1974 when they became engaged to be married. Tommie had a continuing series of strokes over the next ten years, and the marriage never took place. She still possessed the engagement ring at the time of her death in 1984. After her death, Terry brought suit against Tommie's estate to recover the engagement ring. Who has title to the ring?

A Matter of Estate of Lowe, 379 N.W.2d 485 (1985)

10. Robert Lehman and Aki Eveline Lehman were married in 1964. They separated in 1971. They became divorced in 1976. At the time of the separation, Aki retained possession of forty-three art objects that were in the house. Robert and Aki each claimed ownership rights to these objects. Robert claimed that forty-two of the items were either purchased by him or given to him by his father. One item was given to him by Aki. Aki claimed ownership of the items as a result of her purchases made with joint funds, as well as a result of gifts from Robert and Robert's father. Aki took all forty-three items to Paris when she and their children moved there in 1972. Robert demanded that Aki return his property. When she refused, he filed suit against Aki for replevin, conversion, and breach of bailment. At the time the lawsuit was filed, only thirteen items were still in Aki's possession. Aki testified at trial that she didn't know what had happened to the thirty missing items. The court determined that Robert was the exclusive owner of forty of the forty-three items, and Robert and Aki jointly owned the remaining three items. What relief will the court order? Why?

Lehman v. Lehman, 591 F. Supp 1523 (1984)

NOTES

1. P.C. Hoffer, *Law and People in Colonial America* (Baltimore: Johns Hopkins University Press, 1982), pp. 19–24; D. H. Flaherty, *Essays in the History of Early American Law* (Chapel Hill, NC: Institute of Early American History and Culture, 1969), pp. 272–273; B. Schwartz, *The Law in America* (New York: McGraw-Hill Book Co., 1974), pp. 8–18; M. Horwitz, *The Transformation of American Law 1780–1860* (Cambridge, MA: Harvard University Press, 1977), pp. 4–6.

2. Horwitz, pp. 7–9, 84.

3. L. Salmon, *Women and the Law of Property in Early America* (Chapel Hill: University of North Carolina Press, 1986), pp. 18–22.

4. Ibid., pp. 14–15, 22–25.

5. W. Hurst, *Law and the Conditions of Freedom in the Nineteenth Century* (Madison: University of Wisconsin Press, 1967), p. 8.

6. W. E. Nelson, *Americanization of the Common Law* (Cambridge, MA: Harvard University Press, 1975), p. 47; Horwitz, p. 102.

7. Horwitz, p. 35.

8. Nelson, p. 159; Horwitz, p. 36.

9. Horwitz, p. 102; Hurst, pp. 28–29.

10. Hurst, pp. 24–25.

11. *Lochner v. New York,* 198 U.S. 45 (1905).

12. The Uniform Commercial Code is not uniformly adopted from state to state. Each state legislature decides whether to adopt the Uniform Commercial Code, and the extent to which the particular state accepts or modifies its terms. Other differences can arise from judicial interpretations.

13. Many jurisdictions only recognize tenancy by the entirety in conjunction with real property.

14. There are two exceptions to this general rule. A good-faith purchaser of bearer bonds can take title from a thief, and a buyer in the ordinary course of business who purchases goods from a merchant can take title even if the merchant obtained the items from a thief. Public policy reasons support these exceptions because it is very important to the economy that people who buy goods from merchants can rely on the sellers' claims of title to the goods.

15. *Seattle Audubon Society v. Doug Sutherland,* No. C06-1608MJP (W.D. Wash. Aug. 1, 2007).

16. *U.S. v. Causby,* 328 U.S. 256 (1946).

XIII

Administrative Law and Administrative Agencies

CHAPTER OBJECTIVES

1. *Understand the reasons for the creation of administrative agencies.*
2. *Explain the principal ways that federal administrative agencies are structured.*
3. *Explain the importance of an agency's enabling act.*
4. *Describe the powers typically delegated to administrative agencies.*
5. *Understand the limited role of judicial review of administrative decisions.*

A discussion of the U.S. legal system would not be complete without an examination of the government's use of statutory law and administrative rules to regulate business practices. This chapter addresses administrative law and the role of administrative agencies.

THE RISE OF ADMINISTRATIVE AGENCIES

Administrative agencies have existed at the federal level since the early 1800s, when Congress created the U.S. Patent Office (1802),[1] the Bureau of Indian Affairs (1824),[2] and the Army Corps of Engineers (1824).[3] The greatest growth occurred after 1900, however, when approximately two-thirds of current agencies were created.[4] Before President Franklin Roosevelt's New Deal, this country operated on the premise that the federal government should be kept relatively small. That model of government changed during the 1930s in response to the serious social and economic problems associated with the Great Depression. Newly created agencies included the Federal Deposit Insurance Corporation (1933), the Tennessee Valley Authority (1933), the Federal Communications Commission (1933), the Securities and Exchange Commission (1934), and the National Labor Relations Board (1935). More recently, Congress has created agencies to address important social and public welfare goals, such as the Equal Employment Opportunity Commission (1965), the Occupational Safety and Health Review Commission (1970), and the Environmental Protection Agency (1970). These and a multitude of other commissions, boards, authorities, and departments administer legislation that affects many aspects of daily life (see Figure 13.1).

The enactment of the **Administrative Procedure Act (APA)** in 1946 helped to improve and strengthen the administrative regulatory process in the federal system and served as a model for states as well. The APA requirements vis-à-vis rule making, for example, were very influential.

Today, regulatory bodies are well established at both the state and the local levels of government. State administrative agencies monitor environmental pollution, license drivers, determine automobile insurance rates, and oversee public utilities. They also regulate a wide range of professions and occupations, including hairdressers, barbers, teachers, doctors, lawyers, and psychologists. At the local level, administrative agencies operate zoning boards, housing authorities, water and sewer commissions, and historical commissions.

This chapter is concerned with the legal framework for administrative law. It does not include political analyses of the role that ideology and resources play in agency decision making. Nor does this chapter focus on process questions, such as how administrative agencies decide which of competing policy alternatives will be adopted. These most interesting issues are often addressed in conjunction with political science courses.

ORGANIZATION AND CLASSIFICATION OF FEDERAL AGENCIES

Administrative agencies are commonly classified in terms of their organizational structure. Agencies that are organized into commissions and boards and directed by commissioners include the Federal Maritime Commission (FMC), the Federal Reserve Board (FRB), the Interstate Commerce Commission (ICC), the National Labor Relations Board (NLRB), the Nuclear Regulatory Commission (NRC), and the Securities and Exchange Commission (SEC). (See, for example, the SEC organizational chart in Figure 13.2) Agencies that are structured as cabinet-level departments or administrations and are headed by secretaries or administrators include the Department of the Interior, the Department of Agriculture, the Department of Labor, the Department of Homeland Security, and executive agencies such as the Environmental Protection Agency (EPA). (The EPA organizational chart can be seen in Figure 13.3.)

Commissioners, cabinet-level secretaries, and agency head administrators are nominated by the president and are subject to Senate confirmation. In general, commissions and boards are considered to be independent agencies because the commissioners do not serve at the pleasure of the president and can only be removed for cause, such as neglect of duty or inefficiency. In addition, Congress often requires that these agencies be bipartisan. The SEC, for example, has five members. The chairman is chosen by the president and normally is of the president's party. Because the SEC is a bipartisan agency, two Democrats and two Republicans will be chosen for the remaining four seats. Each commissioner serves a five-year staggered term; one term expires each June. Agencies headed by cabinet secretaries and head administrators are not independent, and their leaders serve at the pleasure of the president.

Functions of Administrative Agencies

Administrative agencies came into existence because legislative bodies recognized that they

THE GOVERNMENT OF THE UNITED STATES

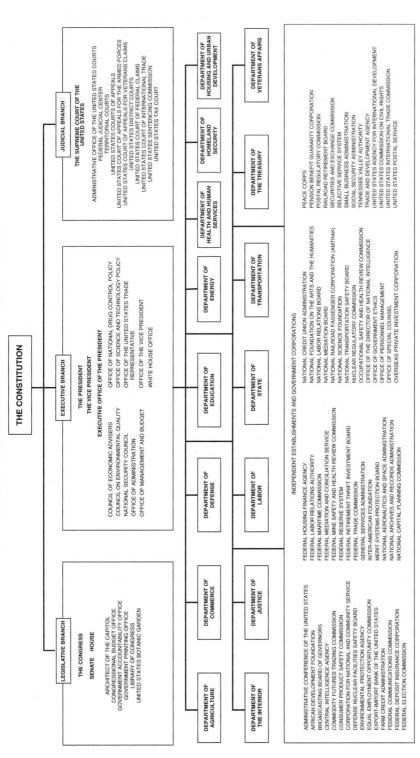

FIGURE 13.1 The Government of the United States

Source: Office of the Federal Register, National Archives and Records Administration, U.S. Government Manual, 2012, p. 22.

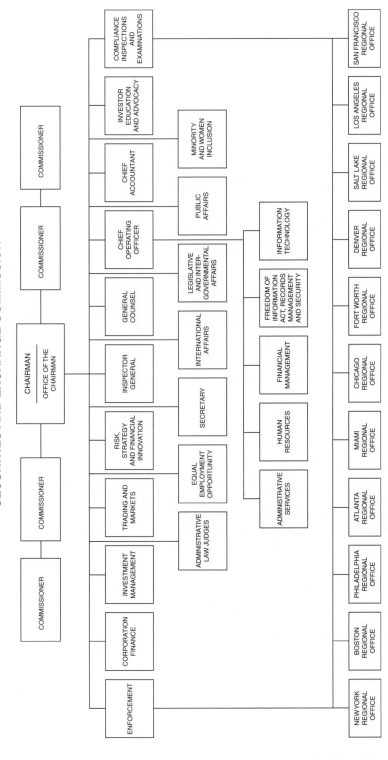

FIGURE 13.2 Securities and Exchange Commission

Source: Office of the Federal Register, National Archives and Records Administration, U.S. Government Manual, 2012, p. 450.

ENVIRONMENTAL PROTECTION AGENCY

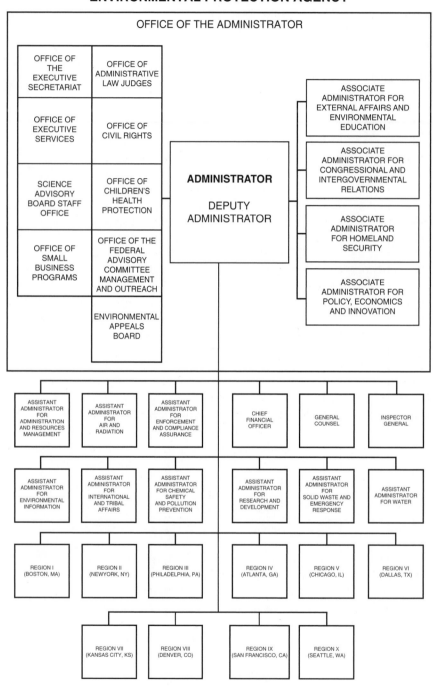

F I G U R E   13.3   Environmental Protection Agency

Source: Office of the Federal Register, National Archives and Records Administration, U.S. Government Manual, 2012, p. 336.

could not achieve desired economic and social goals within the existing governmental structure. Although legislatures could provide general policy direction, they possessed limited subject matter expertise and could not devote continuing attention to the multitude of problems that confront our modern society. Agencies, on the other hand, can assemble experts who focus on one area and work toward achieving legislatively determined objectives.

Legislatures establish an administrative agency by enacting a statute called an **enabling act.** In addition to creating the agency, this act determines its organizational structure, defines its functions and powers, and establishes basic operational standards and guidelines. These standards and guidelines help reviewing courts control the abuse of discretion. Courts also use written directives to assess whether an agency is operating according to the legislature's intent. Administrative agencies also can be created by executive orders authorized by statute.

Agencies perform a variety of functions. For example, they monitor businesses and professions in order to prevent the use of unfair methods of competition and the use of deceptive practices; they help ensure that manufacturers produce pure medications and that food products are safe to consume; and they function to protect society from environmental pollution and insider-stock-trading practices.

ADMINISTRATIVE AGENCY POWERS

Administrative agencies regulate individual and business decision making by exercising legislatively delegated **rule-making, investigative,** and **adjudicative powers.** Although the separation-of-powers doctrine states that the legislative, executive, and judicial functions of government should not exist in the same person or group of persons, the courts have ruled that combining such functions within a single agency does not conflict with the doctrine. Even though a wide range of powers may be delegated to an agency in its enabling act, there are checks on its activities. The creator of the agency, which is

generally the legislature, retains the power to eliminate it or to alter the rules governing it. In addition, agency decisions are subject to judicial review.

Rule-Making Power

The rule-making power of administrative agencies covers a vast range of business and government functions. Rule making often is referred to as the quasi-legislative function of administrative agencies. Agencies that have been granted rule-making powers are authorized to make, alter, or repeal rules and regulations to the extent specified in their enabling statutes. The enabling acts set general standards, authorize the agencies to determine the content of the regulations, and provide general sanctions for noncompliance with the rules. A federal agency possessing the rule-making power is obliged to comply with duly established procedures when making and promulgating rules, and the rules themselves must be necessary for the agency to fulfill its statutory duties.

There are essentially three types of administrative rules: substantive, interpretive, and procedural.

Substantive rules are used to establish and implement policies that assist an agency in accomplishing its statutorily established objectives. Substantive rules normally apply prospectively but not retroactively. If a federal agency properly exercises its rule-making power in developing and promulgating substantive rules and the rules are necessary to achieving the objectives established for it by Congress in the enabling act, the rules will have the same legal force and effect as a statute. The *notice-and-comment process* (which is explained below) is the most common procedure used when agencies develop and promulgate substantive rules. Courts generally uphold substantive rules if they are satisfied that the agency has examined the issues, appropriately reached its decision, followed established procedures, and acted within the scope of its authority.

An **interpretive rule** is used to explain an agency's interpretation of an ambiguous statute, or its understanding of the meaning of an important term that Congress has neglected to define. Interpretive rules are not to be used to make substantive policy changes. Because of an APA exemption, agencies need not follow the notice-and-comment procedures when developing and promulgating interpretive rules. Although interpretive rules are not enforceable to the same extent as laws, courts will often find interpretive rules persuasive if the agency has relied on its own expertise and experience in the rule's development and the agency's actions are within its statutory scope of authority.

Procedural rules are developed to establish standard operating procedures within an agency. These process-oriented rules are devoid of substantive content, and agencies are exempted by the APA from compliance with the notice-and-comment procedures.

Formal and Informal Rule Making

Congress sometimes specifies in an agency's enabling statute that formal rule-making procedures must be followed. The procedural requirements for formal rule making are found in Section 554 of the APA and provide for a trial-like hearing process "on the record," complete with witnesses and recorded testimony, as well as findings of fact and conclusions of law.

More commonly, when an agency seeks to make or promulgate substantive rules, it engages in informal rule making (also known as **notice-and-comment procedures**), pursuant to Section 553 of the APA. In informal rule making, agencies are required to publish proposed rules in the Federal Register, thereby providing notice of the agency's intended action to anyone interested in the matter. Agencies also must accept written submissions from persons interested in commenting on the proposed rule, and in some instances may permit oral presentations. The APA also provides that the agency publish its final version of each rule and an accompanying explanation of the purpose and rationale for the rule in the Federal Register no less than 30 days prior to when the rule takes effect.

Introduction to *National Restaurant Association v. Hilda L. Solis*

Congress, in 1938, enacted a statute called the Federal Labor Standards Act (FLSA). This federal law divides employees paid an hourly wage into two categories: "covered employees," who are entitled to receive the federal minimum hourly wage, and "exempt employees," who are not. Covered hourly employees who make at least $30 per month in tips also are considered to be "tipped employees."

The FLSA was amended in 1966 to provide employers with a "tip-credit" option (29 U.S.C. §203(m)). (In the case below, this is referred to as "section 3(m).") This authorized the employer of a "tipped employee" to pay this worker a subminimum hourly wage if that cash payment and the tips received by the employee equal or exceed the standard federal hourly minimum wage of $7.25. If a tipped employee receives tips that, when added to the employer's cash payment, amounts to less than $7.25 per hour, the employer must make up the shortfall. Food service workers generally are covered by this law, because restaurants are businesses that operate in interstate commerce.

The defendants in the following case are the then-secretary of labor, Hilda Solis, and the U.S. Department of Labor (DOL). In July of 2008 the DOL gave notice in the Federal Register that it was going to propose a new rule impacting the tip credit. The DOL received comments in August and September 2008, and issued its final rule in April 2011, pursuant to its rule-making powers, 29 C.F.R. §531.59(b). The new rule provides that employers wishing to take advantage of the tip-credit option have to inform their employees about the tipped-employee rules. Employers who don't comply are subject to sanctions, which can include forfeiture of the right to make future use of the tip-credit option, and civil and criminal actions.

The plaintiffs—the National Restaurant Association, the country's largest trade association for the restaurant industry, and two other trade associations[5]—challenged the DOL's new rule, claiming that the new regulation violated the APA. The plaintiffs asked the court to vacate the rule and to award it injunctive relief.

Both parties filed motions for summary judgment, and the District Court, after a hearing, issued the Memorandum Opinion that appears below.

National Restaurant Association v. Hilda L. Solis
870 F. Supp. 2d 42
United States District Court for the District of Columbia
May 29, 2012

Amy Berman Jackson, United States District Judge.

Memorandum Opinion
Plaintiffs National Restaurant Association, Counsel of State Restaurant Associations, Inc., and National Federation of Independent Businesses bring this action against defendants Hilda L. Solis, in her official capacity as Secretary of the U.S. Department of Labor; Nancy Leppink, in her official capacity as Acting Administrator of the U.S. Department of Labor; and the U.S. Department of Labor ("the Department" or "DOL")....

I. Background...

A. Statutory and Regulatory Background
In 1966, Congress passed the amendment to FLSA that first enabled employers to take advantage of a tip credit.... The following year, the Department promulgated its first regulation implementing section 3(m)....
As originally enacted, neither section 3(m) nor the implementing regulation required employers to inform employees about the statutory provision before taking the tip credit. That changed in 1974, when Congress again amended FLSA to require employers to inform employees of the provisions of section 3(m) in order to be eligible for the tip credit.... As amended, FLSA provides:

> In determining the wage an employer is required to pay a tipped employee, the amount paid such employee by the employee's employer shall be an amount equal to:
> (1) the cash wage paid such employee which for purposes of such determination shall be not less than the cash wage required to be paid such an employee on August 20, 1996; and
> (2) an additional amount on account of the tips received by such employee which amount is equal to the difference between the wage specified in paragraph (1) and the wage in effect under section 206(a)(1) of this title.
> The additional amount on account of tips may not exceed the value of the tips actually received by an employee. The preceding [two] sentences shall not apply with respect to any tipped employee unless such employee has been informed by the employer of the provisions of this subsection, and all tips received by such employee have been retained by the employee, except that

> this subsection shall not be construed to prohibit the pooling of tips among employees who customarily and regularly receive tips....

B. The Proposed Rule
Although Congress enacted the requirement that employers inform their employees prior to taking the tip credit in 1974, the Department did not initiate further rule making until 2008. On July 28, 2008, the Department published a Notice of Proposed Rule Making ("NPRM"), which stated in its preamble:

> In this proposed rule, the Department of Labor ... proposes to revise regulations issued pursuant to the Fair Labor Standards Act of 1938 (FLSA) ... that have become out of date because of subsequent legislation or court decisions. These proposed revisions will conform the regulations to FLSA Amendments passed in 1974, 1977, 1996, 1997, 1998, 1999, 2000, and 2007....

Updating Regulations Issued Under the Fair Labor Standards Act ("Proposed Rule").... The agency was clear about the broad scope of the undertaking: "The Department requests comments on all issues related to this notice of proposed rule making."...
Section 3(m) was one of several statutory provisions specifically identified in the NPRM as being a particular subject of the announced rule making. The NPRM included a section entitled "Tipped Employees," and the notice expressly referred to the 1974 amendments:

> Section 13(e) of the Fair Labor Standards Act Amendments of 1974 amended the last sentence of section 3(m) by providing that an employer could not take a tip credit unless: "(1) [its] employee has been informed by the employer of the provisions of this subsection...."

... The Tipped Employees section of the NPRM went on to discuss the legislative history of the tip credit, and it also summarized the relevant case law on the need to inform employees under section 3(m)....
... Against this backdrop, the NPRM proposed a new regulation, which stated:

> Pursuant to section 3(m), an employer is not eligible to take the tip credit unless it has informed its employees that it intends to avail itself of the

tip wage credit. Such notice shall be provided in advance of the employer's use of the tip credit; the notice need not be in writing, but must communicate to employees that the employer intends to treat tips as satisfying part of the employer's minimum wage obligation.

... The Department of Labor received comments on the proposed rules from July 28 to September 26, 2008....

C. The Final Rule

On April 5, 2011, the Department of Labor issued a final rule regarding the FLSA's tip credit provision. Updating Regulations Issued Under the Fair Labor Standards Act ("Final Rule")....

... The final rule, which was codified as 29 C.F.R. §531.59(b), provided:

> Pursuant to section 3(m), an employer is not eligible to take the tip credit unless it has informed its tipped employees in advance of the employer's use of the tip credit of the provisions of section 3(m) of the Act, i.e.: The amount of the cash wage that is to be paid to the tipped employee by the employer; the additional amount by which the wages of the tipped employee are increased on account of the tip credit claimed by the employer, which amount may not exceed the value of the tips actually received by the employee; that all tips received by the tipped employee must be retained by the employee except for a valid tip pooling arrangement limited to employees who customarily and regularly receive tips; and that the tip credit shall not apply to any employee who has not been informed of these requirements in this section.

... The rule went into effect on May 5, 2011....

III. Analysis

A. DOL's Notice-and-Comment Procedure Was Sufficient

The APA requires that a notice of proposed rule making must contain "either the terms of substance of the proposed rules or a description of the subjects and issues involved."... The APA's notice-and-comment requirements "serve the salutary purposes of (1) ensur[ing] that agency regulations are tested via exposure to diverse public comment, (2) ensur[ing] fairness to affected parties, and (3) [giving] affected parties an opportunity to develop evidence in the record to support their objections to the rule and thereby enhance the quality of judicial review.' "... Thus, the relevant inquiry in

determining whether notice of a proposed rule was adequate is whether it served those goals....

Because comments received by the agency are expected to shape the outcome of a final rule, a final rule need not be identical to the proposed rule.... Indeed, "[t]he whole rationale of notice and comment rests on the expectation that the final rules will be somewhat different and improved from the rules originally proposed by the agency."...

Plaintiffs claim here, though, that the final rule adopted by the agency "deviates so greatly" from the proposed rule that the notice "failed to appropriately structure the issue and afford the public a reasonable opportunity to comment."... Both plaintiffs and defendants direct the Court to the D.C. Circuit's opinion in *Conn. Light & Power Co. v. Nuclear Reg. Comm'n,* ... which they agree sets out the appropriate test. In that case, the court explained:

> An agency adopting final rules that differ from its proposed rules is required to renotice when the changes are so major that the original notice did not adequately frame the subjects for discussion. The purpose of the new notice is to allow interested parties a fair opportunity to comment upon the final rules in their altered form. The agency need not re-notice changes that follow logically from or that reasonably develop the rules it proposed originally....

Drawing on this language, the parties submit that the question the Court must answer is whether the final rule was the "logical outgrowth" of the rule in the NPRM ... [and] whether the original notice "adequately frame[d] the subjects for discussion."... In other words, the Court's task is not simply to compare the final rule with the text of the originally proposed rule, but more fundamentally, to compare the final rule with the agency's original description of the subject of the upcoming rule making.... Viewed through any of these lenses, DOL's notice of proposed rule making was adequate, and the agency was not required to issue a second notice in this case.

1. The NPRM adequately framed the subject of the rule making

The NPRM [Notice of Proposed Rule Making] adequately framed the subject of the rule making as required by the APA and *Conn. Light & Power*: the notice specifically apprised the public of the agency's intention to promulgate a rule implementing the unambiguous statutory requirement that employers notify employees of the provisions of the statute concerning the tip credit.

On the very first page of the NPRM, the agency announced that the objective of the rule making was to "conform the regulations to FSLA amendments passed in 1974" as well as later amendments.... In the "Tipped Employees" section of the notice, the NPRM again specifically invoked the 1974 amendments and quoted the language of the 1974 legislation that provided: "an employer could not take a tip credit unless ... [its] employee has been informed by the employer of the provisions of this subsection.". . . The agency also reported that under the case law, "while employees must be 'informed' of the employer's use of the tip credit, the employer need not 'explain' the tip credit."... Plaintiffs can hardly complain now that the NPRM was insufficient to put them on notice of what ultimately took place, which was the promulgation of a regulation that requires employers to do just that.... Thus, the Court finds that the NPRM "adequately framed" the issue of how employees should be informed of the provisions of section 3(m) as a subject for discussion in the rule making.

2. The Final Rule was the logical outgrowth and/or a reasonable development of the proposed rule
... [T]he Court must examine the specific facts of this case to determine whether the final rule was a logical outgrowth of the one proposed.

It is true that in this case, the final rule is more specific than the proposed rule in the sense that it requires employers to make five specific disclosures, which were not itemized in the proposed rule....

But as the Court has already observed, the purpose of the rule making was to conform the regulations to the statute. And section 3(m) of FLSA, which is the touchstone for agency rule making on this issue, expressly requires employers to disclose the very provisions that are set out in the final rule. Also, a review of the administrative record reflects that the final rule developed reasonably and logically from the original proposal because—as DOL expressly explained when it issued the final rule—the rule was modified to address concerns that the original proposal could not be squared with the statute....

a. The final rule flows directly from the announced purpose of the rule making.
The purpose of the rule making was "to revise regulations issued pursuant to [FLSA] ... that have become out of date because of subsequent legislation or court decisions."... DOL stated that the revisions would "conform the regulations to [the] FLSA amendments" ... which required employers to inform their employees about the provisions of section 3(m). The agency proposed a rule calling for employers to advise tipped employees of their intent to take advantage of the

credit, and commenters—including representatives of employers—responded that the proposal did not fulfill its stated goal.

Based on comments such as these, DOL revised the proposed rule to track more closely the requirements of section 3(m), which was the purpose the agency announced for the rule making in the first place.... The Court finds that such a revision "follow[s] logically" from and "reasonably develop[s]" the rule the agency originally proposed....

b. The final rule tracks the language of section 3(m).
While defendants acknowledge that the final rule is more detailed than the proposed rule ... they point out that the five disclosures required by the final rule are derived directly from the statutory text of section 3(m)....

In other words, as plaintiffs concede ... the final rule does not require employers to do anything other than what they were already obligated to do under section 3(m), which is "inform employees of the provisions of this subsection."...

c. The purpose of the notice-and-comment process was served here.
As noted above, "[t]he whole rationale of notice and comment rests on the expectation that the final rules will be somewhat different and improved from the rules originally proposed by the agency."... Here, the agency heard from many groups that read the NPRM as an opportunity to weigh in on the proposed form and content of the information to be provided to employees. Organizations speaking on behalf of employees urged the agency to require employers to explain the tip credit requirement, and in some cases, went so far as suggesting that the employers provide a clear written explanation of the tip credit.... As drafted, the Proposed Rule will clearly articulate the required content of the notice, a step that should reduce litigation on this topic." In the Court's view, the final rule that spells out more specifically what must be disclosed under the statute developed logically and reasonably from the rule that was originally proposed, particularly in light of its stated purpose.

B. The Final Rule Is Not Arbitrary and Capricious
Under the APA, a court may set aside agency action that is "arbitrary, capricious, an abuse of discretion, or otherwise not in accordance with law."... Agency action will be upheld if the agency "has considered the relevant factors and articulated a 'rational connection between the facts found and the choice made.' "... The review is "[h]ighly deferential" and "presumes the validity of agency action."... The agency may rely on comments submitted during the notice-and-comment

period as justification for the rule, so long as the submissions are examined critically....

Plaintiffs contend that the final rule is arbitrary and capricious "because it conflicts with the DOL's previously announced positions and established case law[.]..."

In justifying the final rule, DOL stated: "The Department has concluded that notice of the specific provisions of [section] 3(m) is required to adequately inform the employee of the requirements of the tip credit."... Because DOL "considered the relevant factors and articulated a 'rational connection between

the facts found and the choice made,' " the Court finds that the final rule is not arbitrary and capricious....

IV. Conclusion
For the reasons set forth above, the Court will deny plaintiffs' cross motion for summary judgment [Dkt. #24] and will grant defendants' motion to dismiss, or, in the alternative for summary judgment [Dkt. # 15]. Accordingly, judgment will be entered for defendant on Counts I, II, and IV. Count III will be dismissed as conceded. A separate order will issue.

Case Questions

1. What, according to the court, is the primary purpose of the notice-and-comment requirement of the Administrative Procedure Act?
2. What was the plaintiffs' "logical outgrowth" argument?
3. Why did the court reject that argument?

Investigative Power

Agencies cannot operate without access to facts for intelligent regulation and adjudication. Thus, the **investigative power** is conferred on practically all administrative agencies. As regulation has expanded and intensified, the agencies' quest for facts has gained momentum.

Statutes commonly grant an agency the power to use several methods to carry out its fact-finding functions, such as requiring reports from regulated businesses, conducting inspections, and using judicially enforced subpoenas.

The power to investigate is one of the functions that distinguishes agencies from courts. This power is usually exercised in order to perform another pri-

mary function properly. However, some agencies are created primarily to perform the fact-finding or investigative function. Like any other power or function of the government, it must be exercised so as not to violate constitutionally protected rights.

The inspector general of the U.S. Department of Agriculture is statutorily charged with auditing federal programs and exposing fraud and abuse in federal disaster relief programs. In the following case, the inspector general served Ann Glenn and others with subpoenas to turn over specified records, documents, and reports. Glenn and the others, believing that the inspector general did not have the right to subpoena such information, sought relief in the U.S. Court of Appeals for the Eleventh Circuit.

Inspector General of U.S. Department of Agriculture v. Glenn
122 F.3d 1007
U.S. Court of Appeals, Eleventh Circuit
September 18, 1997

Floyd R. Gibson, Senior Circuit Judge.

I. Background
In 1993, in response to a hotline complaint alleging questionable disaster program payments to program participants in Mitchell County, Georgia, the United

States Department of Agriculture's ("USDA") Inspector General audited the Consolidated Farm Service Agency's ("CFSA") Mitchell County disaster program. The Inspector General sought to determine whether CFSA program participants were complying with regulatory payment limitations. As a result of the audit, the

Inspector General determined that $1.3 million in questionable disaster payments were awarded to Mitchell County program participants. As part of the audit, the Inspector General requested various information from appellants to determine their compliance with the payment limitations. When appellants repeatedly refused to provide the requested information, the Inspector General issued subpoenas to require production of the information. The Inspector General sought summary enforcement of the subpoenas in the United States District Court for the Middle District of Georgia. The district court ordered enforcement, and appellants challenge that order on appeal.

II. Discussion

Due to a concern that fraud and abuse in federal programs was "reaching epidemic proportions,"... Congress created Offices of Inspectors General in several governmental departments "to more effectively combat fraud, abuse, waste and mismanagement in the programs and operations of those departments and agencies,"... 5 U.S.C. app. §§1–12 (1994). The Inspector General Act of 1978 ... enables Inspectors General to combat such fraud and abuse by allowing "audits of Federal establishments, organizations, programs, activities, and functions," and by authorizing broad subpoena powers.... We will enforce a subpoena issued by the Inspector General so long as (1) the Inspector General's investigation is within its authority; (2) the subpoena's demand is not too indefinite or overly burdensome; (3) and the information sought is reasonably relevant.... Although appellants recognize that the scope of the Inspector General's subpoena power is broad, they contend that the USDA's Inspector General exceeded the scope of this power when he subpoenaed information as part of a payment limitation review. Appellants argue that a payment limitation review is a "program operating responsibilit[y]" which section 9(a)(2) of the IGA prohibits agencies from transferring to the Inspector General....

The IGA specifically directs the Inspector General to coordinate "activities designed ... to prevent and detect abuse" in departmental programs.... To enable the Inspector General to carry out this function, the IGA authorizes the Inspector General to conduct "audits" ... for the purpose of promoting "efficiency" and detecting "fraud and abuse."... The IGA's legislative history suggests that audits are to have three basic areas of inquiry:

(1) examinations of financial transactions, accounts, and reports and reviews of compliance with applicable laws and regulations,
(2) reviews of efficiency and economy to determine whether the audited is giving due

consideration to economical and efficient management, utilization, and conservation of its resources and to minimum expenditure of effort, and
(3) reviews of program results to determine whether programs or activities meet the objectives established by Congress or the establishment....

To enable the Inspector General to conduct such audits in an effective manner, the IGA provides the Inspector General with broad subpoena power which is "absolutely essential to the discharge of the Inspector ... General's functions," for "[w]ithout the power necessary to conduct a comprehensive audit the Inspector ... General could have no serious impact on the way federal funds are expended."...

This case illustrates the necessity of the Inspector General's auditing and subpoena powers. The Inspector General received a hotline complaint regarding questionable payments in the CFSA's Mitchell County disaster program. The Inspector General appropriately began an investigation of the program to detect possible abuse. As part of the audit, the Inspector General requested information from program participants to determine whether the payments they received were warranted. When appellants, who were program participants, refused to produce the requested information, the Inspector General utilized its subpoena powers to acquire the necessary information. Without this ability to issue subpoenas, the Inspector General would be largely unable to determine whether the program and its benefit recipients were operating in an appropriate manner. Thus, an abuse of the system, which the Inspector General was specifically created to combat, could possibly go undetected, and government waste and abuse could continue unchecked. The subpoena power, which the Inspector General appropriately invoked in this case, is vital to the Inspector General's function of investigating fraud and abuse in federal programs.

Appellants contend that the Inspector General is only authorized to detect fraud and abuse within government programs, and that program administrators are responsible for detecting abuse among program participants. While we agree that IGA's main function is to detect abuse within agencies themselves, the IGA's legislative history indicates that Inspectors General are permitted and expected to investigate public involvement with the programs in certain situations. Congressman Levitas, a co-sponsor of the IGA, stated that the Inspector General's "public contact would only be for the beneficial and needed purpose of receiving complaints about problems with agency administration and in the investigation of fraud and abuse by those persons who are misusing or stealing taxpayer dollars."

... From this statement, we conclude that the Inspector General's public contact in this case was appropriate because it occurred during the course of an investigation into alleged misuse of taxpayer dollars. In sum, we conclude that the subpoenas issued by the Inspector General did not exceed the statutory authority granted under the IGA.

Appellants also claim that the subpoenas were too indefinite and were unduly burdensome. CFSA regulations require participants to retain records for a period of two years following the close of the program year.... Appellants argue that the Inspector General cannot subpoena records which predate the required retention period. We do not agree with appellants' argument. While appellants are not required to retain records beyond the two-year period, no indication exists that records created prior to the retention period should be free from the Inspector General's subpoena powers.

Appellants further contend that the subpoenas are unduly burdensome because the 1990 and 1991 records

sought by the Inspector General "were maintained and controlled by [appellant] J. C. Griffin, Sr., who had no mental capacity to explain the recordkeeping system utilized in 1990 and 1991 in his dealings with the USDA during [that] time period."... We do not believe that Mr. Griffin's mental incapacity has any bearing on the enforceability of the Inspector General's subpoenas. At this stage, the Inspector General is merely requesting information from appellants as part of a large investigation involving many program participants in Mitchell County. The Inspector General has not requested that Griffin explain the contents of his records or his system for maintaining them. Consequently, we are unable to conclude that the subpoenas create an undue burden upon Mr. Griffin or any of the other appellants....

III. Conclusion
For the reasons set forth in this opinion we AFFIRM the district court's decision to enforce the Inspector General's subpoenas.

Case Questions

1. What argument did Glenn make to the appellate court regarding the Inspector General's statutory authority?
2. How did the appeals court rule, and why?
3. Why do you think that the appellants were unsuccessful with their claims that the subpoenas were both indefinite and unduly burdensome?

Adjudicative Power

When an agency's action involves the rule-making function, it need not make use of judicial procedures. The **adjudicative power** delegated to an administrative agency, however, requires it to make determinations of a targeted person's legal rights, duties, and obligations, and for this reason adjudicatory hearings resemble a court's decision-making process. Thus, when an agency is intent on obtaining a binding determination or adjudication that affects the legal rights of an individual or individuals, it must use some of the procedures that traditionally have been associated with the judicial process.

Before sanctions can be imposed, an alleged violator is entitled to an administrative hearing that is conducted according to APA procedures (or other procedures specified in the enabling act) and that complies with the due process requirements of the Fifth and Fourteenth Amendments. This means that the accused

has to receive notice and a fair and open hearing before an impartial and competent tribunal. Parties affected by the agency action must be given the opportunity to confront any adverse witnesses and present oral and written evidence on their own behalf. An agency may confine cross-examination to the essentials, thus avoiding the discursive and repetitive questioning common to courtroom cross-examinations.

Administrative agencies employ **administrative law judges (ALJs)** to conduct adjudicatory hearings. Like judges, ALJs decide both questions of fact and issues of law, and they are limited to the evidence that is established on the record. ALJs are authorized to issue subpoenas, administer oaths, make evidentiary rulings, and conduct hearings. ALJs are not, however, members of the federal judiciary. They perceive their function as that of implementing and administering a legislative purpose rather than as judges impartially deciding between two litigants. In some agencies, ALJs are quite active in questioning witnesses, so that a thorough record of the proceedings will be developed for the benefit of the agency's administrator or board.

However, administrative law judges *are* empowered to make findings of fact and to recommend a decision. The recommendation is sent to the board of final review in the administrative agency, which ultimately decides whether the agency will adopt, alter, or reverse it.

In theory, the decision of an administrative law judge is thoroughly reviewed before the agency's board of final review adopts it as its opinion. In reality, however, because of a board's heavy workload, the review may be delegated to members of its staff, and board members may never even read the administrative law judge's opinion. Although this has been challenged as a lack of due process for the defendant, the courts often permit delegation of review to agency staff members. The courts require only that the board members make decisions and understand the positions taken by the agency.

JUDICIAL REVIEW

Judicial review is a relatively minor aspect of administrative law. In part, this is because judges lack expertise in the very technical and specialized area that is subject to agency regulation. The sheer volume of agency adjudications also makes it unrealistic to expect the judiciary to review more than a small percentage of such decisions. This is one reason why Congress decided to create an adjudicative power within the administrative agencies in stead of substantially increasing the workloads of the federal judiciary. In addition, the expense of obtaining judicial review is a barrier to many potential appellants.

Courts and administrative agencies are collaborators in the task of safeguarding the public interest. Thus, unless exceptional circumstances exist, courts are reluctant to interfere with the operation of a program administered by an agency. As the courts' respect of the administrative process increases, judicial self-restraint also increases.

The petitioner in the next case, the National Mining Association, asked the U.S. Court of Appeals for the D.C. Circuit to review a final rule promulgated by the Federal Mine Safety and Health Administration. The rule came into being after two fatal incidents occurred in West Virginia coal mines in 2006. The Association objected to procedural and substantive provisions of the rule, which had been adopted to help miners survive mining disasters.

National Mining Association v. Mine Safety and Health Administration
512 F.3d 696
United States Court of Appeals, District of Columbia Circuit
January 11, 2008

Randolph, Circuit Judge.
Two fatal accidents at West Virginia coal mines in January 2006 prompted the Mine Safety and Health Administration—MSHA—to adopt emergency safety measures.... MSHA, an agency within the Department of Labor, concluded that the West Virginia miners might have survived if there had been portable oxygen devices ... in the escapeways to protect them from toxic fumes for at least an hour. Acting quickly, MSHA issued an emergency temporary standard requiring mine operators to place such rescue devices, one for each miner, in the primary and emergency escapeways of the mine.... This petition for judicial review, brought by the National Mining Association, seeks to set aside the final rule that replaced the temporary standard.

The Mine Act authorizes MSHA to issue the temporary rules without notice and comment in response to emergencies.... In this case, in order to make its temporary standard permanent, MSHA engaged in notice-and-comment rule making, with the published temporary standard serving as the proposed rule.... The resulting product—the final emergency mine evacuation rule ... —altered the temporary standard with respect to rescue devices.... The final rule required either that one additional device be provided for each miner in each emergency escapeway or that one additional device be provided in a "hardened room" cache located between two adjacent emergency escapeways and accessible from both.... A "hardened room" is a reinforced room built to the "same explosion force criteria as seals" and serviced by an independent, positive pressure source of ventilation from the surface.... The National Mining Association urges us to set the final rule aside. One of its objections is that MSHA failed to give adequate notice of the hardened room option.

The objection rests on §101(a)(2) of the Mine Act. 30 U.S.C. §811(a)(2). This section requires MSHA, in putting out proposed rules for notice and comment, to publish "the text of such rules proposed in their entirety" in the Federal Register.... Because MSHA never published the hardened room option in the Federal Register before issuing the final rule, National Mining concludes that this aspect of the final rule is invalid.

That the final rule differed from the one MSHA proposed is hardly unusual. An agency's final rules are frequently different from the ones it published as proposals. The reason is obvious. Agencies often "adjust or abandon their proposals in light of public comments or internal agency reconsideration."... Whether in such instances the agency should have issued additional notice and received additional comment on the revised proposal "depends, according to our precedent, on whether the final rule is a 'logical outgrowth' of the proposed rule."... While we often apply the doctrine simply by comparing the final rule to the one proposed, we have also taken into account the comments, statements and proposals made during the notice-and-comment period.... In *South Terminal Corp. v. EPA*, the case that gave birth to the "logical outgrowth" formulation, the court did the same ... (1st Cir. 1974). The court held that the final rule was "a logical outgrowth"—not simply of the proposed rule— but "of the hearing and related procedures" during the notice-and-comment period....

Here MSHA's proposed rule—the emergency temporary standard—required that a rescue device be provided for each miner in both the primary and the alternative escapeways. That proposal left open several questions. Where in the escapeways should the devices be stored? How should they be made available to the miners? When the two escapeways are close together, will it suffice to have one common cache of devices rather than two separate caches? Given these considerations, interested persons must have been alerted to the possibility of a hardened room option. And the record shows that they were so alerted. Mine operators inquired about the potential of using a common cache of rescue devices located between adjacent emergency escapeways. They submitted questions to MSHA about whether such a common cache would suffice. Four public meetings were

held as part of the rule making. At each, the MSHA official's opening statement addressed the possibility of a hardened room alternative directly and sought comments from interested parties. A representative of the National Mining Association attended the Washington, D.C., meeting and indicated that his organization would respond to the opening statement by the end of the comment period. The Mining Association never submitted comments, but several interested parties did—including several of the Mining Association's members. MSHA later extended the comment period by thirty days so that "interested parties could adequately address issues contained in MSHA's opening statements."...

The hardened room option was thus a logical outgrowth of the proposed rule, or put differently, the Mining Association had adequate notice. Even if we were less than certain about this conclusion, the actual notice the Mining Association received would have cured any inadequacy....

The Mining Association alleges that the hardened room option—as opposed to an option allowing a common cache with less stringent safeguards—is arbitrary and capricious because MSHA did not sufficiently explain its decision.

The Mine Act incorporates the rule-making requirements of the APA. 30 U.S.C. §811(a).... Under the APA, an agency must "incorporate in the rules adopted a concise general statement of their basis and purpose."... This requirement is not meant to be particularly onerous.... It is enough if the agency's statement identifies the major policy issues raised in the rule making and coherently explains why the agency resolved the issues as it did...MSHA's statement did just that. As to the hardened room option, the main controversy was about whether less stringent common storage measures could be used instead.... The claim was that these less stringent requirements would provide incremental safety benefits over placing the rescue devices in the escapeways and that the options would be cheaper than the hardened room alternative, making common caches feasible for more mines.

MSHA referred to those comments in the preamble to its final rule.... It explained that its primary concern with approving a common cache of devices was that the cache needed to be "secured against damage from explosions in either escapeway."... Underlying MSHA's analysis is the apparent belief that the redundancy provided by having separate sets of devices results in an increased likelihood that at least one set would survive an explosion. Thus, in order to justify collapsing the two sets into one, additional steps are required to ensure that an explosion would not destroy the devices in a common cache. Hardened rooms achieve this end because they are built to more rigorous specifications.... While other options might be cheaper, the hardened room meets the primary concern MSHA identified.

Though MSHA's explanation of its decision is short, it adequately addresses the major policy concerns raised and demonstrates a course of reasoned decision making. The final rule, including the hardened room option, is not arbitrary and capricious.

IV

The Mining Association argues that MSHA failed to comply with the Regulatory Flexibility Act ... because it did not analyze the economic impact of the hardened room option. When promulgating a rule, an agency must perform an analysis of the impact of the rule on small businesses, or certify, with support, that the regulation will not have a significant economic impact on them.... When it published the temporary standard,

MSHA certified that the primary method of compliance —placing a separate set of rescue devices in each emergency escapeway—would not have a significant economic impact on small businesses.... The Mining Association does not challenge the sufficiency of that certification. Since the primary method of compliance did not create a significant economic burden on small businesses, there was no reason for MSHA to undertake an economic analysis of the alternative. If the hardened room option is considerably more expensive, small businesses can simply refuse to choose it. *Compare Envtl. Def. Ctr., Inc. v. EPA*, 344 F.3d 832, 879 (9th Cir. 2003) (noting that the creation of cheaper alternative methods of compliance is one way to minimize the impact on small businesses).

For the foregoing reasons, the petition for review is denied.

So ordered.

Case Questions

1. What were the Association's objections to the final rule?
2. Why did the court deny the petition and sustain the final rule?

INTERNET TIP

The case of *Chao v. Occupational Safety Health Review Commission* has been included in the Chapter XIII materials found on the textbook's website. In that case, the Secretary of the Department of Labor challenged a final ruling made by the Occupational Safety and Health Review Commission. The Review Commission had overturned three Occupational Health and Safety Administration (OSHA) citations issued to a bridge-painting contractor who was removing lead paint from the bridge. OSHA inspectors had issued the citations after inspecting the work site and discovering problems with the protective scaffolding installed at that location. The Secretary asked the U.S. Court of Appeals to reverse the Review Commission's decision with respect to these citations. In this case, the court had to determine whether to defer to a statutory interpretation made by the administrative agency.

Timing of Review

Parties must address their complaints to administrative tribunals and explore every possibility for obtaining relief through administrative channels (i.e., must **exhaust administrative remedies**) before appealing to the courts. The courts generally will not interrupt an agency's procedure until the agency has issued a final decision, because if the administrative power has not been finally exercised, no irreparable harm has occurred; therefore, the controversy is not ripe.

The courts will hear a case before a final agency decision if the aggrieved party can prove that failure to interrupt the administrative process would be unfair. To determine the extent of fairness, the court will consider (1) the possibility of injury if the case is not heard, (2) the degree of doubt of the agency's jurisdiction, and (3) the requirement of the agency's specialized knowledge.

The requirements of exhaustion of administrative remedies and ripeness are concerned with the timing of judicial review of administrative action, but the two requirements are not the same. Finality and exhaustion focus on whether the administrative position being challenged has crystallized and is, in fact, an institutional decision. Ripeness asks whether the issues presented are appropriate for judicial resolution. Although each doctrine has a separate and distinct aim, they frequently overlap.

═══ INTERNET TIP ════════════════════

Readers can find the case of *Sturm, Ruger & Company v. Chao* in the Internet materials for Chapter XIII on the textbook's website. Sturm, Ruger attempted to litigate claims against the Occupational Safety and Health Administration without having first exhausted all of its administrative remedies. The company was unsuccessful in the U.S. District Court, which dismissed their complaint. The company then appealed to the U.S. Court of Appeals for the District of Columbia Circuit. You can read that court's opinion online.
══════════════════════════════════════

Judicial Deference and the Scope of Judicial Review

In general, courts are willing to show **deference** to an agency's competence. Courts will uphold administrative findings if they are satisfied that the agency has examined the issues, reached its decision within the appropriate standards, and followed the required procedures.

It is impossible for a reviewing court to consider more than the highlights of the questions actually argued before an administrative agency, since the fact situations are often complex and technical, and the time available for argument short. Instead, courts rely on an agency's expertise. Even when a court holds an original determination invalid, it usually remands the case for further consideration by the agency, rather than making its own final decision.

The courts have established standards as to the scope of judicial review. In general, questions of law ultimately are determined by courts, but questions of fact are considered only to a very limited extent. Questions of law must be reserved for the courts because the power of final decision on judicial matters involving private rights cannot constitutionally be taken from the judiciary. However, this does not mean that courts will review every issue of law involved in an administrative determination.

Agency findings with respect to questions of fact, if supported by substantial evidence on the record considered as a whole, are conclusive. Substantial evidence exists when the agency's conclusion is reasonably supported by the facts of record. Legal conclusions are judicially reversed only because of arbitrariness, capriciousness, an abuse of discretion, or a denial of due process.

═══ INTERNET TIP ════════════════════

Students may wish to read a case involving the judicial review of a final decision by the Occupational Safety and Health Review Commission to issue citations to one of the contractors involved in the "Big Dig" project in downtown Boston. This case includes discussions of many of the topics addressed in this chapter in the context of an actual dispute. The case is *Modern Continental Construction Co. Inc v. Occupational Safety and Health Review Comm.*, and it can be found on the textbook's website.
══════════════════════════════════════

Introduction to *Ahmed v. Sebelius*

Dr. Ahmed, a Massachusetts dermatologist, was prosecuted in federal court in conjunction with a Medicare-fraud investigation. The prosecution alleged that the doctor had fraudulently falsified and backdated patient documents. Prosecutors claimed that Ahmed intentionally misled CMS (the Centers for Medicare and Medicaid Services), the governmental agency administering Medicare, into paying him for treating patients afflicted with a disease called *pemphigoid*, a malady not covered by Medicare. Ahmed was accused of falsely reporting that some of the pemphigoid patients also were afflicted with a Medicare-authorized disease called *pemphigus*. Ahmed entered a plea of guilty to 1 count of a 15-count indictment and was convicted of feloniously obstructing a health care investigation. Shortly after his conviction and sentencing, Dr. Ahmed's billing privileges were revoked by Medicare.

Dr. Ahmed decided to challenge the billing revocation decision via administrative proceedings.

The first step in the review process involved asking NHIC, Corp., the Medicare contractor that had issued the revocation, to reconsider. A hearing officer reviewed the matter and affirmed the revocation decision. The next step was to request that the Department of Health and Human Services conduct an administrative hearing before an ALJ. The ALJ also sustained the revocation order. The third step was an appeal from the ALJ's decision to the Health and Human Services Department Appeals Board (DAB), which would be the last administrative step. The DAB made the final decision on behalf of the Department and reaffirmed the revocation decision. Having exhausted all administrative remedies, Dr. Ahmed was entitled to seek judicial review, in this case to the U.S. District Court for the District of Massachusetts.

Dr. Ahmed alleged in his complaint that Secretary Sebelius's Department of Health and Human Services had violated the Administrative Procedure Act, the Medicare Act, and the Fifth Amendment's Due Process Clause.

Abdul Razzaque Ahmed v. Kathleen Sebelius
710 F. Supp. 2d 167
United States District Court, District of Massachusetts
May 10, 2010

Douglas Woodlock, District Judge.

Memorandum and Order

I. Background
... Ahmed is a Massachusetts dermatologist who specializes in the diagnosis and treatment of autoimmune skin blistering diseases. Prior to the commencement of the administrative action in this case, Ahmed was an approved Medicare supplier, ... treated Medicare patients, and received reimbursements from Medicare for those treatments.

A. The Medicare Program
The Medicare program provides health insurance benefits to individuals over age sixty-five and to certain disabled persons.... Medicare is administered by the Centers for Medicare and Medicaid Services ("CMS"), an agency of HHS. Congress has granted the Secretary broad authority to issue regulations relating to the administration of Medicare pursuant to Sections 1102 and 1871 of the Social Security Act ... (authorizing the Secretary to "make and publish such rules and regulations ... as may be necessary to the efficient administration of the functions" of Medicare) ... [and] §1395 ... ("The Secretary shall prescribe such regulations as may be necessary to carry out the administration of the [Medicare] insurance programs."...). A physician wishing to participate in Medicare must first enroll in the program to receive Medicare billing privileges and a billing number....

To maintain billing privileges, physicians must complete the applicable enrollment application and revalidate their Medicare enrollment information every five years.... The application requires the physician to list any "final adverse actions" including any felony convictions.... CMS also may perform "off cycle revalidations."... In addition, CMS has regulatory authority to revoke a physician's Medicare enrollment and billing privileges in certain instances.... Relevant to this case is the regulation permitting revocation if, "within the 10 years preceding enrollment or revalidation of enrollment," the physician "was convicted of a Federal or State felony offense that CMS has determined to be detrimental to the best interests of the [Medicare] program and its beneficiaries."...

II. Standard of Review
Any Medicare provider or supplier whose billing privileges are revoked may have a hearing and judicial review under ... 42 U.S.C. §1395cc(j)....

Under the review provision, the district court has the "power to enter, upon the pleadings and transcript of the record, a judgment affirming, modifying, or reversing the decision of the [Secretary], with or without remanding the cause for a rehearing." The Secretary's findings "as to any fact, if supported by substantial evidence, shall be conclusive,"... and must be upheld "if a reasonable mind, reviewing the evidence in the record as a whole, could accept it as adequate to support his conclusion."... Questions of law, however, are reviewed de novo....

III. Discussion
In order for the Secretary to revoke Ahmed's billing privileges properly ... two conditions must be satisfied: first, the supplier must have been convicted of a designated federal or state felony offense that CMS has

determined to be detrimental to the best interests of the Medicare program and its beneficiaries, and second, the conviction must have occurred within the ten years preceding enrollment or revalidation of enrollment. Ahmed challenges the Secretary's decision to revoke his Medicare billing privileges on the grounds that neither condition was met, and that the decision violated his due process rights. I review the Secretary's decision against this challenge and assess whether it is supported by substantial evidence and is legally correct.

A. Relevant Criminal Conduct

1. The designated crimes
Ahmed argues that CMS improperly revoked his Medicare enrollment and billing privileges based on the "erroneous conclusion" that his conviction for obstruction constituted a "financial crime" under 42 C.F.R. §424.535.... That regulation designates "[f]inancial crimes, such as extortion, embezzlement, income tax evasion, insurance fraud and other similar crimes" as offenses that "CMS has determined to be detrimental to the best interests of the [Medicare] program and its beneficiaries."... Obstruction of a criminal investigation of a health care offense, he suggests, is not such an offense. Ahmed attempts to distinguish his felony conviction for obstruction of the criminal investigation of a health care offense from the four financial crimes listed in the regulation, each of which purportedly requires a showing of actual or intended financial harm to another. I agree with the Secretary, however, that the regulation should not be interpreted so narrowly.... The regulation uses nonexclusive, illustrative language to enumerate the various felony convictions that permit revocation of Medicare privileges: "[o]ffenses *include* ... [f]inancial crimes, *such as* extortion, embezzlement, income tax evasion, insurance fraud *and other similar crimes.*"... The DAB [Department Appeals Board] concluded—in my view, correctly—that Ahmed's conviction under §1518 was "similar" to the listed financial crimes, specifically insurance fraud. The obstruction charge for which Ahmed was convicted is a criminal offense that bears the DNA of insurance fraud in the health care setting. Ahmed created and submitted false documents that could support claims for Medicare coverage of his patients' IVIg treatments. The DAB properly concluded that this conduct, as does insurance fraud, "involves a false statement or misrepresentation in connection with a claim or application for insurance or insurance benefits." Moreover, as recited in the DAB decision, Ahmed stated in briefing to the ALJ [administrative law judge] that he had "placed false letters and

immunopathology reports into his patients' files to bolster the reimbursements he received from Medicare." The offense involves the cover up (sic) dimension of criminal conduct striking at the essential financial integrity of the Medicare insurance program.... Ahmed sought to throw investigators off the scent in their pursuit of a core financial fraud. It is not merely similar to insurance fraud; it is of a piece with it.

2. Regulatory revocation versus statutory exclusion
Ahmed also relies on the separate Medicare participation exclusion statute to distinguish obstruction from financial crimes.... The "mandatory exclusion" provision requires the Secretary to exclude individuals who were convicted of certain crimes, including *"a felony relating to fraud,* theft, embezzlement, breach of fiduciary responsibility, *or other financial misconduct,"* from participation in Medicare.... Under the "permissive exclusion" provision, by contrast, the Secretary *may* exclude individuals who have been "convicted, under Federal or State law, in connection with the interference with or *obstruction of any investigation* into" certain criminal offenses, including health care fraud.... Ahmed contends that "Congress's deliberate, separate treatment of obstruction of justice demonstrates that NHIC may not view Dr. Ahmed's actions as falling into the category of 'financial crimes' set forth in 42 CFR §424.535 ... and should not automatically revoke his privileges on that basis."

I reject Ahmed's argument because, as the DAB correctly explained, the regulatory revocation ... and the statutory exclusion ... are "distinct remedial tools, each with its own set of prerequisites and consequences."... Under the revocation provision, the physician is barred from participating in Medicare from the effective date of the revocation until the end of the re-enrollment bar, which ranges between one and three years depending on the severity of the basis for revocation.... To re-enroll after revocation, the physician must complete and submit a new enrollment application and applicable documentation as a new supplier for validation by CMS....

The exclusion of a physician from participation in Medicare also has a finite time period, but the duration of exclusion differs depending on the crime committed. For mandatory exclusion ... based on a felony conviction relating to health care fraud, the minimum period of exclusion is not less than five years.... For permissive exclusion ... for a conviction relating to obstruction of an investigation, the exclusion period is three years, "unless the Secretary determines in accordance with published regulations that a shorter period is appropriate because of mitigating circumstances or that a longer period is appropriate because of aggravating circumstances."... At the end of the exclusion period, the physician may apply to the Secretary for termination of the exclusion, or the Secretary may terminate the exclusion in certain instances....

Although there are a variety of differences in details, a primary difference between revocation and exclusion appears to be in the collateral consequences. Revocation bars a supplier from participation in the Medicare program.... Exclusion extends beyond Medicare to Medicaid and all other federal health care programs.... "Federal health care program" is defined as "any plan or program providing health care benefits, whether directly through insurance or otherwise, that is funded directly, in whole or part, by the United States Government ... or any State health care program."...

3. Detrimental to the best interests of Medicare

In the final analysis, even if Ahmed's felony conviction is somehow conceived as not expressly financial in nature, I am persuaded that his admitted obstruction of a criminal investigation of a health care offense here is the type of similar felony that CMS would properly consider "to be detrimental to the best interests" of Medicare and its beneficiaries because of its financial implications....

I therefore conclude ... that substantial evidence supports the Secretary's determination that Ahmed's conviction ... fell within the scope of relevant financial crimes detrimental to the best interests of Medicare and that the Secretary applied the correct construction of her regulations in reaching this conclusion.

B. Revalidation

Ahmed next argues that even if the Secretary properly determined that he committed a relevant crime, she should not have revoked his Medicare privileges without first engaging in some sort of revalidation process. To revoke Ahmed's Medicare billing privileges, his felony conviction must have occurred "within the 10 years preceding enrollment or revalidation of enrollment."... Neither party disputes that Ahmed's initial enrollment in Medicare occurred over ten years before his felony conviction. Therefore, the issue is whether revalidation occurred.

Section 424.515 outlines two types of revalidations. First, a provider or supplier "must resubmit and recertify the accuracy of its enrollment information every 5 years," and they "are required to complete the applicable enrollment application."... Second, "CMS reserves the right to perform off cycle revalidations in addition to the regular 5-year revalidations and may request that a provider or supplier recertify the

accuracy of the enrollment information when warranted to assess and confirm the validity of the enrollment information maintained by CMS."...

... Specifically, Ahmed objects to the conclusion that "even the passive act of receiving information that a physician was convicted of a felony can constitute revalidation" because that "nonsensical" reading would render the revalidation requirement meaningless. I find, to the contrary, that §424.515 expressly provides for event-triggered revalidation: "[o]ff cycle revalidations may be triggered as a result of random checks, information indicating local health care fraud problems, national initiatives, complaints, or other reasons that cause CMS to question the compliance of the provider or supplier with Medicare enrollment requirements."... That is precisely what happened here and it made a great deal of sense. Ahmed's conviction triggered an off-cycle revalidation in November 2007, when CMS and/or NHIC acquired or reviewed information that Ahmed had pled guilty to a felony related to health care reimbursement. The deliberative process did not end there because the felony conviction did not automatically require revocation; rather the regulation *permits,* but does not require, revocation if a physician is convicted of specified felonies.... The revocation based on Ahmed's felony conviction was assessed by three successive layers of administrative decision makers before reaching finality with the DAB decision. Ahmed was afforded the opportunity to submit materials he believed to bear upon the decision. Given the circumstances, those decision makers understandably did not consider Ahmed's several arguments against revocation compelling. I therefore conclude that the revocation of Ahmed's privileges was well within the Secretary's authority as a procedural matter.

C. Due Process

More broadly, Ahmed contends that his due process rights were violated because a revalidation process did not occur *before* CMS and/or NHIC made the revocation decision. He insists that revalidation is "an important procedural safeguard that provides Medicare participants and their patients with notice and an opportunity to be heard before a provider's billing privileges are revoked." Ahmed claims that if given that opportunity, he would have clarified "the true circumstances of his crime" and demonstrated "that his Medicare patients had access to few, if any, comparable treatment sources." The constitutional right to due process requires notice and a meaningful opportunity to respond.... Both of these requirements were met in this case. With respect to notice, Ahmed received a letter from NHIC on November 8, 2007 before his billing privileges were revoked on December 9, 2007.

That letter also detailed an opportunity for Ahmed to obtain "an independent review" by requesting "an on-the-record reconsideration." With respect to a meaningful opportunity to respond, the Supreme Court "has recognized, on many occasions, that ... where it would be impractical to provide predeprivation process, post-deprivation process satisfies the requirements of the Due Process Clause."... *Gilbert v. Homar*...(1997)...." An important government interest, accompanied by a substantial assurance that the deprivation is not baseless or unwarranted, may in limited cases demanding prompt action justify postponing the opportunity to be heard until after the initial deprivation." *FDIC v. Mallen* ... (1988).... Once Ahmed was convicted of a crime manifesting an intent to manipulate the Medicare reimbursement system and to obstruct the criminal justice system which polices it, there was more than adequate need for prompt action to revoke his privi-

leges to participate in the system. An elaborate pre-revocation process before the initiation of a felony-based revocation is not required for those convicted, as Ahmed was, of any felony within the terms of §424.535(a)(3).... [T]he regulation expressly rejects pre-revocation process for physicians, like Ahmed, whose billing privileges are revoked due to a felony conviction.... The sole remedies are post-revocation administrative and judicial review, which have been pursued vigorously by Ahmed through all their layers and fully satisfy his constitutional right to due process.

IV. Conclusion
For the reasons set forth more fully above, I GRANT the Defendant's motion ... for judgment on the pleadings, or in the alternative, for summary judgment. I DENY the Plaintiff's cross-motion for judgment on the pleadings.

Case Questions

1. Why did Ahmed believe his billing privileges should not have been revoked?
2. Why did the U.S. District Court reject Ahmed's arguments?

ADMINISTRATIVE AGENCIES AND THE REGULATION OF BUSINESS

Congress has neither the time nor the expertise to regulate business. Congress also has decided that the judicial process is not well suited to the task. Instead it has entrusted the day-to-day responsibility for regulating business to administrative agencies. The following material focuses on two administrative agencies and how they perform this function.

Occupational Safety and Health Administration

Historically, the common law provided an employee injured on the job with little recourse against an employer who could use the assumption-of-risk and contributory-negligence defenses. With little incentive for employers to reduce employment-related injuries, the number of industrial injuries increased as manufacturing processes became more complex. Legislation was

passed to improve job safety for coal miners during the late 1800s, and most states had enacted job safety legislation by 1920. Maryland and New York were the first states to establish workers' compensation laws, which have now been adopted in all fifty states. Although these laws modified the common law to enable injured employees to recover, they didn't change the practices that caused the dangerous conditions. Furthermore, state legislatures were reluctant to establish strict safety regulations, fearing that such actions would cause industry to move to other, less restrictive states.

In response to the problem, in 1970 Congress passed the Occupational Safety and Health Act to improve employees' safety and working conditions. The Act established the National Institute of Occupational Safety and Health to conduct research in the area of employee health and safety. The Act also created an administrative agency, called the **Occupational Safety and Health Administration (OSHA),** to set and enforce environmental standards within the workplace.

An employee who suspects a safety violation at his or her place of work can contact the local OSHA office. An OSHA inspector makes an unannounced visit to the premises and conducts an inspection. If the inspection reveals violations, appropriate citations—either civil or criminal—are issued.

For civil citations, OSHA may impose fines up to $70,000 for each willful and repeated violation, and $7,000 for less serious violations. As we saw earlier in this chapter in the case of *Sturm, Ruger & Co., Inc. v. Elaine Chao, Sec., U.S. Dept. of Labor,* an employer may contest an OSHA citation at a hearing before an administrative law judge. The ALJ's decision is appealable to the Occupational Safety and Health Review Commission, whose decision is appealable to the U.S. Court of Appeals.

Criminal prosecutions for OSHA violations are rare; however, when brought they are tried in federal district court. Convicted individual offenders can be fined up to $250,000 for each count and sentenced to a maximum of six months in prison. Corporations can be fined up to $500,000.

OSHA inspectors also have the right to post a job site as imminently dangerous and obtain injunctions where necessary to shut down a work site because of the existence of dangerous working conditions.

Federal Trade Commission and Consumer Credit Protection

The first multiuse, revolving-balance credit cards, Visa and MasterCard, came into existence only in 1959. Initially, businesses that extended credit to consumers were subject to few regulations. They often imposed unduly high interest charges, failed to disclose their interest rates and associated credit charges, and mailed unsolicited credit cards to potential users. Because debt-collection practices were unregulated, consumers often were harassed and threatened at home and at work. As a result, in 1968 Congress passed the **Consumer Credit Protection Act (CCPA).**

Designed to promote the disclosure of credit terms and to establish the rights and responsibilities of both creditors and consumers, the CCPA is much more protective of the consumer than was the common law. Although several agencies share authority for enforcing and controlling the CCPA, the Federal Trade Commission bears primary responsibility for CCPA enforcement.

Under the CCPA, many early credit card and loan practices became illegal. Issuers of credit cards, for example, were no longer permitted to mail unsolicited cards. Many of the questions about the apportionment of duties between the merchants who accepted credit cards and the card-issuing banks were clarified. For example, under the CCPA, a bank may not withdraw funds from a cardholder's savings or checking accounts to cover a credit card charge without the cardholder's authorization. Also, under the CCPA a cardholder's liability for unauthorized charges is limited to $50 in most cases.

The CCPA is extremely lengthy and complex and is better known under its various subsections. Title 1 of the CCPA is known as the Truth in Lending Act. The Fair Credit Reporting Act was added in 1970, the Equal Credit Opportunity Act in 1974, the Fair Credit Billing Act in 1975, and the Fair Debt Collection Practices Act in 1977.

The Truth in Lending Simplification and Reform Act was signed into law in 1980. It primarily regulates the disclosure of credit terms and conditions in conjunction with household purchases and common real estate transactions. Congress intended to make it easier for consumers to shop for credit. Before the passage of this Act, many lenders did not disclose interest rates, finance charges, or other charges in ways that could be compared easily with those of their business competitors. Under the Truth in Lending Act, creditors must disclose information about interest rates and other finance charges in a highly regulated and uniform manner. A willful violator of the Truth in Lending Act may be prosecuted criminally and penalized with fines and incarceration. However, the most effective and most commonly used method of enforcing this Act is through private suit. A successful plaintiff can recover a fine, an award of compensatory damages, and an order that the creditor pay the consumer's attorney fees.

The Fair Credit Reporting Act of 1970 (FCRA) is designed to ensure that consumers are treated fairly by credit-reporting agencies and medical-information businesses. Prior to its enactment, agencies that investigated individuals in order to provide companies with credit, insurance, employment, or other consumer reports were subject to few restraints. Not only did individuals have no right to know the contents of the report, but also businesses had no duty to disclose the fact that a report even existed. Hence, many individuals were denied credit, employment, or other benefits without knowing that an investigation had been made. Consumers now have the right to know the contents of any adverse report used by a business, the name of the agency that compiled the report, and when such information was the basis for an adverse decision. Consumers also can require compiling agencies to investigate disputed facts, correct the report, or include a consumer's own explanation of disputed facts as part of their report. Investigating agencies must follow "reasonable procedures" in compiling the report and comply with provisions intended to protect the consumer's privacy.

The Fair Credit Billing Act (FCBA) provides that a credit cardholder is financially responsible only for the first $50 of unauthorized charges. Many credit card issuers, as a matter of company policy, will even waive a bona fide customer's obligation to make this payment. The FCBA also addresses a cardholder's rights vis-à-vis a creditor where the cardholder has discovered that items purchased with a credit card were received in damaged condition or were of poor quality. In general (and there are exceptions), the FCBA provides a cardholder with the same remedies against the creditor as exist under state law in the cardholder's state (which frequently will include the right to withhold payment) if certain requirements are met. First, the credit card purchase must have cost more than $50; second, the purchase must have been made either in the cardholder's own state or

within 100 miles of his or her home; third, the cardholder must have attempted to resolve the dispute with the merchant; and fourth, the cardholder must have given the credit card issuer a detailed written explanation of the facts within sixty days of receiving the credit card bill containing the disputed charge.

The **Equal Credit Opportunity Act (ECOA)** of 1974 is designed to eradicate discrimination in the granting of credit when the decision to grant it or refuse it is based on an individual's sex, marital status, race, color, age, religion, national origin, or receipt of public assistance. The major effect of this Act had been to eliminate sex discrimination. Under the ECOA, a married woman can now obtain credit in her own name. A prospective creditor may not ask about an individual's marital status, childbearing plans, spouse or former spouse, or other similar criteria. Questions regarding alimony and child support are proper only if the applicant will rely on those sums to repay the obligation.

Because the ECOA is modeled after the Equal Employment Opportunity Act, facially neutral practices that have the effect of discriminating against a protected class also are prohibited.

The ECOA requires creditors to notify consumers of any decision about the extension or denial of credit, along with the creditor's reasons or a statement indicating that the individual is entitled to know the reasons. An individual may bring suit against a creditor for noncompliance with the ECOA to recover actual and punitive damages.

As previously stated, the Federal Trade Commission bears primary responsibility for CCPA enforcement. We see an example of the FTC attempting to enforce one of the various consumer protection acts for which it is responsible in the following case. Trans Union, the appellant, is one of the nation's largest credit-reporting companies. What follows is its appeal of an FTC determination that the Fair Credit Reporting Act prohibits credit-reporting agencies from compiling and selling to marketing firms who deal directly with consumers certain types of information that has been collected for purposes of creditworthiness determinations.

Trans Union Corporation v. Federal Trade Commission
245 F.3d 809
U.S. Court of Appeals, District of Columbia Circuit
April 13, 2001

Tatel, Circuit Judge.

Petitioner, a consumer reporting agency, sells lists of names and addresses to target marketers—companies and organizations that contact consumers with offers of products and services. The Federal Trade Commission determined that these lists were "consumer reports" under the Fair Credit Reporting Act and thus could no longer be sold for target marketing purposes. Challenging this determination, petitioner argues that the Commission's decision is unsupported by substantial evidence and that the Act itself is unconstitutional....

I

Petitioner Trans Union sells two types of products. First, as a credit-reporting agency, it compiles credit reports about individual consumers from credit information it collects from banks, credit card companies, and other lenders. It then sells these credit reports to lenders, employers, and insurance companies. Trans Union receives credit information from lenders in the form of "tradelines." A tradeline typically includes a customer's name, address, date of birth, telephone number, Social Security number, account type, opening date of account, credit limit, account status, and payment history. Trans Union receives 1.4 to 1.6 billion records per month. The company's credit database contains information on 190 million adults.

Trans Union's second set of products—those at issue in this case—are known as target marketing products. These consist of lists of names and addresses of individuals who meet specific criteria such as possession of an auto loan, a department store credit card, or two or more mortgages. Marketers purchase these lists, then contact the individuals by mail or telephone to offer them goods and services. To create its target marketing lists, Trans Union maintains a database known as MasterFile, a subset of its consumer credit database. MasterFile consists of information about every consumer in the company's credit database who has (A) at least two tradelines with activity during the previous six months, or (B) one tradeline with activity during the previous six months plus an address confirmed by an outside source. The company compiles target marketing lists by extracting from MasterFile the names and addresses of individuals with characteristics chosen by list purchasers. For example, a department store might buy a list of all individuals in a

particular area code who have both a mortgage and a credit card with a $10,000 limit. Although target marketing lists contain only names and addresses, purchasers know that every person on a list has the characteristics they requested because Trans Union uses those characteristics as criteria for culling individual files from its database. Purchasers also know that every individual on a target marketing list satisfies the criteria for inclusion in MasterFile.

The Fair Credit Reporting Act of 1970 ("FCRA") ... regulates consumer reporting agencies like Trans Union, imposing various obligations to protect the privacy and accuracy of credit information. The Federal Trade Commission, acting pursuant to its authority to enforce the FCRA, ... determined that Trans Union's target marketing lists were "consumer reports" subject to the Act's limitations....

... Finding that the information Trans Union sold was "collected in whole or in part by [Trans Union] with the expectation that it would be used by credit grantors for the purpose of serving as a factor in establishing the consumer's eligibility for one of the transactions set forth in the FCRA," and concluding that target marketing is not an authorized use of consumer reports ... the Commission ordered Trans Union to stop selling target marketing lists....

Trans Union petitioned for review. In *Trans Union Corp. v. FTC* ... (D.C. Cir. 1996) ("*Trans Union I*"), we agreed with the Commission that selling consumer reports for target marketing violates the Act.... We nevertheless set aside the Commission's determination that Trans Union's target marketing lists amounted to consumer reports.... The Commission, we held, failed to justify its finding that Trans Union's lists, by conveying the mere fact that consumers had a tradeline, were communicating information collected for the purpose of determining credit eligibility. We found that the Commission had failed to provide evidence to support the proposition that "the mere existence of a tradeline, as distinguished from payment history organized thereunder," was used for credit-granting decisions or was intended or expected to be used for such decisions....

On remand, following extensive discovery, more than a month of trial proceedings, and an initial decision by an Administrative Law Judge, the Commission found that Trans Union's target marketing lists contain information that credit grantors use as factors in granting credit. Accordingly, the Commission concluded, the lists are "consumer reports" that Trans Union may not sell for target marketing purposes.... The Commission also rejected Trans Union's argument that such a restriction would violate its First Amendment rights. Applying intermediate scrutiny, the Commission found that the government has a substantial interest in protecting private credit information, that the FCRA directly advances that interest, and that the Act's restrictions on speech are narrowly tailored.... The Commission thus ordered Trans Union to "cease and desist from distributing or selling consumer reports, including those in the form of target marketing lists, to any person unless [the company] has reason to believe that such person intends to use the consumer report for purposes authorized under Section [1681b] of the Fair Credit Reporting Act." *In re Trans Union Corp.*, Final Order, No. 9255 (Feb. 10, 2000). Trans Union again petitions for review.

II

As we pointed out in *Trans Union I*, the first element of the FCRA's definition of consumer report—"bearing on a consumer's credit worthiness, credit standing, credit capacity, character, general reputation, personal characteristics, or mode of living," 15 U.S.C. §§1681a(d) (1)—"does not seem very demanding," for almost any information about consumers arguably bears on their personal characteristics or mode of living.... Instead, Trans Union does not challenge the Commission's conclusion that the information contained in its lists meets this prong of the definition of consumer report.

Whether the company's target marketing lists qualify as consumer reports thus turns on whether information they contain "is used or expected to be used or collected in whole or in part for the purpose of serving as a factor in establishing the consumer's eligibility for [credit]." ... According to the Commission, "a factor in establishing the consumer's eligibility for [credit]," *id.*, includes any type of information credit grantors use in their criteria for "prescreening" or in "credit scoring models."... "Prescreening" involves selecting individuals for guaranteed offers of credit or insurance.... "Credit scoring models" are statistical models for predicting credit performance that are developed by observing the historical credit performance of a number of consumers and identifying the consumer characteristics that correlate with good and bad credit performance.... Applying its prescreening/credit scoring model standard, the Commission found that Trans Union's lists contain the type of information " 'used' and/or 'expected to be used' ... as a factor in establishing a consumer's eligibility for credit."...

Trans Union urges us to reject the Commission's interpretation of the Act in order to avoid what the company calls "serious constitutional questions."... But as we demonstrate in Section III, *infra,* Trans Union's constitutional arguments are without merit, so we have no basis for rejecting the Commission's statutory interpretation on that ground.

Nor has Trans Union offered a basis for questioning the Commission's statutory interpretation on other grounds....

We have the same reaction to the brief's occasional suggestions that the Commission's decision was arbitrary and capricious.... [T]he list of issues presented for review neither mentions the arbitrary and capricious standard nor otherwise questions the reasonableness of the Commission's decision.

We thus turn to the one non-constitutional argument that Trans Union clearly mounts: that the Commission's decision is unsupported by substantial evidence....

Instead of challenging the Commission's findings regarding specific target marketing products, Trans Union points to evidence relating to the general question of whether the information in its target marketing lists is used to determine credit worthiness. This is not the question before us. As we indicate above, the Commission interprets "factors in establishing the consumer's eligibility for credit,"... to include any information considered by lenders in prescreening, which, as two witnesses testified, can involve consideration of criteria other than credit worthiness, e.g., whether a given consumer is likely to respond to an offer of credit. Because Trans Union has not challenged the Commission's interpretation of the statute, its argument that the information the company sells is not actually used to determine credit worthiness is beside the point. Moreover, Trans Union cites no testimony refuting the Commission's finding that the information in its target marketing lists is used in prescreening.

... Trans Union [has] thus failed to mount a proper substantial evidence challenge to the Commission's finding that lenders take list information into account in credit models and prescreening, but we have no doubt that the decision does find support in the record. Consider, for example, Trans Union's "MasterFile/Selects" product line, which allows marketers to request lists based on any of five categories of information: (1) credit limits (e.g., consumers with credit cards with credit limits over $10,000), (2) open dates of loans (e.g., consumers who took out loans in the last six months), (3) number of tradelines, (4) type of tradeline (e.g., auto loan or mortgage), and (5) existence of a tradeline. The Commission cites testimony and other record evidence that support its finding that lenders consider each of these five categories of information in prescreening or credit scoring models.... To support its finding that information about the number of tradelines in a consumer's credit file is a consumer report, the Commission cites the testimony of a vice president in charge of direct mail processing for a bank's credit card department who explained that, in its credit making decisions, her bank considers the number of tradelines consumers possess.... The Commission also points to record evidence demonstrating that Trans Union itself uses the number of tradelines as a predictive characteristic in its credit scoring models.... As to the type of tradeline, the Commission cites the testimony of representatives of companies that design credit models who explained that some credit scoring models, including two used by Trans Union, take into account possession of a bank card.... One witness testified that Trans Union scoring models also consider possession of a finance company loan to be a predictive characteristic. Another witness, this one representing a credit card company, testified that his company's scoring models assign points for possession of a mortgage, retail tradeline, or bank card....

The record also contains sufficient evidence to support the Commission's resolution of the issue remanded by *Trans Union I:* whether mere existence of a tradeline is "a factor in credit-granting decisions."... An employee of a bank that issues credit cards testified that to be eligible for credit, an individual must have at least one tradeline.... The vice president of credit scoring at another credit card issuer testified that the very first question her company asks in prescreening is whether the consumer has a tradeline that has been open for at least a year. Challenging the implications of this testimony, Trans Union argues that banks ask whether consumers have tradelines not because the existence of a tradeline is itself a factor in determining credit eligibility, but because banks want to determine whether there is enough information in consumer files to make credit eligibility determinations. This may be true. But as we explain above, our task is limited to determining whether substantial record evidence supports the Commission's finding that banks consider the existence of a tradeline as a factor in prescreening or credit models. Because the record contains such evidence, we have no basis for questioning the Commission's decision....

III

Trans Union's constitutional challenge consists of two arguments. It claims first that the FCRA is vague, thus running afoul of the due process guarantee of the Fifth Amendment. Trans Union also argues that the statute violates the free speech guarantee of the First Amendment because it restricts its ability to disseminate information.

Beginning with the Fifth Amendment challenge, we are guided by *Village of Hoffman Estates v. Flipside, Hoffman Estates, Inc.* ... (1982). "Laws," the Court said, must not only "give the person of ordinary intelligence a reasonable opportunity to know what is prohibited," but in order to prevent "arbitrary and discriminatory enforcement," they must also "provide explicit standards for those who apply them."... Emphasizing that these principles should not "be mechanically applied," the Court held that "economic regulation is subject to a less strict vagueness test because its subject matter is often more narrow, and because businesses, which face economic demands to plan behavior carefully, can be expected to consult relevant legislation in advance of action."... The "regulated enterprise," the Court added, "may have the ability to clarify the meaning of the regulation by its own inquiry, or by resort to an administrative process."... Finally, "the consequences of imprecision are qualitatively less severe" when laws have "scienter requirements" and "civil rather than criminal penalties."...

Applying this standard, we see no merit in Trans Union's vagueness argument. To begin with, because the FCRA's regulation of consumer reporting agencies is economic, it is subject to "a less strict vagueness test."... Moreover, Trans Union has "the ability to clarify the meaning of the [FCRA]" ... through the Commission's advisory opinion procedures. *See* 16 C.F.R. §§1.1–1.4 (establishing general procedures for obtaining advisory opinions); *id.* §§2.41(d) (establishing procedures for obtaining guidance regarding compliance with FTC orders)....

Trans Union's First Amendment challenge fares no better. Banning the sale of target marketing lists, the company says, amounts to a restriction on its speech subject to strict scrutiny. Again, Trans Union misunderstands our standard of review. In *Dun & Bradstreet, Inc. v. Greenmoss Builders, Inc.* ... (1985), the Supreme Court held that a consumer reporting agency's credit report warranted reduced constitutional protection because it concerned "no public issue." ... "The protection to be accorded a particular credit report," the Court explained, "depends on whether the report's 'content, form, and context' indicate that it concerns a public matter."... Like the credit report in *Dun & Bradstreet,* which the Supreme Court found "was speech solely in the interest of the speaker and its specific business audience,"... the information about individual consumers and their credit performance communicated by Trans Union target marketing lists is solely of interest to the company and its business customers and relates to no matter of public concern. Trans Union target marketing lists thus warrant "reduced constitutional protection."...

We turn then to the specifics of Trans Union's First Amendment argument. The company first claims that neither the FCRA nor the Commission's Order advances a substantial government interest. The "Congressional findings and statement of purpose" at the beginning of the FCRA state: "There is a need to insure that consumer reporting agencies exercise their grave responsibilities with ... respect for the consumer's right to privacy."... Contrary to the company's assertions, we have no doubt that this interest—protecting the privacy of consumer credit information—is substantial.

Trans Union next argues that Congress should have chosen a "less burdensome alternative," i.e., allowing consumer reporting agencies to sell credit information as long as they notify consumers and give them the ability to "opt out."... Because the FCRA is not subject to strict First Amendment scrutiny,

however, Congress had no obligation to choose the least restrictive means of accomplishing its goal.

Finally, Trans Union argues that the FCRA is underinclusive because it applies only to consumer reporting agencies and not to other companies that sell consumer information. But given consumer reporting agencies' unique "access to a broad range of continually-updated, detailed information about millions of consumers' personal credit histories," ... we think it not at all inappropriate for Congress to have singled out consumer reporting agencies for regulation.... To survive a First Amendment underinclusiveness challenge ... "neither a perfect nor even the best available fit between means and ends is required."... The FCRA easily satisfies this standard....

IV
Having considered and rejected Trans Union's other arguments, we deny the petition for review.
So Ordered.

Case Questions

1. What consumer interest was the FTC seeking to protect in ruling as it did vis-à-vis Trans Union?
2. Why did the appeals court uphold the agency's determination that Trans Union's actions were contrary to the requirements of the Fair Credit Reporting Act?

CHAPTER SUMMARY

The chapter began with a historical overview of the evolution of federal administrative agencies and why they came into being. This was followed with a discussion of the ways federal agencies are organized and how agencies are legally delegated rule-making, investigative, and adjudicative powers

in an enabling act. Explanations as to how each of these delegated powers is exercised were then followed by an overview of the judiciary's limited role in reviewing agency decisions. The chapter concluded with a look at how two federal agencies regulate business activity.

CHAPTER QUESTIONS

1. The Secretary of Commerce, pursuant to rule-making authority contained in the Atlantic Tunas Convention Act of 1975 (the ATCA), adopted regulations regarding the use of "spotter aircraft" by fishing-permit holders. The purposes of the ATCA included preventing the overfishing of the Atlantic Bluefin

Tuna (ABT), setting quotas on the ABT catch per country, and increasing ABT scientific research. The regulations prohibited persons holding "general-category" fishing permits from using spotter aircraft to locate ABT, but permitted the use of such planes by persons licensed to catch ABT with harpoons or seine nets. The ABT is a very valuable fish, each one being worth up to $50,000. The Atlantic Fish Spotters Association brought suit, maintaining that this regulation should be overturned. What standard will the plaintiffs have to meet to persuade the U.S. District Court to overturn the regulation? What type of evidence will the plaintiffs need to produce to be successful?

Atlantic Fish Spotters Association v. Dailey, 8 F. Supp. 2d 113 (1998)

2. Faustino Ramos, Michael Beal, and Francisco Marila were employees of Mavo Leasing, Inc. Mavo and the Production Workers Union (PWU) of Chicago were parties to a collective-bargaining agreement that required that all employees pay union dues to the PWU. Mavo discharged the above-named employees for not paying their union dues in accordance with a clause in the collective-bargaining agreement. The three employees claimed that the union had not given them notice of their right to challenge certain union expenditures that were not made in furtherance of collective bargaining. They argued that they did not have to pay dues for nonrepresentation expenses. The employees complained about this lack of notice to the National Labor Relations Board (NLRB). An ALJ heard the complaint and ruled that the union did not have an affirmative obligation to provide the employees with the requested notice. An NLRB three-member appeals panel ruled in favor of the employees and interpreted the National Labor Relations Act as requiring the union to provide the employees with notice of the right to object to paying dues to fund nonrepresentation expenditures, prior to discharge from employment for nonpayment of union dues. The issue was appealed to the U.S. Court of Appeals for the Seventh Circuit. How should the court decide this appeal, and why?

Production Workers Union of Chicago v. N.L.R.B., 161 F.3d 1047 (1998)

3. The Fertilizer Institute (TFI) is a trade organization that represents members of the fertilizer industry. TFI filed suit in U.S. District Court against the EPA, contesting the agency's decision to list nitrate compounds on the toxic release inventory that is compiled by the EPA pursuant to the Emergency Planning and Community Right to Know Act of 1986. The EPA listed these compounds because of evidence that they posed a chronic health threat to human infants. TFI argued that the record did not support the EPA's decision. What evidence would the trial court need to conclude that the EPA had acted arbitrarily in reaching its decision? Why?

Fertilizer Industry v. Browner, 163 F.3d 774 (1998)

4. New York's Aid to Families with Dependent Children (AFDC) program, stressing "close contact" with beneficiaries, requires home visits by caseworkers as a condition for assistance "in order that any treatment or service tending to restore [beneficiaries] to a condition of self-support and to relieve their distress may be rendered and … that assistance or care may be given only in such amount and as long as necessary." Visitation with a beneficiary, who is the primary source of information to welfare authorities about eligibility for assistance, is not permitted outside working hours, and forcible entry and snooping are prohibited. The appellee was a beneficiary under the AFDC program. Although she had received several days' advance notice, she refused to permit a caseworker to visit her home. Following a hearing and advice that assistance would consequently be terminated, she brought suit for injunctive and declaratory relief, contending that home visitation is a search and, when not consented to or supported by a warrant based on probable cause, would violate her Fourth and Fourteenth Amendment rights. The District Court upheld the welfare recipient's constitutional claim. Was the District Court correct? Why or why not?

Wyman v. James, 400 U.S. 309 (1971)

5. Columbia East, Inc., the owner of 34.3 acres of farmland, wanted its zoning changed so it

could develop a mobile home park. The board of zoning appeals granted a preliminary approval of the application for a special exception to develop a mobile home park in an area zoned as agricultural. Final approval by the board of zoning appeals could be granted only after the plans and specifications for the development of the proposed trailer court had been completed and approved by the appropriate agencies. Neighboring landowners filed a suit in court challenging the board's preliminary approval, claiming the decision was made without adequate provision for sewage treatment. What should the court decide?

Downing v. Board of Zoning Appeals, 274 N.E.2d 542 (Ind. 1971)

6. The Occupational Safety and Health Act empowers agents of the Secretary of Labor to search the work area of any employment facility within the Act's jurisdiction. No search warrant or other process is expressly required under the Act. An OSHA inspector entered the customer-service area of Barlow's, Inc., an electrical- and plumbing-installation business, and stated that he wished to conduct a search of the working areas of the business. Barlow, the president and general manager, asked the inspector whether he had received any complaints about the working conditions and whether he had a search warrant. The inspector answered both questions in the negative. The

inspector was denied entry into the working areas. Secretary of Labor Marshall argued that warrantless inspections to enforce OSHA regulations are reasonable within the meaning of the Fourth Amendment, and relied on the Act, which authorizes inspection of business premises without a warrant. Should the court accept Marshall's argument?

Marshall v. Barlow's, Inc., 436 U.S. 307 (1978)

7. Under the U.S. Community Health Centers Act, the Secretary of the Department of Health, Education, and Welfare was empowered to award monetary grants to health centers that complied with federal regulations. Temple University received funds under the Act and was therefore required to meet the federal regulations. In addition, the Pennsylvania Department of Public Welfare and the County Mental Health and Retardation Board were charged with the responsibility of administering county health programs. In 1970, the Temple University Mental Health Center was required to cut back services and impose strict security measures because of campus riots. Members of the surrounding community brought suit against Temple University, charging that the center was not providing required services and that members of the community were deprived of access to the facility. What should the court's decision be?

North Philadelphia Community Board v. Temple University, 330 F. Supp. 1107 (1971)

NOTES

1. *Federal Regulatory Directory* (Washington, DC: Congressional Quarterly, Inc., 1990), p. 621.

2. Ibid., p. 687.

3. Ibid., p. 2.

4. Ibid., p. 3.

5. The plaintiffs in this case were the National Restaurant Association, Counsel of State Restaurant Associations, Inc., and National Federation of Independent Businesses.

XIV

Alternative Dispute Resolution

CHAPTER OBJECTIVES

1. *Understand the rationale supporting the use of alternative dispute resolution (ADR) methods as a substitute for litigation.*

2. *Explain the differences between voluntary and court-annexed arbitration.*

3. *Describe the key features of arbitration, mediation, minitrials, summary jury trials, and private trials.*

Litigation is not the only mechanism available for the resolution of a dispute. Disputants who are unable to negotiate a solution to a pending conflict but who wish to avoid a public court trial can choose what is currently called **alternative dispute resolution (ADR)**. ADR has gained popularity largely because many people are dissatisfied with the workings of the traditional legal system. This dissatisfaction has many origins. Plaintiffs, in particular, dislike litigation's snail-like pace and complain about the volume of cases clogging up the court system and producing gridlock. In federal district courts, for example, 289,969 civil cases were filed in the twelve-month period ending December 31, 2011,[1] up from 244,343 filings in 2006.[2] Dissatisfaction also results when lawyers adopt a strategy of winning by exhausting an opponent's financial resources. Although case preparation generally will not compensate for a weak case, sometimes a weak case can be won if the client has vastly superior resources. An attorney may take such a case to trial in order to drag out the proceedings, dramatically increase the opponent's litigation expenses, and force the opponent to settle the case on unfavorable terms.

As a factual matter, a very small percentage of cases filed actually go to trial. The data from federal courts are illustrative. Of the 305,713 civil cases terminated in U.S. district courts during the twelve-month period ending December 31, 2011, only 1.1 percent actually went to trial.[3] The percentage of federal cases reaching trial was 1.3 percent in 2006 and 2.2 percent in 2000.[4]

Many attorneys, while acknowledging that few cases actually are resolved at trial, continue to prepare each case as if it will be. They over-prepare for a variety of professional and strategic reasons. Because litigation is an adversarial process, lawyers assume that opponents will resort to every legal device to win. Attorneys anticipate a continuing series of battles with the opponent at the pretrial, trial, and appellate stages of a process that can take years to determine an ultimate winner. They know that there are many ways to lose a case, and they worry about malpractice claims. Trial victories require more than good facts and sound legal arguments; they result from careful preparation and thorough discovery. Discovery also consumes large amounts of an attorney's time, which often translates into billable hours paid by the client.

The fact that lawyers become heavily involved in preparing attacks upon their client's opponent often means that they avoid looking at possible weaknesses in their own cases until just before trial. Lawyers often view themselves as their client's champion, and they frequently engage in posturing and puffery. Some refuse to initiate settlement discussions with the opponents because they fear that this might be interpreted by their clients, as well as their client's opponents, as a sign of weakness. If settlement discussions do occur, neither side is likely to be candid and reveal the amount that would be accepted in settlement of the case. Furthermore, an attorney might believe that a tactical advantage can be gained by responding to an opponent's proposal rather than being the first to suggest a settlement figure. This game-like approach to litigation only compounds costs in money and time as the parties prepare for a trial that statistically is unlikely to occur.

Many litigants often find the judicial system's traditional "winner-take-all" approach unsatisfactory because it produces a costly victory. Both parties can lose when the disputants have an ongoing relationship—as in business, labor–management, or child-custody cases—and one party clobbers the other in court. Because ADR methods can often resolve disputes more satisfactorily than trials—at less expense and in less time—some lawyers are required by state supreme court rule to explain the existence of options to litigation to their clients.[5]

Businesses have been looking for ways to resolve disputes that avoid class-action lawsuits and jury trials, which expose them to the possibility of high damage awards. Congress's enactment of the Alternative Dispute Resolution Act (ADRA) in 1998 has increased judicial interest in ADR. In the ADRA, Congress explicitly required all federal agencies, including the federal district courts and courts of appeals, to implement ADR procedures. Its reasoning is clearly explained in the excerpt found in Figure 14.1.

State courts also have been looking for cost-efficient ways to reduce the length of their burgeoning dockets, given the low percentage of their civil cases that actually are tried. Many states have established statewide ADR systems. Some permit local jurisdictions to experiment with ADR if they wish to do so. The extent to which ADR methods are available varies greatly. Some jurisdictions offer a menu of ADR options, while others focus on a preferred procedure, such as mediation or arbitration.

ADR programs generally are classified as either voluntary or court-annexed. **Voluntary ADR** programs serve parties who have elected on their own initiative to try ADR methods to resolve their dispute. **Court-annexed ADR** programs are created by law or court rule, and the parties participate in ADR because it is required by the state or local court rule.

VOLUNTARY ADR

When parties to a dispute decide to avoid the negative aspects of a court trial, they may voluntarily choose to resort to ADR, because often it can produce a fair result faster and at less cost than a public court trial. In fact, several major corporations will contract only with vendors who agree to participate in ADR. Disputants often prefer ADR, because

---

Sec. 651. Authorization of alternative dispute resolution

(a) Definition.—For purposes of this chapter, an alternative dispute resolution process includes any process or procedure, other than an adjudication by a presiding judge, in which a neutral third party participates to assist in the resolution of issues in controversy, through processes such as early neutral evaluation, mediation, minitrial, and arbitration as provided in sections 654 through 658.

(b) Authority.—Each United States district court shall authorize, by local rule adopted under section 2071(a), the use of alternative dispute resolution processes in all civil actions, including adversary proceedings in bankruptcy, in accordance with this chapter, except that the use of arbitration may be authorized only as provided in section 654. Each United States district court shall devise and implement its own alternative dispute resolution program, by local rule adopted under section 2071(a), to encourage and promote the use of alternative dispute resolution in its district.

(c) Existing Alternative Dispute Resolution Programs.—In those courts where an alternative dispute resolution program is in place on the date of the enactment of the Alternative Dispute Resolution Act of 1998, the court shall examine the effectiveness of that program and adopt such improvements to the program as are consistent with the provisions and purposes of this chapter.

(d) Administration of Alternative Dispute Resolution Programs.—Each United States district court shall designate an employee, or a judicial officer, who is knowledgeable in alternative dispute resolution practices and processes to implement, administer, oversee, and evaluate the court's alternative dispute resolution program. Such person may also be responsible for recruiting, screening, and training attorneys to serve as neutrals and arbitrators in the court's alternative dispute resolution program. . . .

FIGURE 14.1 Excerpt from the Alternative Dispute Resolution Act of 1998
Source: Public Law 105-315, 105th Congress.

they can choose the procedure that seems most appropriate to their needs. They also may like having their dispute resolved by a person or persons (*arbitrators* or *neutrals,* discussed below) who have particular expertise in that subject area.

When parties voluntarily participate in ADR, they negotiate a contract that sets forth the rules that will govern the proceedings. They can turn to several agencies for model ADR rules and procedures. This is helpful because attorneys who are inexperienced with ADR are sometimes reluctant to negotiate an ADR agreement with a more-seasoned opponent. Model rules are evenhanded, and their terms provide neither side with an advantage. They establish reasonable and simplified discovery rules and simplified rules of evi-

dence that allow the parties to introduce documents that might otherwise be inadmissible hearsay. The rules also can provide for confidentiality: businesses and individuals often would prefer to deny competitors, the general public, and the news media access to private and potentially embarrassing information that would be revealed in conjunction with public court litigation.[6]

Traditional ADR practitioners and firms often advertise in trade publications and list themselves in many metropolitan-area telephone directories under "arbitration." To attract customers, increasing numbers of automobile manufacturers, local home contractors, businesses, and professionals advertise that they participate in ADR. The American Arbitration Association and the Federal Conciliation and

Mediation Service are prominent examples of institutions that maintain panels of **arbitrators** and impartial third parties (called **neutrals**) who specialize in a particular field such as construction, commercial contracts, real estate, or finance, and can be engaged to provide ADR services. National dispute-resolution firms have offices in major cities, have employed hundreds of retired judges (even state supreme court justices) as arbitrators, and have annual revenues exceeding $40 million.[7]

ONLINE DISPUTE RESOLUTION

In recent years, the Internet explosion and advances in computer hardware and software have contributed to the expansion of online dispute resolution (ODR). Well-known organizations such as the American Arbitration Association and the Better Business Bureau now provide ODR services, as do private companies such as Square Trade and Cybersettle. The speed, flexibility, and relatively low costs of ODR are especially appealing to online retailers seeking another option for handling customer disputes that cannot be resolved easily by customer service representatives.

INTERNET TIP

The American Arbitration Association has a wonderful website explaining both traditional ADR and the expanding ODR options. See http://www.adr.org/

COURT-ANNEXED ADR

Participation in ADR is legislatively or judicially authorized in many jurisdictions. As mentioned above, the federal ADRA, for example, provides for ADR programs in the federal district courts and circuit courts of appeal.

Where federal and state judges claim authority to compel ADR participation, they usually promulgate court rules. Such rules are justified as being a necessary and appropriate exercise of a court's inherent power to manage its docket. Local rules often require that parties participate in nonbinding,

court-annexed ADR programs before they are permitted access to a jury trial. Such programs encourage settlements, reduce court dockets, and lessen the financial burdens on taxpayers, who pay for the operation of the public judicial systems. The ADRA requires every federal district court to adopt at least one ADR method by local rule.

Most ADR methods are undertaken in the expectation that such programs will result in reducing the number of cases that are tried to juries. Any proposals to deny plaintiffs pursuing common law relief access to a trial by jury will collide with the traditional right to a jury trial enshrined in the Seventh Amendment to the U.S. Constitution. The scope of the Seventh Amendment's jury-trial right is deeply rooted in our history. Under our law, the right to a jury trial is recognized for all actions that were tried by English juries at the time of the Constitution's ratification, and for other actions that are closely related to common law claims. There is no jury-trial right for litigants who seek equitable relief or for actions that were unknown to the common law. Compulsory ADR has been structured so that there is no infringement of the right to a jury trial. Litigants are required to participate in pretrial ADR, but they can reject ADR solutions and then proceed to a trial by jury.

Introduction to Delaware Corporation for Open Government v. Strine

The plaintiff in the next case filed suit in federal district court which challenges the constitutionality of a Delaware Statute (Delaware Code Title 10, Section 349) and 3 Delaware Chancery Court rules (96, 97, and 98) which permit regular members of the Chancery Court to act as arbitrators in some commercial disputes. One of the primary benefits to parties participating in these arbitrations was a Chancery Rule provision that the parties could keep the entire process confidential. This absolute confidentiality was an exception to the normal requirements that the public have access to most judicial proceedings. A second benefit of this new "secret court" program is the access the parties get to highly skilled chancery judges who function as arbitrators in these actions, and the enforcement powers of the state judiciary– a most attractive alternative to private arbitrations. The plaintiff's brought suit in the U. S. District Court for the District of Delaware alleging the public's right to access to the proceedings and asserting a constitutional right to know what has transpired in the chancery court.

The district court judge's opinion follows. Readers should know that this case was subsequently appealed to the United States Court of Appeals for the Third Circuit. Unfortunately, no decision has been announced as of August 1, 2013, and it therefore cannot be included in this text.

Delaware Corporation for Open Government v. Honorable Leo E. Strine, Jr.
_____ F. Supp. 2d_____
United States District Court for the District of Delaware
August 30, 2012

McLaughlin, J.

Memorandum
This is a challenge to a confidential arbitration proceeding established by Delaware law and implemented by the Delaware Court of Chancery.... The plaintiff argues that the First Amendment's qualified right of access prevents the defendants from closing this proceeding to the public and press. Both parties have cross-moved for judgment on the pleadings....

I. The Delaware Proceeding
In April of 2009, the Delaware State Legislature amended the rules governing the resolution of disputes in the Court of Chancery.... This law gives the Court of Chancery "the power to arbitrate business disputes when the parties request a member of the Court of Chancery, or such other person as may be authorized under rules of the Court, to arbitrate a dispute."... The arbitration procedure is "intended to preserve Delaware's pre-eminence in offering cost-effective options for resolving disputes, particularly those involving commercial, corporate, and technology matters."...

Access to this arbitration procedure requires the parties' consent. There is no requirement that the parties have an agreement to arbitrate their disputes prior to the dispute arising, but both must consent to participate at the time the dispute is submitted to the court.... In addition, parties must meet certain eligibility criteria to participate.... At least one party must be a "business entity" and one party must be a citizen of the state of Delaware, although the same party can meet both criteria.... Thus both businesses and individuals can utilize the procedure. If the remedy sought includes only monetary damages, the amount in controversy must be more than one million dollars; if any equitable remedy is sought, even in conjunction with monetary damages, there is no amount-in-controversy requirement....

The parties cannot submit their dispute for arbitration if either is a "consumer," defined as an indi-

vidual who purchases or leases merchandise for personal use.... The procedure is accessible for "business disputes" and the law provides no limit to the type of controversy that may be submitted. Because the law allows parties seeking only monetary damages to submit their disputes to the Chancery Court, it allows some cases which would otherwise be excluded under the Chancery Court's limited equitable jurisdiction to be decided by Chancery Court judges....

... To initiate the proceeding, the parties file a petition with the Register in Chancery, stating the nature of the dispute, the claims made, and the remedies sought. The parties must certify that the eligibility criteria described above are met.... Once a petition is filed, the Chancellor appoints a Chancery Court judge to preside over the case as the arbitrator....

Within ten days of the petition's filing, the arbitrator holds a preliminary conference with the parties, and then, as soon as practicable, a preliminary hearing.... At the preliminary hearing, the parties and arbitrator discuss the claims of the case, damages, defenses asserted, legal authorities to be relied upon, the scope of discovery, and the timing, length, and evidence to be presented at the arbitration hearing.... At the preliminary hearing, the parties also consider "the possibility of mediation or other non-adjudicative methods of dispute resolution."...

An arbitration hearing occurs approximately ninety days after the petition's filing.... At any stage of this process, the parties can agree to mediation through the Chancery Court or can seek the assistance of the judge in pursuing and reaching a settlement agreement....

Prior to the arbitration hearing, the parties exchange "information necessary and appropriate for the parties to prepare for the arbitration hearing and to enable the Arbitrator to understand the dispute."... The parties can agree to the scope of information to be exchanged or can have the arbitrator decide the scope of discovery.... Court of Chancery Rules

26 through 37, which govern depositions and discovery in all Chancery Court matters, apply to the arbitration proceeding unless the parties and arbitrator together agree to different rules.... Some discovery matters, such as the procedure for issuing subpoenas, must be created by the parties and the arbitrator.... All parties must participate in the arbitration hearing and at least one representative "with authority to resolve the matter must participate...."...

The arbitrator has the power to issue a final award and to make interim, interlocutory, or partial rulings during the course of the proceeding.... The arbitrator's final award, issued after the hearing, can include "any remedy or relief Chat the Arbitrator deems just and equitable and within the scope of any applicable agreement of the parties."... Finally, "[u]pon the granting of a final award, a final judgment or decree shall be entered in conformity therewith and be enforced as any other judgment or decree."...

Either party may apply to the Supreme Court of Delaware "to vacate, stay, or enforce an order of the Court of Chancery."... The Supreme Court can consider these motions only "in conformity with the Federal Arbitration Act ('FAA')]."... Under the FAA, an arbitration award cannot be vacated on the grounds of legal error. An arbitration judgment can only be vacated if there is a showing of fraud, corruption, undue means in procuring the award; partiality, corruption, or certain misconduct on the part of the arbitrator; or the arbitrator exceeded his powers or failed to make a final award.... Awards can also be modified if there was a material miscalculation of figures, if the arbitrator exceeded his authority, or if the modification would not affect the merits of the controversy....

The Delaware law and Chancery Court Rules governing the arbitration require that the proceeding be conducted out of the public view. The Delaware law provides:

> Arbitration proceedings shall be considered confidential and not of public record until such time, if any, as the proceedings are the subject of an appeal. In the case of an appeal, the record shall be filed by the parties with the Supreme Court in accordance with its rules....

10 Del. C. §349(b).

The Chancery Court Rules require that all parts of the proceeding, including all filings and all contacts between the arbitrator and any party are "confidential and not of public record."... The Register in Chancery does not file the parties' petition on the court's public docketing system.... None of the hearings is open to the public. Only parties are allowed to attend the arbitration hearing unless they agree otherwise.... All "memoranda and work product contained in the case files of

an Arbitrator," and "[a]ny communication made in or in connection with the arbitration that relates to the controversy being arbitrated" are likewise confidential....

The arbitrator's final award is not made public, although a judgment is "entered in conformity therewith."... This judgement is a one-and-a-half page order confirming the arbitration award already entered in favor of the respondents. It contains no information about the nature of the case, except that the suit was originally filed as a civil suit in the Chancery Court and then converted into an arbitration proceeding by consent of the parties....

If the parties apply to the Supreme Court of Delaware for enforcement, stay, or vacatur of the award, then the confidential record of the proceedings "shall be filed by the parties with the Supreme Court in accordance with its Rules."... Once an appeal is filed, at least some of the record will become public.... The Delaware Supreme Court has not yet adopted rules for the procedure, nor is there any public record of an appeal before the Supreme Court.

The question at issue in this case is whether there is a right of access to this proceeding which is violated by the confidentiality requirements of the law and implementing rules.

II. The Right of Access

The First Amendment provides that "Congress shall make no law ... abridging the freedom of speech, or of the press...." U.S. Const, amend. I. The prohibitions of the First Amendment extend to the states through the Fourteenth Amendment and bar government interference with both the speaker and the listener. In 1980, the Supreme Court held that the First Amendment also protects the public's ability to attend criminal judicial proceedings. *Richmond Newspapers. Inc. v. Virginia* ... (1980).

In *Richmond Newspapers*, a Virginia trial court excluded the public and press from a murder trial. In five separate opinions, seven of the eight participating Justices held that the First Amendment prevents the government from denying public access to historically open government proceedings....

Although the Supreme Court has never addressed access to civil judicial proceedings, every Court of Appeals to consider the issue, including the Court of Appeals for the Third Circuit, has held that there is a right of access to civil trials....

In *Publicker Industries*, [*Inc. v. Cohen* (1984)] the Court of Appeals explained why the reasoning of *Richmond Newspapers* applied to civil trials. As with criminal trials, the English and American legal systems have historically presumed that civil proceedings are open to the public....

Many of the same rationales supporting openness in criminal trials apply equally to civil trials. Disputes among private citizens may not be matters of public concern in the same way as criminal prosecutions. But the actions of those charged with administering justice through the judiciary is always a public matter.

Openness of civil trials promotes the integrity of the courts and the perception of fairness essential to their legitimacy. Public dissemination of the facts of a civil trial can encourage those with information to come forward, and public attention can discourage witnesses from perjury. The Court of Appeals for the Third Circuit has summarized the six benefits of open judicial proceedings, both criminal and civil as:

> [1] promotion of informed discussion of governmental affairs by providing the public with the more complete understanding of the judicial system; [2] promotion of the public perception of fairness which can be achieved only by permitting full public view of the proceedings; [3] providing a significant community therapeutic value as an outlet for community concern, hostility and emotion; [4] serving as a check on corrupt practices by exposing the judicial process to public scrutiny; [5] enhancement of the performance of all involved; and [6] discouragement of perjury....

N. Jersey Media Grp., Inc. v. Ashcroft ... (3d Cir. 2002).

In several en banc opinions, the Court of Appeals has declined to extend the right of access to proceedings before the executive branch, which lacked the history and public benefits of openness....

III. Analysis

... The defendants argue that this Court should apply the logic and experience test to determine if commercial arbitration should be subject to the right of access. The plaintiff argues that the Delaware proceeding is essentially a bench trial and *Publicker Industries* governs the state's ability to close the proceeding to the public.

A. Threshold Question

Before this Court can consider the experience and logic test, it must address this threshold question. Has Delaware implemented a form of commercial arbitration to which the Court must apply the logic and experience test, or has it created a procedure "sufficiently like a trial" such that *Publicker Industries* governs?...

1. Arbitration versus litigation.

In many ways, arbitration and civil litigation are similar. Arbitration is "a private system of justice."... Parties select a neutral decision maker, often an expert in the relevant field, to resolve their dispute.... The parties consent to be bound by the decision of the arbitrator, and his resolution of the dispute is constrained by the parties' agreement. This consent is one of arbitration's defining features. The parties' voluntary agreement to resolve their dispute through a decision maker of their choosing is the "essence of arbitration."...

Arbitration differs from litigation because it occurs outside of the judicial process. The arbitrator is not a judicial official.... In litigation, a court can compel an unwilling party. In arbitration, the parties agree to participate in a specified forum....

Parties can craft arbitrations to their specific needs. The parties can specify the scope of the arbitrator's authority and design the applicable procedural rules. Litigation follows the court's procedures and guidelines.

Because they are outside the judicial system, arbitration decisions are ad hoc, lacking any precedential value.... Arbitration tribunals, in "sharp contrast ... are not generally required to apply principles of substantive law or court-established rules of evidence[,] ... arbitrators give no reason for their decision, and the award is generally not open to review by courts for any error in finding facts and applying law."...

The chief advantage of arbitration is the ability to resolve disputes without aspects often associated with the legal system: procedural delay and cost of discovery, the adversarial relationship of the parties, and publicity of the dispute.... As the product of private agreement between the parties, historically, arbitrations have been conducted outside the public view....

2. Arbitrators versus judges.

Because arbitrations offer a private system of remedies that parallels the courts, a judge and arbitrator share many of the same attributes. An arbitrator is [a]n impartial person selected ... to hear the evidence and deliver a final and binding decision as a determination" of parties' dispute....

But an arbitrator and a judge perform very different functions. This distinction is more than just semantic. Arbitrators act as a "private extraordinary Judge[], chosen by the Parties to give Judgments between them."... They are empowered by the parties' consent and limited by the scope of that consent. They serve the parties.

Judges, on the other hand, are empowered by their appointment to a public office. They act according to prescribed rules of law and procedure. They serve the public. The Court of Appeals for the Fifth Circuit described the difference between the judge and arbitrator this way: "The trial judge ... bears a special responsibility in the public interest to resolve the ... dispute, for once the judicial machinery has been set in train, the proceeding takes on a public character in which remedies are devised to vindicate the policies of the [law], not merely to afford private relief....

Even with the proliferation of alternative dispute resolution in courts, judges in this country do not take on the role of arbitrators. States with court-annexed arbitration programs appoint third party neutrals such as attorneys and retired judges, and not sitting judges, to serve as arbitrators.... The California Court of Appeal has held that the judge's public role and obligations prevent a sitting judge from acting as an arbitrator for even consenting parties....

The Alternative Dispute Resolution Act, which creates court-annexed arbitration in the federal courts, seems to allow magistrate judges to serve as arbitrators. But neither the parties nor this Court could find evidence of that practice, and several courts have noted the inherent tension between the role of judge and arbitrator....

A judge bears a special responsibility to serve the public interest. That obligation, and the public role of that job, is undermined when a judge acts as an arbitrator bound only by the parties' agreement.

3. The Delaware proceeding.
The Delaware proceeding, although bearing the label arbitration, is essentially a civil trial.

When the parties file a petition for an arbitration proceeding, the Chancellor, and not the parties, selects the judge who will hear the case. Rather than set rules for arbitration discovery, many of the same rules governing discovery in the Chancery Court apply to the arbitration.

A sitting judge presides over the proceeding. It is this fact which distinguishes the Delaware proceeding from court-annexed arbitrations where third parties sit as arbitrators. Just as in any other civil case, the judge conducts the proceedings in the Chancery courthouse with the assistance of Chancery Court staff. The judges are not compensated privately by the parties; the Chancery Court judge and staff are paid their usual salaries for arbitration work.

In a usual arbitration proceeding, if one party refuses to comply, the other can enforce compliance only by pursuing enforcement through a court. In Delaware, the judge and arbitrator are the same, so the judge's final award results in a judgment enforced by state power. The judge can also issue interim, interloc-

utory, or partial orders and awards.... These orders, and the final arbitration award and judgment, bind the parties much as any court orders would. They are nearly identical to a judge's orders in a civil trial, but with one important difference. Because the Delaware proceedings and awards are confidential, the judge does not publish his rulings or reasoning. The public does not know the factual findings the judge has made or what legal rules the judge is, or should be, applying to these arbitrations.

In the Delaware proceeding, the parties submit their dispute to a sitting judge acting pursuant to state authority, paid by the state, and using state personnel and facilities; the judge finds facts, applies the relevant law, determines the obligations of the parties; and the judge then issues an enforceable order. This procedure is sufficiently like a civil trial that *Publicker Industries* governs....

B. The Experience and Logic Test
Because the Court finds that the Delaware procedure is a civil judicial proceeding, it is not necessary to reiterate the thorough analysis of the experience and logic test performed by the Court of Appeals in *Publicker Industries*.

The public benefits of openness were well described by the Court of Appeals, and this Court does not dwell on them except to note that they are clearly applicable to the Delaware proceeding....

The public benefits of openness are not outweighed by the defendants' speculation that such openness will drive parties to use alternative non-public fora to resolve their disputes. Even if the procedure fell into disuse, the judiciary as a whole is strengthened by the public knowledge that its courthouses are open and judicial officers are not adjudicating in secret.

IV. Conclusion
The Court concludes that the right of access applies to the Delaware proceeding created by section 349 of the Delaware Code. The portions of that law and Chancery Court Rules 96, 97, and 98, which make the proceeding confidential, violate that right.

An appropriate order shall issue.

Case Questions

1. Why did the Delaware Coalition object to the portion of the Delaware statute that made court-annexed arbitrations confidential?
2. In your opinion, how might keeping arbitrations confidential benefit disputing companies?
3. Since companies can arbitrate their suits privately, why should Delaware adopt this new law and duplicate such services within the Chancery Court—isn't it unnecessary? Might the fact that the Delaware law provided the prevailing party in an arbitration with a court judgment be an incentive? Might the fact that other countries have laws similar to Delaware that are "business friendly" and provide for complete confidentiality influence your decision?

INTERNET TIP

The decision of the U.S. Court of Appeals for the Third Circuit in this case was handed down too late for inclusion in this edition. It will be found on the textbook's website.

ADR TECHNIQUES

The demand for trial-avoidance methods to resolve disputes has resulted in increasing reliance on settlement conferences, arbitration, and mediation—three of the oldest and the most popular ADR options—as well as the development of newer techniques such as private trials, minitrials, and summary jury trials.

Settlement Conferences

Rule 1 of the Federal Rules of Civil Procedure states that judges are expected to promote "the just, speedy, and inexpensive determination of every action." This very general charge gives judges considerable flexibility in determining how they will achieve this goal. Many judges use **settlement conferences,** which are a traditional step in the litigation process, as an informal method for resolving a dispute without a trial.[8]

A judge who is willing to be assertive can help parties explore a lawsuit's settlement potential. The judge can initiate the process or respond to a request for assistance from one or more of the parties. This intervention can be helpful when neither of the opposing attorneys is willing to make the first move toward a settlement. The parties, however, often leap at an opportunity to discuss settlement if the judge broaches the subject. An assertive judge may personally convene a settlement conference, carefully review the case, and emphasize each side's weaknesses and strengths. This is important because the evidence is frequently inconclusive. A judge who is knowledgeable about the relevant law can be very influential. He or she can point out the costs of going to trial and emphasize the risks each side incurs by

trying the matter to an unpredictable jury.[9] The judge may know about recent verdicts in similar cases that went to trial and may suggest ADR options that could help each side avoid the necessity of a trial. Some judges, if requested by the parties, will propose a settlement figure. Judges who have the time, skill, and interest to function as mediators may meet privately with each side. They may even request that the clients meet without their attorneys being present. The judge's participation is the key ingredient. It is one thing for an attorney to engage in puffery with a client or an opponent. It is another matter to refuse to acknowledge the weaknesses of one's case to an experienced trial judge. Many judges, however, don't define their role in this way, believing that settlement is a matter to be decided solely by the parties without judicial involvement.

Serious issues arise regarding the judge's proper role in the settlement conference. Many lawyers are concerned that a party who refuses to settle may encounter bias if the matter is subsequently set for trial before the settlement judge. They fear that the judge might rule against the "uncooperative" party on motions and evidence admissibility at trial. One solution to this problem is to make sure that the judge conducting the settlement conference does not sit as the trial judge. Another is to use a lawyer–mediator instead of the judge at the settlement conference.

INTERNET TIP

In *Estate of John Skalka v. Mark Skalka,* the Indiana Court of Appeals decided that a state trial judge had acted improperly when conducting a settlement conference. Readers will find this case included with the Chapter XIV materials on the textbook's website.

Arbitration

Arbitration is the most-used form of ADR[10] and was in existence long before the emergence of the English common law.[11] It was well known in the eighteenth century, and George Washington's will even contained an arbitration clause in the event that disputes arose between his heirs.[12]

American courts traditionally opposed arbitration because the parties were in effect thumbing their noses at the judicial system. Many judges believed that people who chose arbitration over the judicial system should not be entitled to come to the judiciary for enforcement of nonjudicial decisions. In the 1925 **Federal Arbitration Act (FAA),** however, Congress established a national policy favoring the arbitration of commercial transactions. In the Act, Congress provided that arbitration contracts "shall be valid, irrevocable, and enforceable save upon such grounds as exist at law or equity for the revocation of any contract," and required that courts enforce most arbitration awards.[13] Congress subsequently amended the FAA in 1947, 1954, 1970, and 1990 to recognize and enforce arbitration awards involving commercial arbitration agreements between Americans and citizens of other countries. The U.S. Supreme Court generally has gone along with Congress and the executive branch in supporting the expansion of this and other forms of ADR.[14]

Some disputants end up in ADR because it is required by a court-annexed program or because there is an ADR clause in a contract. In the next case we will see what happened when an employer who had contractually agreed to arbitrate disputes with two former employees tried to litigate the disputes in state court in lieu of arbitration.

Introduction to *Nitro-Lift Technologies, L.L.C. v. Howard*

Sometimes a state supreme court will refuse to follow clearly established U.S. Supreme Court precedents with which the state court disagrees. When that occurs, the nation's highest court generally will grant certiorari and correct the state court's error. In the following case, the U.S. Supreme Court insists that Oklahoma's courts comply with the requirements of the Federal Arbitration Act and permit an arbitrator, and not a court, to decide the underlying substantive dispute between the parties.

Nitro-Lift Technologies, L.L.C. v. Eddie Lee Howard
_____ *U.S.* _____
Supreme Court of the United States
November 26, 2012

Per Curiam.
State courts rather than federal courts are most frequently called upon to apply the Federal Arbitration Act (FAA) ... including the Act's national policy favoring arbitration. It is a matter of great importance, therefore, that state supreme courts adhere to a correct interpretation of the legislation. Here, the Oklahoma Supreme Court failed to do so. By declaring the noncompetition agreements in two employment contracts null and void, rather than leaving that determination to the arbitrator in the first instance, the state court ignored a basic tenet of the Act's substantive arbitration law. The decision must be vacated....

This dispute arises from a contract between petitioner Nitro-Lift Technologies, L.L.C., and two of its former employees. Nitro-Lift contracts with operators of oil and gas wells to provide services that enhance production. Respondents Eddie Lee Howard and Shane D. Schneider entered a confidentiality and noncompe-

tition agreement with Nitro-Lift that contained the following arbitration clause:

> Any dispute, difference or unresolved question between Nitro-Lift and the Employee (collectively the "Disputing Parties") shall be settled by arbitration by a single arbitrator mutually agreeable to the Disputing Parties in an arbitration proceeding conducted in Houston, Texas in accordance with the rules existing at the date hereof of the American Arbitration Association....

After working for Nitro-Lift on wells in Oklahoma, Texas, and Arkansas, respondents quit and began working for one of Nitro-Lift's competitors. Claiming that respondents had breached their noncompetition agreements, Nitro-Lift served them with a demand for arbitration. Respondents then filed suit in the District Court of Johnston County, Oklahoma, asking the court to declare the noncompetition agreements null and void and to enjoin their enforcement. The court dismissed the complaint, finding that the contracts contained valid arbitration clauses under which an arbitrator, and not the court, must settle the parties' disagreement.

The Oklahoma Supreme Court retained respondents' appeal and ordered the parties to show cause why the matter should not be resolved by application of Okla. Stat., Tit. 15, §219A (West 2011), which limits the enforceability of noncompetition agreements. Nitro-Lift argued that any dispute as to the contracts' enforceability was a question for the arbitrator. It relied for support—as it had done before the trial court—upon several of this Court's cases interpreting the FAA, and noted that under *Buckeye Check Cashing, Inc. v. Cardegna* ... (2006), "this arbitration law applies in both state and federal courts."...

The Oklahoma Supreme Court was not persuaded. It held that despite the "[U. S.] Supreme Court cases on which the employers rely," the "existence of an arbitration agreement in an employment contract does not prohibit judicial review of the underlying agreement." ... For that proposition, the court relied on the "exhaustive overview of the United States Supreme Court decisions construing the Federal Arbitration Act" in *Bruner v. Timberlane Manor Ltd. Partnership* ... [a case decided by the Oklahoma Supreme Court], which found [United States] Supreme Court jurisprudence "not to inhibit our review of the underlying contract's validity."... Finding the arbitration clauses no obstacle to its review, the court held that the noncompetition agreements were "void and unenforceable as against Oklahoma's public policy," expressed in Okla. Stat., Tit. 15, §219A....

The Oklahoma Supreme Court declared that its decision rests on adequate and independent state grounds.... If that were so, we would have no jurisdiction over this case.... It is not so, however, because the court's reliance on Oklahoma law was not "independent"— it necessarily depended upon a rejection of the federal claim, which was both "'properly presented to'" and "'addressed by'" the state court.... Nitro-Lift claimed that the arbitrator should decide the contract's validity, and raised a federal-law basis for that claim by relying on Supreme Court cases construing the FAA. "'[A] litigant wishing to raise a federal issue can easily indicate the federal law basis for his claim in a state-court petition or brief ... by citing in conjunction with the claim the federal source of law on which he relies or a case deciding such a claim on federal grounds....'"... The Oklahoma Supreme Court acknowledged the cases on which Nitro-Lift relied, as well as their relevant holdings, but chose to discount these controlling decisions. Its conclusion that, despite this Court's jurisprudence, the underlying contract's validity is purely a matter of state

law for state-court determination is all the more reason for this Court to assert jurisdiction.

The Oklahoma Supreme Court's decision disregards this Court's precedents on the FAA. That Act, which "declare[s] a national policy favoring arbitration," *Southland Corp. v. Keating* ... (1984), provides that a "written provision in ... a contract evidencing a transaction involving commerce to settle by arbitration a controversy thereafter arising out of such contract or transaction ... shall be valid, irrevocable, and enforceable, save upon such grounds as exist at law or in equity for the revocation of any contract." 9 U. S. C. §2. It is well settled that "the substantive law the Act created [is] applicable in state and federal courts."... And when parties commit to arbitrate contractual disputes, it is a mainstay of the Act's substantive law that attacks on the validity of the contract, as distinct from attacks on the validity of the arbitration clause itself, are to be resolved "by the arbitrator in the first instance, not by a federal or state court."... For these purposes, an "arbitration provision is severable from the remainder of the contract,"... and its validity is subject to initial court determination; but the validity of the remainder of the contract (if the arbitration provision is valid) is for the arbitrator to decide.

This principle requires that the decision below be vacated. The trial court found that the contract contained a valid arbitration clause, and the Oklahoma Supreme Court did not hold otherwise. It nonetheless assumed the arbitrator's role by declaring the noncompetition agreements null and void. The state court insisted that its "[own] jurisprudence controls this issue" and permits review of a "contract submitted to arbitration where one party assert[s] that the underlying agreement [is] void and unenforceable."... But the Oklahoma Supreme Court must abide by the FAA, which is "the supreme Law of the Land," U. S. Const., Art. VI, cl. 2, and by the opinions of this Court interpreting that law. "It is this Court's responsibility to say what a statute means, and once the Court has spoken, it is the duty of other courts to respect that understanding of the governing rule of law."... Our cases hold that the FAA forecloses precisely this type of "judicial hostility towards arbitration."...

The state court reasoned that Oklahoma's statute "addressing the validity of covenants not to compete, must govern over the more general statute favoring arbitration."... But the ancient interpretive principle that the specific governs the general (generalia specialibus non derogant) applies only to conflict between laws of equivalent dignity. Where a specific statute, for example, conflicts with a general constitutional provision, the latter governs. And the same is true where a specific state statute conflicts with a general federal statute. There is no general-specific exception to the Supremacy Clause, U. S. Const. Art. VI, cl. 2. "'[W]hen state law prohibits outright the arbitration of a particular type of claim, the analysis is straightforward: The conflicting rule is displaced by the FAA.' "... Hence, it is for the arbitrator to decide in the first instance whether the covenants not to compete are valid as a matter of applicable state law....

For the foregoing reasons, the petition for certiorari is granted. The judgment of the Supreme Court of Oklahoma is vacated, and the case is remanded for proceedings not inconsistent with this opinion.

It is so ordered.

Case Questions

1. What was the position of the Oklahoma Supreme Court regarding the arbitration of noncompetition agreements?
2. The Oklahoma Supreme Court, according to the U.S. Supreme Court, violated which constitutional requirement? Explain.

Voluntary Arbitration

Voluntary arbitration is increasingly used to resolve business disputes because it provides prompt decisions at a reasonable cost. The voluntary arbitration process is very different from the judicial process. In voluntary arbitrations, for example, the arbitrator makes a binding decision on the merits of the dispute and can base his or her decision on a lay or business sense of justice rather than on the rules of law that would be applied in court. A private arbitration proceeds pursuant to a contract, in which the parties promise to bind themselves to arbitrate their controversy and abide by the arbitrator's decision (called an **arbitration award**). Because a person who chooses to arbitrate waives the right to a jury trial, arbitration agreements must be in writing to be enforceable in court. Some parties agree to arbitrate their agreements prior to the existence of any dispute.[15] Contracts between unions and management, investors and stockbrokers,[16] and banks and their customers[17] often include arbitration clauses. Many major corporations routinely include arbitration clauses in contracts they make with their suppliers. Arbitration agreements also can be negotiated after a controversy has arisen.

Arbitrators are selected by agreement of the parties. The nonprofit American Arbitration Association has been a supplier of arbitrators since 1926.[18] Arbitrators in business disputes often are chosen because of their expertise in a specific field. This better enables them to render a reasonable and proper decision. This should be contrasted with the trial decisions that are made by a randomly selected judge and jury. The parties can choose a person who they believe will conduct the proceedings fairly and with integrity. However, the legal continuity of the judicial system is not necessarily present in a voluntary arbitration. Arbitrators, for example, do not have to follow precedent in their decision-making process, nor do they have to prepare written explanations for their award (although they often do both).

Each arbitration hearing is convened for the sole purpose of deciding a particular dispute. Arbitration hearings often are conducted in offices or hotel conference rooms and, unlike court trials, generally are not open to the public. Although the formalities of a court proceeding need not be followed, arbitration hearings usually follow the sequence of opening statements by the opposing parties, direct and cross-examination of the witnesses, introduction of exhibits, and closing arguments. Arbitrators base their decisions on the evidence and the arguments made before them. However, they generally are not bound by the rules of evidence used in litigation.

Judicial Review of Arbitration Awards

Either party to an arbitration may institute a court action seeking confirmation (judicial enforcement) or modification of the award. Federal and state laws provide for jurisdiction in specified courts to (1) recognize and enforce arbitration, (2) provide standards of conduct for arbitration hearings, (3) make arbitration agreements irrevocable, and (4) provide that court action cannot be initiated until the arbitration has concluded.

States differ about what powers judges reviewing arbitration awards should possess. Most state courts and the federal courts usually will confirm an arbitration award unless the arbitrator violated the terms of the arbitration contract, the arbitration procedures offended fundamental due process, or the award violated public policy. However, even the traditional rule prohibiting appellate courts from reviewing an arbitrator's findings of fact is subject to reconsideration, as we will see in the following precedent–setting case.

Cable Connection, Inc. v. DIRECTV, Inc.
190 P.3d 586
California Supreme Court
August 25, 2008

Corrigan, J.

This case presents two questions regarding arbitration agreements. (1) May the parties structure their agreement to allow for judicial review of legal error in the arbitration award? (2) Is classwide arbitration available under an agreement that is silent on the matter?...

Defendant DIRECTV, Inc. broadcasts television programming nationwide, via satellite. It contracts with retail dealers to provide customers with equipment needed to receive its satellite signal. In 1996, DIRECTV employed a "residential dealer agreement" for this purpose. A new "sales agency agreement" was used in 1998. Both agreements included arbitration clauses; neither mentioned classwide arbitration.

In 2001, dealers from four states filed suit in Oklahoma, asserting on behalf of a nationwide class that DIRECTV had wrongfully withheld commissions and assessed improper charges. DIRECTV moved to compel arbitration. As the Oklahoma court was considering whether the arbitration could be conducted on a classwide basis, the United States Supreme Court decided *Green Tree Financial Corp. v. Bazzle* (2003).... A plurality in *Bazzle* held that the arbitrator must decide whether class arbitration is authorized by the parties' contract.... Accordingly, the Oklahoma court directed the parties to submit the matter to arbitration in Los Angeles as provided in the sales agency agreement....

After the dealers presented a statement of claim and demand for class arbitration in March 2004, a panel of three AAA [American Arbitration Association] arbitrators was selected. Following the procedure adopted by the AAA in response to *Bazzle*, the panel first addressed whether the parties' agreement permitted the arbitration to proceed on a classwide basis.

After briefing and argument, a majority of the panel decided that even though "the contract is silent and manifests no intent on this issue," arbitration on a class-

wide basis was authorized.... The award emphasized that class arbitration was not necessarily required in this case; it was merely permitted by the contract. Whether the arbitration would actually be maintained on a classwide basis would be the subject of a future hearing....

DIRECTV petitioned to vacate the award, contending (1) the majority had exceeded its authority by substituting its discretion for the parties' intent regarding class arbitration; (2) the majority had improperly ignored extrinsic evidence of contractual intent; and (3) even if the majority had not exceeded the authority generally granted to arbitrators, the award reflected errors of law that the arbitration clause placed beyond their powers and made subject to judicial review.... The trial court vacated the award, essentially accepting all of DIRECTV's arguments.

The Court of Appeal reversed, holding that the trial court exceeded its jurisdiction by reviewing the merits of the arbitrators' decision....

We granted DIRECTV's petition for review.

II. Discussion

A. Contract Provisions for Judicial Review of Arbitration Awards

1. The CAA, the FAA, and prior case law

> In most important respects, the California statutory scheme on enforcement of private arbitration agreements is similar to the FAA [Federal Arbitration Act]; the similarity is not surprising, as the two share origins in the earlier statutes of New York and New Jersey....

> Consistent with that purpose, the CAA [California Arbitration Act] and the FAA provide only limited

grounds for judicial review of an arbitration award. Under both statutes, courts are authorized to vacate an award if it was (1) procured by corruption, fraud, or undue means; (2) issued by corrupt arbitrators; (3) affected by prejudicial misconduct on the part of the arbitrators; or (4) in excess of the arbitrators' powers.... An award may be corrected for (1) evident miscalculation or mistake; (2) excess of the arbitrators' powers; or (3) imperfection in form....

... [I]n *Moncharsh* [v. *Heily & Bliss* (1992] we declared that "in the absence of some limiting clause in the arbitration agreement, the merits of the award, either on questions of fact or of law, may not be reviewed except as provided in the statute."... In the years following the *Moncharsh* decision, our Courts of Appeal have rejected claims that review of the merits was authorized inferentially, by contract clauses stating that "the award will be in the form of a statement of decision".... In each of these cases, however, the courts noted that an expanded scope of review *would* be available under a clause specifically tailored for that purpose....

Nevertheless, when the issue has been squarely presented, no Court of Appeal has enforced a contract clause calling for judicial review of an arbitration award on its merits.... In *Crowell* [v. *Downey Community Hospital Foundation* (2002)] ... the parties' contract included an arbitration clause requiring the arbitrator to make written findings and conclusions "supported by law and substantial evidence."... The award was to be "final, binding and enforceable ... except that upon the petition of any party to the arbitration, a court shall have the authority to review the transcript of the arbitration proceedings and the arbitrator's award and shall have the authority to vacate the arbitrator's award, in whole or in part, on the basis that the award is not supported by substantial evidence or is based upon an error of law."...

The *Crowell* court, in a split decision, decided the statutory bases for vacating and correcting arbitration awards are exclusive, and permitting the parties to expand those grounds by agreement would undermine the purpose of reducing expense and delay....

2. Hall Street and the question of preemption
The *Hall Street* [*Associates v. Mattel* (2008)] case arose from an arbitration agreement negotiated during litigation, to resolve an indemnification claim. The agreement was approved and entered as an order by the trial court. It provided:

> The Court shall vacate, modify or correct any award: (i) where the arbitrator's findings of facts are not supported by substantial evidence, or (ii) where the arbitrator's conclusions of law are erroneous....

The trial court vacated the arbitrator's award and remanded for further consideration; at the time, the Ninth Circuit approved of contract provisions for expanded judicial review.... After the arbitrator ruled a second time, both parties sought modification, and both appealed from the trial court's judgment modifying the award. By that time, the Ninth Circuit had changed its view on the enforceability of judicial review provisions.... It reversed the judgment....

... [T]he Supreme Court granted certiorari. A majority of the court agreed with the Ninth Circuit that the grounds for vacatur and modification provided by sections 10 and 11 of the FAA are exclusive.... First, the majority rejected the argument that the nonstatutory "manifest disregard of the law" standard of review recognized by some federal courts supports the enforceability of contract provisions for additional grounds to vacate or modify an arbitration award....

Next, the *Hall Street* majority disposed of the contention that allowing parties to contract for an expanded scope of review is consistent with the FAA's primary goal of ensuring the enforcement of arbitration agreements.... The majority ... characterized the statutory grounds for review as remedies for "egregious departures from the parties' agreed-upon arbitration," such as corruption and fraud.... It viewed the directive in section 9 of the FAA, that the court "must grant" confirmation "unless the award is vacated, modified, or corrected as prescribed in sections 10 and 11," as a mandatory provision leaving no room for the parties to agree otherwise....

Despite this strict reading of the FAA, the *Hall Street* majority left the door ajar for alternate routes to an expanded scope of review.... "[H]ere we speak only to the scope of the expeditious judicial review under §§9, 10, and 11, deciding nothing about other possible avenues for judicial enforcement of arbitration awards...."

Furthermore, the *Hall Street* majority recognized that the trial court's case management authority under rule 16 of the Federal Rules of Civil Procedure might support its order adopting the parties' agreement to review of the merits. However, it remanded for further proceedings on this point, concluding that it was "in no position to address the question now, beyond noting the claim of relevant case management authority independent of the FAA...."

The dealers in this case urge us to follow the rationale of the *Hall Street* majority. They contend that any other construction of the CAA would result in its preemption by the FAA. Alternatively, they argue that *Hall Street* provides a persuasive analysis of the FAA that should be applied to the similar CAA provisions governing judicial review....

We conclude that the *Hall Street* holding is restricted to proceedings to review arbitration awards under the FAA, and does not require state law to conform with its limitations. Furthermore, a reading of the CAA that permits the enforcement of agreements for merits review is fully consistent with the FAA "policy guaranteeing the enforcement of private contractual arrangements."...

3. Moncharsh and the California Rule

In *Moncharsh* ... [w]e reaffirmed "the general rule that an arbitrator's decision is not ordinarily reviewable for error by either the trial or appellate courts"... and held that the statutory grounds for review were intended to implement that rule.... To that extent, our conclusions were consistent with those of the *Hall Street* majority. However, in several respects *Moncharsh* reflects a very different view of arbitration agreements and the arbitration statutes, as applied to the scope of judicial review. Therefore, we disagree with the dealers' argument that *Hall Street* is persuasive authority for a restrictive interpretation of the review provisions in the CAA.

Moncharsh began from the premise that "[t]he scope of arbitration is ... a matter of agreement between the parties' [citation], and "[t]he powers of an arbitrator are limited and circumscribed by the agreement or stipulation of submission."...

> The policy of the law in recognizing arbitration agreements and in providing by statute for their enforcement is to encourage persons who wish to avoid delays incident to a civil action to obtain an adjustment of their differences by a tribunal of their own choosing.... "Because the decision to arbitrate grievances evinces the parties' intent to bypass the judicial system and thus avoid potential delays at the trial and appellate levels, arbitral finality is a core component of the parties' agreement to submit to arbitration. Thus, an arbitration decision is final and conclusive *because the parties have agreed that it be so.* By ensuring that an arbitrator's decision is final and binding, courts simply assure that the parties receive the benefit of their bargain."...
>
> Thus, both because it vindicates the intentions of the parties that the award be final, and because an arbitrator is not ordinarily constrained to decide according to the rule of law, it is the general rule that, "The merits of the controversy between the parties are not subject to judicial review."...

Our reasoning in *Moncharsh* centered not on statutory restriction of the parties' contractual options, but on the parties' intent and the powers of the arbitrators as defined in the agreement. These factors support the enforcement of agreements for an expanded scope of review. If the parties constrain the arbitrators' authority by requiring a dispute to be decided according to the rule of law, *and* make plain their intention that the award is reviewable for legal error, the general rule of limited review has been displaced by the parties' agreement. Their expectation is not that the result of the arbitration will be final and conclusive, but rather that it will be reviewed on the merits at the request of either party....

We have consistently recognized that "[a]n exception to the general rule assigning broad powers to the arbitrators arises when the parties have, in either the contract or an agreed submission to arbitration, explicitly and unambiguously limited those powers.... Our review in *Moncharsh* of the CAA's legislative history confirms that while the statutory grounds for correction and vacation of arbitration awards do not ordinarily include errors of law, contractual limitations on the arbitrators' powers can alter the usual scope of review.

The current version of the CAA was enacted following a study by the California Law Revision Commission, undertaken at the Legislature's direction....

> The Arbitration Study emphasized that arbitration should be the end of the dispute and that "the ordinary concepts of judicial appeal and review are not applicable to arbitration awards. Settled case law is based on this assumption."... After surveying the state of the law, the report concluded that although the California statutes do not "attempt to express the exact limits of court review of arbitration awards ... no good reason exists to codify into the California statute the case law as it presently exists."... Further, the report recommended that the "present grounds for vacating an award should be left substantially unchanged."... Considering the nature of the revisions incorporated in the CAA, this court concluded that the Legislature intended to "adopt the position taken in case law and endorsed in the Arbitration Study, that is, 'that in the absence of some limiting clause in the arbitration agreement, the merits of the award, either on questions of fact or of law, may not be reviewed except as provided in the statute.' "... *(Moncharsh* ... quoting *Crofoot*....)

The *Crofoot* rule does not suggest that review of the merits must rest on a nonstatutory basis. As discussed below, *Crofoot*'s reference to a limiting clause in the agreement pertains to limits on the arbitrators' powers. Thus, the merits of an award may come within the ambit of the statutory grounds of review for excess of the arbitrators' powers. (§§1286.2, subd. (a)(4); 1286.6, subd. (b).) However, absent such a limitation, the scope of review provided by statute is quite limited. In *Moncharsh,* we noted that section 1286.2 includes no provision for review of the merits like that found in section 1296, governing public construction contract arbitrations.... The *Crowell* court, and the Court of Appeal below, considered section 1296 an indication that the Legislature did not intend to permit review of the merits by agreement.... This view is mistaken. In *Moncharsh* we inferred from section 1296 that "the Legislature did not intend to confer traditional judicial review in private arbitration cases.".... However, the failure to provide for that scope of review *by statute* does not mean the parties themselves may not do so *by contract*.... Our holding in *Moncharsh* that the CAA incorporates the *Crofoot* rule is irreconcilable with the notion that the parties are barred from agreeing to limit the arbitrators' authority by subjecting their award to review on the merits. The history of the FAA, as reviewed by the *Hall Street* majority, includes no similar indication that Congress intended the statutory grounds for review to operate as default provisions, providing only limited review unless the parties agree otherwise.... Therefore, *Hall Street's* FAA analysis is inapposite.

In California, the policy favoring arbitration without the complications of traditional judicial review is based on the parties' expectations as embodied in their agreement, and the CAA rests on the same foundation. "Accordingly, policies favoring the efficiency of private arbitration as a means of dispute resolution must sometimes yield to its fundamentally contractual nature, and to the attendant requirement that arbitration shall proceed *as the parties themselves have agreed.*" ... The scope of judicial review is not invariably limited by statute; rather, "the parties, simply by agreeing to arbitrate, are deemed to accept limited judicial review *by implication.*".... It follows that they may expressly agree to accept a broader scope of review....

The Arbitration Study discussed in *Moncharsh* includes a similar observation. Regarding the statutory ground of review for excess of the arbitrators' powers, the study stated: "Arbitrators may base their decision upon broad principles of justice and equity, but if the submission agreement specifically requires an arbitrator to act in conformity with rules of law, the arbitrator exceeds his authority if his decision is not based on rules of law.".…

A provision requiring arbitrators to apply the law leaves open the possibility that they are empowered to apply it "wrongly as well as rightly.".... As we recently observed:

When parties contract to resolve their disputes by private arbitration, their agreement ordinarily contemplates that the arbitrator will have the power to decide any question of contract interpretation, historical fact or general law necessary, in the arbitrator's understanding of the case, to reach a decision.... Inherent in that power is the possibility the arbitrator may err in deciding some aspect of the case. Arbitrators do not ordinarily exceed their contractually created powers simply by reaching an erroneous conclusion on a contested issue of law or fact, and arbitral awards may not ordinarily be vacated because of such error, for "[t]he arbitrator's resolution of these issues is what the parties bargained for in the arbitration agreement.".…

Therefore, to take themselves out of the general rule that the merits of the award are not subject to judicial review, the parties must clearly agree that legal errors are an excess of arbitral authority that is reviewable by the courts. Here, the parties expressly so agreed, depriving the arbitrators of the power to commit legal error. They also specifically provided for judicial review of such error.... We do not decide here whether one or the other of these clauses alone, or some different formulation, would be sufficient to confer an expanded scope of review. However, we emphasize that parties seeking to allow judicial review of the merits, and to avoid an additional dispute over the scope of review, would be well advised to provide for that review explicitly and unambiguously....

Review on the merits has been deemed incompatible with the goals of finality and informality that are served by arbitration and protected by the arbitration statutes.... However ... those policies draw their strength from the agreement of the parties. It is the parties who are best situated to weigh the advantages of traditional arbitration against the benefits of court review for the correction of legal error....

To the extent the concern with reviewability arises from apprehension that permitting review on the merits would open the door to contracts imposing unfamiliar standards of review, it appears to be unfounded. We have discovered no case where the parties attempted to make the courts apply an unusual standard of review. Instead, as in this case, they have required the arbitrators to apply legal standards, resulting in awards that can be reviewed in traditional fashion.... We need not speculate about provisions calling for bizarre modes of decision, but we note that arbitration agreements are "as enforceable as other contracts, but not more so.".... Thus, just as the parties to any contract are limited in the constraints they may place on judicial review, an arbitration agreement providing that a "judge would review the award by flipping a coin or studying the entrails of a dead fowl" would be unenforceable....

The benefits of enforcing agreements like the one before us are considerable, for both the parties and the courts. The development of alternative dispute resolution is advanced by enabling private parties to choose procedures with which they are comfortable. Commentators have observed that provisions for expanded judicial review are a product of market forces operating in an increasingly "judicialized" arbitration setting, with many of the attributes of court proceedings. The desire for the protection afforded by review for legal error has evidently developed from the experience of sophisticated parties in high stakes cases, where the arbitrators' awards deviated from the parties' expectations in startling ways....

The judicial system reaps little benefit from forcing parties to choose between the risk of an erroneous arbitration award and the burden of litigating their dispute entirely in court. Enforcing contract provisions for review of awards on the merits relieves pressure on congested trial court dockets.... Courts are spared not only the burden of conducting a trial, but also the complications of discovery disputes and other pretrial proceedings. Incorporating traditional judicial review by express agreement preserves the utility of arbitration as a way to obtain expert factual determinations without delay, while allowing the parties to protect themselves from perhaps the weakest aspect of the arbitral process, its handling of disputed rules of law....

There are also significant benefits to the development of the common law when arbitration awards are made subject to merits review by the parties' agreement. "[I]f courts are reduced to the function of merely enforcing or denying arbitral awards, without an opportunity to discuss the reasoning for the arbitral decision, the advancement of the law is stalled, as arbitral decisions carry no precedential value.... Thus, expansion of judicial review gives the courts of first instance the opportunity to establish a record, and to include the reasoning of expert arbitrators into the body of the law in the form of written decisions. This procedure better advances the state of the law and facilitates the necessary beneficial input from experts in the field."...

These advantages, obtained with the consent of the parties, are substantial. As explained in *Moncharsh*, the drafters of the CAA established the statutory grounds for judicial review with the expectation that arbitration awards are ordinarily final and subject to a restricted scope of review, but that parties may limit the arbitrators' authority by providing for review of the merits in the arbitration agreement.... The Court of Appeal erred by refusing to enforce the parties' clearly expressed agreement in this case.

B. The Award Permitting Classwide Arbitration

Two of the three arbitrators below decided the dealers could pursue arbitration on a classwide basis, although the parties' contract did not mention classwide arbitration. The Court of Appeal agreed with this determination. The contract calls for the arbitrators to apply California substantive law, while following the procedural requirements of AAA rules and the FAA....

The Court of Appeal, and the arbitrators in the majority, viewed the right to pursue classwide arbitration as a substantive one.... The court concluded that these cases "give[ ] arbitrators discretion to order classwide arbitration even where the arbitration agreement is silent on that issue, in divergence from the general rules of contract interpretation that terms are not to be inserted into contracts."...

DIRECTV claims that ... the arbitrators in the majority violated a provision of the AAA rules stating: "In construing the applicable arbitration clause, the arbitrator shall not consider the existence of ... AAA rules, to be a factor either in favor of or against permitting the arbitration to proceed on a class basis."...

DIRECTV appears to be correct.... AAA's class arbitration policy is based on the *Bazzle* decision.... The *Bazzle* plurality declared: "[T]he relevant question here is what *kind of arbitration proceeding* the parties agreed to. That question does not concern a state statute or judicial procedures.... It concerns contract interpretation and arbitration procedures. Arbitrators are well situated to answer that question."... We express no view on whether the terms of this arbitration clause are consistent with conducting arbitration on a classwide basis. Instead of deciding that question, the majority arbitrators misapplied AAA rules and policy as well as the *Keating* rule. Under the circumstances, we deem it appropriate to permit the arbitration panel to reconsider the availability of classwide arbitration as a matter of contract interpretation and AAA arbitration procedure.

III. Disposition

We reverse the judgment of the Court of Appeal, with directions to instruct the trial court to vacate the award so that the arbitrators may redetermine whether the arbitration may proceed on a classwide basis.

Case Questions

1. According to the California Supreme Court, what is the general rule regarding the judicial review of the merits of an arbitration award?
2. Why did the California Supreme Court conclude in this case that the court of appeal should have enforced the parties' explicit agreement in the arbitration agreement permitting judicial review of the merits?
3. Why did the California Supreme Court refuse to adopt the U.S. Supreme Court's reasoning in the *Hall Street* case?

Court-Annexed Arbitration

Court-annexed arbitration includes both voluntary and mandatory procedures. Mandatory arbitrations, however, for reasons founded in the right to jury trial contained in both federal and state constitutions, can produce only nonbinding decisions. The types of cases that can be arbitrated increasingly are determined by statute, but in many jurisdictions this is determined pursuant to local court rules. Traditionally, arbitrations are most common in commercial, personal injury, and property damage cases in which the amount does not exceed a designated sum. That sum, called the jurisdictional amount, varies by jurisdiction.

The rules of arbitration often provide for limited discovery and modified rules of evidence. In brief, trial-like hearings lasting only a few hours, attorneys offer documentary evidence, present witness testimony, and cross-examine opposing witnesses. Arbitrators—often retired judges and local attorneys—are selected in various ways. In some

courts, the clerk of court randomly assigns arbitrators. In other jurisdictions the parties participate in the selection process.

Arbitrators listen to the presentations, ask questions of the presenters, and determine the liability and damages issues. They generally do not make findings of fact or conclusions of law (as would judges in bench trials). Depending on local practice, the arbitrator may—or may not—attempt to mediate the dispute, critique the parties, or propose settlement terms.

An arbitrator's award becomes a final judgment unless the parties reject it within a prescribed period of time and demand a traditional jury trial (called a **trial de novo**). Unless the trial judgment exceeds the arbitration award, a party demanding a trial de novo often will be penalized and required to pay the arbitration costs.

The following case contains a discussion of the rights of the parties to a court-annexed arbitration proceeding to reject the arbitrator's decision and insist on a trial de novo.

Allstate Insurance Company v. A. William Mottolese
803 A.2d 311
Supreme Court of Connecticut
August 20, 2002

Sullivan, C. J.
This case is before us on a writ of error brought by the named plaintiff in error, Allstate Insurance Company (plaintiff) ... the insurer of the defendant in the underlying action, seeking reversal of an order of the trial court, *Mottolese. J.,* the defendant in error (trial court), imposing sanctions against the plaintiff pursuant to Practice Book §§14-13. The dispositive issue in this case is whether a party's proper exercise of its right to a trial de novo ... following a nonbinding

arbitration proceeding may serve as the grounds for the imposition of sanctions under Practice Book §§14-13....

The plaintiff claims that the trial court's order of sanctions against it is void because it is not a party to the underlying action and never consented to the court's personal jurisdiction over it. Further, the plaintiff contends that: (1) the trial court violated its due process rights by failing to give notice that court would be considering whether to impose sanctions upon the plaintiff for its refusal to increase its settlement offer;

and (2) the order of sanctions was an improper attempt by the trial court to coerce and intimidate the plaintiff to settle the underlying defendant's case and, as such, violated the underlying defendant's constitutional right of access to the courts. We agree that, under the circumstances of this case, the plaintiff's conduct, which was grounded in its insured's exercise of his right to a trial de novo, cannot serve as the basis for an order of sanctions, and we reverse the order sanctioning the plaintiff.

The record discloses the following relevant facts and procedural history. In December, 1997, Robert Morgan filed the underlying action against David Distasio, the plaintiff's insured, to recover damages for injuries sustained in a December 5, 1995 automobile accident.... After a pretrial conference at which no settlement was reached, the trial court referred the case to nonbinding arbitration ..., the court annexed arbitration program. In December, 1999, the arbitrator issued a memorandum of decision in which he found ... that Distasio negligently had rear-ended Morgan's vehicle, that Morgan had sustained minor physical injuries and property damage, and that judgment should be rendered in favor of Morgan in the amount of $2450. Distasio thereafter timely filed a claim for a trial de novo ... requesting that the trial court vacate the arbitration award and restore the case to the jury trial list.

On April 4, 2001, a pretrial conference was held before the trial court, Mottolese, J. The trial court continued the conference to April 11, 2001, with the instruction that Distasio produce his insurance claims representative on that date. On April 11, 2001, Distasio, Morgan and their respective counsel, along with the claims representative for the plaintiff, Stephen Coppa, appeared before the court in accordance with a written notice of pretrial conference. Coppa acknowledged that the plaintiff had made its initial settlement offer of $2050 to Morgan after evaluating the case, and that, at the time the offer was made, he had told Morgan that the offer was final. After discussion, the trial court found that the plaintiff's refusal "to pay anything more than $2050 ... is conduct which may fairly be characterized as unfair and in bad faith." The trial court further stated that "this court deems [the plaintiff's] refusal to participate in a resolution of this case in a reasonable manner as the functional equivalent of a failure to attend a pretrial," and that "it's unreasonable for any insurance carrier, any tortfeasor, to require judicial resources to be put in place and for thousands and thousands of taxpayers' money to be expended in order to save you, [the plaintiff], $400.00." The trial court held that the plaintiff's conduct was an "unwarranted imposition upon scarce

judicial resources ... a gross abuse of the civil justice system; and [that it made] a mockery of Connecticut's court annexed arbitration program." Accordingly, pursuant to Practice Book §§14-13 ... the trial court awarded Morgan attorney's fees of $250 for the April 4 pretrial conference and $250 for the April 11 hearing.

Distasio moved for articulation, requesting that the trial court clarify whether the ruling on attorney's fees was directed at the plaintiff, Distasio or Distasio's counsel. In response, the trial court appointed H. James Pickerstein, an attorney, "as a special master to conduct discovery on behalf of the court and to assist the court in preparing its articulation." The court ordered that the scope of discovery was to include, but not be limited to, the plaintiff's settlement policies and practices as they related to the underlying case, the extent to which Distasio's counsel had participated in the settlement process, and the policies and practices of the court annexed arbitration program and de novo trials....

... Distasio filed an appeal in the Appellate Court challenging the appointment of the special master.

In the meantime, the plaintiff moved for permission to amend the writ to address the sanction order....

The plaintiff claims that the order of sanctions was an improper attempt to coerce and intimidate it into settling the matter, thereby violating its constitutional right to a trial by jury. Specifically, the plaintiff argues that Distasio's assertion of his statutory right to a trial de novo following the court-ordered nonbinding arbitration proceeding preserved his right to a trial by jury guaranteed by the Connecticut constitution, and that a party's decision not to be bound by an arbitrator's decision regarding settlement cannot be the basis for the imposition of sanctions under Practice Book §§14-13.

Conversely, the trial court argues that, because the arbitrator's award of $2450 in damages was a mere $400 more than the plaintiff was originally willing to pay, the plaintiff took a defiant approach to the settlement process that was interpreted by the trial court as being disrespectful to it, harmful to the opposing party and implicitly contemptuous. The trial court further argues that it is within that court's inherent authority to sanction all who appear before it whose actions may be characterized as unfair and in bad faith.

We agree with the plaintiff and conclude that Distasio's exercise of his right to file for a trial de novo after the completion of arbitration proceedings cannot provide the basis for sanctions pursuant to Practice Book §§14-13. Accordingly, we conclude that the trial court abused its discretion when it sanctioned the plaintiff....

We begin with a review of the nonbinding arbitration program. Section 52-549u permits the judges of the Superior Court to refer certain civil actions to an arbitrator for nonbinding arbitration. The arbitrator's decision, however, is not binding on the parties and does not limit either party's access to a trial.... Pursuant to §§52-549z (d) and Practice Book §§23-66 (c), a party that participated in nonbinding arbitration may appeal from the arbitrator's decision by requesting a trial de novo, in which case the arbitrator's decision becomes null and void.

The statutory right to a trial de novo has its underpinnings in the Connecticut constitution.

> Article IV of the amendments to the constitution of Connecticut provides, inter alia, that the right of trial by jury shall remain inviolate. It is clear that the right to a jury trial may not be abolished as to causes triable to the jury prior to the constitution of 1818, and extant at the time of its adoption.... Nevertheless, such a right may be subjected to reasonable conditions and regulations.... The provision by the legislature for an alternative means of dispute resolution through the use of arbitrators to hear cases claimed for jury trial was but part of an effort to alleviate court congestion.... The right to a trial by jury in these cases is preserved inviolate by General Statutes §§52-549z and Practice Book §§[23-66]. Each of these sections provides for a claim for a trial de novo within twenty days of the filing of the arbitrator's decision. Once a claim for trial de novo is filed in accordance with the rules, a decision of an arbitrator becomes null and void....

Although both parties to the arbitration have an inviolable right to a trial de novo, that right is subject to reasonable conditions and regulations.... Attendance at a pretrial hearing is one such condition. Thus, Practice Book §§14-13 provides in relevant part that "when a party against whom a claim is made is insured, an insurance adjuster for such insurance company shall be available by telephone at the time of such pretrial session unless the judge... in his or her discretion, requires the attendance of the adjuster at the pretrial. If any person fails to attend or to be available by telephone pursuant to this rule, the judicial authority may make such order as the ends of justice require, which may include the entry of a nonsuit or default against the party failing to comply and an award to the complying party of reasonable attorney's fees...."

We further recognize, as the trial court claimed, that "our courts have long been recognized to have an inherent power, independent of any statute, to hold a defendant in contempt of court.... The purpose of the contempt power is to enable a court to preserve its dignity and to protect its proceedings...." The sanction created by Practice Book §§14-13 and relied upon by the trial court in this case, however, was intended to serve a different function, namely to ensure the insurer's presence to assist in the settlement of the case.

Public policy favors and encourages the voluntary settlement of civil suits.... *Krattenstein v. G. Fox & Co.* ... (1967) ("It is a proper exercise of the judicial office to suggest the expediency and practical value of adjusting differences and compromising and settling suits at law. The efficient administration of the courts is subserved by the ending of disputes without the delay and expense of a trial, and the philosophy or ideal of justice is served in the amicable solution of controversies. Our rules specifically provide for the procedure to be followed in pretrial sessions designed to encourage the settlement of cases.") We view with disfavor, however, all pressure tactics, whether employed directly or indirectly, to coerce settlement by litigants, their counsel and their insurers. The failure to concur with what a trial court may consider an appropriate settlement should not result in the imposition of any retributive sanctions upon a litigant, his or her counsel or his or her insurer. As our sister state, New York, has recognized, "the function of courts is to provide litigants with an opportunity to air their differences at an impartial trial according to law.... [The court should not be able] to exert undue pressure on litigants to oblige them to settle their controversies without their day in court."...

We recognize that Practice Book §§14-13 grants the trial court the authority to sanction an insurance company for its failure to attend or be available by telephone at a pretrial session. In this case, however, the plaintiff was not unavailable or otherwise absent from the proceedings. Moreover, its actual presence, through its agent, ... cannot be transformed into the functional equivalent of an absence, as the trial court ruled, ... simply because the insurer decided not to abide by the arbitrator's assessment of damages and to insist, as its insured's agent, on the insured's right to a trial.

Although we sympathize with the trial court's concern that merely attending a pretrial conference while refusing, at the same time, to participate meaningfully in the negotiation or settlement process is not within the spirit of the settlement process, the plaintiff's refusal, on the basis of a validly exercised right to a trial de novo, to abide by the arbitrator's nonbinding decision that the plaintiff should pay $400 more than its original offer does not fall within the parameters of sanctionable behavior under §§14-13. To conclude otherwise would undermine the insured's constitutional right to a trial of the claims. Practice Book §§14-13 authorizes the court to use its discretion to require an insurer to be present or available because the insurer's presence might assist in the settlement of the case. Under these circumstances, however, the failure to negotiate is not equivalent to the failure to appear in court. Distasio indicated, by requesting a trial de novo, that he wanted his dispute to be resolved by trial. The plaintiff's rejection of the arbitration award

evidences the same preference, in accordance with §§52-549z (d) and Practice Book §§23-66 (c). Accordingly, because Distasio properly exercised his statutory right to a trial de novo and the plaintiff properly complied with the trial court's request to be present at the pretrial hearing, we conclude that the trial court abused its discretion when it imposed sanctions....

The writ of error is granted and the matter is remanded with direction to vacate the order of sanctions....

Case Questions

1. What was the arbitrator's decision in this case?
2. Why did Judge Mottolese want to sanction the insurance company in this case for contempt of court?
3. Why did the state supreme court order that the order imposing sanctions be vacated?

JOINTLY USED ADR METHODS

Mediation, minitrials, and arbitration are used with both court-annexed and voluntary ADR. The following discussion briefly examines each of these methods.

Mediation

Mediation is a technique in which one or more neutral parties, called mediators, help disputants to find ways to settle their dispute.[19] Parties often attempt to resolve their disagreements by mediation before participating in binding arbitration or litigation. Informal, unstructured, and inexpensive, mediation focuses on settlement, not on victory at trial. Mediators have no formal power to make a decision: their role is that of facilitator, and different mediators use different styles and techniques to help parties come to an agreement. There is no formal hearing in a mediation. Instead, using joint meetings and private caucuses, mediators (1) help the parties identify their real goals, (2) narrow the issues, (3) look for alternatives and options as well as areas of common interest, and (4) prevent the parties from focusing on only one solution.

Court-annexed mediation often involves using trial attorneys as mediators. Mediators in some jurisdictions are paid and in others are volunteers. The theory is that neutral, experienced trial attorneys

will be able to persuade litigants to look at their cases realistically and moderate their monetary demands. These are important hurdles that often stand in the way of a settlement.

Court-annexed mediation procedures vary. Lawyer-mediators are used in some jurisdictions and three-person panels in others. In complex cases, the court may appoint a person called a special master to serve as a mediator. Mediators vary in their approaches, but they tend to evaluate each case and predict what would happen if the case went to trial. They also indicate what they believe to be the settlement value of the case. These two determinations serve as a catalyst in starting settlement discussions between the parties.

In some jurisdictions the court refers most cases to mediation. In other jurisdictions, mediation occurs pursuant to stipulation or a suggestion from the court. Mediation is nonbinding, and parties retain their rights to attempt other ADR methods and to go to trial.

There is a big difference between the focus of a trial and that of a mediation. Trials exist to produce a winner and a loser. Mediation exists to help the parties settle their dispute in an amicable and expeditious manner. The objective is to find a solution to the dispute that is more acceptable to each party than going to trial. Mediation is more flexible than a trial and can produce a result that is more attuned to the underlying facts. Another advantage to mediation is that there are fewer enforcement problems. Because mediation produces an agreement between the parties, many problems that result when a judgment creditor attempts to enforce a judgment are avoided.

As states have begun to implement court-annexed mediation, questions have arisen regarding the procedures to be employed when using the ADR method. The following case from Tennessee is illustrative.

Team Design v. Anthony Gottlieb
104 S.W.3d 512
Court of Appeals of Tennessee
July 18, 2002

William C. Koch.

This appeal raises important issues regarding the permissible range of court-annexed alternative dispute resolution procedures available under Tenn. S. Ct. R. 31....

Michael J. Bonagura and Kathie Baillie Bonagura perform country music in a group known as "Baillie and the Boys." When the transactions giving rise to this lawsuit arose, they were managed by Anthony Gottlieb, who did business as Morningstar Management. On January 22, 1996, the Bonaguras signed an "Exclusive Artist Agreement" with Intersound Entertainment, Inc. ("Intersound"), a Minnesota corporation whose principal place of business was in Roswell, Georgia. This agreement obligated Intersound to be responsible for the artwork and graphic design for the Baillie and the Boys albums.

With Intersound's knowledge and consent, the Bonaguras hired Harris Graphics, Inc. and Team Design to develop the artwork and graphics for an upcoming album called "Lovin' Every Minute." They believed that Intersound would be responsible for paying for this work. However, unbeknownst to the Bonaguras, Mr. Gottlieb had delivered a letter to Intersound agreeing that the Bonaguras would be responsible for paying for the artwork and graphic design for this album.

When Harris Graphics and Team Design were not paid for their work, they filed suit in the Davidson County General Sessions Court against Intersound and Mr. Gottlieb seeking payment and an injunction against the use of their work until they were paid. The general sessions court later permitted Harris Graphics and Team Design to add the Bonaguras as defendants. Following a hearing, the general sessions court granted Team Design a $4,086.75 judgment against Intersound and the Bonaguras. It also granted Harris Graphics a $2,200 judgment against Intersound and a $2,760 judgment against the Bonaguras.

All the parties perfected de novo appeals to the Circuit Court for Davidson County....

The trial was originally set for September 1998 but, at the trial court's initiative, was continued twice to February 16, 1999. Approximately one month before trial, the lawyer representing the Bonaguras requested his fellow lawyers to agree to preserve the Bonaguras' trial testimony by taking their depositions because Cactus Pete's in Jackpot, Nevada had declined to release them from a previous contractual commitment that conflicted with the rescheduled court date. The lawyers agreed, and the Bonaguras' depositions were scheduled for January 19, 1999. However, before the depositions could be taken, Mr. Gottlieb changed his mind and insisted that the Bonaguras be present at the trial. On January 21, 1999, the Bonaguras filed a motion seeking a continuance and an order enforcing the agreement permitting them to present their testimony by deposition. Team Design and Harris Graphics agreed to the use of the depositions at trial but objected to another continuance.

The trial court conducted a hearing on the Bonaguras' motion on February 5, 1999.... After the trial court agreed to the Bonaguras' request for a continuance, the lawyers and the trial court began discussing another trial date. During this discussion, the trial court offered the alternative of "binding mediation" and stated that it would be available to conduct the mediation on March 11, 1999. The record contains no indication that the trial court informed the parties of the specific procedures that would be used for this mediation or the legal consequences of their agreement to participate in the mediation.... The lawyers for all the parties accepted the court's offer, and on February 16, 1999, the trial court entered an order referring the case to "binding mediation before this Court" on March 11, 1999.

Thereafter, the trial court directed the parties to submit confidential statements outlining their respective positions. When the parties returned to court on

March 14, 1999 … a clerk explained the procedure the trial court intended to follow which consisted of separate meetings with each of the parties and their lawyers in chambers. Over the next four hours, the trial court met separately with each of the parties and their lawyer. According to one of the lawyers, the trial court "made no attempt to seek a mutual agreement as to a resolution of the issues among the parties, but, after the final interview, announced that she would make a decision and enter an order reflecting her decision." On March 19, 1999, the trial court entered an order awarding Team Design a $4,086.75 judgment against Intersound and awarding Harris Graphics a $5,044.45 judgment against Intersound. The trial court also awarded Intersound a judgment against Mr. Gottlieb for one-third of the total amount of Team Design's and Harris Graphics' judgments to be paid from moneys he received from the "Lovin' Every Minute" album. Likewise, the trial court awarded Intersound a judgment against the Bonaguras for one-third of the of Team Design's and Harris Graphics' judgments to be paid from the royalties generated from their "Lovin' Every Minute" album.

On March 31, 1999, Intersound filed a … motion [it is a motion to alter or amend a judgment after it has been rendered] based on its lawyer's assertion that he had understood that the "binding mediation" offered by the trial court would be the sort of mediation authorized by Tenn. S. Ct. R. 31 in which he had previously participated in other cases. He also asserted that he never would have agreed to mediation had he understood the procedure that the court planned to follow. Team Design, Harris Graphics, and Mr. Gottlieb opposed the motion. They argued (1) that all the parties had agreed to "binding mediation," (2) that Intersound had not objected to the procedure prior to the entry of the March 19, 1999 order, and (3) that it would be unfair to permit Intersound to object to the proceeding at this point. The trial court entered an order on April 29, 1999, denying Intersound's post-trial motion. Intersound has perfected this appeal.

II. The Trial Court's Authority to Conduct Binding Mediation

We turn first to the question of a Tennessee trial court's authority to conduct "binding mediation." Intersound asserts that any sort of mediation conducted by a trial court in Tennessee must be consistent with Tenn. S. Ct. R. 31. In response, Team Design, Harris Graphics, and Mr. Gottlieb assert that the parties and the trial court may, by agreement, agree upon an alternative dispute procedure that does not meet all the requirements of Tenn. S. Ct. R. 31 and that the trial court and the parties did precisely that. We have

determined that all court-annexed alternative dispute resolution procedures must be consistent with Tenn. S. Ct. R. 31 and that the "binding mediation" procedure used in this case was not consistent with Tenn. S. Ct. R. 31.

A

Public policy strongly favors resolving disputes between private parties by agreement. Private parties may, of course, decide to submit their disputes to the courts for resolution; however, a broad range of other formal and informal alternatives are available before they resort to litigation. These procedures are, as a practical matter, limited only by the parties' imaginations because the parties themselves may agree on virtually any mutually satisfactory procedure that is not illegal or contrary to public policy. Thus, alternative dispute resolution procedures may range from formal procedures such as arbitration under Tennessee's version of the Uniform Arbitration Act … to far less formal procedures such as "splitting the difference," flipping a coin, or, for that matter, arm wrestling. At least with regard to formal agreements to resolve disputes, the courts will require the parties to follow their agreed-upon dispute resolution procedure as long as they are competent and are dealing at arm's length. When the parties have agreed to be bound by the outcome of their agreed-upon procedure, the courts will require them to accept the result by declining to try their dispute de novo and by limiting the scope of judicial review of the outcome….

The parties' ability to manipulate the contours of the procedure to resolve their disputes narrows considerably once they submit their dispute to the courts for resolution. Judicial proceedings must be conducted in accordance with the ancient common-law rules, applicable constitutional principles, statutes, and court rules.

In Tennessee prior to 1995, traditional litigation was the only procedure available to parties who turned to the courts for resolution of their disputes. The trial courts lacked express authority to provide judicial oversight over pending cases other than the sort of oversight traditionally provided by American judges. They certainly did not have express authority to offer or require the use of alternative dispute resolution procedures. This changed on July 1, 1995, when amendments to Tenn. R. Civ. P. 16 greatly expanded the trial courts' case management authority. For the first time, Tenn. R. Civ. P. 16.03(7) specifically empowered trial courts to discuss "the possibility of settlement or the use of extrajudicial procedures, including alternative dispute resolution, to resolve the dispute." These amendments did not, however, empower trial courts to require the parties to engage in any sort of alternative dispute resolution procedure or to participate in any such procedure themselves. These changes were to come five months later.

On December 18, 1995, the Tennessee Supreme Court filed Tenn. S. Ct. R. 31 establishing procedures for court-annexed alternative dispute resolution in Tennessee's trial courts.... The original version of the rule represented an incremental approach to court-annexed alternative dispute resolution. The procedures ... were intended to be alternatives, not replacements, to traditional litigation....

Under the original version of the rule ... [ADR] procedures became available only after "all parties are before the court."... At that time, any or all of the parties could request authorization to engage in an alternative dispute resolution procedure.... The rule also permitted the trial court, even without the parties' request or consent but after consultation with the lawyers and the parties, ... to require the parties to participate in a judicial settlement conference, a mediation, or a case evaluation.... In addition, with the consent of all parties, the trial court could refer the case for "non-binding arbitration, mini-trial, summary jury trial, or other appropriate alternative dispute resolution proceedings."...

The original version of Tenn. S. Ct. R. 31, like the current version, specifically defined each of the alternative dispute resolution methods contemplated by the rule. Consistent with the Commission's recommendation that court-annexed alternative dispute proceedings should be non-binding ... each of these methods were intended to promote negotiated settlements between the parties themselves. They were not intended to require the parties to relinquish their decision-making right to any third party who would make the decision for them.

The fact that all proposed alternative dispute resolution methods are non-binding is an essential attribute of the court-annexed procedures.... The rule specifically defines mediation as "an informal process in which a neutral person ... conducts discussions among the disputing parties designed to enable them to reach a mutually acceptable agreement among themselves on all or any part of the issues in dispute."... The arbitration permitted by the rule must be "non-binding."... Likewise, a "case evaluation" is advisory only; a "mini-trial" envisions that "the parties or their representatives [will] seek a negotiated settlement of the dispute"... and a "summary jury trial" envisions only an "advisory verdict" followed by a "negotiated settlement."... In 1996, the Tennessee Supreme Court reaffirmed that all court-annexed alternative dispute resolution proceedings permitted

by Tenn. S. Ct. R. 31 were premised on the principle of "self-determination."...

Another essential attribute of alternative dispute resolution is the neutrality and impartiality of the mediators, arbitrators, or other neutral persons conducting the process.... The importance of neutrality is reflected in the fact that Tenn. S. Ct. R. 31 refers to persons conducting court-annexed alternative dispute resolution proceedings as "dispute resolution neutrals."... It is also reflected in the Standards of Professional Conduct for Rule 31 Mediators adopted by the Tennessee Supreme Court ... which state that "integrity, impartiality, and professional competence are essential qualifications of any mediator."...

A third essential attribute of the court-annexed procedures ... is confidentiality. All parties in a mediation proceeding trust that the proceeding will be confidential because these proceedings permit them to "bare their soul" to the mediator and provide them the opportunity to vent which, in some instances, is all that stands in the way of a negotiated settlement.... Accordingly, a vast majority of the proponents of alternative dispute resolution view confidentiality of the proceedings as a central issue....

The Tennessee Supreme Court recognized the importance of confidentiality when it first authorized court-annexed alternative dispute resolution. Tenn. S. Ct. R. 31 ... required that a "mediator, settlement judge, or other dispute resolution neutral shall preserve and maintain the confidentiality of all alternative dispute resolution proceedings except where required by law to disclose the information."...

The principles of self-determination, neutrality, and confidentiality influenced the Tennessee Supreme Court's view of the role trial judges should properly play in court-annexed alternative dispute resolution proceedings. While the court gave trial courts the authority to require litigants, with or without their consent, to participate in a case evaluation, mediation, or judicial settlement conference ... the court carefully limited the trial court's role in these proceedings. First, the court permitted trial judges to participate only in judicial settlement conferences. All other proceedings must be presided over by a "neutral person" or a "neutral panel."... Secondly, with regard to judicial settlement conferences, the court stated clearly that judges presiding over a pending case could not also conduct the judicial settlement conference. The definition of "judicial settlement conference" makes it clear that these proceedings must be "conducted by a judicial officer other than the judge before whom the case will be tried."...

The policy reasons for not permitting the trial judge who could eventually try the case to preside over the mediation or other alternative dispute resolution procedure ... are evident and compelling. A judge who presides over a judicial settlement conference is not acting as a judge but as a neutral.... The success of the settlement "depends largely on the willingness of the parties to freely disclose their intentions, desires, and the strengths and weaknesses of their case" with the neutral.... Thus, a judge conducting a settlement conference becomes a confidant of the parties ... with whom the parties share information that would normally be shared only with their lawyers.

Generally, knowledge gained in a prior judicial proceeding is not a sufficient ground to require the recusal or disqualification of a trial judge in a later judicial proceeding.... However, much of the information imparted during a mediation is not the sort of information that would normally be disclosed to the other parties or the court. Accordingly, should the judge who conducts the judicial settlement conference later be called upon to decide the issues of liability or damages, it is impossible to avoid questions as to whether he or she can disregard the matters disclosed during the conference or put aside any opinions or judgments already formed based on this information....

The Tennessee Supreme Court recognized these confidentiality and predisposition concerns in its September 1996 revisions to Tenn. S. Ct. R. 31. The court added a provision to the rule stating:

> A person serving as a Rule 31 dispute resolution neutral in an alternative dispute resolution proceeding shall not participate as attorney, advisor, judge, guardian ad litem, master or in any other judicial or quasi-judicial capacity in the matter in which the alternative dispute resolution proceeding was conducted....

B

The "binding mediation" proceeding at issue in this case did not comply with... Tenn. S. Ct. R. 31 as it stood in early 1999 in four fundamental particulars. First, [it] ... did not authorize "binding mediation"... as a method for court-annexed alternative dispute resolution.... Second, the procedure actually used by the trial court bore no resemblance to a judicial settlement conference or mediation because the parties' decision-

making rights were supplanted by the trial court, and there was no apparent effort to assist the parties in reaching their own voluntary settlement of their differences.... Third, the proceeding was conducted by the trial judge to whom the case had been assigned notwithstanding the clear requirement... that it be "conducted by a judicial officer other than the judge before whom the case will be tried." Fourth, the judge who conducted the alternative dispute resolution proceeding entered a final order disposing of the parties' claims even though it did not have the authority to do so....

These departures are not just minor deviations from Tenn. S. Ct. R. 31. Each of them is inconsistent with one or more of the fundamental principles that impelled the Tennessee Supreme Court to authorize court-annexed alternative dispute resolution in the first place. They undermined the principles carefully designed to preserve the parties' right of self-determination. They also raised the specter of possible repercussions for the parties who objected to referring the case to alternative dispute resolution or who objected to its outcome. Accordingly, we have concluded that these deviations are substantive and material and that they affected the outcome of this proceeding.

A judgment is considered void if the record demonstrates that the court entering it lacked jurisdiction over either the subject matter or the person, or did not have the authority to make the challenged judgment.... A void judgment lacks validity anywhere and is subject to attack from any angle....

A trial court cannot exercise authority it has not been granted expressly or by necessary implication.... At the time of this proceeding, Tenn. S. Ct. R. 31 did not permit the judge who conducted the judicial settlement conference to enter an order disposing of the case. Accordingly, the order disposing of the parties' claims entered on March 19, 1999, by the judge who conducted the mediation was void, ... and the trial court erred when it declined to grant Intersound's ... motion....

We vacate the March 19, 1999 and April 29, 1999 orders and remand the case to the trial court for further proceedings consistent with this opinion. We tax the costs to Team Design; Harris Graphics, Inc.; Anthony Gottlieb; and Intersound Entertainment, Inc. and its surety for which execution, if necessary, may issue.

Case Questions

1. What was the mediator's decision in this case?
2. Why did the state court of appeals vacate the trial court's orders?

Minitrials

The **minitrial**, used primarily to resolve business disputes, actually isn't a trial at all. It is a process in which each party makes an abbreviated presentation to a panel, generally consisting of a senior manager or decision maker from each side and a judge (in the case of a court-ordered minitrial) or jointly selected neutral (in the case of a voluntary minitrial). The theory behind this process is that the presenters for each side will educate the managers about the dispute.[20] The strength of this process is that the business managers, rather than lawyers, judges, and juries, make the decisions. The managers often can design creative solutions that make it possible to resolve the dispute. They are not restricted to the types of relief that courts can award after a trial. If the managers fail to agree, minitrial rules often require a judge or neutral to forecast what he or she believes would happen if the case were to go to trial and indicate what he or she believes to be a reasonable settlement proposal. The parties in a court-annexed minitrial can reject the judge's proposal, but may incur a penalty. A party who insists on a trial but fails to recover a judgment more favorable than the judge's proposal may be assessed a substantial fine for each day that it takes to try the case.[21] The parties in a voluntary minitrial can reject the neutral's proposal without a penalty.

Some courts schedule minitrials only after the parties agree to participate. Other courts require parties to take part. Minitrials are primarily used in complex, time-consuming cases where the substantial savings of money and time realized by limiting discovery and presentations are strong incentives. Minitrials are most likely to succeed when both parties are serious about resolving the underlying issues with a minimum of acrimony.

The parties in a minitrial have control over the procedures and can disregard the formal rules of civil procedure and evidence that apply in litigation. For example, they can set their own rules regarding the nature and scope of discovery and determine whether position papers will be exchanged prior to the hearing. They also can determine the procedures to be used at the hearing. For example, they can decide whether written summaries will be submitted in lieu of witness testimony, how many hours each side will have to present its case, how long opening statements will be, and whether cross-examination will be allowed.

The typical procedures for a minitrial include an abbreviated presentation of each side's case to a panel of decision makers selected by the parties and the neutral. The decision makers then meet privately after the presentations have concluded and work to negotiate a solution to the dispute.

Summary Jury Trials

An Ohio federal district court judge developed the **summary jury trial (SJT)** process in 1980 as a court-annexed, mandatory procedure. It operates pursuant to local court rules and is used in cases that have proved difficult to settle—primarily damage cases. The key elements in the typical SJT are an advisory jury; an abbreviated, two-hour hearing; and a nonbinding verdict. The SJT procedure can be helpful when parties agree on the defendant's liability but disagree about the damages. In such cases, the plaintiff's attorney doesn't want to settle for less than what he or she estimates a jury will award. Similarly, the defendant's lawyer will not want to settle for more than what a jury would probably require.

SJT procedures are similar to those at trial.[22] A judge presides, and each side has one or two hours to present its case. Case presentations include oral summaries of the evidence and the reading of witness depositions. Each side also has an opportunity to argue the case to the jury, which consists of five or six jurors. The judge gives the jury abbreviated oral instructions. The SJT juries are composed of persons summoned to court but not chosen to sit on a regular trial jury that day.

After the judge's instructions, the SJT jurors retire and deliberate on both liability and damages. The jurors often are asked to discuss the case with the attorneys and clients after they return with a nonbinding verdict. The process works best when the client or some person with settlement authority attends the SJT and participates in this settlement conference.

The SJT process allows the attorneys to have a practice trial and the opportunity to see how a group of regular jurors reacts to each side's presentation. It also gives the parties "a day in court," which helps to satisfy some litigants' emotional needs. The fact that neutral jurors establish a damage figure is an additional plus. The SJT has had an impact on insurance companies, as well as the attorneys and parties. Insurance companies often are more willing to settle after they have seen an SJT jury's verdict because they then have a dollar figure that can serve as a basis for settlement negotiations. If the parties are unable to settle the dispute, the case remains on the calendar for a regular trial.

One criticism of summary jury trials is that SJT presentations compress cases to such an extent that the jurors can't absorb the evidence and argument. In response, a few judges now allow one-week summary "trials." Others permit the use of live witness testimony.

Introduction to *Griffin v. Yonkers*

The plaintiff and defendant in the following case were involved in a motor vehicle collision. The lawyers for both parties stipulated to having the matter decided by a summary jury trial. The plaintiff won the summary jury trial and the defendant filed a motion asking to delay the entry of judgment. The defendant explained that he wanted the court to schedule a hearing and determine whether any third party (such as an insurance company) had a legal obligation to contribute along with the defendant to paying for the plaintiff's damages. The plaintiff urged the court to enter judgment immediately and opposed the defendant's motion, claiming that the motion was forbidden by the judicial district's summary jury trial rules.

Derik Griffin v. Richard A. Yonkers
891 N.Y.S.2d 896
New York Supreme Court, Bronx County
December 21, 2009

Lucindo Suarez, J.
Review of defendant Richard A. Yonkers's motion pursuant to CPLR 4545 (c) for a collateral source setoff with respect to the jury verdict concerning loss of earnings and medical expenses; and same defendant's [motion] ... to stay entry of the judgment pursuant to CPLR 2201 until defendant's motion pursuant to CPLR 4545 (c) for a collateral source hearing is determined.

The issue in these motions to stay enforcement of the judgment until a collateral source hearing is held is whether the court is precluded from conducting such a hearing where the parties have agreed to waive any motions for directed verdicts or to set aside the verdict pursuant to the summary jury trial rules and procedures of the Twelfth Judicial District. This court holds it is not so prevented, as such a motion is not addressed to the validity or sufficiency of the substantive evidence and proof adduced at trial, but to the quantum of compensation pursuant to the verdict; and upon consideration denies the application as defendant has not demonstrated that the relevant portion of the jury's verdict will, with reasonable certainty, be replaced or indemnified from any collateral source.

The underlying action arises from an automobile accident where plaintiff claims various injuries. The attorneys stipulated to a summary jury trial.

A summary jury trial is a voluntary, innovative and streamlined form of alternative dispute resolution that combines the flexibility and cost-effectiveness of arbitration with the structure of a conventional trial. The primary mission of New York's Summary Jury Trial Program is to give cost-conscious litigants a reliable, trial-tested option guaranteed to resolve civil cases fairly, quickly and economically by one-day jury trials. Jury selection is abbreviated, each litigant may offer documentary, demonstrative, and limited testimonial evidence without calling expert witnesses, and the attorneys are permitted to deliver condensed opening and closing statements. The parties may stipulate to a summary jury trial providing for: the extent, dates and period for discovery; the mode and method of the trial; a waiver of the right of appeal and motions directed to the verdict; and high/low verdict parameters. In the absence of agreement of counsel and approval by the trial court, the process provided in the rules of the jurisdiction apply....

The summary jury trial achieves its economy of time by limiting the presentation by each side to one hour, absent a court rule or an agreement to the contrary. During the one hour, each side may call one or two witnesses, who are subject to cross-examination. Other testimony may be presented through deposition transcripts or sworn affidavits. The rules of evidence are relaxed but not abrogated. The key to the saving of time and especially expense is the submission of medical evidence through the affidavits or reports of providers, rather than through live testimony. Police, hospital, and accident reports, as well as other documentary or demonstrative evidence are allowed to be introduced without certification or authentication, subject to all items having been exchanged, and objections to the introduction of evidence and rulings thereto having been made before trial at an evidentiary hearing.

The overarching theme to be borne in mind is that the parties themselves, with the permission of the trial judge, may fashion their own parameters for their summary jury trial, by using, augmenting and/or disregarding the rules existing in the jurisdiction, as well as by creating rules of their choosing. The parties are allowed to shape a format that will allow them to fully explore all the issues or to focus on a particular issue without spending the time and money to bring in myriad witnesses, doctors and other experts.

The parties here did not stipulate to abide by any parameters other than the rules of the Twelfth Judicial District ... with respect to motion practice, which explicitly preclude motions for a directed verdict and motions to set aside the verdict, both of which are addressed to the sufficiency of the substantive evidence and proof at trial.... For example, a trial court may set aside a verdict only if there was "no valid line of reasoning and permissible inferences which could possibly lead rational men to the conclusion reached by the jury on the basis of the evidence presented."...

A motion pursuant to CPLR 4545 (c), however, addresses the sufficiency and propriety of plaintiff's recovery of damages.... It does not question the validity or weight of the substantive evidence adduced at trial. "Under CPLR 4545 (c), if the court finds that any portion of a personal injury award for economic loss 'was or will, with reasonabl[e] certainty, be replaced or indemnified from any collateral source, it shall reduce the amount of the award by such finding.' " (Brewster v Prince Apts. ... [2000].)

The only New York cases answering this question are found in the Fourth Department, emanating from the Eighth Judicial District, the jurisdiction that pio-

neered the use of the summary jury trial in New York State. Although that jurisdiction's summary jury trial rules are essentially similar to those followed in the Bronx, the cases establish that posttrial motion practice is not per se disallowed in the summary jury trial setting. For example, in *Conroe v Barmore-Sellstrom, Inc.* ... [4th Dept 2004]), the court allowed motion practice to challenge the admission into evidence of documents that had not been exchanged pursuant to the summary jury trial rules. In addition, where neither the parties' stipulation to submit the action to summary jury trial nor the administrative judicial materials in the jurisdiction addressed the particular type of motion made in the summary jury trial setting, and while dismissing the appeal, the court stated that it would not have been error to rule on the motion....

Accordingly, as collateral source motions are not specifically excluded by the rules under which the parties stipulated to submit the action to a summary jury trial, defendant's motion may be entertained. Furthermore, "[t]o assure that plaintiffs are fully compensated—but not overcompensated—a 'direct correspondence between the item of loss and the type of collateral reimbursement must exist before the required statutory offset may be made.' " *(Fisher v Qualico Contr. Corp.* ... [2002].... Ordinarily, a hearing would be required to determine the amount of the collateral source offset, if any, from the jury's verdict.

Here, however, movant, pursuant to the court's directive, provided the insurance carrier's denial of benefits of proposed collateral source. As benefits were already denied, and the time to appeal the denial has long since passed, movant has not demonstrated that the relevant portion of the jury's verdict "will, with reasonable certainty, be replaced or indemnified ... from any collateral source."... Therefore, defendant's motion for a stay of enforcement of the judgment is denied as moot.

Accordingly, it is ordered that the motion ... of defendant Richard A. Yonkers for a collateral source hearing and reduction of the verdict by collateral source payment is denied; and it is further ordered, that the motion ... of defendant Richard A. Yonkers for a stay of enforcement of the judgment is denied as moot.

Case Question

1. These parties had three choices. They could have chosen a bench trial, a regular jury trial, or a summary jury trial. Why do you think that the lawyers for both parties stipulated that their dispute be resolved via a summary jury trial as opposed to a regular jury trial?

Private Trials

Parties that have failed to resolve their dispute with mediation or arbitration may choose to litigate in a private court system. Provided by commercial firms that employ retired federal, state, and local judges, such trials are held in hotel conference rooms, law schools, and even office buildings in which courtrooms that replicate public courtrooms have been constructed. These firms exist to provide timely, confidential, and affordable trials. In 13 states, the parties can employ jurors selected from the public jury rolls to hear the case. The **private trial system** allows the parties to select a judge who has experience appropriate to the case. It also allows the parties to conduct their trial in private, an important advantage in many contract, employment rights, professional liability, and divorce actions. The parties to a private trial often contract to use simplified evidentiary and procedural rules and to cooperate in discovery, saving time and money for both parties. The parties also decide whether the decision of the private judge or jury will be final or appealable. Some private court systems even provide for private appeals.

Critics of the private court system maintain that it allows the wealthy to avoid the delays and conditions that others must endure in the public court system. They also express concern that the higher compensation that is paid to private judges could result in a two-tier system of justice. The best judges would handle the litigation of the wealthy in the private sector, while others would litigate before less-able judges in underfunded, overworked public-sector courts.

DOES ADR REALLY WORK?

The question as to the extent to which ADR programs have produced the benefits that were advertised remains unresolved. In 1996, the Rand Corporation evaluated ten ADR pilot programs created pursuant to the Civil Justice Reform Act. Rand found no statistical evidence that the districts with pilot programs had been more successful than ten comparison districts in reducing cost or delay.[23] A 1997 study conducted by the Federal Judicial Center, however, was more favorable and encouraged

continued federal participation.[24] In 2005, the National Arbitration Forum and the American Bar Association surveyed members of two of the ABA's thirty practice-oriented sections, the Tort Trial and Insurance Practice Section (TIPS) and the General Practice Solo and Small Firm Section (GPSolo), to ask their views about and experience with ADR techniques.

When asked about the extent to which they had used ADR techniques to resolve cases in 2004, slightly over 53 percent of the TIPs respondents indicated that they had done so in one to five cases, but only 4.5 percent reported using ADR methods in at least twenty-six cases.

When TIPS respondents were asked if "clients' interests are sometimes served by offering ADR solutions," only 10.6 percent answered in the negative. And when asked about ADR's long-term prospects, almost 60 percent of TIPS respondents believed it would be utilized more frequently in the future.

When GPSolo respondents were asked the same questions as the TIPS respondents, 65.4 percent indicated that they had used ADR techniques to resolve between one and five cases in 2004, but only 1.7 percent reported using ADR methods in at least twenty-six cases. Only 13.8 percent used private trials. GPSolo respondents answered that offering ADR solutions would not benefit their client's interest. And when asked about ADR's long-term prospects, over 66 percent of GPSolo respondents reported they expected it would be utilized more frequently in future years.

It is important to note that the lawyers participating in these two surveys were chosen because of their membership in the targeted ABA sections. Their responses may or may not reflect the views of ABA member lawyers not surveyed. It is also important to note that mediation and arbitration were the only ADR methods explicitly included in either survey's questions. It can be said that most respondents, while including ADR methods in their practices and professing confidence that ADR methods would play a more prominent role in the practice of law in the future, reported having used them infrequently to resolve cases in 2004. There has been no subsequent survey to see what has transpired since 2005.

Statistical Summary: Use and Benefits of Alternative Dispute Resolution by the Department of Justice

	2011	2010	2009
Success Rates for ADR			
Resolved Voluntary ADR	73%	80%	78%
Resolved-Court-Ordered ADR	53%	46%	42%
Cases Benefitted by ADR	**86%**	**73%**	**83%**
Quantified Benefits of ADR			
Discovery or Litigation Expenses Avoided	$12,158,750	$11,662,500	$5,940,287
Litigation Time Saved in Months because of ADR	**1,231**	**930**	**849**

F I G U R E 14.2   Use and Benefits of Alternative Dispute Resolution by the Department of Justice

Source: U.S. Department of Justice, Office of Legal Policy, "Alternative Dispute Resolution at the Department of Justice." http://www.justice.gov/olp/adr/doj-statistics.htm.

The U.S. Department of Justice's (DOJ) Office of Legal Policy (OLP), however, has been collecting data since 2007 on the use of voluntary and court-annexed ADR in DOJ cases. The DOJ's data were derived from "detailed case reports submitted by the lead counsel in all cases in which a private neutral conducted an ADR process in Department litigation...."[25]

The OLP data suggest that cost savings were realized by the DOJ where cases were resolved through the use of ADR instead of through traditional prosecutions. The costs were less because the DOJ's discovery and litigation expenses were reduced. Similarly, the data showed that cases involving ADR techniques were more quickly resolved than litigated cases.[26]

New York State's Unified Court System has established Community Dispute Resolution Centers (CDRCs) in all of its counties. These Centers offer free or low-cost ADR services to interested parties with disputes involving family law, civil law, housing, criminal matters, and commercial law.[27] New York

began collecting data on the effectiveness of these CDRCs in 2007 and publishes annual reports and statistical reports with respect to cases, workloads, and outcomes. The 2011–2012 Annual Report claimed that the CDRCs had served 76,831 people and had provided "16,313 mediations and other dispute resolution processes" during that fiscal year. The report claimed that 74 percent of the disputes in which the CDRC participated were resolved and that the entire process averaged twenty days from intake to resolution.[28] The data also indicated that the average cost incurred for cases involving arbitration, mediation, or conciliation was $314 per case.[29]

INTERNET TIP

Interested readers can find more information about the New York CDRC Program at www.nycourts.gov/ip/adr.

CHAPTER SUMMARY

The chapter began with an explanation of some of the disadvantages of resolving disputes by public court trial. These include the public nature of the

process, the length of time it often takes for a case to get to trial, the cost of preparing for a trial that most likely never will occur, and the potential dissatisfaction with the consequences of litigation's "winner-take-all" approach. Next, the chapter covered the differences between voluntary participation in ADR and participation that is mandated by law (court-annexed ADR). The majority of the chapter focused on explaining various ADR methods such as settlement conferences, arbitration, mediation, minitrials, and summary jury trials. The chapter concluded with a brief discussion of how well ADR works.

CHAPTER QUESTIONS

1. Frances J. Vukasin was employed by D. A. Davidson & Co. in August 1979. The company implemented an annual performance review in 1985, which rated her performance in each of six areas, gave her an overall rating, and indicated a recommended salary increase. Included in Vukasin's 1986 and 1987 performance reviews, directly above the employee's signature line, was a provision that read, "Employment with D. A. Davidson & Co. is subject to arbitration." The review also provided that she or her employer could terminate employment at any time for any reason. There was also a statement that "I [the employee] … acknowledge and agree that any controversy between myself and the Company arising out of my employment or the termination of my employment with the Company for any reasons whatsoever shall be determined by arbitration." On December 12, 1988, Vukasin filed a complaint in a state court against the company. She alleged in the complaint that another employee had assaulted and battered her at the company's offices on April 30, 1988. She claimed damages for mental and emotional distress, pain and suffering, loss of wages, and various medical and therapy expenses. Is the allegation of assault and battery outside the scope of the arbitration clause and appropriate for litigation?

   Vukasin v. D. A. Davidson & Co., 785 P.2d 713 (Mont. 1990)

2. James Clawson contracted with Habitat, Inc., to build a retaining wall and driveway at his home. The contract contained an arbitration clause. A dispute arose regarding the construction, and the matter was submitted to binding arbitration. The parties continued negotiation throughout the arbitration process. When it appeared that they were close to a settlement, they entered into a new agreement. The new agreement provided that the parties would retract the arbitration if they could negotiate a settlement by 3:00 p.m. on October 21, 1988. Clawson and Habitat disagreed about whether an agreement had been reached by that date. The arbitrator's decision was released on November 1, 1988. Both parties filed motions in the circuit court, Habitat to confirm the award, and Clawson to vacate the award. Should the circuit court confirm the award?

   Clawson v. Habitat, Inc., 783 P.2d 1230 (Hawaii 1989)

3. The Medford (Oregon) Firefighters Association and the City of Medford reached a stalemate while negotiating a collective bargaining agreement. They unsuccessfully tried to mediate their dispute. Pursuant to state law, the Oregon Employment Relations Board appointed an arbitrator, who held a hearing, prepared an agreement, and submitted it to the parties. The firefighters petitioned the circuit court for a writ of mandamus when the city refused to sign the agreement. The city claimed that the state law providing for binding arbitration was unconstitutional. Can the state legislature constitutionally delegate legislative power to a private person as an arbitrator?

   Medford Firefighters Association v. City of Medford, 595 P.2d 1268 (1979)

4. Roger Lockhart, a teenager, lost the sight in one of his eyes. He alleged that this was due to the negligence of Dr. Ramon Patel. A summary jury trial was conducted, and the advisory jury awarded the plaintiff $200,000. The court

held several formal and informal settlement conferences following the SJT. The court directed that the defense attorney attend a settlement conference on November 3, 1986, and that he bring with him a representative of Dr. Patel's liability insurance carrier who possessed authority to settle the case. The defense attorney appeared on November 3, but the insurance representative with settlement authority did not. The insurance carrier sent an adjuster instead. The court responded by (1) striking the defendant's pleadings; (2) declaring the defendant in default; (3) setting the trial for the following day, limited to the question of damages; and (4) setting a hearing to show cause why the insurance carrier should not be punished for criminal contempt of court. Does the court have the right to strike the defendant's pleadings because of the insurance carrier's failure to send a representative to attend the settlement conference?

Lockhart v. Patel, 115 F.R.D. 44 (E.D. Ky. 1987)

5. Elizabeth Garfield brought suit against her former employer, Thomas McKinnon Securities, Inc., claiming that McKinnon had discharged her on account of her age in violation of the Age Discrimination in Employment Act (ADEA). McKinnon moved to dismiss the complaint and compel arbitration because Garfield had agreed to arbitrate any controversy arising out of her employment. Garfield responded that she and all registered brokers are required to execute arbitration agreements as a condition of employment. She maintained that Congress did not intend to permit persons to waive their statutory right to sue for ADEA violations in federal court via the execution of an arbitration agreement. Should the court dismiss the complaint and compel arbitration?

Garfield v. Thomas McKinnon Securities, Inc., 731 F. Supp. 841 (N.D. Ill. 1988)

6. Irmis Achong was hired as a nursing attendant by the Cabrini Medical Center. He became a member of Local 1199 of the Drug, Hospital and Health Care Employees Union, which was party to a collective bargaining agreement. On November 4, 1986, a disoriented and distraught patient kicked Achong as he walked by her stretcher. Cabrini claimed that Achong, who had a perfect performance record at the time, responded by cursing the patient and striking her on the leg. Cabrini discharged Achong for abusing the patient. The collective bargaining agreement provided for binding arbitration whenever the union and Cabrini disagreed upon whether an employee was discharged for just cause. Achong's dismissal was submitted to arbitration. The arbitrator made careful and detailed findings and conclusions. He ruled that just cause did not exist for Achong's discharge, because Cabrini failed to establish how hard Achong touched the patient. He believed that summary discharge was too harsh a penalty under the circumstances and based on the limited evidence. He ruled that Achong should be reinstated without back pay (thereby imposing a forfeiture of nine months' pay) and given a warning against future conduct. Cabrini brought an action in federal court to set aside the award, and the union brought an action in state court to confirm. Cabrini removed the state action to federal court, where the two actions were consolidated. Cabrini argued that the award violated public policy based on a statutory provision that patients "shall be free from mental and physical abuse." Should the award be confirmed?

Cabrini Medical Center v. Local 1199 Drug, Hospital and Health Care Employees Union, 731 F. Supp. 612 (S.D.N.Y. 1990)

NOTES

1. Administrative Office of U.S. Courts, Office of Judges Programs, Statistics Division. Federal Judicial Caseload Statistics December 31, 2011, Table C.

2. Administrative Office of the United States Courts. *2009 Annual Report of the Director: Judicial Business of the United States Courts.* Washington, D.C.: U.S. Government Printing Office, 2010.

3. Administrative Office of U.S. Courts, Office of Judges Programs, Statistics Division. Federal Judicial Caseload Statistics December 31, 2011, Table C-4.

4. Administrative Office of U.S. Courts. Judicial Business 2009, Statistical Table for the Federal Judiciary, Tables C-4 and C-4A, September 30, 2009.

5. Massachusetts Supreme Judicial Court Rule 1:18, May 1, 1998. This Massachusetts supreme court rule requires attorneys to file the following certification with the court, indicating they have advised their client of options for alternative dispute resolution:

Commonwealth of Massachusetts

Trial Court Department

UNIFORM COUNSEL CERTIFICATION FOR CIVIL CASES

CASE NAME: _____

DOCKET # _____

I am attorney-of-record for:

_____

plaintiff/defendant/petitioner in the above-entitled matter.

In accordance with Rule 5 of the Supreme Judicial Court Uniform Rules on Dispute Resolution (SJC Rule 1:18) which states in part: "… Attorneys shall: provide their clients with this information about court-connected dispute resolution services; discuss with their clients the advantages and disadvantages of the various methods of dispute resolution; and certify their compliance with this requirement on the civil cover sheet or its equivalent…," I hereby certify that I have complied with this requirement.

_____

Signature of Attorney-of-Record

_____

Print Name

B.B.O. # _____

Date: _____

6. W. H. Schroeder Jr., "Private ADR May Offer Increased Confidentiality," *National Law Journal* (July 25, 1995), pp. C14–C16.

7. J. H. Kennedy, "Merger Aimed at Settling Out of Court," *Boston Globe,* May 16, 1994, pp. 18–19.

8. D. M. Provine, *Settlement Strategies for Federal District Judges* (Washington, DC: Federal Judicial Center, 1986).

9. H. N. Mazadoorian, "Widespread Disgust with Civil Justice Is Boon to ADR," *Corporate Legal Times* (April 1994), p. 17.

10. Ibid.

11. J. W. Keltner, *The Management of Struggle* (Cresskill, NJ: Hampton Press, 1994), p. 152.

12. J. W. Cooley, "Arbitration v. Mediation-Explaining the Differences," 69 *Judicature* 264 (1986).

13. Federal Arbitration Act, 9 U.S.C. §1.

14. See *Eastern Associated Coal Corp. v. United Mine Workers,* 531 U.S. 57 (2000), and *Circuit City Stores, Inc. v. Adams,* 532 U.S. 105 (2001).

15. Some states have, in the past, refused to enforce arbitration agreements entered into before the existence of any dispute.

16. *Shearson Lehman Hutton v. McMahon,* 482 U.S. 220 (1987).

17. R. C. Reuben, "Decision Gives Banking ADR a Boost," *American Bar Association Journal* (December 1994), pp. 32–33.

18. Mazadoorian, p. 17.

19. Cooley, p. 266.

20. J. Davis and L. Omlie, "Mini-trials: The Courtroom in the Boardroom," 21 *Willamette Law Review* 531 (1985).

21. The extent to which judges can order parties to participate in a minitrial remains a hotly contested issue.

22. "Mandatory and Summary Jury Trial Guide-lines for Ensuring Fair and Effective Process," 103 *Harvard Law Review* 1086 (1993).

23. J. S. Kakalik, *Implementation of the Civil Justice Reform Act in Pilot and Comparison Districts* (Santa Monica, CA : Rand Institute for Civil Justice, 1996).

24. Ibid.

25. U.S. Department of Justice, Office of Legal Policy, *Statistical Summary: Use and Benefits of Alternative Dispute Resolution by the Department of Justice,* 2012. http://www.justice.gov/olp/adr/doj-statistics.htm.

26. Ibid.

27. New York Unified Court System, *Alternative Dispute Resolution.* http://www.nycourts.gov/ip/adr/What_is_ADR.shtml.

28. New York Unified Court System, Community Dispute Resolution Centers Program, *Statistical Supplement,* 2011–2012. http://www.nycourts.gov/ip/adr/Publications/Statistical_Supplement/SS2011-12.pdf.

29. New York Unified Court System, Community Dispute Resolution Centers Program, *2011–2012 Annual Report.* http://www.nycourts.gov/ip/adr/Publications/Annual_Reports/AR2011-12.pdf.

Appendices

The Constitution of the United States

We the people of the United States, in order to form a more perfect union, establish justice, insure domestic tranquility, provide for the common defense, promote the general welfare, and secure the blessings of liberty to ourselves and our posterity, do ordain and establish this Constitution for the United States of America.

ARTICLE I

Section 1

All legislative powers herein granted shall be vested in a Congress of the United States, which shall consist of a Senate and House of Representatives.

Section 2

The House of Representatives shall be composed of members chosen every second year by the people of the several States, and the electors in each State shall have the qualifications requisite for electors of the most numerous branch of the State Legislature.

No person shall be a representative who shall not have attained to the age of twenty-five years, and been seven years a citizen of the United States, and who shall not, when elected, be an inhabitant of that State in which he shall be chosen.

Representatives and direct taxes[1] shall be apportioned among the several States which may be included within this Union, according to their respective

---

1. Altered by the 16th Amendment.

numbers, which shall be determined by adding to the whole number of free persons, including those bound to service for a term of years, and excluding Indians not taxed, three fifths of all other persons.[2] The actual enumeration shall be made within three years after the first meeting of the Congress of the United States, and within every subsequent term of ten years, in such manner as they shall by law direct. The number of representatives shall not exceed one for every thirty thousand, but each State shall have at least one representative; and until such enumeration shall be made, the State of New Hampshire shall be entitled to choose three, Massachusetts eight, Rhode Island and Providence Plantations one, Connecticut five, New York six, New Jersey four, Pennsylvania eight, Delaware one, Maryland six, Virginia ten, North Carolina five, South Carolina five, and Georgia three.

When vacancies happen in the representation from any State, the executive authority thereof shall issue writs of election to fill such vacancies.

The House of Representatives shall choose their speaker and other officers; and shall have the sole power of impeachment.

Section 3

The Senate of the United States shall be composed of two senators from each State, chosen by the legislature thereof,[3] for six years; and each senator shall have one vote.

Immediately after they shall be assembled in consequence of the first election, they shall be divided as equally as may be into three classes. The seats of the senators of the first class shall be vacated at the expiration of the second year, of the second class at the expiration of the fourth year and of the third class at the expiration of the sixth year, so that one third may be chosen every second year; and if vacancies happen by resignation, or otherwise, during the recess of the legislature of any

State, the executive thereof may make temporary appointments until the next meeting of the legislature, which shall then fill such vacancies.[4]

No person shall be a senator who shall not have attained to the age of thirty years, and been nine years a citizen of the United States, and who shall not, when elected, be an inhabitant of that State for which he shall be chosen.

The Vice President of the United States shall be President of the Senate, but shall have no vote, unless they be equally divided.

The Senate shall choose their other officers, and also a president pro tempore, in the absence of the Vice President, or when he shall exercise the office of the President of the United States.

The Senate shall have the sole power to try all impeachments. When sitting for that purpose, they shall be on oath or affirmation. When the President of the United States is tried, the chief justice shall preside: And no person shall be convicted without the concurrence of two thirds of the members present.

Judgment in cases of impeachment shall not extend further than to removal from office, and disqualifications to hold and enjoy any office of honor, trust or profit under the United States: But the party convicted shall nevertheless be liable and subject to indictment, trial, judgment and punishment, according to law.

Section 4

The times, places, and manner of holding elections for senators and representatives, shall be prescribed in each State by the legislature thereof: But the Congress may at any time by law make or alter such regulations, except as to the places of choosing senators.

The Congress shall assemble at least once in every year, and such meeting shall be on the first Monday in December, unless they shall by law appoint a different day.

---

2. Altered by the 14th Amendment.

3. Superseded by the 17th Amendment.

4. Altered by the 17th Amendment.

Section 5

Each House shall be the judge of the elections, returns and qualifications of its own members, and a majority of each shall constitute a quorum to do business; but a smaller number may adjourn from day to day, and may be authorized to compel the attendance of absent members, in such manner, and under such penalties as each House may provide.

Each House may determine the rules of its proceedings, punish its members for disorderly behavior, and, with the concurrence of two thirds, expel a member.

Each House shall keep a journal of its proceedings, and from time to time publish the same, excepting such parts as may in their judgment require secrecy; and the yeas and nays of the members of either House on any question shall, at the desire of one fifth of those present, be entered on the journal.

Neither House, during the session of Congress, shall, without the consent of the other, adjourn for more than three days, nor to any other place than that in which the two Houses shall be sitting.

Section 6

The senators and representatives shall receive a compensation for their services, to be ascertained by law, and paid out of the Treasury of the United States. They shall in all cases, except treason, felony, and breach of the peace, be privileged from arrest during their attendance at the session of their respective Houses, and in going to and returning from the same; and for any speech or debate in either House, they shall not be questioned in any other place.

No senator or representative shall, during the time for which he was elected, be appointed to any civil office under the authority of the United States, which shall have been created, or the emoluments whereof shall have been increased, during such time; and no person holding any office under the United States shall be a member of either House during his continuance in office.

Section 7

All bills for raising revenue shall originate in the House of Representatives; but the Senate may propose or concur with amendments as on other bills.

Every bill which shall have passed the House of Representatives and the Senate, shall, before it become a law, be presented to the President of the United States; If he approves he shall sign it, but if not he shall return it, with his objections, to that House in which it shall have originated, who shall enter the objections at large on their journal, and proceed to reconsider it. If after such reconsideration two thirds of that House shall agree to pass the bill, it shall be sent, together with the objections, to the other House, by which it shall likewise be reconsidered, and if approved by two thirds of that House, it shall become a law. But in all such cases the votes of both Houses shall be determined by yeas and nays, and the names of the persons voting for and against the bill shall be entered on the journal of each House respectively. If any bill shall not be returned by the President within ten days (Sundays excepted) after it shall have been presented to him, the same shall be a law, in like manner as if he had signed it, unless the Congress by their adjournment prevent its return, in which case it shall not be a law.

Every order, resolution, or vote to which the concurrence of the Senate and the House of Representatives may be necessary (except on a question of adjournment) shall be presented to the President of the United States; and before the same shall take effect, shall be approved by him, or being disapproved by him, shall be repassed by two thirds of the Senate and House of Representatives, according to the rules and limitations prescribed in the case of a bill.

Section 8

The Congress shall have the power to lay and collect taxes, duties, imposts, and excises, to pay the debts and provide for the common defense and general welfare of the United States; but all duties, imposts, and excises shall be uniform throughout the United States;

To borrow money on the credit of the United States;

To regulate commerce with foreign nations, and among the several States, and with the Indian tribes;

To establish an uniform rule of naturalization, and uniform laws on the subject of bankruptcies throughout the United States;

To coin money, regulate the value thereof, and of foreign coin, and fix the standard of weights and measures;

To provide for the punishment of counterfeiting the securities and current coin of the United States;

To establish post offices and post roads;

To promote the progress of science and useful arts, by securing for limited times to authors and inventors the exclusive right to their respective writings and discoveries;

To constitute tribunals inferior to the Supreme Court;

To define and punish piracies and felonies committed on the high seas, and offenses against the law of nations;

To declare war, grant letters of marque and reprisal, and make rules concerning captures on land and water;

To raise and support armies, but no appropriations of money to that use shall be for a longer term than two years;

To provide and maintain a navy;

To make rules for the government and regulation of the land and naval forces;

To provide for calling forth the militia to execute the laws of the Union, suppress insurrections and repel invasions;

To provide for organizing, arming, and disciplining the militia, and for governing such part of them as may be employed in the service of the United States, reserving to the States respectively, the appointment of the officers, and the authority of training the militia according to the discipline prescribed by Congress.

To exercise exclusive legislation in all cases whatsoever, over such district (not exceeding ten miles square) as may, by cession of particular States and the acceptance of Congress, become the seat of the government of the United States, and to exercise like authority over all places purchased by the consent of the legislature of the State in which the same shall be, for the erection of forts, magazines, arsenals, dockyards, and other needful buildings; and

To make all laws which shall be necessary and proper for carrying into execution the foregoing powers, and all other powers vested by the Constitution in the government of the United States, or any department or officer thereof.

Section 9

The migration or importation of such persons as any of the States now existing shall think proper to admit, shall not be prohibited by the Congress prior to the year one thousand eight hundred and eight, but a tax or duty may be imposed on such importation, not exceeding ten dollars for each person.

The privilege of the writ of habeas corpus shall not be suspended unless when in cases of rebellion or invasion the public safety may require it.

No bill of attainder or ex post facto law shall be passed.

No capitation, or other direct, tax shall be laid, unless in proportion to the census or enumeration hereinbefore directed to be taken.[5]

No tax or duty shall be laid on articles exported from any State.

No preference shall be given by any regulation of commerce or revenue to the ports of one State over those of another: Nor shall vessels bound to, or from, one State be obliged to enter, clear, or pay duties in another.

No money shall be drawn from the treasury, but in consequence of appropriations made by law; and a regular statement and account of the

---

5. Superseded by the 16th Amendment.

receipts and expenditures of all public money shall be published from time to time.

No title of nobility shall be granted by the United States: And no person holding any office of profit or trust under them, shall, without the consent of the Congress, accept of any present, emolument, office, or title, of any kind whatever, from any king, prince, or foreign State.

Section 10

No State shall enter into any treaty, alliance, or confederation; grant letters of marque and reprisal; coin money; emit bills of credit; make any thing but gold and silver coin a tender in payment of debts; pass any bill of attainder, ex post facto law, or law impairing the obligation of contracts, or grant any title of nobility.

No State shall, without the consent of the Congress, lay any imposts or duties on imports or exports, except what may be absolutely necessary for executing its inspection laws: And the net produce of all duties and imposts laid by any State on imports or exports, shall be for the use of the treasury of the United States; and all such laws shall be subject to the revision and control of the Congress.

No State shall, without the consent of the Congress, lay any duty of tonnage, keep troops, or ships of war in time of peace, enter into any agreement or compact with another State, or with a foreign power, or engage in war, unless actually invaded, or in such imminent danger as will not admit of delay.

ARTICLE II

Section 1

The executive power shall be vested in a President of the United States of America. He shall hold his office during the term of four years, and, together with the Vice President, chosen for the same term, be elected as follows:

Each State shall appoint, in such manner as the legislature thereof may direct, a number of electors, equal to the whole number of senators and representatives to which the State may be entitled in the Congress: But no senator or representative, or person holding an office of trust or profit under the United States, shall be appointed an elector.

The electors shall meet in their respective States, and vote by ballot for two persons, of whom one at least shall not be an inhabitant of the same State with themselves. And they shall make a list of all the persons voted for, and of the number of votes for each; which list they shall sign and certify, and transmit sealed to the seat of the government of the United States, directed to the president of the Senate. The president of the Senate shall, in the presence of the Senate and House of Representatives, open all the certificates, and the votes shall then be counted. The person having the greatest number of votes shall be President, if such number be a majority of the whole number of electors appointed; and if there be more than one who have such majority, and have an equal number of votes, then the House of Representatives shall immediately choose by ballot one of them for President; and if no person have a majority, then from the five highest on the list the said House shall in like manner choose the President. But in choosing the President, the votes shall be taken by States, the representation from each State having one vote; a quorum for this purpose shall consist of a member or members from two thirds of the States, and a majority of all the States shall be necessary to a choice. In every case, after the choice of the President, the person having the greatest number of votes of the electors shall be the Vice President. But if there should remain two or more who have equal votes, the Senate shall choose from them by ballot the Vice President.[6]

The Congress may determine the time of choosing the electors, and the day on which they shall give their votes; which day shall be the same throughout the United States.

6. Superseded by the 12th Amendment.

No person except a natural born citizen, or a citizen of the United States, at the time of the adoption of this Constitution, shall be eligible to the office of President; neither shall any person be eligible to that office who shall not have attained to the age of thirty-five years, and been fourteen years a resident within the United States.

In case of the removal of the President from office, or of his death, resignation, or inability to discharge the powers and duties of the said office, the same shall devolve on the Vice President, and the Congress may by law provide for the case of removal, death, resignation or inability, both of the President and Vice President, declaring what officer shall then act as President, and such officer shall act accordingly, until the disability be removed, or a President shall be elected.

The President shall, at stated times, receive for his services a compensation, which shall neither be increased nor diminished during the period for which he shall have been elected, and he shall not receive within that period any other emolument from the United States, or any of them.

Before he enter on the execution of his office, he shall take the following oath or affirmation: "I do solemnly swear (or affirm) that I will faithfully execute the office of President of the United States, and will to the best of my ability, preserve, protect, and defend the Constitution of the United States."

Section 2

The President shall be commander in chief of the army and navy of the United States, and of the militia of the several States, when called into the actual service of the United States; he may require the opinion, in writing, of the principal officer in each of the executive departments, upon any subject relating to the duties of their respective offices, and he shall have power to grant reprieves and pardons for offenses against the United States, except in cases of impeachment.

He shall have power, by and with the advice and consent of the Senate, to make treaties, provided two thirds of the senators present concur; and he shall nominate, and by and with the advice and consent of the Senate, shall appoint ambassadors, other public ministers and consuls, judges of the Supreme Court, and all other officers of the United States, whose appointment are not herein otherwise provided for, and which shall be established by law: But the Congress may by law vest the appointment of such inferior officers, as they think proper, in the President alone, in the courts of law, or in the heads of departments.

The President shall have power to fill up all vacancies that may happen during the recess of the Senate, by granting commissions which shall expire at the end of their next session.

Section 3

He shall from time to time give to the Congress information of the state of the Union, and recommend to their considerations such measures as he shall judge necessary and expedient; he may, on extraordinary occasions, convene both Houses, or either of them, and in case of disagreement between them with respect to the time of adjournment, he may adjourn them to such time as he shall think proper; he shall receive ambassadors and other public ministers; he shall take care that the laws be faithfully executed, and shall commission all the officers of the United States.

Section 4

The President, Vice President, and all civil officers of the United States, shall be removed from office on impeachment for, and conviction of, treason, bribery, or other high crimes and misdemeanors.

ARTICLE III

Section 1

The judicial power of the United States shall be vested in one Supreme Court, and in such inferior courts as the Congress may from time to time ordain and establish. The judges, both of the Supreme and inferior courts, shall hold their offices during good behavior, and shall, at stated times, receive for their services, a compensation, which shall not be diminished during their continuance in office.

Section 2

The judicial power shall extend to all cases, in law and equity, arising under this Constitution, the laws of the United States, and treaties made, or which shall be made, under their authority; —to all cases affecting ambassadors, other public ministers and consuls; —to all cases of admiralty and maritime jurisdiction; —to controversies to which the United States shall be a party;[7] —to controversies between two or more States; —between a State and citizens of another State; —between citizens of different State; —between citizens of the same State claiming lands under grants of different States, and between a State, or the citizens thereof, and foreign States, citizens or subjects.

In all cases affecting ambassadors, other public ministers and consuls, and those in which a State shall be party, the Supreme Court shall have original jurisdiction. In all the other cases before mentioned, the Supreme Court shall have appellate jurisdiction, both as to law and fact, with such exceptions, and under such regulations as the Congress shall make.

The trial of all crimes, except in cases of impeachment, shall be by jury; and such trial shall be held in the State where the said crimes shall have been committed; but when not committed within any State, the trial shall be at such place or places as the Congress may by law have directed.

Section 3

Treason against the United States shall consist only in levying war against them, or in adhering to their enemies, giving them aid and comfort. No person shall be convicted of treason unless on the testimony of two witnesses to the same overt act, or on confession in open court.

The Congress shall have power to declare the punishment of treason, but no attainder of treason shall work corruption of blood, or forfeiture except during the life of the person attained.

ARTICLE IV

Section 1

Full faith and credit shall be given in each State to the public acts, records, and judicial proceedings of every other State. And the Congress may by general laws prescribe the manner in which such acts, records and proceedings shall be proved, and the effect thereof.

Section 2

The citizens of each State shall be entitled to all privileges and immunities of citizens in the several States.[8]

A person charged in any State with treason, felony, or other crime, who shall flee from justice, and be found in another State, shall on demand of the executive authority of the State from which he fled, be delivered up to be removed to the State having jurisdiction of the crime.

No person held to service or labor in one State under the laws thereof, escaping into another, shall in consequence of any law or regulation therein, be discharged from such service or labor, but shall be delivered up on claim of the party to whom such service or labor may be due.[9]

Section 3

New States may be admitted by the Congress into this Union; but no new State shall be formed or erected within the jurisdiction of any other State; nor any State

---

7. Cf. the 11th Amendment.

8. Superseded by the 14th Amendment, Sec. 1.

9. Voided by the 13th Amendment.

be formed by the junction of two or more States, or parts of States, without the consent of the legislatures of the States concerned as well as the Congress.

The Congress shall have power to dispose of and make all needful rules and regulations respecting the territory or other property belonging to the United States; and nothing in this Constitution shall be so construed as to prejudice any claims of the United States, or of any particular State.

Section 4

The United States shall guarantee to every State in this Union a republican form of government, and shall protect each of them against invasion; and on application of the legislature, or of the executive (when the legislature cannot be convened) against domestic violence.

ARTICLE V

The Congress, whenever two thirds of both Houses shall deem it necessary, shall propose amendments to this Constitution, or, on the application of the legislatures of two thirds of the several States, shall call a convention for proposing amendments, which in either case shall be valid to all intents and purposes, as part of this Constitution, when ratified by the legislatures of three fourths of the several States, or by conventions in three fourths thereof, as the one or the other mode of ratification may be proposed by the Congress; Provided that no amendment which may be made prior to the year one thousand eight hundred and eight shall in any manner affect the first and fourth clauses in the ninth section of the first article; and that no State, without its consent, shall be deprived of its equal suffrage in the Senate.

ARTICLE VI

All debts contracted and engagements entered into, before the adoption of this Constitution, shall be as valid against the United States under this Constitution, as under the Confederation.

This Constitution, and the laws of the United States which shall be made in pursuance thereof; and all treaties made, or which shall be made, under the authority of the United States, shall be supreme law of the land; and the Judges in every State shall be bound thereby, any thing in the Constitution or laws of any State to the contrary notwithstanding.

The senators and representatives before mentioned, and the members of the several State legislatures, and all executives and judicial officers, both of the United States and of the several States, shall be bound by oath or affirmation to support this Constitution; but no religious test shall ever be required as a qualification to any office or public trust under the United States.

ARTICLE VII

The ratification of the conventions of nine States shall be sufficient for the establishment of this Constitution between the States so ratifying the same.

Done in Convention by the unanimous consent of the States present the seventeenth day of September in the year of our Lord one thousand seven hundred and eighty-seven, and of the independence of the United States of America the twelfth. In witness thereof we have hereunto subscribed our names. [Names omitted.]

...

Articles in addition to, and amendment of, the Constitution of the United States of America, proposed by Congress, and ratified by the legislatures of the several States, pursuant to the fifth article of the original Constitution.

AMENDMENT I [FIRST TEN AMENDMENTS RATIFIED DECEMBER 15, 1791]

Congress shall make no law respecting an establishment of religion, or prohibiting the free exercise thereof; or abridging the freedom of speech, or of the press; or the right of the people peaceably to assemble, and to petition the government for a redress of grievances.

AMENDMENT II

A well regulated militia, being necessary to the security of a free State, the right of the people to keep and bear arms, shall not be infringed.

AMENDMENT III

No soldier shall, in the time of peace be quartered in any house, without the consent of the owner, nor in time of war, but in a manner to be prescribed by law.

AMENDMENT IV

The right of the people to be secure in their persons, houses, papers, and effects, against unreasonable searches and seizures, shall not be violated, and no warrants shall issue, but upon probable cause, supported by oath or affirmation, and particularly describing the place to be searched, and the persons or things to be seized.

AMENDMENT V

No person shall be held to answer for a capital, or otherwise infamous crime, unless on a presentment or indictment of a grand jury, except in cases arising in the land or naval forces, or in the militia, when in actual service in time of war or public danger; nor shall any person be subject for the same offense to be twice put in jeopardy of life or limb; nor shall be compelled in any criminal case to be a witness against himself; nor be deprived of life, liberty, or property, without due process of law; nor shall private property be taken for public use, without just compensation.

AMENDMENT VI

In all criminal prosecutions, the accused shall enjoy the right to a speedy and public trial, by an impartial jury of the State and district wherein the crime shall have been committed, which district shall have been previously ascertained by law, and to be informed of the nature and cause of the accusation; to be confronted with the witnesses against him; to have compulsory process for obtaining witnesses in his favor, and to have the assistance of the counsel for his defense.

AMENDMENT VII

In suits at common law, where the value in controversy shall exceed twenty dollars, the right of trial by jury shall be preserved, and no fact tried by a jury shall be otherwise reexamined in any court of the United States, than according to the rules of the common law.

AMENDMENT VIII

Excessive bail shall not be required, nor excessive fines imposed, nor cruel and unusual punishments inflicted.

AMENDMENT IX

The enumeration in the Constitution of certain rights shall not be construed to deny or disparage others retained by the people.

AMENDMENT X

The powers not delegated to the United States by the Constitution, nor prohibited by it to the States, are reserved to the States respectively, or to the people.

AMENDMENT XI [RATIFIED JANUARY 8, 1798]

The judicial power of the United States shall not be construed to extend to any suit in law or equity, commenced or prosecuted against one of the United States by citizens of another State, or by citizens or subjects of any foreign State.

AMENDMENT XII [RATIFIED SEPTEMBER 25, 1804]

The electors shall meet in their respective States, and vote by ballot for President and Vice President, one of whom, at least, shall not be an inhabitant of the same State with themselves; they shall name in their ballots the person voted for as President, and in distinct ballots, the person voted for as Vice President, and they shall make distinct lists of all persons voted for as President and of all persons voted for as Vice President, and of the number of votes for each, which lists they shall sign and certify, and transmit sealed to the seat of the government of the United States, directed to the President of the Senate; —The President of the Senate shall, in the presence of the Senate and House of Representatives, open all the certificates and the votes shall then be counted; —The person having the greatest number of votes for President, shall be the President, if such number be a majority of the whole number of electors appointed; and if no person have such majority, then from the persons having the highest numbers not exceeding three on the list of those voted for as President, the House of Representatives shall choose immediately, by ballot, the President. But in choosing the President, the votes shall be taken by States, the representation from each State having one vote; a quorum for this purpose shall consist of a member or members from two thirds of the States, and a majority of all the States shall be necessary to a choice. And if the House of Representatives shall not choose a President whenever the right of choice shall devolve upon them, before the fourth day of March next following, then the Vice President shall act as President, as in the case of the death or other constitutional disability of the President. The person having the greatest number of votes as Vice President shall be the Vice President, if such number be a majority of the whole number of electors appointed, and if no person have a majority, then from the two highest numbers on the list, the Senate shall choose the Vice President; a quorum for the purpose shall consist of two thirds of the whole number of Senators, and a majority of the whole number shall be necessary to a choice. But no person constitutionally ineligible to the office of President shall be eligible to that of Vice President of the United States.

AMENDMENT XIII [RATIFIED DECEMBER 18, 1865]

Section 1

Neither slavery nor involuntary servitude, except as punishment for crime whereof the party shall have been duly convicted, shall exist within the United States, or any place subject to their jurisdiction.

Section 2

Congress shall have power to enforce this article by appropriate legislation.

AMENDMENT XIV [RATIFIED JULY 28, 1868]

Section 1

All persons born or naturalized in the United States, and subject to the jurisdiction thereof, are citizens of the United States and of the State wherein they reside. No State shall make or enforce any law which shall abridge the privileges or immunities of citizens of the United States; not shall any State deprive any person of life, liberty, or property, without due process of law; nor deny to any person within its jurisdiction the equal protection of the laws.

Section 2

Representatives shall be apportioned among the several States according to their respective numbers, counting the whole number of persons in each State, excluding Indians not taxed. But when the right to vote at any election for the choice of electors for President and Vice President of the United States, representatives in Congress, the executive and judicial officers of a State, or the members of the legislature thereof, is denied to any of the male inhabitants of such State, being twenty-one years of age, and citizens of the United States, or in any way abridged, except for participating in rebellion, or other crime, the basis of representation therein shall be reduced in the proportion which the number of such male citizens shall bear to the whole number of male citizens twenty-one years of age in such State.

Section 3

No person shall be a senator or representative in Congress, or elector of President and Vice President, or hold any office, civil or military, under the United States, or under any State, who having previously taken an oath as a member of Congress, or as an officer of the United States, or as a member of any State legislature, or as an executive or judicial officer of any State, to support the Constitution of the United States, shall have engaged in insurrection or rebellion against the same, or given aid or comfort to the enemies thereof. But Congress may by a vote of two thirds of each House, remove such disability.

Section 4

The validity of the public debt of the United States, authorized by law, including the debts incurred for payment of pensions and bounties for services in suppressing insurrection or rebellion, shall not be questioned. But neither the United States nor any State shall assume or pay any debt or obligation incurred in aid of insurrection or rebellion against the United States, or any claim for the loss or emancipation of any slave; but all such debts, obligations, and claims shall be held illegal and void.

Section 5

Congress shall have power to enforce, by appropriate legislation, the provisions of this article.

AMENDMENT XV [RATIFIED MARCH 30, 1870]

Section 1

The right of citizens of the United States to vote shall not be denied or abridged by the United States or by any State on account of race, color, or previous condition of servitude.

Section 2

The Congress shall have power to enforce this article by appropriate legislation.

AMENDMENT XVI [RATIFIED FEBRUARY 25, 1913]

The Congress shall have power to lay and collect taxes on incomes, from whatever source derived, without apportionment among the several States, and without regard to any census or enumeration.

AMENDMENT XVII [RATIFIED MAY 31, 1913]

The Senate of the United States shall be composed of two senators from each State, elected by the people thereof, for six years; and each senator shall have one vote. The electors in each State shall have the qualifications requisite for electors of the most numerous branch of the State legislature.

When vacancies happen in the representation of any State in the Senate, the executive authority of such State shall issue writs of election to fill such vacancies: *Provided,* That the legislature of any State may empower the executive thereof to make temporary appointments until the people fill the vacancies by election as the legislature may direct.

This amendment shall not be so construed as to affect the election or term of any senator chosen before it becomes valid as part of the Constitution.

AMENDMENT XVIII[10] [RATIFIED JANUARY 29, 1919]

After one year from the ratification of this article, the manufacture, sale, or transportation of intoxicating liquors within, the importation thereof into, or the exportation thereof from the United States and all territory subject to the jurisdiction thereof for beverage purposes is thereby prohibited.

The Congress and the several States shall have concurrent power to enforce this article by appropriate legislation.

This article shall be inoperative unless it shall have been ratified as an amendment to the Constitution by the legislature of the several States, as provided in the Constitution, within seven years from the date of the submission hereof to the States by Congress.

AMENDMENT XIX [RATIFIED AUGUST 26, 1920]

The right of citizens of the United States to vote shall not be denied or abridged by the United States or by any State on account of sex.

Congress shall have the power to enforce this article by appropriate legislation.

AMENDMENT XX [RATIFIED JANUARY 23, 1933]

Section 1

The terms of the President and Vice President shall end at noon on the 20th day of January, and the terms of Senators and Representatives at noon on the 3d day of January, of the year in which such terms would have ended if this article had not been ratified; and the terms of their successors shall then begin.

Section 2

The Congress shall assemble at least once in every year, and such meeting shall begin at noon on the 3d day of January, unless they shall by law appoint a different day.

Section 3

If, at the time fixed for the beginning of the term of President, the President-elect shall have died, the Vice President-elect shall become President. If a President shall not have been chosen before the time fixed for the beginning of his term, or if the President-elect shall have failed to qualify, then the Vice President-elect shall act as President until a President shall have qualified; and the Congress may by law provide for the case wherein neither a President-elect nor a Vice President-elect shall have qualified, declaring who shall then act as President, or the manner in which one who is to act shall be selected, and such person shall act accordingly until a President or Vice President shall have qualified.

Section 4

The Congress may by law provide for the case of the death of any of the persons from whom the House of Representatives may choose a President whenever the right of choice shall have devolved upon them, and for the case of the death of any of the persons from whom the Senate may choose a Vice President whenever the right of choice shall have devolved upon them.

Section 5

Sections 1 and 2 shall take effect on the 15th day of October following the ratification of this article.

---

10. Repealed by the 21st Amendment.

Section 6

This article shall be inoperative unless it shall have been ratified as an amendment to the Constitution by the legislatures of three-fourths of the several States within seven years from the date of its submission.

AMENDMENT XXI [RATIFIED DECEMBER 5, 1933]

Section 1

The Eighteenth Article of amendment to the Constitution of the United States is hereby repealed.

Section 2

The transportation or importation into any State, Territory, or possession of the United States for delivery or use therein of intoxicating liquors in violation of the laws thereof, is hereby prohibited.

Section 3

This article shall be inoperative unless it shall have been ratified as an amendment to the Constitution by conventions in the several States as provided in the Constitution, within seven years from the date of the submission thereof to the States by the Congress.

AMENDMENT XXII [RATIFIED MARCH 1, 1951]

No person shall be elected to the office of the President more than twice, and no person who has held the office of President, or acted as President, for more than two years of a term to which some other person was elected President shall be elected to the office of President more than once.

But this article shall not apply to any person holding the office of President when this article was proposed by the Congress, and shall not prevent any person who may be holding the office of President, or acting as President, during the term within which this article becomes operative from holding the office of President or acting as President during the remainder of such term.

This article shall be inoperative unless it shall have been ratified as an amendment to the Constitution by the legislature of three-fourths of the several States within seven years from the date of its submission to the States by the Congress.

AMENDMENT XXIII [RATIFIED MARCH 29, 1961]

Section 1

The District constituting the seat of Government of the United States shall appoint in such manner as the Congress may direct:

A number of electors of President and Vice President equal to the whole number of Senators and Representatives in Congress to which the District would be entitled if it were a State, but in no event more than the least populous State; they shall be in addition to those appointed by the States, but they shall be considered, for the purposes of the election of President and Vice President, to be electors appointed by a State; and they shall meet in the District and perform such duties as provided by the twelfth article of amendment.

Section 2

The Congress shall have power to enforce this article by appropriate legislation.

AMENDMENT XXIV [RATIFIED JANUARY 24, 1964]

Section 1

The right of citizens of the United States to vote in any primary or other election for President or Vice President, for electors for President or Vice President, or for Senator or Representative in Congress, shall not be denied or abridged by the United States or any State by reason of failure to pay any poll tax or other tax.

Section 2

The Congress shall have power to enforce this article by appropriate legislation.

AMENDMENT XXV [RATIFIED FEBRUARY 10, 1967]

Section 1

In case of the removal of the President from office or of his death or resignation, the Vice President shall become President. Whenever there is a vacancy in the office of the Vice President, the President shall nominate a Vice President who shall take office upon confirmation by a majority vote of both Houses of Congress.

Section 3

Whenever the President transmits to the President pro tempore of the Senate and the Speaker of the House of Representatives his written declaration that he is unable to discharge the powers and duties of his office, and until he transmits to them a written declaration to the contrary, such powers and duties shall be discharged by the Vice President as Acting President.

Section 4

Whenever the Vice President and a majority of either the principal officers of the executive departments or of such other body as Congress may by law provide, transmit to the President pro tempore of the Senate and the Speaker of the House of Representatives their written declaration that the President is unable to discharge the powers and duties of his office, the Vice President shall immediately assume the powers and duties of the office as Acting President.

Thereafter, when the President transmits to the President pro tempore of the Senate and the Speaker of the House of Representatives his written declaration that no inability exists, he shall resume the powers and duties of his office unless the Vice President and a majority of either the principal officers of the executive departments or of such body as Congress may by law provide, transmit within four days to the President pro tempore of the Senate and the Speaker of the House of Representatives their written declaration that the President is unable to discharge the powers and duties of his office. Thereupon Congress shall decide the issue, assembling within forty-eight hours for that purpose if not in session. If the Congress, within twentyone days after receipt of the latter written declaration, or, if Congress is not in session, within twenty-one days after Congress is required to assemble, determines by two-thirds vote of both Houses that the President is unable to discharge the powers and duties of his office, the Vice President shall continue to discharge the same as Acting President; otherwise, the President shall resume the powers and duties of his office.

AMENDMENT XXVI [RATIFIED JULY 1, 1971]

Section 1

The right of citizens of the United States, who are eighteen years of age or older, to vote shall not be denied or abridged by the United States or by any State on account of age.

Section 2

The Congress shall have powers to enforce this article by appropriate legislation.

AMENDMENT XXVII [RATIFIED MAY 7, 1992]

No law varying the compensation for the services of the senators and representatives shall take effect until an election of representatives shall have intervened.

E. I. DuPont deNemours & Co., Inc. v. Rolfe Christopher

Author's Comment and Introduction

This case was my favorite. In my own classes it was the first case assigned. I took as much time to teach it as was required. I used it as an introduction to the entire course because it illustrated how *law affects business morality* and how the court has to *balance competing social values* in reaching its decision. Students were immediately confronted with a *tort* case, a *case of first impression*, in a *U.S. District Court*, with *pleadings, motions to dismiss, discovery problems, the* Erie *Doctrine,* and an *interlocutory appeal.* With help they could, to varying degrees, get a preview of the kinds of topics that would be developed in the chapters that followed.

Many who read *DuPont v. Christopher* for the first time will initially find it difficult to understand. Do not despair. Understanding will improve as readers become familiar with the terms and concepts addressed in this case. Turning to the textbook's glossary and index will provide tools that will help with comprehension. Gaining experience in reading case opinions and progressing through the chapters also will help. By the end of the course most readers who reread *DuPont* will ask themselves, "What was it that I found so hard to understand about this case?"

E. I. DuPont deNemours & Co., Inc. v. Rolfe Christopher
431 F.2d 1013
United States Court of Appeals, Fifth Circuit
July 20, 1970

Goldberg, Circuit Judge.

This is a case of industrial espionage in which an airplane is the cloak and a camera the dagger. The defendants-appellants, Rolfe and Gary Christopher, are photographers in Beaumont, Texas. The Christophers were hired by an unknown third party to take aerial photographs of new construction at the Beaumont plant of E. I. DuPont deNemours & Company, Inc. Sixteen photographs of the DuPont facility were taken from the air on March 19, 1969, and these photographs were later developed and delivered to the third party.

DuPont employees apparently noticed the airplane on March 19 and immediately began an investigation to determine why the craft was circling over the plant. By that afternoon the investigation had disclosed that the craft was involved in a photographic expedition and that the Christophers were the photographers. DuPont contacted the Christophers that same afternoon and asked them to reveal the name of the person or corporation requesting the photographs. The Christophers refused to disclose this information, giving as their reason the client's desire to remain anonymous.

Having reached a dead end in the investigation, DuPont subsequently filed suit against the Christophers, alleging that the Christophers had wrongfully obtained photographs revealing DuPont's trade secrets which they then sold to the undisclosed third party. DuPont contended that it had developed a highly secret but unpatented process for producing methanol, a process which gave DuPont a competitive advantage over other producers. This process, DuPont alleged, was a trade secret developed after much expensive and time-consuming research, and a secret which the company had taken special precautions to safeguard. The area photographed by the Christophers was the plant designed to produce methanol by this secret process, and because the plant was still under construction parts of the process were exposed to view from directly above the construction area. Photographs of that area, DuPont alleged, would enable a skilled person to deduce the secret process for making methanol. DuPont thus contended that the Christophers had wrongfully appropriated DuPont trade secrets by taking the photographs and delivering them to the undisclosed third party. In its suit DuPont asked for damages to cover the loss it had already sustained as a result of the wrongful disclosure of the trade

secret and sought temporary and permanent injunctions prohibiting any further circulation of the photographs already taken and prohibiting any additional photographing of the methanol plant.

The Christophers answered with motions to dismiss for lack of jurisdiction and failure to state a claim upon which relief could be granted. Depositions were taken during which the Christophers again refused to disclose the name of the person to whom they had delivered the photographs. DuPont then filed a motion to compel an answer to this question and all related questions.

On June 5, 1969, the trial court held a hearing on all pending motions and an additional motion by the Christophers for summary judgment. The court denied the Christophers' motions to dismiss for want of jurisdiction and failure to state a claim and also denied their motion for summary judgment. The court granted DuPont's motion to compel the Christophers to divulge the name of their client. Having made these rulings, the court then granted the Christophers' motion for an ... appeal ... to allow the Christophers to obtain immediate appellate review of the court's finding that DuPont had stated a claim upon which relief could be granted. Agreeing with the trial court's determination that DuPont had stated a valid claim, we affirm the decision of that court.

This is a case of first impression, for the Texas courts have not faced this precise factual issue, and sitting as a diversity court we must sensitize our Erie antennae to divine what the Texas courts would do if such a situation were presented to them. The only question involved in this interlocutory appeal is whether DuPont has asserted a claim upon which relief can be granted. The Christophers argued both at trial and before this court that they committed no "actionable wrong" in photographing the DuPont facility and passing these photographs on to their client because they conducted all of their activities in public airspace, violated no government aviation standard, did not breach any confidential relation, and did not engage in any fraudulent or illegal conduct. In short, the Christophers argue that for an appropriation of trade secrets to be wrongful there must be a trespass, other illegal conduct, or breach of a confidential relationship. We disagree.

It is true, as the Christophers assert, that the previous trade secret cases have contained one or more of these elements. However, we do not think that the Texas courts would limit the trade secret protection exclusively to these elements. On the contrary, in *Hyde Corporation v. Huffines*, 1958 ... 314 S.W. 2d 763, the Texas Supreme Court specifically adopted the rule found in the Restatement of Torts which provides:

> One who discloses or uses another's trade secret, without a privilege to do so, is liable to the other if
>
> (a) he discovered the secret by improper means, or
>
> (b) his disclosure or use constitutes a breach of confidence reposed in him by the other in disclosing the secret to him....

Thus, although the previous cases have dealt with a breach of a confidential relationship, a trespass, or other illegal conduct, the rule is much broader than the cases heretofore encountered. Not limiting itself to specific wrongs, Texas adopted subsection (a) of the Restatement which recognizes a cause of action for the discovery of a trade secret by any "improper" means....

The question remaining, therefore, is whether aerial photography of plant construction is an improper means of obtaining another's trade secret. We conclude that it is and that the Texas courts would so hold. The Supreme Court of that state has declared that "the undoubted tendency of the law has been to recognize and enforce higher standards of commercial morality in the business world." *Hyde Corporation v. Huffines*, supra 314 S.W.2d at 773. That court has quoted with approval articles indicating that the proper means of gaining possession of a competitor's secret process is "through inspection and analysis" of the product in order to create a duplicate.... Later another Texas court explained:

> The means by which the discovery is made may be obvious, and the experimentation leading from known factors to presently unknown results may be simple and lying in the public domain. But these facts do not destroy the value of the discovery and will not advantage a competitor who by unfair means obtains the knowledge *without paying the price expended by the discoverer. Brown v. Fowler* ... 316 S.W.2d 111 ... (emphasis added).

We think, therefore, that the Texas rule is clear. One may use his competitor's secret process if he discovers the process by reverse engineering applied to the finished product; one may use a competitor's process if he discovers it by his own independent research;

but one may not avoid these labors by taking the process from the discoverer without his permission at a time when he is taking reasonable precautions to maintain its secrecy. To obtain knowledge of a process without spending the time and money to discover it independently is improper unless the holder voluntarily discloses it or fails to take reasonable precautions to ensure its secrecy.

In the instant case the Christophers deliberately flew over the DuPont plant to get pictures of a process which DuPont had attempted to keep secret. The Christophers delivered their pictures to a third party who was certainly aware of the means by which they had been acquired and who may be planning to use the information contained therein to manufacture methanol by the DuPont process. The third party has a right to use this process only if he obtains this knowledge through his own research efforts, but thus far all information indicates that the third party has gained this knowledge solely by taking it from DuPont at a time when DuPont was making reasonable efforts to preserve its secrecy. In such a situation DuPont has a valid cause of action to prohibit the Christophers from improperly discovering its trade secret and to prohibit the undisclosed third party from using the improperly obtained information.

We note that this view is in perfect accord with the position taken by the authors of the Restatement. In commenting on improper means of discovery the savants of the Restatement said:

> f. Improper means of discovery. The discovery of another's trade secret by improper means subjects the actor to liability independently of the harm to the interest in the secret. Thus, if one uses physical force to take a secret formula from another's pocket, or breaks into another's office to steal the formula, his conduct is wrongful and subjects him to liability apart from the rule stated in this Section. Such conduct is also an improper means of procuring the secret under this rule. But means may be improper under this rule even though they do not cause any other harm than that to the interest in the trade secret. Examples of such means are fraudulent misrepresentations to induce disclosure, tapping of telephone wires, eavesdropping or other espionage. A complete catalogue of improper means is not possible. In general they are means which fall below the generally accepted standards of commercial morality and reasonable conduct....

In taking this position we realize that industrial espionage of the sort here perpetrated has become a popular sport in some segments of our industrial community. However, our devotion to free-wheeling industrial competition must not force us into accepting the law of the jungle as the standard of morality expected in our commercial relations. Our tolerance of the espionage game must cease when the protections required to prevent another's spying cost so much that the spirit of inventiveness is dampened. Commercial privacy must be protected from espionage which could not have been reasonably anticipated or prevented. We do not mean to imply, however, that everything not in plain view is within the protected vale, nor that all information obtained through every extra optical extension is forbidden. Indeed, for our industrial competition to remain healthy there must be breathing room for observing a competing industrialist. A competitor can and must shop his competition for pricing and examine his products for quality, components, and methods of manufacture. Perhaps ordinary fences and roofs must be built to shut out incursive eyes, but we need not require the discoverer of a trade secret to guard against the unanticipated, the undetectable, or the unpreventable methods of espionage now available.

In the instant case DuPont was in the midst of constructing a plant. Although after construction the finished plant would have protected much of the process from view, during the period of construction the trade secret was exposed to view from the air. To require DuPont to put a roof over the unfinished plant to guard its secret would impose an enormous expense to prevent nothing more than a school boy's trick. We introduce here no new or radical ethic since our ethos has never given moral sanction to piracy. The market place must not deviate far from our mores. We should not require a person or corporation to take unreasonable precautions to prevent another from doing that which he ought not do in the first place. Reasonable precautions against predatory eyes we may require, but an impenetrable fortress is an unreasonable requirement, and we are not disposed to burden industrial inventors with such a duty in order to protect the fruits of their efforts. "Improper" will always be a word of many nuances, determined by time, place, and circumstances. We therefore need not proclaim a catalogue of commercial improprieties. Clearly, however, one of its commandments does say "thou shall not appropriate a trade secret through deviousness under circumstances in which countervailing defenses are not reasonably available."

Having concluded that aerial photography, from whatever altitude, is an improper method of discovering the trade secrets exposed during construction of the DuPont plant, we need not worry about whether the flight pattern chosen by the Christophers violated any federal aviation regulations. Regardless of whether the flight was legal or illegal in that sense, the espionage was an improper means of discovering DuPont's trade secret.

The decision of the trial court is affirmed and the case remanded to that court for proceedings on the merits....

Jessie Schubert v. August Schubert Wagon Company

Jessie Schubert v. August Schubert Wagon Company
164 N.E. 42
Court of Appeals of the State of New York
November 20, 1928

Cardozo, Ch. J.

Plaintiff while in the highway was struck by the defendant's car and injured. The car causing the hurt was driven by plaintiff's husband, who was then in the defendant's service. His negligence is not disputed. The employer would have been liable if the servant, the driver of the car, had been a stranger to the plaintiff. The question is whether the rule of liability is different where the servant is the husband

We have held that a wife may not maintain an action against a husband, nor a husband against a wife, for personal injuries, whether negligent or willful.... There is no doubt that this was the rule at common law. *Schultz* v. *Schultz*, ... decided in 1882, held that the rule had not been changed by the statutes then in force. The disability was reciprocal, affecting the man as well as the woman, and was based upon the common-law doctrine of the merger of their beings in the unity of marriage. The Legislature, confronted by that decision and by others of like tenor ... has left the applicable statutes unchanged in point of substance. We held very recently that in the absence of amendment the rule thus interpreted must be deemed to have survived....

The disability of wife or husband to maintain an action against the other for injuries to the person is not a disability to maintain a like action against the other's principal or master. There are, indeed, decisions to the contrary by courts of other States (*Maine* v. *Maine & Sons Co.*, 198 Ia. 1278; *Riser* v. *Riser*, 240 Mich. 402; *Emerson* v. *Western Seed & Irrigation Co.*, [Mich.] 216 N.W. Rep. 277). We are unable to accept them. True, of course, it is that a master is not liable for the act of his servant under the rule of *respondeat superior* if the act itself was lawful.... A judgment to that effect in an action against the servant may be pleaded as a bar in an action against the master.... So, accord and satisfaction, or release, will have the same effect as they have upon joint tort feasors generally.... But the master is not exonerated when the servant has ... set up a discharge in bankruptcy, or has escaped liability upon grounds not inconsistent with the commission of a wrong unreleased and unrequited. No doubt one can gather pronouncements from treatise or decision which, taken from their setting, give color of support for an exemption even wider. They have no such effect when related to context and occasion. Few formulas are meant to serve as universals....

An employer commits a trespass by the hand of his servant upon the person of another. The act, let it be assumed, is within the scope either of an express mandate or of an implied one. In either event, if the trespass is not justified, he is brought under a distinct and independent liability, a liability all his own. The statement sometimes made that it is derivative and secondary ... means this and nothing more, that at times the fault of the actor will fix the quality of the act. Illegality established, liability ensues. The defendant, to make out a defense, is thus driven to maintain that the act, however negligent, was none the less lawful because committed by a husband upon the person of his wife. This is to pervert the meaning and effect of the disability that has its origin in marital identity. A trespass, negligent or willful, upon the person of a wife, does not cease to be an unlawful act though the law exempts the husband from liability for the damage. Others may not hide behind the skirts of his immunity. The trespass may be a crime for which even a husband may be punished, but whether criminal or not, unlawful it remains. As well might one argue that an employer commanding a husband to commit a battery on a wife, might justify the command by the victim's disability. The employer must answer for the damage whether there is trespass by direct command or trespass incidental to the business committed to the servant's keeping. In each case the maxim governs that he who acts through another, acts by himself. In all this there is nothing at war with the holding of some cases that the remedy against the husband is denied altogether, and not merely suspended during coverture.... Unlawful the act remains, however shorn of a remedy....

We are told that in the long run the consequences of upholding an action against the master may be to cast the burden on the husband, since the master, if not personally at fault, has a remedy over.... The consequence may be admitted without admitting its significance as a determining factor in the solution of the problem. The master who recovers over against the servant does not need to build his right upon any theory of subrogation to a cause of action once belonging to the victim of the injury. A sufficient basis for his recovery is the breach of an independent duty owing to himself. The servant owes the duty to the master to render faithful service, and must answer for the damage if the quality of the service is lower than the standard....

We find no collision between the principle of liability established in this case and the principle of exemption established in actions against a husband. If such collision, however, could be found, with the result that one or other principle must yield, we agree with HUBBS, P.J., writing in the court below, that the exemption would have to give way as an exception, more or less anomalous, to a responsibility which today must be accepted as the general rule. Domestic Relations Law (Cons. Laws, ch. 14), §57, is explicit that "a married woman has a right of action for an injury to her person, property or character ... as if unmarried." By authority and tradition, an exception has been engrafted upon this rule where the husband is defendant. We are not at liberty to extend it by dubious construction.

The judgment should be affirmed with costs. POUND, CRANE, ANDREWS, LEHMAN, KELLOGG and O'BRIEN, JJ., concur. Judgment affirmed.

August Schubert (holding hat in the front row) and his workers. This is a copy of a family picture, 1885.

Courtesy of Frank August Schubert

Glossary of Selected Terms from *The Law Dictionary* with Augmentation by the Textbook Author*

Acceptance In contract law, the agreement of the offeree to be bound by the terms of the offer.

Accession A natural increase in one's property. Examples include the interest earned on money deposited in a bank account, or crops grown on one's land, or newborn puppies delivered by one's dog.

Accord In contract law, the offer of something different from what was due under the original contract. See also, *accord and satisfaction*, and *satisfaction*.

Accord and Satisfaction An agreement between two (or more) persons, one of whom has a right of action against the others, that the latter should do or give, and the former accept, something in satisfaction of the right of action. When the agreement is executed, and satisfaction has been made, it is called *accord and satisfaction,* and operates as a bar to the right of action. Accord, Restatement (Second) of Contracts §281(1).

Act-of-State Doctrine An issue of *justiciability*. The doctrine provides that American courts should not determine the validity of public acts committed by a foreign sovereign within its own territory.

Actus Reus. An overt wrongful act. See also, *mens rea*.

Additur A motion made by a prevailing party in state court asking that the trial court award the plaintiff an additional sum of money because the jury's verdict is grossly inadequate.

Adjudicative Power A delegated power contained in an *enabling act* authorizing an administrative agency to determine legal rights, duties, and obligations, and to impose sanctions on those subject to its jurisdiction.

Administrative Law Judges (ALJs) Persons employed by administrative agencies to conduct adjudicatory hearings. Like law court judges, ALJs decide questions of fact and issues of law, issue subpoenas, administer oaths, make evidentiary rulings, and conduct hearings. ALJs are not, however, members of the federal judiciary. They perceive their function as that of implementing and administering a legislative purpose rather than as judges impartially deciding between two litigants.

Administrative Procedure Act (APA) A 1946 federal statute enacted to improve and strengthen the administrative process. Section 553 of the APA establishes notice and comment procedures for informal rule making, and Section 554 establishes trial-like procedures for formal rule making.

The Law Dictionary (Cochran's Law Lexicon, Sixth Edition), revised by Wesley Gilmer, Jr., Anderson Publishing Co., Cincinnati. Reprinted by permission. Additional terms have been incorporated into this glossary by the author of this text, Frank A. Schubert.

Adoption A social and a legal process by which the rights and duties accompanying the parent-child relationship are transferred from birth parents to adoptive parents. See also, *agency adoption, independent adoption.*

Adverse Possession Also known as *easement by prescription.* One whose possession of another's realty is open and notorious, hostile, adverse, and continuous for a legally specified period of time can bring a *quiet title action* in court at the end of the time period and, if successful, obtain a marketable title.

Advisory Opinion (1) In some jurisdictions, the formal opinion of a higher court concerning a point at issue in a lower court. (2) The formal opinion of a legal officer, e.g., attorney general, concerning a question of law submitted by a public official. (3) In some jurisdictions, the opinion of a court concerning a question submitted by a legislative body.

Aesthetics The study of beauty.

Affirm An appellate court affirms a lower court when it concludes that the lower court's judgment is valid.

Affirmative Defenses (1) In civil law, defenses pleaded by the defendant in his or her answer to the plaintiff's complaint. Each defense will consist of facts that the defendant contends may bar the plaintiff from recovery. (2) In criminal law, defenses in which a defendant admits to the act but claims that special circumstances mitigate, justify, or excuse the defendant's conduct. Also called *excuse defenses.*

Agency Adoption Birth parents consent to the termination of their parental rights and surrender their child to an adoption agency that selects the adoptive parent(s) and places the child. See also, *adoption, independent adoption.*

Agent A person authorized by another (the principal) to do an act or transact business for him or her, and to bind the principal within the limits of that authority. An agent may be authorized to do all business of a particular kind or limited to one particular act. The agent's power to bind the principal is confined to the scope of his or her authority.

Age of Majority The age at which a minor legally becomes an adult. At present, most states set the age as eighteen, but in three states it is twenty-one. See also, *emancipation.*

Agreement An expression of the parties' willingness to be bound to the terms of a contract.

Alibi Defense A defense in which a criminal defendant proves that he or she was somewhere other than at the scene of the crime on the date and time that the offense allegedly occurred.

Alimony (1) Court order requiring that an economically strong spouse pay financial support to an economically dependent spouse where it is necessary and appropriate. Some jurisdictions deny alimony to a spouse whose marriage ended as a result of that person's marital fault. (2) The term for the support payment ordered by the divorce court.

Alternative Dispute Resolution (ADR) A term that refers to a variety of techniques adherents claim can in some cases resolve disputes more quickly, at less cost, and with less acrimony than would be true if the case were litigated in a court.

Analytical Positivism Adherents of this philosophical approach view law as a self-sufficient system of legal rules that the sovereign issues in the form of commands to the governed. Judgments about the intrinsic morality of the sovereign's commands are viewed as extra-legal.

Annul, Annulment An action in which a marriage partner seeks to prove that no valid marriage ever existed.

Answer (1) A pleading in which a civil defendant responds to the allegations of the complaint and states the defenses on which he or she intends to rely. (2) A statement under oath in response to written interrogatories, i.e., questions, or oral questions.

Appeal A process for obtaining review by a higher court of a lower court's decision.

Appellant A person who initiates an appeal from one court to another.

Appellee The party in a lawsuit against whom an appeal has been taken.

Arbitration A form of *alternative dispute resolution.* The voluntary submission of a matter in dispute to the nonjudicial judgment of one, two, or more disinterested persons, called *arbitrators,* whose decision is binding on the parties.

Arbitration Award An *arbitrator's* decision is called an award.

Arbitrator In the *alternative dispute resolution* proceeding known as *arbitration,* the person or persons who conduct the proceeding and decide the outcome of the dispute. Arbitrators often are persons who specialize in a particular field such as construction, commercial contracts, real estate, finance, etc. See also, *neutrals.*

Arraign, Arraignment To bring a criminally accused person formally before a court for the purpose of having him or her answer charges brought by the prosecution.

Arrest (1) The seizing and detaining of a person in custody by lawful authority. (2) The taking of another into custody for the actual or purported purpose of bringing the other before a court, or of otherwise securing the administration of the law. (3) The seizure and detention of personal chattels, especially ships and vessels libeled (i.e., involved in a lawsuit) in a court of admiralty.

Assault Applies in both civil law, as an *intentional tort,* and criminal law. (1) Strictly speaking, *assault* means threatening to strike or harm. (2) A threatening gesture, with or without verbal communication. If a blow is struck, it is *battery*. (3) Attempting to cause or purposely, knowingly, or recklessly causing bodily injury to another, or negligently causing bodily injury to another with a deadly weapon, or attempting by physical menace to put another in fear of imminent serious bodily injury; also called *simple assault*.

Assignee In contract law, the person to whom an *assignment* of rights is made.

Assignment The transfer of contractual rights to another person.

Assignor In contract law, the person making an *assignment* of rights.

Assumpsit A common-law writ used to remedy some breaches of duty (called undertakings) that had previously been actionable under the old writ of trespass on the case.

Assumption of Risk A defense to a claim for negligent injury to a person or property, i.e., a person who voluntarily exposes himself or his property to a known danger may not recover for injuries thereby sustained.

Attempt An *inchoate crime*. A crime committed by a person who has the intent to commit a substantive criminal offense and does an act that tends to corroborate the intent, under circumstances that do not result in the completion of the substantive crime.

At-Will Doctrine A legal doctrine in employment law that permits an employee who has no contractual rights to employment to quit without notice or be fired by the employer at any time, for any reason or for no reason at all.

Avoidable-Harm Doctrine Also known as the *rule of mitigation,* this rule prevents the recovery of damages that could have been foreseen and avoided by reasonable effort without undue risk, expense, or humiliation.

Bail To set at liberty a person arrested or imprisoned, on written security taken for his appearance on a day and at a place named. The term is applied, as a noun, to the persons who become security for the defendant's appearance; to the act of delivering such defendant to his bondsmen; and also to the bond given by the sureties to secure his release. A person who becomes someone's bail is regarded as his jailer, to whose custody he is committed. The noun "bail" is never used with a plural termination.

Bailee A person who receives goods from another person (the *bailor*) in trust for a specific purpose. See also, *bailment*.

Bailment A broad expression that describes the agreement, undertaking, or relationship that is created by the delivery of personal property by the owner, i.e., the *bailor,* to someone who is not an owner of it, i.e., the *bailee,* for a specific purpose, which includes the return of the personal property to the person who delivered it after the purpose is otherwise accomplished. In a bailment, dominion and control over the personal property usually pass to the bailee. The term is often used to describe, e.g.: (1) The gratis loaning of an automobile for the borrower's use. (2) The commercial leasing of an automobile for a fee. (3) The delivery of an automobile to a repairman for the purpose of having it repaired. (4) The delivery of an automobile to a parking attendant for storage, when the keys are left with the attendant.

Bailor A person who commits goods to another person (the *bailee*) in trust for a specific purpose. See also, *bailment.*

Bar and Merger An issue of *justiciability*. A judicial doctrine that provides that claims made by the plaintiff and claims that could have been made, but were not, merge into the judgment and are extinguished. A subsequent suit against the same defendant based on the same claim is barred.

Battery Applies both in civil law, as an *intentional tort,* and in criminal law. An unlawful touching, beating, wounding, or laying hold, however trifling, of another's person or clothes without his or her consent.

Bench Trial A case is litigated before a judge without a jury.

Benefit In contract law, the acceptance by the promisor of some legal right to which the person had not previously been entitled, which constitutes *consideration* by or on behalf of the promisee.

Benefit Rule When a plaintiff is both damaged and benefitted by the defendant's conduct, the plaintiff's damage award should be reduced by the amount of the benefit conferred.

Best Evidence Rule A rule of evidence that requires the production of original documents in court, rather than photocopies or summaries, unless the originals are unobtainable.

Best-Interests-of-the-Child Doctrine A rule requiring judges to show no gender preference in deciding child custody in divorce proceedings, and to act on ability to provide, and interest in providing, the child with love, a good home, food, clothing, medical care, and education.

Bifurcation A trial is broken up into segments.

Bilateral Contract A contract in which the parties exchange mutual promises to do some future act.

Bill of Attainder A legislative act that declares a person guilty of a crime and imposes punishment (generally capital punishment). Used in lieu of the judicial process. (See also *ex post facto law.*)

Breach of Contract A flexible term for the wrongful failure to perform one or more of the promises that a person previously undertook when he or she made a contract, e.g., failure to deliver goods.

Burden of Proof The duty of proving facts disputed in the trial of a case. It commonly lies on the person who asserts the affirmative of an issue, and is sometimes said to shift when sufficient evidence is furnished to raise a presumption that what is alleged is true. The shifting of the burden of proof is better characterized as the creation of a burden of going forward with the evidence; however, because the total burden of proof is not thereby changed, the burden of going forward with the evidence is apt to revert to the other party and change from time to time.

Business Visitor (Business Invitee) A person who is invited to enter or remain on land for a purpose directly or indirectly connected with business dealings with the possessor of the land.

Canon Law Church law.

Capacity to Contract Where a person is of legal age and is not otherwise so impaired as to be substantially incapable of making decisions for himself or herself.

Capias A writ that orders law enforcement officials to take a person into custody and bring him or her before the court.

Capture A method of obtaining title to previously unowned property such as catching fish on the high seas or netting a butterfly. Capture often requires that the captor purchase a license, such as when one goes hunting or fishing.

Case-in-Chief. In a trial, the party's initial presentation of evidence regarding disputed facts in a case. The party presenting its case-in-chief conducts a direct examination of the witnesses it calls to testify and offers proof that supports its theory of the case. The opposing party cross-examines these witnesses.

Case of First Impression A case presenting a legal question that has not previously been answered in a reported appellate opinion.

Cases and Controversies Article III, Section 2, of the U.S. Constitution requires that a matter must be a "case" or "controversy" to be within the federal judicial power. This means that the parties must truly be adverse, the plaintiff's claims of having suffered legal injuries are real and not hypothetical, and the issues raised are neither abstract nor hypothetical.

Causation An element that must be proved in some, but not all, criminal cases and in negligence and some strict liability cases in tort.

Causation in Fact A causal connection does exist between the defendant and the plaintiff's injuries—i.e., but for the defendant's negligence, the plaintiff's injuries would not have occurred (known as the "but-for" test).

Cause of Action The underlying foundation for a lawsuit. It consists of the legal grounds and alleged facts which, if proved, would constitute all the "elements" required by statute or common law to state a claim for legal relief.

Caveat Emptor Let the buyer beware.

Challenge for Cause Where a party in a jury trial seeks to exclude a prospective juror because the juror has an apparent or potential prejudice or bias against that party or that party's type of claim or defense. See also, *peremptory challenge.*

Chancellor As used in this textbook, an equitable court judge, or a judge exercising the powers of an equitable court judge.

Child Support This term refers to a parent's duty to provide *necessaries* to one's child, and to the sum of money one parent must pay to the other pursuant to a court order in the aftermath of a divorce.

Civil Suit Any legal action other than a criminal prosecution

Civil Union A legally recognized relationship that permits qualifying same-sex partners to obtain economic benefits that in some states are equal to those afforded married people. Only a few states recognize civil unions.

Claim Preclusion An issue of *justiciability*. This doctrine provides that a final decision by a competent court on a lawsuit's merits concludes the litigation of the parties and constitutes a bar (a legal barrier) to a new suit. Irrespective of whether a plaintiff wins his or her lawsuit, the claims that he or she made (and could have made, but didn't) merge into the judgment and are extinguished. Thus no subsequent suit can be maintained against the same defendant based on the same claim. See also, *bar and merger,* and *res judicata.*

Clause A provision in a document such as a contract or constitution containing a subject and a finite verb, for example, the Due Process Clause of the Fourteenth Amendment.

Code Napoleon A civil code developed at the direction of Napoleon Bonaparte in 1804. This code, as amended, is the basis of French law and is still a source of law in Louisiana.

Collusion A term used to describe parties to a lawsuit who are not truly adverse—for example, one party is financing and controlling both sides of a lawsuit.

Common Law This term is used in three different contexts in this textbook. (1) It refers to the right of judges, particularly in contract and tort cases, to declare the law based on principles and precedents established over several centuries in Anglo-American case law. (2) It refers to the system of law established in England and subsequently adopted in most American states that features judge-made law and considers case precedents as an important source of law. This text distinguishes the common law approach to lawmaking from the civil law approach, which is derived from detailed legislative codes rather than judicial precedents. (3) Lastly, this term refers to differences in rights, remedies, and procedures that distinguish the common law courts (law courts) from courts of equity.

Common Law Lien A legally enforceable claim against property recognized under the common law.

Common Law Marriage Informal marriage by agreement that dispenses with licenses and solemnization ceremonies. The parties must have established the relationship of husband and wife, live together as a married couple, and present themselves to the world as being married.

Community Property, Community Property States A system used in some states when apportioning property between the parties in a divorce. The earnings of both spouses and property rights acquired with those earnings during the marriage are lumped together and each party receives a percentage of the whole. State statutes usually exclude from community property any rights acquired prior to marriage and spousal inheritances and gifts received during the marriage.

Comparative Negligence The approach to determining damages in negligence cases followed by most states. These states apportion damages between the plaintiff and defendant in proportion to each party's contributory fault. Thus the trier of fact in a case determines the total damages and then assigns a percentage of the total fault to the plaintiff, as well as the defendant; the plaintiff's total damage award is usually reduced by that percentage. Cf., *contributory negligence*.

Compensatory Damages Damages awarded to compensate the plaintiff for actual monetary losses resulting from the defendant's conduct.

Competent Legally adequate. Evidence must be *competent* to be admissible. Competency is a broad concept. To be competent, witnesses have to take an oath or affirm that they will testify truthfully. A nonexpert witness is limited to testimony about what he or she has heard or seen firsthand (i.e., to facts); the opinions and conclusions of such a witness are "incompetent."

Competent Party A person who has the legal capacity to bind himself or herself contractually.

Complaint Under modern rules of civil and criminal procedure, a pleading that is filed to commence an action.

Concurrent Ownership Property held simultaneously by more than one person.

Concurring Opinion An opinion written by a judge who, while voting with the majority, has additional comments to make that go beyond what is included in the majority opinion.

Condition Precedent (1) A contractual requirement that some specified event must occur before a duty to perform becomes operative. (2) In the *equitable remedy* of *specific performance,* the requirement that the party seeking specific performance must have substantially performed, or be ready to perform, his or her obligations under the contract in order to be entitled to specific performance.

Condition Subsequent A contractual requirement that discharges the parties from their duties if a specified event occurs.

Conflict-of-Laws The variance between the laws of two states or countries relating to the subject matter of a suit brought in one of them, when the parties to the suit, or some of them, or the subject matter, belong to the other. (Also known as the *choice-of-law*.)

Consideration An essential element of contracts. That which is bargained for and given in exchange for another's promise, usually consisting of the performance of an act or promise to do an act, or to refrain from doing an act or to give up a right.

Conspiracy An *inchoate crime*. A crime committed when two or more people agree to commit a criminal act and one or more of the conspirators takes a significant step in furtherance of the intended criminal objective.

Constructive Service Service of a summons and complaint that is accomplished by publishing the notice of summons in the legal announcements section of newspapers. (Cf., *personal service*.)

Construe To interpret the meaning of words.

Consumer Credit Protection Act (CCPA) A statute enacted by Congress in 1968 to promote the disclosure of credit terms and to establish the rights and responsibilities of both creditors and consumers.

Contingent Fee Agreement A method of compensation for lawyers. The lawyer takes a contractually agreed-upon percentage of the damages awarded or collected in a settlement in lieu of other forms of compensation. The attorney receives nothing for his or her time if the client recovers nothing.

Contingent Property Rights Property rights that officially come into being (i.e., become *vested*) only after the occurrence of some specified future event.

Contract A legally enforceable agreement containing one or more promises.

Contributory Negligence (1) The failure to exercise care by a plaintiff, which contributed to the plaintiff's injury. Even though a defendant may have been negligent, in some jurisdictions, contributory negligence will bar a recovery by the plaintiff. (2) Conduct on the part of a plaintiff that falls below the standard to which the plaintiff should conform for his or her own protection, and which is a legally contributing cause cooperating with the negligence of the defendant in bringing about the plaintiff's harm. Cf., *comparative negligence*.

Conversion An *intentional tort*. (1) The wrongful appropriation of the goods of another. (2) An intentional exercise of dominion or control over a chattel that so seriously interferes with the right of another to control it that the actor may justly be required to pay the other the full value of the chattel.

Copyright A type of *intellectual property*. A grant of rights to an author from the federal government. Authors of literary pieces, musical compositions, dramatic works, photographs, graphic works of various types, video and audio recordings, and computer software are protected against most unauthorized uses by placing a prescribed copyright notice on publicly disseminated copies of the work.

Corpus Juris Civilis Sixth-century Roman Code that was promulgated by the Emperor Justinian.

Counterclaim A defendant's claim against the plaintiff, which is usually included in the answer; it is essentially a defendant's "complaint."

Court-Annexed ADR Where either legislation or court rule requires that litigants participate in *alternative dispute resolution* efforts before their case can proceed in a trial court.

Court of Chancery (See also, *equity court*.) Originally a court of equity headed by the Chancellor that came into being in the 14th century in England and lasted until 1875. Today, most states confer on their judges both the powers traditionally exercised by law judges and the powers traditionally exercised by the chancellor in the equity courts.

Covenant (1) A common law writ initially used to enforce agreements pertaining to land and later used to enforce written agreements under seal. (2) A promise contained in a deed or contract.

Creation A method for acquiring title to personalty. A person who manufactures products out of raw materials through physical or mental labor has title to the items created. However, someone who is employed to produce something does not take title to the thing produced.

Creditor Beneficiary A noncontracting person who is the intended beneficiary of a contract entered into between two other people, such as where one of two contracting parties owes a performance to the creditor beneficiary (e.g., to make sure that the creditor's automobile that was damaged by the contracting party is repaired) and contracts with the second contracting party (e.g., an auto repair shop) to repair the vehicle, thereby completing that performance.

Criminal Law Jurisprudence concerning crimes and their punishment.

Criminal Negligence A level of negligence greater than ordinary negligence, in which the actor unconsciously creates risk of harm and grossly deviates from how a reasonable person would have acted under the same circumstances. See Figure 8.2 for a more complete explanation.

Cross-Examine, Cross-Examination. Questioning of a witness at trial by opposing counsel after the attorney for the party who has called the witness completes *direct examination*.

Cruel and Unusual Punishment A clause in the Eighth Amendment to the U.S. Constitution.

Curia Regis A twelfth-century royal court established by Henry I that eventually became known as the Court of King's (or Queen's) Bench.

Custodial Interrogation Police-initiated questioning of a person who has been deprived of his liberty in a "significant" way. This term originated in the famous case of *Miranda v. Arizona*.

Custodial Parent A parent awarded primary physical placement (i.e., custody) of a child.

Damages A flexible term for the reparation in money that is allowed by law on account of damage. *Damages* may be *general*, such as necessarily and by implication of law arise from the act complained of; or *special*, such as under the peculiar circumstances of the case arise from the act complained of, but are not implied by law; *compensatory*, sufficient in amount to cover the loss actually sustained; *exemplary*, *punitive*, or *vindictive*, when in excess of the loss sustained and allowed as a punishment for torts committed with fraud, actual malice, or violence; *nominal*, when the act was wrong, but the loss sustained was trifling; *substantial*, when the loss was serious; *liquidated*, fixed by agreement of the parties, as when it is agreed beforehand what amount one shall receive in case of a breach of contract by the other.

Debt A common law writ used to collect a specific sum of money owed by another.

Declaratory Judgment A determination or decision by a court that states the rights of the parties to a dispute, but does not order or coerce any performance relative to those rights.

Deed In relation to *real property,* a *title* document that indicates ownership of the property.

Defamation (1) An *intentional tort.* A flexible term for the uttering of spoken or written words concerning someone that tend to injure that person's reputation, and for which an action for damages may be brought. (2) To create liability for defamation there must be (a) a false and defamatory statement concerning another, (b) an unprivileged publication to a third party, (c) fault amounting at least to negligence on the part of the publisher, and (d) either actionability of the statement irrespective of special harm or the existence of special harm caused by the publication. See also, *libel* and *slander.*

Default Judgment The failure to plead or otherwise defend an action, by a party against whom a judgment for affirmative relief is sought.

Defendant A person against whom an action is brought, a warrant is issued, or an indictment is found.

Defense of Marriage Act (DOMA). This 1996 federal statute defined the term "effect," a term used in the U.S. Constitution's Full Faith and Credit Clause, as not requiring any state, against its will, to recognize same-sex marriages as valid. Until recently, Section 3 in DOMA prohibited the federal government from recognizing legally married same-sex couples as being married. These same-sex couples also were denied marital benefits under the Social Security and federal income tax laws. Section 3 of DOMA was declared unconstitutional by the U.S. Supreme Court in June of 2013 in the case of *United States v. Perry.*

Delegate (1) A person authorized to act for another (more commonly, a *delegatee*). (2) A person elected to represent others in a deliberative assembly, such as a political convention.

Delegation The transfer of contractual duties to another person.

Demurrer A synonym for *motion to dismiss.*

Deposition A written record of oral testimony, in the form of questions and answers, made before a public officer for use in a lawsuit. Depositions are used for the purpose of discovery of information, or for the purpose of being read as evidence at a trial, or for both purposes.

Detainer A writ requiring that a person be retained in custody.

Detinue A writ used to recover possession of personal property from someone who had possession of another's personal property and refused to return it when requested by the true owner.

Dictum (Plural *Dicta*) A statement by a judge concerning a point of law that is not necessary for the decision of the case in which it is stated. Usually, dictum is not as persuasive as its opposite, i.e., holding.

Directed Verdict A determination by a jury made at the direction of the court, in cases where there has been a failure of evidence, an overwhelming weight of the evidence or where the law as applied to the facts permits only one result.

Direct Examination The initial questioning of a witness by the party who calls that witness.

Disaffirm (a Contract) A party to a contract elects to back out of the agreement.

Discharge (1) A flexible term that connotes finality, e.g., cancellation, rescission, or nullification of a contract. (2) The court order by which a person held to answer a criminal charge is set free. (3) The court order by which a jury is relieved from further consideration of a case.

Discovery A method by which the opposing parties to a lawsuit may obtain full and exact factual information concerning the entire area of their controversy, via pretrial depositions, interrogations, requests for admissions, inspection of books and documents, physical and mental examinations, and inspection of land or other property. The purpose of these pretrial procedures is to disclose the genuine points of factual dispute and facilitate adequate preparation for trial. Either party may compel the other party to disclose the relevant facts that are in his or her possession, prior to the trial.

Discretion The use of private independent judgment; the authority of a trial court that is not controlled by inflexible rules, but can be exercised one way or the other as the trial judge believes to be best in the circumstances. It is subject to review, however, if it is abused.

Dissenting Opinion An opinion written by a judge who disagrees with the court's majority. In the opinion, the dissenting judge explains why he or she believes the majority has decided the case wrongly.

Diversity–of–Citizenship Jurisdiction One of two categories of federal subject-matter jurisdiction. For this type of jurisdiction to exist the lawsuit must be between citizens of different states or between a citizen of a state and an alien, and the amount in controversy must exceed $75,000.

Divorce A term used to describe the entire process of concluding and reordering a couple's marital, parental, and economic relationships.

Divorce *a mensa et thoro* (Latin: "from table and bed," or more colloquially, "from bed and board.") See *legal separation.*

Doctrine of Forum Non Conveniens A judicial policy that permits a court to decline to exercise jurisdiction where it believes that the case can proceed more conveniently in another court.

Doctrine of Substituted Judgment An equitable doctrine that provides that a chancellor in equity has the right to act for an incompetent person in the same manner as the incompetent would if he or she were competent.

Domicile The state in which a person has established his or her permanent home and to which the person returns after temporary absences.

Donative Intent In property law, the requirement that, to prove a valid gift, there must be evidence to show that the person making the gift (the *donor*) wants to relinquish all property rights and expects nothing tangible in return from the person receiving the gift (the *donee*).

Donee In property law, the recipient of a gift. See also, *donor, donative intent.*

Donee Beneficiary A noncontracting person who is intended to receive the benefit of an agreement between the contracting parties, i.e., if *A* contracts with *B* to replace a window in *C*'s house, *C* is the donee beneficiary

Donor In property law, the person making a gift. See also, *donative intent, donee.*

Due Process Clause Clauses found in both the Fifth and Fourteenth Amendments to the U.S. Constitution expressly providing that people are entitled to due process of law when government is seeking to deprive them of "life, liberty or property." The Fifth Amendment Due Process Clause applies to the federal government and the Fourteenth Amendment Due Process Clause applies to the state governments.

Due Process of Law A concept traced back to Magna Carta that has traditionally stood for the notion that government has to treat people fairly when attempting to deprive them of "life, liberty, or property." The determination of what fairness requires in any given context is determined by courts on a case-by-case basis. This principle of due process is included in both federal and state constitutions. This fairness requirement applies in both procedural and substantive contexts.

Duress (1) Imprisonment; compulsion; coercion. (2) Threats of injury or imprisonment.

Easement A nonpossessory property right in land; it is one person's right to use (a portion of) another person's land, for example, to cross the property on a path or road to get to an adjacent property, or cross the property with utility lines or pipes (referred to as *affirmative easements*), or restrict the landowner from, for example, burning trash within a certain distance of the adjacent property (referred to as *negative easement*).

Egoist One who believes it is ethically proper to act on one's own self-interest, irrespective of the consequences to others.

Ejectment A judicial remedy sought by a landowner when a trespasser secures full possession of the land and the owner brings an action to regain possession, as well as damages for the unlawful retention of possession. Formerly a mixed action at common law, which depended on fictions in order to escape the inconveniences in the ancient forms of action. It was a mixed action because it sought to recover both possession of land (a real property claim) and also damages (a personal property claim). Various statutory proceedings for the recovery of land, some of which bear the same name, have taken place in most of the United States.

Emancipation A feature of *domestic relations family law*. A minor who is *emancipated* by a state court assumes most adult responsibilities before reaching the age of majority (usually eighteen). Emancipated minors are no longer considered to be under the care and control of parents—instead, they take responsibility for their own care.

Embezzlement A crime in which a criminal actor who has been entrusted with another person's money or property uses the money or property to his or her own advantage, without permission, and in a manner adverse to the true owner's interests.

Eminent Domain (Power of) The right of the government to take private property for a public purpose over the objection of a landowner. This governmental right is limited by the Fifth and Fourteenth Amendments to the U.S. Constitution, which provide that government must pay just compensation to the objecting landowner whenever property is taken to benefit the public by way of the power of eminent domain.

Enabling Act A statute establishing, defining, and guiding an administrative agency's structure, functions, powers, and objectives.

En Banc All judges assigned to an appellate court hear the case as a group

Entrapment A defense raised in a criminal prosecution where an officer induces a person who was not otherwise so disposed to commit a criminal act. The purpose of this defense is to deter this form of police misconduct.

Epistemology The study or a theory of the nature and grounds of knowledge, especially with reference to its limits and validity.

Equal Credit Opportunity Act (ECOA) A statute enacted by Congress in 1974 to eradicate discrimination in the granting of credit, when the decision to grant it or refuse it is based on an individual's sex, marital status, race, color, age, religion, national origin, or receipt of public assistance.

Equal Protection Clause The Fourteenth Amendment's equal protection clause prohibits discrimination on the basis of race, national origin, gender, or religion.

Equitable Distribution An alternative method for apportioning property in a divorce. The court ignores which party has title to marital property and, based on the totality of the circumstances, treats each divorcing party "fairly," after considering each party's contributions and needs and the duration of the marriage.

Equitable Lien An equitable remedy used to avoid an *unjust enrichment* that would otherwise result because no other lien is provided by statute or under the common law.

Equitable Maxims Short statements of principle used to determine if an equitable remedy should be awarded.

Equitable Remedy A remedy traditionally available in equity but not under the common law. Today, most courts in the United States are empowered to grant both equitable and legal relief as required to achieve justice. Traditionally, courts only grant equitable remedies when the common law remedies are inadequate.

Equity (1) Fairness. A type of justice that developed separately from the common law and that tends to complement it. The current meaning is to classify disputes and remedies according to their historical relationship and development. Under modern rules of civil procedure, law and equity have been unified. Historically, the courts of equity had a power of framing and adapting new remedies to particular cases, which the common law courts did not possess. In doing so, they allowed themselves latitude of construction and assumed, in certain matters such as trusts, a power of enforcing moral obligations that the courts of law did not admit or recognize. (2) A right or obligation attaching to property or a contract. In this sense, one person is said to have a better equity than another.

Equity Court A court with jurisdiction to decide equitable claims and award equitable remedies. Also known as a *court of chancery*.

***Erie* Doctrine** A judicial policy that is applied in federal court when adjudicating state matters. This policy provides that where federal jurisdiction is based on diversity of citizenship, a federal court normally should apply the substantive law that would be applied in the state courts of the district in which the federal court is situated.

Estate in Land The amount of interest a person has in land.

Ethics The study of morality.

Exclusionary Rule A judicial remedy in criminal law that under some circumstances excludes from trial evidence obtained by the prosecution. The evidence is suppressed because it was obtained by the police as a byproduct of infringing a criminal defendant's constitutionally protected rights.

Excuse Defenses The defendant acted unlawfully, but argues that no criminal responsibility should be imposed, given the particular circumstances accompanying the act; examples include duress, insanity, and involuntary intoxication. Also called *affirmative defenses*.

Executed Contract A contract in which both parties have performed as agreed; a completed contract.

Execution (1) The writ, order, or process issued to a sheriff directing him to carry out the judgment of a court. (2) To complete a contract.

Executory Contract A contract where one or both parties have not yet completed their performance obligations.

Exemplary Damages A synonym for *punitive damages*.

Exhaustion of Administrative Remedies In matters relating to the *adjudicative powers* of administrative agencies, a requirement that a person objecting to an administrative agency's decision must pursue to conclusion all opportunities for administrative relief prior to seeking relief from the judiciary.

Ex Parte Injunction An *equitable remedy*. An injunction granted without notice to the party being enjoined. See also, *temporary restraining order (TRO)*.

Ex Post Facto Law An ex post facto law makes acts criminal that were not criminal at the time they were committed.

Express Contract A contract in which none of the terms is implied. Cf., *implied contract*.

Express Warranty In contract law, a warranty created by the parties to the contract. Under UCC Section 2-313, *express warranties* exist whenever a seller affirms facts or describes goods, makes a promise about the goods, or displays a sample model. See also, *implied warranty* and *warranty*.

False Arrest; False Imprisonment (1) In civil law, an *intentional tort* consisting of restraint imposed on a person's liberty, without proper legal authority. (2) In criminal law, false imprisonment is a misdemeanor consisting of knowingly restraining another unlawfully so as to interfere substantially with his or her liberty.

Family There is no single universally accepted legal definition of family. The word generally is defined by statute in operational terms, within a particular context (i.e., to specify which people are entitled to specified economic benefits). Under Social Security, a stepchild sometimes can qualify for family benefits. The traditional notion that a family consists of people sharing kinship and cohabitation is outdated. It is common for people to recognize more than one type of family (notably the nuclear family and the extended family, families with same-sex parents, the nuclear family plus the grandparents, cousins, aunts, and uncles).

Federal Arbitration Act A 1925 federal statute that establishes a policy of favoring the arbitration of disputes over commercial transactions.

Federal Register. This daily publication of the federal government is where administrative agencies give notice of proposed rule making, publish proposed rules, and publish promulgated substantive rules not less than thirty days before the rule's effective date.

Fee Simple The maximum ownership right to land that is permissible by law. A person who holds an *estate in land* in what is known as *fee simple* can pass his or her interest on to heirs. Cf., *life estate.*

Felony Although jurisdictional variations exist, a felony generally is regarded as any criminal offense for which a defendant is subject to execution or may be imprisoned for more than one year.

Feudalism A military, political, and social structure that ordered relationships among people. Under feudalism, a series of duties and obligations existed between a lord and his vassals.

Final Decision A decision that is not or cannot be appealed.

Fixture An article that when purchased was *personal property*, but that, when physically attached to a building or land, became part and parcel of it. Written leases often make specific provisions concerning fixtures.

Forbearance Refraining from doing an act, or giving up a right.

Foreign Laws Those enacted and in force in a foreign state or country.

Foreseeability An individual is responsible in negligence only for the consequences of his or her actions that are reasonably foreseeable. The defendant will not be liable for causing injuries that are so remotely linked to the alleged negligent conduct as to be unreasonably related to that conduct.

Formal Rule Making The procedural requirements that provide for a trial-like hearing process "on the record," complete with witnesses and recorded testimony, as well as findings of fact and conclusions of law.

Forum (1) A court of justice; the place where justice must be sought. (2) Formerly, an open space in Roman cities, where the people assembled, markets were held, and the magistrates sat to transact their business.

Forum State The state in which a lawsuit has been filed.

Foster Care A child-care placement with a family (the foster family) or group home, that is willing to provide an unadopted child with short-term "parenting" in the foster family's home. Some parents voluntarily place their children in foster care for a brief time. Most foster placements, however, result from court intervention because of alleged child abuse or neglect.

Fraud Intentional acts of deception used by one individual to gain an advantage over another.

Full-Faith-and-Credit Requirement The requirement that the public acts, records, and judicial proceedings of every state shall be given the same effect by the courts of another state that they have by law and usage in the state of origin. U.S. Const., Art. IV, Sec. I. Congress has prescribed the manner in which they may be proven.

Fully Integrated In contract law, a term that applies where the document signed by the contracting parties that comprises their agreement contains an express provision that this document constitutes the definitive and complete statement of the agreed-upon terms. See also, *parol-evidence rule*, which prohibits introduction of evidence other than the written agreement to explain the terms of a contract.

Fundamental Liberties, Fundamental Rights Fundamental rights are rights that have been given "heightened protection" by the U.S. Supreme Court. These include most of the protections expressly included in the Bill of Rights. The Court also has added other rights to the list that it has found by implication to be deserving of fundamental constitutional protection. Some examples include the rights to marry, to determine how one's children are raised and educated, to marital privacy, and to abortion.

Fungible Goods Goods of a similar character that may be exchanged or substituted for one another; for example, wheat, corn, lima beans, or currency (money).

Garnishment A judgment enforcement process that results in the debtor's employer being ordered to deduct a percentage of the debtor's earnings from each paycheck.

General Appearance A person makes a *general appearance* by not objecting to in personam jurisdiction and by arguing the substantive facts of the case. Such a person is implicitly consenting to personal jurisdiction.

General Damages Damages that are the natural and necessary result of the wrongful act or omission, and thus can normally be expected to accompany the injury.

General-Intent Crimes Serious offenses such as rape and arson and less serious offenses such as trespass and simple battery. For conviction of a general-intent crime, the prosecution only has to prove that the accused intended to commit the *actus reus*. The common law permitted the trier of fact to infer a wrongful state of mind (*mens rea*) from proof that the actor voluntarily did the act. Cf., *specific-intent crime*.

General or Residual Jurisdiction The authority of a court to hear and decide an action or lawsuit, except for those cases that are within the exclusive jurisdiction of another court.

Genuine Assent Agreement to contract that is not induced because of misrepresentation, fraud, duress, undue influence, or mistake.

Good-Character Defense Defense that proves character traits and argues that the defendant's character is so impeccable that he or she never would have committed the crime as charged.

Good-Faith Excepton Exception to the *exclusionary rule* barring evidence in criminal cases, which applies to allow admission of evidence offered by the prosecution if the police acted reasonably in relying on what subsequently turned out to be a defective warrant in obtaining the evidence.

Governmental Immunity Immunity from prosecution for governmental officials such as executive, legislative, and judicial officers when they are acting within the scope of their authority and in the discharge of their official duties.

Grand Jury A body not less than 12 nor more than 24 persons, freeholders of a county, whose duty it is, on hearing the evidence for the prosecution in each proposed bill of indictment, to decide whether a sufficient case is made out, on which to hold the accused for trial. It is a body that is convened by authority of a court and serves as an instrumentality of the court. It has authority to investigate and to accuse, but it is not authorized to try cases. It is a creature of the common law that was instituted to protect the people from governmental oppression. In a few states, it has been partially abolished, but in others it exists by constitutional mandate. No person shall be held to answer for a capital or otherwise infamous federal crime, unless on a presentment or indictment of a grand jury, except in cases arising in the land or naval forces, or in the militia, when in actual service in time of war or public danger; U.S. Const., Fifth Amendment.

Grantee The recipient of a grant.

Grantor The person making a grant.

Guardian A person appointed by a court to have control or management of the person or property, or both, of another person who is incapable of acting on his or her own behalf, e.g., an infant or a person of unsound mind.

Habeas Corpus (Latin, "you have the body.") A writ used to require that a detained person be brought before the court. The purpose of habeas review is to test the legality of the detention. It is frequently used by prisoners who have been unsuccessful in directly appealing their convictions and who are serving sentences of imprisonment. The writ of habeas corpus was recognized in Article 1, Section 9, of the U.S. Constitution.

Harmless-Error Doctrine A judicial doctrine that provides that a criminal conviction need not be automatically reversed just because it has been proved that constitutional error occurred during the trial. There should be no reversal, according to the U.S. Supreme Court, where the quantity and quality of the factual evidence introduced at trial are consistent with the jury's verdict and are so strong that appellate courts can forecast beyond a reasonable doubt that the error was not included in the jury's calculus in reaching its verdict. Errors of this sort are classified as "harmless."

Hearing A flexible term for a court proceeding or trial.

Hearsay Evidence (Rule) Hearsay is a statement made (or offered to be made) by a witness in court that purports to repeat what another person (especially someone who is not in court or cannot be brought into court) made outside of court, where the quoted statement is offered to prove the truth of the matter asserted. (E.g., "Max told me sometime before he died that he robbed the bank by himself," offered to prove that the now-deceased and unavailable Max was the lone bank robber, not the defendant who is in court.) Under the *hearsay evidence rule,* such evidence usually is inadmissible, but exceptions are made, e.g., in questions of pedigree, custom, reputation, dying declarations, and statements made against the interest of the declarant.

Historical Jurisprudence Adherents of this philosophical approach believe that law is only valid to the extent that the will of the sovereign is compatible with long-standing social practices, customs, and values.

Holder (of a Privilege) A person benefitted by a *privileged communication* is entitled to refuse to testify or to block some other person from testifying as a witness.

Holding The rule of law that the court says applies to the facts of the case.

Hundred The lowest unit of governmental organization in Anglo-Saxon England. Its primary function was judicial. It operated a court that met monthly and handled civil and criminal matters according to local custom. Hundreds were grouped into shires.

Illegal Contract An agreement where the formation or performance is criminal, tortious, or contrary to public policy.

Illegal Per Se A contract that is not legally enforceable because the performance called for is against the law, such as selling the services of a prostitute or selling street drugs.

Illusory Promise When one party to an agreement makes what appears at first glance to be a promise but when on examination no real promise is made. For example, a promise to work for an employer at an agreed rate for as long as the promisor wishes to work is an illusory promise. The promisor is really promising nothing and cannot be bound to do anything.

Immunity Preferential protection from lawsuits.

Immunity Through Contract A type of immunity from prosecution created voluntarily by parties to a contract, where they promise not to sue one another for matters pertaining to performance of the contract. Also known as *hold-harmless* or *exculpatory provisions*.

Impeach (1) To charge a public official with a crime or with misconduct in office. (2) To undermine a witness's testimony by proving lack of veracity, prior inconsistent statement, bias, or that the witness is otherwise unworthy of belief.

Implied Contract Contract presumed by law to have been made from the circumstances and the conduct of the parties. Cf., *express contract*.

Implied Warranty In contract law, a warranty implied by law. See also, *express warranty* and *warranty*.

Implied Warranty of Fitness for a Particular Purpose In contract law, under UCC §2-315, a warranty implied by law when the seller has reason to know some particular (nonordinary) purpose for which the buyer has relied on the seller's skill or judgment in making a selection of the type of product to buy.

Implied Warranty of Merchantability In contract law, under UCC §2-314, a warranty implied by law that goods sold by a merchant are fit for the ordinary purpose for which they are intended and are of average quality and properly labeled and packaged.

Imputed Negligence A person can be held vicariously liable for the negligence of another when one person (the agent) acts for or represents another (the principal) by the latter's authority and to accomplish the latter's ends. In such a scenario, the negligence of the agent can be *imputed* onto the principal, provided the agent is acting within the scope of his or her agency.

In Camera A hearing held in a judge's office or in a closed courtroom (i.e., where no one else is present other than the judge, counsel, and perhaps the parties).

Inchoate Crime The crime of preparing for or attempting to commit a crime—e.g., solicitation, attempt, and conspiracy.

Independent Adoption Birth parent(s) interview and select prospective adoptive parents without agency involvement. Some states prohibit independent adoptions. See also, *adoption, agency adoption*.

Independent Contractor A person who agrees with another to do something for another, in the course of his or her occupation, but who is not controlled by the other, nor subject to the other's right to control with respect to the performance of the undertaking, and is thereby distinguished from an employee or agent.

Indictment A written accusation that one or more persons have committed a crime, presented upon oath, by a grand jury. The person against whom the indictment is returned is said to be indicted.

Infliction of Emotional Distress An *intentional tort* in which the tortfeasor's outrageous conduct intentionally and recklessly subjects someone to severe emotional distress. The tortfeasor's conduct must be serious in nature and cause anguish in the plaintiff's mind. *Note:* Most states also recognize the tort of *negligent* infliction of emotional distress, though proof of damages may be more stringent.

Informal Rule Making Procedural requirements in the Administrative Procedure Act that provide for "notice-and-comment" rule making. In informal rule making, agencies are required to publish proposed rules in the *Federal Register,* so that interested persons can receive notice of the agency's intentions and have an opportunity to submit written submissions in which they comment on the proposed rule and, if the agency so desires, make oral presentations.

Injunction A flexible, discretionary process of preventive and remedial justice, which is exercised by courts that have equity powers. Courts issue injunctions when it appears that the ordinary remedy usually provided by law is not a full, adequate, and complete one. Injunctions are *preventive* if they restrain a person from doing something, or *mandatory* if they command something to be done. They are *temporary* (see also, *temporary restraining order– TRO*), *preliminary, provisional,* or *interlocutory* if they are granted on the filing of a bill, or while the suit is pending, to restrain the party enjoined from doing or continuing to do the acts complained of, until final hearing or the further order of the court. They are *final, perpetual,* or *permanent* if they are awarded after full hearing on the merits, and as a final determination of the rights of the parties.

In Personam Jurisdiction A court's jurisdiction over the persons of the plaintiff and defendant.

In Rem Jurisdiction A court's jurisdiction over property that is the subject of a suit.

Insanity Defendant claims to lack the capacity to commit the crime with which he or she is charged; the meaning of capacity varies by jurisdiction.

Insurance People contract with insurance companies and pay premiums in exchange for economic protection against specified risks. Common examples include automobile, property, life, health, and professional liability insurance.

Intangible Personal Property Personal property that has no physical form. Ownership of intangible property is usually evidenced by some type of legal document that sets forth the ownership rights. For example, a bank account is intangible personal property. Cf., *tangible personal property*.

Intangibles A kind of property that is nonphysical and not subject to being sensed (e.g., touched or felt), but that exists as a concept of people's minds (e.g., promissory notes, bank accounts, and corporate stock).

Integrity Quality of a person whose behavior is consistent with moral principles.

Intellectual Property *Trademarks*, *patents*, and *copyrights*. See also, *intangible personal property*.

Intentional Torts Civil wrongs in which the defendant is alleged to have intentionally interfered with the plaintiff's person, reputation, or property.

Interethnic Adoption Provisions Act (IEP) Federal statute enacted in 1996, amending the 1994 federal statute *Multiethnic Placement Act (MEPA)*. The two acts are generally known as the MEPA–IEP; these laws essentially do the following: (1) Prohibit adoption agencies that receive federal funds from using an aspiring adoptive or foster parent's race, color, or national origin against him or her for purposes of denying such parent the placement of a child. (2) Make it illegal to delay or deny a child an adoptive or foster care placement because of his or her race, color, or national origin. The MEPA–IEP intends that placement decisions be made on a case-by-case basis, and cultural needs cannot routinely be used to prevent white adoptive parents, for example, from adopting nonwhite children.

Interference with Contract Relations An *intentional tort* in which a noncontracting party or third person wrongfully interferes with the contract relations between two or more contracting parties.

Interlocutory Appeal An appeal of a ruling by a trial court that is made before the trial itself has concluded. Most jurisdictions generally prohibit such appeals, requiring parties to wait until the trial has concluded before they challenge any of the decisions made by the judge during that trial. However, many jurisdictions make an exception for decisions that are particularly prejudicial to the rights of one of the parties.

Intermediate Appellate Court An appellate court above trial courts and below the court of last resort in a judicial system.

Interpretive Rule Administrative rule used to explain an agency's interpretation of an ambiguous statute, or its understanding of the meaning of an important term that the legislative body creating the agency has neglected to define. See also, *rule-making power*.

Interspousal Immunity A common law doctrine that husbands and wives were immune from liability for negligence and intentional torts perpetrated against their spouses. In part this policy was a byproduct of the old-fashioned common-law notion that husbands and wives were legally one and the same. During the twentieth century, reformers successfully argued that married persons and unmarried persons should have equivalent legal rights and remedies.

Intestate In property law, where a person dies without leaving a will. See also, *statute of descent*.

Invasion of Privacy An *intentional tort* in which the tortfeasor invades someone's right to be free from unwarranted publicity that places the plaintiff in a false light, intrudes into the plaintiff's private life, discloses embarrassing private facts, or uses the plaintiff's name or likeness for the defendant's gain.

Investigative Power A delegated power contained in an *enabling act* authorizing an administrative agency to engage in fact-finding.

Investigatory Detentions (Stop-and-Frisk) An investigative stop is a warrantless, nonprobable-cause-based seizure of a person by police for investigative purposes. The U.S. Supreme Court approved brief seizures by police for investigative purposes where officers have reasonable suspicion to believe that a person has committed, is about to commit, or is committing a crime. The Court ruled that officers have the right to make such brief stops so that they can engage in brief questioning. The Court has further approved a limited frisk of the detained person if officers can articulate reasonable suspicion to believe that the detained person possesses a weapon. The officers are then permitted to conduct a pat down of the detained person's outer clothing for self-protection while questioning the suspect. If the frisk discloses anything that feels like a weapon, the frisking officer can reach into the detained person's garments to remove the object identified in the frisk. An officer who has finished questioning the detained person is required to return any seized object that was legally possessed and can retain any object that was illegally possessed.

Invitee (1) A person who goes upon land or premises of another by invitation, express or implied. (2) Either a *public* *invitee* or a *business visitor:* (a) A *public invitee* is a person who is invited to enter or remain on land as a member of the public for a purpose for which the land is held open to the public. (b) A *business visitor* (or *business invitee)* is a person who is invited to enter or remain on land for a purpose directly or indirectly connected with business dealings with the possessor of the land.

Involuntary Adoption Adoption that occurs after a court has formally terminated the parental rights of the birth parent(s) on grounds such as abuse, abandonment, or neglect.

Involuntary Intoxication A defense available to a person who is not responsible for having become intoxicated due to the actions of others or circumstances beyond his or her knowledge or control.

Irresistible-Impulse Test This test provides that a criminal defendant is not guilty by reason of insanity if the defendant, although knowing that an act is wrong and aware of the nature and quality of the act, cannot refrain from committing the act due to mental disease or defect. Used to determine insanity in some jurisdictions.

Joint and Several Liability Persons who commit a tort at the same time are both individually and collectively liable for the entire harm.

Joint Custody In *domestic relations law,* where a court grants custody of children of a marriage to both parents instead of just one when spouses divorce. Both parents share decision-making responsibilities in regard to their children's upbringing. The parents, although no longer married to each other, continue to share a family.

Joint Tenancy Each tenant takes an equal, undivided interest in the ownership of property from the same source and at the same time. Includes a right of survivorship, which means that a deceased joint tenant's rights automatically pass to the surviving joint tenants and not through the deceased's will.

Joint Tortfeasors In the tort of *negligence,* if there is more than one person involved in causing a single injury, each possible tortfeasor's actions must be examined to determine whether the injury was caused by *joint tortfeasors* (i.e., in legalese, to see if the acts jointly were so closely related to the damage to have proximately caused the plaintiff's injury).

Judgment A judgment determines the rights of the disputing parties and decides what relief is awarded (if any).

Judgment Creditor Person awarded a money judgment.

Judgment Debtor Person who has been ordered in a judgment to pay money to a *judgment creditor.*

Judicial Deference A court's willingness to show deference to an agency's competence. Courts generally sustain administrative findings if satisfied that the agency has examined the issues, reached its decision appropriately, and followed required procedures.

Jurisdiction The power or authority of a court to determine the merits of a dispute and to grant relief.

Jurisprudence The study of legal philosophy.

Justiciable A case is justiciable if it is well suited for judicial determination.

Justification Defenses Criminal defenses in which the defendant claims to have acted correctly. Examples include self-defense, defense of others, defense of property, necessity—choice of evils, and duress—coercion.

Knowingly An accused person is aware that a prohibited result or harm is very likely to occur as a result of his or her act, but does not consciously intend the specific consequences that result from the act.

Labor Management Relations Act A 1947 federal statute providing for the arbitration of disputes arising from collective bargaining.

Laches An issue of *justiciability.* An equitable doctrine that can be used to bar equitable relief to a plaintiff who has unreasonably delayed filing suit under circumstances that unfairly prejudiced the defendant.

Larceny The unlawful taking and carrying away of another's personal property without color of right, and with intent to deprive the rightful owner of the same. Larceny is commonly classified as grand or petty, according to the value of the object taken. Usually defined and classified by various state statutes.

Leading Object Rule A rule of contract law that applies when determining whether the purpose of the promisor is to become primarily liable or secondarily liable (e.g., for the debts of another). In resolving the issue, courts will look not only to the promise itself, but also to the individual for whose benefit the promise was made. The logic of the rule is that if the leading object of the promise is the personal benefit of the promisor, then the promisor must have intended to become primarily liable. In such a case, the promise will be deemed to be original and need not be in writing to be enforced.

Leading Question A question at trial phrased in such a way that the attorney is suggesting the answer to the witness. This generally is an improper question on direct examination but is allowed on cross-examination or in direct examination of a hostile witness.

Leasehold In general, a possessory interest in real property (i.e., an *estate in land*) for a specified period of time (often a month or year) held by a person who leases property.

Legal Detriment In contract law, the taking on of a legal obligation, the performance of an act, or the giving up of a legal right, which supports a party's contract requirement of *consideration*.

Legal Duty A legal obligation that is created by statute, contract, or case law or that has been voluntarily assumed.

Legal Realists Adherents of this philosophical approach focus on the extent to which actual practices vary from the formal legal rules. They believe that judges are more influenced by their personal convictions than by established and immutable rules.

Legal Separation Granted when lawfully married parties have actually separated and when adequate grounds for a legal separation have been shown. The parties remain married to each other but live apart. During the legal separation, the possibility of reconciliation still exists, as does the option to proceed with a final divorce. The separation period allows the estranged parties to try to work out their difficulties while living apart. Also known as a *divorce a mensa et thoro*.

Legal Sociologists Adherents of this philosophical approach use quantitative methodological tools to explain legal outcomes. They use measurements of such factors as the financial standing, race, social class, respectability, and cultural differences of those involved in disputes to explain why some people win lawsuits and others do not.

Lex Fori. The law of the place where the action was instituted.

Lex Loci Contractus. The law of the state where the last act necessary to complete the contract was done that created a legal obligation.

Lex Loci Delicti Commissi. The substantive law of the place where the last event necessary to make the actor liable takes place or where the person or thing harmed is situated at the time the wrong is committed.

Lex Loci Solutionis. The law of the place where the contract was to be performed.

Libel An *intentional tort*. (1) Defamatory writing; any published matter that tends to degrade persons in the eyes of their neighbors, or to render them ridiculous, or to injure their properties or businesses. It may be published by writing, effigy, picture, or the like. (2) Broadcasting of defamatory matter by means of radio or television, whether or not it is read from a manuscript. See also, *defamation, libel per se.* Cf., *slander.*

Libel Per Se An *intentional tort*. Defamatory writing or broadcast that (1) falsely accuses another of committing a crime of moral turpitude (rape, murder, or selling narcotics); (2) makes false accusations that another person has contracted a morally offensive communicable disease (such as leprosy, syphilis, gonorrhea, or AIDS); or (3) makes defamatory statements that interfere with another person's trade, business, or profession (saying that a banker is dishonest or that a doctor is a "quack"). A plaintiff who proves slander per se is not required to prove special damages because such expressions are almost certain to harm the plaintiff's reputation and produce economic loss. See also, *defamation, libel, slander per se.*

License In property law, a temporary grant of authority to do specified things on the land of another.

Licensee A person who enters or remains on the land of another with express or implied consent.

Lien (a Legally Enforceable Claim) A legal process to secure payment of a debt, by which there is created a right (1) to retain that which is in a person's possession, belonging to another, until certain demands of the person in possession are satisfied; or (2) to charge property in another's possession with payment of a debt, e.g., a vendor's lien.

Life Estate An *estate in land* that is held for the duration of the holder's life but that cannot be passed on to heirs. Cf., *fee simple.*

Lineup A police investigative procedure in which an array of people or an array of photographs of people, including the suspect, is displayed as a group before a victim or witness so the person can attempt to identify the suspect as the perpetrator.

Liquidated Damages A stipulated sum of money that the parties to a contract expressly agree must be paid, or may be collected, in the event of a future default or breach of contract.

Logic The study of correct reasoning.

Long-Arm Statute A state statute that permits the exercise of personal jurisdiction over nonresident defendants who have had sufficient minimum contacts with the forum state.

Magna Carta The first Magna Carta was issued in 1215 by the English monarch King John. It is the original source of the protections imbedded in the Due Process Clauses found in the U.S. Constitution.

Majority Opinion An opinion that explains the court's decision in the case and the majority's reasoning for reaching that outcome.

Mala In Se. Traditional label for criminal offenses that are intrinsically wrong.

Mala Prohibita. Traditional label for illegal acts that are not intrinsically bad. They are criminal only because the law defines them as such.

Malicious Prosecution An *intentional tort* in which the plaintiff alleges that the defendant maliciously and without probable cause instigated a civil or criminal action against the plaintiff. The plaintiff must prevail in the original dispute and must have suffered legal injury due to the groundless nature of the defendant's original allegations.

Malpractice A nonlegal term for a professional person's *negligence*.

Mandamus A writ that commands a public official to perform a nondiscretionary duty.

Mandatory Injunction An *equitable remedy*. A judicial order compelling a person to act in a specified way.

Marital Property Nonseparate property acquired during a marriage that is subject to distribution by a judge in conjunction with a divorce. See also, *community property, separate property*.

Marriage In all fifty states, a state-sanctioned relationship in which two people, after complying with relevant marriage eligibility requirements, become spouses. Each state determines who may marry, the duties and obligations of marriage, and how marriages are terminated. Although eligibility requirements for marriage differ from state to state, they generally include minimum age thresholds, monogamy (it is illegal to marry someone who is already married), competency (neither party can be mentally incompetent), and prohibitions on marriage between close relatives. Parties seeking to marry must be acting voluntarily. They indicate their consent to the marriage by jointly applying for a license. As of June 2013, thirteen states have legalized same-sex marriages, and thirty-seven have do not.

Matching Investigative process in which an agency ranks prospective adoptive parents in terms of how closely they match the agency's conception of the ideal family for the child.

Material *Relevant evidence* that has significant *probative* value.

Material Fact In contract law, a fact without which the contract would not have been entered into.

Maxim An axiom; a general or leading principle.

Mediation A form of *alternative dispute resolution*. The settlement of disputes by the amicable intervention of an outside party who is a stranger to the controversy.

Medical Malpractice An allegation that a physician either has breached a contract or has been professionally negligent in diagnosing or treating a patient.

Mens Rea. Criminal state of mind. See also, *actus reus*.

Mental Competence (to Contract) The mental ability required to enter into a valid contract. A person is said to be incapable of contracting due to mental disabilities or defects when that individual does not understand the nature and consequences of his or her act at the time of entering into an agreement. In such cases, the person lacks capacity, and his or her contracts are either void or voidable.

Metaethics The study of ethical terms and arguments.

Metaphysics The study of the nature of reality or being.

Minitrial A form of *alternative dispute resolution*. A misnomer because it is a process used in business disputes and is an alternative to a trial. In this process each party makes a short presentation to a panel, generally consisting of a senior manager or decision maker from each side and a judge (in the case of a court-ordered minitrial) or jointly selected *neutral* (in the case of a voluntary minitrial). After the presentations are concluded, the panel negotiates a resolution of the dispute.

Misdemeanor Generally, any crime or offense greater than an ordinance violation but not amounting to a felony.

Misprision A common law crime in which the accused failed to tell authorities about the commission of a felony of which the person had knowledge.

Misrepresentation One party to a contract either knowingly or unknowingly misrepresents a material fact that misleads the other contracting party into relying on false information.

Mistake of Fact Where one or both contracting parties unintentionally misunderstand or are ignorant of a fact that is material to their agreement. The mistaken party can be relieved of his or her contractual obligations, provided the mistake relates to a past or present material fact at the time the contract is entered into, and not a mistake as to a future possibility.

M'Naghten Rule Specifies that a criminal defendant is not guilty if they had a diseased mind at the time of the act and were unable to distinguish right from wrong or were unaware of the nature and quality of their act due to a diseased mind.

Modified No-Fault Liability Statutes Statutes enacted by some states in an attempt to correct the injustices and inadequacies of the fault system in automobile accident cases. Under a modified no-fault liability statute, an injured person normally has no right to file suit to recover money damages for personal injuries and lost wages below a statutorily specified threshold. Instead, the injured party is compensated by his or her own insurance company. The amount of compensation paid is determined by dollar ceilings specified in the injured person's insurance policy. All "no-fault" states, however, permit lawsuits for damages where the injured person has been seriously injured.

Money Damages A sum of money claimed by a plaintiff as recompense for injuries sustained as a result of an alleged breach of contract or the commission of a tort.

Moot Case A case that is no longer justiciable because no present case or controversy continues to exist. *Mootness* is an aspect of *ripeness*.

Moral Duty A universally accepted moral obligation.

Motion for Directed Verdict A motion made by the defendant at the end of all the evidence. The motion is granted if the court concludes that evidence favors one side to such an extent that no reasonable juror could find in favor of the other party. This motion is not available to the prosecution in a criminal case but is available to criminal defendants.

Motion For Judgment Notwithstanding the Verdict (JNOV Motion) A motion made after a jury verdict is returned. It is granted when the judge decides that reasonable people could not have reached the verdict that the jury has reached. The acronym "JNOV" comes from the Latin phrase for a judgment *non obstante veridictu*.

Motion for New Trial This motion may be granted by a judge for a variety of reasons, including excessive or grossly inadequate damages, newly discovered evidence, questionable jury verdict, errors in the production of evidence, or simply in the interest of justice.

Motion for Relief from Judgment A motion for relief from judgment is granted only if the judge finds a clerical error in the judgment, newly discovered evidence, or that fraud induced the judgment.

Motion for Summary Judgment A motion made to dispose of controversies that can be decided without a full trial because either no genuine issues of material fact exist or because facts necessary to prove the opponent's case are not provable.

Motion to Dismiss Sometimes also called a *demurrer* or, in federal law, a "Rule 12(b) motion." A motion used to challenge claimed defects in the plaintiff's complaint.

Natural Law Adherents of this philosophical approach believe that every person possesses a moral barometer that gives him or her the capacity to discover independently moral truth.

Natural Parent Birth parent; biological parent.

Necessaries (1) Generally defined as the food, clothing, shelter, and medical care that one spouse is legally responsible for providing the other spouse. (2) What a parent is legally responsible to provide for his or her minor child's subsistence as measured by age, status, and condition in life, such as food, lodging, education, clothing, and medical services.

Negligence (1) A flexible term for the failure to use ordinary care, under the particular factual circumstances revealed by the evidence in a lawsuit. (2) Conduct that falls below the standard established by law for the protection of others against unreasonable risk of harm. It does not include conduct recklessly in disregard of an interest of others.

Negligence Per Se Negligence where the action causing the plaintiff's injury or property damage involved the defendant's violation of a statute concerned with public safety. Once it is decided that such a statute is applicable, most courts hold that an unexcused violation is conclusive as to the issue of negligence. The only issues for the jury are proximate cause and damages. However, some courts hold that the violation of such a statute is only evidence of negligence, which the jury may accept or reject as it sees fit.

Neutrals In *alternative dispute resolution,* persons who conduct the ADR proceeding and decide the outcome of the dispute, or help the parties achieve a resolution. Neutrals often are persons who specialize in a particular field such as construction, commercial contracts, real estate, finance, etc. See also, *arbitrator.*

Nolo Contendere (Latin, "I do not wish to contend.") A plea that can be entered by the accused in a criminal proceeding. The plea of *nolo contendere* ("no contest") is the same as a guilty plea, except that it cannot be used later against the accused as an admission. It is a confession only for the purposes of the criminal prosecution and does not bind the defendant in a civil suit for the same wrong.

Nominal Damages A token sum awarded where a breach of duty or an infraction of plaintiffs' rights is shown, but no substantial injury is proven to have been sustained.

Noncustodial Parent The parent in a custody dispute not awarded primary physical placement of a child.

Nonsuit A trial motion made by the defendant in a civil case at the end of the plaintiff's case-in-chief. It is granted where the court rules that the plaintiff's case is too weak to continue with the trial. The court must conclude that no reasonable person could find in favor of the plaintiff even if all disputed facts are found to be in the plaintiff's favor. If the motion is granted, the court awards a judgment to the defendant.

Normative Ethics The study of whether particular conduct should be classified as moral or immoral.

Notary Public A state official authorized to administer oaths and to authenticate documents.

Notice (1) Information given to a person of some act done, or about to be done; knowledge. Notice may be *actual,* when knowledge is brought home to the party to be affected by it; or *constructive,* when certain acts are done in accordance with law, from which, on grounds of public policy, the party interested is presumed to have knowledge. It may be written or oral, but written notice is preferable to avoid disputes as to its terms. (2) A person has notice of a fact when he or she has actual knowledge of it, or has received a notice or notification of it, or, from all the facts and circumstances known to him or her at the time in question, has reason to know that it exists.

Notice-and-Comment Procedures The rule-making procedure for administrative agencies under the *Administrative Procedure Act,* by which the agency is required to publish proposed rules in the *Federal Register,* thereby providing notice of the agency's intended action to anyone interested in the matter. Agencies also must accept written submissions from persons interested in commenting on the proposed rule and in some instances may permit oral presentations. The APA also provides that the agency must publish its final version of each rule and an accompanying explanation of the purpose and rationale for the rule in the *Federal Register* no less than thirty days prior to when the rule takes effect.

Novation The substitution of a new obligor or obligation for an old one, which is thereby extinguished; e.g., the acceptance of a note of a third party in payment of the original promisor's obligation or the note of an individual in lieu of that of a corporation.

Nuisance A nuisance exists when one person's use of real property injures or infringes on another person's use and/or enjoyment of land or infringes on the general public's rights. See also, *private nuisance, public nuisance.*

Occupational Health and Safety Administration (OSHA) An administrative agency created by Congress in 1970 to set and enforce environmental standards within the workplace that would improve employees' safety and working conditions.

Offer A definite proposal to make a contract that is communicated to another person.

Offeree The recipient of an offer to contract.

Offeror A person who makes an offer to contract.

Open Adoption An adoption in which the adoptive parents permit the birth mother to remain in contact with the adopted child.

Option A contract in which an offeror is bound to hold an offer open for a specified period of time in exchange for consideration, usually a sum of money.

Oral Deposition A discovery tool in which a witness is examined, under oath, by the lawyers for each party, and the testimony is transcribed by a certified court reporter.

Overbreadth Courts will declare unconstitutional statutes and ordinances that are overly broad or too vague. Overbreadth exists where a statute is insufficiently focused. Thus, a disorderly conduct statute would be overly broad if it includes within its scope conduct that is clearly criminal as well as conduct that is protected by the First Amendment.

Pardon The remission by the chief executive of a state or nation of the punishment to which the person to be pardoned has been sentenced.

Parental Immunity Immunity of parents from prosecution by their unemancipated minor children for acts of negligence or intentional torts. First recognized in 1891 by the Mississippi Supreme Court.

Parole Supervised suspension of the execution of a convict's sentence, and release from prison, conditional upon his continued compliance with the terms of parole. Statutes generally specify when and if a prisoner will be eligible to be considered for parole and detail the standards and procedures applicable.

Parol-Evidence Rule Evidence of alleged prior agreements or terms not contained in the written document will be inadmissible if offered to change the terms of the document. See also, *fully* and *partially integrated.*

Patent A type of *intellectual property.* A grant of rights to an inventor from the federal government. The inventor, or owner of the rights, has the exclusive right to make, use, license others to use, and sell an invention for a period of years (twenty years for most inventions). Patents are granted only for inventions that are beneficial, are original, and involve ingenuity.

Penal Statutes Statutes that command or prohibit certain acts and establish penalties for their violation.

Per Curiam Opinion Usually a brief appellate court opinion for the entire court that does not identify any jurist as author. For example, if nine justices of the Supreme Court agree on the outcome of the case but completely disagree as to why that outcome is correct, the Court might announce its decision in a per curiam opinion and then each justice could write a concurring opinion explaining that justice's views as to the rationale supporting the decision.

Peremptory Challenge Where a party in a jury trial seeks to ban a prospective juror because the juror has an apparent or potential prejudice or bias against that party or that party's type of claim or defense. A peremptory challenge may not be based on reasons of the prospective juror's race. See also, *challenge for cause.*

Personal Property Tangible objects that are not realty or fixtures and all intangible rights, duties, and obligations arising out of the ownership of tangible objects. Personal property also includes intangible property, such as money, stocks, and bonds, that are paper substitutes for certain ownership rights. See also, *property, real property.*

Personal Service Delivering the summons and complaint personally to a defendant. (Cf., *constructive service; substituted service.*)

Personalty Personal property.

Petitioner (1) A party wishing to have its case reviewed by the U.S. Supreme Court who has petitioned the Court for a writ of certiorari. (2) Someone who petitions a court.

Physical Custody In *domestic relations law,* physical custody refers to the person with whom a child resides on a more or less permanent basis, generally in association with dissolution of marriage. *Physical custody* is distinct from *legal custody,* which concerns the right of the parent or other person to make major decisions in the child's life. See also, *joint custody.*

Plaintiff A person who initiates a lawsuit.

Plea Bargaining A process by which the accused agrees to enter a plea of guilty, often to a lesser offense, in exchange for a promise by the prosecuting attorney to recommend a lesser sentence or a dismissal of part of the charges.

Pleadings (1) The alternate and opposing written statements of the parties to a lawsuit. The typical pleadings include the complaint, answer, and occasionally a reply. (2) Originally in early (twelfth-century) English law, the plaintiff's oral recitation in court stating the complaint against the defendant, to which the defendant then orally replied.

Plea of *Nolo Contendere.* A plea that is equivalent to a guilty plea, except that it cannot be used as an admission in any subsequent civil action. (Latin, "I do not wish to contend.")

Police Power A flexible term for the authority of state legislatures to enact laws regulating and restraining private rights and occupations for the promotion of public health, safety, welfare, and morals.

Political-Question Doctrine An issue of *justiciability.* The doctrine that political issues should be resolved by the political branches of government and not by the judiciary,

Positive Law Legislated rules or laws.

Possessory Interest The right of possession. Cf., *title.* For example, a *leasehold* allows a tenant to hold *possessory interest* in real property—i.e., the right to occupy or control—as opposed to the ownership interest of the titleholder, who holds the estate in land.

Preliminary Hearing A court hearing at which the prosecution reveals some of its evidence in order to establish the existence of probable cause to believe that a felony was committed and that the accused was the person who committed the crime. This is also where the defense attorney can cross-examine any witnesses who testify for the prosecution and pin them down on their version of the facts.

Pretrial Conference A meeting between the judge and counsel for the parties, preliminary to the trial of a lawsuit. Under modern rules of civil procedure, in any lawsuit the court may in its discretion direct the attorneys for the parties to appear before it for a conference to consider any matters that may aid in the disposition of the lawsuit.

Preventive Detention Preventive detention occurs when criminally accused persons are denied bail because they are alleged to have committed very serious crimes and because they allegedly pose a serious threat of danger to particular individuals or to the public safety in general.

Prima Facie Case; Prima Facie Evidence Proof of a fact or collection of facts from which other facts can be presumed. In most situations the presumed fact(s) can be rebutted by other relevant proof. In criminal law, the minimum amount of evidence of guilt the prosecution has to offer as to every fact that must be proven to obtain a conviction.

Principal (1) The leading, or most important; the original. (2) A person, firm, or corporation from whom an agent derives his authority. (3) A person who is first responsible, and for whose fulfillment of an obligation a surety becomes bound. (4) The chief, or actual, perpetrator of a crime, as distinguished from the accessory, who may assist him. (5) The important part of an estate, as distinguished from incidents, or accessories. (6) A sum of money loaned, as distinguished from the interest paid for its use.

Private Nuisance A tort relating to an owner's use of his or her property that requires proof of an injury that is distinct from that suffered by the general public. (It differs from trespass because the offensive activity does not occur on the victim's property.) A party injured by a private nuisance can obtain both damages and injunctive relief. See also, *nuisance, public nuisance.*

Private Trial System A form of *alternative dispute resolution.* The parties to the dispute contract with a private business to conduct a private trial before a private judge (often well reputed and recently retired) who has experience appropriate to the case or before a private jury. The news media and general public have no right to attend these trials. The parties often use simplified evidentiary and procedural rules, cooperate with discovery, and decide whether the decision of the private judge or jury will be appealable.

Privilege (1) An exceptional right or exemption. It is either (a) personal, attached to a person or office; or (b) attached to a thing, sometimes called real. The exemption of ambassadors and members of Congress from arrest while going to, returning from, or attending to the discharge of their public duties is an example of the first. (2) The fact that conduct which, under ordinary circumstances, would subject an actor to liability under particular circumstances does not subject him or her to liability. A privilege may be based upon (a) the consent of the other affected by the actor's conduct, or (b) the fact that its exercise is necessary for the protection of some interest of the actor or of the public that is of such importance as to justify the harm caused or threatened by its exercise, or (c) the fact that the actor is performing a function for the proper performance of which freedom of action is essential.

Privileged Communication A confidential communication that cannot be introduced at trial because the law recognizes the existence of a *privilege*. Privileges exist to protect legally favored rights (such as the privilege against self-incrimination) and relationships (i.e., attorney–client, doctor–patient, clergy–parishioner). Because privileges permit the withholding of important evidence at trial, they are disfavored by courts.

Privity (1) Participation in, knowledge, or interest. Persons who so participate are called *privies*. See, e.g., *privity of contract*, referring to the parties who actually participate in or have an interest in a contract. (2) An issue of *justiciability*. Privity exists, for example, when there is a relationship between two people that allows one not directly involved in a lawsuit to take the place of the one who is a party. Thus if a person dies during litigation, the executor of the estate may take the deceased person's place in the lawsuit. Privity exists between the person who dies and the executor, so that as far as this litigation is concerned, they are the same person.

Privity of Contract A legal term referring to the existence of a legal relationship between the parties to a contract, allowing them to sue each other for performance of the contract, but preventing a third party from doing so.

Privity of Estate In property law, the direct relationship between grantor and grantee.

Probable Cause (1) A reasonable ground for suspicion, supported by circumstances sufficiently strong to warrant a cautious man to believe that an accused person is guilty of the offense with which he is charged. (2) Concerning a search, probable cause is a flexible, common-sense standard. It merely requires that the facts available to the officer would warrant a person of reasonable caution to believe that certain items may be contraband or stolen property or useful as evidence of a crime; it does not demand any showing that the belief is correct or more likely true than false. All that is required is for there to be a practical, nontechnical probability that incriminating evidence is involved.

Probative (Evidence) Evidence that is not merely *relevant* to the case but that tends to prove something of importance to the case.

Procedural Due Process The premise underlying procedural due process is that justice is more likely to occur if correct procedures are employed when government seeks to deprive someone of life, liberty, or property. The U.S. Supreme Court has ruled that what procedures are due varies with the context. In criminal cases, for example, the procedures are quite extensive and the process is very formal. But when a school board decides to suspend a student for violating school rules, the procedures are much less extensive and the process is much less formal. But irrespective of context it is clear that procedural due process requires at a minimum an "impartial" decision maker, some kind of notice, and some kind of hearing (although the Court has permitted the government in some contexts to take away financial benefits before conducting the requisite hearing).

Procedural Rule Administrative rule used to establish "standard operating procedures" within an agency. See also, *rule-making power*.

Process (1) The means whereby a court enforces obedience to its orders. Process is termed (a) original, when it is intended to compel the appearance of the defendant; (b) mesne, when issued pending suit to secure the attendance of jurors and witnesses; and (c) final, when issued to enforce execution of a judgment. (2) A term sometimes used to refer to the summons served on the defendant along with the complaint (also referred to as *service of process*), generally served by the sheriff or a process server.

Production of Documents (1) A form of pretrial *discovery* in which one party to a lawsuit compels another party (or nonparty) to produce documents or things for inspection by the discovering party. (2) Showing of such documents in a court.

Prohibitory Injunction An *equitble remedy*. A judicial order requiring a person to refrain from acting in a specified way.

Promisee The person to whom a promise is made.

Promisor The person making a promise.

Property Property includes the rights to possess, use, and dispose of things. These may be tangible objects, such as a car, book, or item of clothing, or they may be intangible, e.g., the technology in a camera, a song, or the right of publicity. Although many people refer to the objects themselves as property, "property" actually refers only to ownership rights and interests. See also, *personal property, real property*.

Property Right A person's ownership rights to things or legal interests in things owned by someone else.

Pro Se A person who appears without a lawyer and chooses to represent himself or herself appears pro se.

Prosecutor A person who brings an action against another in the name of the government. A public prosecutor is an officer appointed or elected to conduct all prosecutions on behalf of the government.

Prospective Effect Where a new rule applies to all questions subsequently coming before that court and the lower courts of the jurisdiction.

Proximate Cause (1) Something that produces a result, without which the result could not have occurred. (2) Any original event that, in natural unbroken sequence, produces a particular foreseeable result, without which the result would not have occurred.

Public Invitee A person who is invited to enter or remain on land as a member of the public for a purpose for which the land is held open to the public.

Public Nuisance A tort relating to an owner's use of his or her property. This occurs when a land use poses a generalized threat to the public as a whole or to a substantial segment of the community. An action to redress a public nuisance is brought by government, oftentimes by criminal prosecution and injunctive relief. See also, *nuisance, private nuisance.*

Public Policy (1) A highly flexible term of imprecise definition, for the consideration of what is expedient for the community concerned. (2) The principle of law that holds that no person can do that which has a tendency to be injurious to the public or against the public good.

Punitive Damages Damages awarded in excess of the general damages or economic loss, intended solely to punish the offender. See also, *exemplary damages.*

Purposely A conscious desire to produce a prohibited result or harm.

Quantum Meruit As much as he or she deserves. An equitable means for determining what sum is due where there is no actual agreement between parties but where fairness requires that a contract be implied in order to avoid an unjust enrichment.

Quasi-Contract. An obligation that arises without express agreement between the parties; an implied contract.

Quiet Title, Quiet Title Action A legal proceeding to establish an individual's right to ownership of real property against one or more adverse claimants. Such an action might arise, for example, in a case involving *adverse possession* or *easement by prescription.*

Ratification of Contract An expression or action that indicates an intention to be contractually bound.

Real Property (Realty) Land and things that are attached permanently to land. See also, *property, personal property.*

Recklessly Acts by a person that show utter indifference to the welfare of others and that pose a significant and unjustifiable risk of harm to other people.

Recognizance An unsecured promise to appear in court when so required.

Record A written memorial of the actions of a legislature or of a court.

Recording System The process by which purchasers of realty can evaluate the quality of the seller's title to a parcel, by reviewing documents kept by a local (generally county government) registry of deeds, which contains records of all transactions relating to real property in the jurisdiction of the registry.

Redirect Examination A second direct examination of a witness at trial, conducted by the attorney or party who first called this witness to testify. This examination occurs after the *cross-examination* of the witness by opposing counsel.

Reeve The official heading the *hundred* in Anglo-Saxon England.

Reformation An *equitable remedy.* Reformation is granted when a written agreement fails to express accurately the parties' agreement because of mistake, fraud, or the drafter's ambiguous language. Its purpose is to rectify or reform a written instrument in order that it may express the real agreement or intention of the parties. Cf., *rescission.*

Rehabilitative Alimony A sum of money that a judge may award a dependent spouse in a divorce action so that the recipient can obtain education or training to strengthen job skills.

Relevant (Evidence) Evidence that logically tends to prove or disprove some issue of consequence that is in dispute at the trial or hearing.

Remand Return of a case by an appellate court to a lower court with instructions to the lower court to take further specified action.

Remedy (1) The legal means to declare or enforce a right or to redress a wrong. (2) Any remedial right to which an aggrieved party is entitled.

Remittitur For purposes of this textbook (because it has more than one meaning), *remittitur* refers to a nonprevailing party's postverdict motion to reduce a jury's award of money damages. The motion is granted by a trial or appellate court that has been convinced that the jury's verdict is grossly excessive.

Replevin A judicial remedy; an action to recover possession of personal property wrongfully in the possession of another.

Reply A pleading in which the plaintiff admits, denies, or raises defenses against the factual allegations raised in the defendant's counterclaim.

Request for Admissions or Denials A method of pretrial *discovery* in which one party sends to the other party a request that the other party admit that certain facts are true and/or that specified documents are genuine.

Request for Waiver of Service Defendants who voluntarily waive their right to be formally served with process are allowed sixty days, instead of just twenty days, to respond to the complaint.

Rescission An *equitable remedy*. Rescission is granted when one of the parties consents to a contract because of duress, undue influence, fraud, or innocent misrepresentation or when either or both of the parties made a mistake concerning the contract. Rescission means the court cancels the agreement. If a court orders rescission, each party normally has to return any property or money received from the other party in performance of the agreement (i.e., make *restitution*). Cf., *reformation*.

Residual Jurisdiction A court with residual jurisdiction exercises original jurisdiction over subject matter that has not been assigned by the legislature to a court of original, limited, subject-matter jurisdiction.

Res Ipsa Loquitur (Latin: "the thing speaks for itself.") A judicial doctrine which permits plaintiffs to prove negligence circumstantially if the following facts are proved: (1) the defendant had exclusive control over the allegedly defective product during manufacture; (2) under normal circumstances, the plaintiff would not have been injured by the product if the defendant had exercised ordinary care; and (3) the plaintiff's conduct did not contribute significantly to the accident. From the proved facts, the law permits the jurors to infer a fact for which there is no direct, explicit proof: the defendant's negligent act or omission.

Res Judicata In general, a judicial policy that, once a valid judgment has been rendered on the merits in one jurisdiction, the claims adjudicated in that lawsuit cannot be relitigated by the same parties in some other jurisdiction.

Respondeat Superior This doctrine permits an injured plaintiff, under certain conditions, to hold a company financially responsible for an employee's negligence and intentional torts. Basically, the plaintiff has to prove that the person committed the tortious conduct that caused the plaintiff's injury and that this person an employee of the company to be sued and not by an independent contractor. The plaintiff also has to prove that the tortious conduct occurred while the employee was acting within the scope of his or her employment.

Respondent (1) The name given one of the parties in a case before the U.S. Supreme Court. The petitioner is the party asking the Court to grant a writ of certiorari. The respondent is the party opposing the granting of the petition. (2) The name given a party in any court who is before the court in response to another party's petition.

Restitution An *equitable remedy*. The restoring of property, or a right, to a person who has been unjustly deprived of it.

A *writ of restitution* is the process by which an appellant may recover something of which he has been deprived under a prior judgment.

Restoration in Specie The meaning of this term varies with the context in which it is used. In this textbook it refers to requiring a person wrongfully in possession of property to return the property or its monetary equivalent to the person who rightfully is entitled to possession.

Retroactive Effect Where a new rule applies to causes of action arising before the announcement of the decision.

Reversal An appellate court enters a judgment of reversal when it rules that a lower court's judgment should be overturned.

Ripeness An issue of *justiciability*. A case is ripe if it has developed sufficiently to be before a court for adjudication. If a lawsuit has been filed prematurely, it is not ripe for adjudication.

Rule-Making Power A delegated power contained in an *enabling act* authorizing an administrative agency to make, alter, or repeal rules and regulations covering those activities for which the agency has regulatory responsibility. See also, *interpretive rule, procedural rule, substantive rule*.

Rule of Mitigation An injured person must make a reasonable effort to avoid or minimize damages. Also called the *avoidable harm doctrine*.

Satisfaction (1)The payment of owed money. (2) The agreement to take what is offered in an *accord*. See also, *accord and satisfaction*.

Separate Property In *domestic relations law*, property not classified as *community property* because it was owned prior to the marriage or was received as a gift or inheritance. Cf., *marital property*.

Separation Agreement An agreement between divorcing parties as to the allocation of financial obligations and how property should be divided. It often contains recommendations on how the court should decide child custody and support, spousal support, and visitation rights. Although the court is ultimately responsible for determining each of the aforementioned issues, it is often greatly influenced by the proposals in a separation agreement.

Separation of Powers The federal Constitution delegates the legislative power to the Congress in Article I, the executive power to the president in Article II, and the judicial power to the federal judiciary in Article III. The founders believed that dispersing power in this way would result in a system of checks and balances and prevent abuse.

Settlement Conference A pretrial meeting attended by the lawyers for the contesting parties and sometimes the judge to explore the possiblity of settlement.

Severalty Ownership Property owned by one person.

Shire The term for a county in England.

Significant Relationship Rule The rule that the substantive law of the place that has the most significant contacts with the incident or event in dispute should be the law applied to resolve the dispute.

Slander An *intentional tort*. The malicious defamation of a person in his or her reputation, profession, or business by spoken words. Usually, the truth of the words spoken is a defense. Statutorily defined in many states' statutes. See also, *defamation, slander per se*. Cf., *libel*.

Slander Per Se An *intentional tort*. Defamation by spoken words that (1) falsely accuses another of committing a crime of moral turpitude (rape, murder, or selling narcotics); (2) makes false accusations that another person has contracted a morally offensive communicative disease (such as leprosy, syphilis, gonorrhea, or AIDS); or (3) makes defamatory statements that interfere with another person's trade, business, or profession (saying that a banker is dishonest or that a doctor is a "quack"). See also, *defamation, libel per se, slander*.

Sociological Jurisprudence Adherents of this approach believe that law is not just the formal rules but also the informal rules that actually influence social behavior. The sociological school maintains that law can only be understood when the formal system of rules is considered in conjunction with social realities (or facts).

Solicitation An *inchoate, specific-intent crime* committed by a person who asks, hires, or encourages another to commit a crime.

Sovereign Immunity A rule of law holding that a nation or state, or its political subdivisions, is exempt from being sued, without its consent, in its own courts or elsewhere. Often criticized as being erroneously conceived, anachronistic, and unjust. Occasionally modified by court decisions and various state and federal statutes, e.g., the *Tort Claims Act*.

Sovereignty The supreme authority of an independent nation or state. It is characterized by equality of the nation or state among other nations or states, exclusive and absolute jurisdiction and self-government within its own territorial limits, and jurisdiction over its citizens beyond its territorial limits.

Special Appearance If a person appears in court to challenge a court's in personam jurisdiction, he or she is making a *special appearance* for that limited purpose and is not consenting to personal jurisdiction by arguing that issue.

Special Damages Damages awarded for injuries that arise from the particular circumstances of the wrong.

Special Verdict A verdict that requires the jury to answer specific questions related to certain factual issues in the case.

Specific Intent; Specific-Intent Crime An additional specified level of intent beyond the commission of the *actus reus*. For example, a person who possesses a controlled substance (the *actus reus*) and who at the time of the possession has an intent to sell (an additional specified level of intent beyond the commission of the *actus reus*) has committed a specific-intent crime.

Specific Performance An *equitable remedy*. The actual carrying out of a contract in the particular manner agreed upon. Courts of equity will compel and coerce specific performance of a contract in many cases where damages payable in money, the usual remedy at law, would not adequately compensate for its nonperformance, e.g., in the case of contracts concerning land or for the sale of a unique chattel.

Spontaneous Declarations An exception to the hearsay rule that permits courts to admit in court spontaneous declarations uttered simultaneously with the occurrence of an act.

Spousal Privileges The right to refuse to testify against a spouse in a criminal trial and to refuse to testify about confidential communications that occurred between spouses during their marriage.

Standing An issue of *justiciability*. To have standing to sue, a plaintiff must have a legally sufficient personal stake in the outcome of the litigation and must be adversely affected by the defendant's conduct.

Stare Decisis In general, a judicial policy that guides courts in making decisions. The doctrine normally requires lower-level courts to follow the legal precedents that have been established by higher-level courts.

Status Crimes Status crimes punish people for being in a condition rather than for what they are doing or have done. Examples include being without visible means of support and being found addicted to narcotics.

Statute of Descent In property law, a statutory plan enacted by a state legislature governing the distribution of property of a person who dies without leaving a will (i.e., who dies *intestate*).

Statute of Frauds Various state legislative acts, patterned after a 1677 English act known by the same name. Because of the variations in each state, reference must be made to the specific state statutes. The main object was to take away the facilities for fraud, and the temptation to perjury, that arose in verbal obligations, the proof of which depended upon oral evidence. Its most common provisions are these: (a) all leases, excepting those for less than three years, shall have the force of leases at will only, unless they are in writing and signed by the parties or their agents; (b) assignments and surrenders of leases and interests in land must be in writing; (c) all declarations and assignments of trusts must be in writing, signed by the party (trusts arising by implication of law are, however, excepted); (d) no action shall be brought upon a guarantee, or upon any contract for sale of lands, or any interest in or concerning them, or upon any agreement that is not to be performed within a year, unless the agreement is in writing and signed by the party to be charged or his agent; (e) no contract for the sale of goods for a certain price, or more, shall be good unless the buyer accepts part or gives something in part payment or some memorandum thereof is signed by the parties to be charged or their agents.

Statute of Limitations   An issue of *justiciability*. A time limitation, fixed by different state and federal statutes, within which a lawsuit must be commenced, and after the expiration of which the claimant will be forever barred from the right to bring the action. Generally, a statute of limitations is a procedural bar to a plaintiff's action that does not begin to run until after the cause of action has accrued and the plaintiff has a right to maintain a lawsuit.

Statute of Repose   A statute of repose is similar to a statute of limitation in that it sets a maximum time within which a lawsuit can be brought. A statute of repose, however, is often broader than a statute of limitations in that its cut-off date is rigidly enforced and cannot be "tolled" as can a statute of limitations. For example, a statute of limitations begins to run in a products liability case when the plaintiff is injured as a result of the defendant's breach of a legal duty. By contrast, a statute of repose would begin to run when the plaintiff took possession of the product. If the plaintiff rarely uses a product and then becomes injured years later while using the product, the statute of limitations may not have elapsed because it would start to run on the date of the injury. However, if the state has enacted a statute of repose, it might well have elapsed and would then bar any suit against the product's manufacturer. Statutes of repose are often included in proposals for tort reform in that they absolutely cut off liability on a date certain, irrespective of any other considerations.

Statutory Lien   A lien created by statute, rather than by agreement of the parties.

Strict Construction   A rule of statutory construction, particularly used in criminal cases where the language of a criminal statute is vague. A court should not enlarge the meaning of a criminal statute by implication beyond the fair meaning of the language used nor construe its meaning so as to defeat the obvious intention of the legislature.

Strict Liability Crime   A *mala prohibita* offense that requires no proof of *mens rea*.

Strict Liability in Tort   Where the defendant is held strictly liable for injuries or damage caused by his or her actions, without regard to the defendant's intentions and whether her or she exercised reasonable care. Strict liability in tort is applied in cases involving what the common law recognized as abnormally dangerous activities and, more recently, in certain product liability cases.

Subject–Matter Jurisdiction   Where a court has jurisdiction to decide the merits of a case because it has power over the subject matter..

Subpoena   A writ that requires a person to appear in court to give testimony. Literally, a subpoena "to bring with you."

Subpoena Duces Tecum   A writ requiring that a witness appear in court with a document that is in his or her possession.

Substantive Due Process   A label that is used to refer to the ongoing constitutional debate over what should be included within the scope of the Due Process Clause of the Fourteenth Amendment. At this time, most but not all of the rights enumerated in the Bill of Rights have been incorporated into the Fourteenth Amendment Due Process Clause and made binding on the states. Far more contentious, however, is the debate about which unenumerated rights should also be incorporated into the Fourteenth Amendment Due Process Clause. Students can get a taste of this debate by reading the excerpts from the opinions written by Chief Justice Rehnquist and Justice Souter in the assisted suicide case in Chapter I—*Washington v. Glucksberg.*

Substantive Rule   Administrative rule used to establish and implement policies that assist an agency to accomplish its statutorily established objectives. See also, *rule-making power.*

Substituted Service   The summons and complaint are served on the defendant by a means other than personal service, as provided by law (e.g., by mailing them to the defendant by certified mail, or leaving the documents at the defendant's home with a person who resides there and who is of "suitable age and discretion," or leaving them at the defendant's place of work with someone who is employed there and reasonably can be assumed to be authorized to accept and pass on delivery of the documents, such as a receptionist. Cf., *personal service.*

Summary Jury Trial (SJT)   A form of *alternative dispute resolution.* An abbreviated "practice trial" that allows disputing parties to see how a group of regular jurors reacts to each side's presentation and produces a nonbinding "verdict." Useful when parties agree about liability but disagree as to damages.

Supremacy Clause As a general rule, Article VI, Section 2 of the federal Constitution makes the U.S. Constitution, federal laws, and treaties "the supreme law of the land," taking precedence over state constitutions and laws where a direct conflict exists.

Suspect Classification Legislatively established classifications based on race, religion, national origin, or alienage and classifications that trammel on fundamental rights are likely to violate the provisions of the Equal Protection Clause of the Fourteenth Amendment. Suspect classifications are subject to strict scrutiny and can be justified only by a compelling state interest.

Tangible Descriptive of something that may be felt or touched; corporeal.

Tangible Personal Property Physical objects such as a book, a boat, or a piece of furniture, i.e., objects that are neither *realty* nor *fixtures*. Cf., *intangible personal property*.

Temporary Restraining Order (TRO) An *equitable remedy*. an *ex parte injunction*. This means that it is granted without notice to the defendant. A TRO may not be granted unless irreparable harm would result and there is no time for notice and a hearing. There must be clear evidence on the merits of the case. The court should look at any damage to the defendant that would be noncompensable in money if the plaintiff's relief is later shown to be improper. This consideration must be balanced with the plaintiff's harm if the TRO is not granted. Factors weigh more heavily against the plaintiff, since there is no notice to defendant.

Tenancy by the Entirety A form of property ownership. A tenancy by the entirety is limited to married husbands and wives and is ended only upon death, divorce, or mutual consent. When a tenant spouse dies, title passes to the surviving spouse. If a divorce occurs, the tenancy is converted into a *tenancy in common*.

Tenancy in Common A form of property ownership similar to a joint tenancy; however, there is no automatic passing of the deceased's rights to the surviving tenants (right of survivorship). Instead, the deceased's rights pass according to his or her will.

Tender-Years Doctrine An outdated view that courts should generally award custody of young children to their mother.

Testator A man who makes a will. Cf., *testatrix*.

Testatrix A woman who makes a will. Cf., *testator*.

Title Ownership rights in property.

Tort A wrongful act, not involving a breach of an agreement, for which a civil action may be maintained.

Tortfeasor A person who commits a tort.

Trademark A type of *intellectual property*. A unique symbol, term, phrase, or design that a company uses to help customers identify and distinguish its products from competitors.

Trade Secret A plan, process, tool, mechanism, or compound, known only to its owner and those of his employees to whom it is necessary to confide it, in order to apply it to the uses intended. It is distinguishable from a patent in that it may be used by anyone who is able to discover its nature.

Treason A crime defined only by the Constitution, at Article III, Section 3, clause 1. To commit treason—levying war against the United States or adhering to or giving aid or comfort to its enemies—there must be an overt act and the intent to commit treason.

Trespass (1) At early common law, any offense less than treason, felony, or misprision of either. (2) An *intentional tort,* especially entry on another's land without lawful authority. (3) *Trespass on the case* (see definition below). (4) Criminal trespass is entering or surreptitiously remaining in a building or occupied structure, or separately secured or occupied portion thereof, knowing that he or she is not licensed or privileged to do so.

Trespasser One who enters and remains on the land of another without the possessor's express or implied consent. Licensees or invitees may become trespassers if they venture into an area where they are not invited or expected to venture or remain on the premises for an unreasonable period of time.

Trespass on the Case A statutory writ created by the English Parliament to redress private wrongs not addressed by the writ of trespass where the failure to perform a duty resulted in harm to a victim. Also called *case.*

Trial Court's Jury Instructions The judge's instructions explain to the jury the elements (i.e., the facts that must be proven) of the claims and defenses that were raised by the parties, which party has the burden of proof with respect to each issue, and the forms of verdict being submitted to the jury. After the close of the evidence in a jury trial, the parties will submit suggested jury instructions to the judge. The judge then holds a hearing out of the presence of the jury and, after argument, rules as to which instructions are accepted. The accepted jury instructions are subsequently read to the jury.

Trial De Novo (1) In some jurisdictions, a party who has had a trial in a local court can elect to have a county court with general jurisdiction decide the case afresh. This second trial is called a *trial de novo* because this second trial proceeds "from the beginning" just as if the first trial had not occurred. (2) In an *arbitration*, if permitted by the arbitration agreement (i.e., unless the parties have agreed to binding arbitration), a party can reject the *arbitration award* and request a jury trial, called a *trial de novo*. Unless the trial judgment exceeds the arbitration award, a party demanding a trial de novo often will be penalized and required to pay the arbitration costs.

Unconscionable (Contract or Contract Provision) A contract clause that is too unfair or one-sided. A court may exercise the *equitable remedy* of refusing to enforce such a contract or contract provision if it concludes that enforcement of the contract would "shock the conscience of the court."

Undue Influence The will of a dominant person is substituted for that of the other party, and the substitution is done in an unlawful fashion, resulting in an unfair agreement.

Unenforceable A contract that courts will not enforce. Examples include oral agreements that have not been reduced to writing under circumstances where a writing is required and breach of contract lawsuits that are barred by a statute of limitations.

Uniform Commercial Code (UCC) A model code which has been substantially adopted by all states except Louisiana (which has not adopted those portions of the UCC that are based on common law notions because they are incompatible with that state's civil law approach to commercial law).

Unilateral Contract A contract in which one party makes a promise in exchange for another person performing or refraining from performing an act.

Unjust Enrichment The doctrine that places a legal duty of restitution upon a defendant who has acquired something of value at the expense of the plaintiff.

U.S. Courts of Appeals Normally the courts to which appeals are directed from the federal district courts. There are thirteen federal judicial circuits.

U.S. District Courts Federal courts of original jurisdiction that function as the trial courts for the federal judiciary. Federal district courts are given limited subject-matter jurisdiction by the Constitution and by Congress.

Utilitarian, Utilitarianism A philosophical approach that focuses on the social usefulness of legislation rather than on natural law ideas of goodness and justice.

Vagueness Courts will declare unconstitutional statutes and ordinances that are too vague. Vagueness exists where legislation fails to control the police exercise of discretion and fails to provide citizens with fair notice of what the law prohibits.

Valid Contract A binding and enforceable agreement that meets all the necessary contractual requirements.

Venue The place where judicial authority should be exercised.

Vested Fully effective.

Vicarious Liability Substituted or indirect responsibility, e.g., the responsibility of an employer for the torts committed by his employee within the scope of his employment.

Voidable Contract An agreement in which one of the parties can elect to avoid an obligation created by contract because of the manner in which the contract was brought about (such as fraud, duress, or lack of capacity).

Void Contract No contract because no enforceable legal obligation has been created.

Void-for-Vagueness Doctrine Legislation that is declared unconstitutional because it fails to establish minimal guidelines that structure and confine police discretion or fails to provide citizens with fair notice of what is prohibited. Such legislation is said to violate the requirement of substantive due process.

Voir Dire A pretrial oral examination of prospective jurors conducted to determine their qualifications.

Voluntary Adoption Birth parent(s) consent to the termination of their parental rights and surrender the child either to an agency for placement or to adoptive parents of their choosing.

Voluntary ADR Where parties to a lawsuit (or a prospective lawsuit) voluntarily agree to attempt to resolve their issues through *alternative dispute resolution* before commencing or proceeding with court action. Cf., *court-annexed ADR*.

Waiver The voluntary relinquishment of a legal right.

Wanton Misconduct Behavior that manifests a disposition to perversity. It must be under such circumstances and conditions that the party doing the act, or failing to act, is conscious that his or her conduct will, in all common probability, result in injury.

Warrant A written order from a court to an officer, directing the officer to arrest a person or search specified premises for items subject to lawful seizure.

Warranty In contract law, a contractual obligation that sets a standard by which performance of the contract is measured. An express or implied promise that one of the contracting parties guarantees something in furtherance of the contract, such as a seller's promise that the thing sold is as represented or promised. See also, *express warranty, implied warranty*.

Writ In early English law, administrative letters issued by the king and containing the royal seal. Writs were used to order courts to convene and sheriffs to do justice. Today, a writ is a court's written order, in the name of a state or other competent legal authority, commanding the addressee to do or refrain from doing some specified act.

Writ of Account An old common-law writ used to obtain a reconciliation statement of receipts and payments and to recover any money due.

Writ of Certiorari (1) "To be more fully informed," an original writ or action whereby a cause is removed from an inferior to a superior court for review. The record of the proceedings is then transmitted to the superior court. (2) A discretionary appellate jurisdiction that is invoked by a petition for certiorari, which the appellate court may grant or deny in its discretion. The petition for a writ of certiorari is the legal vehicle used to obtain review from the U.S. Supreme Court.

Writ of Covenant An old common-law writ used to enforce agreements relating to land, especially leases.

Writ of Debt An old common-law writ used to collect a specific sum of money owed.

Writ of Entry An old common-law writ used to regain possession of land.

Writ of Execution A court order commanding the sheriff to take possession of a judgment debtor's nonexempt property so that it can be sold to satisfy a judgment.

Writ of Right A twelfth-century common-law writ that required communal and manorial courts to conduct a trial according to specified royal procedures to determine if the demandant (the previous possessor who sought the writ) had been wrongfully dispossessed.

Writ of Subpoena A writ employed by English chancery judges to speed up the trial process. The writ of subpoena commands a person to appear in court as a witness.

Writ of Summons Usually served on the defendant at the same time as service of the complaint, the writ of summons (or simply the *summons*) warns the defendant that a default judgment can be awarded to the plaintiff unless the defendant responds with a pleading (usually an answer) within a specified period of time. See also, *process*.

Writ of Trespass A common law writ that covered actions for trespass to land, assaults, batteries, the taking of goods, and false imprisonment.

Written Deposition A deposition in which the questions and answers are written down. Written depositions are significantly less expensive than oral depositions but can be useful for third-party discovery.

Written Interrogatories A type of pretrial *discovery* in which written questions propounded on behalf of one party in an action are directed to another party or to someone who is not a party. The person interrogated must give his or her answers in writing, and upon oath.

Year Books Annual series of important cases collected by English lawyers and students during the fourteenth and fifteenth centuries.

Zoning, Zoning Ordinances Laws and regulations that restrict the use of real property. They serve many purposes including protecting housing districts from industrial pollution and preserving historically significant landmarks and agriculture. Zoning also has been used to exclude low-income housing, commercial development, adult-entertainment establishments, and the like and to reduce population density (and therefore the need for such things as additional schools).

Case Index

Subject Index